Lecture Notes in Computer Science 11643

De-Shuang Huang · Vitoantonio Bevilacqua ·
Prashan Premaratne (Eds.)

Intelligent Computing Theories and Application

15th International Conference, ICIC 2019
Nanchang, China, August 3–6, 2019
Proceedings, Part I

Editors
De-Shuang Huang
Tongji University
Shanghai, China

Vitoantonio Bevilacqua
Polytechnic University of Bari
Bari, Italy

Prashan Premaratne
University of Wollongong
North Wollongong, NSW, Australia

ISSN 0302-9743 ISSN 1611-3349 (electronic)
Lecture Notes in Computer Science
ISBN 978-3-030-26762-9 ISBN 978-3-030-26763-6 (eBook)
https://doi.org/10.1007/978-3-030-26763-6

LNCS Sublibrary: SL3 – Information Systems and Applications, incl. Internet/Web, and HCI

This Springer imprint is published by the registered company Springer Nature Switzerland AG
The registered company address is: Gewerbestrasse 11, 6330 Cham, Switzerland

Preface

The International Conference on Intelligent Computing (ICIC) was started to provide an annual forum dedicated to the emerging and challenging topics in artificial intelligence, machine learning, pattern recognition, bioinformatics, and computational biology. It aims to bring together researchers and practitioners from both academia and industry to share ideas, problems, and solutions related to the multifaceted aspects of intelligent computing.

ICIC 2019, held in Nanchang, China, during August 3–6, 2019, constituted the 15th International Conference on Intelligent Computing. It built upon the success of previous ICIC conferences held in Wuhan, China (2018), Liverpool, UK (2017), Lanzhou, China (2016), Fuzhou, China (2015), Taiyuan, China (2014), Nanning, China (2013), Huangshan, China (2012), Zhengzhou, China (2011), Changsha, China (2010), Ulsan, Republic of Korea (2009), Shanghai, China (2008), Qingdao, China (2007), Kunming, China (2006), and Hefei, China (2005).

This year, the conference concentrated mainly on the theories and methodologies as well as the emerging applications of intelligent computing. Its aim was to unify the picture of contemporary intelligent computing techniques as an integral concept that highlights the trends in advanced computational intelligence and bridges theoretical research with applications. Therefore, the theme for this conference was "Advanced Intelligent Computing Technology and Applications." Papers focusing on this theme were solicited, addressing theories, methodologies, and applications in science and technology.

ICIC 2019 received 609 submissions from 22 countries and regions. All papers went through a rigorous peer-review procedure and each paper received at least three review reports. Based on the review reports, the Program Committee finally selected 217 high-quality papers for presentation at ICIC 2019, included in three volumes of proceedings published by Springer: two volumes of *Lecture Notes in Computer Science* (LNCS), and one volume of *Lecture Notes in Artificial Intelligence* (LNAI). This volume of *Lecture Notes in Computer Science* (LNCS) includes 72 papers.

The organizers of ICIC 2019, including Tongji University, Nanchang Institute of Technology, and East China Institute of Technology, as well as Shandong University at Weihai, made an enormous effort to ensure the success of the conference. We hereby would like to thank the members of the Program Committee and the referees for their collective effort in reviewing and soliciting the papers. We would like to thank Alfred Hofmann, executive editor from Springer, for his frank and helpful advice and guidance throughout, and for his continuous support in publishing the proceedings. In particular, we would like to thank all the authors for contributing their papers. Without the high-quality submissions from the authors, the success of the conference would not have been possible. Finally, we are especially grateful to the International Neural Network Society, and the National Science Foundation of China for their sponsorship.

June 2019

De-Shuang Huang
Vitoantonio Bevilacqua
Prashan Premaratne

ICIC 2019 Organization

General Co-chairs

De-Shuang Huang, China
Shengqian Wang, China

Program Committee Co-chairs

Kang-Hyun Jo, South Korea
Phalguni Gupta, India

Organizing Committee Co-chairs

Chengzhi Deng, China
Zhikai Huang, China
Yusen Zhang, China

Organizing Committee Members

Shumin Zhou, China
Wei Tian, China
Yan Li, China
Keming Liu, China
Shaoquan Zhang, China
Liling Zhang, China

Award Committee Chair

Vitoantonio Bevilacqua, Italy

Tutorial Chair

M. Michael Gromiha, India

Publication Chair

Ling Wang, China

Special Session Chair

Abir Hussain, UK

Special Issue Chair

Kyungsook Han, South Korea

International Liaison Chair

Prashan Premaratne, Australia

Workshop Co-chairs

Jair Cervantes Canales, Mexico
Michal Choras, Poland

Publicity Co-chairs

Valeriya Gribova, Russia
Laurent Heutte, France
Chun-Hou Zheng, China

Exhibition Contact Chair

Di Wu, Tongji University, China

Program Committee Members

Abir Hussain	Dah-Jing Jwo	Tianyong Hao
Khalid Aamir	Shaoyi Du	Mohd Helmy Abd Wahab
Kang-Hyun Jo	Dunwei Gong	Hao Lin
Angelo Ciaramella	Xiaoheng Deng	Hongmin Cai
Wenzheng Bao	Meng Joo Er	Xinguo Lu
Binhua Tang	Eros Pasero	Hongjie Wu
Bin Qian	Evi Syukur	Jianbo Fan
Bingqiang Liu	Fengfeng Zhou	Jair Cervantes
Bin Liu	Francesco Pappalardo	Junfeng Xia
Li Chai	Gai-Ge Wang	Juan Carlos
Chin-Chih Chang	LJ Gong	Figueroa-Jiangning Song
Wen-Sheng Chen	Valeriya Gribova	Joo M. C. Sousa
Michal Choras	Michael Gromiha Maria	Ju Liu
Xiyuan Chen	Naijie Gu	Ka-Chun Wong
Jieren Cheng	Guoliang Li	Kyungsook Han
Chengzhi Liang	Fei Han	Seeja K. R.

Yoshinori Kuno
Laurent Heutte
Xinyi Le
Bo Li
Yunxia Liu
Zhendong Liu
Hu Lu
Fei Luo
Haiying Ma
Mingon Kang
Marzio Pennisi
Gaoxiang Ouyang
Seiichi Ozawa
Shaoliang Peng
Prashan Premaratne
Boyang Qu
Rui Wang
Wei-Chiang Hong
Xiangwei Zheng
Shen Yin
Sungshin Kim

Surya Prakash
TarVeli Mumcu
Vasily Aristarkhov
Vitoantonio Bevilacqua
Ling Wang
Xuesong Wang
Waqas Haider Khan
Bangyal
Bing Wang
Wenbin Liu
Weidong Chen
Wei Jiang
Wei Wei
Weining Qian
Takashi Kuremoto
Shitong Wang
Xiao-Hua Yu
Jing Xiao
Xin Yin
Xingwen Liu
Xiujuan Lei

Xiaoke Ma
Xiaoping Liu
Xiwei Liu
Yonggang Lu
Yongquan Zhou
Zu-Guo Yu
Yuan-Nong Ye
Jianyang Zeng
Tao Zeng
Junqi Zhang
Le Zhang
Wen Zhang
Qi Zhao
Chunhou Zheng
Zhan-Li Sun
Zhongming Zhao
Shanfeng Zhu
Quan Zou
Zhenran Jiang

Additional Reviewers

Huijuan Zhu
Yizhong Zhou
Lixiang Hong
Yuan Wang
Mao Xiaodan
Ke Zeng
Xiongtao Zhang
Ning Lai
Shan Gao
Jia Liu
Ye Tang
Weiwei Cai
Yan Zhang
Yuanpeng Zhang
Han Zhu
Wei Jiang
Hong Peng
Wenyan Wang
Xiaodan Deng
Hongguan Liu
Hai-Tao Li

Jialing Li
Kai Qian
Huichao Zhong
Huiyan Jiang
Lei Wang
Yuanyuan Wang
Biao Zhang
Ta Zhou
Wei Liao
Bin Qin
Jiazhou Chen
Mengze Du
Sheng Ding
Dongliang Qin
Syed Sadaf Ali
Zheng Chenc
Shang Xiang
Xia Lin
Yang Wu
Xiaoming Liu
Jing Lv

Lin Weizhong
Jun Li
Li Peng
Hongfei Bao
Zhaoqiang Chen
Ru Yang
Jiayao Wu
Dadong Dai
Guangdi Liu
Jiajia Miao
Xiuhong Yang
Xiwen Cai
Fan Li
Aysel Ersoy Yilmaz
Agata Giełczyk
Akila Ranjith
Xiao Yang
Cheng Liang
Alessio Ferone
José Alfredo Costa
Ambuj Srivastava

Mohamed Abdel-Basset
Angelo Ciaramella
Anthony Chefles
Antonino Staiano
Antonio Brunetti
Antonio Maratea
Antony Lam
Alfredo Pulvirenti
Areesha Anjum
Athar Ali Moinuddin
Mohd Ayyub Khan
Alfonso Zarco
Azis Ciayadi
Brendan Halloran
Bin Qian
Wenbin Song
Benjamin J. Lang
Bo Liu
Bin Liu
Bin Xin
Guanya Cai
Casey P. Shannon
Chao Dai
Chaowang Lan
Chaoyang Zhang
Chuanchao Zhang
Jair Cervantes
Bo Chen
Yueshan Cheng
Chen He
Zhen Chen
Chen Zhang
Li Cao
Claudio Loconsole
Cláudio R. M. Silva
Chunmei Liu
Yan Jiang
Claus Scholz
Yi Chen
Dhiya AL-Jumeily
Ling-Yun Dai
Dongbo Bu
Deming Lei
Deepak Ranjan Nayak
Dong Han
Xiaojun Ding

Domenico Buongiorno
Haizhou Wu
Pingjian Ding
Dongqing Wei
Yonghao Du
Yi Yao
Ekram Khan
Miao Jiajia
Ziqing Liu
Sergio Santos
Tomasz Andrysiak
Fengyi Song
Xiaomeng Fang
Farzana Bibi
Fatih Adıgüzel
Fang-Xiang Wu
Dongyi Fan
Chunmei Feng
Fengfeng Zhou
Pengmian Feng
Feng Wang
Feng Ye
Farid Garcia-Lamont
Frank Shi
Chien-Yuan Lai
Francesco Fontanella
Lei Shi
Francesca Nardone
Francesco Camastra
Francesco Pappalardo
Dongjie Fu
Fuhai Li
Hisato Fukuda
Fuyi Li
Gai-Ge Wang
Bo Gao
Fei Gao
Hongyun Gao
Jianzhao Gao
Jianzhao Gao
Gaoyuan Liang
Geethan Mendiz
Geethan Mendiz
Guanghui Li
Giacomo Donato
   Cascarano

Giorgio Valle
Giovanni Dimauro
Giulia Russo
Linting Guan
Ping Gong
Yanhui Gu
Gunjan Singh
Guohua Wu
Guohui Zhang
Guo-Sheng Hao
Surendra M. Gupta
Sandesh Gupta
Gang Wang
Hafizul Fahri Hanafi
Haiming Tang
Fei Han
Hao Ge
Kai Zhao
Hangbin Wu
Hui Ding
Kan He
Bifang He
Xin He
Huajuan Huang
Jian Huang
Hao Lin
Ling Han
Qiu Xiao
Yefeng Li
Hongjie Wu
Hongjun Bai
Hongtao Lei
Haitao Zhang
Huakang Li
Jixia Huang
Pu Huang
Sheng-Jun Huang
Hailin Hu
Xuan Huo
Wan Hussain Wan Ishak
Haiying Wang
Il-Hwan Kim
Kamlesh Tiwari
M. IkramUllah Lali
Ilaria Bortone
H. M. Imran

Ingemar Bengtsson
Izharuddin Izharuddin
Jackson Gomes
Wu Zhang
Jiansheng Wu
Yu Hu
Jaya Sudha
Jianbo Fan
Jiancheng Zhong
Enda Jiang
Jianfeng Pei
Jiao Zhang
Jie An
Jieyi Zhao
Jie Zhang
Jin Lu
Jing Li
Jingyu Hou
Joe Song
Jose Sergio Ruiz
Jiang Shu
Juntao Liu
Jiawen Lu
Jinzhi Lei
Kanoksak
 Wattanachote
Juanjuan Kang
Kunikazu Kobayashi
Takashi Komuro
Xiangzhen Kong
Kulandaisamy A.
Kunkun Peng
Vivek Kanhangad
Kang Xu
Kai Zheng
Kun Zhan
Wei Lan
Laura Yadira
Domínguez Jalili
Xiangtao Chen
Leandro Pasa
Erchao Li
Guozheng Li
Liangfang Zhao
Jing Liang
Bo Li

Feng Li
Jianqiang Li
Lijun Quan
Junqing Li
Min Li
Liming Xie
Ping Li
Qingyang Li
Lisbeth Rodríguez
Shaohua Li
Shiyong Liu
Yang Li
Yixin Li
Zhe Li
Zepeng Li
Lulu Zuo
Fei Luo
Panpan Lu
Liangxu Liu
Weizhong Lu
Xiong Li
Junming Zhang
Shingo Mabu
Yasushi Mae
Malik Jahan Khan
Mansi Desai
Guoyong Mao
Marcial Guerra de
 Medeiros
Ma Wubin
Xiaomin Ma
Medha Pandey
Meng Ding
Muhammad Fahad
Haiying Ma
Mingzhang Yang
Wenwen Min
Mi-Xiao Hou
Mengjun Ming
Makoto Motoki
Naixia Mu
Marzio Pennisi
Yong Wang
Muhammad Asghar
 Nadeem
Nadir Subasi

Nagarajan Raju
Davide Nardone
Nathan R. Cannon
Nicole Yunger Halpern
Ning Bao
Akio Nakamura
Zhichao Shi
Ruxin Zhao
Mohd Norzali Hj Mohd
Nor Surayahani Suriani
Wataru Ohyama
Kazunori Onoguchi
Aijia Ouyang
Paul Ross McWhirter
Jie Pan
Binbin Pan
Pengfei Cui
Pu-Feng Du
Kunkun Peng
Syed Sadaf Ali
Iyyakutti Iyappan
 Ganapathi
Piyush Joshi
Prashan Premaratne
Peng Gang Sun
Puneet Gupta
Qinghua Jiang
Wangren Qiu
Qiuwei Li
Shi Qianqian
Zhi-Xian Liu
Raghad AL-Shabandar
Rafał Kozik
Raffaele Montella
Woong-Hee Shin
Renjie Tan
Rodrigo A. Gutiérrez
Rozaida Ghazali
Prabakaran
Jue Ruan
Rui Wang
Ruoyao Ding
Ryuzo Okada
Kalpana Shankhwar
Liang Zhao
Sajjad Ahmed

Sakthivel Ramasamy
Shao-Lun Lee
Wei-Chiang Hong
Hongyan Sang
Jinhui Liu
Stephen Brierley
Haozhen Situ
Sonja Sonja
Jin-Xing Liu
Haoxiang Zhang
Sebastian Laskawiec
Shailendra Kumar
Junliang Shang
Wei-Feng Guo
Yu-Bo Sheng
Hongbo Shi
Nobutaka Shimada
Syeda Shira Moin
Xingjia Lu
Shoaib Malik
Feng Shu
Siqi Qiu
Boyu Zhou
Stefan Weigert
Sameena Naaz
Sobia Pervaiz
Somnath Dey
Sotanto Sotanto
Chao Wu
Yang Lei
Surya Prakash
Wei Su
Qi Li
Hotaka Takizawa
FuZhou Tang
Xiwei Tang
Li-Na Chen
Yao Tuozhong
Qing Tian
Tianyi Zhou
Junbin Fang
Wei Xie
Shikui Tu
Umarani Jayaraman
Vahid Karimipour
Vasily Aristarkhov

Vitoantonio Bevilacqua
Valeriya Gribova
Guangchen Wang
Hong Wang
Haiyan Wang
Jingjing Wang
Ran Wang
Waqas Haider Bangyal
Pi-Jing Wei
Wei Lan
Fangping Wan
Jue Wang
Minghua Wan
Qiaoyan Wen
Takashi Kuremoto
Chuge Wu
Jibing Wu
Jinglong Wu
Wei Wu
Xiuli Wu
Yahui Wu
Wenyin Gong
Wu Zhang
Zhanjun Wang
Xiaobing Tang
Xiangfu Zou
Xuefeng Cui
Lin Xia
Taihong Xiao
Xing Chen
Lining Xing
Jian Xiong
Yi Xiong
Xiaoke Ma
Guoliang Xu
Bingxiang Xu
Jianhua Xu
Xin Xu
Xuan Xiao
Takayoshi Yamashita
Atsushi Yamashita
Yang Yang
Zhengyu Yang
Ronggen Yang
Xiao Yang
Zhengyu Yang

Yaolai Wang
Yaping Yang
Yue Chen
Yongchun Zuo
Bei Ye
Yifei Qi
Yifei Sun
Yinglei Song
Ying Ling
Ying Shen
Yingying Qu
Lvjiang Yin
Yiping Liu
Wenjie Yi
Jianwei Yang
Yu-Jun Zheng
Yonggang Lu
Yan Li
Yuannong Ye
Yong Chen
Yongquan zhou
Yong Zhang
Yuan Lin
Yuansheng Liu
Bin Yu
Fang Yu
Kumar Yugandhar
Liang Yu
Yumin Nie
Xu Yu
Yuyan Han
Yikuan Yu
Yong Wang
Ying Wu
Ying Xu
Zhiyong Wang
Shaofei Zang
Chengxin Zhang
Zehui Cao
Tao Zeng
Shuaifang Zhang
Yan Zhang
Liye Zhang
Zhang Qinhu
Sai Zhang
Sen Zhang

Shan Zhang
Shao Ling Zhang
Wen Zhang
Wei Zhao
Bao Zhao
Zheng Tian
Sijia Zheng
Zhenyu Xuan
Fangqing Zhao
Zhao Fangqing

Zhipeng Cai
Xing Zhou
Xiong-Hui Zhou
Lida Zhu
Ping Zhu
Qi Zhu
Zhong-Yuan Zhang
Ziding Zhang
Junfei Zhao
Zhe Li

Juan Zou
Quan Zou
Qian Zhu
Zunyan Xiong
Zeya Wang
Yatong Zhou
Shuyi Zhang
Zhongyi Zhou

Contents – Part I

Contents – Part II

Contents – Part III

Solving Symmetric and Asymmetric Traveling Salesman Problems Through Probe Machine with Local Search

Md. Azizur Rahman and Jinwen Ma[⊠]

Department of Information Science, School of Mathematical Sciences
and LMAM, Peking University, Beijing 100871, People's Republic of China
mdazizur201171@pku.edu.cn, jwma@math.pku.edu.cn

Abstract. Combinatorial optimization problems emerge extensively in the different fields and traveling salesman problem (TSP) is certainly one of the most representative and hardest (i.e., NPC) combinatorial optimization problems. In this paper, we propose a dynamical route construction algorithm to solve both symmetric and asymmetric TSP's, which uses probe concept to generate the better routes step by step. Specifically, a reasonable value of filtering proportion is set in each step such that the worst routes are filtered out. On the other hand, a set of local search operators are further implemented on the retained routes for their variations and improvements. Actually, our proposed algorithm is tested on various TSP instances taken from TSPLIB and compared with the best-known results reported by the data library as well as the other four recent state-of-the-art algorithms. It is demonstrated by the experimental results that our proposed algorithm can achieve the best results in certain cases and generally get the results close to the best-known results within a reasonable period of time. In addition, the proposed algorithm outperforms in some cases and obtains superior results than the best-known results, and even performs better than the recent state-of-the-art algorithms.

Keywords: Probe machine · Symmetric and asymmetric TSP · Filtering proportion value · Local search · Combinatorial optimization

1 Introduction

Routing problems are widely studied among combinatorial problems that have been proven to be in the class of NP-hard [1]. The TSP is undoubtedly the most prominent elements of these routing problems, and it cannot be solved easily by using traditional optimization techniques. Generally, the problems aim at optimizing a route for a traveling person who travels around a list of cities with each city being visited only once and returning back to a point of departure. Mathematically, the problem can be stated as to find the shortest Hamiltonian cycle from a complete graph $G = (V, E)$, where V is the set of vertices, and E is the set of edges, also a distance matrix $D = (d_{ij})$ associated with E. The distance from one node to another is same as its reverse order i.e., $d_{ij} = d_{ji} \ \forall i, j$ for the symmetric problem, whereas the asymmetric problem corresponds to the case with $d_{ij} \neq d_{ji}$ for at least one edge in E. Although the TSP problems

© Springer Nature Switzerland AG 2019
D.-S. Huang et al. (Eds.): ICIC 2019, LNCS 11643, pp. 1–13, 2019.
https://doi.org/10.1007/978-3-030-26763-6_1

can be easily formulated in mathematically, it offers all the features of combinatorial optimization. Moreover, many practical applications are modeled as TSP such as computer wiring, vehicle routing and scheduling, control of robots, and so on. Therefore, developing an efficient and effective algorithm for this family of TSP is not only academic interest but also has important engineering and practical significance.

Due to the importance and applicability, an immense number of approaches have been developed to tackle the TSP problems. However, most of these approaches perform the optimizing task that are based on metaheuristics and heuristics. Basically, the metaheuristic algorithms start with a set of randomly generated complete routes and then improve the routes iteratively using different techniques. Although these algorithms have the ability to supply good quality solutions, many parameters are used which are very hard to understand and need to be fitted. As a result, the procedures are often time consuming as well as problem-specific. On the other hand, the route of heuristic approaches is enhanced consecutively and the portion of the route that has already been created remains unchanged in every step during the process. These greedy algorithms take a reasonable computational time but easily fall into the trapped of local optimization.

To overcome the difficulties of traditional heuristic approaches, Lau *et al.* [2] developed a dynamic route construction approach in 2001. It can be observed that the benefit of this technique is to modify the part of route, which has been already constructed during the searching process. However, it is limited to a very small number of cases (8-city problem). Considering the limitations of existing approaches, we have introduced a consecutive route filtering approach to solve the symmetric TSP [8] in 2018, where the route is built consecutively with the help of probe concept. In addition, the worse routes are filtered out in every step of the procedure based on a filtering proportion value. In this work, we take an attempt to enhance the performance of our earlier algorithm [8] for solving both symmetric and asymmetric TSP. For this reason, in every step of the working process, a set of local search operators are applied consecutively on each of the filtered routes for their modification and improvement. The remainder of this paper is structured as follows: we review some recent work in Sect. 2. Section 3 describes some useful operators. In Sect. 4, we provide an explanation of our proposed framework in details. Experimental results with discussion present in Sect. 5 and the final section gives the conclusion.

2 Recent Work

To inspect the performance of the proposed algorithm, we consider four different recently publish state-of-the-art algorithms namely, improved discrete bat algorithm (IBA), discrete symbiotic organisms search (DSOS) algorithm, hybrid variable neighborhood search (HVNS) algorithm, and discrete water cycle algorithm (DWCA). A brief description of these algorithms are given below:

In [3], Osaba *et al.* reported a discrete bat algorithm to solve both symmetric and asymmetric TSP. The BA performs the optimizing search based on the echolocation characteristics of microbats. Generally, the original BA works for continuous problems and they addressed a discrete version of the original algorithm. In addition, two local search operators (2-opt. and 3-opt.) have been used in the algorithm to create the new generation from the old. On the other hand, Ezugwu *et al.* [4] concentrated on another optimization technique based on the symbiotic organisms search (SOS) for solving the symmetric TSP. This optimization technique is inspired by the mutual interaction strategies adopt by the organisms to survive and propagate in the ecosystem. Basically, the search process begins with a random generation and update the generations itera-tively based on three mutual interaction of the organism namely, mutualism, com-mensalism, and parasitism. To represent the solution in discrete form from continuous, they used a set of local search operators in every step of mutual interaction scheme.

An improvement of variable neighborhood search technique has been revealed by Hore *et al.* [5] to solve both symmetric and asymmetric TSP. They accomplished the optimizing search task in two stages – firstly generate an initial solution based on a greedy approach, and then improve the initial solution iteratively by using various neighborhood structure. As opposed to that, Osaba *et al.* [6] paid their attention to apply water cycle algorithm to solve both symmetric and asymmetric problems. The WCA is a nature stimulated powerful optimization technique based on the observation of water cycle and, how rivers and streams flow downhill towards the sea in the real world. They reported a discrete form of the original algorithm and integrated two local search operators to modify the location of the streams.

3 Some Useful Operators

This section consists of the description of some operators that incorporate to our algorithm to rid of from local optimum during the search process, which are as follows:

3.1 Probe Concept

Generally, the probe operator uses to find out something properly. In [7], Xu intro-duced a probe machine in which he addressed two types of the probe for solving Hamiltonian and graph coloring problems. Based on his concept we developed a new type of the probe in our earlier work [8]. This paper also uses a similar concept of the probe as [8] to solve the family of TSP. In fact, each of the route (sub or complete) consider as the probe in which the outer two edges of the route are treated as wings of the probe. Using these two wings, the probe can add automatically two unvisited cities on the route at every step of the route construction process. In this way, each of the probes consecutively enhances on both sides in each step until form a complete route. A sample of 3-city, 5-city, and n-city probe together with their wings are displayed in Fig. 1.

3.2 Filtering Proportion Value

The proportion value is an important operator adopt in our algorithm that helps to filter out the worse probe and keep the potential probe at every step of the searching process. Actually, it's a very crucial task to fit a suitable filtering proportion value dynamically in the algorithm because an inappropriate proportion value not only provides a worse solution but also takes more computational time. This paper uses proportion value same as [8], which is defined for δ^{th} step as:

$$\alpha_{2\delta+1} = \frac{c}{N+\sqrt{\delta}}; \delta = 1, 2, \cdots \cdots \cdots \cdots, \left[\frac{N}{2}\right] \qquad (1)$$

where δ is the step number, N represents the scale of the problem, and c is the constant need to be tuned. In fact, the values of c depend on N and adjust it by the experiments. For the results of this paper, the values of c lie within the interval $\left[\frac{2N+2}{N^3-3N^2+2N}, \frac{800N+800}{N^3-3N^2+2N}\right]$ for symmetric TSP and $\left[\frac{N+1}{N^3-3N^2+2N}, \frac{100N+100}{N^3-3N^2+2N}\right]$ found in case of asymmetric.

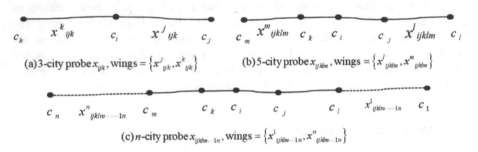

(a) 3-city probe x_{ijk}, wings $= \left\{x^j_{ijk}, x^k_{ijk}\right\}$

(b) 5-city probe x_{ijklm}, wings $= \left\{x^j_{ijklm}, x^m_{ijklm}\right\}$

(c) n-city probe $x_{ijklm\cdots1n}$, wings $= \left\{x^1_{ijklm\cdots1n}, x^n_{ijklm\cdots1n}\right\}$

Fig. 1. A sample of 3-city, 5-city, and n-city probe with the wings

3.3   Local Search Operators

Actually, a set of local search operators apply consecutively on each of the filtered probes to improve the probe quality at every step except the first of searching procedure. These local search operators are briefly described in the followings:

2-Optimization

The 2-opt. operator eliminates two edges from the existing probes and reconnects the new two paths created. Let, $<c_i, c_{i+1}>$ and $<c_j, c_{j+1}>$ be two selected edges, then the 2-opt. delete these edges and add new two edges, and finally reverse the part between the cities c_{i+1} and c_j. The 2-opt. is controlled by the following decision function:

$$DF_{2-opt.} : \left\{d(c_i, c_{i+1}) + d(c_j, c_{j+1})\right\} > \left\{d(c_i, c_j) + d(c_{i+1}, c_{j+1})\right\}; \qquad (2)$$
$$1 \leq i \leq N-2; \; i+2 \leq j \leq N$$

Inversion

The inversion operator simply inverse the part of the probe between the cities c_i and c_j where $c_i \neq c_j$. So, firstly select two cut points on the probe and then reverse the sub-tour between the cut points. The inversion is measured by Eq. (3):

$$DF_{Inverse} : \{d(c_{i-1}, c_i) + d(c_j, c_{j+1})\} > \{d(c_{i-1}, c_j) + d(c_i, c_{j+1})\};$$
$$1 \leq i \leq N - 1; \; i + 1 \leq j \leq N \qquad (3)$$

Swap

Generally, the swap operator selects two cities from probe and exchange the position of the cities. Let, c_i and c_j be the two cut point, and the swap operator interchange the position between c_i and c_j. The swap is examined by Eq. (4):

$$DF_{swap} : \begin{cases} \{d(c_{i-1}, c_i) + d(c_i, c_{i+1}) + d(c_{j-1}, c_j) + d(c_j, c_{j+1})\} > \\ \{d(c_{i-1}, c_j) + d(c_j, c_{i+1}) + d(c_{j-1}, c_i) + d(c_i, c_{j+1})\}; \; If \; j - i \neq 1 \\ \{d(c_{i-1}, c_i) + d(c_j, c_{j+1})\} > \{d(c_{i-1}, c_j) + d(c_i, c_{j+1})\}; \; If \; j - i = 1 \end{cases} ;$$
$$1 \leq i \leq N - 1; \; i + 1 \leq j \leq N$$
$$(4)$$

Insertion

In insertion, first need to select two position c_i and c_j from the probe with $c_i \neq c_j$, and then c_i is inserted into the c_j back position. The decision function for insertion is:

$$DF_{Insertion} : \begin{cases} \{d(c_{i-1}, c_i) + d(c_i, c_{i+1}) + d(c_j, c_{j+1})\} > \\ \{d(c_{i-1}, c_{i+1}) + d(c_j, c_i) + d(c_i, c_{j+1})\}; \; If \; i < j \\ \{d(c_{j-1}, c_j) + d(c_{i-1}, c_i) + d(c_i, c_{i+1})\} > \\ \{d(c_{j-1}, c_i) + d(c_i, c_j) + d(c_{i-1}, c_{i+1})\}; \; If \; i > j \end{cases} ; \qquad (5)$$
$$1 \leq i \leq N; \; 1 \leq j \leq N; \; i \neq j$$

The details working mechanism of the local search operators are given below:

(1) Select a filtered probe $< c_1, c_2, \cdots, c_i, c_{i+1}, \cdots, c_j, c_{j+1}, \cdots, c_N >$, $N \geq 5$
(2) Choose c_i from the probe as the first cut point. For N-city probe, if $i = 1$, then $i - 1 = N$
(3) Choose c_j from the probe as the second cut point. For N-city probe, if $j = N$, then $j + 1 = 1$
(4) Calculate the decision function (DF) of the operators mentioned in Eqs. (2)–(5). If the decision function is satisfied, then execute the operation; otherwise go to (5), and the modified probe is only acceptable if it better than the older one
(5) Increase j as $j + 1$ and if the values of j exceed the maximum value, go to (6); otherwise go to (3).
(6) Increase i as $i + 1$ and if the values of i don't exceed the maximum value, go to (2); otherwise exit the process

4 Proposed Framework

In our earlier work [8], we reported a consecutive route filtering approach in which the process performs two tasks in each step. In this paper, we integrate the local search operators with the earlier work to improve the filtered probes. In fact, to complete the searching procedure, the algorithm needs to perform $\lceil \frac{N}{2} \rceil$ steps, and in each step except first it accomplishes three tasks; where $\left[\frac{N}{2}\right]$ equal to $\frac{N}{2}$ for even N, and $\frac{N-1}{2}$ in case of odd. That is, it firstly produces possible probes based on probe concept, then keep the potential probes with the help of proportion value, and finally utilizes local search operators to improve the potential probes. The process of working mechanism can be described as the following steps:

Step-1: Let, c_i be the position of a city and $A(c_i)$ be the set of cities adjacent to c_i. Then, the set of all two-paths with internal city $c_i (i = 1, 2, \cdots, N)$ [7, 8] is defined as:

$$E^2(c_i) = \left\{ c_k c_i c_j \triangleq x_{ijk} : c_j, \ c_k \in A(c_i); \ i \neq j, k; \ j \neq k; \ j, k = 1, 2, \cdots, N \right\} \quad (6)$$

where x_{ijk} is the two-paths with internal city c_i and adjacent cities c_j, c_k. Consequently, the set of all two-paths generates for N-city problem can be constructed as:

$$X_3 = \bigcup_{i=1}^{N} E^2(c_i) \quad (7)$$

As each two-paths contain 3-city, we consider it a 3-city probe. The number of such types of probe produces in this step will be $\frac{N(N-1)(N-2)}{2}$ for the symmetric problem and $N(N-1)(N-2)$ in asymmetric cases. Then, the probe's rank is calculated based on Euclidean distance, for example, the rank of the lowest distance probe 1, second lowest distance probe's rank 2, and in this manner. After that, a proportion value uses to keep the good probes from the generated probes. If we choose α_3 as the proportion value, then the set of good probes can be made as:

$$G_3 = \left\{ x_{ijk} : x_{ijk} \in X_3; \ \text{rank of} \ (x_{ijk}) \leq \alpha_3 N_3; \ N_3 = |X_3| \right\} \quad (8)$$

Step-2: This step constructs 5-city probe based on the set of good probes G_3 obtain from step-1. In fact, each good probe enhances the route on both sides through the wings. Therefore, the set of the 5-city probe can be formed as follows:

$$X_5 = \left\{ c_m c_k c_i c_j c_l \triangleq x_{ijklm} : \forall \ x_{ijk} \in G_3; \ x_{kim}, x_{jli} \in X_3; \ l \neq m; \ l, m \neq i, j, k \right\} \quad (9)$$

In the same way of step-1, calculate the probe's rank and select the proportion value α_5 to keep the potential probes from the produces probes. Thus, the set of filtered probes is:

$$P_5 = \left\{ x_{ijklm} : x_{ijklm} \in X_5; \ \text{rank of} \ (x_{ijklm}) \leq \alpha_5 N_5; \ N_5 = |X_5| \right\} \quad (10)$$

After that, the local search operators applied consecutively on each of the filtered probes of P_5 to make better the quality of the probe. So, the set of filtered probe P_5 updated as the set of good probes G_5 as:

$$G_5 = \left\{ LS(x_{ijklm}) : \forall x_{ijklm} \in P_5; \ \text{distance of} \ (LS(x_{ijklm})) \leq \text{distance of} \ x_{ijklm} \right\} \quad (11)$$

where LS indicates the local search operators and the number of probes in G_5 is the same as P_5.

Step- $(\delta + 1)$: Let, $G_{2\delta+1}$ be the set of good $(2\delta+1)$-city probe obtain from δ-step, and based on it the set of $(2\delta+3)$-city probe is constructed as:

$$
X_{2\delta+3} = \left\{
\begin{array}{c}
\overbrace{c_h \underbrace{c_v c_t \cdots c_m c_k c_i c_j c_l \cdots c_s c_u}_{(2\delta+3)-\text{cityprobe}} c_g}^{(2\delta+1)-\text{citygoodprobe}} \triangleq x_{ijklm\cdots stuvgh} : \\
\forall x_{ijklm\cdots stuv} \in G_{2\delta+1};\ x_{ugs}, x_{vth} \in X_3;\ h \neq g; h, g \neq v, \cdots, u
\end{array}
\right\} \quad (12)
$$

After creating possible probes apply the same procedure as previous steps i.e., keep the potential probes with the help of proportion value $\alpha_{2\delta+3}$, and implement the local search operators one by one on each filtered probes to find the good probes. Thus, the set of filtered probes is:

$$
P_{2\delta+3} = \left\{
\begin{array}{c}
x_{ijklm\cdots stuvgh} : x_{ijklm\cdots stuvgh} \in X_{2\delta+1}; \\
\text{rank of } (x_{ijklm\cdots stuvgh}) \leq \alpha_{2\delta+3} N_{2\delta+3};\ N_{2\delta+3} = |X_{2\delta+3}|
\end{array}
\right\} \quad (13)
$$

whereas, the set of $(2\delta+3)$-city good probes is built as follows:

$$
G_{2\delta+3} = \left\{
\begin{array}{c}
LS(x_{ijk\cdots vgh}) : \forall x_{ijk\cdots vgh} \in P_{2\delta+3}; \\
\text{distance of } (LS(x_{ijk\cdots vgh})) \leq \text{distance of} (x_{ijk\cdots vgh})
\end{array}
\right\} \quad (14)
$$

In this fashion, the procedure of probe construction, probe filtering, and probe quality improvement continue until complete all of the steps. Finally, the best complete route seeks out from the good probes found in the last step. It needs to highlight that one city left to add in the last step of even number of problem, the probe uses any one wing to include the remaining city in this situation. The pseudocode and flowchart of the proposed algorithm are shown in Algorithm 1 and Fig. 2 respectively.

Algorithm 1. Pseudocode of the proposed algorithm

Input: Distance matrix of TSP, $D_{N \times N}$, Dynamic filtering proportion value, $\alpha_{2\delta+1}$
Output: Best probe X_{best}, the distance of best probe F_{best}
1: Generate 3-city probes set X_3 considering all of two paths
2: Calculate the Euclidean distance of each 3-city probe $x_3 \in X_3$, and determine the rank of the probe
3: Based on proportion value α_3 find the good probes set G_3
4: For step, $\delta = 2$ to maximum step, $\left[\frac{N}{2}\right]$
5: Create new probe set $X_{2\delta+1}$ based on good probe set $G_{2\delta-1}$
6: Compute Euclidean distance of each $(2\delta+1)$-city new probe $x_{2\delta+1} \in X_{2\delta+1}$, and determine the rank
7: Make the set of filtered probes $P_{2\delta+1}$ based on filtering proportion value $\alpha_{2\delta+1}$
8: For each filtered probes, $l = 1$ to $|P_{2\delta+1}|$
9: Improve the filtered probe by applying
    (a) 2-optimization operators (b) Insertion operators (c) Inversion operators (d) Swap operators
10: Update the filtered probe as the good probe
11: End for
12: The set of filtered probe $P_{2\delta+1}$ improved as the set of good probes $G_{2\delta+1}$
13: End for
14: Search out the best probe X_{best} from the set of good probes $G_{2\left[\frac{N}{2}\right]+1}$ that found in the last step and its distance F_{best}

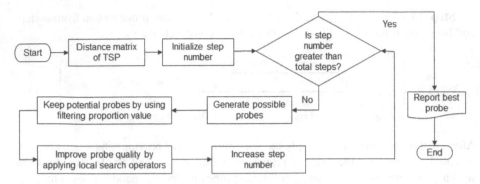

Fig. 2. The flowchart of the proposed framework.

5 Experimental Results and Discussion

To verify the effectiveness and efficiency of the proposed algorithm, we have carried out a number of experiments in this subsection based on symmetric and asymmetric TSP benchmark instances taken from well-known TSPLIB [9] with cities scale from 14 to 1655. Actually, the proposed algorithm is implemented in MATLAB R2016b software and executed on a computer system with specifications of Intel Core i-5 at 3.30 GHz CPU and 8 GB RAM with a 64-bit platform under Windows 10 operating system for most of the tested instances. A few numbers of instances namely d493, p654, fl1400, d1655, rbg323, rbg403 and rbg443 run with 4 core GPU system due to requiring high computational resources. Each of the instances run independently 10 consecutive times to measure the average runtime. The percentage deviation of simulated results to the best-known result is calculated by the following formula:

$$\text{Error} = \frac{\text{Our result} - \text{Best known result}}{\text{Best known result}} \times 100\% \tag{15}$$

5.1 Discussion of Simulated Results

The experimental results of 55 different TSP instances are presented in Table 1. The results show that in some cases namely pr144, u159, and tsp225, the proposed algorithm produces the optimal values with negative error, which indicates the strong search capability of the algorithm. It is noticeable that the proposed algorithm provides optimal results in 58.54% of the symmetric instances (24 out of 41), and in 57.14% of the asymmetric instances (8 out of 14). Besides that, the approach yields optimal values with maximum error 2.54% in symmetric instances (2.11% in asymmetric instance), where less than 1% error has been occurred in 11 cases (3 for asymmetric) and only 6 (3 for asymmetric) cases more than 1% error is found. On the other hand, it's observed that when the number of cities are up to 280, the algorithm takes on average 8.49 s, whereas, the average 5.70 min require for solving up to 1400 cities instances. Therefore, the algorithm proposed in this paper is a promising optimization technique that provides better quality solutions within a reasonable computational time. The obtained optimal routes of the proposed technique for some instances are displayed in Figs. 3, 4, 5 and 6.

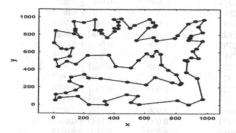

Fig. 3. Obtained optimal tour of rd100.

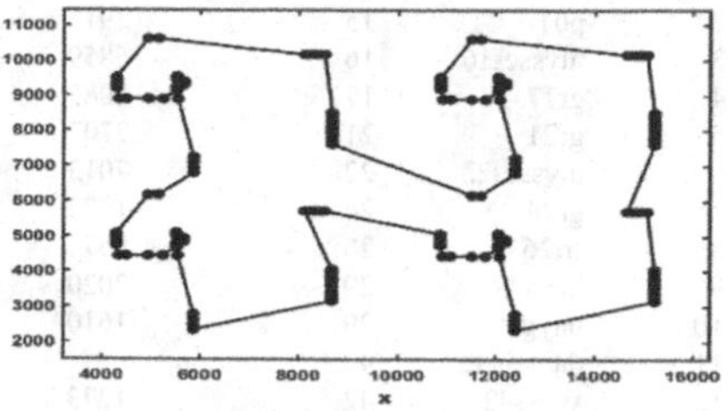

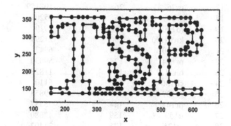

Fig. 4. Obtained optimal tour of pr144.

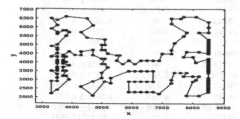

Fig. 5. Obtained optimal tour of u159.

Fig. 6. Obtained optimal tour of tsp225.

5.2 Comparison of the Results with Other Algorithms

In this research, four recent state-of-the-art algorithms such as DSOS, HVNS, IBA, and DWC are considered to compare the results of the proposed algorithm. The comparison of the results of 33 selected symmetric instances with the results of DSOS and HVNS are presented in Table 2. It's clear from Table 2 that the results of the proposed algorithm are better than the best results of DSOS and HVNS in almost all of the selected instances except ch130, ch150, and pcb442. In fact, HVNS performed well in two cases (pcb442 and ch130) while in one case (ch150) of DSOS found better result. In these three instances, the obtained results of our method are better than the best results of DSOS in case of pcb442 and HVNS for ch150 as well as the average result for ch130 of HVNS. In terms of optimal solution, the overall performance of the proposed algorithm is better than the HVNS algorithm in 93.94% cases and better than in 94.12% cases of DSOS algorithm.

Table 1. Obtained optimization results of the proposed algorithm for 41 symmetric and 14 asymmetric TSP benchmark instances.

SI No.	Instances	No. of cities	Optimum	Our results	Error (in %)	CPU time (in seconds)
Symmetric Traveling Salesman Problem (STSP)						
1	burma14	14	3323	**3323**	0.000	0.0084 ± 0.0057
2	p01	15	291	**291**	0.000	0.0071 ± 0.0027
3	ulysses16	16	6859	**6859**	0.000	0.0401 ± 0.0028
4	gr17	17	2085	**2085**	0.000	0.0082 ± 0.0023
5	gr21	21	2707	**2707**	0.000	0.0622 ± 0.0038
6	ulysses22	22	7013	**7013**	0.000	2.2655 ± 0.0918
7	gr24	24	1272	**1272**	0.000	0.6605 ± 0.0168
8	fri26	26	937	**937**	0.000	0.0290 ± 0.0055
9	bays29	29	2020	**2020**	0.000	0.0301 ± 0.0046
10	bayg29	29	1610	**1610**	0.000	0.0354 ± 0.0046
11	dantzig42	42	699	**699**	0.000	0.2756 ± 0.0034
12	swiss42	42	1273	**1273**	0.000	0.1643 ± 0.0060
13	gr48	48	5046	**5046**	0.000	0.7807 ± 0.0215
14	att48	48	10628	**10628**	0.000	0.4748 ± 0.0147
15	hk48	48	11461	**11461**	0.000	0.7198 ± 0.0117
16	brazil58	58	25395	**25395**	0.000	0.1338 ± 0.0067
17	pr76	76	108159	**108159**	0.000	1.8875 ± 0.0150
18	gr96	96	55209	55430	0.400	1.4731± 0.0272
19	rd100	100	7910	**7910.4**	0.000	1.2026 ± 0.0257
20	kroD100	100	21294	**21294**	0.000	5.7436 ± 0.0403
21	gr120	120	6942	6982	0.570	6.2058 ±0.0719
22	pr124	124	59030	**59030**	0.000	7.4098 ± 0.4505
23	bier127	127	118282	118293.52	0.009	7.7001 ± 0.0584
24	ch130	130	6110	6145.47	0.580	9.4239 ± 0.0859
25	gr137	137	69853	70152	0.428	5.8932 ± 0.0794
26	pr144	144	58537	**58535**	-0.003	0.8857 ± 0.0203
27	u159	159	42080	**42075.67**	-0.010	4.6058 ± 0.2350
28	si175	175	21407	21422	0.070	18.1207±0.3951
29	brg180	180	1950	**1950**	0.000	10.8813±0.5731
30	rat195	195	2323	2351	1.205	37.4649±0.3577
31	gr202	202	40160	40560	0.996	32.3021±0.3731
32	ts225	225	126643	126645.93	0.002	38.9138±0.4916
33	tsp225	225	3916	**3867.35**	-1.245	41.4955±2.0795
34	gr229	229	134602	135544	0.699	14.9488±0.2086
35	gil262	262	2378	2413.28	1.483	36.8047± 0.1419
36	a280	280	2579	2594	0.583	81.3576±0.4412
37	rd400	400	15281	15537.98	1.681	200.4097±3.396
38	d493	493	35002	35772	2.200	172.008±2.1113
39	si535	535	48450	48588	0.284	323.9820±7.9858
40	p654	654	34643	35257	1.772	729.0827±56.017
41	fl1400	1400	20127	20638	2.539	15492.00±1522.1
	Average percentage error:				**0.34739**	
Asymmetric Traveling Salesman Problem (ATSP)						
1	br17	17	39	**39**	0.000	0.0089 ± 0.0027
2	ftv33	34	1286	**1286**	0.000	0.1910 ± 0.0068
3	ftv35	36	1473	**1473**	0.000	0.3845 ± 0.0099
4	ftv38	39	1530	**1530**	0.000	10.9092±0.2784
5	p43	43	5620	**5620**	0.000	0.1820 ± 0.0069
6	ftv47	48	1776	1807	1.746	1.5388± 0.0366
7	ry48p	48	14422	**14422**	0.000	0.8516±0.01570
8	ftv55	56	1608	**1608**	0.000	1.6315±0.01650
9	ft70	70	38673	39291	1.598	7.4144±0.17960
10	ftv70	71	1950	1954	0.205	1.4152± 0.0159
11	kro124p	100	36230	**36230**	0.000	4.3164 ± 0.0943
12	rbg323	323	1326	1354	2.111	269.1746±22.242
13	rbg403	403	2465	2469	0.162	498.2370±12.142
14	rbg443	443	2720	2721	0.036	731.2116±22.265
	Average percentage error:				**0.4188429**	

Note: Optimum indicates the best known results reported by TSPLIB

Table 3 shows the comparison of selected 15 symmetric and asymmetric TSP instances with the results of IBA and DWC. It's observed that in 100% cases of the symmetric problems, the proposed algorithm produces better results than the best results of IBA. Besides that, the generated results are better than the best of DWC algorithm in 4 cases out of 6. In the remaining two cases (pr152 and pr264), the produced route lengths are little bit higher than the best route lengths of DWC but lower than the average values. As opposed to, in case of asymmetric, our algorithm is better than the other two algorithms (IBA and DWC) in all of the considered instances except ftv47.

Table 2. Comparison of the proposed algorithm with DSOS and HVNS algorithms on 33 symmetric TSP instances.

Instances				DSOS [4], 2017		HVNS [5], 2018		Our Results
S/N	Name	Scale	Optimum	Average	Best	Average	Best	
1	pr76	76	108159	NA	108159	108159	108159	108159
2	rat99	99	1211	1228.37	1224	1241.26	1240.38	1219.2
3	rd100	100	7910	NA	NA	7918.6	7910.4	7910.4
4	kroD100	100	21294	21493.10	21294	21490.62	21294.29	21294
5	pr124	124	59030	59429.10	59030	59051.82	59030.74	59030
6	bier127	127	118282	NA	NA	119006.39	118974.6	118293.52
7	ch130	130	6110	NA	NA	6153.72	6140.66	6145.47
8	pr136	136	96772	97673.20	97437	97985.84	97979.11	97189
9	pr144	144	58537	58817.10	58565	58563.97	58535.22	58535
10	ch150	150	6528	6552.58	6542	6644.95	6639.52	6555.5
11	kroA150	150	26524	NA	NA	26947.17	26943.31	26727
12	kroB150	150	26130	NA	NA	26537.04	26527.57	26275
13	pr152	152	73682	74785.70	74013	73855.11	73847.6	73821
14	u159	159	42080	NA	NA	42467.61	42436.23	42075.67
15	rat195	195	2323	NA	NA	2453.81	2450.14	2351
16	kroA200	200	29368	29651.23	29477	30339.67	30300.56	29453
17	tsp225	225	3916	NA	3877	NA	NA	3867.35
18	gil262	262	2378	NA	NA	2501.86	2492.85	2413.3
19	pr264	264	49135	52798.90	50454	51197.14	51155.38	49390
20	pr299	299	48191	50335.20	49162	50373.12	50271.69	48212.75
21	lin318	318	42029	42972.42	42201	43964.93	43924.08	42189
22	rd400	400	15281	NA	NA	16250.21	16155.91	15537.98
23	fl417	417	11861	NA	NA	12183.14	12180.78	12010
24	pcb442	442	50778	NA	51418	50800.24	50783.55	51362
25	rat575	575	6773	7117.32	7073	7362.51	7349.81	6964.7
26	u724	724	41910	NA	NA	45729.71	45725.39	43175
27	rat783	783	8806	9102.67	9045	9707.364	9707.166	9042
28	pr1002	1002	259045	278381.51	272381	280563.9	280368.2	269766.40
29	pcb1173	1173	56892	NA	NA	63435.95	63354.82	59446
30	d1291	1291	50801	NA	NA	56095.33	56088.31	54267
31	rl1323	1323	270199	NA	NA	295611.2	295607.3	280750
32	fl1400	1400	20127	NA	NA	21085.98	21040.65	20638
33	d1655	1655	62128	NA	NA	70337.23	69992.49	64707

Note: 'NA' means that the original references did not provide any result

Table 3. Comparison of the proposed algorithm with IBA and DWC on 9 symmetric and 6 asymmetric TSP instances.

Instances				IBA [3], 2016		DWC [6], 2018		Our Results
S/N	Name	Scale	Optimum	Average	Best	Average	Best	
Symmetric traveling salesman problem (STSP)								
1	kroD100	100	21294	21593.4	21294	21529.6	21361	21294
2	pr124	124	59030	59412.1	59030	59338.9	59030	59030
3	pr136	136	96772	99351.2	97547	98761.4	97488	97189
4	pr144	144	58537	58876.2	58537	58734.6	58537	58535
5	pr152	152	73682	74676.9	73921	74202.6	73682	73821
6	pr264	264	49135	50908.3	49756	49528.6	49310	49390
7	pr299	299	48191	49674.1	48310	NA	NA	48212.75
8	pr439	439	107217	115256.4	111538	NA	NA	109330
9	pr1002	1002	259045	274419.7	270016	NA	NA	269766.4
Asymmetric traveling salesman problem (ATSP)								
1	ftv47	48	1776	1863.6	1796	1827.8	1776	1807
2	ry48p	48	14422	14544.8	14422	14517.8	14429	14422
3	ft70	70	38673	40309.7	39901	40111.1	39669	39291
4	ftv70	71	1950	2233.2	2111	2126.2	2014	1954
5	kro124p	100	36230	39213.7	37538	39252.8	37412	36230
6	rbg323	323	1326	1640.9	1615	NA	NA	1354

Note: 'NA' means that the original references did not provide any result

6   Conclusion

We have established a promising optimization technique for searching the optimal solution of the family of TSP that uses a proportion value to filter out the worse probes. It also utilizes a set of local search operators to enhance the quality of filtered probes in each steps. Generally, local search operators are applied on a complete route to improve the route iteratively. In contrast, we have adopted these operators at every step of the working process in an efficient manner rather than the traditional ones. The proposed algorithm produces the same result in each run because there is no randomness in the procedure and no fine-tune parameters except filtering proportion value that are the benefits over the existing methods. Furthermore, the proposed algorithm can able to solve the asymmetric problem with almost equal flexibility of symmetric problem except in the first step. The experimental results suggest that the proposed algorithm can reach the optimal point for a mentionable number of instances and usually provide an approximate solution closer to the best known solution within a reasonable CPU running time. In addition, the algorithm generates the results that are superior to the best-known results reported by the data library in some cases, and outperforms than the other four recent state-of-the-art algorithms for selected instances.

Acknowledgment. This work is supported by the Natural Science Foundation of China for Grant 61171138.

References

1. Garey, M.R., Johnson, D.S.: Computers and Intractability: A Guide to the Theory of NP-Completeness. W. H. Freeman, New York (1979)
2. Lau, S.K., Shue, L.Y.: Solving travelling salesman problems with an intelligent search approach. Asia Pac. J. Oper. Res. **18**(1), 77–88 (2001)
3. Osaba, E., Yang, X.S., Diaz, F., Lopez-Garcia, P., Carballedo, R.: An improved discrete bat algorithm for symmetric and asymmetric traveling salesman problems. Eng. Appl. Artif. Intell. **48**, 59–71 (2016)
4. Ezugwu, A.E.S., Adewumi, A.O.: Discrete symbiotic organisms search algorithm for travelling salesman problem. Expert Syst. Appl. **87**, 70–78 (2017)
5. Hore, S., Chatterjee, A., Dewanji, A.: Improving variable neighborhood search to solve the traveling salesman problem. Appl. Soft Comput. **68**, 83–91 (2018)
6. Osaba, E., Del Ser, J., Sadollah, A., Bilbao, M.N., Camacho, D.: A discrete water cycle algorithm for solving the symmetric and asymmetric traveling salesman problem. Appl. Soft Comput. **71**, 277–290 (2018)
7. Xu, J.: Probe machine. IEEE Trans. Neural Netw. Learn. Syst. **27**(7), 1405–1416 (2016)
8. Rahman, Md.A., Ma, J.: Probe machine based consecutive route filtering approach to symmetric travelling salesman problem. In: Shi, Z., Pennartz, C., Huang, T. (eds.) ICIS 2018. IAICT, vol. 539, pp. 378–387. Springer, Cham (2018). https://doi.org/10.1007/978-3-030-01313-4_41
9. TSPLIB. http://elib.zib.de/pub/mp-testdata/tsp/tsplib/tsplib.html. Accessed 07 Mar 2019

An Evolutionary Algorithm Based
on Multi-operator Ensemble
for Multi-objective Optimization

Chao Wang, Ran Xu, and Xingyi Zhang[✉]

School of Computer Science and Technology, Anhui University,
Hefei 230601, China
xyzhanghust@gmail.com

Abstract. For the multi-objective optimization problems with complex decision space, the main challenge is how to choose the most suitable operator for the effective search in the complex decision space. To address this issue, an evolutionary algorithm based on multi-operator ensemble (EAMOE) is proposed for multi-objective optimization. The core idea of the proposed algorithm is to design a multi-operator ensemble strategy based on subpopulations. To be specific, a performance evaluation indicator is first constructed based on the ratio and the fitness improvement of each subpopulation. Then this indicator is used to update the size of each subpopulation in order to reward or punish the weights of operators. Experimental results on UF test suite demonstrate that EAMOE has competitive performance in comparison with existing state-of-the-art algorithms for multi-objective optimization problems with complex decision space.

Keywords: Multi-objective optimization · Complex decision space ·
Multi-operator ensemble · Performance evaluation indicator ·
Subpopulation update

1 Introduction

Evolutionary algorithms (EAs) for solving complex MOPs have been attracting great attention over the past few decades and have proven to be effective for large-scale optimization [1], combinatorial optimization [2, 3], interval optimization [4] and many-objective optimization [5, 6].

However, MOPs with complex decision space are still a challenge for EAs using a single operator [7]. Multi-operator strategy is one of the most effective methods for solving this type of problems. The common approaches select an operator from the operator pool based on some stochastic rules. For example, Elhossini et al. [8] proposed hybrid EA-PSO algorithms in which the solution is first generated by the PSO operator

© Springer Nature Switzerland AG 2019
D.-S. Huang et al. (Eds.): ICIC 2019, LNCS 11643, pp. 14–24, 2019.
https://doi.org/10.1007/978-3-030-26763-6_2

and then improved by the GA operator. Li et al. [9] developed a method of randomly combining multiple DE mutation operators to improve the reproduction procedure under the MOEA/D framework. Luo et al. [10] proposed a hybrid multi-objective PSO-EDA algorithm, which reproduces new offspring by using two types of operators. Some pioneering works use an adaptive operator selection according to the evolution status, which determines the use rates of different operators in an online manner based on their recent performances. Khan et al. [11] studied the effect of the use of two crossover operators in MOEA/D-DRA, and the selection probability of each operator at each generation is updated in an adaptive way. Mashwani et al. [12] developed a novel hybrid multi-objective evolutionary algorithm derived by combining NSGA-II with adaptive multiple operator selection strategy. Li et al. [13] proposed a bandit-based adaptive operator selection method, which considers the recent fitness improvement rates and the number of times used of operators simultaneously. However, this type of method can't make full use of multiple operators to obtain the complementary effect. Therefore, an evolutionary algorithm based on multi-operator ensemble (EAMOE) is proposed for multi-objective optimization problems with complex decision space, which can adaptively assign the weights of different operators in the evolutionary process. The main contributions of this paper are as follows:

1. A multi-operator ensemble strategy based on subpopulations is proposed to make all operators exist simultaneously in the whole evolutionary process that can improve the search ability for complex decision space by cooperating and complementing each other.
2. A performance evaluation indicator is first constructed to evaluate the performance of each operator from both local and global improvements and then used to update the subpopulations to reward or punish the weights of operators.

The rest of this paper is organized as follows. Section 2 describes the technical details of the proposed algorithm step by step. Afterwards, Sect. 3 details experimental settings and gives an analysis of the obtained results. Finally, Sect. 4 concludes with a summary.

2 The Proposed Algorithm

The basic procedure of the proposed algorithm is similar to most Pareto-based MOEAs. The main difference is that multiple operators are used to produce offspring at every iteration. Algorithm 1 gives the general framework of EAMOE. First, an initial parent population P with the size of N is randomly generated, then P is randomly divided to K subpopulations with equal size. Second, for each subpopulation P_k^t, an offspring population *offspring*(k) is generated by using operator op_k, and then all the *offspring*(k) are merged into the offspring population Q. Using the environmental selection of NSGA-II [15], the N elite solutions are survived and added into P'. Third, the proposed performance evaluation indicator θ is employed to evaluate the recent performance of operators, and the subpopulations $P_1^t, P_2^t, \cdots, P_K^t$ are updated by θ and P'. Fourth, the weights of operators are reset equal every iteration number T to prevent the algorithm from using a single operator all the time. This procedure repeats until a termination condition is met.

Algorithm 1: Framework of EAMOE

Input: t_{max} (maximum number of iterations); N (population size);

        op (operators pool); T (period)

Output: $P^{t_{max}}$ (final population)

1. $P \leftarrow Population\_initialization$ (N);

2. $t \leftarrow 0$;

3. Randomly divide P into $\{P_1^t, P_2^t, \cdots P_K^t\}$ with equal size;

4. **while** $t < t_{max}$ **do**

5.   **for** k=1 to K **do**

6.   *offspring*(k) is generated by subpopulation P_k^t using the operator $op(k)$;

7.   **end for**

8. $Q \leftarrow$ *offspring*(1) $\cup \cdots \cup$ *offspring*(K);

9. $S \leftarrow P \cup Q$;

10. $P' \leftarrow Environmental\_selection(S)$;

11. $\{\theta_1, \theta_2, \cdots, \theta_K\} \leftarrow Performance\_evaluation(P', \{P_1^t, P_2^t, \cdots P_K^t\})$;

12. $\{P_1^t, P_2^t, \cdots P_K^t\} \leftarrow Subpopulation\_update(P', \{\theta_1, \theta_2, \cdots, \theta_K\})$;

13. $t \leftarrow t + 1$;

14.   **if** $mod(t, T) == 0$ **then**

15.   Randomly divide P into $\{P_1^t, P_2^t, \cdots P_K^t\}$ and each subpopulation with equal size;

16.   **end if**

17. **end while**

18. **return** $P^{t_{max}}$

2.1   Performance Evaluation of Operators

Since the function of different kinds of operators may vary from different stages of optimization, how to determine the weights according to the recent performance of each operator is a key for multi-operator ensemble. To address this issue, a performance evaluation indicator θ is constructed based on the ratio and the fitness improvement of each subpopulation.

First, the survival numbers of individuals generated by different operators after the environmental selection can reflect the global performance of operators. That is, the larger size of the subpopulation produced by the operator $op(k)$ indicates that the weight of operator $op(k)$ should be increased; otherwise, the weight should be decreased. So, the subpopulation ratio ΔH_k is defined as follows:

$$\Delta H_k = \frac{|P'_k|}{|P'_1| + \cdots + |P'_K|} \tag{1}$$

Where P'_k is the subpopulation that is generated by the operator $op(k)$ in the population P'.

Second, maybe one subpopulation can keep the high survival rate in every generation but has no the fitness improvement. Hence, we calculate the fitness difference value between the current subpopulation and the last subpopulation to reflect the local performance of operators. The fitness improvement rate ΔF_k of a subpopulation is defined as follows:

$$\Delta F_k = \frac{\sum_{i=1}^{|P_k|} F^i_{P_k}}{|P_k|} - \frac{\sum_{i=1}^{|P'_k|} F^i_{P'_k}}{|P'_k|} \tag{2}$$

Where F^i_P is the sum of the normalized objective values of the i-th individual in the population P. P_k is the parent subpopulation and P'_k is the offspring subpopulation. When the fitness improvement value ΔF_k is larger, the weight of this operator is more likely to be rewarded; otherwise, it should be given a punishment.

Finally, in order to dynamically consider these above two aspects simultaneously in different stages, the performance evaluation indicator θ is constructed as follows:

$$\theta_k = \Delta H_k * \Delta F_k \tag{3}$$

Noting that the value of θ_k can be large only if both ΔH_k and ΔF_k values are large or one of them is large significantly, it indicates that the performance of the operator $op(k)$ is higher in the current optimization stage. The value of θ_k fluctuates slightly when ΔH_k and ΔF_k change very little, it indicates that the operator has a general performance in the current optimization stage.

2.2   Subpopulation Update

In order to promote the evolution of the population, we updated the subpopulation through the performance evaluation indicator θ to reward or punish the weights of operators. In detail, the size of subpopulation according to the well-performing operator should be increased, and the size of subpopulation according to the poor-performing operator should be reduced. The update method is shown in Fig. 1 and the details of the process are as follows:

Some individuals in the subpopulation may be have no promising for producing high-quality offspring over time, which should be eliminated. The set of inferior individuals P_k^- in the subpopulation P_k is obtained by the environmental selection. Then all the eliminated individuals are stored in the *Poor Archive*. The number of eliminated individuals in $|P_k^-|$ is calculated by:

$$|P_k^-| = |P_k| - |P_k| \cdot \theta_k \tag{4}$$

When the value of θ_k is larger, it indicates that the better the operator $op(k)$ performance is, so fewer individuals are eliminated from subpopulation P_k; otherwise, more individuals should be eliminated.

Maybe the inferior individuals could produce the high-quality offspring by using the other operator. Each subpopulation P_k selects $|P_k^+|$ individuals from the *Poor Archive* and adds them into P_k. The selection method is through random selection, but the priority of individuals in other subpopulation is greater than that in subpopulation P_k. The number of individuals added $|P_k^+|$ is calculated by:

$$|P_k^+| = (|P_1^-| + \cdots + |P_K^-|) \cdot \frac{\theta_k}{(\theta_1 + \cdots + \theta_K)} \tag{5}$$

When the θ_k is larger, more individuals selected from the *Poor Archive* is added into the subpopulation P_k; otherwise, less individuals are added.

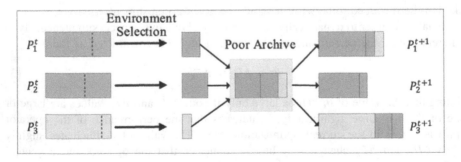

Fig. 1. Illustration of subpopulation update.

3   Experimental Results

This section presents the evaluation of the proposed EAMOE. First, we describe the benchmark suite, the quality indicator and the experimental settings. Then, we verify the validity of the multi-operator strategy in EAMOE. Finally, we analyze the performance of EAMOE compared with HNSGA [12], FRRMAB [13], MOEA/D [14], NSGA-II [15] and NSGA-III [16] based on the experimental results.

3.1   Experimental Settings

Benchmark Suites. Ten unconstrained MOP test instances (UF 1 to UF 10) with various characteristics proposed in [17] are used in experimental studies. The UF instances have nonlinear PSs with arbitrary shapes in the decision space, different instances have different PS shapes. The number of decision variables of the UF instances is set to 30, where UF1 to UF7 instances with two objectives and UF8 to UF10 instances with three objectives.

Performance Metrics. In our empirical studies, the inverted generational distance (IGD) [18] is employed to measure the convergence and diversity of solutions simultaneously. A smaller IGD value indicates a better performance of the algorithm. For calculating IGD, roughly 10,000 reference points on the Pareto front of each test instance are first sampled by the Das and Dennis's approach with two layers.

Parameter Settings. The population size $N = 600$ for 2-objective test instances, $N = 1000$ for 3-objective test instances. 30 independent runs are conducted for each algorithm on each test instance. The maximum number of function evaluations is fixed to be 300,000. For MOEA/D [14] and FRRMAB [13], the neighborhood size is set to 20 and the neighborhood selection probability is 0.9. For EAMOE, the period $T = 60,000$.

Operator Settings. In this paper, we select three DE operators [19] and SBX operator [20]. All multi-operator algorithms use the following operators and give the parameter settings.

(1) *DE-rand*-1: The scaling factor $F = 1$, the crossover rate $CR = 0.1$;
(2) *DE-rand*-2: The scaling factor $F = 1$, the crossover rate $CR = 0.9$;
(3) *DE-current-to-rand*: The scaling factor $F = 1$;
(4) *SBX*: distribution indices $\eta_c = 20$ and the crossover probability is $p_c = 1.0$. The mutation probability is $p_m = 1/V$ and its distribution indicator is $\eta_m = 20$, where V denotes the length of decision variables.

In the following experimental analysis, *DE1*, *DE2*, and *DE3* respectively represent *DE-rand*-1, *DE-rand*-2, and *DE-current-to-rand*.

3.2   Validity of EAMOE

In this section, the effectiveness of EAMOE in dealing with multi-objective optimization problems with complex decision spaces is verified. Since EAMOE is basically similar to NSGA-II [15] except the multi-operator ensemble strategy, this experiment uses NSGA-II with single operator (*DE1* or *SBX*) as comparison while EAMOE uses the ensemble of *DE1* and *SBX*.

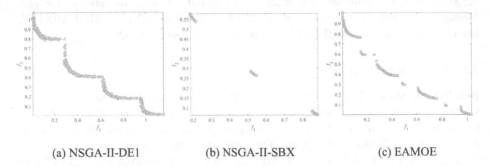

(a) NSGA-II-DE1   (b) NSGA-II-SBX   (c) EAMOE

Fig. 2. The non-dominated solution sets obtained by three algorithms on UF1.

Figure 2 shows the distribution of non-dominated solution sets for NSGA-II-DE1, NSGA-II-SBX, and EAMOE in dealing with UF1 instance. It can be clearly observed that the non-dominated solution set obtained by NSGA-II-DE1 cannot effectively converge to the true PF, but the distribution is relatively good due to the global search capability of the *DE1* operator. The non-dominated solution set obtained by NSGA-II-SBX falls into the local optimal due to the excessive exploitation of the *SBX* operator. While the non-dominated solution set obtained by EAMOE has significant advantages than the other two algorithms in terms of convergence and diversity.

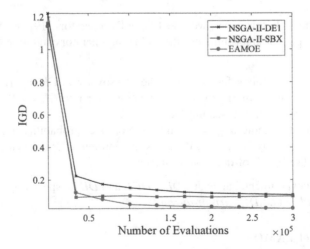

Fig. 3. The trend of IGD values for the NSGA-II-DE1, NSGA-II-SBX and EAMOE on UF1.

The trend of IGD values for the three algorithms is shown in Fig. 3. It can be seen that NSGA-II-SBX almost stagnates in the late stage although converges quickly in the early stage. NSGA-II-DE1 focuses on the exploration, so the convergence speed is slow. EAMOE uses the ensemble of operators *SBX* and *DE1* and can take the advantage of both of them by giving the proper weight according to the performance of each operator, so the convergence speed is fast and the global search is also emphasized in the whole optimization process.

3.3 Simulation Results and Comparisons

The comparison results of EAMOE with MOEA/D [14], NSGA-II [15], NSGA-III [16], HNSGA [12] and FRRMAB [13] on the UF instances are shown in Table 1. Among them, FRRMAB, HNSGA and EAMOE use the operators pool composed of *SBX*, *DE1*, *DE2* and *DE3*. In addition, to test the differences for statistical significance, the Wilcoxon rank sum test is applied with a 5% significance level is performed between EAMOE and each of the compared algorithms over each test instance. Symbols '+', '−' and '≈' indicate that the compared algorithm performs significantly better than, worse than, and equivalent to EAMOE in the corresponding column, respectively.

Table 1. Average and standard deviation of the IGD values obtained by the six algorithms on UF test instances. Best result is highlighted in bold.

	MOEA/D	NSGA-II	NSGA-III	HNSGA	FRRMAB	EAMOE
UF1	2.2945e−1	3.5517e−2	4.0606e−2	4.6007e−2	**5.8133e−3**	3.1893e−2
	(7.79e−2) −	(7.84e−4) ≈	(1.03e−3) −	(8.11e−4) −	**(7.99e−4) +**	(6.58e−3)
UF2	1.3487e−1	2.0455e−2	2.4676e−2	2.6055e−2	**5.5486e−3**	1.5381e−2
	(4.63e−2) −	(2.01e−3) −	(2.32e−3) −	(1.71e−3) −	**(1.10e−3) +**	(8.69e−4)
UF3	3.2472e−1	6.7754e−2	8.3179e−2	1.1008e−1	2.7269e−2	**1.3347e−2**
	(1.04e−2) −	(9.04e−3) −	(1.50e−2) −	(7.48e−3) −	(1.35e−2)−	**(7.22e−3)**
UF4	8.4556e−2	7.7127e−2	7.0261e−2	7.4642e−2	6.7774e−2	**5.5263e−2**
	(3.18e−3) −	(3.30e−3) −	(2.26e−3) −	(2.31e−3) −	(2.36e−3) −	**(1.34e−3)**
UF5	1.2472e+0	7.4887e−1	1.2583e+0	1.1624e+0	4.0166e−1	**3.9653e−1**
	(5.15e−2) −	(1.03e−1) −	(4.54e−2) −	(7.82e−2) −	(1.10e−1) ≈	**(6.18e−2)**
UF6	4.0649e−1	3.0843e−1	4.2240e−1	4.0734e−1	3.8977e−1	**2.5391e−1**
	(4.26e−2)−	(1.18e−2) −	(1.36e−2) −	(1.67e−2) −	(1.14e−2)−	**(1.78e−1)**
UF7	4.1936e−1	2.1466e−2	2.2790e−2	2.2250e−2	**4.4307e−3**	1.5678e−2
	(1.11e−1) −	(1.83e−3) −	(1.53e−3) −	(9.73e−4) −	**(3.97e−4) +**	(2.84e−4)
UF8	3.5545e−1	1.2591e−1	1.4467e−1	1.6314e−1	**5.4893e−2**	1.0458e−1
	(3.00e−1) ≈	(9.20e−3) −	(5.42e−3) −	(4.37e−3) −	**(5.75e−3) +**	(4.33e−3)
UF9	4.0886e−1	1.5432e−1	1.7191e−1	1.3094e−1	1.8437e−1	**1.1107e−1**
	(1.97e−2) −	(7.69e−2) ≈	(6.14e−2) ≈	(8.52e−3) ≈	(5.77e−4) ≈	**(7.35e−3)**
UF10	2.2749e+0	2.3107e+0	2.3973e+0	2.5459e+0	1.1641e+0	**6.6110e−1**
	(1.45e−1)−	(2.01e−1) −	(6.41e−2) −	(1.66e−1) −	(1.18e−1) −	**(4.67e−2)**

Table 1 shows the average IGD values of the six algorithms on UF1 to UF10. From the experimental statistics, the overall performance of EAMOE is better than the other five algorithms. Compared with MOEA/D, NSGA-II, and NSGA-III algorithms using a single operator, EAMOE outperforms these three algorithms in all test instances. It shows that multi-operator ensemble strategy can effectively deal with multi-objective optimization problems with complex decision space. This is due to the fact that the abilities of the operators at different stages of the search process are different, and the optimization effect can be maximized by the ensemble of operators. Compared with HNSGA and FRRMAB algorithms using multiple operators, EAMOE outperforms HNSGA in all test instances and is superior to FRRMAB in UF3-6 and UF9-10 test instances. The reason is that EAMOE uses the evaluation indicator to fully consider the global and local performance of the operator in the evolution process. Moreover, the adopted multiple operators in EAMOE exist in every generation with the different weights that can produce the complementary effects of operators.

To make a deeper understanding of the behavior of EAMOE, we investigate the ensemble situation during the whole search process. For this purpose, we divide the whole search process (i.e., 300,000 function evaluations) into 250 consecutive phases, each of which consists of 1200 function evaluations. And the subpopulation is reset every 60,000 function evaluations. We have calculated the proportion of each operator's subpopulation during each phase and illustrated in Fig. 4.

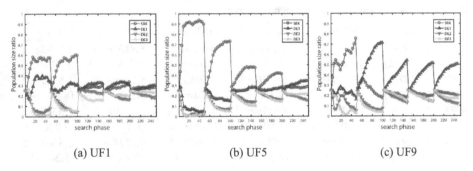

(a) UF1   (b) UF5   (c) UF9

Fig. 4. Operator adaptation trajectories of EAMOE on UF1, UF5 and UF9 instances.

From Fig. 4, we can observe that no single operator can dominate over the whole search process. Furthermore, the search process for each test instance can be divided into several stages, each of which is primarily dominated by a single or multiple operators. For example, on UF1, the search phases 1–100 constitute the first stage, where *SBX* operator plays a leading role that accelerate the convergence of the population. In the second stage of search phases 100–200, *DE1* plays the dominant role because the population almost converges to PF and the diversity of the population need promoted. While in the third stage of search phases 200–250, *SBX* and *DE1* intersect to dominate. Since *DE2* and the *DE3* also have global search capabilities, the according subpopulations are also relatively bigger in the late search phase. These observations show that the proposed ensemble strategy can adaptively adjust the weights of operators in different search phases and effectively switch from one operator to another. So we can include that EAMOE is able to solve the problems with complex decision spaces.

4 Conclusion

In this paper, we have presented an evolutionary algorithm based on multi-operator ensemble for multi-objective optimization problem with complex decision space, termed EAMOE. In the proposed algorithm, we use the multi-operator ensemble strategy to adaptively adjust the weights of operators in different search phases for the complex decision space. More specifically, the performance evaluation indicator is first constructed based on the ratio and the fitness improvement of each subpopulation. And based on it, the size of subpopulation can be updated for rewarding or punishing the weights of operators, which can contribute to the coevolution of subpopulations. To prove the validity, we have made an experimental comparison of EAMOE with five state-of-the-art algorithms on the UF test suite with different types of PSs. The results show that the effectiveness of the proposed algorithm.

Acknowledgement. This work was supported in part by National Nature Science Foundation of China under Grant 51779050, 61603073, 61672033, 61822301, U1804262, State Key Laboratory of Synthetical Automation for Process Industries under Grant PAL-N201805, and Anhui Provincial Natural Science Foundation for Distinguished Young Scholars under Grant 1808085J06.

References

1. Zhang, X., Tian, Y., Cheng, R., Jin, Y.: A decision variable clustering-based evolutionary algorithm for large-scale many-objective optimization. IEEE Trans. Evol. Comput. **22**(1), 97–112 (2018)
2. Cai, X., Li, Y., Fan, Z., Zhang, Q.: An external archive guided multiobjective evolutionary algorithm based on decomposition for combinatorial optimization. IEEE Trans. Evol. Comput. **19**(4), 508–523 (2015)
3. Zhang, Y., Gong, D., Cheng, J.: Multi-objective particle swarm optimization approach for cost-based feature selection in classification. IEEE/ACM Trans. Comput. Biol. Bioinf. **14**(1), 1545–1563 (2017)
4. Gong, D., Sun, J., Ji, X.: Evolutionary algorithms with preference polyhedron for interval multi-objective optimization problem. Inf. Sci. **233**, 141–161 (2013)
5. Tian, Y., Cheng, R., Zhang, X., Cheng, F., Jin, Y.: An indicator-based multiobjective evolutionary algorithm with reference point adaptation for better versatility. IEEE Trans. Evol. Comput. **22**(4), 609–622 (2018)
6. Zhang, X., Tian, Y., Jin, Y.: A knee point-driven evolutionary algorithm for many-objective optimization. IEEE Trans. Evol. Comput. **19**(6), 761–776 (2015)
7. Li, H., Zhang, Q.: Multiobjective optimization problems with complicated Pareto sets, MOEA/D and NSGA-II. IEEE Trans. Evol. Comput. **13**(2), 284–302 (2009)
8. Elhossini, A., Areibi, S., Dony, R.: Strength Pareto particle swarm optimization and hybrid EA-PSO for multi-objective optimization. Evol. Comput. **18**(1), 127–156 (2010)

9. Li, Y., Zhou, A., Zhang, G.: An MOEA/D with multiple differential evolution mutation operators. In: 2014 IEEE Congress on Evolutionary Computation (CEC), pp. 397–404. IEEE, July 2014
10. Luo, J., Qi, Y., Xie, J., Zhang, X.: A hybrid multi-objective PSO-EDA algorithm for reservoir flood control operation. Appl. Soft Comput. **34**, 526–538 (2015)
11. Khan, W., Zhang, Q.: MOEA/D-DRA with two crossover operators. In: 2010 UK Workshop on Computational Intelligence (UKCI), pp. 1–6. IEEE, September, 2010
12. Mashwani, W.K., Salhi, A., Yeniay, O., Hussian, H., Jan, M.A.: Hybrid non-dominated sorting genetic algorithm with adaptive operators selection. Appl. Soft Comput. **56**, 1–18 (2017)
13. Li, K., Fialho, A., Kwong, S., Zhang, Q.: Adaptive operator selection with bandits for a multiobjective evolutionary algorithm based on decomposition. IEEE Trans. Evol. Comput. **18**(1), 114–130 (2014)
14. Zhang, Q., Li, H.: MOEA/D: a multiobjective evolutionary algorithm based on decomposition. IEEE Trans. Evol. Comput. **11**(6), 712–731 (2007)
15. Deb, K., Agrawal, S., Pratap, A., Meyarivan, T.: A fast elitist non-dominated sorting genetic algorithm for multi-objective optimization: NSGA-II. In: Schoenauer, M., et al. (eds.) PPSN 2000. LNCS, vol. 1917, pp. 849–858. Springer, Heidelberg (2000). https://doi.org/10.1007/3-540-45356-3_83
16. Deb, K., Jain, H.: An evolutionary many-objective optimization algorithm using reference-point-based nondominated sorting approach, part I: solving problems with box constraints. IEEE Trans. Evol. Comput. **18**(4), 577–601 (2014)
17. Zhang, Q., Zhou, A., Zhao, S., Suganthan, P.N., Liu, W., Tiwari, S.: Multiobjective optimization test instances for the CEC 2009 special session and competition. University of Essex, Colchester, UK and Nanyang Technological University, Singapore, Special Session on Performance Assessment of Multi-objective Optimization Algorithms, Technical report, 264 (2008)
18. Bosman, P.A., Thierens, D.: The balance between proximity and diversity in multiobjective evolutionary algorithms. IEEE Trans. Evol. Comput. **7**(2), 174–188 (2003)
19. Storn, R., Price, K.: Differential evolution–a simple and efficient heuristic for global optimization over continuous spaces. J. Glob. Optim. **11**(4), 341–359 (1997)
20. Deb, K., Agrawal, R.B.: Simulated binary crossover for continuous search space. Complex Syst. **9**(3), 1–15 (1994)

Water Evaporation Optimization Algorithm Based on Classification and Unbiased Search

Yanjiao Wang and Xiangyang Che[✉]

College of Electrical Engineering, Northeast Electric Power University,
Jilin 132012, China
y_9890@126.com

Abstract. The existing water evaporation optimization algorithm has some disadvantages, such as slow convergence speed, poor accuracy and so on. In order to accelerate WEO's convergence and improve its accuracy, in this paper, we propose a water evaporation optimization algorithm based on classification and unbiased search (CUS-WEO). In this algorithm, different learning objects are selected for better and poorer individuals in monolayer evaporation phase, which can balance the algorithm's exploration ability and exploitation ability. Meanwhile, the unbiased search information is taken as the base vector, and the number of disturbance terms and the search direction are increased in droplet evaporation phase, which can improve the convergence accuracy. To verify the performance of this algorithm, a series of experiments are carried out on 15 benchmark functions and compared with WEO algorithm. The results show that the proposed algorithm can obtain global optimal solutions with higher accuracy and speed up the convergence.

Keywords: Water evaporation optimization · Classification · Unbiased search · Global optimization

1 Introduction

In the recent decades, many metaheuristics with different philosophy and characteristics have been developed and played an important role in productive practice. In terms of how they have been inspired, meta-heuristic algorithms can be divided into swarm algorithms, evolutionary algorithms and physical algorithms. Among them, physical algorithm is inspired by a certain physical law or phenomenon. For example, Gravitational Search Algorithm (GSA) of Rashedi et al. which mimics gravitational phenomena, Water Cycle Algorithm (WCA) of Eskandar et al. based on the basic principles of river generation and water inflow into the ocean and Collision Body Optimization (CBO) of Kaveh et al. which is inspired by one-dimensional collision law, have been accepted as most prevalent algorithms.

In 2016, Kaveh et al. proposed water evaporation optimization algorithm that mimics the evaporation of a tiny amount of water molecules adhered on the solid surface with different wettability which can be studied by molecular dynamics simulations. Experiments show that the water evaporation optimization algorithm has the characteristics of simple operation and strong ability to maintain population diversity,

© Springer Nature Switzerland AG 2019
D.-S. Huang et al. (Eds.): ICIC 2019, LNCS 11643, pp. 25–34, 2019.
https://doi.org/10.1007/978-3-030-26763-6_3

but similar to other new algorithms, WEO algorithm also has some shortcomings, such as blindness in the selection of learning objects in the early stage of evolution, poor search benchmark and narrow search range in the later stage and so on. To improve the optimization performance of WEO algorithm, this paper presents a water evaporation optimization algorithm based on classification and unbiased search (CUS-WEO). Firstly, it selects two different learning objects for better and poorer individuals to balance the local and global search capabilities in monolayer evaporation phase; secondly, it takes unbiased search information as the base vector and increase the number of disturbance terms and the search direction to improve the convergence accuracy in droplet evaporation phase. A series of experiments are carried out on the 15 benchmark test functions. The results show that the CUS-WEO algorithm achieves better performance than WEO algorithms in terms of convergence speed and accuracy.

The rest of this paper is organized as follows. Section 2 presents a brief description of WEO. Section 3 illustrates the proposed algorithm. Section 4 gives benchmark test functions, experimental results and analysis. Finally, Sect. 5 makes a conclusion.

2 Water Evaporation Optimization Algorithm Description

As we all know, with the gradual decrease of the wettability of the solid surface, the aggregation form of water molecules on the solid surface gradually changes from a flat single-layer molecule sheet to a sessile droplet like a spherical cap, and the corresponding evaporation rates of water molecules vary greatly. In order to further study, Wang et al. carried out molecular dynamics simulation on the evaporation of nanoscale water aggregation on a solid substrate with different surface wettability at room temperature. It was found that the water evaporation velocity was affected by the substrate interaction energy $Esub$ and the contact angle θ respectively under different aggregation forms, and the corresponding mathematical models were given.

Inspired by the physical phenomenon of water evaporation in the experiments carried out by Wang et al., the factors affecting water evaporation rate are simulated as individual fitness, and the water evaporation rate is abstracted as individual renewal probability (called evaporation probability matrix) to participate in individual evolution, and the water evaporation optimization algorithm is proposed. In view of the fact that different forms of water molecule aggregation correspond to two models of water evaporation rate, WEO corresponds to the establishment of "monolayer evaporation phase" and "droplet evaporation phase" in the early and late evolution stages. The following is an example of minimization problem that illustrates the specific principle of WEO algorithm.

2.1 Monolayer Evaporation Phase

Firstly, the evaporation rate $J(i)$ of the ith individual is calculated via formula (1).

$$J(i) = \exp(E_{sub}(i)), \tag{1}$$

where $E_{sub}(i)$ is called the substrate interaction energy of the ith individual. In each iteration, $E_{sub}(i)$ can be calculated according to the following formula (2).

$$E_{sub}(i) = \frac{(E_{max} - E_{min}) \times (Fit_i - \text{Min}(Fit))}{(\text{Max}(Fit) - \text{Min}(Fit))} + E_{min}, \tag{2}$$

where Fit_i is the fitness value of tth individual; $\text{Max}(Fit)$ and $\text{Min}(Fit)$ are the maximum and minimum fitness values of the current set of individuals, respectively, and corresponding to the MD simulation result, E_{max} and E_{min} are -3.5 and -0.5, respectively.

Then, the Monolayer Evaporation Probability matrix (MEP) of the current population is constructed according to formula (3), as follows.

$$MEP_{ij} = \begin{cases} 1 & if \quad rand_{ij} < J(i) \\ 0 & if \quad rand_{ij} \geq J(i) \end{cases}, \tag{3}$$

where $rand_{ij}$ is a random number with uniform distribution in $[0, 1]$; MEP_{ij} is the updating probability for the jth variable of the ith individual.

Finally, the current population WM is updated according to formula (4).

$$WM = WM + S \times MEP, \tag{4}$$

where S is a random permutation based step size, and its calculation method is shown in formula (5).

$$S = rand(0, 1) \times (WM[permute1(i)] - WM[permute2(i)]), \tag{5}$$

where $permute1$ and $permute2$ represent two different random vectors with the number of population N as dimensions, respectively.

Obviously, the better the original individual is, the smaller the $Esub$ value is, thus the smaller the evaporation rate $J(i)$ is, the easier the corresponding updating probability of its genes is to be 0, therefore, the more genes it will retain to its offspring.

2.2 Droplet Evaporation Phase

In the droplet evaporation phase, the evaporation rate of individual is calculated according to formula (6). Then, construct the evaporation probability matrix and update the population in the same way as the monolayer evaporation phase.

$$J(\theta(i)) = J_0 \times \left(\frac{2}{3} + \frac{\cos^3(\theta(i))}{3} - \cos(\theta(i)) \right)^{-2/3} (1 - \cos(\theta(i))), \tag{6}$$

where J_0 is $1/2.6$; $\theta(i)$ is the corresponding contact angle of the ith individual, as shown in formula (7).

$$\theta(i) = \frac{(\theta_{max} - \theta_{min}) \times (Fit_i - \text{Min}(Fit))}{(\text{Max}(Fit) - \text{Min}(Fit))} + \theta_{min}, \tag{7}$$

where Max(Fit) and Min(Fit) are the maximum and minimum fitness values of the current set of individuals, respectively, and corresponding to the MD simulation results, θ_{max} and θ_{min} are $-50°$ and $-20°$, respectively.

It can be seen from formula (6) and (7) that the better the ith individual is, the smaller the corresponding contact angle is, similarly, the smaller the corresponding evaporation rate is, the more likely the corresponding updating probability of its genes is to be 0 in the current evaporation probability matrix, which is constructed by formula (3), so the more genes it retains in its offspring.

To further understand the working principle of WEO algorithm, Fig. 1 shows its specific operation process.

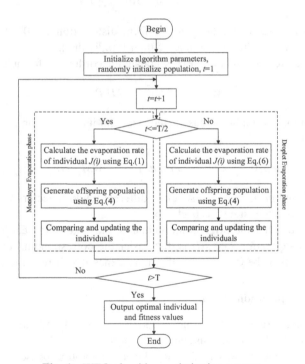

Fig. 1. WEO algorithm optimization process.

3 The Proposed Algorithm CUS-WEO

3.1 Monolayer Evaporation Phase Based on Classification Strategy

As shown in formula (4), the original individuals realize mutual communication and self-updating through the step size matrix S. Obviously, the calculation method of the step size determines the individual update mode, which has a greater impact on the performance of the algorithm. It can be seen from formula (5) that the step size S consists of two random individuals, from which the original individual learns. The search will inevitably be blindness, although a variety of populations will be produced. In other words, the original calculation method of the step size makes the algorithm's exploration ability stronger and the exploitation ability weaker, which is not conducive to improving the overall convergence speed and accuracy.

Since monolayer evaporation phase is the early stage of overall evolution, the effective balance between exploration and exploitation is the key to improve the convergence speed and accuracy of the algorithm. In order to take both abilities into account in the phase, the better individuals should learn from the best individual and carry out fine search around it to improve the algorithm's exploitation ability, while the poorer individuals should learn from a random individual to maintain the diversity of the population and explore the unknown areas.

Based on the above considerations, two different calculation methods of the step size for better and poorer individuals are designed in this paper, so as to improve the individual update mode and the overall performance of the algorithm. Taking the minimization problem as an example, the specific operations of the proposed algorithm are as follows:

① If $Fit(i) \leq Fitave$, the calculation method of step size is shown in formula (8):

$$S_{i,j} = rand \times \left(WM_{\text{best},j} - WM_{i,j}\right) + rand \times \left(WM_{r1,j} - WM_{i,j}\right), \qquad (8)$$

where $Fit(i)$ denotes the fitness value of the ith individual, and $Fitave$ denotes the average fitness value of all individuals, $r1$ is a random number selected from $\{1, 2...N\}$, and $r1 \neq best \neq i$.

② If $Fit(i) > Fitave$, the step size is calculated as shown in formula (9):

$$S_{i,j} = \phi_{i,j} \times \left(WM_{r2,j} - WM_{i,j}\right), \qquad (9)$$

where $r2 \in \{1, 2...N\}$ and $r2 \neq i$, and $\phi_{i,j}$ is a random number between $[-1, 1]$.

Compared with formula (5), the proposed classification strategy using formula (8) and (9) to calculate the step size of better and worse individuals has the following advantages: Firstly, the evolution information of the optimal individual is introduced in formula (8), so that the better individuals can strengthen the fine search around it, which enhances the ability of local exploitation and speeds up convergence; Secondly, by formula (9), the worse individuals can learn from random other individuals and the step factor is changed from rand to a random number in $[-1, 1]$, which is beneficial to increase random disturbance and improve the ability of global exploration.

3.2 Droplet Evaporation Phase Based on Unbiased Search Strategy

In the droplet evaporation phase, i.e. the later evolution stage, new individuals are found in the region with the original individual as the center and the step size S as the scope, by the formula (4) as well. Due to the difference between individuals, the search area centers determined by the base vectors may not be good enough, and because the original step size S consists of a disturbance term and the unidirectional disturbance factor rand, it will cause the disadvantage that the search range is closer to the base vector in many cases. Therefore, it is bound to be difficult to improve the convergence speed and accuracy in the late evolution.

In order to meet the requirements of improving solution accuracy at this stage, under the premise of avoiding premature maturity, the leading role of the optimal individual should be fully exerted, and new individuals should be generated in excellent areas. Usually, the best individual are surrounded by the best regions found at present, but if new individuals are searched directly based on the best individual, it will inevitably result in a smaller search area and all new individuals being very similar to the best individual, which is not conducive to achieving the desired results. In order to avoid over-biasing the mining area to the optimal individual or the current individual, the coordination between the optimal individual and the current individual can be considered to form the center of the excellent region. In addition, in view of improving the convergence accuracy and maintaining the diversity of the population, the number of disturbance terms and the search direction should be increased to expand the search scope centered on excellent individuals.

Based on the above ideas, an individual update strategy is designed for the droplet evaporation phase in this paper, as shown in formula (10).

$$WM_{inew,j} = \frac{WM_{best,j} + WM_{i,j}}{2} + S_{i,j} \times DEP_{i,j}, \tag{10}$$

$$S_{i,j} = \phi_{k1,j} \times \left(WM_{k1,j} - WM_{i,j}\right) + \phi_{k2,j} \times \left(WM_{k2,j} - WM_{i,j}\right), \tag{11}$$

Compared with the formula (4) for original droplet evaporation phase, the new search strategy proposed in this paper has the following advantages: Firstly, in Formula (10), the base vector composed of the optimal individual and the current individual is taken as the search benchmark, so the convergence speed is speeded up to some extent and the search is not biased in any direction, which is helpful to reduce the risk of premature. Secondly, in Formula (11), a new step size S consisting of two disturbance terms and multi-direction disturbance factors can expand the search range, so convergence accuracy and maintain population diversity can be improved.

3.3 CUS-WEO Algorithm Flow

The specific implementation steps of the water evaporation optimization algorithm based on classification and unbiased search are as follows:

Step 1. Set the size of the population to N, the dimension to d, the maximum number of iterations to T;
Step 2. Generate initial population individuals by using random method;
Step 3. Evaluate individuals, update the optimal individual and calculate the average fitness value of the current population;

Step 4. Perform the monolayer evaporation phase based on classification strategy in Sect. 2.1, to generate new population, compare old and new individuals, and select the fittest;

Step 5. Judge whether the number of iterations is greater than $T/2$, if so, proceed to Step 6, if not return to Step 3;

Step 6. Perform the droplet evaporation phase based on unbiased search strategy in Sect. 2.2, to generate new population, compare old and new individuals, and select the fittest;

Step 7. Judge whether the number of iterations reaches T, if reached, the fitness value of the optimal solution is output, if not return to *Step 6*.

4 Experiment and Result Analysis

To demonstrate the performance of the proposed algorithm, a series of comparative experiments in terms of convergence accuracy are carried out between CUS-WEO algorithm and WEO algorithm. Ten extendible benchmark functions f_1—f_{10} with diverse high dimensions and five benchmark functions f_{11}—f_{15} with the fixed low dimension are selected to make the experiment more representative.

The CUS-WEO algorithm and WEO algorithm are independently run on each function for 30 times. To make a fair comparison, the population size N of both algorithms is set to 50 and the max number of function evaluation on diverse high dimensional functions and fixed low dimensional functions is set to 80 000 and 8 000 respectively. The results are reported in Table 1, and for the sake of clarity, the best mean value results are highlighted in boldface.

Table 1. The results of convergence accuracy on all functions.

Function	Alg	d	Minimum	Mean	Maximum	SD
f_1 Sphere	WEO	30	0.0012	0.0025	0.0052	9.4139e−04
		50	0.3422	0.6838	1.1450	0.1973
		100	76.6477	103.9979	152.0910	17.7811
	CUS-WEO	30	1.2256e−46	**5.0548e−45**	3.4824e−44	8.9036e−45
		50	2.4749e−27	**1.8119e−26**	8.8777e−26	2.0320e−26
		100	2.4374e−11	**1.8394e−10**	6.3706e−10	1.3461e−10
f_2 Schwefel 2.22	WEO	30	0.0611	0.0995	0.1632	0.0264
		50	0.8599	1.1113	1.4723	0.1571
		100	10.8143	12.5294	14.9678	1.1284
	CUS-WEO	30	2.9146e−23	**1.4498e−22**	5.0342e−22	1.1775e−22
		50	5.7398e−14	**1.6249e−13**	4.8167e−13	1.0240e−13
		100	4.7697e−06	**1.0742e−05**	2.8310e−05	5.2724e−06

(*continued*)

Table 1. (*continued*)

Function	Alg	d	Minimum	Mean	Maximum	SD
f_3 SumSquares	WEO	30	1.7046e−04	3.4023e−04	7.4931e−04	1.3367e−04
		50	0.0496	0.1445	0.2724	0.0474
		100	28.6369	40.0878	62.1117	6.9008
	CUS-WEO	30	1.0605e−47	**6.9352e−46**	5.0821e−45	1.1941e−45
		50	3.0443e−28	**2.3322e−27**	9.5159e−27	1.8841e−27
		100	2.0740e−11	**6.8160e−11**	1.9253e−10	4.8416e−11
f_4 Dixon-Price	WEO	30	7.0717	11.3488	16.2929	2.5565
		50	120.6244	162.1387	206.8723	19.1729
		100	1.6651e+03	1.8632e+03	2.0381e+03	86.3717
	CUS-WEO	30	0.0082	**0.2257**	0.9501	0.2002
		50	1.2586	**3.7317**	12.0158	2.0852
		100	111.8371	**169.8576**	245.3166	33.8241
f_5 Elliptic	WEO	30	1.5703	5.4283	13.2616	2.7109
		50	649.8478	1.2963e+03	2.0060e+03	353.0935
		100	1.2469e+05	1.8427e+05	2.8148e+05	3.4679e+04
	CUS-WEO	30	1.2771e−43	**9.5403e−42**	8.6713e−41	1.6337e−41
		50	3.0263e−24	**3.8363e−23**	2.9410e−22	5.9410e−23
		100	3.4130e−08	**2.3393e−07**	9.3232e−07	2.1433e−07
f_6 Step	WEO	30	3.4847e−06	7.6627e−06	1.5081e−05	3.0927e−06
		50	0.0012	0.0019	0.0029	4.7421e−04
		100	0.1757	0.2719	0.4268	0.0600
	CUS-WEO	30	0	**4.1087e−34**	1.2326e−32	2.2504e−33
		50	6.1784e−30	**5.3502e−29**	3.8703e−28	7.1929e−29
		100	1.1059e−13	**4.2194e−13**	9.6181e−13	2.2943e−13
f_7 Griwank	WEO	30	0.0110	0.0485	0.0995	0.0258
		50	0.4857	0.6432	0.8050	0.0870
		100	1.6877	2.1276	2.4758	0.2145
	CUS-WEO	30	0	**6.6692e−09**	1.2510e−07	2.5430e−08
		50	0	**1.4869e−11**	3.0587e−10	5.6619e−11
		100	8.4092e−11	**0.0014**	0.0123	0.0033
f_8 Ackley	WEO	30	0.0592	0.1031	0.1957	0.0350
		50	0.4590	0.7189	1.0871	0.1426
		100	3.2522	3.5606	4.1596	0.2182
	CUS-WEO	30	6.2172e−15	**3.6944e−09**	1.0770e−07	1.9648e−08
		50	3.1086e−14	**1.1469e−13**	2.7267e−13	6.0736e−14
		100	1.3942e−06	**3.9821e−06**	1.0436e−05	1.7451e−06
f_9 Generalized penalizeed1	WEO	30	98.8108	1.2256e+05	7.7857e+05	2.0326e+05
		50	1.3028e+06	1.0033e+07	5.2056e+07	1.0240e+07
		100	1.8671e+07	8.6584e+07	2.3793e+08	5.4368e+07
	CUS-WEO	30	1.3498e−32	**7.3249e−04**	0.0110	0.0028
		50	2.2472e−22	**3.165e+03**	9.1437e+04	1.6676e+04
		100	67.0441	**5.4516e+06**	2.3140e+07	6.5602e+06

(*continued*)

Table 1. (*continued*)

Function	Alg	d	Minimum	Mean	Maximum	SD
f_{10} Generalized penalized2	WEO	30	0.0235	0.1411	0.4651	0.0851
		50	0.2528	0.5277	0.9029	0.1839
		100	1.4102	2.6415	4.0172	0.5620
	CUS-WEO	30	1.5705e−32	**1.5705e−32**	1.5705e−32	5.5674e−48
		50	1.1365e−29	**4.1883e−28**	1.8585e−27	5.4725e−28
		100	3.4590e−13	**1.3727e−09**	3.8254e−08	6.9704e−09
f_{11} Booth	WEO	2	1.0499e−08	5.0170e−07	3.6970e−06	7.4163e−07
	CUS−WEO	2	2.4250e−26	**2.3306e−23**	2.1957e−22	5.1236e−23
f_{12} Boachevsky111	WEO	2	2.0859e−06	1.7497e−04	0.0025	4.5174e−04
	CUS-WEO	2	0	**0**	0	0
f_{13} Boachevsky3	WEO	2	3.4127e−06	3.1993e−04	0.0017	4.2568e−04
	CUS−WEO	2	0	**0**	0	0
f_{14} Schaffer	WEO	2	3.7109e−04	0.0084	0.0097	0.0030
	CUS−WEO	2	3.6361e−06	**0.0016**	0.0097	0.0029
f_{15} Easom	WEO	2	−1.0000	−0.7333	0	0.4497
	CUS-WEO	2	−1	**−1.0000**	−1.0000	5.6055e−11

As shown in Table 1, on all benchmark functions and no matter how many dimensions the function is, the CUS-WEO achieves better results than WEO algorithm. CUS-WEO finds the global optimal solutions in some of the 30 runs on f_6 at $d = 30$, on f_7 at $d = 30, 50$, and on f_{15} at $d = 2$, and is able to find the global optimal solutions for all 30 runs on f_{12}, f_{13} at $d = 2$. Similarly, for remaining functions excluding f_4, f_9 at both $d = 50$ and 100, the solutions found by CUS-WEO are very close to their corresponding global optimal solutions. In contrast, the solution accuracy of WEO algorithm on these test functions is not ideal, indicating that the optimization ability of the algorithm needs to be improved.

The convergence curve by CUS-WEO and WEO algorithm on functions f_1, f_7, f_{10} at $d = 30$ are illustrated in Fig. 2, where the abscissa denotes the number of function evaluation (FES) and the ordinate represents the objective function value obtained by the algorithms under the FES. The steeper the curve is, the faster the convergence is. It is obvious that CUS-WEO has faster convergence speed than WEO algorithm on all functions.

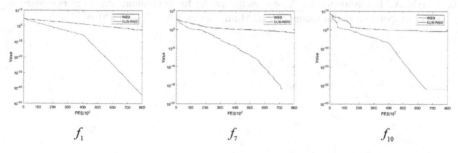

f_1 f_7 f_{10}

Fig. 2. The convergence curve of CUS-WEO and WEO algorithm on functions at $d = 30$.

5 Conclusion

In this paper, we proposed a water evaporation optimization algorithm based on classification and unbiased search. The algorithm has the following characteristics: (1) in monolayer evaporation phase, design two different calculation methods of the step size for better and poorer individuals to balance the local and global search capabilities of the algorithm; (2) in droplet evaporation phase, take unbiased search information consisting of the optimal individual and the current individual as the base vector and increase the number of disturbance terms and the search direction to improve the convergence accuracy in the late evolution. And in Sect. 3, a series of experiments are carried out on the 15 benchmark test functions. The experimental results show that the proposed algorithm is superior to WEO algorithms in terms of solution quality. Therefore, CUS-WEO algorithm has certain value in solving the engineering optimization problem.

References

1. Rashedi, E., Nezamabadi-pour, H., Saryazdi, S.: GSA: a gravitational search algorithm. Inf. Sci. **179**(13), 2232–2248 (2009)
2. Eskandar, H., Sadollah, A., Bahreininejad, A., Hamdi, M.: Water cycle algorithm–a novel metaheuristic optimization method for solving constrained engineering optimization problems. Comput. Struct. **110–111**(10), 151–166 (2012)
3. Kaveh, A., Mahdavi, V.R.: Colliding bodies optimization method for optimum discrete design of truss structures. Adv. Eng. Softw. **139**(7), 43–53 (2014)
4. Sun, W., Lin, A., Yu, H., Liang, Q., Wu, G.: All-dimension neighborhood based particle swarm optimization with randomly selected neighbors. Inf. Sci. **405**(C), 141–156 (2017)
5. Osaba, E., Diaz, F., Onieva, E.: Golden ball: a novel meta-heuristic to solve combinatorial optimization problems based on soccer concepts. Appl. Intell. **41**(1), 145–166 (2014)
6. Kaveh, A., Bakhshpoori, T.: Water evaporation optimization: a novel physically inspired optimization algorithm. Comput. Struct. **167**, 69–85 (2016)
7. Saha, A., Das, P., Chakraborty, A.K.: Water evaporation algorithm: a new metaheuristic algorithm towards the solution of optimal power flow. Eng. Sci. Technol. Int. J. **20**(6), 1540–1552 (2017)
8. Liang, Z., Hu, K., Zhu, Q., Zhu, Z.: An enhanced artificial bee colony algorithm with adaptive differential operators. Appl. Soft Comput. J. **58**, 480–494 (2017)
9. Kaveh, A., Bakhshpoori, T.: An accelerated water evaporation optimization formulation for discrete optimization of skeletal structures. Comput. Struct. **177**, 218–228 (2016)
10. Kaveh, A., Bakhshpoori, T.: A new metaheuristic for continuous structural optimization: water evaporation optimization. Struct. Multi. Optim. **54**(1), 23–43 (2016)

A Discrete Sine Cosine Algorithm
for Community Detection

Yongqi Zhao, Feng Zou[⊠], and Debao Chen

Huaibei Normal University, Huaibei 235000, China
zfemail@163.com

Abstract. As an important research area in complex networks, community detection problems (CDPs) have aroused widespread concern among researchers. Many heuristic optimization algorithms have been successfully utilized to solve CDPs. As a recently proposed heuristic optimization algorithm, the sine cosine algorithm has been successfully applied in many fields and achieved better performance compared with other algorithms. In this paper, a new discrete sine cosine algorithm (DSCA) is developed to solve community detection problems. DSCA are compared with FM, BGLL and GA on four real-world benchmark networks. Extensive experiments verify that our algorithm is effective and promising.

Keywords: Community detection · Sine cosine algorithm

1 Introduction

Complex systems in many cases are considered as complex networks [1], such as the ecological network, the neural network in the organism, and the political and economic networks among countries, and those of transportation and power that are closely related to daily life as well as the social relationship networks which are more complicated. A complex network includes a set of network vertices, which are closely connected within the community and sparsely connected among the communities. As an important structural feature of complex networks, the community structure is of great significance for understanding network functions, studying network topology, revealing the existing laws in networks and predicting network evolution.

With the in-depth research of community detection problems (CDPs) in complex networks, various algorithms have been developed. Traditional community detection algorithms include graph-based segmentation methods such as Kernighan-Lin (LK) algorithm [2] and spectral bisection method [3], and the hierarchical methods such as the Label Propagation Algorithm (LPA) [4] and the GN Algorithm [5]. Moreover, a fast modularity maximization algorithm [6] was also proposed to deal with community detection problems (CDPs).

Since the end of last century, the research on complex networks has developed rapidly in many disciplinary fields (such as finance, social science, computer science, ecology, etc.) due to its close relations to people's life and production. Specially, CDPs have aroused widespread concern among researchers and many evolutionary computing and swarm intelligent optimization algorithms have been utilized to work out

© Springer Nature Switzerland AG 2019
D.-S. Huang et al. (Eds.): ICIC 2019, LNCS 11643, pp. 35–44, 2019.
https://doi.org/10.1007/978-3-030-26763-6_4

CDPs in complex networks. To achieve a good detection performance, a new particle swarm optimizer was proposed by Cai et al. to optimize the modularity function [7]. Utilizing the new initialization and mutation strategies, a new discrete fireworks algorithm was developed by Guendouz et al. for solve CDPs [8]. To deal with CDPs, a new genetic algorithm with efficient initialization and searching strategies was employed by Guerrero et al. [9]. Inspired by the krill population optimization algorithm, Ahmed et al. proposed a discrete krill population optimization algorithm (AKHSO) by dynamically defining the number of communities [10]. Noveiri et al. integrated ant colony algorithm with fuzzy clustering to solve CDPs [11].

As a new intelligent optimization algorithm, due to its simple structure and easy to implement characteristics, Sine cosine algorithm and its variants have been widely developed in many disciplinary fields [12–15]. However, as far as we know, there is no research of using the SCA algorithm to detect the communities in complex networks till now. Based on these considerations, in this paper, a new discrete variant of sine cosine algorithm (DSCA) is developed to handle CDPs. The rest of the paper is structured as follows: CDPs are given in Sect. 2 and a brief description of SCA is given in Sect. 3. Section 4 presents a new discrete variant of SCA for solving CDPs. Simulation experiments are executed on several benchmark networks and the results of DSCA are compared with those of some other algorithms in Sect. 5. Conclusions are given in Sect. 6.

2 Community Detection Problems

On the basis of the nature of CDPs in complex networks, a graph structure G(V, E) is adopted to represent a complex network. Here $V = (v_1, v_2, \cdots, v_n)$ denotes vertices from the graph G and $E = \{e = (i,j) | i, j \in V\}$ denotes edges from the graph G. Any two vertices in V maybe correspond to an edge in E. Further, CDPs can be considered as: achieve a set of closely connected communities G_i subject to $G_1 \cup \ldots G_i \ldots \cup G_k = G$ and $G_1 \cap \ldots G_i \ldots \cap G_k = \emptyset$. Hence, CDPs can also be considered as a clustering problem, and they can be solved by utilizing clustering algorithms.

To evaluate the performance metric of community partitions, an appropriate quality function needs to be designed and utilized to guide the searching process of the community detection algorithm. The common quality metric is the modularity (Q) metric [6]. Modularity Q is a famous quality function developed by Girvan and Newman. Assume that the graph has a partition $\Omega = \{V_1, V_2, \cdots, V_C\}$ and V_i is the vertex set of subgraph $G_i (i = 1, 2, \cdots, C)$, the modularity (Q) density of this partition $\Omega = \{V_1, V_2, \cdots, V_C\}$ [16, 17] can be represented below:

$$Q = \sum_{c=1}^{c} \frac{L(V_i, V_i) - L(V_i, \overline{V_i})}{|V_i|} \tag{1}$$

where $L(V_1, V_2) = \sum_{i \in V_1, j \in V_2} A_{ij}$, $L(V_1, \overline{V_2}) = \sum_{i \in V_1, j \in \overline{V_2}} A_{ij}$, $\overline{V_2} = \Omega - V_2$.

3 Sine Cosine Algorithm

Sine cosine algorithm (SCA) [18] makes use of the mathematical model of sines and cosines functions to obtain the best solution. SCA can obtain a better balance of exploration and exploitation by using the random and/or adaptive parameters so as to avoid falling into local optima. In SCA, each individual is represented as $X_i = (x_{i1}, \ldots, x_{ij} \ldots, x_{iD})$ in the D-dimensional search space, the best individual in the t-th generation is expressed as P_j, and then the updating equation of this individual X_i is given as follows:

$$X_i^{t+1} = \begin{cases} X_i^t + [r_1 \times \sin(r_2) \times \left| r_3 P_j^t - X_i^t \right|, & r_4 < 0.5 \\ X_i^t + [r_1 \times \cos(r_2) \times \left| r_3 P_j^t - X_i^t \right|, & r_4 \geq 0.5 \end{cases} \tag{2}$$

where X_i^t represents the position of the search space in the t-th generation, and the parameter r_2 is a random number $[0, 2\pi]$. Parameters r_3 and r_4 are a random number of $[0, 2]$ and $[0, 1]$, respectively. Parameter r_1 is a linear decreasing function, and its expression is:

$$r_1 = a - a\frac{t}{T} \tag{3}$$

where a is generally set to 2, T is the maximum iteration times and t represents the current iteration number.

In SCA, parameter r_1 is used to obtain a better balance of exploration and exploitation. When $r_1 > 1$, the next individuals appears outside the current solution and target solution (exploration stage), and when $r_1 < 1$, the next generation of individuals appears between the current solution and target solution (exploitation stage). The parameter r_2 determines the step size of the next generation. When the parameter $r_3 > 1$, it indicates that the effect of the current optimal solution is enhanced; when the parameter $r_3 < 1$, it indicates that the effect of the current optimal solution is weakened. When the parameter r_4 is less than 0.5, the algorithm is iterated in a sine manner; otherwise, it is iterated in a cosine manner.

4 Proposed DSCA for Community Detection

This section detailed describes a new discrete variant of sine cosine algorithm (DSCA) for solving CDPs. First, a population with N individuals is initialized by a question-based random initialization strategy. Moreover, new trial individuals are generated by defining new updating rules. Furthermore, the better individual is maintained through greedy selection. Finally, when the termination demands are met, the above process ends; otherwise, the next generation updating process is performed.

Community detection problems usually involve dividing a network into subsets of vertices based on their similarity or other features linked with vertices and edges of graphs. Therefore, the most intuitive encoding scheme is to encode an individual into a real integer vector in which each element represents the clustering identification of this corresponding vertex. In addition, if the cluster of a vertex is equal to that of another one, these two vertices subject to the same community. Otherwise, they subject to different communities. Hence, each individual stands for a partition of the network. Assume that a network includes N vertices, and then an individual X_i can be shown as follows:

$$X_i = (X_{i1}, \ldots, X_{ij}, \ldots, X_{iN}) \tag{4}$$

where X_{ij} is the clustering identification of vertex j in X_i and it is initialized to a random integer in the range [1, N]. If vertex j and vertex k come from the same community, $X_{ij} = X_{ik}$.

In DSCA, a heuristic method based on label propagation [19] is utilized to initialize individuals. Figure 1 shows the example of discrete individual representation.

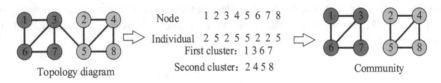

Fig. 1. An example of discrete individual representation

Assume that *Best* is defined as the best individual of the population, and then the searching process of the proposed DSCA algorithm is redesigned and its expression is given as follow:

$$X_i^{t+1} = \begin{cases} X_i^t \Phi[S(r_1 \times \sin(r_2) \times (r_3 \times Best \oplus X_i^t))], & r_4 < 0.5 \\ X_i^t \Phi[S(r_1 \times \cos(r_2) \times (r_3 \times Best \oplus X_i^t))], & r_4 \geq 0.5 \end{cases} \tag{5}$$

where $\oplus$ stands for XOR operation, and S function is describes in the following.

Suppose $Y = (y_1, y_2, \cdots, y_N)$ and $X = (x_1, x_2, \cdots, x_N)$, then $Y = S(X)$ in Eq. (5) can be calculated as follows:

$$y_i = \begin{cases} 1, & if \ rand(0, 1) < sigmoid(x_j) \\ 0, & otherwise \end{cases} \quad j = 1, 2, \ldots, N \tag{6}$$

where the sigmoid function [20] is expressed as follows:

$$sigmoid(x) = \frac{1}{1 + e^x} \tag{7}$$

The Φ operator is the important and key process to generate new individuals, and a Φ good operation process can help guide the searching process of the detection algorithm.

Suppose $Y = (y_1, y_2, \cdots, y_N)$ and $X = (x_1, x_2, \cdots, x_N)$, $Z = X\Phi Y$ can be defined as follows [21]:

$$Z_j = \begin{cases} x_j, & if\ y_i = 0 \\ Nbest_j, & otherwise \end{cases} \tag{8}$$

where $NBest_j$ stands for the label identifier that most neighborhood individuals in the j-th vertex have.

In addition, the locus-based adjacency mutation is utilized to maintain the diversity of individuals.

5 Simulation Experiment

To test the validity of DSCA, four real-world networks were simulated and compared with some representative detection algorithms based on modularity optimization such as FM [6], BGLL [22] and GA [23]. In FM, each vertex is an isolated vertex of a community and then the two communities whose amalgamation produces the largest modularity are merged. The algorithm is repeated until no further improvement can be achieved. In BGLL, the vertices or the communities of the network are merged with their neighbors when the modularity is the largest. The algorithm is repeated until no further improvement can be achieved. In GA, a special locus-based adjacency encoding scheme is used to represent the community partitions and this encoding scheme enables the algorithm to determine the number of communities adaptively and automatically. All algorithms were independently run for 20 times to reduce statistical errors. For GA and DSCA, the population size is 100 and the algorithm terminates when the maximum iterative times reach 500. For GA, the crossover probability is 0.8, and the mutation probability is 0.2.

5.1 Real-World Networks

In this paper, four real-world benchmark networks are utilized to assess the detection performance of DSCA and they are described as the following. Karate network consists of 34 karate club members [24]. During these two years, the club was split into two nearly identical groups as a result of disagreements between the manager and the coach. Dolphins network involves 62 bottlenose dolphins that have spent seven years in New Zealand's fantastic fjords, and it is established on the basis of social acquaintance [25]. Networks naturally fall into two broad categories: males and females. Football network consists of 12 American college football teams and it includes 115 vertices and 616 sides [26]. Polbooks network represents a network of online booksellers that buy books about American politics from amazon and it include 105 vertices represented 105 books [27].

5.2 Comparison of Simulation Results

In this section, DSCA algorithm is compared with classical community detection algorithms (i.e., FM, BGLL and GA) for four real-world benchmark networks. Modularity Q obtained by all detection algorithms are given in Table 1.

Table 1. Modularity Q obtained for four real-world networks.

Algorithm	Q	Karate	Dolphins	Football	Polbooks
FM	Mean	0.3807	0.5014	0.5766	0.5024
	Std	0.0000	0.0000	0.0000	0.0000
BGLL	Mean	**0.4211**	0.5188	**0.6046**	0.4986
	Std	0.0000	0.0000	0.0000	0.0000
GA	Mean	0.4142	0.4983	0.5882	0.5154
	Std	0.0044	0.0046	0.0073	0.0087
DSCA	Mean	0.4198	**0.5266**	0.5519	**0.5261**
	Std	0.0000	0.0012	0.0098	0.0011

According to Table 1, for the Karate network, Modularity Q value obtained by BGLL is the largest and it is 0.4211. It indicates that BGLL algorithm has the best optimization result for Karate network. Modularity Q value obtained by DSCA is 0.4198, and it is better than 0.3807 and 0.4142 obtained by FM and GA, respectively. The structure with the highest Q value obtained by DSCA is shown in Fig. 2. From Fig. 2, it can be seen that the Karate network can be divided into four communities when Modularity Q has the highest for DSCA.

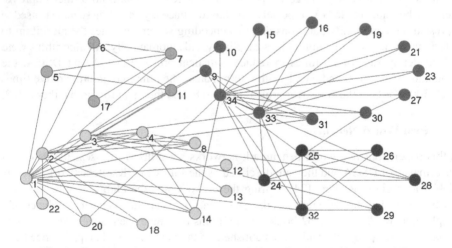

Fig. 2. Karate network structure with the largest Q value obtained by DSCA

According to Table 1, for the Dolphins network, Modularity Q obtained by DSCA is 0.5266. It indicates that DSCA can find the strongest community structure for the Dolphins network. Modularity Q values obtained by FM, BGLL and GA were 0.5014, 0.5188 and 0.4983 respectively and they are lower than that of DSCA. The structure with the highest Q value obtained by DSCA is shown in Fig. 3. From Fig. 3, it can be seen that the Dolphins network can be divided into four communities when Modularity Q has the highest for DSCA.

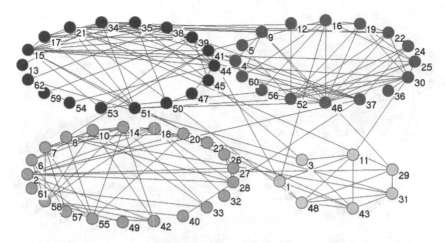

Fig. 3. Dolphins network structure with the highest Q value obtained by DSCA

According to Table 1, for the Football network, BGLL has the largest Modularity Q with 0.6046 and it indicates that it finds the strongest community structure. Modularity Q values obtained by FM, GA and DSCA are 0.5766, 0.5882 and 0.5519, respectively. It is obvious that our proposed DSCA has the worst performance for this network. The structure with the highest Q value obtained by DSCA is shown in Fig. 4. From Fig. 4, it can be seen that the Dolphins network can be divided into eleven communities when Modularity Q has the highest for DSCA.

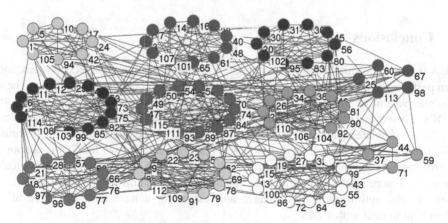

Fig. 4. Football network structure with the highest Q value obtained by DSCA

According to Table 1, for the Polbooks network, DSCA has the largest value in term of Modularity Q with 0.5261. It indicates that it can find the strongest community structure. FM, BGLL and GA can obtain Modularity Q values with 0.5024, 0.4986 and 0.5154 respectively. The structure with the highest Q value obtained DSCA is shown in Fig. 5. From Fig. 5, it can be seen that the Polbooks network can be divided into four communities when Modularity Q has the highest for DSCA.

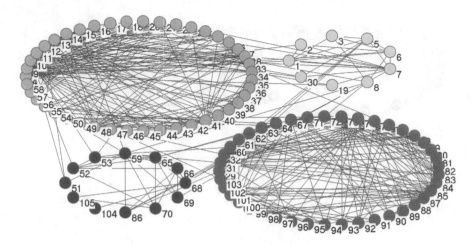

Fig. 5. Polbooks network structure with the highest Q value obtained by DSCA

Based on the above analysis, we can observe that DSCA can obtain the best partition for Dolphins and Polbooks networks, and it is better than FM and GA for all networks except the Football network. In additional, BGLL is better than DSCA for Karate and Football networks. This may be due to the fact that the search strategy of the algorithm needs to be further improved. Hence, it is clearly known that DSCA is a feasible and effective method for CDPs in complex networks, although DSCA may be not always the best performance compared with BGLL and GA.

6 Conclusions

SCA is one of the simple and effective population-based optimization technologies, and can perform well when solving many complex optimization issues. In this paper, a new discrete variant of sine cosine algorithm (DSCA) has been employed to deal with CDPs. To test and evaluate the efficiency of DSCA, four real-world benchmark networks are simulated and the results are compared with those of some other algorithms. The experimental results show that DSCA is feasible and effective for CDPs, although it still needs to be improved compared with BGLL for Karate network and Football network. Future works should include modifying the updating operators of DSCA to improve the optimization performance and extending a new multi-objective SCA algorithm to deal with CDPs.

Acknowledgment. This research was partially supported by National Natural Science Foundation of China (61572224), Anhui Provincial Natural Science Foundation (1708085MF140), the Natural Science Foundation in colleges and universities of Anhui Province (Grant No. KJ2019A0593) and Graduate Innovation Foundation of Huaibei Normal University (ycx201901007).

References

1. Amaral, L.A.N., Ottino, J.M.: Complex networks. Eur. Phys. J. B **38**(2), 147–162 (2004)
2. Ezhilarasi, G.A., Swarup, K.S.: Network decomposition using Kernighan-Lin strategy aided harmony search algorithm. Swarm Evol. Comput. **7**, 1–6 (2012)
3. Pothen, A., Simon, H.D., Liou, K.P.: Partitioning sparse matrices with eigenvectors of graphs. SIAM J. Matrix Anal. Appl. **11**(3), 430–452 (1990)
4. Zhang, X.K., Fei, S., Song, C., et al.: Label propagation algorithm based on local cycles for community detection. Int. J. Mod. Phys. B **29**(05), 1550029 (2015)
5. Girvan, M., Newman, M.: Community structure in social and biological networks. Proc. Natl. Acad. Sci. **99**(12), 7821–7826 (2002)
6. Clauset, A., Newman, M.E.J., Moore, C.: Finding community structure in very large networks. Phys. Rev. E **70**(6), 066111 (2004)
7. Cai, X., et al.: An algorithm Q-PSO for community detection in complex networks. In: 2017 16th International Symposium on Distributed Computing and Applications to Business, Engineering and Science (DCABES), pp. 76–79. IEEE Computer Society (2017)
8. Guendouz, M., Amine, A., Hamou, R.M.: A discrete modified fireworks algorithm for community detection in complex networks. Appl. Intell. **46**(2), 373–385 (2016)
9. Guerrero, M., Montoya, F.G., Baños, R., et al.: Adaptive community detection in complex networks using genetic algorithms. Neurocomputing **266**, 101–113 (2017)
10. Ahmed, K., Hafez, A.I., Hassanien, A.E.: A discrete krill herd optimization algorithm for community detection. In: 11th International Computer Engineering Conference (ICENCO), pp. 297–302. IEEE (2015)
11. Noveiri, E., Naderan, M., Alavi, S.E.: Community detection in social networks using ant colony algorithm and fuzzy clustering. In: International Conference on Computer & Knowledge Engineering, pp. 73–79. IEEE (2015)
12. Attia, A.-F., El Sehiemy, R.A., Hasanien, H.M.: Optimal power flow solution in power systems using a novel Sine-Cosine algorithm. Int. J. Electr. Power Energy Syst. **99**, 331–343 (2018)
13. Rajesh, K.S., Dash, S.S.: Load frequency control of autonomous power system using adaptive fuzzy based PID controller optimized on improved sine cosine algorithm. J. Ambient Intell. Human. Comput. **10**, 2361–2373 (2018)
14. Reddy, K.S., Panwar, L.K., Panigrahi, B., et al.: A new binary variant of sine–cosine algorithm: development and application to solve profit-based unit commitment problem. Arab. J. Sci. Eng. **43**(8), 4041–4056 (2017)
15. Rizk-Allah, R.M.: An improved sine–cosine algorithm based on orthogonal parallel information for global optimization. Soft Comput. **23**, 7135–7161 (2019)
16. Li, Z., Liu, J.: A multi-agent genetic algorithm for community detection in complex networks. Physica A **449**, 336–347 (2016)
17. Gong, M., et al.: Community detection in networks by using multiobjective evolutionary algorithm with decomposition. Physica A: Stat. Mech. Appl. **391**(15), 4050–4060 (2012)
18. Mirjalili, S.: SCA: a sine cosine algorithm for solving optimization problems. Knowl.-Based Syst. **96**, 120–133 (2016)
19. Gong, M., et al.: An improved memetic algorithm for community detection in complex networks. In: Evolutionary Computation, pp. 1–8. IEEE (2012)
20. Kennedy, J., Eberhart, R.C.: A discrete binary version of the particle swarm algorithm. In: IEEE International Conference on Systems, Man, and Cybernetics. Computational Cybernetics and Simulation, vol. 5, pp. 4104–4108. IEEE (1997)

21. Radicchi, F., et al.: Defining and identifying communities in networks. Proc. Natl. Acad. Sci. USA **101**(9), 2658–2663 (2003)
22. Blondel, V.D., Guillaume, J.L., Lambiotte, R., Lefebvre, E.: Fast unfolding of communities in large networks. J. Stat. Mech.: Theory Exp. **10**, P10008 (2008)
23. Shi, C., Yan, Z.Y., Wang, Y., et al.: A genetic algorithm for detecting communities in large-scale complex networks. Adv. Complex Syst. **13**(1), 3–17 (2010)
24. Ji, J., Jiao, L., Yang, C., et al.: A multiagent evolutionary method for detecting communities in complex networks. Comput. Intell. **32**(4), 587–614 (2016)
25. Lusseau, D., Schneider, K., Boisseau, O.J., et al.: The bottlenose dolphin community of doubtful sound features a large proportion of long-lasting associations. Behav. Ecol. Sociobiol. **54**(4), 396–405 (2003)
26. Li, W.: Visualizing network communities with a semi-definite programming method. Inf. Sci. **321**, 1–13 (2015)
27. Atzmueller, M., Doerfel, S., Mitzlaff, F.: Description-oriented community detection using exhaustive subgroup discovery. Inf. Sci. **329**, 965–984 (2016)

Automatical Pulmonary Nodule Detection by Feature Contrast Learning

Jie Chang[1,2], Minquan Ye[2], Naijie Gu[1(✉)], Xiaoci Zhang[1],
Chuanwen Lin[3], and Hong Ye[1]

[1] School of Computer Science and Technology,
University of Science and Technology of China,
Hefei 230000, People's Republic of China
{cjfuture, zxiaoci, yh}@mail.ustc.edu.cn,
gunj@ustc.edu.cn
[2] Research Center of Health Big Data Mining and Applications,
Wannan Medical College, Wuhu 241002, Anhui, People's Republic of China
ymq@wnmc.edu.cn
[3] Department of Computer Science and Technology, Hefei University,
Hefei 230601, People's Republic of China
lcw@mail.ustc.edu.cn

Abstract. With regard to pulmonary nodule detection, due to the similar texture and shape as particular tissues, it is difficult for Computer-Aided Detection (CAD) system in detecting pulmonary nodule with both high accuracy and sensitivity. To address this problem, we design a 3D automated pulmonary nodule detection where a auxiliary 3D generative adversarial network is embedded. This well-trained auxiliary component that fully learns volumetrically contextual information of nodule and non-nodule structure, is exploited for each input sample of detection model to generate a derivative which only preserve background context by removing all the nodules. By learning the feature contrast between each input and its derivative, our detection model achieves competitive performance to state-of-the-art approaches for the pulmonary nodule detection task.

Keywords: Pulmonary nodule detection · Generative adversarial network · Multi-scale features

1 Introduction

According to the latest statistics from world health organization (WHO), lung cancer is the cancer disease with the highest morbidity and mortality, which brings a great threat to human survival and life. In 2017, there are about 800,000 new patients with lung cancer in China, and the death toll was 700,000, accounting for 19% and 20.8% of the total cancer incidence and mortality. The lesions of lung cancer, which appear nodular, typically originate in the lung parenchymal area. Accordingly, detecting pulmonary nodules with low-dose computed tomography (CT) at early stage is significant for a good prognosis of the disease. Although manually screening CT images has proven effective in expediting pulmonary tumor prognosis and diagnosis, radiologists are apt

© Springer Nature Switzerland AG 2019
D.-S. Huang et al. (Eds.): ICIC 2019, LNCS 11643, pp. 45–53, 2019.
https://doi.org/10.1007/978-3-030-26763-6_5

to be overwhelmed by this time-consuming and repeatable workload. This demonstrates the necessity to develop a competent CAD system.

Since Krizhevsky and Hinton [1] prove the potential of deep neural network in image processing area. 'Feature engineering' is prone to 'network engineering' which can extract more abstract non-linear features without parametric distribution hypothesis.

A classic method proposed by Setio et al. observes nodule candidates from 9 different directions and provides diagnosis by synthesizing all the information [2]. Ding et al. attempted to merge the adjacent 3 CT slices to detect lung nodule with high recall, and reduced false positives with the 3D information around the candidate nodules [4]. However, models fed by non-3D images might loss the 3D context information of CT images [5]. The development of high speed and large capacity computing resources for the past few years makes 3D convolutional networks possible. Dou et al. employs 3D fully convolutional network (FCN) to generate proposals and a 3D CNN based binary classifier for candidate screening with online sample filtering scheme [6]. Zhu et al. [13] designs a 3D Faster RCNN based on the 3D U-net architecture to propose candidate region firstly, then trains a classifier for false positive screening.

Automatic pulmonary nodule detection suffers from two hardships in achieving the performance of radiologists with years of training and experience. Firstly, it is difficult to distinguish nodules from the similar tissues in appearance. Variations of nodule size, shape, density and anatomical context set up the second obstacle.

To this end, we made efforts on designing a perceptive architecture which can perceive distinguishable features between nodules and non-nodules. Experiments showed that our model can operate with high sensitivity while preserving high specificity.

2   Methods

Our framework incorporates two parts: 3D GAN model and 3D detector model. For each input patch of the detector, 3D GAN model induces a derivative, which is fabricated by nodule-to-background generator tt to remove all nodules if input patch has any.

2.1   3D GAN

Generative Adversarial Network (GAN) proposed by Ian Goodfellow [7], typically consists of a generator and a discriminator. The generator captures the potential distribution of real data samples and generates new samples into input sample space of discriminator, which is a classifier that discriminates whether the input is real or fake. In our 3D Generative Adversarial Network (3D GAN), the generator G maps a $32 \times 32 \times 32$ nodule cube z to an object $G(z)$ in the same size, which only preserve background information of z. The discriminator D determines whether input y is counterfeited by the generator with a confidence value $D(y)$.

The optimization process of GAN is a minmax game process with the optimization function presented as:

$$\min_{G} \max_{D} V(D, G) = E_{x \sim p_{background}}[\log D(x)] + E_{z \sim p_{nodule}}[\log(1 - D(G(z)))] \quad (1)$$

where x is a $32 \times 32 \times 32$ cube without any nodule, and z is a $32 \times 32 \times 32$ cube with a nodule in the center. By optimizing generator and discriminator against each other iteratively, the results of V would finally converge to Nash equilibrium point.

Enlightened by Radford et al. [8], the generator and discriminator are all composed of convolutional and deconvolutional layers as shown in the left of Fig. 1. The framework of generator is encoder-decoder-like with five convolutional and three deconvolutional layers. The first three convolutional layers serve as encoder part while the last three deconvolutional ones as decoder part with a Tanh activation function at the end. The discriminator's architecture includes 4 convolutional layers with a sigmoid activation function at the end for binary classification. Except for the last layer, the other convolutional and deconvolutional layers in two architecture are followed by Leaky ReLU [10]. Leaky parameter is set to 0.05. More structure details is listed in Table 1.

Table 1. Architecture of 3D GAN

Generator			Discriminator		
Kernel	Stride	Padding	Kernel	Stride	Padding
conv 4 $\times$ 4 $\times$ 4 $\times$ 64	2	1	conv 4 $\times$ 4 $\times$ 4 $\times$ 64	2	1
conv 4 $\times$ 4 $\times$ 4 $\times$ 128	2	1	conv 4 $\times$ 4 $\times$ 4 $\times$ 128	2	1
conv 4 $\times$ 4 $\times$ 4 $\times$ 256	2	1	conv 4 $\times$ 4 $\times$ 4 $\times$ 256	2	1
conv 3 $\times$ 3 $\times$ 3 $\times$ 256	1	1	conv 4 $\times$ 4 $\times$ 4 $\times$ 1	1	0
conv 3 $\times$ 3 $\times$ 3 $\times$ 256	1	1			
deconv 4 $\times$ 4 $\times$ 4 $\times$ 128	2	1			
deconv 4 $\times$ 4 $\times$ 4 $\times$ 64	2	1			
deconv 4 $\times$ 4 $\times$ 4 $\times$ 1	2	1			

2.2 3D Detector Model

The detector model we chose is based on Single Shot Multi-box Detector (SSD) [11]. This U-net-like structure illustrated in the right of Fig. 1, integrates region proposal network and binary classifier network into one-stage framework in an more effective and efficient way. The input samples of the detector are $96 \times 96 \times 96$ cubes cropped from preprocessed CT images. This architecture can learn the multi-scale features for varied nodule detection task. As the feature maps are downsampling first and then upsampling, the shortcuts between corresponding layers can not only fuse the multi-level and multi-scale features, thus saving the memory consumption, but avoid gradient vanishing in deep architecture as well.

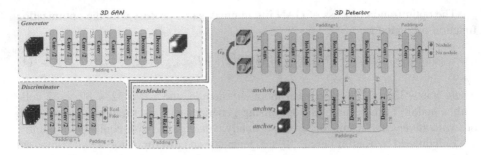

Fig. 1. 3D detector model

Just like the 3D GAN model, the detector architecture only consists of convolutional and deconvolutional layers, each of which is followed by residual module except for last two convolutional layers. The encoder part uses convolutional layers with stride two instead of pooling layers. Deconvolution layers are employed in the decoder part. Dropout tactic is used for the second last convolutional layer with dropout probability 0.5. Last layer is used for voxel-wise classification and regression. According to spheroidal property of nodules and the distribution of nodules' diameter as presented by Fig. 2, anchors with three scales ([5, 10, 20]) and a single aspect ratio [1:1:1] are chosen.

During training session, according to overlap ratio between each anchor and ground-truth bounding boxes, each anchor is allocated with three flag values [1, 0, 1], two of which ([0, 1]) for binary classification. Anchors with the highest intersection over union (IoU) or IoU higher than 0.6 are labeled with 1 as positive samples while those with IoU less than 0.1 are consider as negative with label 0. The other anchors are labeled with 1 and ignored during the training process. Noticeably, each input of detector has its background derivative generated by 3D GAN. Obviously, each anchor from derivative, which has not any nodule, is labeled 0. We only choose anchors whose corresponding anchors in the other input are labeled 1. These anchors are considered to incorporate context information around nodules.

For each anchor i, the prediction consists of five elements. The first one, denoted as p_i, indicates the probability for the anchor being positive. The remaining four elements, denoted as t_i and defined as Eq. 2, stand for nodule relative position and size.

$$t_i = \left(\frac{x - x_a}{d_a}, \frac{y - y_a}{d_a}, \frac{z - z_a}{d_a}, \log\left(\frac{d}{d_a}\right) \right) \qquad (2)$$

where (x, y, z, d) stand for three coordinates of the predicted nodule's center and its diameter in 3D volume space. (x_a, y_a, z_a, d_a) denote the coordinates and scale of the anchor i.

Accordingly, the multi-task loss function L for the anchor i is defined as:

$$L(p_i, t_i) = \gamma L_{cls}(p_i, p_i^*) + p_i^* L_{reg}(t_i, t_i^*) \tag{3}$$

$$t_i^* = \left(\frac{x^* - x_a}{d_a}, \frac{y^* - y_a}{d_a}, \frac{z^* - z_a}{d_a}, \log\left(\frac{d^*}{d_a}\right) \right) \tag{4}$$

where classification loss L_{cls} quantifies whether the current box is a nodule or not, while regression loss L_{reg} is calculated on nodule relative position and size. pi is the predicted probability for anchor i being a nodule while p^* is the ground truth label. The tradeoff super parameter γ is set to 0.5. (x^*, y^*, z^*, d^*) are the ground-truth coordinates and diameter of the nodule. For L_{cls}, we used binary cross entropy loss function. For L_{reg}, we used smooth L_1 regression loss function.

3 Experiments

3.1 Datasets

LUNA16 dataset is a subset of the LIDC-IDRI dataset [12], which is the largest public dataset for pulmonary nodules. For facilitating nodule detection, LUNA16 dataset removes 130 deficient CTs (such as those slice thickness greater than 2.5 mm, slice spacing inconsistent or slices missed) from 1018 samples of LIDC-IDRI dataset. Afterward, LUNA16 explicitly gives the patient-level 10-fold cross validation split of 888 CTs set. For lowering difficulty in the small target detection, nodules smaller than 3 mm are ignored in evaluation system.

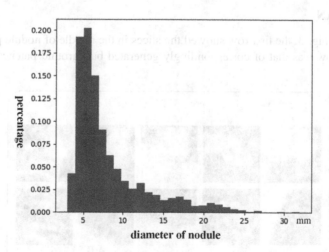

Fig. 2. Diameter distribution of nodules

We perform 10-fold cross validation on both models with training set derived from LUNA16 dataset According to the distribution of nodules' diameter as shown in Fig. 2, we choose $32 \times 32 \times 32$ as the input size of 3D GAN. Half of training samples are cropped from LUNA16 with nodule at the center while the other half without nodules are cropped in size $32 \times 32 \times 32$ directly from non-nodule regions. Due to the GPU memory limitation, $96 \times 96 \times 96$ is chosen as input size of the detector model. Samples in training set are cropped in this size directly from CT samples of LUNA16. On each training epoch of detection model, 3D GAN model replaces every nodule region within input data patch of detection model with generated background cubes

3.2 Configuration

Our architectures are implemented on the GPU server with eight Nvidia K40 GPU. The only augmentation method for 3D GAN is random rotation from 0 to 360° along any of the three axis. In 3D detector model, several popular augmentation methods are applied (e.g., flipping, randomly scale from 0.75 to 1.25). Rotation is not adopted lest a nodule at the corner might be lost. For 3D GAN model, during 4×10^4 epochs of training stage, each epoch includes both discriminator's and generator's gradient updates using Adam optimization with their initial learning rate both set as 0.0001 and β as [0.5, 0.999]. Learning rates are reduced to one tenth per 5,000 iterations. The training of 3D detector model iterates for 200 epochs using SGD optimization with 0.9 of momentum and 1×10^{-4} of weight decay. The initial learning rate is 0.01, then decreased to one tenth per 50 epochs.

4   Results

4.1   3D GAN

As shown in Fig. 3, the first row showed the slices in the middle of nodule patches and the second row was that of correspondingly generated background patches.

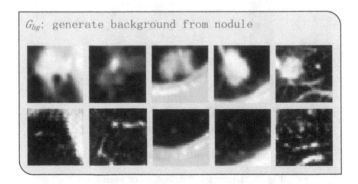

Fig. 3. Background generated: the first row shows the slices in the middle of nodule patches and the second row is that of correspondingly generated background patches.

From the second image of the fifth column, 3D GAN could preserve features of vessels below the nodule in the first image. In order to make generated cubes more indistinguishable, 3D GAN was opt to replace the nodule region with diffuse bubble texture, which was the most common feature of lung parenchyma.

3D GAN could accurately remove nodule-related data and only preserve context information. Noticeably, the model was capable of handling the overlap between nodule and lung wall presented in the first column of Fig. 3.

4.2   3D Detector

Officially LUNA16 considered a predicted candidate as a true positive if its center was located inside a true nodule. The evaluation metric for LUNA16 dataset was called free receiver operation characteristic (FROC), which measured the detection recall rate at seven average false positive rates per scan, specifically, 0.125, 0.25, 0.5, 1, 2, 4, 8. The average of the seven detection recall rates was considered as a competition performance metric (CPM) score that is used to evaluate the performance of models.

Some other three state-of-the-art architectures were used as baselines. 3D RES and 3D DPN [13] both proposed by Zhu et al. achieved comparable performance as top-ranked detector designed by Dou et al. [6]. The FROC performances of these models on LUNA16 was visualized in Fig. 4. All the seven recall rates in the FROC and CPM score were presented in Table 2. From Table 2, the ranking of CPM scores of all models kept consistent with AUC (Area Under Curve) of FROCs showed in Fig. 4. Intrinsically two-stage framework such as Dou et al. were more flexible in adjusting the trade-off between sensitivity and specificity than those without any false positive nodule reduction stage as the other three. 3D DPN was superior to Dou et al. in CPM scores due to the former achieved better performance in three rate points, 0.125, 0.25 and 0.5. This phenomenon indicated that the feature descriptors generated by 3D DPN architecture had more specificity and less generalization quality. Comparatively, the performance of ours is more convincing at last five points of the average number of false positives. It was worth noting that the input of architecture was the main contrast between 3D RES and ours. Our model can extract features from one input with nodules and the other only with the context of the nodules. The superiority of our model justify effective learning from the contrast between these features.

Table 2. FROC points and CPM score

Model	0.125	0.25	0.5	1	2	4	8	CPM score
Dou et al.	0.659	0.745	0.819	0.865	0.906	0.933	0.946	0.839
3D RES	0.662	0.746	0.815	0.864	0.902	0.918	0.932	0.834
3D DPN	**0.692**	**0.769**	0.824	0.865	0.893	0.917	0.933	0.842
Ours	0.667	0.744	**0.840**	**0.881**	**0.915**	**0.940**	**0.960**	**0.859**

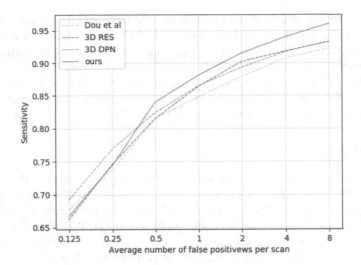

Fig. 4. FROC of four models

5 Conclusion

In this work, we presented a 3D SSD-based model with auxiliary nodule-removing GAN for computer-aided detection of pulmonary nodules from volumetric CT scans. It is shown that learning the feature contrast between each input and its derivative without nodules, can reinforce capability of distinguishing 3D multi-level contextual information of nodule structure from other similar tissues. Experiment on the LUNA16 challenge demonstrate impressive efficacy of the proposed approach for the nodule detection.

Acknowledgement. This work was supported by the National Natural Science Foundation of China [Grant numbers 61672386]; the Anhui Provincial Natural Science Foundation of China [Grant numbers 1708085MF142]; the Major Research Project Breeding Foundation of Wannan Medical College [Grant numbers WK2017Z01]; ANHUI Province Key Laboratory of Affective Computing and Advanced Intelligent Machine [Grant numbers ACAIM180202]; the Anhui Provincial Humanities and Social Science Foundation of China [Grant numbers SK2018A0198].

References

1. Krizhevsky, A., Sutskever, I., Hinton, G.E.: ImageNet classification with deep convolutional neural networks. In: Advances in Neural Information Processing Systems, pp. 1097–1105 (2012)
2. Setio, A.A.A., et al.: Pulmonary nodule detection in ct images: false positive reduction using multi-view convolutional networks. IEEE Trans. Med. Imaging **35**(5), 1160–1169 (2016)
3. Tang, H., Kim, D.R., Xie, X.: Automated pulmonary nodule detection using 3D deep convolutional neural networks. In: 2018 IEEE 15th International Symposium on Biomedical Imaging (ISBI 2018), pp. 523–526. IEEE (2018)

4. Ding, J., Li, A., Hu, Z., Wang, L.: Accurate pulmonary nodule detection in computed tomography images using deep convolutional neural networks. In: Descoteaux, M., Maier-Hein, L., Franz, A., Jannin, P., Collins, D.L., Duchesne, S. (eds.) MICCAI 2017. LNCS, vol. 10435, pp. 559–567. Springer, Cham (2017). https://doi.org/10.1007/978-3-319-66179-7_64
5. Zhang, L., et al.: Online modeling of esthetic communities using deep perception graph analytics. IEEE Trans. Multimedia 20(6), 1462–1474 (2018)
6. Dou, Q., Chen, H., Jin, Y., Lin, H., Qin, J., Heng, P.-A.: Automated pulmonary nodule detection via 3D ConvNets with online sample filtering and hybrid-loss residual learning. In: Descoteaux, M., Maier-Hein, L., Franz, A., Jannin, P., Collins, D.L., Duchesne, S. (eds.) MICCAI 2017. LNCS, vol. 10435, pp. 630–638. Springer, Cham (2017). https://doi.org/10.1007/978-3-319-66179-7_72
7. Goodfellow, I., et al.: Generative adversarial nets. In: Advances in Neural Information Processing Systems, pp. 2672–2680 (2014)
8. Radford, A., Metz, L., Chintala, S.: Unsupervised representation learning with deep convolutional generative adversarial networks. arXiv preprint arXiv:1511.06434 (2015)
9. Ioffe, S., Szegedy, C.: Batch normalization: accelerating deep network training by reducing internal covariate shift. arXiv preprint arXiv:1502.03167 (2015)
10. He, K., Zhang, X., Ren, S., Sun, J.: Delving deep into rectifiers: surpassing human-level performance on ImageNet classification. In: Proceedings of the IEEE International Conference on Computer Vision, pp. 1026–1034 (2015)
11. Liu, W., et al.: SSD: single shot MultiBox detector. In: Leibe, B., Matas, J., Sebe, N., Welling, M. (eds.) ECCV 2016. LNCS, vol. 9905, pp. 21–37. Springer, Cham (2016). https://doi.org/10.1007/978-3-319-46448-0_2
12. Armato III, S.G., et al.: The lung image database consortium (LIDC) and image database resource initiative (IDRI): a completed reference database of lung nodules on CT scans. Med. Phys. 38(2), 915–931 (2011)
13. Zhu, W., Liu, C., Fan, W., Xie, X.: DeepLung: deep 3D dual path nets for automated pulmonary nodule detection and classification. arXiv preprint arXiv:1801.09555 (2018)
14. Shrivastava, A., Gupta, A., Girshick, R.: Training region-based object detectors with online hard example mining. In: Proceedings of the IEEE Conference on Computer Vision and Pattern Recognition, pp. 761–769 (2016)
15. Lin, T.-Y., Goyal, P., Girshick, R., He, K., Dollár, P.: Focal loss for dense object detection. IEEE Trans. Pattern Anal. Mach. Intell.

Unsupervised Cross-Domain Person Re-identification Based on Style Transfer

Yanwen Chong[1], Chengwei Peng[1], Jingjing Zhang[2],
and Shaoming Pan[1(✉)]

[1] State Key Laboratory of Information Engineering in Surveying,
Mapping and Remote Sensing, Wuhan University, Wuhan 430079, China
pansm@whu.edu.cn
[2] School of Electrical Engineering and Automation, Anhui University,
Hefei 230601, China

Abstract. Person re-identification (person Re-ID) is mostly viewed as an image retrieval problem across different cameras. Most of existing models have achieved significant improvement on single-domain setting but failed to generalize to new domain due to the image style variations between domains. In this work, we aim to adapt a model trained on source domain to unlabeled target domain without significant performance drop. Thus, a novel style transfer framework that allows us to separate image style from content is proposed in Re-ID. Firstly, the source domain image is transferred to the target style while retaining the ID information. Then the source domain images and transferred images are combined to train a style-independent Re-ID model. Experiments show that we achieved higher performance of unsupervised cross-domain person Re-ID on the Market-1501 and DukeMTMC-reID datasets.

Keywords: Person Re-ID · Unsupervised cross-domain · Style transfer · Image retrieval · Deep learning

1 Introduction

Person re-identification (Re-ID) is a retrieve task on non-overlapping surveillance camera views. In other words, given an interesting people image under one camera, Re-ID returns all possible images that belong to the same people under other cameras [1]. With the development of deep learning, supervised single domain Re-ID has made great progress [2, 3]. However, supervised learning Re-ID is impractical for real-world owing to the heavy work of manually labeling a large scale dataset.

Recent researches show models trained in one domain may fail to generalize to another [4, 5]. The main reason is the difference in data distribution between domains. For example, Market-1501 [6] dataset was collected in summer in Tsinghua University and DukeMTMC-reID [7] dataset was taken at Duke University in winter. The light, clothes and background between the two datasets have significantly difference. The performance by directly applying the source-trained model on the target domain will drops significantly due to domain bias [8].

© Springer Nature Switzerland AG 2019
D.-S. Huang et al. (Eds.): ICIC 2019, LNCS 11643, pp. 54–64, 2019.
https://doi.org/10.1007/978-3-030-26763-6_6

To explicitly overcome this problem, recent studies have paid attention to unsupervised cross-domain person Re-ID [4, 9–13]. In unsupervised cross-domain person Re-ID setting, the source domain has ID annotation, while the target domain only contains unlabeled images. Style transfer [4, 9], attribute recognition [10] and target-domain label estimation [11–13] have shown their effectiveness in overcoming domain bias.

In this work, we followed the idea of style transfer. Previous style transfer methods translate the labeled source dataset to target domain based on CycleGAN [14]. Then the translated images are used to train the Re-ID model. The CycleGAN-based style transfer methods need to add peculiar constraint to ensure person ID information preserved during image translate. Although some methods have been adopted [4, 9], it is difficult to represent ID information in CycleGAN. Our proposed approach is different significantly from existing style transfer methods in Re-ID, in which we separate the image style from content expression [15]. In the process of image transfer, we can weigh the reconstruction of image content and style to obtain a variety of images whose style between the source domain and target domain. Furthermore, we propose a Re-ID base model with very strong generalization performance. The source domain images and translated images are combined to fed into the powerful Re-ID model to learn the style-independent features. Extensive experiments are conducted based on datasets commonly used in Re-ID. The results show that our approach achieves higher performance.

2 Related Work

2.1 Supervised Deep Learning Person Re-ID

Person Re-ID aims to search people images with the same ID in a large gallery. CNN-based deep learning models show their powerful performance in this field. Most of existing person Re-ID deep models are based on supervised learning that is given all the images and their corresponding ID annotation during training. During the test, the retrieval results are obtained by calculating the feature distance or similarity between the query image and each gallery image. Person Re-ID model mainly contain feature extraction and similarity metric. For similarity metric, contrastive loss [16, 17], triplet loss [18], quadruplet loss [19] are proposed. For feature extraction, the local-based feature method, attention-based method and pose estimation assistant method show their effectiveness. BPM [2] used ResNet50 [20] to extract the global feature of image and then split it into several part-informed features for discriminative local feature learning. PAN [21] proposed an alignment based on attention mechanism to reduce the size and position difference caused by misalignment. Both Zheng et al. [22] and Zhao et al. [23] used pose estimation algorithm to obtain human pose information and then train deep models. Although these methods have achieved good performance, they are not suitable for real-world scenarios because it is expensive to manually annotate a large dataset.

2.2   Unsupervised Cross-Domain Person Re-ID

For the reason of expensive annotating, we expect a model trained on one annotated domain which can be direct transferred or adapted to another unlabeled domain. Hand-craft features [24–26] can be directly employed for unsupervised person Re-ID. But Hand-craft features do not fully exploit rich information from data distribution, resulting in poor performance. Recent works pay attention to style transfer [4, 9], attribute recognition [10] and target-domain label estimation [11–13]. Both SPGAN [4] and PTGAN [9] use CycleGAN with different constraints to transfer source domain images to target domain style. Then use these generate images to train a Re-ID model. TJ-AIDL [10] use additional person attribute information to learn feature for unlabeled target domain. The label estimation methods [11–13] can be obtained by using clustering to estimate target domain pseudo labels for supervised learning. This work is inspired by style transfer. Unlike previous CycleGAN-based transfer, we separate the image representation into content and style to explicitly consider the intra-domain image style variations to learn discriminative re-ID model for target domain.

3   Proposed Method

Unsupervised Cross-Domain Person Re-ID Problem Definition. For unsupervised cross-domain person Re-ID, we have two datasets called the source domain and the target domain. The source domain $S = \{X_s, Y_s\}$ contains N_s person images x_s and corresponding labels y_s. We also have N_t unlabeled images x_t from the target domain $T = \{X_t\}$. The goal of this work is to use $\{X_s, Y_s\}$ and $\{X_t\}$ to learn a model that performs well on the target domain.

3.1   Preview

Figure 1 shows our framework's pipeline, which consists of two steps, i.e., source-target image transfer, and feature learning for person Re-ID. By separating the image style and content, we obtain a style transfer model in step one. Style transfer model alters the style of each image in the source domain to generate new images while keeping the person ID information unchanged. Then the generated image and source domain image are combined and fed into the Re-ID model to learn discriminative style-independent features. In the following section, we will illustrate the structure of the two components in detail.

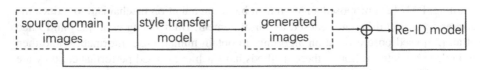

Fig. 1. The pipeline of our framework. First, through the style transfer model, the source domain image is transformed into a new image with a different style but the same ID. Then, the generated images and the source domain images are combined together and fed into the Re-ID model for feature learning.

3.2   Style Transfer Model

The goal of the style transfer model is to generate new images that are similar to the target domain style while retaining the original ID information. Previous study [27] showed that deep learning processes information through layers, processing image color and texture information at the low-level layer, and extracting semantic information at the high-level layer. Thus, the low-level features over all images in the target domain can be regard as the "style" of the target domain and the high-level features of the source domain images can be regard as the representation of ID information.

The structure of our style transfer model is shown in Fig. 2. In the training phase, style transfer model is divided into two part, i.e., source-target transfer network G and loss network F. The given image $x_s \in X_s$ input to G to generate new image $\tilde{x} = G(x_s)$, where G is a deep residual convolutional neural network [20] and roughly follow the architectural guidelines set forth by Justin et al. [28]. F is a VGG19 [29] pre-trained on ImageNet [30] dataset. We input x_s and $\tilde{x}$ to F, $M_l \in \mathbb{R}^{C_l \times H_l \times W_l}$ and $\tilde{M}_l \in \mathbb{R}^{C_l \times H_l \times W_l}$ are their respective feature representation in layer l. In order to the ID information in x_s and $\tilde{x}$ to be consistent, we encourage their features M_l and $\tilde{M}_l$ to be as close as possible, so the ID-related loss function is defined as:

$$L_{ID-related} = \frac{1}{C_l H_l W_l} \sum_{i=1}^{C_l} \sum_{j=1}^{H_l} \sum_{k=1}^{W_l} \left(M_{l_{i,j,k}} - \tilde{M}_{l_{i,j,k}} \right)^2 \tag{1}$$

where the l is "relu2_1" layer in F.

The "style" of an image is often thought of as an overall pattern of the image so it is composed of correlations between the responses of different filters. We followed Gatys [15] to calculate this correlation using a gram matrix $\tilde{G}_l \in \mathbb{R}^{C_l \times C_l}$, where $\tilde{G}_{l_{m,n}}$ is the inner product between the vectorized feature maps m and n in layer l:

$$\tilde{G}_{l_{m,n}} = \sum_{i=1}^{H_l W_l} \tilde{M}_{l_{m,i}} \tilde{M}_{l_{n,i}} \tag{2}$$

Then the style loss is defined as:

$$L_{style} = \frac{1}{4H_l^2 W_l^2} \sum_{l \in L} weight_l \sum_{i=1}^{C_l} \sum_{j=1}^{C_l} \left(\tilde{G}_{l_{i,j}} - \overline{Q}_{l_{i,j}} \right)^2 \tag{3}$$

where L is composed by "relu1_2", "relu2_1", "relu3_4", "relu4_3" and "relu5_3" layers, $\overline{Q}_l$ is the average of the gram matrix value over all images in the target domain and $weight_l$ represent the weight of layer l.

Finally, the overall loss function to be minimized is:

$$L_{total} = L_{ID-related} + \alpha L_{style} \tag{4}$$

where α is the weight to balance ID information and style matching. During training, the parameters of F are fixed and the parameters of G are updated through SGD algorithm. After several iterations, we will obtain a trained source-target transfer network G.

In practice, we trained multiple source-target transfer G under the different value of α. The proposed method has several advantages as follows:

1. Style transfer is a domain adaptation method in the image pixel space, which enables model trained on source domain to generalize well to target domain.
2. Different source-target transfer network G will generate multiple images with same ID information and their "style" is between the source and target domains, which enables Re-ID model to learn style-independent features.
3. The combination of generated images and the original images can be regarded as the new training data for the person Re-ID model. Using additional data is non-trivial to avoid model overfitting.

The impact of different number of source-target transfer on the Re-ID performance will be tested in Sect. 4.3.

3.3   Re-ID Model

In this work, DenseNet [31] pre-trained on ImageNet dataset is used as the base model. We modified the final pooling layer to the global average pooling (GAP) layer to obtain a 1024-dim feature map. Afterwards, we added a 512-dimensional fully connected layer, followed by the batch normalization [32] and dropout layer. Finally, we use a fully connected layer to get the prediction that output dimension is the number of training identities. The cross-entropy loss is applied for classification, which can be defined as follows:

$$L_c = \sum_{i=1}^{C} -p_i \log(\hat{p}_i) \tag{5}$$

where p is the ground truth label and $\hat{p}$ is the output of the Re-ID model after softmax conversion.

Our experiments show that the performance of this model greatly exceeds Resnet50 [20] on unsupervised cross-domain re-identification. During testing, given an input image, we can extract the GAP vector for retrieval under the Euclidean distance.

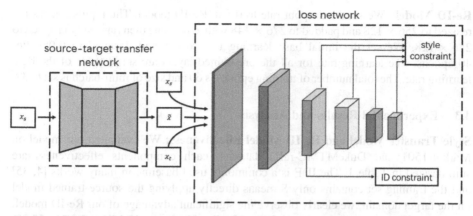

Fig. 2. The architecture of style transfer model. Given a source domain image, we use the source-target transfer network to generate a new image. Loss network is a pre-trained network to extract feature, then the style and ID information constraint are applied on the feature.

4 Experiment

4.1 Datasets

We evaluate our model on two large-scale person re-identification datasets. i.e., Market-1501 [6] and DukeMTMC-reID [7]. Market-1501 [6] was captured by six cameras, including 1,501 identities and 32,668 annotated bounding boxes which were obtained by DPM [33] detector. Market-1501 is typically divided into two parts, 751 identities for training and another 750 for testing. DukeMTMC-reID [7] contains 36,411 images of 1,404 identities, which was captured by eight cameras. Similar to the diversion of Market-1501, the training dataset has 702 identities, the test dataset contains another 702 identities. We adopt rank-k accuracy and mAP for model evaluation [6].

4.2 Experiment Settings

Style Transfer Model: For source-target transfer network G, the shape of input and output are both $3 \times 256 \times 128$. The network starts with three convolutional layers, in which the first convolutional layer with 9×9 kernel and stride-1, and the other two layers with 3×3 kernel and stride-2. The feature map is sampled down to 64×32 through these layers. Then the feature map pass through the five residual blocks [20], and the output size remains unchanged. Finally, G use two upper sampling layers to enlarge the feature map to the size of the original input image, then obtained the output image by a convolution layer with 9×9 kernel. The corresponding $weight_l$ of "relu1_2", "relu2_1", "relu3_4", "relu4_3" and "relu5_3" layer is 1e2, 1e4, 1e4, 5e3 and 1e4 respectively. We set α to 10, 0.1 and 0.001 for training and used the resulting three different G to transform the style of source domain image. Our proposal is implemented on Pytorch framework. The mini-batch SGD algorithm with Adam [34] is exploited to optimize the model. The batch size is 4, the learning rate is 0.001 and maximum iteration number is 30k.

Re-ID Model: We set the dropout rate to 0.5 in Re-ID model. The inputs images are resized to 256×128 and padded to 276×148 with zero value then randomly cropped to 256×128. We set the initial base learning rate to 0.5 and decayed to 0.05 after 40 epochs. The learning rate for all the pre-trained layers are set to $0.1\times$ of the base learning rate. The total number of training epochs is 60 and size of mini-batch is set to 32.

4.3   Experimental Results and Analysis

Style Transfer Model and Re-ID Model Effectiveness: We evaluated our model on Market-1501 and DukeMTMC-reID datasets, each components effectiveness are summarized in Table 1. The IDE is a commonly used baseline in many works [4, 35] and the training set contains only S means directly applying the source-trained model on the target domain, we clearly observe the significant advantage of our Re-ID model: rank-1 on two datasets increases from 32.9%, 44.6% to 40.1% (+7.2%), 55.2% (+10.6%) and mAP increases from 16.9%, 20.6% to 22.0% (+5.1%), 25.8% (+5.2%), respectively. Further combined with the generated images, the performance of our model exceeded the strong Re-ID model and achieves rank-1 52.3% (+12.2%), 62.3% (+7.1%) and mAP 29.2% (+7.2%), 31.6% (+5.8%) on the two datasets. This comparison proves the effectiveness of the two components. Some visual examples of source-target image translation are shown in Fig. 3.

Fig. 3. Visual examples of source-target image translation. The left two columns map Market-1501 images to the DukeMTMC-reID style, and the right two columns map DukeMTMC-reID images to the Market-1501 style. From top to bottom: (a) original image, (b) output of source-target transfer network with $\alpha = 10$.

Table 1. Comparison of various methods on the unsupervised cross domain person re-identification. Where $S_{T_{\alpha_i}}$ represents new images converted from source domain by G, which is trained under the parameter α_i. As describe in Sect. 4.2, we set α_1, α_2, α_3 to 10, 0.1, 0.001 respective.

	Train set	Source: Market Target: Duke		Source: Duke Target: Market	
		Rank-1	mAP	Rank-1	mAP
IDE	S	32.9	16.9	44.6	20.6
STReID (m = 0)	S	40.1	22.0	55.2	25.8
STReID (m = 1)	$S + S_{T_{\alpha_1}}$	49.4	28.5	59.1	27.4
STReID (m = 2)	$S + S_{T_{\alpha_1}} + S_{T_{\alpha_2}}$	51.9	29.0	61.8	31.4
STReID (m = 3)	$S + S_{T_{\alpha_1}} + S_{T_{\alpha_2}} + S_{T_{\alpha_3}}$	52.3	29.2	62.3	31.6

Comparison with State-of-the-Art Methods: In Tables 2 and 3, we compare the proposed method with the state-of-the-art unsupervised cross-domain person re-identification methods on Market-1501 and DukeMTMC-reID. For the hand-crafted features based methods, we compare our model with LOMO [25] and BoW [6]. For unsupervised method, there are UMDL [36], the Progressive Unsupervised Learning (PUL) [5] and the Clustering-based Asymmetric Metric Learning (CAMEL) [37]. In addition, four unsupervised domain adaptation methods are compared, including PTGAN [9], SPGAN [4], TJ-AIDL [10], HHL [35]. Our model outperforms these model in Rank-1, Rank-5, Rank-10, and mAP on Market-1501 and DukeMTMC-reID.

Table 2. Comparison with the state-of-the-art unsupervised cross-domain person re-identification methods on Market-1501.

Methods	R-1	R-5	R-10	mAP
LOMO [25]	12.3	21.3	26.6	4.8
BoW [6]	17.1	28.8	34.9	8.3
UMDL [36]	18.5	31.4	37.6	7.3
PTGAN [9]	27.4	–	50.7	–
PUL [5]	30.0	43.4	48.5	16.4
SPGAN [4]	41.1	56.6	63.0	22.3
TJ-AIDL [10]	44.3	59.6	65.0	23.0
HHL [35]	46.9	61.0	66.7	27.2
STReID (Ours)	**52.3**	**65.9**	**71.1**	**29.2**

Table 3. Comparison with the state-of-the-art unsupervised cross-domain person re-identification methods on DukeMTMC-reID.

Methods	R-1	R-5	R-10	mAP
LOMO [25]	27.2	41.6	49.1	8.0
BoW [6]	35.8	52.4	60.3	14.8
UMDL [36]	34.5	52.6	59.6	12.4
PTGAN [9]	38.6	–	66.1	–
PUL [5]	45.5	60.7	66.7	20.5
SPGAN [4]	51.5	70.1	76.8	22.8
CAMEL [37]	54.5	–	–	26.3
TJ-AIDL [10]	58.2	74.8	81.1	26.5
HHL [35]	62.2	78.8	84.0	31.4
STReID (Ours)	**62.3**	**79.1**	**84.4**	**31.6**

5 Conclusion

In this paper, we propose STReID, a novel unsupervised cross-domain person re-identification method. Due to the gap between source domain and target domain, directly applying the source-trained model on the target domain will lead to poor performance. To improve performance in the new dataset, we propose a source-target image transfer model to reduce the domain gap. The images generated by the source-target transfer model are combined with source domain images to enable the model adapt to the target domain and learn style-independent features. Further, we propose a new Re-ID baseline model with better generalization ability. The proposed STReID effectively combines source-target domain style transfer with a strong Re-ID model, achieving the higher performance on Market-1501 and DukeMTMC-reID datasets.

Acknowledgments. This work is supported by the National Science Foundation for China (Nos. 61572372, 41671382), State Key Laboratory for Information Engineering in Surveying, Mapping and Remote Sensing Special Research Funding, Anhui Provincial Natural Science Foundation (grant number 1608085MF136).

References

1. Zheng, L., et al.: Person re-identification: past, present and future. arXiv preprint arXiv:1505.06821 (2016)
2. Sun, Y., Zheng, L., Yang, Y., Tian, Q., Wang, S.: Beyond part models: person retrieval with refined part pooling (and a strong convolutional baseline). In: Ferrari, V., Hebert, M., Sminchisescu, C., Weiss, Y. (eds.) ECCV 2018. LNCS, vol. 11208, pp. 501–518. Springer, Cham (2018). https://doi.org/10.1007/978-3-030-01225-0_30
3. Zhang, X., et al.: AlignedReID: surpassing human-level performance in person re-identification. arXiv preprint (2017)
4. Deng, W., et al.: Image-image domain adaptation with preserved self-similarity and domain-dissimilarity for person re-identification. In: CVPR (2018)

5. Fan, H., et al.: Unsupervised person re-identification: clustering and fine-tuning. ACM Trans. Multimedia Comput. Commun. Appl. **14**, 83 (2018)
6. Zheng, L., et al.: Scalable person re-identification: a benchmark. In: ICCV (2015)
7. Zheng, Z., Zheng, L., Yang, Y.: Unlabeled samples generated by GAN improve the person re-identification baseline in vitro. In: ICCV (2017)
8. Torralba, A., Efros, A.A.: Unbiased look at dataset bias. In: CVPR (2011)
9. Wei, L., et al.: Person transfer GAN to bridge domain gap for person re-identification. In: CVPR (2018)
10. Wang, J., et al.: Transferable joint attribute-identity deep learning for unsupervised person re-identification. In: CVPR (2018)
11. Liu, Z., Dong, W., Lu, H.: Stepwise metric promotion for unsupervised video person re-identification. In: ICCV (2017)
12. Lv, J., et al.: Unsupervised cross-dataset person re-identification by transfer learning of spatial-temporal patterns. In: CVPR (2018)
13. Li, M., Zhu, X., Gong, S.: Unsupervised person re-identification by deep learning tracklet association. In: Ferrari, V., Hebert, M., Sminchisescu, C., Weiss, Y. (eds.) ECCV 2018. LNCS, vol. 11208, pp. 772–788. Springer, Cham (2018). https://doi.org/10.1007/978-3-030-01225-0_45
14. Zhu, J., et al.: Unpaired image-to-image translation using cycle-consistent adversarial networks. In: ICCV (2017)
15. Gatys, L.A., Ecker, A.S., Bethge, M.: A neural algorithm of artistic style. Nat. Commun. (2015)
16. Varior, R.R., Haloi, M., Wang, G.: Gated Siamese convolutional neural network architecture for human re-identification. In: Leibe, B., Matas, J., Sebe, N., Welling, M. (eds.) ECCV 2016. LNCS, vol. 9912, pp. 791–808. Springer, Cham (2016). https://doi.org/10.1007/978-3-319-46484-8_48
17. Varior, R.R., Shuai, B., Lu, J., Xu, D., Wang, G.: A Siamese long short-term memory architecture for human re-identification. In: Leibe, B., Matas, J., Sebe, N., Welling, M. (eds.) ECCV 2016. LNCS, vol. 9911, pp. 135–153. Springer, Cham (2016). https://doi.org/10.1007/978-3-319-46478-7_9
18. Hermans, A., et al.: In defense of the triplet loss for person re-identification. In: Computer Vision and Pattern Recognition, arXiv (2017)
19. Chen, W., et al.: Beyond triplet loss: a deep quadruplet network for person re-identification. In: CVPR (2017)
20. He, K., et al.: Deep residual learning for image recognition. In: CVPR (2016)
21. Zheng, Z., et al.: Pedestrian alignment network for large-scale person re-identification. IEEE Trans. Circ. Syst. Video Technol. 1 (2018)
22. Zheng, L., et al.: Pose invariant embedding for deep person re-identification. In: CVPR (2017)
23. Zhao, H., et al.: Spindle net: person re-identification with human body region guided feature decomposition and fusion. In: CVPR (2017)
24. Gray, D., Tao, H.: Viewpoint invariant pedestrian recognition with an ensemble of localized features. In: Forsyth, D., Torr, P., Zisserman, A. (eds.) ECCV 2008. LNCS, vol. 5302, pp. 262–275. Springer, Heidelberg (2008). https://doi.org/10.1007/978-3-540-88682-2_21
25. Liao, S., et al.: Person re-identification by local maximal occurrence representation and metric learning. In: CVPR (2015)
26. Matsukawa, T., et al.: Hierarchical Gaussian descriptor for person re-identification. In: CVPR (2016)
27. Gatys, L.A., Ecker, A.S., Bethge, M.: Texture synthesis using convolutional neural networks. In: NIPS (2015)

28. Johnson, J., Alahi, A., Fei-Fei, L.: Perceptual losses for real-time style transfer and super-resolution. In: Leibe, B., Matas, J., Sebe, N., Welling, M. (eds.) ECCV 2016. LNCS, vol. 9906, pp. 694–711. Springer, Cham (2016). https://doi.org/10.1007/978-3-319-46475-6_43
29. Simonyan, K., Zisserman, A.: Very deep convolutional networks for large-scale image recognition. In: ICLR (2015)
30. Deng, J., et al.: ImageNet: a large-scale hierarchical image database. In: CVPR (2009)
31. Huang, G., et al.: Densely connected convolutional networks. In: CVPR (2017)
32. Ioffe, S., Szegedy, C.: Batch normalization: accelerating deep network training by reducing internal covariate shift. In: ICML (2015)
33. Felzenszwalb, P.F., et al.: Object detection with discriminatively trained part-based models. IEEE Trans. Pattern Anal. Mach. Intell. **32**, 1627–1645 (2010)
34. Kingma, D.P., Ba, J.: Adam: a method for stochastic optimization. In: ICLR (2015)
35. Zhong, Z., Zheng, L., Li, S., Yang, Y.: Generalizing a person retrieval model hetero- and homogeneously. In: Ferrari, V., Hebert, M., Sminchisescu, C., Weiss, Y. (eds.) ECCV 2018. LNCS, vol. 11217, pp. 176–192. Springer, Cham (2018). https://doi.org/10.1007/978-3-030-01261-8_11
36. Chen, H., et al.: Deep transfer learning for person re-identification. In: IEEE International Conference on Multimedia Big Data (2018)
37. Peng, P., et al.: Unsupervised cross-dataset transfer learning for person re-identification. In: CVPR (2016)

Improving Object Detection by Deep Networks with Class-Related Features

Shoutao Xu[✉] and Zhong-Qiu Zhao

School of Computer Science and Information Engineering,
HeFei University of Technology, Hefei, China
xust930@mail.hfut.edu.cn

Abstract. Context is an important additional information for object detection. Class-related features which mainly focus on the coexistence of various classes objects in a single image is a kind of context information. In this paper, we propose an object detection algorithm that makes use of the class-related features. Specifically, in order to improve the performance of object detection, we propose an end-to-end network which introduces the attention mechanism to learn the class-related features and combine it with convolutional neural network (CNN) visual features. The experimental results on PASCAL VOC and MS COCO show that our method get a better performance than the baseline method (Faster R-CNN). The introduction of spatial attention module and channel-wise attention module captures the class-related features greatly. Furthermore, the Gated Recurrent Unit (GRU) which is adopted to combine class-related features and visual features works well in our model.

Keywords: Object detection · Class-related features · Context information

1 Introduction

As one of the important and fundamental computer vision problems, object detection has a series of breakthroughs due to the advance of convolutional neural network (CNN) in recent years [8, 16, 26]. Some neural networks are proposed to extract rich semantic features to improve the precision of classification, such as ZFNet [24], VGG [17], GoogLenet [18], ResNet [10] and so on. Girshick et al. [9] adopt CNN in object detection firstly. For improving the performance on large-scale datasets, many scholars focus on how to improve CNN object detection models in different ways, such as replacing the backbone with a better one, combining coarse and high layer features and taking advantage of the context information around objects or global scene.

Most of existing methods pay attention to semantic information of region of interest (RoI). Methods which utilize context information take into account surrounding scene of objects or global scene. However, another kind of context information, which we called class-related features was left out in recent years. Class-related features focus on whether various classes of objects can coexist in an image. Figure 1 shows an example of class-related features intuitively. In Fig. 1(a), there are 3 classes of objects—person, motorcycle and skateboard. Moreover, a person slides on a skateboard and a person rides a motorcycle. So that skateboard and motorcycle are related to person. Figure 1

© Springer Nature Switzerland AG 2019
D.-S. Huang et al. (Eds.): ICIC 2019, LNCS 11643, pp. 65–76, 2019.
https://doi.org/10.1007/978-3-030-26763-6_7

(b) illustrates some bowls and a spoon which are put on a dinner table. Obviously, bowls and spoons are closely related. If there is a bowl or a spoon in an image, the chance of existence another one would be higher. Meanwhile, because of the existence of bowls and spoons, the existence possibility of a bus or an airplane should be almost 0 in a single image. Therefore, utilizing the class-related features reasonably can effectively improve the performance of object detection.

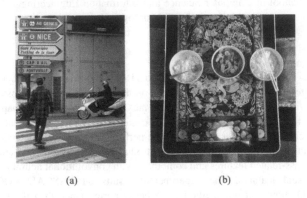

(a)   (b)

Fig. 1. Two examples of class relationship. (a) Includes a person ride on a motorcycle and a person play on a skateboard, (b) includes a spoon which is put on a bowl.

For learning the class-related features, it is natural to be associate with attention mechanism. Spatial attention mainly focus on specific region where objects are probably presence. And channel-wise attention makes each channel being related to objects belong to a certain class.

In this paper, we introduce a model, which is aimed at capturing the class-related features and combining it with visual features for a better performance on object detection. We take Faster R-CNN as the main network of our model, then we add a branch network for capturing the class-related features. In this branch network, two attention modules are proposed to learn spatial and class sensitive features. Then, a class relationship module is adopted to learn class-related features. At last, we add a Gated Recurrent Unit (GRU) for extracting the fusion features.

In summary, our main contributions are as follows:

(1) We design a branch network which learned class-related features by the introduction of attention mechanism and class relationship module.
(2) We design an end-to-end network based on Faster R-CNN for object detection. A GRU [4] is proposed to fuse the class-related features learned from branch network and the visual features learned from each RoI.
(3) We comprehensively evaluate our method on PASCAL VOC and MS COCO datasets, which are well-known in object detection task. We get better performance than the baseline method (Faster RCNN).

2   Related Work

2.1   Object Detection

Object detection problem focus on detecting and classifying all objects which annotated in training dataset from images. Therefore, a classical model of object detection, which divided into two stage: candidate boxes selection, feature extraction and classification was naturally proposed [20]. Before CNN are widely used in object detection, the candidate boxes are obtained by some region proposal algorithms (e.g. Selective Search [19] and Edgebox [28]), or even by a exhaustive strategy that scanning the whole image with multi-scale sliding windows [7]. Besides, the features are extracted by some manually engineered low-level descriptors, such as HOG [5], SIFT [6] and Haar-like features [13]. Girshick et al. [9] proposed the first object detection framework R-CNN which based on CNN, which greatly improved the detection accuracy on common dataset. Compared with the hand-engineered low-level features, CNN features are quite more discriminative representations. Ren et al. [16] proposed an end-to-end object detection framework—Faster R-CNN, which contain a region proposal network (RPN) to replace region proposal algorithm in R-CNN. And it has achieved impressive improvements in both accuracy and efficiency. Different from these two-stage methods, one-stage methods like SSD [15] have been proposed for real-time object detection. In this type of methods, the region proposal algorithm is eliminated and a single stage end-to-end detector is trained directly.

However, these methods treat object detection as an isolated task. The classification and localization of a object is determined by its CNN features which lead to a low recall and omission of small objects.

2.2   Context Information

In order to solve these problems, some methods that take advantage of additional information are proposed [1]. For example, Bell et al. [2] proposed a model which utilize recurrent neural network (RNN) to extract the context features and fuse multi-level features for better performance. Zeng et al. [25] proposed a gated bi-directional CNN to pass message between features of different support regions around objects. Different from existing methods, our model make use of class-related features sufficiently. It is similar to human visual cognition. Besides shape, color and texture, the information of surrounding classes and scene is helpful when we classify a small object in an image.

2.3   Attention Mechanism

The visual attention mechanism that is unique to human is signal processing mechanism. By quickly scanning the global image, people obtain the regions that need to be focused on, which is the focus of attention, and then pay more attention to these regions to obtain more detailed information about the objects. With these considerations in mind, the attention mechanism in computer vision has been proposed. Xu et al. [21] proposed the first visual attention model in image caption. In general, they used hard pooling to selects the most probably attentive region, or soft pooling to averages the spatial features with attentive weights. In recent years, various types of attention mechanisms have been proposed (e.g., spatial attention [22] and semantic attention [23]). In our model, a spatial attention and a channel-wise attention module which proposed in [3] are adopted to capture the class-related features.

3   Method

In this section, we describe the details of our method. The purpose of the method is that improving the precision of object detection, especially the impact on small objects. The whole framework of our method is depicted in Fig. 2. In this framework, we consider the Faster R-CNN based on ResNet as the main network. In additional, we design a branch network which learns the class-related features. Specifically, a channel-wise attention CNN and a spatial attention CNN are used as the class-related features to implement the multi-label classification. Moreover, a GRU is used to connect the main net and branch network. Then the confidence scores of region proposals which amended by class-related features can be inferred by the GRU unit. The whole network is trained in an end-to-end manner.

3.1   Spatial Attention

As we know that the region proposals are classified independently in Faster R-CNN. However, the relationship between various objects and scene contextual information in whole image have counted for a lot in object detection, especially for small objects. In order to utilize these additional information, we design a branch network for learning the class-related features. Specifically, we take advantage of the channel-wise attention and spatia attention feature maps in our branch network.

   We propose to decouple semantic in this branch network, we adopt a spatial attention module that can be embedded in a traditional convolutional neural network. Instead of considering each image pixel equally, the spatial attention model try to pay more attention to the semantic-related region. As previously stated, the spatial attention model learned more appropriate weights so that the region of original images or CNN features could be more concerned. Here, we adopt the spatial attention module which is similar as that in [3]. The architecture of the spatial attention module is shown in Fig. 2.

   As shown in Fig. 2, the input of spatial attention module f^k is the CNN features extracted from the ResNet because of the sufficient semantic features. And the superscript of f^k donate the number of feature channels. We define $f^k_{(x,y)} \in \mathbb{R}^k$ as the feature in spatial location (x,y). As to any spacial location (x,y) of f^k, the spatial attention module θ can be defined as follow:

$$S_{(i,j)} = \Phi_S\left(w_{S(i,j)}, b_{S(i,j)}, f^k_{(i,j)}\right) = \text{softmax}\left(w_{S(i,j)} f^k_{(i,j)} + b_{S(i,j)}\right) \qquad (1)$$

where $w_{S(i,j)} \in \mathbb{R}^k$ is a transform matrix, and $b_{S(i,j)} \in \mathbb{R}^1$ is the bias of model in spatial location (i,j). According to Eq. 1, we can get spatial attention weights

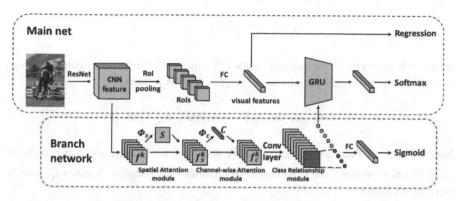

Fig. 2. The framework of our method is divided into two parts: main net and branch network. The structure of main net is illustrated in the blue dashed border. In main net, we extract the CNN features by a ResNet. The main net utilize RPN network and Non-Maximum Suppression (NMS) algorithm to extract a certain number of proposals. And the visual features are captured by a RoI pooling layer and a fully connected layer. In addition, we add a branch network after the ResNet. The structure of branch network is shown in the red dashed border. In our branch network, the class-related features are captured by a spatial attention module, a channel-wise attention module and a class relationship module. We combine these features by a GRU. The main net and branch network can be trained by an end-to-end manner. (Color figure online)

$S = \left[\left[S_{(1,1)}, \ldots, S_{(1,w)} \right], \ldots, \left[S_{(h,1)}, \ldots, S_{(h,w)} \right] \right]$. Then the output of spatial attention module f_s^k can be described as: $f_s^k = f^k \otimes S$ where $\otimes$ is an element-wise multiplication for regions of each feature map channel $f_s^{(i)}$ and its corresponding region attention weights S.

3.2   Channel-Wise Attention

Note that the output of the spatial attention module in Eq. 1 are semantic-related visual features. However, in order to get the class-related feature, the class-related features are what we need to learn in this branch network. Hence, we introduce a channel-wise attention module which is proposed in [3]. It is worth noting that each CNN kernel performs as a pattern detector, and each channel of a feature map in CNN is a response activation of the corresponding convolutional kernel. Therefore, applying an attention mechanism in channel-wise manner can be viewed as a process of selecting semantic-related features. The details of channel-wise attention module structure are shown in Fig. 2.

Different from the spatial attention module, we will handle the feature maps by a channel-wise manner in this module. Specifically, we consider $f_s^k = \left[f_s^{(1)}, f_s^{(2)}, \ldots, f_s^{(k)} \right]$, where $f_s^{(i)} \in \mathbb{R}^{w \times h}$ is the i-th channel of the feature maps f_s^k. Then we apply a global average pooling for each channel $f_s^{(i)}$ to get a channel feature f':

$$f_C' = \left[f^{(1)}, f^{(2)}, \ldots, f^{(k)}\right] \tag{2}$$

where $f^{(1)}$ is the mean of the channel vector $f_s^{(i)}$. Similar to the spatial attention module, the definition of channel-wise attention weights C is as follows:

$$C = \Phi_C\left(w_C, b_C, f_C'\right) = \text{softmax}\left(w_C f_C' + b_C\right) \tag{3}$$

where $w_C \in \mathbb{R}^k$ is the transformation matrix and $b_C \in \mathbb{R}^1$ is the bias term. Similar to spatial attention module, the i-th channel of channel-wise attention features $f_C^{(i)}$ can be described as follows:

$$f_C^{(i)} = f^{(i)} \odot f_s^{(i)} \tag{4}$$

where $\odot$ in Eq. 4 donate that each element of $f_s^{(i)}$ is multiplied by $f^{(i)}$. According to Eq. 4, we can get the output of channel-wise attention module $f_C^k = \left[f_C^{(1)}, f_C^{(2)}, \ldots, f_C^{(k)}\right]$. Our channel-wise attention module is aimed at changing the weights of feature maps so that the feature maps are consistency in a channel-wise way. Particularly, each channel of the feature maps $f_C^{(i)}$ is simply focus on a certain class. As illustrated in Fig. 3, the class activation maps show the activation of a channel of features.

3.3 Class-Related Features Learning for Object Detection

The features learned from above modules provide abundant semantic information. And the spatial information in our attention features can be located in each channel as well. However, the features we have captured are mutual independent. So we aim at learning the relationships features in class-level, especially the coexistence relationships between multiple classes.

In order to capture the class-related features, we adopt a class relationship module which is introduced in [27]. The structure of the class relationship module is shown in Fig. 2. For the attention feature f_C, we add 1024 convolution kernels with size $1 \times 1 \times k$ to extract the spatial relationship f_C' between various classes. In order to obtain the class-related features, we add four single-channel CNN filters for each channel of f_C'. In general, objects that belong to a single class is generally closely related to a few classes. Most of the relationships between various are not strongly related. Meanwhile, because of the structure of this class relation module, the number of the parameters is greatly reduced. After the single-channel CNN filters, we added a fully connected layer to predict the possibility of classes existed in an image. The branch network can be trained by a supervised manner. More details of training is mentioned in Sect. 3.4.

For purpose of combining class-related features and visual features from main net, we introduce the Gated Recurrent Unit (GRU) which is a variant of Long short-term memory (LSTM) [11]. The architecture of GRU is shown in Fig. 4. The update gate z selects whether the hidden state $f_v^{(t+1)}$ is to be updated with a new hidden state $\tilde{f}$. The

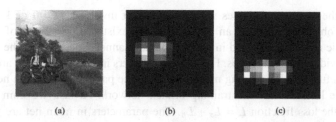

    (a)   (b)   (c)

Fig. 3. The class activation of channel-wise attention features. (a) and (b) Is the different classes activation maps from different channel. (b) Illustrate the person activation maps. And (c) is the activation maps related to motorcycle.

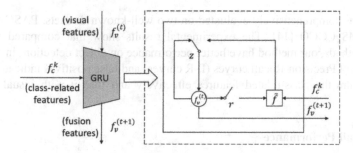

Fig. 4. The framework of GRU. The update gate z decide that whether $f_v^{(t+1)}$ is updated. The reset gate r choose that how much the previous state is ignored.

reset gate r decides whether the previous hidden state $f_v^{(t)}$ is ignored. In our GRU, we consider the visual features of each region of proposal (RoI) f_v as the initial state.

3.4 Training Schema

For getting a better performance on object detection, we combine the visual features from RoI and the class-related features that captured from the branch network. As same as Faster R-CNN, the loss function of object classification and localization is defined as follow:

$$L_\alpha = L_{cls} + L_{loc} \qquad (5)$$

where L_{cls} is a softmax cross entropy loss function and L_{loc} is a smooth L_1 loss function proposed in [16].

Meanwhile, in the branch network, we add a fully connected layer and supervised train with the class labels of an image. To solve this multi-label classification problem, we utilize the sigmoid cross entropy loss function as follow:

$$L_\beta = -\frac{1}{C} \sum_{i=1}^{C} (l_i \ln p_i + (1 - l_i) \ln(1 - p_i)) \qquad (6)$$

where C is the number of classes where the dataset involved, $l_i = 0$ or 1 depend on whether i-th object is existed in an image, p_i is the existence possibility of i-th object.

The whole network is trained in an end-to-end manner. Specifically, the strategy of training is divided into three steps. First, the parameters in branch network are fixed and L_α is the loss function for training main net. Then, the parameters in main net are fixed and L_β is the loss function for training branch network. At last, we train the whole network by the loss function $L = L_\alpha + L_\beta$. The parameters in main net are pre-trained on ImageNet.

4   Experiments

Our model is comprehensively evaluated on two well-known datasets, PASCAL VOC [27] and MS COCO [14]. The experimental results show that compared with the baseline methods, our method have better performance on object detection. In addition, the analysis of Precision-Recall curves (P-R curves) and false positives indicate that our model capture the class-related features effectively and fuse it with visual features greatly.

4.1   Overall Performance

PASCAL VOC
Our model has been evaluated on the PASCAL VOC. PASCAL VOC is a dataset which involves 20 categories. In object detection task, the performance is evaluated by mean average precision (mAP). We trained our model on VOC2007 and VOC2012. Besides, VOC2007 is consist of trainval images and test images, each of which contain about $5k$ images. And VOC2012 is consist of $11k$ trainval images and $11k$ test images. We take VOC2007 and VOC2012 trainval images as the training set and take VOC2012 test images as validation set. The parameters of main net based on ResNet101 are pre-trained on ImagNet. The training strategy has been detailed in Sect. 3.4. First, we train the main net with a learning rate of 10^{-3} for $80k$ iteration. Then we train the branch network with the same learning rate for $50k$. At last, we train the whole network with a learning rate of 10^{-4} for $30k$. As shown in Table 1, our method achieve 2.9% improvement in mAP. Moreover, we get a great improvement in some small objects, such as bottle and chair.

MS COCO
Different from PASCAL VOC, MS COCO is a lager and more challenging dataset which focus on computer vision tasks. MS COCO involves 80 categories. Our model is trained on COCO2014 trainval35k and test on COCO2014 minival. First, we train the main net with a learning rate of 10^{-3} for $350k$ iteration. Then we train the branch network with the same learning rate for $100k$. At last, we train the whole network with a learning rate of 10^{-4} for $140k$. According to Table 2, our method achieves 27.3% on test-dev score, which is 3.1% higher than the AP of baseline. And our method get a better average recall (AR) as well.

4.2 Ablation Study

Attention Mechanism

For illustrating the effectiveness of the attention mechanism in more model, we use the analytical tools proposed by [12]. The false positives analysis of our method and baseline is shown in Table 3. It is obvious that the percentage of confusion with similar objects and confusion with other VOC objects is decreasing. And it suggests that our visual features combined with class-related features is more discriminative in object detection.

Moreover, we calculate the mAP and recall in a situation of IoU = 0.5. The P-R curves of our method and baseline are shown in Fig. 5. From Fig. 5, we can know that our methods get a better precision when the recall is equal, and our recall is higher than baseline when the precision is same. This fact indicates that the class-related features obtained by spatial and channel-by-channel attention features can assist the detector at improving the confidence of the correct category.

Feature Connection

We introduced a GRU when combine the visual features of the RoIs and the class-related features. It selectively accommodates information about the relationships between various classes through three gating functions. Compared with concatenating vector directly, it seems that our method is more reasonable. The experimental result on PASCAL VOC validate our hypothesis. As shown in Table 4, the directly concatenating method gain a little benefit in our model. In fact, the visual features learned from RoIs take a decisive role in object detection. Since the dimension of the two kind of features are equal, this directly concatenating method may have negative effect on the detect results.

Table 1. PASCAL VOC2012 test detection results. Legend: mAP: mean average precision

Methods	mAP	Areo Table	Bike Dog	Bird Horse	Boat Bike	Bottle Person	Bus Plant	Car Sheep	Cat Sofa	Chair Train	Cow Tv
Baseline	73.8	86.5	81.6	77.2	58.0	51.0	78.6	76.6	**93.2**	48.6	80.4
		59.0	**92.1**	85.3	84.8	80.7	48.1	77.3	66.5	84.7	65.6
SSD321	75.4	**87.9**	82.9	73.7	61.5	45.3	81.4	75.6	92.6	57.4	78.3
		65.0	90.8	**86.8**	85.8	81.5	50.3	78.1	**75.3**	85.2	72.5
YOLOv2	73.4	86.3	82.0	74.8	59.2	51.8	79.8	76.5	90.6	52.1	78.2
		58.5	89.3	82.5	83.4	81.3	49.1	77.2	62.4	83.8	68.7
ION	76.4	87.5	**84.7**	76.8	**63.8**	58.3	**82.6**	**79.0**	90.9	**57.8**	**82.0**
		64.7	88.9	86.5	84.7	**82.3**	51.4	**78.2**	69.2	85.2	**73.5**
Ours	**76.7**	85.3	83.8	**79.4**	62.6	**60.2**	78.2	78.8	91.8	56.1	79.3
		65.1	90.4	86.2	**85.9**	81.9	**52.2**	77.9	**69.8**	**85.5**	72.1

Table 2. Comparative results on MS COCO test-dev set.

Methods	AP	AP^{50}	AP^{75}	AP^S	AP^M	AP^L	AR^1	AR^{10}	AR^{100}	AR^S	AR^M	AR^L
Baseline	24.2	45.3	23.5	7.7	26.4	37.1	23.8	34.0	34.6	12.0	38.5	54.4
ION	26.8	46.5	27.8	8.7	28.9	41.9	24.8	37.5	39.8	14.0	43.5	59.0
Ours	**27.3**	**46.8**	**28.1**	**9.2**	**29.3**	**42.1**	**25.1**	**37.9**	**40.3**	**14.2**	**43.8**	**59.2**

Table 3. Analysis of false positives. Legend: Cor: correct. Loc: poor location. Sim: similar objects. Bg: confusion with background. Oth: confusion with other objects.

Methods	Cor	Loc	Sim	Bg	Oth
Baseline	73.8	13.6	6.2	4.7	1.5
Ours	75.7	13.6	5.2	4.4	1.1

Table 4. Comparison of feature confusion methods. Legend: mAP: mean average precision, Ours + concate: confusing two features by concatenating, Ours + GRU: confusing two features by GRU.

Methods	mAP
Baseline	73.8
Ours + concate	74.2
Ours + GRU	75.7

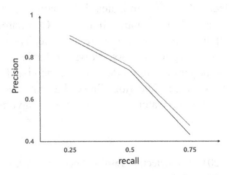

Fig. 5. The precision-recall curves. Legend: Blue line: baseline. Red line: our method. (Color figure online)

5   Conclusion

In this paper, we capture the class-related features by spatial and channel-wise attention modules, and combine it with visual features from RoIs for improving the performance of object detection. The whole network can be trained in an end-to-end manner. The evaluation on PASCAL VOC and MS COCO datasets shows that our class-related features can achieve a better results than baseline method. The analysis of the error types of negative samples indicate that our model can significantly reduce the possibility of false positives.

Acknowledgments. This research was supported by the National Natural Science Foundation of China (No. 61672203), and AnHui Natural Science Funds for Distinguished Young Scholar (No. 170808J08).

References

1. Alexe, B., Heess, N., Teh, Y.W., Ferrari, V.: Searching for objects driven by context. In: Advances in Neural Information Processing Systems. pp. 881–889 (2012)
2. Bell, S., Zitnick, C.L., Bala, K., Girshick, R.B.: Inside-outside net: detecting objects in context with skip pooling and recurrent neural networks. In: Computer Vision and Pattern Recognition, pp. 2874–2883 (2016)
3. Chen, L., et al.: SCA-CNN: spatial and channel-wise attention in convolutional networks for image captioning. In: Proceedings of the IEEE Conference on Computer Vision and Pattern Recognition, pp. 5659–5667 (2017)
4. Cho, K., Van Merrienboer, B., Bahdanau, D., Bengio, Y.: On the properties of neural machine translation: encoder–decoder approaches. In: Empirical Methods in Natural Language Processing, pp. 103–111 (2014)
5. Dalal, N., Triggs, B.: Histograms of oriented gradients for human detection. In: International Conference on Computer Vision & Pattern Recognition (CVPR 2005), vol. 1, pp. 886–893. IEEE Computer Society (2005)
6. Lowe, D.G.: Distinctive image features from scale-invariant keypoints. Int. J. Comput. Vis. **60**(2), 91–110 (2004)
7. Felzenszwalb, P.F., Girshick, R.B., McAllester, D., Ramanan, D.: Object detection with discriminatively trained part-based models. IEEE Trans. Pattern Anal. Mach. Intell. **32**(9), 1627–1645 (2010)
8. Girshick, R.B.: Fast R-CNN. In: International Conference on Computer Vision, pp. 1440–1448 (2015)
9. Girshick, R.B., Donahue, J., Darrell, T., Malik, J.: Rich feature hierarchies for accurate object detection and semantic segmentation. In: Computer Vision and Pattern Recognition, pp. 580–587 (2014)
10. He, K., Zhang, X., Ren, S., Sun, J.: Deep residual learning for image recognition. In: Computer Vision and Pattern Recognition, pp. 770–778 (2016)
11. Hochreiter, S., Schmidhuber, J.: Long short-term memory. Neural Comput. **9**(8), 1735–1780 (1997)
12. Hoiem, D., Chodpathumwan, Y., Dai, Q.: Diagnosing error in object detectors. In: Fitzgibbon, A., Lazebnik, S., Perona, P., Sato, Y., Schmid, C. (eds.) ECCV 2012. LNCS, vol. 7574, pp. 340–353. Springer, Heidelberg (2012). https://doi.org/10.1007/978-3-642-33712-3_25
13. Lienhart, R., Maydt, J.: An extended set of haar-like features for rapid object detection. In: Proceedings. International Conference on Image Processing, vol. 1, p. I. IEEE (2002)
14. Lin, T.-Y., et al.: Microsoft COCO: common objects in context. In: Fleet, D., Pajdla, T., Schiele, B., Tuytelaars, T. (eds.) ECCV 2014. LNCS, vol. 8693, pp. 740–755. Springer, Cham (2014). https://doi.org/10.1007/978-3-319-10602-1_48
15. Liu, W., et al.: SSD: single shot multibox detector. In: Leibe, B., Matas, J., Sebe, N., Welling, M. (eds.) ECCV 2016. LNCS, vol. 9905, pp. 21–37. Springer, Cham (2016). https://doi.org/10.1007/978-3-319-46448-0_2
16. Ren, S., He, K., Girshick, R., Sun, J.: Faster R-CNN: towards real-time object detection with region proposal networks (2015)
17. Simonyan, K., Zisserman, A.: Very deep convolutional networks for large-scale image recognition. international conference on learning representations (2015)
18. Szegedy, C., et al.: Going deeper with convolutions. In: Proceedings of the IEEE Conference on Computer Vision and Pattern Recognition, pp. 1–9 (2015)

19. Uijlings, J.R., Van De Sande, K.E., Gevers, T., Smeulders, A.W.: Selective search for object recognition. Int. J. Comput. Vis. **104**(2), 154–171 (2013)
20. Vedaldi, A., Gulshan, V., Varma, M., Zisserman, A.: Multiple kernels for object detection. In: 2009 IEEE 12th International Conference on Computer Vision, pp. 606–613. IEEE (2009)
21. Xu, K., et al.: Show, attend and tell: neural image caption generation with visual attention. In: International Conference on Machine Learning, pp. 2048–2057 (2015)
22. Yang, Z., He, X., Gao, J., Deng, L., Smola, A.: Stacked attention networks for image question answering. In: Proceedings of the IEEE Conference on Computer Vision and Pattern Recognition, pp. 21–29 (2016)
23. You, Q., Jin, H., Wang, Z., Fang, C., Luo, J.: Image captioning with semantic attention. In: Proceedings of the IEEE Conference on Computer Vision and Pattern Recognition, pp. 4651–4659 (2016)
24. Zeiler, M.D., Fergus, R.: Visualizing and understanding convolutional networks. In: Fleet, D., Pajdla, T., Schiele, B., Tuytelaars, T. (eds.) ECCV 2014. LNCS, vol. 8689, pp. 818–833. Springer, Cham (2014). https://doi.org/10.1007/978-3-319-10590-1_53
25. Zeng, X., Ouyang, W., Yang, B., Yan, J., Wang, X.: Gated bi-directional CNN for object detection. In: Leibe, B., Matas, J., Sebe, N., Welling, M. (eds.) ECCV 2016. LNCS, vol. 9911, pp. 354–369. Springer, Cham (2016). https://doi.org/10.1007/978-3-319-46478-7_22
26. Zhao, Z., Zheng, P., Xu, S., Wu, X.: Object detection with deep learning: a review. IEEE Trans. Neural Netw. 1–21 (2019)
27. Zhu, F., Li, H., Ouyang, W., Yu, N., Wang, X.: Learning spatial regularization with image-level supervisions for multi-label image classification. In: Proceedings of the IEEE Conference on Computer Vision and Pattern Recognition, pp. 5513–5522 (2017)
28. Zitnick, C.L., Dollár, P.: Edge boxes: locating object proposals from edges. In: Fleet, D., Pajdla, T., Schiele, B., Tuytelaars, T. (eds.) ECCV 2014. LNCS, vol. 8693, pp. 391–405. Springer, Cham (2014). https://doi.org/10.1007/978-3-319-10602-1_26

Dynamic Neural Network for Business and Market Analysis

Javier de Arquer Rilo[1]([⊠]), Abir Hussain[1]([⊠]), May Al-Taei[2],
Thar Baker[1]([⊠]), and Dhiya Al-Jumeily[1]

[1] Department of Computer Science, Liverpool John Moores University,
Liverpool L33AF, UK
javierdearquer@gmail.com, {A.Hussain, T.baker,
D.Aljumeily}@ljmu.ac.uk
[2] College of Technological Innovation, Zayed University, Abu Dhabi, UAE
may.Altaei@zu.ac.ae

Abstract. The problem of predicting nonlinear and nonstationary signals is complex since the physical law that controls them is unknown and it is complicated to be considered. In these cases, it is necessary to devise nonlinear models that imitate or learn the rules of behavior of the problem and can be developed based on historical data. For this reason, neural networks are useful tools to deal with this type of problem due to their nonlinearly and their capacity of generalizing. This paper aims at exploring various types of neural network architectures and study their performance with time series predictions. Predictions on two sets of data (of a very different nature) will be made using three neural networks including multilayer perceptrons, recurrent neural network and long-short term memory varying some important parameters: input neurons, epochs and the anticipation with which the predictions are made. Then, all results will be compared using standard metrics.

As a conclusion, the influence of the type of series under study is more important than the parameters considered in what concerns the performance. The management of the memory in the networks is a key to its success in the prediction of S&P 500 and electrical power time series.

Keywords: ANN · Long short-term memory · Neural Turing Machine

1 Introduction

Forecasting techniques can be classified by the data used: qualitative or quantitative methods. Fundamental analysis looks for factors that include on the time series that is being analysed. Knowing the main process that gives value to a certain stock (the supply chain, the sales and distribution) allows knowing better how a certain series will behave and therefore make good predictions [1].

This prediction method considers measures and quantities and relevant qualitative information (i.e. news). The interpretation and combination of all this information is very complex and is difficult to put together. Nevertheless, this huge amount of data can make quite precise predictions in the hands of an expert [2].

© Springer Nature Switzerland AG 2019
D.-S. Huang et al. (Eds.): ICIC 2019, LNCS 11643, pp. 77–87, 2019.
https://doi.org/10.1007/978-3-030-26763-6_8

Econometric forecasting, so called technical analysis, studies the past stock price to analyse the stock convenience. Technical analysis considers trending nature of prices, traded volume, confirmation and divergence [3].

It assumes that all the data available is contained in real time prices of stocks. This is a widely accepted hypothesis in market analysis. Trends in price and volume are identified by analysts who rely on historical data to predict future outcomes.

The main criticism that this technique faces is that, although based on numerical data, the final decision is subjective, and therefore different experts can extract different results from the same data.

Predictions can also be made with machine learning, which is a branch of computer science where algorithms learn from data. These systems are trained with historical data from which they learn the nature of the problem, which allows them to generalize and make predictions. Thus, this algorithm resembles the natural process of operation of a stockbroker [4].

Due to the huge amount of data available and growing computing capacity, this seems to be the technique with the best future projection. This work focuses on the study of neural networks as a technique to make predictions, using two datasets which are the S&P 500 stock market data set and the electrical power price dataset.

The reminder of this paper is organised as follows. Section 2 shows the utilised network structure including the long-short memory network and the recurrent neural network. Section 3 shows the method used in this research, while Sect. 4 shows illustrates the simulation results. The final section is Sect. 5 which concludes the paper.

2   Network Architecture

2.1   Long Short-Term Memory (LSTM)

One of the most prevalent typologies to make predictions is the Long short-term memory (LSTM) introduced by Hochreiter and Schmidhuber in 1997 [5]. The authors introduce the concept of "memory cell" that replaces the previously seen neuron to solve the problem of gradient fading. In Fig. 1(a), it can be seen a memory cell and the parts that compose it.

The name LSTM suggests the addition of short-term memory (STM) since neural networks already have long-term memory in the weights of the connections but in this structure also has STM in the possible connections between memory cells. Variations such as the peephole connections have been proposed on the memory cell. These loop closure connections improve performance since they need not to go through the activation function, thus saving computation.

This typology has a great diffusion and extensively used nowadays with multiple layers and their computational cost is reasonable.

(a)

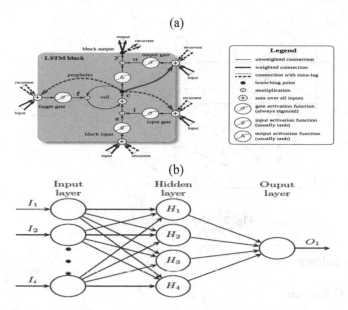

(b)

Fig. 1. (a) LSTM - memory cell [5], (b) LSTM - network layout utilised in this research.

A network consisting of 1 hidden-layer of 4 LSTM neurons is used in this research as illustrated in Fig. 1(b). The output layer is made of one neuron that weights the values of the 4 previous neurons.

2.2 Recurrent Neural Network (RNN)

Recurrent neural networks (RNNs) give better long-range memory due to the huge amount of states they can store. It should be noted that besides the connections between layers are the feedbacks. These stored states grow exponentially with the number of neurons but the complexity of inference and training grow only quadratically [6].

RNNs ability to compute arbitrary problem has been proved because they can simulate a universal Turing machine [7]. Its great advantage over other systems that can solve complex problems is that it can learn and generalize for cases not covered in their training.

Recurrent network with a hidden layer of 4 neurons is utilised in this research that will deliver its output to the next layer and its input in the next time-step. The structure of the network can be shown in Fig. 2.

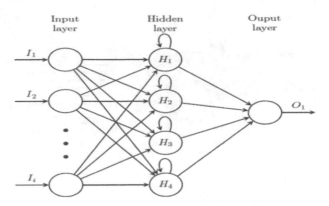

Fig. 2. RNN - network layout

3 Methodology

3.1 Data Collection

Two data sets are used for our experiments which are the reference hourly power demand of electricity in Spain (in MW) and monthly values of the S&P 500 index.

The electricity dataset is made of 8760 values from an average reference year (365 days/24 h). The S&P 500 values are from May 1954 to August 2016. Figure 3 shows the utilised time series for this research paper. The data sets are split so that 70% is used for training and the remaining 10% is used for testing with 20% used for validation.

The Electricity hourly power is published by Red Electrica de Espana (REE) which is a partly state owned and public limited Spanish corporation. REE operates the national electricity grid in Spain, where it operates the national power transmission system. As shown in Fig. 4, although the dispersion of the values in the histogram is quite uniform, two peaks can be seen: one in the vicinity of 23,000 MW and another close to 31,000 MW.

The auto-correlogram allows us seeing the extent the signals are random: the closer to 0 the values are, the more random the signal.

In Fig. 5, it can be seen that between values 24 h apart there is a high correlation. This will be considered in the seasonality analysis of the series. The time series of Standard & Poor's 500 (S&P 500) is used in many prediction studies. Unlike the electricity hourly power, with a clear seasonality and with no tendency, this series has the nature of most stock series: it is stochastic and nonstationary. Because of the differences between both series, it is possible to compare the behaviour of networks in different environments. Forecasting (of currency exchanges or shares) is interesting because benefits could be easily obtained with reliable automated systems. Figure 6 shows the histogram of the S&P 500 time series while Fig. 7 shows its auto-correlogram which indicates that the auto-correlogram does not go to zero until a very small value of the lags indicating a nonstationary behaviour.

(a)

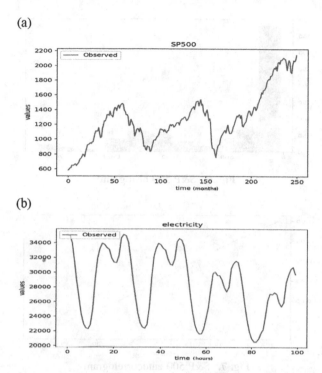

(b)

Fig. 3. Time series studied: (a) S&P 500 index, (b) electricity hourly power demand of reference

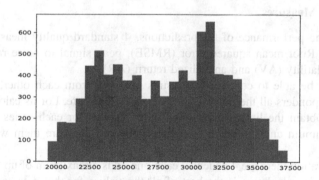

Fig. 4. Electricity power histogram

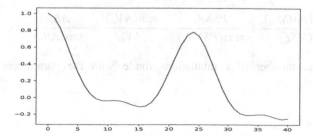

Fig. 5. Electricity power autocorrelogram

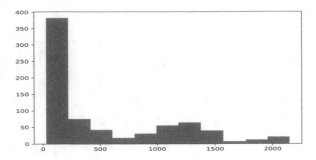

Fig. 6. S&P 500 histogram

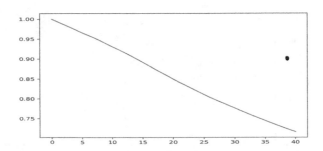

Fig. 7. S&P 500 autocorrelogram

3.2 Quality Measures

To compare the performance of the predictions, 4 standard quality measures will be used, namely: Root mean squared error (RMSE), peak signal to noise ratio (PSNR) annualized volatility (AV) and annualized return (AR).

Finally, to be able to compare the results obtained from each other, a metric is proposed that ponders all the previous ones. It is called score. For its calculation, it is necessary to obtain the limit values of all other metrics for each series of data and network (maximum and minimum as appropriate) and compare them with the case under study.

In the operation there are 4 addends, each one adds a maximum of up to 1 point in case the value in calculation is the best of all the values for that data series and that network. As explained, the operation performed is:

$$Score_i = \frac{min(RMSE_n)}{RMSE_i} + \frac{PSNR_i}{max(PSNR_n)} + \frac{min(AV_n)}{AV_i} + \frac{AR_i}{max(AR_n)} \forall n \in (1, \ldots, 36)$$

Where n is the number of combinations made with the parameters i, p and e (36 in total).

3.3 Prediction Parameters

Each network will be studied by varying certain characteristics to know how they affect the performance. This is also made to compare the best performances of each network that might not be obtained with the same parameters. These parameters are:

- The number of input neurons (i) will be varied. This value can be 5, 10, 15 or 20.
- Predictions are made 1, 5 or 10 steps ahead (p). In this way, it can be seen the ability to predict the events that the network has and where it behaves best.
- The number of epochs (e) will be varied, being able to take the values 20, 100 and 1000. Each epoch consists on one forward pass and one backward pass of all the training examples.

The studied networks are: Multilayer perceptrons (used for benchmarking purposes), RNN and LSTM are used as illustrated in Sect. 2.

4 Results and Discussion

All the procedures are implemented in Tensor Flow (test, train, neurons, etc.), a python library developed by Google. Keras which is a high-level library that enables fast experimentation was also used. To benchmark our results, Multilayer perceptrons (MLP) was implemented in our experiments. Table 1 summarizes the network results.

Table 1. Best 3 MLP typologies

i	p	e	SP500					i	p	e	elec				
			RAISE	PSNR	AV	AR	Score				RMSE	PSNR.	AV	AR	Score
5	1	1000	97	25.8	743	0.0625	3.1	10	1	1000	481	37.4	336452	230	3.2
15	1	1000	100	25.9	808	0.0498	2.9	15	1	1000	457	37.9	332820	230	3.2
10	1	1000	96	26	768	1.0509	2.9	20	1	1000	439	38.2	335102	230	3.2

Figure 8, shows the negative influence that the number of epochs has for the series of S&P 500 when using RNN. The influence of this parameter is lower in the electrical series where a slight improvement is observed as more neurons are in the input layer. However, the parameter that most influences this metric for the electrical power is the anticipation with which the prediction is made: indeed the closer prediction is in the future (i.e. the step ahead prediction), the better it will be.

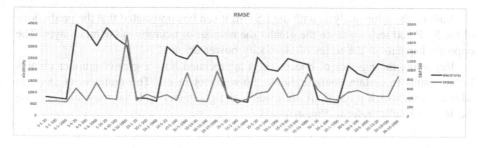

Fig. 8. RMSE obtained with RNN

With respect to the peak signal-to-noise ratio (see Fig. 9) of the predictions made, the increase in the number of neurons in the input layer: positively influences subtlety for the electrical data series, while for the S&P 500 series it does not seem to have any influence.

For the electric series, better values (higher) are obtained as the number of epochs increases: the greater the training, the more consistent is the response of the network. In absolute terms it can be seen that the noise is very small compared to the signal because in most cases, values are obtained in the range from 20 dB to 35 dB. However, for the series S&P 500, the number of neurons in the input layer does not seem to influence and the increase of epochs seems to be counterproductive and the prediction anticipation does not either seem to have the influence discussed above either.

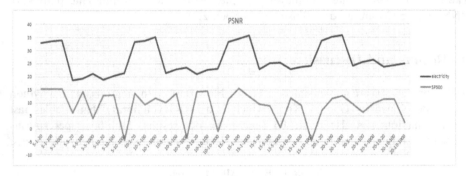

Fig. 9. PSNR obtained with RNN

Table 2 summarizes the configurations that, for each series of data, obtain the best score.

Table 2. Best 3 RNN typologies

i	p	e	SP500					i	p	e	elec				
			RMSE	PSNR	AV	AR	Score				RMSE	PSNR	AV	AR	Score
5	1	1000	294	15.4	512	0.0453	3.34	15	1	1000	579	36	342827	237	3.46
20	1	1000	349	12.53	430	0.0440	3.04	20	1	1000	583	36	339729	237	3.46
15	1	100	287	15.5	521	0.0295	3.01	20	1	100	634	35	342847	236	3.35

Making the same analysis with the LSTM, it can be appreciated that the predictions of the S&P 500 series worsen the greater the number of neurons in the input layer. The opposite happens in the series of electricity power demand.

Regarding the number of epochs, it is appreciated how a greater number obtains better results in certain configurations although not in all. The numbers of steps in advance with which predictions are made is the parameter with the most influence on the RMSE results (refer to Fig. 10).

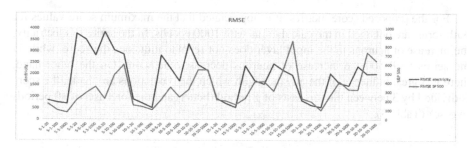

Fig. 10. RMSE obtained with LSTM

Regarding the peak signal-to-noise ratio of the predictions made, there seems to be a small relationship between the number of neurons in the input layer and the value of the input layer: with the S&P 500 series, worse values of PSNR (lower) are obtained the more neurons the input layer has, unlike what happens with the electric power series.

While it is true, the parameter that most influences this metric is the number of steps before the prediction: the larger this number is, the worse the results are. It should be noted that the PSNR is much better in the electrical series than in the S&P 500. Also, increasing the number of epochs produces stronger responses: improves the result for predictions few steps to the future (where the result is better in all cases) and makes it worse when the predictions are much in advance.

Regarding volatility, the two data series show different behaviours. In the series of S&P 500 it can be argued that the fewer epochs are made, the lower volatility is obtained, whereas in the electricity series it cannot always be shown. In the case of the electricity series, the increase of neurons in the input layer seems very harmful when increasing the volatility, while in the series S&P 500 no influence is seen. Again, the idea is insisted that this metric is not adequate for the electricity series given the high values it achieves.

In Fig. 11, it can be shown that the different parameters influence the annualized rate of return. The increase of neurons in the input layer is significantly positive for the results of the electricity series, quite the opposite as for the series of S&P 500. On the other hand, the maximum values are obtained in cases with 1000 epochs (the maximum number proposed for this work). It should be noted that as in the previous cases, that different scales are used for the two series since the metrics in the electric power series are several orders of magnitude higher than those of the stock series.

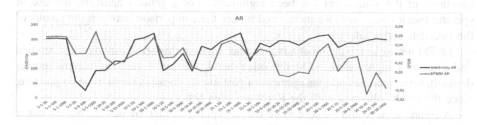

Fig. 11. AR obtained with LSTM

For the proposed score metrics, it is appreciated that the maximum score values for both series are obtained in the calculations with 1000 epochs. In the series of electricity, the increase of neurons in the input layer does not seem to influence the score, while in the series S&P 500 the increase of neurons decreases the score. On the other hand, there is a great influence of the advance with which the predictions are made: the score is divided by 3 between the forecasts of 1 period (better) and the forecasts of 10 periods (worse) (Table 3).

Table 3. Summarizes the configurations that obtain the best score for each series of data. All of them are predictions at 1 step of time (as it has been seen, it is one of the most influential parameters) and with a high number of epochs that always enhance the characteristics of the network (for better or for worse). It is appreciated that for predictions of the S&P 500 series it is not necessary to consider many past time steps, while for the series of electrical power the more time steps are considered the better the predictions are.

i	p	e	SP5Q0					i	p	e	elec				
			RMSE	PSNR	AV	AR	Score				RMSE	PSNR	AV	AH	Score
5	1	1000	77	28.3	801	0.0472	3.45	10	1	1000	516	36.8	335925	222	3.4
5	1	100	102	25.8	768	1.0478	3.16	15	1	1000	525	36.8	336583	225	3.42
10	1	1000	104	26.2	751	0.0469	3.15	20	1	1000	539	36.6	330600	221	3.37

5 Conclusion

Artificial Neural networks learn easy from data and adapt to multiple problems. With the series used there are possibilities to make stock market predictions as seen on S&P 500 values but also predictions can be made in other areas of interest for industry and society. One day ahead stock market prediction seems to be promising because of the superb results in term of AR.

On one hand, although precision of stock predictions is small, the tendency is what makes ANN big and what can make money from predictions. On the other hand, electricity power predictions are more accurate due to its stationarity and absence of a trend.

For new applications, the number of layers, neurons, and the amount of training data should be chosen to try with different combinations. As seen with the results, the amount of training data available is important for better performance, to allow the net to generalize. Then, the error that will be committed in the predictions should be delimited.

The inability of the annualized return, and the annualized volatility to represent the goodness of the adjustment has been significant. For a general analysis, the use of specific metrics such as those mentioned makes the comparison between the results of the two data series difficult.

LSTM networks are the most advanced networks in this sense among those studied and present a higher Score. On the other hand, for series such as electric power demand, better storage and management of past events does not seem to be so positive, since the results obtained with the RNN are even better.

A future work would explore more recent typologies that, by design, have a better ability to memorize, such as Neural Turing Machines [8].

References

1. Brockwell, P.J., Davis, R.A.: Introduction to Time Series and Forecasting. Springer, New York (2016). https://doi.org/10.1007/b97391
2. Sapankevych, N.I., Sankar, R.: Time series prediction using support vector machines: a survey. IEEE Comput. Intell. Mag. **4**(2), 24–38 (2009)
3. Dey, H.S., Kabir, M.A., Wadud, Z., Khan, S.I., Azad, M.A.K.: Econometric modeling and forecasting of natural gas demand for power sector in Bangladesh. In: TENCON 2011, pp. 1383–1386 (2011)
4. Liu, X.Q., Ang, B.W., Goh, T.N., Forecasting of electricity consumption: a comparison between an econometric model and a neural network model. In: IEEE International Joint Conference on Neural Networks, pp. 1254–1259 (1991)
5. Hochreiter, S., Schmidhuber, J.: Long short-term memory. Neural Comput. **9**(8) (1997). https://doi.org/10.1162/neco.1997.9.8.1735
6. Lipton, Z.C.: A critical review of recurrent neural networks for sequence learning. CoRR, abs/1506.00019 (2015)
7. Siegelmann, H.T., Sontag, E.D.: Turing computability with neural nets. Appl. Math. Lett. **4**(6) (1991). https://doi.org/10.1016/0893-9659(91)90080-F
8. Graves, A., et al.: Hybrid computing using a neural network with dynamic external memory. Nature **538**, 471–476 (2016)

ψ-type Synchronization of Memristor-Based Competitive Neural Networks with Time-Varying Delays via Nonlinear Feedback Control

Yue Chen, Zhenkun Huang$^{(\boxtimes)}$, and Chao Chen

School of Science, Jimei University, Xiamen 361021, China
hzk974226@jmu.edu.cn

Abstract. This paper is concerned with the ψ-type synchronization of memristive-based competitive neural networks with time-varying delays. A nonlinear feedback controller and Lyapunov-Krasovskii function are constructed properly, as well as using corresponding differential inclusions theory and lemmas, the ψ-type synchronization of coupled neural networks is obtained. The results of this paper are general, and they also extend and complement some previous results. A simulation example is carried out to show the effectiveness of theoretical results.

Keywords: Competitive neural network · ψ-type synchronization · Nonlinear feedback control · Lyapunov-Krasovskii functional

1 Introduction

In the past few decades, neural networks have given a lot of attention for they have extensive applications in image processing, associative memory, optimization problems, and so on [1–4]. Memristor-based neural networks have been paid much attention of researchers for the memristor's memory characteristic and nanometer dimensions, as a special kind of neural network. Memristor was introduced by Chua [5] in 1971 and was first realized by the Hewlett-Packard (HP) Laboratory team in 2008 [6, 7]. From the previous work, it proved that the memristor exhibits features just as the neurons in the human brain. Because of this feature, more and more researchers construct a new model of neural networks to emulate the human brain through replacing the resistor by the memristor, and analysis the dynamical behaviors of memristor-based neural networks for the purpose of realizing its successful applications [8–11].

Since MeyerBase et al. proposed the competitive neural networks with time scales in [12], the synchronization problem of competitive neural networks have been a hot topic. In this paper, we introduce memristor-based competitive neural networks with different time scales, which has two different state variables: the short-term memory (STM) variable describing the fast neural activity and the long-term memory (LTM) variable describing the slow unsupervised synaptic modifications. In addition, the switched memristor-based competitive neural networks (SMCNNs) can exhibit

© Springer Nature Switzerland AG 2019
D.-S. Huang et al. (Eds.): ICIC 2019, LNCS 11643, pp. 88–97, 2019.
https://doi.org/10.1007/978-3-030-26763-6_9

some undesirable system behaviour, e.g. oscillations, may happen when the parameters and time delays are appropriately chosen [13]. The SMCNNs model are with discontinuous right-hand sides and they generalize the conventional neural networks [14–17]. It is well known that the SMCNNs model has more flexibility compared with the conventional neural networks in associative memory and optimization problems. Thus, it is great significance to investigate it.

Although nonlinear feedback control was used in early publications [18–20], so far there is little work on synchronization of SMCNNs via nonlinear feedback control. In [14, 15], exponential synchronization of neural networks is obtained by linear control while in this paper we discuss ψ-type synchronization. However, the ψ-type synchronization studied in this paper is in a general framework and it contains exponential synchronization, polynomial synchronization, and other synchronization as its special cases. Motivated by the above discussions, we will use some lemmas and construct a nonlinear controller to realize the ψ-type synchronization of SMCNNs with time-varying delays via a nonlinear controller. It should be noted that the ψ-type synchronization is in a general framework and it can only be obtained with our nonlinear controller exhibits special construction.

The structure of this paper is outlined as follow. In Sect. 2, the model formation and some preliminaries are given. In Sect. 3, sufficient criteria are obtained by using our control strategy. Section 4, A numerical example is given to describe the effectiveness of the proposed results. Finally, the conclusion is drawn in Sect. 5.

2 System Formulation and Preliminaries

The following notations will be used. $\|x\| = \sqrt{x^T x}$ is the Euclidean norm of $x \in R^n$. $co\{\underline{a}_i, \bar{a}_i\}$ denotes the convex hull of $\{\underline{a}_i, \bar{a}_i\}$, $\underline{a}_i, \bar{a}_i \in R$. R^n and $R^{n \times n}$ denote the n-dimensional Euclidean space and the set of all $n \times n$ real matrixes, respectively. $P > 0$ means that is a real positive definite matrix. $C([-\tau, 0], R^n)$ denote the Banach space of all continuous functions $\phi : [-\tau, 0] \to R^n$.

In this paper, we propose SMCNNs with time-varying delays as following:

$$STM : \varepsilon \dot{x}_i(t) = -x_i(t) + \sum_{j=1}^{n} a_{ij}(x_i) f_j(x_j(t)) + \sum_{j=1}^{n} b_{ij}(x_i(t - \tau(t))) f_j(x_j(t - \tau(t))) + H_i s_i(t), j = 1, 2, \ldots, n, \quad (2.1)$$

$$LTM : \dot{s}_i(t) = -s_i(t) + f_i(x_i(t)), i = 1, 2, \ldots, n,$$

where a_{ij} and b_{ij} denote the connection weight between the i th neuron and the j th neuron and the synaptic weight of delayed feedback.

$$a_{ij}(x_i(t)) = \begin{cases} \hat{a}_{ij}, |x_i(t)| > T_i, \\ \check{a}_{ij}, |x_i(t)| \le T_i, \end{cases}$$

$$b_{ij}(x_i) = b_{ij}(x_i(t - \tau(t))) = \begin{cases} \hat{b}_{ij}, |x_i(t - \tau(t))| > T_i, \\ \check{b}_{ij}, |x_i(t - \tau(t))| \le T_i, \end{cases}$$

the switching jumps $T_i > 0, \hat{a}_{ij}, \breve{a}_{ij}, \hat{b}_{ij}, \breve{b}_{ij}$ are all constant numbers and $\tau(t)$ corresponds to the transmission delay and satisfies $0 \leq \tau(t) \leq \tau$, where $\varepsilon > 0$ is the time scale of STM state; n denotes the number of neuron, $x(t) = (x_1(t), x_2(t), \ldots, x_n(t))^T, x_i(t)$ is the neuron current activity level. $f_j(x_j(t))$ is the output of neurons, $f(y(t)) = (f_1(x_1(t)), f_2(x_2(t)), \ldots, f_n(x_n(t)))^T$. $s_i(t)$ is the synaptic efficiency, $s(t) = (s_1(t), s_2(t), \ldots, s_n(t))^T$. H_i is the strength of the external stimulus. The following assumptions are given for system (2.1).

H1: The neuron activation function f_j is bounded and there exists a diagonal matrix $L : L = diag(l_1, l_2, \ldots, l_n)$ satisfying

$$\left| f_j(s_1) - f_j(s_2) \right| \leq l_j |s_1 - s_2|,$$

for all $s_1, s_2 \in R, j = 1, 2, \ldots, n$.

H2: The transmission delay $\tau(t)$ is a differential function and there exists constants $\tau > 0, \mu > 0, \beta > 0$ such that

$$0 \leq \tau(t) \leq \tau, \dot{\tau}(t) < \mu \leq \beta < 1,$$

for all $t \geq 0$.

Definition 2.1 [21]. Let $E \subset R^n, x \mapsto F(x)$ be called a set-valued map from $E \rightarrow R^n$. If for each point x of a set $E \subset R^n$, there corresponds a nonempty set $F(x) \subset R^n$.

Definition 2.2 [21]. For a system with discontinuous right-hand sides

$$\frac{dx}{dt} = g(x), \ x(0) = x_0, \ x \in R^n, \ t \geq 0, \tag{2.2}$$

A set-valued map is defined as

$$\varphi(x) = \bigcap_{\delta > 0} \bigcap_{\mu(N) = 0} \overline{co}[g(B(x, \delta)) \backslash N],$$

where $B(x, \delta) = \{y : \|y - x\| < \delta, x, y \in R^n, \delta \in R^+\}$ and $N \in R^n, \overline{co}[E]$ is the closure of the convex hull of set $E, E \subset R^n, \mu(N)$ is a Lebesgue measure of set N. A solution in Filippovs sense of the Cauchy problem for this system with initial condition $x(0) = x_0 \in R^n$ is an absolutely continuous function $x(t), t \in [0, T]$ which satisfies $x(0) = x_0$ and the differential inclusion:

$$\frac{dx}{dt} \in \phi(x), \quad \text{for a.e. } t \in [0, T]$$

By applying the theories of set-valued maps and differential inclusions above, there exist $\tilde{a}_{ij} \in co\{\hat{a}_{ij}, \breve{a}_{ij}\}$, $\tilde{b}_{ij} \in co\{\hat{b}_{ij}, \breve{b}_{ij}\}$, such that the memristor-based neural networks (2.1) can be written as the following differential inclusion:

$$STM : \varepsilon\dot{x}_i(t) = -x_i(t) + \sum_{j=1}^{n} \tilde{a}_{ij}f_j(x_j(t)) + \sum_{j=1}^{n} \tilde{b}_{ij}f_j(x_j(t - \tau(t))) + H_is_i(t), \; j = 1, 2, \ldots, n,$$

$$LTM : \dot{s}_i(t) = -s_i(t) + f_i(x_i(t)), \; i = 1, 2, \ldots, n,$$

(2.3)

Consider system (2.3) as the drive system and the corresponding response system can be constructed as following:

$$STM : \varepsilon\dot{y}_i(t) = -y_i(t) + \sum_{j=1}^{n} \tilde{a}_{ij}f_j(y_j(t)) + \sum_{j=1}^{n} \tilde{b}_{ij}f_j(y_j(t - \tau(t))) + H_ir_i(t) + u_i(t), \; j = 1, 2, \ldots, n,$$

$$LTM : \dot{r}_i(t) = -r_i(t) + f_i(y_i(t)), \; i = 1, 2, \ldots, n,$$

(2.4)

where $y(t) \in R^n$ is the state vector of response system, $u(t)$ is the control input to be designed. Define the synchronization error as $e(t) = (e_1(t), e_2(t), \ldots, e_n(t))^T$ where $e(t) = y(t) - x(t)$ and $h(t) = r(t) - s(t)$. Then the synchronization error system is given as following:

$$STM : \varepsilon\dot{e}_i(t) = -e_i(t) + \sum_{j=1}^{n} \tilde{a}_{ij}g_j(e_j(t)) + \sum_{j=1}^{n} \tilde{b}_{ij}g_j(e_j(t - \tau(t))) + H_ih_i(t) + u_i(t), \; j = 1, 2, \ldots, n,$$

$$LTM : \dot{h}_i(t) = -h_i(t) + g_i(e_i(t)), \; i = 1, 2, \ldots, n,$$

(2.5)

where $g(e(t)) = f(y(t)) - f(x(t)), g(e(t - \tau(t))) = f(y(t - \tau(t))) - f(x(t - \tau(t)))$.

Lemma 2.1 [22]. The function $g(x)$ of system (2.2) is local bounded, if there exist a differential function $V(t, x) : R_+ \times R^n \to R_+$ and positive constants λ_1, λ_2 for system (2.2) such that for $V(t, x) \in R_+ \times R^n$

$$(\lambda_1 \|x\|)^2 \leq V(t, x),$$

$$\frac{V(t, x)}{dt} \leq -\delta V(t, x) + \lambda_2\zeta(t),$$

where $x(t)$ is a solution of system (2.2), $\delta > 0$ and $\zeta(t) \in C(R, R^+)$. Then the solution $x(t)$ of system (2.2) is ψ-type stable and the convergence rate is $\frac{\delta}{2}$.

Lemma 2.2 [23]. For any vector $x, y \in R^n$ and a positive constant q, the following matrix inequality holds

$$2x^Ty \leq qx^Tx + q^{-1}y^Ty.$$

3 Main Results

In this paper, the nonlinear controller in the response system (2.4) is considered as follows:

$$u(t) = we(t) + K_1 e(t - \tau(t)) - \frac{\varepsilon \|e(t)\|^2 e(t)}{2\left(\|e(t)\|^2 + \zeta(t)\right)}, \tag{3.1}$$

where w and K_1 are the controller gains to be determined, $w = (w_1, w_2, \ldots, w_n)^T$, w_i is a constant, $i = 1, 2, \ldots, n$. To prove our main results, we construct the following Lyapunov functional:

$$V(t) = e^T(t)e(t) + h^T(t)h(t) + \frac{1}{1-\mu} \int_{t-\tau(t)}^t e^T(s)Qe(s)ds + \int_{-\tau}^0 \int_{t+\xi}^t e^T(s)Qe(s)dsd\xi. \tag{3.2}$$

where Q is a positive diagonal matrix. Then from (3.2), there always exists a scalar $\sigma > 1$ such that

$$\|e(t)\|^2 \leq V(t) \leq \sigma \|e(t)\|^2 + \frac{\sigma}{\lambda_{\min}(T)} \int_{t-\tau}^t e^T(s)Qe(s)ds, \tag{3.3}$$

where

$$\lambda_{\min}(T) > 0,$$

$$T = \frac{2I}{\varepsilon} - \frac{2}{\varepsilon}AL - \frac{r_1}{\varepsilon}(BL)^T BL - \frac{r_2}{\varepsilon}H^T H - \frac{2w}{\varepsilon} - \frac{r_3}{\varepsilon}K_1^T K_1 - \frac{1}{r_4}L^T L - \frac{Q}{1-\mu} - Q\tau > 0 \tag{3.4}$$

and $A = (\tilde{a}_{ij})_{n \times n}, B = (\tilde{b}_{ij})_{n \times n}, H = diag(H_1, H_2, \ldots, H_n), L = (l_1, l_2, \ldots, l_n)^T$.

Theorem 3.1. Under the assumptions H1–H2, if there exist a constant $\sigma > 1$, $r_1, r_2, r_3, r_4 > 0$, diagonal matrix $Q > 0$ and K_1, K_2 such that

$$\delta\sigma < \lambda_{\min}(T), \ T > 0, \tag{3.5}$$

where $\delta > 0$, then systems (2.3) and (2.4) are ψ-type synchronization with the non-linear feedback controller and the convergence rate is $\frac{\delta}{2}$ when the error $e(t)$ approaches to zero.

Proof. Calculating the derivative of Lyapunov-Krasovskii function (3.2), along (2.5) we have

$$\dot{V}(t, e(t)) \leq 2e^T(t)\dot{e}(t) + 2h^T(t)\dot{h}(t) + \frac{1}{1-\mu}e^T(t)Qe(t) - \frac{1-\dot{\tau}(t)}{1-\mu}e^T(t-\tau(t))Qe(t-\tau(t))$$

$$+ e^T(t)Q\tau e(t) - \int_{t-\tau}^t e^T(s)Qe(s)ds$$

$$= \frac{2}{\varepsilon}e^T(t)[-e(t) + Ag(e(t)) + Bg(e(t-\tau(t))) + Hh(t) + u(t)] + 2h^T(t)[-h(t)$$

$$+ g(e(t))] + \frac{1}{1-\mu}e^T(t)Qe(t) - \frac{1-\dot{\tau}(t)}{1-\mu}e^T(t-\tau(t))Qe(t-\tau(t))$$

$$+ e^T(t)Q\tau e(t) - \int_{t-\tau}^t e^T(s)Qe(s)ds \tag{3.6}$$

By Lemma 2.2 and H1, there exist positive scalars $r_1, r_2, r_3, r_4 > 0$ such that

$$2e^T(t)Bg(e(t-\tau(t))) \leq r_1 e^T(t)(BL)^T BLe(t) + \frac{1}{r_1}e^T(t-\tau(t))e(t-\tau(t)), \tag{3.7}$$

$$2e^T(t)Hh(t) \leq r_2 e^T(t)(H)^T He(t) + \frac{1}{r_2}h^T(t)h(t), \tag{3.8}$$

$$2e^T(t)K_1 e(t-\tau(t)) \leq r_3 e^T(t)(K_1)^T K_1 e(t) + \frac{1}{r_3}e^T(t-\tau(t))e(t-\tau(t)), \tag{3.9}$$

$$2h^T(t)g(e(t)) \leq r_4 h^T(t)h(t) + \frac{1}{r_4}e^T(t)L^T Le(t). \tag{3.10}$$

Substituting (3.7)–(3.10) into (3.6) we have

$$\dot{V}(t, e(t)) \leq -e^T(t)\left[\frac{2I}{\varepsilon} - \frac{2}{\varepsilon}AL - \frac{r_1}{\varepsilon}(BL)^T BL - \frac{r_2}{\varepsilon}H^T H - \frac{2w}{\varepsilon} - \frac{r_3}{\varepsilon}K_1^T K_1 - \frac{1}{r_4}L^T L - \frac{Q}{1-\mu} - Q\tau\right]e(t)$$

$$+ e^T(t-\tau(t))\left[\frac{I}{\varepsilon r_1} + \frac{I}{\varepsilon r_3} - \frac{1-\beta}{1-\mu}Q\right]e(t-\tau(t)) + h^T(t)\left[-2 + \frac{I}{\varepsilon r_2} + r_4\right]h(t)$$

$$- \int_{t-\tau}^t e^T(s)Qe(s)ds - \frac{\|e(t)\|^4}{\|e(t)\|^2 + \zeta(t)}. \tag{3.11}$$

Le $T = \frac{2I}{\varepsilon} - \frac{2}{\varepsilon}AL - \frac{r_1}{\varepsilon}(BL)^T BL - \frac{r_2}{\varepsilon}H^T H - \frac{2w}{\varepsilon} - \frac{r_3}{\varepsilon}K_1^T K_1 - \frac{1}{r_4}L^T L - \frac{Q}{1-\mu} - Q\tau > 0$,
$\frac{1-\beta}{1-\mu}Q = \frac{1}{\varepsilon r_1} + \frac{1}{\varepsilon r_3}, \frac{1}{\varepsilon r_2} + r_4 - 2 < 0$, we have

$$\dot{V}(t, e(t)) \leq -e^T(t)Te(t) + \|e(t)\|^2 - \frac{\|e(t)\|^4}{\|e(t)\|^2 + \zeta(t)} - \int_{t-\tau}^t e^T(s)Qe(s)ds$$

$$= -e^T(t)Te(t) + \frac{\|e(t)\|^2\zeta(t)}{\|e(t)\|^2 + \zeta(t)} - \int_{t-\tau}^t e^T(s)Qe(s)ds. \tag{3.12}$$

By using the inequality $0 \leq \frac{b\rho(t)}{b+\rho(t)} \leq \rho(t), \forall b > 0, \rho(t) > 0$, we have

$$
\begin{aligned}
\dot{V}(t, e(t)) &\leq -e^T(t)Te(t) + \zeta(t) - \int_{t-\tau}^t e^T(s)Qe(s)ds \\
&\leq -\lambda_{\min}(T)e^T(t)e(t) + \zeta(t) - \int_{t-\tau}^t e^T(s)Qe(s)ds.
\end{aligned}
\tag{3.13}
$$

Then, from (3.3) and (3.12), we have

$$
\begin{aligned}
\dot{V}(t) + \delta V(t) &\leq -\lambda_{\min}(T)e^T(t)e(t) + \zeta(t) - \int_{t-\tau}^t e^T(s)Qe(s)ds + \delta \left[\sigma \|e(t)\|^2 + \frac{\sigma}{\lambda_{\min}(T)} \int_{t-\tau}^t e^T(s)Qe(s)ds \right] \\
&= (\delta\sigma - \lambda_{\min}(T))\|e(t)\|^2 + \left(\frac{\delta\sigma}{\lambda_{\min}(T)} - 1 \right) \int_{t-\tau}^t e^T(s)Qe(s)ds + \zeta(t) \\
&\leq \zeta(t)
\end{aligned}
\tag{3.14}
$$

which leads to

$$
\dot{V}(t) \leq -\delta V(t, x) + \zeta(t)
$$

From Lemma 2.1, the error system (2.5) is ψ-type stable. Consequently, systems (2.3) and (2.4) are ψ-type synchronized via the nonlinear feedback controller (3.1). The convergence rate that the error e(t) approaches to zero is $\frac{\delta}{2}$. The proof is completed.

Corollary 3.1. Under the assumption H1–H2, let $\zeta(t) = e^{-\alpha t}$, $\alpha > 0$, $\psi(t) = e^t$, if there exist constants $\delta > 0, \sigma > 1$ such that

$$
\delta\sigma < \lambda_{\min}(T), \quad T > 0,
\tag{3.15}
$$

where $\lambda_{\min}(T)$, T are defined as in (3.4). Then systems (2.3) and (2.4) are exponentially synchronized with the nonlinear feedback controller (3.1). The exponential convergence rate of the error $e(t)$ approaches to zero is $\frac{\delta}{2}$.

Corollary 3.2. Under the assumption H1–H2, let $\zeta(t) = (t+1)^{-\alpha}$, $\alpha > 0$, $\psi(t) = t+1$, if there exist constants $\delta > 0, \sigma > 1$ such that

$$
\delta\sigma < \lambda_{\min}(T), \quad \delta < \alpha - 1, \quad T > 0,
\tag{3.16}
$$

where $\lambda_{\min}(T)$, T are defined as in (3.4). Then systems (2.3) and (2.4) are polynomial synchronized with the nonlinear feedback controller (3.1). The polynomial convergence rate of the error $e(t)$ approaches to zero is $\frac{\delta}{2}$.

4 A Numerical Example

In this section, we give a example to verify the effectiveness of the synchronization scheme obtained in the previous section. Consider the following SMCNNs with time-varying delays:

$$STM : \varepsilon \dot{x}_i(t) = -x_i(t) + \sum_{j=1}^{n} \tilde{a}_{ij} f_j(x_j(t)) + \sum_{j=1}^{n} \tilde{b}_{ij} f_j(x_j(t - \tau(t))) + H_i s_i(t), \; j = 1, 2, \ldots, n,$$

$$LTM : \dot{s}_i(t) = -s_i(t) + f_i(x_i(t)), \; i = 1, 2, \ldots, n, \tag{4.1}$$

Let $\varepsilon = 0.8, \; \tau(t) = 0.5|\cos t|, \tau = 1, f_j(x_j(t)) = \tanh(x_j(t)), H_1 = 1.4, H_2 = 0.5,$
$l_1 = l_2 = 1,$
$K_1 = diag(1, 1), \; \dot{\tau}(t) < \mu = \beta = 0.25.$ The initial values $x_1(\theta) = -0.7, x_2(\theta) = 1,$
$s_1(\theta) = 0.8, s_2(\theta) = -0.8, \forall \theta \in [-0.8, 0].$

$$a_{11}(x_1) = \begin{cases} 3.0, |x_1(t)| > 1, \\ 2.5, |x_1(t)| \leq 1, \end{cases} a_{12}(x_1) = \begin{cases} -0.3, |x_1(t)| > 1, \\ -0.25, |x_1(t)| \leq 1, \end{cases}$$

$$a_{21}(x_2) = \begin{cases} -0.5, |x_2(t)| > 1, \\ -0.3, |x_2(t)| \leq 1, \end{cases}$$

$$a_{22}(x_2) = \begin{cases} 1, |x_2(t)| > 1, \\ 1.1, |x_2(t)| \leq 1, \end{cases} b_{11}(x_1(t - \tau(t))) = \begin{cases} -3, |x_1(t)| > 1, \\ -2.5, |x_1(t)| \leq 1, \end{cases}$$

$$b_{12}(x_1(t - \tau(t))) = \begin{cases} -0.3, |x_1(t)| > 1, \\ -0.15, |x_1(t)| \leq 1, \end{cases}$$

$$b_{21}(x_2(t - \tau(t))) = \begin{cases} -0.5, |x_2(t)| > 1, \\ -0.4, |x_2(t)| \leq 1, \end{cases} b_{22}(x_2(t - \tau(t))) = \begin{cases} -3, |x_2(t)| > 1, \\ -2, |x_2(t)| \leq 1, \end{cases}$$

Consider (4.1) as the drive system, then the corresponding response system is as follows:

$$STM : \varepsilon \dot{y}_i(t) = -y_i(t) + \sum_{j=1}^{n} \tilde{a}_{ij} f_j(y_j(t)) + \sum_{j=1}^{n} \tilde{b}_{ij} f_j(y_j(t - \tau(t))) + H_i r_i(t) + u_i(t), \; j = 1, 2, \ldots, n,$$

$$LTM : \dot{r}_i(t) = -r_i(t) + f_i(y_i(t)), \; i = 1, 2, \ldots, n, \tag{4.2}$$

with initial values $y_1(\theta) = 0.5, y_2(\theta) = -1, r_1(\theta) = 0.5, r_2(\theta) = -0.8, \forall \theta \in [-1, 0].$
$w_1 = -9.5, w_2 = -10.5, \zeta(t) = e^{-0.1t}, \phi(t) = e^t,$

$$u_1(t) = -9.5e_1(t) + e_1(t - \tau(t)) - \frac{\varepsilon \|e(t)\|^2 e_1(t)}{2\left(\|e(t)\|^2 + e^{-0.1t}\right)},$$

$$u_2(t) = -10.5e_2(t) + e_2(t - \tau(t)) - \frac{\varepsilon \|e(t)\|^2 e_2(t)}{2\left(\|e(t)\|^2 + e^{-0.1t}\right)}.$$

The constants δ and σ can be chosen as 0.08 and 6, respectively. Then the conditions of Corollary 3.1 are satisfied. It has shown that the drive system (4.1) and the response system (4.2) are exponentially synchronized with the nonlinear controller. Figures 1 and 2 depict the synchronization errors of state variables between drive and response systems, which can check that the convergence rate of error e(t) approaches to zero is 0.04.

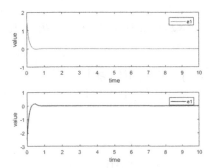

Fig. 1. Shows the synchronization errors $e_1(t)$, $e_2(t)$

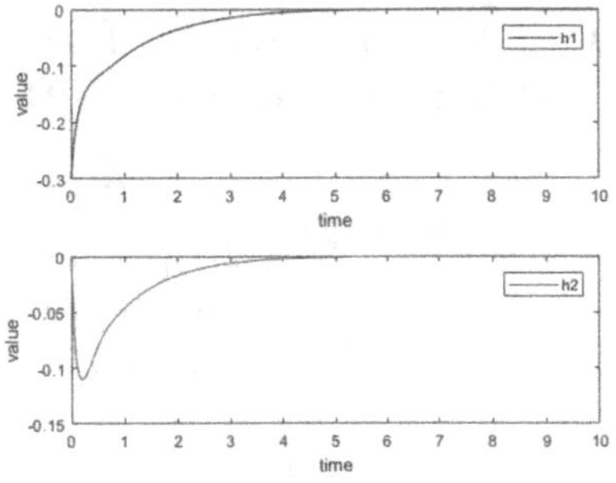

Fig. 2. Shows the synchronization errors $h_1(t)$, $h_2(t)$.

5   Conclusion

In this paper, we have considered the ψ-type synchronization problem for switch memristor-based competitive neural networks with time-vary delays. By using some lemmas and constructing a proper Lyapunov-Krasovskii functional, a nonlinear feedback controller is designed to achieve the ψ-type synchronization of SMCNNs. Our results are general and can be considered as the complement and extension of the previous works on exponential synchronization of neural networks.

References

1. Zeng, Z., Wang, J.: Analysis and design of associative memories based on recurrent neural networks with linear saturation activation functions and time-varying delays. Neural Comput. **19**(8), 2149–2182 (2007)
2. Cheng, L., Hou, Z.G., Lin, Y.: Recurrent neural network for non-smooth convex optimization problems with application to the identification of genetic regulatory networks. IEEE Trans. Neural Netw. **22**(5), 714–726 (2011)

3. Chua, L.O., Yang, L.: Cellular neural networks: applications. IEEE Trans. Circ. Syst. **35**(10), 1273–1290 (1988)
4. Huang, Z.K., Cao, J.D., Li, J.M.: Quasi-synchronization of neural networks with parameter mismatches and delayed impulsive controller on time scales. Nonlinear Anal. Hybrid Syst. **33**, 104–115 (2019)
5. Chua, L.: Memristor-The missing circuit element. IEEE Trans. Circ. Theory **18**(5), 507–519 (1971)
6. Strukov, D.B., Snider, G.S., Stewart, D.R.: The missing memristor found. Nature **453**(7191), 80–83 (2008)
7. Itoh, M., Chua, L.O.: Memristor oscillators. Int. J. Bifurcation Chaos **18**(11), 3183–3206 (2008)
8. Wu, A., Zeng, Z., Zhu, X.: Exponential synchronization of memristor-based recurrent neural networks with time delays. Neurocomputing **74**(17), 3043–3050 (2011)
9. Corinto, F., Ascoli, A., Gilli, M.: Nonlinear dynamics of memristor oscillators. IEEE Trans. Circ. Syst. I: Regul. Pap. **58**(6), 1323–1336 (2011)
10. Milanovic, V., Zaghloul, M.E.: Synchronization of chaotic neural networks and applications to communications. Int. J. Bifurcation Chaos **06**(12b), 2571–2585 (1996)
11. Merrikh-Bayat, F., Shouraki, S.B.: Memristor-based circuits for performing basic arithmetic operations. Procedia Comput. Sci. **3**, 128–132 (2011)
12. Meyer-Bäse, A., Ohl, F., Scheich, H.: Singular Perturbation Analysis of Competitive Neural Networks with Different Time-Scales. MIT Press, Cambridge (1996)
13. Nie, X., Cao, J.: Multistability of competitive neural networks with time-varying and distributed delays. Nonlinear Anal. Real World Appl. **10**(2), 928–942 (2009)
14. Cheng, C.J., Liao, T.L., Yan, J.J.: Exponential synchronization of a class of neural networks with time-varying delays. IEEE Trans. Syst. Man Cybern. Part B Cybern. **36**(1), 209–215 (2006)
15. Lu, H., Leeuwen, C.V.: Synchronization of chaotic neural networks via output or state coupling. Chaos Solitons Fractals **30**(1), 166–176 (2006)
16. Chen, G., Zhou, J., Liu, Z.: Global synchronization of coupled delayed neural networks and applications to chaotic cnn models. Int. J. Bifurcation Chaos **14**(07), 2229–2240 (2004)
17. Cui, B., Lou, X.: Synchronization of chaotic recurrent neural networks with time-varying delays using nonlinear feedback control. Chaos Solitons Fractals **39**(1), 288–294 (2009)
18. Cheng, G., Peng, K.: Robust composite nonlinear feedback control with application to a servo positioning system. IEEE Trans. Ind. Electron. **54**(2), 1132–1140 (2007)
19. Deng, M., Inoue, A., Ishikawa, K.: Operator-based nonlinear feedback control design using robust right coprime factorization. IEEE Trans. Autom. Control **51**(4), 645–648 (2006)
20. Tang, Y., Gao, H., Zou, W.: Distributed synchronization in networks of agent systems with nonlinearities and random switchings. IEEE Trans. Syst. Man Cybern. Part B Cybern. Publ. IEEE Syst. Man Cybern. Soc. **43**(1), 358–370 (2012)
21. Filippov, A.F.: Differential Equations With Discontinuous Right-Hand Sides. Kluwer Academic, Dordrecht (1988)
22. Wang, L., Shen, Y., Zhang, G.: Synchronization of a class of switched neural networks with time-varying delays via nonlinear feedback control. IEEE Trans. Cybern. **46**(10), 2300–2310 (2016)
23. Shi, Y., Zhu, P.: Synchronization of memristive competitive neural networks with different time scales. Neural Comput. Appl. **25**(5), 1163–1168 (2014)

A Computer Immune Optimization Algorithm Based on Group Evolutionary Strategy

Fan Yang[1,2(✉)] ⓘ, Hua-li Zhang[1], and Lu Peng[1]

[1] City College of Wuhan University of Science and Technology,
Wuhan 430083, China
18341029@qq.com
[2] Computer School of Wuhan University, Wuhan 430072, China

Abstract. Computer Immune Optimization Algorithm (CIOA) has the advantages of high success rate and good individual diversity compared with other intelligent optimization algorithms. However, it also has the disadvantages of premature convergence and local optimality. To address these shortcomings, this paper proposes a new algorithm, called ESCIOA, which enhances the mutation operation in CIOA, by introducing Recombination Operator and Mutation Operator of Group Evolution Strategy (GES), to achieve more accurate local optimization and faster global optimization. At the same time, this paper describes the implementation steps of ESCIOA, proves the convergence of the algorithm, and gives the comparative experiment. The results show that ESCIOA absorbs the advantages of CIOA and ES, and has the characteristics of not being easy to fall into local extremum, high precision of solution and fast convergence.

Keywords: Computer Immune Optimization Algorithm ·
Optimization problem · Group Evolutionary Strategy ·
Recombination operator · Mutation operator

1 Introduction

Optimization Problem is a theoretical and practical problem that exists widely in the fields of science, technology and engineering [1]. Many problems can be modeled with optimization method or transformed into optimization problems. As the complexity of the problem increases, such as the increasing of the variable dimensionality, discontinuity, non-differentiation, or even unable to describe it with a mathematical expression, traditional methods based on derivatives (or gradients) encounter great difficulties. Therefore, people simulate some systems and rules in the natural world, and propose new intelligent algorithms, which open up new ideas and inject new vitality for solving optimization problems, and also attract the attention of many researchers. We call these intelligent algorithms bio-heuristic algorithms.

Foundation project: School-level Key Research Project (2017CYZDKY006); Scientific Research Program Guiding Project of Hubei Provincial Department of Education (B2016589).

D.-S. Huang et al. (Eds.): ICIC 2019, LNCS 11643, pp. 98–110, 2019.
https://doi.org/10.1007/978-3-030-26763-6_10

Bio-inspired algorithms are being accepted, disseminated, promoted and applied gradually in their development. There are two main reasons for this: First, Bio-inspired algorithms can produce the necessary and better solutions while the traditional methods became invalid; Second, it can avoid detailed descriptions or understandings of biological systems or biology itself. However, as the optimization problem becomes more complex, simple abstraction or simulated biological systems are no longer able to adapt to the complexity of the problem. The main challenges faced by bio-inspired computing systems are slow convergence and easy to fall into local optimal solutions, such as genetic algorithms and evolutionary strategies, but they do not have theories and methods to effectively overcome these defects [2–4].

It is thought that Computer Immune Algorithm (CIA) is a new second generation bio-inspired algorithm [5], which are closer to biological essence. The human or animal immune system can provide people with rich inspiration in the ways of learning, adaptability, and memory mechanisms for different computing tasks. Inspired by the immune system, many researchers have proposed various computer immune algorithms [6]. CIA is an intelligent method which simulated the function of natural immune system; it has the potential to provide novel solutions to problems, because it learns the natural defense mechanism of the organism to the external matter, provides immune mechanisms such as noise tolerance, no teacher learning, self-organization, memory, etc., combines with the advantages of Classifier, Artificial Neural Networks and Machine Reasoning; and it has become another new research hotspot of Artificial Intelligence after Artificial Neural Network, Fuzzy Logic Inference and Evolutionary Computation [7–10].

As an interdisciplinary subject, Group Evolutionary Strategy (GES) provides a theoretical basis for solving problems in Biology and Genetics [11]. The core idea of GES is variation, Because Charles Robert Darwin believes that all organisms are mutated, some of which can be inherited to offspring and others not. The concept of Cauchy mutation in GES has important implications for CIA which is widely studied nowadays.

According to the characteristics of CIA and GES, this paper proposes a Computer Immune Optimization Algorithm based on GES, called ESCIOA. The algorithm draws on the advantages of GES and introduces the concept of Cauchy Mutation Operator, so that the antibody is divided into local competition and global competition according to the principle of clonal expansion and receptor editing, and implements a Two-tier Search Mechanism. In addition, the algorithm emphasizes the excellent antibody retention of immune memory.

2 Backgrounds and Problem Statement

2.1 Biological Mechanism of Immune System

The immune system is the most important defense barrier of the organism. It is a multi-layer, distributed, and autonomous rejection system [12]. It can detect internal environmental fluctuations caused by foreign bodies such as foreign pathogenic microorganisms, remove foreign matter, adaptively maintain the dynamic balance of the body and maintain the life of the organism. It is the most effective weapon for the body to defend against pathogen invasion. The vertebrate defense system is a multi-layered structure consisting of the skin and mucous membranes, the body fluid environment and the immune system, as shown in Fig. 1.

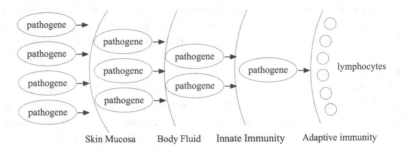

Fig. 1. Multi-layer structure of biological immune system.

When pathogenic microorganisms such as bacteria and viruses, collectively referred to as "pathogens", enter the organism, the innate immune system first plays a role. Various cells in the innate immune system, including macrophages, complement, neutrophils, and nature killer cells, etc., can destroy most pathogens by phagocytosis, conditioning, and killing.

Although the innate immune system can effectively kill most pathogens, there are always new variants that are not within the scope of identification of innate immune cells. However, the innate immune system can still perceive the "danger" caused by invasion. After the danger is perceived, the innate immune system begins to activate the adaptive immune system and respond to these intrusions.

How is the adaptive immune system activated? Antigen presenting cells (APCs) capture fragments of pathogens or infected cells, and display these protein fragments containing pathogenic DNA on the surface with a primary histocompatibility complex, in order to activate helper T cells (T-Helper, TH). Activated helper T cells then activate naive B cells or primary killer T cells (T-Killer, also known as CTL) to initiate an adaptive immune response [13, 14].

2.2   Background of Group Evolution Strategy

The evolution of any species is a process of self-improvement of complex systems and is an optimized process. Therefore, in terms of computer bionics, it has direct reference. It constitutes the basic idea and algorithm form of evolutionary strategy. Evolutionary operator is the direct imitation of biological evolution. Therefore, evolution is one of the sources of evolutionary computation [15, 16].

The working process of GES includes the problem of expression, the initial population generated, the calculation of fitness, the implementation of reorganization, mutation, the selection of new groups, etc., after repeated iterations, the optimal solution is gradually obtained [17–20].

Figure 2 shows the workflow of the evolution strategy. In the figure, Gen represents the evolutionary order. In the 0th generation, according to the problem, the expression is a two- or three-tuple method, and μ initial individuals are randomly generated, and their fitness is calculated. Recombination and mutation operations are then performed in sequence to generate new individuals. Recombination and mutation are performed λ times. Produce λ new individuals. Then, the fitness of the new individual is calculated, and then according to the selection strategy, μ individuals are selected from $(\mu + \lambda)$ individuals or λ new individuals to form a new group. In this way, a generation of evolution is completed. This evolutionary process is repeated until the termination condition is met.

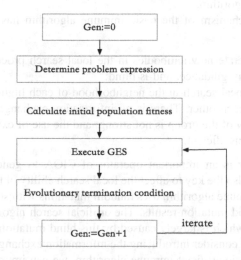

Fig. 2. Group Evolution Strategy work steps

In a nutshell, the procedure of GES included 4 steps. First, determine how the problem is expressed. Second, randomly generate the initial population and calculate its fitness. Third, according to the evolution strategy, the following operations are used to generate new groups:

(1) **Reorganization.** *The two parent individuals exchange target variables and random factors to produce new individuals.*
(2) **Mutation.** *A random amount is added to the recombined individual to produce a new individual.*
(3) **Calculate.** *Calculate the fitness of new individuals.*
(4) **Choice.** *According to the selection strategy, select good individuals to form the next generation group.*

Final, repeated execution "Third" until the termination condition is reached, and the best individual is selected as the result of the evolution strategy.

2.3   Problem Statement

The evolutionary chain of CIOA can be described as: *Antibody Population* → *Immune Selection* → *Cell Cloning* → *High-frequency Variation* → *Clonal Inhibition* → *Population Refresh* → *New-antibody Population*. There are two operations for generating new antibodies: Population Refresh and High-frequency Variation. Population Refresh is to replace the inferior antibody in the original antibody population with a random new antibody, which is a means to maintain antibody diversity; and the mutation operator mutates the antibody clone result obtained by the cloning operator to generate affinity. Mutation, local search, is an important operator in CIOA to generate potential new antibodies, to achieve regional search, and has a great impact on the performance of the algorithm.

Local Search mechanism of the basic immune algorithm has the following two problems.

(1) The way to generate new antibodies in the local search process is random variation, without any guidance, and is blind;
(2) The process of local search in the neighborhood of each high-quality antibody is independent of each other. There is no information exchange in the search process, the sociality of the group is not strong, and the use of existing search results of the group is insufficient.

Mutation operator is an important operator of CIOA to generate potential new individuals, and it is also the key to affect the local search ability of the algorithm. Since the basic artificial immune algorithm uses random mutations with strong blindness, it is difficult to ensure good mutation results. The artificial search algorithm's local search ability is not strong, which is largely caused by this blind mutation operation.

In summary, if we consider introducing the information exchange mechanism in the local search of the basic artificial immune algorithm, we can improve the sociality of the antibody population, and make better use of the group search results to provide guidance for the local search, and then Local Search will have a certain promotion. These formed the idea of ESCIOA.

3   ESCIOA Design

According to the biological mechanism of the immune system in the previous section, we found that similar to Darwin's biological evolution principle, there are also evolutionary phenomena in Immune System. We can describe the biological principles of immune system from the perspective of evolution. When an antigen invades the body, the B cell population produces antibodies by the following evolutionary process to destroy the antigen.

(1) B cells having a high affinity for antigen are selected.
(2) Under the action of helper T cells, the B cells divide and proliferate, producing a large number of B cells, called Clonal Expansion. B cells generate a large number of sub-B cells in a small range in the shape space by clonal amplification to search for B cells with higher affinity in a local range.

(3) Some low affinity B-cells delete their receptors and generate new receptors, Receptor Editing. Receptor editing allows sub-B cells to mutate into a point farther away from their shape space to search for more affinity B cells globally. Other sub-B cells with low affinity die, while the bone marrow produces a portion of new B cells to increase population diversity.

(4) After several generations of selection, clonal expansion, receptor editing, and bone marrow production of new B cell processes, B cells with high affinity are eventually produced to destroy the antigen.

According to the evolutionary mechanism of the immune system described above, the design of ESCIOA mainly considers four aspects, including Antibody Selection, Antibody Recombination, Antibody Mutation and Antibody Update. The flow chart of the algorithm is shown in Fig. 3.

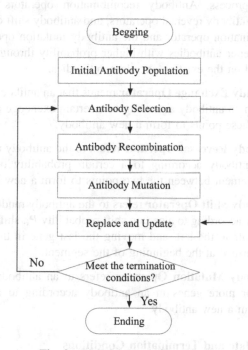

Fig. 3. ESCIOA Work-flow Chart

3.1 Initial Antibody Population & Antibody Selection

Initial Antibody Population. The n real-coded antibodies were generated as the initial population A, and at the first iteration, the antibodies were typically generated in a random manner in the solution space.

Antibody Selection Operation. Calculate the affinity value of each antibody in population A, and calculate the concentration of the antibody, select the m antibody-based population B (where $m < n$) based on the probability formula of the antibody concentration, and maximize the $m1$ affinity in the population A. The antibody is retained as an immunological memory antibody ($m1 < m$). The selection method based on the antibody concentration is:

Calculate the cumulative probability $q_k = \sum_{j=1}^{k} P_s(v_j)$, where $k = 1, 2, ., n$, and let $q_0 = 0$. A uniformly distributed random number w is generated on the interval $[0, 1]$. If $q_{k-1} < w < q_k$, the antibody v_k is selected, and m such random numbers are generated, and m antibodies are selected to the population B.

3.2   Antibody Recombination and Mutation

Because the antibody is in the process of affinity maturation, the receptor editing and somatic high frequency variation are the main methods. This paper uses the recombination operator and mutation operator of the evolutionary strategy to realize the affinity maturation process. Antibody recombination operators include antibody exchange operators, antibody reversal operators, and antibody shift operators. Through the antibody recombination operator and the antibody mutation operator, the original algorithm can find better antibodies with higher probability through the affinity maturation process based on the existing excellent antibodies.

Definition 1. Antibody Exchange Operator means that an antibody randomly selects two or more points in an antibody according to a certain exchange probability P_c, and exchanges genes at these points to form a new antibody.

Definition 2. Antibody Reversal Operator refers to the antibody randomly selecting two points in the antibody according to a certain probability of reversal P_i, and inverting the gene segment between the two points to form a new antibody.

Definition 3. Antibody Shift Operator refers to the antibody randomly selecting two points in the antibody according to a certain shift probability P_s, shifting the gene cycle between the two points to the left, and moving the last gene in the gene segment to A new antibody is formed at the beginning of the segment.

Definition 4. Antibody Mutation Operator refers to an antibody that is randomly replaced with one or more genes in an antibody according to a certain mutation probability P_m to form a new antibody.

3.3   Antibody Update and Termination Conditions

Antibody Update. The $m1$ antibodies with the lowest affinity in population D were replaced with the immunological memory antibodies in step 3 to form a new generation population A.

Termination Conditions. If a new generation of population A has an antibody that meets the requirements, the optimal antibody is output and the algorithm ends; otherwise, go to step 2 and repeat.

4 Algorithm Convergence Analysis

The antibody population sequence X of ESCIOA constitutes a random sequence. Let the population size of the algorithm be N, all approximate solutions in the algorithm population are regarded as one point in the state space F_1, and all approximate solutions of the intermediate group are regarded as one point in the state space F_2, when it is not necessary to distinguish between F_1 and When F_2, F can be used to indicate the state space. $F_i \in F$ represents the i-th state in F, V_n^i indicating that the random variable V is in state F_i at the n-th generation. Let f be the optimized objective function whose domain is I, then define the global optimal solution set of F^* as Eq. (1).

$$F^* = \{x \in I | f(x) = min_{x_i \in I} f(x_i)\} \tag{1}$$

This can define the convergence of the algorithm.

Definition 1. Let F_k be the optimal antibody in the population at time k, and F* is the antigen to be solved. If $\lim_{k \to \infty} P(F_k = F^*) = 1$, and only if it is established, the ESCIOA is globally convergent.

Definition 2. A is an $n \times n$ square matrix.

(1) If all $I, j, a_{ij} \geq 0$, denoted as $A \geq 0$, said A is non-negative;
(2) If a is non-negative, and for all i, $\sum_{j=1}^{n} a_{ij} = 1$, then A is stochastic;
(3) if A is non-negative, and the row and column in A are replaced to obtain the form
$\begin{bmatrix} C & 0 \\ R & T \end{bmatrix}$ (C, T is a square matrix), then A is reducible.

Theorem 1. Let P be an approximate random matrix, $P = \begin{bmatrix} C & 0 \\ R & T \end{bmatrix}$, where C is a positive m-order random matrix, R, $T \neq 0$, then

$$P^\infty = \lim_{k \to \infty} \begin{bmatrix} C^k & 0 \\ \sum_{i=0}^{k-1} T^i R C^{k-i} & T^k \end{bmatrix} = \begin{bmatrix} C^\infty & 0 \\ R^\infty & 0 \end{bmatrix} \tag{2}$$

Theorem 2. The ESCIOA converges according to probability 1.

Proof: The crossover operation in the algorithm crosses the two gene positions on a selected pair of antibodies with a probability P_c. The mutation operation is to mutate each gene position of the antibody independently of each other with a probability P_m. Then the n-step state transition of the algorithm steps (1 to 5) can be represented by the state transition matrix P = (p_{ij}), and $p_{ij} \in [0, 1]$, $\sum_{j=1}^{n} p_{ij} = 1$. According to Definitions 1 and 2, the state transition matrix P is random.

The states of the transfer matrix P are arranged by permutation as follows: the first state is the global optimal solution; the second state is the global suboptimal solution; and so on, the n-th state is the global worst solution. Then, the update operation in the algorithm step (6) can be regarded as: for any state i, according to $p_{ii} + \sum_{j=i+1}^{n}$ $p_{ij} \to p_{ii}$ and $p_{ij} = 0$, any $j > i$ is added to the transfer matrix to generate a new transfer matrix P^*.

$$P^* = \begin{bmatrix} 1 & 0 & \cdots & 0 \\ p_{21} & p_{22} & \cdots & 0 \\ \cdots & \cdots & \cdots & \cdots \\ p_{n1} & p_{n2} & \cdots & p_{nn} \end{bmatrix} = \begin{bmatrix} C & 0 \\ R & T \end{bmatrix} \tag{3}$$

Here, $R = \begin{bmatrix} p_{21} \\ \vdots \\ p_{n1} \end{bmatrix}$, $T = \begin{bmatrix} p_{22} & \cdots & 0 \\ \cdots & \cdots & \cdots \\ p_{n2} & \cdots & p_{nn} \end{bmatrix}$, $R, T \neq 0$, is a first-order positive

random matrix, and by definition, the state transition matrix P is approximating. According to Theorem 1.

$$P^\infty = \lim_{k \to \infty} P^{*\infty} = \begin{bmatrix} C^\infty & 0 \\ R^\infty & 0 \end{bmatrix} = \begin{bmatrix} 1 & 0 \\ R^\infty & 0 \end{bmatrix} \tag{4}$$

The limit probability of the first state of P^* is 1, that is $\lim_{k \to \infty} P(F_k = F^*) = 1$, from **definition** 1, the ESCIOA is globally convergent.

5 Simulation Experiments and Conclusions

The convergence of ESCIOA has been proved theoretically. This section compares ESCIOA with ordinary CIOA in terms of convergence effect and convergence speed. For the extremum, this section selects the following three typical functions as test functions.

Function 1. $f_1(x_1, x_2) = -4x_1^2 + 2.1x_1^4 - \frac{1}{3}x_1^6 + 4x_2^2 - 4x_2^4$, $f_{max} = 1.03163$;

Function 2. $f_2(x_1, x_2) = 21.5 + \sin(4\pi x_1) - x_2^2$, $f_{max} = 22.5$;

Function 3. $f_3(x_1, x_2) = 20 \exp\left[-0.2 \cdot \sqrt{\frac{1}{2}(x_1^2 + x_2^2)}\right] + \exp\left\{\sqrt{\frac{1}{2}} \cdot [\cos(2\pi x_1) + \cos(2\pi x_2)]\right\} - 20 - e$, $f_{max} = 0$.

The parameters in the algorithm are set to $n = 20$, $m = 10$, $m1 = 5$, and the algorithm is iterated 100 times. The algorithm is compared with the general computer immune algorithm for function optimization. The dotted line in the figure below represents the curve of CIOS, and the solid line represents the curve of ESCIOS.

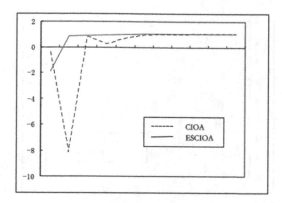

Fig. 4. Function 1 optimization comparison

For **function 1**, as shown in Fig. 4, it can be seen that the function value obtained by the first iteration of ESCIOA quickly approaches the optimal solution, and the Relative Error is an order of magnitude smaller than CIOA. The curve of the function value of CIOA is very unstable, and the beating is obvious; the ESCIOA curve does not appear to jump as CIOA, and the iteration evolves smoothly in a better direction.

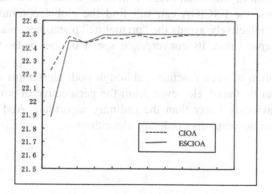

Fig. 5. Function 2 optimization comparison

For **function 2**, as shown in Fig. 5, it can be seen that the test function f_2 has multiple optimal solutions, and the ESCIOA relative error is smaller than CIOA. Although the function value curve is close before and after improvement, the relative error of the algorithm before the improvement is iterated many times before it approaches zero. The change of the variable x_1 before and after the change is very large, because the variable x_1 causes the test function f_2 to have multiple optimal solutions, but the change of the variable x_2 before the improvement is still large, and the modified curve of the variable x_2 is stabilized very quickly after several iterations.

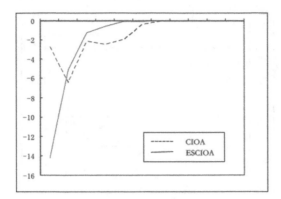

Fig. 6. Function 3 optimization comparison

For **function 3**, as shown in Fig. 6, it can be seen that the function value obtained by the first iteration of the algorithm before the improvement is closer to the optimal solution than the improved one, but because it is the reason for jumping into the local optimal solution, it is far away from the optimal solution. The function value becomes smaller than the improved one. Although the improved relative difference curve appears to be jumping, it quickly settles down.

In the optimization of such multimodal functions, although the function has many local extreme values, the ESCIOA can still find the global optimal solution faster, which shows that it effectively avoids the "premature" phenomenon and is not easy to fall into local extreme value. Its convergence speed is also better than the general algorithm.

In the optimization of such functions, although both algorithms are effective, the optimal solution can be found. However, from the perspective of convergence speed, the ESCIOA is obviously faster than the ordinary algorithm. And its optimization results are also more accurate than ordinary algorithms.

6   Conclusion

In summary, ESCIOA can simultaneously search for antibodies with higher affinity in the local range and global range of excellent antibodies in the population. The reorganization operation performs a wide-range search within the specified range, so that in the region where the global search affinity is high, it is a rough search. When the rough search finds a region with a high affinity, the mutation operation seeks a high-precision solution by performing a local fine search. The algorithm searches through coarse and thin two layers to ensure its global optimization and local accuracy. It can be seen that the ESCIOA is not easy to fall into local extremum, and it still has certain advantages in terms of convergence speed and accuracy.

The main follow-up work of this paper is as follow 2 aspects.

(1) Study the influence of parameters on the performance of Computer Immune Algorithm, and summarize the basic methods of parameter selection for different types of problems.
(2) Study the hybrid mechanism of other intelligent algorithms and Computer Immune Algorithm, such as comprehensively applying several intelligent optimization algorithms to form an optimization problem processing model, and strengthen the optimization search ability.

References

1. Cedersund, G., Samuelsson, O., Ball, G., et al.: Optimization in biology parameter estimation and the associated optimization problem. In: Geris, L., Gomez-Cabrero, D. (eds.) Uncertainty in Biology. Springer, Cham (2016). https://doi.org/10.1007/978-3-319-21296-8_7
2. Branke, J.: MCDA and multi-objective evolutionary algorithms. In: Greco, S., Ehrgott, M., Figueira, J. (eds.) Multiple Criteria Decision Analysis. Springer, New York (2016). https://doi.org/10.1007/978-1-4939-3094-4_23
3. Cofnas, N.: Judaism as a group evolutionary strategy: a critical analysis of Kevin Macdonald's theory. Hum. Nat. 29(2), 1–23 (2018)
4. Bharathi, C., Rekha, D., Vijayakumar, V.: Genetic algorithm based demand side management for smart grid. Wirel. Pers. Commun. 93(2), 481–502 (2017)
5. Read, M., Andrews, P.S., Timmis, J.: An introduction to artificial immune systems. In: Rozenberg, G., Bäck, T., Kok, J.N. (eds.) Handbook of Natural Computing. Springer, Heidelberg (2012). https://doi.org/10.1007/978-3-540-92910-9_47
6. Aickelin, U., Dasgupta, D., Gu, F.: Artificial immune systems. In: Burke, E.K., Kendall, G. (eds.) Search Methodologies, pp. 187–211. Springer, New York (2014). https://doi.org/10.1007/978-1-4614-6940-7_7
7. Zandieh, M., Ghomi, S.M.T.F., Husseini, S.M.M.: An immune algorithm approach to hybrid flow shops scheduling with sequence-dependent setup times. Appl. Math. Comput. 180(1), 111–127 (2006)
8. Endoh, S., Toma, N., Yamada, K.: Immune algorithm for n-TSP. In: IEEE International Conference on Systems (1998)
9. Chun, J.S., Jung, H.K., Hahn, S.Y.: A study on comparison of optimization performances between immune algorithm and other heuristic algorithms. IEEE Trans. Magn. 34(5), 2972–2975 (1998)
10. Aydin, I., Karakose, M., Akin, E.: A multi-objective artificial immune algorithm for parameter optimization in support vector machine. Appl. Soft Comput. 11(1), 120–129 (2011)
11. Anderson, R.E., Sogin, M.L., Baross, J.A.: Evolutionary strategies of viruses, bacteria and archaea in hydrothermal vent ecosystems revealed through metagenomics. PLOS ONE 9, e109696 (2014)
12. Murphy, K.P., Travers, P., Walport, M., et al.: Janeway's Immunobiology (2014)
13. Traggiai, E., Chicha, L., Mazzucchelli, L., et al.: Development of a human adaptive immune system in cord blood cell-transplanted mice. Science 304(5667), 104–107 (2004)

14. Ranganathan, S.: Adaptive immune system. In: Encyclopedia of Systems Biology, pp. 10–11 (2016)
15. Hoyle, F., Wickramasinghe, N.C.: Biological evolution. Astrophys. Space Sci. **268**(1–3), 55–75 (1999)
16. Grant, P.R., Grant, B.R.: Evolution of character displacement in Darwin's finches. Science **313**(5784), 224–226 (2006)
17. Hansen, N.: The CMA evolution strategy: a comparing review. Stud. Fuzziness Soft Comput. **192**, 75–102 (2006)
18. Hansen, N.: The CMA evolution strategy: a tutorial (2005)
19. Liem, K.F.: Evolutionary strategies and morphological innovations: cichlid pharyngeal jaws. Syst. Biol. **22**(4), 425–441 (1973)
20. Huemmer, C., Hofmann, C., Maas, R., et al.: The elitist particle filter based on evolutionary strategies as novel approach for nonlinear acoustic echo cancellation. In: 2014 IEEE International Conference on Acoustics, Speech and Signal Processing (ICASSP), pp. 1315–1319. IEEE (2014)

Sound Field Reproduction in Reverberant Room Using the Alternating Direction Method of Multipliers Based Lasso and Regularized Least-Square

Jiaming Zhang, Maoshen Jia(✉), Changchun Bao, and Qi Wang

Faculty of Information Technology, Beijing University of Technology,
Beijing 100124, China
jiamaoshen@bjut.edu.cn

Abstract. This paper presents a three-dimensional (3D) sound-field reproduction (SFR) method based on the Pressure-Matching (PM) approach. The desired sound field is modeled to be reverberation field to approximate a real conference room through the image-source model and the reflection model of the incoherent rough room surfaces. The whole reproduction procedure can be divided into two parts. At the first step, a large number of candidate loudspeaker positions for selecting, and the most efficient active loudspeaker is chosen based on the Alternating Direction Method of Multipliers (ADMM) based Lasso. During the second step, all the selected active loudspeaker weights are calculated via regularized Least-Square (LS) method. Simulation results shows that the proposed SFR approach outperforms the existing PM-based SFR method in most cases for reverberation environment, and the runtime is far less than the reference methods, which means that the proposed approach is especially suited for low latency sound field synthesis in reverberant rooms.

Keywords: Sound field reproduction ·
Alternating direction method of multipliers · Lasso · Image source

1 Introduction

Sound Field Reproduction (SFR) aims at synthesizing a desired sound field in a region of interest (listening area) by the array of limited numbers of loudspeakers. The SFR system can offer one or more listeners the impression of being immersed in a realistic sound environment, typical applications include home theatre system, audio-visual conferencing, etc. The purpose of SFR is to find the solution of loudspeaker weight vector (i.e. the driven signal of loudspeakers) while minimizing the reproduction error. So far, the implementation of SFR mainly utilizes Wave Field Synthesis (WFS) [1] method, Higher Order Ambisonics (HOA) [2] technique, and Pressure-Matching (PM) [3] approach.

PM-based SFR, which is the focus of this work, is designed to minimize the approximation error between the reproduced field and the original desired field at a set of spatially distributed matching points. The Least-Square (LS) constraint regularized

© Springer Nature Switzerland AG 2019
D.-S. Huang et al. (Eds.): ICIC 2019, LNCS 11643, pp. 111–120, 2019.
https://doi.org/10.1007/978-3-030-26763-6_11

with the l_2-norm of the loudspeaker weights is a traditional numerical method to compute the driven signal of loudspeakers under power limitation. However, this approach requires a large number of loudspeakers [4] and may lead to a blurry spatial sound image [5]. Alternatively, the loudspeaker weights could be penalized with convex l_1-norm instead of l_2-norm, namely, the Least-absolute shrinkage and selection operator (Lasso). This result in sparse representation of the desired field and convert the SFR problem to convex optimization problem, hence, the solution of loudspeaker locations and their corresponding weight signals are globally optimal. Nevertheless, Lasso-based SFR are performed in the absence of power constraint. In [6, 7], the authors proposed two-stage Lasso-LS for 2D multizone SFR through the control of both linear loudspeaker locations and their total power. Unfortunately, the major difficulty of the aforementioned approaches is the high computational complexity of Lasso. In our previous work [8], a SFR scheme via the Alternating Direction Method of Multipliers (ADMM) based Lasso plus regularized LS (AL-LS) was proposed for jointly optimizing the loudspeaker locations and weights in three-dimensional (3D) environment by using planar array. The simulation results demonstrated that the performance of the proposed SFR method outperforms several existing PM-based SFR, and the execution speed of the loudspeaker location optimization is much faster than the reference methods. Therefore, the computational complexity and time delay of SFR can be reduced to the great extent. However, this approach leaves the problem that the sound sources and the loudspeakers radiated in free-field, the Acoustic Transform Function (ATF) is modeled to be free space Green's function, which is unsuitable for practical reverberant environment.

This paper expands on the contributions in [8], a novel 3D SFR approach for synthesizing the desired sound field is proposed in this work. This approach is also based on the AL-LS framework whilst utilizing Image Source Model (ISM) [9] for simulating room reflections, in order to model a sound field in a real environment as far as possible. Unlike [8], the SFR approach proposed in this paper optimizes the loudspeaker placement strategy from all candidate loudspeakers and their complex weights in a reverberant room. At the first step, the desired field is treated as the superposition of the virtual source and its image sources, and the active loudspeaker selection is performed by the ADMM based Lasso. During the second step, regularized LS is employed to calculate the weightings for the selected loudspeakers.

The reminder of this paper is organized as follows: Sect. 2 presents the proposed 3D SFR structure for reverberant room in detail. Simulation results are described and discussed in Sect. 3, while the conclusion is given in Sect. 4.

2 Proposed 3D SFR Approach

2.1 Sound Field Modeling of the Room

Consider the SFR structure using planar array shown in Fig. 1, where the number of matching points and the number of candidate loudspeakers are M and N, respectively. In this work, ISM is utilized to model wall reflections, which allows the calculation of sound behavior using ray propagation assumptions, travelling directly from the source to matching points but also reflecting specularly.

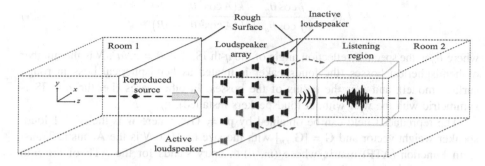

Fig. 1. Illustration of the proposed 3D SFR system in reverberant room

In terms of the desired field generated by a monopole virtual source in reverberant room, which can be expressed as a sum of two components:

$$\mathbf{p}^d = \mathbf{p}^s + \sum_{q=1}^{Q} \mathbf{p}^i_q \tag{1}$$

where $\mathbf{p}^i_q = \left[p^i_{q,1}, p^i_{q,2}, \cdots, p^i_{q,M}\right]^T$ is the pressure at all matching points emitted by the q-th Image Source (IS) and $\mathbf{p}^s = \left[p^s_1, p^s_2, \cdots, p^s_M\right]^T$ is equivalent to the omnidirectional point source radiating in free field. The m-th element of $\mathbf{p}^s$ can be expressed as free space Green's function (suppose the source located at $\mathbf{s} = (s_x, s_y, s_z)$ with complex amplitude of A):

$$p^s_m = A \cdot \frac{1}{4\pi} \cdot \frac{e^{-jk\|\mathbf{s}-\mathbf{y}_m\|_2}}{\|\mathbf{s}-\mathbf{y}_m\|_2} \tag{2}$$

where $k = 2\pi f/c$ is the wave number, $c = 343$ m/s is the sound propagation speed, and $\mathbf{y}_m$ is the coordinate of m-th matching point. Recall the Eq. (1), the $\mathbf{p}^i_q$ is defined as:

$$\mathbf{p}^i_q = r_q \cdot \frac{e^{-jk\mathbf{R}_q}}{4\pi\mathbf{R}_q} \tag{3}$$

where $\mathbf{R}_q$ is the $M \times 1$ vector contains the distance between the q-th IS and all matching points, r_q is the room reflection coefficient corresponding to the q-th IS. In our SFR system, the loudspeakers are installed on the wall, hence, the wall should be regarded as rough surface and such reflections are incoherent. When the q-th IS is symmetric with respect to the wall where the loudspeakers are installed, we let

$r_q = r \cdot l_q(k)$, where r represents the reflection coefficient of smooth room surface and $l(k)$ can be calculated according to [10]:

$$l_q(k) = \frac{j\cos\theta_q - k(A\cos^2\theta_q - B)}{j\cos\theta_q + k(A\cos^2\theta_q - B)} \tag{4}$$

where θ_q is the specular reflection angle of the q-th IS, $A = B = \pi N a^3$, N is the number of hemispherical bosses (the loudspeaker is treated as hemispherical boss in rough surface model), and a is the radius of the bosses. In other cases (i.e. the q-th IS is symmetric with the wall without loudspeakers installed), $r_q = r$.

The reproduced field can be obtained by $\mathbf{p}^r = \mathbf{Gw}$, where $\mathbf{w}$ is the $N \times 1$ loudspeaker weight vector and $\mathbf{G} = [G_{m,n}]$ with the size of $M \times N$ is the Acoustic Transform Function (ATF) matrix whose (m, n)-th entry stands for the ATF of the n-th loudspeaker at m-th matching point:

$$G_{m,n} = \frac{e^{-jk\|\mathbf{x}_n - \mathbf{y}_m\|_2}}{4\pi\|\mathbf{x}_n - \mathbf{y}_m\|_2} + \sum_{q=1}^{Q} r_q \cdot \frac{e^{-jk\|\mathbf{x}_n^q - \mathbf{y}_m\|_2}}{4\pi\|\mathbf{x}_n^q - \mathbf{y}_m\|_2} \tag{5}$$

where $\mathbf{x}_n$ and $\mathbf{x}_n^q$ are the positions of the n-th loudspeaker and the q-th IS of the n-th loudspeaker, respectively.

2.2 ADMM-Based Active Loudspeaker Selection

The conventional SFR methods based on regularized LS allocate power to all loudspeakers, which fall short in limiting the number of simultaneously active loudspeaker. However, we hope to use as few loudspeakers as possible in realistic SFR scenarios. Hence, selecting the most efficient loudspeaker locations out of N candidate positions is indispensable. In this work, the procedure of obtaining the loudspeaker weights is modeled to be sparse linear regression problem (i.e. Lasso estimator):

$$\hat{\mathbf{w}}_{\text{Lasso}} = \arg\min_{\mathbf{w}} \frac{1}{2}\|\mathbf{Gw} - \mathbf{p}^d\|_2^2 + \lambda\|\mathbf{w}\|_1 \tag{6}$$

where $\|\cdot\|_1$ is the vector one-norm and λ is the positive tuning parameter, which essentially controls the sparsity (or the complexity) of the estimated coefficients. In other words, larger values of λ cause fewer nonzero loudspeaker weights in $\hat{\mathbf{w}}_{\text{Lasso}}$ (i.e. decrease the number of active loudspeaker). The formula (6) can be solved by classical algorithms such as Coordinate Descent (CD) method or Least-Angle Regression Solver (LARS), but these optimization algorithms are usually slow in convergence and expensive in computational complexity. To deal with the problems, we propose to solve (6) using the ADMM algorithm for speeding up the procedure of optimal loudspeaker position selection (i.e. l_1-minimazation process).

ADMM has been widely used to solve structured or large-scale convex optimization problems such as compressed sensing [11] and machine learning [12]. It have dealt with problems involving real variables and cannot be directly applied for complex case.

In the proposed SFR scheme, the complex-valued sparse recovery algorithms is employed, because each element of all variables and the ATF matrix $\mathbf{G}$ are complex value. The extension of the Lasso to the complex setting is to consider the original complex variable as a $2N$ dimensional real-valued variable. This mapping process can be written in the following form:

$$\bar{\mathbf{w}} \triangleq \begin{bmatrix} \mathbf{w}_R \\ \mathbf{w}_I \end{bmatrix} \quad \bar{\mathbf{p}}^{\mathrm{d}} \triangleq \begin{bmatrix} \mathbf{p}_R^{\mathrm{d}} \\ \mathbf{p}_I^{\mathrm{d}} \end{bmatrix} \quad \bar{\mathbf{G}} \triangleq \begin{bmatrix} \mathbf{G}_R & -\mathbf{G}_I \\ \mathbf{G}_I & \mathbf{G}_R \end{bmatrix} \tag{7}$$

where the subscript R and I denote the real and imaginary parts of a complex number, respectively.

The basic idea of the ADMM approach is to decompose a harder problem into a set of simpler ones. As far as the SFR problem, (6) can be re-formulated as the ADMM form:

$$\begin{aligned} &\text{minimize} f(\bar{\mathbf{w}}) + g(\bar{\mathbf{z}}) \\ &\text{subject to } \bar{\mathbf{w}} - \bar{\mathbf{z}} = 0 \end{aligned} \tag{8}$$

where $f(\bar{\mathbf{w}}) = (1/2)\|\bar{\mathbf{G}}\bar{\mathbf{w}} - \bar{\mathbf{p}}^{\mathrm{d}}\|_2^2$, $g(\bar{\mathbf{z}}) = \lambda\|\bar{\mathbf{z}}\|_1$, and $\bar{\mathbf{z}}$ is the intermediate variable when splitting the original problem (6). The functions f and g are assumed to be convex, such that the formula (8) can be expressed as the form of augmented Lagrangian function:

$$L_\rho(\bar{\mathbf{w}}, \bar{\mathbf{z}}, \bar{\boldsymbol{\eta}}) = f(\bar{\mathbf{w}}) + g(\bar{\mathbf{z}}) + \bar{\boldsymbol{\eta}}^{\mathrm{T}}(\bar{\mathbf{w}} - \bar{\mathbf{z}}) + \frac{\rho}{2}\|\bar{\mathbf{w}} - \bar{\mathbf{z}}\|_2^2 \tag{9}$$

where $\bar{\boldsymbol{\eta}}$ is dual variable and $\rho > 0$ is the augmented Lagrangian parameter. The ADMM algorithm for solving (8) requires K iterations, the whole updating procedure is summarized as the following steps:

Algorithm1: ADMM algorithm for obtaining the positions and weights of the active loudspeakers

---

Set $\bar{\mathbf{w}}^0 = \bar{\mathbf{z}}^0 = \bar{\mathbf{u}}^0 = \mathbf{0}$ and $i = \sqrt{-1}$, where $\bar{\mathbf{u}} = (1/\rho)\bar{\boldsymbol{\eta}}$ is the the scaled version of the dual variable.

repeat

$$\bar{\mathbf{w}}^{k+1} \leftarrow (\bar{\mathbf{G}}^{\mathrm{T}}\bar{\mathbf{G}} + \rho\mathbf{I})^{-1}[\bar{\mathbf{G}}^{\mathrm{T}}\bar{\mathbf{p}}^{\mathrm{d}} + \rho(\bar{\mathbf{z}}^k - \bar{\mathbf{u}}^k)]$$

$$\bar{\mathbf{z}}^{k+1} \leftarrow S_{\lambda/\rho}(\bar{\mathbf{w}}^{k+1} + \bar{\mathbf{u}}^k)$$

$$\bar{\mathbf{u}}^{k+1} \leftarrow \bar{\mathbf{u}}^k + \bar{\mathbf{w}}^{k+1} - \bar{\mathbf{z}}^{k+1}$$

until stopping criterion is satisfied.

for $j=1$: N **do**

$$\hat{\mathbf{w}}_{\text{Lasso}}(j) = \bar{\mathbf{w}}(j) + i \cdot \bar{\mathbf{w}}(j+N)$$

end for

return $\hat{\mathbf{w}}_{\text{Lasso}}$

It should be noted that the adjustment of the Lasso regularization parameter λ and the augmented Lagrangian parameter ρ, the definition of the soft thresholding function $S_{\lambda/\rho}(\cdot)$ and the termination criterion for iteration are elaborated in [8] Sect. III-C. The nonzero elements in $\hat{w}_{\text{Lasso}}$ is then counted as N_a, which determines the number of active loudspeakers to be used in the second step. In general, the first step completes the procedure of selecting N_a active loudspeakers out of N candidate positions.

2.3 Loudspeaker Weight Estimation Using Regularized LS

Power constraints exist in all practical SFR systems, since no real system can draw infinite power. During the second step, the pre-selected N_a active loudspeakers is used for SFR under power constraints. Recall that the sparse vector $\hat{w}_{\text{Lasso}} = \left\{ \hat{w}^i_{\text{Lasso}} \right\}^N_{i=1}$ whose indexes of non-zero items is denoted as n_b (b = 1, 2, ..., N_a). Afterwards, the n_b-th column of the ATF matrix $\mathbf{G}$ is successively extracted and merged to form a new matrix $\mathbf{G_a}$, which containing the ATF of all active loudspeakers at all matching points with the size of $M \times N_a$.

The ultimate loudspeaker weights are attained by minimizing the squared error between the desired and reproduced sound field with power limitation, i.e.,

$$\hat{\mathbf{w}}_{\text{LS}} = \arg\min_{\mathbf{w}} \left\| \mathbf{G_a w} - \mathbf{p}^d \right\|^2_2 + \delta \|\mathbf{w}\|^2_2 \tag{10}$$

where $\delta > 0$ is the LS regularization factor and $\|\mathbf{w}\|^2_2$ is the total loudspeaker power. The closed-form solution is obtained by:

$$\hat{\mathbf{w}}_{\text{LS}} = \left(\mathbf{G_a^H G_a} + \gamma \mathbf{I} \right)^{-1} \mathbf{G_a^H p}^d \tag{11}$$

Finally, the monochromatic reproduced sound field from active loudspeakers at all matching points is given by:

$$\mathbf{p}^r = \mathbf{G_a} \hat{\mathbf{w}}_{\text{LS}} \tag{12}$$

3 Experimental Results

Our simulation is based on the 3D SFR structure depicted in Fig. 1, where the size of room 1 and room 2 are both 7 m (width) $\times$ 3 m (height) $\times$ 5 m (depth). In order to approximate a real conference room, the room reflection coefficient r is set to be 0.6 thus the reverberation time $T_{60} = 0.1611 \cdot V/(S \cdot r) = 0.2$ s (V and S are the volume and the surface area of the room, respectively). In our experiments, three image sources are adopted in each direction of the original virtual source, thus the total number of image source $Q = (2 \times 3 + 1)^3 - 1 = 342$. The reason behind selecting this value is that the greater the number of image sources leads to the greater degree of accuracy in reverberation time estimate calculation. Each wall itself produces an image source and a second-order image source is produced by the combined reflection off the two walls giving us four effective sources instead of one. This can be extended to a desired number of image sources and we balanced the actual scenario and the computational cost to calculate a reasonable number of image source.

The first experiment is to examine the SFR performance of the proposed approach and the reference methods. The Loudspeaker Array (LA) is a 3 m × 3 m square centered at the wall on the xy-plane, while the listening volume occupies 1 m × 1 m × 1 m cube and located 1 m away from the LA. The omni-directional monochromatic source is placed 8 m away from the LA (the coordinate is $(0, 0, -8)$) with complex amplitude $A = 8 \angle 0°$. All matching points are distributed uniformly throughout the listening region with a Cartesian spacing 0.2 m, so the number of matching point is $M = 125$. Besides, the number of candidate positions on LA and active loudspeakers are determined to be $N = 625$ and $N_a = 25$, respectively. For quantitative analysis, the Normalized Mean Square Error (NMSE) is employed to describe the reproduced error in this paper, which is defined as follows:

$$\text{NMSE(dB)} = 10 \cdot \lg\left(\frac{\left\|(\mathbf{p}^d)_{M_1} - (\mathbf{p}^r)_{M_1}\right\|_2^2}{\left\|(\mathbf{p}^d)_{M_1}\right\|_2^2}\right) \tag{13}$$

where $(\bullet)_{M_1}$ means the sound field sampled at M_1 matching points and $M_1 = 125000$ to ensure the error field is comfortably over-sampled. The position and driven signal of active speakers only optimized at $f = 800$ Hz (i.e. the single source frequency) under the maximum available power $P_{\max} = 2$, and the interested reproduced frequency range is [200, 2000] Hz. We investigate the NMSE of the four SFR methods – benchmark, Singular Value Decomposition (SVD) [13], Constrained Matching Pursuit (CMP) [14], and the proposed method. It is need to emphasize that the benchmark configuration is defined as N_a active loudspeakers uniformly placed in the LA, that is, the distance between the arbitrary adjacent loudspeaker is 75 cm. SFR error analysis results are shown in Fig. 2.

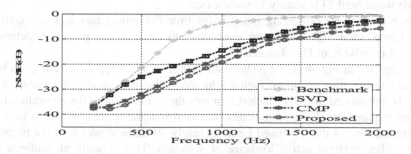

Fig. 2. The NMSE of the proposed SFR method and the comparative SFR methods for monochromatic source under $P_{\max} = 2$. The interested frequency range is [200, 2000] Hz with the interval of 100 Hz.

According to Fig. 2, it is observed that the NMSE increases as the frequency raises, all SFR systems perform well at very low frequency. However, the proposed SFR method outperforms the tested approaches over the frequency range [300, 2000]. The reason is that the process of solving Lasso is a convex optimization problem, and the solution of (6) owns global optimality, which leads to the selected active loudspeakers are the most suitable for SFR.

In our test, we also consider the circumstance of multiple sources. Suppose there are two virtual sources with $f = 800$ Hz located on $(-1, 0, -2)$ and $(1, 0, -2)$. The remaining experimental conditions are the same as the previous test and results are shown in Fig. 3.

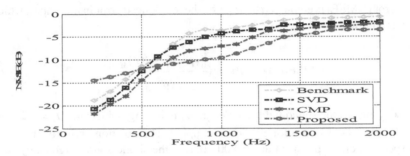

Fig. 3. Reproduction error of the Benchmark SFR, SVD-based SFR, CMP-based SFR and the proposed SFR method for two primary sources. The other experimental settings are maintain the same as the previous simulation.

By checking the Fig. 3, the proposed SFR method has the lowest NMSE among the three reference methods when $f > 600$ Hz but little inferior when $f \leq 600$ Hz. The probable cause may be the most active speakers are located in the central part of the speaker array and perhaps they are allocated excessive power. This phenomenon may degrade the overall SFR quality to some extent.

Since the process of solving Lasso is the time-consuming task in many conventional Lasso-based SFR, hence, the execution efficiency of the proposed method is presented intuitively in Fig. 4 at last.

As depicted in Fig. 4(a), the ADMM algorithm for loudspeaker selecting has been finished after iterating 56 times. Figure 4(b) shows that the convergence curve of the residuals (introduced in [15]) which determines the termination of the algorithm. Each iteration requires 0.004 s approximately, the total runtime is about 0.2 s. In contrast, the iteration time of the CD-based Lasso is nearly 40 times slower than the proposed method when perform active loudspeaker selection. This experiment confirms that ADMM-based Lasso is more advantageous in practical large-scale or low-latency SFR applications.

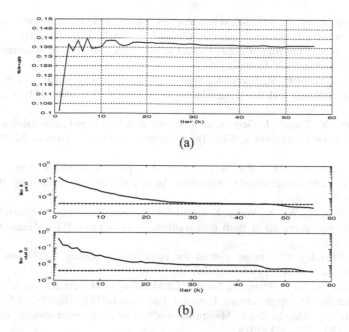

Fig. 4. The convergence curve of (a) the objective function of the ADMM-based Lasso and (b) the primal and dual residuals (defined in [15]) during the iteration processing.

4   Conclusion

This paper aims at 3D SFR applications, which is a continuation work of our previous proposed AL-LS SFR framework. In sound field design phase, the image source model is employed for simulate the room reflections. Afterwards, the active loudspeaker is chosen based on the ADMM-based Lasso algorithm in order to use a relatively small number of loudspeakers for archiving a better reproduction quality. Finally, all active loudspeaker weightings are calculated by regularized LS to control the total power. Numerical simulation experiments prove that the proposed method outperforms the benchmark, SVD, and CMP approaches in most frequency bands and the execution efficiency is much higher than the traditional algorithm, which is demonstrated to be applied in low delay and reverberant SFR scene.

Acknowledgement. This research is supported by National Natural Science Foundation of China (No. 61831019).

References

1. Ahrens, J., Spors, S.: Sound field reproduction using planar and linear arrays of loudspeakers. IEEE Trans. Audio Speech Lang. Process. **18**(8), 2038–2050 (2010)
2. Jia, M., Wang, W., Yang, Z.: 2.5 D sound field reproduction using higher order loudspeakers. Cybern. Inf. Technol. **15**(6), 5–15 (2015)

3. Gauthier, P., Berry, A.: Sound-field reproduction in-room using optimal control techniques: simulations in the frequency domain. J. Acoust. Soc. Am. **2**, 662–678 (2005)
4. Radmanesh, N.: Multizone wideband sound field reproduction. Ph. D. dissertation, RMIT Univ., Melbourne, VIC, Australia (2013)
5. Gauthier, P., Lecomte, P., Berry, A.: Source sparsity control of sound field reproduction using the elastic-net and the lasso minimizers. J. Acoust. Soc. Am. **141**(4), 2315–2326 (2017)
6. Radmanesh, N., Burnett, I.: Generation of isolated wideband sound fields using a combined two-stage Lasso-LS algorithm. IEEE Trans. Audio Speech Lang. Process. **21**(2), 378–387 (2013)
7. Radmanesh, N., Burnett, I., Rao, B.D.: A Lasso-LS optimization with a frequency variable dictionary in a multizone sound system. IEEE/ACM Trans. Audio Speech Lang. Process. **24** (3), 583–593 (2016)
8. Jia, M., Zhang, J., Wu, Y., Wang, J.: Sound field reproduction via the alternating direction method of multipliers based lasso plus regularized least-square. IEEE Access **6**, 54550–54563 (2018)
9. Allen, J., Berkley, D.: Image method for efficiently simulating small-room acoustics. J. Acoust. Soc. Am. **65**, 943–950 (1979)
10. Siltanen, S., Lokki, T., Tervo, S., Savioja, L.: Modeling incoherent reflections from rough room surfaces with image sources. J. Acoust. Soc. Am. **131**(6), 4606–4614 (2012)
11. Yin, P., Lou, Y., He, Q., Xin, J.: Minimization of l_{1-2} for compressed sensing. SIAM J. Sci. Comput. **37**(1), 536–563 (2015)
12. Zhang, R., Kwok, J.: Asynchronous distributed ADMM for consensus optimization. In: International Conference on Machine Learning, Beijing, China, pp. 1701–1709, June 2014
13. Khalilian, H., Bajic, I.V., Vaughan, R.G.: Towards optimal loudspeaker placement for sound field reproduction. In: Proceedings IEEE International Conference Acoustics, Speech Signal Processing, Vancouver, BC, Canada, pp. 321–325, May 2013
14. Khalilian, H., Bajic, I.V., Vaughan, R.G.: Comparison of loudspeaker placement methods for sound field reproduction. IEEE/ACM Trans. Audio Speech Lang. Process. **24**(8), 1364–1379 (2016)
15. Boyd, S., Parikh, N., Chu, E., Peleato, B., Eckstein, J.: Distributed optimization and statistical learning via the alternating direction method of multipliers. Found. Trends® Mach. Learn. **3**(1), 1–122 (2011)

Improvement of Image Reconstruction Algorithm Based on CS

Tongxu Zhou[1](✉) and Li Wang[2]

[1] College of Mechanical and Vehicle Engineering, West Anhui University,
Lu'an 237012, China
13966300049@163.com
[2] Electrical Engineering and Automation, Anhui University,
Hefei 230601, China
liwang1002@163.com

Abstract. Nowadays, Compressed sensing as a new type of signal processing theory has been widely used to image compression codec. The development of reconstruction algorithm is core issue of CS. The original orthogonal matching pursuit algorithm will bring Gaussian noise when reconstructing the image, which seriously affects the accuracy of image reconstruction. Aiming at this problem, this paper propose an adaptive hard threshold approach that based on orthogonal matching pursuit algorithm. The image reconstructed by the original OMP algorithm is transformed into a domain, and it is further processed by the adaptive hard threshold algorithm, and then to inverse transform and recovery the image. The simulation results show that the proposed reconstruction algorithm has a better performance in terms of reconstruction quality compared with original OMP algorithm.

Keywords: Compressed sensing · Reconstruction algorithm · OMP · Adaptive hard threshold

1 Introduction

Compressed sensing (CS) is an emerging technique in the field of signal processing in recent years. The concept was proposed by Donoho [1] and Candes [2] et al. in 2006. As we all known, the traditional Nyquist [3]/Shannon [4] sampling theorem requires that the sampling rate of the signal must be twice as high as the maximum signal rate. Compressed sensing offers an alternative to the traditional Nyquist theory for sampling signals. In compressed sensing, if a signal is sufficiently sparse, a small number projections onto random vectors is enough to reconstruct the signal. That is signal can be reconstructed under the rate that much lower than that of the Nyquist.

It combines the processes of sampling and compressing into one step by measuring minimum samples that include maximum information about the signal which is sampled at much lower than the Nyquist sampling rate.

Figure 1 shows that traditional sampling at Nyquist rate condition. The process mainly includes four parts: sampling, compression, transmission and decompression. In this traditional codec method, due to the sampling rate of the signal not less than twice

© Springer Nature Switzerland AG 2019
D.-S. Huang et al. (Eds.): ICIC 2019, LNCS 11643, pp. 121–130, 2019.
https://doi.org/10.1007/978-3-030-26763-6_12

the signal bandwidth, making that the corresponding hardware equipment is facing a lot of sampling pressure, and the process of high-speed sampling and then compression is indeed a waste of sampling resources.

Figure 2 shows that the process of data acquisition and signal reconstruction in the framework of compressed sensing theory. Unlike traditional signal acquisition and processing, it combines the processes of sampling and compressing into one step by measuring minimum samples that include maximum information about the signal which is sampled at much lower than the Nyquist sampling rate. Therefore, reducing the cost of collecting information hardware, and speeding up the transmission and reconstruction of information.

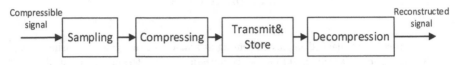

Fig. 1. Traditional signal processing system

Fig. 2. CS signal processing system

This new idea of improving sampling efficiency has aroused widespread concern in academia, and CS is highly concerned in the fields of digital signal processing [5], optical imaging [6], medical imaging [7], radio communication [8], radar imaging [9], pattern recognition [10] and so on.

Compressed sensing focuses on study of the three aspects: (1) Signal sparse transformation, the sparse transformation of the signal usually has the Fourier transform (FT) [11], the discrete cosine transform (DCT) [12] and the wavelet transform (DWT) [13]. (2) The design of the measurement matrix, the measurement matrix contains random measurement matrix [14, 15] and deterministic measurement matrix [16, 17]. (3) Reconstruction algorithm, such as Basis Pursuit (BP) algorithm [18, 19], Matching Pursuit (MP) algorithm [20] and Orthogonal Matching Pursuit (OMP) algorithm [21, 22].

The traditional OMP algorithm generates Gaussian noise when reconstructing images, which seriously reduces the accuracy of image reconstruction. The focus of this paper is to optimize and improve the reconstruction algorithm, an adaptive hard threshold method based on OMP algorithm is proposed. This paper is organized as follows: Sect. 1 Introduce the background, development and prospects of the theory of compressed sensing. Section 2 Summarize the theory of compressed sensing and its related theory. Section 3 Simulation experiments and analysis of image reconstruction. Section 4 Summary and prospect.

2 Overview of Theory

2.1 Theoretical Framework of Compressed Sensing

The theoretical framework of compressed sensing consists of three main parts: sparse transformation, encoding measurement, signal reconstruction. That shows in Fig. 3.

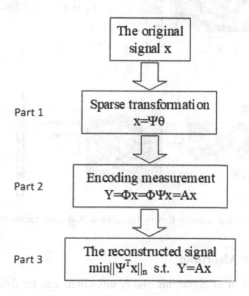

Fig. 3. Compressed sensing theory framework

Signal x of length N converts to spares signal θ by using transform domain Ψ, which is expressed by,

$$x = \Psi\theta \quad \text{or} \quad \theta = \Psi^{-1}x \tag{1}$$

Then the signal is encoded by measurement matrix and obtain measurement value Y,

$$Y = \Phi x = \Phi\Psi\theta \tag{2}$$

$$A = \Phi\Psi \tag{3}$$

$$\Rightarrow Y = A\theta \tag{4}$$

A is called sensing matrix. The final step is to reconstruct the original signal from the measurement value Y. The problem is transformed into obtaining optimal sparse solution θ by using any optimization techniques. Figure 4 is the process of linear measurement and signal reconstruction of compressed sensing, the images can clearly describe the changes of signal dimension.

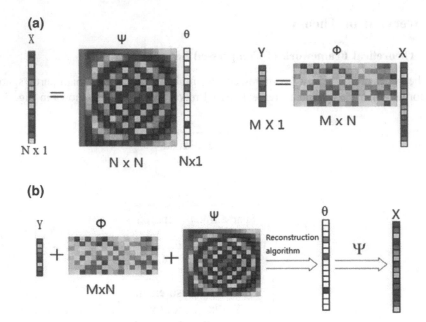

Fig. 4. a. Compressed sensing theory framework b. Signal reconstruction process

2.2   Reconstruction Algorithm

For any linear system of M equations and N unknowns can be defined as,

$$y = \Phi x \tag{5}$$

Which y is a column vector of length M, Φ is a matrix of $M \times N$, x is a column vector of length N. According to the theory of linear algebra, when $M \geq N$, if the linear system is solvable, we can use the method of the general algebraic iteration to solve it. However, in the theory of compressed sensing, $M \ll N$, this is a system of undefined equations and don't have unique solution. But, because x is K-sparse, Candes et al. proved that the CS problem can be solved by solving the l_0 optimization problem. But directly solving the l_0 optimization problem is an NP-hard problem [23] and the value of the solution is unstable. Later it was proved that when the measurement matrix satisfies the RIP condition [24], the problem of solving the minimum l_0 norm can be transformed into solving the minimum l_1 norm problem, and the approximate solution can be obtained with high probability. The following will introduce a commonly used reconstruction algorithm of CS.

OMP Algorithm. OMP [21, 22] algorithm is a classical iterative greedy algorithm based on MP algorithm. The essence of the OMP algorithm that it selects the columns of the sensing matrix in a greedy iteration and the column selected in each iteration has maximum correlation to the current redundant vector, then subtracting the relevant parts from the measurement vector and iterating it repeatedly. Until the number of iterations reaches the sparse K, the iteration is forced to stop. The OMP algorithm guarantees the optimality of each iteration and reduces the number of iterations. Although OMP algorithm has a simple structure, it also introduces noise in the reconstruction process, so it is difficult to improve the reconstruction accuracy (Table 1).

Table 1. The OMP algorithm

Input: Sensing matrix A, Sparseness K
Output: Sparse representation θ
Initialize: Residual $r_0 = y$, Index set $\Lambda_0 = \emptyset, t = 1$
Loop performs the following five steps: (1) Find out λ: $\lambda_t = \arg\max_{j=1,\cdots,N}\|\langle r_{t-1}, \alpha_j\rangle\|$; (2) Update the index set: $\Lambda_t = \Lambda_{t-1} \cup \{\lambda_t\}$,   Reconstruction of atomic collection: $A_t = [A_{t-1}, \alpha_\lambda]$; (3) Least square method: $\theta_t = \arg\min\|y - A_t x\|_2$; (4) Update the residual: $r_t = y - A_t\theta_t, t = t + 1$; (5) Judgment: if $t > K$ stop the iteration, or go to step(1)

3 Simulation Analysis

In this paper, there are three natural scenes images for experiment and the images size is 256 × 256. This experiment completed in WIN7 ultimate system under the Matlab7.0 environment.

3.1 Improvement of Reconstruction Algorithm

In fact, the image reconstructed directly by the OMP algorithm will produce additional noise, resulting in poor reconstruction accuracy. In order to eliminate some noise, the adaptive hard threshold algorithm [25, 26] is introduced in this paper.

The adaptive hard threshold algorithm is by setting a threshold value. If the coefficient is greater than the threshold, it is retained, whereas it is discarded. The advantage of this scheme is that the threshold is set by referring to the coefficients of the whole. According to the distribution of coefficients, the coefficient of energy in the majority can be retained. For the energy-dispersed images, the retention of coefficients will be increased, and for the energy-concentrated images, the retention of coefficients will be reduced accordingly. The following is the function of the adaptive hard threshold:

$$x^{i+1} = \begin{cases} x^i, & |x^i| \geq \tau^i, \\ 0, & else \end{cases} \tag{6}$$

Where τ^i represents the threshold value of the ith iteration threshold function, which is calculated as follows:

$$\tau^i = \lambda \sigma^i \sqrt{2 \log K} \tag{7}$$

Where λ is the constant factor that controls the rate of convergence, K represents the number of the transformation coefficient, σ^i is the signal standard variance which is obtained by the median estimate:

$$\sigma^i = \frac{median(|x^i|)}{0.6745} \tag{8}$$

3.2   Experiment

In this section, we will verify the reconstruction performance of the proposed algorithm by comparing experiments. The experimental flow of the two sets of algorithms is shown in Fig. 5.

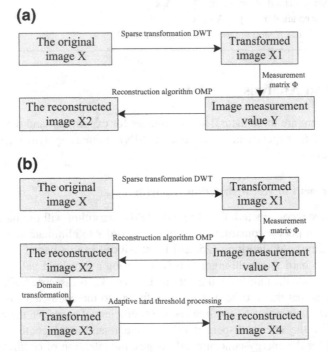

Fig. 5.   a. The original OMP algorithm flow chart b. Adaptive hard threshold algorithm flow chart

As shown in Fig. 5a: First of all, the original image is transformed by the discrete wavelet transform (DWT) to obtain the transformed image X1. Then, encoding the transformed image X1 by measurement matrix and getting the observed value Y. Finally, to reconstruct the image by using orthogonal matching pursuit algorithm.

As shown in Fig. 5b: The former steps are the same as the first experiment. The difference is that applied adaptive hard threshold algorithm based on the first experiment. After the former steps, the domain of the reconstructed image X2 is transformed and getting transformed image X3, then the image X3 is processed by adaptive hard threshold algorithm, last, recovering image by domain inverse transform.

3.3   Simulation Results

Figure 6 shows that the images are reconstructed by the two different algorithms. The sampling rate (*M/N*) is 0.5 and the measurement matrix is the Gaussian random matrix.

Fig. 6. Reconstruction of different algorithms (from left to right: Original, OMP, Proposed)

From Fig. 6, we can visually see the effects of images reconstruction of the two algorithms. The effects of the improved algorithm reconstruction image is better than that the original algorithm. Especially in the complex texture, the edge is more fuzzy, the reconstruction effect is more perfect. To illustrate the experimental results of Fig. 6

from the data, Table 2 shows the PSNR and SSIM values of the reconstructed images of each algorithm when the sampling rate is 0.5.

As shown in Table 2, the PSNR and SSIM values of the images reconstructed by the improved algorithm are greater than those of the images reconstructed by the original OMP algorithm under the same sampling rate.

Table 2. Different algorithms reconstruct natural image effect

Test images	Algorithms	PSNR/dB	SSIM
Monarch	OMP	20.99	0.6515
	Proposed	24.45	0.7238
lena	OMP	28.26	0.8245
	Proposed	31.06	0.9091
peppers	OMP	25.22	0.7675
	Proposed	29.78	0.8774
house	OMP	26.34	0.7110
	Proposed	29.51	0.8277

In order to further verify the advantages of the improved algorithm proposed in this paper, the images are reconstructed with the above two algorithms at different sampling rates. Sampling rate is 0.3–0.7, the changes of PSNR values of the reconstructed images are shown in Fig. 7.

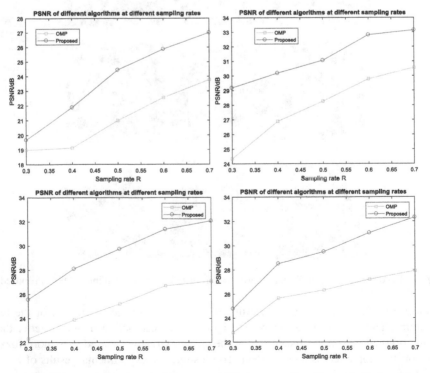

Fig. 7. The PSNRs of reconstructed images at different sampling (from clockwise: Monarch, lena, peppers, house)

As can be seen from Fig. 7, with the increase of the sampling rate, the reconstruction precision of the image is also improved. Indicating that the more image data is measured, the more accurate the reconstructed image information is. Moreover, when the sampling rate in 0.3–0.7, the PSNR curve of the improved algorithm is always above the original algorithm curve. The results show that under the same conditions, the performance of the improved algorithm is always better than that of the original algorithm.

4 Conclusion

How to improve the accuracy of signal reconstruction has always been an important part of CS research field. In this paper, an improved algorithm is proposed for 2D image reconstruction, adaptive hard threshold algorithm is applied on the basis of original OMP algorithm. The experimental analysis shows that the proposed algorithm is superior to the original OMP algorithm, both from the objective visual reconstruction effect of the image and the PSNR and SSIM values of the reconstructed image. But there are still some problems, such as the stability and complexity of the reconstruction algorithm. In the next work, I will further study its optimization problem.

References

1. Donoho, D.L.: Compressed sensing. IEEE Trans. Inf. Theory 52(4), 1289–1306 (2006)
2. Candes, E.J., Romberg, J., Tao, T.: Robust uncertainty principles: exact signal reconstruction from highly incomplete frequency information. IEEE Trans. Inf. Theory 52(2), 489–509 (2006)
3. Mishali, M., Eldar, Y.C.: From theory to practice: Sub-Nyquist sampling of sparse wideband analog signals. IEEE J. Sel. Top. Signal Process. 4(2), 375–391 (2010)
4. Unser, M.: Sampling-50 years after Shannon. Proc. IEEE 88(4), 569–587 (2000)
5. Hariri, A., Babaie-Zadeh, M.: Compressive detection of sparse signals in additive white Gaussian noise without signal reconstruction. Signal Process. 131, 376–385 (2017)
6. Usala, J.D., Maag, A., Nelis, T., et al.: Compressed sensing spectral imaging for plasma optical emission spectroscopy. J. Anal. At. Spectrom. 31(11), 2198–2206 (2016)
7. Chen, Y., Ye, X., et al.: A novel method and fast algorithm for MR image reconstruction with significantly under-sampled data. Inverse Probl. Imaging 4(2), 223–240 (2017)
8. Lv, S.T., Liu, J.: A novel signal separation algorithm based on compressed sensing for wideband spectrum sensing in cognitive radio networks. Int. J. Commun. Syst. 27(11), 2628–2641 (2014)
9. Bu, H., Tao, R., Bai, X., et al.: A novel SAR imaging algorithm based on compressed sensing. IEEE Geosci. Remote Sens. Lett. 12(5), 1003–1007 (2017)
10. He, Z., Zhao, X., Zhang, S., et al.: Random combination for information extraction in compressed sensing and sparse representation-based pattern recognition. Neurocomputing 145(18), 160–173 (2014)
11. Kajbaf, H., et al.: Compressed sensing for SAR-based wideband three-dimensional microwave imaging system using non-uniform fast Fourier transform. IET Radar Sonar Navig. 7(6), 658–670 (2013)

12. Li, Q., Han, Y.H., Dang, J.W.: Image decomposing for inpainting using compressed sensing in DCT domain. Front. Comput. Sci. **8**(6), 905–915 (2014)
13. Zhang, J., Xia, L., Huang, M., et al.: Image reconstruction in compressed sensing based on single-level DWT. In: IEEE Workshop on Electronics, Computer & Applications. IEEE (2014)
14. Monajemi, H., Jafarpour, S., Gavish, M., et al.: Deterministic matrices matching the compressed sensing phase transitions of Gaussian random matrices. Proc. Natl. Acad. Sci. U.S.A **110**(4), 1181–1186 (2013)
15. Lu, W., Li, W., Kpalma, K., et al.: Compressed sensing performance of random Bernoulli matrices with high compression ratio. IEEE Signal Process. Lett. **22**(8), 1074–1078 (2015)
16. Li, X., Zhao, R., Hu, S.: Blocked polynomial deterministic matrix for compressed sensing. In: International Conference on Wireless Communications Networking & Mobile Computing. IEEE (2010)
17. Yan, T., Lv, G., Yin, K.: Deterministic sensing matrices based on multidimensional pseudo-random sequences. Circ. Syst. Signal Process. **33**(5), 1597–1610 (2014)
18. Boyd, S., Vandenberghe, L.: Convex optimization. IEEE Trans. Autom. Control **51**(11), 1859 (2006)
19. Mota, J.F.C., et al.: Distributed basis pursuit. IEEE Trans. Signal Process. **60**(4), 1942–1956 (2012)
20. Mallat, S.G., Zhang, Z.: Matching pursuits with time-frequency dictionaries. IEEE Trans. Signal Process. **41**(12), 3397–3415 (1993)
21. Tropp, J.A., Gilbert, A.C.: Signal recovery from random measurements via orthogonal matching pursuit. IEEE Trans. Inf. Theory **53**(12), 4655–4666 (2007)
22. Sahoo, S.K., Makur, A.: Signal recovery from random measurements via extended orthogonal matching pursuit. IEEE Trans. Signal Process. **63**(10), 2572–2581 (2015)
23. Natarajan, B.: Sparse approximate solutions to linear systems. SIAM J. Comput. **24**(2), 227–234 (1995)
24. Candès, E.J.: The restricted isometry property and its implications for compressed sensing. Comptes rendus - Mathématique **346**(9), 589–592 (2008)
25. Donoho, D.L.: De-noising by soft-thresholding. IEEE Trans. Inf. Theory **41**(3), 613–627 (2002)
26. Gavish, M., Donoho, D.L.: The optimal hard threshold for singular values is $4/\sqrt{3}$. IEEE Trans. Inf. Theory **60**(8), 5040–5053 (2014)

Automatic Badminton Action Recognition Using CNN with Adaptive Feature Extraction on Sensor Data

Ya Wang[1], Weichuang Fang[2], Jinwen Ma[1(✉)], Xiangchen Li[3(✉)], and Albert Zhong[4]

[1] Department of Information Science, School of Mathematical Sciences and LMAM, Peking University, Beijing 100871, China
wangyachn@pku.edu.cn, jwma@math.pku.edu.cn
[2] Academy for Advanced Interdisciplinary Studies, Peking University, Beijing 100871, China
f.weichuang@pku.edu.cn
[3] China Institute of Sport Science, Beijing 100061, China
lixiangchen@ciss.cn
[4] Hangzhou Zhidong Sports Co., Ltd., Hangzhou 310052, China
zhongll1978@outlook.com

Abstract. With the fast development of sensor technology, a sensor chip can be easily inserted into the badminton racket so that the data of the activity of the badminton player can be recorded continuously. It has become a very challenging problem whether we can use these sensor-based data to effectively recognize the badminton actions. Although there have been some researches on the general human action recognition such as sitting, walking and running, there is few result or public dataset concerning badminton action recognition. In order to investigate the problem of badminton action recognition, we implement a specialized sensor chip being inserted into the badminton racket to collect the data of ten major badminton actions. On such a dataset, a deep convolutional neural network (CNN) can get a much better result of badminton action recognition than the conventional methods, but its recognition accuracy is not good enough for practical applications. The key difficulty is that the attributes recorded as time series in the sensor data have different measures and magnitudes so that the conventional feature normalization cannot work effectively in this complicated situation. In order to overcome this difficulty, we propose a specific block of adaptive feature extraction to enhance the performance of CNN for badminton action recognition. It is demonstrated by the experimental results on the sensor dataset that our proposed CNN with the adaptive feature extraction block can get 98.65% action recognition accuracy and outperforms the competitive methods remarkably.

Keywords: Action recognition · Sensor data · Time series · CNN

© Springer Nature Switzerland AG 2019
D.-S. Huang et al. (Eds.): ICIC 2019, LNCS 11643, pp. 131–143, 2019.
https://doi.org/10.1007/978-3-030-26763-6_13

1 Introduction

The fast development of artificial intelligence has motivated the progress of human action recognition. According to different data sources, researches on action recognition can be divided into two categories, video-based and sensor-based action recognition. The video-based action recognition has recently attracted much attention because the breakthrough of deep learning makes it possible to recognize the actions from the videos. However, the accuracy of video-based action recognition is relatively low and severely affected by various factors such as the setting of cameras (perspective, focal length, exposure, etc.), background and obstruction. Besides, it is very hard to design a real-time system with video data because of the high computational complexity. The sensor-based action recognition is more reliable and practical in comparison with the video-based action recognition. Hussain et al. [1] utilized multiple sensors to recognize human actions, such as sitting, walking and running. However, it will make a human more uncomfortable and inconvenient to wear multiple sensors on the body, which strongly limits the practical application of the multi-sensor recognition system. To overcome this problem, we utilize a single sensor for badminton action recognition. Although it is much more difficult than multi-sensors due to the lack of information, it is convenient for the implementation and can be widely applied in practice.

In literature, the main machine learning algorithms for sensor-based action recognition include C4.5, SVM, HMM as well as their fusion algorithms, but deep learning has not been effectively adopted in this field. In fact, those conventional machine learning methods need to extract the features artificially. But the quality of these features has great influence on the recognition accuracy. In this paper, we aim to use a specific deep learning method to extract the spatial and temporal features from the sensor data of badminton actions automatically, which can make use of the original information as much as possible. Since the sensor data are a kind of practical time series, CNN can cause a serious problem called "big attributes engulf small attributes" in feature extraction. The reason is that, time series classification is quite different from image processing because the pixels of an image have the same or similar physical meaning, while different attributes of time series data have their own measures and magnitudes.

Moreover, in order to make the badminton action recognition more effective, we also propose an Adaptive Feature Extraction Block (AFEB) for previous feature extraction by a two-layer feedward neural network and then integrate it to a classical CNN, AlexNet, to construct the AFEB-AlexNet framework for badminton action recognition. The experimental results on a practically collected Badminton Single Sensor (BSS) dataset demonstrate that the AFEB can effectively adjust the original sensor data to the input of CNN to deal with the feature extraction problem, and further improve the recognition accuracy remarkably.

The rest of this paper is organized as follows. Firstly, we review the related work on human action recognition and CNN. We then analyze the "dislocation" phenomenon in the sensor data of badminton actions. We further propose the AFEB-AlexNet framework for badminton action recognition. Furthermore, the experimental results are summarized and analyzed. Finally, we make a brief conclusion.

2 Related Work

2.1 Sensor-Based Action Recognition

Human action recognition based on accelerometer has been widely studied using machine learning algorithms. Ling et al. [2] used multiple accelerometers to collect data from different parts of human body, and then used them to identify the daily actions, like running, walking and climbing stairs. In this work, C4.5 achieved the best effect with the overall accuracy about 84%. Dernbach et al. [3] tested Multi-layer Perceptron, Naïve Bayes, Bayesian network and Decision Tree for its task, showed that simple actions such as biking could be easily recognized by sensor data of smart phone, but the performance of these models on complex actions was poor. Ward et al. [4] used HMM to identify the screwing, opening a drawer and other movements of the assembly workers. Yang et al. [5] were also aimed to identify the human's daily actions, and it showed that weighted SVM had the best performance in this task. Among these machine learning algorithms for human action recognition, SVM is most popularly used. Wang et al. [6] identified the actions of drinking, phoning, writing and so on. In this task, the SVM performed better than C4.5. Song et al. [7] used SVM to identify the daily activity of the elder. On a dataset of 9 classes, it achieved a 96% recognition accuracy. He et al. [8] used SVM to recognize 17 gestures based on single three-dimensional accelerometer mounted on a cell phone and the average recognition accuracy were 89.89%

However, most of this works were designed based on the conventional features and a classifier specified for their own task. The features, which perform well in one task, may act badly in another task. Here, we are devoted to making the action recognition free from artificial feature extraction. How to make this process adaptive? The key point is to use an automatic mechanism to extract features, as deep learning methods do. Inspired by it, we propose the AFEB-AlexNet algorithm, whose input is original sensor data. In this framework, A convolutional neural network is used as a classifier, it can adaptively extract deep features both spatially and temporally.

2.2 Convolutional Neural Network

Convolution neural networks have been investigated since the 1980 s, and there were related works on small scale image-based task, such as handwritten character recognition [9] and face recognition [10]. With the arrival of big data era and rapid development of computing capabilities, convolution neural networks have been applied to many large scale images-based tasks. In 2012, AlexNet was used in ImageNet Visual Challenge Race [11], and became the leading algorithm at that time. It was the first time that the convolution neural network was applied to large scale data recognition. AlexNet contains 5 convolution layers and 3 fully connected layers. It uses ReLU and dropout technology to make itself more robust as well as reducing the over fitting of the fully connected layers. After that, the proposed VGGNet [12] and GoogLeNet [13] greatly increased the depth of convolution network and reduced the number of parameters in each convolution layer. On ImageNet dataset, they achieved rather better results compared with their own competitors. Though AlexNet, VGGNet, GoogLeNet perform very well, they can only accept fixed size input. To break the limitation, SPP-net [14] was proposed to make different sizes of input produce the same size of output. The model adds a spatial pyramid pooling between the last convolution layer and the first full connection layer of CNN. ResNet [15] was proposed to solve the gradient disappearance and explosion problem of convolution networks. Now, the convolution networks are successfully used in many big data tasks, such as image classification [11, 15], face recognition [16].

To some extent, the form of badminton sensor data is similar to images, however one of the most remarkable differences is that the number of attributes is very small in comparison with the width of images, which causes that the receptive field of a shallow network can cover total attributes. Therefore, we use a classical shallow CNN, Alex-Net, to identify badminton actions. However, as for sensor data, the attributes of records in them have different measures and magnitudes, which will degrade the performance of CNN. In order to solve this problem, we further propose a specific block called adaptive feature extraction block in our framework.

3   Dislocation of Sensor Data

Let the sensor dataset denoted as $\{X^i\}_{i=1}^{N}$, where $X^i = \left[x_{jk}^i\right]_{L_i \times K}$. That is, X^i is a sample of sensor data, being formatted as a matrix, whose jth row contains K attributes at the jth time. Each attribute has its own measures and physical meanings, for example, in the badminton sensor dataset, some of attributes represent spatial attitude angles (including pitch, yaw and roll), others represent acceleration and the position of racket. We now describe the "dislocation" of sensor data using an example below.

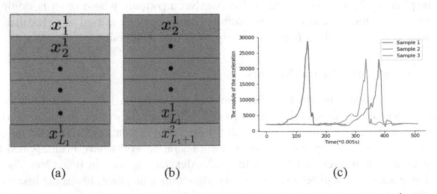

       (a)   (b)   (c)

Fig. 1. An example of "dislocation" phenomenon in sensor data. (a): Sample X^1 with L_1 records. (b): Sample X^2 with the same number of records as X^1. The blue part of X^1 shares the same value of the blue part of X^2, The yellow part of X^1 and the green part of X^2 are unique. (c): A real-world example of "dislocation" in BSS dataset. Actually, sample 1, sample 2 and sample 3 represent the same action, which is called backhand lift (Color figure online).

As shown in Figs. 1(a) and 2(b), there are two samples $X^1 = \left[x_1^1, x_2^1, \cdots, x_{L_1}^1\right]^T$ and $X^2 = \left[x_1^2, x_1^1, x_2^1, \cdots, x_{L_1-1}^1\right]^T$, where X_j^i denotes the j_{th} row of X^i. Suppose $x_i^1 \neq x_i^1 + 1, \forall i \in \{1, 2, \cdots, L_1 - 1\}$ and $x_{L_1}^1 \neq x_{L_1}^2 + 1$, then the Euclidean distance $d(X^1, X^2)$ between X^1 and X^2 is extremely large, but X^1 and X^2 differ from each other only at the starting and ending records. That is, if L_1 is large enough, the most parts of X^1 and X^2 are the same, so they usually belong to the same class. We call this phenomenon the "dislocation" of data.

The "dislocation" phenomenon is ubiquitous, and even inevitable in some real-world sensor datasets. Figure 1(c) shows a practical example of our BSS dataset. It sketches the modules of three-dimensional acceleration of three random samples. They are recorded when a player repeats the same action three times with the same equipment, however, the locations of the peak values and the lengths of these samples are different from each other. As a result, the Euclidean distance between any pair of sample 1, sample 2 and sample 3 is large, which contradicts the similarity among them.

4 Methodology

4.1 Adaptive Feature Extraction Block

As we talk above, CNN is competent to deal with the "dislocation" phenomenon, because both convolution and pooling are local operators and not sensitive to the locations of pixels. However, if CNN is applied to recognize sensor-based activities directly, another problem will arise. Since different attributes have their own measures and magnitudes, the attributes with larger magnitudes will "engulf" the smaller ones when passing through convolution and pooling layers, so that the larger ones affects the classification results much more significantly than the smaller ones, which will degenerate the classification process.

To overcome the problem of "big attributes engulf small attributes", Min-Max normalization, Z-Score, PCA and other feature normalization strategies are usually used to preprocess data in most types of data. However, they do not work in sensor data. The reason is that in feature normalization process, our goal is to enhance the separability among different samples, rather than the separability among all records. So it is clear that we should perform statistical analysis on samples instead of records of all samples.

The general calculation process of traditional feature normalization strategies can be described as four parts. Firstly, each multidimensional sample is converted to a one-dimensional vector. Secondly, calculate the mean, variance or other statistics based on all samples. Thirdly, construct an affine transformation according to these statistics. Fourthly, apply the affine transformation on the one-dimensional vector. Unfortunately, as for the sensor data, due to the ubiquity of "dislocation" phenomenon in it, we cannot effectively calculate these statistics. Therefore, the traditional feature normalization strategy cannot be applied to sensor data.

In order to balance the magnitudes of all attributes, we should make an affine transformation on the columns of sample data, that is

$$\hat{X}_i = X^i W + b, \quad i = 1, 2, \cdots, N \tag{1}$$

where X^i is an $L_i \times K$ matrix, denotes the i_{th} sample. Each row of X^i is a record. W is a $K \times K_2$ dimensional matrix, represents the scale and rotation transformation. b is a $1 \times K_2$ dimensional row vector, represents the offset residual. The addition operator between matrix $X^i W$ and vector b is broadcast along the rows. Conventional feature normalization strategies calculate W and b from the distribution of samples in the dataset, which is not available because of the "dislocation" phenomenon. Instead, we use back-propagation algorithm to "end-to-end" optimize their values together with the parameters of CNN, which agrees better with the subsequent AlexNet classifier. It should be noted that, the transformation in Eq. 1 contains not only feature normalization but also linear combination of original attributes, because W is not necessarily diagonal.

Based on the idea above, we further improve the process. The above process is only a linear combination of original K features, but more general nonlinear transformations, such as the transformation from the acceleration vectors to the module, cannot be fitted by it. However, as we know, the module of three-dimensional acceleration is an important feature of badminton actions. In order to extract these kinds of features, inspired by [17], we improve the transformation Eq. 1 by adding a hidden layer

$$\hat{X}^i = \delta\left(X^i W_1 + b_1\right) \tag{2}$$

$$\tilde{X}^i = \delta\left(\hat{X}^i W_2 + b_2\right) \tag{3}$$

for all $i = 1, 2, \cdots, L_i$. Here $\delta(\cdot)$ is an activation function, we take ReLU instead of a squashing function here. W_1 and W_2 are $K \times K_1$ and $K_1 \times K_2$-dimensional matrices respectively, b_1 and b_2 are $1 \times K_1$-dimensional and $1 \times K_2$-dimensional row vectors, respectively. Obviously, the $\tilde{X}^i$ is an $L \times K_2$-dimensional matrix, whose rows represent reformed records obtained by feature extraction. As Eq. 1 does, the addition operators in Eqs. 2 and 3 are both broadcast along the rows. It should be noted that the AFEB structure is different from the fully connected layers in CNN. It only works on the columns of raw data, so the parameters in AFEB is few. A two layers AFEB has only $(K+1)K_1 + (K_1 + 1)K_2$ parameters, it is few because K, K_1 and K_2 are usually small.

4.2   AFEB-AlexNet

Theoretically, AFEB can be integrated with any kind of CNN. Here, we take a shallow CNN, AlexNet, as the classifier for our task. As shown in Fig. 2, in the network we designed, firstly original data X^i is reformed to $\tilde{X}^i$ by AFEB. $\tilde{X}^i$ and X^i have the same numbers of records, but the records of them have different attributes. Every record of $\tilde{X}^i$

comes from the transformation of original record of X^i. Then AlexNet classifier is used to get the predicted class from $\tilde{X}^i$. We call the network AFEB-AlexNet.

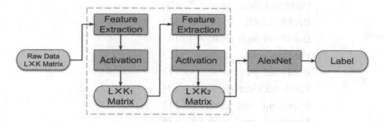

Fig. 2. The overall framework of the AFEB-AlexNet algorithm. The component surrounded by the orange dotted line is the AFEB architecture.

AFEB is composed with only two affine transformations and two activation functions, so the back propagation formula can be derived easily.

5 Experimental Results

5.1 BSS Dataset

In order to reduce the influence on actions of players, we fix a specialized sensor on badminton racket. As shown in Fig. 3, the badminton rocket is composed of four parts. The LED, controller and sensor are fixed on the racket. The frequency of sensor is 200 Hz, which means that the sensor collects 200 records per second. The data of each record includes acceleration in a three-dimensional orthogonal system and spatial attitude angles (roll angle, pitch angle, and yaw angle).

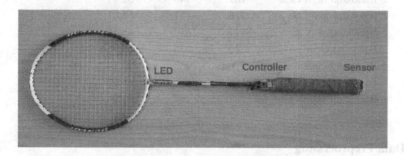

Fig. 3. The badminton racket used to collect data.

Table 1 shows the numbers of samples in BSS dataset. The collected data include ten major actions, such as backhand hook diagonal, forehand clear and backhand high clear. On average, each action contains about 113 samples.

Table 1. The numbers of samples in BSS dataset

Action	Number of samples
Backhand hook diagonal	115
Forehand clear	100
Backhand lift	123
Backhand high clear	103
Forehand play	123
Backhand play	118
Forehand clear service	104
Backhand clear service	111
Forehand smash high lift	176
Backhand smash high lift	57

The number of records in a badminton action sample is determined by the starting and ending time of the sensor. The collection process is controlled artificially, so this procedure is very subjective. Table 2 demonstrates that samples from different actions, even the same action, have significantly different numbers of records. For example, in backhand lift, the shortest sample has 269 records, while the longest one has 719 records. In this experiment, we randomly select 4/5 data of them as the training set and the remaining 1/5 of them as the testing set.

Table 2. The numbers of records in all samples

Action	Minimum	Maximum	Standard deviation
Backhand hook diagonal	213	461	47.67
Forehand clear	453	654	41.54
Backhand lift	269	719	71.08
Backhand high clear	187	445	32.91
Forehand play	318	851	66.81
Backhand play	277	610	46.15
Forehand clear service	240	635	63.98
Backhand clear service	176	933	93.14
Forehand smash high lift	156	645	68.75
Backhand smash high lift	147	267	21.24

5.2 Data Preprocessing

The raw data contain many redundant records, such as those indicating athlete's preparation or swing racket after the end of shot. We use the Sliding Window and Bottom-Up (SWAB) [18] method to eliminate these redundant records. Then, linear interpolation and compression are applied to adjust the numbers of records in all samples.

Removal of Redundant Records With SWAB

SWAB combines sliding window [19] and Bottom-up method [20]. It uses some piecewise linear segments to fit an arbitrary curve, then locates breakpoints of the curve according to the slopes of these segments. A fixed-size buffer is reserved to store enough data to create about 5 or 6 segments. In each loop, firstly, it uses the Bottom-Up method to perform piecewise linear fitting on the data in buffer. Secondly, it outputs the leftmost segment and removes it from the buffer in order to read more data. The number of data points read in depends on the distribution of incoming data. Then, sliding window method is used to add data one by one until the value of error function reaches the threshold. After that, this segment is merged into the buffer and Bottom-Up method is applied again. In this way, it loops until all data are processed.

In order to reduce the impact of "dislocation" phenomenon, we remove the redundant records of the BSS dataset based on SWAB. In badminton action recognition, the module of acceleration can effectively represent the changes of different actions. Therefore, we extract the acceleration module, which is a vector whose length is equal to the number of records. Then, the SWAB algorithm is used to fit the curve of acceleration module with some piecewise linear segments, and the slope of each segment is calculated. In general, the absolute value of slopes of redundant data are quite different from that of valid data. The former is smaller, while the latter is larger. Therefore, we can eliminate redundant data based on these slopes. After that, the redundant parts before and after the valid records are removed effectively. The overall framework of the algorithm is shown in Fig. 4.

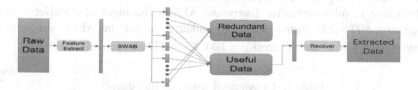

Fig. 4. The framework of removing redundant records with SWAB.

Unification of Sample Length

After the elimination operation, we need to unify the lengths of all samples, because the input of AlexNet should be fixed. We apply linear interpolation and linear compression to original data, so that the reformatted samples have the same number of records. Assume that the current data is $X^i = \left\{X_1^i, X_2^i, \cdots, X_{L_i}^i\right\}$, and the number of output records is L' (here we take $L' = 600$).

If $L \leq L'$, we use linear interpolation to fill in X^i. Let output variable be $X^i = \left\{X_1^i, X_2^i, \cdots, X_L^i\right\}$, then the interpolation formula is:

$$X_j^{\prime i} = \left(s + 1 - \frac{jL}{L'X_s^i}\right) + \left(\frac{jL}{L'} - s\right)X_{s+1}^i \tag{4}$$

where X' is the reformatted sample.

$$S = \begin{cases} 1 & \frac{iL}{L'} < 1 \\ \lfloor \frac{iL}{L'} \rfloor & 1 \le \frac{iL}{L'} \le L \\ L & \frac{iL}{L'} > L \end{cases} \tag{5}$$

If $L > L'$, we compress the data with a linear compression. The formula is the same as Eq. 4.

5.3 Results and Comparisons

We implement the AFEB-AlexNet on the Badminton action dataset and compare it with AlexNet, LSTM, SVM and VLAD-SVM on the BSS dataset. Among them, both SVM and VLAD-SVM need to manually extract features. As for the SVM algorithm, we use the sliding window strategy with a window length of 10 records and a step size of 5 records, then extract the maximum and minimum values of each attributes, along with its mean, variance, skewness and kurtosis. The features of all windows are then flatten to a vector. In order to reduce the influence of "dislocation" phenomenon, we firstly select the peak point of the acceleration norm as the initial point, then alternately slide windows left and right from the initial point. As for the VLAD-SVM algorithm, we use sliding windows with length of 6 records and a step size of 2 records during training codebooks and generating codebook features. The LSTM algorithm contains 128 hidden layers. Its loss function is computed only according to the output of the last loop. The dropout of the AlexNet algorithm and the AFEB-AlexNet algorithm is 0.5. In order to enhance the generalization ability of AlexNet and AFEB-AlexNet, we use a ℓ_2 regularization in fully connected layers and AFEB. The input of AlexNet is transformed to a 600×227 matrix with zero padding. As for the AFEB structure, the column numbers of $\hat{X}^i$ and $\tilde{X}^i$ are $K_1 = 100$, $K_2 = 227$ respectively.

Table 3. Experimental results on BSS dataset

Algorithm	Accuracy	Time $(10^{-4}\,\text{s})$
LSTM	0.8518	0.1114
SVM	0.2297	0.5445
VLAD-SVM	0.2568	**0.1078**
AlexNet	0.9024	2.5886
AFEB-AlexNet	**0.9865**	2.5953

The experimental results are described in Table 3. Both SVM and VLAD-SVM perform badly in this experiment, while VLAD-SVM benefits from the codebook features which can deal with "dislocation" phenomenon to some extent, therefore the recognition accuracy of it is better than SVM by 2.71%. Dynamic LSTM, AlexNet and AFEB-AlexNet achieve much better recognition accuracy. AlexNet outperforms LSTM. The reason, we think, is that the number of records is fixed to 600. It makes the loops of LSTM too large, further causes the degeneration of gradient descent process. The recognition accuracy of AFEB-AlexNet is 98.65%, 8.41% better than AlexNet.

Fig. 5. Six records nearby the position of peak values in acceleration module curve. "Zero Padding" is a part of reformatted sample, which is the input of AlexNet. "AFEB Layer 1" and "AFEB Layer 2" represent $\hat{X}^i$ and $\tilde{X}^i$ respectively. In order to draw the images of these records, we scale the values of them to $[0, 1]$.

Figure 5 demonstrates the mechanism of AFEB structure. The difference of attribute magnitudes in original data is significant. In the first layer of AFEB, $\hat{X}^i$, the fixed attributes of raw sample is broadcasted to many other columns and the magnitudes gaps of adjacent columns are diluted a little. The second layer of AFEB further makes the magnitudes of each column more similar to its neighbors. This mechanism has a great effect on the convolution and pooling processes.

6   Conclusion

We have proposed an adaptive feature extraction block (AFEB) for previous feature extraction and then constructed the AFEB-AlexNet framework for badminton action recognition. Specifically, the AFEB is proposed to deal with the problem of "big attributes engulf small attributes" appearing in CNN on the sensor data of badminton actions. Actually, this architecture can balance the measures and magnitudes of different attributes. At the same time, it can pre-extract some effective features of different attributes for CNN. It is similar to PCA process for one-dimensional data, but it can extract nonlinear features from the original sensor data, which cannot be processed by PCA. In addition, as a kind of neural network, the AFEB can be trained in an end-to-end way together with the subsequent CNN. Moreover, the experimental results demonstrate that the AFEB is really effective and the AFEB-AlexNet method can obtain 98.65% badminton action recognition accuracy and outperforms the competitive methods remarkably. Although our experiments are based on a dataset with 10 categories, the AFEB can be combined with more complex CNN networks such as Resnet and ResNeXt for more complex and extensive senor-based action recognition problems.

Acknowledgment. This work in supported by the Joint Laboratory of Intelligent Sports of China Institute of Sport Science (CISS).

References

1. Hussain, S.M.A., Rashid, H.U.: User independent hand gesture recognition by accelerated DTW. In: International Conference on Informatics, Electronics & Vision, pp. 1033–1037 (2012)
2. Bao, L., Intille, S.S.: Activity recognition from user-annotated acceleration data. In: Ferscha, A., Mattern, F. (eds.) Pervasive 2004. LNCS, vol. 3001, pp. 1–17. Springer, Heidelberg (2004). https://doi.org/10.1007/978-3-540-24646-6_1
3. Dernbach, S., Das, B., Krishnan, N.C., Thomas, B.L., Cook, D.J.: Simple and complex activity recognition through smart phones. In: International Conference on Intelligent Environments, pp. 214–221 (2012)
4. Ward, J.A., Lukowicz, P., Troster, G., Starner, T.E.: Activity recognition of assembly tasks using body-worn microphones and accelerometers. IEEE Trans. Pattern Anal. Mach. Intell. 28(10), 1553–1567 (2006)
5. Yang, J., Wang, S., Chen, N., Chen, X.: Wearable accelerometer based extendable activity recognition system. In: IEEE International Conference on Robotics and Automation, pp. 3641–3647 (2010)
6. Wang, S., Yang, J., Chen, N., Chen, X.: Human activity recognition with user-free accelerometers in the sensor networks. In: International Conference on Neural Networks and Brain 2005, ICNN & B, pp. 1212–1217 (2005)
7. Song, S., Jang, J., Park, S.: An efficient method for activity recognition of the elderly using tilt signals of tri-axial acceleration sensor. In: Helal, S., Mitra, S., Wong, J., Chang, CK., Mokhtari, M. (eds.) ICOST 2008. LNCS, vol. 5120, pp. 99–104. Springer, Heidelberg (2008). https://doi.org/10.1007/978-3-540-69916-3_12
8. He, Z.: Accelerometer based gesture recognition using fusion features and SVM. J. Softw. 6 (6), 1042–1049 (2011)
9. Nebauer, C.: Evaluation of convolutional neural networks for visual recognition. IEEE Trans. Neural Netw. 9(4), 685–696 (1998)
10. Lawrence, S., Giles, C.L., Tsoi, A.C., Back, A.D.: Face recognition: a convolutional neural-network approach. IEEE Trans. Neural Netw. 8(1), 98–113 (1997). https://doi.org/10.1109/72.554195
11. Krizhevsky, A., Sutskever, I., Hinton, G.E.: ImageNet classification with deep convolutional neural networks. In: International Conference on Neural Information Processing Systems, pp. 1097–1105 (2012)
12. Simonyan, K., Zisserman, A.: Very deep convolutional networks for large-scale image recognition. CoRR abs/1409.1556 (2014). http://arxiv.org/abs/1409.1556
13. Szegedy, C., et al.: Going deeper with convolutions, pp. 1–9 (2014)
14. He, K., Zhang, X., Ren, S., Sun, J.: Spatial pyramid pooling in deep convolutional networks for visual recognition. IEEE Trans. Pattern Anal. Mach. Intell. 37(9), 1904–1916 (2015)
15. He, K., Zhang, X., Ren, S., Sun, J.: Deep residual learning for image recognition, pp. 770–778 (2015)
16. Schroff, F., Kalenichenko, D., Philbin, J.: FaceNet: a unified embedding for face recognition and clustering, pp. 815–823 (2015)
17. Hornik, K.: Approximation capabilities of multilayer feedforward networks. Neural Netw. 4 (2), 251–257 (1991)
18. Keogh, E., Chu, S., Pazzani, M.: An online algorithm for segmenting time series. In: ICDM, pp. 289–296 (2001)

19. Ishijima, M., Shin, S.B., Hostetter, G.H., Sklansky, J.: Scan-along polygonal approximation for data compression of electrocardiograms. IEEE Trans. Biomed. Eng. BME **30**(11), 723–729 (1983)

20. Hunter, J., McIntosh, N.: Knowledge-based event detection in complex time series data. In: Horn, W., Shahar, Y., Lindberg, G., Andreassen, S., Wyatt, J. (eds.) AIMDM 1999. LNCS (LNAI), vol. 1620, pp. 271–280. Springer, Heidelberg (1999). https://doi.org/10.1007/3-540-48720-4_30

A Deep Learning Model for Multi-label Classification Using Capsule Networks

Diqi Pan, Yonggang Lu[(✉)], and Peiyu Kang

School of Information Science and Engineering, Lanzhou University,
Lanzhou 730000, Gansu, China
ylu@lzu.edu.cn

Abstract. During the past few years, single-label classification has been extensively studied. However, in public datasets, the number of multiple-labeled images is much larger than the number of single-labeled images, which means that the study of multi-label image classification is more important. Most of the published network for multi-label image classification uses a CNN with a sigmoid layer, which is different from the single-label classification network using a CNN with a softmax layer. The binary cross entropy is often used as loss function for multi-label image classification. But due to the complex underlying object layout and feature confusion caused by multiple tags, the effect of CNN with a sigmoid layer on multi-label image classification is not satisfactory. Recently, in order to break some restrictions of CNN, the concept of capsule networks has been proposed. In this paper, a capsule network layer has been used to replace the traditional fully-connected layer and the sigmoid layer in the CNN network to improve the effect of multi-label image classification. In order to solve the deep network's convergence problem due to insufficient training data, fine-tuning DCNNs techniques have been applied to the capsule network architecture. In the experiments, three datasets, PASCAL VOC 2007, PASCAL VOC 2012 and NUS-WIDE, have been used. The proposed CNN+Capsule architecture has been compared with the traditional CNN+FullyConnected architecture. It has been shown that with different parameter settings the proposed CNN+Capsule architecture can consistently achieve better performance than the CNN+FullyConnected architecture.

Keywords: CNN · Multi-label image classification · Capsule networks

1 Introduction

Single-label image classification, which aims to get the unique label from a predefined set to an image [1], has been studied for a long time. This kind of datasets includes the AR dataset [2] for face recognition [3] and the MNIST dataset [4] for handwriting recognition [5]. However multi-label image classification is a more general and practical problem, since real-world images contain more semantic information such as objects, parts, scenes and their interactions [6]. For a typical multi-label image, several objects are located at various positions with different scales and poses. Furthermore, these objects in an image may have various interaction and occlusion problems with others, which increases the complexity of the classification task [7]. For examples, for

© Springer Nature Switzerland AG 2019
D.-S. Huang et al. (Eds.): ICIC 2019, LNCS 11643, pp. 144–155, 2019.
https://doi.org/10.1007/978-3-030-26763-6_14

the picture shown on the left of Fig. 1, it is easy for people to interpret it, but difficult for the computer to distinguish the person inside the image, because the content of the mountains in the picture is dominant. And for the picture shown on the right of Fig. 1, the computer usually cannot identify the chair due to the occlusion of the cat. So, compared with single-label image classification, the multi-label image classification is more challenging.

Person & mountain   **cat & chair**

Fig. 1. Two multi-label examples from Pascal VOC 2007 [21]. The left picture has the problem that the content of two objects is imbalance, and the right has the problem that the chair has been almost completely blocked by the cat.

Deep convolutional neural network (CNN) has been successfully applied to single-label image classification. Using a CNN with several layers, the classification accuracy for the MNIST dataset can reach 95%, and some state-of-the-art models can also produce excellent results for some high dimensional datasets (For example, VGG-16 [8] gains 71.5% accuracy and InceptionV3 [9] gains 78.2% accuracy on ImageNet dataset [1]). It is natural for people to study how to repeat the success of CNN on single-label image classification to the multi-label image classification. It has been found that replacing the softmax layer by the sigmoid layer at the end of CNN and replacing the categorical cross entropy by the binary cross entropy as loss function, the CNN network can be applied to multiple-label classification. However, replacing the activation function in the last layer of CNN also bring some side-effects. It reduces the contribution of negative tags, which may slow the network convergence and reduce the classification accuracy.

Furthermore, the traditional CNN methods can't solve the feature confusion problem caused by multiple label objects in an image [7]. To address this challenging problem, some improved methods [10–12] have been proposed by using ground-truth bounding box information in CNN training, and others like CNN-RNN [13] and HCP [7] have employed the state-of-the-art object detection techniques, e.g., binarized normed gradients (BING) [14] or EdgeBoxes [15] in CNN structure. These methods do improve performance on multi-label image classification, but they also add a lot of overheads.

Recently, Hinton et al. proposes the capsule network [16]. Each layer in this network has been divided into many small groups of neurons called "capsules". The vector stored in the "capsules" can express more information than the CNN neurons in the operation. The capsule network has shown its potential by achieving a state-of-the-art result of 0.25% test error on MNIST dataset without data augmentation such as rotation and scaling. Furthermore, the capsule network also works well on complex data (71.50% accuracy on CIFAR10) [17], this also shows the prospect of capsule network in high-dimensional data classification. In this work, the benefits of capsule network have been exploited in multi-label classification. After analyzing the properties of multi-label image classification, a new architecture that combines a capsule network with CNN has been designed. In the traditional CNN, a fully connected layer is connected after the convolution layer, but in this new architecture, a capsule network layer is connected after the convolution layer. Compared to the fully connected network, the capsule network can better utilize several additional pose parameters (e.g., position, orientation, scaling, and skewness) in the classification, which is conducive to the multiple label classification [18].

2   Multi-label Image Classification with CNN

The scene of multi-label image classification is as below. Giving a set of training images $x = (x_1; x_2; \ldots; x_N)$ and their categories $c = (c_1; c_2; \ldots; c_N)$, each image can contain one or more category. After transforming the label to binary, the label of an image will have the form of $y = [a_1, a_2, \ldots, a_k]$. The value of a_j only can be 1 (when the image contains the category c_j) or 0 (when the image does not contain the category c_j). The goal of learning is training the data to make the learner more responsive to the positive label of the testing images. By transforming the activation function in the last layer and modifying the loss function, CNN can be modified to produce output values for each label separately. More specifically, replacing the softmax layer with the sigmoid layer at the end of CNN and replacing the categorical cross entropy with the binary cross entropy as loss function, the CNN network can be applied to multi-label image classification.

2.1   Softmax and Sigmoid

In the case of image x_i, we assume that $f_j^l(x_i)$ represents the input of neuron in layer l and this neuron representing the class j. For single-label image classification, the softmax activation function is usually used by the neurons in the last layer [6]. The posterior probability of an image x_i and class j can be expressed as:

$$p_{i,j}^l = \frac{\exp\left(f_j^l(x_i)\right)}{\sum\limits_{k=1}^{c} \exp\left(f_k^l(x_i)\right)} \tag{1}$$

In this function, it's obviously that the sum of the layer's outputs will be 1, which equals to the number of positive labels:

$$p_i^l = \sum_{k=1}^{c} p_{i,k}^l = 1 \tag{2}$$

But different from single label classification, multiple-label-classified images have more than one positive labels. So, in multiple-label classification network, it's inappropriate to use softmax activation function in the last layer. Instead, the sigmoid activation function is usually used, which can be expressed as:

$$p_{i,j}^l = \frac{1}{1 + \exp\left(-f_j^l(x_i)\right)} \tag{3}$$

This function lets the activation value perform a dichotomous task (is positive label or not) independently, which enables the outputs on multiple labels to be 1 simultaneously.

2.2 Categorical Cross Entropy and Binary Cross Entropy

In general, if the last layer is connected to softmax function as the classification probability output, categorical cross entropy will be used as the loss function. The function of categorical cross entropy is as follows:

$$loss = -\sum_{i=1}^{n}\sum_{j=1}^{m} \hat{y}_{ij} \log y_{ij} \tag{4}$$

where y_{ij} is the output of the i-th sample on the j-th class and $\hat{y}_{ij}$ is the target of the i-th sample on the j-th class. The parameter n is the number of samples, and m is the count of categories. Each category in one image will gain the same loss calculated by this function.

In multiple-label-classification, since the sigmoid function has been used as activation function, the loss function needs to be changed to binary cross entropy function:

$$loss = -\sum_{i=1}^{n} \hat{y}_i \log y_i + (1 - \hat{y}_i) \log(1 - \hat{y}_i) \tag{5}$$

Unlike the categorical cross entropy, it is independent for each vector component (class), meaning that the loss computed for every vector component is not affected by other component values.

3 The Capsule Network

A capsule is a set of neurons that individually activate for various properties of an object, such as position, size and hue. Formally, a capsule is a set of neurons that collectively produce an activity vector, with one element of each neuron to hold that neuron's instantiation value. The probability of an entity's presence in a specific input is represented by the vector's length, while the vector's orientation describes the capsule's properties [19]. Different from the neuron network, the capsule network uses the squash function as the activate function and the margin loss as the loss function. The dynamic routing algorithm is used to calculate the correlation between the capsules.

3.1 The Squash Function

The length of the output vector of a capsule represents the probability of the category represented by the capsule. The "squash" function has been used to calculate outputs of every capsules. This function is as follow [7]:

$$v_j = \frac{\|s_j\|^2}{1 + \|s_j\|^2} \frac{s_j}{\|s_j\|} \tag{6}$$

where s_j and v_j are the input vector and the output vector of the capsule j.

3.2 Network Connection Mode

Figure 2 shows the connection mode of the capsule network, the capsules on the left is the bottom capsule and the capsule on the right is the top capsule, in which s_j is calculated by [7]:

$$s_j = \sum_i c_{ij} \hat{u}_{j|i}, \hat{u}_{j|i} = w_{ij} u_i \tag{7}$$

where parameter u_j is the output of the upper layer of the capsule network, and w_{ij} is an element of the weight matrix. It can be seen that each capsule neuron in the upper layer connects to a certain neuron in the next layer with different connection strength. The parameter c_{ij} is the coupling coefficient which is calculated by [7]:

$$c_{ij} = \frac{\exp(b_{ij})}{\sum_k \exp(b_{ik})} \tag{8}$$

The above equation can be viewed as a softmax function of the parameter b_{ij} which is updated by dynamic routing algorithm as described in the next subsection.

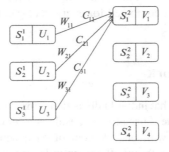

Fig. 2. The connection mode of a capsule network.

3.3 Dynamic Routing

Capsule network uses parameter b_{ij} to describe the connection between a capsule and a parent capsule in the previous layer. In the first iteration, b_{ij} is initialized to 0 and the coupling coefficient c_{ij} will be the same for different capsules in a layer. Then, the value of $\hat{u}_{j|i}$ and v_j is updated with (6) and (7). In the latter iterations, the parameter b_{ij} is updated by $\hat{u}_{j|i}$ and v_j as follow [7]:

$$b_{ij} = b_{ij} + \hat{u}_{j|i} \cdot v_j \qquad (9)$$

When the dot product of $\hat{u}_{j|i}$ and v_j is positive, the value of b_{ij} will be larger after updated using (9). A larger value of b_{ij} will produce a larger value of c_{ij} using (8), which results in a larger value of s_j and v_j, that eventually strengthens the connection between capsule i and capsule j. On the contrary, if the dot product of $\hat{u}_{j|i}$ and v_j is negative, the connection between capsule i and capsule j will be diminished.

3.4 Margin Loss

Except that the coupling coefficient C is updated through dynamic routing, other convolution parameters in the capsule network need to be updated according to the loss function. The capsule network uses the margin loss which is usually seen in Support Vector Machine to update the parameters. The loss function of a capsule network is as follows [7]:

$$L_c = T_k \max(0, m^+ - \|v_k\|)^2 + \lambda(1 - T_k)\max(0, \|v_k\| - m^-)^2 \qquad (10)$$

where T_k is 1 whenever class k is actually present, and 0 otherwise. Hyper parameters m^+, m^-, and λ need to be selected before the learning process. The parameter settings $(T_k = 1, m^+ = 1, m^- = 1, \lambda = 0.5)$ are used in the Hinton's digit experiment [7], and they are also used in our experiments.

4 Method

4.1 The Selected Architecture of CNN

The Xception model [20] and the InceptionResNetV2 model [9] have been used in our experiments as the selected CNN models. The Xception architecture has 36 convolutional layers, and the 36 convolutional layers are structured into 14 modules, all of which have linear residual connections between them, except for the first and the last modules [20].

4.2 Fine-Tuning of CNN

The dimension of the data in multi-label image datasets is usually much larger than the data in most single-label image datasets. For example, an image in PASCOL VOC

2007 have a size of 500 × 300, while the MNIST dataset contains images with the size of 28 × 28. As a result, deep CNN is desired for multi-label image classification, since more convolution kernels need to be used to extract features and more pooling layers need to be used to reduce data dimension. In order to make the network converge, we use a pretrained DCNN model in network and fine-tune the weights of the pre-trained DCNN by back propagation.

4.3   Details of the Network Model

The summary of our proposed model (illustrated in Fig. 3) is as follows:

1. The first part of our model architecture is the Inputs. The dimensions of the input image are arbitrary, however in order to training conveniently, the dimension of all input images is transformed to 224 × 224 × 3.
2. The second part is a pretrained CNN model. The last pooling layer of pretrained model has been thrown away, and the output of this part is the feature maps. If the Xception model is used, the output of this layer is 2,048 feature maps of size 16 × 16.
3. The third part is a Primary Capsule layer. The input of this layer is the feature maps produced by the second part of the network. This layer consists of 2,048 capsules with dimension of 16, each of which has feature maps of size 16 × 16. These capsules will be using to calculate the contribution of each category.
4. The fourth part of our architecture is the Class Capsule layer. Capsules in this layer contain the vectors from the Primary Capsule layer, which are calculated by the dynamic routing process mentioned in Sect. 3. The length of vector in capsule can be set artificially, and if the output from Primary Capsule layer is long, the length of vectors in Class Capsule layer needs to be large. The number of Class Capsules in this part depends on the total number of categories. For example, if the dataset using for training contains 20 labels, the number of Class Capsules also needs to be 20.
5. The final part of our architecture is the output layer. This layer contains the length of the instantiation vector in Class Capsules. The length represents the probability that a capsule's entity is present in the image, and it will be used to calculate the loss using the margin loss function.

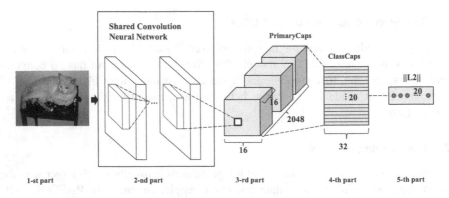

Fig. 3. Proposed model architecture for multi-label classification.

5 Experimental

5.1 Experimental Setup

The proposed architecture has been compared with the traditional CNN model on three public multi-label classification datasets: VOC PASCAL 2007 dataset, VOC PASCAL 2012 dataset and NUS-WIDE dataset. The CNN architecture for comparison has used the same convolution layers with the proposed architecture, and followed with three fully connected layers with size of 1024, 512 and 256 respectively. In each comparison, the selected types of optimization algorithms and other parameters of the two architectures are the same. To deal with the fluctuation of the experimental results, the 5-fold cross-validation has been used. All experiments are conducted on a NVIDIA GTX 1080ti GPU with 11 GB memory.

5.2 The PASCAL VOC 2007 Dataset

PASCAL Visual Object Classes Challenge (VOC) [21] usually used as the dataset for image detection, image segmentation and multi-label classification. The VOC 2007 dataset contains 9,963 images with 20 categories. In each experiment, 7,970 images are used for training and 1,993 images are used for testing. The mAP metric method has been used for PASCAL VOC dataset, since it has been used in the VOC challenge. The results of VOC 2007 dataset are shown in Table 1:

Table 1. Classification results (AP in %) on VOC 2007 test.

Networks	InceptionResNet V2+FC	InceptionResNet V2+Capsule	Xception+ FC	Xception+ Capsule
Aero	92.2	94.2	95.6	97.3
Bike	76.1	83.3	84.5	90.3
Bird	86.3	89.6	90.2	94
Boat	71.2	85	86.4	91.4
Bottle	37.6	42.2	52.2	62.2
Bus	54.8	69.6	79.4	82.1
Car	86.3	88	87.8	89.2
Cat	82.9	86.8	90.1	92.7
Chair	60.1	65.4	68.5	74.9
Cow	55.6	62.9	80.1	78.3
Table	58.4	64.5	76.3	74.1
Dog	81	84.3	86.5	91.2
Horse	84.3	86.5	92.4	91.4
mbike	81.7	83.6	86.7	89.8
Person	93.8	91.5	92.5	94.2
Plant	44.4	49.1	54.4	61.8
Sheep	67	72.5	83.1	93.2
Sofa	54.2	61.4	65.2	76.4
Train	92.4	91	95.2	94.4
Tv	67.2	72.4	74	80.3
mAP	71.4	**76.2**	81.1	**85**

Table 1 shows the details of the comparison between tradition CNN architecture and the proposed architecture on the VOC 2007 dataset. It can be seen that, based on the capsule network, the classification performance can be improved by 4.3%. Figure 4 shows an example of the testing results based on different architecture. There are three ground-truth categories in the given image, i.e., person, dog, chair. In the architecture of Xception+FullyConnected, only the person and the dog gain the high output, but in the architecture of Xception+Capsule, all of the categories has been identified.

5.3   The PASCAL VOC 2012 Dataset

The VOC 2007 dataset contains 22,531 images with 20 categories. In each experiment, 18,024 images are used for training and 4,507 images are used for testing. The results of VOC 2012 dataset are shown in Table 2:

Table 2. Classification results (AP in %) on VOC 2012 test.

Networks	InceptionResNetV2 +FC	InceptionResNetV2 +Capsule	Xception +FC	Xception +Capsule
Aero	80.6	95.2	95.3	96.1
Bike	71.6	78.5	71.1	76.4
Bird	87.5	90.5	91.1	91.7
Boat	74.4	81.6	81.7	87.3
Bottle	46.9	48.9	51	55.3
Bus	86.2	88.9	85.7	90.5
Car	74.6	74.5	71.8	76.7
Cat	93.8	93.1	93.5	93.5
Chair	55.7	59.8	54.7	63.6
Cow	74.2	76.3	80.1	79.6
Table	60.9	64.6	64.9	70.3
Dog	90	89.8	89.9	90.5
Horse	69.2	68.6	63.3	73.7
mbike	70.1	74.4	75.1	79.6
Person	97	97.3	96.7	98.7
Plant	56.6	58	46.3	54.6
Sheep	81.8	84.3	79.6	77.7
Sofa	52.9	56.8	54	56
Train	94.6	95.4	95	95.4
Tv	68.8	65.4	61.8	70.2
mAP	74.4	**77.1**	75.1	**78.9**

Table 2 shows similar results as Table 1 that the proposed architecture can outperform the tradition architecture with about 3.7% improvement in mAP. Comparing the results of the Tables 1 and 2, it can be found that the pretrained CNN model has a great impact on the results in Table 1, but it not appears in Table 2. The reason may be that the InceptionResNetV2 model is deeper than the Xception model, so the InceptionResNetV2 model works well on large dataset, but not on small dataset. The results of NUS-WIDE dataset are also consistent with this explanation, which will be shown in the next subsection.

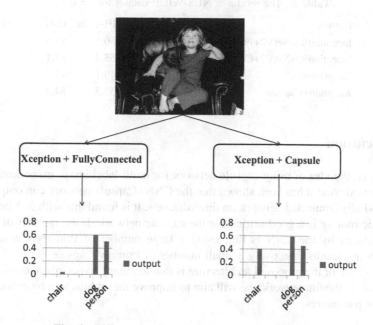

Fig. 4. Different predict results with two architectures.

5.4 The NUS-WIDE Dataset

NUS-WIDE dataset is a web image dataset that contains 269,648 images and 5,018 tags from Flickr [22]. By removing noisy and rare tags, these images are further manually annotated into 81 concepts. For convenience, these 81 concepts are used as the classification labels. For this dataset, the precision and recall of the generated labels are employed as evaluation metrics. For each image, the category which corresponds to an output bigger than a threshold t will be selected as its label. The precision is the proportion of correctly annotated labels to annotated labels, and the recall is the proportion of correctly annotated labels to ground-truth labels. In order to measure overall performance, the mAP and F1 score which is the geometrical average of the precision and recall scores are also computed.

Table 3 shows the results of NUS-WIDE dataset. We can see from Table 3, with $t = 0.3$ the architecture of Xception+Capsule can outperform about 5% F1-score to the architecture of Xception+FullyConnected. Both the precision and recall values of the Xception+Capsule architecture are higher than the architecture of Xception +FullyConnected, means that our new architecture has a full advancement of the tradition architecture. Furthermore, it can be seen that the architecture of IncionResNetV2 model is outperform to Xception which demonstrates applicability of InceptionResNetV2 model to larger data.

Table 3. The results of NUS-WIDE dataset for t = 0.3.

Networks	Precision	Recall	F1-score	mAP
InceptionResNetV2+FC	45.5	56.8	50.5	51.6
InceptionResNetV2+Capsule	50.1	61.9	**55.4**	**57.1**
Xception+FC	44.8	54.4	49.1	49.7
Xception+Capsule	48.3	59.5	**53.3**	**54.2**

6   Conclusion

In this paper, the idea of using capsule network for multi-label image classification has been proposed. And it has been shown that the CNN+Capsule network can outperform the CNN+FullyConnected network on three datasets. It is found that with 3–5 iterations of dynamic routing is a good setting for the capsule network. If the number of feature maps produced by the CNN is big, using a large number of Primary Capsule can produce better results than using a small number of Primary Capsule.

A drawback of the proposed architecture is that too many hyper-parameters need to be adjusted. In the future work, we will aim to improve the architecture by reducing the number of parameters.

References

1. Deng, J., Dong, W., Socher, R., et al.: ImageNet: a large-scale hierarchical image database. In: 2009 IEEE Conference on Computer Vision and Pattern Recognition. IEEE (2009)
2. Martínez, A., Benavente, R.: The AR face database. CVC Technical report (1998)
3. Zhao, W., Chellappa, R., Krishnaswamy, A.: Discriminant analysis of principal components for face recognition. In: IEEE International Conference on Automatic Face & Gesture Recognition (2002)
4. LeCun, Y., Cortes, C., Burges, C.J.C.: The MNIST database of handwritten digits (1998)
5. Cao, J., Ahmadi, M., Shridhar, M.: Recognition of handwritten numerals with multiple feature and multistage classifier. Pattern Recogn. **28**(2), 153–160 (1995)
6. Gong, Y., Jia, Y., Leung, T., et al.: Deep convolutional ranking for multilabel image annotation (2013)
7. Wei, Y., Xia, W., Lin, M., et al.: HCP: a flexible CNN framework for multi-label image classification. IEEE Trans. Pattern Anal. Mach. Intell. **38**, 1901–1907 (2016)
8. Simonyan, K., Zisserman, A.: Very deep convolutional networks for large-scale image recognition. In: ICLR (2015)
9. Szegedy, C., Vanhoucke, V., Ioffe, S., et al.: Rethinking the inception architecture for computer vision. In: 2016 IEEE Conference on Computer Vision and Pattern Recognition (CVPR) (2016)

10. Song, Z., Chen, Q., Huang, Z., et al.: Contextualizing object detection and classification (2011)
11. Dong, J., Xia, W., Chen, Q., et al.: Subcategory-aware object classification. In: IEEE 2013 IEEE Conference on Computer Vision and Pattern Recognition (CVPR) (2013)
12. Oquab, M., Bottou, L., Laptev, I., et al.: Learning and transferring mid-level image representations using convolutional neural networks. In: 2014 IEEE Conference on Computer Vision and Pattern Recognition (CVPR). IEEE Computer Society (2014)
13. Wang, J., Yang, Y., Mao, J., et al.: CNN-RNN: a unified framework for multi-label image classification (2016)
14. Cheng, M.M., Liu, Y., Lin, W.Y., et al.: BING: binarized normed gradients for objectness estimation at 300 frames per second. Comput. Vis. Media **5**, 3–20 (2018)
15. Zitnick, C.L., Dollár, P.: Edge boxes: locating object proposals from edges. In: Fleet, D., Pajdla, T., Schiele, B., Tuytelaars, T. (eds.) ECCV 2014. LNCS, vol. 8693, pp. 391–405. Springer, Cham (2014). https://doi.org/10.1007/978-3-319-10602-1_26
16. Sabour, S., Frosst, N., Hinton, G.E.: Dynamic routing between capsules (2017)
17. Xi, E., Bing, S., Jin, Y.: Capsule network performance on complex data (2017)
18. Afshar, P., Mohammadi, A., Plataniotis, K.N.: Brain tumor type classification via capsule networks (2018)
19. Srihari, S.: Capsule Nets (PDF). University of Buffalo (2017)
20. Chollet, F.: Xception: deep learning with depthwise separable convolutions (2016)
21. Everingham, M., Van Gool, L., Williams, C.K., et al.: The pascal visual object classes (VOC) challenge (2010)
22. Chua, T.S., Tang, J., Hong, R., et al.: NUS-WIDE: a real-world web image database from national university of Singapore. In: Proceedings of the ACM International Conference on Image and Video Retrieval, p. 48. ACM (2009)

Bundled Round Bars Counting Based
on Iteratively Trained SVM

Chang Liu$^{(\boxtimes)}$, Liyao Zhu, and Xin Zhang

School of Information Science and Engineering, Shenyang Ligong University,
Shenyang 110159, China
syliuch@126.com, 1511759094@qq.com, 363668289@qq.com

Abstract. Bundled bars counting is difficult in the cases of overlap or varied illumination. An iteratively trained SVM method is proposed to count bundled round bars from a bottom side image. Using Hough transformation, the sizes of bars are extracted and normalized. A SVM classifier using HOG features of the image are applied to determine the center points of bars. These center points generate central regions corresponding to bars. By counting the number of connected regions with great area in the image, the number of bars is obtained. In SVM training process, sample selection affects the classifier significantly. From an iteratively selection process, typical samples are selected and used for training the SVM classifier. The experimental results showed this strategy improved the performance of SVM classifier effectively, and the method works well in overlapped or varied illumination situation.

Keywords: Computer vision · SVM · Machine learning · HOG feature

1 Introduction

Many kinds of bars have the characteristics of round bottom surface, such as round steel bars, round aluminum bars, round wood bars, etc. A counting process is generally needed before storage or delivery for production enterprises. How to count the bundled bars automatically is a task for quality test departments of these enterprises. In recent years, with the development of computer vision, many image processing methods have been proposed and gradually applied to bar counting problems. Typical methods include connected region method [1–4], Hough transformation method [5–7], template matching method [8, 9], etc.

The basic principle of the connected region method is to extract the connected regions of the bottom surfaces according to the gray difference between the bottom surfaces of bars and the background of the image firstly, and then count the number of connected regions as the number of bars. To improve the region segment results, binarization with fixed or varied thresholds [1, 2], morphological method [3], concave point matching method [4] are generally used. These methods work well when the

Supported by Provincial Natural Science Foundation of Liaoning Province, China. (Grant No. 20170540792).

borders of bar are clear. But if the bars are overlapped and occlude each other, they generally count a wrong number. Hough transformation is used to vote the centers of the bars from the edge points [5, 6], or gradient directions of the edge points of the image [7]. In the case of low illumination, incomplete edge information can easily lead to counting errors. Template matching method is widely used in counting problems. According to the similarity between the detection window and the standard template, whether the window includes a bar or not is determined. For bar counting problem, round template, octagonal template, square template, and line template can all be used [8, 9]. The disadvantage of template matching is its performance is easily affected by illumination and binarization.

In this paper, a method of iteratively trained SVM (Support Vector Machine) was applied to the counting problem of bundled bars. Using HOG (Histogram of Oriented Gradient) features, a SVM classifier model was established to recognize the center points of bottom surfaces of bars. The number of bars was determined by counting the connected regions consisted of center points. In SVM training process, we adopted an iterative process. In each iteration, those samples far from the separating hyperplane of SVM were replaced by misclassified samples from the training image set. From this strategy, the performance of SVM classifier improved quickly. Using the finial optimized classifier, the accuracy of counting result improved greatly.

2 Size Normalization

Generally, the size of bars in an image might vary due to different sizes of real bars or camera position. In order to simplify the process of bar recognition, the image needs to be firstly zoomed so that the bars have an uniform size. Here we suppose the bars of one bundle have a same diameter. We firstly used Canny operator to extract the edge points of the image. These edge point might come from real bar edges and background. Each real bar edges has a circle feature. Then we used Hough transformation to extract the diameter of the circles in the image. It is unnecessary to extract every circle accurately because we are only interested in the diameter of the bars, but not the location of each bar in the image. Using the acquired diameter, we can zoom the image to make every bar in the zoomed image have a fixed size. In this paper, we zoomed their diameter to 34 pixels.

3 SVM Method for Bar Counting

The key of bar counting method here is to accurately determine the central points of each bar. For a given size detection window (In this paper we defined its size 40×40 pixels), we need to determine whether the window includes a bar or not. If it does, we can mark the center of the window as a center point of the bar. This is a classification problem. In recent years, many classification models based on machine learning have been successfully applied to target detection problems [10–12]. In this paper, a SVM classifier model using HOG features was adopted.

3.1   HOG Features Extraction

HOG feature is not sensitive to the variance of illumination and can easily express the gradient distribution of a target. We extracted the HOG features as follows.

Step 1. Calculate gradient magnitude and direction. Using gradient operators $[-1, 0, 1]$ and $[-1, 0, 1]^T$, the gradient components $G_u(u, v)$ in horizontal directions and $G_v(u, v)$ in vertical directions at each pixel point (u, v) were computed from a convolution process. Then the gradient magnitude and direction of each pixel are calculated from

$$\begin{cases} G(u, v) = \sqrt{(G_u^2(u, v) + G_v^2(u, v))} \\ \theta(u, v) = \tan^{-1}(G_v(u, v)/G_u(u, v)) \end{cases}. \tag{1}$$

Step 2. Construct directional gradient histogram of cell. Here the size of the detection window is 40×40 pixels. As shown in Fig. 1, it was divided into 10×10 regions which are all 4×4 pixels in size. We call the small regions cells. The range of gradient direction was divided into 9 intervals, each of which contains $20°$ angle interval. In each cell, the gradient direction intervals were voted, and the value of voting was the gradient magnitude of each pixel. Then we got a 9-dimensional vector which is the directional gradient histogram of the cell.

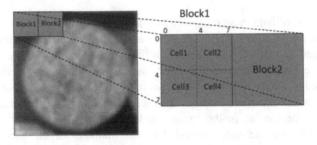

Fig. 1. Principle of HOG features extraction

Step 3. Construct HOG vector. 4 cells adjacent to each other in the window were grouped into 1 block. The 4 feature vectors of the cells in the block are connected orderly into a 36-dimensional block feature vector. We normalized the block feature vector to reduce the influence of illumination and contrast changing. At last we connected the 25 normalized block feature vectors orderly into a 900-dimensional HOG vector of the detection window.

3.2   SVM Classifier

SVM is a supervised learning model for binary classification problems. Given a training dataset $\{(x_i, y_i)|i = 1, 2, \ldots, N_S\}$, in which x_i is the feature vector corresponding to the i-th sample, and $y_i = 1$ means it is a positive sample while $y_i = -1$

represents negative, an optimal separating hyperplane can be calculated to classify the positive and negative samples. This process is called SVM training. For a new undetermined sample, we only calculate the distance from the sample to the separating hyperplane. If the distance is positive, the sample is classified positive, otherwise it is negative. In the case that the training dataset is linear inseparable, the feature can be mapped to a high dimensional space using a kernel function. The linear SVM classifier can be transformed into a non-linear classifier which extends the application fields of SVM.

For the counting problem in this paper, when HOG features are used to describe the detection window, it is linear inseparable. Here we used a SVM classification model with Gaussian kernel. The form of Gaussian kernel function is

$$K(x, z) = \exp\left(-\frac{\|x - z\|^2}{2\sigma^2}\right), \tag{2}$$

where x and z are both feature vectors of samples. We selected $\sigma = 3.85$.

3.3 Datasets Construction

Datasets generally include a training dataset for training the classifier, and a test dataset to test the performance of the classifier. We selected some bundled round wood bars as counting targets and used the following method to construct the datasets.

Step 1. Image acquisition

We bundled 100 bars together, and used a camera to catch 200 images of the bottom side of the bars in different conditions, such as different illumination, different position relationship, different background, etc. Then using the method in Sect. 2, we extracted the diameter of the bars in each image, and normalized all the images. These images simulate real scenes of bar counting. Finally we divided the 200 images into two sets. Each set includes 100 images selected from 200 randomly. One set is called training image set, in which the images are used for training the classifier. Another set is called test image set, in which the images are used for test.

Step 2. Center points marking and training dataset construction

For each image in the training image set, we marked the center point of each bar manually. Because the bundle includes 100 bars, we marked $100 \times 100 = 10000$ points totally. Each marked point corresponds to a square window in the normalized image. The point is just the center of the window. So we obtained 10000 positive samples. Considering the computing cost, we randomly select $S_P = 1500$ samples from them as initial positive training samples for SVM.

To select initial negative training samples, we randomly selected $S_N = 4500$ points from normalized images. The distances from any one of these points to all marked points in the same image are far from $0.7r$, where $r = 17$ is the radius of the bar circle. Some of initial training samples are shown in Fig. 2.

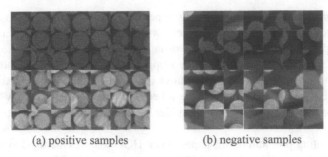

(a) positive samples   (b) negative samples

Fig. 2. Some initial training samples for SVM

In above procedure, each sample is a 40 × 40 pixels window, it also corresponds to a point in the image. Once a sample was determined, its corresponding HOG vector could be constructed by the method in Sect. 3.1. After all training samples were determined, they were used to train the SVM classifier. It needs to be mentioned we defined two types of datasets here. One is training dataset which consisted of samples. This dataset is used to train the SVM classifier directly. Another type is training image set and test image set which consisted of images. They are used to optimize and test the performance of counting algorithm respectively.

3.4   Bar Counting

Bar counting process includes two steps. The first is to detect the central points of the bars in the image using the trained SVM classifier by sliding detection window on the image. To save computing cost, we hopped 1 pixel at every movement of the detection window. Figure 3 shows a part of an image after detection of central points, where the white dots are identified bar centers. The results show the SVM classifier can correctly determine the bar centers in most cases even though the bars are overlapped. These center points formed some isolate connected regions. We can also find there are some wrong classified points in the image which are marked inside a white square, but these wrong points generally exist as isolate points.

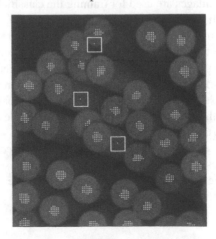

Fig. 3. Results of central point detection using SVM classifier

The second step is to count the number of connected regions. By setting an appropriate area threshold T_S, a connected region can be classified whether it expresses a bar. We described the area of a connected region using the total pixel number of the region. If the area of a connected region is greater than T_S, we believe it corresponds to a bar, otherwise it is a noise region. Then the number of connected regions with great area is the number of bars inside the bundle. T_S is a super parameter of the algorithm. It can be optimized from the training image set according to the performance evaluation criterion following.

3.5 Counting Performance Evaluation Criterion

Precision, recall and F measure are generally used to evaluate the performance of a classifier. These criterion are calculated based on a dataset. For bar counting problem, we used CA (Counting Accuracy) and MB (Mean Bias) to evaluate the counting algorithm's performance. Counting accuracy was defined as

$$CA = \frac{M}{N}, \tag{3}$$

where M denotes the number of images correctly counted, and N is the number of images in an image set. Mean bias was defined as

$$MB = \frac{1}{N} \sum_{i=1}^{N} \frac{\left| N_C^{(i)} - N_A^{(i)} \right|}{N_A^{(i)}}, \tag{4}$$

where $N_C^{(i)}$ and $N_A^{(i)}$ denote the counting result and accurate number of bars for the i-th image in the image set. Both counting accuracy and mean bias are based on an image set.

4 Iteratively Training Strategy

In the previous sample selecting procedure in Sect. 3.3, we only selected the very central points of bars as candidate positive samples. In fact, if a point is not far from a center of a bar, it can also be treated as a positive sample. The amount of negative samples from the training image set is also great because any point far from all bar centers can be looked as a negative sample. From this point of view, the 1500 positive and 4500 negative samples we initially selected for training SVM are only small parts of the total. On the other hand, because we selected the samples randomly, the SVM classifier trained from these samples might not have the best performance. To improve the performance of the classifier, we presented an iteratively training method. It includes some key strategies as follows.

4.1 Training Samples Replacement

Support vectors are critical for the SVM, while those samples far from the separating hyperplane have nearly no effect on the training results. In each iteration, we like to replace those without influence by new samples which are possibly more typical.

(1) *typical positive sample.*

  After SVM classifier training in each iteration, the classifier was applied to every image in the training image set to detect the central points and counting. For each marked center point of the bar which was not correctly counted, we defined a square region (the size is 5×5 pixels here) whose center is just the market point. For each point in the region, if it was classified as a non-center point, we defined it a typical positive sample. It had chance to join the training dataset for next iteration. We denoted the number of these samples $M_P^{(k)}$, where k is the iteration number.

(2) *typical negative samples.*

  Similarly, we defined another square region (here the size is 24×24 pixels) for each real center point. For each point out of any regions in a image, if it was classified as a center point, we defined it a typical negative samples. It also had chance for training SVM in the next iteration. We denoted the number of these samples $M_N^{(k)}$.

(3) *samples replacement strategy.*

  Here we defined a replacement ratio T_R. After each iteration of training, the absolute distance from each training sample to the separating hyperplane was calculated and sorted from far to near. Those ranked high will be replaced by new typical samples. Here exists following two cases.

   Case one. If $M_P^{(k)} > S_P T_R$, we randomly selected $S_P T_R$ from $M_P^{(k)}$ new samples for replacement.

   Case two. If $M_P^{(k)} \leq S_P T_R$, $M_P^{(k)}$ old samples ranked highest were replaced.

The replacement strategy for negative samples is similar to the positive.

4.2 Termination Condition

In each iteration, the latest trained SVM classifier was applied to the training image set. The area threshold T_S can be optimized for the best counting. Here we use the criteria CA defined in Sect. 3.5 to optimize T_S, and use CA and MB to evaluate the classifier. If the performance of the counting algorithm has no obvious improvement on both CA and MB, we terminate the iteration. The final trained SVM classifier and the area threshold T_S are the optimal gotten from the training image set.

5 Experiment and Results

The camera we used to acquire images is Basler's acA640-90gm equipped with a 25 mm fixed focal lens. The captured gray image size is 640×480 pixels. The diameter of real bars is about 5 mm, The distance between the bundled bars and the camera is about 0.7 m.

We firstly tested the evolution of the algorithm performance with iterations. Here we set the replacement ratio $T_R = 20\%$. The classifiers were tested on the training image set and the test image set respectively. Table 1 shows the experimental results.

From Table 1, the counting performance using the SVM from initial training samples which were randomly selected is not good. With the iterations of samples replacement and training, the optimized area threshold T_S was stable, and the algorithm's performance on CA and MB improved rapidly both on the training and the test image set. The results verified the efficiency of the method we presented.

Table 1. Algorithm performance on each iteration

Iteration	Training dataset				Training image set		Test image set	
	Precision	Recall	F	T_S	CA	MB	CA	MB
0	100%	100%	100%	9	39%	3.56%	31%	1.13%
1	100%	100%	100%	4	72%	0.34%	83%	0.20%
2	100%	100%	100%	5	83%	0.22%	86%	0.15%
3	100%	100%	100%	4	89%	0.15%	91%	0.09%
4	100%	100%	100%	3	93%	0.11%	84%	0.16%
5	100%	100%	100%	4	91%	0.13%	89%	0.11%
6	100%	100%	100%	4	92%	0.12%	91%	0.09%

On the other hand, when the SVM classifiers on each iteration was tested by the corresponding samples and evaluated by traditional criterion, precision, recall or F measure, they were all excellent. But when they were tested by the training and the test image set, and evaluated by CA and MB, the differences among them were great. The results show the limitation of traditional classifier's evaluation criterion for the counting problem here.

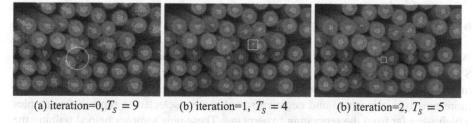

(a) iteration=0, $T_S = 9$ (b) iteration=1, $T_S = 4$ (b) iteration=2, $T_S = 5$

Fig. 4. Results of central point detection from classifiers in different iterations

Figure 4 shows the results of central point detection to the same part of an image from the training image set using the classifiers in different iterations. In initial iteration the results were not good. There were many misclassified points. The bar which was marked in the white circle was wrongly counted because the number of detected center points in the connected region was less than the area threshold. With the replacement of samples and repeated training, the performance of classifier became better and better. Those misclassified points marked in white squares are less and isolate. The algorithm not only modified many misclassified points, but also successfully distinguished the bar which was missed at the beginning.

We secondly tested the replacement ratio's effect to the algorithm performance. Using the same initial training samples, we selected $T_R = 10\%$ and $T_R = 30\%$, and repeated the above iterations respectively. The SVM classifiers on every iteration were also applied to the training and the test image set. The test results of the performance with iterations are shown in Fig. 5. We can find their evolution speeds are similar to each other in the cases different T_R were selected. It shows the algorithm's performance is not sensitive to this super parameter.

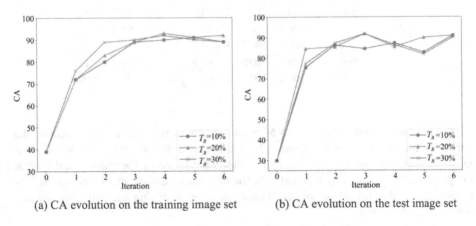

(a) CA evolution on the training image set   (b) CA evolution on the test image set

Fig. 5. Replacement ratio's effect to the algorithm

6   Conclusion

We presented a bundled bars counting method from a bottom side image based on SVM classifier using HOG features. An iteratively training strategy was used to improve the classifier's performance. By a sample replacement procedure, more and more new typical positive and negative samples were selected to replace the samples which were far from the separating hyperplane. These new samples helped training the SVM classifier and improving its performance effectively. The experimental results showed the efficiency of the approach.

References

1. Okumoto, M., Nakamura, S.: Algorithm to automatically count the number of steel pipes. J. Fukui Natl. Coll. Technol. **41**, 25–28 (2007)
2. Liu, X.H., Ouyang, J.N.: Research on steel bar detection and counting method based on contours. In: Proceedings International Conference on Electronics Technology, Chengdu, China, pp. 294–297 (2018)
3. Wang, J.Z., Chen, H., Xu, X.Q.: Pattern recognition for counting of bounded bar steel. In: Proceedings 4th International Conference on the Applications of Digital Information and Web Technologies, Stevens Point, Wisconsin, USA, pp. 173–176 (2011)
4. Wu, Y., Zhou, X.F., Zhang, Y.C.: Steel bars counting and splitting method based on machine vision. In: Proceedings 5th Annual IEEE International Conference on Cyber Technology in Automation, Shenyang, China, pp. 420–425 (2015)
5. Ghazali, M.F., Wong, L.-K., See, J.: Automatic detection and counting of circular and rectangular steel bars. In: Ibrahim, H., Iqbal, S., Teoh, S.S., Mustaffa, M.T. (eds.) 9th International Conference on Robotic, Vision, Signal Processing and Power Applications. LNEE, vol. 398, pp. 199–207. Springer, Singapore (2017). https://doi.org/10.1007/978-981-10-1721-6_22
6. Xing, Y., Xue, W., Yuan, P.X., et al.: Research on an automatic counting method for steel bars' image. In: Proceedings International Conference on Electrical & Control Engineering, Wuhan, China, pp. 1644–1647 (2010)
7. Zhao, J.Y., Xia, X.X., Wang, H.D., et al.: Design of real-time steel bars recognition system based on machine vision. In: Proceedings 8th International Conference on Intelligent Human-Machine Systems and Cybernetics, Hangzhou, China, pp. 505–509 (2016)
8. Hou, W.Y., Duan, Z.W., Liu, X.D.: A template-covering based algorithm to count the bundled steel bars. In: Proceedings 4th International Congress on Image and Signal Processing, Shanghai, China, pp. 1813–1916 (2011)
9. Yan, X., Chen, X.Q.: Research on the counting algorithm of bundled steel bars based on the features matching of connected regions. In: Proceedings 3rd International Conference on Image, Vision and Computing, Chongqing, China, pp. 11–15 (2018)
10. Llorca, D.F., Arroyo, R., Miguel, Á.S.: Vehicle logo recognition in traffic images using HOG features and SVM. In: Proceedings Intelligent Transportation Systems Conference, Hague, Netherlands, pp. 2229–2234 (2013)
11. Yao, C., Wu, F., Sun, H.J., et al.: Traffic sign recognition using HOG-SVM and grid search. In: Proceedings 12th International Conference on Signal Processing, Hangzhou, China, pp. 962–965 (2014)
12. Dalal, N., Triggs, B.: Histograms of oriented gradients for human detection. In: Proceedings International Conference on Computer Vision and Pattern Recognition, San Diego, USA, pp. 886–893 (2005)

Combining LSTM Network Model and Wavelet Transform for Predicting Self-interacting Proteins

Zhan-Heng Chen[1,2], Zhu-Hong You[1,2(✉)], Li-Ping Li[1],
Zhen-Hao Guo[1,2], Peng-Wei Hu[3], and Han-Jing Jiang[1,2]

[1] The Xinjiang Technical Institute of Physics and Chemistry,
Chinese Academy of Sciences, Urumqi 830011, China
zhuhongyou@ms.xjb.ac.cn, zhuhongyou@gmail.com
[2] University of Chinese Academy of Sciences, Beijing 100049, China
[3] Department of Computing,
Hong Kong Polytechnic University, Hong Kong, China

Abstract. With the explosive growth of protein sequences generated by biological experiment in the post-genomic era, more and more researchers pay particular attention to the development of approaches for the prediction of protein interactions and functions from sequences. In addition, elucidation of the self-interacting proteins (SIPs) play significant roles in the understanding of cellular process and cell functions. This work explored the use of deep learning model, Long-Short Term Memory (LSTM), for the prediction of SIPs directly from their primary sequences. More specifically, the protein sequence is firstly converted to Position Specific Scoring Matrix (PSSM) by exploiting the Position Specific Iterated BLAST method, in which the evolutionary information is contained. Then, the wavelet transform algorithm is used on PSSM to extract discriminative feature. Finally, based on the knowledge of known self-interacting and non-interacting proteins, LSTM model is trained to recognize SIPs. The prediction performance of the proposed method is evaluated on yeast dataset, which achieved an accuracy rate of 92.21%. The experimental results show that the proposed method outperforms other six existing methods for SIPs prediction. Achieved results demonstrate that the proposed model is an effective architecture with SIPs detection, and would provide a useful supplement for the proteomics research.

Keywords: Self-interacting proteins · PSSM · Wavelet transform · LSTM

1 Introduction

Cells are the main structural and functional units in the organisms. A cell contains tens of thousands of proteins. Therefore, proteins play essential roles in the cell functions and living organisms. They also can provide the energy for the life activities. To be functionally active, proteins should interact with other components [1–4]. The interactions which have drawn more attention of researchers. Many researchers have contributed to the protein-protein interactions (PPIs) data by implementing a large number

© Springer Nature Switzerland AG 2019
D.-S. Huang et al. (Eds.): ICIC 2019, LNCS 11643, pp. 166–174, 2019.
https://doi.org/10.1007/978-3-030-26763-6_16

of experiments, which establish the proteome-wide PPI networks [5]. This will provide help for discovering the self-interacting proteins (SIPs). SIPs represent that two or more copies can interact with each other. Knowing whether proteins could self-interact that can better understand the theory of protein interaction networks (PINs) [6–10]. From the past years, many studies show that homo-oligomerization must play an important role in many biological processes, such as gene expression regulation, signal transduction, enzyme activation and immune response [11, 12].

So far, there is a large previous methods on the PPIs detection have been proposed [13–24]. For instance, Wang et al. used the probabilistic classification vector machines model (PCVM) combined with a Zernike moments (ZM) descriptor to predict PPIs from protein sequences [25]. Xia et al. presented a sequence-based multiple classifier system that employed autocorrelation descriptor to code an interaction protein pair and chose rotation forest as classifier to infer PPIs [26]. You et al. proposed an efficient ensemble learning method to predict PPIs by integrating protein primary sequence and evolutionary information [27]. However, these approaches could be applied to detect PPIs well [28, 29], but they are not good enough to predict SIPs. It is becoming more and more important to develop an effective calculation method to predict SIPs.

2 Methods and Materials

2.1 Dataset

As we all know that the PPIs related information can be achieved from many different types of resources, including DIP [30], BioGRID [31], IntAct [32], InnateDB [33] and MatrixDB [34]. In this study, the datasets constructed in the experiment which contains 710 yeast SIPs and 5511 yeast non-SIPs [35].

We need to select the dataset mainly includes three steps [35]: (1) We removed the protein sequences which may be fragments, and retained the length of protein sequences more than 50 residues and less than 5000 residues; (2)To build the yeast positive dataset, we chose a high quality SIPs data which should conform to one of the following conditions: (a) The self-interactions were revealed by at least one small-scale experiment or two sorts of large-scale experiments; (b) The protein has been announced as homo-oligomer (containing homodimer and homotrimer) in UniProt; (c) It has been reported by more than two publications for the self-interactions; (3) For the yeast negative dataset, we removed all the types of SIPs from the whole yeast proteome (including proteins annotated as 'direct interaction' and more extensive 'physical association') and SIPs detection in UniProt database.

2.2 Position Specific Scoring Matrix

In our achievements, Position Specific Scoring Matrix (PSSM) is a helpful tool which was applied to detect distantly related proteins [36–39]. Accordingly, a PSSM was converted from each protein sequence information by employing the Position Specific

Iterated BLAST (PSI-BLAST) [40]. And then, a given protein sequence can be transformed into an H × 20 PSSM which can be announced as follow:

$$M = \{M_{\alpha\beta} \, \alpha : 1 = 1 \cdots H, \, \beta = 1 \cdots 20\} \tag{1}$$

where the rows H of the matrix is the length of a protein sequence, and the columns represent the number of amino acids because of each protein gene was constructed by 20 types of amino acids. The score $C_{\alpha\beta}$ represents the β-th amino acid in the position of α which can be distributed from a PSSM. Thus, the score $C_{\alpha\beta}$ can be defined as:

$$C_{\alpha\beta} = \sum\nolimits_{k=1}^{20} p(\alpha, \, k) \times q(\beta, \, k) \tag{2}$$

where $p(\alpha, \, k)$ denotes the appearing frequency value of the k-th amino acid at position of α with the probe, and $q(\beta, \, k)$ is the value of Dayhoff's mutation matrix between β-th and k-th amino acids.

In conclusion, to get a high degree and a wide range of homologous sequences, the E-value parameter of PSI-BLAST was set to be 0.001 which reported for a given result represents the number of two sequences' alignments and chose three iterations in this process. As a result, the PSSM can be denoted as a 20-dimensional matrix which compose of $M \times 20$ elements, where the rows M of the matrix is the number of residues of a protein, and the columns of the matrix denote the 20 amino acids.

2.3   Wavelet Transform

In signal processing, Wavelet Transform (WT) [41] is an ideal tool for signal time-frequency analysis and processing. The main point is that transformation can adequately highlight some aspects of the problems, and any details of signal can be focused. It solved the difficult problem of Fourier transform. And then, WT has been a major breakthrough in the scientific method since the Fourier transform. Wavelet Transform (WT) [42] was applied to decompose the image. WT also can be employed in many fields, such as signal processing [43], speech processing [44] and non-linear science [45]. The main feature is that some characteristics of the problem can be fully highlighted by transformation, and then it can focus on any details of the problem.

In bioinformatics and genomics, a protein can be treated as a series of digital signals, and then, we can applied WT method to analyses them [46–48]. In virtue of each protein sequence has different amount of amino acids, we cannot directly transform a PSSM into a feature vector, which will bring about different length of feature vectors. Hence, we multiplied the transpose of PSSM by PSSM to get 20 × 20 matrix, and employed the feature extraction method of wavelet transform to generate feature vectors from the 20 × 20 matrix. Afterwards, each protein sequence of yeast dataset was converted into a 400-dimensional vector by applying WT method. In order to reduce the influence of unimportant information and increase the prediction accuracy, we used the Principal Component Analysis (PCA) approach to remove noisy features from yeast dataset. So that we can reduce the dimension of the two datasets from 400 to 150. Furthermore, reducing the dimensionality of the dataset could use a small number of features to represent the information and push the complexity into smaller, so as to improve the generalization error.

2.4   Long-Short Term Memory

Long-Short Term Memory (LSTM) is a recurrent network architecture in conjunction with an appropriate gradient-based learning algorithm, which motivated overcome the error flow problems [49–52]. The same as RNNs, with the exception of hidden layer. We use purpose-built memory cells to replace the hidden layer of LSTM. A single LSTM memory cell is shown Fig. 1.

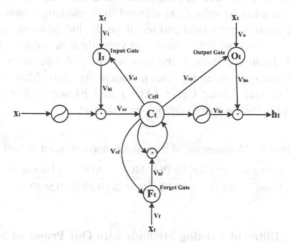

Fig. 1. A single LSTM cell

The specific achievement process of LSTM cell is gave out as follow:

$$I_t = Sig(V_i x_t + V_{hi} h_{t-1} + V_{ci} C_{t-1} + b_i)$$

$$F_t = Sig(V_f x_t + V_{hf} h_{t-1} + V_{cf} C_{t-1} + b_f)$$

$$C_t = F_t c_{t-1} + I_t \tanh(V_{xc} x_t + V_{hc} h_{t-1} + b_c)$$

$$O_t = Sig(V_o x_t + V_{ho} h_{t-1} + V_{co} C_t + b_o)$$

$$h_t = O_t \tanh(C_t)$$

where *Sig* is the logistic sigmoid function which is used on the output to predict the binary value, I_t represents the input gate's activation vector, F_t stands for the forget gate activation vector, O_t is the output gate activation vector, and C_t is the cell state vector. The subscripts of weight matrix *V* have the meaning as the name suggests. For instance, V_i represents the input gate weight matrix, V_{hi} is the hidden-input gate weight matrix, V_{ci} is the cell-input gate weight matrix ect. The *b* is bias vector parameters.

3 Experimental Results

3.1 Performance on Yeast Dataset

The performance of the proposed method is estimated on yeast dataset. From the LSTM model, in view of the over-fitting problems, we only separate the datasets into training and test dataset except for validation dataset. Further, described it in details, we cut the dataset into five non-overlapping pieces, and the training set was randomly chosen in 4/5 of characteristic values and selected the remaining values as independent test set. Then, we training our model and test it on the independent set.

Afterwards, we test our prediction model on yeast dataset, and got the results of the dataset in Table 1. From the Table 1, the data is observed that our proposed method exhibited the outcomes of Accuracy (Acc), Specificity (Sp), Matthews Correlation Coefficient (MCC), Area Under Curve (AUC) and F1-score of 92.21%, 98.72%, 0.5628, 0.8945 and 0.5689 respectively on yeast dataset.

Table 1. Measurement of proposed method on yeast dataset

Datasets	Acc (%)	Sp (%)	MCC	AUC	F1-score
Yeast	92.21	98.72	0.5628	0.8945	0.5689

3.2 Comparing Different Existing Methods with Our Proposed Method

In the process of practice, we measured the quality of proposed model named LSTM-WT with other existing methods based on the yeast dataset to further testify that our approach can achieve good results. We listed a clear statement of account in Table 2, which are the comparison results on yeast dataset. From Table 2, it is obvious that the LSTM-WT model achieved the highest accuracy of 92.21% than the other six methods (range from 66.28% to 87.46%) on yeast dataset. At the same instant, it is clear to see that the other six methods got lower MCC (range from 0.1577 to 0.2842) than our proposed model of 0.8945 on the same dataset. This fully illustrates that a good feature extraction method and a suitable classifier are very important for predicting model. It is further illustrated that the proposed method is superior to the other six approaches and quite suitable for predicting SIPs.

Table 2. Measure the quality of proposed model and the other methods on yeast dataset

Model	Acc (%)	Sp (%)	MCC	AUC	F1-score
SLIPPER [53]	71.90	72.18	0.2842	0.7723	0.3616
DXECPPI [54]	87.46	94.93	0.2825	0.6934	0.3489
PPIevo [55]	66.28	87.46	0.1801	0.6728	0.2892
LocFuse [56]	66.66	68.10	0.1577	0.7087	0.2753
CRS [35]	72.69	74.37	0.2368	0.7115	0.3305
SPAR [35]	76.96	80.02	0.2484	0.7455	0.3454
Proposed method	**92.21**	**98.72**	**0.5628**	**0.8945**	**0.5689**

As mentioned above, It is apparent that our method can receive good effect of SIPs detection because of the appropriate feature extraction and classifier. The presented feature extraction technique plays a critical part in enhancing the calculation accuracy. The specific reasons can be summed up in the following three aspects: (1) PSSM could describe the protein sequence in the form of numerical values. It can be employed to find an amino acid that matches a specific location to give the score in a target protein sequence. Not only can it represents the information of protein sequence, but also it preserves useful enough information as much as possible. Accordingly, A PSSM contains almost the whole major information of one protein sequence for detecting SIPs. (2) The wavelet transform (WT) feature extraction method of protein sequence can further optimize the performance of our proposed model. (3) In order to drop the negative influence of noise, Principal Component Analysis (PCA) method was used to reduce the dimension of data on the condition of the integrity of WT feature vector, thus the helpful information in the data will be mined. In a few words, experimental results revealed that our presented model is extreme fit for SIPs prediction.

4 Conclusion

In this study, a deep learning-based model was proposed to detect SIPs directly from protein primary sequence. Experimental results measured by the proposed model on yeast dataset, which achieved an accuracy rate of 92.21%. It is revealed that our method is much better than other existing approaches. The improvements are attributable to the following reasons: (1) An efficient deep learning model, Long-Short Term Memory (LSTM), is designed for the prediction of SIPs. (2) The protein sequence is transformed to Position Specific Scoring Matrix (PSSM) by exploiting the Position Specific Iterated BLAST method, in which the evolutionary information is contained. (3) Wavelet transform algorithm is a reasonable feature extraction method which can improve prediction performance by capturing the main useful information. For the future work, there will be more effective feature extraction methods and deep learning techniques explored for detecting SIPs.

Acknowledgement. This work is supported in part by the National Science Foundation of China, under Grants 61373086, 61572506, The authors would like to thank all the guest editors and anonymous reviewers for their constructive advices.

References

1. Zhu, L., You, Z.-H., Huang, D.-S., Wang, B.: t-LSE: a novel robust geometric approach for modeling protein-protein interaction networks. PLoS ONE **8**, e58368 (2013)
2. You, Z.-H., Zhou, M., Luo, X., Li, S.: Highly efficient framework for predicting interactions between proteins. IEEE Trans. Cybern. **47**, 731–743 (2017)
3. Wang, L., et al.: Using two-dimensional principal component analysis and rotation forest for prediction of protein-protein interactions. Sci. Rep. **8**, 12874 (2018)

4. Huang, Y.-A., You, Z.-H., Chen, X., Chan, K., Luo, X.: Sequence-based prediction of protein-protein interactions using weighted sparse representation model combined with global encoding. BMC Bioinform. **17**, 184 (2016)
5. Natali, A., et al.: Clustering of insulin resistance with vascular dysfunction and low-grade inflammation in type 2 diabetes. Diabetes **55**, 1133–1140 (2006)
6. Li, J.-Q., You, Z.-H., Li, X., Ming, Z., Chen, X.: PSPEL: in silico prediction of self-interacting proteins from amino acids sequences using ensemble learning. IEEE/ACM Trans. Comput. Biol. Bioinform. (TCBB) **14**, 1165–1172 (2017)
7. Wang, Y.-B., You, Z.-H., Li, X., Jiang, T.-H., Cheng, L., Chen, Z.-H.: Prediction of protein self-interactions using stacked long short-term memory from protein sequences information. BMC Syst. Biol. **12**, 129 (2018)
8. Chen, Z.-H., You, Z.-H., Li, L.-P., Wang, Y.-B., Wong, L., Yi, H.-C.: Prediction of self-interacting proteins from protein sequence information based on random projection model and fast Fourier transform. Int. J. Mol. Sci. **20**, 930 (2019)
9. You, Z., Lei, Y., Ji, Z., Zhu, Z.: A novel approach to modelling protein-protein interaction networks. In: Tan, Y., Shi, Y., Ji, Z. (eds.) ICSI 2012. LNCS, vol. 7332, pp. 49–57. Springer, Heidelberg (2012). https://doi.org/10.1007/978-3-642-31020-1_7
10. Huang, Y.-A., et al.: Construction of reliable protein–protein interaction networks using weighted sparse representation based classifier with pseudo substitution matrix representation features. Neurocomputing **218**, 131–138 (2016)
11. Hu, T., Liu, C., Tang, Y., Sun, J., Xiong, H., Sung, S.Y.: High-dimensional clustering: a clique-based hypergraph partitioning framework. Knowl. Inf. Syst. **39**, 61–88 (2014)
12. Chen, Z.-H., You, Z.-H., Li, L.-P., Wang, Y.-B., Li, X.: RP-FIRF: prediction of self-interacting proteins using random projection classifier combining with finite impulse response filter. In: Huang, D.-S., Jo, K.-H., Zhang, X.-L. (eds.) ICIC 2018. LNCS, vol. 10955, pp. 232–240. Springer, Cham (2018). https://doi.org/10.1007/978-3-319-95933-7_29
13. Huang, Q., You, Z., Zhang, X., Zhou, Y.: Prediction of protein-protein interactions with clustered amino acids and weighted sparse representation. Int. J. Mol. Sci. **16**, 10855–10869 (2015)
14. Huang, Y.-A., You, Z.-H., Chen, X., Yan, G.-Y.: Improved protein-protein interactions prediction via weighted sparse representation model combining continuous wavelet descriptor and PseAA composition. BMC Syst. Biol. **10**, 120 (2016)
15. Lei, Y.-K., You, Z.-H., Dong, T., Jiang, Y.-X., Yang, J.-A.: Increasing reliability of protein interactome by fast manifold embedding. Pattern Recogn. Lett. **34**, 372–379 (2013)
16. Li, J., Shi, X., You, Z., Chen, Z., Lin, Q., Fang, M.: Using weighted extreme learning machine combined with scale-invariant feature transform to predict protein-protein interactions from protein evolutionary information. In: Huang, D.-S., Bevilacqua, V., Premaratne, P., Gupta, P. (eds.) ICIC 2018. LNCS, vol. 10954, pp. 527–532. Springer, Cham (2018). https://doi.org/10.1007/978-3-319-95930-6_49
17. Li, L.-P., Wang, Y.-B., You, Z.-H., Li, Y., An, J.-Y.: PCLPred: a bioinformatics method for predicting protein-protein interactions by combining relevance vector machine model with low-rank matrix approximation. Int. J. Mol. Sci. **19**, 1029 (2018)
18. Li, Z.-W., You, Z.-H., Chen, X., Gui, J., Nie, R.: Highly accurate prediction of protein-protein interactions via incorporating evolutionary information and physicochemical characteristics. Int. J. Mol. Sci. **17**, 1396 (2016)
19. Luo, X., et al.: A highly efficient approach to protein interactome mapping based on collaborative filtering framework. Sci. Rep. **5**, 7702 (2015)
20. Wang, L., et al.: An ensemble approach for large-scale identification of protein-protein interactions using the alignments of multiple sequences. Oncotarget **8**, 5149 (2017)

21. Wang, Y.B., et al.: Predicting protein-protein interactions from protein sequences by a stacked sparse autoencoder deep neural network. Mol. BioSyst. **13**, 1336–1344 (2017)
22. Wen, Y.-T., Lei, H.-J., You, Z.-H., Lei, B.-Y., Chen, X., Li, L.-P.: Prediction of protein-protein interactions by label propagation with protein evolutionary and chemical information derived from heterogeneous network. J. Theor. Biol. **430**, 9–20 (2017)
23. Wong, L., You, Z.-H., Ming, Z., Li, J., Chen, X., Huang, Y.-A.: Detection of interactions between proteins through rotation forest and local phase quantization descriptors. Int. J. Mol. Sci. **17**, 21 (2015)
24. Zhu, L., Deng, S.-P., You, Z.-H., Huang, D.-S.: Identifying spurious interactions in the protein-protein interaction networks using local similarity preserving embedding. IEEE/ACM Trans. Comput. Biol. Bioinform. (TCBB) **14**, 345–352 (2017)
25. Wang, Y., You, Z., Li, X., Chen, X., Jiang, T., Zhang, J.: PCVMZM: using the probabilistic classification vector machines model combined with a Zernike moments descriptor to predict protein-protein interactions from protein sequences. Int. J. Mol. Sci. **18**, 1029 (2017)
26. Xia, J.-F., Han, K., Huang, D.-S.: Sequence-based prediction of protein-protein interactions by means of rotation forest and autocorrelation descriptor. Protein Pept. Lett. **17**, 137–145 (2010)
27. You, Z.-H., Huang, W., Zhang, S., Huang, Y.-A., Yu, C.-Q., Li, L.-P.: An efficient ensemble learning approach for predicting protein-protein interactions by integrating protein primary sequence and evolutionary information. IEEE/ACM Trans. Comput. Biol. Bioinform. **16**, 809–817 (2018)
28. An, J.Y., You, Z.H., Chen, X., Huang, D.S., Yan, G., Wang, D.F.: Robust and accurate prediction of protein self-interactions from amino acids sequence using evolutionary information. Mol. BioSyst. **12**, 3702 (2016)
29. An, J.Y., et al.: Identification of self-interacting proteins by exploring evolutionary information embedded in PSI-BLAST-constructed position specific scoring matrix. Oncotarget **7**, 82440–82449 (2016)
30. Salwinski, L., Miller, C.S., Smith, A.J., Pettit, F.K., Bowie, J.U., Eisenberg, D.: The database of interacting proteins: 2004 update. Nucleic Acids Res. **32**, D449–D451 (2004)
31. Chatr-Aryamontri, A., et al.: The BioGRID interaction database: 2017 update. Nucleic Acids Res. **45**, D369–D379 (2017)
32. Orchard, S., et al.: The MIntAct project—IntAct as a common curation platform for 11 molecular interaction databases. Nucleic Acids Res. **42**, D358–D363 (2013)
33. Breuer, K., et al.: InnateDB: systems biology of innate immunity and beyond—recent updates and continuing curation. Nucleic Acids Res. **41**, D1228–D1233 (2012)
34. Clerc, O., et al.: MatrixDB: integration of new data with a focus on glycosaminoglycan interactions. Nucleic Acids Res. **47**, D376–D381 (2018)
35. Liu, X., Yang, S., Li, C., Zhang, Z., Song, J.: SPAR: a random forest-based predictor for self-interacting proteins with fine-grained domain information. Amino Acids **48**, 1655–1665 (2016)
36. Jones, D.T.: Protein secondary structure prediction based on position-specific scoring matrices. J. Mol. Biol. **292**, 195–202 (1999)
37. Gao, Z.G., Lei, W., Xia, S.X., You, Z.H., Xin, Y., Yong, Z.: Ens-PPI: a novel ensemble classifier for predicting the interactions of proteins using autocovariance transformation from PSSM. Biomed. Res. Int. **2016**, 1–8 (2016)
38. Li, Z.W., et al.: Accurate prediction of protein-protein interactions by integrating potential evolutionary information embedded in PSSM profile and discriminative vector machine classifier. Oncotarget **8**, 23638 (2017)

39. Wang, Y.-B., You, Z.-H., Li, L.-P., Huang, Y.-A., Yi, H.-C.: Detection of interactions between proteins by using legendre moments descriptor to extract discriminatory information embedded in pssm. Molecules **22**, 1366 (2017)
40. Altschul, S.F., Koonin, E.V.: Iterated profile searches with PSI-BLAST - a tool for discovery in protein databases. Trends Biochem. Sci. **23**, 444–447 (1998)
41. Daubechies, I.: The wavelet transform, time-frequency localization and signal analysis. IEEE Trans. Inf. Theory **36**, 961–1005 (1990)
42. Lewis, A.S., Knowles, G.: Image compression using the 2-D wavelet transform. IEEE Trans. Image Process. **1**, 244–250 (1992)
43. Sahambi, J.S., Tandon, S.N., Bhatt, R.K.P.: Using wavelet transforms for ECG characterization - an on-line digital signal processing system. IEEE Eng. Med. Biol. Mag. **16**, 77–83 (1997)
44. Ranjan, S.: A discrete wavelet transform based approach to hindi speech recognition. IEEE (2010)
45. Staszewski, W.J.: Identification of non-linear systems using multi-scale ridges and skeletons of the wavelet transform. J. Sound Vib. **214**, 639–658 (1998)
46. Chen, Z.-H., Li, L.-P., He, Z., Zhou, J.-R., Li, Y., Wong, L.: An improved deep forest model for predicting self-interacting proteins from protein sequence using wavelet transformation. Front. Genet. **10**, 90 (2019)
47. Jia, J., Liu, Z., Xiao, X., Liu, B., Chou, K.-C.: Identification of protein-protein binding sites by incorporating the physicochemical properties and stationary wavelet transforms into pseudo amino acid composition. J. Biomol. Struct. Dyn. **34**, 1946–1961 (2016)
48. Jia, J., Liu, Z., Xiao, X., Liu, B., Chou, K.-C.: iPPI-Esml: an ensemble classifier for identifying the interactions of proteins by incorporating their physicochemical properties and wavelet transforms into PseAAC. J. Theor. Biol. **377**, 47–56 (2015)
49. Graves, A., Schmidhuber, J.: Framewise phoneme classification with bidirectional LSTM and other neural network architectures. Neural Netw. **18**, 602–610 (2005)
50. Hochreiter, S., Schmidhuber, J.: Long short-term memory. Neural Comput. **9**, 1735–1780 (1997)
51. Balducci, C., et al.: Synthetic amyloid-β oligomers impair long-term memory independently of cellular prion protein. Proc. Natl. Acad. Sci. **107**, 2295–2300 (2010)
52. Yi, H.-C., et al.: ACP-DL: a deep learning long short-term memory model to predict anticancer peptides using high efficiency feature representation. Mol. Ther. Nucleic Acids **17**, 1–9 (2019)
53. Liu, Z., et al.: Proteome-wide prediction of self-interacting proteins based on multiple properties. Mol. Cell. Proteomics **12**, 1689–1700 (2013)
54. Du, X., Cheng, J., Zheng, T., Duan, Z., Qian, F.: A novel feature extraction scheme with ensemble coding for protein-protein interaction prediction. Int. J. Mol. Sci. **15**, 12731–12749 (2014)
55. Zahiri, J., Yaghoubi, O., Mohammad-Noori, M., Ebrahimpour, R., Masoudi-Nejad, A.: PPIevo: Protein-protein interaction prediction from PSSM based evolutionary information. Genomics **102**, 237–242 (2013)
56. Zahiri, J., et al.: LocFuse: human protein-protein interaction prediction via classifier fusion using protein localization information. Genomics **104**, 496–503 (2014)

Coarse-to-Fine Supervised Descent Method
for Face Alignment

Xijing Zhu[✉], Zhong-Qiu Zhao, and Weidong Tian

School of Computer Science and Information Engineering,
HeFei University of Technology, Hefei, China
zhuxijing@mail.hfut.edu.cn

Abstract. Supervised Descent Method (SDM) is an efficient and accurate approach for facial landmark locating and face alignment. In the training phase, it requires a large amount of training samples to learn the descent directions and get the corresponding regressors. Then in the test phase, it uses the corresponding regressors to estimate the descent directions and locate the facial landmarks. However, when the facial expression or direction changes too much, generally SDM cannot obtain good performance due to the large variation between the initial shape (the initial shape of SDM is the mean shape of the training samples) and the target shape. Therefore, we propose a coarse-to-fine SDM (CFSDM) method to improve the accuracy of the test results. This method predicts the approximate coordinates of the facial landmarks with a simple CNN (Convolutional Neural Network) network (here we introduce the channel-wise attention mechanism, which can predict the coordinates of the landmarks more accurately with a relatively simple structure) in advance, and then SDM will take the coordinates as its initial shape's coordinates, which reduces the distance between the initial shape and the target shape, thereby solving the problem that SDM cannot achieve good results when the facial expression or direction changes greatly.

Keywords: Face alignment · Coarse-to-fine · SDM · Attention mechanism

1 Introduction

Face alignment means that the key feature points (such as the eyes, the tip of the nose, the corners of the mouth, the eyebrows, and so on) of the face are automatically located according to the input face image, as shown in the Fig. 1. It is widely used in many facial analysis tasks, such as face recognition [1], expression analysis [2], face tracking, face animation [3] and facial attributes analysis [4]. Face alignment still faces many challenges due to many factors, like different poses, expressions, lighting, and occlusion.

SDM (Supervised Descent Method) [5] is a very representative method based on cascaded regression model. It evolved from Newton Descent Method with high efficiency and precision. The SDM starts with the initial shape (the mean shape of the training samples) and iterates through a series of regressors to bring the initial shape closer to the true shape. One of the drawbacks of the cascaded regression model is that

© Springer Nature Switzerland AG 2019
D.-S. Huang et al. (Eds.): ICIC 2019, LNCS 11643, pp. 175–186, 2019.
https://doi.org/10.1007/978-3-030-26763-6_17

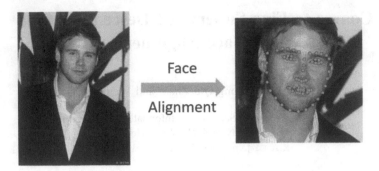

Fig. 1. The task of face alignment.

its final result is highly dependent on its initial shape. When in simple conditions, SDM can often achieve better results due to its superior performance, but when under extreme conditions, such as a large head pose, or a facial expression is too exaggerated, the initial is too different from the true shape, at this time, it is very difficult to make the initial shape approximate to the true shape by several iterations.

After 2013, the methods based on deep learning began to be widely used in face alignment and achieved remarkable results. These methods generally do not rely on initialization. But under the premise of achieving high precision, they often show a complex structure and a time-consuming process.

To solve the above problems, we propose a coarse-to-fine SDM (CFSDM) method. We first use a simple CNN (Convolutional Neural Network) network (we added the channel-wise attention mechanism to the CNN network, so that the position of the landmarks will be predicted more accurately with a relatively simple structure) to predict the approximate location of the facial landmarks, and the resulting coordinates of the landmarks are assigned to SDM as its average face coordinate (i.e., the initial shape at the time of testing), thus the initialization of SDM will be optimized. This method provides a good initialization for SDM and is not easy to fall into local optimum, thus improves the results.

2   Related Work

2.1   Face Alignment

Traditional Methods
Traditional face alignment methods include ASM [6], AAM [7], CLM [8], etc. ASM is an active shape model, it model the facial landmarks labeled in the training set, and then search for the best matching points on the test set and locate the facial landmarks. AAM is an active appearance model. AAM is based on ASM, it further statistical model the texture, and merge the two statistical models of shape and texture into appearance models. CLM inherits the advantages of ASM and AAM respectively, it

gets a balance between the efficiency of ASM and the accuracy of AAM, and models the patch of the local texture around the facial landmarks on the basis of ASM rather than the global texture method of AAM.

Recently, the cascade shape regression model has made a major breakthrough in face alignment task. These methods use a regression model to learn the mapping function directly from the appearance of the face to the shape of the face (or the parameters of the face shape model), then establish a correspondence from the appearance to the shape. Such methods do not require complex face shape and appearance, and achieve good results in controllable scenes (human faces collected under laboratory conditions) and non-controllable scenes (network face images, etc.). In 2010, Dollar proposed CPR (Cascaded Pose Regression) [9], CPR gradually refines a specified initial prediction value through a series of regressors. ESR [10] adopted boosted regression and two-level cascade regression. CFSS [11] began with a coarse search over a shape space that contains diverse shapes, and employs the coarse solution to constrain subsequent finer search of shapes. LBF (Regressing Local-Binary Features) [12] learned sparse binary features in local regions based on random forest regression model. SDM [5] used supervised gradient descent method to solve non-Linear least squares problem, and learns a series of regressors for locating facial landmarks. In general, the cascade shape regression methods are very sensitive to the starting point of the regression process.

CNN Based Methods
Deep learning has been widely used in the field of computer vision [24, 25], face alignment methods based on deep learning have also achieved remarkable results. Sun et al. [13] used CNN for face alignment for the first time, they proposed a three-layer network structure, and each layer contains multiple independent CNN models, which are responsible for predicting some or all key points. Wu et al. [14] found that the cnn network is hierarchical, and the deeper network extracted features can reflect the position of the facial landmarks more accurately, so they proposed TCNN (Twaned Convolutional Neural Networks). MTCNN [15] used three CNN cascades to simultaneously perform face detection and face alignment. SAN [16] predicted facial landmarks by simultaneously inputting the original face image and the style aggregate image, and solves the problem caused by the change of the image's style. LAB [17] used a network to extract boundary of the face and fuses the information of boundary into face alignment. TCDCN [18] used multi-task learning to optimize facial landmark locating with a set of related tasks. In summary, in order to achieve accuracy, the deep learning methods generally use a cascaded depth model to gradually improve the estimation, which leads to more complicated calculations.

We propose a coarse-to-fine SDM (SDM) method, which takes advantage of the fact that the deep learning methods do not depend on initialization, reduces the complexity of the cnn structure, optimizes the initialization of SDM, and improves the final result.

2.2 Attention Mechanism

In recent years, the study of deep learning has become more and more extensive, and many breakthroughs have been made in various fields. Neural networks based on the attention mechanism have become a hot topic in recent neural network research. Mnih et al. [19] used the attention mechanism on the RNN model for image classification. Bahdanau et al. [20] first proposed the application of the attention mechanism to the NLP field. In order to make the i-th channel only related to the position of the i-th landmark, We use a channel-wise attention module which proposed in [21] in our method.

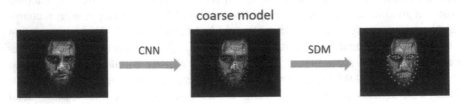

Fig. 2. The overall process of our CFSDM. The coarse shape is estimated by CNN network, and it is the initial shape of SDM during test phase.

3 Method

During the test phase, SDM starts with the initial shape (the average shape of the training samples) and iterates with a series of regressors to gradually approximate the initial shape to the true shape. It is easy to find that its final result is very dependent on the initial shape. When the facial expression or the head pose changes too much, since the variation between the initial shape and the real shape is too large, generally SDM cannot obtain good performance. So we propose a coarse-to-fine SDM (CFSDM) method. We utilize a simple CNN network (the channel wise attention mechanism is introduced here) to predict the approximate position of the facial landmarks in advance, and then the obtained coordinates are given to SDM as its initial shape coordinates, which optimize the initialization of SDM, and then the initial shape will be closer to the real shape through the regressors that be learned. The overall process of the method is shown in Fig. 2.

3.1 Coarse Localization Based on CNN

Architecture of CNN Network

Figure 3 shows the detailed structure of CNN network. We take the first 13 layers of VGG-16 [22] as our backbone. VGG is simple and practical, and it performs very well in both image classification and object detection. The size of convolutional filters' receptive field is 3×3, which is the smallest size to capture the left/right, up/down and center. The stride of the convolution is fixed to 1 pixel. The padding of the convolution layer is used to maintain the spatial resolution of the image after convolution.

The second, the fourth, the seventh and the tenth convolutional layer are followed with a max-pooling layer respectively. Max-pooling is performed over a 2 × 2 pixel window, with stride 2.

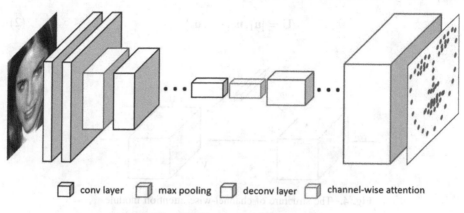

conv layer   max pooling   deconv layer   channel-wise attention

Fig. 3. The structure of CNN network.

It is well known that the bottleneck of VGG-16 is that there are too many parameters in the fully connected layer, and the speed is very slow, so we give up the fully connected layer of VGG-16. We adopt a structure with fewer parameters and higher efficiency, that is, a deconvolution layer. We revert the obtained CNN feature maps to the input size through the deconvolution layer. Each channel of the final output is equivalent to a probability map that predicts where a landmark is most likely to exist. For example, to predict the location of 68 landmarks for a face image in Helen dataset, the final output of our network contains also 68 channels. In order to make the i-th channel only related to the position of the i-th landmark, we have added the channel-wise attention module. We will introduce the specific structure of channel-wise attention module in Sect. 3.1.

Our CNN network is trained with an end-to-end manner. We take the mean square error as the loss function,

$$\mathbf{L}_{\text{MSE}} = \frac{\sum_{i=1}^{n} \left((x_i - x_i')^2 + (y_i - y_i')^2 \right)}{n} \tag{1}$$

where x_i and y_i are the ground truth coordinate of the i-th landmark, x_i' and y_i' are the predicted coordinate of the i-th landmark.

Channel-Wise Attention
The different channels of the feature maps are essentially features extracted by different filters, and the different filters may extract different emphases. It is possible that one filter extracts more features of the tip of the nose, and another filter extracts more features of the eye. So it is required a weight, that is, channel-wise weight. To a certain

extent, channel-wise attention can be seen as semantic attention which focuses on different objects in the image. Figure 4 shows the structure of channel-wise attention module.

At first, the feature maps **V** which extracted from our convolutional filters are reshaped to get the channel-wise vectors,

$$U = [u_1, u_2, \cdots, u_c] \tag{2}$$

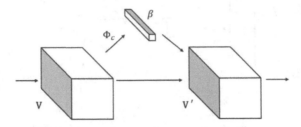

Fig. 4. The structure of channel-wise attention module.

where $u_i \in \mathbb{R}^{W \times H}$ is the i-th channel of feature maps and c is the number of the CNN feature channels. Then the average pooling is performed on each channel to obtain the vector

$$V = [v_1, v_2, \cdots, v_C] \tag{3}$$

which characterizes the information of different channels. And the final weight calculation is expressed as:

$$b = \tanh(W_c \otimes v + b_c) \tag{4}$$

$$\beta = \mathrm{softmax}(W_i b + b_i) \tag{5}$$

$$V' = V \odot \beta \tag{6}$$

where W_c, W_i are transformation matrices we prepared to learn, and $\otimes$ represents the outer product of vectors, b_c, b_i are bias terms and $\odot$ donate that each channel of **V** is multiplied by β.

3.2   Fine Localization Based on SDM

SDM is a commonly used method to solve complex Non-linear Least Squares (NLS) problems. SDM gets a initial shape after training, and it uses the initial shape as the staring point of the test, see Fig. 5. The initial shape of SDM is obtained by averaging the coordinates of all the training samples. But in our CFSDM, the initial shape is estimated by the CNN network. Such initialization is more beneficial to the results.

Let us review the derivation of SDM. Given an image $\mathbf{d} \in \mathbb{R}^{m \times 1}$ of m pixels, $\mathbf{d(x)} \in \mathbb{R}^{p \times 1}$ represents p landmarks in the image. $\mathbf{h}$ is a nonlinear feature extraction function, such as $\mathbf{h(d(x))} \in \mathbb{R}^{128p \times 1}$ can denote the SIFT features extracted from p landmarks. Given the initial shape x_0, the goal is to make x_0 more and more close to the correct shape x_* of the face by regression. In order to achieve this goal, it is required to find the Δx that minimizes the following function

$$f(x_0 + \Delta x) = \|\mathbf{h(d}(x_0 + \Delta x)) - \Phi_*\|_2^2 \qquad (7)$$

where $\Phi_* = \mathbf{h(d}(x_*))$ represents the SIFT values in the manually labeled landmarks of the face. Of course, the above is the target of testing. We only have the initial x_0 in the prediction, and we do not know Δx and Φ_*.

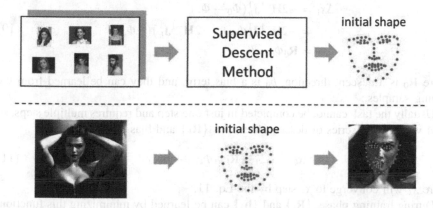

Fig. 5. The initial shape of SDM (the above is the training phase, and the following is the test phase).

In training phase, the Δx and Φ_* are known, and the good regressors need to be trained from the training samples, so that it can return the initial x_0 step by step to the correct unknown shape. In general, the initial x_0 is the mean shape of the true shape of all known samples.

For regressing the same initial shape of each image to the true shape of there face, we extracted different SIFT features from different images. Although the initial shape is same, the SIFT features extracted from different images are completely different, that is Φ_0 is different. This allows the initial shape to be regressed to the true shape through regressors. This can also be seen in Eq. 7.

The next thing to do is to get a series of regressors that can be used to regress an initial shape to a real shape, that is to learn the correct regressors to get the best Δx. Of course, if you want to regress the initial shape to the real shape step by step, it is generally impossible to do it by only one Δx, because it is very difficult to achieve the final goal in just one step. So we have to learn to get a series of different regressors, they will regress in turn, and a series of Δx will be learned, so x_0 will converge to x_* in the training data by $x_{k+1} = x_k + \Delta x_k$ (k is the number of regressors or iterations).

The Taylor expansion of the objective function Eq. 7 is described as:

$$f(x_0 + \Delta x) \approx f(x_0) + \mathbf{J}_f(x_0)^\mathrm{T} \Delta x + \frac{1}{2} \Delta x^\mathrm{T} \mathbf{H}(x_0) \Delta x \tag{8}$$

where $\mathbf{J}_f(x_0)$ and $\mathbf{H}(x_0)$ are the Jacobian and Hessian matrices of f evaluated at x_0. Differentiating Eq. 8 with respect to Δx and setting it to 0 gives us the first update for x,

$$\Delta x_1 = -\mathbf{H}^{-1} \mathbf{J}_f = -2\mathbf{H}^{-1} \mathbf{J}_h^\mathrm{T} (\Phi_0 - \Phi_*) \tag{9}$$

where $\Phi_0 = \mathbf{h}(\mathbf{d}(x_0))$ denotes the SIFT features extracted from the initial shape x_0. Let $\mathbf{R}_0 = -2\mathbf{H}^{-1} \mathbf{J}_h^\mathrm{T}$, and Φ_* is unknown but fixed during the test stage, so Eq. 9 can be rewritten as follows:

$$\begin{aligned}
\Delta x_1 &= -2\mathbf{H}^{-1} \mathbf{J}_h^\mathrm{T} (\Phi_0 - \Phi_*) \\
&= -2\mathbf{H}^{-1} \mathbf{J}_h^\mathrm{T} \Phi_0 + \left(-2\mathbf{H}^{-1} \mathbf{J}_h^\mathrm{T}\right)(-\Phi_*) \\
&= \mathbf{R}_0 \Phi_0 + b_0
\end{aligned} \tag{10}$$

where $\mathbf{R}_0$ is a descent direction, b_0 is a bias term, and they can be learned from the training samples.

Usually the task cannot be completed in just one step and requires multiple steps, so SDM will learn a series of descent directions $\{\mathbf{R}_k\}$ and bias terms $\{b_k\}$,

$$x_k = x_{k-1} + \mathbf{R}_{k-1} \Phi_{k-1} + \mathbf{b}_{k-1} \tag{11}$$

where x_k will converge to x_* step by the Eq. 11.

During training phase, $\{\mathbf{R}_k\}$ and $\{\mathbf{b}_k\}$ can be learned by minimizing this function:

$$\min_{\mathbf{R}_k, \mathbf{b}_k} \sum_{d^i} \sum_{x_k^i} \left\| \Delta x_*^{ki} - \mathbf{R}_k \Phi_k^i - b_k \right\|^2 \tag{12}$$

where $\Delta x_*^{ki} = x_*^i - x_k^i$, and i indicates the number of landmarks.

During test stage, the initial shape x_0 is determined by CNN network, and it will be more and more close to the true shape x_k through the learned $\{\mathbf{R}_k\}$ and $\{\mathbf{b}_k\}$.

4   Experiment

In this section, we evaluate the performance of the proposed method and compare it with several existing state-of-the-art methods on four datasets: LFPW, Helen, IBUG, and 300W.

LFPW (68 landmarks) contains 1432 face images, in which 1132 are for training and 300 are for testing. Since only image URLs are available and some links disappeared as time passed, we used a reduced version of 1035 images (each annotated with 68 landmarks), 811 of which are for training and the rest 224 for testing. The challenges are Large variations in illuminations, expressions, poses and occlusion.

Helen (68 landmarks) contains 2330 high resolution and accurately labeled face images, 2000 of which are for training and 330 are for testing. The challenges are large variations in expressions, poses and occlusion.

IBUG (68 landmarks) contains 135 accurately labeled face images. The challenges are extremely large variations in illuminations, expressions, poses and occlusion.

Multiple (68 landmarks) contains 150 people, and 10 facial expressions for each person. Each image is annotated with 68 landmarks. We select 225 images as training set, and 100 images as test set.

We use the Normalized Mean Error (NME) as a metric to measure the shape estimation error

$$NME = \frac{100}{N} \sum_{i=1}^{N} \left(\frac{1}{\|w_i^g\|_1} \sum_{l=1}^{L} \left(\frac{w_i^g(l) \cdot \|x_i(l) - x_i^g(l)\|}{d_i} \right) \right) \qquad (13)$$

Table 1. Error of face alignment methods on four datasets.

Methods	LFPW	Helen	IBUG	Multiple
LBF	5.36	5.41	11.98	5.93
CFAN	5.44	5.53	16.78	5.98
SDM	5.67	5.67	15.40	6.01
CFSDM	4.92	5.03	11.36	5.15

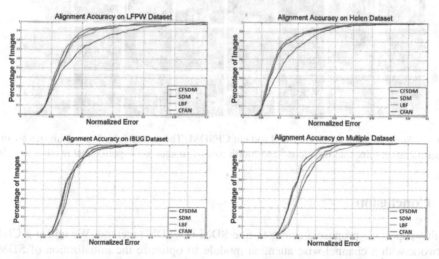

Fig. 6. The curves of percentage of test images vs normalized error of various approaches on four datasets: LFPW, Helen, IBUG, and 300W.

It computes the euclidean distance between the ground-truth and estimated land-mark positions normalized by d_i. Table 1 shows the face alignment performance of our CFSDM and those of several excellent methods: LBF [12], CFAN [23], SDM [5] as well. From Table 1, it can be seen that our CFSDM outperforms the other methods, and it has a great improvement compared with SDM, especially in challenging datasets like IBUG and Multiple. Figure 6 plots the curves of percentage of images versus nor-malized error, it shows that our CFSDM performs the best on most of the test images. Some example results of SDM and our CFSDM are displayed in Fig. 7.

In order to prove that the CNN network and the channel-wise attention module are both beneficial for the improvement of the final result, we performed an ablation experiment, see Table 2.

Table 2. Error of SDM, SDM+CNN (without the channel-wise attention module) and our CFSDM on four datasets.

Methods	LFPW	Helen	IBUG	Multiple
SDM	5.67	5.67	15.40	6.01
SDM+CNN	5.35	5.29	12.51	5.39
CFSDM	4.92	5.03	11.36	5.15

Fig. 7. Some example results of SDM and our CFSDM. The first and third row of images are our experimental results, and the second and fourth row of images are experimental results of SDM.

5   Conclusion

In this paper, we propose a coarse-to-fine SDM (CFSDM) method. We utilize a CNN network with a channel-wise attention module to optimize the initialization of SDM, which reduces the distance between the initial shape and the real shape in the test phase of SDM. It solves the problem that SDM can't achieve good results when the facial expression or direction changes greatly. The evaluation on four datasets shows that our CFSDM improves the accuracy of traditional SDM method and outperforms some other excellent methods.

Acknowledgments. This research was supported by the National Natural Science Foundation of China (No. 61672203), and AnHui Natural Science Funds for Distinguished Young Scholar (No. 170808J08).

References

1. Chen, C., Dantcheva, A., Ross, A., et al.: Automatic facial makeup detection with application in face recognition. In: International Conference on Biometrics, pp. 1–8 (2013)
2. Ashraf, A.B., Lucey, S., Cohn, J.F., et al.: The painful face - pain expression recognition using active appearance models. Image Vis. Comput. 27(12), 1788–1796 (2009)
3. Thies, J., Zollhofer, M., Stamminger, M., et al.: Face2Face: real-time face capture and reenactment of RGB videos. In: Computer Vision and Pattern Recognition, pp. 2387–2395 (2016)
4. Datta, A., Feris, R., Vaquero, D.: Hierarchical ranking of facial attributes. In: Face and Gesture 2011, pp. 36–42. IEEE (2011)
5. Xiong, X., De la Torre, F.: Supervised descent method and its applications to face alignment. In: Computer Vision and Pattern Recognition, pp. 532–539 (2013)
6. Cootes, T.F., Taylor, C.J., Cooper, D.H., et al.: Active shape models—their training and application. Comput. Vis. Image Underst. 61(1), 38–59 (1995)
7. Cootes, T.F., Edwards, G.J., Taylor, C.J., et al.: Active appearance models. IEEE Trans. Pattern Anal. Mach. Intell. 23(6), 681–685 (2001)
8. Cristinacce, D., Cootes, T.F.: Feature detection and tracking with constrained local models. In: British Machine Vision Conference, pp. 929–938 (2006)
9. Dollar, P., Welinder, P., Perona, P., et al.: Cascaded pose regression. In: Computer Vision and Pattern Recognition, pp. 1078–1085 (2010)
10. Cao, X., Wei, Y., Wen, F., et al.: Face alignment by explicit shape regression. Int. J. Comput. Vis. 107(2), 177–190 (2014)
11. Zhu, S., Li, C., Loy, C.C., et al.: Face alignment by coarse-to-fine shape searching. In: Computer Vision and Pattern Recognition, pp. 4998–5006 (2015)
12. Ren, S., Cao, X., Wei, Y., et al.: Face alignment at 3000 FPS via regressing local binary features. In: Computer Vision and Pattern Recognition, pp. 1685–1692 (2014)
13. Sun, Y., Wang, X., Tang, X., et al.: Deep convolutional network cascade for facial point detection. In: Computer Vision and Pattern Recognition, pp. 3476–3483 (2013)
14. Wu, Y., Hassner, T., Kim, K., et al.: Facial landmark detection with tweaked convolutional neural networks. IEEE Trans. Pattern Anal. Mach. Intell. 40(12), 3067–3074 (2018)
15. Zhang, K., Zhang, Z., Li, Z., et al.: Joint face detection and alignment using multitask cascaded convolutional networks. IEEE Signal Process. Lett. 23(10), 1499–1503 (2016)
16. Dong, X., Yan, Y., Ouyang, W., et al.: Style aggregated network for facial landmark detection. In: Computer Vision and Pattern Recognition, pp. 379–388 (2018)
17. Wu, W., Qian, C., Yang, S., et al.: Look at boundary: a boundary-aware face alignment algorithm. In: Computer Vision and Pattern Recognition, pp. 2129–2138 (2018)
18. Zhang, Z., Luo, P., Loy, C.C., Tang, X.: Facial landmark detection by deep multi-task learning. In: Fleet, D., Pajdla, T., Schiele, B., Tuytelaars, T. (eds.) ECCV 2014. LNCS, vol. 8694, pp. 94–108. Springer, Cham (2014). https://doi.org/10.1007/978-3-319-10599-4_7
19. Mnih, V., Heess, N., Graves, A., et al.: Recurrent models of visual attention. In: Neural Information Processing Systems, pp. 2204–2212 (2014)
20. Bahdanau, D., Cho, K., Bengio, Y., et al.: Neural machine translation by jointly learning to align and translate. In: International Conference on Learning Representations (2015)

21. Chen, L., Zhang, H., Xiao, J., et al.: SCA-CNN: spatial and channel-wise attention in convolutional networks for image captioning. In: Computer Vision and Pattern Recognition, pp. 6298–6306 (2017)
22. Simonyan, K., Zisserman, A.: Very deep convolutional networks for large-scale image recognition. In: International Conference on Learning Representations (2015)
23. Zhang, J., Shan, S., Kan, M., Chen, X.: Coarse-to-fine auto-encoder networks (CFAN) for real-time face alignment. In: Fleet, D., Pajdla, T., Schiele, B., Tuytelaars, T. (eds.) ECCV 2014. LNCS, vol. 8690, pp. 1–16. Springer, Cham (2014). https://doi.org/10.1007/978-3-319-10605-2_1
24. Zhao, Z.Q., Zheng, P., Xu, S., Wu, X.: Object detection with deep learning: a review. IEEE Trans. Neural Netw. Learn. Syst. (2018). https://doi.org/10.1109/tnnls.2018.2876865
25. Zhao, Z.Q., Hu, J., Tian, W., Ling, N.: Cooperative adversarial network for accurate super resolution. In: Asian Conference on Computer Vision (ACCV) (2018)

Prediction of Chemical Oxygen Demand in Sewage Based on Support Vector Machine and Neural Network

Jian Zhou[1], Qian-Jing Huang[1], Xiao-Feng Wang[2(✉)], and Le Zou[2]

[1] Department of Environmental Engineering, Hefei University, Hefei 230601, Anhui, China
[2] Anhui Provincial Engineering Laboratory of Big Data Technology Application for Urban Infrastructure, Department of Computer Science and Technology, Hefei University, Hefei 230601, China
xfwang@hfuu.edu.cn

Abstract. Aiming at the problem that the detection accuracy of effluent COD (chemical oxygen demand) in sewage treatment needs to be further improved, a combined model based on support vector machine and neural network is proposed to predict effluent COD. It can reduce the influence of local optimum on the global scope so as to improve the accuracy of prediction. Firstly, the sample data are divided into two categories by support vector machine. Then the BP neural network model and the Echo State Network (ESN) model are established on two sub-samples respectively. Compared with single neural network model, the mean absolute error and root mean square error of combined model are both reduced. Besides, the proposed model has better comprehensive prediction performance and can meet the actual demand of effluent COD prediction in sewage treatment.

Keywords: COD · Support vector machine · BP neural network · Echo State Network

1 Introduction

In the process of sewage treatment, COD (chemical oxygen demand) is an important index to measure the content of organic substances in water. The accurate detection of COD is of great significance to the optimal control of the follow-up sewage treatment system. Due to the complex process of sewage treatment system, there are numerous factors affecting the measurement of effluent COD, such as influent COD, dissolved oxygen concentration, pH value, influent ammonia nitrogen concentration, water load and so on. The traditional COD measurement methods are often difficult to meet the requirements of accuracy, environmental protection, economy and real-time. So, it is necessary to establish a high-quality effluent COD prediction model.

In the 1940s, foreign scholars began to study sewage treatment models. At the end of 1980s, the International Water Quality Association (IAWQ) launched Activated Sludge Model 1 (ASM1) [1] on the basis of previous studies. Since the 21st century, data-driven models have attracted more and more attention. Support Vector Machine

D.-S. Huang et al. (Eds.): ICIC 2019, LNCS 11643, pp. 187–196, 2019.
https://doi.org/10.1007/978-3-030-26763-6_18

(SVM) and Artificial Neural Network (ANN) are the most widely used data-driven models. Huang [2] established the soft-sensing model of effluent BOD (biochemical oxygen demand) and effluent COD in the sewage treatment process by using the least square support vector machine. Further, the particle swarm optimization algorithm was used for global optimization, which made the soft sensing accuracy higher. Xu [3] put forward a model combining fuzzy monotone increasing algorithm with correlation vector machine algorithm, and established the soft sensing prediction model for effluent BOD and COD. Zhang [4] used BP neural network model to predict the dissolved oxygen concentration. Cao [5] used the generalized regression neural network (GRNN) to predict effluent COD. Hu [6] established an online prediction model based on adaptive fuzzy artificial neural network for effluent NH4N-N of A/A/O process. An [7] used the improved BP neural network to predict the dissolved oxygen concentration in sewage. However, the training sample size of the above models are small, the measurement of influent parameters did not take the lag into account. Hence, there might be under-fitting for the massive data, which leads to the poor prediction accuracy in actual application.

Based on activated sludge process [8], this paper presents a prediction model of SVM combined with BP and Echo State Network (ESN) models. Indexes such as influent COD, pH value, ORP (oxidation-reduction potential), influent NH4-N (ammonia nitrogen concentration), TP (total phosphorus), DO (dissolved oxygen) are selected as the input [9] and effluent COD as the output. This model can make the network learn the COD concentration which changes in a certain range, and reduce the influence of local optimum on the global scope. Compared with the single neural network model, the prediction effect of the proposed model is more prominent, which achieves much accurate prediction for effluent COD.

The remaining of this paper is as follows: Sect. 2 describes the modeling process of the combined model based on support vector machine and neural network. In Sect. 3, the model is tested on real data and compared with the single neural network model, which proves the validity of the model. Section 4 summarizes the whole paper.

2   Prediction of Effluent COD Based on Support Vector Machine Combined with Neural Network

In the process of sewage treatment, the effluent COD value sometimes varies greatly, and there are different effluent COD value data with similar water quality. If we use a single neural network, the training data sample may fall into the local minimum, which will affect the accuracy of the final effluent COD value prediction. In this paper, SVM is used to classify the effluent COD firstly, and then the neural network is used to learning the effluent COD concentration changes within a certain range to reduce the impact of local optimum on the global range, so as to improve the prediction performance of the model.

2.1 Data Preprocessing

In this paper, the time series data of each index in sewage data are used. Due to possible influences in the data collecting operation such as abnormal detector, abnormal weather and power failure, incomplete data may be obtained. Since the missing data may contain some important architecture information, the stability of the prediction model and the reliability of the prediction results cannot be guaranteed. Therefore, it is necessary to complete the missing data before establishing the prediction model.

Based on the analysis of the time series characteristics of sewage data, in view of the lack of the time series data, the mean value of n moments before and after is used as the missing data:

$$f(t) = \frac{f(t-n) + f(t-n+1)\ldots + f(t-1) + f(t+1) + f(t+2) + \cdots + f(t+n)}{2n}$$

(1)

where $f(t)$ is the sewage data filling value at the moment of t.

Through correlation analysis of data sample indexes, 7 indexes with relatively strong correlation with effluent COD are selected as input data, which are PH, DO, ORP, influent NH4-N, influent COD, influent TP and cumulative inflow. The output data is effluent COD value. The correlation calculation formula is as follows:

$$R(X, Y) = \frac{\sum_{i=1}^{n}(x_i - \bar{x})(y_i - \bar{y})}{\sqrt{\sum_{i=1}^{n}(x_i - \bar{x})^2}\sqrt{\sum_{i=1}^{n}(y_i - \bar{y})^2}}$$

(2)

Due to the large difference between the input variables of sewage treatment and the different attributes, the training data must be normalized before training. At the last, the inverse normalization operation is performed in the simulation prediction.

The normalization formula is as follows:

$$X^* = \frac{X_i - X_{min}}{X_{max} - X_{min}}$$

(3)

The inverse normalization formula is as follows:

$$X' = X_{min} + X^*(X_{max} - X_{min})$$

(4)

2.2 Construction of Model

The combined model proposed in this paper is based on SVM, BP neural network and echo state network. The construction process of each model will be introduced separately as follows.

2.2.1 Construction of Support Vector Machine Model

Before training the SVM model, the classification threshold was predicted according to the data distribution of effluent COD in the sample. The class whose COD value is lower than the classification threshold is labeled as class '0', and the class whose COD value was higher than the classification threshold is labeled as class '1'. The sample data are divided into training data and test data according to the ratio of 8:2. RBF function is selected as the kernel function of the SVM model. The formula is shown in Eq. (5):

$$k(x, y) = exp\left(\frac{-\|x - y\|^2}{2g^2}\right) \tag{5}$$

In the process of SVM model training, the variation of kernel function coefficient g plays an important role in the distribution dimension of samples in high-dimensional space, which determines the complexity of the optimal classification surface and the dimension of sample space. Error penalty factor C can regulate the confidence interval of SVM and the penalty degree of misjudgment sample data. Therefore, the selection of C and g is of great importance. Here, we select the grid search method for parameter optimization. In the orthogonal coordinate system, the penalty factor C and the parameter g are two coordinate axes respectively. The two parameters changes within a certain range of parameters for a given step. Using cross-validation method [10], the data sets are randomly divided into k groups, one of which is used as test data each time, and the remaining $k - 1$ groups are used as training data. The parameters C and g at that time are used for model training, and the average classification accuracy of K models is obtained. The search range and the search step size are adjusted continuously, selecting the best parameters of cross validation accuracy as optimal parameters.

SVM model is selected here for sewage data classification due to the following advantages: (1) It is based on the principle of structural risk minimization, which avoids over-learning and has strong generalization ability. It can make the classification result of sewage data more reliable. (2) SVM algorithm is eventually transformed into a convex quadratic programming problem, the local optimal solution must be the global optimal solution, which can reduce the influence of the local optimal problem of the neural network method. (3) Sewage data has the characteristics of strong non-linearity. SVM can use inner product kernel function instead of non-linear mapping to high-dimensional space to avoid the 'dimensional disaster'.

2.2.2 Construction of BP Neural Network

BP neural network has the advantages of strong generalization ability and easy adjustment. Thus, it can achieve a good approximation performance to the predicted sample data. It is suitable for sewage treatment modeling because of its good non-linear mapping ability. The modeling process of BP neural network is as follows.

Firstly, the network was initialized. According to the input and output matrix (X, Y), the number of input nodes m, the number of hidden layers n and the number of output nodes q are determined. The weight values w_{ij} and w_{jk} between the input layer, hidden layer and output layer were then initialized. The threshold values of hidden layer and output layer are initially set to $T1$ and $T2$ respectively. The learning rate and excitation function were initially determined.

Here, because the increase of the hidden layer of BP neural network will only increase the training time of the model, resulting in over-fitting state of the model and reducing the prediction accuracy. Therefore, we adopted a three-layer structure of one input layer, one hidden layer and one output layer. According to Kolmogorov theorem, the number of hidden layer nodes is about two times the number of input indicators plus one. The sigmoid function is used in both the excitation function of the hidden layer and the output layer, as shown in formula (6).

$$f(x) = \frac{1}{1+e^{-x}} \tag{6}$$

Then, the output of the hidden layer is as follows:

$$H_j = f\left(\sum_{i=1}^{n} w_{ij}x_i - T1_j\right), j = 1, 2, \cdots, l \tag{7}$$

The output of the output layer is as follows:

$$Y_k = \sum_{j=1}^{l} H_j w_{jk} - T2_k, k = 1, 2, \cdots, m \tag{8}$$

The mean square error of the model is as follows:

$$E_{AV} = \frac{1}{2N} \sum_{j=1}^{N} \sum_{jec} e_j^2(n) \tag{9}$$

The BP neural network model is established on the classified sample class '0'. The selected seven influent indexes are regarded as input, effluent COD as output, 80% of sample class '0' as training data and 20% as prediction data to train the BP neural network.

2.2.3   Construction of Echo State Network

The ESN neural network model is used on the classified sample class '1'. ESN network is a special recursive neural network. Because its hidden layer is composed of a large number of sparsely connected neurons, ESN network has the function of short-term memory. Compared with BP neural network, ESN network is more suitable for time series prediction and has outstanding performance in dealing with complex non-linear system problems. ESN network is composed of input layer, dynamic reservoir (DR) and output layer. The dynamic reservoir is the core part of the network, which is composed of a large number of sparsely connected neurons [11] (usually between 100 and 1000).

Suppose the input vector u(n), the dynamic reservoir state vector x(n) and the output vector y(n) at the moment of n are respectively:

$$u(n) = [u_1(n), u_2(n), \ldots, u_K(n)]^T$$
$$x(n) = [x_1(n), x_2(n), \ldots, x_N(n)]^T \tag{10}$$
$$y(n) = [y_1(n), y_2(n), \ldots, y_L(n)]^T$$

Then the state update equation and output update equation of the neural network are as follows respectively:

$$x(n+1) = f(W_{in}u(n+1) + Wx(n) + W_{back}y(n)) \tag{11}$$

$$y(n+1) = f^{out}(W_{out}u(n+1), x(n), y(n)) \tag{12}$$

Here, f is the activation function of neurons in the hidden layer, usually being sigmoid function shown in formula (6). f^{out} is the activation function of the output layer, which is generally taken as a linear function. W_{in} are the connection weights from input layer to hidden layer. W are the connection weights of neurons in the hidden layer. W_{out} are the connection weights from the hidden layer to the output layer. W_{back} are the connection weights from the output layer to the hidden layer.

Among the parameters of the ESN neural network, only the connection weights from the hidden layer to the output layer need to be adjusted by learning algorithm, and the connection weights of other layers are fixed and kept unchanged by randomly assigning initial values at the beginning of training process. In order to ensure the echo characteristics of the network, the dynamic reservoir must be kept at a sparsity of 1%–5%, and the spectral radius γ of its weight matrix W is less than 1.

PH, DO, ORP, influent NH4-N, influent COD, influent TP and cumulative inflow of the sample class '1' are selected as input, effluent COD as output, 80% of sample class '1' as training data and 20% as prediction data to train the ESN model.

Set the number of neurons in the dynamic reservoir as 300 and the ESN network structure is 7-300-1. The spectral radius is set to 0.6. W_{in}, W and W_{back} are randomly initialized. The training process only needs to adjust the connection weight of output layer W_{out}, and the adjustment of W_{out} can be realized by least square method.

The root mean square error RMSE and mean absolute error MAE are used to evaluate the model:

$$RMSE = \left(\frac{1}{n}\sum_{i=1}^{n} (y_i - y_{testi})^2\right)^{\frac{1}{2}} \tag{13}$$

$$MAE = \frac{1}{n}\sum_{i=1}^{n} |y_i - y_{testi}| \tag{14}$$

2.2.4   Structure of the Combined Model

The complete structure of the combined model proposed in this paper is shown in Fig. 1. For the data to be predicted, the selected seven characteristic indexes are used as input. Firstly, the trained SVM model is used to classify the data. Then, according to the classification situation, the trained BP neural network or ESN neural network is used to obtain the predicted the effluent COD value. BP neural network is suitable for the treatment of sewage treatment process with complicated internal mechanism because of its strong non-linear mapping ability. ESN can be used in time series prediction data because of its short-term memory characteristics.

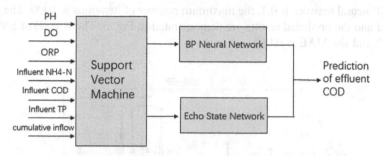

Fig. 1. Structure of the combined model

3 Results and Analysis

The experimental data in this paper are from the sewage index data of a sewage treatment plant in Hefei City from January 1 to January 18 in 2017. The data were collected every minute, and a total of 25,920 groups of sample data were collected. In order to estimate the classification threshold of effluent COD and train SVM, the distribution of effluent COD data from original data is shown in Fig. 2.

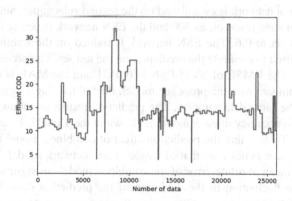

Fig. 2. Distribution of effluent COD data

Based on the data distribution of COD in effluent, we use the average value of effluent COD 12.4 mg/L as the classification threshold. The range of the penalty factor C and the kernel function parameter g is initialized as [log − 2, log2] by the grid search method. The initial parameters are divided into 10 parts on average, and the best parameter pairs were obtained through cross validation. When the final results C = 100 and g = 0.599 is achieved, the classification accuracy of the test set reached the best 94.12%.

A three-layer BP neural network is then established on the first sub-sample, and the number of nodes in the hidden layer is determined as 17 according to the input layer. That is, the structure of the established BP neural network is 7-15-1. The initial learning rate of BP neural network is 0.1, the maximum number of iterations is 1000. The model is trained and the predicted results are demonstrated in Fig. 3. The RMSE of SVM-BP is 0.1102 and the MAE is 0.067.

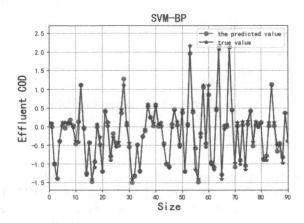

Fig. 3. Prediction results of SVM-BP

The ESN neural network is established on the second subsample. Set the number of neurons in the dynamic reservoir as 300 and the ESN network structure is 8-300-1. The spectral radius is set to 0.6. The ESN network is trained on the training set, and the trained model is used to continue the prediction on the test set. The predicted results are shown in Fig. 4. The RMSE of SVM-ESN is 0.0851 and the MAE is 0.062.

In order to compare with the proposed model, the trained single neural network are used to predict the same data samples. The prediction results are shown in Fig. 5.

The prediction accuracy of each model is shown in the Table 1. It can be seen from Figs. 3, 4, 5 and Table 1 that the prediction effect of combined model based on SVM and neural network is better than that of single neural network model. The root mean square error and mean absolute error of the combined model are significantly reduced. There is no large fluctuation in the deviation of the prediction data. Because of the advantages of ESN in processing time series, the performance of the model is better than that of BP neural network. Since the SVM algorithm is eventually transformed into a convex quadratic programming problem with linear constraints, the local optimal solution must be the global optimal solution, which can reduce the influence of the local optimal problem of the neural network method. Besides, SVM has good generalization performance. Therefore, the combined model of SVM and neural network proposed in this paper has achieved better prediction effect.

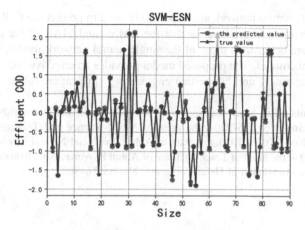

Fig. 4. Prediction results of SVM-ESN

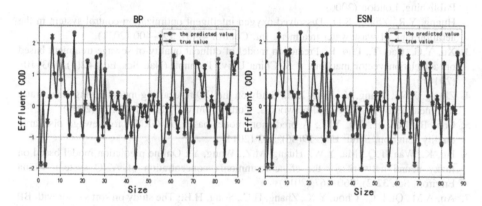

Fig. 5. Prediction results of single neural network

Table 1. RSME and MAE Comparison

	RMSE	MAE
SVM-BP	0.1102	0.067
SVM-ESN	0.0851	0.062
BP	0.1452	0.084
ESN	0.1411	0.082

4 Conclusion

In order to solve the problem of local optimum and contradictory data in the learning process of neural network and improve the prediction accuracy for effluent COD, a combined model based on SVM and neural network is proposed. SVM is used to conduct dichotomous classification of COD concentration data, and then BP neural network and ESN neural network are respectively used to predict the COD value of the water. The experimental results show that the RMSE and MAE of the proposed prediction models are better than those of the single neural network model, which proves the validity of this model. The proposed model provides an effective solution to predict effluent COD accurately and has certain engineering application value.

Acknowledgements. This work was supported by the grant of the National Natural Science Foundation of China, No. 61672204, the grant of Major Science and Technology Project of Anhui Province, No. 17030901026, the grant of Anhui Provincial Natural Science Foundation, No. 1908085MF184, the grant of Teaching Team of Anhui Province, No. 2016jxtd101, the grant of Natural Science Foundation of Hefei University, No. 0391648022.

References

1. Henzm, M.: Activated Sludge Models ASM1, ASM2, ASM2d and ASM3, pp. 13–15. IW-A Publishing, London (2000)
2. Huang, Y.R., Zhang, S.D.: Dissolved oxygen intelligent optimization control system in the aeration tank of wastewater treatment. Inf. Control **40**(3), 393–400 (2011)
3. Xu, Y.G., Cao, T., Luo, F.: Prediction model of effluent quality of sewage treatment based on correlation vector machine. J. S. China Univ. Technol. (Nat. Sci. Ed.) **42**(5), 103–108 (2014)
4. Zhang, X.W., Wang, Y., Feng, L.H.: Study on the DO forecasting model during wastewater treatment based on BP neural network. J. Yunnan Univ. **31**(S2), 103–105 (2009)
5. Cao, B., Luo, F., Xu, Y.G.: A prediction model based on GRNN for sewage discharge quality. Environ. Sanit. Eng. **19**(S6), 1–3 (2011)
6. Hu, K., Wan, T.Q., Ma, Y.W., Huang, M.Z., Wang, Y.: Online prediction model based on fuzzy neural network for the effluent ammonia concentration of A2/O system. China Environ. Sci. **32**(2), 260–267 (2012)
7. An, A.M., Qi, L.C., Chou, Y.X., Zhang, H.C., Song, H.B.: The study on soft sensor with BP neural network and its application to dissolved oxygen concentration. Comput. Appl. Chem. **33**(S1), 117–121 (2016)
8. Gu, R.N.: On treatment method of urban domestic sewage in China. Environ. Prot. **09**, 46–47 (2001)
9. Lu, R.L.: Several often neglected technical problems affecting chemical oxygen demand (COD) in wastewater biochemical treatment. Green Technol. **2015**(8), 227–228 (2015)
10. Yang, Z.X., Tian, Y.J., Deng, N.Y.: Leave-one-out bounds for support vector ordinal regression machine. Neural Comput. Appl. **15**, 750–782 (2009)
11. Jaeger, H., Haas, H.: Harnessing nonlinearity: predicting chaotic system and saving energy in wireless tele-communication. Science **304**(5667), 78–80 (2004)

Relaxed 2-D Principal Component Analysis by L_p Norm for Face Recognition

Xiao Chen[1], Zhigang Jia[1(⊠)], Yunfeng Cai[2], and Meixiang Zhao[1]

[1] Jiangsu Normal University, Xuzhou 221116, China
zhgjia@jsnu.edu.cn
[2] Cognitive Computing Lab, Baidu Research, Beijing 100193, China

Abstract. A relaxed two-dimensional principal component analysis (R2DPCA) approach is proposed for face recognition. Different to the 2DPCA, 2DPCA-L_1 and G2DPCA, the R2DPCA utilizes the label information (if known) of training samples to calculate a relaxation vector and presents a weight to each subset of training data. A new relaxed scatter matrix is defined and the computed projection axes are able to increase the accuracy of face recognition. The optimal L_p-norms are selected in a reasonable range. Numerical experiments on practical face databased indicate that the R2DPCA has high generalization ability and can achieve a higher recognition rate than state-of-the-art methods.

Keywords: Face recognition · G2DPCA · Relaxed 2DPCA · Optimal algorithms · Generalized total scatter criterion

1 Introduction

The principal component analysis (PCA) [1, 2], has become one of the most powerful approaches of face recognition [2–6]. Recently, many robust PCA (RPCA) algorithms are proposed with improving the quadratic formulation, which renders PCA vulnerable to noises, into L_1-norm on the objection function, e.g., L_1-PCA [7], R_1-PCA [8], and PCA-L_1 [9]. Meanwhile, sparsity is also introduced into PCA algorithms, resulting in a series of sparse PCA (SPCA) algorithms [10–13]. A newly proposed robust SPCA (RSPCA) [14] further applies L_1-norm both in objective and constraint functions of PCA, inheriting the merits of robustness and sparsity. Observing that L_2-, L_1-, and L_0-norms are all special L_p-norm, it is natural to impose L_p-norm on the objection or/and constraint functions, straightforwardly; see PCA-L_p [15] and generalized PCA (GPCA) [16] for instance.

To preserve the spatial structure of face images, two-dimensional PCA (2DPCA), proposed by Yang et al. [17], represents face images with two-dimensional matrices rather than one-dimensional vectors. The computational problems bases on 2DPCA are of much smaller scale than those based on traditional PCA, and the difficulties caused by low rank are also avoided.

© Springer Nature Switzerland AG 2019
D.-S. Huang et al. (Eds.): ICIC 2019, LNCS 11643, pp. 197–207, 2019.
https://doi.org/10.1007/978-3-030-26763-6_19

This image-as-matrix method offers insights for improving above RSPCA, PCA-L_p, GPCA, etc. As typical examples, the L_1-norm-based 2DPCA (2DPCA-L_1) [18] and 2DPCA-L_1 with sparsity (2DPCAL$_1$-S) [19] are improvements of PCA-L_1 and RSPCA, respectively, and the generalized 2DPCA (G2DPCA) [20] imposes L_p-norm on both objective and constraint functions of 2DPCA. Recently, the quaternion 2DPCA is proposed in [21] and applied to color face recognition, where the red, green and blue channels of a color image is encoded as three imaginary parts of a pure quaternion matrix. To arm the quaternion 2DPCA with the generalization ability, Zhao, Jia and Gong [22] proposed the sample-relaxed quaternion 2DPCA with applying the label information (if known) of training samples. The structure-preserving algorithms of quaternion eigenvalue decomposition and singular value decomposition can be found in [23–30]. More applications of the quaternion representation and structure-preserving methods to color image processing can be found in [31] and [32].

Both PCA and 2DPCA are unsupervised methods and omit the potential or known label information of samples. They are often applied to the training set and thus the computed projections will maximize the scatter of projected training samples. That means the scatter of projected testing samples are not surely optimal, and certainly, so are the whole (training and testing) projected samples. Inspired by this observation, we proposed a new relaxation two-dimensional principal component analysis (R2DPCA) in this paper. R2DPCA sufficiently utilizes the labels (if known) of training samples, and can enhance the total scatter of whole projected samples. This approach is a generalization of G2DPCA [20], and will reduce to G2DPCA if the label information is unknown or unused.

The rest of this paper is organized as follows. In Sect. 2, we present a new relaxed two-dimensional principal component analysis (R2DPCA) approach for face recognition. In Sect. 3, we compare the R2DPCA with the state-to-the-art approaches, and indicate the efficiencies of the R2DPCA. In Sect. 4, we sum up the contribution of this paper.

2   The Relaxed 2DPCA by L_p Norm

In this section, we introduce a relaxed two-dimensional principal component analysis (R2DPCA) method by L_p-norm. R2DPCA includes three parts: relaxation vector generation, objective function relaxation, and projection relaxation.

2.1 Relaxation Vector

Suppose that training samples $X_1, X_2, \ldots, X_n \in R^{h \times w}$ can be partitioned into m classes and each class contains n_j samples:

$$X_1^1, \cdots, X_{n_1}^1 | X_1^2, \cdots, X_{n_2}^2 | \cdots | X_1^m, \cdots, X_{n_m}^m,$$

where X_i^j denotes the i-th sample of the j-th class, $i = 1, \ldots, n_j$, $j = 1, \ldots, m$. Define the mean of training samples from the j-th class as $M_j = \frac{1}{n_j} \sum_{i=1}^{n_j} X_i^j \in R^{h \times w}$, and the j-th within-class covariance matrix of the training set as

$$C_j = \frac{1}{n_j} \sum_{i=1}^{n_j} \left(X_i^j - M_j \right)^T \left(X_i^j - M_j \right) \in R^{w \times w}, \tag{1}$$

where $j = 1, \ldots, m$, $\sum_{j=1}^{m} n_j = n$ and $i = 1, \ldots, n_j$. The within-class covariance matrix C_j is a symmetric and positive semi-definite matrix. Its maximal eigenvalue, denoted by $\lambda_{max}(C_j)$, represents the variance of training samples $X_1^j, \ldots, X_{n_j}^j$ in the principal component. In general, the larger $\lambda_{max}(C_j)$ is, the better scattered of the training samples of j-th class are. A very small $\lambda_{max}(C_j)$ indicates that $X_1^j, \ldots, X_{n_j}^j$ are not well scattered samples to represent the j-th class. Extremely, if $\lambda_{max}(C_j) = 0$ then all of training samples from the j-th class are same, and then the contribution of the j-th class to the covariance matrix of training set should be controlled by a small factor. To this aim, we define a *relaxation vector* of training classes,

$$\mathbf{v} = [v_1, \cdots, v_m]^T \in R^m, \tag{2}$$

where $v_j = \frac{f(\lambda_{max}(C_j))}{\sum_{i=1}^{m} f(\lambda_{max}(C_i))}$ is a relaxation factor of the j-th class with a function, $f : R \rightarrow R^+$. A relaxation factor of each training sample of j-th class is defined as v_j/n_j.

2.2 Objective Function Relaxation

Let **M** denote the mean of training samples, i.e.,

$$\mathbf{M} = \frac{1}{n} \sum_{i=1}^{n} X_i = \frac{1}{n} \sum_{j=1}^{m} \sum_{i=1}^{n_j} X_i^j.$$

With computed relaxation vector $\mathbf{v} = [v_1, \cdots, v_m]^T$ in Sect. 2.1, we define a *relaxed criterion* as

$$J(\mathbf{w}) = \gamma \mathbf{G} + (1-\gamma)\tilde{\mathbf{G}}, \tag{3}$$

where $\gamma \in [0,1]$ is a relaxation parameter, $\mathbf{w} \in R^w$ is a unit vector under L_p norm, $\mathbf{G} := \sum_{i=1}^{n} \left\| (X_i - M)w \right\|_s^s$ and $\tilde{\mathbf{G}} := \sum_{j=1}^{m} \sum_{i=1}^{n_j} \left\| \frac{v_j}{n_j}(X_i^j - M)w \right\|_s^s$. R2DPCA finds its first projection vector $\mathbf{w} \in R^w$ by solving the optimization problem with equality constraints:

$$\max_{w \in R^w} J(w), \, s.t. \|w\|_p^p = 1, \tag{4}$$

where the criterion $J(\mathbf{w})$ is defined as in (3). Notice that (4) reduces to (8) if $\gamma = 1$, and thus, the first projection vector of R2DPCA is the same as that of G2DPCA. When $\gamma = 0$, (4) is simplified as

$$\max_{w \in R^w} \sum_{j=1}^{m} \sum_{i=1}^{n_j} \left\| \frac{v_j}{n_j}(X_i^j - M)w \right\|_s^s, \, s.t. \|w\|_p^p = 1. \tag{5}$$

If first j projection vectors $\mathbf{W} = [w_1, w_2, \ldots, w_j]$ have been obtained, the $(j+1)$-th projection vector w_{j+1} can be calculated similarly on the deflated samples [33]:

$$X_i^{deflated} = X_i(I - WW^T), i = 1, 2, \ldots, n. \tag{6}$$

From each iterative step, we also obtain a maximized objective function value corresponding to w_j,

$$f_j = \gamma \sum_{i=1}^{n} \left\| (X_i - M)^{deflated} w_j \right\|_s^s + (1-\gamma) \sum_{j=1}^{m} \sum_{i=1}^{n_j} \left\| \frac{v_j}{n_j}(X_i^j - M)^{deflated} w_j \right\|_s^s.$$

With the relaxed criterion defined in (3), first r optimal projection vectors of R2DPCA solve the optimal problem with equality constraints:

$$\{w_1, \ldots, w_r\} = \arg \max J(w), \quad s.t. \begin{cases} \|w_i\|_p^p = 1, \\ w_i^T w_j = 0, i \neq j, \end{cases} i, j = 1, \cdots, r. \tag{7}$$

We propose Algorithm 3.1 to compute first r optimal projection vectors and corresponding optimal objective function values.

Algorithm 3.1. (R2DPCA)

Require: $X_1, X_2, \cdots, X_n$, $s \in [1, \infty)$, $p \in (0, \infty]$, r, m, w, γ, $n_1, \ldots, n_m$, tol.

Ensure: $W = [w_1, \cdots, w_r]$, $D = diag(f_1, \cdots, f_r)$.

   Initialize $W = [\ ]$, $D = [\ ]$. $v = relaxvec(X_1, X_2, \cdots, X_n, m, w)$.

   Homogenized training samples.

   for $t = 1, 2, \cdots, r$ **do**

      Initialize $k = 0$, $\delta = 1$, *arbitrary* w^0 *with* $\|w^0\|_p = 1$.

$$f_0 = \gamma \sum_{i=1}^{n} \|X_i w^0\|_s^s + (1 - \gamma) \sum_{j=1}^{m} \sum_{j=1}^{n_j} \|\frac{v_j}{n_j} X_i^j w^0\|_s^s.$$

      While $\delta > tol$ *do*

$$v^k = \gamma \sum_{i=1}^{n} X_i^T \left[|X_i w^k|^{s-1} \circ sign(X_i w^k) \right] +$$

$$(1 - \gamma) \sum_{j=1}^{m} \sum_{j=1}^{n_j} (\frac{v_j}{n_j} X_i^j)^T \left[\left|\frac{v_j}{n_j} X_i^j w^k\right|^{s-1} \circ sign\left(\frac{v_j}{n_j} X_i^j w^k\right) \right].$$

      Case 1: $0 < p < 1$. $u^k = |w^k|^{2-p} \circ v^k$, $w^{k+1} = \dfrac{u^k}{\|u^k\|_p}$.

      Case 2: $p=1$. $j = arg\,max_{i \in [1,w]} |v_i^k|$, $\quad w_i^{k+1} = \begin{cases} sign(v_j^k), i = j, \\ 0, i \neq j. \end{cases}$

      Case 3: $1 < p < \infty$. $q = p/(p-1)$, $u^k = |v^k|^{q-1} \circ sign(v^k)$,

$$w^{k+1} = \frac{u^k}{\|u^k\|_p}.$$

      Case 4: $p = \infty$. $w^{k+1} = sign(v^k)$.

$$f_{k+1} = \gamma \sum_{i=1}^{n} \|X_i w^{k+1}\|_s^s + (1 - \gamma) \sum_{j=1}^{m} \sum_{j=1}^{n_j} \|\frac{v_j}{n_j} X_i w^{k+1}\|_s^s.$$

      $\delta = |f_{k+1} - f_k|/|f_k|$.

      $k \leftarrow k + 1$.

   end while

   $W \leftarrow [W, w^k]$. $D = diag(D, f_k)$. $X_i = X_i(I - WW^T), i = 1, 2, \cdots, n$.

   end for

2.3 Projection Relaxation

In Sect. 2.2, we obtain r pairs of optimal values and projection vectors: $(f_1, w_1), \ldots, (f_r, w_r)$. Define the *feature image* of X_i under W as

$$P_i = (X_i - M)W \in R^{w \times r}, i = 1, \cdots, n. \tag{8}$$

Each column of P_i is called the *principal component (vector)*. Now we use a nearest neighbor classifier for face recognition. For a given testing sample $\mathbf{X}$, compute its feature image, $\mathbf{P} = (\mathbf{X} - \mathbf{M})\mathbf{W}$. Find out the nearest training sample $X_i(1 \leq i \leq n)$ whose feature image minimizes $||(P_i - P)D||_2$. Such X_i is output as the person to be recognized.

The distance, $||(P_i - P)D||_2 = ||(X_i - X)WD||_2$, is called *relaxed distance* between X_i and $\mathbf{X}$. Compared with originally defined distance, such as in [20], each projection axe w_j is relaxed by f_j in classification process, $j = 1, \cdots, r$.

2.4   Mathematical Theory of R2DPCA

R2DPCA is a generalization of G2DPCA [20]. As one of PCA-based methods, G2DPCA does not use the labels of data which possibly can impair class discrimination. To improve this, R2DPCA utilizes labels of training samples and variances within class to generate a relaxation vector, computes optimal projections maximizing the relaxes criterion, and thus enhances the class discrimination.

The working principle of R2DPCA can be clearly explained through a special case that p = s = 2. The relaxed criterion with L_2-norm is also called *generalized total scatter criterion*, and has the form:

$$J(W) = trace\left(W^T \left(\gamma G + (1 - \gamma)\tilde{G}\right)W\right) = \sum_{i=1}^r w_i^T \left(\gamma G + (1 - \gamma)\tilde{G}\right)w_i, \tag{9}$$

where

$$G = \frac{1}{n} \sum_{i=1}^n (X_i - M)^T (X_i - M), \quad \tilde{G} = \sum_{j=1}^m \left(\frac{v_j}{n_j} \sum_{i=1}^{n_j} (X_i^j - M)^T (X_i^j - M)\right),$$

and $W = [w_1, \ldots w_r]$ has orthogonal columns and each column is unitary under L_p-norm, v_j is the j-th element of the relaxation vector $\mathbf{v}$. Here $\sum_{j=1}^m n_j = n$. Let $W^{opt} = \left[w_1^{opt}, \ldots, w_r^{opt}\right]$ be the optimal projection, where $w_1^{opt}, \ldots, w_r^{opt}$ solve the optimal problem (7). These optimal projection axes are in fact the orthogonal eigenvectors of $\gamma G + (1 - \gamma)\tilde{G}$ corresponding to first r largest eigenvalues. Since the matrix $\gamma G + (1 - \gamma)\tilde{G}$ is symmetric and positive semi-definite, J(W) is nonnegative.

3   Experiments

In this section, we present numerical experiments to compare the proposed relaxed two-dimensional principle component analysis by L_p-norm (R2DPCA) with state-of-the-art algorithms on face recognition. Three famous databases are utilized:

(a)   Faces95 database (1440 images from 72 subjects, twenty images per subject),
(b)   Color Feret database (3025 images from 275 subjects, eleven images per subject),

(c) Grey Feret database (1400 images from 200 subjects, seven images per subject).

All of face images are cropped and resized, and each image is of 80×80 size. The numerical experiments are performed with MATLAB-R2016 on a personal computer with Intel(R) Xeon(R) CPU E5-2630 v3 @ 2.4 GHz (dual processor) and RAM 32 GB.

Example 3.1. In this experiment, we compare R2DPCA with 2DPCA, 2DPCAL$_1$, 2DPCAL$_1$-S, and G2DPCA. We randomly select 10 and 5 images of each person from Faces95 database and Color Feret face database as the training set, respectively, and the remaining as the testing set. As in [20] we set

$$\Omega = \{(s,p)|s = 1.0:0.1:3.0, \, p = 0.9:0.1:3.0\}$$

for G2DPCA and R2DPCA. The parameter ρ of 2DPCAL$_1$-S relates to the λ in [10] via $\lambda = 10^{-\rho}$ is tuned, consistent with [19]. The optimal ρ value is selected from $[-3.0:0.1:3.0]$. Here, the relaxed parameter of criterion in (3) is set as $\gamma = 0$ and the number of eigenfaces is fixed as $r = 10$.

The face recognition rate (Accuracy) and corresponding optimal parameter are listed in Table 1. The reasonable trend of the classification accuracies according to different choices of s and p is presented in Fig. 1. These numerical results indicate that R2DPCA performs better than other four state-of-art algorithms.

Table 1. Classification accuracies of five algorithms

Algorithms	Optimal parameters		Accuracy	
	Faces95	Color Feret	Faces95	Color Feret
2DPCA	-	-	0.8729	0.5982
2DPCA-L$_1$	-	-	0.8708	0.5985
2DPCAL$_1$-S	$\rho = -0.5$	$\rho = -0.3$	0.8785	0.6236
G2DPCA	$s = 2.7, p = 2.2$	$s = 2.8, p = 2.6$	0.9451	0.6918
R2DPCA ($\gamma = 0$)	$s = 1, p = 2.2$	$s = 3, p = 2.2$	**0.9493**	**0.7085**

Example 3.2. In this experiment, we research the effort of the parameter γ of R2DPCA on the classification accuracy. The first 10 and 5 images of each person are selected as the training sets of the Faces95 and Color/Gray Feret face databases, respectively; and $r = 10$ features are selected.

The results with several representative values γ are shown in Tables 2 and 3. We can see that the Faces95 and Color Feret databases are not sensitive to γ, and however, we can see the validity of the parameters γ on the Gray Feret database.

Example 3.3. In this experiment, we test the effect of numbers of chosen features on the classification accuracy. We randomly select 10, 5 images of each subject as training samples and the remaining as testing samples on the Faces95 and Color Feret databases, respectively. The whole procedure is repeated two times and the average accuracies are listed. Based on the optimal parameters s, p of R2DPCA with $\gamma = 0$ in Example 3.1, we set $s = 1$, $p = 2.2$ and $s = 3$, $p = 2.2$.

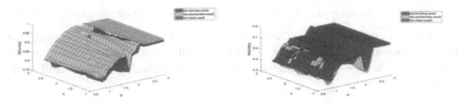

Fig. 1. Classification accuracies with s, p on Faces95 (left) and Color Feret (right).

Table 2. Classification accuracies according to different γ on Faces95 and Color Feret.

Database	γ	Optimal parameters	Accuracy
Faces95	0:1/4:1	s = 1.1, p = 2.2	**0.8861**
Color Feret	0:1/4:3/4	s = 3, p = 2.2	0.7673
	1	s = 3, p = 2.2	**0.7733**

Table 3. Classification accuracies according to different γ on Gray Feret.

γ	Optimal parameters	Accuracy
0	s = 1.8, p = 1.7	0.6075
1/4	s = 1.9, p = 1.7	0.6075
1/2	s = 2.3, p = 1.6	**0.6112**
3/4	s = 2.4, p = 1.6	0.6088
1	s = 2.6, p = 1.8	0.5837

In Fig. 2, we show the classification accuracies of G2DPCA and R2DPCA with different feature numbers in the range of $[1, 30]$ on the Faces95 database and Color Feret database, respectively. From these results, we can see that the classification accuracies of R2DPCA are higher and more stable than G2DPCA. When $k = 1$ the classification accuracies of G2DPCA and R2DPCA are the same, which consists to the theory.

Example 3.4. We test the accuracies of the Gray Feret database with the number of training samples in this example. We randomly select $tr = 3$ trainimg samples from each subject and the remaining images as testing samples, and choose 10 feature numbers. In order to be consistent with the previous experimental parameters, we set $\gamma = 0$. The classification accuracies are shown in Fig. 3. We can see that the classification accuracies of relaxed versions are higher than those in original versions.

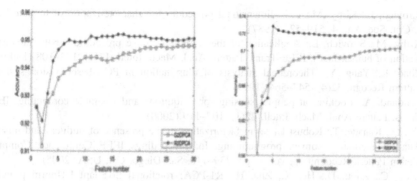

Fig. 2. Classification accuracies of R2DPCA and G2DPCA with k = 1:30 on Faces95 (left) and Color Feret (right).

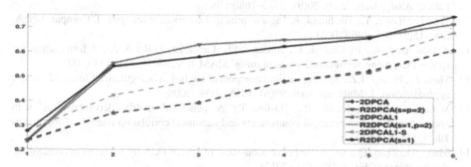

Fig. 3. Accuracy with the number of training samples on Gray Feret database.

4 Conclusion

In this paper, we present a relaxed two-dimensional principal component analysis (R2DPCA) approach for face recognition, with applying the label information of the training data. The R2DPCA is a generalization of 2DPCA, 2DPCA-L$_1$ and G2DPCA, and has higher generalization ability. Since utilizing the label information, the R2DPCA can be seen as a new supervised projection method, but it is totally different to the two-dimensional linear discriminant analysis (2DLDA) [34, 35]. In future, we will consider the comparison between R2DPCA and LDA and generalize the TV-Stokes model in [36, 37] into quaternion skew field for color images restoration.

Acknowledgments. This paper is supported in part by National Natural Science Foundation of China under grant 11771188.

References

1. Jolliffe, I.: Principal Component Analysis. Springer, New York (2004)
2. Turk, M., Pentland, A.: Eigenfaces for recognition. J. Cogn. Neurosci. **3**(1), 71–86 (1991)

3. Sirovich, L., Kirby, M.: Low-dimensional procedure for characterization of human faces. J. Opt. Soc. Am. **4**, 519–524 (1987)
4. Kirby, M., Sirovich, L.: Application of the Karhunen-Loeve procedure for the characterization of human faces. IEEE Trans. Pattern Anal. Mach. Intell. **12**(1), 103–108 (1990)
5. Zhao, L., Yang, Y.: Theoretical analysis of illumination in PCA-based vision systems. Pattern Recogn. **32**(4), 547–564 (1999)
6. Pentland, A.: Looking at people: sensing for ubiquitous and wearable computing. IEEE Trans. Pattern Anal. Mach. Intell. **22**(1), 107–119 (2000)
7. Ke, Q., Kanade, T.: Robust L_1 norm factorization in the presence of outliters and missing data by alternative convex programming. In: Proceedings IEEE Conference Computer Vision Pattern Recognition, vol. 1, pp. 739–746, San Diego, CA, USA (2005)
8. Ding, C., Zhou, D., He, X., Zha, H.: R1-PCA: rotational invariant L1-norm principal component analysis for robust subspace factorization. In: Proceedings 23rd International Conference Machine Learning, pp. 281–288, Pittsburgh, PA, USA (2006)
9. Kwak, N.: Principal component analysis based on L_1-norm maximization. IEEE Trans. Pattern Anal. Mach. Intell. **30**(9), 1672–1680 (2008)
10. Zou, H., Hastie, T., Tibshirani, R.: Sparse principal component analysis. J. Comput. Graph. Stat. **15**(2), 265–286 (2006)
11. d'Aspremont, A., El Ghaoui, L., Jordan, M.I., Lanckriet, G.R.: A direct formulation for sparse PCA using semidefinite programming. SIAM Rev. **49**(3), 434–448 (2007)
12. Shen, H., Huang, J.Z.: Sparse principal component analysis via regularized low rank matrix approximation. J. Multivar. Anal. **99**(6), 1015–1034 (2008)
13. Witten, D.M., Tibshirani, R., Hastie, T.: A penalized matrix decomposition, with applications to sparse principal components and canonical correlation analysis. Biostatistics **10**(3), 515–534 (2009)
14. Meng, D., Zhao, Q., Xu, Z.: Improve robustness of sparse PCA by L_1-norm maximization. Pattern Recogn. **45**(1), 487–497 (2012)
15. Kwak, N.: Principal component analysis by L_p-norm maximization. IEEE Trans. Cybern. **44**(5), 594–609 (2014)
16. Liang, Z., Xia, S., Zhou, Y., Zhang, L., Li, Y.: Feature extraction based on L_p-norm generalized principal component analysis. Pattern Recogn. Lett. **34**(9), 1037–1045 (2013)
17. Yang, J., Zhang, D., Frangi, A.F., Yang, J.Y.: Two-dimensional PCA: a new approach to appearance-based face representation and recognition. IEEE Trans. Pattern Anal. Mach. Intell. **26**(1), 131–137 (2004)
18. Li, X., Pang, Y., Yuan, Y.: L_1-norm-based 2DPCA. IEEE Trans. Syst. Man Cybern. B Cybern. **40**(4), 1170–1175 (2010)
19. Wang, H., Wang, J.: 2DPCA with L_1-norm for simultaneously robust and sparse modelling. Neural Netw. **46**, 190–198 (2013)
20. Wang, J.: Generalized 2-D principal component analysis by L_p-Norm for image analysis. IEEE Trans. Cybern. **46**(3), 792–803 (2016)
21. Jia, Z.-G., Ling, S.-T., Zhao, M.-X.: Color two-dimensional principal component analysis for face recognition based on quaternion model. In: Huang, D.-S., Bevilacqua, V., Premaratne, P., Gupta, P. (eds.) ICIC 2017. LNCS, vol. 10361, pp. 177–189. Springer, Cham (2017). https://doi.org/10.1007/978-3-319-63309-1_17
22. Zhao, M., Jia, Z., Gong, D.: Sample-relaxed two-dimensional color principal component analysis for face recognition and image reconstruction. arXiv.org/cs/arXiv:1803.03837v1 (2018)
23. Jia, Z., Wei, M., Ling, S.: A new structure-preserving method for quaternion Hermitian eigenvalue problems. J. Comput. Appl. Math. **239**, 12–24 (2013)

24. Ma, R., Jia, Z., Bai, Z.: A structure-preserving Jacobi algorithm for quaternion Hermitian eigenvalue problems. Comput. Math Appl. **75**(3), 809–820 (2018)
25. Jia, Z., Ma, R., Zhao, M.: A new structure-preserving method for recognition of color face images. Comput. Sci. Artif. Intell. 427–432 (2017)
26. Jia, Z., Wei, M., Zhao, M., Chen, Y.: A new real structure-preserving quaternion QR algorithm. J. Comput. Appl. Math. **343**, 26–48 (2018)
27. Jia, Z., Cheng, X., Zhao, M.: A new method for roots of monic quaternionic quadratic polynomial. Comput. Math Appl. **58**(9), 1852–1858 (2009)
28. Jia, Z., Wang, Q., Wei, M.: Procrustes problems for (P, Q, η)-reflexive matrices. J. Comput. Appl. Math. **233**(11), 3041–3045 (2010)
29. Zhao, M., Jia, Z.: Structured least-squares problems and inverse eigenvalue problems for (P, Q)-reflexive matrices. Appl. Math. Comput. **235**, 87–93 (2014)
30. Jia, Z., Ng, M.K., Song, G.: Lanczos method for large-scale quaternion singular value decomposition. Numer. Algorithms (2018). https://doi.org/10.1007/s11075-018-0621-0
31. Jia, Z., Ng, M.K., Song, G.: Robust quaternion matrix completion with applications to image inpainting. Numer. Linear Algebra Appl. (2019). https://doi.org/10.1002/nla.2245. http://www.math.hkbu.edu.hk/∼mng/quaternion.html
32. Jia, Z., Ng, M.K., Wang, W.: Color image restoration by saturation-value (SV) total variation. SIAM J. Imaging Sci. (2019). http://www.math.hkbu.edu.hk/∼mng/publications.html
33. Mackey, L.: Deflation methods for sparse PCA. Proceedings Advances in Neural Information Processing Systems 21, pp. 1017–1024, Whistler, BC, Canada(2008)
34. Ye, J.: Characterization of a family of algorithms for generalized discriminant analysis on undersampled problems. Mach. Learn. Res. **6**, 483–502 (2005)
35. Liang, Z.Z., Li, Y.F., Shi, P.F.: A note on two-dimensional linear discriminant analysis. Pattern Recogn. Lett. **29**, 2122–2128 (2008)
36. Chang, Q., Jia, Z.: New fast algorithms for a modified TV-Stokes model. Sci. Sinica Math. **44**(12), 1323–1336 (2014). (in Chinese)
37. Jia, Z., Wei, M.: A new TV-Stokes model for image deblurring and denoising with fast algorithms. J. Sci. Comput. **72**(2), 522–541 (2017)

Palm Recognition Using the Adaptive LWT Based Sparse Representation Method

Li Shang[1(✉)], Yan Zhou[1], and Zhan-li Sun[2]

[1] Department of Automation, College of Electronic Information Engineering,
Suzhou Vocational University, Suzhou 215104, Jiangsu, China
{sl0930,zhyan}@jssvc.edu.cn
[2] School of Electrical Engineering and Automation, Anhui University,
Hefei 230039, Anhui, China
zhlsun2006@126.com

Abstract. To extract the essential features from a relatively small number of sampling set and further improve the feature recognition precision of images, a novel palm recognition method using the adaptive lifting wavelet transform (ALWT) based sparse representation (SR) algorithm is proposed here. This lifting wavelet behaves local texture features in spatial and the fast operation speed. While SR method can effectively represent structure features of images and behaves adaptive denoising characteristics. First, the ALWT method is used to extract high frequency coefficient set and low frequency coefficient set of test images, and then, respectively using the high frequency and low frequency set as the input samples of SR model, the high frequency dictionary denoised and low sparse dictionary can be learned. Furthermore, the high and low frequency dictionaries are fused by weighted coefficient, the sparse dictionary behaved texture features can be obtained. Here the SR model is selected as the one based on fast sparse coding (FSC). Finally, using several classical classifiers to test the validity of extracted features. In test, all palmprint images are selected randomly from the PolyU palmprint database. Experimental results testify the better recognition performance of the proposed algorithm compared with PCA and the common SR model.

Keywords: Lift wavelet · Local detail features · Sparse representation · Palmprint images · Feature recognition

1 Introduction

In palmprint recognition task, the key problem is how to extract better palmprint features so that one person can be easily discriminated from others [1, 2]. Traditional palmprint feature methods are mainly divided into four categories, such as ones based on palmprint structure features, statistical features, subspace features, coding features and so on. Currently, many palmprint feature extraction methods based on wavelet transform idea have been developed and used widely in application, such as discrete wavelet transform (DWT) based methods, curvelet based methods [3], contourlet based methods [4], Bandlet based methods [5, 6] and so on. In these methods, curvelet transform and contourlet transform can provide more choice of direction and increase

© Springer Nature Switzerland AG 2019
D.-S. Huang et al. (Eds.): ICIC 2019, LNCS 11643, pp. 208–217, 2019.
https://doi.org/10.1007/978-3-030-26763-6_20

the number of high frequency sub-bands, but they are not adaptive and behave certain redundancy. Bandlet transform can adaptively track the geometric regular direction of an image for high frequency sub-bands of classical wavelet, but its computation is very complex and it is very difficult to implement. However, above methods are limited in application, especially when training samples are small, and their feature recognition precision are not high. In recent years, SR model [7, 8] based image feature extraction have been the research hot. This method can represent effectively the sparse structure and has been used widely image classification fields. And the K-singular value decomposition (K-SVD) model is thought as the classical SR model in application. In this paper, the K-SVD model is selected as the modified one based on fast sparse coding (FSC). The FSC algorithm is based on iteratively solving two convex optimization problems, namely the L_1-regularized and the L_2-constrained least squares problem. While this feature recognition method based on the modified K-SVD model is robust to noise and occlusion and can well find a linear representation of an image, but it doesn't behave the prior feature information of images, so the recognition precision is still not satisfied in feature recognition task. To represent palmprint information effectively and improve the feature classification precision, the adaptive lifting wavelet transform (ALWT) is used as the preprocessed stage of feature extraction in this paper. The ALWT not only inherits the above-mentioned wavelet transform's advantages [9, 10], but also overcome its limitations of the time-frequency localization. Moreover, this wavelet can save the computer memory and the number of computation required is also reduced hardly. The ALWT method is first used to extract high frequency coefficient set and low frequency coefficient set of test images, and then, respectively using the high frequency and low frequency set as the input samples of SR model, the high frequency dictionary denoised and low sparse dictionary can be learned. Furthermore, the high and low frequency dictionaries are fused by weighted coefficient, the sparse dictionary behaved texture features can be obtained. Furthermore, three classifiers used widely in practice, such as the Euclidean distance classifier, the radial basis function neural network (RBFNN) classifier and the extreme learning machine (ELM) classifier, are utilized to testify the validity of the ALWT based SR method in image feature extraction task. In test, all palmprint images are selected from the PolyU database [11] used commonly in palmprint image processing. Compared with DWT transform, Contourlet transform and SR without feature information, in the same test condition, experimental results testify that our method proposed here can extract image features efficiently and has quicker convergence speed, as well as higher recognition rate.

2   Adaptive Lifting Wavelet Transform

2.1   Lifting Wavelet Transform (LWT)

The basic principle of the lifting scheme is to factorize the polyphase matrix of a wavelet filter into a sequence of alternating upper and lower triangular matrices and a diagonal matrix [12, 13]. This leads to the wavelet implementation by means of banded matrix multiplications [14]. The WT method is a well-developed mathematical tool for vibration signal processing. LWT is proposed by Sweldens in 1998 [15], which can construct wavelet coefficient without relying on Fourier transform and provides low computation compared with filter banks used in regular DWT. Also, LWT has integer to integer computation, which provides ease in implementation in hardware compared to DWT. The major three steps of LWT are summarized as follows:

Step 1: Splint. Split is to build a simple lazy wavelet, where the input set $X_N(x,y)$ is separate into small subsets, odd and even samples denoted respectively by $X_o(x,y) = X(2x+1,y)$, $X_e = X(2x,y)$, namely, $X_N = (X_o, X_e)$.

Step 2: Predict. Predict is a dual lifting process, which can improve the odd set X_o. Because the odd set and even set are correlative, the odd set can be predicted by the even set X_e, and the calculated detail coefficient matrix is written as $H(x,y) = X_o(x,y) - \sum_l p_l X_e(x,y)$, where p_l is the predicted coefficient selected.

Step 3: Update. Due to the nonlinearity changing in image pixels, even samples interposed the odd ones cannot be taken directly as they need to be updated with the differences computed in predict steps. Update aims at preserving the resolution character of input samples and obtaining a sub samples. Using the approximated set $H(x,y)$ to update the even set, the updated formula is written as $L(x,y) = X_e(x,y) + \sum_l u_l H(x,y)$, where u_l is the updated coefficients.

After predict and update processes, the even set denotes the approximate of LWT, and the odd set denotes the image detail.

2.2 Adaptive Direction LWT

Considered the deviation degree concept of the pixel matrices of images in this paper, the prediction scheme of image texture direction is constructed. Assumed that the deviation degree between matrix G and matrix P is denoted as $E(G,P)$, and the size of matrix G and matrix P is $m \times n$. Then $E(G,P)$ is defined as follows:

$$E(G,P) = \frac{\|G - P\|}{mn} \tag{1}$$

where the sign $\|*\|$ denotes a certain norm. And $E(G,H)$ behaves the following properties:

$$\begin{cases} E(G,P) \geq 0 \\ E(\alpha G, \alpha P) = |\alpha| E(G,P) \\ E(G,P) \leq E(G,C) + E(C,P) \end{cases} \tag{2}$$

Where α is the real or plural parameter, and the matrix deviation degree represents the direction information of the image transformation's maximum part, so the image texture and edge can be estimated.

In application, an image first is blocked according to certain directions. Assumed that $C_e(i,j)$ is the center of each image patch B_k, then all possible direction angles $\theta(i,j)$ comprised by the center $C_e(i,j)$ are written as follows:

$$\theta(i,j) = \begin{cases} \arctan(x - j/n - i) & n \neq i \\ \pi/2 & n = i \end{cases}, \quad (n,m) \in B_k \tag{3}$$

So, for given pixel (i,j), an image is divided into image patches with fixed pixel size according to the angle θ, and then the bias between adjacent two image patches can be calculated. Because the bias reflects the image's flat degree and the adjacent pixels' drastic variation degree. The more flat the image is, the smaller the bias. Therefore, the largest bias value's direction θ is selected as the directions of image patches located near pixel point (i,j). Then, on the basis of LWT method, in the adaptive LWT method, the updated image signal with low frequency information can be written as:

$$\hat{L}(x,y) = X_e(x,y) + \sum_j u_j H(x + sign(j)tg(\theta), y + j) \tag{4}$$

Then, using the results of adaptive LWT as the input set of sparse representation algorithm, the spare dictionary can be learned.

3 Modified SR Model

3.1 KSVD Model

The sparse representation (SR) has been successfully applied to many other related inverse problems in image processing, such as denoising and restoration, often improving on the state-of-the-art [7, 16], especially, it is effective in image SR reconstruction. This method can represent sparsely and linearly test samples by using original training samples, and realizes the classification task according to linear class reconstruction errors [7, 16]. The K-SVD algorithm is in fact one of sparse representation algorithms [16]. Currently, the theory of sparse representation has been used widely in image research field. Its basic idea is that a natural signal can be represented by compressed methods or by the liner combination of prototype atoms [17]. Usually, these atoms are chosen from a so called over-complete dictionary $D \in \mathfrak{R}^{N \times K}$. Supposed that $x \in \mathfrak{R}^N$ is the observed signal, then utilized the sparse representation's idea, x can approximately represented as $x \approx Ds$, satisfying $\|x - Ds\|_p \leq \varepsilon$, where $s \in \mathfrak{R}^K$ is a vector with very few ($\ll K$) nonzero entries [15]. In common application, this sparsest representation is the solution of the following formula:

$$(P_0) \quad \min_s \|s\|_0 \quad subject \quad to \|x - Ds\|_2^2 \leq \varepsilon \tag{5}$$

where the symbol $\|\cdot\|_0$ and $\|\cdot\|_2$ are respectively the l^0 and l^2 norm, counting the nonzero entries of a vector. Assumed that x_h and x_l denote respectively a HR and LR image patch vector, according to Eq. (1), x_h can be approximated by the equation of $x_h \approx D_h s$, and x_l can be approximated by $x_l = \Gamma x_h \approx \Gamma D_h s$, here T is the mapping matrix. Thus, the LR dictionary D_l can be calculated by $D_l = T D_h$. Namely, the HR image patch x_h can be restored by using the equation of $x_h = D_h s$. Generally, for an image, to improve its reconstructed version's quality, it is randomly sampled L times with $p \times p$ image patch to obtain the image patch set $X = \{x_1, x_2, \cdots, x_L\} \in \mathfrak{R}^{N \times L}$, thus, the dictionary D can be learned from X, and the optimized problem is described as follows:

$$\{D, S\} = \arg \min_{D,S} \|X - DS\|_F^2 + \lambda \|S\|_1 \tag{6}$$

subject to $\|d_k\|_2^2 \le 1$ ($k = 1, 2, 3, \cdots, K$), and d_k is the kth column atoms of the dictionary D, and S denotes the sparse coefficient matrix.

3.2 Fast Sparse Coding Model

The fast sparse coding (FSC) algorithm is as the same as the standard sparse coding (SC) algorithm, which is a sparse representation method and can model the receptive fields of neurons in the visual cortex in brain of human, however, it has a faster convergence speed than the existing SC model [16–19]. This algorithm is based on iteratively solving two convex optimization problems, the L_1-regularized and the L_2-constrained least squares problem. And L_1 regularization is known to produce sparse coefficients and can be robust to irrelevant features. The maximum a posteriori estimate of bases and coefficients is the solution to the following optimization problem:

$$\text{minimize} \quad J = \frac{1}{2\sigma^2} \|X - DS\|_F^2 + \beta \sum_{i,j} \phi\left(s_j^i\right) \tag{7}$$

where s_j is the jth column vector of the coefficient matrix S and $\phi(\cdot)$ is a sparsity function and β is a constant.

The basis feature vectors and sparse coefficients are updated in turn. Keeping the bases fixed, the sparse coefficient matrix S can be solved by optimizing each $s_j^{(i)}$ individually [18]:

$$\text{minimize} \quad J1 = \left\| x^{(i)} - \sum_j d_j s_j^{(i)} \right\|_2^2 + (2\sigma^2 \beta) \sum_j \left| s_j^{(i)} \right| \tag{8}$$

The learning process of $s_j^{(i)}$ is called feature-sign search algorithm. This algorithm converges to a global optimum in a finite number of steps. Given fixed sparse coefficients S, the bases D can be learned by the following problem [18]:

$$\|X - DS\|_2^2 \tag{9}$$

Subject to $\sum_{i=1}^{k} D_{i,j}^2 \le c$, $\forall j = 1, 2, 3, \cdots, n$. This is a least squares problem with quadratic constraints. Using a Lagrange dual, this problem can be much more efficiently solved. The optimal basis vectors are deduced as follows:

$$D^T = \left(S S^T + \Lambda\right)^{-1} \left(X S^T\right)^T \tag{10}$$

The advantage of solving the dual is that it uses significantly fewer optimization variables than the primal. And note that the dual formulation is independent of the sparsity function, and can be extended to other similar models.

3.3   K-SVD Model Based on Modified FSC

Based on the FSC idea and K-SVD model, a new K-SVD method is proposed and used in this paper. To reduce the redundancy between column vectors of dictionary D to improve the convergence speed in training, in the base of Eq. (8), the modified FSC model is defined by us in this paper:

$$\min_s \|s_k\|_0 \quad s.t. \quad \left\| x^{(i)} - \sum_j d_j s_j^{(i)} \right\|_2^2 + \lambda \sum_j \varphi(s_j) + \alpha \sum_j \left(d_j^T d_j\right) \tag{11}$$

subject to the constraints: $\alpha, \lambda > 0$ and $\|d_k\| = 1 (k = 1, 2, \cdots, K)$, and the sparse constraint function $\varphi(s_j)$ is selected to be the negative logarithm form of the Laplace density function $|s_j|$. In the learning of Eq. (11), it is key to determine the sign of s_j. Once the sign of s_j is selected, the sparse coefficients can be learned by the gradient descent algorithm:

$$\begin{cases} s_j(t+1) = s_j(t) + d_j^T \left(X - \sum_j d_j s_j \right) \\ s_j(t+1) = s_j(t+1) \big/ \|s_j(t+1)\|_2 \end{cases} \tag{12}$$

And this algorithm converges to a global optimum in a finite number of steps.

Fixed sparse coefficient matrix S, matrix D can be learned by the Lagrangian form:

$$D\left(\begin{matrix} r \\ \lambda \end{matrix} \right) = trace\left[X^T X - X S^T \left(S S^T + \Lambda\right)^{-1} \left(X S^T\right)^T + \delta\left(D^T D\right) - c\Lambda \right] \tag{13}$$

Using the Newton's method or the conjugate gradient, the Lagrange dual Eq. (13) can be optimized. The optimal basis vectors are deduced as follows:

$$\hat{D} = \left[\left(SS^T + diag\left(\begin{matrix} r \\ \lambda \end{matrix} \right)\right)^{-1} \left(X S^T\right)^T + \eta D \right]^T \tag{14}$$

and the advantage of solving the dual is that it uses significantly fewer optimization variables than the primal. And note that the dual formulation is independent of the sparsity function, and can be extended to other similar models. Clearly, as the same as SC and ICA, the features of FSC behave the distinct sparsity, locality and orientation.

4 Experimental Results and Analysis

4.1 Data Preprocessing and Feature Basis Training

In image recognition task, the PolyU palmprint database is used to verify the LWT based SR model proposed in this paper. Here 600 palmprint images with the size of 384×284 from 100 individuals are chosen. Several images of one class of palmprint images were shown in Fig. 1. Each person's first three images are used as training samples, while the remaining ones are treated as testing samples. Using the ALWT method, the low frequency sub-band image and high frequency detail coefficients in different directions, namely, the low horizontal and low vertical (LL) sub-band image, low horizontal and high vertical (LH) sub-band image, high horizontal and low vertical (HL) sub-band image, and high horizontal and high vertical (HH) sub-band image, can be obtained, and these detail images are respectively shown in Fig. 1.

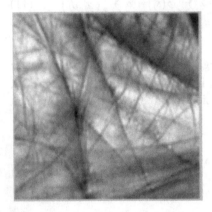
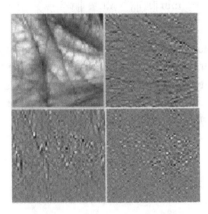

(a) The original palm image of one class.

(b) Sub-images decomposed by ALWT method. The first line: the left is the LL sub-image, and the right is the LH sub-image. The second line: the left is the HL sub-image, and the right is the HH sub-image.

Fig. 1. One class of original palmprint images selected randomly from PolyU database.

For all test images, the ALWT method is used to extract high frequency coefficient set and low frequency coefficient set, and then, using the high frequency and low frequency set as the input samples of SR method based on K-SVD model, and the noise existed in high frequency sub-images can be denoised self-adaptively. Thus the high frequency dictionary denoised and low sparse dictionary can be learned. Furthermore, the two dictionaries are fused by weighted coefficient, the sparse dictionary behaved local features can be obtained. Here, considered the different number of features, the feature basis images can be obtained. Limited by the length of this paper, only some feature basis images corresponding to the dimensions of 36 and 64 are shown in Fig. 2. And it is clear to see that feature basis images behave distinct local and direction property.

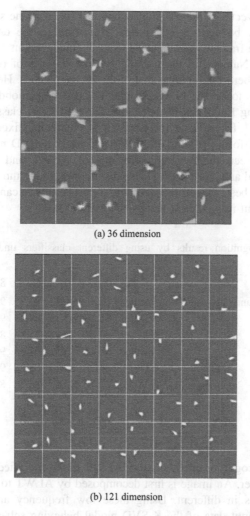

(a) 36 dimension

(b) 121 dimension

Fig. 2. Considering different feature dimensions, feature basis images obtained by ALWT based K-SVD model.

4.2 Feature Recognition

Utilizing sparse dictionary trained, the feature coefficients can be represented. And then the palmprint recognition task can be implemented by these feature coefficients. Here, two types of classifiers, i.e., the Euclidean distance classifier and extreme learning machine (ELM) classifier [17, 18] were considered. Euclidean distance classifier used widely is the simplest distance-matching algorithm among classifiers. While ELM learning behaves a much faster learning speed with the higher generalization performance, especially in the pattern recognition, so ELM is very suitable for classification problems. Moreover, many documents published have been proved to be the high efficiency of ELM classifier now [17]. Otherwise, in palmprint test, each image is converted a column vector in the training set and test set. And the size of the two sets are both changed to be 4096 × 300 pixels. Referring to the document [14], the palmprint recognition framework is selected to be the independent component analysis (ICA) framework I. Namely, in the training set, the number of rows is that of the features and the number of columns is that of the image patches. Here, let the number of feature dimensions to be 36, 49, 64, 81 and 121, the corresponding feature recognition results by using Euclidean distance classifier and ELM classifier were respectively listed in Table 1. From Table 1, it is easy to see that when fixed the classifier, our method clearly outperform methods of ALWT and basic K-SVD model. But there is little difference between the recognition results of ALWT and K-SVD methods. Moreover, when fixed an algorithm, it is also distinct to see that the recognition rate of ELM classifier is the best. Therefore, according to test results, it can be concluded that our method is efficient in palmprint feature recognition task.

Table 1. Feature recognition results by using different classifiers under different feature dimensions.

Algorithms		36	49	64	81	121
Euclidean distance classifier	Our method	82.36	86.13	90.75	92.34	92.33
	K-SVD	81.43	83.33	89.81	90.05	91.33
	ALWT	80.21	81.42	85.83	87.83	89.52
ELM classifier	Our method	88.43	89.51	91.35	93.33	96.33
	K-SVD	83.53	84.13	88.26	90.17	93.42
	ALWT	81.72	83.57	86.36	89.18	91.56

5   Conclusions

A new palmprint recognition method using ALWT based modified K-SVD model is discussed in this paper. An image is first decomposed by ALWT to get low frequency and high sub-images in different. Using these low frequency and high frequency coefficients as the input data of the K-SVD model behaving self-adaptive denoising property, the sparse dictionary responding to low frequency and high frequency fields are obtained. Further, fused the low frequency and high frequency dictionaries, the palmprint feature coefficients of the training set and test set are obtained. And then, using two classical classifiers of ELM and Euclidean distance to test the validity of extracted features. In test, the PolyU database used widely in image classification is selected, and the palmprint features extracted by our method are proved to be efficient in the image reconstruction task. Otherwise, the classification results of methods of ALWT and K-SVD are also given to compare with the method proposed by us. Experimental results prove that our method behaves the best recognition rate. Especially, when use the ELM classifier, the recognition result is satisfied.

Acknowledge. This work was supported by the grants from National Nature Science Foundation of China (Grant No. 61373098), the "333" Project Scientific Research Foundation of Jiangsu Province of China and the Qinlan project of Jiangsu Province.

References

1. Connie, T., Teoh, A., Goh, M., et al.: Palmprint recognition with PCA and ICA. Image Vis. Comput. NZ **3**, 227–232 (2003)
2. Zhang, D., Hong, W.-K., You, J.: Online palmprint identification. IEEE Trans. Pattern Anal. Mach. Intell. **25**(9), 1041–1050 (2003)
3. Liu, S., Fang, Y.: A contourlet-transform based sparse ICA algorithm for blind image separation. J. Shanghai Univ. (English Edition) **11**, 464–468 (2007)
4. Li, W., David, Z., Xu, Z.: Palmprint identification by Fourier transform. Int. J. Pattern Recogn. Artif. Intell. **16**(4), 417–432 (2002)
5. Shang, L., Huai, W., Dai, G., Chen, J., Du, J.: Palmprint recognition using 2D-Gabor wavelet based sparse coding and RBPNN classifier. In: Zhang, L., Lu, B.-L., Kwok, J. (eds.) ISNN 2010. LNCS, vol. 6064, pp. 112–119. Springer, Heidelberg (2010). https://doi.org/10.1007/978-3-642-13318-3_15
6. Lian, Q., Zhang, J., Chen, S., et al.: Single image super-resolution algorithm based on two-stage and multi-frequency-band dictionaries. ACTA Automatica Sinica **39**(8), 1310–1320 (2013)
7. Rubinstein, R., Bruckstein, A., Elad, M.: Dictionaries for sparse representation modeling. IEEE Proc. **98**(6), 1045–1057 (2010)
8. Li, Y.R., Dai, D.Q., Shen, L., et al.: Multiframe super-resolution reconstruction using sparse directional regularization. IEEE Trans. Circuits Syst. Video Technol. **20**(7), 945–956 (2010)
9. Zhang, J., Cheng, L., Yang, H., et al.: Adaptive lifting wavelet transform and image compression via texture. Chin. J. Comput. **33**(1), 184–192 (2010)
10. Zhao, D., Pan, X., Liu, X., et al.: Palmprint recognition based on lift wavelet and deep learning. Comput. Simul. **33**(10), 338–342 (2016)
11. Claypoole, R.L., Baraniukm, R.G., Nowark, R.D., et al.: Adaptive wavelet transform via lifting scheme. In: Proceedings IEEE Conference on Acoustics, Speech and Signal Processing, Phoenix, USA, vol. 12, pp. 1513–1518 (1998)
12. Sweldens, W.: The lifting scheme: a construction of second generation wavelets. SJAM J. Math. Anal. **29**(2), 511–546 (1996)
13. Kim, K.L., Ra, S.W.: Performance improvement of the SPIHT coder. Signal Process. Image Commun. **19**, 29–36 (2004)
14. Fan, W., Chen, J., Zhen, J.: SPIHT algorithm based on fast lifting wavelet transform in image compression. In: Hao, Y., et al. (eds.) CIS 2005. LNCS (LNAI), vol. 3802, pp. 838–844. Springer, Heidelberg (2005). https://doi.org/10.1007/11596981_122
15. Daubechies, I., Sweldens, W.: Factoring wavelet transforms into lifting steps. J. Fourier Anal. Appl. **4**(3), 245–267 (1998)
16. Aharon, M., Elad, M., Bruckstein, A.: K-SVD: an algorithm for designing overcomplete dictionaries for sparse representation. IEEE Trans. Signal Process. **54**(11), 4311–4322 (2006)
17. Yang, J., Wang, Z., Lin, Z., et al.: Coupled dictionary training for image super-resolution. IEEE Trans. Image Process. **21**(8), 3467–3478 (2012)
18. Thiagarajan, J.J., Ramamurthy, K.N., Spanias, A.: Multiple Kernel sparse representations for supervised and unsupervised learning. IEEE Trans. Image Process. **23**(7), 2905–2915 (2014)
19. Lee, H., Battle, A., Raina, R.: Efficient sparse coding algorithms. In: The Proceedings of Neural Information Processing Systems (NIPS2007), pp. 801–808, Vancouver, B.C., Canada (2007)

Dislocation Theory Based Level Set Image Segmentation

Fan Zhang[1(✉)], Boyan Zhang[2], and Xinhong Zhang[3]

[1] School of Computer and Information Engineering, Henan University,
Kaifeng 475001, China
zhangfan@henu.edu.cn
[2] School of Mechanical, Electrical and Information Engineering,
Shandong University at Weihai, Weihai 264209, China
[3] School of Software, Henan University, Kaifeng 475001, China
zxh@henu.edu.cn

Abstract. Dislocation theory of material science is introduced into the level set method. The curve evolution of level set method is viewed as the slipping of edge dislocation, and the curve evolution is driven by the dislocation configuration force which is derived based on the dislocation dynamics mechanism. In the image segmentation, the proposed algorithm can effectively avoid the phenomenon that level set function stop evolution because of the abnormal image gradient, and the phenomenon of boundary leakage because of the smaller image gradient. Experimental results show that the proposed algorithm has better segmentation performance for images with weak boundaries.

Keywords: Image segmentation · Dislocation ·
Distance regularized level set method

1 Introduction

Image segmentation is the process of partitioning a digital image into multiple segments (sets of pixels). The goal of segmentation is to simplify or change the representation of an image into something that is more meaningful and easier to analyze. Many image segmentation algorithms have been proposed in recent decades [1]. Generally, image segmentation can be divided into the following categories: the threshold based segmentation method, the edge based segmentation method [2], the region based segmentation method [3], and the energy based segmentation method.

Level set method has been applied in many fields [4]. Li et al. proposes a region based method for image segmentation, which is able to deal with intensity inhomogeneity in the segmentation [5]. Li et al. proposed a distance regularized level set evolution (DRLSE) method [6]. In this model, the level set evolution is derived as the gradient flow which minimizes an energy functional with a distance regularization term and an external energy that drives the motion of the zero level set toward desired locations. In this paper, the dislocation theory is introduced into level set method. The curve evolution of level set method is viewed as the slipping process of dislocation lines, and a new level set method is proposed based on the dislocation dynamics theory.

© Springer Nature Switzerland AG 2019
D.-S. Huang et al. (Eds.): ICIC 2019, LNCS 11643, pp. 218–227, 2019.
https://doi.org/10.1007/978-3-030-26763-6_21

2 Dislocation Theory

In the material science, the dislocation is a kind of special atom configuration, refers to the local irregular sort between atoms (crystallographic defects). A crystalline material consists of a regular array of atoms, arranged into lattice planes. However, because of the influence of the external or internal stress, the deformation of atoms array and the slipping of atom lattice planes may occurs (the dislocation occurs). In this case, the crystal no longer conforms to a regular crystal lattice and forms a linear defect. From the perspective of geometric, the dislocation is a boundary between the slipped and no-slipped parts of crystal planes. The dislocation is also called as the line defects. Analyzing from aspects of mathematical theory, the dislocation is a defect on the topology structure of materials.

The dislocation subjects to a force on the slipping plane which is perpendicular to dislocation line. When the force is sufficient to overcome the movement resistance, the dislocation will move along the direction of force. The direction and the magnitude of slipping is characterized by the Burgers vector of dislocation. The Burgers vector is a physical quantity which reflects the size of the lattice distortion caused by dislocation. Mode of Burgers vector indicates the degree of distortion, so the Burgers vector is also known as the dislocation strength. When the dislocation movement lead to slip, the magnitude of distortion is the Burgers vector, and the slipping direction is the direction of Burgers vector.

Under the effect of shear stress, the dislocation line will move if the shear stress is greater than the yield value of crystal stress. In the edge dislocation, the direction of dislocation movement is always perpendicular to the dislocation line. Assuming that there is a virtual force which is perpendicular to the dislocation line and causes the dislocation movement, we named it the dislocation configuration force $\mathbf{F_d}$. If we view the dislocation (the atomic configuration) as a physical construct, the configuration force $\mathbf{F_d}$ is the force acting on the physical construct and it can drive the physical construct move.

Assuming that the stress of slipping surface is τ. When the dislocation line moves a distance ds, the crystal just slip a Burgers vector $\mathbf{b}$. Assuming that the shear stress on this slipping surface makes the crystal slipping a distance b, the shear stress does work W_1,

$$W_1 = \tau \cdot (l\mathrm{d}s) \cdot b. \tag{1}$$

Assuming the configuration force $\mathbf{F_d}$ does work W_2,

$$W_2 = \mathbf{F_d} \cdot (l\mathrm{d}s). \tag{2}$$

According to the principle of virtual work, $W_1 = W_2$.
So the force acting on dislocation line is $\mathbf{F_d}$,

$$\mathbf{F_d} = \tau \cdot b. \tag{3}$$

It can be seen from Eq. 3, for any dislocation line, if a uniform stress τ acts on the slipping plane along the direction of the Burgers vector, then the dislocation line per unit length will subject to a configuration force $\mathbf{F_d}$. The magnitude of configuration force is τb, and the direction is the normal direction of this point. The dislocation line will move when the force $\mathbf{F_d}$ is greater than a yield value.

In the active contour model, the speed function drives the active curve evolution along the normal direction of curve. In the level set method, the image gradient and the edge indicator function g drive the zero level set function evolution. Both of the curve movement in active contour models and in level set method are similar to the movement of dislocation lines in dislocation theory. In the edge dislocation, the dislocation line is driven by the configuration force $\mathbf{F_d}$.

3 Dislocation Theory Based Level Set Method

The distance regularized level set evolution method greatly reduces the dependence of the initial contour selection, and can get a better segmentation result by choosing a simple form of initial contour. The introduction of penalty term can avoid the problem of large computational complexity which is caused by the need of continual re-initialization.

In order to solve the problem of weak boundaries image segmentation, the dislocation theory is introduced. In the proposed algorithm, the curve evolution of level set method is regarded as the slipping process of dislocation line. Using the dislocation mechanism, especially including elastic properties, energy and dislocation dynamics theory, we put forward a virtual dislocation configuration force which drives the initial contour moving.

According to ideas of level set method for image segmentation, we put a two-dimensional image plane into a three-dimensional space, and then define the curve energy in three-dimensional space [7]. Parameterize the curve $\gamma(s)$ in three dimensional space, and the curve energy related with $\gamma(s)$ is,

$$E(\gamma) = \min \int \frac{1}{2}\|\mathbf{w}(x, y, z)\|^2 \mathrm{d}x\mathrm{d}y\mathrm{d}z, \tag{4}$$

The stress $\mathbf{W}$ can be solved as follows,

$$\mathbf{w}(x, y, z) = -\frac{1}{4\pi}\int_\gamma \frac{\mathbf{r} \times \mathbf{dl}}{r^3} \tag{5}$$

where $\mathbf{dl}$ is a line element of the curve γ. $\mathbf{r} = (x - x(s), y = y(s), z - z(s))$ is the vector between the point (x, y, z) and the point $(x(s), y(s), z(s))$. And r is the distance between the two points.

The curve line element dl can be expressed as,

$$\mathbf{dl} = \tau\delta(\gamma)dxdydz = \nabla\phi\delta(\phi)dxdydz. \tag{6}$$

then,

$$\mathbf{w}(x, y, z) = -\frac{1}{4\pi}\int_{\gamma}\frac{\mathbf{r} \times \nabla\phi\delta(\phi)}{r^3}dxdydz. \tag{7}$$

Driving by dislocation configuration force $\mathbf{F_d}$, dislocation line will move along the normal direction of curve. Let $I(x, y)$ is intensity of image, the direction of an object boundary can be defined as,

$$\mathbf{n} = \frac{\nabla(G_{\sigma} * I)}{|\nabla(G_{\sigma} * I)|}. \tag{8}$$

Then the dislocation configuration force $\mathbf{F_d}$ can be expressed as follows,

$$\mathbf{F_d} = \mathbf{w}(x, y, z) \times \mathbf{n} = -\frac{1}{4\pi}\int_{\gamma}\frac{\mathbf{r} \times \nabla\phi\delta(\phi)\nabla(G_{\sigma} * I)}{r^3|\nabla(G_{\sigma} * I)|}dxdydz. \tag{9}$$

The dislocation line or the zero level set curve Φ moves along the normal direction of curve driven by the dislocation configuration force $\mathbf{F_d}$. When the point (x, y) is inside an object, then $\mathbf{F_d} > 0$, and when the point (x, y) is outside an object, then $\mathbf{F_d} < 0$. When the dislocation line is close to object boundary, the image gradient becomes larger, and the dislocation configuration force $\mathbf{F_d}$ also becomes stronger. When the dislocation line is not close to object boundary, the dislocation configuration force $\mathbf{F_d}$ will becomes weaker.

In the dislocation theory based level set method, we replace the $\nabla\phi/|\nabla\phi|$ with the dislocation configuration force. Then, the new evolution equation of level set function based on the dislocation theory is shown as Eq. 10.

$$\frac{\partial\phi}{\partial t} = \mu\mathrm{div}\big(d_p(|\nabla\phi|)\nabla\phi\big) + \alpha g\delta_{\varepsilon}(\phi) + \lambda\delta_{\varepsilon}(\phi)\mathrm{div}(g\mathbf{F_d}). \tag{10}$$

In the proposed level set method based on the dislocation theory, the evolution of level set function is mainly determined by the dislocation configuration force. The dislocation configuration force $\mathbf{F_d}$ contains more image information. $\nabla(G_{\sigma} * I)$ represents the image gradient information. γ represents the distance information between the active curves, and it also reflects the effective range of the dislocation configuration force $\mathbf{F_d}$. In the region near the dislocation line (active curve), $\mathbf{F_d}$ will be larger, on the contrary, it will be smaller. The integral part represents the stress of dislocation line (active curve), and also reflects the energy of active curve. This force or curve energy can constrain the shape of curve.

According to the new distance regularized level set evolution equation, the zero level set curve Φ evolves along the normal direction of curve driven by the dislocation configuration force $\mathbf{F}_d$. The dislocation configuration force not only depends on the gradient information of images, but also depends on the energy information of curve and the effective range of the dislocation configuration force. So the dislocation theory based level set method can effectively avoid the phenomenon that the level set function stop evolution because of the abnormal image gradient, and the phenomenon of boundary leakage because of the smaller image gradient.

4   Experimental Results

In order to verify the validity of proposed algorithm, some image segmentation experiments are carried out in this section. And in this section, we also compare the experimental results of our algorithm with other conventional level set algorithms. Part of the test images come from the database of University of California, Berkeley.

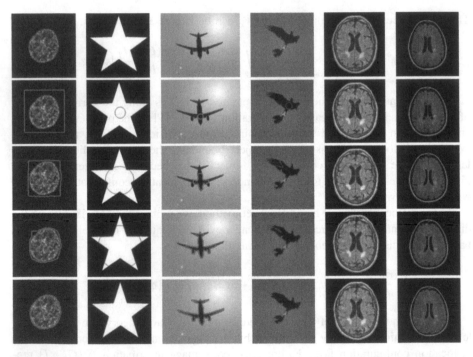

Fig. 1. Segmentation result of proposed algorithm. Row 1: The test images. Row 2: Initial contour on the original images. The other rows show the evolution results. Column 1: Nucleus image. Column 2: Simulated pentagram image. Column 3: Aircraft image. Column 4: Eagle image. Column 5 and 6: Medical images.

The implementation of proposed algorithm consists of the following steps:

Step 1: Initializing the level set function Φ, and setting the default value of specific parameters, μ, λ and α etc.

Step 2: Computing the dislocation configuration force $\mathbf{F}_d$ according to Eq. 9 and the speed stopping function g.

Step 3: Updating the level set function Φ according to the level set evolution equation Eq. 10.

Step 4: If the stopping condition is satisfied, stopping evolution, otherwise, go to step 2 and continue the iterative process.

The stopping condition: The curve evolution stops if either of the following conditions is satisfied:

(1) The speed stopping function g is approaches to zero and no longer changes.
(2) A pre-specified maximum number of iterations is reached.

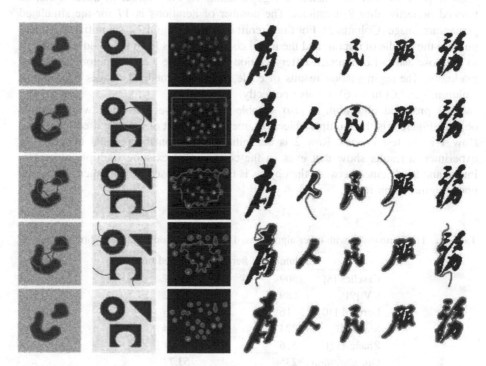

Fig. 2. Multiple objects segmentation result of the proposed algorithm. Row 1: The test images. Row 2: Initial contour on the original images.

In Eq. 10, there are three specific parameters, μ, λ and α. The level set regularization term μ weights the influence of the regularization of the shape of level set function, the default value is set to 0.005. The parameter λ weights the influence of the regularization of the evolving curve, the default value is set to 1. Nonzero parameter α gives additional external force to drive the motion of curve, but the resulting final contour may slightly deviate from the true object boundary due to the shrinking or expanding effect of the third term of Eq. 10. In our experiments, if the initial contour is put inside of the target object, we set $\alpha = -1$, otherwise, we set $\alpha = 1$. In our experiments, we set the standard deviation of the Gaussian kernel $\sigma = 9$ and the time step $\Delta t = 0.2$.

In Eq. 8, G_σ is the two-dimensional Gaussian function with mean zero and standard deviation σ. In our experiments, the deviation of Gaussian function takes the value of $\sigma = 4$.

Figure 1 is the image segmentation results of the proposed algorithm. Row 1 is the test images. Row 2 shows the initial contour on the original images. The other rows show the level set evolution process and the final image segmentation results. The test images include nucleus image (Column 1), simulated pentagram image (Column 2), aircraft image (Column 3), eagle image (Column 4) and medical images (Column 5 and Column 6). Experimental results show that the proposed algorithm can track the target contour perfectly. For the nucleus image (Column 1), the contour of nucleus can be tracked perfectly after 8 iterations. The number of iterations is 17 for the simulated pentagram image (Column 2). For the aircraft images (Column 3), the initial contour is put into the middle of aircraft and the initial contour extends from the middle of aircraft to the nose and tail of aircraft. After iteration tracking, the aircraft contour is tracked gradually. The segmentation results of eagle image and medical images (Column 4, Column 5 and Column 6) are also perfectly.

The proposed algorithm is also suitable for image segmentation with multiple objects. Figure 2 is the multiple objects segmentation result of the proposed algorithm. Row 1 is the test images. Row 2 is the initial contour on the original images. The experimental results show that even in the condition of existing multiple objects in image and the distance between the objects is far, the proposed algorithm can also get a good segmentation result.

Table 1. The comparison with other algorithms. The segmentation results are shown as Fig. 3.

	Number of iterations	Elapsed time (s)
Caselles [8]	1509	60.07
CV [9]	689	29.72
Bernard [10]	16	128.23
Shi [11]	224	57.44
Zhang [12]	526	83.61
Our algorithm	235	53.77

We also compare the image segmentation results of our algorithm with other conventional level set algorithms. Those conventional level set algorithms include Caselles algorithm [8], CV (Chan-Vese) model [9], Bernard algorithm [10], Shi algorithm [11]. Figure 3 is the comparison between the proposed algorithm and other conventional algorithms. The original test image is a mobile phone image (500×347). (a) shows the experimental result of Caselles algorithm [8]. The convergence threshold is set to 2, and the propagation term is set to 1, which acts as a balloon force pushing the contour either inward or outward. (b) shows the experimental result of CV algorithm [9]. The convergence threshold takes the value of 2, and the curvature term is set to 0.2, which weights the influence of the regularization. (c) shows the experimental result of Bernard algorithm [10]. The convergence threshold is set to 2, and the scale factor that allows to select the degree of smoothness of the evolving contour is set to 1. (d) shows the experimental result of Shi algorithm [11]. The number of iteration in the data dependent cycle is set to 300; The number of iteration in the regularization cycle is set to 30; The variance of the Gaussian filter is set to 4. (e) shows the experimental result of Zhang algorithm [12]. (f) shows the experimental result of our algorithm. The value of parameters is as follows, $\lambda = 1$, $\mu = 0.005$, $\alpha = -1$, $\sigma = 9$, $\Delta t = 0.2$.

Fig. 3. The comparison with other algorithms. (a) Caselles algorithm [7]. (b) CV algorithm [8]. (c) Bernard algorithm [9]. (d) Shi algorithm [10]. (e) Zhang algorithm [11]. (f) Our algorithm. The number of iterations and elapsed time are given in Table 1.

The number of iterations and elapsed time of the contrast experiment shown in Fig. 3 are given in Table 1. The experimental results show that CV algorithm, Bernard algorithm, Shi algorithm and our algorithm successfully track the mobile phone contour, in which the contour tracked by our algorithm is smoothest and complete.

In the conventional level set algorithms, the process of level set evolution is achieved by the minimization of curve energy function, and the curve evolution mainly depends on image gradient information, such as Caselles algorithm and DRLSE algorithm, etc. In the image with weak boundaries, the image gradient is small in the weak boundaries regions, and the level set algorithm based on image gradient information is difficult to achieve a good image segmentation results. In the proposed algorithm, the dislocation line or the zero level set function ϕ is driven by the dislocation configuration force $\mathbf{F}_d$. Because the dislocation configuration force is combined with image gradient, curve energy and distance information, so the proposed algorithm is more effective for the segmentation of weak boundaries image.

Figure 4 shows the experimental results for the segmentation of weak boundaries image. We compare the experimental results of our algorithm with other conventional algorithms. In Fig. 4, the test image is an experimental blood vessel image (335 × 429). (a) shows the experimental result of Caselles algorithm [8]. (b) shows the experimental result of CV algorithm [9]. (c) shows the experimental result of Bernard algorithm [10]. (d) shows the experimental result of Shi algorithm [11]. (e) shows the experimental result of DRLSE algorithm [6]. (f) shows the experimental result of Wang algorithm [13]. (g) shows the experimental result of Zhang algorithm [12]. The experimental result of our algorithm is shown as (h). The experimental results show that the DRLSE algorithm, the Wang algorithm, the Zhang algorithm and our algorithm tracks the contour of blood vessels completely. According to the experimental results, the number of iterations, the elapsed time, the Area Overlap Error and the Boundary Mean Distance of our algorithm are better than that of the DRLSE algorithm, the Wang algorithm and the Zhang algorithm.

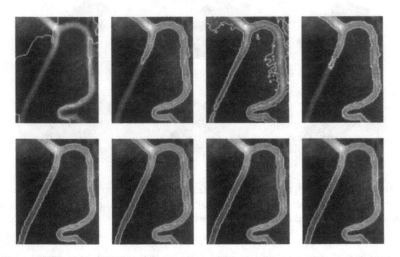

Fig. 4. The comparison with other algorithms. (a) Caselles algorithm [8]. (b) CV algorithm [9]. (c) Bernard algorithm [10]. (d) Shi algorithm [11]. (e) DRLSE algorithm [6]. (f) Wang algorithm [13]. (g) Zhang algorithm [12]. (h) Our algorithm.

5   Conclusions

The contribution of this paper is to propose a new level set method based on dislocation theory, which can effectively solve the problem of weak boundaries image segmentation. The dislocation theory of materials science is introduced into level set method. The curve evolution of level set method is viewed as the slipping process of dislocation lines, and a new evolution equation of level set function is constructed. This paper presents a virtual dislocation configuration force to drive the curve evolution of level set. The dislocation configuration force not only includes the gradient information of image, but also includes the energy information of level set curve and the effective range of the dislocation configuration force. This paper refers to the distance regularized level set method. The regularity of level set function is intrinsically maintained during the level set evolution. The distance regularization effect eliminates the need for re-initialization and thereby avoids its induced numerical errors.

Acknowledgment. This research was supported by the Natural Science Foundation of China (No. 61771006 and No. U1504621), the Natural Science Foundation of Henan Province (No. 162300410032).

References

1. Jiang, H., Zhang, G., Wang, H., Bao, H.: Spatio-temporal video segmentation of static scenes and its applications. IEEE Trans. Multimedia **17**(1), 3–15 (2015)
2. Koo, H.I.: Segmentation and rectification of pictures in the camera-captured images of printed documents. IEEE Trans. Multimedia **15**(3), 647–660 (2013)
3. Cheng, M., Mitra, N.J., Huang, X., Torr, P.H., Hu, S.: Global contrast based salient region detection. IEEE Trans. Pattern Anal. Mach. Intell. **37**(3), 569–582 (2015)
4. Thomas, B., Joachim, W.: Level set segmentation with multiple regions. IEEE Trans. Image Process. **15**(10), 3213–3218 (2006)
5. Li, C., Huang, R., Ding, Z., Gatenby, J.C., Metaxas, D., Gore, J.: A level set method for image segmentation in the presence of intensity inhomogeneities with application to mri. IEEE Trans. Image Process. **20**(7), 2007–2016 (2011)
6. Li, C., Xu, C., Gui, C., Fox, M.D.: Distance regularized level set evolution and its application to image segmentation. IEEE Trans. Image Process. **19**(12), 3243–3254 (2010)
7. Luo, Y., Chung, A.C.: Nonrigid image registration with crystal dislocation energy. IEEE Trans. Image Process. **22**(1), 229–243 (2013)
8. Caselles, V., Kimmel, R., Sapiro, G.: Geodesic active contours. Int. J. Comput. Vision **22**(1), 61–79 (1997)
9. Chan, T.F., Vese, L., et al.: Active contours without edges. IEEE Trans. Image Process. **10**(2), 266–277 (2001)
10. Bernard, O., Friboulet, D., Thevenaz, P., Unser, M.: Variational b-spline level-set: a linear filtering approach for fast deformable model evolution. IEEE Trans. Image Process. **18**(6), 1179–1191 (2009)
11. Shi, Y., Karl, W.C.: A real-time algorithm for the approximation of level-set-based curve evolution. IEEE Trans. Image Process. **17**(5), 645–656 (2008)
12. Zhang, F., Zhang, X.: Distance regularized level set image segmentation algorithm by means of dislocation theory. Acta Automatica Sinica **44**(5), 178–187 (2018)
13. Wang, X.F., Min, H., Zou, L., Zhang, Y.G.: A novel level set method for image segmentation by incorporating local statistical analysis and global similarity measurement. Pattern Recogn. **48**(1), 189–204 (2015)

Out-of-Stock Detection Based
on Deep Learning

Jun Chen, Shu-Lin Wang$^{(\boxtimes)}$, and Hong-Li Lin

College of Computer Science and Electronics Engineering, Hunan University,
Changsha 410082, Hunan, China
smartforesting@163.com

Abstract. Out-of-stock (OOS) problem is a significant reason of the decline of goods sales in offline supermarkets since the frequent lack of goods on the shelves can reduce the enthusiasm of shoppers. For this purpose, it is necessary to effectively detect the OOS situation, which can ensure that the products are replenished in time. In this paper, an out-of-stock detection method based on deep learning is proposed. We first introduce the Faster R-CNN algorithm to obtain location information. Then the Faster R-CNN algorithm is followed by three out-of-stock detection methods: canny operator, gray level co-occurrence matrix, and color features for out-of-stock detection. The experimental results show that the method based on canny operator performs better, which can achieve a recall rate of 83.9%, a precision rate of 91.7% and a F1-Measure of 87.6% in real scene dataset.

Keywords: Deep learning · Out-of-stock detection · Canny operator

1 Introduction

Out-of-stock (OOS) problem could be defined as the absence of products on the shelf, which can lead consumers not to purchase what they want. When OOS occurs frequently, customers will have a poor purchase experience, thus reducing the loyalty of customer and affecting sales volume. Efficient Consumer Response studies indicate that the industry suffers an economic loss of 4 billion euros per year due to OOS. According to research by Corsten and Gruen [1], retailers did not put enough effort on checking their own shelves, and they can improve their revenue by solving OOS problem. However, many retailers do not pay attention to this issue. When faced with OOS, customers may 1. buy the item at another store, 2. do not purchase the item, 3. delay their purchase. These situations will reduce sales volume to some extent. Fernie and Grant [2] have conducted a thorough research of different retail stores and found that the loyalty to a store is even more important than the loyalty to a brand. The emergence of OOS can reduce customers' loyalty and ultimately affect the sales volume of retail stores. Therefore, the proposal of OOS detection method is of great significance.

© Springer Nature Switzerland AG 2019
D.-S. Huang et al. (Eds.): ICIC 2019, LNCS 11643, pp. 228–237, 2019.
https://doi.org/10.1007/978-3-030-26763-6_22

2 Related Work

In a retail store, the OOS detection is usually performed by salesmen. The inspectors regularly count the goods on the shelves and replenish the goods in time. However, this method is labor-intensive and inefficient [3]. With the rapid development of computer technology, computer-aided detection is gradually replacing the manual detection method. An automatic method to detect OOS based on the inventory information stored in the computer has been proposed to measure whether the goods on the shelf is out-of-stock. However, this method cannot accurately detect OOS since 30% of products are not on the shelves. Papakiriakopoulos [4] proposed a rule-based decision support system based on machine learning technology to solve OOS problem by using some data such as sales-data, ordering information or product assortment. However, different store data with the same rules will make different results. The fact that each retail store has to develop specific rules makes this approach less robust. At present, merchants are detecting OOS by deploying embedded sensor networks [5]. Unfortunately, the method of embedded sensor network is difficult to deploy and cannot be popularized yet. R. Moorthy and S. Behera used the SURF algorithm (Speeded-Up Robust Features) to describe the features of the target image and then compare it with the features of the reference image to detect products. However, this method is not universal because the location of products is different and the merchants need to recalculate the reference images. Kejriwal [6] designed a method by installing a camera on a mobile robot to acquire an image, and then identified the product by using the nearest neighbor search method for the image template in the database. Obviously, this method also requires a lot of data. Therefore, there is a need for an efficient method to detect OOS.

This paper proposes an out-of-stock detection method based on deep learning, which does not rely on the deployment of additional equipment (such as sensors and robots), nor does it require a large amount of database information or product template information. First, the product images are identified by using the method of object detection. Next, we use the identified location information of certain commodities to determine all unknown areas (potential out-of-stock areas). After obtaining the unknown areas, the out-of-stock detection algorithm is utilized in these specific areas. In this method, the number of out-of-stock products can be counted while detecting the out-of-stock areas. In particular, the location of the potential out-of-stock areas does not require high recall rate and precision rate.

3 The Proposed Methods

Figure 1 shows overall flowchart of the proposed method. First, the object detection network Faster R-CNN is used to identify the position of products on the shelf. Then, the unknown areas are located according to the position of products. Finally the OOS detection is performed in the unknown areas.

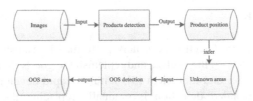

Fig. 1. Overall flow chart

3.1 Products Detection

In products detection, there exists the problem of image multi-scale due to the different scales of products in real scenes. Therefore, two-stage object detection algorithm is used in products detection. Faster R-CNN [7] is a two-stage object detection algorithm, which is improved on RCNN [8] and Fast R-CNN [9]. The Faster R-CNN network can be regarded as the combination of Region Proposal Network (RPN) and Fast R-CNN networks. The network structure of the Faster-RCNN is shown in Fig. 2. The Fast R-CNN uses the RPN network instead of the original region generation algorithm, which greatly accelerates the detection speed of the network. Meanwhile, the anchor of the RPN network structure can effectively solve the problem of image multi-scale. For our research purposes, Faster R-CNN is used to train the Nestle milk powder product model.

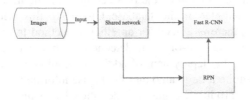

Fig. 2. Faster R-CNN network structure diagram

3.2 Out-of-Stock Detection

In this paper, we focus on out-of-stock detection in the actual retail store scene. The problems of camera angle of the shelf image, lighting, shelf type and product placement will result in the inconsistency of the size, illumination and background of the out-of-stock areas. When deep learning method is used for location recognition directly, the detection effect is poor. In addition, it is difficult to mark the images. Fortunately, the trained Faster R-CNN model can be used to identify and locate the goods. The goods shelves are arranged in a regular way, and according to the detected positions of goods, all other unknown positions of goods can be deduced. Then, we carry out-of-stock detection for these positions. In the following parts, three out-of-stock detection methods will be discussed respectively. 1. The canny operator based on edge detection. 2. The method of texture feature-based gray level co-occurrence matrix. 3. The similarity measurement method based on color feature.

3.2.1   Out-of-Stock Detection Based on Canny Operator

The canny operator is employed for edge detection [10]. When the canny operator is used for edge detection, the edge information that can be detected is relatively less since there is no product in the out-of-stock area. However, a large amount of edge information can be detected in the product area. We first calculate the ratio of pixels value (s1) of edge information by using the canny operator for unknown areas to pixels value (S) of the whole region. Then, a threshold value is set to determine whether the area is truly out-of-stock. Less edge information means that the region is more likely to be out-of-stock. So the confidence of unknown areas is defined as follows in Eq. (1).

$$\text{score} = 1 - \frac{s_1}{S} \tag{1}$$

3.2.2   Out-of-Stock Detection Based on Gray Level Co-occurrence Matrix

The statistical method of gray level co-occurrence matrix (GLCM) [11] was proposed by R. Haralick in the early 1970s. It is an extensive texture analysis method proposed under the assumption that the spatial distribution relationship of each pixel in the image contains the image texture information. It's obvious that out-of-stock area and area with product are different in texture features. The former basically has no texture features, while the latter has. Therefore, we use gray level co-occurrence matrix to extract texture features of unknown areas. Next, we calculate key features such as entropy, angular second moment (ASM), contrast and correlation by using GLCM, where entropy represents the non-uniform degree or complexity of texture in the image. ASM reflects the grayscale distribution and texture thickness of the image. The contrast indicates the sharpness of the image and the depth of the texture furrow. The correlation reflects consistency of the texture of the image. These features are input as texture features into SVM [12] for classification. Finally, the out-of-stock detection is completed.

3.2.3   Out-of-Stock Detection Based on Color Feature

Color feature is a general feature that describes the whole information of the image. In this paper, the method of color histogram is used to extract the color feature of the image since the color histogram method has the advantages of low computational cost and features are invariable under rotation, shifting and scaling. Obviously, the color characteristics of the area where the commodities exist are quite different from the stock-out area. The color of the out-of-stock area is mostly gray, while the color of the commodity area is relatively bright. In our experiments, six color histograms of typical out-of-stock areas are selected as the local feature database. When carrying out the stock-out detection, the color histogram calculation is performed on the unknown areas, and the calculated information is used as the feature to compare the similarity with the features in the local feature database. Usually, an unknown area is considered more likely to be out-of-stock if the unknown area features is more similar to local features.

4 Experiment

4.1 Data Set

In order to verify the recognition performance of the proposed method, the images of shelf goods in real scenes are collected. In the dataset, there are 1000 images of shelves containing a total of 139 different categories of merchandise. The images of the test set contain approximately 400 unknown areas. The shelf images in the data set present different angles, lighting and pixels, which can effectively represent the actual scene. Two images in the dataset are shown in Fig. 3.

Fig. 3. Shelf goods images

4.2 Products Detection and Recognition Result

The Faster R-CNN with Inception_v2 model is used for products detection. The learning rate was initially set to 10^{-3}, and then decreased by a factor of 10 when the number of training steps reached 100K and 150K. In total, the learning rate was decreased 2 times, and the learning was stopped after 200K itcrations. For example, Fig. 4 shows the results of the products detection on two shelves. In this example, the products identified are marked by the green bounding boxes. It can be seen that some products have not been detected. According to the products detection information (bounding box), the position of all unknown areas could be inferred. Corresponding to Fig. 4, the unknown areas are shown in Fig. 5, in which all unknown areas are marked by the yellow bounding boxes.

Fig. 4. Products detection results (Color figure online)

Fig. 5. Unknown areas corresponding to Fig. 4 (Color figure online)

4.3 Analysis of OOS Detection Recognition Result

The most commonly measures are recall rate, precision rate and F1-Meature, which are used to evaluate the performance of the method. Recall rate denotes the ratio of the correct number of predictors in the class to all the numbers of the positive class, and precision rate is the ratio of the correct number of predictors in the class to the number of all the predicted numbers in the class. F1-Measure is a composite index of recall and precision, which is the weighted harmonic average of precision and recall.

Table 1 shows the experimental results of out-of-stock detection based on the canny operator. The pixel value s1 of the edge information and the total pixel value S of the unknown area are obtained. Assuming that s1 < S *threshold is true, an unknown area is judged to be out-of-stock. Some of the out-of-stock areas might contain background, so these areas might also contain a small amount of edge information. However, the product area has abundant edge information. When setting a low threshold, a part of the out-of-stock areas with background might be judged as products, increasing omission rate. When setting a high threshold, some product areas might be judged to be out-of-stock areas, adding the error rate. Therefore, a compromise threshold should be selected. Different thresholds have been tried in this experiment, including 0.1, 0.15, 0.2, 0.25 and 0.3. As shown in Table 1, it is obvious that the threshold of 0.2 obtains the best experimental result.

Table 1. Canny operator detection results

Threshold	Recall	Precision	F1
0.1	43.1%	100%	60.3%
0.15	66.7%	100%	80.0%
0.2	83.9%	91.7%	87.6%
0.25	92.2%	74.1%	82.2%
0.3	96.6%	47.5%	63.7%

We compare the results obtained by out-of-stock detection based on gray level co-occurrence matrix, with the combination of different texture features (such as Energy, ASM, Contrast, Correlation). Table 2 shows the corresponding experimental results. The experimental results have the best performance when combining energy and correlation features. However, the detection results based on gray level co-occurrence matrix are generally poor. Because of the variety of goods, the low definition of some images and the complex background of the out-of-stock areas, it is difficult to form uniform features, which leads to poor detection results. Various out-of-stock areas are shown in Fig. 6. It can be seen that the background of the out-of-stock areas are complicated due to the type of shelves, lighting, angle, and image pixels.

Fig. 6. Various OOS areas

Table 2. GLCM detection results

GLCM	Feature				Recall	Precision	F1
	Energy	ASM	Contrast	Correlation			
1		√		√	50.4%	83.8%	63.0%
2		√	√	√	51.8%	68.6%	59.0%
3	√	√		√	40.7%	93.9%	56.8%
4	√	√	√	√	41.1%	92.0%	56.8%

Table 3 shows the results of the out-of-stock detection method based on color features. We have selected six typical out-of-stock areas to extract color histograms as local feature database. We measure the similarity between the local features and the color histogram features of unknown areas. When the similarity exceeds a certain threshold, an unknown area is considered to be out-of-stock area. When the threshold value is too small, some areas of products that are blurry or have a darker background are judged to be out-of-stock areas, which increases error rate. When the threshold value is too large, some out-of-stock areas with background or bright light are judged as product areas, which increases the omission rate. Therefore, a suitable threshold should be selected. In this experiment, the threshold values selected are as follows: 0.4, 0.5, 0.6, 0.7 and 0.8. The experiment shows that the OOS detection result is best when the threshold is set to 0.5. It is noted that increasing the local feature database does not cause significant changes in the calculation of amount. Thus, it is expected to improve recall rate and precision rate by increasing the feature database of out-of-stock and setting a higher similarity threshold simultaneously.

Table 3. Color detection results

Threshold	Recall	Precision	F1
0.4	80.5%	68.4%	74.0%
0.5	76.6%	73.9%	75.2%
0.6	61.1%	80.2%	69.3%
0.7	58.9%	85.7%	69.8%
0.8	51.9%	80.0%	62.9%

Table 4 compares the results of three kinds of out-of-stock detection methods in the best case. The comparison results show that the out-of-stock detection based on canny operator gets the best result, which indicates that the edge information is a better feature for judging whether the shelf is out-of-stock. In addition, the color feature can also indicate the products are out-of-stock to some extent.

Table 4. Results of three OOS detection methods

Detection methods	Recall	Precision	F1
GLCM	50.4%	83.8%	63.0%
Color	76.6%	73.9%	75.2%
Canny	83.9%	91.7%	87.6%

Figure 7 shows some of the recognition results. The blue bounding boxes in the figure represent the areas that are ultimately identified as out-of-stock. The method proposed in this paper can not only detect the location of out-of-stock areas, but also count the number of out-of-stock areas.

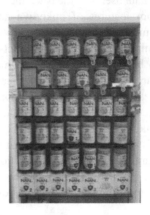

Fig. 7. OOS detection results (Color figure online)

5   Conclusion

This paper proposes an out-of-stock detection method based on deep learning, which is easy to implement and does not require a large amount of statistical information (such as inventory information, etc.). The experimental results show that the proposed method can achieve the high recall rate and precision rate on the real scene dataset. Furthermore, we compared three different out-of-stock detection methods and found that the edge feature and color feature could describe the OOS areas in a better way. However, due to the problem of camera angle, shelf type and lighting, it is difficult to detect certain type of out-of-stock areas by use of only one feature effectively. Therefore, in future several features, especially the edge information and color information of the out-of-stock areas, should be combined to achieve a better result.

Acknowledgement. This work was supported by the grants of the National Science Foundation of China (Grant Nos. 61472467 and 61672011) and the National Key R&D Program of China (2017YFC1311003).

References

1. Corsten, D., Gruen, T.: On shelf availability: an examination of the extent, the causes, and the efforts to address retail out-of-stocks. In: Doukidis, G.J., Vrechopoulos, A.P. (eds.) Consumer Driven Electronic Transformation, pp. 131–149. Springer, Heidelberg (2005). https://doi.org/10.1007/3-540-27059-0_9
2. Fernie, J., Grant, D.B.: On-shelf availability: the case of a UK grocery retailer. Int. J. Logist. Manag. **19**(3), 293–308 (2008)
3. Moorthy, R., Behera, S., Verma, S., Bhargave, S., Ramanathan, P.: Applying image processing for detecting on-shelf availability and product positioning in retail stores. In: Proceeding of the Third International Symposium on Women in Computing and Informatics (Wci-2015), pp. 451–457 (2015)
4. Papakiriakopoulos, D., Pramatari, K., Doukidis, G.: A decision support system for detecting products missing from the shelf based on heuristic rules. Decis. Support Syst. **46**(3), 685–694 (2009)
5. Frontoni, E., Mancini, A., Zingaretti, P., Contigiani, M., Di Bello, L., Placidi, V.: Design and test of a real-time shelf out-of-stock detector system. Microsyst. Technol.-Micro-and Nanosyst.-Inf. Storage Process. Syst. **24**(3), 1369–1377 (2018)
6. Kejriwal, N., Garg, S., Kumar, S.: Product counting using images with application to robot-based retail stock assessment. In: 2015 IEEE International Conference on Technologies for Practical Robot Applications (Tepra) (2015)
7. Ren, S.Q., He, K.M., Girshick, R., Sun, J.: Faster R-CNN: towards real-time object detection with region proposal networks. IEEE Trans. Pattern Anal. Mach. Intell. **39**(6), 1137–1149 (2017)
8. Girshick, R., Donahue, J., Darrell, T., Malik, J.: Rich feature hierarchies for accurate object detection and semantic segmentation. In: 2014 IEEE Conference on Computer Vision and Pattern Recognition (CVPR), pp. 580–587 (2014)
9. Girshick, R.: Fast R-CNN. In: 2015 IEEE International Conference on Computer Vision (ICCV), pp. 1440–1448 (2015)
10. Canny, J.F.: A computation approach to edge detection. IEEE Trans. Pattern Anal. Mach. Intell. **8**, 679–698 (1986)
11. Aksoy, S., Haralick, R.M.: Textural features for image database retrieval. In: Proceedings of IEEE Workshop on Content-Based Access of Image and Video Libraries, pp. 45–49 (1998)
12. Joachims, T.: Making large-scale SVM learning practical. Technical reports, vol. 8, no. 3, p. 499-5 (1998)

A Fractional-Order Variational Residual CNN for Low Dose CT Image Denoising

Miao Chen, Yi-Fei Pu$^{(\boxtimes)}$, and Yu-Cai Bai

College of Computer Science, Sichuan University, Chengdu 610065, China
15071454440@163.com

Abstract. In this paper, a Fractional-order Variational Residual CNN (FVCNN) for Low Dose CT (LDCT) denoising is proposed. Recently, the trade-off between the radiation dose and the quality of CT image has become a challenging study. To this end, inspired on the rapid development and on the application of deep learning and fractional calculus, this paper combines CNN and fractional-order total variation to propose a new algorithm for LDCT image denoising. At first, a Fractional-order Total Variational (FTV) item is introduced into the loss function for texture enhancement. Secondly, a FVCNN with residual connection is constructed aiming at denoising. Finally, the capability of removing noise and preserving texture details of the proposed method is validated by experimental analysis. According to the experimental analysis, the fractional order regularization item can preserve the critical texture details while suppressing noise, generating high-quality CT image for radiologists' judgment. Compared with the state-of-the-art method, our method achieved better details preserving in vision as well as in numerical calculation. The promising results obtained by our extensive experiments will significantly improve the availability of LDCT images.

Keywords: Deep learning · Fractional calculus · Fractional-order regularization · Image denoising · Low Dose CT

1 Introduction

Computed Tomography (CT) scanning uses X-ray and detector to repeatedly scan a part of the patient under test, and then input the data acquired by the detector to the computer for processing, and complete the reconstruction of the voxel in a certain part of the patient through data transformation [1]. High-dose CT examination will cause a certain degree of harm to human health, while reducing the dose of CT scanning will seriously affect the effect of CT imaging, which may further affect the diagnosis of the patient's condition [2]. The Low Dose CT (LDCT) technique can reduce the number of photons received by the detector when the tube current is lowered while other scanning parameters remain unchanged, thus producing "photon starvation effect" [3].

LDCT image denoising algorithms are mainly divided into three categories: (1) sinogram domain filtration. Typical projection domain denoising methods include Penalty Weighted Least Squares (PWLS) [4] and adaptive convolution filtering [5]. (2) Iterative reconstruction algorithm [6], such as Adaptive Statistical Iterative Reconstruction (ASIR) algorithm. (3) Image denoising algorithm like Non-Local Mean

© Springer Nature Switzerland AG 2019
D.-S. Huang et al. (Eds.): ICIC 2019, LNCS 11643, pp. 238–249, 2019.
https://doi.org/10.1007/978-3-030-26763-6_23

algorithm (NLM) [7] and three-Dimensional Block Matching filtering algorithm (BM3D) [8]. Different from the raw data, the noise distribution in the image domain does not conform to a certain statistical model [9]. As a result, the denoising effects of these traditional methods are not ideal. Recently, some LDCT image denoising algorithms based on neural network [10–14] have been proposed. However, the most common loss function in the-state-of-art methods is Mean Square Error (MSE), which may loss many texture details while denoising and reduce quality of the denoised image.

After years of development and research, fractional calculus has been applied to LDCT [15]. Pu demonstrated that fractional calculus has unique properties and inherent advantages in terms of long-term memory, non-locality, and weak singularity in signal processing and image processing [16], which can preserve texture details while removing noise to the maximum extent. Motivated by the network structure of [17] and the application of residual learning [18], this paper proposes a denoising model based on the encoder-decoder structure and skip connection as well as fractional order variational regularization item, which is a major contribution to extending the application of fractional calculus to LDCT images denoising in residual CNN, especially for the parts rich in texture details.

This paper is organized as follows: In Sect. 2, the definitions of fractional calculus and related theories are introduced. In Sect. 3, the network structure and fractional-order loss function are introduced. In Sect. 4, the model is evaluated through experimental comparison. Furthermore, we conclude our works in the last section.

2 Mathematical Background

In this section, we introduced the classical definition of fractional calculus.

There are three classical definition expressions, including Grumwald - Letnikov (G-L), Riemann - Liouville (R-L) and Capotu definition. We mainly use the G-L definition of fractional calculus in our proposed model. The fractional-order differential expression based on G-L definition is as follows.

$$D_{G-L}^{v} s(x) = \frac{d^{v}}{[d(x-a)]^{v}} s(x)|_{G-L} = \lim_{N \to \infty} \left\{ \frac{\left(\frac{x-a}{N}\right)^{-v}}{\Gamma(-v)} \sum_{k=0}^{N-1} \frac{\Gamma(k-v)}{\Gamma(k+1)} s\left(x - k\left(\frac{x-a}{N}\right)\right) \right\}.$$

(1)

where the duration of signal s(x) is [a, x], and v is any real number (including fraction). G-L definition is directly derived from the integral calculus function, the only needed coefficient in (1) is the discrete sampling of s(x − k(x − a)/N) and the derivative or integral value of signal s(x) is not required.

Actually, according to G-L definition, we get (2), where n and v are any numbers.

$$\frac{d^n}{dx^n} \frac{d^v}{[d(x-a)]^v} s(x) = \frac{d^{n+v}}{[d(x-a)]^{n+v}} s(x). \tag{2}$$

3 FVCNN for LDCT

3.1 Construction of Loss Function

In this subsection, the noise model and the construction of loss function are introduced.

Assuming that X is a low dose CT (LDCT) image and Y is a corresponding normal dose CT (NDCT) image, the relational model between them can be defined as (3).

$$X = \sigma(Y) \tag{3}$$

where σ denotes the noise pollution caused by the dose reduction.

Denoising algorithm based on deep learning used to be independent in the statistical distribution of image noise, to implement the end-to-end mapping between images. The main function of the proposed network is to generate the fitting map between the noise image X and the residual image R, F(X): X→R. The denoised image is obtained by adding to LDCT image X: R + X.

As the optimizing target of a model, the loss function plays a critical role in deep learning. The loss function of the proposed method is (4), constructed by an average Euclidean error of each point, between the denoised image and the corresponding target image, adding to a fractional-order regularization item, representing the fractional order differentiation of the denoised image in 8 different directions.

$$Loss = L_E + \lambda L_{FTV} = \frac{1}{WH} \sum_{w=1}^{W} \sum_{h=1}^{H} \|Y - M(X)\|^2 + \lambda \sum_{w=1}^{W} \sum_{h=1}^{H} \left(\left|D_{x-}^v X'\right| + \left|D_{y-}^v X'\right| + \left|D_{x+}^v X'\right| \right.$$
$$\left. + \left|D_{y+}^v X'\right| + \left|D_{LDD}^v X'\right| + \left|D_{RUD}^v X'\right| + \left|D_{LUD}^v X'\right| + \left|D_{RDD}^v X'\right| \right). \tag{4}$$

where W and H denote the width and length of the image, M(X) denotes the final result, defined by X + F(X). F(X) denotes the fitting function trained by the proposed network. X' denotes the final denoised image, namely M(X). x^-, y^-, x^+, y^+, LDD, RUD, LUD and RDD represent the negative direction of the X-axis, the negative direction of the Y-axis, the positive direction of the X-axis, the positive direction of the X-axis, the left-down direction, the right-up direction, the left-up direction and the right-down direction. D_{x-}^v represents the derivative in x^- direction.

The experiments in [16] proved that the texture preserving and enhancing of the first order total variation is not satisfactory. Inspired by the fractional order calculus theory and the application fractional order differentiation in image processing [19], we further introduced fractional-order total variational regularization item into the loss function to improve model in texture preserving and enhancing.

In order to control the diffusion rate of the image in 8 directions, fractional mask operators in 8 directions were adopted. In [20], Pu proved that the yifeipu-2 operator has the best retention effect on texture details of the image, with the best convergence and accuracy compared with other operators. And it works best when the mask size is 7 * 7. In this paper, yifeipu-2 of template 7 * 7 was selected to construct fractional derivatives of 8 directions around each pixel in the image.

Because the integer-order total variation only consider the derivative of the x direction and y direction, ignoring the self-correlation between adjacent pixels, could lose part of the texture details information and cause "stair-casing". In this paper, we fully consider the eight directions around each pixel to keep the details by introducing the fractional order total variation. We proposed the fractional-order 1 norm of 8 directions, shown in (5).

$$L_{FTV} = \sum_{w=1}^{W}\sum_{h=1}^{H}\left(\left|D_{x-}^{v}X'\right| + \left|D_{y-}^{v}X'\right| + \left|D_{x+}^{v}X'\right| + \left|D_{y+}^{v}X'\right| + \left|D_{LDD}^{v}X'\right| + \left|D_{RUD}^{v}X'\right| + \left|D_{LUD}^{v}X'\right| + \left|D_{RDD}^{v}X'\right|\right)\right).$$

(5)

As for nx * ny digital gray image s(x, y) and n * n differential mask, fractional derivative of an image can be implemented numerically through convolutional filters respectively on the 8 symmetrical directions. The calculation processes of 8 directions are shown in [14]. The concrete structure of the fractional-order differential mask operators in 8 directions is shown in [20].

Actually, some of previous CNN model [21–23] mostly only used the 2nd norm, the average Euclidean error of each point, to be a loss function. Typical loss function is shown in (6).

$$L_E = \frac{1}{WH}\sum_{w=1}^{W}\sum_{h=1}^{H}\|Y - M(X)\|^2.$$

(6)

In order to suppress image artifacts, some other methods introduce the total variational regularization term into the loss function. The calculation method is as follows (7).

$$L_{TV} = \sum_{w=1}^{W}\sum_{h=1}^{H}\sqrt{(X'(w+1,h) - X'(w,h))^2 + (X'(w,h+1) - X'(w,h))^2}.$$ (7)

Particularly, when suppose v = 1, if we choose only two directions (x+ coordinate direction and y+ coordinate direction), (5) can be rewritten as (8), equal to (7). It indicates that fractional order total variation is a generalization of integral order.

$$L = \sum_{w=1}^{W} \sum_{h=1}^{H} \left(|D_{x^+}^1 X'| + |D_{y^+}^1 X'| \right)$$

$$= \sum_{w=1}^{W} \sum_{h=1}^{H} \sqrt{(X'(w+1,h) - X'(w,h))^2 + (X'(w,h+1) - X'(w,h))^2} \qquad (8)$$

Finally, as for the proposed loss function (4), the Euclidean distance is used to learn the pixel value of each pixel of the image, and the fractional total variation is related to the details of the image as a whole. λ is the weight of fractional total variational item, used to control the importance of the fractional order total variation in the optimization process, which should be greater than 0 and far less than 1.

3.2 Implementation of FVCNN

In this subsection, the concrete structure of FVCNN is proposed.

Compared with the original "red-net" [17], the proposed network added batch normalization layer BN between Conv and Relu layers except the first and the last layer. The overall architecture is shown in Fig. 1, with 7 convolution layers and 7 deconvolution layers. Each ConvBlock block is composed of three groups of conv-bn-relu, and each DeconvBlock block is composed of three groups of deconv-bn-relu. The concrete structures of the ConvBlock block and the DeconvBlock block are shown in Fig. 2. The second ConvBlock output is connected to the first DeconvBlock block. And there is a skip connection between the input and the last activation function layer, shown in Fig. 3.

In the network, the proposed network rejected the pooling layers of the original encoder to avoid details loss and added the BN layer before activation function. The input of the activation function can be normalized to a certain range, preventing gradient disappeared and accelerating the convergence speed of the network to improve the performance of network.

In order to solve two problems: details losing and gradient vanishing as network deepens, we use residual connection [13, 18], and add skip connection between corresponding convolution block and deconvolution block. The residual structure is shown in the Fig. 1, the longer arrow. There are two reasons for using residual connection. First, network training is difficult for the gradient vanishing problem mentioned above, and the combination of residual connection makes network training easier. Second, when the network depth increases, more details will be lost, making it more difficult to recover details by deconvolution layers. In addition, residual connection can make the network carry more details and improve the final output quality of the network.

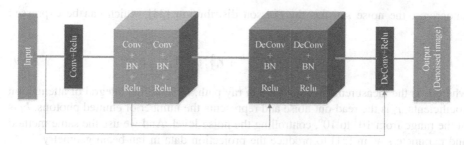

Fig. 1. Schematic of the network.

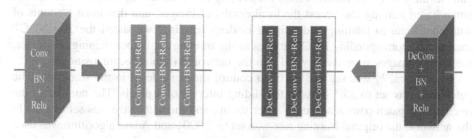

Fig. 2. Structure of ConvBlock and DeConvBlock.

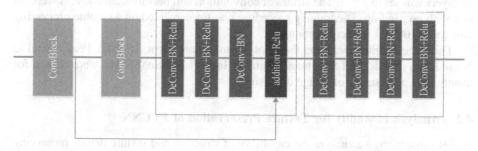

Fig. 3. Structure of the skip connection between blocks.

4   Experiments and Analysis

4.1   Numerical Achievement of FVCNN

This subsection studies the numerical achievement of FVCNN.

The normal-dose CT images are downloaded from the public datasets The Cancer Imaging Archive (TCIA). Adding the Poison noise into the sinograms by the fan-beam projection transformation, we can generate the corresponding LDCT images. In the sinograms, the noise satisfies the Poisson distribution [24], which can be expressed as (9).

$$z_i \sim Poisson\{b_i e^{-l_i} + r_i\}, i = 1, \ldots, I. \tag{9}$$

where z_i is the measurement along the i-th ray path, l_i is the line integral of attenuation coefficients, r_i is the read-out noise and represents the number of emitted photons. b_i is in the range from 10^4 to 10^6, controlling the noise level. And we use the same method and parameters as in [21] to produce the projection data in fan-beam geometry.

In our experiment, we chose 200 NDCT images and corresponding LDCT images as the training set with different parts of the human body for diversity while 100 image pairs as the testing set, different from the training set. Considering the great benefit that patch-based training can access the local details of images, and that large amounts of data contribute to learning and training in deep learning, we sliced the 200 NDCT images and corresponding LDCT images in the training set before training. However, the testing images were directly fed into the network without decomposition.

In addition, b_i was set to $5 * 10^4$ to control the noise level in the sinogram. The patch size was set to $55 * 55$ with the sliding interval of 4 pixels. The number of the overlapping patch pairs reached 10^6 after slicing and the batch size was set to 128. In the network, the original learning rate was set to 0.0001 and Adam algorithm was used to optimize the network. The convolution and deconvolution kernels were initialized with random Gaussian distributions with zero mean and standard deviation 0.01. The filter number of last layer was set to 1 and the others were set to 64. The kernel size of all layers was set to $3 * 3$. The strides of convolution and deconvolution layers were set to 1 with no padding. The training procedure was implemented on a graphic processing unit card (1080Ti) for acceleration.

The three metrics, including the Root Mean Square Error (RMSE), Peak Signal to Noise Ratio (PSNR) and Structural Similarity Index Measure (SSIM), were chosen for quantitative assessment of image denoising.

4.2   Analysis of Ability for Texture Preservation of FVCNN

In this subsection, we analyze the capability of structure and texture details preserving of FVCNN as well as contrast enhancing.

We tried $v = 0.5, 0.8, 0.85, 0.9, 0.95, 1, 1.05, 1.25, 2.25$ in the experiments. Figure 4 showed the comparison of denoising effect, the zoomed regions of interest (ROIs) in a lung picture.

In Fig. 4(b), the white part was blurred by noise pollution. To be honest, RED-CNN and the proposed method with different fractional orders have all suppressed the noise to a large extent. Figure 4(c) shown the denoised result of RED-CNN, which smoothened some essential small structures. By contrast, results in Fig. 4(d)–(l) have preserved more texture structure details to various degrees while removing noise and artifacts.

In Fig. 4(c), when removing the noise, the parts in the dashed circles and the bright spot pointed by the arrow have inevitably been treated as noise and tended to be suppressed. It is obviously that FVCNN with different order are much clear than RED-

CNN. In particular, as for the area marked by a red circle and the bright spot pointed by the blue arrow, in Fig. 4(c) they were almost invisible. The part marked by a red circle in Fig. 4(d), (h), (j) is clear, preserving the structure while removing most noise around. And the corresponding area in Fig. 4(e), (f), (k), (l) are not very clear though removing

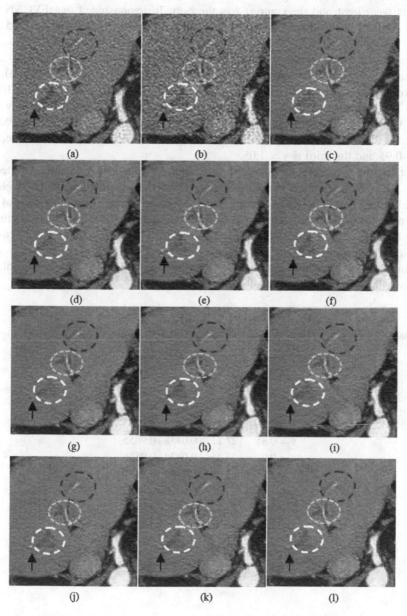

Fig. 4. Zoomed parts of a lung picture. (a) NDCT, (b) LDCT, (c) RED-CNN, (d) v = 0.5, (e) v = 0.8, (f) v = 0.85, (g) v = 0.9, (h) v = 0.95, (i) v = 1, (j) v = 1.05, (k) v = 1.25, (l) v = 2.25. (Color figure online)

most noise. Therefore, as for this kind of structure detail, FVCNN can gain better effect of details preserving and noise removing when v = 0.5, 0.95, 1.05. Regard as the low-contrast lesions marked by a purple dashed circle and a yellow dashed circle, there were some extra white artifacts in Fig. 4(c), while they were much less or even inexistent in Fig. 4(a) and Fig. 4(d)–(l). It can be seen that when v = 0.85 and 1.05, the artifacts were least and the contrast was the best. It demonstrated that FVCNN can reduce artifacts while denoising and enhancing contrast especially for v = 0.85 and 1.05.

Besides, the bright spot pointed by the blue arrow has been vanished after denoising in Fig. 4(c). By contrast, FVCNN with v = 0.8 and 1.05 in Fig. 4(e) and (j) were well-preserved when denoising. Other orders still look a little better than RED-CNN. The quantitative results for the whole image are listed Table 1. As shown in Table 1, all fractional-order methods have better values than RED-CNN on PSNR, SSIM and RMSE. Particularly, v = 0.5 has the best values of three metrics. The second is v = 0.95 and the third is v = 1.05.

Totally, the average values of 100 images in the whole testing dataset are listed in Table 2. It is evident that all fractional order methods outperformed the RED-CNN and integral order in numerically. According to Fig. 4, experiments shown that v = 0.4 can retain most texture and structure details and v = 0.85 can improve the contrast better in vision because of long-term memory, non-locality, and weak singularity of fractional calculus.

However, for the whole test dataset, the overall denoising effect in numerically is the best when v = 1.05 in terms of each of the metrics.

Table 1. Quantitative results with RED-CNN and FVCNN with different orders for Fig. 4

	PSNR	RMSE	SSIM
LDCT	24.856	0.0572	0.9736
RED-CNN	26.869	0.0453	0.9847
v = 0.5	**27.291**	**0.0432**	**0.9860**
v = 0.8	27.217	0.0436	0.9857
v = 0.85	27.172	0.0438	0.9855
v = 0.9	27.254	0.0434	0.9858
v = 0.95	27.280	0.0433	0.9860
v = 1	27.212	0.0436	0.9857
v = 1.05	27.234	0.0435	0.9858
v = 1.25	27.232	0.0435	0.9858
v = 2.25	27.189	0.0437	0.9856

Table 2. Quantitative results (mean) with different algorithms

	PSNR	RMSE	SSIM
LDCT	26.285	0.0518	0.9706
RED-CNN	30.128	0.0325	0.9901
v = 0.5	31.999	0.0255	0.9937
v = 0.8	31.846	0.0260	0.9934
v = 0.85	31.032	0.0254	0.9938
v = 0.9	31.977	0.0256	0.9937
v = 0.95	31.988	0.0255	0.9937
v = 1	31.943	0.0256	0.9937
v = 1.05	**32.089**	**0.0250**	**0.9939**
v = 1.25	31.966	0.0256	0.9937
v = 2.25	32.068	0.0253	0.9938

4.3 Multi-scale Denoising Analysis for FVCNN

In this subsection, we evaluate the robustness of FVCNN.

According to the experiments above, the method with fractional FTV has better results than ITV, which can preserve more structure and texture details while denoising. The reason is that fractional order differential value is not zero at the starting point of the gray scale step or slope, strengthening the high frequency information.

To sum up, FVCNN with different orders obtained different results for LDCT denoising. Especially for regions rich in structure and texture details, fractional differential plays a critical role in preserving more structures information to improve the quality of LDCT images visually, enhancing radiologists' judgment.

We used fixed noise level in the training of our experiments. In practice, the robustness to noise is really critical property because it is inevitable to suffer different noise level. We combine different noise levels in the training and testing datasets to evaluate the robustness of FVCNN. RED-CNN+ and FVCNN+ represent the same

Table 3. Comparision of different methods with different noise level

b_0	RED CNN	FVCNN			RED CNN+	FVCNN+		
		v = 1	v = 0.95	v = 1.05		v = 1	v = 0.95	v = 1.05
$5 * 10^5$	27.930	27.873	28.027	28.052	27.667	28.004	**28.112**	28.100
	0.0433	0.0435	0.0427	0.0426	0.0453	0.0427	**0.0422**	0.0422
	0.9818	0.9814	0.9820	0.9821	0.9793	0.9819	**0.9823**	0.9823
10^5	27.201	27.268	27.384	**27.417**	26.873	27.247	27.279	27.291
	0.0472	0.0468	0.0462	**0.0460**	0.0497	0.0468	0.0467	0.0466
	0.9786	0.9787	0.9792	**0.9793**	0.9753	0.9785	0.9784	0.9787
10^4	27.182	27.263	27.380	**27.407**	26.885	27.248	27.284	27.285
	0.0473	0.0469	0.0462	**0.0461**	0.0496	0.0469	0.0467	0.0466
	0.9785	0.9787	0.9792	**0.9792**	0.9754	0.9785	0.9784	0.9787

networks as RED-CNN and FVCNN with randomly mixed training dataset for $b_0 = 5 * 10^4$, $b_0 = 10^5$ and $b_0 = 5 * 10^5$. The average results for 100 denoised images randomly selected are listed in Table 3. For each b_0 in Table 3, the values of each row represented PSNR, RMSE and SSIM respectively. FVCNN (v = 1.05) and FVCNN+ (v = 0.95) obtained the best performance. Even if the noise level is fixed in training, FVCNN still has good robustness to noise with different levels, especially v = 1.05.

5 Conclusion

In this paper, we proposed a new network structure with a new loss function. We made full use of the unique strengths of fractional calculus in terms of long-term memory, non-locality, and weak singularity and the ability of a fractional differential to enhance the complex textural details of an image in a nonlinear manner, to construct a fractional-order variational item. Particularly, we extended the integral-order regularization item to fractional order and applied it on LDCT images. Experimental results show that the unique property of fractional differentiation to preserve texture details while removing noise can improve the effect visually and numerically. In the future, we will further study the properties of research, which is required to determine the image-dependent optimal fractional calculus in digital image processing, and further study the characteristics of LDCT. For example, further value of v or make it adaptive. It will be discussed in my future work.

References

1. Templeton, A.W., et al.: A 57 cm X-ray image intensifier digital radiography system. In: Lemke, H., Rhodes, M.L., Jaffee, C.C., Felix, R. (eds.) Computer Assisted Radiology/Computergestützte Radiologie, pp. 276–281. Springer, Heidelberg (1985). https://doi.org/10.1007/978-3-642-52247-5_45
2. Mastora, I., Remyjardin, M., Suess, C., Scherf, C., Guillot, J.P., Remy, J.: Dose reduction in spiral CT angiography of thoracic outlet syndrome by anatomically adapted tube current modulation. Eur. Radiol. 11(4), 590 (2001)
3. Mori, I., Machida, Y., Osanai, M., Iinuma, K.: Photon starvation artifacts of X-ray CT: their true cause and a solution. Radiol. Phys. Technol. 6(1), 130–141 (2013)
4. Wang, J., Li, T., Lu, H., Liang, Z.: Penalized weighted least-squares approach to sinogram noise reduction and image reconstruction for low-dose X-Ray computed tomography. IEEE Trans. Med. Imaging 25(10), 1272–1283 (2006)
5. Kachelriess, M., Watzke, O., Kalender, W.A.J.M.P.: Generalized multi-dimensional adaptive filtering for conventional and spiral single-slice, multi-slice, and cone-beam CT. Med. Phys. 28(4), 475–490 (2001)
6. Elbakri, I.A., Fessler, J.A.: Efficient and accurate likelihood for iterative image reconstruction in x-ray computed tomography. In: Proceedings of SPIE, vol. 5032 (2003)
7. Li, Z., et al.: Adaptive nonlocal means filtering based on local noise level for CT denoising. Med. Phys. 41(1), 011908 (2014)
8. Fumene, F.P., Vinegoni, C., Gros, J., Sbarbati, A., Weissleder, R.: Block matching 3D random noise filtering for absorption optical projection tomography. Phys. Med. Biol. 55 (18), 5401 (2010)

9. Whiting, B.R.: Signal statistics in x-ray computed tomography. In: Medical Imaging 2002: Physics of Medical Imaging, pp. 53–60. International Society for Optics and Photonics (2002)

10. Bevilacqua, V., et al.: Metallic artifacts removal in breast CT images for treatment planning in radiotherapy by means of supervised and unsupervised neural network algorithms. In: Huang, D.-S., Heutte, L., Loog, M. (eds.) ICIC 2007. LNCS, vol. 4681, pp. 1355–1363. Springer, Heidelberg (2007). https://doi.org/10.1007/978-3-540-74171-8_138

11. Dong, C., Chen, C.L., He, K., Tang, X.: Image super-resolution using deep convolutional networks. IEEE Trans. Pattern Anal. Mach. Intell. 38(2), 295–307 (2016)

12. Oyedotun, O.K., El Rahman Shabayek, A., Aouada, D., Ottersten, B.: Training very deep networks via residual learning with stochastic input shortcut connections. In: Liu, D., Xie, S., Li, Y., Zhao, D., El-Alfy, E.S. (eds.) International Conference on Neural Information Processing. LNCS, vol. 10635, pp. 23–33. Springer, Cham (2017). https://doi.org/10.1007/978-3-319-70096-0_3

13. Srivastava, R.K., Greff, K., Schmidhuber, J.: Training very deep networks. Computer Science (2015)

14. Xie, J., Xu, L., Chen, E.: Image denoising and inpainting with deep neural networks. In: Advances in Neural Information Processing Systems, pp. 341–349 (2012)

15. Liao, Z.: Low-dosed X-ray computed tomography imaging by regularized fully spatial fractional-order Perona-Malik diffusion. Adv. Math. Phys. 2013(1), 2093 (2013)

16. Pu, Y.F., Zhou, J.L., Yuan, X.: Fractional differential mask: a fractional differential-based approach for multiscale texture enhancement. IEEE Trans. Image Process. 19(2), 491–511 (2010)

17. Mao, X.-J., Shen, C., Yang, Y.-B.: Image restoration using very deep convolutional encoder-decoder networks with symmetric skip connections. In: Advances in Neural Information Processing Systems (2016)

18. He, K., Zhang, X., Ren, S., Sun, J.: Deep residual learning for image recognition. In: IEEE Conference on Computer Vision and Pattern Recognition, pp. 770–778 (2015)

19. Pu, Y.F., et al.: A fractional-order variational framework for retinex: fractional-order partial differential equation based formulation for multi-scale nonlocal contrast enhancement with texture preserving. IEEE Trans. Image Process. 27(3), 1214–1229 (2017)

20. Pu, Y.F.: Fractional-order Euler-Lagrange equation for fractional-order variational method: a necessary condition for fractional-order fixed boundary optimization problems in signal processing and image processing. IEEE Access 4, 10110–10135 (2016)

21. Chen, H., et al.: Low-dose CT with a residual encoder-decoder convolutional neural network (RED-CNN). IEEE Trans. Med. Imaging 36, 2524–2535 (2017)

22. Chen, H., et al.: Low-dose CT denoising with convolutional neural network. In: 14th International Symposium on Biomedical Imaging, pp. 143–146 (2017)

23. Chen, H., et al.: Low-dose CT via convolutional neural network. Biomed. Opt. Express 8(2), 679 (2017)

24. Dong, Z., et al.: A simple low-dose X-ray CT simulation from high-dose scan. IEEE Trans. Nucl. Sci. 62(5), 2226–2233 (2015)

CNN-SIFT Consecutive Searching and Matching for Wine Label Retrieval

Xiaoqing Li, Jiansheng Yang, and Jinwen Ma$^{(\boxtimes)}$

Department of Information Science,
School of Mathematical Sciences and LMAM,
Peking University, Beijing 100871, China
xiaoqing_li@pku.edu.cn, {yjs,jwma}@math.pku.edu.cn

Abstract. Wine label retrieval is key to automatic wine brand search through the web or mobile phone in our daily life. In comparison with the general image retrieval tasks, it is a rather challenging problem with a huge number of unbalanced wine brand images. In this paper, we propose a CNN-SIFT Consecutive Searching and Matching (CSCSM) framework for wine label retrieval. In particular, a CNN is trained to recognize the main-brand (manufacturer) for narrowing the searching range, while the SIFT descriptor is improved by adopting the RANSAC and TF-IDF mechanisms to match the final sub-brand (item attribute under the manufacture). The experiments are conducted on a dataset containing approximately 548k images of wine labels with 17, 328 main-brands and 260, 579 sub-brands. It is demonstrated by the experimental results that our proposed CSCSM method can solve the wine label retrieval problem effectively and efficiently and outperform the competitive methods.

Keywords: Wine label retrieval · CNN · SIFT descriptor

1 Introduction

Nowadays, wine label retrieval becomes very important and popular with the improvement of living standard. In order to solve this problem, we need to construct an effective and efficient automatic wine label image retrieval system which can return the wine brand in an input wine label image so that the related information about the wines of this brand can be provided to the user or recommendation system. The interest of this paper is in the wine label retrieval, i.e., to recognize the brand of the wine via a query wine label image from a dataset. In comparison with the general image retrieval problems, it has two major challenges. Firstly, there is a huge number of wine label images with large numbers of main-brands and sub-brands, which makes the recognition task very difficult. Secondly, the numbers of the samples in different sub-brands are quite different so that the actual classes are rather unbalanced. Moreover, there is even a significant difference among the wine label images of one sub-brand, as shown in Fig. 1, which makes the classification more difficult.

As far as we know, most of the existing methods for wine label retrieval are realized by recognizing the texts on the images [1]. They firstly segment each character on the image, and then identify those single segmented characters, respectively.

© Springer Nature Switzerland AG 2019
D.-S. Huang et al. (Eds.): ICIC 2019, LNCS 11643, pp. 250–261, 2019.
https://doi.org/10.1007/978-3-030-26763-6_24

(a)   (b)   (c)   (d)

Fig. 1. Typical examples of wine label images. (a) and (b) two pairs of examples with different main-brands and sub-brands, but the examples in (b) have very similar overall styles; (c) two examples with the same main-brand but different sub-brands; (d) two examples with the same main-brand and sub-brand, but there is a distant difference between them.

Clearly, the character recognition relies heavily on the character segmentation. If the fonts are standard and the layouts are similar, the segmentation can perform well and thus the retrieval accuracy can keep high. However, the realistic situation is that the font style is changeable and the sizes of characters are quite different, which makes the segmentation effect degrade severely. Other methods try to utilize some conventional features to deal with the recognition or matching problem [2]. Actually, those methods perform well on datasets with a small number of brands. However, as the number of brands is large, the recognition accuracy will decrease sharply, because those conventional features have limited ability to retrieve a large number of images. Besides, the retrieval time of each image will increase rapidly in a large dataset. To overcome these disadvantages, we propose a CNN-SIFT Consecutive Searching and Matching (CSCSM) framework for wine label retrieval with a large number of brands. This method firstly utilizes an advanced deep CNN to shrink the searching range by recognizing the main-brand in a supervised learning mode, and then apply an improved SIFT descriptor based on the combination of the RANSAC and TF-IDF mechanisms to match the final sub-brand. It can not only increase the retrieval accuracy, but also speed up the retrieval process in a large dataset. Finally, we conduct the experiments on a real-world dataset to demonstrate the effectiveness and efficiency of our proposed CSCSM method for wine label retrieval.

The main contributions of this paper lie in three aspects:

– It presents a two-phase retrieval framework, which can not only retrieve the main-brand but also find out the sub-brand.
– The deep network is combined with the conventional feature descriptor to improve the retrieval accuracy and efficiency.
– The Term Frequency-Inverse Document Frequency (TF-IDF) [3, 4] mechanism and the Random Sample Consensus (RANSAC) mechanism are adopted to reduce certain defects emerged in the conventional SIFT matching.

This paper is organized as follows. Section 2 gives a review of the related work. We present the CSCSM framework in Sect. 3. Section 4 summarizes the experimental results. We make a brief conclusion in Sect. 5.

2   Related Work

2.1   SIFT Descriptor

SIFT descriptor [5] is widely used in the fields of image retrieval [6], image recognition, and 3D reconstruction [7] for its excellent functions, such as the invariances of scale, rotation, brightness and perspective. Although the SIFT features can lead to high retrieval accuracy, their computing time and storage space are too large. This disadvantage makes it not very competitive to the image retrieval task for a large dataset. In order to reduce the storage space complexity of the SIFT descriptor, Sivic [8] proposed an algorithm combining the Bag of Words (BOW) algorithm. Similarly, Jegou [6] proposed another algorithm with the Vector of Locally Aggregated Descriptors (VLAD) strategy. Both of these algorithms were aimed at quantifying the SIFT features using a codebook. They were able to reduce the storage space complexity of SIFT descriptors while maintain the retrieval accuracy to some extent. However, the retrieval results are not good enough when they are applied to a wine label image dataset whose numbers of the main-brands and the sub-brands are large.

Here, we try to combine the mechanisms of RANSAC and TF-IDF in the SIFT descriptor. Actually, the RANSAC mechanism can effectively remove the wrong SIFT matching pairs, while the TF-IDF mechanism improves the matching process according to the importance of each descriptor. In order to reduce training time and space storage, instead of using BOW strategy to quantify the SIFT features [9], we redefine a new SIFT distance function based on the importance of each descriptor.

2.2   CNN for Supervised Classification

Deep convolutional neural network is considered as a breakthrough in the field of supervised classification. AlexNet [10] was proposed in the ImageNet classification competition, it achieved the best accuracy and was much better than its competitors. After that, it was found that deeper CNN performed better than shallower ones under the premise of similar structure. VGG [11] was constructed with much more convolutional layers than AlexNet, and improved the classification accuracy in ImageNet by 7.3%. However, deeper neural networks are more difficult to train because of the diffusion and explosion of gradient. He [12] proposed a "ShortCut" connection to ease the training of deeper networks, then proposed the ResNet. It was widely used in image classification, scene segmentation, etc. Based on ResNet, ResNeXt [13] was proposed combined with inception strategy [14]. It could achieve almost the same accuracy with about half parameters, compared with ResNet.

We employ ResNeXt to retrieve main-brand of the query image. Even if a transfer learning strategy is used, it still requires that each main-brand has enough labeled samples, but this is too harsh for wine label image dataset where lots of main-brands have only 10 labeled samples. In order to ensure the retrieval accuracy, CNN is not used to return one main-brand, but a certain number (It will be introduced in Sect. 3.2 in detail.) of main-brands to narrow the searching range. The left work is assigned to improved SIFT matching. This strategy can get higher accuracy using less retrieval time.

3   CSCSM Framework

In this section, we present the CSCSM framework in detail. As shown in Fig. 2, when a query image is input to the CSCSM system, the Fully Convolutional Networks (FCN) is utilized to segment the label area and remove the background. Then, the fine-tuned ResNeXt network based on the given labeled dataset returns a number of possible main-brands. The improved SIFT matching is conducted on all the wine label samples with the possible main-brands to get the most similar sub-brands.

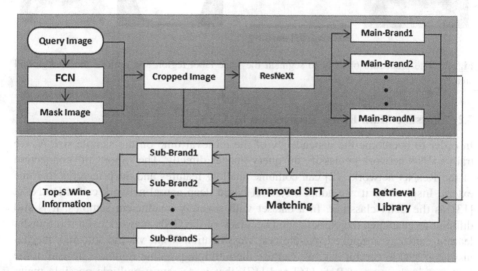

Fig. 2. The sketch of the CSCSM framework. The blue part is for the identification of the main-brands, while the pink part is for the retrieval of the sub-brands. (Color figure online)

3.1   Segmentation of Wine Label by FCN

In order to reduce the interference of background factors in a wine label image, we need to separate the wine label or bottle region from the background area, which is essentially a binary semantic segmentation problem. Actually, FCN [15] is effective for semantic segmentation. Its segmentation procedure is shown in Fig. 3. With the strategy of transfer learning, we firstly get the FCN which is based on VGG16 and pre-trained on the VOC2012 dataset, and then fine-tune it to obtain the mask image of the image, so as to segment the label region from the wine label image and remove the background area.

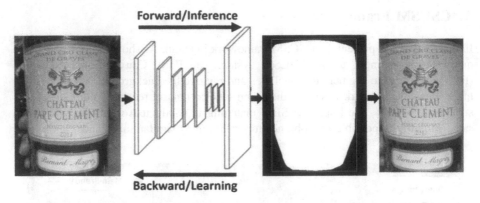

Fig. 3. The procedure of FCN to segment the wine label region and remove the background area.

3.2 Possible Main-Brand Recognition by CNN

In order to overcome the dependency of the retrieval time on the sample size N, we train a CNN network to classify the query images directly. The "ShortCut" connection of the ResNet network [12] can combine shallow features and deep features to some extent. Inspired by it, we adopt a ResNet based deep neural network called ResNeXt [13] as the CNN classifier. In a dataset with severely insufficient samples, it is still difficult to guarantee the classification accuracy of the CNN network even if a transfer learning strategy is applied. As the best classification result via the soft-max mechanism can lead to certain risk, we can use the multiple possible solutions instead of the best one in the way of Refs [16] and [17], that is, to return multiple possible main-brands at the same time. In the light of this idea, we have the following adaptive strategy.

Let the probabilities that the query image x_i belongs to each main-brands be p_j^i, where $1 \leq j \leq Z$ and Z is the number of main-brands. Without loss of generality, let $p_1^i \geq p_2^i \geq \cdots \geq p_Z^i$.

In order to ensure the accuracy of retrieval, we set the number of returned main-brands by

$$M_1 = argmin\{z | s_z \geq \delta\} \tag{1}$$

where $s_z = \sum_{j=1}^{z} p_j^i, z = 1, 2, \cdots, Z$ and δ is the threshold value set by experience. In some cases, for example, x_1 and x_2 represent two query samples with $p_1^1 = p_2^1 = \cdots = p_Z^1$ and $\delta/2 \approx p_1^2 > p_2^2 = \cdots = p_Z^2 \approx 0$, respectively. If δ is large, then M_1 is too large for x_2. In this case, too many main-brands will be returned, which will cause the following SIFT matching accuracy to decrease seriously; Conversely, if the threshold δ is small, M_1 is also small. The probability that the ground-truth of x_1 is in the returned main-brand sets is $P = M_1/n$. As a result, P will be small, which affect the accuracy of the method. So, δ is quite important and should be carefully selected. In the experiments of this paper, we set δ to 95%.

In order to alleviate the above difficulty, we set the upper bound of the number of main-brands to be a finite number M_2 for the query image. And, this value is also determined by experience. Finally, The number of main-brands returned by the CNN is determined by the minimum of M_1 and M_2

$$M = min\{M_1, M_2\} \tag{2}$$

3.3 Improved SIFT Matching for Sub-brands

After getting the most possible main-brands of the query image by the deep CNN, the improved SIFT matching is further used to retrieve the possible sub-brands. In order to prove the retrieval accuracy, we combine the RANSAC and TF-IDF mechanisms into the SIFT descriptor.

The mis-matching points extracted by the SIFT descriptor can cause serious interference to the subsequent image matching. Applying the RANSAC algorithm to the SIFT matching [18], we can successfully delete some mis-matching point pairs, and then obtain the features with scale, rotation, certain affine invariance and anti-jamming, as shown in Fig. 4.

Fig. 4. The left and right subfigures illustrate the SIFT feature matching results without and with the RANSAC mechanism, respectively.

Term Frequency-Inverse Document Frequency (TF-IDF) is one of the most popular weighting technique in information retrieval. It uses numerical statistic to reflect the importance of a word to a document in a corpus. The weight of a word increases proportionally to the number of times it appears in the document and is negatively correlated with the frequency of it in the corpus.

We can also adopt the TF-IDF mechanism into the SIFT feature matching. In fact, a SIFT descriptor can be regarded as a visual word while an image can be regarded as a document. TF-IDF is employed to determine the weight of each SIFT descriptor in the feature matching. In this way, we can further improve the possibility of seeking out the true sub-brand of the query image.

Let x_0 be the query image and $\{x_1, x_2, \cdots, x_N\}$ be the image dataset. For each image, we extract the first K SIFT descriptors according to the degree of saliency. $\{s_1^i, s_2^i, \cdots, s_K^i\}$ denotes the SIFT descriptors of x_i. Let d_{pk}^j be the Euclidean distance between the p_{th} SIFT descriptor of x_0 and the k_{th} SIFT descriptor of x_j. Without loss of generality, let $d_{p1}^j < d_{p2}^j < \cdots < d_{pK}^j$. In the image retrieval, if the SIFT descriptor s_p^0 is noise, such as salt and pepper noise, usually $d_{p1}^j / d_{p2}^j \ll 1$; if s_p^0 is the real feature point of x_0, such as contour folding, then $d_{p1}^j / d_{p2}^j \approx 1$. Given the facts above, we define the matching result in s_p^0 and s_k^j as an indicator function by

$$\theta_{pk}^j = \begin{cases} 1, & k \in G_P^j \\ 0, & k \notin G_P^j \end{cases} \tag{3}$$

where

$$G_P^j = \{k | d_{pk}^j = \min_l \{d_{pl}^j\}, d_{pr}^j = \min_{l \neq k} \{d_{pl}^j\}, d_{pk}^j / d_{pr}^j \geq \epsilon\} \tag{4}$$

and $\epsilon \in (0, 1]$ is the threshold parameter. Denote

$$TF_P = \frac{\delta\left(s_p^0\right)}{\sum_k \delta\left(s_k^0\right)} \tag{5}$$

where $\delta(\cdot)$ is an indicator function and $\delta\left(s_k^0\right) = 1$ if $s_k^0 \in \{s_1^0, s_2^0, \cdots, s_K^0\}$, otherwise $\delta\left(s_k^0\right) = 0$.

Obviously, TF_P represents the frequency that the p_{th} SIFT descriptor of x_0 appears in the image. Since each SIFT descriptor of the image is unique, $TF_P = 1/K$.

As for the query image x_0, the IDF of the p_{th} SIFT descriptor is denoted as $IDF_P = N/c_p$, where c_p indicates the number of images containing s_p^0. In order to avoid a real number divided by zero, let $c_p = 1$ if there is not eligible image. In summary, $c_p = \max\left\{\left|\left\{j | s_p^0 \in \left\{s_1^j, s_2^j, \cdots, s_K^j\right\}\right\}\right|, 1\right\}$. An improved SIFT-based distance function is utilized to represent the difference between x_0 and x_j

$$d_j = \sum_{p=1}^K TF_P IDF_P \sum_{k=1}^K \theta_{pk}^j \tag{6}$$

For the convenience of calculation, a simplified notation is used as a substitution for d_j

$$D_j = \sum_{p=1}^K \frac{1}{c_p} \sum_{k=1}^K \theta_{pk}^j \tag{7}$$

which is called the improved SIFT distance.

We use the improved SIFT distance to measure the degree of difference between the query image x_0 and the other images in the retrieval library. It is very beneficial to improve matching the ground-truth main-brands and sub-brands of wine images. The details of the algorithm are shown in Algorithm 1.

Algorithm 1. the Improved SIFT Matching Algorithm

Input: query image x_0, retrieval library $\{x_1, \cdots, x_N\}$
Output: S best matching images
1: set $i = 1$
2: Extract the SIFT descriptors of x_0 and correct SIFT matching of x_0 and x_i with RANSAC.
3: Calculate θ_{pk}^i, where $p, k = 1, 2, \cdots, K$
4: Calculate the improved distance D_i
5: If $i < N$, then $i = i + 1$ and go to step 2, otherwise go to the next step.
6: Sort $D_1, D_2, \cdots, D_N$ in descending order.
7: Take the first S ones and return the matching images.

---

4   Experimental Results

In this section, we evaluate our proposed CSCSM wine label retrieval approach on a real world dataset, being compared with competitive methods. Without specification, we implement our above experiments based on Python code in Ubuntu 16.04. The hardware configuration is as follows: NVIDIA Tesla M40 graphics card, 24 GB GPU memory.

4.1   Wine Label Image Dataset

In the experiment, we verify the effectiveness and efficiency of the CSCSM method in a real-world wine label image dataset provided by Ruixun Science and Technology (Beijing) Limited Company in China. It contains 17,328 main-brands, 260,579 sub-brands and 547,857 wine images. Table 1 shows the sample sizes of the main-brands and sub-brands.

Table 1. The number of samples in main-brands and sub-brands

Number$_{images}$	Number$_{main-brands}$	Number$_{images}$	Number$_{sub-brands}$
11~20	8974	1	129932
21~30	3359	2	71257
31~50	2811	3	24993
51~100	1473	4~10	32802
101~1371	711	11~371	1595

All of the images in wine label image dataset are manually taken by mobile phones. The size of the images is 500×375 and all the images are formatted into RGB. It contains many interference factors, such as background, light changes, local highlight, marginal highlight, image rotation and so on. Each image is labeled with a sub-brand belong to a main-brand.

4.2 Data Preprocessing

In the experiment, we firstly perform the data enhancement including adding Gaussian blur, changing contrast, sharpness, saturation, brightness, and tilt. After that, the FCN is implemented to segment the wine label region and remove the background area so that we can reduce the interference from the background.

4.3 Improved SIFT Matching

We further evaluate the retrieval effect of the improved SIFT matching method against the conventional one on a subset of wine label image dataset. For clarity, the improved SIFT matching method is referred to as SIFT+RANSAC+TF-IDF, while the SIFT matching with the RANSAC algorithm is referred to as SIFT+RANSAC. The selected subset contains 400 retrieval library images and 100 query images. In order to reduce the influence of noise and other interference factors, we extract only the first 500 SIFT keypoints in the descending order of significance. The experimental results are listed in Table 2.

Table 2. The experimental results of the improved SIFT matching method on wine label image dataset

Algorithm	MA	SA	Time(s)
SIFT	0.58	0.48	**19.9538**
SIFT+RANSAC	0.74	0.69	25.1209
SIFT+RANSAC+TF-IDF	**0.82**	**0.76**	25.9183

MA: The average retrieval accuracy of the main-brands.
SA: The accuracy of the sub-brands.
Time(s): Instead of the best The average time spent when each image is retrieved.

It can be found from Table 2 that the accuracy of the conventional SIFT matching method is very low when the number of samples to be retrieved is large. The SIFT +RANSAC matching method introduces the RANSAC process so that the retrieval time is increased by 25.90% relative to the pure SIFT matching. But the MA is increased by 16% and the SA is increased by 21%. In comparison with SIFT+RAN-NSAC, SIFT+RANSAC+TF-IDF increases MA by 8%, and SA by 7% with the retrieval time being increased by 3.17%.

4.4 Retrieval Results and Comparison on a Small Dataset

In this subsection, we implement the CSCSM method and compare it with competitive algorithms, including our improved SIFT descriptor, the BOW and VLAD algorithms with our improved SIFT descriptors, and the CNNfeat-SVM algorithm [19]. Taking into account that the BOW and VLAD algorithms need using the K-means algorithm to establish the codebook. The time complexity is $O(NKT)$, where N, K, T denote the number of training samples, the codebook length and the times of iteration, respectively. If the training is implemented on the total wine label image dataset, the time cost is too long. So, as in the previous section, we take a subset of the wine label image dataset. This subset contains 13813 training images. For the BOW and VLAD algorithms, we set the length of the codebook to be 800 and 100 respectively. In order to speed up the retrieval of query images, we use the Ball-Tree algorithm for the codebooks of BOW and VLAD algorithms, which reduces the time complexity of each image retrieval from $O(N)$ to $O(logN)$. For the CNNfeat-SVM algorithm, we fine-tune the ResNeXt-50 network trained in the ImageNet dataset and extract the CNN features from the last fully connected layer. Finally, we use SVM for classification. The multiple classification strategy is 1-VS-1 in SVM. In order to compare the ability of CNN fully-connected layer features to express the main-brands and sub-brands, we conduct two experiments on the CNN-SVM algorithm, namely CNNfeat-SVM1 and CNNfeat-SVM2. Training labels are classified according to the main-brands and sub-brands, respectively. The sub-brand recognition of the Improved SIFT algorithm is accurate, but the calculation time is too long. The computational time of BOW and VLAD is significantly improved compared to the Improved SIFT algorithm, but the loss of information brought by recoding makes the algorithm seriously reduce the retrieval accuracy of the main-brands and sub-brands. CNNfeat-SVM1 has a recognition accuracy of 91.67% for the main-brands. It benefits from the less number of main-brands than that of sub-brands. On average, the algorithm uses only 0.0734 s for per query image. The disadvantage is that it cannot be used to identify sub-brands, which makes it unusable to wine label retrieval. Compared with CNNfeat-SVM1, CNNfeat-SVM2 can identify sub-brands, but the accuracy of main-brands recognition is reduced. Our CSCSM method is the best in the recognition accuracy of main-brands as well as sub-brands, reaching 92.85% and 79.76%, respectively. The calculation time is much less than the Improved SIFT algorithm. A more detailed result is shown in Table 3.

Table 3. The comparison among CSCSM and the competitive methods

Method	MA	SA	Time(s)
Improved SIFT	0.9074	0.7619	355.7199
BOW(800)	0.1547	0.0476	0.8327
VLAD(100)	0.7500	0.5476	0.6126
CNNfeat-SVM1	0.9167	–	**0.0734**
CNNfeat-SVM2	0.7976	0.1905	5.2899
CSCSM	**0.9285**	**0.7976**	3.5819

4.5 Retrieval Result on the Real World Wine Label Image Dataset

We finally implement the CSCSM method on the real world wine label image dataset. As shown in Sect. 4.1, the total number of images in the dataset is very large. As a result, most of the methods we mentioned above cannot work for this retrieval task.

According to Table 2, the retrieval times per query images of the pure SIFT matching, SIFT+RANSAC matching and SIFT+RANSAC+TF-IDF matching are recorded to be 6.07 h, 7.65 h and 7.89 h, respectively. Therefore, the retrieval time of these SIFT matching methods is intolerable. As for the SIFT matching using the BOW and VLAD strategy, the retrieval time maybe is acceptable, while as we find, the training time of codebooks is very long and intolerable. So, we give up the experiment of them. The CNNfeat-SVM1 cannot be used for this task, because it is incompetent in retrieving sub-brands. As for the CNNfeat-SVM2, the accuracy of sub-brands retrieval will less than that in Table 3, because each sub-brand just has 2.10 examples in the wine label image dataset. It is far from satisfied for the training process. Therefore, as we know, the only practical method mentioned in this paper is CSCSM. In order to test the influence of the number M of the main-brands returned in Fig. 2, we carry out three experiments, return one, three and five main-brands respectively. The number S of sub-brands returned is fixed to five. The result is shown in Table 4. As the increase of M, the accuracy of main-brands retrieval rises, while the rate of rising decays. The best accuracy of sub-brands retrieval is achieved by CSCSM(M3), not CSCSM(M5), because the former has a narrower range of retrieval in SIFT matching processing.

Table 4. The results of the CSCSM method in the real world wine label image dataset

Method	MA	SA	Time(s)
CSCSM(M1)	0.8125	0.6932	**2.5286**
CSCSM(M3)	0.9063	**0.8014**	7.2658
CSCSM(M5)	**0.9107**	0.7846	9.5657

"M1" means returning 1 main-brand, similar to "M3" and "M5"

5   Conclusion

We have proposed a CNN-SIFT Consecutive Searching and Matching (CSCSM) framework for wine label retrieval. This framework is a two-phase system of consecutive searching and matching. Specifically, it utilizes a CNN to be trained for main-brand classification to narrow the searching range, and improved SIFT descriptor which combines the RANSAC and TF-IDF mechanisms to retrieve the final sub-brand more effectively. This strategy makes the retrieval time complexity independent on the number of samples in the retrieval dataset. It is demonstrated by the experiments on a real-world wine label image dataset that the CSCSM method has the best retrieval accuracy and efficiency on both main-brands and sub-brands in comparison with the competitive methods.

Acknowledgment. This work is supported by the Natural Science Foundation of China for Grand U1604153.

References

1. Lim, J., Kim, S., Park, J.H., Lee, G.S., Yang, H.J., Lee, C.W.: Recognition of text in wine label images. In: Chinese Conference on Pattern Recognition, pp. 1–5 (2009)
2. Wu, M.Y., Lee, J.H., Kuo, S.W.: A hierarchical feature search method for wine label image recognition. In: International Conference on Telecommunications and Signal Processing, pp. 568–572 (2015)
3. Joachims, T.: Text categorization with support vector machines: learning with many relevant features. In: Nédellec, C., Rouveirol, C. (eds.) ECML 1998. LNCS, vol. 1398, pp. 137–142. Springer, Heidelberg (1998). https://doi.org/10.1007/BFb0026683
4. Wu, H.C., Luk, R.W.P., Wong, K.F.: Interpreting TF-IDF term weights as making relevance decisions. ACM Trans. Inf. Syst. **26**(3), 13 (2008)
5. Lowe, D.G.: Distinctive image features from scale-invariant keypoints. Int. J. Comput. Vision **60**(2), 91–110 (2004)
6. Jegou, H., Douze, M., Schmid, C., Perez, P.: Aggregating local descriptors into a compact image representation. In: IEEE Conference on Computer Vision and Pattern Recognition, pp. 3304–3311 (2010)
7. Peng, K., Chen, X., Zhou, D., Liu, Y.: 3D reconstruction based on SIFT and Harris feature points. In: 2009 IEEE International Conference on Robotics and Biomimetics, pp. 960–964 (2009)
8. Sivic, J., Zisserman, A.: Video Google: a text retrieval approach to object matching in videos. In: Proceedings Ninth IEEE International Conference on Computer Vision, p. 1470 (2003)
9. Zhou, W., Li, H., Hong, R., Lu, Y., Tian, Q.: BSIFT: toward data-independent codebook for large scale image search. IEEE Trans. Image Process. **24**(3), 967–979 (2015)
10. Krizhevsky, A., Sutskever, I., Hinton, G.E.: ImageNet classification with deep convolutional neural networks. In: Advances in Neural Information Processing Systems, pp. 1097–1105 (2012)
11. Simonyan, K., Zisserman, A.: Very deep convolutional networks for large-scale image recognition. CoRR abs/1409.1556 (2014). http://arxiv.org/abs/1409.1556
12. He, K., Zhang, X., Ren, S., Sun, J.: Deep residual learning for image recognition. In: IEEE Conference on Computer Vision and Pattern Recognition, pp. 770–778 (2016)
13. Xie, S., Girshick, R., Dollar, P., Tu, Z., He, K.: Aggregated residual transformations for deep neural networks. In: IEEE Conference on Computer Vision and Pattern Recognition, pp. 1492–1500 (2017)
14. Szegedy, C., Vanhoucke, V., Ioffe, S., Shlens, J., Wojna, Z.: Rethinking the inception architecture for computer vision. In: IEEE Conference on Computer Vision and Pattern Recognition, pp. 2818–2826 (2016)
15. Long, J., Shelhamer, E., Darrell, T.: Fully convolutional networks for semantic segmentation. In: IEEE Conference on Computer Vision and Pattern Recognition, pp. 3431–3440 (2015)
16. Swets, D.L., Weng, J.J.: Using discriminant eigenfeatures for image retrieval. IEEE Trans. Pattern Anal. Mach. Intell. **18**(8), 831–836 (1996)
17. Tieu, K., Viola, P.: Boosting image retrieval: special issue on content-based image retrieval. Int. J. Comput. Vision **56**(1–2), 17–36 (2004)
18. Wei, W., Jun, H., Yiping, T.: Image matching for geomorphic measurement based on SIFT and RANSAC methods. In: 2008 International Conference on Computer Science and Software Engineering, vol. 2, pp. 317–320 (2008)
19. Azizpour, H., Razavian, A.S., Sullivan, J., Maki, A., Carlsson, S.: Factors of transferability for a generic convnet representation. IEEE Trans. Pattern Anal. Mach. Intell. **38**(9), 1790–1802 (2015)

Image Denoising via Multiple Images Nonlocally Means and Residual Tensor Decomposition

Pengfei Guo and Lijuan Shang[(✉)]

Academy of Computer Science and Technology, Neusoft Institute Guangdong,
Foshan 528200, China
shanglijuan@nuit.edu.cn

Abstract. The nonlocal means and iterate filtering techniques have attracted much research effort due to their superior performances. In this paper, the two approaches are combined into a framework to perform denoising based on residual tensor decomposition in loop of iteration. The search of accurate similar patches is essential for image denoising, to reconstruct the damaged part, we utilize multiple images nonlocal means method to exploit the image nonlocal self-similarity and obtain accurate weight, thus eliminate the interference of unsimilar patches. Although the degraded or lost slight structure of the image due to imperfect denoising methods, we propose the use of iterating residual image to compensate the sharpness of image texture via patch-based tensor decomposition, which can describe the intrinsic geometrical structure of there similar data. We use standard test images and multi-frame video test sequences to illustrate that the proposed denoising algorithm outperforms the leading algorithms such as weighted nuclear norm minimization (WNNM), BM3D and NCSR in terms of the quantitative and perceptual evaluation.

Keywords: Nonlocal means · Multiple images · Residual image ·
Tensor decomposition · Iterate filtering

1 Introduction

Image denoising [1] is a fundamental restoration problem in image processing, which reconstructs original image from observed image corrupted by zero mean additive gaussian white noise, which can be generally formulated by

$$\mathbf{Y} = \mathbf{X} + \mathbf{N} \tag{1}$$

A variety of algorithms for image denoising have already been put forward to reveals a better prior knowledge on natural image. For example, Buades et al. [2], presented the Non-Local Means (NLM) based on a nonlocal averaging of its all local neighborhood pixels in the image, however, the same weight cause that image textures are often blurred. In order to get accurate similar patches, some complicated nonlocal methods were presented such as K means based Singular Value Decomposition (K-SVD) [3] and Block-Matching and 3D filtering (BM3D) [4]. Since weight function

© Springer Nature Switzerland AG 2019
D.-S. Huang et al. (Eds.): ICIC 2019, LNCS 11643, pp. 262–273, 2019.
https://doi.org/10.1007/978-3-030-26763-6_25

has attracted a lot of attention in recent years, Zhong et al. [5] also presented a new weight for nonlocal means exploited the nonlocal similarities of residual image in method noise. In order to get more accurate similitude, Wang et al. [6] extended weight for nonlocal means method and proposed multiple noised images which are two different noisy images but with the same standard deviation to improve the performance of NLM method.

In image processing, there exists a few small coefficients and slight structure to be degraded or lost texture, we can use residual image to compensate the missing edge information. In [7], He et al. used residual learning framework to ease the training of networks and show that these residual networks are easier to optimize. The methods above are limited to refactor linear structure and can't capture nonlinearities, in [8], Özdemir et al. proposed a multiscale tensor decomposition to construct hierarchical low-rank structure by dividing the tensor into subtensors sequentially and fitting a low-rank model to better deal with intrinsic nonlinearities.

In this paper, we unify the nonlocal means, multiple images and the Tucker tensor decomposition to perform denoising based on residual tensor decomposition iteration. In the proposed framework, we first obtain the pre-denoised image $\mathbf{X}_M$ and residual image $\mathbf{R}_1$ by multiple images nonlocal means, then exploit them to redesign new weight and implemented nonlocal means algorithm again to get final denoised image $\mathbf{X}_N$. To reserve abundant detail information in edge area, residual image $\mathbf{R}_1$ can be calculated by noisy image and pre-denoised image $\mathbf{X}_M$. Next, Tucker tensor decomposition to obtain a refined observation $\mathbf{X}_T$ and residual image $\mathbf{R}_2$ between noisy image and $\mathbf{X}_T$. Finally, the four parts $\mathbf{X}_N$, $\mathbf{R}_1$, $\mathbf{X}_T$ and $\mathbf{R}_2$ are mixed to finely remove noise iteration by iteration based on tensor decomposition.

We summarize the main contribution of this paper as follows:

- Applying multiple images nonlocal means method to confirm the accurate similar patches and combine pre-denoised image and residual image to redesign new weigh.
- Tensor structured form a patch cluster of a nature image, the data processing method of the visual perception based on tensor can maintain data internal manifold structure and low-rank properties.
- Combining residual image not only can find accurate nonlocal similar patches, but also compensate the missing edge information effectively.

The rest of this paper is organized as follows. Section 2 introduces the proposed denoising algorithm in detail. In Sect. 3, we evaluate experimental results with others competing methods. Conclusions are given in Sect. 4.

2 Methods

Throughout the paper, to simplify the notation, we use lowercase letters for scalars, e.g., a. Boldface lowercase letters for vectors, e.g., $\mathbf{a}$. Boldface capital letters for matrices, e.g., $\mathbf{A}$. Boldface Euler script letters for higher-order tensors (order three or higher), e.g., $\mathcal{X}$.

2.1　Multiple Images Nonlocal Means

In the practical imaging system, the gray value of observation image patch can be formulated as:

$$\mathbf{y}_i = \mathbf{x}_i + \mathbf{n}_i \tag{2}$$

Where i is the pixel index, $\mathbf{x}_i$ and $\mathbf{y}_i$ denote the noise free and noisy image patches centered at pixel i index, respectively. $\mathbf{n}_i$ is the zero mean additive gaussian white noise.

The basic ideology of the nonlocal means denoising is to replace the noisy gray value y_i of the i-pixel with a weighted average of its all local neighborhood pixels. The estimated gray value x_i is defined as the follow:

$$\hat{x}_i = \frac{\sum_{j \in S_i} w_{ij} y_j}{\sum_{j \in S_i} w_{ij}} \tag{3}$$

where S_i is the search window, w_{ij} is the weight of pixels i and j, which is calculated by

$$w_{ij} = \exp\left(-\frac{\|\mathbf{y}_i - \mathbf{y}_j\|_2^2}{h^2}\right) \tag{4}$$

where h is a smoothing filtering parameter, it controls the attenuation of weights. Judging from the Eq. (4), the accuracy of similar patches computation is an important issue is influenced by priori information of damaged image.

Method noise, i.e., the difference between the noisy image and its denoised version, often contains residual image information due to imperfect denoising methods. Here the method noise is denoted as:

$$\hat{n}_i = y_i - \hat{x}_i \tag{5}$$

Some edge information are removed and left in the method noise, it implies that it's yet necessary to exploit the nonlocal similarities in method noise for better weight.

The noise free pixel value x_i can be written again as:

$$x_i = y_i - n_i = \hat{x}_i + \hat{n}_i - n_i = \hat{x}_i + \Delta x_i \tag{6}$$

where $\Delta x_i = \hat{n}_i - n_i$ implies the residual image signal in method noise. But we can't get good denoising result by adding Δx_i back to $\hat{x}_i$, since Δx_i contains noise.

The Euclidean norm $\|\mathbf{x}_i - \mathbf{x}_j\|_2^2$ denotes the similarity between noise free patches $\mathbf{x}_i$ and $\mathbf{x}_j$, can be expressed by

$$
\begin{aligned}
\|\mathbf{x}_i - \mathbf{x}_j\|_2^2 &= \sum_k \left(x_i^k - x_j^k\right)^2 = \sum_k \left[\left(\hat{x}_i^k + \Delta x_i^k\right) - \left(\hat{x}_j^k + \Delta x_j^k\right)\right]^2 \\
&= \|\hat{\mathbf{x}}_i - \hat{\mathbf{x}}_j\|_2^2 + \|\Delta \mathbf{x}_i - \Delta \mathbf{x}_j\|_2^2 + 2\sum_k \left(\hat{x}_i^k - \hat{x}_j^k\right)\left(\Delta x_i^k - \Delta x_j^k\right)
\end{aligned}
\tag{7}
$$

where k is the pixel index in the patch, if the residual signal is not zero, which implies the nonlocal similarity of the residual signal and its relationship with the pre-denoised image.

We replace $\|\mathbf{y}_i - \mathbf{y}_j\|_2^2$ with $\|\mathbf{x}_i - \mathbf{x}_j\|_2^2$ can obtain better similarity, so w_{ij} can be written again as:

$$w_{ij} = \exp\left(-\frac{\|\mathbf{x}_i - \mathbf{x}_j\|_2^2}{h^2}\right) \tag{8}$$

In order to calculate the similarity accurately, we utilize two noisy images to find the true similar patches. In actual operation, we add noise to the original clean image $\mathbf{I}$, the same action twice obtain two different noisy images $\mathbf{N}_1$ and $\mathbf{N}_2$, they hold same noise standard deviation. The next step, we utilize obtained pre-denoised image and residual image to accurately detect the similar patches and then redesign a new weight to implement nonlocal means algorithm again. The new weight can be obtained by

$$w_{i_1 j_1} = \exp\left(-\frac{\|\mathbf{x}_{i_1} - \mathbf{x}_{j_1}\|_2^2}{h_1^2} - \frac{\|\mathbf{x}_{i_2} - \mathbf{x}_{j_2}\|_2^2}{h_2^2}\right) \tag{9}$$

where h_1 and h_2 are filtering parameters, we utilize three noisy images or more can get more accurate similitude, but it will waste of running time.

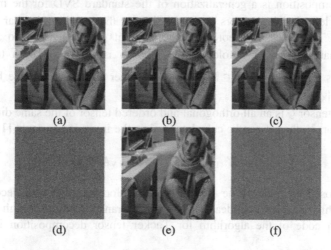

(a)   (b)   (c)

(d)   (e)   (f)

Fig. 1. Image denoising using multiple images nonlocal means (a) latent image $\mathbf{I}$, (b) noisy image $\mathbf{N}_1$, (c) pre-denoised image $\mathbf{X}_M$, (d) the residual image R_1 between (b) and (c), (e) denoised image $\mathbf{X}_N$, (f) the residual image R_2 between (c) and (e).

Figure 1 shows the example image *Barbara* with the noise level $\sigma = 20$, we can see that although residual image Fig. 1(d) contains more details than Fig. 1(f), it also contains more noise, so we utilize residual image $\mathbf{R}_2$ in Subsect. 2.3 to offset missing detail and texture. The specific implementation flow chart of multiple images nonlocal means is shown in Fig. 2.

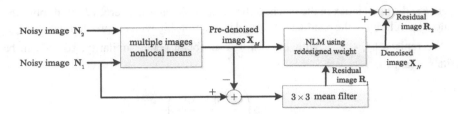

Fig. 2. The flow chart of multiple images nonlocal means

2.2 Denoising via Tensor Decomposition

Tensor is a multidimensional array [9], give a N-th order tensor $\mathcal{X} \in \mathbb{R}^{I_1 \times I_2 \times \cdots \times I_N}$ the Tucker tensor decomposition of $\mathcal{X}$ is

$$\mathcal{X} = \mathcal{G} \times_1 \mathbf{A}^{(1)} \times_2 \mathbf{A}^{(2)} \cdots \times_N \mathbf{A}^{(N)} = \left[\left[\mathcal{G}; \mathbf{A}^{(1)}, \mathbf{A}^{(2)}, \cdots, \mathbf{A}^{(N)}\right]\right] \tag{10}$$

where '$\times_n$' is the n-mode product of a tensor by matrix. $\mathbf{A}^{(n)} \in \mathbb{R}^{I_n \times I_n} (n = 1, 2, \ldots, N)$ are orthogonal matrices, they can be obtained by

$$\mathbf{X}_{(n)} = \mathbf{U}\mathbf{S}\mathbf{V}^T = \mathbf{A}^{(n)}\mathbf{S}\mathbf{V}^T \tag{11}$$

This decomposition is a generalization of the standard SVD for the matrix $\mathbf{X}_{(n)}$, whereby the left singular vectors corresponding to the smallest singular values are ignored [10]. The process of reordering the elements of the tensor into a matrix is known as matricization or unfolding, the mode-n matricization of a tensor $\mathcal{X} \in \mathbb{R}^{I_1 \times I_2 \times \cdots \times I_N}$ is denoted by $\mathbf{X}_{(n)} \in \mathbb{R}^{I_n \times \prod_{j \neq n} I_j}$. In other words, $\mathbf{A}^{(n)}$ is the leading left singular matrix of $\mathbf{X}^{(n)}$.

The core tensor $\mathcal{G}$ is an all-orthogonal and ordered tensor of the same dimension as the data tensor $\mathcal{X}$, then it can be calculated using the inversion formula [11, 12]

$$\mathcal{G} = \mathcal{X} \times_1 \mathbf{A}^{(1)T} \times_2 \mathbf{A}^{(2)T} \cdots \times_N \mathbf{A}^{(N)T} \tag{12}$$

The proposed method will be referred to as nonlocal linear tensor decomposition (NLL-TD) which enables us to deal with linear low-rank structure for high-order data.

A pseudo code of the algorithm for Tucker tensor decomposition is given in Algorithm 1.

In the step of thresholding, τ is the threshold [13]. The hard threshold step can be formulated as

$$\text{Thresh}\,(z, \tau) = \begin{cases} z & |z| > \tau \\ 0 & |z| \leq \tau \end{cases} \tag{13}$$

where $\tau = \eta\sigma\sqrt{2\log_{10}\left(\prod_{n=1}^{N} I_n\right)}$ is the universal threshold [14], η is a decay parameter.

Then the denoised tensor $\tilde{\mathcal{X}}$ is formed by mapping as follow

$$\tilde{\mathcal{X}} = \tilde{\mathcal{G}}_{\times 1}\mathbf{A}^{(1)}_{\times 2}\mathbf{A}^{(2)}_{\times 3}\mathbf{A}^{(3)} \tag{14}$$

Algorithm 1: Denoising by Tucker tensor decomposition

Input: nonlocal similar patches $\{\mathbf{y}_i\}$, the noise standard deviation σ .

Output: denoised tensor $\tilde{\mathcal{X}}$

1 Initialization: $\mathbf{x} = \mathbf{y}$

2 Patch clustering: search a set of K similar patches for each exemplar patch

and create tensor $\mathcal{X}_i$ for each cluster

   3 Tensor decomposition: $TD(\mathcal{X}_i) = \left[\mathcal{G}_i; \mathbf{A}^{(1)}, \mathbf{A}^{(2)}, \mathbf{A}^{(3)}\right]$

   4 Thresholding: $\tilde{\mathcal{G}}_i \leftarrow \text{Thresh}(\mathcal{G}_i, \tau)$

   5 Tensor reconstruction: $\tilde{\mathcal{X}} \leftarrow \tilde{\mathcal{G}}_i{}_{\times 1}\mathbf{A}^{(1)}{}_{\times 2}\mathbf{A}^{(2)}{}_{\times 3}\mathbf{A}^{(3)}$

   6 Return: $\tilde{\mathcal{X}}$

In this work, we use the Tucker tensor decomposition to remove noise while preserve image detail at the same time. There are two superiorities: firstly, the tensor decomposition is a convincing generalization of the matrix SVD and discussed ways to more efficiently compute the leading left singular vectors of $\mathbf{X}_{(n)}$. Secondly, tensor-based multilinear data analysis is capable to take advantage of signal correlations across tensor frames in order to achieve better noise reduction and provide more accurate understanding.

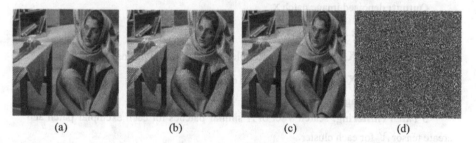

    (a)   (b)   (c)   (d)

Fig. 3. Image denoising using Tucker tensor decomposition (a) latent image, (b) noisy image, (c) denoised image $\mathbf{X}_T$, (d) the residual image $\mathbf{R}_T$ between (b) and (c).

Figure 3 shows the denoised result using Tucker tensor decomposition. By denoised image (Fig. 3(c)) and residual image (Fig. 3(d)) we can see that there remains a lot of noise, however, residual image (Fig. 3(d)) indicates more abundant slight textures are conserved at the same time.

2.3 Denoising Based on Residual Tensor Iteration

The N-th order tensor $\mathcal{X}$ is denoised using tensor decomposition as Algorithm 1 which yields an updated tensor $\tilde{\mathcal{X}}^{(1)}$, the residual tensor can be computed as

$$\mathcal{R}^{(1)} = \mathcal{X} - \tilde{\mathcal{X}}^{(1)} \tag{15}$$

We adapted the idea of iterative regularization that updated $\tilde{\mathcal{X}}$ and residual tensor $\mathcal{R}^{(1)}$ to a combined tensor $\tilde{\mathcal{X}}^{(2)}$ which obtained as

$$\begin{aligned}
\mathcal{X}^{(2)} &= \tilde{\mathcal{X}}^{(1)} + \lambda \mathcal{R}^{(1)} \\
&= (1 - \lambda)\tilde{\mathcal{X}}^{(1)} + \lambda \mathcal{X}
\end{aligned} \tag{16}$$

where $\lambda \in [0, 1]$ is the relaxation parameter, if it is set too big, $\hat{\sigma}$ is big, then shrinkage operator is big, the texture will lost in the denoised image. If it is set too small, the noise will not be removed enough. In this work [15], selects $\lambda = 0.5$ for all noise levels.

In order to improve the performance of image denoising, herein we propose a new method to perform denoising combine four parts $\mathbf{X}_N$, $\mathbf{R}_2$, $\mathbf{X}_T$ and $\mathbf{R}_T$ by using the recursive regularization as in [16]. We construct new input image

$$\mathbf{X}^* = \alpha(\mathbf{X}_N + \lambda \mathbf{R}_2) + \beta(\mathbf{X}_T + \lambda \mathbf{R}_T) \quad s.t. \quad \alpha + \beta = 1 \tag{17}$$

The ultimate image denoising algorithm unified multiple images nonlocal means and tensor decomposition based on residual iteration is summarized in Algorithm 2, where "Med" in re-estimate noise standard deviation indicates median operator.

Algorithm 2: Iterative Residual Tensor Decomposition for the Entire Image Denoising

Input: nonlocal similar patches $\{\mathbf{y}_i\}$, the noise standard deviation σ . η , α , β , λ , Maximum iterations Max-Iteration.

Output: denoised image patch $\mathbf{X}_i$

1 Initialization: $\mathbf{X}_i = \mathbf{y}_i$

2 Stage 1: Get $\mathbf{X}_N$ and $\mathbf{R}_2$ using multiple images nonlocal means

3 Stage 2: Get $\mathbf{X}_T$ and $\mathbf{R}_T$ using tensor decomposition

4 Solve $\mathbf{X}^*$ using Eq. (13)

5 Patch clustering: search a set of K similar patches for each exemplar patch and create tensor $\mathcal{X}_i$ for each cluster

for $k = 1$ to Max-Iteration do

> Tensor decomposition: $TD(\mathcal{X}_i) = \left[\mathcal{G}_i ; \mathbf{A}^{(1)}, \mathbf{A}^{(2)}, \mathbf{A}^{(3)} \right]$;
>
> Thresholding: $\tilde{\mathcal{G}}_i \leftarrow \text{Thresh}(\mathcal{G}_i, \tau)$;
>
> Tensor reconstruction: $\tilde{\mathcal{X}} \leftarrow \tilde{\mathcal{G}}_i \times_1 \mathbf{A}^{(1)} \times_2 \mathbf{A}^{(2)} \times_3 \mathbf{A}^{(3)}$;
>
> Re-estimate noise standard deviation: $\hat{\sigma} = \lambda\sqrt{\sigma^2 - Med(\|\mathcal{X} - \tilde{\mathcal{X}}\|)}$;

6 Return: denoised image patch $\mathbf{X}_i$

---

3 Experiments

In this section we will compare the performance of the proposed approach with several state-of-the-art denoising methods, including WNNM [17], BM3D and Nonlocally Centralized Sparse Representation for Image Restoration (NCSR) [18].

3.1 Evaluation Criteria

In order to evaluate the performance of the proposed method objectively, we use peak signal to noise ratio (PSNR) and structural similarity (SSIM) indices [19] as quantitative measure for restoration image quality. PSNR is defined as

$$PSNR = 10 \log_{10} \left(\frac{(2^k - 1)^2}{MSE} \right) \tag{18}$$

where the pixels are represented using k bits per sample, here $k = 8$. The MSE is the mean squared error, which is defined as

$$MSE = \frac{1}{H \times W} \sum_{i=0}^{H-1} \sum_{j=0}^{W-1} \|\mathbf{X}(i,j) - \mathbf{Y}(i,j)\|^2 \tag{19}$$

where $\mathbf{X}$ is original image and $\mathbf{Y}$ is restored image, H and W are the height and width of the image, respectively. A larger PSNR stands for better image quality.

Another image evaluation criteria is SSIM, the definition of local similarity index of two different windows x and y is computed as [20]

$$ssim(x,y) = \frac{(2\mu_x\mu_y + c_1)(2\sigma_{xy} + c_2)}{(\mu_x^2 + \mu_y^2 + c_1)(\sigma_x^2 + \sigma_y^2 + c_2)} \tag{20}$$

where μ_x, μ_y are the average of x, y; σ_x^2, σ_y^2 are the variances; σ_{xy} is covariance of x, y; and c_1, c_2 are two variables to stabilize the division with weak denominator. Through the mean of local similarity indexes, we can obtain overall SSIM

$$SSIM(\mathbf{X}, \mathbf{Y}) = \frac{1}{N} \sum_{i=1}^{N} ssim(x_i, y_i) \tag{21}$$

where x_i, y_i are corresponding windows indexed by i, and N is the number of windows, the size of window is 8×8. The SSIM conforms with the quality perception of the human visual system. If the SSIM value is closer to 1, the characteristic of restored image is more similar to the original image.

3.2   Parameters Setting

We use 6 natural images with resolution 512×512 [pixel] as clean test images. The basic parameters setting of the proposed method is as follow: h_1 and h_2 are smoothing filtering parameters are typically regulated manually, we set them as 20 when $\sigma = 20$. The patch size is 8×8 and the number of similar patches $K = 30$. In this paper, we empirically set η, α, β as 0.5. Max-Iteration is set 7 to 12 according to the difference noise standard deviation.

Table 1 shows the PSNR and SSIM compared by different methods, the highest PSNR and SSIM result for each image and on each noise level is highlighted in bold, we can see that the superiority of our method than the other methods for all the test images. For example, for *Barbarn* image, the PSNR gains of our method over WNNM, BM3D, NCSR are 1.12 dB, 1.66 dB and 1.63 dB, respectively, when $\sigma = 10$; the PSNR gains of our method over WNNM, BM3D, NCSR are 2.01 dB, 2.57 dB and 2.80 dB, respectively, when $\sigma = 50$. It means our method has better performance when bigger noise standard deviation.

Table 1. Comparison of PSNR and SSIM for noisy images and restored images by applying different methods

Images	Methods	$\sigma = 10$		$\sigma = 20$		$\sigma = 30$		$\sigma = 50$	
		PSNR	SSIM	PSNR	SSIM	PSNR	SSIM	PSNR	SSIM
Barbarn	Proposed	**36.64**	**0.953**	**33.92**	**0.929**	**32.26**	**0.909**	**29.80**	**0.866**
	WNNM	35.52	0.945	32.20	0.911	30.33	0.882	27.79	0.821
	BM3D	34.98	0.942	31.78	0.905	29.81	0.869	27.23	0.795
	NCSR	35.01	0.942	31.78	0.905	29.62	0.867	27.00	0.789
Lean	Proposed	**38.12**	**0.940**	**35.68**	**0.913**	**34.08**	**0.893**	**31.80**	**0.859**
	WNNM	36.98	0.930	33.87	0.891	32.17	0.865	29.92	0.820
	BM3D	36.80	0.928	33.78	0.890	31.94	0.857	29.70	0.813
	NCSR	36.71	0.927	33.68	0.890	31.74	0.859	29.55	0.818
Boats	Proposed	**35.37**	**0.916**	**32.65**	**0.861**	**31.02**	**0.827**	**28.89**	**0.774**
	WNNM	34.08	0.890	30.99	0.826	29.23	0.781	26.97	0.709
	BM3D	33.92	0.888	30.88	0.826	29.12	0.780	26.78	0.705
	NCSR	33.91	0.888	30.78	0.820	28.94	0.772	26.67	0.697
Hill	Proposed	**35.12**	**0.914**	**32.38**	**0.852**	**30.84**	**0.807**	**28.86**	**0.740**
	WNNM	33.81	0.890	30.81	0.806	29.24	0.751	27.33	0.678
	BM3D	33.62	0.883	30.72	0.804	29.16	0.750	27.19	0.675
	NCSR	33.69	0.886	30.65	0.801	28.97	0.743	26.99	0.662
Couple	Proposed	**35.44**	**0.928**	**32.57**	**0.881**	**30.88**	**0.845**	**28.58**	**0.786**
	WNNM	34.13	0.910	30.80	0.844	28.97	0.795	26.64	0.714
	BM3D	34.04	0.909	30.76	0.848	28.87	0.795	26.46	0.707
	NCSR	34.00	0.909	30.60	0.840	28.58	0.783	26.20	0.695
Fingerprint	Proposed	**34.45**	**0.980**	**31.10**	**0.957**	**29.08**	**0.935**	**26.55**	**0.891**
	WNNM	32.83	0.971	29.08	0.934	27.11	0.900	24.77	0.842
	BM3D	32.46	0.969	28.81	0.934	26.83	0.894	24.53	0.831
	NCSR	32.68	0.970	28.96	0.931	26.92	0.894	24.48	0.822

The implementation of the exact same pictures acquisition is hard due to the speed of camera is limited, so we use multi-frame video sequences to test our algorithm, when we denoising a frame image, we can use the next frame as its similar image. Every video has its last frame image, we can use its previous frame as its similar image. Figure 4 shows three pairs multi-frame video sequences images, the particulars of rapidly photoelectricity, spoondrift and Scrollable soccer are different, nevertheless, our algorithm is applicable to them. Table 2 shows the PSNR and SSIM compared by different methods when we use multi-frame video sequences.

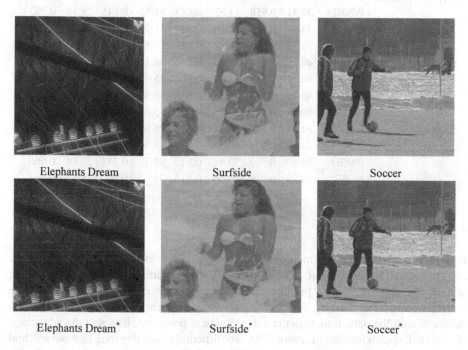

| Elephants Dream | Surfside | Soccer |
| Elephants Dream* | Surfside* | Soccer* |

Fig. 4. Three pairs multi-frame video sequences images, '*' denotes the next frame image.

Table 2. Comparison of PSNR and SSIM for multi-frame video sequences images by applying different methods

Images	Methods	$\sigma = 10$		$\sigma = 20$		$\sigma = 30$		$\sigma = 50$	
		PSNR	SSIM	PSNR	SSIM	PSNR	SSIM	PSNR	SSIM
Elephants dream	Proposed	36.97	0.946	**33.68**	**0.893**	**32.04**	**0.859**	**29.69**	**0.805**
	WNNM	**37.31**	**0.950**	33.34	0.886	31.54	0.846	29.37	0.793
	BM3D	36.87	0.947	33.11	0.886	31.30	0.844	29.06	0.791
	NCSR	36.79	0.944	31.51	0.881	31.16	0.841	28.99	0.792
Surfside	Proposed	**40.29**	**0.950**	**37.85**	**0.935**	**36.17**	**0.923**	**33.68**	**0.903**
	WNNM	40.12	0.949	37.12	0.927	35.51	0.914	33.38	0.890
	BM3D	40.27	**0.950**	37.41	0.929	35.57	0.909	33.43	0.889
	NCSR	39.90	0.947	37.27	0.932	35.48	0.918	33.57	**0.903**

(*continued*)

Table 2. (*continued*)

Images	Methods	$\sigma = 10$		$\sigma = 20$		$\sigma = 30$		$\sigma = 50$	
		PSNR	SSIM	PSNR	SSIM	PSNR	SSIM	PSNR	SSIM
Soccer	Proposed	**34.34**	**0.915**	**30.72**	**0.824**	**28.90**	**0.761**	26.79	0.674
	WNNM	34.28	0.911	30.67	0.821	28.84	0.750	**27.02**	**0.679**
	BM3D	34.09	0.908	30.45	0.813	28.74	0.751	26.84	0.667
	NCSR	34.24	0.912	30.56	0.816	28.73	0.750	26.79	0.664
Elephants dream[*]	Proposed	36.97	0.946	**33.66**	**0.893**	**32.01**	**0.860**	**29.67**	**0.805**
	WNNM	**37.31**	**0.950**	33.33	0.885	31.53	0.845	29.35	0.792
	BM3D	36.87	0.946	33.10	0.885	31.29	0.844	29.04	0.790
	NCSR	36.77	0.943	33.02	0.881	31.11	0.840	28.96	0.792
Surfside[*]	Proposed	**40.29**	**0.950**	**37.82**	**0.935**	**36.12**	**0.923**	**33.73**	**0.904**
	WNNM	40.11	0.949	37.07	0.927	35.42	0.913	33.37	0.890
	BM3D	40.28	**0.950**	37.39	0.928	35.52	0.909	33.49	0.888
	NCSR	39.88	0.947	37.26	0.931	35.45	0.918	33.55	0.903
Soccer[*]	Proposed	**34.34**	**0.913**	**30.74**	**0.823**	28.92	**0.760**	26.80	0.675
	WNNM	34.29	0.909	30.69	0.819	**28.96**	0.758	**27.07**	**0.679**
	BM3D	34.10	0.907	30.49	0.812	28.78	0.751	26.88	0.666
	NCSR	34.25	0.910	30.60	0.816	28.77	0.749	26.83	0.664

4   Conclusions

In this paper we combine multiple images nonlocally means and residual tensor decomposition to implement denoising. Exploiting multiple images can increase accuracy of finding similar patches, and residual image contains abundant texture information to offset missing detail. Using tensor can extract essential attribute of the hidden within the data, thus to better solve practical problems, it is also the advantage of low-rank approximation of tensor. The experimental result illustrate that our method can outperform the state-of-the-art denoising methods in the terms of the quantitative and perceptual evaluation. The major shortcoming of this paper is that if we're going to process images, we must use very fast camera to continuous capture dynamic scenery or ensure camera absolutely motionless to continuous capture static scenery. In the future, we will extend the proposed algorithm to other image processing tasks and video sequences visualizations.

References

1. Frosio, I., Kautz, J.: Statistical nearest neighbors for image denoising. IEEE Trans. Image Process. **28**(2), 723–738 (2019)
2. Buades, A., Coll, B., Morel, J.-M.: A non-local algorithm for image denoising. In: 2005 IEEE Computer Society Conference on Computer Vision and Pattern Recognition (CVPR), vol. 2, pp. 60–65. IEEE (2005)

3. Aharon, M., Elad, M., Bruckstein, A.: K-SVD: an algorithm for designing overcomplete dictionaries for sparse representation. IEEE Trans. Signal Process. **54**(11), 4311–4322 (2006)
4. Dabov, K., Foi, A., Katkovnik, V., Egiazarian, K.: Image denoising by sparse 3-D transform-domain collaborative filtering. IEEE Trans. Image Process. **16**(8), 2080–2095 (2007)
5. Zhong, H., Yang, C., Zhang, X.: A new weight for nonlocal means denoising using method noise. IEEE Signal Process. Lett. **19**(8), 535–538 (2012)
6. Wang, X., Wang, H., Yang, J., et al.: A new method for nonlocal means image denoising using multiple images. PLoS One **11**(7), e0158664 (2016)
7. He, K., Zhang, X., Ren, S., et al.: Deep residual learning for image recognition. In: Proceedings of the IEEE Conference on Computer Vision and Pattern Recognition, pp. 770–778 (2016)
8. Özdemir, A., Iwen, M.A., Aviyente, S.: Multiscale tensor decomposition. In: 2016 50th Asilomar Conference on Signals, Systems and Computers, pp. 625–629. IEEE (2016)
9. McCullagh, P.: Tensor Methods in Statistics: Monographs on Statistics and Applied Probability. Chapman and Hall/CRC, Boca Raton (2018)
10. Kolda, T.G., Bader, B.W.: Tensor decompositions and applications. SIAM Rev. **51**(3), 455–500 (2009)
11. Vasilache, N., Zinenko, O., Theodoridis, T., et al.: Tensor comprehensions: framework-agnostic high-performance machine learning abstractions. arXiv preprint arXiv:1802.04730 (2018)
12. Huffman, N., Bennett, I.: White matter integrity and subclinical depression: a diffusion tensor imaging study. UC Riverside Undergraduate Res. J. **12**(1) (2018)
13. Hu, W., Xie, Y., Zhang, W., et al.: Image denoising via nonlocally sparse coding and tensor decomposition. In: Proceedings of International Conference on Internet Multimedia Computing and Service, p. 283. ACM (2014)
14. Donoho, D.L., Johnstone, J.M.: Ideal spatial adaptation by wavelet shrinkage. Biometrika **81**(3), 425–455 (1994)
15. Özdemir, A., Iwen, M.A., Aviyente, S.: A multiscale approach for tensor denoising. In: 2016 IEEE Statistical Signal Processing Workshop (SSP), pp. 1–5. IEEE (2016)
16. Osher, S., Burger, M., Goldfarb, D., et al.: An iterative regularization method for total variation based image restoration. In: IEEE International Conference on Imaging Systems and Techniques, pp. 170–175. IEEE (2011)
17. Gu, S., Zhang, L., Zuo, W., et al.: Weighted nuclear norm minimization with application to image denoising. In: Proceedings of the IEEE Conference on Computer Vision and Pattern Recognition, pp. 2862–2869 (2014)
18. Dong, W., Zhang, L., Shi, G., et al.: Nonlocally centralized sparse representation for image restoration. IEEE Trans. Image Process. **22**(4), 1620–1630 (2013)
19. Wang, Z., Bovik, A.C., Sheikh, H.R., et al.: Image quality assessment: from error visibility to structural similarity. IEEE Trans. Image Process. **13**(4), 600–612 (2004)
20. Lou, Y., Zeng, T., Osher, S., et al.: A weighted difference of anisotropic and isotropic total variation model for image processing. SIAM J. Imaging Sci. **8**(3), 1798–1823 (2015)

Identification of Apple Tree Trunk Diseases Based on Improved Convolutional Neural Network with Fused Loss Functions

Jie Hang[1], Dexiang Zhang[1], Peng Chen[2(✉)], Jun Zhang[1], and Bing Wang[3(✉)]

[1] School of Electrical Engineering and Automation, Anhui University, Hefei 230601, Anhui, China
[2] Institutes of Physical Science and Information Technology, Anhui University, Hefei 230601, Anhui, China
pchen.ustc10@foxmail.com
[3] School of Electrical and Information Engineering, Anhui University of Technology, 243032 Ma'anshan, Anhui, China
wangb@ahut.edu.cn

Abstract. Apple tree disease is a main threat factor to apple quality and yield. This paper proposed an improved convolutional neural network model to classify apple tree diseases. It took the advantages of neural network to extract the deep characteristics of disease parts, and used deep learning to classify target disease areas. In order to improve the classification accuracy and speed up the convergence of the network model, the center loss and focal loss functions were fused, instead of the traditional softmax loss function, which was especially important for our classification network model. Experimental results on our apple trunk dataset showed that our model achieved an accuracy of 94.5%. Therefore our method is feasible and effective for apple tree disease identification.

Keywords: Apple trunk disease · Convolutional neural network · Loss function

1 Introduction

The ring disease and rot disease of apple trunks are worldwide disaster for apple. It has occurred in many countries such as Japan, North Korea and the United States, especially in China, whose northern area produced the largest apple yields. In general, the incidence of ring disease in orchards is above 20%, and in some orchards it can reach more than 50%. Apple tree disease has affected the quality and yield of apples, causing serious economic losses to fruit farmers.

Traditional machine learning methods have been used in the prediction of plant diseases more and more widely [6–8]. Tan *et al*. Established a multi-layer BP neural network model to realize the disease identification of soybean leaves, by calculating the chromaticity values of the leaves [1]. By extracting the color and texture characteristics of grape disease leaves, Tian *et al*. used a support vector machine (SVM) recognition method that achieved better results than neural network [2]. Wang *et al*. developed a

© Springer Nature Switzerland AG 2019
D.-S. Huang et al. (Eds.): ICIC 2019, LNCS 11643, pp. 274–283, 2019.
https://doi.org/10.1007/978-3-030-26763-6_26

discriminant analysis method to identify cucumber lesions, by extracting the characteristics of leaf lesion color, shape and texture, as well as combining with environmental information [3]. Zhang *et al.* also extracted the color, shape and texture features of lesion after segmentation, and then used them to identify the five types of corn leaves by K-nearest neighbor (KNN) classification algorithm [4].

Deep learning was originally proposed by Hinton [5] and has been successfully applied in the fields of handwriting recognition and face recognition. Sladojevic [9], Brahimi [10] and Amara [11] used convolutional neural networks for plant leaf disease identification. Yang et al. proposed a new rice disease identification method based on deep convolutional neural networks [12]. Sun *et al.* proposed an improved convolutional neural network which achieved an accuracy of 99.35% on a test dataset containing 54,306 images, with 26 diseases in 14 different plants [13]. Moreover, the PASCAL VOC Challenge [14] and the recent Large Scale Visual Recognition Challenge (ILSVRC) [15] based on the ImageNet dataset [16] have been widely used as benchmark for many visualization related issues in computer vision, including object classification. In 2012, a convolutional neural network called Alexnet [17] reduced the top5 error rate of the 1000 categories of classified images to 16.4% on imagenet, and in the next three years, with advanced deep learning methods, the error rate was reduced to 3.57%.

This work focused on five different convolutional neural network architectures, Alexnet [17], VGGNet [18], GoogLeNet [19], ResNet [20] and SENet [21], which participated in ImageNet Large Scale Recognition Challenge (ILSVRC) from 2012 to 2017, and achieved good classification results. On our dataset of apple tree diseases, the above five convolutional neural network structures and our proposed VGGNet were investigated, by replacing the last loss function and then comparing the traditional Softmax loss function and the Centerloss loss function. In combination with the characteristics of our dataset, our proposed model obtained the highest classification accuracy of 94.5% compared with other convolutional neural network structures. Figure 1 shows a flow chart for the classification of apple tree diseases.

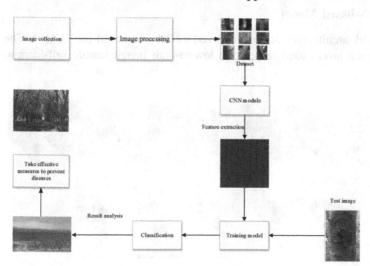

Fig. 1. Flowchart of apple tree trunk diseases classification.

2 Materials and Methods

2.1 Data Preprocessing and Augmentation

The experimental dataset of trunk diseases were collected from apple orchards. In our dataset, we collected 607 images, which consisted in 200 round sickness, 202 rot and 205 healthy trunks.

To adopt CNN in the identification of apple trunk diseases, our relatively small size of trunk image dataset were augmented. First, trunk images were adjusted so that the length and width of images are the same, which were randomly cut to 224×224. Then, since trunk images were always taken by different image acquisition devices with different shooting locations in apple orchards, it is difficult to take apple tree disease images from all angles. Therefore, in order to fully test and construct adaptive CNN-based model, all images were extended using flip transform in horizontal and vertical as well as mirror symmetry. To prevent redundancy in the dataset, noise technique was adopted to ensure the validity of the data.

After the data augmentation, the apple trunk dataset was expanded to contain 3,035 images, of which 2,435 are for training and 600 for test. Table 1 lists the number of images in each class.

Table 1. Apple trunk dataset.

Class	Number of training images	Number of testing images
Ring disease	800	200
Rot disease	810	200
Healthy	825	200
Total	2435	600

2.2 CNN-Based Model

The network architecture of our improved model was based on VGG19. The first 16 convolutional layers used to perform low-to-high image feature self-learning on the

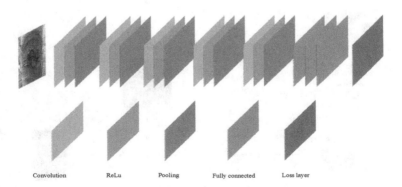

Convolution   ReLu   Pooling   Fully connected   Loss layer

Fig. 2. the structure of the convolutional neural network of VGG19.

training images, where the deeper convolution layer reduces the resolution of feature maps and extracts more abstract high-level features, the last two fully connected layer FC6 and FC7 can obtain complex comprehensive feature information. Experiments in this work were based on the 5 CNN models. For each model, the last layer of the network was replaced by different fully connected (FC) layers with 3 outputs (the number of the prediction categories), instead of 1,000. Figure 2 shows we applied the structure of the convolutional neural network of VGG19.

2.3 Loss Function

2.3.1 Softmax Loss Function

In solving classification problems, deep learning usually used softmax layer to produce final results. In addition, depth metric learning typically optimized distance loss to produce more discriminant features, such as triplet loss [6] and center loss [22], which are generally used for image classification, such as face recognition [23].

In most deep neural networks for classification tasks, they always adopted softmax loss function as the objective function, which can be expressed as:

$$L_s = -\frac{1}{N}\sum_i \log\left(\frac{e^{s_{y_i}}}{\sum_j e^{s_j}}\right), \tag{1}$$

where y_i represents the label of the i-th sample and s_j represents the j-th element of the classification score vector s.

2.3.2 Centerloss Loss Function

In literature [22], Wen et al. proposed a loss function called face recognition center loss. Combining center loss with softmax loss can make deep neural networks achieving more discriminating features.

The definition of central loss is as follows:

$$L_c = \frac{1}{2}\sum_{i=1}^m \|x_i - c_{y_i}\|_2^2, \tag{2}$$

where y_i represents the label of the i-th sample, x_i represents i-th extracted feature, and c_{yi} represents the class of the i-th sample.

The center loss was combined directly with the softmax loss:

$$L = (1 - \lambda)L_s + \lambda L_c, \tag{3}$$

where L_s represents the softmax loss function, L_c represents the central loss function and λ is a weight that balances the two loss functions.

2.3.3 Focalloss Loss Function

The Focalloss function was modified based on the standard cross-entropy loss function. The traditional cross entropy loss function for binary classification is shown as below:

$$CE(p, y) = \begin{cases} -\log(p) & if \ y = 1 \\ -\log(1 - p) & otherwise \end{cases}, \tag{4}$$

where $p \in [0, 1]$ is the estimated probability for the class.

For two-classesclass problem, the value of y is positive 1 or negative 0, and p ranges from 0 to 1. To explain the problem conveniently, let P_t replace p, so the formula is rewritten as follows:

$$P_t = \begin{cases} p & if \ y = 1 \\ 1 - p & otherwise \end{cases}. \tag{5}$$

Then the above cross-entropy loss function in Eq. (4) can be rewritten as $CE(p, y) = CE(Pt) = -log(Pt)$.

In order to control the weights of samples that are difficult to be classified and those easily classified samples, a modulating factor $(1 - Pt)^\gamma$ was added to the cross entropy loss, so that the easily classified samples were assigned small weights and thus CNN model paid more attentions in those difficult classified samples. The focalloss function is shown as follows:

$$FL(P_t) = -(1 - P_t)^\gamma \log(P_t), \tag{6}$$

where $(1 - P_t)^\gamma$ denotes modulation factor and $\gamma \geq 0$.

2.4   Experimental Framework

Our model was based on the VGG19 model with integrating multiple loss functions. The model was trained by a stochastic gradient descent optimization method. The initial learning rate is set to 0.001. This step of the pre-training phase is called fine-tuning and needs to decide which layers of the original network must be frozen, and which layers are allowed to continue learning, and at what rate. Usually, the first few layers are frozen because the low-level features can be better adapted to different problems. We choose a momentum of 0.9 and a weight attenuation of 0.0005.

3   Experimental Results

All of our experiments were performed on NVDIA TITANX GPUS. The experimental software environment is Ubuntu 16.04 LTS 64-bit system, with using Caffe [24] deep learning open source framework and Python as programming language. The prediction results of the five CNN architectures are listed in Table 2.

Figure 3 shows the cases of convolution diagrams for our proposed network, which can be better understanding how the CNN network learns the characteristics of the input image by visualizing various convolutional layers. They are for visual feature maps of conv1, conv3 and conv5, respectively. Through the visualization, it can be found that the features learned by CNN are hierarchical.

Table 2. Classification accuracy (in percent) of five CNN-Based models.

CNN	Design	Test accuracy
Alexnet	Fine-Turing	0.896
VGG16	Fine-Turing	0.913
Goolenet	Fine-Turing	0.92
VGG19	Fine-Turing	0.925
VGG19+Centerloss	Fine-Turing	0.938
VGG19+Focalloss	Fine-Turing	0.945
Resnet-50	Fine-Turing	0.916
SE-Resnet-50	Fine-Turing	0.915

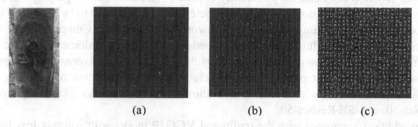

(a)   (b)   (c)

Fig. 3. Visualization of feature maps from different convolutional layers of our proposed network (a): conv1; (b) conv3; (c) conv5.

4   Results and Analysis

4.1   Effect of Feature Extraction Networks

Observing from Table 2 can be seen a conclusion that different convolution depths of the trained models produced different classification results on the test set. In general, the more layers of convolutional network, the more complex features the network can be learned from the original images. Figure 4 shows prediction comparison among CNN models, where the shallow network, such as Alexnet, took an unsatisfactory

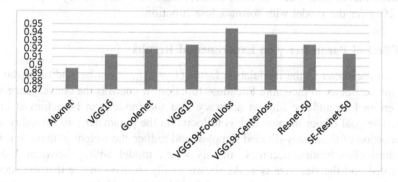

Fig. 4. Performance comparison among CNN models.

learning effect on extracting target features from images. The shallow Alexnet network achieved an accuracy of 0.896 on the test set; while the deep networks, GoogLeNet, VGGnet-19, ResNet-50 and SE-ResNet-50 yielded test accuracies of 0.92, 0.925, 0.916 and 0.915 on the test set, respectively. The fundamental reason is that feature maps extracted by deep networks contained more feature information. This means that deeper networks can extract more feature information and semantic information, and thus achieved better results than shallow networks.

4.2   Effect of Loss Functions

Different loss functions produced different predictions on different models. Generally, the final loss layer of traditional convolutional neural network is softmax loss function. Softmax function can make the probability of prediction class to be ranging in [0, 1]. In regression and classification problems, parameters of network have to be sought so that the best prediction performance of the network was obtained. Compared with the traditional softmax loss function, our developed focalloss loss function can increase the classification accuracy on our dataset up to 94.5% on the VGG19 convolutional neural network. Moreover, our proposed model achieved an improvement of accuracy by nearly 2%, compared with classic convolutional neural networks like GoogLeNet, ResNet-50, and SE-ResNet-50.

In addition, compared with the traditional VGG19 model with softmax loss function, the model with centerloss function increased an accuracy of 1.3%, while that with focalloss function increased an accuracy of 2% too. Figure 5 illustrates trends in the performance of the VGG19 network structure with respect of different loss functions on the test set.

From the Fig. 5, It can be intuitively observed that the model with softmax loss function had sharp jitters on our dataset, which made the convergence curve poor, so that it is difficult to be converged when the final iteration of the model is completed. Compared with the model with softmax loss function, the convergence curve of that with centerloss function is smoother, but still contains some small jitters in the iteration process. Focalloss can make the loss curve smooth and stable. The instability of these samples that are difficult to be classified will make more severe Loss jitters. Focal Loss is equivalent to the cross entropy loss function with adding the modulation factor. This mechanism makes Loss's decline more stable, resulting in an accuracy improvement of nearly 2% over the model with softmax loss function.

4.3   Effect of Parameter γ on Experimental Results

The γ is a parameter in the modulation factor $(1 - P_t)^\gamma$. It can be said to be the most important parameter in the entire Focalloss function. It controls the convergence speed of the entire loss and the highest accuracy that the model can be achieved on our dataset. The goal of our training task is to focus on the parameter γ to smoothly adjust the proportion of these easy-divided samples, and reduce the weight of them to achieve the highest classification accuracy. In this work, model with γ between 1–5 was investigated and the step size is 1. As shown in Fig. 6, we can see that the accuracy almost decreases as γ increases. The model achieved the highest accuracy of 94.5%

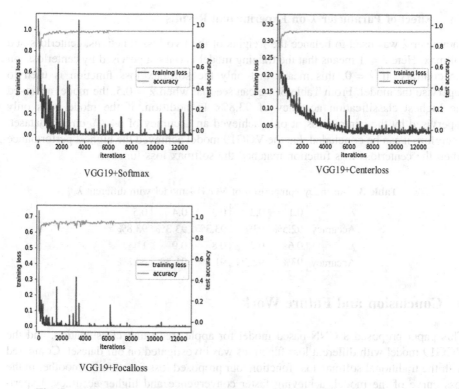

VGG19+Softmax

VGG19+Centerloss

VGG19+Focalloss

Fig. 5. Performance comparison of VGG19 model with different loss functions.

when $\gamma = 1$. It is easy to understand that γ reduces the loss contribution of easily classified samples, as γ increases, the probability of correct classification $(1 - P_t)$ decreases, which increases the weight of samples that are difficult to be classified, so that the model focuses on the difficultly classified samples that makes the classification accuracy decreased.

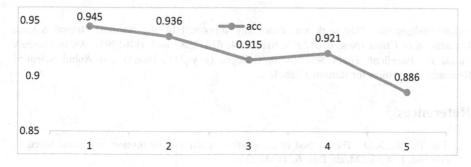

Fig. 6. Performance comparison for VGG19 model with different parameter γ.

4.4   Effect of Parameter λ on Experimental Results

Parameter λ was used to balance the weights of the two loss functions, centerloss and softmax. Here $\lambda = 1$ means that the training model is only supervised by centerloss, on the contrary, if $\lambda = 0$, this means that only the softmax loss function is used to supervise the model. From Table 3, we can see that when $\lambda = 0.5$, the model achieved the highest classification accuracy of 93.8%. In addition, if the model was only supervised by the central loss, it only achieved an accuracy of 64.8% on our dataset. Therefore it can be concluded that the VGG19 model achieved the highest performance when the centerloss loss function matched the softmax loss function.

Table 3. Accuracy comparison of VGG19 model with different λ.

λ	0.1	0.2	0.3	0.4	0.5
Accuracy	92.5%	93%	93.3%	93.3%	93.8%
λ	0.6	0.7	0.8	0.9	1
Accuracy	93%	92.3%	91.8%	91.3%	64.8%

5   Conclusion and Future Work

This paper proposed a CNN-based model for apple tree trunk classification, and the VGG19 model with different loss functions was investigated on our dataset. Compared with the traditional softmax loss function, our proposed loss function is smoother in the loss curve of the model, achieving faster convergence and higher accuracy. Experimental results on our dataset showed that our VGG19-based model with the improved loss function obtained the highest classification accuracy compared with other basic CNN models.

However, some aspects in this work should be improved in the future.

(1) The apple trunk disease database needs to be expanded by taking images from crop fields, data collection for websites and image augmentation techniques.
(2) For the images in classes that are difficult to be classified, the quality of the images needs to be improved manually to suit for CNN models, so as to obtain higher classification accuracy.

Acknowledgement. This work was financially supported by the National Natural Science Foundation of China (Nos. 61672035, 61872004, 61472282 and 31401293), Anhui Province Funds for Excellent Youth Scholars in Colleges (gxyqZD2016068) and Anhui Scientific Research Foundation for Returned Scholars.

References

1. Tan, F., Ma, X.D.: The method of recognition of damage by disease and insect based on laminae. J. Agric. Mech. Res. **6**, 41–43 (2009)
2. Tian, Y.W., Li, T.L., Li, C.H.: Method for recognition of grape disease based on support vector machine. Trans. Chin. Soc. Agric. Eng. **23**(6), 175–180 (2007)

3. Wang, X.F., Zhang, S.W., Wang, Z.: Recognition of cucumber diseases based on leaf image and environmental information. Trans. Chin. Soc. Agric. Eng. **30**(14), 148–153 (2014)
4. Zhang, S.W., Shang, Y.J., Wang, L.: Plant disease recognition based on plant leaf image. J. Anim. Plant Sci. **25**, 42–45 (2015)
5. Lecun, Y., Bengio, Y., Hinton, G.: Deep learning. Nature **521**, 436–444 (2015)
6. Es-Saady, Y., Massi, I.E., Yassa, M.E., Mammass, D., Benazoun, A.: Automatic recognition of plant leaves diseases based on serial combination of two SVM classifiers. In: Proceedings of the 2nd International Conference on Electrical and Information Technologies, pp. 561–566 (2016)
7. Gavhale, M.K.R., Gawande, U.: An overview of the research on plant leaves disease detection using image processing techniques. IOSR J. Comput. Eng. **16**(1), 10–16 (2014)
8. Wang, G., Sun, Y., Wang, J.X.: Automatic image based plant disease severity estimation using deep learning. Comput. Intell. Neurosci. **2017**, 8 p. (2017). Article ID 2917536
9. Sladojevic, S., Arsenovic, M., Anderla, A.: Deep neural networks based recognition of plant diseases by leaf image classification. Comput. Intell. Neurosci. **2016**, 11 p. (2016). Article ID 3289801
10. Brahimi, M., Boukhalfa, K., Moussaoui, A.: Deep learning for tomato diseases: classification and symptoms visualization. Appl. Artif. Intell. **31**(4), 299–315 (2017)
11. Amara, J., Bouaziz, B., Algergawy, A., et al.: A deep learning based approach for banana leaf diseases classification. In: BTW (Workshops), pp. 79–88 (2017)
12. Yang, L., Shu, J.Y., Nian, Y.Z., Yu, R.L., Yong, Z.: Identification of rice diseases using deep convolutional neural networks. Neurocomputing **267**, 378–384 (2017)
13. Sun, J., Tan, W.J., Mao, H.P., Wu, X.H., Chen, Y., Wang, L.: Identification of leaf diseases of various plants based on improved convolutional neural network. Agric. Eng. Newspaper **33**(19), 209–215 (2017)
14. Everingham, M., Van Gool, L., Williams, C.K., Winn, J., Zisserman, A.: The pascal visual object classes (VOC) challenge. Int. J. Comput. Vision. **88**, 303–338 (2010)
15. Deng, J., Dong, W., Socher, R., et al.: ImageNet: a large scale hierarchical image database. In: 2009 IEEE Computer Society Conference on Computer Vision and Pattern Recognition (CVPR 2009), Miami, Florida, USA, 20–25 June 2009. IEEE (2009)
16. Russakovsky, O., Deng, J., Su, H., et al.: ImageNet large scale visual recognition challenge. Int. J. Comput. Vision **115**, 211–252 (2012)
17. Krizhevsky, A., Sutskever, I., Hinton, G.E.: ImageNet classification with deep convolutional neural networks. In: Advances in Neural Information Processing Systems, pp. 1106–1114 (2017)
18. Simonyan, K., Zisserman, A.: Very deep convolutional networks for large-scale image recognition. Computer Science (2014)
19. Szegedy, C., et al.: Going deeper with convolutions (2015)
20. He, K., Zhang, X., Ren, S., Sun, J.: Deep residual learning for image recognition. In: Proceedings of the IEEE Conference on Computer Vision and Pattern Recognition, pp. 770–778 (2015)
21. Hu, J., Shen, L., Sun, G.: Squeeze-and-Excitation Networks. arXiv preprint arXiv:1709.01507 (2017)
22. Wen, Y., Zhang, K., Li, Z., Qiao, Yu.: A discriminative feature learning approach for deep face recognition. In: Leibe, B., Matas, J., Sebe, N., Welling, M. (eds.) ECCV 2016. LNCS, vol. 9911, pp. 499–515. Springer, Cham (2016). https://doi.org/10.1007/978-3-319-46478-7_31
23. Schroff, F., Kalenichenko, D., Philbin, J.: FaceNet: a unified embedding for face recognition and clustering. In: Proceedings of the IEEE Conference on Computer Vision and Pattern Recognition, pp. 815–823 (2015)
24. Jia, Y., et al.: Caffe: convolutional architecture for fast feature embedding. In: MM. ACM (2014)

Mirror PCA: Exploiting Facial Symmetry for Feature Extraction

Jian-Xun Mi[1,2(✉)] and Yueru Sun[1,2]

[1] Chongqing Key Laboratory of Image Cognition,
Chongqing University of Posts and Telecommunications,
Chongqing 400065, China
mijianxun@gmail.com
[2] College of Computer Science and Technology,
Chongqing University of Posts and Telecommunications,
Chongqing 400065, China

Abstract. Feature extraction technique aiming at obtaining discriminative information from high-dimensional face images is of great importance in face recognition. One widely used method for extracting primary feature is Principal Component Analysis (PCA), which uses projection matrix for dimensionality reduction. There are many improvements of PCA but no one pays attention to the fact that both facial images and facial expression are symmetrical to some degree. Facial symmetry is a helpful characteristic, which benefits of feature extraction. In this paper, Mirror Principal Component Analysis (Mirror PCA) method is proposed for extracting representative facial features, which takes advantage of the facial symmetry in a face image. In order to verify the effectiveness of the proposed method, we compare the Mirror PCA method with other four methods on four famous face databases. The experimental results indicate that the representation capacity of our method is superior to others.

Keywords: Feature extraction · Principal component analysis · Facial symmetry

1 Introduction

In recent years, face recognition (FR) has been extensively studied for its broad application prospects, such as authentication and payment system. The primary task of FR consists of feature extraction and classification [1–7]. Since there is rich redundancy in face images, using this concise feature alleviates the computational cost and could improve the recognition performance of classifiers.

Principal component analysis (PCA) [8] is one of the most popular methods used to deal with high-dimensional data. In traditional PCA method, the 2D face image matrices have to be transformed into 1D image vectors. The spatial structural information in the original face images is ignored when all face images are arranged as a column vector in pixels. It is in this context that two-dimensional principal component analysis (2DPCA) for image representation was proposed by Yang et al. [9] in 2004. Kong et al. [10] proposed bilateral projection-based 2-DPCA (B2-DPCA) combining

© Springer Nature Switzerland AG 2019
D.-S. Huang et al. (Eds.): ICIC 2019, LNCS 11643, pp. 284–295, 2019.
https://doi.org/10.1007/978-3-030-26763-6_27

rows and columns information of the matrix. In addition, 2DPCA has been widely used for face recognition or image reconstruction [9–11]. Block PCA is another improved method based on conventional PCA method, which was proposed by Kim et al. [12] in 2007. In BPCA, each image is supposed to be divided into several blocks preciously. BPCA is a generalization of 2DPCA in the sense that BPCA turns out to be 2DPCA if the blocks are taken as the row vectors [13]. Besides, the objective function of the traditional PCA is minimized by L2-norm, which is sensitive to outliers, because the influence of the large errors is exaggerated by L2-norm [14, 15]. To cope with this issue, plenty of improved robust PCA methods with more robustness have been proposed, such as L1-PCA [16], R1-PCA [17], PCA-L1 [18] etc. Recently, there have been others robust PCA methods based on L1-norm. Nie et al. [19] presented a non-greedy iterative algorithm to solve the PCA-L1, while Pang et al. [20] proposed L1-norm based on tensor analysis (TPCA-L1).

It is obvious that both the facial structure and the facial expression are approximately symmetrical [21–25], which is a useful natural characteristic of facial images. Xu et al. [24] proposed an algorithm for face recognition, which generated "symmetrical" face images as new samples and devise a representation-based method to perform face recognition. The SPCA uses the facial symmetry to expand the volume of training samples for face recognition, then combing the traditional PCA method with the even-odd decomposition principle proposed in [25]. However, no matter the facial structure or the facial expression are not symmetrical completely, the synthetic face images generated in are not natural enough.

In this paper, we propose a novel algorithm called Mirror principal component analysis (Mirror PCA), which uses the symmetrical structure of face images for feature extraction. The feature we extracted from our proposed model consists of two parts: a projection matrix corresponding to the left face samples, an error matrix denoting the difference between the left and right parts of the face. The contributions of this paper are as follows:

(1) Mirror PCA exploits the spatial information of face images by leveraging the symmetrical structure of face images;
(2) Mirror PCA method succeeds in obtaining low-dimensional structure of the left face image, and the error matrix between the left face images and the right face images.
(3) The experimental results prove that Mirror PCA method has provable recovery guarantee;

The method we proposed is superior to other PCA based method on storage space. By utilizing facial symmetry, the feature extracted from this method has greater compressibility.

The remainder of this paper is organized as follows: In Sect. 2, the idea of the proposed Mirror PCA method and its algorithm are described. In Sect. 3, details about the optimization procedure of Mirror PCA will be provided. In Sect. 4, the experimental results on four public face databases will be discussed. Section 5 concludes our work.

2 Mirror Principal Component Analysis (Mirror PCA)

In this section, a new technique called Mirror principal component analysis (Mirror PCA) is proposed for feature extraction. Mirror PCA takes the face symmetry into consideration. On this basis, we reform the objection function of traditional PCA method, which minimizing the reconstruction error between the original face image and the reconstruction face image.

We first introduce some steps used for prepossessing the training samples based on the face symmetry before we put forward our method. Suppose that there are N face images in data samples, that is $A = \{A_1, A_2, \cdots, A_N\}$. Suppose that the original face image matrix has m rows and n columns, and $A_i = (a_{i(1)}, a_{i(2)}, \cdots, a_{i(n)})$ denotes the $i - th$ training sample in the form of image matrix. The a_i denotes the $i - th$ column vector in image matrix A_i, and the size of a_i is $m \times 1$, $i \in (1, 2, \cdots, n)$.

(1) First of all, we should divide the face image matrix into two parts according to the center axis of every face picture. That is the left and the right part of A_i is denoted as $A_i^L = [a_{i(1)}, a_{i(2)}, \cdots, a_{i(n/2)}]$ and $A_i^R = [a_{i(n/2+1)}, a_{i(n/2+2)}, \cdots, a_{i(n)}]$;

(2) Denote a mirror function $g(\cdot)$ for generating the mirror image of original image. For example, $g(A_i^R) = [a_{i(n)}, a_{i(n-1)}, \cdots, a_{i(n/2+1)}]$ denotes the mirror right face of the $i - th$ face image;

(3) Convert each left face image A_i^L and mirror right face image $g(A_i^R)$ into column vector x_i^L, $g(x_i^R)$ respectively represent t column vector form of A_i^L and $g(A_i^R)$, and the size of x_i^L and $g(x_i^R)$ are all $(m \times n/2) \times 1$;

(4) Finally, the left face data set is $X^L = (x_1^L, x_2^L, \cdots, x_N^L)$, and the mirror right faces in data set are represented as $g(X^R) = (g(x_1^R), g(x_2^R), \cdots, g(x_N^R))$.

In this method, we also propose a minimization problem based on the reconstruction error, which is similar to the idea of traditional PCA method. Besides, the L1-norm was used to make sure that the residual matrix between the left and the right face is sparse enough. Finally, the objective function is described as follows:

$$J = \sum_{i=1}^{N} \left\{ \|x_i^L - x_i^{L'}\|_2^2 + \lambda_1 \|\|x_i^R - x_i^{R'}\|_2^2 + \lambda_2 \|e_i\|\|_1 \right\} \tag{1}$$

where λ_1 is a certain coefficient used to express the weight of the reconstruction error of the right face, λ_2 is another coefficient used to control the sparsity of $e_i \cdot x_i^L$ and x_i^R are all column vector mentioned above. $x_i^{L'}$ and $x_i^{R'}$ denote the reconstructed sample points of the left and right faces respectively.

In addition, we define a new variable $e_i = x_i^{L'} - g(x_i^{R'})$ to represent the difference between the left part and the right part of the $i - th$ reconstructed face image. Then the right side of the reconstruct face image is denoted as $g(x_i^{R'}) = x_i^{L'} - e_i$. So, the Eq. (1) is reformulated as follows:

$$J = \sum_{i=1}^{N} \left\{ \left\| x_i^L - x_i^{L'} \right\|_2^2 + \lambda_1 \left\| g(x_i^R) - (x_i^{L'} - e_i) \right\|_2^2 + \lambda_2 \left\| e_i \right\|_1 \right\} \qquad (2)$$

According to the conventional PCA method, the reconstructed sample point of x_i will be obtained by $x_i' = WW^T x_i$, where $W = (w_1, w_2, \cdots w_d)$ represents for the projection matrix corresponding to the samples $X = (x_1, x_2, ..x_N)$. Similarly, the reconstructed left sample point is expressed as $W_L W_L^T x_i^L$, where W_L represents for the projection matrix of the left face sample points and $X^L = (x_1^L, x_2^L, ..x_N^L)$ is the left face sample points. Thus, it is obviously to know that the optimization problem in Eq. (2) is denoted as follows through equivalent transformation:

$$J = \sum_{i=1}^{N} \left\{ \left\| x_i^L - W_L W_L^T x_i^L \right\|_2^2 + \lambda_1 \left\| g(x_i^R) - (W_L W_L^T x_i^L - e_i) \right\|_2^2 + \lambda_2 \left\| e_i \right\|_1 \right\} \qquad (3)$$

Finally, the optimization problem is formulated as:

$$\underset{W_L, E=(e_1,e_2,\cdots,e_N)}{\arg\min} \sum_{i=1}^{N} \left\{ \left\| x_i^L - W_L W_L^T x_i^L \right\|_2^2 + \lambda_1 \left\| g(x_i^R) - (W_L W_L^T x_i^L - e_i) \right\|_2^2 + \lambda_2 \left\| e_i \right\|_1 \right\}$$
$$s.t \ W_L W_L^T = I$$
$$\qquad (4)$$

3 Algorithm of the Mirror PCA

In this section, we use an efficient iterative algorithm to solve the optimization problem in Eq. (4). The objection function in Eq. (4) is divided into two sub-problems by optimizing W_L and e_i alternately. We update W_L when e_i is fixed, and update e_i with W_L fixed. The alternative optimization is to find the desired projection matrix W_L and the error matrix $E = (e_1, e_2, \cdots, e_N)$.

3.1 Update of $E = (e_1, e_2, \cdots, e_N)$

Based on the assumption that the projection matrix W_L is fixed, and the objection function in Eq. (4) is consequently transformed into a soft thresholding algorithm to calculate $E = (e_1, e_2, \cdots e_N)$. We could compute e_i class by class. When the initial value of W_L is given, the objective function in Eq. (4) is rewritten as:

$$\underset{e_i}{\arg\min} \ const_1 + \lambda_1 \left\| \mathbf{e}_i - const_2 \right\|_2^2 + \lambda_2 \left\| \mathbf{e}_i \right\|_1 \qquad (5)$$

Further, Eq. (5) is simplified as follows:

$$\arg\min_{e_i}\|e_i - const_2\|_2^2 + \frac{\lambda_2}{\lambda_1}\|e_i\|_1 \tag{6}$$

where $const_1 = \left\|x_i^L - W_L W_L^T x_i^L\right\|_2^2$ and $const_2 = W_L W_L^T x_i^L - g(x_i^R)$ are all constant. The initial value of W_L is computed by the traditional PCA method. Next, we could solve Eq. (6) by applying the soft thresholding algorithm. The soft threshold function can be used to solve the following optimization problems:

$$\arg\min_x \|X - B\|_2^2 + \lambda\|X\|_1 \tag{7}$$

where $X = [x_1, x_2, \cdots, x_N]^T$, $B = [b_1, b_2, \cdots, b_N]^T$. The solution to the above optimization problems is described as:

$$soft(B, \lambda/2) = \begin{cases} B + \lambda/2 & , & B < -\lambda/2 \\ 0 & , & |B| < \lambda/2 \\ B - \lambda/2 & , & B > \lambda/2 \end{cases} \tag{8}$$

Equation (8) can be employed to solve Eq. (6) with some equivalent transformation, which is formulated as:

$$e_i = soft(const_2, \frac{\lambda2}{2 * \lambda1}) = \begin{cases} const_2 + \frac{\lambda2}{2*\lambda1} & , & const_2 < -\frac{\lambda2}{2*\lambda1} \\ 0 & , & |const_2| < \frac{\lambda2}{2*\lambda1} \\ const_2 - \frac{\lambda2}{2*\lambda1} & , & const_2 > \frac{\lambda2}{2*\lambda1} \end{cases} \tag{9}$$

Finally, we iterate each step through Eq. (9) the details of the process of obtaining the $E = (e_1, e_2, \cdots e_N)$ is described in Algorithm 1.

Algorithm1   Update of $E\_temp = (e_1, e_2, ..., e_N)$

Inputs: coefficients λ_1, λ_2, the termination condition parameters T

Initialization: $W_L = W_{L(0)}$ and $t = 1$

While convergence is not reached T do

　　$t = t+1$

　　For $i = 1, 2, 3, ..., N$

　　　　calculate the e_i class by class by using Eq.(9), $e_i = soft(const_2, \frac{\lambda_2}{2 * \lambda_1})$

　　　　where $soft(\bullet)$ is a soft thresholding operator, $const_2 = W_L W_L^T x_L^i - g(x_R^i)$

　　End For

　　Updating $E\_temp^{(t)} = (e_1, e_2, ..., e_N)$

　End while

Return $E = E\_temp^{(t)}$.

3.2   Update of W_L

In this part, we will elaborate on how to update $W_L = (W_{L(1)}, W_{L(2)}, \cdots W_{L(d)})$ when e_i is fixed. The objective function in Eq. (4) is reduced when the initial value of e_i is given. First of all, we will initialize e_i by using the algorithm described in Sect. 4.1. On this basis, the optimization problem is rewritten as

$$L(W_L) = \left\| x_i^L - W_L W_L^T x_i^L \right\|_2^2 + \lambda_1 \left\| W_L W_L^T x_i^L - e_i - g(x_i^R) \right\|_2^2 + \xi(W_L^T W_L - I) \quad (10)$$

by using the Lagrange multiplier method on the condition of $W_L W_L^T = I$. It is obviously that Eq. (10) is an equation with only one unknown quantity W_L. So, we can take the derivative of Eq. (10) with respect to W_L, which is shown as

$$\frac{\partial L(W_L)}{\partial(W_L)} = -2x_i^L(x_i^L)^T W_L + \lambda_1(2x_i^L(x_i^L)^T W_L - 2x_i^L C^T W_L - 2C(x_i^L)^T W_L) + 2\xi W_L \quad (11)$$

where $C = e_{i\_}temp + g(x_i^R)$. Let $\frac{L(W_L)}{\partial(W_L)} = 0$, then we obtain another equation:

$$[x_i^L(x_i^L)^T - \lambda_1(x_i^L(x_i^L)^T - x_i^L C^T - C(x_i^L)^T)]W_L = \xi W_L \quad (12)$$

we define a new variable $A = x_i^L(x_i^L)^T - \lambda_1(x_i^L(x_i^L)^T - x_i^L C^T - C(x_i^L)^T)$, the equation is rewritten as:

$$A W_L = \xi W_L \quad (13)$$

It is obviously that Eq. (13) is the equation of the characteristic equation. Therefore, we just need to decompose the eigenvalues for matrix A, to sort the eigenvalues $\lambda_1 \geq \lambda_2 \geq \cdots \geq \lambda_d$. Finally, we obtain the eigenvectors of the first d eigenvalues to make up $W_L = (W_{L(1)}, W_{L(2)}, \cdots, W_{L(d)})$.

Algorithm2 **Update of** $W_L\_temp = (W_{L(1)}, W_{L(2)}, ..., W_{L(d)})$

1. **Inputs:** coefficients λ_1, λ_2, the termination condition parameters T
2. **Initialization:** $E_L = E_{L(0)}$ and $t = 1$
3. **While** convergence is not reached T do
   t=t+1
   calculate the matrix A in Eq. (12)
   Eigenvalue decomposition of matrix
   $A = x_i^L(x_i^L)^T - \lambda_1(x_i^L(x_i^L)^T - x_i^L C^T - C(x_i^L)^T)$
   Obtain the eigenvectors corresponding to the first d largest eigenvalues
   $W_L\_temp = (W_{L(1)}, W_{L(2)}, ..., W_{L(d)})$
   End while
4. **Return** $W_L = W_L\_temp^{(t)}$.

---

4   Experiment Results

In this section, the performances of Mirror PCA are evaluated via extensive experiments in which we compare Mirror PCA with four PCA-based methods, including PCA [8], PCA-L1 [16], R1-PCA [17], and PCA-L1 non-greedy [18]. We will give the reconstructed error of the proposed method and the other four PCA based methods. In general, the reconstruction error in this experiment is defined as:

$$error = \frac{1}{N} \left\| X - X' \right\|_F \tag{14}$$

where N represents the number of samples in the training set, X is the original data sample, and X' is the reconstructed data sample. For Mirror PCA, the reconstruction error is split into the left part and the right part. The left part of reconstructed face is expressed as: $X^{L'} = W_L W_L^T X^L$, and the reconstructed right face could be expressed as:

$$X^{R'} = X^{L'} - E = W_L W_L' X^L - E \tag{15}$$

Therefore, the reconstructed sample in Mirror PCA method could be finally expressed as: $[X^{L'}, X^{R'}]$. For the other four methods, the reconstructed sample matrix X is expressed as: $X' = WW^T X$

4.1   Feature Extraction Without Occlusion

AR Database. The AR face database [26] consists of more than 4000 facial images from 126 individuals. For each individual, the first four face images in session 1 and session 2 are used as training set. Figure 1 shows the reconstructed errors of PCA, R1-PCA, PCA-L1 greedy, PCA-L1 non-greedy, and our proposed Mirror PCA methods with varying features number. It is clear that the performance of our proposed method is always far superior to the other four PCA based methods.

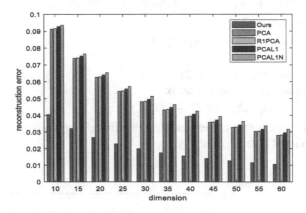

Fig. 1. Reconstruction error on AR database

Extended Yale B Database. The Extended Yale B database contains 2414 frontal face images collected from 38 individuals under varying illuminations [27]. We use 31 subjects in the data set as a gallery, each of which has 64 frontal facial images under different illuminations. According to different lighting intensities, the images in database are divided into five subsets. Figure 2 shows that the reconstruction error of our method is much lower than other five methods, which means the proposed method can deal with varying illuminations greatly.

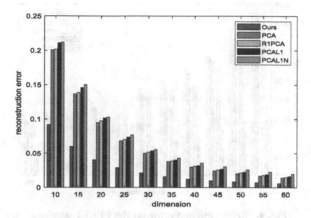

Fig. 2. Reconstruction error on Extended Yale B database

ORL Database. ORL database contains 40 subjects and each individual provides 10 face images [28], which includes rich gesture variations. We used first three images as experiment dataset, and all images were down sampled to 50×40. Figure 3 shows that the reconstruction error of Mirror PCA method keeps the smallest among the four PCA-based methods, and PCA-L1 non-greedy performs worse than other methods.

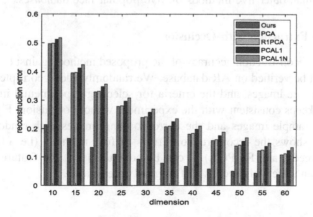

Fig. 3. Reconstruction error on the ORL database

FERET Database. FERET database [29] is a public database with plenty of face images. In the experiment, we selected a subset of it containing 200 subjects from the database. Each category has 7 images with different angles, and the first, third and fourth images in each category were selected as experiment dataset. All images were sampled down to 40×40. The experimental results are shown in Fig. 4. It is obvious that the reconstruction capacity of Mirror PCA method is superior than that of PCA-L1, L1-PCA non-greedy and R1-PCA.

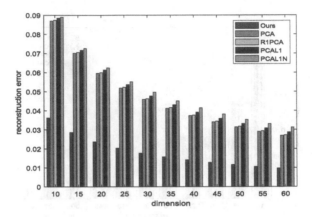

Fig. 4. Reconstruction error on the FERET database

Discussions. From the results of the four above experiments, we can conclude that the proposed PCA method is consistently better than other five PCA-based methods with the number of features keeping increasing, which is probably result from that the features extracted by Mirror PCA can represent the original face images more accurately. In addition, the performance of PCA, R1-PCA, PCA-L1, PCA-L1 non-greedy are similar with each other. Since our proposed method combined the objective function with facial symmetry, the reconstruction error of the proposed consistently much smaller than other five methods on five popular face databases.

4.2   Feature Extraction with Occlusion

In this section, reconstruction accuracy of the proposed method against to random pixel corruption will be verified on AR database. We randomly added corrupted 30% pixels in the original face images, and the criteria for selecting experimental images in each face database keeps consistent with the experiment without occlusion. Figure 5 shows some original sample images and the corresponding images with random pixel corruption Fig. 6 shows the reconstruction errors of four methods (i.e. PCA, PCA-L1, PCA-L1 no-greedy, and R1-PCA). It can be concluded that the feature extracted by Mirror PCA can effectively reconstruct original face images.

Fig. 5. Some images of the AR face database. The first row shows the original images, and the second row shows the images with random corrupted 30% pixels on the original facial images.

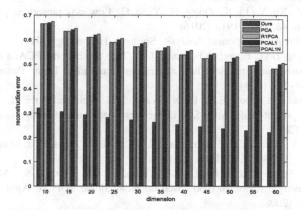

Fig. 6. Reconstructed error on AR database with random pixel corruption

5   Conclusions

In this paper, we proposed a novel PCA algorithm for feature extraction, leveraging the symmetrical structure of face images. Compared to traditional PCA method, the algorithm of our method calculates the reconstruction error of a face image from the left and right face respectively. It is in this context, we only need to obtain the projection matrix corresponding to the half of the face, which means that the size of the projection matrix in our model is just the half of other PCA methods based on the whole face image. In addition, considering that there are no perfectly symmetrical face images in practical world, the differences of the left and the right face will be taken into consideration in the proposed model. And L1-norm was used in the objective function to guarantee the sparsity of the differences. Experimental results on four open face databases show the performance of Mirror PCA is superior to other four PCA based methods.

References

1. Kirby, M., Sirovich, L.: Application of the Karhunen-Loeve procedure for the characterization of human faces. IEEE Trans. Pattern Anal. Mach. Intell. **12**, 103–108 (1990)
2. Fang, X., et al.: Approximate low-rank projection learning for feature extraction. IEEE Trans. Neural Netw. Learn. Syst. **29**, 1–14 (2018)

3. Xu, Y., Zhang, D.: Represent and fuse bimodal biometric images at the feature level: complex-matrix-based fusion scheme. Opt. Eng. **49**, 037002 (2010)
4. Elgallad, E.A., Charfi, N., Alimi, A.M., Ouarda, W.: Human identity recognition using sparse auto encoder for texture information representation in palmprint images based on voting technique. In: Computer Science & Information Technology (2018)
5. Reza, M.S., Ma, J.: ICA and PCA integrated feature extraction for classification. In: IEEE International Conference on Signal Processing (2017)
6. Yoo, C.H., Kim, S.W., Jung, J.Y., Ko, S.J.: High-dimensional feature extraction using bit-plane decomposition of local binary patterns for robust face recognition. J. Vis. Commun. Image Represent. **45**, 11–19 (2017)
7. Lu, Y., Lai, Z., Xu, Y., Li, X., Zhang, D., Yuan, C.: Low-rank preserving projections. IEEE Trans. Cybern. **46**, 1900–1913 (2016)
8. Jolliffe, I.: Principal Component Analysis. Springer, Heidelberg (2011)
9. Yang, J., Zhang, D.D., Frangi, A.F., Yang, J.-y.: Two-dimensional PCA: a new approach to appearance-based face representation and recognition. IEEE Trans. Pattern Anal. Mach. Intell. **26**, 131–137 (2004)
10. Kong, H., Wang, L., Teoh, E.K., Li, X., Wang, J.-G., Venkateswarlu, R.: Generalized 2D principal component analysis for face image representation and recognition. Neural Netw. **18**, 585–594 (2005)
11. Li, X., Pang, Y., Yuan, Y.: L1-norm-based 2DPCA. IEEE Trans. Syst. Man Cybern. Part B (Cybern.) **40**, 1170–1175 (2010)
12. Kim, Y.-G., Song, Y.-J., Chang, U.-D., Kim, D.-W., Yun, T.-S., Ahn, J.-H.: Face recognition using a fusion method based on bidirectional 2DPCA. Appl. Math. Comput. **205**, 601–607 (2008)
13. Kim, C., Choi, C.-H.: Image covariance-based subspace method for face recognition. Pattern Recogn. **40**, 1592–1604 (2007)
14. Wang, H.: Block principal component analysis with L1-norm for image analysis. Pattern Recogn. Lett. **33**, 537–542 (2012)
15. Ng, A.Y.: Feature selection, L 1 vs. L 2 regularization, and rotational invariance. In: Proceedings of the Twenty-First International Conference on Machine Learning, p. 78. ACM (2004)
16. Ke, Q., Kanade, T.: Robust L/sub 1/norm factorization in the presence of outliers and missing data by alternative convex programming. In: 2005 IEEE Computer Society Conference on Computer Vision and Pattern Recognition (CVPR 2005), pp. 739–746. IEEE (2005)
17. Ding, C., Zhou, D., He, X., Zha, H.: R 1-PCA: rotational invariant L 1-norm principal component analysis for robust subspace factorization. In: Proceedings of the 23rd International Conference on Machine Learning, pp. 281–288. ACM (2006)
18. Kwak, N.: Principal component analysis based on L1-norm maximization. IEEE Trans. Pattern Anal. Mach. Intell. **30**, 1672–1680 (2008)
19. Nie, F., Huang, H., Ding, C., Luo, D., Wang, H.: Robust principal component analysis with non-greedy ℓ1-norm maximization. In: Twenty-Second International Joint Conference on Artificial Intelligence (2011)
20. Pang, Y., Li, X., Yuan, Y.: Robust tensor analysis with L1-norm. IEEE Trans. Circuits Syst. Video Technol. **20**, 172–178 (2010)
21. Ekman, P., Hager, J.C., Friesen, W.V.: The symmetry of emotional and deliberate facial actions. Psychophysiology **18**, 101–106 (1981)
22. Saha, S., Bandyopadhyay, S.: A symmetry based face detection technique (2007)
23. Saber, E., Tekalp, A.M.: Frontal-view face detection and facial feature extraction using color, shape and symmetry based cost functions. Pattern Recogn. Lett. **19**, 669–680 (1998)

24. Xu, Y., Zhu, X., Li, Z., Liu, G., Lu, Y., Liu, H.: Using the original and 'symmetrical face' training samples to perform representation based two-step face recognition. Pattern Recogn. **46**, 1151–1158 (2013)

25. Yang, Q., Ding, X.: Symmetrical PCA in face recognition. In: Proceedings of International Conference on Image Processing, pp. II-II. IEEE (2002)

26. Martínez, A., Benavente, R.: The AR face database. Cvc Technical report 24 (1998)

27. Kuang-Chih, L., Jeffrey, H., Kriegman, D.J.: Acquiring linear subspaces for face recognition under variable lighting. IEEE Trans. Pattern Anal. Mach. Intell. **27**, 684–698 (2005)

28. Samaria, F.S., Harter, A.C.: Parameterisation of a stochastic model for human face identification. In: IEEE Workshop on Applications of Computer Vision (1994)

29. Huang, J.: The FERET database and evaluation procedure for face recognition. Image Vis. Comput. J. **16**, 295–306 (1998)

Face Image Super-Resolution via Sparse Representation and Local Texture Constraints

Bao-Cheng Wang[1,2(✉)] and Bo Li[1,2]

[1] School of Computer Science of Technology, Wuhan University of Science
of Technology, Wuhan 430065, Hubei, China
1623956251@qq.com
[2] Hubei Province Key Laboratory of Intelligent Information Processing
and Real-Time Industrial System, Wuhan 430065, Hubei, China

Abstract. In order to solve the problem brought by low-resolution images and to make better use of low-resolution images, this paper proposed a face super-resolution image reconstruction method based on sparse representation and local texture constraints. In the proposed method, sparse representation is used to reconstruct the super-resolution of face image. Moreover, the local texture of the reconstructed image is also used twice before and after reconstruction as constraints to obtain better details and make the reconstructed face image clearer. Experimental results show that this method can effectively reconstruct the corresponding high-resolution images from low-resolution images.

Keywords: Super representation · Local texture · Face image ·
Super-resolution · Image reconstruction

1 Introduction

With the development of society, surveillance camera system has been established in most cities. Although the city surveillance camera network is expanding, the role it can play is often limited due to the inherent low resolution of the video surveillance system. The resolution of the surveillance system resulted in the low resolution of the image and the poor quality of the picture, which affects its normal use. In some cases, low-resolution images especially human face images, lacking of features in details, which may not be helpful for image analysis and recognition [1, 2]. Therefore, how to improve the image resolution is an urgent problem. Super-resolution (SR) is very important and numerous algorithms have been proposed in recent years. The goal of SR is to generate a high-resolution (HR) image from one or more low-resolution (LR) images. SR algorithm can be broadly classified into three main categories: interpolation-based algorithms, learning-based algorithms, and reconstruction-based algorithms. Interpolation-based algorithms [3–5] are fast but the results may lack some of the fine details. In learning-based algorithms [6, 7], detailed textures are elucidated by searching through a training set of LR/HR image, but they require large amounts of data and training costs. Reconstruction-based algorithms [1, 8–10] apply various smoothness priors and impose the constraint so that when properly down-sampled, the HR image should reproduce the original LR image. In this paper, we mainly focus on

© Springer Nature Switzerland AG 2019
D.-S. Huang et al. (Eds.): ICIC 2019, LNCS 11643, pp. 296–303, 2019.
https://doi.org/10.1007/978-3-030-26763-6_28

super-resolution reconstruction of face image, and generate HR images form LR face images by learning the relationship between HR face images and LR face images training pairs, thus the face images with SR reconstruction can restore more details [11]. Baker *et al.* [12] proposed "face hallucination" to infer the HR face image from an input LR one based on a parent structure with the assistance of LR and HR training samples. Liu *et al.* [13] described a two-step approach integrating a global parametric Gaussian model and a local nonparametric Markov random field (MRF) model. In the process of image reconstruction, Li *et al.* [14] used the gray level co-occurrence matrix [15] for local constraints to restored the reconstructed image detailed feature and enhanced the robustness of reconstruction.

In this paper, we use the super resolution reconstruction method to reconstruct a single face image, and optimize the problem of the image super-resolution reconstruction. In the process of reconstruction of face image super-resolution, Nonnegative Matrix Factorization (NMF) [16] is used to enlarge the face image to the appropriate medium resolution image, where local texture constraints are used to enhance the texture extraction. Then the local sparsity prior is used to reconstruct the face image. After reconstruction, reconstruction constraint and local texture constraint are added to achieve more texture feature extraction and reconstruction.

2 Related Works

2.1 Image Super-Resolution from Sparsity

Let $D \in R^{n \times K}$ be an over-complete dictionary of K atoms ($K > n$), and suppose a signal $x \in R^n$ can be represented as a sparse linear combination with respect to D. That is, the signal x can be written as $x = D\alpha_0$, where $\alpha_0 \in R^K$ is the sparse representation coefficients. In the experiment, the face image we observed is

$$y = Lx = LD\alpha_0 \tag{1}$$

where $L \in R^{K \times n}$ with $K < n$ is a projection matrix. In the paper, x is a high-resolution image patch, while y is its low-resolution counterpart.

If the dictionary D is over-complete, $x = D\alpha$ is underdetermined for the unknown coefficient α, and $y = LD\alpha$ is even more dramatically underdetermined, which is caused ill-posed problem. Two constraints are modeled in this work to solve the ill-posed problem: (1) reconstruction constraint and (2) sparsity prior.

(1) Reconstruction constraint: The reconstructed high-resolution image X can reproduce the low-resolution image Y as

$$Y = SHX \tag{2}$$

where H represents a blurring filter, and S represents the down sampling operator.

(2) Sparsity prior: The patches x of the high-resolution image X can be represented as a sparse linear combination in a dictionary D_h trained from high-resolution patches sampled from training images

$$x \approx D_h\alpha \quad s.t. \ \|\alpha\|_0 \ll K \tag{3}$$

It can be solved by the image patches y of the low-resolution image Y.

2.2   Local Model from Sparse Representation

For this local model, there are two dictionaries as D_h and D_l, which are trained to obtain the same sparse representations for each high-resolution and low-resolution image patch pair. The problem of finding the sparsest representation of y can be formulated as

$$\min\|\alpha\|_0 \ s.t. \ \|FD_l\alpha - Fy\|_2^2 \le \varepsilon \tag{4}$$

where F is a feature extraction operator. As long as the desired coefficients are sufficiently sparse, they can be efficiently recovered as follows

$$\min\|\alpha\|_1 \ s.t. \|FD_l\alpha - Fy\|_2^2 \le \varepsilon \tag{5}$$

Lagrange multipliers can offer an equivalent formulation

$$\min_{\alpha}\|FD_l\alpha - Fy\|_2^2 + \lambda\|\alpha\|_1 \tag{6}$$

where λ is the penalty parameter. It cannot guarantee the compatibility between adjacent patches. Thus we enforce compatibility between adjacent patches as

$$\min\|\alpha\|_1 \quad s.t. \ \begin{aligned} \|FD_1\alpha - Fy\|_2^2 \le \varepsilon_1 \\ \|PD_h\alpha - w\|_2^2 \le \varepsilon_2 \end{aligned} \tag{7}$$

where P extracts the region of overlap between the current target patch and previously reconstructed high-resolution image, w contains the value of the overlapping high-resolution image. The final constrained optimization problem can be formulated as

$$\min_{\alpha}\|\tilde{F}\alpha - \tilde{y}\|_2^2 + \lambda\|\alpha\|_1 \tag{8}$$

where $\tilde{F}=\begin{bmatrix} FD_l \\ \beta PD_h \end{bmatrix}, \tilde{y} = \begin{bmatrix} Fy \\ \beta w \end{bmatrix}, \beta = 1$. Denote the optimal solution α^*, the HR patch can be reconstructed as $x = D_h\alpha^*$. But it does not satisfy the reconstruction constraint: $Y = SHX$, We eliminate this discrepancy by projecting X_0 onto the solution space of $Y = SHX$:

$$\arg\min_{X}\|SHX - Y\|_2^2 + \mu\|X - X_0\|_2^2 \tag{9}$$

3 Methods

For face image super-resolution reconstruction, the basic idea is first to use the face prior to zoom the input to a reasonable medium resolution and then recover the details using local sparse prior model. There are two main steps: (1) global model: reconstruction constraint is used to recover medium high-resolution face image; (2) local models: local sparse model is introduced to recover image in details.

3.1 Nonnegative Matrix Factorization

Nonnegative Matrix Factorization (NMF): The common subspace method in face image super-resolution reconstruction is principal component analysis (PCA). However the PCA bases are holistic, the PCA reconstruction is hard to interpret, therefore NMF [16] is used. NMF seeks a representation of the given signals, and formulated as the following optimization problem:

$$\arg\min_{U,V}\|X - UV\|_2^2 \quad s.t. \quad U \geq 0, V \geq 0 \tag{10}$$

where $U \in R^{n\times r}$ is the basis matrix and $V \in R^{r\times m}$ is the coefficient matrix. The problem of face image reconstruction can be expressed as

$$\min_{c}\|SHUc - Y\|_2^2 + \eta\rho(Uc) \\ s.t. \ c \geq 0 \tag{11}$$

where $\rho(Uc)$ is the regularization term, $c \in R^{r\times 1}$ is the coefficient matrix, η is a penalty factor. Let δ denote a matrix performing high-pass filtering, the final formulation is

$$\min_{c}\|SHUc - Y\|_2^2 + \eta\|\delta Uc\|_1 \\ s.t. \ c \geq 0 \tag{12}$$

In order to reconstruct HR image with more details, a texture constraint is applied to the reconstruct HR image with better quality:

$$\arg\min_{c}\|SHUc - Y\|_2^2 + \eta\|\delta Uc\|_1 \\ s.t. \ c \geq 0 \ and \ \|\psi Uc - \psi Y\|_2^2 \leq \varepsilon \tag{13}$$

Using Lagrange multipliers, an equivalent formulation can be offered

$$\min\|SHUc - Y\|_2^2 + \eta\|\delta Uc\|_1 + \lambda\|\psi Uc - \psi Y\|_2^2 \tag{14}$$

where ψ extracts the textural features. The medium high-resolution image is $\bar{x} = Uc^*$. Then the texture constraint is added again.

$$\min\|SHX - \bar{x}\|_2^2 + \mu\|X - X_0\|_2^2 + \gamma\|\psi X - \psi\bar{x}\|_2^2 \tag{15}$$

Thus final estimated HR image can be obtained.

3.2 Local Binary Patterns

LBP which has obvious advantages such as rotation invariance and grayscale invariance, is an operator used to describe the local texture features of the image in the field of machine vision. LBP is a simple but very effective texture operator, and the robustness of the grayscale change caused by the change of light is the most important attribute. The process of extracting LBP is to convert the original image into LBP diagram, then the LBP histogram of LBP diagram is calculated, and the original image is represented by the histogram of this vector. LBP can be defined as:

$$LBP(x_c, y_c) = \sum_{p=0}^{p-1} 2^p s(i_p - i_c) \tag{16}$$

where (x_c, y_c) denotes central pixel with intensity i_c and i_p is the intensity of the neighbor pixel. s is the sign function defined as:

$$s(x) = \begin{cases} 1 & if\ x \geq 0 \\ 0 & else \end{cases} \tag{17}$$

Then the histogram of the image is calculated, after which the histogram is normalized. Finally, the statistical histogram is connected to an eigenvector. By applying the eigenvector into SR process, the reconstructed HR image can better maintain textural details and edge information.

4   Experiment Results

In our experiment, we tested multiple images to verify the effectiveness of the proposed method. The experiments are conducted on the FEI face database.

4.1   Database and Experimental Setting

The FEI face database contains 200 persons, 100 men and 100 women. Each person has two images: one with normal expression and the other with smile expression, we used normal expression in the experiment. The HR images are down-sampled to generate LR image. 100000 patch pairs are randomly selected to learn dictionaries.

The LR patch size is set to be 3 × 3, the size of medium resolution image patch and HR patch is 6 × 6 and 9 × 9, respectively. After the reconstruction images were obtained, then it uses the reconstruction constraints and local texture constraints to carry out the constraint optimization, and the final reconstructed image was obtained. We compared our method with bicubic interpolation [4], Yang *et al.* [10] and ASDS by Dong *et al.* [17]. In the experiment, we set the parameter $\lambda = 0.1$, $\beta = 1$.

4.2 Results

The results are shown in Fig. 1, where the images followed are image one to image five. From the experimental results, it can be seen that the ASDS method can produce artifacts in some details, especially in the reconstruction of the eyes, affecting the experiment results. Bicubic interpolation method, especially before the image has no uniform size, lacks some corresponding details and contours, but for the regular images, the experimental results are still relatively clear visually. Sparse representation and the method of this paper produce similar experimental results, but in this paper, local texture constraints are added, which has better reconstruction in some places.

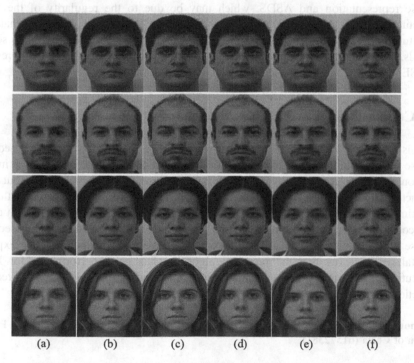

(a)　　　　　(b)　　　　　(c)　　　　　(d)　　　　　(e)　　　　　(f)

Fig. 1. Comparison between the proposed methods with other methods. From left to right: (a) low-resolution image, (b) sparse representation, (c) bicubic interpolation, (d) ASDS, (f) our method

In order to evaluate the results of various methods, we utilize two indexes i.e., the Structural Similarity Index (SSIM) and the Root Mean Square Error (RMSE). Table 1 shows the experimental results of each method.

Table 1. The experimental results of different methods

Picture	Indexes	Sparse representation	Bicubic interpolation	ASDS	Our method
One	RMSE	6.195070	4.340443	23.086793	**3.010353**
	SSIM	0.912978	0.951196	0.933413	**0.983135**
Two	RMSE	6.507765	4.610660	22.974624	**3.224335**
	SSIM	0.899768	0.945200	0.923767	**0.979615**
Three	RMSE	5.956770	5.200605	22.678918	**2.959204**
	SSIM	0.922658	0.951622	0.939353	**0.983527**
Four	RMSE	7.256012	4.944189	22.869193	**3.527873**
	SSIM	0.891131	0.934894	0.883674	**0.974377**

As seen from the table, the bicubic interpolation method has better result than the sparse representation and ASDS, which may be due to the regularity of the face structure. The SSIM of ASDS are good, but the RMSE are poor, indicating that the structure of the reconstruct image of the ASDS method remains good, but lacks some details. Due to the local texture constraints, the method of this paper get a better result, RMSE and SSIM are better than the bicubic interpolation.

5   Conclusions

In this paper, we proposed a face super-resolution reconstruction method based on sparse representation and local texture constraint to extract better local texture information, not only retains the advantages of sparse representation reconstruction, but also extract the local texture information to achieve a better result. Compared with the learning method with a large amount of data and the interpolation method which does not consider the texture information, the face super resolution algorithm based on sparse representation and local texture constraint has more advantages. The experimental results show that the proposed algorithm has good performance for low-resolution reconstruction from qualitative and quantitative analysis of image reconstruction results.

Acknowledgments. This work was partly supported by the grants of Natural Science Foundation of China (61572381).

References

1. Zou, W.W.W., Yuen, P.C.: Very low resolution face recognition problem. IEEE Trans. Image Process. **21**(1), 327–340 (2012)
2. Jiang, J., Ma, X., Cai, Z., Hu, R.: Sparse support regression for image super-resolution. IEEE Photonics J. **7**(5), 1–11 (2015)
3. Fattal, R.: Image upsampling via imposed edge statistics. ACM Trans. Graph. **26**(3), 951–958 (2007)
4. Hou, H.S., Andrews, H.C.: Cubic spline for image interpolation and digital filtering. IEEE Trans. Signal Process. **26**(6), 508–517 (1978)
5. Mallat, S., Yu, G.: Super-resolution with sparse mixing estimators. IEEE Trans. Image Process. **19**(2), 2889–2900 (2010)
6. Freeman, W.T., Jones, T.R., Pasztor, E.C.: Example-based super-resolution. IEEE Comput. Graph. Appl. **22**(2), 56–65 (2002)
7. Glasner, D., Bagon, S., Irani, M.: Super-resolution from a single image. In: Proceedings of IEEE International Conference on Computer Vision, pp. 349–356 (2009)
8. Sun, J., Sun, J., Xu, Z., Shum, H.Y.: Gradient profile prior and its applications in image super-resolution and enhancement. IEEE Trans. Image Process. **20**(6), 1529–1542 (2011)
9. Donoho, D.L.: For most large underdetermined systems of linear equations, the minimal l_1-norm near-solution approximates the sparsest near-solution. Commun. Pure Appl. Math. **59**(7), 907–934 (2006)
10. Yang, J., Wright, J., Huang, T.S., Ma, Y.: Image super-resolution via sparse representation. IEEE Trans. Image Process. **19**(11), 2861–2873 (2010)
11. Wang, N., Li, J., Tao, D., Li, X., Gao, X.: Heterogeneous image transformation. Pattern Recogn. Lett. **34**(1), 77–84 (2013)
12. Baker, S., Kanade, T.: Limits on super-resolution and how to break them. IEEE Trans. Pattern Anal. Mach. Intell. **24**(9), 1167–1183 (2002)
13. Liu, C., Shum, H.Y., Zhang, C. S.: A two-step approach to hallucinating faces: global parametric model and local nonparametric model. In: Proceedings of CVPR, pp. 192–198 (2001)
14. Li, W., Li, B.: Image super-resolution via sparse representation and local texture constraint. In: ICIEA, pp. 1041–1046 (2016)
15. Baraldi, A., Parmiggiani, F.: Investigation of the textural characteristics associated with gray level cooccurrence matrix statistical parameters. IEEE Trans. Geosci. Remote Sens. **33**(2), 293–304 (1995)
16. Lee, D.D., Seung, H.S.: Learning the parts of objects by non-negative matrix factorization. Nature **401**, 788–791 (1999)
17. Dong, W., Zhang, L., Shi, G., Wu, X.: Image deblurring and super-resolution by adaptive sparse domain selection and adaptive regularization. IEEE Trans. Image Process. **20**(7), 1838–1857 (2011)

Convolutional Capsule-Based Network for Person Re-identification

Andong Li[1(✉)], Di Wu[1], De-Shuang Huang[1], and Lijun Zhang[2,3]

[1] Institute of Machine Learning and Systems Biology,
School of Electronics and Information Engineering, Tongji University,
Shanghai, China
li_andong@yeah.net
[2] Collaborative Innovation Center of Intelligent New Energy Vehicle,
Shanghai, China
[3] School of Automotive Studies, Tongji University, Shanghai, China

Abstract. Person re-identification is yet a critical challenging task in video surveillance domain. It aims to match the same person across different cameras. Practically, pedestrian's appearances may vary greatly due to the complex background. Most deep learning methods rely on convolutional neural network to extract the feature of the pedestrian. But most of them lose the crucial details of the pedestrian and are sensitive to the viewpoints of the camera. To remedy this problem, we propose using capsule network as the feature extractor and introduce an improved loss function for the network. The experiment results on the Market-1501 dataset show the effectiveness of the proposed method.

Keywords: Pedestrian re-identification · Capsule network · Loss fusion

1 Introduction

Person re-identification is a task of re-identifying the pedestrian captured by different cameras. Figure 1 is an intuitive explanation for pedestrian re-identification from academic angle. The purpose is to automatically find the target of interest on the left side from extensive image library with multiple views and periods on the right [1, 2].

Generally, pedestrian recognition is divided into two parts: feature representation designing [3, 4] and distance metric learning [5, 6]. We use A to represent the query image,and $\{N_1, N_2, \cdots, N_K, \cdots N_n\}$ to represent the images in the gallery set. The feature representations of A and $\{N_1, N_2, \cdots, N_K, \cdots N_n\}$ can be formulated as $f(A)$ and $\{f(N_1), f(N_2), \cdots, f(N_k), \cdots f(N_n)\}$, respectively.

The process of re-identification [7, 8] can be written as:

$$Res = argmin(dis(f(N_k), f(A))) \tag{1}$$

Where Res represents the most similar picture with A $dis()$ is a suitable distance metric.

At present, the difficulties of pedestrian recognition are: (1) the appearances of pedestrians and the surrounding environment change due to the different camera angles

© Springer Nature Switzerland AG 2019
D.-S. Huang et al. (Eds.): ICIC 2019, LNCS 11643, pp. 304–311, 2019.
https://doi.org/10.1007/978-3-030-26763-6_29

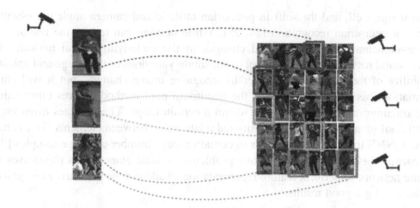

Fig. 1. Pedestrian re-identification

[9, 10]; (2) background spots and obstructions [11, 12]; (3) different time and place, pedestrians [13, 14].

This paper proposes a deep and multi-loss fusion method for Person re-identification, using capsule network as the reference network and combining two losses to joint train network.

2 Related Work

The traditional pedestrian recognition firstly uses the feature representation method to extract the features of the pedestrian image and then uses the appropriate similarity measure to measure the pedestrian characteristics. Then Use the large-scale data set to train the metric discrimination and feature extraction model. Finally, using the target image of interest, and matching the pedestrian image in the image collection collected under the monitoring system, obtained the sorted list of feature distances from near to far [15, 16], thereby finding the target image and realizing the pedestrian recognition process.

There are some drawbacks when combining the feature extraction with metric learning. Individually, the feature extraction method cannot adjust adaptively according to the requirements of metric learning. Two components are still independent [17–19]. The lack of interaction between feature extraction and metric learning makes person re-identification systems separated [20, 21].

Recently, deep learning person re-identification methods have shown their strengths over traditional methods. Feature extraction and metric learning can be combined as an entirety. Convolutional neural networks are considered as feature extractor, and loss functions such as triplet loss are considered as metric learning [22, 23]. Networks can adjust adaptively according to the requirements of the loss function through back-propagation.

However, the commonly used convolutional neural networks and their variants have two problems. A single convolution operation cannot cope with various changes of the image well, and the shift in pedestrian attitude and camera angle are essential issues for pedestrian recognition [24, 25]. While pooling can reduce the response of high-level neural networks to local changes in the underlying neural network, the whole neural network can better adapt to the subtle variations of the image and enhance the ability of the convolutional layer to recognize image changes, but it will cause information loss [26]. For example, the maximum pool method ignores other values while retaining a maximum amount within a certain range. These values often imply essential information, such as the positional relationship between elements. To a certain extent, CNN's training set still needs to contain a large number of image samples [27]. The capsule network solves the above problems to some extent. This paper uses the capsule network to perform feature representation to address the pedestrian recognition problem and get good results.

3   CapsuleReIdNet

The concept of capsules is not anything new, because Hinton, the dominant figure in deep learning field, has been thinking about it for a while (see for example [28], although the idea goes back several decades ago, according to Hinton himself). It just never worked before, up until the dynamic routing algorithm was proposed [29]. In what follows, the concept of Convolutional capsule network (CapsNet) will be presented in more details.

First of all, a capsule is a group of neurons whose outputs are interpreted as various properties of the same object. Each capsule has two ingredients: a pose matrix, and an activation probability. These are like activities of a standard neural network. The length of the output vector of a capsule can be interpreted as the probability that the entity represented by the capsule is present in the current input [30]. There can be several layers of capsules. In our architecture, we used a layer of primary capsules (re-shaped and squashed output of the last convolutional layer) and a layer of ReIDCaps [31] (i.e. capsules representing kinds of the pedestrian).

Each capsule in the primary capsule layer connects to every other capsule in ReIDCaps layer [32]. However, an algorithm, called routing-by-agreement, enables better learning, as compared to the max-pooling routing. Routing-by-agreement is a feedback algorithm which increases the contribution of those capsules that agree most with the parent output [33]. Thus, even more, strengthening its contribution.

The above-mentioned squashing function is a multi-dimensional alternative to the one-dimensional activation functions in conventional neural networks and is calculated as follows [34]:

$$v_j = \frac{\| s_j \|^2}{1 + \| s_j \|^2} \frac{s_j}{\| s_j \|} \tag{2}$$

Where v_j is the vector output of capsule j, and s_j is its total input (Fig. 2).

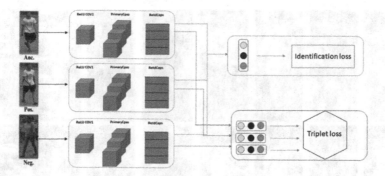

Fig. 2. Network architecture

Its original margin loss can only solve the classification task, which is not enough. In this paper, we treat the person Reid as a combination of classification task [35] and ranking task [36]. The two tasks are complementary to each other. We use the triplet and softmax losses to optimize the network simultaneously, leveraging the additional advantages of this two losses. The ReIdCaps are concatenated together as the final part-based representation and send to the identification loss and triplet loss. The overall loss function of the network can be formulated is:

$$L = \alpha_1 l_1 + \alpha_2 l_t \tag{3}$$

where α_1, α_2 are the weighting parameter that balance the loss functions.

4   Experiment

4.1   Dataset

The Market1501 dataset was first published in the 2015 ICCV paper [37] and is one of the widely used large-scale pedestrian recognition datasets to date. The dataset was collected in front of a Tsinghua University supermarket using six cameras (5 high resolutions, one low resolution). To ensure cross-camera search, there is overlap between different cameras, and each marked pedestrian is guaranteed to come from at least two cameras. More specifically, the data set includes a total of 32,668 pictures of 1501 pedestrians. The public dataset provided on the Internet has divided 32,668 images into training and test sets, including 19,732 images in the test set folder and 12,936 images in the training set folder. Also, a total of 3368 pictures (750 IDs, up to 6 IDs per ID) of one ID pedestrian randomly selected by each camera are separately separated as a candidate set. In the experiment, we can further subdivide the test set into test sets and validation sets (Fig. 3).

Fig. 3. Market1501 dataset

4.2 Implementation Details

Adam optimizer [38] with parameter 0.0001was used to train the entire network. The threshold parameter margin of the triple loss is set to 0.5. the weighting factors α_1, α_2 of the classification loss and the triple loss are set to 0.69 to 0.01, respectively.

4.3 Result

This paper compares the performance of the proposed model with the other 11 representative work on the Market-1501 dataset. According to the dataset setup, the training set contains 12,936 images of 751 pedestrians, and the test set includes images of 19,722 750 pedestrians. The average accuracy (mAP), Rank-1 and Rank-5 performance values are shown in Table 1. It can be seen from Table 1 that the accuracy of mAP, Rank-1, and Rank-5 of the proposed model reach to 70.10% 86.60% and 94.60%, respectively, achieving the good experimental result

Table 1. Experimental results on the market1501 dataset (% in the table)

Method	mAP	Rank-1	Rank-5
BoW + KISSME [13]	20.76	44.42	-
SL [17]	26.35	51.90	-
DNS [6]	35.68	61.02	-
Gated Siamese [18]	39.55	65.88	-
LOMO+TMA [5]	22.30	47.90	-
Deep Transfer [9]	65.50	83.70	-
CAN [11]	35.90	60.30	-
CNN Embedding [20]	59.87	79.51	90.91
CNN+DCGAN [13]	56.23	78.06	-
IDE(R)+ML (re-ra) [27]	63.63	77.11	-
TriNet [28]	69.14	84.92	94.21
CapsuleReIdNet	70.10	86.60	94.60

5 Conclusion

A convolutional capsule network was presented to solve the Person Reid problem, and we combine the identification loss and triplet loss to replace its original loss and achieve a good result on market101 dataset. In the future, a more in-depth analysis will be performed to optimize the architecture, i.e. number of convolutional layers, dimensions of capsules in primary and ReIdCaps layers.

Acknowledgements. This work was supported by the grants of the National Science Foundation of China, Nos. 61672203, 61572447, 61772357, 31571364, 61861146002,61520106006, 61772370, 61702371, 61672382, and 61732012, China Post-doctoral Science Foundation Grant, No. 2017M611619, and supported by "BAGUI Scholar" Program and the Scientific & Technological Base and Talent Special Program, GuiKe AD18126015 of the Guangxi Zhuang Autonomous Region of China.

References

1. Cai, Y., Takala, V., Pietikainen, M.: Matching groups of people by covariance descriptor. In: 2010 20th International Conference on Pattern Recognition, pp. 2744–2747. IEEE (2010)
2. Huang, D.-S., Chi, Z., Siu, W.-C.: Computation: a case study for constrained learning neural root finders. Appl. Math. Comput. **165**, 699–718 (2005)
3. Zheng, W.-S., Li, X., Xiang, T., Liao, S., Lai, J., Gong, S.: Partial person re-identification. In: Proceedings of the IEEE International Conference on Computer Vision, pp. 4678–4686 (2015)
4. Huang, D.-S., Du, J.-X.: A constructive hybrid structure optimization methodology for radial basis probabilistic neural networks. IEEE Trans. Neural Netw. **19**, 2099–2115 (2008)
5. Zhao, R., Ouyang, W., Wang, X.: Unsupervised salience learning for person re-identification. In: Proceedings of the IEEE Conference on Computer Vision and Pattern Recognition, pp. 3586–3593 (2013)
6. Huang, D.-S., Horace, H.I., Ken, C.L., Chi, Z., Wong, H.-S.: Computation: a new partitioning neural network model for recursively finding arbitrary roots of higher order arbitrary polynomials. Appl. Math. Comput. **162**, 1183–1200 (2005)
7. Zhao, R., Ouyang, W., Wang, X.: Learning mid-level filters for person re-identification. In: Proceedings of the IEEE Conference on Computer Vision and Pattern Recognition, pp. 144–151 (2014)
8. Huang, D.-S., Ip, H.H., Chi, Z.J.: A neural root finder of polynomials based on root moments. Neural Comput. **16**, 1721–1762 (2004)
9. Su, C., Yang, F., Zhang, S., Tian, Q., Davis, L.S., Gao, W.: Multi-task learning with low rank attribute embedding for person re-identification. In: Proceedings of the IEEE International Conference on Computer Vision, pp. 3739–3747 (2015)
10. Huang, D.-S., Ip, H.H.-S., Law, K.C.K., Chi, Z.J.: Zeroing polynomials using modified constrained neural network approach. IEEE Trans. Neural Netw. **16**, 721–732 (2005)
11. Barbosa, I.B., Cristani, M., Del Bue, A., Bazzani, L., Murino, V.: Re-identification with RGB-D sensors. In: Fusiello, A., Murino, V., Cucchiara, R. (eds.) ECCV 2012. LNCS, vol. 7583, pp. 433–442. Springer, Heidelberg (2012). https://doi.org/10.1007/978-3-642-33863-2_43

12. Huang, D.-S.: Beijing: Systematic theory of neural networks for pattern recognition. J. Publishing House Electron. Ind. China **201** (1996)
13. Takač, B., Catala, A., Rauterberg, M., Chen, W.: People identification for domestic non-overlapping RGB-D camera networks. In: 2014 IEEE 11th International Multi-Conference on Systems, Signals & Devices (SSD14), pp. 1–6. IEEE (2014)
14. Huang, D.-S.: A constructive approach for finding arbitrary roots of polynomials by neural networks. IEEE Trans. Neural Netw. **15**, 477–491 (2004)
15. Oliver, J., Albiol, A., Albiol, A.: 3D descriptor for people re-identification. In: Proceedings of the 21st International Conference on Pattern Recognition (ICPR 2012), pp. 1395–1398. IEEE (2012)
16. Huang, D.-S.: Radial basis probabilistic neural networks: model and application. Int. J. Pattern Recogn. Artif. Intell. **13**, 1083–1101 (1999)
17. Hoi, S.C., Liu, W., Lyu, M.R., Ma, W.-Y.: Learning distance metrics with contextual constraints for image retrieval. In: 2006 IEEE Computer Society Conference on Computer Vision and Pattern Recognition (CVPR 2006), pp. 2072–2078. IEEE (2006)
18. Li, B., Zheng, C.-H., Huang, D.-S.: Locally linear discriminant embedding: an efficient method for face recognition. J. Pattern Recogn. **41**, 3813–3821 (2008)
19. Shang, L., Huang, D.-S., Du, J.-X., Zheng, C.-H.: Palmprint recognition using FastICA algorithm and radial basis probabilistic neural network. Neurocomputing **69**, 1782–1786 (2006)
20. Guillaumin, M., Verbeek, J., Schmid, C.: Multiple instance metric learning from automatically labeled bags of faces. In: Daniilidis, K., Maragos, P., Paragios, N. (eds.) ECCV 2010. LNCS, vol. 6311, pp. 634–647. Springer, Heidelberg (2010). https://doi.org/10.1007/978-3-642-15549-9_46
21. Wang, X.-F., Huang, D.-S., Xu, H.: An efficient local Chan-Vese model for image segmentation. Pattern Recogn. **43**, 603–618 (2010)
22. Yu, J., Tian, Q., Amores, J., Sebe, N.: Toward robust distance metric analysis for similarity estimation. In: 2006 IEEE Computer Society Conference on Computer Vision and Pattern Recognition (CVPR 2006), pp. 316–322. IEEE (2006)
23. Wang, X.-F., Huang, D.-S.: A novel density-based clustering framework by using level set method. IEEE Trans. Knowl. Data Eng. **21**, 1515–1531 (2009)
24. Roth, Peter M., Hirzer, M., Köstinger, M., Beleznai, C., Bischof, H.: Mahalanobis distance learning for person re-identification. In: Gong, S., Cristani, M., Yan, S., Loy, C.C. (eds.) Person Re-Identification. ACVPR, pp. 247–267. Springer, London (2014). https://doi.org/10.1007/978-1-4471-6296-4_12
25. Zhao, Z.-Q., Huang, D.-S., Sun, B.-Y.: Human face recognition based on multi-features using neural networks committee. Pattern Recogn. Lett. **25**, 1351–1358 (2004)
26. Sharif Razavian, A., Azizpour, H., Sullivan, J., Carlsson, S.: CNN features off-the-shelf: an astounding baseline for recognition. In: Proceedings of the IEEE Conference on Computer Vision and Pattern Recognition Workshops, pp. 806–813 (2014)
27. Robinson, P.: The CNN Effect: The Myth of News. Foreign Policy and Intervention. Routledge, Abingdon (2005)
28. Sabour, S., Frosst, N., Hinton, G.E.: Dynamic routing between capsules. In: Advances in Neural Information Processing Systems, pp. 3856–3866 (2017)
29. Hinton, G.E., Sabour, S., Frosst, N.: Matrix capsules with EM routing (2018)
30. Wang, D., Liu, Q.: An optimization view on dynamic routing between capsules (2018)
31. Zhao, W., Ye, J., Yang, M., Lei, Z., Zhang, S., Zhao, Z.: Investigating capsule networks with dynamic routing for text classification (2018)
32. Xi, E., Bing, S., Jin, Y.: Capsule network performance on complex data (2017)
33. Neill, J.O.: Siamese capsule networks (2018)

34. Iesmantas, T., Alzbutas, R.: Convolutional capsule network for classification of breast cancer histology images. In: Campilho, A., Karray, F., ter Haar Romeny, B. (eds.) ICIAR 2018. LNCS, vol. 10882, pp. 853–860. Springer, Cham (2018). https://doi.org/10.1007/978-3-319-93000-8_97

35. Chen, Z., Crandall, D.: Generalized capsule networks with trainable routing procedure (2018)

36. Shen, Y., Gao, M.: Dynamic routing on deep neural network for thoracic disease classification and sensitive area localization. In: Shi, Y., Suk, H.-I., Liu, M. (eds.) MLMI 2018. LNCS, vol. 11046, pp. 389–397. Springer, Cham (2018). https://doi.org/10.1007/978-3-030-00919-9_45

37. Zheng, L., Shen, L., Tian, L., Wang, S., Wang, J., Tian, Q.: Scalable person re-identification: a benchmark. In: Proceedings of the IEEE International Conference on Computer Vision, pp. 1116–1124 (2015)

38. Kingma, D.P., Ba, J.: Adam: a method for stochastic optimization (2014)

Plant Leaf Recognition Based on Conditional Generative Adversarial Nets

Zhihao Jiao[1]([⊠]), Lijun Zhang[2,3], Chang-An Yuan[4], Xiao Qin[4],
and Li Shang[5]

[1] Institute of Machine Learning and Systems Biology,
School of Electronics and Information Engineering, Tongji University,
Shanghai, China
Jiaozhihao17@163.com

[2] Collaborative Innovation Center of Intelligent New Energy Vehicle,
Shanghai, China

[3] School of Automotive Studies, Tongji University, Shanghai, China

[4] Science Computing and Intelligent Information Processing of GuangXi Higher
Education Key Laboratory, Nanning Normal University,
Nanning, Guangxi, China

[5] Department of Communication Technology,
College of Electronic Information Engineering,
Suzhou Vocational University, Suzhou 215104, Jiangsu, China

Abstract. Plants play an important role in human life, Identifying and protecting plants has far-reaching implications for the sustainable development of the ecological environment. Plant leaves can often reflect important characteristics of plants, so it is scientific and feasible to effectively identify plant species through plant leaves.

With the rapid development of deep learning in recent years, it has been widely applied in plant leaf recognition. Compared with the traditional method, deep learning based plant leaf recognition algorithm can extract plant leaf features more effectively and can greatly improve the performance. Based on the detailed analysis of the structural characteristics of three classical convolutional neural network models, this paper comprehensively compares the recognition performance of three convolutional neural network models on ICL plant leaf datasets. The experimental results show that the Conditional Generative Adversarial Net with optimized output layer has better recognition results on the plant leaf dataset than other convolutional neural network models.

Keywords: Convolutional neural network · Plant leaf recognition ·
Deep learning · Generative adversarial nets

1 Introduction

The automatic classification technology of plants is of great significance for people to study and protect plants. In recent years, with the rapid development of computer vision technology, the automatic classification technology of plants has also made great

© Springer Nature Switzerland AG 2019
D.-S. Huang et al. (Eds.): ICIC 2019, LNCS 11643, pp. 312–319, 2019.
https://doi.org/10.1007/978-3-030-26763-6_30

progress. Plant leaves, due to their strong discrimination, are important basis for plant automatic classification techniques to identify plant types.

The plant leaf recognition technology based on traditional methods is mainly based on the different characteristics of plant leaves, [1] and the feature vector extraction algorithm is constructed. At present, these feature vector extraction algorithms are mainly aimed at the leaf shape, vein and texture of plant leaves. The feature vector extraction method for the blade shape mainly simulates and represents the contour shape of the leaf by the feature vector [2]. For example, Neto et al. extracted the shape of the blade shape by elliptic Fourier analysis to distinguish different kinds of plants. Later, they proposed two shape modeling methods based on the invariant moment and the centroid radius model. Du et al. proposed a method combining geometric features and invariant moment features to extract the morphological structure of the leaves. Texture features are another important feature often used in plant leaf recognition techniques. By analyzing the distribution law of regional pixel points in the image of plant leaves, the texture features of the surface of plant leaves are extracted [3]. For example, multi-fractal dimensions are applied to plant leaf classification. Cope et al. extracted texture features of plant leaves based on a Gabor filter.

Since the GAN network excels in the field of computer vision, this paper introduces an optimized version of cGAN for the field of plant leaf recognition, [1] and replaces the output layer of the discriminator model with the softmax classifier. The experimental results show that the proposed model has a significant effect on ICL plant leaf data, and the recognition rate is 2.89% higher than that of the ResNet50 benchmark model.

2 Materials and Methods

In this section, we will introduce the dataset we use, as well as the architecture of cGAN and our optimization of plant leaf identification issues, and discuss in detail its advantages in plant leaf identification.

2.1 Dataset

We conducted experiments on the ICL plant leaf dataset. The open dataset of ICL plant leaves is established by the Institute of Machine Learning and Systems Biology of Tongji University and the Hefei Botanical Garden. It can be downloaded free of charge by relevant researchers on the ICL website. The data set contains 220 categories, a total of 16,851 plant picture samples, each type of leaf contains 26 to 1078 pieces of inequality. The image format in the dataset is in JPG compression format with a scan accuracy of 300 dpi and both are 24-bit white background images. A sample of some data sets is shown:

2.2 Generative Adversarial Nets

The Generative Adversarial Nets (GAN) consists of two models, [4] Generator G and Discriminator D, Random noise z Generate a sample G(z) that passes the real data distribution Pdata as much as possible through G, [7]. The discriminant model D can determine whether the input sample is real data x or the generated data G(z) [5]. Both G and D can be nonlinear mapping functions, such as multilayer perceptrons [6].

The algorithm of the GAN core principle is described as follows:

First, in the case given by the generator, the discriminator is optimized [20]. The discriminator is a two-class model, and the training discriminator is a process to minimize cross entropy. E(•) is the calculation of the expected value, x is sampled in the real data distribution P(x), [12] and z is sampled in the prior distribution P(z) [10]. In order to learn the distribution of the data x, the generator constructs a mapping space G (z; θ) from the a priori noise distribution P(z) [25]. The corresponding discriminator mapping function is D(x; θ), [11] and outputs a scalar to represent the probability that x is real data.

$$\min_{G} \max_{D} V(D, G) = E_{x \sim P_{\text{data}(x)}}[\log D(x)] + E_{z \sim P_{z(z)}}[\log(1 - D(G(z)))]$$

The purpose of G is to make the generated sample as close as possible to the real sample, that is, the closer D(G (z)) is to 1, the better, then V(D, G) will become smaller; and the purpose of D is to let D(x) Close to 1, and D(G (z)) is close to 0, at which point V(D, G) will increase.

Compared with other generation models, from the actual results, G AN can produce a better sample.

However, there are many problems with the original G AN [7]. Training G AN needs to reach Nash equilibrium, and training G AN model is unstable. In addition, it is difficult to learn to generate discrete data. In order to obtain "victory" generator, it will be easy to generate. Sample.

2.3 Conditional Generative Adversarial Nets

The conditional generated confrontation network (CGAN) is an extension of the original GAN. Both the generator and the discriminator add additional information y to the condition, and y can make arbitrary information, [8] such as category information, or other modal data. The condition GAN is achieved by feeding additional information y to the discriminant model and generating the model as part of the input layer. In the generation model, the a priori input noise p(z) and the condition information y combine to form a joint hidden layer representation. The confrontational training framework is quite flexible in terms of the composition of the hidden layer representation. Similarly, the objective function of the condition GAN is a two-player minimax game with conditional probability [16].

$$\min_{G} \max_{D} V(D, G) = E_{x \sim P_{\text{data}}(x)}[\log D(x|y)] + E_{z \sim P_{z}(z)}[\log(1 - D(G(z|y)))].$$

2.4 Conditional Generative Adversarial Net with Optimized Output Layer

The logic of using GAN in semi-supervised learning is as follows.

Unmarked samples do not have category information and cannot be trained on classifiers;

After introducing the GAN, [11] the generator can generate a pseudo sample from the random signal;

In contrast, the original unmarked samples have an artificial category: true [21]. The classifier can be trained with pseudo samples.

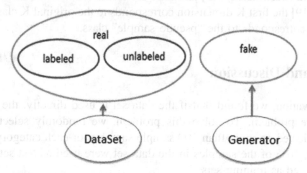

When applying GAN to a semi-supervised classification task, only a slight modification to the structure of the original GAN is required, [24] that is, the output layer of the discriminator model is replaced with the softmax classifier. Assuming that the training data has class c, then when training the GAN model, the sample simulated by the generator can be classified as the c + 1 class, [15] and the softmax classifier is also

added with an output neuron to indicate that the input of the discriminator model is "
The probability of "false data", [26] here "false data" refers specifically to the sample
generated by the generator. [23] Because the model can use tagged training samples, it
can also learn from unlabeled generated data, so it is called "semi-supervised" classification. Define the loss function as follows [17, 22]

$$L = - \mathrm{E}_{x,y \sim p_{\mathrm{data}}(x,y)}[\log p_{\mathrm{model}}(y|x)] - \mathrm{E}_{x \sim G}[\log p_{\mathrm{model}}(y = K+1|x)]$$

$$= L_{\mathrm{supervised}} + L_{\mathrm{unsupervised}}, \text{where}$$

$$L_{\mathrm{supervised}} = - \mathrm{E}_{x,y \sim p_{\mathrm{data}}(x,y)} \log p_{\mathrm{model}}(y|x, y < K+1)$$

$$L_{\mathrm{unsupervised}} = - \left\{ \mathrm{E}_{x \sim p_{\mathrm{data}}(x)} \log[1 - p_{\mathrm{model}}(y = K+1|x)] + \mathrm{E}_{x \sim G} \log[p_{\mathrm{model}}(y = K+1|x)] \right\}$$

Here, the classifier is used instead of the discriminator.

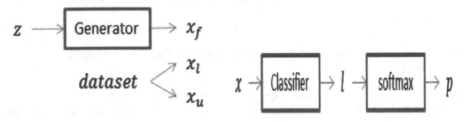

The training set contains a label sample xl and an unlabeled sample xu [18].

The generator generates a pseudo sample If from random noise [27].

The classifier accepts the sample I. For the K class classification problem, [14] the
K + 1 dimension is estimated, [23] and then the softmax function is used to obtain the
probability p: [19] the first K dimension corresponds to the original K class, [9] and the
last dimension corresponds to the "pseudo sample" class.

3   Results and Discussion

Through observation, we found that if the data set is used directly, the sample has a
large imbalance problem. To solve this problem, we randomly selected 150 plant
samples and selected no more than 100 sample samples for each category of plants. In
the experiment, 10% of the samples in the data set were used as test sets and 90% of
samples were used as training sets.

The following figure shows the trend of loss function values during the training of
four network models. Each network model iterates 100 epochs. It can be seen from the
figure that the loss of the cGAN model is relatively fast.

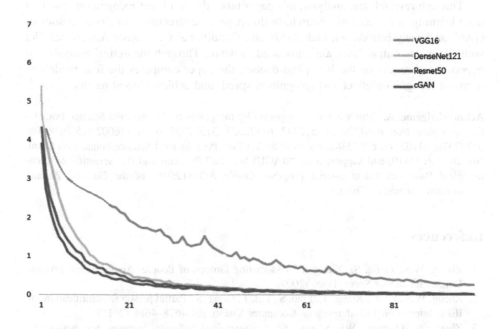

In this experiment, VGG16, ResNet50, DenseNet121 and cGAN were selected for model comparison experiments, in which the input picture size was 224 × 224. The experiment uses batch training. The size of each batch is set to 64, the learning rate is set to 0.01, the network model parameters are optimized using the Momentum algorithm, the momentum value is set to 0.9, and the weight decay value is set to 0.000005, the training phase and the test phase of the experiment were completed on two Nvidia Tesla K80 graphics cards, and the memory of each graphics card was 24G.

Model	Top1 (%)	Top4 (%)	Test time(s)
VGG16	88.32	92.67	0.051
ResNet50	93.12	96.48	0.040
DenseNet121	93.16	96.54	0.055
cGAN	93.41	96.63	0.043

4   Conclusion

Plants play an important role in human production and life. Identifying and protecting plants has far-reaching implications for the development of natural sciences. However, most people have little understanding of plants. Under this premise, the need for automatic identification of plants through pictures has emerged. Since plant leaves often reflect important characteristics of plants, it is feasible and worthwhile to classify plants by plant leaves.

Through research and analysis, this paper takes the plant leaf recognition based on deep learning as the core of research. In this paper, the structure and characteristics of GAN are briefly introduced, and cGAN and Conditional Generative Adversarial Net with optimized output layer are introduced in detail. Through theoretical analysis and experimental results on the ICL plant dataset, the paper compares the four models in terms of recognition effect and recognition speed, and achieves good results.

Acknowledgements. This work was supported by the grants of the National Science Foundation of China, Nos. 61672203, 61572447, 61772357, 31571364, 61861146002,61520106006, 61772370, 61702371, 61672382, and 61732012, China Post-doctoral Science Foundation Grant, No. 2017M611619, and supported by "BAGUI Scholar" Program and the Scientific & Technological Base and Talent Special Program, GuiKe AD18126015 of the Guangxi Zhuang Autonomous Region of China.

References

1. Zheng, W.S., Gong, S., Xiang, T.: Associating Groups of People. Active Range Imaging Dataset for Indoor Surveillance (2009)
2. Zheng, W.S., Li, X., Xiang, T., Liao, S., Lai, J., Gong, S.: Partial person re-identification. In: IEEE International Conference on Computer Vision, pp. 4678–4686 (2015)
3. Zhao, R., Ouyang, W., Wang, X.: Unsupervised salience learning for person re-identification. In: Computer Vision and Pattern Recognition, pp. 3586–3593 (2013)
4. Zhao, R., Ouyang, W., Wang, X.: Learning mid-level filters for person re-identification. In: Computer Vision and Pattern Recognition, pp. 144–151 (2014)
5. Su, C., Yang, F., Zhang, S., Tian, Q., Davis, L.S., Gao, W.: Multi-task learning with low rank attribute embedding for person re-identification. In: IEEE International Conference on Computer Vision, pp. 3739–3747 (2015)
6. Barbosa, I.B., Cristani, M., Del Bue, A., Bazzani, L., Murino, V.: Re-identification with RGB-D sensors. In: Fusiello, A., Murino, V., Cucchiara, R. (eds.) ECCV 2012. LNCS, vol. 7583, pp. 433–442. Springer, Heidelberg (2012). https://doi.org/10.1007/978-3-642-33863-2_43
7. Munaro, M., Basso, A., Fossati, A., Van Gool, L., Menegatti, E.: 3D reconstruction of freely moving persons for re-identification with a depth sensor. In: 2014 IEEE International Conference on Robotics and Automation (ICRA), pp. 4512–4519. IEEE (2014)
8. Takac, B., Catala, A., Rauterberg, M., Chen, W.: People identification for domestic non-overlapping RGB-D camera networks. In: 2014 11th International Multi-Conference on Systems, Signals & Devices (SSD), pp. 1–6. IEEE (2014)
9. Oliver, J., Albiol, A., Albiol, A.: 3D descriptor for people re-identification. In: 2012 21st International Conference on Pattern Recognition (ICPR), pp. 1395–1398. IEEE (2012)
10. Wang, X.F., Huang, D.S., Xu, H.: An efficient local Chan-Vese model for image segmentation. Pattern Recogn. 43(3), 603–618 (2010)
11. Li, B., Huang, D.S.: Locally linear discriminant embedding: an efficient method for face recognition. Pattern Recogn. 41(12), 3813–3821 (2008)
12. Huang, D.S.: Systematic Theory of Neural Networks for Pattern Recognition. Publishing House of Electronic Industry of China (1996). (in Chinese)
13. Huang, D.S., Du, J.-X.: A constructive hybrid structure optimization methodology for radial basis probabilistic neural networks. IEEE Trans. Neural Netw. 19(12), 2099–2115 (2008)

14. Huang, D.S.: Radial basis probabilistic neural networks: model and application. Int. J. Pattern Recognit. Artif. Intell. **13**(7), 1083–1101 (1999)
15. Wang, X.-F., Huang, D.S.: A novel density-based clustering framework by using level set method. IEEE Trans. Knowl. Data Eng. **21**(11), 1515–1531 (2009)
16. Shang, L., Huang, D.S., Du, J.-X., Zheng, C.-H.: Palmprint recognition using fast ICA algorithm and radial basis probabilistic neural network. Neurocomputing **69**(13-15), 1782–1786 (2006)
17. Zhao, Z.-Q., Huang, D.S., Sun, B.-Y.: Human face recognition based on multiple features using neural networks committee. Pattern Recogn. Lett. **25**(12), 1351–1358 (2004)
18. Huang, D.S., Ip, H.H.S., Chi, Z.-R.: A neural root finder of polynomials based on root moments. Neural Comput. **16**(8), 1721–1762 (2004)
19. Huang, D.S.: A constructive approach for finding arbitrary roots of polynomials by neural networks. IEEE Trans. Neural Netw. **15**(2), 477–491 (2004)
20. Huang, D.S., Chi, Z., Siu, W.C.: A case study for constrained learning neural root finders. Appl. Math. Comput. **165**(3), 699–718 (2005)
21. Huang, D.S., Ip, H.H.S., Law, K.C.K., Chi, Z.: Zeroing polynomials using modified constrained neural network approach. IEEE Trans. Neural Netw. **16**(3), 721–732 (2005)
22. Huang, D.S., Horace, H.I., Ken, C.L., Chi, Z., Wong, H.S.: A new partitioning neural network model for recursively finding arbitrary roots of higher order arbitrary polynomials. Appl. Math. Comput. **162**(3), 1183–1200 (2005)
23. Huang, D.S., Zhao, W.B.: Determining the centers of radial basis probabilistic neural networks by recursive orthogonal least square algorithms. Appl. Math. Comput. **162**(1), 461–473 (2005)
24. Huang, D., Ip, H.H.S., Chi, Z., Wong, H.S.: Dilation method for finding close roots of polynomials based on constrained learning neural networks. Phys. Lett. A **309**(5–6), 443–451 (2003)
25. Huang, D.S.: Application of generalized radial basis function networks to recognition of radar targets. Int. J. Pattern Recognit. Artif. Intell. **13**(6), 945–962 (1999)
26. Huang, D.S.: The local minima free condition of feed forward neural networks for outer-supervised learning. IEEE Trans. Syst. Man Cybern. **28B**(3), 477–480 (1998)
27. Huang, D.S.: The united adaptive learning algorithm for the link weights and the shape parameters in RBFN for pattern recognition. Int. J. Pattern Recognit. Artif. Intell. **11**(6), 873–888 (1997)
28. Huang, D.S., Ma, S.D.: Linear and nonlinear feedforward neural network classifiers: a comprehensive understanding. J. Intell. Syst. **9**(1), 1–38 (1999)

Leaf Recognition Based on Capsule Network

Yang Zheng[1(⊠)], Chang-An Yuan[2], Li Shang[3], and Zhi-Kai Huang[4]

[1] Institute of Machine Learning and Systems Biology,
School of Electronics and Information Engineering,
Tongji University, Shanghai, China
`Zy_yang6354@126.com`

[2] Science Computing and Intelligent Information Processing of GuangXi Higher
Education Key Laboratory, Nanning Normal University,
Nanning, Guangxi, China

[3] Department of Communication Technology, College of Electronic Information
Engineering, Suzhou Vocational University, Suzhou 215104, Jiangsu, China

[4] College of Mechanical and Electrical Engineering,
Nanchang Institute of Technology, Nanchang 330099, Jiangxi, China

Abstract. Plant is an indispensable part of human life, so it is very important to identify and protect plants. Convolutional neural network is a commonly used neural network for image recognition. However, convolutional neural network has huge defects. In order to avoid the defects of convolutional neural network, this paper adopts a new type of neural network: capsule neural network to complete plant leaf recognition. The experiment shows that the capsule neural network has a more effective recognition rate than the common neural network in plant leaf recognition.

Keywords: Convolutional neural network · CNN · Capsule networks · CapsuleNet · Squash function · Leaf classification

1 Introduction

Everybody knows the importance of plant, so it is also important to build an automatic system to recognize plant. In these years image classification has been developed faster as an effiention recongnition method As an effective recognition method, image classification has always been an important research field in computer networks. In recent years, various convolutional neural network architectures have been proposed, and more and more in-depth. Dense convolutional network is a structure form proposed in recent years. It was inspired by the concept of a convolutional network – one that can be significantly deeper, easier to train, and more precise when the links between the input and output layers are shorter.

The selection of training model is of great significance to the training and precision of deep neural network. Traditional neural network for image recognition for CNN as well as a variety of variations of the neural network (CNN), convolution is one of the important part of CNN, although there exist various convolution layer and way of improvement, but as a result of various convolution layer is good at recognition in a different direction, today did not exist can completely replace convolution layer

© Springer Nature Switzerland AG 2019
D.-S. Huang et al. (Eds.): ICIC 2019, LNCS 11643, pp. 320–325, 2019.
https://doi.org/10.1007/978-3-030-26763-6_31

training. Capsule neural network (Capsule_net) is the father of deep learning hinton and in 2017 put forward a new neural network, the network in the direction of handwritten numerals recognition test results. Since capsule network is similar to CNN in nature, it is a feasible scheme to replace CNN with capsule network.

In this paper, a new type of neural network is adopted: capsule neural network for the classification of the blade, we evaluated the different capsule on ICL database leaves the effectiveness of the network parameters, then capsule on network in ICL leaf database testing effect is optimum parameters, and the final test results comparing with test results of different neural network.

CNN is mainly used to identify images with invariable deformation forms such as translation and scaling [3, 4]. Since CNN is a feature of gradual detection data, it does not directly extract features [7] for learning, but implicitly trains itself. With the deepening of CNNs, a new problem arises: CNN's image processing is limited to the analysis of the shape characteristics of corresponding graphs in the image, while ignoring the position relationship between the graphs in the image.

CapusleNet's main inspiration was to use vectors to save the shape features of the image graphics while preserving the position relationship between the graphics in the image. Then the vector was aggregated using the dynamic routing algorithm and the final vector was compressed through the squash function. After viewing it, the length of the vector was regarded as the probability value of the corresponding feature.

CapsuleNet also has advantages of reducing parameters and making network training easier. Because of the unsupervised algorithm, it avoids the excessive use of supervised learning. Traditional network architectures transfer state from layer to layer. Each layer makes its own changes to the state when forwarding information that should be retained. But Capsule takes a different approach. It replaces some supervised training parameters with unsupervised ones, and eliminates the pooling layer, which reduces the number of parameters.

The CapsuleNet structure consists of two convolutional layers, a sub-capsule layer, a dynamic routing layer and a high-level capsule layer. Among them, the secondary capsule layer is reconstructed from the convolution result of the convolutional layer. The specific reconstruction method is to expand the convolution result of the convolutional layer to obtain the secondary capsules, and then conduct the dimensional expansion and dynamic routing algorithm of the secondary capsules to obtain the final advanced capsules. Then the final senior Capsule after activation function, the compression of the compressed vector length is the probability value of the corresponding characteristics, connect the secondary Capsule into the layer at the same time, will reconstruct the results into the size of the input image after the reconstruction of image difference with the original image is calculated and then get the loss function of refactoring difference, Capsule of network structure as shown in Fig. 1.

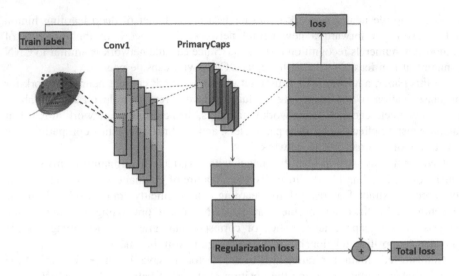

Fig. 1. The network structure of Capsule

2 Squash Activation Function and Dynamic Routing Algorithm

The selection of activation functions in the deep networks has an important impact on the training process and task accuracy. Currently, Rectified Linear Unit (ReLU) is the most successful and popular activation function. It has been shown that ReLU can largely improve the training performance of deep networks.

But due to the special nature of capsule nerve cell network, the nerve cell is different from other forms of neural network in the scalar vector, resulting in the capsule network activation function only as Squash function, is the main purpose of this function will be part of the capsule at the top of neural network output compression, the length down to less than 1, then the length of the compressed vector as the final output of the network. The squash activation function is shown in formula (1)

$$V_j = \frac{\|s_j\|}{1 + \|s_j\|} \frac{s_j}{\|s_j\|} \tag{1}$$

In this formula, s_j represents the vector that finally appears after the dynamic routing algorithm, and when the length of s_j is far greater than 1, the length of the vector can be minimized through the squash function.

Dynamic routing algorithm is an indispensable part from the bottom capsule to the capsule, and its function is to classify multiple capsules as a vector into one capsule. In this process, there is no problem of training, which is an unsupervised classification process.

3 Performance Evaluation

The ICL leaf database contains more than 200 plants, with 60 samples per plant. Each image size of the leaf is 224 by 224, and each image has three channels. We randomly selected 130 leaves for the experiment. Firstly, the ICL leaf database is extended. Data enhancement operations include cropping and flipping. After data expansion, each leaf has 600 images. The dimensions of each image are 160 by 160. To further reduce the number of architecture parameters and speed up the training process, we adjusted the image size to 32 × 32.

In the training process, we randomly selected 100 images of each leaf as the test data set, and the remaining images as the training data set. The architectural details are shown in Table 1.

Table 1. Experiment network architecture

Layers	Output size	CapsuleNet
Convolution layer (1)	32 × 32 × 256	7 × 7 conv, stride 2
Convolution layer (2)	32 × 32 × 256	7 × 7 conv, stride 2
PrimaryCapsule	16384 × 16	Reshape 32 × 32 × 256 to 16384 × 16
w	16384 × 8	16 × 8
PlanCapsule	130 × 8	Dynamic routing algorithm

Three experiments were performed on the ICL leaf database, respectively DcsnseNet, ResNet and CapsuleNet. The experimental results are shown in Table 2.

Table 2. Experiment results

	DesnseNet	ResNet	CapsuleNet
Train precision	0.89	0.88	0.90
Test precision	0.85	0.84	0.88

4 Conclusion

A novel neural network CapsuleNet was used in this paper for leaf recognition. Experimental results show that californienet has a better effect on location recognition than conventional convolutional neural network. The practice on ICL leaf database also shows that this architecture can accomplish the task of leaf classification well.

Acknowledgements. This work was supported by the grants of the National Science Foundation of China, Nos. 61672203, 61572447, 61772357, 31571364, 61861146002,61520106006, 61772370, 61702371, 61672382, and 61732012, China Post-doctoral Science Foundation Grant, No. 2017M611619, and supported by "BAGUI Scholar" Program and the Scientific & Technological Base and Talent Special Program, GuiKe AD18126015 of the Guangxi Zhuang Autonomous Region of China.

References

1. Huang, G., Liu, Z., et al.: Densely connected convolutional networks. In: Proceedings of the IEEE Conference on Computer Vision and Pattern Recognition, vol. 1, no. 2 (2017)
2. Ramachandran, P., Zoph, B., Le, Q.V.: Swish: a self-gated activation function. arXiv preprint arXiv:1710.05941 (2017)
3. Wang, X.F., Huang, D.S., Xu, H.: An efficient local Chan-Vese model for image segmentation. Pattern Recognit. **43**(3), 603–618 (2010)
4. Li, B., Huang, D.S.: Locally linear discriminant embedding: an efficient method for face recognition. Pattern Recognit. **41**(12), 3813–3821 (2008)
5. Huang, D.S.: Systematic Theory of Neural Networks for Pattern Recognition. Publishing House of Electronic Industry of China, Beijing (1996)
6. Huang, D.S., Du, J.-X.: A constructive hybrid structure optimization methodology for radial basis probabilistic neural networks. IEEE Trans. Neural Netw. **19**(12), 2099–2115 (2008)
7. Hinton, G.E., Salakhutdinov, R.R.: Reducing the dimensionality of data with neural network. Science **313**(5786), 504–507 (2006)
8. Won, Y., Gader, P.D., Coffield, P.C.: Morphological shared-weight networks with applications to automatic target recognition. IEEE Trans. Neural Netw. **8**(5), 1195–1203 (1997)
9. Serre, T., Riesenhuber, M., Louie, J., Poggio, T.: On the role of object-specific features for real world object recognition in biological vision. In: Bülthoff, H.H., Wallraven, C., Lee, S.-W., Poggio, T.A. (eds.) BMCV 2002. LNCS, vol. 2525, pp. 387–397. Springer, Heidelberg (2002). https://doi.org/10.1007/3-540-36181-2_39
10. Huang, D.S.: Radial basis probabilistic neural networks: model and application. Int. J. Pattern Recognit Artif Intell. **13**(7), 1083–1101 (1999)
11. Wang, X.-F., Huang, D.S.: A novel density-based clustering framework by using level set method. IEEE Trans. Knowl. Data Eng. **21**(11), 1515–1531 (2009)
12. Shang, L., Huang, D.S., Du, J.-X., Zheng, C.-H.: Palmprint recognition using fast ICA algorithm and radial basis probabilistic neural network. Neurocomputing **69**(13-15), 1782–1786 (2006)
13. Zhao, Z.-Q., Huang, D.S., Sun, B.-Y.: Human face recognition based on multiple features using neural networks committee. Pattern Recognit. Lett. **25**(12), 1351–1358 (2004)
14. Simonyan, K., Zisserman, A.: Very deep convolutional networks for large-scale image recognition. arXiv preprint arXiv:1409.1556 (2014)
15. Srivastava, R.K., Greff, K., Schmidhuber, J.: Training very deep networks. In: Advances in Neural Information Processing Systems (2015)
16. He, K., et al.: Deep residual learning for image recognition. In: Proceedings of the IEEE Conference on Computer Vision and Pattern Recognition (2016)
17. Huang, D.S., Ip, H.H.S., Law, K.C.K., Chi, Z.: Zeroing polynomials using modified constrained neural network approach. IEEE Trans. Neural Netw. **16**(3), 721–732 (2005)
18. Huang, G., Sun, Y., Liu, Z., Sedra, D., Weinberger, K.Q.: Deep networks with stochastic depth. In: Leibe, B., Matas, J., Sebe, N., Welling, M. (eds.) ECCV 2016. LNCS, vol. 9908, pp. 646–661. Springer, Cham (2016). https://doi.org/10.1007/978-3-319-46493-0_39
19. Larsson, G., Maire, M., Shakhnarovich, G.: FractalNet: ultra-deep neural networks without residuals, arXiv preprint arXiv:1605.07648 (2016)
20. Huang, D.S., Zhao, W.-B.: Determining the centers of radial basis probabilistic neural networks by recursive orthogonal least square algorithms. Appl. Math. Comput. **162**(1), 461–473 (2005)

21. Huang, D.S.: Application of generalized radial basis function networks to recognition of radar targets. Int. J. Pattern Recognit Artif Intell. **13**(6), 945–962 (1999)
22. Huang, D.S., Ma, S.D.: Linear and nonlinear feedforward neural network classifiers: a comprehensive understanding. J. Intell. Syst. **9**(1), 1–38 (1999)
23. Sabour, S., Frosst, N., Hinton, G.E.: Dynamic routing between capsules (2017)
24. Wu, J., Yu, Y., Huang, C., Yu, K.: Deep multiple instance learning for image classification and auto-annotation. In: Proceedings of the IEEE Conference on Computer Vision and Pattern Recognition, pp. 3460–3469 (2015)
25. Van de Sande, K.E., Uijlings, J.R., Gevers, T., Smeulders, A.W.: Segmentation as selective search for object recognition. In: 2011 IEEE International Conference on Computer Vision (ICCV), pp. 1879–1886 (2011)
26. Zitnick, C.L., Dollár, P.: Edge boxes: locating object proposals from edges. In: European Conference on Computer Vision, pp. 391–405 (2014)
27. Gao, Z., Ruan, J.: Computational modeling of in vivo and in vitro protein-DNA interactions by multiple instance learning. Bioinformatics **33**(14), 2097–2105 (2017)
28. Annala, M., Laurila, K., Lähdesmäki, H., Nykter, M.: A linear model for transcription factor binding affinity prediction in protein binding microarrays. PLoS ONE **6**, e20059 (2011)
29. Maron, O., Ratan, A.L.: Multiple-instance learning for natural scene classification. In: Fifteenth International Conference on Machine Learning, pp. 341–349 (1998)
30. Park, Y., Kellis, M.: Deep learning for regulatory genomics. Nat. Biotechnol. **33**, 825–826 (2015)
31. Glorot, X., Bordes, A., Bengio, Y.: Deep sparse rectifier neural networks. In: Proceedings of the Fourteenth International Conference on Artificial Intelligence and Statistics, pp. 315–323 (2011)

Image Segmentation Based on Local Chan-Vese Model Combined with Fractional Order Derivative

Le Zou[1,2,3], Liang-Tu Song[1,2], Xiao-Feng Wang[3(✉)], Yan-Ping Chen[3], Chao Tang[3], and Chen Zhang[3]

[1] Hefei Institute of Intelligent Machines, Hefei Institutes of Physical Science, Chinese Academy of Sciences, P.O. Box 1130, Hefei 230031, Anhui, China
[2] University of Science and Technology of China, Hefei 230027, Anhui, China
[3] Anhui Provincial Engineering Laboratory of Big Data Technology Application for Urban Infrastructure, Department of Computer Science and Technology, Hefei University, Hefei 230601, China
xfwang@hfuu.edu.cn

Abstract. Image segmentation plays a significant role in computer vision and image processing. In this paper, we proposed a novel Local Chan–Vese (LCV) image segmentation model. The new model combined classical LCV model with fractional order magnitude image. We used absolute value instead of square root operation to approximate the magnitude of fractional order gradient, and constructed the eight directions 5×5 fractional differential masks. We can get a novel fractional order difference image and drive a new local image fitting term. We also presented a new distance regularized term. The new distance regularization term was defined by a potential function. We used the spectral residual method for getting the saliency map of the given image. The initial level set function was driven based on saliency map to accelerate the convergence speed. The experiments were given to show the effectiveness of the new image segmentation model.

Keywords: Image segmentation · Level set · Fractional order derivative image · Saliency map

1 Introduction

Image segmentation is an essential problem in the field of image processing and computer vision. Image segmentation can provide effective image feature information for image analysis and image understands. In the last decades, hundreds of the image segmentation models have been investigated, such as region growing, watershed algorithm, thresholding, edge detection segmentation, clustering segmentation, graph cut, and active contour models (ACMs) and so on [1, 2]. Active contour models have been widely studied in the field of image segmentation by many scholars [2]. Based on curve evolution and level set image segment theories, ACMs have many advantages such as automatically topological change, which can deal with noise image and inhomogeneous images.

© Springer Nature Switzerland AG 2019
D.-S. Huang et al. (Eds.): ICIC 2019, LNCS 11643, pp. 326–336, 2019.
https://doi.org/10.1007/978-3-030-26763-6_32

In general, the existing image segmentation algorithms based on level set can be roughly divided into three categories: the edge-based models, the region-based models and the hybrid level set image segmentation models. The edge-based method uses gradient information of an image to identify object boundaries and to stop the evolution of the contour. The edge-based model is sensitive to the initial level set position and the level set can easily leak through weak edges. Compared with the edge-based level set model, the region-based method employ the regional information to control contour evolution, which can overcome the shortcoming of the edge based models. The most famous region based model is the Chan-Vese (CV) model [3], which is a particular case of the Mumford-Shah (MS) model. The CV model is powerless when the given image with intensity inhomogeneity [4]. To overcome this disadvantage, many hybrid level set image segment models have been presented to improve the performance of segmenting images with intensity inhomogeneity. Wang et al. [4] proposed a local Chan-Vese model (LCV) by introducing the kernel function and constructing the difference image. Some algorithm of the model LCV were studied by many scholars [5–7]. Li et al. [8] presented a local binary (LBF) fitting model by combining a gauss kernel function to construct a local binary fitting energy functional.

Recently, fractional order differentiation was introduced in the field of image processing and analysis [9]. It shows that the active contour models based on fractional order differential [9] have better performance than the above region-based model. Ren [10] presented an active contour model with fractional order fitting energy functional. Zhang et al. [11] proposed a region-scalable fitting (RSF) model based on fractional order fitting energy. A fractional order differential method can enhance weak edges and textures of the original image. So image segmentation is more accurate. During the contour evolution, to ensure the level set function can be used as a signed distance function (SDF), reinitialization is necessary. In order to avoid periodically initializing the level set function, some authors proposed the penalizing energy terms [1, 12, 13]. Saliency detection [14] is an important method for image analysis and image understands. Hou et al. [14] presented a spectral residual (SR) method for getting the saliency map of the given image. Automatic segmentation is a very important image segmentation method. Many scholars [15–18] have studied the level set image segmentation model by combing the active contour model with saliency detection. For Automatic segmentation of organs at risk in head Magnetic Resonance Images (MRI), Bevilacqua et al. [19] proposed a modified Gradient Vector Flow (GVF) Snake algorithm. Owing to the automatic tuning of the GVF snake parameters, the algorithm shows a remarkable performance. In this paper, we construct a new differences image combined with the Grünwald-Letnikov (G-L) fractional order derivative. We propose a novel distance regularized energy term. We utilize a saliency map to distinguish the desired object from the image. The saliency map was used as the initial level set, which can ensure the contour evolution carried out around the target. Experiments were given to demonstrate the efficiency of the proposed image segment model.

The remaining of this paper is organized as follows: In Sect. 2, the improved Local Chan-Vese model based on fractional order magnitude is constructed, the initial level set function and the new distance regularized energy functional is given. In Sect. 3, some examples are presented to show the effectiveness of the proposed improved Local Chan-Vese model. Finally, we present some conclusions in Sect. 4.

2 The Proposed Improved Local Chan-Vese Model Based on Fractional Order Magnitude

In this section, we present an improved Local Chan-Vese model, which is constructed by combing classical LCV model with fractional order magnitude image. We propose a new distance regularized term to avoid the reinitialize level set. Its numerical algorithm based on the gradient descent method is driven.

2.1 Data Fitting Energy Functional Term

Let $u_0(x, y) : \Omega \to \Re$ be the intensity image. We propose a novel variational level set image segmentation model, in which fractional-order magnitude difference image energy term and a different regularization term are used. In the proposed model, we use the global information to fit the original image and fit the fractional order magnitude difference image by local image information. The energy functional is as follows

$$E^F(c_1, c_2, d_1, d_2, \phi) = \int_\Omega \alpha_1 |u_0(x, y) - c_1|^2 H(\phi) dxdy + \alpha_2 |u_0(x, y) - c_2|^2 (1 - H(\phi)) dxdy$$

$$+ \int_\Omega \beta_1 |g_k * u_0(x, y) - \nabla^v u_0(x, y) - d_1|^2 H(\phi) dxdy$$

$$+ \int_\Omega \beta_2 |g_k * u_0(x, y) - \nabla^v u_0(x, y) - d_2|^2 (1 - H(\phi)) dxdy$$

$$\tag{1}$$

$$\nabla^v u_0(x, y) = \frac{|u_{0x}^v(x, y)| + |u_{0y}^v(x, y)|}{2} \tag{2}$$

where $\nabla^v u_0(x, y)$ is the fractional order gradient magnitude of the original image, $u_{0x}^v(x, y)$, $u_{0y}^v(x, y)$ are fractional differential masks in the x and y directions, respectively, v is the fractional order number. In numerical operations, to simplify the operation, the fractional derivative is approximately the first M term of approximate expression of partial differential difference of G-L fractional order. One can construct a $M \times M$ fractional differential mask. In this paper, we set $M = 5$. α_1, α_2, β_1, β_2 are four nonnegative constants. The meaning of c_1 and c_2 are the intensity means of the evolving contour as the same as that of CV model [3]. d_1 and d_2 are the intensity means of $g_k * u_0(x, y) - \nabla^v u_0(x, y)$ inside and outside of the evolving contour. Here g_k computes the averaging convolution in a $k \times k$ size window, $H(z)$ is the Heaviside function, we set $k = 3$.

For a fixed level set function $\phi(x, y)$, we minimize the energy functional in (1) concerning two pairs of constants: c_1 and c_2, d_1 and d_2. By calculus of variations, for a fixed function $\phi(x, y)$, the constant functions c_1, c_2, d_1 and d_2 are given by Eq. (3)–(6)

$$c_1(\phi) = \frac{\int_\Omega u_0(x, y) H_\varepsilon(\phi(x, y)) dxdy}{\int_\Omega H_\varepsilon(\phi(x, y)) dxdy}, \tag{3}$$

$$c_2(\phi) = \frac{\int_\Omega u_0(x,y)(1 - H_\varepsilon(\phi(x,y)))dxdy}{\int_\Omega (1 - H_\varepsilon(\phi(x,y)))dxdy}, \tag{4}$$

$$d_1(\phi) = \frac{\int_\Omega (g_k * u_0(x,y) - \nabla^\alpha u_0(x,y))H_\varepsilon(\phi(x,y))dxdy}{\int_\Omega H_\varepsilon(\phi(x,y))dxdy}, \tag{5}$$

$$d_2(\phi) = \frac{\int_\Omega (g_k * u_0(x,y) - \nabla^\alpha u_0(x,y))(1 - H_\varepsilon(\phi(x,y)))dxdy}{\int_\Omega (1 - H_\varepsilon(\phi(x,y)))dxdy} \tag{6}$$

Where $H_\varepsilon(z)$ are the regularization form of the Heaviside function.

2.2 Regularization Energy Term

In order to avoid the reinitialization step of the proposed model, we construct a new distance penalty term, which can keep the evolving level set function as a signed distance function.

We use the following function as the new distance penalty energy term, which can preserve the level set function $\phi(x,y)$ being a signed distance function (SDF) during the evolution of the contour

$$R(\phi) = \int_\Omega Pdxdy \tag{7}$$

$$P(s) = \frac{1}{4}(s - 2)^2 + \ln(s + 1) - (\frac{1}{4} + ln2) \tag{8}$$

where $P(s)$ is a new potential function. By utilizing distance regularization penalty energy term in (7) and (8), the level set function $\phi(x,y)$ can be maintained as an SDF [1, 9] in evolution process.

We also use length energy term as Eq. (9) to restrict small and isolated curves happening in the final segmentation result.

$$L(\phi) = \int_\Omega \delta(\phi(x,y))|\nabla\phi(x,y)|dxdy \tag{9}$$

Thus, the final regularization energy term E^R of our method was driven in Eq. (10)

$$E^R(\phi) = \mu \cdot L(\phi) + \eta \cdot R(\phi)$$
$$= \mu \cdot \int_\Omega \delta(\phi(x,y))|\nabla\phi(x,y)|dxdy + \eta \cdot \int_\Omega P(|\nabla\phi(x,y)|)dxdy \tag{10}$$

where μ and η are constants, which can control the length penalization effect and signed distance function maintaining effect separately.

2.3   Level Set Formulation for Proposed Model

Due to the introduction of distance regularization energy term in (8) and length regularization energy (9), the total energy functional is reformulated as follows:

$$
E(c_1, c_2, d_1, d_2, \phi) = \int_\Omega \alpha_1 |u_0(x,y) - c_1|^2 H(\phi) dxdy + \alpha_2 |u_0(x,y) - c_2|^2 (1 - H(\phi)) dxdy
$$
$$
+ \int_\Omega \beta_1 |g_k * u_0(x,y) - \nabla^\nu u_0(x,y) - d_1|^2 H(\phi) dxdy
$$
$$
+ \int_\Omega \beta_2 |g_k * u_0(x,y) - \nabla^\nu u_0(x,y) - d_2|^2 (1 - H(\phi)) dxdy
$$
$$
+ \eta \int_\Omega (\frac{1}{4}(\phi(x,y) - 2)^2 + \ln(\phi(x,y) + 1) - (\frac{1}{4} + \ln2)) dxdy
$$
$$
+ \mu \int_\Omega \delta(\phi(x,y)) |\nabla \phi(x,y)| dxdy
$$
$$
(11)
$$

Like other methods, the calculus of variations and the gradient descent method are used to minimize the energy function, the level set function ϕ can be updated according to Eq. (11):

$$
\frac{\partial \phi}{\partial t} = \delta_\varepsilon(\phi)[-\alpha_1 (u_0(x,y) - c_1)^2 - \beta_1 (g_k * u_0(x,y) - \nabla^\nu u_0(x,y) - d_1)^2
$$
$$
+ \alpha_2 (u_0(x,y) - c_2)^2 + \beta_2 (g_k * u_0(x,y) - \nabla^\nu u_0(x,y) - d_2)^2]
$$
$$
+ \mu \delta_\varepsilon(\phi) div\left(\frac{\nabla \phi}{|\nabla \phi|}\right) + \eta (div(\frac{1}{2} - \frac{1}{|\nabla \phi| + 1}) \nabla \phi)
$$
$$
(12)
$$

where $\delta_\varepsilon(x)$ is the regularized approximation of the Dirac delta function. We use the finite difference scheme to solve the above equation as the same as the traditional level set image segmentation methods.

2.4   Initialization

Initialization is the first step in level set image segmentation. Inappropriate initial contours will increase the number of iterations and the evolution time, and even get the incorrect segmentation results. Most of the existing level set image segmentation models are sensitive to the initial level set. As is well-known, the saliency region can quickly get the location of the desired object in the given image. In order to better combine the improved Local Chan-Vese model based on fractional order image, we first binarized saliency map of spectral residual (SR) method for the given image, and the thresholds was driven by using the maximum interclass variance method. To further refine the obtained saliency map, we used the morphological smoothing operation. The saliency map is eroded (dilated) with a kernel of width 4 to obtain a marker map, then we can get the initial level set function of contour evolution.

3 Experimental Results

In this section, to demonstrate the performance of the improved Local Chan-Vese model, we shall provide some experiments of the proposed model on several synthetic and real images. The proposed model was programmed using MATLAB 2016a and performed on an Intel Core (TM) i7-6700 2.6 GHz CPU, 16G RAM, and 64 bit Windows 10 operating system. We use LCVSR and CVSR to indicate the CV and LCV model with the initial contour extracted based on SR saliency map respectively. The parameters of the proposed model are chosen as follows: $\varepsilon = 1$, $\alpha_1 = \alpha_2 = 1$, $\beta_1 = \beta_2 = 0.1$, $\sigma = 40$, $\Delta t = 0.1$, $\mu = 0.1 * 255 * 255$, $\eta = 1$, $v = 0.7$ unless mentioned otherwise. For LCV model, LBF model, CV model, the parameters are set according to source code. For the LCVSR model, $\varepsilon = 1$, $\alpha_1 = \alpha_2 = 1$, $\beta_1 = \beta_2 = 0.1$, $\sigma = 35$, $\Delta t = 0.1$, $\mu = 0.001 * 255 * 255$, $v = 0$ for all experiments. For the CVSR model, we use the same parameters as CV model. We use the green line for the initial contour and the red line to represent the final evolution results.

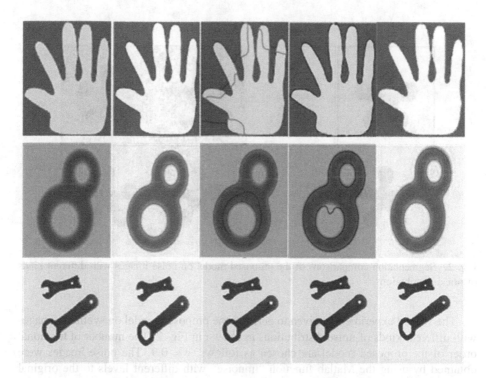

Fig. 1. Segmentation results of the proposed model, LBF, LCV and CV model on synthetic images.

Firstly, we presented an example to show the effectiveness of our model on several synthetic images. For the model LBF, LCV and CV, the center of the circle is in the middle of the image. The first column is the original image, the second column is the final segment result of the proposed model with only four iterations. The final evolving contours of LBF, LCV and CV model are shown in the last three columns of Fig. 1. It shows that our model can achieve remarkable performance on the synthetic image. But the model LBF, LCV and CV could not obtain the right segmentation results.

Fig. 2. Segmentation comparisons of the proposed model on noise images with different kinds of noise distributions.

The second experiment is given to perform the proposed model on synthetic images with different kinds of noise distributions as shown in Fig. 2. The number of fractional order of the proposed model are chosen as follows: $v = 0.9$. The noise images were obtained by using the Matlab function "imnoise" with different levels to the original image. The first row is the original image, the first one is the original image, the second one is the image with 0.75 Gauss noise and the third one is the image with 0.19 speckle noise. The fourth one is the image with Gauss noise 0.3 and speckle noise 0.1. The second row shows the initial contours extracted based on SR saliency map. The third column shows the fractional differential gradient images. The fourth column shows the final segment results of the proposed model. The fractional gradient magnitude have good performance in preserving and enhancing the low frequency information. It can restrain noise to some extent. Because of the fractional order fitting term in the proposed model, the force of curve evolution was strengthened. We can find that the proposed method can give remarkable segmentation results with different kinds of noise distributions.

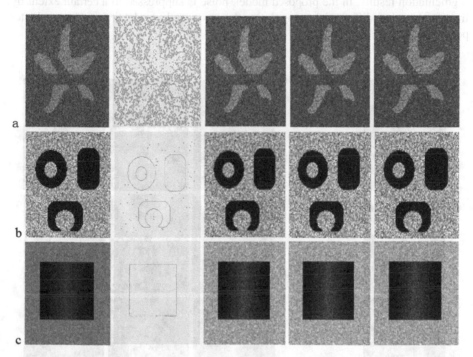

Fig. 3. Segmentation comparisons of the proposed model, CVSR and LCVSR model on synthetic images.

Table 1. A comparison of the computation cost (times(s))/iteration numbers of the proposed model and CVSR, LCVSR on noise images in Fig. 3

	a	b	c
Proposed model	25.05/190	2.26/70	0.67/4
CVSR	6.22/60	0.89/60	1.64/120
LCVSR	33.64/240	3.41/240	0.51/20

The third experiment demonstrated the performance of the proposed model, CVSR and LCVSR model on three noise images (as shown in Fig. 3). The first column shows the original images. The second column shows the initial contours based on salient map. The third column shows the final segment results of the proposed model. The final evolving contours of CVSR and LCVSR models are presented in the last two columns of Fig. 3. We also give the iteration number and computation cost (times(s)) in Table 1 for the three models. It can be seen that saliency detection can only provide a rough outline of the object and SR saliency map contains the noise information of the image. It cannot give the right outline of the target. Therefore, we use it as the initial contour of level set method in order to get an accurate boundary of the object. Due to the influence of noise, CVSR model and LCVSR model models cannot give better segmentation results. In the proposed model, noise is suppressed to a certain extent by fractional order differential image. So the proposed model can achieve better performance.

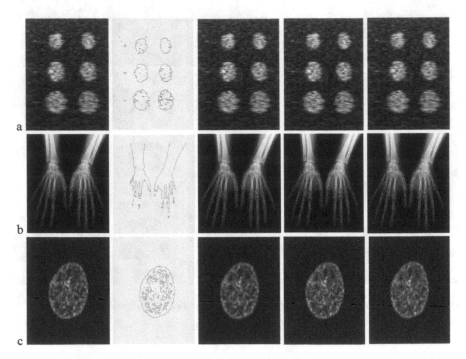

Fig. 4. Segmentation comparisons of the proposed model, CVSR and LCVSR model on synthetic images.

Table 2. A comparison of the computation cost (times(s))/iteration numbers of the proposed model and CVSR, LCVSR model on medical images in Fig. 4

	a	b	c
Proposed model	20.207535/100	3.686963/30	2.692465/80
CVSR	15.420809/140	4.809129/140	3.307429/240
LCVSR	21.368082/190	6.377980/190	2.605783/190

The fourth experiment is to perform the proposed model on three medical images as shown in Fig. 4. For the image (a) and (c), the parameters are set as described earlier. For the image (b), the parameters of the presented model are chosen as follows: $\mu = 0.001 * 255 * 255, \nu = 0.9$. The first column shows the original images, the second column shows the initial contours, the third column are the final segment results of the proposed model. The final evolving contours of CVSR and LCVSR model are presented in the last two columns of Fig. 4. Table 2 shows a comparison of the iteration number and computation cost (times(s)) for the three models. The initial level set function extraction based on spectral residual saliency detection method can obtain the potential position of the object. So iteration numbers is very few and the segmentation speed is greatly improved. Moreover, the initial curves are provided automatically and it is located near the object, which can avoid manual setting the parameters of initial level set contour and position. Because of the advantages of fractional order derivative image, the proposed model outperforms other models in terms of accuracy, segmenatation time and iteration numbers.

4   Conclusion

In this paper, we have presented a novel active contour model image segmentation model based on fractional order differentiation. By introducing the fractional order differentiation into level set method, we have presented an improved local Chan-Vese image segmentation model. We also used the saliency map as the initial level set function. The initial curve which was driven by SR saliency detection, it is near the edge of the object area, which significantly saves the segmentation time and improves the accuracy of the segmentation. The fractional gradient magnitude has good performance in preserving and enhancing the low frequency information. Particularly, in our proposed method, the new initialization method and new distance penalty energy term are introduced. Moreover, compared with Chan-Vese method and Local Chan-Vese method based on SR saliency map, the proposed method has much higher convergent speed and gives a much better segmentation performance.

Acknowledgements. The authors would like to express their thanks to the referees for their valuable suggestions. This work was supported by the grant of the National Natural Science Foundation of China, Nos. 61672204, 61806068, the grant of Anhui Provincial Natural Science Foundation, No. 1908085MF184, the grant of the key Scientific Research Foundation of Education Department of Anhui Province, Nos. KJ2018A0555, KJ2018A0556, the grant of Major Science and Technology Project of Anhui Province, No. 17030901026, the grant of Key Technologies R&D Program of Anhui Province, No. 1804a09020058, the grant of Teaching Team of Anhui Province, No.2016jxtd101.

References

1. Wang, X.F., Min, H., Zou, L., Zhang, Y.G., Tang, Y.Y., Philip Chen, C.L.: An efficient level set method based on multi-scale image segmentation and hermite differential operator. Neurocomputing **188**, 90–101 (2016)
2. Malladi, R., Sethian, J.A., Vemuri, B.C.: Shape modeling with front propagation: a level set approach. IEEE Trans. Pattern Anal. Mach. Intell. **17**(2), 158–175 (1995)
3. Chan, T.F., Vese, L.A.: Active contours without edges. IEEE Trans. Image Process. **10**(2), 266–277 (2001)
4. Wang, X.F., Huang, D.S., Xu, H.: An efficient local Chan-Vese model for image segmentation. Pattern Recognit. **43**(3), 603–618 (2010)
5. Zou, L., et al.: A fast algorithm for image segmentation based on local chan vese model. In: Huang, D.-S., Jo, K.-H., Zhang, X.-L. (eds.) ICIC 2018. LNCS, vol. 10955, pp. 54–60. Springer, Cham (2018). https://doi.org/10.1007/978-3-319-95933-7_7
6. Boutiche, Y., Abdesselam, A.: Fast algorithm for hybrid region-based active contours optimisation. IET Image Process. **11**(3), 200–209 (2017)
7. Li, Z., Zeng, L., Wang T.: Image segmentation based on local Chan-Vese model optimized by max-flow algorithm. In: IEEE/ACIS International Conference on Software Engineering, Artificial Intelligence, Networking and Parallel/Distributed Computing, pp. 213–218. IEEE (2016)
8. Li, C.M., Kao, C.Y., Gore, J.C., Ding, Z.H.: Minimization of region-scalable fitting energy for image segmentation. IEEE Trans. Image Process. **17**, 1940–1949 (2008)
9. Chen, B., Huang, S., Liang, Z., Chen, W., Pan, B.: A fractional order derivative based active contour model for inhomogeneous image segmentation. Appl. Math. Model. **65**, 120–136 (2019)
10. Ren, Z.: Adaptive active contour model driven by fractional order fitting energy. Sig. Process. **117**, 138–150 (2015)
11. Zhang, G., Xu, J., Liu, J.: A new active contour model based on adaptive fractional order. J. Comput. Res. Dev. **54**(5), 1045–1056 (2017)
12. Li, M., Liu, L.: Forward-and-backward diffusion-based distance regularized model for image segmentation. Appl. Res. Comput. **33**(5), 1596–1600 (2016)
13. Sun, L., Meng, X., Xu, J., Zhang, S.: An image segmentation method based on improved regularized level set model. Appl. Sci. **8**(12), 1–19 (2018)
14. Hou, X., Zhang, L.: Saliency detection: a spectral residual approach. In: 2007 IEEE Conference on Computer Vision and Pattern Recognition, pp. 1–8. IEEE Computer Society (2007)
15. Liu, G., Li, C.: Active contours driven by saliency detection for image segmentation. In: Liu, D., et al. (eds.) ICONIP 2017, Part III, LNCS, vol. 10636, pp. 416–424. Springer, Heidelberg (2017). https://doi.org/10.1007/978-3-319-70090-8_43
16. Zhi, X., Shen, H.: Saliency driven region-edge-based top down level set evolution reveals the asynchronous focus in image segmentation. Pattern Recognit. **80**, 241–255 (2018)
17. Bai, X., Wang, W.: Saliency snake: a unified framework with adaptive initial curve. Opt.-Int. J. Light. Electron Opt. **125**(23), 6972–6976 (2014)
18. Zhao, Y., et al.: Saliency driven vasculature segmentation with infinite perimeter active contour model. Neurocomputing **259**, 201–209 (2017)
19. Bevilacqua, V., Piazzolla, A., Stofella, P.: Atlas-based segmentation of organs at risk in radiotherapy in head MRIs by means of a novel active contour framework. In: Huang, D.-S., Zhang, X., Reyes García, C.A., Zhang, L. (eds.) ICIC 2010. LNCS (LNAI), vol. 6216, pp. 350–359. Springer, Heidelberg (2010). https://doi.org/10.1007/978-3-642-14932-0_44

Deep Learning Based Fluid Segmentation in Retinal Optical Coherence Tomography Images

Xiaoming Liu[1,2(✉)], Dong Liu[1,2], Bo Li[1,2], and Shaocheng Wang[1,2]

[1] College of Computer Science and Technology, Wuhan University of Science and Technology, Wuhan 430065, China
lxmspace@gmail.com
[2] Hubei Province Key Laboratory of Intelligent Information Processing and Real-Time Industrial System, Wuhan 430065, China

Abstract. Macular Edema (ME) is the accumulation of fluid in the macular region of the eye, and it may lead to the distortion of center vision. It often occurs in diabetic retinopathy. It is important to measure fluid accumulation in ME patients for disease monitor. Segmentation of the fluid region in the retinal layer is an essential step for quantitatively analysis. However, manual segmentation is time consuming and also subjective. In this paper, a new deep learning based segmentation method is proposed. The attention mechanism is introduced to automatically locate the fluid region, which can reduce the number of parameters compared to typical two-stage approaches. In addition, dense skip connection makes the segmentation result more accurate. Joint losses are used, including cross entropy loss, dice loss and regression loss. The proposed method is evaluated on a public available dataset, results show that the proposed method can adapt to the OCT scans acquired by various imaging scanning devices, and this method is more effective than other methods.

Keywords: OCT · Fluid region segmentation · Deep learning ·
Attention mechanism · Regression loss

1 Introduction

Macular Edema (ME) is the fluid accumulation due to disruptions in blood retinal barrier [1]. It can distort the center vision of a patient. Figure 1 shows the retinal images with macular edema, first row is the retinal OCT image with macular edema, and the second row is the mask of the cyst fluid region labeled by the expert. In order to monitor the development of the disease, it is required to segment the fluid region in OCT images.

Manual segmentation of fluid region is often a time consuming and subjective process. Several automated segmentation methods have been proposed in recent years. The earliest methods are based on basic image processing methods [2, 3]. Machine learning-based methods typically transform segmentation problems into classification or regression tasks, including unsupervised or semi-supervised methods [4–7]. Compared to image processing-based methods, machine-based learning methods could

© Springer Nature Switzerland AG 2019
D.-S. Huang et al. (Eds.): ICIC 2019, LNCS 11643, pp. 337–345, 2019.
https://doi.org/10.1007/978-3-030-26763-6_33

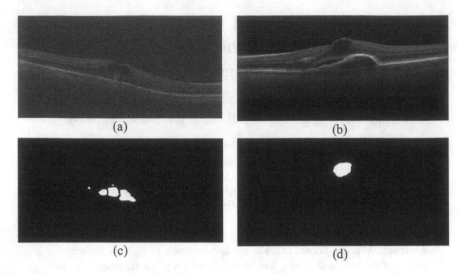

Fig. 1. Retinal OCT images with macular edema. (a) (b) are the retinal OCT images with macular edema; (c) (d) are the mask of the cyst fluid region labeled by an expert.

better consider the characteristic of medical image and design suitable classifiers. In recent years, deep learning, especially convolutional neural networks (CNN), has been succeed applied to computer vision tasks [8, 9]. It has also been investigated in fluid segmentation problem. In our previous work [10], a CNN-based on binary classification was trained to distinguish fluid and surrounding region. Lee et al. [11] proposed an automatic segmentation methodology using CNN. Schlegl et al. [12] used a neural network comprising of two processing components. These deep learning-based methods greatly improve the segmentation accuracy of the fluid region segmentation task.

However, the above deep learning-based methods have some shortcomings. They need to train several networks to detect and segment fluids which increases the complexity of training. In addition, most methods cannot separate closely located fluid regions, which may affect the analysis of disease development. In this paper, we designed a modified u-net network architecture for fluid region segmentation. The proposed network architecture is an integration of improved u-net and attention gates. Different to the work [13], we introduce the attention gates to learn where to look for the fluid region instead of two separate networks. In addition, similar to refine-net [14], we use dense skip connection to fuse the missing information in the down sampling to produce a high resolution predicted image. In this way, coarse high-level semantic features and fine-grained underlying features can be better utilized. To deal with the problem of wrongly merging of closely located fluid regions, regression loss is introduced. The segmentation network is trained by minimize a joint loss function that combining cross entropy, dice loss, and regression loss.

2 The Proposed Approach

In order to segment fluid region automatically, we designed an improved u-net alike network. The architecture of the network is shown in Fig. 2.

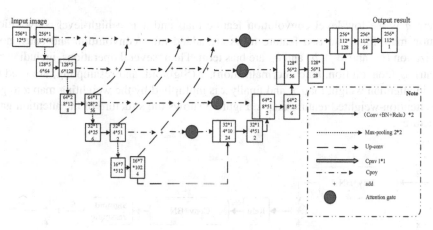

Fig. 2. The network structure of proposed method

2.1 Network Architecture

As shown in Fig. 2, the proposed network consists of an encoder and a decoder. The encoder uses OCT image as input. Then decoder uses extracted feature maps to generate the prediction map as the segmentation result.

The encoder is formed by four down-sample blocks. In each down-sample block, there is one convolution block and a maximum pooling layer. The convolution block contains a convolutional layer with 1 padding, followed by a bath normalization layer and a ReLU layer. After two consecutive convolutional blocks, there is a max-pooling layer with 2 strides.

Similar to the encoder, the decoder also has four up-sampling blocks. The up-sampling block contains a deconvolution block and a convolution block. The deconvolution block consists of one up-sampling layer, one convolutional layer, one batch normalization layer, and one ReLU layer.

There are skip connections between encoder and decoder. Different from general U-Net, the dense skip connection similar to RefineNet [14] is used to replace the simple single-scale direct connection. Besides, the attention structure is introduced between the encoder and the decoder to automatically locate the fluid region.

2.2 Attention Gate

We uses the additive attention mechanism [15] to obtain the gating coefficient. Although this is computationally more expensive than the multiplication attention mechanism, experiments have shown that it can achieve higher accuracy [16]. It is formulated as:

$$q_{att} = \psi(\sigma_1(W_x x + W_g g + b_g)) + b_\psi \tag{1}$$

$$\alpha = \sigma_2(q_{att}(x, g, \theta_{att})) \tag{2}$$

$$\hat{x} = a * x \tag{3}$$

where g is the low-level convolution feature map and x is a high-level convolution feature map. First, the two feature maps are added after convolution and batch normalization (W_x and W_g), b_g and b_ψ are bias term. Then, several operations, including σ_1 (Relu), ψ (convolution, batch normalization), α (Sigmoid, and resampling) are used to obtain attention weight map α, and finally x is multiplied by the weighting map α to get the attention-weighted feature map $\hat{x}$. Figure 3 shows the structure of the attention gate structure.

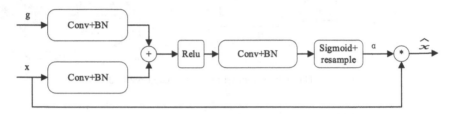

Fig. 3. Attention gate structure diagram

2.3 Loss Function

The segmentation network is trained via minimizing a jointly loss function:

$$L_s = \alpha L_{mce} + \beta L_{dice} + \gamma L_{regression} \tag{4}$$

where L_{mce}, L_{dice}, $L_{regression}$ denote the cross entropy, dice loss and the designed regression loss, α, β, γ are user defined parameters. The loss will be described in detail below.

Cross entropy loss is commonly used in deep learning which is employed to minimize the empirical risk. Given a pixel i in image X_n, its formulation is defined as:

$$L_{mce} = -\sum_{i \in X_n} Y_n^{(i)} \log(P_n^{(i)}) \tag{5}$$

L_{mce} will push the prediction $P_n^{(i)}$ made by the segmentation network to be close to the ground truth label $Y_n^{(i)}$.

The second loss term is the Dice loss. The dice score coefficient is an important measure to evaluate segmentation performance. We use a derivable dice loss that proposed in [17]:

$$L_{dice} = 1 - 2 \frac{\sum_{i \in X_n^{(c)}} P_n^{(i)(c)} Y_n^{(i)(c)}}{\sum_{i \in X_n^{(c)}} (P_n^{(i)(c)} + Y_n^{(i)(c)})} \tag{6}$$

where $P_n^{(i)(c)}$ is the probability of pixel i belongs to the class c, $Y_n^{(i)(c)}$ is the ground truth of pixel i.

We further integrate a regression loss [18] into the loss function. For each image to be segmented, calculate the distance map of the gold standard mask map, and the distance map of the predicted graph obtained by the model prediction, and finally define the regression loss id defined as:

$$L_{regression} = \frac{1}{m * n} \sum_{i,j} (B_{dist}[i,j] - \hat{B}_{dist}[i,j])^2 \tag{7}$$

where m and n is the height and width of the image, the mean square error of the ground truth distance map and the predicted distance map is calculated to represent the regression loss.

3 Experimentation and Results

3.1 Dataset

The used data set in this paper contains 500 scans from four OCT scan devices (cirrus, nidek, spectralis, topcon) [19]. The scans of four devices are 57, 159, 53 and 231. Three quarters of them are used to network train, one quarter is used as test. In addition, image enhancement is also used to maintain the balance of different devices. The image sizes of the four devices are different, we resampled all to 1024 * 512.

3.2 Comparative Methods and Metric

In addition to demonstrating the results of the proposed method on different scanning device data, in this experiment, the method of this paper is also compared with several advanced fluid region segmentation algorithms, which are (1) patch-based CNN segmentation proposed in the previous work. Method [10]; (2) U-net direct segmentation method based on Dice loss [11]; (3) Based on FCN and U-net The two-step strategy segmentation method [13].

We uses the Dice coefficient as a comparison indicator, which is used as a metric in many segmentation papers. The Dice coefficient depends on the overlap between the segmentation result and the gold standard. The formula is defined as follows:

$$dice = \frac{2|P \cap Y|}{|P| + |Y|} \tag{8}$$

Where P and Y respectively represent the fluid area prediction results and the gold standard.

3.3   Comparison of Experimental Result by Different Methods

This section presents qualitative and quantitative segmentation results analysis for different methods. The segmentation results of several methods on different images are shown in Fig. 4, and the quantitative results based on the dice coefficient are shown in Table 1.

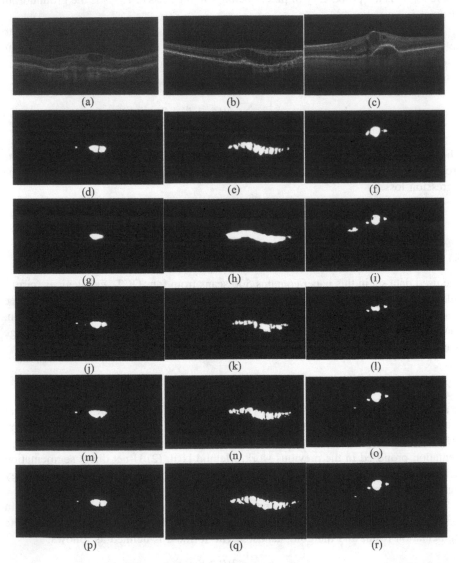

Fig. 4. Comparison of different method segmentation results. (a)–(c) are segmented images with lesions; (d)–(f) are gold standard for experts; (g)–(i) are segmentation results for block-based CNN methods; (j)–(l) The result is segmented by the U-net method based on Dice loss; (m)–(o) is the segmentation method based on the two-step strategy. Segmentation result; (p)–(r) proposed method segmentation results.

Table 1. quantitative results of different methods of segmentation results

	Cirrus	Nidek	Spectralis	Topcon	Mean	Standard deviation
Patch-based CNN segmentation method [10]	0.721	0.645	0.682	0.764	0.703	0.051
U-net segmentation method based on Dice loss [11]	0.755	0.703	0.755	0.799	0.758	0.039
Two-step strategy segmentation method based on FCN and U-net [13]	0.821	0.795	0.825	0.806	0.811	**0.013**
The proposed method	**0.836**	**0.805**	**0.841**	**0.837**	**0.829**	0.016

In Fig. 4, the first row is the original image, the second row is ground truth, and the third to seventh row are the results of patch-based CNN methods, based on the Dice loss U-net method, segmentation method based on two-step strategy and the proposed method. It can be clearly seen from the result graph that the third-row patch-based CNN method has the roughest segmentation result. The method can segment the independent small-area fluid region to some extent as shown in (g) and (i). When the area fluid area or a plurality of independent fluid areas exist, the effect is poor, and the separated fluid areas are merged into one whole. Because the patch-based CNN method simply converts the segmentation problem into a binary classification problem, and does not pay attention to the specific feature information of the fluid region, the segmentation result is relatively rough. The fourth row is based on the U-net method with Dice loss. Compared with the patch-based CNN method, the segmentation result is more elaborate, and a large number of continuous fluid regions are segmented, as shown in (k), but the details of the segmentation result are lost, and the segmentation result is not complete. The results of the latter two segmentation methods are not much different, only differing in the segmentation details. The method proposed is closer to ground truth. Moreover, the method proposed is different from the two-step segmentation strategy, which introduces attention with less time complexity.

Quantitative comparison results are shown in Table 1, which shows the results of the Dice coefficient analysis of the four methods on the four devices (cirrus, nidek, spectralis, topcon) scans. As shown in the table, all four methods can perform fluid segmentation task on all device scans. Among the listed comparison methods, the patch-based CNN segmentation method and the U-net segmentation method based only on Dice loss training have poor segmentation performance, because the two methods are relatively simple to model and no more image features are utilized. Information cannot solve the problem of segmentation of complex fluid regions. It is worth mentioning that the performance gap between the latter two methods is not large, but the method proposed still achieves the best segmentation performance on the test data set. The data shows that the strategy of segmentation in two steps is also good, and all statistics are ranked second.

4 Conclusion

The segmentation of the fluid region on the retinal OCT image layer is essential for quantitatively analysis. This paper proposes a fluid region segmentation method based on deep learning, which can quickly and accurately segment the macular edema fluid region. The proposed method used a network structure improved from U-net, the attention structure is introduced to automatically focus on the fluid area. The network is trained through a joint loss, joint loss including cross entropy loss, Dice loss and introduced regression loss, The result shows that the proposed method can achieve better segmentation performance.

Acknowledgment. This work is partially supported by the National Natural Science Foundation of China (No. 61403287, No. 61472293, No. 61572381), and the Natural Science Foundation of Hubei Province (No. 2014CFB288).

References

1. Marmor, M.F.: Mechanisms of fluid accumulation in retinal edema. In: Wolfensberger, T. J. (ed.) Macular Edema, pp. 35–45. Springer, Heidelberg (2000). https://doi.org/10.1007/978-94-011-4152-9_4
2. Roychowdhury, S., Koozekanani, D.D., Radwan, S., Parhi, K.K.: Automated localization of cysts in diabetic macular edema using optical coherence tomography images. In: International Conference of the IEEE Engineering in Medicine and Biology Society, vol. 2013, pp. 1426–1429 (2013)
3. Wilkins, G.R., Houghton, O.M., Oldenburg, A.L.: Automated segmentation of intraretinal cystoid fluid in optical coherence tomography. IEEE Trans. Biomed. Eng. **59**(4), 1109–1114 (2012)
4. Liu, X., Liu, D., Fu, T., Pan, Z., Hu, W., Zhang, K.: Shortest path with backtracking based automatic layer segmentation in pathological retinal optical coherence tomography images. In: Multimedia Tools and Applications, pp. 1–22 (2018)
5. Pilch, M., et al.: Automated segmentation of pathological cavities in optical coherence tomography scans. Investig. Ophthalmol. Vis. Sci. **54**(6), 4385–4393 (2013)
6. Lang, A., et al.: Automatic segmentation of microcystic macular edema in OCT. Biomed. Opt. Express **6**(1), 155–169 (2015)
7. Chiu, S.J., Allingham, M.J., Mettu, P.S., Cousins, S.W., Izatt, J.A., Farsiu, S.: Kernel regression based segmentation of optical coherence tomography images with diabetic macular edema. Biomed. Opt. Express **6**(4), 1172–1194 (2015)
8. Liu, X., et al.: Automated layer segmentation of retinal optical coherence tomography images using a deep feature enhanced structured random forests classifier. IEEE J. Biomed. Health Inform. **PP**(99) (2018)
9. Liu, X., et al.: Semi-supervised automatic segmentation of layer and fluid region in retinal optical coherence tomography images using adversarial learning. IEEE Access **7**, 3046–3061 (2019)
10. Liu, D., Liu, X., Fu, T., Yang, Z.: Fluid region segmentation in OCT images based on convolution neural network. In: Ninth International Conference on Digital Image Processing (ICDIP 2017), vol. 10420, p. 104202A. International Society for Optics and Photonics (2017)

11. Lee, A.Y., Rokem, A., Tyring, A.J., Lee, C.S., Deruyter, N.P., Wu, Y.: Deep-learning based, automated segmentation of macular edema in optical coherence tomography. Biomed. Opt. Express **8**(7), 3440 (2017)
12. Schlegl, T., et al.: Fully automated detection and quantification of macular fluid in OCT using deep learning. Ophthalmology **125**(4), S0161642017314240 (2017)
13. Venhuizen, F.G., et al.: Deep learning approach for the detection and quantification of intraretinal cystoid fluid in multivendor optical coherence tomography. Biomed. Opt. Express **9**(4), 1545 (2018)
14. Lin, G., Milan, A., Shen, C., Reid, I.: RefineNet: multi-path refinement networks with identity mappings for high-resolution semantic segmentation (2016)
15. Bahdanau, D., Cho, K., Bengio, Y.: Neural machine translation by jointly learning to align and translate. In: ICLR (2015)
16. Luong, T., Pham, H., Manning, C.D.: Effective approaches to attention-based neural machine translation. In: Proceedings of the 2015 Conference on Empirical Methods in Natural Language Processing, pp. 1412–1421 (2015)
17. Milletari, F., Navab, N., Ahmadi, S.A.: V-Net: fully convolutional neural networks for volumetric medical image segmentation. In: Fourth International Conference on 3D Vision, pp. 565–571 (2016)
18. Naylor, P., Laé, M., Reyal, F., Walter, T.: Segmentation of nuclei in histopathology images by deep regression of the distance map. IEEE Trans. Med. Imaging **38**(2), 448–459 (2019)
19. Wu, J., et al.: Multivendor spectral-domain optical coherence tomography dataset, observer annotation performance evaluation, and standardized evaluation framework for intraretinal cystoid fluid segmentation. J. Ophthalmol. **2016**, 1–8 (2016)

An Authentication Scheme in VANETs Based on Group Signature

Xinxin Liu[⊠], Yanyan Yang, Erfeng Xu, and Zhijuan Jia

School of Information Science and Technology, Zhengzhou Normal University,
Zhengzhou 450044, China
liuxinxin325@163.com

Abstract. Anonymous authentication is an effective way to achieve vehicle privacy protection in Vehicular Ad-Hoc Networks (VANETs). On the basis of group signature, this paper proposes a vehicle group signature authentication mechanism suitable for vehicle networking. The scheme provides the dynamic joining and revocation of vehicles, and provides the security privacy protection for vehicle in-formation. When the vehicle joins to the group, the group administrator generates a group member certificate for signing the message without changing other vehicle keys and certificates in the group; when the vehicle quits to the group, the group administrator prevents the revoked member from continuing to use the group membership by updating the synchronization primer. The performance analysis shows that the scheme has lower computational overhead in the process of message signing and signature verification, which improves the overall signature efficiency and is suitable for real-time and efficient computing requirements of VANETs.

Keywords: VANETs · Authentication · Group signature ·
Synchronization primer

1 Introduction

Vehicular Ad-Hoc Networks (VANETs) is a special mobile internet network that can implement various applications such as security alarms and assisted driving [1]. However, due to the large scale of the network, rapid changes in network topology, and frequent network segmentation, it is vulnerable to various security attacks such as communication information tampered, traffic routes tracked, causing safety hazards to drivers. Anonymous authentication relies on public key cryptography to achieve the security needs for VANETs, but may reveal private information. The group signature can effectively authenticate the user's identity without revealing the user's true identity. By using the group member key to send the message, the certifier can determine the user's origin by verifying the group member key, and cannot verify the specific identity of the member. While protecting the actual identity of the group member, the user can be authenticated to ensure the legitimacy of user identity.

Group signature is a special digital signature with unique security features such as anonymity, no association, and joint attack resistance [2]. Group signature was first proposed by Chaum and Heyst [3], but did not give a specific group signature security

© Springer Nature Switzerland AG 2019
D.-S. Huang et al. (Eds.): ICIC 2019, LNCS 11643, pp. 346–355, 2019.
https://doi.org/10.1007/978-3-030-26763-6_34

model. In 2003, Bellare, Micciancio, Warinschi proposed the first strict definition of static group signatures and a formal security model [4]. This security model is called the BMW model. However, the group signature security model is a static group signature model, which does not consider the dynamic joining process of members. That is, once the group signature system is established, new members cannot join the group. In order to join a new member, the system must regenerate the new group public key and issue a new signed private key to each member. Thereafter, in 2005, Bellare, Shi and Zhang proposed the BSZ security model and its formal definition [5]. In this model, they consider the case where users dynamically join a group. However, the revocation of group members is not considered in the model.

Subsequently, many scholars began to study the revocation of group members in group signature [6–12]. In 2009, T. Nakanishi et al. proposed a group signature scheme with constant complexity for signature and verification [13]. In this scheme, the group members can be revoked, while the group unrevoked members do not have to update their keys. However, the length of the verification public key increases linearly with the number of members of the whole group, and the number of members of the whole group must be predetermined. Thereafter, in 2011, Fan, et al. proposed a group signature scheme for revocable members based on accumulation factor techniques [14]. In this scheme, the group administrator calculates new parameters for each unrevoked member, the computational cost is N (N is the total number of members), and the private key issuer of the trusted member is required.

Literature [15] proposed a GSIS scheme for VANETs based on group signature technology. Literature [16] proposed that the RSU as a group manager to manage the vehicles of the group. RSU knows the user's private key, and once RSU compromises, the vehicle's privacy will be disclosed. Therefore, literature [17] proposed that RSU should be credible by using CA to issue certificates for RSU. However, because the rapid changes of vehicles and the management limited of scope in RSU, the RSU is not appropriate to establish and manage the group.

Based on the bilinear pairing and zero-knowledge proof protocol, this paper proposes a group signature authentication scheme for VANETs. In this scheme, it mainly uses certificate and synchronization primer to authenticate group members. First. The trusted authority TA manages vehicles within its coverage and generates anonymous identities certificates for vehicles, then when the identity authentication is performed, the verification message and the synchronization primer are signed. When the message is received, the verification process is completed by checking the correctness of the message and synchronization primers. Finally When revoking members, only updating synchronization primers can ensure that revoked members can not pass group membership authentication. Which can reduce the performance consumption of group member authentication after revoking group members.

2 System Model and Preliminaries

2.1 System Model

In this paper, the system model of VANETs consists of the certificate authority CA, the vehicle service provider SP, the trusted authority TA, the RSU, and OBUs. As shown in Fig. 1.

TA (Trusted Authority): The manager of the group in the network that is responsible for issuing group user certificates for OBUs.

CA (Certificate Authority): A trusted third party in the network that is responsible for issuing the public key and private key for OBUs.

SP (Service Provider): It is responsible for providing various services to OBUs in the network, and authenticates the identity of the OBUs.

RSU (Road-Side Unit): A fixed unit deployed in the network, which communicates with the TA through a wired network, and communicates with the vehicle OBUs through the wireless network.

OBUs (On-Board Unit): Periodically broadcast messages such as speed and direction of travel et al with OBUs and RSU, and can use the service provided by SP to exchange data between RSU and SP

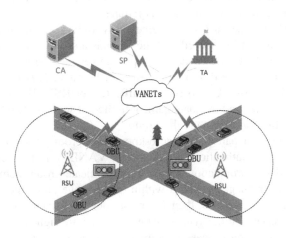

Fig. 1. The system model of VANETs.

2.2 Bilinear Mapping

Bilinear mapping is defined as $e : G \times G \rightarrow G_T$, where G and G_T are q-order prime cycle groups. It satisfies the following properties:

(1) Bilinearity: $\forall g, h \in G, a, b \in Z_q^*, e(g^a, h^b) = e(g, h)ab$.
(2) Non-degenerate: $\forall g, h \in G$, let $e(g, h) \neq 1$.
(3) Computability: $\forall g, h \in G$, computes $e(g, h) \in G_T$.

2.3 Hash Function

Hash function is defined as $h : \{0, 1\}^* \rightarrow \{0, 1\}^n$, where $\{0, 1\}^*$ denotes a bit string of arbitrary length, $\{0, 1\}^n$ indicates a string of length with n. A one-way hash function is considered to be secure if it satisfies the following properties.

(1) Given m, it is easy to calculate $H(m) = y$. While conversely, given $y = H(m)$, it is infeasible to compute m.
(2) Given m and m', it is infeasible to compute $H(m) = H(m')$.

2.4 Zero Knowledge Proof Protocol

Zero Knowledge Proof Protocol is performed as (P, V), where P is prover and V is verifier. P can be verified by verifier V to prove that P has a kind of knowledge. Zero Knowledge Proof Protocol is defined as follows:

First, P chooses randomly public parameters $g_1, \eta, \pi, \tau \in G_1$ and $g_2, \omega_1, \omega_2 \in G_2$, where g_2 is a generator of G_2 and $\gamma, \beta \in Z_P$, which satisfies $\varphi(g_2) = g_1$, $\omega_1 = g_2^{\gamma}$, $\omega_2 = g_2^{\beta}$. Suppose that P has a tuple (R, x, y), where $R = g_1^{(x+\gamma)^{-1}(y+\beta)}$, $x, y \in Z_P$ satisfied $e(R, \omega_1 \cdot g_2^x) \cdot e(g_1, g_2^{-y}) = e(g_1, \omega_2)$. P chooses randomly parameters $\zeta_1, \zeta_2 \in Z_P$ and $v_\zeta, v_x, v_y, v_{\xi_1}, v_{\xi_2} \in Z_P$, takes tuple (R, x, y) as input, computes and sends commitment values $(C_1, C_2, C_3, D_1, D_2, D_3)$ to verifier V.

Then V chooses randomly c as challenge value after receiving the commitment values, and sends to P. P computes $r_\zeta, r_x, r_y, r_{\xi_1}, r_{\xi_2}$ as the response value of V.

Finally, V computes D'_1, D'_2, D'_3 by C_1, C_2, C_3 and $r_\zeta, r_x, r_y, r_{\xi_1}, r_{\xi_2}$. If the equation $D_i - D'_i$ holds, the proof passes.

3 Proposed Scheme

In this paper, the scheme consists of the following parts: CA (Certificate Authority), TA (Trusted Authority), and SP (Service Provider). CA is responsible for issuing the public key and private key for OBUs; TA is responsible for creating and managing the group, and hiring multiple SPs to provide services for VANETs, and SP can be hired by multiple TA and provide services to the TA-managed groups. TA has an SP employment list S_{SP}, and each entry in the list $SP_k(k = 1, \ldots, k)$ indicates the SP that can be accessed by the TA-managed group. Each SP_k has a list L_{SPg} that stores the group identity and synchronization primer of the TA that have access to the service.

The idea of the scheme is as follows: TA generates a member private key C_i for each user U_i of the group. In order to access service provider SP_k, the user U_i generates the signature RM of the message M by C_i and the message M provided by SP_k. And then U_i sends RM to SP_k, SP_k verifies whether U_i is a group member in L_{SPg} by verifying RM.

The group signature authentication process includes six parts as follows: initialization, employment service, joining, service verification, opening and revocation

3.1 Initialization

TA generates group public key and group private key making use of the algorithm as follows:

Let G_1, G_2, G_T are the q-order prime multiplicative cycle groups, $\varphi : G_2 \rightarrow G_1$ is a computable linear isomorphism on G_1 and $G_2 \cdot g_1 \in G_1$ and $g_2 \in G_2$ are generators of G_1 and G_2, such that $\varphi(g_2) = g_1$. $e : G_1 \times G_2 \rightarrow G_T$ is a bilinear map and $H : \{0, 1\}^* \rightarrow Z_p^*$ is a collision-resistant hash function.

TA chooses randomly $\eta, \pi, \tau \in G_1$, $\alpha, \beta \in Z_p^*$ and $\lambda_1, \lambda_2 \in Z_p^*$, satisfied $\eta^{\lambda_1} = \pi^{\lambda_1} = \tau$, computes $\omega_1 = g_1^\alpha$, $\omega_2 = g_2^\beta$, and then obtains the group public key PK_{TA} and the group private key SK_{TA} according as formula (1) and (2):

$$PK_{TA} = (g_1, g_2, \varphi, \eta, \pi, \tau, \omega_1 = g_1^\alpha, \omega_2 = g_2^\beta) \tag{1}$$

$$SK_{TA} = (SK_{TA1}, SK_{TA2}) = ([\alpha, \beta], [\lambda_1, \lambda_2]) \tag{2}$$

Where SK_{TA1} is mainly used to generate the private key of the group member, and SK_{TA2} is mainly used to open the group signature to reveal the true identity of the group members. Then TA chooses randomly $T_0 \in G_1$ as the synchronization primer of the group.

3.2 Employment Service

TA employs SP to provide services to group members making use of the algorithm as follows:

TA sends (PK_{TA}, T, R) to SP, where $(T = T_0)$ and R is the signature of TA on T by SK_{TA}. SP verifies the signature R by PK_{TA}. If it is true, SP adds (ID_{TA}, PK_{TA}, T) to its own access list L_{SPg}, where ID_{TA} is id with TA. TA adds SP to its SP employment list S_{SP}.

3.3 Joining

In this paper, it is supported that vehicle user U_i wants to join to the group of TA. Assume that U_i is the ith user joining the group, and $PK_{UID}[i]$ is the public key and $SK_{UID}[i]$ is the private key. U_i joins to the group making use of the algorithm as follows:

(1) (1) U_i chooses randomly a secret value $y_i \in Z_p^*$ and $b_i \in Z_p^*$, computes $g_1^{y_i}$. U_i sends $(g_1^{y_i}, PK_{UID}[i], S_i, b_i)$ to TA, where S_i is the signature of U_i on $g_1^{y_i}$ by $SK_{UID}[i]$.

(2) TA verifies the signature S_i by $PK_{UID}[i]$. If it is true, TA chooses randomly $x_i \in Z_p^*$, and then computes $K_i = (g_1^{y_i} \cdot \varphi(\omega_2))^{(x_i + \gamma_i)^{-1}} = g_1^{(y_i + \beta)(x_i + \gamma_i)^{-1}}$. TA sends (PK_{TA}, K_i, x_i, T) to U_i, and $C_i = (K_i, x_i, y_i, b_i, T_i)$ is the certificate of user U_i, where $T = T_i$ is the synchronization primer of the group. TA adds $(K_i, g_1^{y_i}, x_i, b_i, S_i, PK_{UID}[i])$ to the list L_{UG}.

(3) TA sends (T, b_i) to other members in the group. The other members in the group U_j update the synchronization primer T_j in his certificate. If the certificate is

$C_j = (K_j, x_j, y_j, b_j, T_j)$ of U_j, then U_j computes the new synchronization primer with $T'_j = T_i \cdot T_j^{b_i - b_j}$. So, the new certificate of the U_j is $C_j = (K_j, x_j, y_j, b_j, T'_j)$.

(4) TA computes $T' = T_i^{b_i} \cdot T_i^{\alpha}$ with the private key α. TA sends (ID_{TA}, T') to SP_K, SP_K update the synchronization primer T' to its own access list L_{SPg}.

3.4 Service Verification

The authentication process between group user U_i and SP_k making use of the algorithm as follows:

The user U_i sends ID_{TA} to SP_k, and SP_k views the T of the list L_{SPg}, and then generates a random reply message M to U_i.

After U_i received M, U_i chooses randomly $\zeta_1, \zeta_2, v_\zeta, v_x, v_y, v_{\xi_1}, v_{\xi_2}$ in Z_P, and computes the Median according to the following Eqs. (3) by the private key $C_i = (K_i, x_i, y_i, b_i, T_i)$ and the group public key $PK_{TA} = (g_1, g_2, \varphi, \eta, \pi, \tau, \omega_1 = g_1^\alpha, \omega_2 = g_2^\beta)$.

$$
\begin{aligned}
&C_1 = \eta^{\zeta_1}, C_2 = \pi^{\zeta_2}, C_3 = K_i \tau^{\zeta_1 + \zeta_2} \\
&D_1 = C_1^{v_x} \cdot \eta^{-v_{\xi_1}}, D_2 = C_2^{v_x} \cdot \pi^{-v_{\xi_2}} \\
&D_3 = e(C_3, g_2)^{v_x} \cdot e(\tau, \omega_1)^{v_\zeta} \cdot e(\tau, g_2)^{-v_{\xi_1} - v_{\xi_2}} \cdot e(g_1, g_2)^{v_y} \\
&t = T_i^{g_1^{b_i}} \cdot T_i^{\omega_1} \\
&c = H(M, t, C_1, C_2, C_3, D_1, D_2, D_3)
\end{aligned}
\tag{3}
$$

And then computes $r_\zeta = v_\zeta - c(\zeta_1 + \zeta_2)$, $r_x = v_x + cx_i$, $r_y = v_y - cy_i$, $r_{\xi_1} = v_{\xi_1} + cx_i\zeta_1$, $r_{\xi_2} = v_{\xi_2} + cx_i\zeta_2$, so $RM = (C_1, C_2, C_3, c, r_\zeta, r_x, r_y, r_{\xi_1}, r_{\xi_2})$ is the signature on M.

SP_k computes following equations by PK_{TA} and signature pair (RM, M, T).
$D'_1 = C_1^{r_x} \cdot \eta^{-r_{\xi_1}}$, $D'_2 = C_2^{r_x} \cdot \pi^{-r_{\xi_2}}$,

$$
D'_3 = e(C_3, g_2)^{r_x} \cdot e(\tau, \omega_1)^{r_\zeta} \cdot e(\tau, g_2)^{-r_{\xi_1} - r_{\xi_2}} \cdot e(g_1, g_2)^{r_y} \cdot e(C_3, \omega_1)^c \cdot e(g_1, \omega_2)^{-c}
$$

$$
t' = T^{g_1}, c' = H(M, t', C_1, C_2, C_3, D', D'_2, D'_3),
$$

If the equation $c' = c$ holds, it can be confirmed that U_i is the member of the group. And SP_k accepts U_i access request, or refuses.

3.5 Opening

SP_k sends the signature RM to TA, and TA computes $K = C_3/(C_1^{\lambda_1} \cdot C_2^{\lambda_2})$. TA views the list L_{UG}. If the equation $K_i = K$ holds, and then TA can reveal the real identity $PK_{UID}[i]$ of K_i.

3.6   Revocation

In order to revoke the user U_i, TA computers the new synchronization primer $T' = T^{(\alpha+b_i)^{-1}}$, TA sends (ID_{TA}, T') to SP_K, SP_K update the synchronization primer T' to its own access list L_{SPg}.

TA sends (T', b_i) to the other members in the group. The other members in the group U_j update the synchronization primer T_j to T'_j, $T'_j = (T_j \cdot T'^{-1})^{(b_i-b_j)^{-1}}$.

4   Security and Performance Analysis

4.1   Correctness Analysis

SP_k computes the following equations as formula (4):

$$
\begin{aligned}
D'_1 &= C_1^{r_x} \cdot \eta^{-r_{\xi_1}} = \eta^{\zeta_1 v_x + cx\zeta_1} \cdot \eta^{-v_{\xi_1} - cx\zeta_1} = \eta^{\zeta_1 v_x} \cdot \eta^{-v_{\xi_1}} = D_1 \\
D'_2 &= C_2^{r_x} \cdot \pi^{-r_{\xi_2}} = \pi^{\zeta_2 v_x + cx\zeta_2} \cdot \pi^{-v_{\xi_2} - cx\zeta_2} = \pi^{\zeta_2 v_x} \cdot \pi^{-v_{\xi_2}} = D_2 \\
t' &= T^{g_1} = (T_i^{b_j} \cdot T_i^{\alpha})^{g_1} = T_i^{b_j g_1} \cdot T_i^{\alpha g_1} = T_i^{b_i g_1} \cdot T_i^{\omega_1} = t \\
D'_3 &= e(C_3, g_2)^{r_x} \cdot e(\tau, \omega_1)^{r_\zeta} \cdot e(\tau, g_2)^{-r_{\xi_1} - r_{\xi_2}} \cdot e(g_1, g_2)^{r_y} \cdot e(C_3, \omega_1)^c \cdot e(g_1, \omega_2)^{-c} \\
1_{G_T} &= e(C_3, g_2)^{cx} \cdot e(\tau, \omega_1)^{-c(\zeta_1 + \zeta_2)} \cdot e(\tau, g_2)^{-cx(\zeta_1 + \zeta_2)} \cdot e(g_1, g_2)^{-cy} \cdot e(C_3, \omega_1)^c \cdot e(g_1, \omega_2)^{-c}
\end{aligned}
$$
$$(4)$$

If the equation $D'_3 = D_3$ holds, it proves that U_i is the member of the group.

4.2   Security Analysis

(1) Anonymity proof

In the process of certificate generation, blind certificate signature technology is applied to this scheme. In addition to group administrators, the attackers cannot infer the real identity of group members based on blind certificates. In addition, the relationship between the generation of the group member private key and the membership is irrelevant, and even if the attacker obtains the member's secret key, the real identity cannot be inferred.

(2) Traceability

If a group member needs to be identified, TA computes $K = C_3/(C_1^{\lambda_1} \cdot C_2^{\lambda_2})$ to obtain the random signature K_i of the member, checks the group member list to obtain the member public key $PK_{UID}[i]$, checks the CA obtains the true identity of the member.

(3) Unforgeability

When the group member U_i registers with the group administrator, the U_i only sends the blind value $g_1^{y_i}$ of the y_i to the TA, and the private key information y_i does not inform the group administrator that the group administrator can't obtain the group member private key. Therefore, the group administrator cannot pretend to be a member of the group to sign.

U_j gets the signature information from the received signature and forges the signature. Assuming that the U_i receives the signature RM_i of the member U_i, it uses the signature information (C_1, C_2, C_3, c) to forge the signature. Because of U_i does not know the private key $C_i = (K_i, x_i, y_i, b_i, T_i)$, it is unable to perform $r_x, r_y, r_{\xi_1}, r_{\xi_2}$ calculation. Therefore, U_j cannot successfully use other member signature information to forge signatures.

After the U_j is revoked, the signature is forged by modifying its signature and verification information. When U_j is revoked, the synchronization factor T is updated, and its stored T does not the newest synchronization factor issued by the current group, resulting in failure to pass the verification. Therefore, U_j cannot forge a signature by modifying the information.

4.3 Performance Analysis

This section will give a performance analysis of the scheme. The analysis mainly includes the computational cost of signature and verification in the scheme, The calculation overheads of the k-bottom index in the bilinear groups G_1, G_2, and G_T are denoted as $E_{k,1}$, $E_{k,2}$, $E_{k,T}$, and P is used to represent the computational cost of the bilinear pair. The performance analysis as shown as follows:

The calculation cost of the user U_i is the exponentiation calculation in $4G_1$, and the multi- exponential calculation of 4-bottoms on $1G_T$. The calculation cost of service provider SP verification is the exponential calculation of 2-bottoms on $2G_1$, the exponential calculation of 2-bottoms on $1G_2$, the exponential calculation of 4-bottoms on $1G_T$, and one pair of operations.

A computational cost comparison between our proposed scheme and others is made as Table 1, where SC and VC represent signature calculation overhead and verification computation overhead.

Table 1. Computational cost comparison

Schemes	SC	VC
BBS [18]	$3E_{1,1} + E_{4,T}$	$4E_{2,1} + E_{2,1} + E_{4,T} + P$
P [19]	$3E_{1,1} + E_{4,T}$	$2E_{2,1} + E_{3,1} + E_{2,2} + E_{4,T} + P$
HL [20]	$3E_{1,1} + 3E_{3,1} + E_{8,T}$	$4E_{2,1} + E_{4,1} + E_{2,2} + E_{7,T} + P$
Ours	$3E_{1,1} + E_{4,T}$	$2E_{2,1} + E_{2,2} + E_{4,T} + P$

The results from the table show that the scheme has higher efficiency and lower computational cost of signature and verification.

5 Conclusion

VANETs is an important branch of the Internet of Things (IOT) technology. However, with the expansion of VANETs scale, the openness of the communication channel, and predictability of moving trajectory, vehicles are facing the various network attacks and security threats. In particular, the leakage of vehicle identity in VANETs will cause more serious security problems. In order to protect the safety and privacy of vehicles, conditional anonymous authentication is required in VANETs. Based on the group signature technology, this paper proposes an anonymous authentication scheme suitable for VANETs. In this scheme, the bilinear pairing technique is used to generate the group public key and the group members key, and the zero-knowledge proof protocol is used for the group members authentication. Meanwhile, the manage r can open the group signatures to reveal the real identity of group member and ensure the safety of the other users.

Acknowledgments. This work was supported by the National Natural Science Funds (U1304614, U1204703), the construct program of the key discipline in Zhengzhou Normal University, aid program for Science and Technology Innovative Research Team of Zhengzhou Normal University, Henan Province Education Science Plan General Topic "Research on Trusted Degree Certification Based on Blockchain" ((2018)-JKGHYB-0279).

References

1. Zhang, C., et al.: An efficient identity-based batch verification scheme for vehicular sensor networks. In: The 27th Conference on Computer Communications, INFOCOM 2008. IEEE (2008)
2. Liu, M.: Efficient special group signature scheme. Central South University (2013)
3. Chaum, D., van Heyst, E.: Group signatures. In: Davies, D.W. (ed.) EUROCRYPT 1991. LNCS, vol. 547, pp. 257–265. Springer, Heidelberg (1991). https://doi.org/10.1007/3-540-46416-6_22
4. Bellare, M., Micciancio, D., Warinschi, B.: Foundations of group signatures: formal definitions, simplified requirements, and a construction based on general assumptions. In: Biham, E. (ed.) EUROCRYPT 2003. LNCS, vol. 2656, pp. 614–629. Springer, Heidelberg (2003). https://doi.org/10.1007/3-540-39200-9_38
5. Bellare, M., Shi, H., Zhang, C.: Foundations of group signatures: the case of dynamic groups. In: Menezes, A. (ed.) CT-RSA 2005. LNCS, vol. 3376, pp. 136–153. Springer, Heidelberg (2005). https://doi.org/10.1007/978-3-540-30574-3_11
6. Camenisch, J., Groth, J.: Group signatures: better efficiency and new theoretical aspects. In: Blundo, C., Cimato, S. (eds.) SCN 2004. LNCS, vol. 3352, pp. 120–133. Springer, Heidelberg (2005). https://doi.org/10.1007/978-3-540-30598-9_9
7. Camenisch, J., Kohlweiss, M., Soriente, C.: An accumulator based on bilinear maps and efficient revocation for anonymous credentials. In: Jarecki, S., Tsudik, G. (eds.) PKC 2009. LNCS, vol. 5443, pp. 481–500. Springer, Heidelberg (2009). https://doi.org/10.1007/978-3-642-00468-1_27
8. Camenisch, J., Lysyanskaya, A.: Dynamic accumulators and application to efficient revocation of anonymous credentials. In: Yung, M. (ed.) CRYPTO 2002. LNCS, vol. 2442, pp. 61–76. Springer, Heidelberg (2002). https://doi.org/10.1007/3-540-45708-9_5

9. Jin, H., Wong, D.S., Xu, Y.: Efficient group signature with forward secure revocation. In: Ślęzak, D., Kim, T., Fang, W.-C., Arnett, K.P. (eds.) SecTech 2009. CCIS, vol. 58, pp. 124–131. Springer, Heidelberg (2009). https://doi.org/10.1007/978-3-642-10847-1_16

10. Nakanishi, T., Funabiki, N.: Efficient revocable group signature schemes using primes. J. Inf. Process. **16**, 110–121 (2008)

11. Nakanishi, T., Kubooka, F., Hamada, N., Funabiki, N.: Group signature schemes with membership revocation for large groups. In: Boyd, C., González Nieto, J.M. (eds.) ACISP 2005. LNCS, vol. 3574, pp. 443–454. Springer, Heidelberg (2005). https://doi.org/10.1007/11506157_37

12. Nakanishi, T., Sugiyama, Y.: A group signature scheme with efficient membership revocation for reasonable groups. In: Wang, H., Pieprzyk, J., Varadharajan, V. (eds.) ACISP 2004. LNCS, vol. 3108, pp. 336–347. Springer, Heidelberg (2004). https://doi.org/10.1007/978-3-540-27800-9_29

13. Nakanishi, T., Fujii, H., Hira, Y., Funabiki, N.: Revocable group signature schemes with constant costs for signing and verifying. In: Jarecki, S., Tsudik, G. (eds.) PKC 2009. LNCS, vol. 5443, pp. 463–480. Springer, Heidelberg (2009). https://doi.org/10.1007/978-3-642-00468-1_26

14. Fan, C.-I., Hsu, R.-H., Manulis, M.: Group signature with constant revocation costs for signers and verifiers. In: Lin, D., Tsudik, G., Wang, X. (eds.) CANS 2011. LNCS, vol. 7092, pp. 214–233. Springer, Heidelberg (2011). https://doi.org/10.1007/978-3-642-25513-7_16

15. Lin, X., Sun, X., Ho, P.H., et al.: GSIS: Secure vehicular communications with privacy preserving. IEEE Trans. Veh. Technol. **56**(6), 3442–3456 (2007)

16. Zhang, L., Wu, Q., Solanas, A., Domingo-Ferrer, J.: A scalable robust authentication protocol for secure vehicular communications. IEEE Trans. Veh. Technol. **59**(4), 1606–1617 (2010)

17. Hao, Y., Chengcheng, Y., Zhou, C., Song, W.: A distributed key management framework with cooperative message authentication in VANETs. IEEE J. Sel. Areas Commun. **29**(3), 616–629 (2011)

18. Boneh, D., Boyen, X., Shacham, H.: Short group signatures. In: Franklin, M. (ed.) CRYPTO 2004. LNCS, vol. 3152, pp. 41–55. Springer, Heidelberg (2004). https://doi.org/10.1007/978-3-540-28628-8_3

19. Delerablée, C., Pointcheval, D.: Dynamic fully anonymous short group signatures. In: Nguyen, Phong Q. (ed.) VIETCRYPT 2006. LNCS, vol. 4341, pp. 193–210. Springer, Heidelberg (2006). https://doi.org/10.1007/11958239_13

20. Hwang, J.Y., Lee, S., Chung, B.H., et al.: Group signatures with controllable linkability for dynamic membership. Inf. Sci. **222**, 761–778 (2013)

Malware Detection in Android System Based on Change Perception

Hua-li Zhang[✉], Hua-yong Yang, Fan Yang, and Wei Jiang

City College, Wuhan University of Science and Technology,
Wuhan 430083, China
zhanghuali@foxmail.com

Abstract. The existing detection methods of Android mobile malware mainly include signature scanning, heuristic method and behavior monitoring method. These traditional detection methods have a common limitation: they are not adaptive. The detection methods based on artificial immune system, such as dendritic cell algorithm, have some self-adaptability, but they depend too much on artificial experience, and the self-adaptability is obviously insufficient. Therefore, in order to overcome the lack of self-adaptability of existing detection methods, this paper introduces a change perception method based on danger theory to detect malicious software by looking for change in Android mobile phone system, that is, danger signal. When studying the generation of dangerous signal, this paper uses the method of describing the law of function change in mathematics to describe the change in smartphone system with the concept of differential, and then defines and expresses dangerous signal. Considering the discrete type of data in Android mobile phone system, this paper realizes the expression of dangerous signal based on the theory of numerical differentiation, and puts forward the method of calculating dangerous signal in Android system.

Keywords: Android · Danger theory · Change perception · Malware detection

1 Introduction

With the rapid development of wireless network and the improvement of mobile communication technology, mobile smart phones with complete functions and powerful processing capabilities have become an indispensable social and office tool in people's daily life. At present, Android and IOS are the main operating systems of mobile smartphones in the market. According to the statistics of Ministry of Industry and Information Technology, the popularization rate of mobile phones in China reached 97.9/100 in the second quarter of 2018. According to Gartner, the authoritative statistical agency in Table 1, global sales of mobile smartphones were 380 million in the first quarter of 2018.

This research was financially supported by the Science and Technology Research Program of Hubei Provincial Department of Education (B2017424).

© Springer Nature Switzerland AG 2019
D.-S. Huang et al. (Eds.): ICIC 2019, LNCS 11643, pp. 356–366, 2019.
https://doi.org/10.1007/978-3-030-26763-6_35

Table 1. Worldwide Smartphone scales to end users by operating system in 2Q18 (thousands of units).

Operating system	2Q18 units	2Q18 market share (%)	2Q17 units	2Q17 market share (%)
Android	329,503.4	88.0	321,848.2	87.8
IOS	44,715.1	11.9	44,314.8	12.1
Other OS	112.1	0.0	433.1	0.1
Total	374,330.6	100.0	366,596.1	100.0

Android system is an open source operating system based on Linux kernel. It has become the largest mobile terminal platform in the market. The openness of Android makes it the largest platform for malicious software development. In 2018, the number of malicious mobile Internet programs captured by the National Internet Emergency Response Center and acquired by manufacturers for Android platform ranked first [1]. With the increasing share of Android malware [2, 3], how to quickly and efficiently analyze and detect it has become a research hotspot.

2 Android System Security

2.1 Native Primary Privilege Mechanism of Android

Android is a free and open source operating system based on Linux. The components of the overall architecture are divided into four layers: application layer, application framework layer, core library layer, runtime layer and Linux kernel layer. Android's native privilege mechanism can be divided into sandbox mechanism, signature mechanism and privilege mechanism (see Fig. 1) [4, 5].

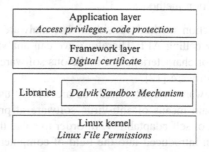

Fig. 1. Native privilege mechanism of Android

Although Android's privilege mechanism can play a good protective role, its own shortcomings still provide an opportunity for criminals and a breeding ground for malware. First of all, the privilege mechanism is complex and cumbersome. For those who have professional knowledge, it is still difficult to distinguish, and ordinary users do not understand the specific meaning of permission information. According to a survey, only 17% of Android users noticed the privilege prompt before the software was installed, while only 3% of Android users correctly understood the meaning of each privilege declaration. Secondly, the privilege mechanism lacks flexibility. For users, there are only two choices: one is that the installation software agrees to grant full permission, the other is to abandon the installation. Users are in a very passive state, unable to selectively authorize or withdraw authorization unless the software is uninstalled.

2.2   Traditional Malware Detection Method

For mobile operating system, traditional malware detection methods mainly include three categories [6, 7]: signature-based detection method, heuristic detection method and behavior-based detection method.

- Signature-based detection method

The signature-based detection method is mainly to analyze malware code, extract the features and store them in the feature library [8], scan the software to be detected, and determine whether it contains the code matching the feature string in the feature library [9].

- Heuristic detection method

Heuristic detection methods are divided into static heuristic method and dynamic heuristic method [10]. Static heuristic method scans and analyses the instructions in the detected objects to determine whether they contain some malicious instructions by simple decompilation without running the software [11]. Dynamic heuristic method builds a simulated running environment for software, such as sandbox or virtual machine, simulates the execution process of code, and judges whether the software will perform some malicious behavior.

- Behavior-based detection method

Behavior-based detection method considers that malware mainly affects system resources maliciously by calling API. Therefore, we can analyze the API calls of the system to get the behavior characteristics of malicious software and apply them to the detection of malicious software [12].

These traditional malware detection methods are widely used by major anti-virus software, and are the main means of anti-virus software at present, but they have a common limitation: lack of self-adaptability. In order to solve this problem, Biological immune system has been introduced into the field of computer security.

3   Mechanisms of AIS

Biological immune system (AIS) is a kind of security defense mechanism of organisms [13]. It uses self-learning, adaptive and evolutionary methods to resist foreign hazards, and can maintain the stability of organisms in the changing environment. AIS is an intelligent method to solve practical problems based on the idea of biological immune system. AIS has a strong ability of self-adaptation, which can be achieved by stimulating the change of its operating parameters through the change of information environment [14].

3.1 Danger Theory

In 1994, Polly Matzinger put forward the Danger Theory (DT) of immune recognition. According to danger theory, the immune system does not recognize self and nonself, but harmful self and harmful nonself. More important for immune recognition is the danger of invasion rather than the exoticism. It's not nonself that the immune system has to guard against, but danger, a danger signal. Nonself can not induce immune response, only dangerous signals can induce the activation of effector cells and induce immune response in the body [15, 16].

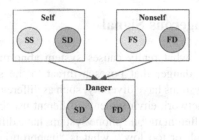

Fig. 2. Danger theory model

There are factors that promote risk in nonself, and there are such factors in Self. As shown in Fig. 2, SS is the normal factor in self and SD is the risk factor in self, such as non-benign mutation of human gene and proliferation of cancer cells. FS is a normal factor in nonself, such as food intake, and FD is a risk factor in nonself. The immune system recognizes SD in self and FD in nonself, namely danger.

The danger theory expounds the working principle of the immune system from different angles. The immune system is not defending against nonself, but against potential dangers. The objects identified by the immune system is the "dangerous antigen". Some outstanding problems in body immunology are well explained.

3.2 Change Perception

According to danger theory, what really causes system abnormalities or pathological changes is the potential danger that poses a threat to the system [17, 18]. The function of the immune system is to find out the change of the system environment caused by invasive antigens, to detect whether the "change" poses a threat to the system, and then to suppress harmful change (danger) and ignore harmless change (safety), so as to complete the evolution and learning of the immune system.

Danger is not a sudden occurrence, its occurrence has inevitable causes and consequences. The process of system state migration is a large number of minor changes, which slowly accumulate and lead to essential changes in the system, that is, the so-called "quantitative change causes qualitative change". These small changes are the direct cause of the system from normal to abnormal, which is the danger signal in immunology. What causes qualitative change is danger, in the form of co-stimulus signals that activate lymphocytes, prompt lymphocytes to recognize antigens and initiate adaptive immune responses.

A static system will not cause danger. When the system is damaged, such as being attacked by malicious software [19], the balance of the system is broken. Various indicators of the system change, indicating the emergence of danger, that is, change is the main cause of danger [20]. Therefore, to study the danger theory in smartphone system is essentially to find out the change that leads to the abnormal system, that is, danger signal, and then complete the adaptive adjustment of the smartphone immune system to the balance.

4 Definition of Dangerous Signal

According to risk theory, what really causes system abnormalities or "pathological changes" is the potential danger that poses a threat to the system. Like biological individuals, smartphone systems have diversity, such as different hardware and software configurations, different network environments, different usage habits and so on. Individual differences make different mobile phone systems have different judgments of risk. The definition of "too high or too low", what is "inappropriate" and what is "unexpected" are different, so for different individuals, the danger signals are also different.

It is assumed that a system will remain stationary without any change. In a nutshell, the system is safe. If the system is at risk, it must have changed. Regardless of whether the system is open or not, as long as the reference frame is selected, the division of "change" and "invariability" can be determined. Therefore, for the definition of smartphone dangerous signal, we can start with the change of the system and learn from the method of differential calculus to study the change.

- System variable V

System variable V is a set of system variables representing the state of smartphone system. $V = \{v_i \mid i \in N\}$, Where v_i represents a system state variable.

Setting R be the reference frame for observing system variables, which can be time, events, data, etc. and can be selected according to the object of study.

The set of System Variable $V = G(R) = \{g_1(R), g_2(R), \ldots, g_n(R)\}$, Of which $v_1 = g_1(R)$, $v_2 = g_2(R)$, $\ldots$, $v_n = g_n(R)$. The change of V relative to reference system R can be expressed as:

$$\frac{dV}{dR} = \frac{d\{v_1, v_2, \ldots, v_n\}}{dR} = \{\frac{dv_1}{dR}, \frac{dv_2}{dR}, \ldots, \frac{dv_n}{dR}\} \tag{1}$$

- System state SS

System state is a snapshot of a system at a certain time. It is a function $SS = f(V)$ of multiple system variables.

- System State Change SC

Changes in the overall system state can be described as follows:

$$SC = dSS = \frac{df(V)}{dv} = \frac{\partial SS}{\partial v_1}\Delta v_1 + \frac{\partial SS}{\partial v_2}\Delta v_2 + \ldots + \frac{\partial SS}{\partial v_n}\Delta v_n \qquad (2)$$

- Danger signal DS

The dangersignal is the set $DS = \{dS_i \mid i \in N\}$ of all the changes of system variables related to system imbalance, and it is the subset $DS \subseteq dV$ of the changes of system variables. In this paper, all the changes of system variables are considered as possible danger signals, that is $DS = dV$. The changes of system variables independent of danger are screened out, and the changes independent of danger are eliminated naturally.

$$DS = dV = \{dv_1, dv_2, \ldots, dv_n\} = \{dg_1(R), dg_2(R), \ldots, dg_n(R)\} \qquad (3)$$

Danger signal is a set of variable values of multiple system variables. Referring to the calculation method of numerical differentiation, the values of danger signals can be expressed by forward, backward and central difference methods respectively.

1. Approximate expression of danger signal by forward difference

$$ds_i \approx g_i(R_{i+1}) - g_i(R_i) \qquad (4)$$

$$DS \approx \{(g_1(R_{i+1}) - g_1(R_i)), (g_2(R_{i+1}) - g_2(R_i)), \ldots, (g_n(R_{i+1}) - g_n(R_i))\} \qquad (5)$$

ds_i represents the danger signal of a specific system variable.

2. Approximate expression of dangerous signal by backward difference

$$ds_i \approx g_i(R_i) - g_i(R_{i-1}) \qquad (6)$$

$$DS \approx \{(g_1(R_i) - g_1(R_{i-1})), (g_2(R_i) - g_2(R_{i-1})), \ldots, (g_n(R_i) - g_n(R_{i-1}))\} \qquad (7)$$

3. Approximate Central Difference Expression of Dangerous Signals

$$ds_i \approx \frac{g_i(R_{i+1}) - g_i(R_{i-1})}{2} \qquad (8)$$

$$DS \approx \{\frac{g_1(R_{i+1}) - g_1(R_{i-1})}{2}, \frac{g_2(R_{i+1}) - g_2(R_{i-1})}{2}, \ldots, \frac{g_n(R_{i+1}) - g_n(R_{i-1})}{2}\} \quad (9)$$

Change perception method considers that change is the main cause of danger. Therefore, the first step of presenting danger signal should be to find changes in the system.

5 Extraction of Danger Signals

In this paper, the danger signal is expressed as the differential value of various system variables in Android system. The change is the change of system variables relative to a reference system. This paper takes time as the reference system.

Considering that the granularity level of sample points at a single time is too low to reflect the state of the system correctly, the change of system variables in a period of time is a meaningful reference. In this paper, the sliding window based on the time axis is selected as the specific reference frame, and the differential value of Android system variables is calculated by the change extraction method based on distance.

5.1 Selection of Reference System

In different operation stages, under different operation conditions, and when running different software, the values of variables of Android system are different. The equilibrium state of smartphone system is actually relatively static state. When measuring change in a relatively static system, the frame of reference should also be relative. This paper takes the sliding window [21] based on time as a reference frame, as shown in Fig. 3.

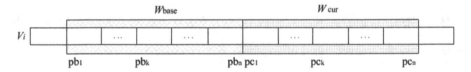

Fig. 3. Time-based sliding window as reference frame.

W represents sliding window, $Wbase$ represents benchmark window, and $Wcur$ represents current window. The reference window $Wbase$ and the current window $Wcur$ are two adjacent windows, and the difference between the values of system variables in the two windows is used as a danger signal. Let the size of sliding window be w. When the calculation of dangerous signal is completed, the two windows slide forward together, the $Wcur$ window slides forward w, and the $Wbase$ slides forward w to the position of the $Wcur$ window.

v_i represents the ith system variable. Sampling the system variable v_i according to the sampling time t, several sample points $P\{p_k \mid k \in N\}$ are obtained. Let window

w contain n sample points, that is $w = n \times t$. Sample point numbers in *Wbase* and *Wcur* are *pbk* and *pck*, $k \in (1, n)$. The danger signal *dsi* of system variable v_i is the difference of sample points in two adjacent windows *Wbase* and *Wcur*. With the sliding of the window, comparing the values of the two windows, we can dynamically calculate the changes of system variables in different time periods, so as to get the dangerous signals of each system variable.

5.2 Variation Calculation Method

Common distance calculation methods include Euclidean Distance, Absolute Distance, Hausdorff Distance and Canberra Distance. Distance-based danger signal extraction method regards n sample points in sliding window W as points in n-dimensional space, and two windows *Wbase* and *Wcur* are regarded as points in two n-dimensional space to find distance. Distance represents the difference between states, that is, the danger signal to be extracted in this paper.

- Danger signal calculation based on Euclidean distance

$$ds_i = \sqrt{\sum_{k=1}^{n} (pc_k - pb_k)^2} \tag{10}$$

- Danger signal calculation based on absolute distance

$$ds_i - \sum_{k=1}^{n} |pc_k \quad pb_k| \tag{11}$$

- Hausch Distance Based Danger Signal Computation

$$ds_i = max(h(A,B), h(B,A)) \tag{12}$$

Where $h(A, B) = max(a \in A)min(b \in B)\|a\text{-}b\|$, $h(B, A) = max(b \in B)min(a \in A)\|b\text{-}a\|$ and $A = \{pb_1, pb_2, ..., pb_n\}$, $B = \{pc_1, pc_2, ..., pc_n\}$.

- Calculating Danger Signals Based on Rand Distance

$$ds_j = \sum_{h=1}^{n} |pc_k - pb_k|/(pc_k + pb_k) \tag{13}$$

ds_i is a danger signal generated by a system variable, $DS = \{ds_i \mid i \in n\}$, and so on.

6 Malware Detection Experiment

The main purpose of this experiment is to verify the validity of the proposed smart-phone malware detection model based on change perception. In order to achieve this goal, I have implemented a smartphone malware detection prototype system based on change perception, and designed four groups of experiments.

1. Collecting data when the smartphone is in normal condition and the application program is not running (Normal group);
2. Collecting data (SMS&Call group) when the smartphone is running normal applications (sending short messages and calling);
3. Collect data of BgServ embedded in smartphone operation (BgServ group);
4. Collect the data when the smartphone runs Secret SMS Replicator (Replicator group).

The results of the four groups of experiments are shown in Table 2.

Table 2. Table of experimental result.

	Normal	SMS&Call	BgServ	Replicator
Quotation times	2	12	32	49
Quotation rate	0.02	0.21	0.46	0.75

As can be seen from Table 2, the alarm rate of the group with malicious software is higher than that of the reference group. Through the observation of the alarm, we can find that the alarm of the reference group is sporadic, and there is no aggregation; while in the group with latent software, the alarm is relatively centralized and can be followed regularly. Thus, the model designed in this paper is feasible for detecting malicious software in smartphones.

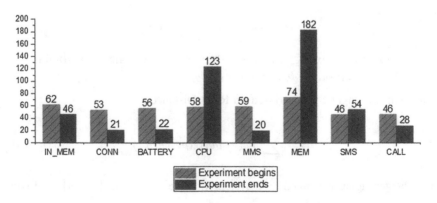

Fig. 4. Experimental results of TLR distribution.

As shown in Fig. 4, TLR is uniformly distributed at the beginning of the calculation. After the calculation, the distribution of TLR has changed greatly. Among them, the top three TLR receptors are mem (RAM memory utilization), CPU (CPU utilization), SMS (short message transmission frequency). This is because every time Secret SMS Replicator finds a short message, it calls the short message sending API and secretly forwards the short message to the monitoring phone. In this process, it consumes a lot of memory and CPU. Therefore, for mobile phones with Secret SMS Replicator installed, the changes of memory occupancy and CPU occupancy are very obvious at the moment of receiving short messages. At the same time, the frequency of SMS transmission also changed slightly. Therefore, in the calculation process, TLR receptors that recognize MEM, CPU and SMS are retained, the number of TLR receptors increases, while other receptors are eliminated and the number of TLR receptors decreases.

In conclusion, the APC population will adjust adaptively with the different states of the current system. The proportion of TLR receptors that can recognize danger signals in the current system state increases, and the proportion of TLR receptors that can not recognize dangerous signals decreases. Therefore, the distribution of TLR receptors is different for different malware and different stages of the same software. It can be proved that the model designed in this paper is adaptive in detecting malware.

7 Conclusion

Danger theory is a research branch of biological immune system. At present, dendritic cell algorithm has been widely studied in risk theory. However, the dendritic cell algorithm has a heavy artificial manipulation trace in signal selection, value selection and so on. Although it has a certain degree of self-adaptability, it is lack of self-adaptability.

In this paper, aiming at the lack of self-adaptability of the existing detection methods for malicious software in smart phones, a change-awareness method based on risk theory is introduced. By searching for change in smart phone systems, that is, dangerous signals, the purpose of detecting malicious software is achieved.

References

1. Xie, L., Shuang, L.I.: Android malware detection model based on Bagging-SVM. J. Comput. Appl., 3 (2018)
2. Onwuzurike, L., Almeida, M., Mariconti, E., et al.: A family of droids: analyzing behavioral model based android malware detection via static and dynamic analysis (2018)
3. Wei, W., Zhao, M., Wang, J.: Effective android malware detection with a hybrid model based on deep autoencoder and convolutional neural network. J. Ambient. Intell. Hum. Comput. 1, 1–9 (2018)
4. Betarte, G., Campo, J., Gorostiaga, F., et al.: A certified reference validation mechanism for the permission model of android. In: International Symposium on Logic-Based Program Synthesis & Transformation (2017)

5. Xin, J., Liu, M., Yang, K., et al.: A security sandbox approach of android based on hook mechanism. Secur. Commun. Netw. **2018**, 1–8 (2018)
6. Ping, Y., Zheng, Y.: A survey on dynamic mobile malware detection. Softw. Qual. J., 1–29 (2017)
7. Liang, X., Li, Y., Huang, X., et al.: Cloud-based malware detection game for mobile devices with offloading. IEEE Trans. Mob. Comput. **16**(10), 2742–2750 (2017)
8. Biedermann, S., Katzenbeisser, S.: Detecting computer worms in the cloud. In: Camenisch, J., Kesdogan, D. (eds.) iNetSec 2011. LNCS, vol. 7039, pp. 43–54. Springer, Heidelberg (2012). https://doi.org/10.1007/978-3-642-27585-2_4
9. Kim, J.Y., Bu, S.J, Cho, S.B.: Zero-day malware detection using transferred generative adversarial networks based on deep autoencoders. Inf. Sci. (2018). https://www.sciencedirect.com/science/article/pii/S0020025518303475
10. Ma, Z., Ge, H., Liu, Y., et al.: A combination method for android malware detection based on control flow graphs and machine learning algorithms. IEEE Access **PP**(99), 1 (2019)
11. Gao, T., Peng, W., Sisodia, D., et al.: Android malware detection via Graphlet sampling. IEEE Trans. Mob. Comput. **PP**(99), 1 (2018)
12. Narayanan, A., Chandramohan, M., Chen, L., et al.: A multi-view context-aware approach to Android malware detection and malicious code localization. Empir. Softw. Eng. **6**, 1–53 (2017)
13. King, R.L., Lambert, A.B., Russ, S.H., Reese, D.S.: The biological basis of the immune system as a model for intelligent agents. In: Rolim, J., et al. (eds.) IPPS 1999. LNCS, vol. 1586, pp. 156–164. Springer, Heidelberg (1999). https://doi.org/10.1007/BFb0097896
14. Banirostam, T., Fesharaki, M.N.: Immune system simulation with biological agent based on capra cognitive framework. In: UKSIM International Conference on Computer Modelling & Simulation (2011)
15. Sulaiman, N.F., Jali, M.Z., Abdullah, Z.H., et al.: A study on the performances of danger theory and negative selection algorithms for mobile spam detection. Adv. Sci. Lett. **23**(5), 4586–4590 (2017)
16. Zhang, Z., Lun, L., Zhang, R.: Danger theory based micro immune optimization algorithm solving probabilistic constrained optimization. In: IEEE International Conference on Computational Intelligence & Applications (2017)
17. Secker, A., Freitas, A.A., Timmis, J.: A danger theory inspired approach to web mining. In: Timmis, J., Bentley, Peter J., Hart, E. (eds.) ICARIS 2003. LNCS, vol. 2787, pp. 156–167. Springer, Heidelberg (2003). https://doi.org/10.1007/978-3-540-45192-1_16
18. Hashim, F., Munasinghe, K.S., Jamalipour, A.: A danger theory inspired survivability framework for the next generation mobile network. IEEE Lat. Am. Trans. **8**(4), 358–369 (2010)
19. Weigold, T., Kramp, T., Hermann, R., et al.: The Zurich trusted information channel—an efficient defence against man-in-the-middle and malicious software attacks. In: International Conference on Trusted Computing & Trust in Information Technologies: Trusted Computing-challenges & Applications (2008)
20. Park, C.S., Lee, J.H., Seo, S.C., et al.: Assuring software security against buffer overflow attacks in embedded software development life cycle. In: International Conference on Advanced Communication Technology (2010)
21. Lin, X., Yuan, Y., Wang, W., et al.: Stabbing the sky: efficient skyline computation over sliding windows. In: International Conference on Data Engineering (2005)

Model Analysis and Prediction of People's Travel Behaviors Under no Shared Bicycles

Guoquan Liu[✉], Wenhui Yi, Zehui Lin, and Yiming Chen

Jiangxi Province Engineering Research Center of New Energy Technology
and Equipment, East China University of Technology,
Nanchang 330013, Jiangxi Province, China
gqlecit@hotmail.com

Abstract. As the development of sharing economics, the sharing bicycles rapidly grow domestically and overseas. However, there are some problems together with the shared bicycles, such as traffic congestion, bicycles are hard to park, etc. This paper will discuss the changes of people's traffic behaviors without sharing bikes, by combining wavelet analysis with Back Propagation (BP) neural network and established a traffic behavior prediction model based on wavelet analysis method. First, the model selected the BP as network and the Morlet wavelet as the hidden layer excitation function, then take the data of New York City in October 2018 as an example to apply in the prediction model to solve this problem. The simulation results show that the prediction model has accurate precise the urban traffic change trend, with a fast convergence speed, and has high practical application value. Lastly, if there are no shared bicycles, a small number of people will choose to walk or take a taxi, most people are more willing to take the bus to finish the "last mile".

Keywords: Shared bicycles · Wavelet analysis · Back propagation algorithm · Traffic behavior

1 Introduction

With the sustainable development of cyber link, shared bicycles have received more and more attentions in recent years [1]. Due to its advantages of reducing environmental pollution and enhance traffic quality, many cities already introduced sharing bikes to help relieve traffic problems. Shared bicycles are now an integral part of the transport system. Apart from the advantages of sharing bikes, we also know that there are some new problems such as the traffic congestion and the difficulty in parking the bicycles, besides, it's also hard to get the refund of deposits. Based on these problems, this paper mainly discussed about people's traffic behaviors without shared bicycles.

Recently, many scholars have interests in issues on shared bicycles. On the one hand, for example, Zhu, Ma, Wang and Wen studied the optimal bicycle scheduling problem based on BP neural network for demand forecasting and analyzes the shared bicycle supply and demand gap [2]. Ding, Yang, Lu and Liu investigated the impact of shared bikes on urban transportation carbon emissions in literature [3]. Due to the increasing complex situations, traditional methods cannot satisfy the demand of all

© Springer Nature Switzerland AG 2019
D.-S. Huang et al. (Eds.): ICIC 2019, LNCS 11643, pp. 367–376, 2019.
https://doi.org/10.1007/978-3-030-26763-6_36

kinds of problems. Zhang and Benveniste first discovered the structure of Wavelet Neural Networks [5]. Since then, wavelet neural networks have been widespread. Furthermore, Yong, Wong, Liao and Chen realized the online synthesis of wavelet neural network with recursive least squares criterion training network [6] and used Bayesian criterion [7] to determine the optimal wavelet number in training, which proved that the method can adapt to the changes of system parameters and approximate unknown system functions. In the literatures mentioned, they are all applied wavelet analysis method to establish the model on traffic problems. Li studied the influence of shared bicycles on traffic congestion in Beijing based on the previous work in literature [4]. Those researchers empirically analyzed the effects of shared bicycles on traffic congestion by establishing a time series regression model. So far, wavelet analysis method has established a complete theoretical system. Due to the superior characteristics, wavelet analysis method is widely used in many fields [8, 9, 11].

On the other hand, however, there seems no literatures that focus on the circumstance that there are no sharing bicycles. In order to discuss the travel behaviors of people with no sharing bicycles, this paper establishes a traffic travel prediction model based on wavelet analysis method. The model selected the BP as network and the Morlet wavelet as the hidden layer excitation function, then take the data of New York City in October 2018 [10] as an example to apply in the prediction model to draw the conclusion. The traveler's trip duration, user type, gender, and age factors are used as the input variables of the model. Then, the travel mode is selected as the output variable of this paper. Use the test data as the input, then test and train the model, and use the actual data as input into the trained model. In the end, the final predicted output is obtained.

This paper makes the following two main contributions to the topic:

However, there is little research literature on the issue of people's traffic behavior without shared bicycles. Therefore, it is meaningful to study the travel behavior of people without shared bicycle.

(1) In this paper, the authors are trying to combine the BP algorithm with the wavelet analysis, the BP neural network is selected as the neural network in the prediction model of traffic mode selection and the Morlet wavelet is selected as the hidden layer excitation function.

(2) In this paper, a reasonable model is proposed to predict people's traffic behavior under a city without sharing bicycle.

The structure of this article arranges mainly as follows. In the second section, the wavelet neural network and some preparatory work are introduced. In the third section, this paper verifies the validity and practicability of the model through a numerical simulation. Finally, the proposed conclusion is in the fourth section.

2 Preliminaries

In the paper, assuming that the destination can be reached by six means of transportation, besides, it can be seen from Fig. 1 that the six means of transportations depend on the travel distance. In this paper, we mainly discuss about the short-distance travel, there are four types of main short-distance transportation: walking, cycling, bus and taxi. If there are no shared bicycles, the related data is eliminated from the population travel data [10], and the remaining data samples are divided into the experimental data. Through the inner motivation of people's traffic behavior, and then find the interconnection of motivation, and finally predict the changes of people's traffic behaviors.

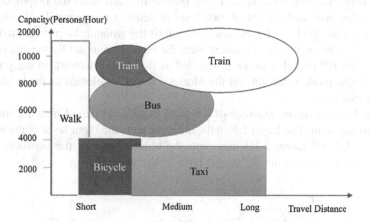

Fig. 1. The transportations for people depending on distance.

2.1 The Wavelet Theory

The wavelet analysis is based on the insufficiency of Fourier transform. The Fourier transform is the widely used analysis method in signal processing field. However, it has a s shortcoming that the transformation discards the time information, and the transformation result cannot determine when a signal occurs. The wavelet is with a limited length and an average of 0. It has the following characteristics:

The time domain has a tight support set or an approximate compact support set.

The DC (Direct Current) portion is 0.

The wavelet transform is to transform a basic wavelet function into b, and then inner product with the signal $x(t)$ to be analyzed under different scales a.

$$WT_x(a,b) = \frac{1}{\sqrt{a}} \int x(t)\varphi^* \left(\frac{t-b}{a}\right) dt = \int x(t)\varphi_{a,b}^*(t) dt = \langle x(t), \varphi_{a,b}(t) \rangle \quad (1)$$

where $\varphi^*(\cdot)$ means conjugate form, $\varphi(t)$ is the wavelet function, a stands for contraction-expansion factor and b is the shift factor.

2.2 The BP Theory

The BP neural network is known as a typical feedforward network. A feedforward neural network is referred as a signal direct neural network. Each neuron starts at the input layer and gets the previous input, then get the outputs to the next stage until the information transmits to output layer. There isn't any connection between neurons in the same layer, and the information transmits between layers is only in single direction.

The BP neural network is also called feedforward neural network with connection propagation adjustment using backpropagation learning algorithm. The adjustment of its weight and threshold is precisely achieved by the inverse calculation of the error. In the training part of the model, the total error of the whole sample data is calculated by the multi-layer network method, and then pushed forward from the output layer network. The threshold and weight of each layer of neurons are generally obtained layer by layer using the gradient descent method. Adjust the amount, loop iteration, stop the operation when the network parameters meet the requirements set by the algorithm. In this paper, the BP neural network is selected as the neural network in the prediction model of traffic mode selection and the Morlet wavelet is selected as the hidden layer excitation function.

Figure 2 visualizes an example of a typical three-layer neural network model for forward propagation. The Layer L1 on the left represents the input layer of the network, the Layer 2 L2 and Layer 3 L3 represents the hidden layer of the network, and the Layer 4 Layer L4 represents the output layer of the network.

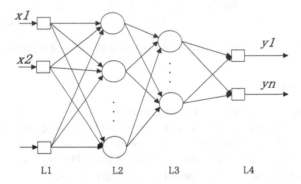

Fig. 2. The typical neural network model

2.3 Wavelet Analysis Method

The purpose of the wavelet neural network is to replace the traditional excitation function of the hidden layer nodes of the conventional single hidden layer neural network with the wavelet function. The corresponding input layer to hidden layer, hidden layer to the weight of output layer and the threshold of hidden layer are respectively determined by the scale and translation parameters of the wavelet function. The wavelet neural network has more degrees of freedom than wavelet transform, which makes the function approximation ability more flexible and effective. By selecting the suitable parameters, the wavelet neural network composed of fewer terms of series can achieve excellent approximation effects. Therefore, the wavelet method owns the better function approximation feature, which is the best mode identification ability. Due to the model is different from the BP algorithm of the grape neural network, it can effectively overcome the inherent defects in the universal artificial neural network mode. Besides, the prediction model can perform better prediction results.

The basis function used is the Morlet mother wavelet basis function. The mathematical formula is:

$$\psi(t) = e^{-t^2/2} \cos ct, \tag{2}$$

where e is the natural log, and cos stands for cosine function.

The wavelet neural network output layer calculation formula is as follows:

$$y(k) = \Sigma \omega_{ik} h(i), \quad k = 1, 2, \cdots, m, \tag{3}$$

where ω_{ik} stand for the weight values, and $h(i)$ stand for hidden layers.

The weight parameter modification of wavelet, method algorithm is similar to the BP neural network weight correction algorithm. The gradient correction network weight and basis parameters are used to make the wavelet neural network prediction output continuously approximate the expected output. The wavelet correction process is illustrated below:

Calculate the prediction error:

$$e = \sum yn(k) - y(k). \tag{4}$$

Based on prediction error e, to correct the wavelet neural network weights and basis coefficients, that is:

$$w_{n,k}^{i+1} = w_{n,k}^{i} + \Delta w_{n,k}^{i+1}, \tag{5}$$

$$a_k^{i+1} = a_k^i + \Delta a_k^{i+1}, \tag{6}$$

$$b_k^{i+1} = b_k^i + \Delta b_k^{i+1}, \tag{7}$$

$$\Delta w_{n,k}^{i+1} = -\eta \Delta \frac{\partial e}{\partial w_{n,k}^i}, \tag{8}$$

$$\Delta a_k^{i+1} = \eta \Delta \frac{\partial e}{\partial a_k^i}, \tag{9}$$

$$\Delta b_k^{i+1} = -\eta \Delta \frac{\partial e}{\partial b_k^i}, \tag{10}$$

where η is the study rate, and $\Delta w_{n,k}^{i+1}, \Delta a_k^{i+1}, \Delta b_k^{i+1}$ can be calculated according to (5)–(7).

2.4   Working Process of Prediction Model

Next, the design procedure is shown below and the flowchart is given in Fig. 3.

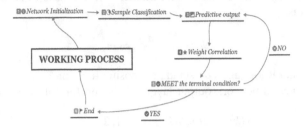

Fig. 3. The flowchart of the working process

Step1: Network initialization. Randomly initialize the scaling factors of the wavelet function, the translation factors, together with the network connection weights, then assign the learning speed.

Step2: Sample cluster. Divide the samples into two parts, one is training samples and the other is testing samples. Apply the training samples to the network and use the network samples to test the prediction accuracy of the network.

Step3: Predictive output. Input the training data into the network, predict the network output, besides, calculate the error and the expected output.

Step4: Weight value correction. According to the error value, to correct the network weight values, and the wavelet function parameters, those values are the network prediction approximates the expected value.

Step5: Detect if the process ends, if not, return to **Step 3.**

3   Numerical Simulation

In the previous sections, the methods were illustrated. In this section, to test the precision of the model and solve the problem, we finished the following work.

3.1   Experimental Data Selection

(1) Data acquire calibration

The data in this paper comes from [10]. In this experiment, we made a pre-proceed to the data, then eliminated some data form it which is not suitable. Finally, the data in the data sheet about the sharing bike.

(2) Data calibration

The experimental data cannot be used for research directly, and the data requires to be calibrated. For example, when "Walk" is the travel mode, it is calibrated to 1. When the travel mode is "Bus", it is calibrated to 3, etc. The specific calibration situation is shown in Table 1.

Table 1. Data calibration

Travel mode	Corresponding value
Walk	1
Bike	2
Bus	3
Taxi	4

(3) Input and output variables

The mode of urban transportation is related to quantities of factors. However, the internal factors are taken the majority proportion, namely, the conscious activity of the traveler. Therefore, the traveler's **TRIPDURATION**, **USERTYPE**, **GENDER**, and **AGE** are selected as the main influencing factors and take these four factors as the model's input variables. The main topic to be solved of this article is the travel mode, together with the selection of the way of travel, as the output variable of this paper.

(4) Determination of model parameters

The value of each parameter processes a huge impact on the output of the wavelet neural network. In this paper, considering the influencing factors in many aspects, and finally select 6 hidden layer nodes, the first learning probability is 0.1, the first learning probability is 0.01, and the iteration times is 100.

3.2 Test Results and Discussion

(1) Division of experimental data

According to the different properties of the input and output vectors, divide the experimental data of the group into two groups, namely, the input data of a group of groups. Another set of output data for the 92975 group. Then, the first group of input data is selected as the test input data of the model, and the latter group data is used as the actual input data; the first 70000 groups of the output data are selected as the test input data of the model, and the latter 22975 sets of data are used as the actual input data. The group information is displayed in Table 2.

Table 2. Experimental data

Type of data	Quantity
Input_test	70000×4
Input	22975×4
Output_test	70000
Output	22795

(2) Experimental result

The result is shown in Fig. 4.

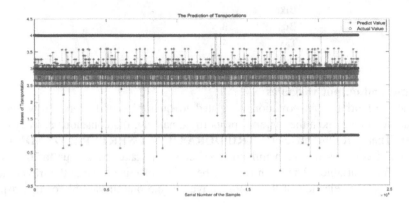

Fig. 4. The prediction of transportation

In the experiment, both the test data and the actual data was input into the network, and the blue line is the actual data while the red line stands for the predict value.

According to Fig. 4, it can be known that the main mode of transportation for people is walking when there are no shared bicycles.

(3) Verification

A *Test indicator.*

To verify the veracity of the prediction results, the mean absolute error (*MAE*), the root mean square error (*RMSE*) and the mean absolute error (*MSE*) were used as the evaluation criteria of the model. The *MAE*, *RMSE*, and *MSE* calculation formulas are expressed as follows:

$$MAE = \frac{1}{N} \sum_{i=1}^{N} |(f_i - y_i)|, \tag{11}$$

where N is the amount the sample, $observed_t$ is the current value of samples, $predicted_t$ is the predicted values of the samples.

$$MSE = \frac{1}{N} \sum_{i=1}^{N} (observed_t - predicted_t)^2, \tag{12}$$

where N is the amount the sample, $observed_t$ is the current value of samples, $predicted_t$ is the predicted value of the samples.

$$RMSE = \sqrt{\frac{1}{N} \sum_{i=1}^{N} (observed_t - predicted_t)^2}, \tag{13}$$

where N is the amount the sample, $observed_t$ are the current values of sample, $predicted_t$ are the predicted values of the sample.

. It's obviously that if the model is more precise, the accuracy is higher.

B *Verification results.*

The *RMSE*, *MAE* and *MSE* values of the result data were obtained, as illustrated in Table 3.

Table 3. Three evaluation indicators

Evaluation index	Value
MSE	1.3624
MAE	0.9264
RMSE	1.6498

Note: It can be known from Table 3 that the *RMSE*, *MAE* and *MSE* values are not so large, indicating that the model established in this paper can predict more accurately the way people travel when there is no shared bicycle.

4 Discussion and Future Work

4.1 Discussion

This paper discussed about people's traffic behaviors without sharing bicycles. A traffic behavior prediction model was established based on BP neural network. In the solution, according to a numerical simulation example, it can be concluded that most travelers will choose to take the bus to solve the "last mile" problem without sharing bicycles. In the end, the predict result shows the feasibility and practically.

Moreover, the work in this paper is valuable. As the sharing bikes is a new-born thing, and it need time to be accepted by the market and the public, so our work can be more meaningful in the future when the sharing economic develops and the sharing bikes be accepted by more and more people.

4.2 Future Work

The influence of shared bicycles on urban traffic is a complex issue involving multiple factors. However, there is still something that needs to be explored.

The data used in the model is only comes from New York City. If it is provided in other regions or even other countries, more unknown factors need to be considered, and the model should be improved according to local conditions,

When considering the travel mode of the traveler, the experiment only extracts the four most important influence components and cannot achieve a comprehensive and accurate assessment. Therefore, how to combine and enrich new and improve the evaluation model is the direction that needs further research.

Acknowledgement. This work is supported by the Start-up Foundation for Doctors of East China University of Technology (No. DHBK2012201), the Foundation of Jiangxi Educational Committee (GJJ170484), the Science and Technology Foundation of Jiangxi Province (No. 20181BAB202019) and the National Natural Science Foundation of China (Nos. 51567001, 11565002).

References

1. Jin, J., Shi, J.X.: Research on problems and countermeasures of government in governing shared bicycles. Foreign Trade **01**, 114–116 (2018). In Chinese
2. Zhu, Y., Ma, Z.X., Wang, S.Y., Wen, Z.L.: The problem of shared bicycle optimization scheduling based on BP neural network. Netw. Secur. Technol. Appl. **11**, 44–45 (2018). In Chinese
3. Ding, N., Yang, J.X., Lu, X.H., Liu, J.R.: Shared bicycle life cycle assessment and its impact on urban transportation carbon emissions: a case study of Beijing. Acta Scientiae Circumstantiae, 1–14 (2018, in Chinese)
4. Li, Y.G.: Research on the impact of shared bicycles on traffic congestion in Beijing. Beijing Jiaotong University (2018, in Chinese)
5. Akca, H., Al-Lail, M., Covachev, V.: Survey on wavelet transform and application in ODE and wavelet networks. Adv. Dyn. Syst. Appl. **1**, 129–162 (2006)
6. Wang, Y., Wong, K., Liao, X., Chen, G.: A new chaos-based fast image encryption algorithm. Appl. Soft Comput. **11**, 514–522 (2011)
7. Chen, J., Chen, Z.: Extended Bayesian information criteria for model selection with large model spaces. Biometrika **95**(3), 759–771 (2008)
8. Zhang, S., Chang, T., Lin, D.: A preliminary study on a hybrid wavelet neural network model for forecasting monthly rainfall. EURASIA J. Math. Sci. Technol. Educ. **14**(5), 1747–1757 (2018)
9. Gao, M.J., Tian, J.W., Zhou, S.R.: Simulation study of oil and water migration modeling based on wavelet neural network. In: Proceedings of the 2009 International Conference on Wavelet Analysis and Pattern Recognition, Baoding, 12–15 July 2009
10. https://s3.amazonaws.com/tripdata/index.html
11. Dai, H., Xue, G., Wang, W.: An adaptive wavelet frame neural network method for efficient reliability analysis. Comput.-Aided Civ. Infrastruct. Eng. **29**, 801–814 (2014)

Research on Security Vulnerabilities Based on Artificial Intelligence

Qian Zhu[1(✉)] and Liang Liang[2]

[1] City College of Wuhan University of Science and Technology,
Wuhan 430083, China
zhuqian722@163.com
[2] Accelink Technologies Co., Ltd., Wuhan 430205, China

Abstract. Security vulnerability research is the core content of information security research. Faced with the increasing scale of software, security vulnerabilities have brought unprecedented severe challenges, artificial methods have been unable to meet the demand of the research. How to apply artificial intelligence technology such as machine learning and natural language processing to security vulnerability research has become an urgent issue. This paper summarizes the common research methods of vulnerability, expounds the key technology of intelligent vulnerability research, points out that intelligent vulnerability mining is the focus of research on security vulnerability based on artificial intelligence, analyzes and summarizes the latest research results in related fields in recent years, puts forward the existing problems, and gives the corresponding solutions.

Keywords: Security vulnerability · Vulnerability mining ·
Artificial intelligence · Machine learning

1 Introduction

Security vulnerability refers to various forms of defects of information technology and related products in various levels and links of the information system. These defects directly affect the normal operation of the entire information system. Once maliciously exploited, it will seriously damage the integrity, confidentiality and availability of the information system. Therefore, the research on security vulnerability is one of the core contents of information security research [1]. Faced with the severe challenges brought by security vulnerabilities, how to achieve automated and efficient vulnerability mining, vulnerability utilization, vulnerability assessment and vulnerability repair are all urgent issues to be solved.

In recent years, artificial intelligence technology has been developed very well. Artificial intelligence technology can be used to mine and predict vulnerabilities, automate the processing of program code, extract effective information, and realize intelligent research on security vulnerabilities. Machine learning and natural language processing technologies in the field of artificial intelligence will be widely used in the field of security vulnerability research.

© Springer Nature Switzerland AG 2019
D.-S. Huang et al. (Eds.): ICIC 2019, LNCS 11643, pp. 377–387, 2019.
https://doi.org/10.1007/978-3-030-26763-6_37

2 Common Vulnerability Research Methods

The research of security vulnerability is mainly divided into vulnerability mining, vulnerability utilization, vulnerability assessment, vulnerability repair and so on.

Vulnerability mining refers to security researchers using various technologies and tools to review software or system code, analyze software execution processes, and find defects in computer systems, which is the key content of information security. Vulnerability mining technology can be divided into static analysis technology and dynamic analysis technology. Static analysis technology refers to the analysis and detection of the target program without running the program, so as to find the possible security vulnerabilities in the target program. Static analysis technology can efficiently and quickly complete the inspection of program code, and its code coverage rate is high, and there are fewer missed reports. However, due to the lack of runtime data and dynamic testing process and fine-grained security assessment, static analysis technology has low accuracy and more false positives. Dynamic analysis technology discovers vulnerabilities by observing the abnormalities of running state and register state in the process of program running. Dynamic analysis technology has high accuracy of vulnerability mining, but its code coverage is relatively low. When the condition is not satisfied, the code will not be able to execute, and there are omissions. Therefore, the current mainstream security vulnerability research method is to combine static and dynamic analysis for vulnerability mining.

Vulnerability exploitation refers to the further analysis of the defects found in software or system to confirm whether the vulnerability is a security vulnerability or not. If it is a security vulnerability, further determine the type of vulnerability and develop a proof-of-concept. It is an important way to obtain system control permission by triggering a vulnerability through a program with a payload and overriding the program limit of the vulnerable program to control the running process of the code in the target system. Research on vulnerability utilization is to find the exploitable points of confirmed vulnerabilities, but most vulnerabilities have not found the corresponding exploitable points.

Vulnerability assessment can also be called vulnerability grading. It refers to the evaluation of security vulnerabilities. According to the relevant attributes of vulnerabilities, we can obtain the threat severity of security vulnerabilities by synthetically measuring relevant vulnerability threat assessment indicators, analyze the harmfulness and impact scope of the vulnerabilities, and provide guidance for vulnerability repair. Vulnerability classification methods can be divided into qualitative and quantitative methods. Common vulnerability quantitative system is the common vulnerability scoring system (CVSS) [2]. CVSS is an open and free quantitative risk assessment system for security vendors to assess the severity of security vulnerability threats. CVSS scoring process includes three scoring items: basic index, temporary index and environmental index. Each index contains a set of different measures and scoring criteria. Finally, the corresponding scoring results are weighted to obtain a score used to measure the severity of security vulnerability threat. Generally speaking, the CVSS score between 0 and 3.9 indicates low-level vulnerabilities, 4 to 6.9 indicates medium vulnerabilities, and 7 to 10 indicates serious vulnerabilities. According to these scoring results, it is preferred to repair and deal with serious vulnerabilities.

Vulnerability repair will be based on the level of vulnerability assessment for vulnerability repair, priority to repair high-level vulnerabilities. In general, there are three kinds of fixes: (1) if the type of vulnerability is known and recorded, the developer will continue to analyze the code related to the vulnerability, design and implement a solution, and then use the technology to identify the vulnerability for testing until the security vulnerability is fixed; (2) if the vulnerability type is known and recorded by the core security team, but no such security vulnerability has been encountered before, then the development team and the core security team shall cooperate to analyze and identify the vulnerability and design corresponding solutions; (3) if the vulnerability type is unknown, the core security team will collaborate with experts and developers from different fields to develop a common solution for the vulnerability. At present, the main method of vulnerability repair is manual.

3 Intelligent Vulnerability Research

Common security vulnerability research methods often require security researchers to have enough professional knowledge, and this artificial research method is often very inefficient. Applying artificial intelligence technology to security vulnerability research and realizing intelligent vulnerability research will greatly improve the efficiency of security protection.

3.1 Intelligent Vulnerability Mining

The application of machine learning to vulnerability mining has always been concerned by security researchers. The essence is to treat vulnerability mining as a program classification problem or clustering problem, to distinguish the program containing the vulnerability from the normal program or to aggregate the program containing the vulnerability. In recent years, security researchers have deeply studied the principle of vulnerability generation and the conditions of vulnerability generation, and constructed different vulnerability mining models using various learning algorithms.

Vulnerability Mining Model Based on Software Metrics. Software metrics is a continuous quantitative process for data definition, collection and analysis of software development projects, processes and their products, aiming at understanding, predicting, evaluating, controlling and improving development projects. Software metrics is a quantitative representation of software specific entity attributes, which can provide various information of software and can be acquired through software tools. Therefore, software metrics has become one of the feature choices for security researchers to mine vulnerabilities. Common software metrics include complexity, code churn, coupling, cohesion and developer activity, etc.

Complexity metrics is the primary choice for security researchers. Software with higher complexity is more vulnerable to loopholes. In this paper, the performance of the model around Mozilla Firefox is poor, and the impact of complexity metrics changes due to project changes. At the same time, correlation analysis shows that the correlation between security vulnerabilities and software complexity is weak, which also confirms the experimental results of low recall rate of complexity measurement.

Code change metrics are defined as changes in the number of lines of code between software versions. Code changes are directly related to software defects, which is likely to produce security vulnerabilities, so researchers use this metric for vulnerability mining. The results show that the correlation between code change metrics and vulnerabilities is weak, which restricts the validity of these software metrics.

Coupling and cohesion are the criteria for measuring the degree of module independence. Coupling degree refers to the degree of information or parameter dependence between modules in a program. Cohesion refers to the degree to which functionally relevant programs are grouped into modules. Literature [3, 4] combines complexity, coupling and cohesion for vulnerability mining. Experimental results show that low-coupling and high-cohesion files are not prone to generate vulnerabilities, while high-coupling and low-cohesion files are more prone to generate vulnerabilities.

In general, the selection of software metrics for vulnerability mining still cannot meet the research needs. Although coupling, cohesion, developer activities and other metrics can reflect which files may contain vulnerabilities to a certain extent, the performance of the vulnerability mining model built by software metrics is still low. Therefore, it is not appropriate to use software metrics for vulnerability mining. Only by starting from the vulnerability itself and developing code characteristics combining security vulnerabilities, can machine learning be better applied to vulnerability mining.

Code attributes are different from software metrics. It is a further development of software metrics, but it is not a generalization of the software's overall information, but a combination of specific knowledge of a certain type of vulnerability, requiring researchers to fully develop the vulnerability. The understanding of this type of exploits has in-depth research, and can be statistically analyzed at the code level, using this information as a feature for vulnerability mining. Code attributes are based on the relevant information of security vulnerabilities, and can be counted at the code level, linking the program code with security vulnerabilities, so that better detection results can be achieved. However, the determination of code attributes involves professional knowledge areas, requiring expert experience to determine the corresponding feature selection. Although code attributes are an effective feature of vulnerability mining, the current research on code attributes mainly focuses on Web vulnerabilities and buffer overflow vulnerabilities. Whether new code attributes can be developed to improve the performance of existing vulnerability mining models needs further exploration. At the same time, the application scope of code attributes is too narrow, and different types of vulnerabilities have different requirements for code attributes. Whether the code attributes suitable for mining other types of vulnerabilities can be found still needs researchers' continuous research. Finally, code attributes are selected according to expert experience, and these characteristics tend to have a certain subjectivity, which will affect the effect of machine learning model. Therefore, this paper can alleviate this situation by letting multiple experts define the features that they think are important, and then select features that can effectively improve efficiency. However, this will bring more heavy work. Therefore, it is necessary to select features objectively and automatically and realize vulnerability mining, so that experts can get rid of the tedious work of manually defining vulnerability detection features. Automated vulnerability feature selection in software metrics is a long-term process. At this stage, we need to rely on expert experience to improve the performance of vulnerability mining model.

Vulnerability Mining Model Based on Grammatical and Semantic Features. The vulnerability mining model based on grammatical and semantic features can be divided into grammar-based vulnerability mining model and semantic-based vulnerability mining model.

Grammar-based vulnerability mining model mainly uses AST to represent program grammar for security vulnerability mining. AST is a tree-like representation of the abstract grammatical structure of source code. Each node on the tree represents a structure in the source code. Literature [5, 6] combines AST with program analysis technology to exploit vulnerabilities and improve the accuracy of vulnerability mining. Literature [7] combines the abstract syntax tree, control flow graph and data dependency graph of the program to form a code property map to better characterize the structure information of the program. The automatic vulnerability mining is realized by traversing code attributes graph according to rules, and good results have been achieved. However, the compilation of rules relies heavily on security experts. Whether the combination of machine learning and code attributes graph can be used to mine vulnerabilities is a topic worth discussing.

Semantic-based vulnerability mining model mainly uses text mining technology to obtain semantic information in program source code. Text mining refers to the process of extracting valuable knowledge from text files and using this knowledge to better organize information. There are two main aspects in applying text mining to vulnerability mining. Firstly, it analyses the development documents or annotations of programs and excavates the possible vulnerabilities. According to the statistics in this paper, there is no research in this field. Literature [8] utilizes natural language technology to effectively mine vulnerabilities, and it is worth paying attention to whether natural language processing technology can be used to process development documents or annotations and conduct vulnerability mining accordingly. Secondly, text mining of source code is carried out to extract the effective information of source code to mine vulnerabilities.

N-gram semantic model can record collocation information between adjacent words in context, and infer sentence structure by the probability of N words appearing. In general, the larger N is, the better the semantic effect can be provided. However, when N > 3, it will cause feature explosion, which increases the burden of machine learning on data processing and limits the performance of the vulnerability mining model. In addition, only relying on word frequency statistics and N-gram semantic model vulnerability mining model only extracts rough semantic information from program source code, lacking in deep extraction of code semantic information, and introducing some unnecessary code elements, which reduces the effectiveness of the model. Word2Vec Semantic Model is a new type of Semantic Model commonly used in natural language processing in recent years. It can map words to a continuous real-valued vector, thus facilitating the digitization of natural language and automatically realizing the comparison of word semantics similarity, which provides a new idea for code similarity calculation. However, there are few studies on the application of the Word2Vec semantic model to vulnerability mining.

In addition, literature [9–11] used the concept of vulnerability extrapolation for vulnerability mining. Vulnerability extrapolation refers to the use of known vulnerability patterns to guide code audit and identify programs with similar patterns. These literatures, starting from the API mode, AST mode, data propagation mode, etc., combined with machine learning for vulnerability mining, have found some unknown vulnerabilities, which shows the effectiveness of their methods. However, the use of vulnerability extrapolation for vulnerability mining often requires professional security personnel to conduct in-depth research on known vulnerabilities, and determining the use model often requires in-depth analysis of certain types of vulnerabilities. At the same time, each vulnerability extrapolation method is only suitable for a certain mode, and can not detect other vulnerabilities, which has greater limitations.

Combination of Machine Learning and Programming Analysis. Literature [12–15] combines vulnerability mining model with program analysis technology to improve the performance of program analysis technology. Static analysis technology and dynamic analysis technology play a very important role in common vulnerability mining methods. However, both static analysis and dynamic analysis technology have corresponding defects. Using machine learning to alleviate or eliminate these defects and improve the performance of program analysis technology is a very good research direction.

Static stain analysis technology often requires large space overhead and high false alarm rate. Machine learning can process a large number of samples quickly. Combining machine learning to reduce false alarm rate is a feasible method. A key problem of symbolic execution is the problem of path execution space explosion. This paper determines the set of suspicious functions through machine learning. Using the set of suspicious functions to guide symbol execution can effectively reduce the number of paths, slow down the space explosion of path execution, and improve the performance of symbol execution. Fuzzing tests need to generate more efficient test samples to effectively trigger vulnerabilities, and machine learning can improve the effectiveness of Fuzzing tests. At the same time, using artificial intelligence technology can effectively improve the code coverage, and then effectively carry out vulnerability mining. It can be seen that machine learning can not only be used to mine vulnerabilities, but also its classification results can be used to guide program analysis technology to exploit vulnerabilities and improve the efficiency of vulnerability mining. Combining machine learning with program analysis technology to solve the problems of static analysis such as high false alarm, low accuracy, high dynamic analysis missed alarm rate and low code coverage provides a new way to alleviate the problems of large space overhead, difficulty in solving constraints and space explosion of path execution. Combining machine learning with static analysis technology and dynamic analysis technology for vulnerability mining is also a direction that can be explored.

Deep Learning Applied to Vulnerability Mining. Based on the empirical proof that deep learning has better performance than other "shallow" machine learning algorithms in image recognition and malware detection, many researchers try to introduce deep learning into the field of vulnerability mining. Deep learning can be applied to vulnerability mining in two aspects. On the one hand, deep learning model can be used for automatic selection of vulnerability features. In this aspect, deep learning can be combined with grammatical and semantic features for vulnerability mining. On the other hand, deep learning is used for vulnerability mining.

The use of deep learning for vulnerability mining needs to consider: (1) How to represent programs as a vector representation suitable for the deep learning model. Applications have rich features, such as AST, function calls, etc. These features can not be directly used as input of deep learning model. Therefore, these features need to be transformed into vector representation suitable for deep learning model. (2) Granularity of vulnerability mining. Different feature information has different granularity. At the same time, the granularity of vulnerability mining is related to vulnerability location. Fine-grained vulnerability mining can better locate vulnerabilities. (3) Whether it can mine multiple types of vulnerabilities. Different types of security vulnerabilities have different requirements for security researchers. Professional security researchers often perform deep mining for certain types of security vulnerabilities. It is a very interesting question whether deep learning algorithm can be used to mine multiple vulnerabilities at the same time. (4) How to choose a deep learning model. There are many kinds of deep learning models. How to build an appropriate deep learning model to obtain the best performance of vulnerability mining is also a problem.

At present, the application of deep learning to vulnerability mining is still in the preliminary stage. Firstly, literature [16, 17] shows that depth model can achieve better research performance than "shallow layer". There are few studies on how to improve the mining effect by combining software metrics or grammatical and semantic features with deep learning. Secondly, fine-grained vulnerability mining can identify the location of vulnerabilities, which undoubtedly expands the ability of vulnerability mining. Vulnerability positioning under the premise of ensuring the effect of vulnerability mining is also a research direction in the future. In addition, literature [18] adopted the deep learning model to mine two kinds of vulnerabilities. The experimental results show that deep learning can mine both kinds of vulnerabilities at the same time, but whether there is an upper limit of this ability does not give a clear answer. Finally, different deep learning models need to be compared. Different neural networks on the same data set will produce different mining effects, which may be related to the type of features selected, and there is still little research in this area. From this perspective, deep learning can improve the effect of "shallow" learning algorithm to a certain extent, and relying on the powerful ability of deep learning model to exploit vulnerability mining may become the main way of vulnerability mining in the future.

3.2 Intelligent Vulnerability Utilization

It is a complicated process to realize automatic generation of vulnerability utilization. Firstly, the location of vulnerabilities should be located, and the path of the exploitable points of input vulnerabilities should be quickly found by using symbolic execution technology. Secondly, the stack layout information of the actual running program can be obtained through dynamic monitoring process. Finally, the vulnerability utilization and verification can be generated by using the above information. SemFuzz framework is the first time to used NLP technology to extract relevant semantic information, such as key functions and variables from CVE and Git logs to guide the automatic generation of PoC, and at the same time expanded the types of processing vulnerabilities. The research shows that it is feasible to apply NLP to the automated generation of vulnerability utilization. In addition, the literature [19, 20] used machine learning algorithm to predict the exploitability of vulnerabilities from the aspects of code characteristics.

The artificial intelligence technology is introduced into the automatic generation field of vulnerability utilization. Firstly, the security vulnerability report is extracted to contain the software name, version number, involved functions, vulnerability type and other information related to the vulnerability. This information can preliminarily install software and roughly locate vulnerabilities. Secondly, the combination of artificial intelligence technology and programming technology can accelerate the analysis process. In fact, there are still some problems in automatic vulnerability generation, such as incomplete information of vulnerability, low utilization rate of information and low success rate of vulnerability generation. Major security websites and security forums provide information about configuration, software dependencies, etc., which can also assist in the automated generation of vulnerability utilization. This paper argues that the use of NLP technology to comprehensively deal with vulnerability-related information sources, so as to achieve automatic vulnerability generation, which will become a new method of automatic vulnerability utilization. Through the research on automatic generation of vulnerability utilization, it is of great significance to promote vulnerability mining and analysis.

3.3 Intelligent Vulnerability Assessment

Assessment of security vulnerabilities can help people establish standards to measure the severity of vulnerabilities and determine the priority of vulnerability repair. CVSS classifies the severity of vulnerabilities into three levels, which provides the basis for automating vulnerability assessments. At the same time, CVE vulnerability library can also provide more feature selection for machine learning application vulnerability assessment, such as data sets, vulnerability keywords, vulnerability description and so on.

Researchers extracted effective information from vulnerability reports for vulnerability assessment, and achieved certain results. However, these studies only focused on the information of the vulnerability report, and did not consider the statistics information of major security websites. In this paper, in addition to the above factors related to vulnerability reporting, we should also consider the application scope of the software. The wider the application scope of the software, the greater the impact it will have. Secondly, the complexity of the software should be considered. The more complex the software is, the more difficult it is to maintain and the longer the vulnerability lasts, the greater harm it will cause. Therefore, CVSS provides an open and free risk assessment system for the severity assessment of security vulnerabilities. However, the indicators are often complex and it is difficult to implement vulnerability assessment quickly. Combining natural language processing with machine learning to process vulnerability reports and other vulnerability information sources can quickly realize intelligent evaluation of security vulnerabilities.

3.4   Intelligent Vulnerability Repair

The repair of security vulnerabilities is the best way to reduce the loss of property due to exposure to security breaches. From the perspective of the security attack time in recent years, due to the fact that the update speed of the manufacturer could not catch up with the propagation speed of the vulnerability PoC, it failed to timely repair the vulnerability, thus causing great losses to computer users. To realize the automatic repair of bugs is helpful to make up the bugs quickly, reduce the loss of users' property and play a significant role in promoting the ecological security of the computer.

It is still difficult to apply machine learning to vulnerability automatic repair. Firstly, accurate location of vulnerability is a difficulty that needs to be solved urgently. Literature [21] studies complexity metrics and other metrics, such as whether process metrics can be used for vulnerability location. Secondly, the patching method of the vulnerability is more complicated. It is necessary to determine the type of trigger vulnerability, modify the program accordingly, and ensure that the patched program can run normally and other vulnerabilities will not be generated. Finally, because the current program analysis technology can not conduct a comprehensive analysis of the software, it also requires manual vulnerability repair. Ben et al. [22] identified eight categories of 65 factors that affect vulnerability repair time. Their work can improve the vulnerability repair process, allocate the vulnerability repair resources more reasonably, and improve the effectiveness of vulnerability repair. Some vulnerabilities such as integer overflow vulnerability and format string vulnerability can be patched by fault repair. It can be seen that manual vulnerability patching is still the mainstream method of vulnerability patching, and it requires researchers to invest a lot of research to realize the automation of vulnerability patching.

4   Conclusion

With the continuous development of artificial intelligence technology, the intelligent analysis of security vulnerabilities using artificial intelligence technology has become an important direction in the field of security research. This paper summarizes the application of artificial intelligence technology in security vulnerability research, summarizes its existing problems, and discusses its solutions in depth. Using the deep learning model to study security vulnerabilities will play a strong role in promoting, and the new vulnerability features will also play an active role in improving the accuracy of existing vulnerability mining models. At the same time, this paper also analyzes and discusses the problems of false negatives and false positives in vulnerability mining and vulnerability positioning, so as to improve the important role of artificial intelligence technology in security vulnerability research, which has a significant impact and significance on promoting intelligent vulnerability research.

Acknowledgement. This paper is supported by Hubei Provincial Education Department of Scientific Research Project of B2017420.

References

1. Zhang, Y.Q., Gong, Y.F., Wang, H.: Vulnerability identification and description specification. National Information Security Standardization Technical Committee
2. Mell, P., Scarfone, K., Romanosky, S.: Common vulnerability scoring system. IEEE Secur. Priv. **4**(6), 85–95 (2006)
3. Chowdhury, I., Zulkernine, M.: Using complexity, coupling and cohesion metrics as early indicators of vulnerabilities. J. Syst. Arch. **57**(3), 294–313 (2011)
4. Chowdhury, I., Zulkernine, M.: Can complexity, coupling and cohesion metrics be used as early indicators of vulnerabilities, pp. 1963–1969 (2010)
5. Meng, Q., Wen, S., Zhang, B.: Automatically discover vulnerability through similar functions, pp. 3657–3661 (2016)
6. Medeiros, I., Neves, N., Correia, M.: Detecting and removing web application vulnerabilities with static analysis and data mining. IEEE Trans. Reliab. **65**(1), 54–69 (2016)
7. Yamaguchi, F., Maier, A., Gascon, H.: Automatic inference of search patterns for taint-style vulnerabilities. In: 2015 IEEE Symposium on Security and Privacy (SP), pp. 797–812 (2015)
8. Wang, D., Lin, M., Zhang, H.: Detect related bugs from source code using bug information. Computer Software and Applications Conference (COMPSAC), pp. 228–237 (2010)
9. Yamaguchi, F., Lottmann, M., Rieck, K.: Generalized vulnerability extrapolation using abstract syntax trees. In: The 28th Annual Computer Security Applications Conference, pp. 359–368 (2012)
10. Yamaguchi, F., Wressnegger, C., Gascon, H.: Chucky: exposing missing checks in source code for vulnerability discovery. In: The 2013 ACM SIGSAC Conference on Computer & Communications Security, pp. 499–510 (2013)
11. Meng, Q., Wen, S., Zhang, B.: Automatically discover vulnerability through similar functions. In: Progress in Electromagnetic Research Symposium (PIERS), pp. 3657–3661 (2016)
12. Meng, Q., Zhang, B., Feng, C.: Detecting buffer boundary violations based on SVM. In: 3rd International Conference on Information Science and Control Engineering (ICISCE), pp. 313–316 (2016)
13. Heo, K., Oh, H., Yi, K.: Machine-learning-guided selectively unsound static analysis. In: The 39th International Conference on Software Engineering, pp. 519–529 (2017)
14. Grieco, G., Grinblat, G.L., Uzal, L.: Toward large-scale vulnerability discovery using machine learning. In: The Sixth ACM Conference on Data and Application Security and Privacy, pp. 85–96 (2016)
15. Godefroid, P., Peleg, H., Singh, R.: Learn&Fuzz: machine learning for input fuzzing. In: The 32nd IEEE/ACM International Conference on Automated Software Engineering, pp. 50–59 (2017)
16. Pang, Y., Xue, X., Wang, H.: Predicting vulnerable software components through deep neural network. In: The 2017 International Conference on Deep Learning Technologies, pp. 6–10. (2017)
17. Wu, F., Wang, J., Liu, J.: Vulnerability detection with deep learning. In: 3rd IEEE International Conference on Computer and Communications (ICCC), pp. 1298–1302 (2017)
18. Li, Z., Zou, D., Xu, S.: VulDeePecker: a deep learning-based system for vulnerability detection (2018)
19. Younis, A., Malaiya, Y., Anderson, C.: To fear or not to fear that is the question: code characteristics of a vulnerable function with an existing exploit. In: The Sixth ACM Conference on Data and Application Security and Privacy, pp. 97–104 (2016)

20. Allodi, L., Massacci, F.: A preliminary analysis of vulnerability scores for attacks in wild: the EKITS and SYM datasets. In: The 2012 ACM Workshop on Building Analysis Datasets and Gathering Experience Returns for Security, pp. 17–24 (2012)
21. Shin, Y., Meneely, A., Williams, L.: Evaluating complexity, code churn and developer activity metrics as indicators of software vulnerabilities. IEEE Trans. Softw. Eng. **37**(6), 772–787 (2011)
22. Ben, O.L., Chehrazi, G., Bodden, E.: Factors impacting the effort required to fix security vulnerabilities. In: International Information Security Conference, pp. 102–119 (2015)

Privacy Preservation Based on Key Attribute and Structure Generalization of Social Network for Medical Data Publication

Jie Su[1,2(✉)], Yi Cao[1,2], and Yuehui Chen[1,2]

[1] School of Information Science and Engineering,
University of Jinan, Jinan 250022, China
ise_suj@ujn.edu.cn
[2] Shandong Provincial Key Laboratory of Network Based
Intelligent Computing, University of Jinan, Jinan 250022, China

Abstract. Protection of privacy data published in health care field is the research to prevent the problem of disclosing sensitive data in healthcare. The Health Insurance Portability and Accountability Act (HIPPA) in the USA is the current practice regulation of privacy protection. Recently, however, the Institute of Medicine Committee on Health Research and the Privacy of Health Information concluded that HIPPA cannot adequately safeguard privacy and allow researchers to effectively use them for discoveries at the same time. Privacy protection method based on clustering is the process of developing methods and algorithm to ensure that the published data remains useful and protected. In this paper, we purposed an algorithm based on greedy clustering to group the data points according to the attributes and the connective information of the nodes in the published social network. During the procedure of clustering, we handled the loss of information, and evaluated the proposed approach in terms of classification accuracy and information loss rates on real medical datasets. The experimental results in our proposed approach show that the data privacy can be protected with less information loss. Finally we show a visualization process for the clustering.

Keywords: Privacy protection · Cluster · K-anonymity · Medical data

1 Introduction

In the United States, HIPAA requires that any entity must adhere to the Privacy Rule when sharing data collected in the context of clinical activities. However, the Privacy Rule can't entirely protect the patients' health records, partly because of the widespread use of social networks. People are always connected with each other through social networking tools such as Facebook, Twitter, and micro-blog. When the social network is released, we are trying to protect the sensitive information and social relations, while the attackers of the social network are trying to find the sensitive information in social network through data mining methods. A famous lawyer, Lori Andrews, published a book named "I know you and I know what you are doing" in 2015. This book pointed out the death of privacy in social networking era. According to a survey from a security

© Springer Nature Switzerland AG 2019
D.-S. Huang et al. (Eds.): ICIC 2019, LNCS 11643, pp. 388–399, 2019.
https://doi.org/10.1007/978-3-030-26763-6_38

software company, users in social network are more likely to encounter the loss of financial information, steal of their identity information, and the security threats for software. Besides these, integration and fusion of data based on linkage also results in privacy disclosure, which is demonstrated in the Fig. 1. The data source 1 is the anonymous published medical data. The attributes of gender, age, zip codes, and marriage status were anonymized. The data source 2 is the data published in social network, which also has the attributes of gender, age, zip codes, and marriage status. However, attackers can figure out the privacy information (such as the diagnosis), by integrating the data source 1 with data source 2.

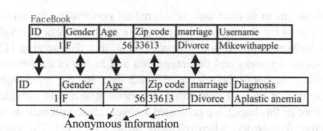

Data source2: open social network

Fig. 1. Privacy disclosure caused by integration and fusion

Therefore, technical efforts are highly encouraged to make published health data both privacy preserving and useful. Limited release technique selectively publishes data according to specific circumstances by using data generalization and anonymity techniques. For sensitive data, it publishes data with low accuracy or does not publish the data. The aim is to find a balance between data availability and risk of privacy leakage. It ensures that the released data has greater value, while the sensitive data privacy leaking risk is controlled within a reasonable range. These kinds of algorithms have high versatility and wide adaptability. However, the problem with these techniques is that published data will have a variant degree of information loss.

The existing algorithms of privacy protection are either based on interactive approaches or non-interactive approaches. In a non-interactive framework, the owner of the database first anonymizes the raw data and then releases the anonymized version for public usage [1]. Anonymity is the technique aiming to hidden or fuzzy data and data sources. This kind of techniques generally apply some methods to anonymize the data, such as suppression, generalization, analysis, slicing, and separation. Data privacy protection technology in social network is divided into 2 categories: clustering-based method and graph structure modification method. When we use clustering-based method, we divide the nodes and edges of the graph into super nodes and edges, and we hide the sensitive information of nodes and edges in their super classes. Graph structure modification method is similar to K-anonymous, which prevents attackers from using network structure as the background knowledge [2].

The data in social network contains large amounts of sensitive information such as link node attributes, node tags, and graph structure features. Attackers can use the active attack model and passive attack model to deduce and discover sensitive information. Social network is released in the form of graph. In a graph, each node is described with the entity attribute set. There is a unique identifier for each node. Due to the advantages of graphs, some researchers are using them as the tools to study the problem of safety protection [3]. A clustering approach for data and structural anonymity in social networks was discussed in [4]. Literature [5] introduced how to reserve the privacy of sensitive relationships in graph data. Literature [6] examined the problem of vertex re-identification from anonymized graphs. Literatures [7] showed that the true anonymous level of graphs was lower than that implied by measures such as k-anonymity.

The wide deployment of electronic health record systems has brought convenience to our lives. The need for sharing health data among multiple parties is evident in many areas, such as decision support, policy development, and data mining [1]. The widespread use of social networks and the integration and fusion of data based on linkage have posed privacy threats to the release of health data. Recent research has indicated that the present models are still vulnerable to various attacks and provide insufficient privacy protection. In this paper, we presented a novel privacy protection method based on non-interactive framework, when releasing healthy data [8]. The contributions of this article are:

(1) To prevent attacks on network structure, we provided a partition-based privacy models, which made use of background knowledge. A k-anonymous greedy clustering algorithm was proposed. In this algorithm, we defined a method of evaluating information loss. It significantly reduces the risk of privacy exposure and at the same time ensures data availability. Moreover, the algorithm is computationally efficient.

(2) The proposed privacy protection algorithm is based on a generalization technique. The graph theory is applied as the tool in this algorithm. The connections between nodes and nodes represent social background information in the graph, while the node attributes represent information of social individuals. Node links represent connections between social individuals. The method of evaluating information loss evaluates the balance between data availability and risk of privacy leakage.

(3) The experimental results demonstrate that our algorithm can dynamically control the clustering by evaluating the information loss while preserving privacy. The provided visualization method of the clustering demonstrated the complexity of the algorithm.

2   The Key Attribute of Medical Data in Social Network

When the data in the social network is released, each data set contains a plurality of tuples, and each tuple corresponds to a specific individual member in the society. Considering the attribute function and the main object of privacy protection, the attribute information is divided into three categories: The first is unique identifier attribute. Namely this attribute can uniquely identify a specific individual member of the community through identity, such as ID number, driver license number, or social security number SSN etc. This kind of attributes has been hidden before being released to the social network. The second one is the approximate identity attribute, which must be presented in a list of published data sheets and external data sources, such as a postal code, home address, etc. The third one is sensitive attribute, which is the secret attribute, such as the family, the income, or medical history. In the social network, the difficulty of privacy protection is increased because these three kinds of attribute information described above are often interrelated and mutually influenced. In the published and shared data table, people often directly remove unique identifies because the unique identifier attributes can clearly identify the individual members of the society with private information. However, when the open shared data tables are released, there are zip codes, genders, birthdays and other similar identities. An attacker can often link these data obtained by the approximate identity attributes and other channels, and can easily identify all the data of the individual member in the data. According to statistics, about 87% of the citizens in United States can be recognized by means of the identity attributes such as zip codes, genders, dates of birth, etc.

Because of the need for statistics, research, or some other purposes, hospitals need to release some of the patient's data. Table 1 is patient's medical information table, in which the sensitive attribute is {disease} and the approximate properties are {postal codes, ages}. Table 2 is the publicly available individual information data table.

Table 1. Patient medical information (privacy table)

	Postcode	Age	Disease
2	273212	33	Heart disease
3	273215	45	Heart disease
4	273203	23	Influenza
5	273211	29	Heart disease
6	273207	50	Cancer
7	273206	20	Influenza
8	273221	31	A-dis

Table 2. Disclosed personal information

	Name	Sex	Postcode	Age
1	Mary	Mail	273209	29
2	Alice	Fe-mail	273212	33
3	David	Mail	273211	29
4	Sam	Fe-mail	273207	50
5	Bob	Mail	273206	20
6	Angle	Fe-mail	273221	31

The current practice of preventing the leakage of the patient's privacy information primarily relies on policies and guidelines, such as HIPAA in the USA [9]. However, the result is that patients' health records are not absolutely protected while researchers cannot effectively use them for discoveries. Theoretically, the hospitals have deleted the unique identifiers of the individual information, and de-identified the unique identity attributes. It has protected the individual privacy to a certain extent. However, the attackers can still obtain individual privacy information by connecting the approximate identity attributes in Table 1 and the released relevant information in Table 2. For example, if the attacker wants to know Sam's disease, by using the information of his ZIP code and age, it may be inferred that Sam suffered from the disease "cancer". This is a simple link attack. To solve this problem, an attribute information-based clustering algorithm is used in our method.

During the process of social network releasing, trying to change the identification information of nodes or the structure information through adding or deleting edges is the basic theory of privacy protection. Because a large number of historically released data could be collected easily and information of nodes can be collected in a certain time when the destination node is inserted into the network, attacks can happen by recognizing the target node in the distribution network. Anonymous methods for preventing such attacks include K degree-anonymity method, K neighborhood anonymous method, and the anonymous method of k sub graph isomorphism [10–12]. These three kinds of methods need evaluation of information loss when reconstructing social network graph.

3 Construction of Anonymous Network for Medical Data Publication

3.1 Describe of Anonymous Network

K-anonymity is realized through using generalization technology and hiding technology. These two techniques are different from distortion, disturbance, and randomization because they can maintain the authenticity of the data. Attribute-based generalization method can reduce the damage to the original structure, and reduce information loss.

Network is expressed with a dynamic graph G, where $G = (V, E)$, and $|V| = N$. V is a set of nodes, and E is a set of edges, and N is the number of the nodes. Each node expresses an individual. There is an attribute set for each node, and the attribute set is expressed with AT. Clustering is to get an optimal partition. Each set has k nodes with similar attributes, while minimizing information loss.

We record the V with a ordered sequence $\{v_0, v_1, \ldots, v_N\}$. The adjacency relationship between nodes is represented by an adjacency matrix $A = \{a_{i,j}\}$, where $i = 1, 2, \ldots, N$ and $j = 1, 2, \ldots, N$. When there is direct connection between v_i and v_j, $a_{i,j} = 1$ and otherwise $a_{i,j} = 0$. The neighborhood can be retrieved. We use symmetric binary distance measurement for this matrix.

3.2   Definition of Distance

The distance between node v_i and node v_j is defined as (1).

$$\forall v_i \text{ and } \forall v_j, Dis(v_i, v_j) = d(v_i, v_j)/|d(v_i, v_j)| \tag{1}$$

Where $d(v_i, v_j)$ is the shortest path between nodes v_i and v_j.

The distance between nodes $v_i (v_i \notin Coll_k)$ and collection $Coll_k$ is defined as (2).

$$\forall v_j \in Coll_k, Dis(v_i, Coll_k) = \left(\sum\nolimits_{v_j \in Coll_k} Dis(v_i, v_j)\right)/|Coll_k| \tag{2}$$

The distance between nodes and the distance between nodes and a cluster are in the interval of [0, 1]. For the graph G, the node with the maximum degree is selected to be the center of new cluster, and $k - 1$ unallocated nodes with the minimize distance between nodes and the structure are selected to form the new cluster. The node distance is represented with the $Dis(v_i, v_j)$, and the structure distance is represented with $Dis(v_i, coll_k)$.

3.3   Construction of Anonymous Network

The anonymized network is created by using generalization information and edge intra-cluster generation. When social network is evolving, we first evaluate the change of structure in the published social network. Clustering process is based on two factors: the attributes of the nodes and structure information. We define two functions to control the clustering process according paper [10]. One is GIL that is used to evaluate generalization information loss [13], and the other is SIL that is used to evaluate structure information loss [14].

Definition 1. GIL

$$GIL(G, CL) = \frac{\sum_{j=1}^{m}(|Coll_j| \cdot (Attr(Coll_j, N) + Cate(Coll_j, C))}{n \cdot (p+q)}, \tag{3}$$

where $S = \{Coll_1, Coll_2, \cdots, Coll_m\}$ is a partition, $|Coll_j|$ is the cardinality of cluster $Coll_j$, $N = \{N_1, N_2, \cdots, N_p\}$ and $C = \{C_1, C_2, \cdots, C_q\}$ are the sets of numerical attributes and the sets of categorical attributes. $Attr(Coll_j, N)$ and $Cate(Coll_j, C)$ are the generalization information loss factors caused by generalizing attributes of the $Coll_j$ sets to $gen(Coll_j)$, and they are defined as:

$$Attr(Coll_j, N) = \sum\nolimits_{k=1}^{p} \frac{size(gen(Coll_j)[N_k])}{(max_{X \in N}(X[N_k]) - min_{X \in N}(X[N_k]))} \tag{4}$$

$$Cate(Coll_j, C) = \sum\nolimits_{k=1}^{q} \frac{height(M(gen(Coll_j)[C_k]))}{height(H_{C_k})} \tag{5}$$

where $\text{gen}(Coll_j)$ is the generalization information of cluster $Coll_j$, and it contains the values for each attribute, numerical or categorical, the most specific common generalized value for all the values of attributes from $Coll_j$ sets. $\text{gen}(Coll_j)[N_k]$ is the interval of $[\min\{X^1[N_k], \cdots, X^u[N_k]\}, \max\{X^1[N_k], \cdots, X^u[N_k]\}]$. The hierarchy attribute associated with the classification is defined as H_{C_k}, and $\text{gen}(Coll_j)[C_k]$ is defined as H_{C_k} of the recent ancestors, satisfying Eq. (6)

$$\text{size}\big(\text{gen}(Coll_j)[N_k]\big) = \max\{X^1[N_k], \cdots, X^u[N_k]\} - \min\{X^1[N_k], \cdots, X^u[N_k]\} \quad (6)$$

$M\big(\text{gen}(Coll_j)[C_k]\big)$ is H_{C_k} when $\text{gen}(Coll_j)[C_k]$ as the root of the sub layer, Height (H_{C_k}) is H_{C_k} sub layer height. Parameter α and β are set by the users and they are used to control the relative information importance of nodes and structure.

Definition 2. SIL

$$\text{SIL}(G, \text{CL}) = \frac{\sum_{j=1}^{m} \big(\text{intraSL}(Coll_j)\big) + \sum_{i=1}^{m} \sum_{j=i+1}^{m} \big(\text{interSL}(Coll_i, Coll_j)\big)}{(n \cdot (n-1)/4)} \quad (7)$$

SIL is based on the partition $\text{CL} = \{Coll_1, Coll_2, \cdots, Coll_m\}$, and includes all inter-cluster and intra-cluster structural information loss. $\sum_{j=1}^{m} \big(\text{intraSL}(Coll_j)\big)$ is the intra-cluster structural information loss and $\sum_{i=1}^{m} \sum_{j=i+1}^{m} \big(\text{interSL}(Coll_i, Coll_j)\big)$ is the inter-cluster structural information loss, satisfying (8) and (9)

$$\text{intraSL}(Coll_j) = 2 \cdot |E_{Coll_j}| \cdot \left(1 - |E_{Coll_j}| \Big/ \left(\binom{|Coll_j|}{2}\right)\right) \quad (8)$$

$$\text{interSL}(Coll_i, Coll_j) = 2 \cdot |E_{Coll_i, Coll_j}| \cdot \left(1 - |E_{Coll_i, Coll_j}| / (|Coll_i| \cdot |Coll_j|)\right) \quad (9)$$

By the conditions (10) we can find, when $|E_{Coll_i, Coll_j}| = \frac{(|Coll_i| \cdot |Coll_j|)}{2}$, the $Coll_i$ and $Coll_j$ class structure loss gets the maximum value $|Coll_i| \cdot |Coll_j|$. The maximum loss and anonymous graph construction process in the class structure is defined as the maximum loss formula (10) and (11).

$$\max\left(\sum_{j=1}^{m} \text{intraSL}(Coll_j)\right) = \sum_{j=1}^{m} \left(\frac{|Coll_j| \cdot (|Coll_j| - 1)}{4}\right)$$

$$= \frac{1}{4} \sum_{j=1}^{m} |Coll_j|^2 - \frac{1}{4} \left(\sum_{j=1}^{m} |Coll_j|\right) \quad (10)$$

$$\max\left(\sum_{i=1}^{m} \sum_{j=i+1}^{m} \big(\text{interSL}(Coll_i, Coll_j)\big)\right) = \sum_{i=1}^{m} \sum_{j=i+1}^{m} \left(\frac{|Coll_i| \cdot |Coll_j|}{4}\right)$$

$$(11)$$

SIL(G, CL) will be a value in interval $[0, 1]$.

From an initial social network G, we can obtain a partition $S = \{Coll_1, Coll_2, \cdots,$
$Coll_m\}$ using the graph anonymous cluster algorithm. $\{S_1, S_2, \cdots, S_m\}$ is the focus
node set corresponding to the cluster set $\{Coll_1, Coll_2, \cdots, Coll_m\}$ and $S_i =$
$[gen(Coll_i), (|Coll_i|, |E_{Coll_i}|)]$, where $(|Coll_i|, |E_{Coll_i}|)$ is the intra-cluster generalization
pair, $S_i \cap S_j = \emptyset$ and $i, j = 1..m, i \neq j$. The masked social network is defined as

$$G_m = (\{S_1, S_2, \cdots, S_m\}, \{S_1, S_2, \cdots, S_m\} \times \{S_1, S_2, \cdots, S_m\}) \tag{12}$$

In the above definition, $\forall e\ (v_k, v_p), v_k \in Coll_i$ and $v_p \in Coll_j$, there is a edge
$(S_i, S_j) \in \{S_1, S_2, \cdots, S_m\} \times \{S_1, S_2, \cdots, S_m\}$.

Graph anonymous cluster algorithm for social network is shown as the following.

Algorithm 1. Graph anonymous cluster algorithm

Input raw graph G, k, parameters α and β, initial cluster set S = $\emptyset$;

Output cluster set S = $\{Coll_1, Coll_2, \cdots, Coll_m\}$

1. m=|S|=0; // The number of clusters
2. n=|V|;
3. while(n $\neq$ 0) //n is the number of nodes not allocated to any cluster
       //travel the raw graph to find the seed for cluster
4.   Seed= v_i, where v_i is the node with maximum degree of d_i ;
5. $Coll_j$={ v_i }; // the cluster j with one node v_i
6.   V=V- v_i ;
7.   while(| $Coll_j$ |<k)
8. $MinLoss(\alpha \cdot GIL(G_j, S_j) + \beta \cdot D(v, Coll_j))$; //v is the node with minimal loss,
      GIL$(G_j, S_j)$is the   generalization information loss caused by clustering when v is
      added, G_j is the subgraph including $Coll_j$ and v, S_j is a partition of $Coll_j$ and v,
      $D(v, Coll_j)$ is the distance between v and cluster $Coll_j$;
9. $Coll_j = Coll_j \cup v$;
10.   n = n − |v|;
11.   if(n == 0)
12.   return;
13.   end if;
14.   end while;
15.   if(| $Coll_j$ |<k)
16. $\forall v \in Coll_j$, find the $Coll_p$, p $\neq$ j, where $Coll_p$ has the minimal loss when add v to
      $Coll_p$;
17. $Coll_p = Coll_p \cup v$;
18.   else
19.   S = S $\cup \{Coll_p\}$;
20.   m=m+1;
21.   end if;
22.   end while.

---

4 Experiments

We sampled a part data from disclosed network, which is shown as in Fig. 2.

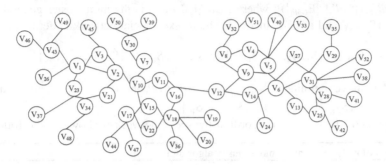

Fig. 2. Part data of networks

The medical data used for cancer diagnosis have 6 attributes, ID, Gender, Age, Zip code, Marriage Status and Diagnosis. The unique identifiers such as driver license and SSN have been removed. However, there are still some quasi-identifiers such as age, gender, zip code, marriage status. To protect the privacy of patients, anonymous method is used. The attribute sets can be denoted as $Al = \{N_1, C_1, C_2, C_3\}$, where $P = 1, Q = 3, N_1 = $ Age. C_1, C_2 and C_3 are hierarchical structure of attribute Gender, marriage, Zip code respectively. $\{C_1, C_2, C_3\} = \{\{F, M\}, \{Marrige, Single, Divorce\}$ $\{\{32556 : 32868\}, \{33102 : 33709\}, \{34565 : 34813\}, \{75211 : 75868\}\}, \}.$

Figure 3 shows the cluster result using our algorithm, where $k = 4$ and $a = 0.5$.

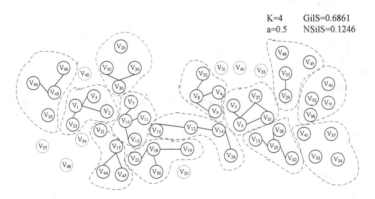

Fig. 3. The clustering result using our algorithm

Figure 4(a) shows the information loss caused by generalization and Fig. 4(b) shows the structural information losses for the anonymous cluster, where the k is 2, 8, 14, 20, 26 respectively and parameter a is 0, 0.5, 1 respectively. When the parameter *a* is selected, the bigger the *k*, the more the information loss caused by generalization. When the parameter *k* is selected, the smaller the parameter a, the more the information loss caused by generalization. When the parameter *a* is selected, the bigger the *k*, the more the structural information loss.

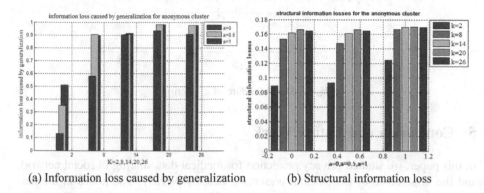

(a) Information loss caused by generalization   (b) Structural information loss

Fig. 4. Evaluation of loss

The clustering result is shown as Fig. 5. (a) is the result of clustering when a = 0 and *k* = 2. (b) is the result of clustering when a = 0.5 and *k* = 8.

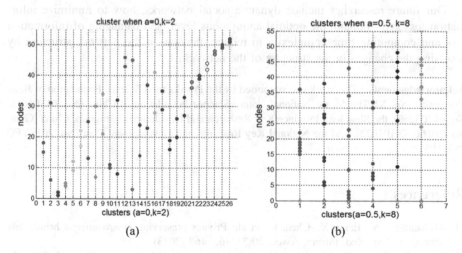

(a)   (b)

Fig. 5. The results of clustering

The procedure of clustering for the sub-network of social network shown in Fig. 2 is demonstrated in Fig. 6, where a = 0.5 and *k* = 26.

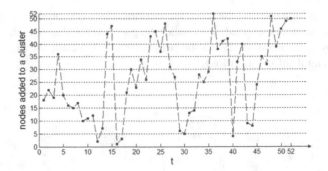

Fig. 6. The procedure of clustering.

5   Conclusion and Future Work

In this paper, we studied privacy protection for medical data sharing in social network and the importance of attributes in preserving healthy privacy. The nodes in the network were classified according to the relationship among the attributes. Then a K-anonymous method based on attributes clustering was provided, which estimated the information loss during privacy preservation process. Graphic methods were used in our work. Information loss estimation algorithm for anonymous clustering method in social network is proposed to deal with the information loss in the reconstruction of anonymous graphs.

Our future researches include dynamic social networks, how to minimize information loss and to obtain the optimal anonymous level, and balancing of information loss and computing time complexity to reduce damage on the network structure by assessing the changes in the structure of the network.

Acknowledgements. This work was supported by the Postdoctoral Science Foundation of Jinan University (No. XBS1905), the National Nature Science Foundation of China (No. 61305015, No. 61203269), the Shandong Province Key Research and Development Program, China (Grant No. 2016GGX101022), and the National Key Research and Development Plan (No. 2018YFC 0831105).

References

1. Mohammed, N., Jiang, X., Chen, R., et al.: Privacy-preserving heterogeneous health data sharing. J. Am. Med. Inform. Assoc. **20**(3), 462–469 (2013)
2. Meng, X., Zhang, X.: Big data privacy management. J. Comput. Res. Dev. **52**, 265–281 (2015)
3. Luo, Z.-Y., You, B., Xu, J.-Z., Liang, Y.: Automatic recognition model of intrusive intention based on three layers attack graph. J. Jilin Univ. **44**(5), 1392–1397 (2014)
4. Campan, A., Traian, M.: A clustering approach for data and structural anonymity in social networks. In: Privacy, Security, and Trust in KDD Workshop (PinKDD), pp. 33–54 (2008)

5. Zheleva, E., Getoor, L.: Preserving the privacy of sensitive relationships in graph data. In: Bonchi, F., Ferrari, E., Malin, B., Saygin, Y. (eds.) PInKDD 2007. LNCS, vol. 4890, pp. 153–171. Springer, Heidelberg (2008). https://doi.org/10.1007/978-3-540-78478-4_9

6. Aggarwal, C.C., Li, Y., Yu, P.S.: On the hardness of graph anonymization, pp. 1002–1007 (2011)

7. Campan, A., Truta, T.M.: Data and structural k -anonymity in social networks. In: Aggarwal, C. (ed.) Social Network Data Analytics. LNCS, vol. 5456, pp. 33–54. Springer, Heidelberg (2008). https://doi.org/10.1007/978-3-642-01718-6_4

8. Fung, B.C.M., Wang, K., Chen, R., et al.: Privacy-preserving data publishing: a survey of recent developments. ACM Comput. Surv. **42**(4), 2623–2627 (2010)

9. Standards for privacy of individually identifiable health information. Final Rule, 45 CFR parts 160 and 164. http://www.hhs.gov/ocr/privacy/hipaa/administrative/privacyrule/adminsimpregtext.pdf. Accessed 20 Feb 2012

10. Liu, K., Terzi, E.: Towards identity anonymization on graphs. In: Proceedings of the 2008 ACM SIGMOD International Conference on Management of Data, pp. 93–106. ACM (2008)

11. Cheng, J., Fu, A.W., Liu, J.: K-isomorphism: privacy preserving network publication against structural attacks. In: Proceedings of the 2010 ACM SIGMOD International Conference on Management of data, pp. 459–470. ACM (2016)

12. Hay, M., Miklau, G., Jensen, D., et al.: Resisting structural re-identification in anonymized social networks. VLDB J. **19**(6), 97–823 (2010)

13. Byun, J.-W., Kamra, A., Bertino, E., Li, N.: Efficient *k*-anonymization using clustering techniques. In: Kotagiri, R., Krishna, P.R., Mohania, M., Nantajeewarawat, E. (eds.) DASFAA 2007. LNCS, vol. 4443, pp. 188–200. Springer, Heidelberg (2007). https://doi.org/10.1007/978-3-540-71703-4_18

14. Han, J., Pei, J., Kamber, M.: Data Mining: Concepts and Techniques. Elsevier, Amsterdam (1999)

EmoSens – The Proposal of System for Recognition of Emotion with SDK Affectiva and Various Sensors

Martin Magdin[✉], Michal Kohútek, Štefan Koprda,
and Zoltán Balogh

Department of Computer Science, Faculty of Natural Science,
Constantine the Philosopher University in Nitra,
Tr. Andreja Hlinku 1, 949 74 Nitra, Slovakia
mmagdin@ukf.sk

Abstract. The face recognition and subject emotion classification is also an important area of current studies in psychology, with many potential uses and applications. Correctly assessing and recognizing subject's emotion can lead to better understanding its behavior. However the used methods in present often have had a multitude of disadvantages. Therefore, we have set upon creating a solution that is modular and invariant from surrounding light conditions, which in the past represented the biggest problem. We can do so by using an array of data resources (localization of eye pupil) and data from sensors that complement each other, diminishing their disadvantages and reinforcing confidence. These data we can measure using to human physiological properties – pulse (heart rate sensor) and skin response (GSR). To verify of our proposed solution, we realized a simple experiment (displaying the various video clips to 50 participants). This experiment showed that the using SDK Affdex and the particular sensors, we achieved greater classification success rate (90.79%) than with alone SDK Affdex (85.04%).

Keywords: Emotional state · Sensors · Affectiva · Valence · Classification

1 Introduction

Recognition and emotion classification is an important object of studies in today's psychology, with many potential uses and applications [1]. Previous implementations of emotion recognition technology often have had a multitude of disadvantages, which prohibited its daily and widespread usage. Therefore, we have set upon creating a solution that is modular, reasonable to wear for prolonged durations of time and still maintains a degree of reliability in captured data. We can do so by using an array of data resources that complement each other, diminishing their disadvantages and reinforcing confidence.

The rest of the paper is structured as follows: Sect. 2 contains the related work of emotional state detection, extraction, and classification which consists of historical development, analysis of similar research and current approaches in the examined field. Section 3 contains the materials and methods of technical and software solutions that

© Springer Nature Switzerland AG 2019
D.-S. Huang et al. (Eds.): ICIC 2019, LNCS 11643, pp. 400–411, 2019.
https://doi.org/10.1007/978-3-030-26763-6_39

influence the process of the emotional state classification. Subsequently, the last section contains the conclusion and future work. We have designed and realized this solution because we must not to rely only on the detection of emotional states that are characterized by external expression (change of facial expression). In the present it is important also unearth the internal states that cause these emotional states. According to [1], we can then better understand the student and adapt the learning process to his needs.

2 Related Work

In 2015 was published a paper on a system using EEG (Electroen-cephalography) signals as input (electrophysiological monitoring method to record electrical activity of the brain). They observed better results for clustering of EEG and ECG (Electrocardiography) data stream (process of producing an electrocardiogram - a graph of voltage versus time - of the electrical activity of the heart using electrodes placed on the skin) [2]. The main difference in their approach is that they first applied EMD (Empirical Mode Decomposition) strategy to split EEG signals into a series of intrinsic mode functions, which were then fed as sample entropies and as feature vectors into SVM (Support Vector Machine) classifier for testing and training. With this approach, they claim to have reached accuracy levels of 94.98% for binary-class tasks and 93.20% for the multi-class task on DEAP database (A Database for Emotion Analysis using Physiological Signals) [3]. Also in 2016, was demonstrated an emotional recognition technique using functional MRI (Magnetic Resonance Imaging) with results, that brain-based models may, in future, allow us deeper understanding and assessing emotional status in clinical settings, particularly in individuals incapable of providing self-report of their own emotional experience [4].

Another indicator of the subject's emotional state is the heartbeat. In 2013 was shown compelling data gathering by means of ECG and shown differences in ECG signal in subjects in chosen emotional states, limited only to sadness, fear and anger [5]. A more complex approach was taken by researchers at the University of Calabria in collaboration with Washington State University. Instead of applying a single or a few sensors to study physiological states, they used a whole BSN (Body Sensor Network, specialized Wireless Sensor Network applied to the whole human body) such networks can include accelerometers, gyroscopes, pressure sensors for body movements and applied forces, skin/chest electrodes (for electrocardiogram (ECG), electromyogram (EMG), galvanic skin response (GSR), and electrical impedance plethysmography (EIP)), (PPG) sensors, microphones (for voice, ambient, and heart sounds), scalp-placed electrodes for electroencephalogram (EEG) [6]. Albeit they were not focusing primarily on emotion recognition, this survey shows consequential advancement in the state-of-the-art body data collection, especially in the data fusion techniques. A similar approach using a variety of sensors and data sources was also taken by Mosciano to reasonably accurately classify the two dimensions of affect both normal and simulated critical working conditions [7].

An interesting approach to emotion detection and classification is based upon speech patterns and variations and are better suited for emotions, which are otherwise hard to physiologically measure, such as sadness and joy. One study shows, that speech signal and feature distances of letters and words vary depending on the mood and emotional state of the subject [8].

In terms of evaluating arousal, respiration-based emotion recognition shows promise. A study in China showed, that using respiration data to evaluate valence and arousal levels of Russel theory, they reached classification accuracy of valence and arousal at 73.06% and 80.78%, respectively [9].

A study on the thermal behavior of anger, disgust, fear, joy, and sadness was carried out in 2014. When an emotion occurs a change in facial temperature appears due to the blood flow that the body emits through blood vessels in the subcutaneous area [10]. For example, research focused on the emotion of joy, in other words, when a subject is smiling, it has been found that the temperature of the nose and forehead decreases during this event [11]. Biomedical thermal images of the facial expressions of 44 subjects were captured experiencing the five studied emotions, with results of this test at 89.9% success rate [12].

Another novel approach represents created a software touch keyboard that was installed on Android smartphones, which they have been collecting sensor data while users were typing on the keyboard. As they have been typing, he or she were prompted to indicate their current emotional state, which then tagged the sensor data collected for the particular user. Afterward, the data was classified by multiple machine learning algorithms to find the best classification method [13].

One approach seems to be very promising, especially due to its implementation in commercial solutions and services. One such research has used Microsoft Kinect for 3D face modeling with a goal to computationally recognize facial expressions of seven basic emotional states: neutral, joy, surprise, anger, sadness, fear and disgust. The subjects of the experiment were six men aged 26–50 years, told to mimic expressions shown on the screen. Researchers used nearest neighbor classifier (3-NN) and two-layer neural network classifier (MLP) with 7 neurons in the hidden layer with output accuracy rate of 96% for a random division of data and 73% for "natural" division of data [14].

One of the more recent (and less explored) approaches taken in affective computing is gaze and pupil tracking. This builds on classic theories [15, 16] and tries to implement eye-tracking techniques to investigate the emotional state and behavior of subjects. For example, eye fixation in some direction related to head inclination, depending on a particular experience, may indicate embarrassment, pride or fear [17]. Nowadays, the eye fixation and pupil localization research are mostly applied to the eye tracking are, where problems related to neuromarketing, reader literacy, and others are being solved. However, research into emotional facial expressions as dynamic multimodal behavioral patterns also points to some new, interesting and unanswered questions [18]. Over time, it has been found that the way in which scientists studied human emotions in laboratories was wrong [19]. Emotions studied under laboratory conditions have been instructed and, to a large extent, induced. Often, these emotional expressions for classification databases were created by actors and thus fake "laboratory" stimuli were being created, which did not reflect emotional states during various events in real life. That is why not only other classifications were sought but, in particular, ways of undisturbed observation of human behavior in real life situations.

For example, a low-cost prototype of a headset with a scene camera (left) and eye camera and IR LED (right) was created [20]. A similar system based upon the localization of pupils, although designed to identify driver's fatigue was conducted by Kim [21]. The principle of pupil localization and capturing the front view (surrounding world) can also be used in games or for computer graphics applications [22]. The next researchers [23] examined the ability to use Google Glass with the QTM sensor (Affectiva Inc.) through Bluetooth. In this way is possible to realize continuous measurement and visualization of the captured emotional states. They did not prioritize capturing the pupil (although the Google glass allowed for it) but focused on other physiological properties of humans (body temperature, blood pressure, heart rate, brain waves, etc.) to determine their emotional state. They based their research on the work of Picard, who was a co-author of a team that in 1999 wrote Expression Glasses: A Wearable Device for Facial Expression Recognition [24]. They were successful in distinguishing between emotions, albeit having to limit them from the core seven to four. The accuracy of their recognition ranged in the interval from 80 to 90% [25].

2.1   Current Approaches to Face Recognition and Emotion Classification

Currently consequently, the number of dependable SDK (Software Development Kit) and API (Application programming interface) grows rapidly and these contains the methods and algorithms, which was previously proposed and successfully used for the detection, extraction and classification phases.

Emotient has developed the FACET SDK. This SDK allows the to track and analyze the emotional responses of users in real-time, detecting and tracking expressions of primary emotion, as well as overall positive, negative and neutral sentiments and blended composites of two or more emotions. In 2016 Emotient got acquired by Apple and their website is no longer online.

Eyeris EmoVu - it's a closed-source, multi-platform SDK and API. Their pricing starts with a free license that covers the analysis of 500 frames per month. It's declared various features (e.g. Face and Emotion Recognition, Gender and Age Recognition, Facial Tracker, Engagement and Mood metrics). EmoVu's main drawback is the lack of clear information about the SDK availability since they only mention it on their website in unclear terms and the pricing only mentions API.

InSight SDK is facial recognition C++ toolbox developed by Sightcorp in collaboration with the University of Amsterdam (Theo Gevers, Roberto Valenti). It boasts a large set of features, apart from face detection and emotion recognition, it uncovers gaze estimation, head pose estimation, and motion tracking features. InSight does not provide academic trials, therefore we could not evaluate their performance. The aim of the authors is the implementation of this SDK to the virtual reality environment of Second Life.

Affectiva by 2018, they analyzed over 6 million faces from 87 countries. They have built their massive data set of facial expressions by analyzing millions of face videos, of people engaged in various activities, such as watching media content (i.e., ads, movie trailers, television shows, and online viral campaigns), driving cars, people in conversational interactions. Those images cover different lighting conditions, both genders, various poses of participants, etc. Via the SDK, the application can access and read multiple metrics (7 emotion metrics, 20 facial expression metrics, 13 emojis and 4 appearance metrics). Apart from the 7 emotional states, the SDK surfaces also the Engagement - a measure of facial muscle activation that illustrates the subject's expressiveness. The range of values is from 0 to 100. SDK further it includes also Valence metric. The Valence metric is a measure of the positive or negative nature of the recorded person's experience. The range of values is from −100 to 100. Affectiva's mapping of expressions onto emotions builds on EMFACS mapping, developed by Friesen and Ekman [26].

3 Materials and Methods

In this paper, we present our solution, it consists of two parts: technical (hardware) and software. From the point of view of the technical solution, it is the use of previously known components in the form of several sensors which can measure human physiological response - heart rate sensors and galvanic skin response (GSR). These sensors are combined with special glasses containing 3 cameras front view camera (capturing what the subject's gaze is looking at), IR camera for determining right pupil location and the IR camera for determining left pupil location.

As we've demonstrated, there are a great many approaches to take and physiological markers to explore. Due to the nature of our desired use-case, we've decided to omit those physiological signs and pertaining sensors that would excessively constrain and disturb the user. Therefore, we did not use EEG, fMRI scanning, neither thermal imaging, neither speech recognition. For our body sensors, we have chosen a simple, inexpensive optical heart rate sensor, GSR sensor and Arduino to read and resend the collected data. Furthermore, we used a Pupil headset (https://pupil-labs.com) with two high-speed (200 Hz) infrared cameras and one 1920 × 1080 "world" camera connected together to a computer using USB-A to USB-C connector. To provide referential emotion values, we used a regular 720p web camera and processed the camera feed with modified Affdex sample OpenCV application. The research has been done using two different computers: Desktop workstation (hexa-core AMD FX-6300 clocked at 4.0 GHz, 8 GB of RAM and Radeon 7750 GPU) and laptop (quad-core Intel Core i7-4770HQ, 16 GB of RAM and NVidia 860 M GPU). We have also tried to run the modified Affdex sample application on Raspberry Pi 3B with official IR camera, however, we found out, that the single board computer was greatly lacking computing power and would freeze, hang and drop frames with even one face detected on the video feed. Powerful hardware was needed not only for the use of Affectiva SDK but also for the Pupil Capture software, supplied by the manufacturer of our headset. These two applications taxed both our computers close to peak load, although since our EmoSens (The name of own programmed application) data collection application requires very few resources; it did not negatively impact our experiments.

The heart rate data was gathered by Pulse Sensor Amped SEN-11574, a plug-and-play heart rate sensor for Arduino and Raspberry Pi. We did find out, that it requires tight strapping to subject's skin, otherwise, the data collected has been inconsistent with reality. The Galvanic Skin Response data was collected using Groove GSR sensor. The Groove GSR sensor we connected straight to Arduino's GPIO pins. Both of these sensors were sewn into a fingerless glove and wired to Arduino Due connected via USB cable to computer. In the realization phase of this technical solution, we are using out from similarly oriented research and technical solutions [27–30].

The software solution is the usage and modification (additional programming) some applications in the form of:

1. Application using Affdex SDK by Affectiva for classification of emotional states,
2. Software for the headset to localize the pupils,
3. Programming our own application to determine the valence of emotional states while wearing the heart rate and the GSR sensors.

Both development and experiments took place on computers running Ubuntu 16.04. To create the data collection software, we have used the Qt5 application framework. The modified Affdex webcam application is written in C++, albeit due to the incompatibilities with newer compilers was compiled in GNU GCC 4.8. This leads us to the unexpected setback that we came across. Both Affectiva and Pupil use OpenCV 2.4, but Affectiva forked its version and when building with CMake on a recent operating system, it will either fail or overwrite shared libraries, thus breaking QT5 and Pupil. Since Affectiva's license agreement prohibits its integration with a copyleft open source licensed projects we have modified the sample OpenCV application to send out data serialized in message pack over ZeroMQ [31, 32]. This has added benefit in that our project is, therefore, modular and can use any and all face or other emotion recognition SDK with little to no changes to our source code. The message pack by design solves the problem of interprocess communication, especially if the processes are written in different languages, or are even running on different platforms. For our project, we opted to use the Publish-Subscribe pattern, with Pupil Capture and Affectiva being the Publishers and our application serving as a Subscriber to their messages serialized with MessagePack. For visualization of collected data, we have used two QT libraries (the QtCharts library and the QCustomPlot) for plotting and data visualization as vectorized PDF files and rasterized pictures in PNG, JPG and BMP.

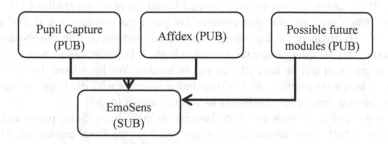

Fig. 1. Simplified diagram of the data flow

In Fig. 1 is shown the block diagram of the EmoSens application. After the start of the application, the main window is shown. Here, the user can choose whether to collect data or to visualize previously collected data. The QLineEdit on the right is auto-filled with the computer's IP address. If a user is running Pupil Capture and Affectiva application on another computer on the local area network, he or she can change the IP address of the server. When opened, the Data Collection Dialog polls the selected IP by sending a request at port 5020, where Pupil Capture is listening. Since ZeroMQ can send millions of messages per second, we decided to omit most of them and to save only one every 50 ms. The dialog runs a timer and every 50 ms will save the current state of pupils, heart rate, galvanic skin resistance and facial expressions (Fig. 2).

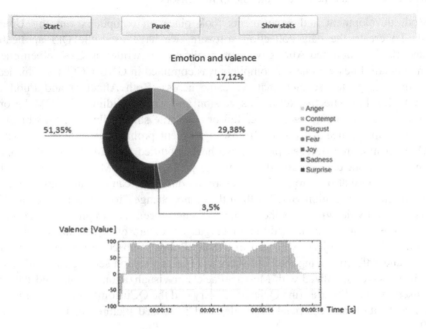

Fig. 2. Data collection in progress

The 50 ms sampling rate was determined based on previous studies [33], which show that when the gaze position changes the pupil can refocus in a 0.39-2 s time interval (0.5 Hz frequency), depending on the focal distance of the observed object. Even though this sampling rate may seem too high, it is preferable to collect a larger amount of data that can be later filtered out as needed. We have used the Pupil Labs software to locate the pupils, which is distributed together with the Pupil headset. The pupil localization can be accomplished in several ways [34, 35].

As shown in Fig. 2, there are three buttons on this screen. Start, pause and show stats. The pie chart shows current emotion derived from the facial expression. The last chart on the screen shows the subject's emotion valence.

The User can, at any time, use the "show stats" button to reveal the average or current ratio of emotions up until the push of the button, represented as a bar graph. All addictions we can export as a chart to vector PDF or rasterized image file such as PNG or JPEG.

4   Results - Calibration of EmoSens

Using the supplied software, we can only locate the pupils, but not classify emotions. In order to classify emotional states, we launched the Affdex process in the background. Affectiva's Affdex SDK is primarily designed for facial recognition and subsequent classification of the emotional state using a webcam. Since Affdex uses SVM (Support Vector Machine), the classification of two different symptoms was performed using the Affdex SDK. At the same time, we compared the value of valence from Affdex to the valence value obtained from the Heart Rate and Galvanic Skin Response sensors. The value of emotion valence is of great importance. In the previous section, we have indicated that we can also determine the value of emotional state changes (valence) from Heart Rate and Galvanic Skin Response. Affdex also works with this value. By constantly comparing values from sensors to valence values from Affectiva, we can determine which emotions are real and which have been caused by ambient noise (for example, incorrect grip or sensor fixation). A precondition for the realization of this solution was the fact, that several authors confirmed our assumption - emotions can manifest through the eyes [25, 34]. That's why, from the data gained by Affdex, we've filtered out those unrelated to the pupils. This solution enabled us to classify individual emotional states in our own way.

The system calibration was realized according to the methodology Maskeliunas and Raudonis [25]. For our experiment, we have gathered 50 participants, with equal sex ration. The participants were aged 25–65 years, with various education background and upbringing. The experiment we've conducted consisted of having the participant watch a 4-minute collection of videos in 7 categories (Anger, Contempt, Disgust, Fear, Joy, Sadness, Surprise), depending on the emotion, they were supposed to induce. Before the experiment, we have explained to the participants the categories and that they should act naturally. During the experiment, they were told not to look around himself, concentrating on the screen of the laptop (Fig. 3). The whole experience was observed and their behavior was documented with hand-written notes.

Fig. 3. The experiment

The first part of the shown video was an array of amusing videos. It was a collection of various popular "fail" clips on Youtube. The second part, disgust, was a long
clip of an epidermoid cyst being extracted by a dermatologist. The third part was a
scary video clip of a ghost jumping in the window of a car in a snowstorm. The last
segment was an erotic clip. The segments were divided by a few seconds of a blank
screen to allow participants' emotion to return to neutral. After the experiment, we have
questioned the participants about their feelings and emotions. We analyzed this video
clip by using a psychologist. The psychologist provided us a detailed explanation of
each scene and the predicted emotion. After conducting the experiment, we were
received with a lot of data. For each tested participant, we focused on Gaze position,
Pupil diameter, Biometric information and Valence.

If we filtered these values and use only data from Affdex, we have achieved in the
experiment the success rate of classification 85.04%. On the bases of those data which
we in real time compared with values from Affdex, we created a graph of current
emotional state or also complete emotion graph (Fig. 4). This complete emotion graph
contains all classified emotion during the experiment, data from sensors, gaze position,
pupil diameter, and valence. On the basis of evaluation of the individual parameters
(expected emotion versus real emotion), we have achieved the value of the system's
average success rate. The total average percentage of success rate of our designed
system EmoSens in emotional recognition is 90.79%.

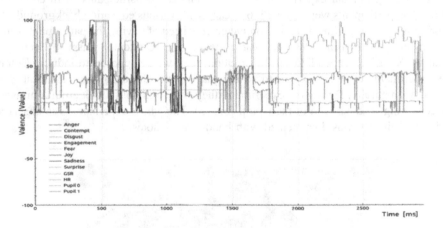

Fig. 4. Example of complete emotion graph

Today, it is not important to classify emotional status on the basis of one parameter
(by extracting features of the face) but various parameters (GSR, EEG, ECG and pupils
localization) for the most relevant information and the subsequent classification of the
emotional states. From the perspective of psychology [1], it is very important that we
do not focused only on the external features of the emotional state that we are able to
capture through the web camera, but also on the detection of internal states that subsequently cause specific emotions. We can only determine internal states based on
sensors such as GSR, EEG or ECG. However, if we added to them the localization of

the pupils, we obtain an extremely powerful tool to detect and classify emotional states that would otherwise be hidden. Although the difference is only 5.75%, we assume that the difference could be even greater for a larger sample of participants.

5 Conclusion

Currently, there are different technical solutions as well as methods by which it is possible to classify the emotional state of the user. Each of these approaches uses a different way of gaining and processing data. Ultimately, however, there is a point where all the solutions meet - valence, the value which represents the magnitude of the change in the emotional state. We have also used this fact in our proposed solution while collecting and comparing data based on different approaches. The first approach was to determine emotional state and valence using GSR and heart rate sensors. The second approach was capturing subject's facial expressions, extracting individual facial features using multi-point mask and subsequent classification of emotional state as well as determining valence by tools provided in Affdex SDK. By comparing the valence values we have been able to determine which emotional states are classified correctly. At the same time, we have also applied the third approach - capturing the position of pupils. Based on the data we've obtained from the exact location of pupils and linking the data from the previous two approaches we have classified our solution using Pupil headset. In further research, we want to focus on determining the impact of individual sensors and the pupil headset in relation to the overall outcome of the classification phase.

Acknowledgments. This paper was created with the financial support of the projects: 1. Research and Innovation for the project Fake news on the Internet - identification, content analysis, emotions (code: NFP313010T527). 2. The project UGA: Gathering data on understanding of study materials based upon the students' pupil movement (code: VII/9/2019). 3. The project KEGA 036UKF-4/2019, Adaptation of the learning process using sensor networks and the Internet of Things.

References

1. Makransky, G., Terkildsen, T., Mayer, R.: Role of subjective and objective measures of cognitive processing during learning in explaining the spatial contiguity effect. Learn. Instr. **61**, 23–34 (2019). https://doi.org/10.1016/j.learninstruc.2018.12.001
2. Lahane, P., Kumar Sangaiah, A.: An approach to EEG based emotion recognition and classification using kernel density estimation. Pap. Present. Procedia Comput. Sci. **48**(C) 574–581 (2015). https://doi.org/10.1016/j.procs.2015.04.138
3. Zhang, Y., Ji, X., Zhang, S.: An approach to EEG-based emotion recognition using combined feature extraction method. Neurosci. Lett. **633**, 152–157 (2016). https://doi.org/10.1016/j.neulet.2016.09.037
4. Kragel, P.A., Knodt, A.R., Hariri, A.R., LaBar, K.S.: Decoding spontaneous emotional states in the human brain. PLoS Biol. **14**(9) (2016). https://doi.org/10.1371/journal.pbio.2000106

5. Baby, S.T., Vanitha, L.: Emotion detection in human beings using ECG signals. Int. J. Eng. Trends Technol. (IJETT) **4**(5), 1337–1342 (2013)
6. Gravina, R., Alinia, P., Ghasemzadeh, H., Fortino, G.: Multi-sensor fusion in body sensor networks: state-of-the-art and research challenges. Inf. Fusion **35**, 1339–1351 (2017). https://doi.org/10.1016/j.inffus.2016.09.005
7. Mosciano, F., Mencattini, A., Ringeval, F., Schuller, B., Martinelli, E., Di Natale, C.: An array of physical sensors and an adaptive regression strategy for emotion recognition in a noisy scenario. Sens. Actuators A: Phys. **267**, 48–59 (2017). https://doi.org/10.1016/j.sna.2017.09.056
8. Davletcharova, A., Sugathan, S., Abraham, B., James, A.P.: Detection and analysis of emotion from speech signals. Pap. Present. Procedia Comput. Sci. **58**, 91–96 (2015). https://doi.org/10.1016/j.procs.2015.08.032
9. Zhang, Q., Chen, X., Zhan, Q., Yang, T., Xia, S.: Respiration-based emotion recognition with deep learning. Comput. Ind. **92–93**, 84–90 (2017). https://doi.org/10.1016/j.compind.2017.04.005
10. Ioannou, S., Gallese, V., Merla, A.: Thermal infrared imaging in psychophysiology: potentialities and limits. Psychophysiology **51**(10), 951–963 (2014). https://doi.org/10.1111/psyp.12243
11. Salazar-López, E., et al.: The mental and subjective skin: emotion, empathy, feelings and thermography. Conscious. Cogn. **34**, 149–162 (2015). https://doi.org/10.1016/j.concog.2015.04.003
12. Cruz-Albarran, I.A., Benitez-Rangel, J.P., Osornio-Rios, R.A., Morales-Hernandez, L.A.: Human emotions detection based on a smart-thermal system of thermographic images. Infrared Phys. Technol. **81**, 250–261 (2017). https://doi.org/10.1016/j.infrared.2017.01.002
13. Zualkernan, I., Aloul, F., Shapsough, S., Hesham, A., El-Khorzaty, Y.: Emotion recognition using mobile phones. Comput. Electr. Eng. **60**, 1–13 (2017). https://doi.org/10.1016/j.compeleceng.2017.05.004
14. Tarnowski, P., Kołodziej, M., Majkowski, A., Rak, R.J.: Emotion recognition using facial expressions. Pap. Present. Procedia Comput. Sci. **108**, 1175–1184 (2017). https://doi.org/10.1016/j.procs.2017.05.025
15. Hess, E.H.: The tell-tale eye: how your eyes reveal hidden thoughts and emotions. Van Nostrand Reinhold (1975)
16. Beatty, J., Lucero-Wagoner, B.: The pupillary system. In: Berntson, G., Tassinar, L.G. (eds.) Handbook of Psychophysiology, 2nd edn., pp. 142–162 Cambridge University Press, Hillsdale (2000)
17. Keltner, D., Cordaro, D.T.: Understanding multimodal emotional expressions: recent advances in basic emotion theory. Emotion Researcher (2015). http://emotionresearcher.com/understanding-multimodal-emotional-expressions-recent-advances-in-basic-emotion-theory/
18. Aviezer, H., Trope, Y., Todorov, A.: Body cues, not facial expressions discriminate between intense positive and negative emotions. Science **338**(6111), 1225–1229 (2012)
19. Abramson, L., Marom, I., Petranker, R., Aviezer, H.: Is fear in your head? A comparison of instructed and real-life expressions of emotion in the face and body. Emotion **17**(3), 557–565 (2017). https://doi.org/10.1037/emo0000252
20. Schneider, N., Bex, P., Barth, E., Dorr, M.: An open-source low-cost eye-tracking system for portable real-time and offline tracking. Paper presented at the ACM International Conference Proceeding Series (2011). https://doi.org/10.1145/1983302.1983310

21. Kim, J., Lee, E.C., Lim, J.S.: A new objective visual fatigue measurement system by using a remote infrared camera. Paper presented at the Proceedings of the 2011 8th International Joint Conference on Computer Science and Software Engineering, JCSSE 2011, pp. 182–186. (2011). https://doi.org/10.1109/jcsse.2011.5930117

22. Mantiuk, R., Kowalik, M., Nowosielski, A., Bazyluk, B.: Do-it-yourself eye tracker: low-cost pupil-based eye tracker for computer graphics applications (2012). https://doi.org/10.1007/978-3-642-27355-1_13

23. Hernandez, J., Picard, R.W.: SenseGlass: using Google glass to sense daily emotions. Paper presented at the UIST 2014 - Adjunct Publication of the 27th Annual ACM Symposium on User Interface Software and Technology, pp. 77–78 (2014). https://doi.org/10.1145/2658779.2658784

24. Scheirer, J., Fernandez, R., Picard, R.W.: Expression glasses: a wearable device for facial expression recognition. Paper presented at the Conference on Human Factors in Computing Systems - Proceedings, pp. 262–263 (1999). https://doi.org/10.1145/632716.632878

25. Maskeliunas, R., Raudonis, V.: Are you ashamed? Can a gaze tracker tell? PeerJ Comput. Sci. (8) (2016). https://doi.org/10.7717/peerj-cs.75

26. Ekman, P., Rosenberg, E.L.: What the face reveals: basic and applied studies of spontaneous expression using the facial action coding system (FACS). What the face reveals: basic and applied studies of spontaneous expression using the facial action coding system (FACS), pp. 1–672. (2012). https://doi.org/10.1093/acprof:oso/9780195179644.001.0001

27. Quazi, M.T., Mukhopadhyay, S.C.: Continuous monitoring of physiological parameters using smart sensors. Paper presented at the Proceedings of the International Conference on Sensing Technology, ICST, pp. 464–469 (2011). https://doi.org/10.1109/icsenst.2011.6137022

28. Quazi, M.T., Mukhopadhyay, S.C., Suryadevara, N.K., Huang, Y.M.: Towards the smart sensors based human emotion recognition. Paper presented at the 2012 IEEE I2MTC - International Instrumentation and Measurement Technology Conference, Proceedings, pp. 2365–2370 (2012). https://doi.org/10.1109/i2mtc.2012.6229646

29. Silva, F., Olivares, T., Royo, F., Vergara, M.A., Analide, C.: Experimental study of the stress level at the workplace using an smart testbed of wireless sensor networks and ambient intelligence techniques (2013). https://doi.org/10.1007/978-3-642-38622-0_21

30. Wiem, M.B.H., Lachiri, Z.: Emotion recognition system based on physiological signals with raspberry pi III implementation. Paper presented at the 2017 3rd International Conference on Frontiers of Signal Processing, ICFSP 2017, pp. 20–24 (2017). https://doi.org/10.1109/icfsp.2017.8097053

31. Hintjens, P.: ZeroMQ: Messaging for Many Applications. O'Reilly Media, Sebastopol (2013). Incorporated

32. Akgul, F.: ZeroMQ. Packt Publishing (2013). ISBN 178216104X, 9781782161042

33. Oliva, M., Anikin, A.: Pupil dilation reflects the time course of emotion recognition in human vocalizations. Sci. Rep. 8(1) (2018). https://doi.org/10.1038/s41598-018-23265-x

34. Duque, A., Sanchez, A., Vazquez, C.: Gaze-fixation and pupil dilation in the processing of emotional faces: the role of rumination. Cogn. Emot. 28(8), 1347–1366 (2014). https://doi.org/10.1080/02699931.2014.881327

35. Saha, R., et al.: A brief study on evolution of iris recognition system. Paper presented at the 2017 8th IEEE Annual Information Technology, Electronics and Mobile Communication Conference, IEMCON 2017, pp. 685–688. (2017). https://doi.org/10.1109/iemcon.2017.8117234

Smart-Scrolling: Improving Information Access Performance in Linear Layout Views for Small-Screen Devices

Chuanyi Liu[1(✉)] ⓘ, Ningning Wu[1], Hao Mao[2], and Wei Su[1]

[1] School of Information Science & Engineering, Lanzhou University, Lanzhou, China
liuchuanyi96@hotmail.com, {wunnl6,suwei}@lzu.edu.cn
[2] Fiberhome Telecommunication Technologies Co., LTD, Wuhan, China
hmao@fiberhome.com

Abstract. We proposed an adaptive auto-scrolling technique, Smart-Scrolling, which determined the scanned information region and hid it automatically in a linear layout view. An experiment was conducted with 15 participants to explore the usability of the technique under various application conditions of different interaction methods, information list lengths, and screen sizes. The experimental results revealed that Smart-Scrolling outperformed the baseline with an improvement in task completion speed of 9.4% and accuracy of 42.9%, and reducing 51.4% manual scrolling. Smart-Scrolling performed better than the baseline under various application conditions of different interaction methods, information list lengths, and screen sizes.

Keywords: Adaptive · Auto-scrolling · Mobile devices

1 Introduction

Mobile devices are common for most people and their proliferation is ceaseless. These devices promise to facilitate our daily life in many aspects. They are not only used for communication, but also for information processing. But the conditional metaphors designed for a full-screen desktop environment are not completely suitable for the small-screen mobile devices; and interaction efficiency on small displays is half less than on normal-sized desktop screens [1]. For easy information access, the information should be displayed with good readability and the orientation of information pieces should be facilitated. The former requires a sufficiently large font size and a low information density; while the latter requires presenting maximum information per screen and a large preview [2]. The two requirements are obviously contradictory for a small screen.

There are two types of methods to address these issues, i.e., redesigning contents to fit small screens [3–8], or finding out better information retrieval methods for small screens [7, 9–17]. Interface redesign imposes extra work on the existing applications, and the present researches only focus on menu [5, 7] or web [4, 6, 8] redesign, how to better present other contents on small displays has rarely been concerned. Suitable information retrieval methods are most of Around Device Interaction (ADI), which typically needs

© Springer Nature Switzerland AG 2019
D.-S. Huang et al. (Eds.): ICIC 2019, LNCS 11643, pp. 412–423, 2019.
https://doi.org/10.1007/978-3-030-26763-6_40

additional devices or sensors. ForceEdge [17] proposed a novel auto-scrolling technique, but it relied on some special force-sensing devices which are rare in mobile market.

We proposed a novel Smart-Scrolling technique acting in all linear layout interfaces, which are common when we send short messages to multiple contacts, file files or directories, etc. A quantitative experiment revealed that our proposed technique outperformed the baseline in various application contexts.

2 Related Work

The metaphors for a desktop screen are not completely suitable for a small-screen computing device, and user performance with a small screen is typically 50% less than with a normal-sized one [1]. There are many studies for improving interaction performance with small screens. Some of these researches aimed at finding out better information presentation methods [3–8], others at better information retrieval [7, 9–17].

2.1 Information Presentation

Kamba et al. [3] proposed that combining semi-transparent widgets with delayed response could improve user performance on information retrieval with small screens. Users took more time to perform information search tasks on a small screen interface than on a normal-sized desktop one [4]. Albers and Kim [6] explored how text-based design, screen size, and cumbersome interfaces of small-screen devices affected information search and retrieval, and identified issues for research on this topic. Dou and Sundar [8] found out that horizontal swiping technique positively affected users' behavioral intentions to use a website.

Besides information presentation of a website, menu design [5, 7] also had a significant effect on user performance interacting with small screens. Wang et al. [7] proposed that a hierarchical menu was more efficient than a scrolling menu. Tang [5] found out that menu design with visual momentum was helpful for users to develop effective mental maps of a menu structure.

2.2 Information Retrieval

Around Device Interaction (ADI) [9–16] allows users to interact with a small device using outer space around it. ADI gives a larger input space and addresses the issue of occlusion of the display when using direct touch on a mobile device. But additional devices or sensors are necessary for ADI.

With infra-red proximity sensors [9, 11, 14, 15], users performed off-screen mid-air gestures in the space around a device. Users gained more freedom and were free from the hand occlusion issue which is typically with direct touch. Magnetic sensors were also utilized in ADI [10, 13]. Users interacted with smart phones through both the magnetic sensors integrated in the mobile devices and outside permanent magnets. Outside cameras were also used for ADI with mobile devices [12, 15, 16].

Besides the aforementioned information retrieval techniques with ADI, there are some other retrieval techniques for mobile devices. ForceEdge [17] was a novel auto-scrolling technique to alleviate the issues related to auto-scrolling on the screen of a mobile device. This technique relied on touch surfaces with force-sensing capabilities, but these surfaces are not common for most mobile devices. Being different from ForceEdge, our proposed Smart-Scrolling technique is suitable for all direct touch devices. Plessas et al. [18] evaluated several contact retrieval methods with a context-aware mobile app; and found out that an alphabetical ordering of prediction matches best served the users, while the hybrid interface designs provided the users with a modest benefit for non-successful predictions.

2.3 Performance Measurements

Some researchers presented their studies of performance measurements with small screens [1, 2, 7, 19]. Some of the researches [1, 7] were for normal users, and others [2, 19] aimed at the older. These research results found out the existing issues and offered some useful design guidelines for small-screen interfaces. Jung et al. [20] determined that list search interfaces outperformed list interfaces when pool sizes over 60 for touchscreen smartwatches.

3 The Smarting-Scrolling Technique

There are many application contexts where the objects are listed in a linear layout, e.g., when we are sending short messages to multiple contacts, or filing photos, files, or directories, the contacts, photos, files, and directories are all in a linear layout. We typically retrieve or process information in a linear layout view in such an order: from top to bottom and from front to back.

Fig. 1. Three partitions in a linear layout view.

In these scenarios, we can divide a mobile view into three partitions (see Fig. 1): Scanned Region (*SR*), Being Processed Item (*BPI*), and Not Scanned Region (*NSR*).

BPI is the current item being processed, *SR* is the region before *BPI*, and *NSR* is the rest region following *BPI*. We suppose that a user has not omitted any useful information before *BPI*, then the information in both *SR* and *BPI* can be hidden after an appropriate time point. The typical operation to point or select an object is tapping on it. The moment when the user lifts her finger from *BPI* (*MFBPI*) is the appropriate time point to hide information in both *SR* and *BPI*. The information scrolls upward to present the item next to *BPI* in the top of the view. The upward scrolling is conducted adaptively by a mobile device at *MFBPI*. This technique is referred to as Smart-Scrolling. Smart-Scrolling has the potential to reduce manual scrolling times and improve interaction performance when a user retrieves information in a linear layout view.

4 Experiment

4.1 Participants and Apparatus

Fifteen computer master students, 10 males and 5 females, aged from 22 to 32, were recruited from the local university. They all had normal or corrected to normal vision. All of them were regular smart phone users and right-handed. None of them had experience of using adaptive techniques.

The experiment was conducted on three smartphones: MI Redmi 2 (screen size = 4.7", resolution = 1280 × 720 pixels), MI Redmi 4 (screen size = 5.5", resolution = 1920 × 1080 pixels), and MI Max2 (screen size = 6.44", resolution = 2160 × 1080 pixels). The processors of the three devices varied between 1.5 GHz and 2.11 GHz, and the memories between 1 GB and 4 GB. But these differences did not introduce significant bias of task time, since the experimental software conducted minute computation (only recorded a trial time and completion correct or not when an item was tapped) during time recording.

The experimental software was developed with Android SDK and the programming language was Java.

4.2 Hypotheses and Dependent Measures

Having obtained insights into Smart-Scrolling, we were to test the following hypotheses in our experiment:

- H1 Smart-Scrolling totally reduces information retrieval time.
- H2 Smart-Scrolling facilitates information access by reducing manual scrolling.
- H3 Smart-Scrolling improves task accuracy.
- H4 Smart-Scrolling acts in various sizes of mobile devices.
- H5 Smart-Scrolling works for information lists with various lengths.
- H6 Smart-Scrolling is helpful for a user whenever she manipulates a mobile device one-handed or two-handed.

There were five dependent measures in our experiment: Time, Wrong Selection (*WrongSel*), Missing Selection (*MissSel*), Upward Scrolling (*ScrollUp*), and Downward Scrolling (*ScrollDown*). Time was the whole time a user spent in selecting an item, and it was the time took the user to lift her finger up from the last item to from the current one.

A *WrongSel* occurred when a non-target item was tapped. A *MissSel* happened if there was an item omitted before the next target was tapped. *ScrollUp* was the times the user manually scrolled the view upward during a target selection. *ScrollDown* was the times the user manually scrolled the view downward during a target selection, and it only happened when a target was omitted.

4.3 Procedure and Tasks

The experiment was a part of a university statistical course for the participants. Before the formal experiment, all the participants were asked to familiarize themselves with the experimental tasks in 5 min each. For the formal experiment, the participants were asked to complete the experimental tasks as quickly and accurately as possible. The participants were allowed to have a rest between each two experimental conditions, and a longer break was mandatory between two blocks. It took each participant approximately one hour and a half to complete the whole experiment. After the quantitative testing, the participants were asked to complete a questionnaire.

Prior to formal experimental trials, an initial view was used to set an experimental condition (Fig. 2). The timing began as soon as the "submit" button in the initial view was tapped. In the full-screen task view, 20 targets were pseudo-randomly arrayed in a list. The participants were required to select the targets one by one in the list from top to bottom. Each target was filled with yellow background, while the others with black. The participants were asked to select a target by tapping on it. Its background turned into green if a target was selected; while if a non-target was selected, its background turned into red accompanying with an audio alarm. If a non-target was selected, one time of *WrongSel* was recorded. Its background also turned into red accompanying with an audio alarm if a target was selected but the last one had not, and one time of *MissSel* was recorded. The next trial would not begin until a *WrongSel* or *MissSel* mistake was corrected. During a

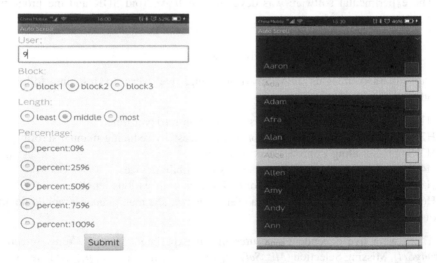

Fig. 2. Experimental interfaces: the initial view (left) and the task view (right). (Color figure online)

trial time, the number of times that participant manually scrolled the view upward or downward was recorded as *ScrollUp* or *ScrollDown*, respectively.

4.4 Design

We conducted a full factorial within-subjects design experiment. There were 5 factors: *Block* (*B*, 3 levels), *Percentage* (*PT*, 5 levels), *Interaction* (*I*, 2 levels), *Length* (*L*, 3 levels), and *Screen* (*S*, 3 levels). The 5 levels of *PT* were: 0%, 25%, 50%, 75%, and 100%, which represented the proportion of Smart-Scrolling functioned top region in the full screen, e.g., 50% stood for that Smart-Scrolling acted only in the top half screen. The first level (0%) was the baseline. The 2 levels of *I* were: one- and two-handed interaction methods. The factor *Length* was the length of the list, which was presented in the task view (Fig. 2), and its 3 levels were 100, 150, and 200. And the factor *Screen* was the screen sizes of the three experimental mobile devices, and its 3 levels were: 4.7", 5.5", and 6.44", which are three popular screen-size levels in mobile market.

A 5×5 Latin square was used to counterbalance order effects of the *PT* levels. The orders of other factor levels were randomized between subjects. A participant correctly selected 20 targets in each condition. Totally, there were: 15 subjects × 3 *B*s × 5 *PT*s × 2 *I*s × 3 *L*s × 3 *S*s × 20 trials = 81000 correct selections in the experiment.

5   Results

A 3 *B*s × 5 *PT*s × 2 *I*s × 3 *L*s × 3 *S*s RM-ANOVA was conducted on mean data of all the experimental measures. The confidence interval was adjusted by Bonferroni. The statistical summarization of the 5 performance measures was shown in Table 1.

Table 1. Statistical results for performance measures.

Measures		Time		WrongSel		MissSel		ScrollUp		ScrollDown	
Factors	df	F	p	F	p	F	p	F	p	F	p
B	2,28	79.3	**	1.08	.35	0.82	.45	1.46	.25	17.8	**
PT	4,56	45.8	**	2.75	*	0.93	.45	237	**	8.74	**
I	1,14	86. 6	**	0.04	.85	0.45	.52	3703	**	111687	**
L	2,28	529	**	0.65	.53	1.35	.28	450	**	14.2	**
S	2,28	61.9	**	4.23	*	0.91	.42	86.9	**	37.5	**
PT × B	8,112	1.5	.16	1.04	.41	1.18	.32	0.83	.58	12.7	**
PT × I	4,56	6.1	**	0.86	.49	0.49	.74	0.08	.99	5.11	**
PT × L	8,112	0. 8	.61	0.48	.86	1.36	.22	0.79	.61	15.0	**
PT × S	8,112	3.9	**	0.54	.82	1.35	.23	2.48	.02	16.2	**

Significant effects are shown with ** for $p < .0001$, and with * for $p < .05$; "×" means interaction effects.

5.1   Time

All the 5 experimental factors had significant effects on task completion time at $p < 0.0001$. As shown in Fig. 3a, task time decreased with the increase of PT. Time reduced 9.4% from $PT = 0\%$ (1366 MS) to $PT = 100\%$ (1238 MS): supporting H1. The results of contrasts showed that the difference between the levels 0% (the baseline) and 25% was not significant ($p = .23$). All the other 3 levels of PT were significantly different from the baseline. The results of pairwise comparisons revealed that there was a significant difference between all levels except 0% vs. 25% and 75% vs. 100%. This indicated that Smart-Scrolling performed significantly when its impacted region over 25% of the screen area and achieved the best speed effect when its impacted region over 75% of the screen area or more.

Figure 3 shows that Smart-Scrolling positively affected task time under various application conditions, i.e., across different interaction methods, list lengths, and screen sizes (H4, H5, and H6 supported). The significant interaction effect between PT and S (F (8,112) = 3.9, $p < .0001$) indicated that Smart-Scrolling acted differently on different sizes of screens. As shown in Fig. 3d, the proposed techniques performed the best on the largest screen.

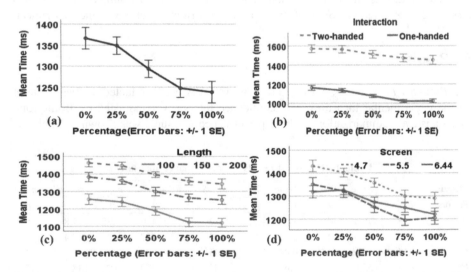

Fig. 3. Mean completion time per trial by percentage (a), across interaction methods (b), list lengths (c), and screen sizes (d).

5.2   Accuracy

Wrong Selection. As shown in Fig. 4, PT (F (4,56) = 2.75, $p < 0.05$) and S (F (2,28) = 4.23, $p < .05$) had significant effects on error rates of wrong selection, while the other 3 experimental factors had not. Figure 4a shows that wrong selection decreased with the increase of percentage. Wrong selection decreased 42.9% from $PT = 0\%$ (0.7%) to $PT = 100\%$ (0.4%): supporting H3. We can see from Fig. 4 that

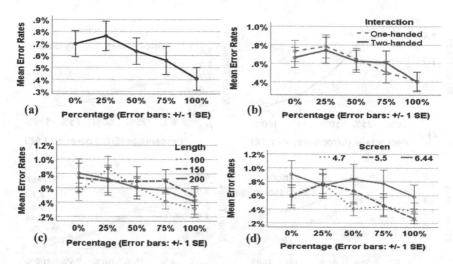

Fig. 4. Mean error rates of wrong selection per trial by percentage (a), across interaction methods (b), list lengths (c), and screen sizes (d).

under different application conditions of interaction methods, list lengths, and screen sizes, Smart-Scrolling all afforded positive effects on task accuracy in terms of wrong selection (H4, H5, and H6 supported). The insignificant effects of I and L revealed that Smart-Scrolling performed positively all the same with different interaction methods and list lengths. The results of contrasts showed that merely the level $PT = 100\%$ was significantly different from the baseline. This indicated that it performed the best in terms of accuracy when Smart-Scrolling impacted the whole screen.

Missing Selection. As shown in Table 1, all the effects of the 5 experimental factors and interaction effects of PT between other factors were not significant in terms of error rates of missing selection.

5.3 Manual Scrolling

Upward Scrolling. All the experimental factors except block had significant effects at $p < .0001$, but the interaction effects of percentage vs. the other factors were not significant. Figure 5a shows that the number of upward scrolling times decreased with the increase of percentage. Manual upward scrolling decreased 42.9% from $PT = 0\%$ (1.4) to $PT = 100\%$ (0.8). The results of pairwise comparisons revealed that all the differences between levels of percentage were significant at $p < .05$, except $PT = 0\%$ vs. $PT = 25\%$. We can infer from the results that Smart-Scrolling acted significantly when PT is not less than 50%, and its performance achieved the best effect when it acted in the whole screen in terms of manual upward scrolling. Figure 5 reveals that Smart-Scrolling was helpful according to manual upward scrolling under different application conditions of different interaction methods, list lengths, and screen sizes.

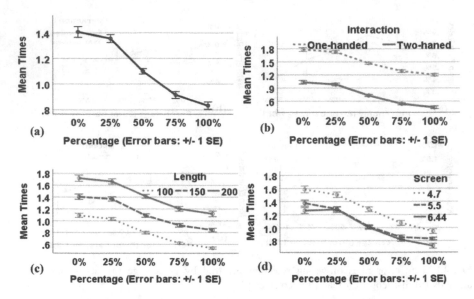

Fig. 5. Mean times of upward scrolling per trial by percentage (a), across interaction methods (b), list lengths (c), and screen sizes (d).

Downward Scrolling. As shown in Table 1, all the 5 experimental factors had significant effects on the number of manual downward scrolling at $p < .0001$. We can see from Fig. 6a that downward scrolling totally decreased accompanying the increase of

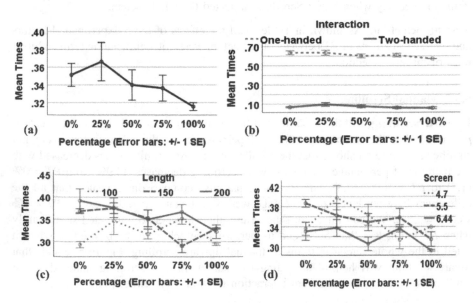

Fig. 6. Mean times of downward scrolling per trial by percentage (a), across interaction methods (b), list lengths (c), and screen sizes (d).

PT. But the results of contrasts revealed significant difference between the other levels of *PT* and the baseline merely after *PT* = 75%, and the difference between the last two levels was not significant (p = .62) in terms of manual downward scrolling. We can infer from the results that Smart-Scrolling acted significantly better than the baseline only when its impacted region covering the top 75% region or more of the whole screen according to manual downward scrolling. Manual downward scrolling decreased 8.6% from *PT* = 0% (0.35) to *PT* = 100% (0.32). Figure 6 reveals that Smart-Scrolling performed better than the baseline under various application conditions of different interaction methods, list lengths, and screen sizes.

Totally, manual scrolling decreased 51.4%, *PT* = 100% vs. *PT* = 0%, with the help of Smart-Scrolling (H2 supported).

5.4 Subjective Comments

The participants were conducted to complete a questionnaire to comment Smart-Scrolling and the baseline with three subjective measures: usability, fatigue, and personal preference. The participants were asked to rate each measure with a 1–7 rating levels (1 representing the worst and 7 the best).

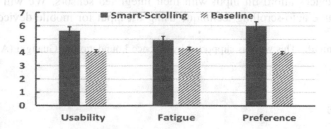

Fig. 7. Subjective comments.

As shown in Fig. 7, the participants rated Smart-Scrolling higher across the 3 measures. All the participants thought that Smart-Scrolling possessed better usability and they expressed higher preference for the proposed technique. They felt that Smart-Scrolling was less fatigue-prone for both hands and eyes since it reduced manual scrolling and visual-seeking area for a target.

6 Discussion

Smart-Scrolling improved information access performance by reducing 9.4% task completion time and 42.9% wrong selection, because of 51.4% decrease in manual scrolling with it vs. the baseline. Auto-hiding the scanned information also reduced visual-seeking area in the process of information retrieval, and this further led to improvement of both task completion speed and accuracy.

Smart-Scrolling was adaptive, and the participants did not need to study new skill for this novel technique. All the participants grasped how to work efficiently with this technique in a short time.

Smart-Scrolling can be used directly in any linear layout interfaces. We need not adapt the existing interfaces to accommodate the technique.

7 Conclusion and Future Work

In this paper, we present an adaptive auto-scrolling technique, Smart-Scrolling, which acts in linear layout views of small-screen mobile devices. The experiment revealed that Smart-Scrolling improved 9.4% task completion speed and 42.9% accuracy vs. the baseline by reducing 51.4% manual scrolling. The proposed technique performed better under various application conditions of different interaction methods, information list lengths, and screen sizes. The participants performed the best when the percentage was 75% or more in terms of task completion time and manual downward scrolling. But in terms of error rates of wrong selection and manual upward scrolling, the participants performed the best when the percentage was 100%. Totally, the best performance was achieved when Smart-Scrolling acted in the whole interface.

Mobile devices afford tilt input with their integrated sensors. We will investigate another adaptive auto-scrolling technique using tilt input for mobile devices.

Acknowledgement. This work is supported by Science Foundation of Guangxi (AA17204096, AD16380076).

References

1. Jones, M., Marsden, G., Mohd-Nasir, N., Boone, K., Buchanan, G.: Improving web interaction on small displays. Comput. Netw. **31**(11), 1129–1137 (1999)
2. Ziefle, M.: Information presentation in small screen devices: the trade-off between visual density and menu foresight. Appl Ergon. **41**(6), 719–730 (2010)
3. Kamba, T., Elson, S.A., Harpold, T., Stamper, T., Sukaviriya, P.: Using small screen space more efficiently. In: Proceedings of the SIGCHI Conference on Human Factors in Computing Systems: Common Ground, pp. 383–390. ACM, Vancouver (1996)
4. Kim, L., Albers, M.J.: Web design issues when searching for information in a small screen display. In: Proceedings of the 19th Annual International Conference on Systems Documentation Communication in the New Millenium, pp. 193–200. Association for Computing Machinery, Santa Fe (2001)
5. Tang, K.H.: Menu design with visual momentum for compact smart products. Hum. Factors **43**(2), 267–277 (2001)
6. Albers, M., Kim, L.: Information design for the small-screen interface: an overview of web design issues for personal digital assistants. Tech Commun. **49**(1), 45–60 (2002)
7. Wang, A.-H., Lai, Y.-Y., Sun, C.-T.: Effect of PDA scrolling- and hierarchy-menu design on users' operating performance. Displays **25**(2), 109–114 (2004)
8. Dou, X., Sundar, S.S.: Power of the swipe: why mobile websites should add horizontal swiping to tapping, clicking, and scrolling interaction techniques. Int. J. Hum.-Comput. Interact. **32**(4), 352–362 (2016)

9. Butler, A., Izadi, S., Hodges, S.: SideSight: multi-"touch" interaction around small devices, pp. 201–204. In: Proceedings of the 21st Annual ACM Symposium on User Interface Software and Technology. ACM, Monterey (2008)

10. Harrison, C., Hudson, S.E.: Abracadabra: wireless, high-precision, and unpowered finger input for very small mobile devices. In: Proceedings of the 22nd Annual ACM Symposium on User Interface Software and Technology, pp. 121–124. ACM, Victoria (2009)

11. Kratz, S.G., Rohs, M.: Hoverflow: exploring around-device interaction with ir distance sensors. In: Proceedings of the 11th International Conference on Human-Computer Interaction with Mobile Devices and Services, MobileHCI 2009, pp. 1–4. ACM, Bonn (2009)

12. Wang, Q., Hsieh, T., Paepcke, A.: Piles across space: Breaking the real-estate barrier on small-display devices. Int. J. Hum.-Comput. Stud. **67**(4), 349–365 (2009)

13. Ketabdar, H., Yüksel, K.A., Roshandel, M.: MagiTact: interaction with mobile devices based on compass (magnetic) sensor. In: Proceedings of the 15th International Conference on Intelligent User Interfaces, IUI 2010, Hong Kong, China, pp. 413–414 (2010)

14. Jones, B.R., Sodhi, R., Forsyth, D.A., Bailey, B.P., Maciocci, G.: Around device interaction for multiscale navigation. In: Proceedings of the 16th International Conference on Human-Computer Interaction with Mobile Devices and Services Adjunct, MobileHCI 2012, San Francisco, CA, USA, pp. 83–92 (2012)

15. Kratz, S.G., Rohs, M., Guse, D., Müller, J., Bailly, G., Nischt, M.: PalmSpace: continuous around-device gestures vs. Multitouch for 3D rotation tasks on mobile devices. In: Proceedings of the 2012 International Conference on Advanced Visual Interfaces, AVI 2012, pp. 181–188. ACM, Capri Island (2012)

16. Hasan, K., Ahlström, D., Irani, P.: AD-binning: leveraging around device space for storing, browsing and retrieving mobile device content. In: Proceedings of the SIGCHI Conference on Human Factors in Computing Systems, pp. 899–908. ACM, Paris (2013)

17. Antoine, A., Malacria, S., Casiez, G.: ForceEdge: controlling autoscroll on both desktop and mobile computers using the force. In: Proceedings of the 2017 CHI Conference on Human Factors in Computing Systems, pp. 3281–3292. ACM, Denver (2017)

18. Plessas, A., Stefanis, V., Komninos, A., Garofalakis, J.D.: Field evaluation of context aware adaptive interfaces for efficient mobile contact retrieval. Pervasive Mob. Comput. **35**(2017), 51–64 (2017)

19. Arning, K., Ziefle, M.: Barriers of information access in small screen device applications: the relevance of user characteristics for a transgenerational design. In: Stephanidis, C., Pieper, M. (eds.) UI4ALL 2006. LNCS, vol. 4397, pp. 117–136. Springer, Heidelberg (2007). https://doi.org/10.1007/978-3-540-71025-7_9

20. Jung, J.G., Lee, S., Ahn, S., Lee, G.: Auto-switching list search interface for touchscreen smartwatches. In: Proceedings of the 20th International Conference on Human-Computer Interaction with Mobile Devices and Services, MobileHCI 2018, pp. 45:41–45:10. ACM, Barcelona (2018)

Scalable Distributed Genetic Algorithm Using Apache Spark (S-GA)

Fahad Maqbool[1(✉)], Saad Razzaq[1], Jens Lehmann[2,3], and Hajira Jabeen[2]

[1] University of Sargodha, Sargodha, Pakistan
{fahad.maqbool,saad.razzaq}@uos.edu.pk
[2] Bonn University, Bonn, Germany
{lehmann,jabeen}@cs.uni-bonn.de
[3] Fraunhofer IAIS, Sankt Augustin, Germany

Abstract. In this era of big data with facilities for advanced real-time data acquisition, the solutions to large-scale optimization problems are strongly desired. Genetic Algorithms are efficient optimization algorithms that have been successfully applied to solve a multitude of complex problems. The growing need for large-scale optimization, and inherent parallel evolutionary nature of the algorithms calls for new solutions exploiting existing parallel, in-memory, distributed computing frameworks like Apache Spark. In this paper, we present an algorithm for Scalable Genetic Algorithms using Apache Spark (S-GA). S-GA makes liberal use of rich APIs offered by Spark. We have tested S-GA on several numerical benchmark problems for large-scale continuous optimization containing up to 3000 dimensions, 3000 population size, and one billion generations. S-GA presents a variant of island model and minimizes the materialization and shuffles in RDDs for minimal and efficient network communication. At the same time it maintains the population diversity by broadcasting the best solutions across partitions after specified Migration Interval. We have tested and compared S-GA with the canonical Sequential Genetic Algorithm (SeqGA). S-GA has been found to be more scalable and it can scale up to large dimensional optimization problems while yielding comparable results.

Keywords: Apache Spark · Parallel genetic algorithms · Function optimization · Hadoop Map Reduce

1 Introduction

Owing to inherently decentralized nature of Genetic Algorithms (GA), a multitude of variants of Parallel GA (PGA) have been introduced in the literature [1, 2]. However, their application has remain limited to moderately sized optimization problems and the research focused mostly on speeding up the performance of otherwise time-consuming and inherently complex applications e.g. assignment and scheduling [11–13], or prediction [8], tasks. To deal with large-scale optimization problems multi-core systems and standalone clusters architectures have been proposed by Zheng et al. [6]. They have used distributed storage file system or distributed processing framework like Apache Hadoop, to achieve scalability in PGA [3–6]. Hadoop Map Reduce [7], is a

© Springer Nature Switzerland AG 2019
D.-S. Huang et al. (Eds.): ICIC 2019, LNCS 11643, pp. 424–435, 2019.
https://doi.org/10.1007/978-3-030-26763-6_41

reliable, scalable and fault tolerant framework for large scale computing. Hadoop requires writing data to HDFS after each iteration to achieve its resilience. In case of CPU bound iterative processing, e.g. in case of Genetic Algorithms, this I/O overhead is undesirable and substantially dominates the processing time. PGA has been explored for numerous interesting applications like software fault prediction [8], test suite generation [9], sensor placement [10], assignment and scheduling [11–13], dynamic optimization [23], adapting offspring population size and number of islands [24].

Researchers have made significant efforts to explore the intrinsically parallel nature of genetic algorithms using island model [16], and other PGA models [18]. A lot of efforts have also been made by implementing and testing these models on Hadoop framework [8, 17, 18, 25], by using map reduce strategy to improve scalability. PGAs have been implemented using distributed frameworks and the effectiveness is evaluated in terms of execution time, computation effort, solution quality in comparison with Sequential Genetic Algorithm (SeqGA). However, the above mentioned efforts have been tested on simple problems which have been solved using limited population size and small number of generations overlooking the scalability that can be achieved by using these frameworks to solve large-scale optimization problems. Apache Spark [14] is an open source distributed cluster computing framework that has gained popularity in recent years. It has been shown to be faster than Hadoop for large scale optimization problems. it especially works better for iterative processing [14]. Contrary to Hadoop, Spark keeps data in memory and uses lineage graphs to achieve resilience and fault tolerance. This makes computing faster and eliminates the I/O overhead of read/write to the Hadoop distributed file system (HDFS) incurred in case of map-reduce. Spark provides APIs for generic processing in addition to specialized libraries for SQL like operations [29], stream processing using concepts of mini-batches [26], iterative machine learning algorithms [30], and a Graph processing library [15]. Spark's efficient data processing has proven to be 100 times faster for in-memory operations and 10 times faster for disk operations when compared to Hadoop MapReduce [25].

In this paper, we propose a Scalable GA (S-GA) for large-scale optimization problems using Apache Spark. S-GA aims to reduce the communication overhead of Apache Spark by optimal resource utilization for large scale optimization tasks. This is contrary to the traditional island model [16], of PGA, where communication among different subpopulation islands is directly proportional to the population and solution size. In S-GA, the communication is independent of the population size and is limited by the *Migration Rate* and *Migration Interval*. Hence, reducing a significant amount of data transfer between parallel computations making it scalable and applicable to large scale problems. We have compared S-GA with SeqGA for continuous numerical optimization problems. The experiments have been performed on five different large scale benchmark problems. The results of S-GA have been compared with GA and found to be more efficient.

The paper is structured as follows: In Sect. 2, related work is discussed. SeqGA and proposed S-GA is explained in Sects. 3 and 4 respectively. Experiments and evaluations are discussed in Sect. 5. Finally, we discuss the Conclusions and future work in Sect. 6.

2 Related Work

Generally, there are three main models to parallelize GA i.e. global single-population master-slave (global model), single-population fine-grained (grid model), multiple-population coarse-grained (island model) [1]. Mostly, PGA divides a population into multiple sub-populations. Each population independently searches for an optimal solution using stochastic search operators like crossover and mutation. The **Global Model** works like SeqGA with one population. The master is responsible for handling the population by applying GA operators while slave manages the fitness evaluation of individuals. In **Grid Model**, GA operators are applied within each sub-population and each individual is assigned to only one sub-population. This helps in improving the diversity. However, this model suffers from the problem of getting stuck in a local optima, and it has high communication overhead due to frequent communication between the sub-populations. **Island Model**, [16] uses a large population divided among different sub-populations called islands. GA operates on these islands independently with the ability to exchange/migrate some of the individuals. This helps in increasing the diversity of chromosome and avoid to get stuck in a local optima. **SeqGA** uses single large population pool and apply stochastic operators on them. Details about SeqGA, is given in Sect. 3.2. Whitley et al. [16], expected that Island model would outperform SeqGA, because of the diversity of chromosomes and migration of individuals among several islands. However, results revealed that Island model may perform better only if migration among sub-populations is handled carefully.

A comparison of Hadoop Map Reduce based implementation of three main PGA models, global single-population master-slave GAs (global model), single-population fine-grained (grid model), multiple-population coarse-grained (island model) is discussed by Ferrucci et al. [8]. They observed that overhead of Hadoop distributed file system (HDFS) make Global and Grid models less efficient as compared to Island model for parallelizing GA for because of HDFS access, communication and execution time. Island model performs less HDFS operations, resulting in optimized resource utilization and efficient execution time. However, they reported experimental results of Global, Grid, and Island models on population size of 200 only, with 300 generations on smaller problems with a limited number of dimensions (only up to 18). Their results concluded that distributed frameworks provide efficient support for data Distribution, parallel processing, and memory management but they incur significant overhead of communication delays.

Verma et al. [17], used Hadoop MapReduce framework to make GA scalable. Their experiments were performed on OneMax problem and they addressed the scalability and convergence as decreasing time per iteration, by increasing the number of resources while keeping the problem size fixed. Keco and Subasi [18] discussed PGA using Hadoop MapReduce. Their focus was to improve final solution quality and cloud resource utilization. They obtained improved performance and fast convergence but there were no improvements in the solution quality due to lack of communication among the subpopulations. Edgar et al. [19], proposed a diversity based parent selection mechanism for speeding up the multi-objective optimization using Evolutionary Algorithm. This novel parent selection mechanism helped to find the Pareto front faster than the classical approaches. Osuna et al. [19], focused on individuals having high diversity located in poor explored areas of the search space. Gao et al. [20], contributed to maximizing the diversity of population in GA, by favoring the solutions whose fitness value is better than a given threshold. They worked on OneMax and Leading One's [27], problems. The results revealed that algorithm efficiently maximized the diversity of a population. They have presented a theoretical framework and haven't addressed the contribution of diversity in large-scale optimization problems.

PGA using Apache Spark framework [9], was proposed for the pairwise test suite generation. Parallel operations were used for fitness evaluation and genetic operations. They did not address the large scale data problems and only focused on test suite size generation. Results were compared with SeqGA on synthetic and real-world datasets [9].

Both, GA and PGAs are widely used in several applications. Junior et al. [21], applied parallel biased random-key GA with multiple populations on irregular strip packing problem. In this problem, items of variable length and fixed width need to be placed in a container. For an efficient layout scheme, they used collision-free region as a partition method along with a meta-heuristic and a placement algorithm. Gronwald et al. [22], determined location and amount of pollutant source in air by using Backward Parallel Genetic Algorithm (BPGA). A concentration profile was compiled by considering the readings from different points in an area. BPGA utilized multiple guesses in a generation, and the best one was determined by a fitness function. This best guess was used in the reproduction of next generation.

Previously proposed parallel implementations of GA majorly differ in structuring the population and subpopulations named as the topology. The topology of PGA determines the sub-population model and the sharing of solutions (i.e. sending and receiving solutions from each other) among these subpopulations. These models, when executed using distributed frameworks like Apache Spark, suffer from substantial communication and network overhead. On one hand there is substantial parallelism intrinsic in Genetic Algorithms, and on the other hand, the desired communication hinders the ideal speed-up that could be achieved by using parallel/distributed techniques. There exists a tradeoff between sub-population communication and solution quality (due to population stagnation, getting stuck in the local optima and the lack of diversity).

In conclusion, there is a strong need to develop fundamental new approaches for parallel and distributed GA, while keeping in view the I/O, network, and communication overhead present in the existing distributed large scale computing frameworks. In order to exploit the existing frameworks, the implementation must make optimal resource utilization to gain the ideal speedup.

3 Background

3.1 Apache Spark

Apache Spark [28] was introduced by RAD Lab at the University of California in 2009 in order to overcome the limitations of Hadoop MapReduce. It has been designed for faster in-memory computation for interactive queries and iterative algorithms while achieving efficient fault recovery and compliance with the Hadoop stack. At its core, Spark is a "computational engine" that is responsible for scheduling, distributing, and monitoring applications consisting of many computational tasks across many worker machines, or a computing cluster. Apache Spark provides data distribution using resilient distributed datasets (RDDs), which are Spark's main programming abstraction. RDDs represent a collection of items distributed across many compute nodes that can be manipulated in parallel. RDD supports two types of operations: (i) Transformations, (ii) Actions. Transformations are lazy operations that create a new RDD from existing data in RDD. Lazy evaluation means that transformations are not executed, and an execution graph is created instead, until an action is called. The actions materialize the lazy evaluations and perform operations (e.g. aggregation) that transfer data from worker nodes to the master node. In order to efficiently work with RDDs it is important to be aware of the internal working details of RDDs, use of narrow transformations and dependencies, reducing the number of actions etc. in order to achieve better speed up with the parallel computing.

3.2 Sequential Genetic Algorithm (SeqGA)

SeqGA [11–13, 16, 18, 20], also known as Canonical GA is a stochastic search method that is used to find the optimal solution for a given optimization problem using the Darwinian's principal of evolution "Survival of the Fittest". It creates a single pool of possible solutions population (panmixia) and applies stochastic operators (i.e. Selection, Crossover, Mutation, and Survival Selection) to create a new evolved population. This process of new population evolution continues until the population has converged to an optimal solution, or desired time/effort has elapsed. For large scale, or complex problems, SeqGA may require more computational effort like more memory and long execution time (for large population size and more generations).

Algorithm 1 explains the working of SeqGA. (Line 3), *Select Parents* specifies the individual selection mechanism for reproduction or recombination. *Crossover* (Line 4) helps to explore the search space by generating new solutions after recombination, while M*utation* (Line 5) exploits the solutions for improvement by random perturbation of the selected solution. The *Survival Selection* scheme decides the number of individuals to be selected from parents and offspring's for the next generation.

Algorithm 1. Sequential Genetic Algorithm

1.P ← *Generate Initial Population*

2.**While** Stopping Criteria not met **do**

3. *P'← Select Parents (P)*

4. *P' ← Crossover (P')*

5. P' ← *Mutate (P')*

6. P' ← *Survival –Selection (P U P')*

7. P ← P'

end while

---

4 Scalable Distributed Genetic Algorithm Using Apache Spark (S-GA)

S-GA creates an initial random population of solutions and distributes them on different partitions as an RDD. The GA operators and fitness evaluations are performed within each partition, independent of the other partitions. We have used roulette wheel selection operator, uniform crossover, interchange mutation operation, and weak parent survival selection, for creation of new offspring's for the next generation.

In S-GA each partition (corresponding to an island in island model) replaces its weakest solution by the fittest solutions broadcasted by other partitions. **Migration Size** *(Ms)* specifies the number of solutions to be broadcasted to other partitions during each migration step. S-GA significantly reduces the communication overhead by minimizing the actions on RDD.

The pseudo code of S-GA is elaborated in Algorithm 2. The population is randomly initialized at line (1) then distributed among m partitions at line (2). Solutions are evolved using stochastic operators at line (6–12). It is worth mentioning here that we have used operations that calculate and sort the fitness within each partition (MapPartitionsWithIndex), therefore reducing the communication overhead and achieving efficient performance. At line (14), SGA broadcasts evolved best solutions (s) to other partitions and the weak solutions from the partitions are replaced with the new broadcasted solutions at line (6). Migration Interval *(Mi)* defines the number of generations after which S-GA broadcasts the fittest individual (s) of each partition to other partitions. This helps achieving diversity in each subpopulation while searching for the better solutions. The size of the broadcast and Migration Interval contribute to the network communication delay, and directly affect the performance and convergence. We have experimented with several values in our evaluations. Finally the above steps are iterated until the stopping criteria is met. Figure 1 explains the idea of Migration, Migration Size and Migration Interval with an example.

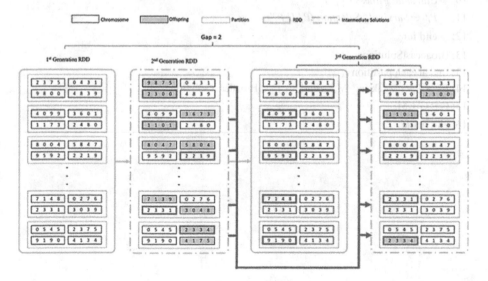

Fig. 1. Evolution process of S-GA

Let's assume value of $Mi = 2$, $Ms = 1$, and fitness function as sphere (i.e., $f(xi) = \sum_{i=1}^{n} x_i^2$. Initial RDD is created using a population of random solutions. These initial solutions are then evolved using crossover and mutation operators. After every 2nd generation (as $Mi = 2$), best solution (as $Ms = 1$) from each partition is migrated to other partitions. As the solution migrates, each partition at the start of very next generation picks all the migrated solutions and replaces them with its weakest solutions at each partition.

Algorithm 2.   Pseudo-code-of-S-GA

N: Population Size
P: Population
P_i: Sub-Population at partition i
D: Dimensions
G: Generations
m: Number of Partitions
M_i: Migration Interval / gap
f: Fitness Function
M_s: Migration Size

1: Randomly initialise population of size P

2: Distribute P among m partitions

3: $G = 0+$

4: **while** stopping criteria not met **do**

5: at each partition i

6:     **for** k: 1 to M_i **do**

7:     P_i'' ←Select Parents (P_i')

8:     P_i'' ←*Crossover (P_i')*

9:     P_i'' ←*Mutate (P_i')*

10   *Calculate Fitness (P_i'')*

11:    P_i' ← *Survival_ Selection (P_i' ∪ P_i'')*

12:    **end for**

13: BroadcastSolutions

13: End at each partition i

14. $P_{i'} = (P_i - ($ weak $(m* M_s)$ solutions)) ∪ BroadcastSolutions

15: $G = G + M_i$

16: **end while**

---

5 Experiments

5.1 Experimental Setup

The experiments are performed on a three node cluster: DELL PowerEdge R815, 2x AMD Opteron 6376 (64 Cores), 256 GB .RAM, 3 TB SATA RAID-5 with spark-2.1.0 and Scala 2.11.8. Both S-GA and SeqGA used Crossover scheme: Uniform, Mutation: Interchange, Replacement Scheme: Weak parent, Selection Scheme: Roulette Wheel, Crossover Probability: 0.5, Mutation Probability: 0.05, P = D, and Function: Griewank as configuration parameters. While S-GA also used m: 24 and M_s: 2 as configuration parameters.

5.2 Evaluation Matrics

Speed Up: It is the ratio of sequential execution time to the parallel execution time. It reflects how much parallel algorithm is faster than a sequential algorithm. Table 1 reflects speed up for all the cases where SeqGA and S-GA converge to VTR (Value To Reach). VTR defines the threshold for convergence. We have used $\frac{1}{Number\ of\ Dimensions}$ as VTR in experimentations.

In Table 1, we with different values of Migration Interval and Migration Size. it can be seen that for large Migration Interval and Migration Size, a high speedup was achieved.

Execution Time: The execution time of SeqGA and S GA was measured using system clock time. This time was recorded for a maximum of 1 billion generations. Table 2 shows average execution time over 5 runs for each configuration of S-GA. We can observe that execution time reduces significantly when we increase M_i from 50000 to 100000, however fitness error also decreases significantly. This difference in time reduces with an increase in the number of partitions. Migration overhead defines the total number of migrated individual (s) by all partitions after M_i. Increase in m and M_i results in increased network overhead ($m*M_i$) and hence execution time. But on the other hand this also helps S-GA to converge in a lesser number of generations. Table 2 lists the execution time of Sphere, Ackley, Griewank, Rastrigin, Zakharov, and Sum-of-Different-Power-functions for optimization upto 3000 dimensions (D). For simplicity population size (N) has been assumed to be equivalent to the number of dimensions. G represents the number of generations that have been consumed using specified configurations. VTR as mentioned earlier, is reciprocal to D. Hence VTR would be lesser for 3000 dimensions compared to 2000 and 1000 dimensions. Bold values in Table 2 represents the fitness error that has decreased beyond the specified threshold i.e. VTR.

Table 1. Experimental results of S-GA and SeqGA.

D	SeqGA						S-GA			Speed up
	G	Time	Error	M_i	m	M_s	G	Time	Error	
1000	748	2476999	2.45e-4	25000	18	1	106850000	712	8.25e-4	–
						2	39050000	352	9.28e-4	–
						3	27275000	327	1.4e-4	–
					24	1	46050000	356	6.68e-4	–
						2	22675000	263	8.08e-4	–
						3	19925000	311	9.55e-4	–
					30	1	37500000	328	2.87e-4	–
						2	15750000	228	2.33e-4	1.08
						3	13150000	269	7.01e-4	–
				50000	18	1	194500000	650	2.79e-4	–
						2	86500000	393	7.99e-4	–
						3	54850000	317	4.15e-4	–
					24	1	92800000	565	9.37e-5	–
						2	44250000	262	2.52e-4	–
						3	38750000	311	3.69e-4	–
					30	1	81850000	344	3.42e-4	–
						2	33550000	244	2.01e-5	1.01
						3	30350000	309	3.24e-4	–
2000	989	1064	2.03e-4	25000	18	1	242650000	3479	1.94e-4	–
						2	95400000	1845	4.17e-4	–
						3	62225000	1472	1.67e-4	–
					24	1	127075000	2112	2.65e-4	–
						2	61875000	1466	3.22e-4	–
						3	36650000	1061	3.51e-4	1.002
					30	1	95950000	1714	1.88e-4	–
						2	41250000	1042	2.64e-4	1.02
						3	26275000	970	1.65e-4	1.1
				50000	18	1	448200000	3309	1.5e-4	–
						2	179300000	1713	2.37e-4	–
						3	133200000	1541	4.15c-5	–
					24	1	246500000	2162	3.62e-4	–
						2	120250000	1429	2.47e-4	–
						3	74300000	1052	1.37e-4	1.01
					30	1	185250000	1837	2.91e-4	–
						2	78900000	1076	3.2e-4	–
						3	54900000	989	2.56e-4	1.07

Table 2. Experimental Results of S-GA.

| f | Mi | D = 1000 | | | D = 2000 | | | D = 3000 | | |
| | | VTR = 0.001 | | | VTR = 5.0 E-4 | | | VTR = 3.33 E-4 | | |
		G	Time	Error	G	Time	Error	G	Time	Error
Sphere	50000	1e9	556	8.28	1e9	11531	0.004	1e9	18904	0.017
	100000	1e9	282	265.05	1e9	5932	0.003	1e9	12227	5.967
Ackley	50000	1e9	5616	0.009	1e9	11799	0.095	1e9	17609	1.27
	100000	1e9	2613	0.02	1e9	5819	0.015	1e9	9456	2.07
Griewank	50000	4.4e7	262	**2.52e-4**	1.2e8	1429	**2.47e-4**	2.1e9	3917	**1.25e-4**
	100000	9.6e7	277	**6.23e-4**	2.4e6	1417	**1.41e-4**	4.1e9	3732	**2.47e-4**
Rastrigin	50000	1e9	5339	0.024	1e9	11513	1.443	1e9	18594	0.067
	100000	1e9	2623	2.081	1e9	5809	0.907	1e9	9447	52.45
Zakharov	50000	1e9	5575	17035.15	1e9	11779	33111.93	1e9	16048	10249.73
	100000	1e9	2896	16803.21	1e9	5783	33205.55	1e9	9036	50674.89
Sum of Diff Powers	50000	200000	6	**4.59e-4**	250000	10	**3.16e-4**	700000	19	**1.6e-4**
	100000	400000	6	**2.82e-4**	400000	8	**4.5e-4**	600000	11	**1.42e-4**

It can be seen from Table 2 that for higher values of M_i (i.e. 100000), each function consumes less time in most of the cases. Broadcasts are also important as they help each sub-population P_j to increase it's diversity and helps each P_j to get out of local optima. Increased M_i values reduces frequent broadcasts and hence the network overhead. In case of higher M_i, more number of iterations may not improve the optima significantly, due to reduced diversity in the particular sub population. Table 2 reveals the discussed fact as Error is less for M_i = 50000 as compared to M_i= 100000 in most of the cases.

6 Conclusion

In this paper, we have proposed initial results for S-GA using Apache Spark for large-scale optimization problems. The results have been compared with SeqGA. We have tested S-GA for Sphere, Ackley, Griewank, Rastrigin, Zakharov, and Sum-of-Different-Powers functions that are typical benchmarks for continuous optimization problems. We have used population size of up to 3000, Dimensions of up to 3000, Partition Size up to 30, Migration Size up to 03, and Migration Interval to 100000. For few cases S-GA has outperformed SeqGA for higher Population, Partitions, Migration Size, and Migration Interval in term of execution time. In future, we plan to extend S-GA and evaluate different migration and distribution strategies for larger scale and more complex optimization problems.

Acknowledgment. This work was partly supported by the EU Horizon2020 projects Boost4.0 (GA no. ~ 780732), LAMBDA (GA no. ~ 809965), SLIPO (GA no. ~ 731581), and QROWD (GA no. ~ 723088).

References

1. Luque, G., Alba, E.: Parallel Genetic Algorithms: Theory and Real-World Applications. Springer, Heidelberg (2011)
2. Knysh, D.S., Kureichik, V.M.: Parallel genetic algorithms: a survey and problem state. J. Comput. Syst. Sci. Int. **49**(4), 579–589 (2010)
3. Chávez, F., et al.: ECJ + HADOOP: an easy way to deploy massive runs of evolutionary algorithms. In: Squillero, G., Burelli, P. (eds.) EvoApplications 2016. LNCS, vol. 9598, pp. 91–106. Springer, Cham (2016). https://doi.org/10.1007/978-3-319-31153-1_7
4. Di Geronimo, L., Ferrucci, F., Murolo, A., Sarro, F.: A parallel genetic algorithm based on hadoop MapReduce for the automatic generation of JUnit test suites: In: IEEE International Conference on Software Testing, Verification and Validation (2012)
5. Salza, P., Ferrucci, F., Sarro, F.: Develop, deploy and execute parallel genetic algorithms in the cloud. In: Genetic and Evolutionary Computation Conference (GECCO) (2016)
6. Zheng, L., Lu, Y., Ding, M., Shen, Y., Guoz, M.: Architecture-based performance evaluation of genetic algorithms on multi/many-core systems. In: IEEE International Conference on Computational Science and Engineering (2011)
7. Hashem, I.T., Anuar, N.B., Gani, A.Y., Xia, F., Khan, S.U.: MapReduce review and open challenges. Scientometrics **109**, 389–422 (2016)
8. Ferrucci, F., Pasquale, S., Federica, S.: Using hadoop MapReduce for parallel genetic algorithm: a comparison of the global, grid and island models. Evol. Comput. Early Access **26**(4), 535–567 (2017)
9. Qi, R.Z., Wang, Z.J., Li, S.-Y.: A parallel genetic algorithm based on spark for pairwise test suite. J. Comput. Sci. Technol. **31**(2), 417–427 (2016)
10. Hu, C., Ren, G., Liu, C., Li, M., Jie, W.: A spark-based genetic algorithm for sensor placement in large-scale drinking water distribution systems. Cluster Comput. J. Netw. Softw. Tools Appl. **20**(2), 1089–1099 (2017)
11. Lim, D., Ong, Y.-S., Jin, Y., Sendhoff, B., Lee, B.-S.: Efficient hierarchical parallel genetic algorithm using grid computing. Future Gener. Comput. Syst. **23**(4), 658–670 (2007)
12. Liu, Y.Y., Wang, S.: A scalable parallel genetic algorithm for the generalized assignment problem. Parallel Comput. **46**, 98–119 (2015)
13. Trivedi, A., Srinivasan, D., Biswas, S., Reindl, T.: Hybridizing genetic algorithm with differential evolution for solving the unit commitment scheduling problem. Swarm Evol. Comput. **23**, 50–64 (2015)
14. Gu, L., Li, H.: Memory or time performance evaluation for iterative operation on hadoop and spark. In: High-Performance Computing and Communications and IEEE International Conference on Embedded and Ubiquitous Computing (HPCC EUC) (2013)
15. Wani, M.A., Jabin, S.: Big data: issues, challenges, and techniques in business intelligence. In: Aggarwal, V.B., Bhatnagar, V., Mishra, D.K. (eds.) Big Data Analytics. AISC, vol. 654, pp. 613–628. Springer, Singapore (2018). https://doi.org/10.1007/978-981-10-6620-7_59
16. Whitley, D., Rana, S., Heckendorn, R.B.: The island model genetic algorithm: on separability, population size, and convergence. CIT J. Comput. Inf. Technol. **7**(1), 33–47 (1999)
17. Verma, A., Llorà, X., Goldberg, D.E., Campbell, R.H.: Scaling simple, compact and extended compact genetic algorithms using MapReduce. Illinois Genetic Algorithms Laboratory (Illinois) report no. 2009001, illegal, University of Illinois, Urbana-Champaign (2009)
18. Ke˘co, D., Subasi, A.: Parallelization of genetic algorithms using hadoop Map/Reduce. SouthEast Eur. J. Soft Comput. **1**(2), 56–59 (2002)

19. Osuna, E.C., Gao, W., Neumann, F., Sudholt, D.: Speeding up evolutionary multi-objective optimization through diversity-based parent selection. In: Genetic and Evolutionary Computation Conference, Berlin, Germany (2017)
20. Gao, W., Neumann, F.: Runtime analysis of maximizing population diversity in single-objective optimization. In: Genetic and Evolutionary Computation Conference, Vancouver, Canada (2014
21. Junior, B.A., Pinheiro, P.R., Coelho, P.V.: A parallel biased random-key genetic algorithm with multiple populations applied to irregular strip packing problems. Math. Probl. Eng. **2017**, 11 (2017)
22. Gronwald, F., Chang, S., Jin, A.: Determining a source in air dispersion with a parallel genetic algorithm. Int. J. Emerg. Technol. Adv. Eng. **7**(8), 174–185 (2017)
23. Lissoni, A., Witt, C.: A runtime analysis of parallel evolutionary algorithms in dynamic optimization. Algorithmica **78**(2), 641–659 (2017)
24. Lässig, J., Sudholt, D.: Adaptive population models for offspring populations and parallel evolutionary algorithms. In: 11th Workshop Proceedings on Foundations of Genetic Algorithms, Schwarzenberg, Austria (2011)
25. Shoro, A.G., Soomro, T.R.: Big data analysis: apache spark perspective. Global J. Comput. Sci. Technol. **15**(1), 09–14 (2015)
26. Zaharia, M., et al.: Apache spark: a unified engine for big data processing. Commun. ACM **59**(11), 56–65 (2016)
27. Witt, C.: Runtime analysis of the (μ + 1) EA on simple pseudo-Boolean functions. Evol. Comput. **14**(1), 65–86 (2006)
28. Zaharia, M., et al.: Apache spark: a unified engine for big data processing. Commun. ACM **59**(11), 59–65 (2016)
29. Armbrust, M., et al.: Spark sql: relational data processing in spark. In: Proceedings of the 2015 ACM SIGMOD International Conference on Management of Data, pp. 1383–1394. ACM, May 2015
30. Meng, X., et al.: MLlib: machine learning in apache spark. J. Mach. Learn. Res. **17**(1), 1235–1241 (2016)

EEG-Based Seizure Diagnosis
Using Discriminative Fractal Features
from Feature Selection

Su Yang[1,3]($\boxtimes$), Gang Li[2], Jing Lu[2], Yi Sun[1], and Zhengyu Huang[2]

[1] Shanghai Key Laboratory of Intelligent Information Processing,
School of Computer Science, Fudan University, Shanghai 201203, China
suyang@fudan.edu.cn
[2] Department of Neurology, East Hospital,
Tongji University School of Medicine, Shanghai 200120, China
[3] School of Computer Science, Xi'an University of Technology, Xi'an, China

Abstract. EEG classification has received much attention in computer-aided diagnosis for seizure. However, the present feature extraction strategies lead to uninterpretable features to which human vision is not sensitive, and due to the lack of explicit knowledge consistent with human intuition in such features, their usage in clinic diagnosis is limited. Inspired by human perception of seizure patterns, from a morphological point of view, we propose to make use of blanket-covering dimensions for seizure diagnosis, which act as a morphological lens of waveform complexity to enable visually straightforward features consistent with human perception. Moreover, we apply feature selection to mine the relevant features for seizure diagnosis from a pool of blanket-covering dimensions computed by combining different scales. The fractal dimensions computed as such combined with multifractals lead to 97.72% precision in classifying healthy people, seizure-inactive patients, and seizure-active patients on a public benchmark.

Keywords: Fractal dimension · Multifractal · Chaos · Feature selection · Computer-aided diagnosis

1 Introduction

EEG classification for seizure diagnosis has received much attention in the context of signal processing and machine learning. So far, a variety of techniques in terms of feature extraction and pattern classification have been proposed in the literature: The existing features fall into the following categories: Time-domain features like zero-crossing intervals in time series [22] and 1-dimensional local binary pattern [21], spectra based features [3, 7, 8], time-frequency analysis and wavelet transform based features [4, 10–13, 24], high order statistics [17], sparse representation based features [1], and nonlinear features such as approximate entropy [3], Lyapunov exponents [4, 5], fractal dimensions [18], multifractal features [16], statistics over locally linear embedding [23], and zero-crossing statistics on Poincare surfaces of section [6]. Meanwhile, the machine learning methods can be sorted into the following categories:

© Springer Nature Switzerland AG 2019
D.-S. Huang et al. (Eds.): ICIC 2019, LNCS 11643, pp. 436–447, 2019.
https://doi.org/10.1007/978-3-030-26763-6_42

neural networks [5, 10, 13], support vector machines [3, 4, 8], neuro-fuzzy inferences systems [11], Gaussian mixture models [22], and ensemble methods [7, 12]. Besides, feature selection is a common practice to obtain highly relevant features prior to classification [20].

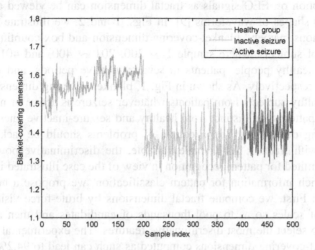

Fig. 1. Blanket-covering dimension computed at two selected scales for 3 groups: Healthy, inactive seizure, and active seizure.

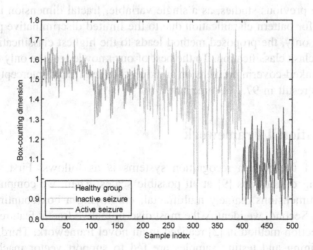

Fig. 2. Box-counting dimension computed at all scales for 3 groups: Healthy, inactive seizure, and active seizure

The existing works are limited in that the present feature description makes no sense for human perception nor is interpretable such that the doctors cannot see explicit knowledge from machine diagnosis. In practice, human experts distinguish seizure patterns in EEG signals according to morphological characteristics since human vision is sensitive to graphics, not numerical strings. This motivates us to study fractal-based feature description on EEG signals as fractal dimension can be viewed as a morphological lens of shapes of waveforms [9]. In Figs. 1 and 2, we illustrate two types of fractal dimensions, namely, blanket-covering dimension and box-counting dimension, for 3 groups of subjects, where sample $1 \sim 200$, $201 \sim 400$, and $401 \sim 500$ correspond with healthy people, patients in seizure-inactive periods, and patients with active seizure, respectively. As shown in Fig. 1, blanket-covering dimension is able to distinguish healthy subjects from patients whatever seizure is active or not. In Fig. 2, active seizure patterns are distinct from healthy and seizure-inactive ones in the sense of box-counting dimension. Yet, a couple of problems should be tackled for EEG classification with fractals: As a single variable, the discriminative power of fractal dimension is limited for pattern recognition in view of the case illustrated in Figs. 1 and 2. To obtain rich information for pattern classification, we propose a new computational strategy: First, we compute fractal dimensions by brute-force visiting different combination of scales so as to pool thousands of candidates and then apply feature selection [2] to select the most discriminative features. The experimental results show that the blanket-covering dimensions computed as such can lead to 94.2% accuracy in classifying the 3 classes by using support vector machine as classifier [15]. If multi-fractals including box-counting dimension, information dimension, and correlation dimension are taken into account [14], the classification precision can be improved to 97.72%. In the previous studies, as a single variable, fractal dimension is rarely used independently for pattern classification due.to the limited discriminative power. Using fractal features only, the proposed method leads to the highest classification accuracy, 97.72%, for 3-class classification. To the best of our knowledge, the only competitor is [18], where blanked-covering dimension and the so-called fractal intercept computed as multiple scales result in 97.13% precision.

2 Computational Framework

The pipeline of the pattern recognition systems is as follows: First, we compute blanket-covering dimensions [9] at all possible scales. Then, we compute the generalized fractal dimensions, namely multifractal, employing a box-counting based fast algorithm [14]. Second, we identify the most discriminative fractal features referring to the feature selection method in [2] realized in an novel framework. Third, the selected features of training and testing samples are fed to support vector machine [15] for classification.

2.1 Blanket-Covering Dimension

For a time sequence $f(n)$: $n = 1, 2, \ldots, N$, perform the dilation operation in terms of morphology to form an upper envelope $Ur(n)$ and a lower envelope $Lr(n)$ at a given scale r:

$$U_r(n) = \max\{U_{r-1}(n-1), U_{r-1}(n)+1, U_{r-1}(n+1)\} \tag{1}$$

$$L_r(n) = \min\{L_{r-1}(n-1), L_{r-1}(n)-1, L_{r-1}(n+1)\} \tag{2}$$

$$U_0(n) = L_0(n) = f(n) \tag{3}$$

The fractal measure at scale r is defined as

$$A_r = \sum_{n=1}^{N} [U_r(n) - L_r(n)] \tag{4}$$

Once the fractal measures at two given scales i and j are obtained, the blanket-covering dimension can be computed:

$$D_{ij} = 1 - \left[\log(A_i) - \log(A_j)\right] / [\log(i) - \log(j)] \tag{5}$$

By trying every possible combination of two scales, we can obtain a set of features $\{D_{ij} | i, j \in [1, R] \wedge i \neq j\}$, where R refers to the predefined maximum scale.

2.2 Generalized Fractal Dimension from Box Counting

For a time sequence $f(n)$: $n = 1, 2, \ldots, N$, we reformat it into a 2-dimensional point set as follows:

$$X_n = n/N \tag{6}$$

$$Y_n = f(n) / \sum_{n=0}^{N} f(n) \tag{7}$$

Then, Yn is normalized through the following operation:

$$Y_n - \min_{n}\{Y_n\} \rightarrow Y_n \tag{8}$$

We partition the 2-dimensional space spanned by $\{(Xn, Yn)|n = 1, 2, ..., N\}$ into grid and compute the probability that the points falling into every box as:

$$P_i(r) = S_i(r)/\sum_{i=1}^{M} S_i(r) \tag{9}$$

where $S_i(r)$ denote the number of the points falling into box i, M the number of the boxes enclosing at least one point, and r the box size applied to grid partition. The fractal measure at scale r is defined as follows:

$$Z_r(q) = \begin{cases} \sum_{i=1}^{M} P_i(r).\log P_i(r) & q = 1 \\ \sum_{i=1}^{M} [P_i(r)]^q & q \neq 1 \end{cases} \tag{10}$$

Then, the generalized fractal dimension can be computed by performing least-squared fitting over $\{[\log r, \log Z_r(q)] \,|r\in[r_{min}, r_{max}]\}$ and the exact definition is:

$$D_q = \begin{cases} \lim_{r\to 0} Z_r(q)/\log r & q = 1 \\ \frac{1}{q-1}\lim_{r\to 0} \frac{\log Z_r(q)}{\log r} & q \neq 1 \end{cases} \tag{11}$$

D_0, D_1, and D_2 correspond with the 3 well-known fractal dimensions, namely, box-counting dimension, information dimension, and correlation dimension, which act as the multifractal features in this study.

2.3 Feature Selection Based on Run Covering

The algorithm is based on computing the discriminative possibility of each sample at each dimension through the run length defined below, and counting how many samples correspond with the best discrimination at each dimension.

Definition 1 (Run): Provided the feature values at dimension k has been sorted in ascending order: $F_{k1} \leq F_{k2} \leq ... \leq F_{kL}$, the class labels of which are $[C(F_{k1}), C(F_{k2}), ..., C(F_{kL})]$, a run is defined as a subsequence of the feature values whose class labels are identical.

Definition 2 (Support of Run): If $C(F_{k,j-1}) \neq C(F_{kj}) = C(F_{k,j+1}) = ... = C(F_{k,j+T-1}) \neq C(F_{k,j+T})$, where $F_{k,j-1} \leq F_{kj} \leq F_{k,j+1} \leq ... \leq F_{k,j+T-1} \leq F_{k,j+T}$, then, $\{F_{kl} \mid l \in [j, j + T-1]\}$ forms a run with support of T. Here, the support is defined as the length of the run.

Algorithm 1:

Input:

F_{kl}: Feature value at the ith dimension of the jth data sample for $k=1,2,...K$ and $j=1,2,...,L$.

$C(F_{kl})$: Class label of F_{kl}.

Output:

I: Indices of selected features

Algorithm:

1. For each dimension $k \in [1,K]$, sort the feature values in ascending order to satisfy $F'_{k1} \leq F'_{k2} \leq ... \leq F'_{kL}$, where $F'_{kj} \in \{F_{k1}, F_{k2}, ..., F_{kL}\}$ for $j=1,2,...,L$

2. Compute the runs of the data samples with identical class labels at each dimension, and each data sample at a given dimension is marked with the support of the run to which the data sample belongs, which is denoted as $\{O(F'_{kj}) \mid k \in [1,K]; j \in [1,L]\}$.

3. For each data sample $j \in [1,L]$, compute the maximum run length to cover it taking into account the K dimensions: $M_j = \max\{O(F'_{kj}) \mid k \in [1,K]\}$.

4. Initialize a flag matrix S: $\{S_{kj}=0 \mid k \in [1,K]; j \in [1,L]\}$.

5. Scanning S and let $S_{kj}=1$ if $S_{kj}= M_j \wedge M_j \geq thre$, where *thre* is a predefined hyper parameter acting as a threshold to filter out the perturbation of short runs.

6. Call Algorithm 2 to get feature selection result I from S.

Algorithm 1:

Input:

$S=\{S_{kj} \mid k \in [1,K]; j \in [1,L]\}$.

Output:

I: Set of indices of features.

Algorithm:

Initialize I as an empty set;

while true

Let $S_k = \sum_{j=1}^{L} S_{kj}$ for $k=1,2,...,K$;

$V=\max\{S_k \mid k=1,2,...,K\}$;

$i=\arg \max\{S_k \mid k=1,2,...,K\}$;

if $V>0$

$I=I \cup i$;

$D=\{j \mid S_{ij}=0 \wedge j \in [1,L]\}$;

Scan S to let $S_{kj}=0$ for $j \in D \wedge k \in [1,K]$;

else

quit;

end if

end while

Note that when computing runs in Algorithm 1, if $C(F_{k,j}) \neq C(F_{kl}) \wedge F_{k,j} = F_{kl}$, $j \in [1, L]$ and $l \in [1, L]$, we let $C(F_{k,j}) = C(F_{kl}) = 0$ to mark such data samples as indistinguishable such that they will be exclude from the counting of run length. Besides, *thre* defines the minimum run length to have enough members spanning a pattern.

A higher value of run length (the support of a run) corresponds with a better case for pattern classification as the samples from the same class distribute in a more homogeneous manner. For data sample $j \in [1, L]$, in general, it belongs to one run per dimension and there are K runs to cover it taking into account the K dimensions, where the run with the maximum support among the K runs represents the best case for classifying this data sample. If the best case for classifying data sample j as mentioned before appears at feature index k, we let $S_{kj} = 1$ to represent such a case in S. Therefore, S_k counts how many data samples correspond with the best cases in terms of pattern classification at dimension k. The goal of the feature selection algorithm is to iteratively find the dimension corresponding with the maximum value of S_k in each epoch. Note that when dimension k has been added to the set of selected features, all the data samples corresponding with $S_{kj} = 1$, which means the samples with the best discrimination at dimension k, should be removed without any further consideration in the subsequent procedure, that is, we turn the flags of all such data samples into $S_{kj} = 0$ and such samples will not appear in any other dimension to take part in feature selection.

3   Experimental Results

We use the data developed in [19] to evaluate the performance of the proposed feature for EEG classification. This data set is composed of 5 classes of EEG signals denoted as Z, O, N, F, S, each of which contains 100 samples of 23.6 s duration with 173.61 Hz sampling rate. The data length of every signal is 4097. A bandpass filter of 0.53–80 Hz is applied prior to data sampling. The description of the 5 classes is provided in Table 1.

Table 1. Description of data

Name of classes	Description
Z	5 healthy persons with eye open
O	5 healthy persons with eye close
N	5 patients in seizure-free intervals with signals from epileptogenic zone
F	5 patients in seizure-free intervals with signals from the opposite zone
S	5 patients during seizure-active period

For every class, 50% samples are selected randomly to train the classifier while the other samples are used for testing. Test as such is repeated 10 times with randomly selected training and testing samples with regard to each run. The performance data reported in the following is the average over the 10 tests. We use the classification accuracy as the performance index, which is the ratio of the number of the correctly classified samples to that of the total samples for each class. For support vector machine (SVM) [15], we apply 5-fold cross validation on the training data to obtain the best parameters for SVM.

In Table 2, we list the performance of different features for 3-class classification, where ZC, LLE, Fractal+FS, and Fractal2+FS refer to the zero-crossing feature proposed in [6], the LLE feature proposed in [23], the blanket-covering dimensions resulting from the feature selection, and the feature selection granted features from both blanket-covering dimensions and multifractals. The latter two solutions have been described in Sect. 2, where the parameter in computing blanket-covering dimension is set as $R = 50$, which leads to 1225 features. Along with the multifractal features D_0, D_1, and D_2 computed via box counting, three are 1228 fractal features in total. For feature selection, we let *thre* = 10. We see that the solution Fractal2+FS leads to 97.72% precision, close to that of ZC but better than that of LLE. Except for the aforementioned 4 solutions, in Table 3, we add 2 new solutions, that is, the zero-crossing features output by the feature selection algorithm, denoted as ZC+FS, and the selected features resulting from the feature selection over the combination of blanket-covering dimensions, multifractals, and zero-crossing features, denoted as Fractal2_ZC +FS. The Fractal+FS and Fractal2+FS solutions lead to 79.88% and 83.44% precision for 5-class classification, which are obviously lower than that of ZC. To examine whether the fractal features provide extra information over the chaotic feature [6], we perform classification based on the combined chaotic and fractal features resulting from the features selection, that is, Fractal2_ZC+FS. Such solution leads to 95.28% precision, which outperforms using either chaotic or fractal features alone with the performance improvement of 0.6% at least. This proves that the fractal features can provide complementary information to augment the chaotic feature based solution. To check whether the higher performance is attributed to feature selection only, it is compare to the solution based on the feature selection over the zero-crossing features, which leads to 94.12% precision, even inferior to the case without feature selection. This shows that the improved performance does result from incorporating fractal features into the existing solution [6].

Table 2. 3-class classification using SVM (%)

	Z&O	N&F	S	Ave.
ZC	99.9	99.5	98.4	99.27
LLE	97.5	96.2	90.6	94.77
Fractal+FS	97.3	94.9	90.4	94.2
Fractal2+FS	98.2	97.2	97.8	97.72

Table 3. 5-class classification using SVM (%)

	Z	O	N	F	S	Ave.
ZC	92.8	89.4	94.6	98.8	97.8	94.68
ZC+FS	95.4	86.6	94.6	96.4	97.6	94.12
LLE	83.2	83.4	75	63.4	91.2	79.24
Fractal+FS	90	91.4	71.6	56.4	90	79.88
Fractal2+FS	94	91.6	68.4	65	98.2	83.44
Fractal2-ZC+FS	94.2	90.6	95	98	98.6	95.28

Table 4. Classification precision (%) against feature dimension

Method	3 Classes		5 Classes	
	#Feature	%	#Feature	%
Fraclta2+FS+SVM	72	97.72	65	83.44
Fraclta2+SVM	1228	97.17	1228	81.88
Fractal2_ZC+FS+SVM	33	98.92	55	95.28
Fraclta2+FS+1NN	72	96.12	65	81
Fraclta2+1NN	1228	93.23	1228	75.6
Fractal2_ZC+FS+1NN	33	98.76	55	92.8

In Table 4, we evaluate the effect of the feature selection on the performance of the fractal features in terms of 3-class and 5-class classification, respectively. For 3-class classification with SVM, the feature selection improves the accuracy from 97.17% to 97.72% but the feature dimensionality is greatly reduced from 1228 to 72. For nearest neighbor (1NN) based 3-class classification, the performance improvement by means of the feature selection is more apparent, from 93.23% to 96.12%. For 5-class classification, SVM and 1NN improve the classification precision from 81.88% to 83.44% and from 75.6% to 81%, respectively, while the feature dimensionality is reduced from 1228 to 65. These results show that the feature selection leads to not only remarkable dimensionality reduction but also obvious performance improvement in terms of classification accuracy. Since the applied feature selection algorithm belongs to the filter category, not subject to classifier, the performance improvement can be observed using either SVM or 1NN. In Table 4, we also list the performance of the solution of Fractal2_ZC+FS for both SVM and 1NN classifier in terms of 3-class and 5-class classification. We can see that the feature selection method can find the best feature set of 33 and 55 features for 3-class and 5-class classification, respectively, with 98.92% and 95.28% precision using SVM classifier, and 98.76% and 92.8% precision using 1NN classifier.

Table 5. Comprehensive performance comparison for 3-class classification (Z, F, S)

Authors	Method	Year	%
Güler etc. [5]	Lyapunov exponents-Recurrent neural network	2005	96.79
Übeyli [12]	Wavelet-Mixture of expert network	2008	93.17
Sadati etc. [10]	Discrete wavelet transform-Adaptive neural fuzzy network	2006	85.9
Liang etc. [3]	Approximate entropy, spectra-SVM	2010	98.67
Tzallas etc. [13]	Time-frequency analysis-ANN	2009	100
Duque-Muñoz etc. [24]	STFT-SVM	2014	100
Kaya etc. [21]	One-dimensional local binary patterns- Bayes network	2014	95.67
Yang etc. [6]	ZC-SVM	2017	99.27
Wang etc. [18]	Fractal+SVM	2013	97.13
This work	**Fractal2+FS+SVM (#Feature = 72)**		**97.72**

Table 6. Comprehensive performance comparison for 5-class classification (Z, O, N, F, S)

Authors	Method	Year	%
Güler etc. [11]	Wavelet transform- Adaptive neuro-fuzzy inferences system	2005	98.68
Güler etc. [4]	Wavelet transform, Lyapunov exponents-SVM	2007	99.28
Übeyli etc. [7]	Spectra-Modified mixture of expert model	2007	98.60
Übeyli [8]	Spectra-SVM	2008	98.30
Liang etc. [3]	Approximate entropy, spectra-SVM	2010	85.9
Tzallas etc. [13]	Time-frequency analysis-ANN	2009	89
Yang etc. [6]	ZC-SVM (#Feature = 45)	2017	94.68
This work	**Fractal2+FS+SVM (#Feature = 65)**		**83.44**
	Fractal2-ZC+FS+SVM (#Feature = 55)		**95.28**

Further, we compare the performance of the proposed method with those of the state-of-the-art works in Tables 5 and 6 in terms of 3-class and 5-class classification, respectively. For 3-class classification, we see that the proposed method is comparable to the existing methods. In the context of fractal feature based classification, the proposed method outperforms the method proposed in [18] slightly, where the precision comparison is 97.72% against 97.13%. However, the authors of [18] do not report 5-class classification accuracy but the proposed method leads to 83.44% precision using fractal features only. For 5-class classification, although the fractal features do not lead to high classification precision. However, incorporating such fractal features can augment the existing solutions. One example is: The combination of ZC and the proposed solution gains advantage over using either scheme alone, where the performance has been improved from 94.68% to 95.28%. Note that such performance improvement does not lead to much higher data dimensionality. Here, the feature number of the ensemble solution is only 55 following feature selection, which is comparable to the feature number of 45 in ZC based solution.

The previous performance comparisons show that the proposed solution based on fractal features and feature selection can lead to satisfactory performance for 3-class classification while augment the existing solutions for 5-class classification.

Table 7. SVM based 5-class classification against parameter for feature selection

thre	5	10	15
#Feature	107	65	33
Precision (%)	82.92	83.44	83.08

To check the impact of the parameter *thre* on feature selection, we list in Table 7 the results of 5-class classification using SVM classifier against different values of the parameter, where *thre* = 10 is the best one and the performance changes little since *thre* ≥ 10.

4 Concluding Remarks

We propose to make use of blanked-covering dimensions and generalized fractal dimensions computed via box counting to characterize the morphological patterns of EEG signals for seizure diagnosis. Computer aided diagnosis based on morphological features is consistent to human intuition, so it is more practical for clinic usage by enabling human experts to understand the knowledge fed by machine decision. As a one-dimensional variable, classical fractal dimension cannot provide enough rich information for pattern classification. Thus, we propose to compute fractal features by trying every pair of scales and apply feature selection to identify the relevant features truly contributive to distinguish different classes of EEG signals. The classification accuracy is 97.72% for 3-class classification, which is an acceptable performance in practice.

As for feature selection, unlike most of the existing methods, the proposed method can determine the dimensionality of feature selection automatically. By using the length of the run covering each data sample as the measure of discriminative power, the best case for each sample is marked in the corresponding feature dimension, and the feature dimension corresponding with as more as possible data samples in terms of the best discrimination is iteratively selected. The experiments show that the feature selection algorithm can lead to performance improvement with considerable dimensionality reduction.

Acknowledgment. This work is supported by Shanghai Science and Technology Commission (grant No. 17511104203) and NSFC (grant NO. 61472087).

References

1. Nagaraj, S.B., Stevenson, N.J., Marnane, W.P., Boylan, G.B., Lightbody, G.: Neonatal seizure detection using atomic decomposition with a novel dictionary. IEEE Trans. Biomed. Eng. **61**(11), 2724–2732 (2014)
2. Yang, S., Liang, J., Wang, Y., Winstanley, A.: Feature selection based on run covering. In: Chang, L.-W., Lie, W.-N. (eds.) PSIVT 2006. LNCS, vol. 4319, pp. 208–217. Springer, Heidelberg (2006). https://doi.org/10.1007/11949534_21
3. Liang, S.F., Wang, H.C., Chang, W.L.: Combination of EEG complexity and spectral analysis for epilepsy diagnosis and seizure detection. EURASIP J. Adv. Signal Process. **2010**, 62 (2010)
4. Guler, I., Ubeyli, E.D.: Multiclass support vector machines for EEG-signals classification. IEEE Trans. Inf Technol. Biomed. **11**(2), 117–126 (2007)
5. Güler, N.F., Ubeyli, E.D., Güler, I.: Recurrent neural networks employing Lyapunov exponents for EEG signals classification. Expert Syst. Appl. **29**(3), 506–514 (2005)
6. Yang, S., Zhang, A., Zhang, J., Zhang, W.: A new chaotic feature for EEG classification based seizure diagnosis. In: 2017 IEEE International Conference on Acoustics, Speech and Signal Processing (ICASSP), pp. 4651–4655. IEEE (2017)
7. Ubeyli, E.D., Güler, I.: Features extracted by eigenvector methods for detecting variability of EEG signals. Pattern Recogn. Lett. **28**(5), 592–603 (2007)

8. Ubeyli, E.D.: Analysis of EEG signals by combining eigenvector methods and multiclass support vector machines. Comput. Biol. Med. **38**(1), 14–22 (2008)
9. Maragos, P., Sun, F.K.: Measuring the fractal dimension of signals: morphological covers and iterative optimization. IEEE Trans. Signal Process. **41**(1), 108 (1993)
10. Sadati, N., Mohseni, H.R., Maghsoudi, A.: Epileptic seizure detection using neural fuzzy networks. In: 2006 IEEE International Conference on Fuzzy Systems, pp. 596– 600. IEEE (2006)
11. Güler, I., Ubeyli, E.D.: Adaptive neuro-fuzzy inference system for classification of EEG signals using wavelet coefficients. J, Neurosci. Methods **148**(2), 113–121 (2005)
12. Ubeyli, E.D.: Wavelet/mixture of experts network structure for EEG signals classification. Expert Syst. Appl. **34**(3), 1954–1962 (2008)
13. Tzallas, A.T., Tsipouras, M.G., Fotiadis, D.I.: Epileptic seizure detection in EEGs using time–frequency analysis. IEEE Trans. Inf Technol. Biomed. **13**(5), 703–710 (2009)
14. Meisel, L., Johnson, M., Cote, P.: Box-counting multifractal analysis. Phys. Rev. A **45**(10), 6989 (1992)
15. Chang, C.C., Lin, C.J.: LIBSVM: a library for support vector machines. ACM Trans. Intell. Syst. Technol. (TIST) **2**(3), 27 (2011)
16. Ghosh, D., Dutta, S., Chakraborty, S.: Multifractal detrended cross-correlation analysis for epileptic patient in seizure and seizure free status. Chaos, Solitons Fractals **67**, 1–10 (2014)
17. Alam, S.S., Bhuiyan, M.I.H.: Detection of seizure and epilepsy using higher order statistics in the EMD domain. IEEE J. Biomed. Health Inf. **17**(2), 312–318 (2013)
18. Wang, Y., Zhou, W., Yuan, Q., Li, X., Meng, Q., Zhao, X., Wang, J.: Comparison of ictal and interictal EEG signals using fractal features. Int. J. Neural Syst. **23**(06), 1350028 (2013)
19. Andrzejak, R.G., Lehnertz, K., Mormann, F., Rieke, C., David, P., Elger, C.E.: Indications of nonlinear deterministic and finite-dimensional structures in time series of brain electrical activity: dependence on recording region and brain state. Phys. Rev. E **64**(6), 061907 (2001)
20. Dhiman, R., Saini, J., et al.: Genetic algorithms tuned expert model for detection of epileptic seizures from EEG signatures. Appl. Soft Comput. **19**, 8–17 (2014)
21. Kaya, Y., Uyar, M., Tekin, R., Yıldırım, S.: 1D-local binary pattern based feature extraction for classification of epileptic EEG signals. Appl. Math. Comput. **243**, 209–219 (2014)
22. Zandi, A.S., Tafreshi, R., Javidan, M., Dumont, G.A.: Predicting epileptic seizures in scalp eeg based on a variational bayesian gaussian mixture model of zero-crossing intervals. IEEE Trans. Biomed. Eng. **60**(5), 1401–1413 (2013)
23. Yang, S., Shen, I.-F.: Manifold analysis in reconstructed state space for nonlinear signal classification. In: Huang, D.-S., Heutte, L., Loog, M. (eds.) ICIC 2007. LNCS, vol. 4681, pp. 930–937. Springer, Heidelberg (2007). https://doi.org/10.1007/978-3-540-74171-8_94
24. Duque-Muñoz, L., Espinosa-Oviedo, J.J., Castellanos-Dominguez, C.G.: Identification and monitoring of brain activity based on stochastic relevance analysis of short–time EEG rhythms. Biomed. Eng. Online **13**(1), 123 (2014)

Classifying Mixed Patterns of Proteins in High-Throughput Microscopy Images Using Deep Neural Networks

Enze Zhang[1,2], Boheng Zhang[3], Shaohan Hu[4], Fa Zhang[1(✉)],
and Xiaohua Wan[1]

[1] High Performance Computer Research Center, Institute of Computing
Technology, Chinese Academy of Sciences, Beijing, China
{zhangenze,zhangfa,wanxiaohua}@ict.ac.cn
[2] University of Chinese Academy of Sciences, Beijing, China
[3] Department of Automation, Tsinghua University, Beijing, China
zbh17@mails.tsinghua.edu.cn
[4] School of Software, Tsinghua University, Beijing, China
hush17@mails.tsinghua.edu.cn

Abstract. Proteins contribute significantly in most body functions within cells, and are essential to the physiological activities of every creature. Microscopy imaging, as a remarkable technique, is applied to observe and identify proteins in different kinds of cells, by which the analysis results are critical to the biomedical studies. However, as the development of high-throughput microscopy imaging, images of protein microscopy are generated in a faster pace ever, making it harder for experts to manually identify them. For better digging and understanding the information of the proteins in those huge amounts of images, it is urgent for methods to identify the mixed-patterned proteins within various cells automatically and accurately. Here in this paper, we design some novel and effective data preparation and preprocessing methods for high-throughput microscopy protein datasets. We propose ACP layer and "buffering" layers, using them to design customized architectures for some typical CNN classifiers with new inputs and head parts. The modifications let the models be more adaptive and accurate to our task. We train the models in more effective and efficient optimization strategies that we design, e.g., cycle learning with learning rate scheduling. Besides, greedy selection of thresholds and multi-sized models ensembling in the post-process stage are proposed to further improve the prediction accuracy. Our experimental results based on Human Protein Atlas datasets demonstrates that the proposed methods show an excellent performance in mixed-patterned protein classifications to date, even beyond the state-of-the-art architecture GapNet-PL by 0.02 to 0.03 in F1 score. The whole work reveals the usefulness of our methods for high-throughput microscopy protein images identification.

Keywords: Protein classification · Deep learning · Mixed patterns of proteins · High-throughput microscopy images

© Springer Nature Switzerland AG 2019
D.-S. Huang et al. (Eds.): ICIC 2019, LNCS 11643, pp. 448–459, 2019.
https://doi.org/10.1007/978-3-030-26763-6_43

1 Introduction

Proteins perform their function in different types and forms within distinct cells. Understanding various protein structures in different cell types of highly different morphology is fundamental in understanding processes of human body. Protein identification was restricted to one pattern in certain types of cells. However, the models are expected to recognize multi-patterns that are mixed together among various types of cells. The identification of some specific patterns of proteins may reveal the contacts and relations of them and help us knowing better about biological features, such as diseases or evolution, of ourselves.

Recently, the Human Protein Atlas is determined to create a smart-microscopy system to classify the proteins and localize their positions from high-throughput images using methods capable of classifying mixed patterns of proteins in cellular microscopy images (see Fig. 1). Generally, human experts can identify proteins based on those high-throughput microscopy images [1]. However, it is considered as high-cost and time-consuming because there are lots of extremely similar and confusing patterns in those images. Therefore, high performance in classifying proteins is expected by applying deep learning methods since the HPA project has provided plenty of protein microscopy images with annotations as our data for training neural network models [7].

Fig. 1. Some random protein microscopy images from HPA Cell Atlas datasets.

DNNs methods have become popular in image analysis and other tasks currently as they can learn features automatically. Especially, CNNs have been strong tools for image classification, localization, detection, segmentation and so on, e.g., FCNs [3], VggNet [6], InceptionNet [3], ResNet [4], DenseNet [5]. Currently, CNNs have also been applied to analyze biological images, medical images, and microscopy images. However, these classification networks cannot be applied to these high-throughput microscopy data directly due to some certain characteristics such as the complex patterns in the data, relatively high resolution with random sizes, and high noise.

GapNet-PL [7] is a state-of-the-art CNN architecture that has been designed to tackle the characteristics of high-throughput fluorescence microscopy imaging data and uses global averages of filters at different abstraction levels. The architecture can achieve an excellent performance on datasets provided by HPA project. For better accuracy, we came up with some novel methods of dataset preprocessing, which helped to improve the performance. We utilized some typical CNNs feature extractors and built our networks by combining these normal encoders with the novel customized head parts. Moreover, we came up with some new optimization strategies. Greedy selection of thresholds and multi-sized model ensembling in postprocessing are designed to further improve the scores of the models. Our experimental results show that the proposed methods make our models achieve higher accuracy than all baseline approaches. In the following, we will explain our datasets that are applied to the experiments and the proposed methods in details.

2   Methods

2.1   Dataset Preparation and Preprocessing

All experiments were conducted on datasets released for the "Human Protein Atlas Image Classification" challenge by Human Protein Atlas [8]. The main dataset contains around 30000 samples for training and 11500 samples for testing from part of the HPA Cell Atlas led by Dr. Emma Lundberg. And we also adopt around 70000 external data from the HPA Cell Atlas [9]. Therefore, we have around 100000 samples for training and validating, and about 30000 for testing. We removed about 6000 duplicated samples which seem extremely similar by image hashing to avoid label distribution shifting problem.

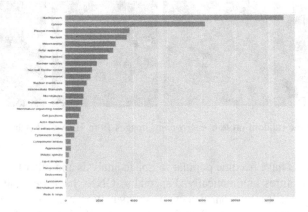

Fig. 2. The categories and calculated distribution of 28 protein classes (Color figure online).

There are 28 distinct classes (or types) of proteins in the dataset. The data is collected via the confocal microscopy approach. However, the dataset includes 27 various cell types of highly different morphology, and this could influence the protein patterns of the distinct organelles. Every sample in the dataset is formed of 4 image channels, red, green, blue and yellow. Each channel filter is stored as an individual file. The red channel represents for the microtubules, green for protein, blue for nucleus, and yellow for reticulum. Obviously, the green channel files should be used as the labels, and other channels could also be utilized for references. We use all filter information for our inputs. Moreover, there is extreme label imbalance in the dataset (see Fig. 2). Some type of proteins may take most part of the whole dataset, e.g., Nucleoplasm, Cytosol. Rare classes, like Rods & rings, are hard to train and predict but play an important role in the score. Therefore, we adopted multilabel stratification particularly to balance the inconsistent distributions of training and validation data when splitting the whole training dataset. The training samples were randomly split into a training (90%, 80% when 5-folds CV) set and a validation (10%, 20% when 5-folds CV) set by different random seeds (Fig. 3).

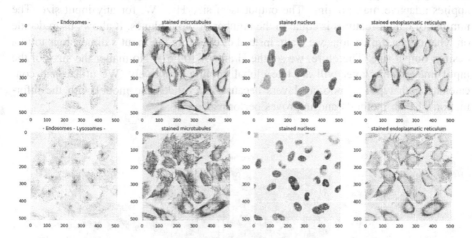

Fig. 3. The figure illustrates some protein images (green) related to Endosomes together with other three filter channels. The first row shows a sample that only contains Endosomes proteins. The second row displays another sample which contains two mixed types of protein. (Color figure online)

The data was provided as two versions of the same images, a scaled set of 512×512 PNG files and full-sized original images (a mix of 2048×2048 and 3072×3072 TIFF files). However, there are only full-sized images for our external data. To obtain more accurate prediction results, full size original images were adopted. Though the original images are with high quality, we must find a balance between model efficiency and accuracy. Therefore, we resized every image to 768×768 or 1024×1024 depending on its original size. And we randomly crop 512×512 patches from 768×768 images (or cropping 768×768 patches from 1024×1024 images) when training time augmentations before feeding images to the models.

2.2 Customized Architectures

We design our architectures inspired by some typical classification networks, improving them with more targeted, accurate and adaptive head parts, as well as new input layers. We implement these architectures with two parts, encoders and heads. We adopt some encoders from the widely utilized classifiers, as they have been proved advanced and effective in many situations. We change the input layers to ones with 4 channels because all four filters (red, green, blue, yellow) of each image are utilized.

The head part is key to the task. The high-throughput microscopy images of proteins are often related with various sizes, high resolution and complex patterns. Therefore, we drop the GAP (global average pooling) layers at the beginning of other typical heads (see Fig. 4(a)). Instead we propose and build up an ACP (adaptive concatenate pooling) layer by concatenating two kinds of pooling layers, an adaptive average pooling layer and an adaptive max pooling layer, together in channel dimension (see Fig. 4(b)). An adaptive average pooling layer applies adaptive average pooling over an input signal composed of several input planes, while an adaptive max pooling layer applies adaptive max pooling. The output is of size H × W, for any input size. The number of output features is equal to the number of input planes. It allows us to decide on what output dimensions we want, instead of choosing the input's dimensions to fit a desired output size. Therefore, we set the H and W to be 1. No matter the sizes of the input images, this layer will act like global pooling adaptively. We utilize and concatenate both types of pooling layers because it provides the model with the information of both methods and improves performance.

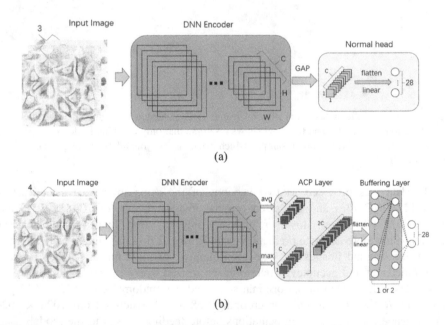

(a)

(b)

Fig. 4. The comparison between (a) typical CNN classifier with normal input and head part, and (b) proposed architecture with customized head and input layer (Color figure online).

We assume that the channel number of output features by a general encoder is C. After our adaptive concatenate pooling, the channel number will be 2C, usually a relatively large number. Instead of directly cutting or shrinking the channel number to the target channel number as usual classifiers do, which would lose much information we have got from encoded features, we added one or two middle linear layers which we call "buffering layers", with channel numbers distributed from C to C/4, to maintain the original feature information as much as possible (see Fig. 4(b)). Both the adaptive concatenate pooling and buffering layers help to let the classifiers be more accurate on their specific task. The modification of the input layers also matters.

2.3   Optimization Strategies

Although we may have designed good architectures, we discover it's rather hard and inefficient to train networks on this dataset so we cannot get an ideal result. Therefore, we design some more effective and efficient optimization strategies. While training our models, we divide our networks to 2 different layer groups (see Fig. 5(a)). The first group consists of the layers of encoders and the second group includes the layers of heads. Therefore, we can apply multi learning rates on different layer groups. It has been proven that building CNNs based on pre-trained architectures usually performs better than building ones from scratch. Obviously, when adapted to a new task, the weights of top layers need the most changing since they are newly initialized and present more high-level object features and those deeper-level (encoder part) layers need less change since they are already well-trained to recognize some primary features like lines and corners. Since the images in HPA datasets are quite different from ImageNet that only include normal and daily pictures, we decrease the learning rate for first layer group (encoder part) only by 2 to 3 times. Therefore, models are trained with [lr/2, lr] where lr denotes the learning rate.

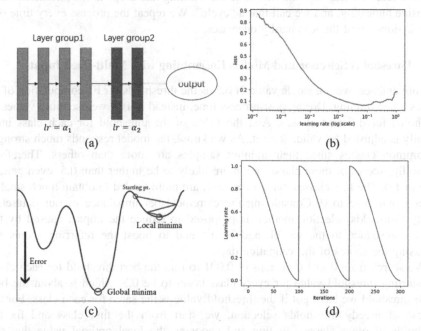

Fig. 5. (a) The network is divided with 2 layer groups with separate learning rate (b) The function of batch loss and learning rate when find the optimal starting lr (the best lr is around 1e −3 to 1e−2). (c) Some condition where the loss might be stuck at local minima as the learning rate keeps dropping during training. (d) An example of cycle learning with cosine annealing and cycle repetition (lr restart).

As for choosing the starting learning rates, we no longer try the learning rate from a larger one to a small one, or conversely. We begin with finding the optimal initial learning rate. In this method, at first, we train our networks with a relative low learning rate (around 1e−6). Then we gradually increase it exponentially with each batch, and the loss is recorded in an array for each learning rate at the same time (see Fig. 5(b)). The current optimal learning rate is the value found where the learning rate is highest yet the loss is still dropping.

After choosing the starting optimal learning rate, we adopted cycle learning with learning rate scheduling to train our models (see Fig. 5(d)). The cycle learning, inspired by Leslie Smith's work [10], contains two key factors which are cosine annealing and cycle repetition. Along the process of training, the total loss of the architecture should be closer and closer to the minimum (local or global). However, it is often found hard to converge as the loss gets closer to its minimum value. Cosine annealing solves the problem by decreasing the learning rate following the mode of cosine function with each batch of data. We start at a high-level of learning rate, and drop the learning rate based on a cosine function. We found this mode of learning rate decreasing works very well with the convergence problem in this task. Moreover, it is very likely for loss to be trapped at its local minimum instead of the global one during training (see Fig. 5(c)). Therefore, if we increase the learning rate suddenly, the current loss may find its way toward the global minimum by "jumping" out of the local minimum with a bigger step. We reset the learning rate each time the learning rate drops to it's minimum value by cosine annealing, and we call that a "cycle". We repeat the process every time one cycle is done, until the loss hardly decreases.

2.4   Thresholds Selection and Models Ensembling with Multi-sized Inputs

For convenience, we use single value of 0.5 as the thresholds for F1 computation of all classes when training. During post-process time, instead of 0.5, we use multi values as thresholds for different classes. And the value of the threshold for each class individually is adjusted by validation set. As we know, the model responds much strongly to common classes since their training samples are more than others. Therefore, probability scores of these classes are more likely to be higher than 0.5, even getting close to 1.0. The rare classes, on the contrary, are more tended to obtain much smaller scores even close to 0. Considering the extreme label imbalance of our dataset, a greedy thresholds selection method is proposed to reduce the impact caused by the sample imbalance to the model, and in the end to boost the referring scores via increasing the scores of the validation data.

We search from 0 to 1.0 in steps of 0.001 to find the best threshold for each class. The starting threshold value for every class is set to be 0.3, which is about the best single threshold we have got if the threshold value is the same for each class. For the process of greedy thresholds selection, we start from the first class and fix the thresholds of other classes, finding and choosing the local optimal value that can achieve the highest score on validation set. Then we move on to the second class and fix the thresholds of other classes, exploring the local optimal value. The searching process continues until we finish the last class. In the end we obtain an array of "greedy optimal" thresholds for 28 classes using the threshold strategy, and it works well in the experiments.

Apart from ensembles of N-folds from CV (cross validation), we ensemble the models with different architectures and input sizes (512×512, 768×768) while predicting. Generally, every kind of network has its advantages. If we adopt a few networks and take advantages from each one, the model would be more general and robust. Meanwhile, the models with larger inputs may do better in details classification and the models with smaller input sizes are more stable to a dataset and easier to train. By averaging the predicting scores of various models with different input sizes, we achieve a much better final performance. The experiment and evaluation results will be showed and analyzed in the next section.

3 Experiments and Results

3.1 Models Designing and Training Settings

The whole experiments are implemented with Python3.6 under the framework of PyTorch1.0 library [11]. To conduct a fair comparison we re-implemented all methods, including all baselines and ours, and optimized the relevant hyperparameters and even structures for each method. As it is a multi-class and multi-label classification task with 28 classes, the final output layers of all networks contain 28 units. Apart from the GapNet, all models are optimized by Focal loss with γ set by 2. The batch sizes for the models depends on their memory consumption. They are set as large as possible to fit on 4 NVIDIA GTX 1080 Ti GPU with around 11 GB memory for each. We use Adam with default settings as the optimizer of our models except GapNet.

VGG19. A modified version is adopted where a BN (batch normalization) layer follows every time there is a convolutional layer in the original VGG, which makes the training easier.

ResNet18. The optimal learning rate is discovered around 3e−4, and it grows a little with new head part to 4e−4. We use 3e−4 with learning rate scheduling to train the original ResNet18, after replacing its old GAP layer to fit the new input size. For the modified ResNet18, we use cycle learning with a cycle length of 5 epochs, optimized by learning rates of [2e−4, 4e−4]. We decrease the learning rate by a half every cycle. After about 20 epochs the training process stops. The number of buffering layers is set to be one with 1024 units. We use the large inputs of 768×768 to feed the networks. Since it is a small network, a batch size of 128 is adopted.

ResNet50. For modified ResNet50, cycle learning with length of 4 epochs is used, and we apply the learning rates of [1e−4, 2e−4] to train for 3 or 4 cycles where we find the performance is the best. One buffering layer of 1024 units with 0.5 dropout ratio is employed following the flattened ACP layer of 4096 units. We use 512×512 crops to feed the networks and adopt a batch size of 74 as after several attempts.

ResNet101. Since we have enough data for feeding this large network, the model shall be solid. The alteration of ResNet101 is the same as ResNet50 except that the ACP layer is followed by two buffering layers with 4096 units, 0.25 dropout ratio and 1024 units, 0.5 dropout ratio separately.

InceptionV4. InceptionV4 is proposed recently and has been widely applied. Though it improves memory consumption problem existing on InceptionV3, it is still space consuming. Therefore, we use a batch size of 48 with the input size of 512×512. The channel number of the encoder outputs is 1536, and it becomes 3072 after ACP layer. We add one buffering layer with 1024 units for a little information maintaining, followed by 50% dropout.

GapNet-PL. This architecture has a relatively simple structure and low number of parameters. To achieve its best performance, we add some convolutional blocks in its first step, thus passing more features to its second stage. Large input size of 768×768 is fed, since we want to test its best capability on the dataset. The Stochastic Gradient Descent (SGD) with momentum of 0.9 is kept as well as its original initial learning rate of 0.01. To avoid overfitting the following regularization techniques are applied: L1 norm of 1e−7, L2 norm of 1e−5, which is the same as the original settings. The dropout rate in the fully connected layers is still 30%, and we use a bigger batch size of 128.

3.2   Evaluation and Results

For performance evaluation, we use F1-score as our evaluating metric. As it is a task for multilabel classification, the version of Macro F-Score is adopted. It calculates the F1 score for each label, and then finds their unweighted mean. The computing method is as follows:

$$R = \frac{TP}{TP + FN} \tag{1}$$

$$P = \frac{TP}{TP + FP} \tag{2}$$

$$F1 = \frac{2PR}{P + R} \tag{3}$$

$$F1\ macro = \frac{\sum_{i=1}^{N} F1_i}{N} \tag{4}$$

where R denotes the Recall score of one certain class and P denotes the Precision of a class. TP, FP and FN denote the number of true positive, false positive and false negative correspondingly. The F1 score (single class) is computed by harmonic average of Recall and Precision. At last the Macro F1 score that measuring the classification accuracy of all classes can be obtained by unweighted average of F1 for each class.

Usually, when evaluating the performance of a classification task, a confusion matrix can be utilized to help understand. However, as this is a multi-class classification with multi labels for each sample, it is a bit hard to say which class is mistaken for another if you contain two or more classes in the label of one sample. Therefore, we use three tables to demonstrate the evaluation results of the proposed methods.

Table 1. Comparison of model performance (F1) with various methods combination

Model	Original	Original+Opt	Customized	Customized+Opt
ResNet50 (fold 0)	0.737	0.742	0.750	0.759
ResNet50 (fold 1)	0.729	0.738	0.734	0.747
ResNet50 (fold 2)	0.735	0.737	0.746	0.751
ResNet50 (fold 3)	0.731	0.733	0.741	0.746
ResNet50 (fold 4)	0.726	0.731	0.730	0.735
InceptionV4 (single fold)	0.736	0.743	0.749	0.758
VGG19_BN (single fold)	0.721	0.727	0.736	0.745
ResNet18 (random fold 1)	0.725	0.728	0.737	0.743
ResNet18 (random fold 2)	0.719	0.730	0.725	0.734
ResNet18 (random fold 3)	0.728	0.734	0.741	0.748
ResNet101 (single fold)	0.742	0.749	0.758	**0.766**

In Table 1, we can see that both the proposed customized architectures (Customized) and our optimization strategies (Opt) help to improve the performance of identifying those mixed patterns of protein microscopy images, compared with the original classifiers (Original). We can even see a relatively large increase of F1 by even 0.02 to 0.03 in some customized models. Except of the proposed ACP layer and buffering layer, the new input layers which can help the networks utilize all provided cellular landmarks also matter.

Table 2. Scores of models applied with methods above and threshold selection (except GapNet)

Model	Macro F1
ResNet50 (fold 0)	0.773
ResNet50 (fold 1)	0.766
ResNet50 (fold 2)	0.769
ResNet50 (fold 3)	0.762
ResNet50 (fold 4)	0.754
InceptionV4 (single fold)	0.776
VGG19_BN (single fold)	0.761
ResNet18 (random fold 1)	0.758
ResNet18 (random fold 2)	0.747
ResNet18 (random fold 3)	0.763
ResNet101 (single fold)	**0.780**
GapNet-PL	0.763

In Table 2, we list performances of all customized single fold models trained with proposed strategies and applied with thresholds selection. And we also list the f1 score of GapNet-PL for comparison. We can see that our thresholds optimization algorithm is significant to the performance of models. The F1 increase 0.01-0.02 after thresholds selection compared with scores in Table 1. Moreover, we can find out that many single fold models equipped with the proposed methods can perform better than GapNet-PL. Especially the ResNet101, could achieve around 0.02 higher scores than GapNet-PL, and it can still perform a little better than GapNet-PL even without thresholds selection according to Tables 1 and 2.

Table 3. Performance comparison of models with different ensembles and the GapNet-PL

Model	Input size	Macro F1
ResNet50 (5-folds)	512	0.783
ResNet18 (3-random folds)	768	0.768
5 (ResNet50) + 3 (ResNet18)+ 1 (ResNet101)+ 1 (InceptionV4) + 1 (VGG19)	512, 768	**0.791**
5 (ResNet50) + 3 (ResNet18)+ 1 (ResNet101)+ 1 (InceptionV4)	512, 768	0.789
5 (ResNet50) + 1 (ResNet101)+ 1 (InceptionV4)+ 1 (VGG19)	512, 768	0.788
5 (ResNet50) + 3 (ResNet18)	512, 768	0.784
GapNet-PL	768	0.763

In Table 3, we demonstrate the performance of 6 ensembled models for further comparison. We notice that though the scores of VGG and ResNet18 are relatively low, the performance improves a little after ensembled with other models with 512×512 inputs. For example, there would be a 0.002 drop, from 0.791 to 0.789, on F1 without ensemble of VGG, according to the third and fourth row of the table. Since the VGG19_BN and Resnet18 are both fed with 768×768 inputs and others are with 512×512 input sizes, we can conclude that the ensemble of models with multi-sized inputs do help to improve the accuracy.

Finally we can obtain some models with excellent performance as seen in tables above, based on all proposed methods. The score of the best model comes to 0.791, even a 0.028 higher than the state-of-the-art model GapNet-PL on Macro F1 score.

4   Conclusion and Discussion

In this paper, we propose some effective methods on identifying proteins with mixed patterns in high-throughput microscope images based on datasets provided by Human Protein Atlas. We design some customized typical CNN architectures with new input layers and novel top parts. Several data preparation and preprocessing methods are proposed to solve data distribution problems and improve total performance. And by proposing "resize and crop" method mapping the original huge sized high-throughput microscopy images to different smaller sizes, we find a balance between efficiency and accuracy on processing this kind of data. Meanwhile, some optimization strategies are proposed to improve the training performance and the accuracy of models, which is implemented by layer group division, optimal learning rate probing and cycle learning.

Some postprocess strategies have been designed to further upgrade the scores of our models.

The evaluation results based on our experiments demonstrate that our methods do improve the performances of regular CNNs, and the best-performing models based on our methods outperform all baselines and the state-of-the-art architecture with their best settings on HPA datasets. The work reveals the usefulness of our methods for high-throughput microscopy protein images identification.

In the future work, we may try different combinations of input channels instead of using all provided channel filters. We would adopt larger input crops if more computing resources are available.

Acknowledgments. This research is supported by the Strategic Priority Research Program of the Chinese Academy of Sciences Grant (No. XDA19020400), the National Key Research and Development Program of China (No. 2017YFE0103900 and 2017YFA0504702, 2017YFE 0100500), Beijing Municipal Natural Science Foundation Grant (No. L182053), the NSFC projects Grant (No. U1611263, U1611261 and 61672493).

References

1. Swamidoss, I.N., et al.: Automated classification of immunostaining patterns in breast tissue from the human protein atlas. J. Pathol. Inf. 4(Suppl) (2013)
2. Long, J., Shelhamer, E., Darrell, T.: Fully convolutional networks for semantic segmentation. In: Proceedings of the IEEE Conference on Computer Vision and Pattern Recognition, pp. 3431–3440 (2015)
3. Szegedy, C., Ioffe, S., Vanhoucke, V.: Inception-v4, inception-resnet and the impact of residual connections on learning. CoRR, abs/1602.07261 (2016)
4. He, K., Zhang, X., Ren, S., Sun, J.: Deep residual learning for image recognition. In: IEEE Conference on Computer Vision and Pattern Recognition (CVPR) (2015)
5. Huang, G., Liu, Z., van der Maaten, L., Weinberger, K.Q.: Densely connected convolutional networks. In: 2017 IEEE Conference on Computer Vision and Pattern Recognition (CVPR), pp. 2261–2269. IEEE (2017)
6. Simonyan, K., Zisserman, A.: Very deep convolutional networks for large-scale image recognition. In: ICLR (2015)
7. Rumetshofer, E., Hofmarcher, M., Röhrl, C., Hochreiter, S., Klambauer, G.: Human-level protein localization with convolutional neural networks. In: ICLR (2019)
8. Human Protein Atlas Image Classification Challenge . https://www.kaggle.com/c/human-protein-atlas-image-classification
9. The Human Protein Atlas. http://www.proteinatlas.org/
10. Smith, L.N.: Cyclical learning rates for training neural networks. In: 2017 IEEE Winter Conference on Applications of Computer Vision (WACV), pp. 464–472. IEEE (2017)
11. PyTorch 1.0 library. https://pytorch.org/. Accessed 23 Feb 2019

Integration of Multimodal Data
for Breast Cancer Classification
Using a Hybrid Deep Learning Method

Rui Yan[1,2], Fei Ren[2], Xiaosong Rao[5], Baorong Shi[3], Tiange Xiang[4],
Lingling Zhang[5], Yudong Liu[2], Jun Liang[5(✉)], Chunhou Zheng[1(✉)],
and Fa Zhang[2(✉)]

[1] College of Computer Science and Technology, Anhui University, Hefei, China
zhengch99@126.com
[2] High Performance Computer Research Center, Institute of Computing
Technology, Chinese Academy of Sciences, Beijing, China
zhangfa@ict.ac.cn
[3] School of Computer Science, Wuhan University, Wuhan, China
[4] School of Computer Science, The University of Sydney, Sydney, Australia
[5] Department of Pathology, Peking University International Hospital,
Beijing, China
liangjun1959@aliyun.com

Abstract. Although the application of deep learning has greatly improved the performance of benign and malignant breast cancer classification algorithm, the accuracy of classification using only the pathological image has been unable to meet the requirements of clinical practice. Inspired by the real scene when the pathologist read the pathological image for diagnosis, in this paper, we propose a new hybrid deep learning method for benign and malignant breast cancer classification. From the perspective of multimodal data fusion, our method combines pathological image and structured data in the clinical electronic medical record (EMR) to further improve the accuracy of breast cancer classification. Thus, the proposed method can be useful for breast cancer diagnosis in real clinical practice. Experimental results based on our datasets show that the proposed method significantly outperforms the state-of-the-art methods in terms of overall classification accuracy.

Keywords: Breast cancer classification · Pathological image ·
Electronic medical record · Deep learning · Multimodal data fusion

1 Introduction

Nowadays, even with the rapid advances in medical sciences, the analysis of pathological image remains the most widely used method for breast cancer diagnosis. However, the complexity of histopathological images and the dramatic increase in workload make this task time consuming, and the results may be subject to pathologist subjectivity. Facing this problem, the development of automatic and precise diagnosis methods is challenging but also essential for the field [1].

© Springer Nature Switzerland AG 2019
D.-S. Huang et al. (Eds.): ICIC 2019, LNCS 11643, pp. 460–469, 2019.
https://doi.org/10.1007/978-3-030-26763-6_44

Recently, deep learning methods have made great progress and achieved remarkable performance in the field of computer vision and image processing [2]. This has also inspired many scholars to apply this technique to pathological image analysis. In spite of this, the accuracy of the benign and malignant classification of breast cancer using only the pathological image data of single mode cannot be improved to meet the requirements of clinical practice [3].

Although it is not possible to obtain high accuracy only by using pathological image, pathological image provides a rich environment to integrate data from EMR, making novel information accessible and quantifiable. In particular, the raw pathological images are highly dimensional information. It requires less human labor to obtain but it contains a large amount of potentially undiscovered information. The clinical information extracted by clinicians from EMR have fewer feature dimensions, but they usually provide more instructional information for diagnosis.

Therefore, we proposed a fusion method to mimic diagnosis tasks in clinical practice. From the perspective of multimodal data fusion, we try to combine pathological image and structured data in EMR to further improve the accuracy of breast cancer diagnosis. This is also consistent with the pathologist's actual scenario of reading pathological images for diagnosis. When reading pathological images, pathologists will repeatedly refer to the relevant information in patients' EMR as a priori until the final diagnosis is made.

There is almost no literature that classifies breast cancer using multimodal data, but the approach of multimodal fusion in other areas of medicine (text, images, genomics) has yielded good results. Although their fusion method has achieved good results than traditional methods, it still has some problems, such as the feature representation of image is not rich enough, information fusion is insufficient, especially the loss of high-dimensional information before data fusion is not addressed.

In this paper, we proposed a hybrid deep neural network to integrate multimodal data for breast cancer classification. The main contributions of our work are as follows:

(1) To the best of our knowledge, this is by far the first time integrate multimodal data to diagnose breast cancer, and the multimodal network significantly outperforms methods using any single source of information alone.
(2) In order to make pathological image can be integrated more sufficient with structured data in EMR, we proposed a method to extract richer feature representation of the pathological image from multiple convolutional layers.
(3) In order not to lose the information of each mode before data fusion, we use the method of low-dimensional data amplification instead of reducing the high-dimensional data to the low-dimensional data before data fusion.

2   Related Work

Multimodal Data Fusion: Recently, deep learning has demonstrated excellent performance in the medical imaging field such as pathological image classification. Bayramoglu et al. [4] proposed a magnification-independent deep learning method for the breast cancer pathological image classification task, with a classification accuracy of approximately 83%. However, such classification accuracy is not enough to be used in clinical practice. Inspired by the actual situation of the pathologist in diagnosis, the method of multimodal data fusion provides a good opportunity. Moreover, many research results show that the performance of multimodal fusion is better than that of single modal. Although the fusion of multiple modes has achieved good results, each modality of multi-modal objects has different characters with each other, leading to the complexity of heterogeneous data. Therefore, heterogeneous data poses another challenge in multimodal deep learning methods.

Richer Feature Representation: The precondition of multi-mode fusion is feature extraction of single-mode data. The current deep learning method enables to learn very good feature representation from some unstructured data, such as pathological images. This also makes the deep learning method achieve good results in tasks such as classification, detection and segmentation.

However, different tasks have different characteristics, which makes it necessary to adjust the required feature representation according to specific tasks. For example, in the field of semantic segmentation and edge detection, more multi-level features have a better impact on the final result. Xie et al. [5] proposed a method, holistically-nested edge detection, to automatically learns rich hierarchical representations that are important in order to resolve the challenging ambiguity in object boundary detection.

For the multimodal fusion task, the key factor is whether the fusion between different modes is sufficient or not. Therefore, it is necessary for each mode to learn rich enough feature representation before fusion, so as to provide a fertile environment for full multi-mode fusion. However, the current classification method using original deep learning (such as CNN) does not enable each mode (such as pathological image) to learn enough rich feature representation.

High-Dimensional and Low-Dimensional Data Fusion: High-dimensional data (unstructured data) generally have high dimensions of feature representation. In contrast, the dimension of structured data is inherently low. How to solve the problem of fusing high-dimensional data and low-dimensional data will have a significant impact on the final result of fusion.

According to the level of fusion, information fusion technology can be divided into three categories: data-level, feature-level and decision-level fusion [6]. Generally speaking, the larger the amount of information, the smaller the information loss, the more sufficient the information fusion, and the better the final fusion result. From the existing studies, the accuracy of this viewpoint is also demonstrated, especially that the feature-level fusion achieves better results than the decision-level fusion. This indicates that the information of each mode, especially the high-dimensional information, should be kept as complete as possible before fusion, and then reduced to the required level after fusion. So, they are enough effective to capture the complex correlations over different modalities for heterogeneous data.

At present, most data fusion is image and image or image and text, and these data are all of high dimension, so fusion is relatively simple. Zhang et al. [7] introduce the semantic knowledge of medical images from diagnostic reports to provide an inspirational network training and an interpretable prediction mechanism with their proposed novel multimodal neural network, namely TandemNet.

For the fusion of low-dimensional structured data and high-dimensional unstructured data, there was little early work involved. Xu et al. [8] first reduced the high-dimensional image data to low-dimensional, and then merged with the low-dimensional structured data. This approach has yielded good results. However, in this way, a lot of information is lost before the fusion, making the fusion insufficient.

3 Method

In this section, we describe our proposed method for breast cancer classification. For simplicity, we first present an overview of our method framework. And then introduce our innovation points from two aspects: richer feature representation and high-dimensional and low-dimensional data fusion, respectively.

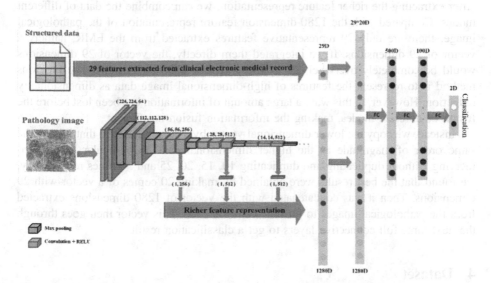

Fig. 1. The framework of our proposed method. (1) In terms of structured data, 29 representative features were extracted from EMR, which are closely related to the diagnosis of breast cancer. We copy this 29-dimensional vector 20 times on average (29D * 20); (2) In terms of pathological image, the third, fourth and fifth convolution layers were extracted from VGG16 network (1280-dimensional) as richer feature representation; (3) Finally, the vector of 29D * 20 dimensions extracted from the structured data was concatenated with the vector of 1280D dimensions extracted from the pathological images to form a vector of 1860D. This vector then goes through the next three full connective layers to get a classification result.

3.1 Richer Feature Representation

Since objects in pathological images possess various scales and high complexity, learning the rich hierarchical representations is very critical for fusion of multimodal data. CNN has been proved to be effective for this task. In addition, the convolutional features in CNN gradually become coarser with the increase of the convolutional layers. Inspired by these observations, we attempt to use richer convolutional features in such a challenging fusion task. Richer convolutional features provide richer representations compared to features just extracted from the final fully connected layer. Because multi-level convolutional layer retained complementary information such as local textures and fine details lost by higher levels.

We extract the third, fourth and fifth feature map of VGG16 network, and then use average pooling to compress the original 56 * 56 * 256, 28 * 28 * 512 and 14 * 14 * 512 into 1 * 256, 1 * 512 and 1 * 512. Then concatenate the three vectors into a 1280 (512 + 512 + 256) dimension vector, which was used as the richer feature representation of the pathological image. The specific fusion process is shown in Fig. 1.

3.2   High-dimensional and Low-dimensional Data Fusion

After extracting the richer feature representation, we can combine the data of different modes. Compared with the 1280-dimension feature representation of the pathological image, there are only 29 representative features extracted from the EMR, namely a vector of 29 dimensions. If we integrated them directly, the vector of 29 dimensions would be completely overwhelmed by the vector of 1280 dimensions. The previous method is to represent the features of high-dimensional image data as dimensionality reduction. However, in this way, a large amount of information has been lost before the fusion of different modes, making the information fusion insufficient.

Instead, we copy the lower dimensional vector by a certain ratio, so that it is on the same order of magnitude as the higher dimensional data. In particular, by experimenting without duplicating and duplicating 10, 15, 20, 25 and 30 times respectively, we found that the best results were obtained by making 20 copies of a vector with 29 dimensions. Then it was concatenated with the vector of 1280 dimensions extracted from the pathological images to form a vector of 1860. This vector then goes through the next three full connective layers to get a classification result.

4   Dataset

In this work, we collected a new dataset with pathological images and pairwise multiple types of features extracted from EMR for breast cancer classification.

Pathological Image: We collected the medical records of 185 breast cancer patients (82 benign, 103 malignant), and for each patient we selectively cropped 2–10 representative image areas from WSI (whole slide image). In the end, we collected a total of 3764 high resolution (2048 × 1536 pixels) H&E stained pathological images (1332 benign, 2432 malignant). Each image is labeled as benign or malignant according to the main cancer type in each image. Figure 2 shows the example of pathological images in the dataset and summarizes the image distribution.

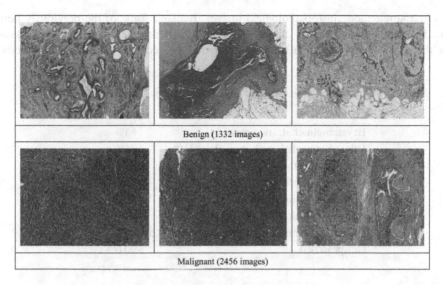

Fig. 2. Examples of pathological images in our collected dataset.

Structured Data in EMR: After consulting with pathologists, 29 representative features were extracted from EMR, which are closely related to the diagnosis of breast cancer, and used as structured data to represent the clinical condition description of a patient. Specifically, these 29 features include Age, Gender, Disease Course Type, Pectoral Muscle Adhesion, Personal Tumor History, Family Tumor History, Prophase Treatment, Neoadjuvant Chemotherapy, Dimple Sign, Orange Peel Appearance, Redness And Swelling Of Skin, Skin Ulcers, Tumor, Breast Deformation, Nipple Change, Nipple Discharge, Axillary Lymphadenectasis, Swelling of Lymph Nodes, Tumor Position, Tumor Number, Tumor Size, Tumor Texture, Tumor Border, Smooth Surface, Tumor Morphology, Activity, Capsules, Tenderness and Skin Adhesion.

5 Experiments

In this section, we present the performance of our proposed algorithm on our collected dataset. The 80% of the datasets are randomly selected to train the model and the remaining 20% to test. All experiments in this paper are finished on an NVIDIA Tesla K40 GPU using the TensorFlow framework [9].

5.1 Accuracy Comparison with Previous Methods

The performance of our proposed method is shown in Table 1. For the 2-class classifications, our method achieved 90.6% average accuracy. The structured data in EMR only plays an auxiliary role, and the pathological images are the gold standard for the final diagnosis in clinical practice. Therefore, there is currently almost no paper that classifies breast cancer using only clinical EMR, we only compare it with the method only use single-mode histopathological images. Because some of the previously published papers reported 2-class classification and others reported 4-class classification. For the comprehensive comparison, we compared the accuracy with all the methods.

Table 1. Comparation of accuracy with previous methods.

Methods	Accuracy
Bayramoglu et al. (two-class) [4]	83%
Fabio A. Spanhol et al. (two-class) [10]	85%
Araujo et al. (two-class) [11]	83.3%
Rakhlin et al. (four-class) [12]	87.2%
Yeeleng S. Vang et al. (four-class) [13]	87.5%
Aditya Golatkar et al. (four-class) [14]	85%
Aresta, Guilherme et al. (BACH contest) [15]	87%
Our proposed	90.6%

5.2   Accuracy Comparison Using Different Dimensional Fusion

For our proposed methods with different strategies to integrate low-dimensional structured data and high-dimensional unstructured data, we compare their overall performance via average classification accuracy in Table 2. When only structured data from EMR were used, the classification accuracy was not very high, only 81.5% on the test set. This is a reasonable result. Because the structured data in EMR only plays an auxiliary role, the pathological image is the gold standard for the final diagnosis in clinical practice. In addition, Due to the small amount of structured data in EMR and the large amount of pathological image data, especially after the enhancement of pathological image data, the use of structured data alone is the only case in which the phenomenon of overfitting exists.

When we used VGG16 to classify pathological images, we got a relatively high accuracy of 83.6%. Although the accuracy of using only structured data is not high, the leverage of structured data can improve the accuracy of pathological image classification. We got 87.9% accuracy when integrated 29-dimensional structured data and 29-dimensional feature representation of pathological images. We added a full connectivity layer with 29 nodes at the end of the VGG network, thus obtaining the 29-dimensional feature representation of pathological images.

Further, we compared two different fusion methods of high-dimensional pathological images and low-dimensional structured data. The experimental results show that it is better to first reduce the 4096-dimensional vector extracted from the last full connected (FC) layer of VGG16 to 29 dimensions, and then fuse it with the 29-dimensional structured data. This strategy is better than directly integrated 29-dimensional structured data with 4096-dimensional feature representation of pathological image. Because the dimension of the 29-dimensional is too low compared to the 4096-dimensional. In this fusion, the higher-dimensional vectors completely overwhelm the lower-dimensional ones.

Finally, after trying different multiples of the amplification, a 20-fold amplification of structured data yields best results. When the amplification of structured data is 10 times, the overall accuracy is barely changed. The reason for this is that the amplification is insufficient. However, if amplification too much on low-dimensional structured data, the results will go down.

Table 2. Comparation of accuracy using different dimensional fusion of structured data and pathological image.

Method	Accuracy (train)	Accuracy (test)
Structured data only (29D)	89.3%	81.5%
Pathological image only (VGG16)	84.5%	83.6%
Structured data (29D) + Pathological image (29D)	88.2%	87.9%
Structured data (29D) + Pathological image (4096D)	85.1%	84.2%
Structured data (29D * 10) + Pathological image (4096D)	86.2%	84.8%
Structured data (29D * 20) + Pathological image (4096D)	92.3%	90.1%
Structured data (29D * 30) + Pathological image (4096D)	85.5%	85.2%

5.3 ROC Comparison Using Richer Feature Representation

We can further improve our model using richer convolutional features extracted from different convolutional layers of VGG16. After trying fusion different number of convolutional layers, we get our best model by integrating 29-dimensional structured data and the third, fourth and fifth convolution layers extracted from VGG16 network (1860-dimensional). And Fig. 3 shows the Area Under Curve (AUC) using different fusion method based on Receiver Operating Characteristic (ROC) analysis.

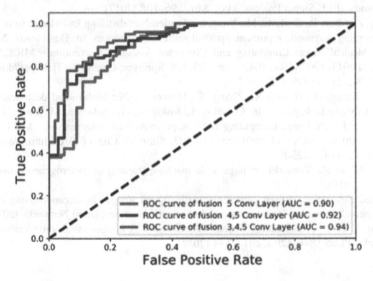

Fig. 3. ROC curves were compared integrating different convolutional layers of VGG16.

6 Conclusions

In this paper, we utilized a new method to integrate highly heterogeneous data to leverage structured data of EMR to improve pathological images classification accuracy. Therefore, the application of automatic classification algorithm in clinical practice becomes possible. Due to the generality of the proposed fusion workflow, it can be straightforwardly extended to other fusion of structured data and unstructured data.

Acknowledgement. This research is supported by the National Key Research and Development Program of China (No. 2017YFE0103900 and 2017YFA0504702), the NSFC projects Grant (No. U1611263, U1611261, 61502455 and 61672493), Peking University International Hospital Research Grant (No. YN2018ZD05), Beijing Municipal Natural Science Foundation Grant (No. L182053) and Special Program for Applied Research on Super Computation of the NSFC-Guangdong Joint Fund (the second phase).

References

1. Holzinger, A., et al.: Towards the augmented pathologist: challenges of explainable-ai in digital pathology (2017)
2. Lecun, Y., Bengio, Y., Hinton, G.: Deep learning. Nature **521**(7553), 436 (2015)
3. Litjens, G., et al.: A survey on deep learning in medical image analysis. Med. Image Anal. **42**(9), 60–88 (2017)
4. Bayramoglu, N., Kannala, J., Heikkilä, J.: Deep learning for magnification independent breast cancer histopathology image classification. In: International Conference on Pattern Recognition (2017)
5. Xie, S., Tu, Z.: Holistically-Nested Edge Detection. Int. J. Comput. Vis. **125**(1–3), 3–18 (2017)
6. Ramachandram, D., Taylor, G.W.: Deep multimodal learning: a survey on recent advances and trends. IEEE Signal Process. Mag. **34**(6), 96–108 (2017)
7. Zhang, Z., Chen, P., Sapkota, M., Yang, L.: TandemNet: distilling knowledge from medical images using diagnostic reports as optional semantic references. In: Descoteaux, M., et al. (eds.) Medical Image Computing and Computer Assisted Intervention − MICCAI 2017 MICCAI 2017. LNCS, vol. 10435, pp. 320–328. Springer, Cham (2017). https://doi.org/10.1007/978-3-319-66179-7_37
8. Xu, T., Zhang, H., Huang, X., Zhang, S., Metaxas, D.N.: Multimodal deep learning for cervical dysplasia diagnosis. In: Ourselin, S., Joskowicz, L., Sabuncu, M., Unal, G., Wells, W. (eds.) Medical Image Computing and Computer-Assisted Intervention – MICCAI 2016 MICCAI 2016. LNCS, vol. 9901, pp. 115–123. Springer, Cham (2016). https://doi.org/10.1007/978-3-319-46723-8_14
9. Abadi, M., et al.: TensorFlow: large-scale machine learning on heterogeneous distributed systems (2016)
10. Spanhol, F.A., et al.: Breast cancer histopathological image classification using convolutional neural networks. In: International Joint Conference on Neural Networks (2016)
11. Araújo, T., et al.: Classification of breast cancer histology images using convolutional neural networks. PLoS ONE **12**(6), e0177544 (2017)

12. Rakhlin, A., Shvets, A., Iglovikov, V., Kalinin, Alexandr A.: Deep convolutional neural networks for breast cancer histology image analysis. In: Campilho, A., Karray, F., ter Haar Romeny, B. (eds.) ICIAR 2018. LNCS, vol. 10882, pp. 737–744. Springer, Cham (2018). https://doi.org/10.1007/978-3-319-93000-8_83
13. Vang, Y.S., Chen, Z., Xie, X.: Deep learning framework for multi-class breast cancer histology image classification. In: Campilho, A., Karray, F., ter Haar Romeny, B. (eds.) ICIAR 2018. LNCS, vol. 10882, pp. 914–922. Springer, Cham (2018). https://doi.org/10.1007/978-3-319-93000-8_104
14. Golatkar, A., Anand, D., Sethi, A.: Classification of breast cancer histology using deep learning. In: Campilho, A., Karray, F., ter Haar Romeny, B. (eds.) ICIAR 2018. LNCS, vol. 10882, pp. 837–844. Springer, Cham (2018). https://doi.org/10.1007/978-3-319-93000-8_95
15. Aresta, G., et al.: BACH: grand challenge on breast cancer histology images (2018)

Liver Segmentation in CT Images
with Adversarial Learning

Yuxuan Chen, Suiyi Li, Su Yang[(✉)], and Wuyang Luo

Shanghai Key Laboratory of Intelligent Information Processing,
School of Computer Science, Fudan University, Shanghai 201203, China
suyang@fudan.edu.cn

Abstract. Liver diseases, especially liver cancer, are a major threat to human health. In order to assist doctors in efficiently diagnosing the condition and developing treatment plans, automatic segmentation of the liver from CT images has a strong clinical need. However, it is difficult to design an accurate segmentation algorithm because of the blurred boundary of CT images and the great difference of pathological changes. In this paper, we propose a cascade model for liver segmentation from CT images, which uses cascade U-nets with adversarial learning to obtain more accurate segmentation results. The experimental results show that the proposed algorithm is competitive and its dice value reaches 0.955.

Keywords: Automatic liver segmentation · CT images · Cascade model · Adversarial learning

1 Introduction

1.1 Motivation

Liver is the largest abdominal organ in human body, which is often threatened by diseases and drug damage. According to the Global Hepatitis Report 2017 released by the World Health Organization, about 325 million people worldwide are infected with chronic hepatitis B virus or hepatitis C virus, which can lead to chronic infection for life and eventually lead to progressive liver damage. CT image is a very convenient way to detect abdominal organs. Radiologists often need to observe the shape and texture of patients' liver through CT images to find visible lesions. However, it is tedious and inefficient to analyze abdominal CT images manually by radiologists. Therefore, it is very important to study the automatic liver segmentation technique in CT images. However, as shown in Fig. 1, this task faces many challenges, such as great variation of size and shape, unclear boundaries and different degrees of lesions, so automatic segmentation technology has not yet entered the clinical stage.

1.2 Related Work

Traditional manual segmentation requires extensive radiology experience and is very time consuming. In order to help radiologists improve their work efficiency, researchers

© Springer Nature Switzerland AG 2019
D.-S. Huang et al. (Eds.): ICIC 2019, LNCS 11643, pp. 470–480, 2019.
https://doi.org/10.1007/978-3-030-26763-6_45

have turned their attention to automatic liver segmentation technology. In recent years, many automatic segmentation methods have been proposed. Pham et al. [16] proposed a method based on grayscale and texture. This method includes global threshold, region growth, voxel classification and edge detection, but it is easy to segment along the blurred boundary, resulting in boundary leakage. Chan et al. [1] proposed a variational semi-automated liver segmentation method, which employs prior knowledge and morphological features into account. Zheng et al. [22] and Zhang et al. [21] proposed a point-based statistical shape model (SSM), which can obtain higher accuracy in the case of small amount of data.

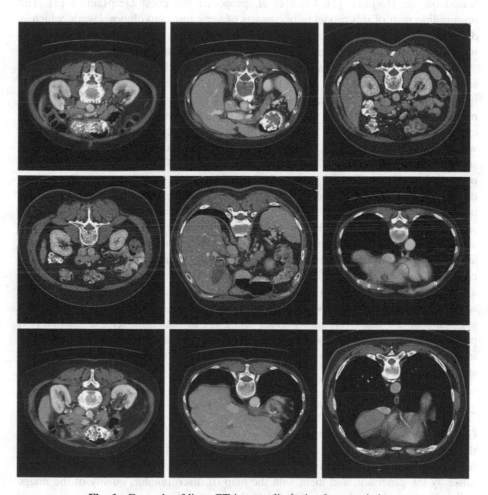

Fig. 1. Example of liver CT images displaying large variations

2 Background

2.1 Image Segmentation Network

The fully convolutional network (FCN) [13] is the basic architecture for many semantic segmentation tasks, which consists of cascaded downsampling path and upsampling path. The U-net [18] extends FCN by introducing skip connection between downsampling path and corresponding upsampling path. The skip connection improves the network performance by facilitating the transmission of information. The DeepLab architecture [12] involved atrous convolutions and poolings into the CNN architecture. Based on the DeepLab [2], Chen et al. proposed the latest DeepLabV3 [3]. The upsampling path of this model only consists of very few convolution layers, which is different from the upsampling path used in the FCN and the U-net. Jegou et al. [10] introduces the Dense connection [8] into FCN for segmentation tasks.

In recent years, fully convolutional network has developed rapidly in the field of semantics segmentation, and has achieved remarkable results in the competition of image segmentation. Exploration of this new segmentation method has begun for medical image segmentation. Christ et al. [4] and Vorontsov et al. [19] proposed a cascaded fully convolutional network, which combines two fully convolutional networks. The first network is used to segment liver, and the second network is used to segment liver lesions on the basis of the first network. The segmentation results are processed by 3D conditional random field to make results more accurate. The authors of [5] proposed a deeply supervised network for liver segmentation. The input of the network is part of the 3D bounding box, which has to be slid on a target scan during the test time. In order to alleviate the problem of vanishing gradient, the network uses additional deconvolution layers to generate feature maps from two intermediate layers, and the gradients of loss are calculated from several branches. A three-dimensional convolutional neural network is proposed in [7]. This method contains two steps. First, a deep 3D CNN is trained to learn prior map of the liver. Then, in order to optimize segmentation result, both global and local appearance information from the prior segmentation are adaptively incorporated into a segmentation model. Rafiei et al. [17] proposed a 3D-2D fully convolutional network, which makes full use of the spatial information in CT volume to segment the liver while computation and memory consuming are moderate.

2.2 GAN

GAN [6] has achieved great success in the field of image generation. It is inspired by the theory of zero-sum game. It regards generation problem as conflict and cooperation between two players: Discriminator and generator. First, images will be generated from noise by the generator, and then, with the help of discriminator, quality of the image will be improved step by step. CGAN [14] has gained impressive results in various image-to-image conversion problems, such as image super-resolution [11], image inpainting [15], and style transfer [12]. CGAN regards original image as a constraint, feeding it into the network along with noise as input, and adding conditional variables into loss functions of both generator and discriminator. Under this circumstance, the generated image is of higher quality and closer to the real image. Zhang et al. [20] firstly proposed a stacking model of GAN called StackGAN. The model can be divided into two stages: The first stage generates a coarse image mainly containing primitive shapes and colors based on the given text description. Then, the second stage takes the coarse image and text description as input, to generate high-resolution images gradually. Huang et al. [9] designed a stacked GAN, which is trained to invert the hierarchical representations of a bottom-up discriminative network. Each GAN in this stacked model learns to generate lower-level representations that are conditional on higher level representations in order to generate more qualified images.

3   Method

In this paper, we propose a cascade model with adversarial learning for liver segmentation. The algorithm is able to segment the liver accurately and efficiently from CT slices. It consists of two stages: In the first stage, the 2D slice images are fed into the first stage U-net segmentation network, and the segmentation results of the first stage are obtained. In the second stage, CT slices are concatenated with the results of the first U-net, and then input into the second stage U-net segmentation network to obtain more accurate segmentation results. The training of the above two stages utilizes the adversarial loss. The model is illustrated in the Fig. 2.

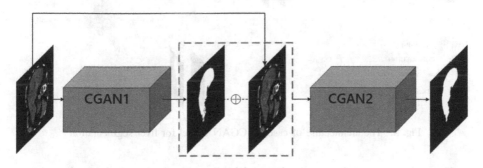

Fig. 2. The proposed cascade model

3.1   Model

Generative Adversarial Networks (GANs) consists of two components: a generator G and a discriminator D. The two components are competing in a zero-sum game, in which the generator G aims to produce a realistic image given an input z, that conforms to a certain distribution. The discriminator D is forced to distinguish if a given image is generated by G or it is indeed a real one from the dataset. The adversarial competition enables the generator and the discriminator to achieve better performance, whilst making it hard for D to differentiate generation of G from the real data. Conditional Generative Adversarial Networks (CGANs) extends GANs by introducing an additional observed information, namely conditioning variable, to both the generator G and the discriminator D.

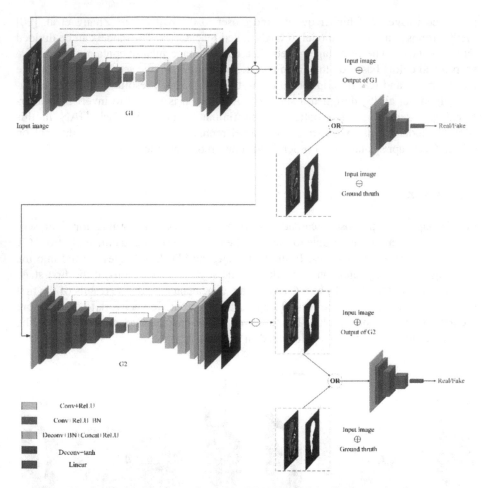

Fig. 3. The architecture of cascade CGAN model for liver segmentation

The architecture of the proposed model is shown in the Fig. 3. It consists of two stacked CGANs: CGAN1(G1, D1), CGAN2(G2, D2), with the second stacked on top of the first. CGAN is an extension of GAN. It introduces additional conditional variables for both generator and discriminator. In the proposed model, CT slice is the conditional variable. The architectures of the generator G and discriminator D (ignoring BN and ReLU) can be seen in Tables 1 and 2, respectively.

Table 1. Architecture of the generator G.

Type	Kernel	Stride	Output size	Output channels
conv.	5×5	2×2	128×128	64
conv.	5×5	2×2	64×64	128
conv.	5×5	2×2	32×32	256
conv.	5×5	2×2	16×16	512
conv.	5×5	2×2	8×8	512
conv.	5×5	2×2	4×4	512
conv.	5×5	2×2	2×2	512
conv.	5×5	2×2	1×1	512
deconv.	5×5	2×2	2×2	1024
deconv.	5×5	2×2	4×4	1024
deconv.	5×5	2×2	8×8	1024
deconv.	5×5	2×2	16×16	1024
deconv.	5×5	2×2	32×32	512
deconv.	5×5	2×2	64×64	256
deconv.	5×5	2×2	128×128	128
deconv.	5×5	2×2	256×256	1
Sigmoid	–	–	256×256	1

Table 2. Architecture of the discriminator D.

Type	Kernel	Stride	Output size	Output channels
conv.	5×5	2×2	128×128	64
conv.	5×5	2×2	64×64	128
conv.	5×5	2×2	32×32	256
conv.	5×5	1×1	32×32	512
Linear	–	–	1	–
Sigmoid	–	–	1	–

Both the generator G1 and the discriminator D1 of the first CGAN are added with condition, the CT image x. G1 is trained to produce mask G1 (z, x) corresponding to CT image. y denotes the ground truth corresponding x.

The objective function of the CGAN1 is:

$$\mathcal{L}_{adversarial_1}(G_1, D_1) = E_{x,y \sim p_{data}(x,y)}[logD_1(x,y)]$$
$$+ E_{x \sim p_{data}(x), z \sim p_z(z)}[log(1 - D_1(x, G_1(x)))] \tag{1}$$

In order to obtain deterministic results from G1, we eliminate random noise and simplify the formula as follows:

$$\mathcal{L}_{adversarial_1}(G_1, D_1) = E_{x,y \sim p_{data}(x,y)}[log D_1(x, y)]$$
$$+ E_{x \sim p_{data}(x)}[log(1 - D_1(x, G_1(x)))] \tag{2}$$

In addition to adversarial loss, L1 loss is also applied to obtain more accurate pixel-level classification results:

$$\mathcal{L}_{data_1}(G_1) = E_{x,y \sim p_{data}(x,y)}||y - G_1(x)|| \tag{3}$$

So, the final objective function of CGAN1 is:

$$\mathcal{L}_{CGAN_1} = \mathcal{L}_{adversarial_1} + \lambda \mathcal{L}_{data_1} \tag{4}$$

λ is L1 loss weighted coefficient. For CGAN2, it consists of G2 and D2. We use similar objective functions. The adversarial loss of CGAN2 is:

$$\mathcal{L}_{adversarial_2}(G_2, D_1|G_1) = E_{x,y,r \sim p_{data}(x,y,r)}[log D_2(x, y, r)]$$
$$+ E_{x \sim p_{data}(x)}[log(1 - D_2(x, G_1(x), G_2(x, G_1(x))))] \tag{5}$$

The difference is that CGAN2 combines CT slices and the output of CGAN1 as input. Finally, the objective function of the whole model is:

$$\mathcal{L}_{total} = \lambda \min_{G_1,G_2} \max_{D_1,D_2} \mathcal{L}_{data_1}(G_1) + \lambda \mathcal{L}_{data_2}(G_2|G_1) + \mathcal{L}_{adversarial_1}(G_1, D_1)$$
$$+ \mathcal{L}_{adversarial_1}(G_2, D_2|G_1) \tag{6}$$

The output of CGAN1 is fed into CGAN2 as a prior knowledge to help it get more accurate segmentation results.

3.2   Training

Training is divided into two phases. The first phase employs an alternating training scheme. Specifically, each time a mini-batch CT slices is fed into model, firstly, update G1, D1, with G2, D2 fixed. Then, update G2, D2, and fix G1, D1. After 10 epochs training, enter the second stage. In the second phase, the entire model is end-to-end trained for several epochs updating CGAN1 and CGAN2 simultaneously.

4   Experiment

4.1   Dataset

We employ dataset provided by Liver Tumor Segmentation Challenge (LiTS) which is organized by ISBI and MICCAI in conjunction to evaluate the proposed method. The open dataset includes 131 CT volumes and corresponding expert standard labels. The dataset was collected from six different clinical sites using different scanners and scanning methods with different slice resolutions and slice spacings. We randomly divided the data set into 10 folds, each with about 13 volumes, and a fold is used for validation, while the others for training, namely 10-fold cross validation. For data preprocessing, we crop the image intensity values of all volumes to the range of [−200, 250] HU, in order to reduce irrelevant information.

4.2 Implementation

The proposed model was implemented based on tensorflow1.12.0. All experiments were performed on workstations equipped with two Intel Xeon E5-2609 processors, 64G RAM and one NVIDIA TITAN XP GPU.

We use the Adam solver to train the CGAN1 and CGAN2 with a mini-batch size of 8. The model was trained for 15 epochs and the initial learning rate was set to 0.0002. In the second phase of training, the learning rate is divided by 10. In our experiments, λ is set to 100.

5 Comparison with Other Methods

The proposed model is compared with two baseline methods. U-net is widely used in biomedical image segmentation tasks. A 3D-2D model proposed in [17] makes full use of volume's 3D spatial information.

Dice is employed for evaluating our model. The Dice score is defined as:

$$Dice = \frac{2|X \cap Y|}{|X| + |Y|} \tag{7}$$

where |X| and |Y| are the pixel values of predicted result and ground truth respectively, and the Dice score is in the interval [0,1]. A perfect segmentation yields a Dice score of 1. Dice is usually divided into Dice per case and Dice global where Dice per case score refers to an average Dice score per volume while Dice global score is the Dice score evaluated by combining all datasets into one. In this paper, we employ Dice per case score to evaluate liver segmentation performance.

Some quantitative results of several methods are shown in Table 3 through cross validation. It is observed that our model has achieved more accurate segmentation results. This is because we introduced adversarial loss, which can be seen as a high-level loss that provides more global optimization information for the model. On the other hand, the cascade structure can help the model to further improve performance. Using the output of the first stage as the prior knowledge of the second stage can provide more reliable information for the second stage CGAN and help it achieve more accurate segmentation. Some results are demonstrated in Fig. 4.

Table 3. Quantitative comparison between the proposed method and other methods

Methods	Dice score
U-net [18]	0.924
3D-2D FCN [17]	0.935
only $CGAN_1$	0.943
Cascade model	**0.955**

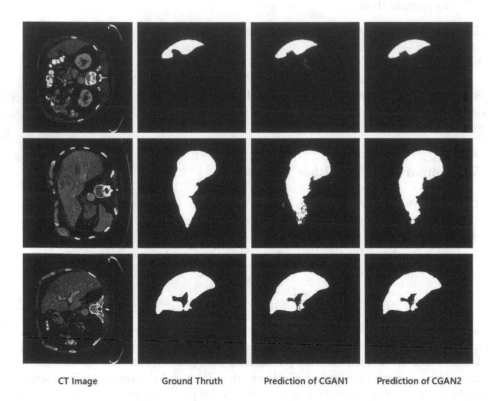

| CT Image | Ground Thruth | Prediction of CGAN1 | Prediction of CGAN2 |

Fig. 4. Results of the proposed method

6 Conclusion

In this paper, we propose a cascade model for liver segmentation with adversarial. This model is able to segment the liver accurately and efficiently from CT slice images. It consists of two stages: In the first stage, the 2D CT slice image is input into the first-level CGAN segmentation network to obtain the segmentation result of the first stage. In the second stage, the CT slice image is concatenated with the corresponding segmentation results of the first stage as input of the second stage CGAN2 to obtain more accurate segmentation results. The main contributions of this work are the followings: First, the generative adversarial method is introduced into the liver segmentation task in CT images. Compared with the traditional L1 and L2 losses, adversarial loss can get a clear prediction result and reduce the ambiguity of the segmentation results. Second, due to the cascade structure, the segmentation result of the first phase can provide a prior knowledge for the second phase. Thus, more accurate segmentation results can be obtained. Further research can explore more efficient CGAN cascading methods.

Acknowledgement. This work is supported by Shanghai Science and Technology Commission (grant No. 17511104203) and NSFC (grant NO. 61472087).

References

1. Chan, T.F., Vese, L.A.: Active contours without edges. IEEE Trans. Image Process. **10**(2), 266–277 (2001)
2. Chen, L.C., Papandreou, G., Kokkinos, I., Murphy, K., Yuille, A.L.: Semantic image segmentation with deep convolutional nets and fully connected crfs. arXiv preprint arXiv: 1412.7062 (2014)
3. Chen, L.C., Papandreou, G., Schroff, F., Adam, H.: Rethinking atrous convolution for semantic image segmentation. arXiv preprint arXiv:1706.05587 (2017)
4. Christ, P.F., et al.: Automatic liver and lesion segmentation in CT using cascaded fully convolutional neural networks and 3D conditional random fields. In: Ourselin, S., Joskowicz, L., Sabuncu, Mert R., Unal, G., Wells, W. (eds.) MICCAI 2016. LNCS, vol. 9901, pp. 415–423. Springer, Cham (2016). https://doi.org/10.1007/978-3-319-46723-8_48
5. Dou, Q., Chen, H., Jin, Y., Yu, L., Qin, J., Heng, P.-A.: 3D deeply supervised network for automatic liver segmentation from CT volumes. In: Ourselin, S., Joskowicz, L., Sabuncu, Mert R., Unal, G., Wells, W. (eds.) MICCAI 2016. LNCS, vol. 9901, pp. 149–157. Springer, Cham (2016). https://doi.org/10.1007/978-3-319-46723-8_18
6. Goodfellow, I., et al.: Generative adversarial nets. In: Advances in neural information processing systems, pp. 2672–2680 (2014)
7. Hu, P., Wu, F., Peng, J., Liang, P., Kong, D.: Automatic 3D liver segmentation based on deep learning and globally optimized surface evolution. Phys. Med. Biol. **61**(24), 8676 (2016)
8. Huang, G., Liu, Z., Van Der Maaten, L., Weinberger, K.Q.: Densely connected convolutional networks. In: Proceedings of the IEEE Conference on Computer Vision and Pattern Recognition, pp. 4700–4708 (2017)
9. Huang, X., Li, Y., Poursaeed, O., Hopcroft, J., Belongie, S.: Stacked generative adversarial networks. In: Proceedings of the IEEE Conference on Computer Vision and Pattern Recognition, pp. 5077–5086 (2017)
10. Jégou, S., Drozdzal, M., Vazquez, D., Romero, A., Bengio, Y.: The one hundred layers tiramisu: fully convolutional densenets for semantic segmentation. In: Proceedings of the IEEE Conference on Computer Vision and Pattern Recognition Workshops, pp. 11–19 (2017)
11. Ledig, C., et al.: Photo-realistic single image super-resolution using a generative adversarial network. In: Proceedings of the IEEE Conference on Computer Vision and Pattern Recognition, pp. 4681–4690 (2017)
12. Li, C., Wand, M.: Precomputed real-time texture synthesis with markovian generative adversarial networks. In: Leibe, B., Matas, J., Sebe, N., Welling, M. (eds.) ECCV 2016. LNCS, vol. 9907, pp. 702–716. Springer, Cham (2016). https://doi.org/10.1007/978-3-319-46487-9_43

13. Long, J., Shelhamer, E., Darrell, T.: Fully convolutional networks for semantic segmentation. In: The IEEE Conference on Computer Vision and Pattern Recognition (CVPR), June 2015
14. Mirza, M., Osindero, S.: Conditional generative adversarial nets. arXiv preprint arXiv:1411.1784 (2014)
15. Pathak, D., Krahenbuhl, P., Donahue, J., Darrell, T., Efros, A.A.: Context encoders: feature learning by inpainting. In: Proceedings of the IEEE Conference on Computer Vision and Pattern Recognition, pp. 2536–2544 (2016)
16. Pham, M., Susomboon, R., Disney, T., Raicu, D., Furst, J.: A comparison of texture models for automatic liver segmentation. In: Medical Imaging 2007: Image Processing, vol. 6512, p. 65124E. International Society for Optics and Photonics (2007)
17. Rafiei, S., Nasr-Esfahani, E., Soroushmehr, S., Karimi, N., Samavi, S., Najarian, K.: Liver segmentation in CT images using three dimensional to two dimensional fully connected network. arXiv preprint arXiv:1802.07800 (2018)
18. Ronneberger, O., Fischer, P., Brox, T.: U-Net: convolutional networks for biomedical image segmentation. In: Navab, N., Hornegger, J., Wells, W.M., Frangi, A.F. (eds.) MICCAI 2015. LNCS, vol. 9351, pp. 234–241. Springer, Cham (2015). https://doi.org/10.1007/978-3-319-24574-4_28
19. Vorontsov, E., Tang, A., Pal, C., Kadoury, S.: Liver lesion segmentation informed by joint liver segmentation. In: 2018 IEEE 15th International Symposium on Biomedical Imaging (ISBI 2018), pp. 1332–1335. IEEE (2018)
20. Zhang, H., et al.: StackGAN: text to photo-realistic image synthesis with stacked generative adversarial networks. In: Proceedings of the IEEE International Conference on Computer Vision, pp. 5907–5915 (2017)
21. Zhang, X., Tian, J., Deng, K., Wu, Y., Li, X.: Automatic liver segmentation using a statistical shape model with optimal surface detection. IEEE Trans. Biomed. Eng. 57(10), 2622–2626 (2010)
22. Zheng, S., et al.: A novel variational method for liver segmentation based on statistical shape model prior and enforced local statistical feature. In: 2017 IEEE 14th International Symposium on Biomedical Imaging (ISBI 2017), pp. 261–264. IEEE (2017)

Cascade Dense-Unet for Prostate Segmentation in MR Images

Suiyi Li, Yuxuan Chen, Su Yang$^{(\boxtimes)}$, and Wuyang Luo

Shanghai Key Laboratory of Intelligent Information Processing,
School of Computer Science, Fudan University, Shanghai 201203, China
suyang@fudan.edu.cn

Abstract. Automatic prostate segmentation from magnetic resonance images can assist in diagnosis and radiological planning. The extensive clinical application of this task has attracted the attention of researchers. However, due to noise, blurred boundaries and scale variation, it is very challenging to segment prostate from magnetic resonance images. We propose a cascade method for prostate segmentation. The model consists of two stage. In the first stage, a dense-unet model are used to obtain the initial segmentation results. In the second stage, the segmentation result of the first stage is used as prior knowledge, and another dense-unet is used to obtain more accurate segmentation results. The experimental results show that the proposed method can obtain more accurate segmentation results.

Keywords: Automatic prostate segmentation · Magnetic resonance images · Cascade Dense-unet

1 Introduction

1.1 Motivation and Challenge

The prostate is part of the male reproductive system and is about the size of a walnut. Twenty-five percent of men aged 55 and over are affected by prostate diseases, while the proportion of men aged 70 and over has risen to 50 percent. The three major prostate diseases are prostatitis, non-cancerous enlargement of the prostate (BPH) and prostate cancer. According to the statistics of the World Cancer Research Foundation, 1.3 million new cases of prostate cancer were reported in 2018. Prostate cancer is the second most common type of cancer in men and the fourth most common type of cancer. Early detection and accurate diagnosis of prostate cancer can significantly improve the cure rate of prostate cancer, so there is an urgent need for reliable computer-aided diagnosis (CAD) solutions to diagnose and treat prostate diseases. Compared with transrectal ultrasound images and CT images, magnetic resonance images (MRI) can present the prostate and its surrounding soft tissue structure more clearly and in more details, so MRI has become the main tool for diagnosis and evaluation of prostate diseases. Prostate segmentation from magnetic resonance images is an essential prerequisite for detecting prostate diseases, especially prostate cancer [1]. Prostate segmentation can accurately locate the boundary of the prostate, which can be

© Springer Nature Switzerland AG 2019
D.-S. Huang et al. (Eds.): ICIC 2019, LNCS 11643, pp. 481–490, 2019.
https://doi.org/10.1007/978-3-030-26763-6_46

used to formulate radiotherapy plans to limit damages to surrounding tissues. Prostate volume can be estimated by prostate segmentation [2], which is mainly used to assess the extent of prostate diseases. There are two limitations to the traditional manual segmentation method: First, it relies on radiologists with strong professional knowledge; Second, the manual segmentation method is time-consuming. Therefore, automatic segmentation of prostates in MRI images has become a hot research field. However, there are many challenges to accurate and efficient prostate segmentation methods:

1. The size of prostate gland varies greatly from patient to patient. Even in the same patient's MRI volume, the size and shape of the prostate gland presented in the slices at different locations are very different, as shown in Fig. 1.
2. Different MR protocols, distortion of the MR images, noises, and the pixel intensities make the appearances of prostates different.
3. The prostate and adjacent tissues are usually very similar, so the boundaries between them are often very blurred and difficult to locate accurately.

Although much progress has been made, there are still some challenges that have not yet been fully addressed, which has led to a gap between clinical needs and automatic segmentation performance.

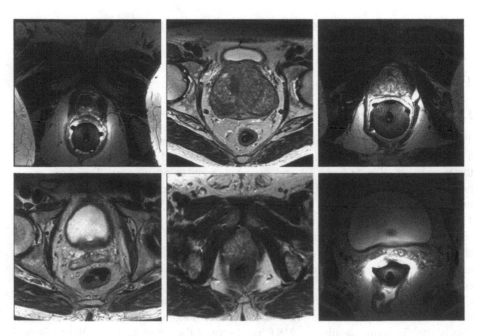

Fig. 1. Example of prostate MR images exhibiting large variations

1.2 Previous Work

Many automatic prostate segmentation methods have been proposed for MR images. Because the trend of neural networks has been rekindled in recent years, many computer vision research fields, including image segmentation, have shown dramatic performance improvement by using deep neural networks. We divide the automatic prostate segmentation method into non-deep learning methods and deep learning-based methods. Non-deep learning methods can be further divided into atlas based methods [3–6], deformable model based methods [7–9], graph based method [10–12]. Klein et al. [3] employed multi-atlas matching and localized mutual information for prostate in 3D MR images. Pasquier et al. [7] used active shape models (ASMs) to locate the prostate boundaries of prostates by strong gradients. Makni et al. [8] combined deformable model and a probabilistic framework to identify the prostate region. Both the ASM and active appearance model (AAM) are limited by the use of landmarks. To eliminate the restriction of landmarks, Toth et al. [9] proposed a novel landmark-free AAM to overcome the difficulty of setting landmarks in ASMs. Moschidis et al. [10] combines graph cut and random forest (RF) classifiers for prostate segmentation. Zouqi et al. [11] employed graph cuts and domain knowledge for prostate segmentation from ultrasound images. Tian et al. [12] proposed a superpixel-based 3D graph cut algorithm to obtain the prostate surface.

In the era of deep learning, many deep neural network models have been proposed to solve the automatic segmentation task of the prostate. Guo et al. [13] learned the high-level features by a stacked sparse auto-encoder (SSAE) and integrated them into a deformable model. Jia et al. [14] proposed an ensemble deep convolutional neural network for fine prostate segmentation. Milletari et al. [15] proposed a 3D convolutional neural network for prostate segmentation. Yu et al. [16] introduced the mixed residual connections into 3D convolutional neural network. Yan et al. [17] proposed an automated model that extracts and combines multi-level features in a deep neural network to segment prostates on MR images.

2 Background: Medical Image Segmentation

In the field of medical image processing, automatic segmentation technology can provide very useful information for computer-aided diagnosis and treatment of diseases. Because convolutional neural networks have hierarchical feature extraction capabilities, they have achieved success in many areas of computer vision, such as classification, object detection, and segmentation. Convolutional neural networks have proven to be very robust, which has prompted people to apply them in the field of medical image processing. Ronneberger et al. [18] proposed u-net for biomedical image segmentation. It is based on fully convolutional networks (FCN), introducing skip connections between downsampling paths and up-sampling paths. Zhu et al. [19] proposed a new network with bidirectional convolution recurrence layer for MRI images of prostates, extracting intra-slice and inter-slice information as well as context information of slices for auxiliary segmentation. Li et al. [20] proposed a hybrid model referred to as H-DenseUNet for the liver segmentation problem. The model takes densenet as backbone, whose densely connected paths improved information flow and parameters efficiently, which greatly alleviates the difficulty for training. Moreover, this model makes UNet connections between encoder and decoder, preserving low-level spatial features of the slices for better intra-slice context exploration. Yu et al. [21] proposed a novel densely connected volumetric convolutional neural network referred to as DenseVoxNet, to automatically segment cardiac and vascular structures from 3D cardiac MR images. Chen et al. [22] proposed a voxel residual network (VoxResNet) on the task of volumetric brain segmentation. By seamlessly integrating the low-level image appearance features, implicit shape information and high-level context together, it improves the volumetric segmentation performance.

3   Method

In this paper, we propose a cascade dense-unet model for prostate segmentation. Its architecture is shown in Fig. 2. The method can segment prostates from magnetic resonance images accurately and efficiently. It consists of two stages: In the first stage, the 2D slice images are fed into the first stage dense-unet segmentation network, and the preliminary segmentation results are obtained. In the second stage, the slice images and the corresponding first-stage segmentation results are concatenated together as the input of the second-stage dense-unet segmentation network to obtain a more accurate segmentation result.

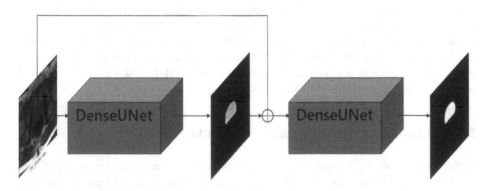

Fig. 2. The architecture of the proposed model

3.1   Network Architecture (Dense-Unet)

In order to more accurately segment prostates, this paper designed a dense-unet network model, as illustrated in the Fig. 3(a).

We carefully extend the densenet [23] architecture to unet for semantic segmentation. The architecture follows the encoder-decoder design concept of FCN and u-net, which consists of a down-sampling path and an up-sampling path. The downsampling path extracts the semantic information of the input images, layer by layer through continuous convolution and down-sampling operations, from low-level to high-level.

Up-sampling path expands the resolution of feature map by deconvolution operation until the resolution of input images is completely restored. Up-sampling path and down-sampling are composed of dense block and transition layer, which connects adjacent dense blocks. Their structure is shown in Fig. 3(b).

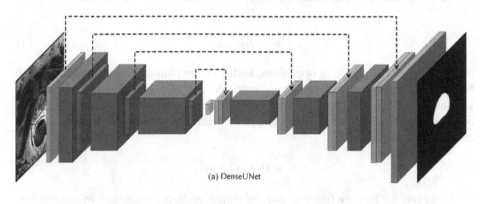

(a) DenseUNet

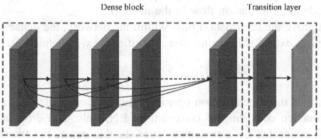

(b) Dense block and Trasition layer

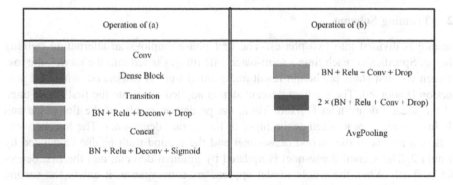

Fig. 3. Dense block and transition layer

Both up-sampling path and down-sampling path are composed of 4 dense blocks and 4 transition layers. A dense block consists of n consecutive convolution layers of the same resolution, each followed by a batch normalization (BN) rectified linear units (ReLU) and dropout layer. The Lth convolution layer takes the feature maps of all the previous layers as input.

In a convolutional neural network, x_l is defined as the output of the lth layer, and x_l can be computed by a transformation $H_l(x)$ from the output of the previous layer, x_{l-1} as:

$$x_l = H_l(x_{l-1}) \tag{1}$$

where $H_l(x)$ is a sequence of operations, such as Convolution (Conv), Pooling, Batch Normalization (BN) or rectified linear unit (ReLU), etc. To boost training against vanishing gradients, ResNet [24] introduces the skip connection which integrates the output of $H_l(x)$ with the identity mapping of the feature maps from the previous layer to enhance information flow:

$$x_l = H(x_{l-1}) + x_{l-1} \tag{2}$$

However, the identity function and the output of H_l are combined by summation, which may impede the information flow in the network.

To further improve the information flow within the network, the dense connection [23] is introduced to extend skip connection. Specifically, x_l is defined as:

$$x_l = H_l([x_{l-1}, x_{l-2}, \ldots, x_0]) \tag{3}$$

where [...] represents the concatenation operation. In this case, H denotes a nonlinear transformation function consisting of convolution, BN, Relu, and dropout. The two dense blocks are connected by a transition layer. In this paper, the transition layer consists of a BN layer, a 1 * 1 convolutional layer, followed by a subsequent 2 * 2 average pooling layer.

3.2   Training Scheme

Training is divided into two phases. The first phase employs an alternating training scheme. Specifically, each time a mini-batch MR images is fed into the model, the loss between the first stage prediction result and ground truth is calculated, where L1 loss function is adopted. The gradient descent step is applied to update the first dense-unet, and the second dense-unet is fixed. Then, the prediction results of the first stage and MR images are concatenated as the input of the second dense-unet. The loss between prediction results of the second dense-unet and the ground truth is also calculated by formula 2. The second dense-unet is updated by gradient descent, and the first dense-unet is fixed. When the whole model approaches convergence, it enters the second phase of training, and the first and second dense-unet are trained in an end-to-end training manner.

4   Experiments

4.1   Dataset and Pre-processing

The proposed method is validated on the MICCAI Prostate MR Image Segmentation (PROMISE12) challenge dataset [25]. The open dataset contains 50 volumes of transverse T2-weighted MR images and the corresponding expert-annotated standard segmentation results. We randomly divided the data set into 5 folds, each with 10 volumes, using a fold for testing, and the rest for training, namely 5-fold cross validation.

These MR images are collected from different hospitals and equipments, which results in large differences in voxel size, dynamic range, position, resolution, field of view, anatomic appearance, and contrast, which will directly affect the performance of the model. In data processing, we first remove noise in data pre-processing. Specifically, sort the pixel values of each slice. Then, set an interval [min, max], only 2% of the pixels in the slice are smaller than min, and only 2% of the pixels are larger than max. Values outside the interval are clipped to the interval edges. Finally, all the pixel values are mapped to 0–255 and all CT/MR slices are resized to 256 * 256.

4.2   Implementation

The proposed model was implemented based on tensorflow. All the experiments were performed on the workstations equipped with CPU, memory, and NVIDIA TITAN XP GPU. We use the Adam solver to train the model with a mini-batch size of 8. The model was trained for 500 epochs and the initial learning rate was set to 0.0002. The learning rate is divided by 10 when training 50% of the total training epoch number.

4.3   Comparison with Other Methods

The proposed model is compared with two baseline models (u-net, v-net). u-net is widely used in biomedical image segmentation tasks, and v-net can be regarded as a 3D extended version of u-net.

Table 1. Quantitative comparison between the proposed method and other methods.

Methods	Dice score
u-net [18]	0.820
v-net [15]	0.830
dense-unet	0.845
cascade dense-unet	0.856

In order to evaluate the performance of our model, we used Dice score as the metrics to measure the overall region and shape similarity of the segmentation results, respectively. The Dice score is calculated as Eq. 4, which is usually used in two ways. The first is called Dice per case score, which averages the Dice score calculated in each

CT volume. The second is Dice global score. This Dice score is calculated over the entire data set. In our experiments, we employed Dice per case score to evaluate prostate segmentation performance. As can be seen from the formula, the Dice score is distributed between 0 and 1.

$$dice = \frac{2|X \cap Y|}{|X| + |Y|} \qquad (4)$$

Some quantitative results of several methods are shown in Table 1 through cross validation. It is observed that our model has achieved more accurate segmentation results. This is because we introduced a dense connection in the proposed model, which has implicit deep supervision and enables better information transfer between layers. On the other hand, the cascade structure can help the model further improve performance. Some predictions of our model are shown in Fig. 4.

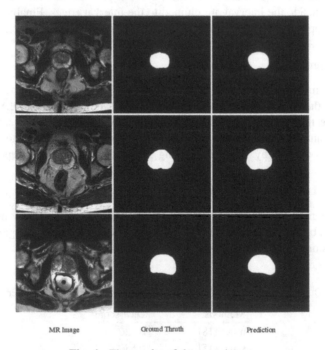

MR Image   Ground Thruth   Prediction

Fig. 4. The results of the experiments

5   Conclusion

In this paper, we propose a cascade dense-uent model for automatic prostate segmentation from MR images. The main contributions are the followings: First, a dense-unet model suitable for this task is designed based on unet and densenet. Second, due to the cascade architecture, the segmentation results of the first phase can provide prior knowledge for the second phase, resulting in more accurate segmentation. Future investigations to be conducted include extending the model to more biomedical segmentation tasks, and exploring more efficient cascade structures.

Acknowledgement. This work is supported by Shanghai Science and Technology Commission (grant No. 17511104203) and NSFC (grant NO. 61472087).

References

1. Vos, P., Barentsz, J., Karssemeijer, N., Huisman, H.: Automatic computer-aided detection of prostate cancer based on multiparametric magnetic resonance image analysis. Phys. Med. Biol. **57**(6), 1527 (2012)
2. Toth, R., et al.: Accurate prostate volume estimation using multifeature active shape models on T2-weighted MRI. Acad. Radiol. **18**(6), 745–754 (2011)
3. Klein, S., vander Heide, U., Lipps, I., Vulpen, M., Staring, M., Pluim, J.: Automatic segmentation of the prostate in 3-D MR images by atlas matching using localized mutual information. Med. Phys. **35**(4), 1407–1417 (2008)
4. Martin, S., Daanen, V., Troccaz, J.: Automated segmentation of the prostate 3-D MR images using a probabilistic atlas and a spatially constrained deformable model. Med. Phys. **37**(4), 1579–1590 (2010)
5. Ou, Y., Doshi, J., Erus, G., Davatzikos, C.: Multi-atlas segmentation of the prostate: a zooming process with robust registration and atlas selection. In: 2012 MICCAI Grand Challenge: Prostate MR Image Segmentation (2012)
6. Yan, P., Cao, Y., Yuan, Y., Turkbey, B., Choyke, P.L.: Label image constrained multi-atlas selection. IEEE Trans. Cybernet. **45**(6), 1158–1168 (2015)
7. Pasquier, D., Lacornerie, T., Vermandel, M., Rousseau, J., Lartigau, E., Betrouni, N.: Automatic segmentation of pelvic structures from magnetic resonance images for prostate cancer radiotherapy. Int. J. Radiat. Oncol. Biol. Phys. **68**(2), 592–600 (2007)
8. Makni, N., Puech, P., Lopes, R., Dewalle, A.: Combining a deformable model and a probabilistic framework for an automatic 3-D segmentation of prostate on MRI. Int. J. Comput. Assisted. Radiol. Surg. **4**(2), 181–188 (2009)
9. Toth, R., Madabhushi, A.: Multifeature landmark-free active appearance models: Application to prostate MRI segmentation. IEEE Trans. Med. Imag **31**(8), 1638–1650 (2012)
10. Moschidis E., Graham, J.: Automatic differential segmentation of the prostate in 3-D MRI using random forest classification and graph cuts optimization. In: Proceedings of the IEEE International Symposium on Biomedical Imaging, pp. 1727–1730 (2012)
11. Zouqi M., Samarabandu, J.: Prostate segmentation from 2-D ultrasound images using graph cuts and domain knowledge. In: Proceedings of the Conference on Computer and Robot Vision, pp. 359–362 (2008)
12. Tian, Z., Liu, L., Zhang, Z., Fei, B.: Superpixel-based segmentation for 3D prostate MR images. IEEE Trans. Med. Imaging **35**(3), 791–801 (2016)
13. Guo, Y., Gao, Y., Shen, D.: Deformable MR prostate segmentation via deep feature learning and sparse patch matching. IEEE Trans. Med. Imaging **35**(4), 1077–1089 (2016)
14. Jia, H., Xia, Y., Song, Y., Cai, W., Fulham, M., Feng, D.D.: Atlas registration and ensemble deep convolutional neural network-based prostate segmentation using magnetic resonance imaging. Neurocomputing **275**, 1358–1369 (2017)

15. Milletari, F., Navab, N., Ahmadi, S.-A.: V-Net: fully convolutional neural networks for volumetric medical image segmentation. In: 2016 Fourth International Conference on 3D Vision (3DV), pp. 565–571. IEEE (2016)

16. Yu, L., Yang, X., Chen, H., Qin, J., Heng, P.-A.: Volumetric ConvNets with mixed residual connections for automated prostate segmentation from 3D MR images. In: AAAI, pp. 66–72 (2017)

17. Yan, K., Wang, X., Kim, J., et al.: A propagation-DNN: deep combination learning of multi-level features for MR prostate segmentation. Comput. Methods Programs Biomed. **170**, 11–21 (2019)

18. Ronneberger, O., Fischer, P., Brox, T.: U-Net: convolutional networks for biomedical image segmentation. In: Navab, N., Hornegger, J., Wells, W.M., Frangi, A.F. (eds.) MICCAI 2015. LNCS, vol. 9351, pp. 234–241. Springer, Cham (2015). https://doi.org/10.1007/978-3-319-24574-4_28

19. Zhu, Q., Du, B., Turkbey, B., Choyke, P., Yan, P.: Exploiting interslice correlation for MRI prostate image segmentation, from recursive neural networks aspect. Complexity, vol. 10 (2018)

20. Li, X., Chen, H., Qi, X., Dou, Q., Fu, C., Heng, P.: H-DenseUNet: hybrid densely connected UNet for liver and liver tumor segmentation from CT volumes. IEEE Trans. Med. Imaging **37**(12), 2663–2674 (2018)

21. Yu, L., Cheng, J.-Z., Dou, Q., Yang, X., Chen, H., Qin, J., Heng, P.-A.: Automatic 3D cardiovascular MR segmentation with densely-connected volumetric ConvNets. In: Descoteaux, M., Maier-Hein, L., Franz, A., Jannin, P., Collins, D.L., Duchesne, S. (eds.) MICCAI 2017. LNCS, vol. 10434, pp. 287–295. Springer, Cham (2017). https://doi.org/10.1007/978-3-319-66185-8_33

22. Chen, H., Dou, Q., Yu, L., Heng, P.-A.: VoxResNet: deep voxelwise residual networks for volumetric brain segmentation. arXiv preprint arXiv:1608.05895 (2016)

23. Huang, G., Liu, Z., Weinberger, K.Q., van der Maaten, L.: Densely connected convolutional networks. CoRR, abs/1608.06993 (2016)

24. He, K., Zhang, X., Ren, S., Sun, J.: Deep residual learning for image recognition. In: CVPR, pp. 770–778 (2016)

25. Litjens, G., et al.: Evaluation of prostate segmentation algorithms for MRI: the PROMISE12 challenge. Med. Image Anal. **18**(2), 359–373 (2014)

A Percolation Algorithm to Discover Emerging Research Topics

Rong-Qiang Zeng[1(✉)] and Li-Yuan Xue[2]

[1] School of Mathematics, Southwest Jiaotong University, Chengdu 610031,
Sichuan, People's Republic of China
zrq@swjtu.edu.cn
[2] EHF Key Laboratory of Science, School of Electronic Engineering,
University of Electronic Science and Technology of China,
Chengdu 611731, Sichuan, People's Republic of China
xuely2013@gmail.com

Abstract. With the fast growth of the scientific papers, it is vital to discover the implicit knowledge from the enormous information accurately and efficiently. To achieve this goal, we propose a percolation algorithm to discover emerging research topics based on SPO predications, which constructs a three-level SPO-based semantic relation network in the research area of stem cells. We perform the experiments on the scientific papers of stem cells from 2013 to 2015, and the experimental results indicate that the proposed approach can effectively and accurately discover the emerging research topics of stem cells.

Keywords: Emerging research topics · Stem cells ·
SPO-based semantic relation network · Percolation algorithm ·
Community detection

1 Introduction

The emerging research topics represent the newly developing areas of science and technology, in which the scientists are highly concerned. In fact, it is very significant to explore the emerging research topics through the scientific papers for scientific research and policy making [8].

With the fast growth of scientific papers, it has become a huge challenge to efficiently and accurately discover the implicit knowledge from the enormous information in a credible way. Then, Knowledge Discovery in Biomedical Literature (KDiBL) has become an important research area. Actually, it is very interesting and useful to combine the semantic networks with scientometrics for KDiBL.

In this paper, we propose a percolation algorithm to discover emerging research topics based on Subject-Predication-Object (SPO) predications, which represent the semantic relationships among the knowledge units and consist of a subject argument (noun phrase), an object argument (noun phrase) and the relation that binds them (verb phrase) [5]. The experiments are carried out on the scientific papers of stem cells from 2013 to 2015, and the computational results indicate that the proposed algorithm can effectively and accurately discover the emerging research topics of stem cells.

D.-S. Huang et al. (Eds.): ICIC 2019, LNCS 11643, pp. 491–500, 2019.
https://doi.org/10.1007/978-3-030-26763-6_47

The remaining parts of this paper is organized as follows. Section 2 briefly describes the previous works related to the discovery of emerging research topics. In Sect. 3, we present a percolation algorithm to discover the emerging research topics based on SPO predications. Afterwards, we provides the experimental results and the performance analysis of the proposed algorithm in Sect. 4. The concluding remarks are given in the last section.

2   Related Works

In this section, we present the literature reviews related to the emerging research topics.

In [1], the authors proposed two effective clustering algorithms unsupervised Expectation Maximization (EM) and Distribution Based (DB) clustering approach, which are used to cluster web videos based on the video meta-objects of large scale web such as length, view counts, numbers of comments, rating information. These two algorithms are dedicated to automatically forming three types of clusters for further knowledge discovery. The resultant clusters are analyzed to discover popular video cluster, average popular video cluster and non-popular video clusters.

In [3], to the study of a scientific field, the authors proposed a multi-level structural variation approach, which is motivated by an explanatory and computational theory of transformative discovery. With the novel structural variation metrics derived from the theory, they integrated the theoretical framework with a visual analytic process, which enables an analyst to study the literature of a scientific field across multiple levels of aggregation and decomposition, including the field as a whole, specialties, topics and predicates.

In [4], based on Human Phenotype Ontology (HPO), the authors presented a novel method named RelativeBestPair to measure similarity from the query terms to hereditary diseases and rank the candidate diseases. In order to evaluate the performance, they carried out the experiments on a set of patients based on 44 complex diseases by adding noise and imprecision to be closer to real clinical conditions. In comparison with seven existing semantic similarity measures, RelativeBestPair significantly outperformed all other seven methods in the simulated dataset with both noise and imprecision, which might be of great help in clinical setting.

In [7], the authors proposed method of discovering uncommercialized research fronts, which compares the structures of citation networks of scientific publications with those of patents by citation analysis and measures the similarity between sets of academic papers and sets of patents by natural language processing. In order to discover research fronts that do not correspond to any patents, they performed a comparative study to measure the semantic similarity between academic papers and patents. As a result, cosine similarity of term frequency-inverse document frequency (tfidf) vector was found to be the best way of discovering corresponding relationships.

3 Percolation Algorithm

In our research, we propose a percolation algorithm to discover the emerging research topics based on the SPO predications, which is a three-level SPO-based semantic relation network in the research area of stem cells. There is an example of the SPO-based semantic relation network with thousands of vertices and edges in the research areas of stem cells presented in Fig. 1, in which the vertices with different colors denotes the different verbs in the semantic relation and the size of the vertex denotes the frequency of this word.

In order to effectively detect the communities from the SPO-based semantic relation network, the percolation algorithm employs the widely used modularity function defined in [6]:

$$Q = \frac{1}{2m} \sum_{vw} \left[A_{vw} - \frac{k_v k_w}{2m} \right] \delta(C_v, C_w).$$ (1)

Suppose that the vertices are divided into different communities such that the vertex v belongs to the community C denoted by C_v. In Formula 1, A is the adjacency matrix of the network G. $A_{vw} = 1$ if one vertex v is connected to another vertex w, otherwise $A_{vw} = 0$. The δ function $\delta(i,j)$ is equal to 1 if $i = j$ and 0 otherwise. The degree k_v of a vertex v is defined to be $k_v = \sum_v A_{wv}$, and the number of edges in the network is $m = \sum_{wv} A_{wv}$.

According to the modularity function optimization [2], the percolation algorithm presented in Algorithm 1 is a heuristic approach to find the communities in the large networks.

Algorithm 1. The Percolation Algorithm

1: **Input:** SPO-based semantic relation network G
2: **Output:** Sequence of communities
3: Initialization (G)
4: Calculating the the average weighted degree d of G
5: Calculating the weight of each edge of G multiplies by a random number with theprobability $1 - 1/d$
6: $P = \{x^1, \dots, x^p\} \leftarrow$ Random_Initialization (P)
7: **repeat:**
8:     $x^i \leftarrow$ Local_Search (x^i)
9: **until** a stop criterion is met

Based on the SPO-based semantic relations, we initialize the network into a directed weighted graph in Algorithm 1. Afterwards, we calculate the average weighted degree d of the generated graph, in which the weight of each edge multiplies by a random number with the probability $1-1/d$. With the modularity function value, the local search procedure is executed until the modularity function value does not improve any more. At last, we obtain the communities in the considered network. Actually, the time complexity of the proposed algorithm is $O(n^2)$.

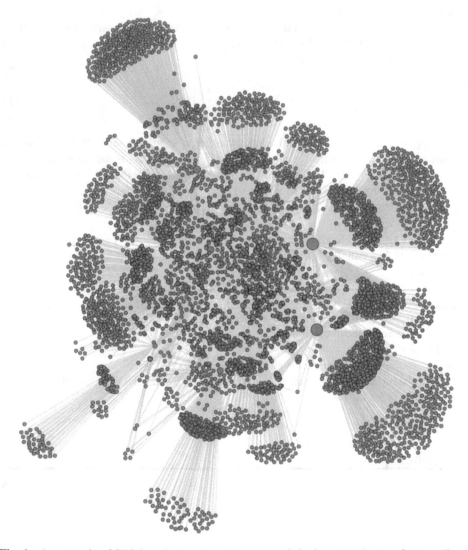

Fig. 1. An example of SPO-based semantic relation network in the research area of stem cells.

An example of the communities in the SPO-based semantic relation network detected by the percolation algorithm is presented in Fig. 2, in which the communities are denoted with different colors.

4 Experiments

For the stem cells research, it is of great significance to explore the research frontiers from the vast scientific literatures. In this section, we perform our proposed approach to the field of stem cells research, then provide the experimental results and performance analysis.

4.1 Data Information

In order to conduct the experiments, we obtain the data from the PubMed Database by inputting the key words "stem cells" from 2013 to 2015. Then, we select the papers retrieved by the Semantic Medline Database by filtering "Systematic Review", "Meta-Analysis" and "Review". The exact data information is presented in Table 1.

Table 1. The information of the constructed SPO-based semantic relation network.

Year	Number of subjects	Number of object	Number of verbs
2013	2028	2670	45
2014	5473	5143	45
2015	3993	3992	45

In this table, we have retrieved 9, 463 papers and obtained 19, 710 SPO-based semantic relations, which consists of 12, 160 subjects, 11, 538 objects and 45 verbs in total. With these information, we can construct the SPO-based semantic relation network for the research topics discovery.

4.2 Experimental Results

In this subsection, we provide the experimental results in the research area of stem cells. The selected research topics from the SPO-based semantic relation network in 2013, 2014 and 2015 are respectively presented in Figs. 3, 4 and 5.

In these figures, the different communities detected by the percolation algorithm are depicted with different colors, and the frequency of each SPO is proportional to the size of the vertex in the SPO-based semantic relation network.

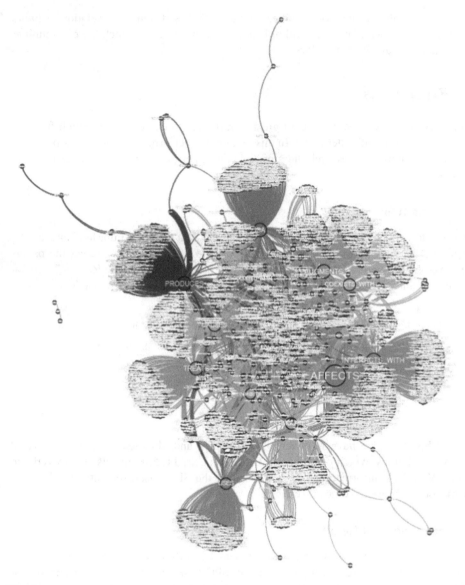

Fig. 2. An example of the communities detected by the percolation algorithm in the SPO-based semantic relation network.

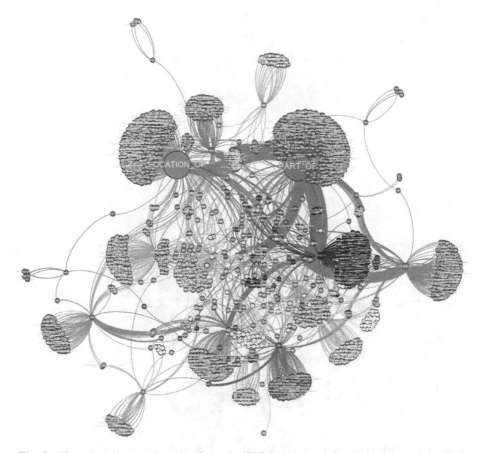

Fig. 3. The selected research topics from the SPO-based semantic relation network in 2013.

Moreover, we can clearly observe that the community "PART OF" by which the corresponding SPO is linked has strong relation with other communities and high frequency of the corresponding SPO in Figs. 3 and 4.

On the other hand, the community "LOCATION OF" has weak relation with other communities in Fig. 3. Moreover, in Fig. 4. However, the frequency of the SPO in the community "PART OF" is almost the same as the frequency of the SPO in the community "LOCATION OF".

Fig. 4. The selected research topics from the SPO-based semantic relation network in 2014.

In Fig. 5, the community "AFFECTS" by which the corresponding SPO is linked has the obvious advantages both in the strength of the relations with other communities and in the frequency of the corresponding SPO in the year 2015. Actually, we can discover the emerging research topics from these three figures, which is useful to recognize the current research trends of the stem cells.

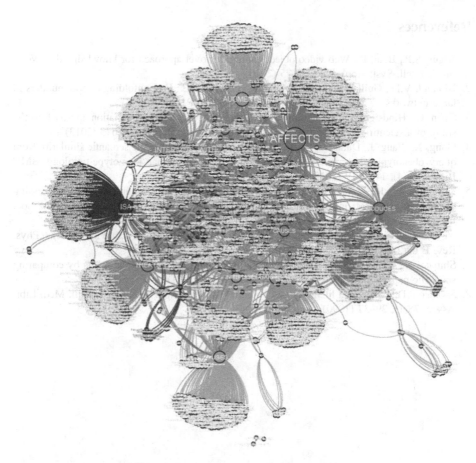

Fig. 5. The selected research topics from the SPO-based semantic relation network in 2015.

5 Conclusions

In this paper, we have investigated a percolation approach to discovering the emerging research topics from the SPO-based semantic relation network. Then, we perform the experiments in the research area of stem cells. The experimental results indicate that our proposed approach can significantly identify the research topics and the current research trends in the considered area.

Acknowledgments. The work in this paper was supported by the Fundamental Research Funds for the Central Universities (Grant No. 2682017CX05).

References

1. Algur, S.P., Bhat, P.: Web video object mining: a novel approach for knowledge discovery. Int. J. Intell. Syst. Appl. **8**(4), 67–75 (2016)
2. Blondel, V.D., Guillaume, J., Lambiotte, R., Lefebvre, E.: Fast unfolding of communities in large networks. J. Stat. Mech: Theory Exp. **2008**(10), P10008 (2008)
3. Chen, C.: Hindsight, insight, and foresight: a multi-level structural variation approach to the study of a scientific field. Technol. Anal. Strateg. Manag. **25**(6), 619–640 (2013)
4. Gong, X., Jiang, J., Duan, Z., Lu, H.: A new method to measure the semantic similarity from query phenotypic abnormalities to diseases based on the human phenotype ontology. BMC Bioinf. **19**(4), 111–119 (2018)
5. Keselman, A., Rosemblat, G., Kilicoglu, H.: Adapting semantic natural language processing technology to address information overload in influenza epidemic management. J. Am. Soc. Inf. Sci. Technol. **61**(12), 2531–2543 (1990)
6. Newman, M.E.J., Girvan, M.: Finding and evaluating community structure in networks. Phys. Rev. E **69**(2), 026113 (2004)
7. Shibata, N., Kajikawa, Y., Sakata, I.: Detecting potential technological fronts by comparing scientific papers and patents. Foresight **13**(5), 51–60 (2011)
8. Swanson, D.R.: Medical literature as a potential source of new knowledge. Bull. Med. Libr. Assoc. **78**(1), 29–37 (1990)

Designing and Implementing Mobile Robot Navigation Based on Behavioral Programming

Zuohua Ding$^{(\boxtimes)}$, Bing Liu, and Haibang Xia

School of Information Science and Technology, Zhejiang Sci-Tech University,
Hangzhou 310018, China
zouhuading@hotmail.com, liubing1994@outlook.com,
xhbswitch@163.com

Abstract. If we want to add a new functionality to a software system, we usually need to modify the software design and the code. One of the big challenges to complete such work in the traditional way is to handle the interactions between the new parts and the existing parts. Mistakes can be easily made during this processing, especially in the programming, thus intensive regression testing is required to detect the bugs. In this paper, we attempt to solve this issue by using behavioral programming technique. Behavioral programming approach is an incremental software development approach. By using this technique, the coupling of components is low, and the removing or redefining of a behavior module only needs a small amount of code change. That means that our design become simpler, and the testing become easier. We apply this technique to mobile robot programming by decoupling the global path planning and the local path planning. Simulation experiments show the effectiveness of the proposed method.

Keywords: Behavioral programming · Decoupling · Mobile robot ·
Path planning

1 Introduction

Nowadays software systems become more complicated as more functions have been added to the systems, which leads to the hard maintenance. One of the challenges to add a new functionality to the software system is to consider the interactions between the new parts and the existing parts from design and implementation aspects since most of our software systems are designed based on components. In addition, mistakes can be easily made by our human, so that an intensive regression testing is required. We hope that the couplings between components or subsystems we de-signed are as low as possible, and the behaviors of functions are less dependent, so that the implementation and maintenance become easier [16].

To address the above issues, we try to employ behavioral programming approach [3, 5, 9]. Roughly speaking, it can be used as a "scenario" based design technique. The behavioral programming approach is based on the specific functional behavior and scene requirements, using the scene coding technology and design method to incrementally construct the reaction system from the expected behavior of the reaction

D.-S. Huang et al. (Eds.): ICIC 2019, LNCS 11643, pp. 501–510, 2019.
https://doi.org/10.1007/978-3-030-26763-6_48

system. The main advantages of behavioral programming approach include self-made behavior, positive and negative increments, early partial execution, and consolidation of the same execution requirements [4, 6, 8].

As an application, we apply the behavioral programming method to the navigation system of mobile robots. We divide the behavior of the navigation system of a mobile robot into global path planning behavior and local path planning behavior, and independently code the program based on the behavior. The global path planning is implemented by using the A* algorithm, and the local path planning is implemented by using fuzzy logic. The simulation experiments show the effectiveness and convenience of behavioral programming method in mobile robot programming. Our work has the following contributions:

1. We find a new application of behavioral programming method to the navigation system of mobile robots.
2. We can incrementally add new scenes to the existing navigation system.
3. We can reduce code changes when we implement new functions to the navigation system.

The rest of the paper is structured as follows. Section 2, for self-contained reason, describes some fundamental concepts of behavioral programming and its current applications. In Sect. 3, we explain how to design a mobile robot's navigation system using behavioral programming technique. Section 4 shows how to implement the navigation functions based on behavioral programming methods. Section 5 is a simulation the and the analysis of the results. The last section, Sect. 6, is the conclusion of the paper.

2 Preliminaries

In this section, we provide some of the prerequisites used in this paper. We first explain the basic theoretical background of behavioral programming and the applications in the current scene, and then describe how to model behavior thread.

Behavioral programming is a method that advocates not combining expected and undesired scenes according to system structure [1, 11]. This method is a planned execution protocol and coordination mechanism through the event sequence set, which can well control the behavior in the scene. Figure 1 illustrates the execution mechanism of these behavior threads.

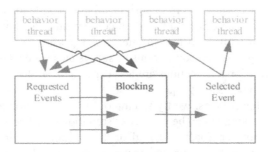

Fig. 1. The sequence of executions of the behavior thread is controlled by an event set. Only the behavior thread that is not blocked and selected can be executed.

Behavioral programming approach have been applied in many directions. For example, in [7], the behavioral programming approach is applied in distributed systems to solve some of the challenges associated with a truly distributed or decentralized approach. In [10, 12], behavioral programming approaches are used to solve conflicts and unclear scenarios in the early development of Java programs. The behavioral programming approach is selected to achieve adaptive system development in [20].

2.1 Behavior Thread

Based on the principle of behavioral programming, we formalize the behavior thread execution mechanism by marking the transition system [21]. The mark transition system based on behavior thread is defined as a quaternion $\langle S, E, \rightarrow, init \rangle$ [4]. Where S is a set of behavior thread states, E is a set of events, "$\rightarrow$" is an event-based state transition, $init \in S$ and $init$ is the initial state. This relational conversion system operates in the form of $s_0 \xrightarrow{e_1} s_1 \xrightarrow{e_2} \cdots \xrightarrow{e_i} s_i \cdots$ where $s_0 = init$. For all $i = 1, 2, \cdots$ have $s_{i-1} \xrightarrow{e_i} s_i$, where $s_i \in S$, $e_i \in E$.

A behavior thread (marked as b-thread) can be described by a model below.

$$(S, E, \rightarrow, init, R, B) \tag{1}$$

where R is a collection event of the request thread, and B is a collection event of the block thread $R \in S$, $B \in E$.

Runs of a set of b-threads models as

$$\{(S_i, E_i, \rightarrow_i, init_i, R_i, B_i)\}_{i=1}^{n} \tag{2}$$

Where $S = S_1 \times \cdots \times S_n$, $E = \cup_{i=1}^{n} E_i$, and $init = (init_1, \cdots, init_n)$, "$\rightarrow$" is a transition $(s_1, \cdots, s_n) \xrightarrow{e} (s_1', \cdots, s_n')$, iff:

$$e \in \bigcup_{i=1}^{n} R_i(s_i) \wedge e \notin \bigcup_{i=1}^{n} B_i(s_i) \tag{3}$$

and

$$\bigwedge_{i=1}^{n} ((e \in E_i \Rightarrow s_i \xrightarrow{e} s_i') \wedge (e \notin E_i \Rightarrow s_i = s_i')) \tag{4}$$

3 A Design Framework of Navigation of Mobile Robots

In this section, we introduce how to design the mobile robot navigation framework based behavioral programming approach.

3.1 Navigation Design Based on Behavioral Programming

According to the division of navigation behavior, we design three behavior threads, namely navigation control behavior thread, global path planning behavior thread, and local path planning behavior thread. The requirement of the entire navigation system is that the navigation control behavior thread completes the scheduling of the two path planning behavior threads. The global path planning behavior thread completes the function of global static route planning. The local path planning behavior thread completes the function of the local dynamic path planning.

Navigation Control Behavior Thread: The purpose of the navigation control behavior thread is to coordinate the behavior thread requesting this event through the blocking of events and the observation of events. Name the navigation control behavior thread *NavigationCtrl*, we define the model of the navigation control behavior thread by (1).

$$NavigationCtrl = (S_N, E_N, \rightarrow_N R_N, B_N) \tag{5}$$

where,

1. S_N is the *NavigationCtrl* state collection, the expression is

$$S_N = \{init_{GL1}, q_{GL2}, q_{GL3}\} \tag{6}$$

where $init_{GL1}$, q_{GL2}, and q_{GL3} are the behavior thread *NavigationCtrl* order change states.

2. R_N is request a collection of events, B_N is the collection of blocking events, E is the set of request events and blocking events, $R_N \in E_N$, $B_N \in E_N$, R_N and B_N expression is

$$R_N = \{\phi\}$$
$$B_N = \{LParthEvent, GParthEvent\} \tag{7}$$

where *LParthEvent* is the local path planning event, and *GParthEvent* is the global path planning event.

3. $\rightarrow_N$ is the state transition. Its state transition expression is

$$init_{GL1} \overset{e_{GL1}}{\rightarrow} q_{GL2} \overset{e_{GL2}}{\rightarrow} q_{GL3} \tag{8}$$

when *LParthEvent* $\notin e_{GL1}$, where the initial state $init_{GL1}$ enters the next state q_{GL2}, when *GParthEvent* $\notin e_{GL2}$, enters the next state q_{GL3}.

Path Planning Behavior Threads: After the navigation control behavior thread is established, then we create the behavior thread of the global path planning and the behavior thread of the local path planning. Name the global path planning thread

GlobalPathPlanning, Name the local path planning thread LocalPathPlanning, We define the model of the global path planning behavior thread and the behavior thread of the local path planning by (1) and (2).

$$\{GlobalPathPlanning, LocalPathPlanning\} = \\ \{(S_G, E_G, \rightarrow_G, init_G, R_G, B_G), (S_L, E_L, \rightarrow_L, init_L, R_L, B_L)\} \tag{9}$$

where,

1. S_G is the *GlobalPathPlanning* state collection, S_L is the *LocalPathPlanning* state collection, the expression is

$$S_G = \{init_{G1}, q_{G2}\} \tag{10}$$

where $init_{G1}$ and q_{G2} are the behavioral thread *GlobalPathPlanning* order change state.

2. B_G is a collection of blocking events. E_G is the set of request events and blocking events, $R_G \in E_G$, $B_G \in E_G$, R_G and B_G its expression is

$$R_G = \{GParthEvent\} \\ B_G = \{\phi\} \tag{11}$$

where *GParthEvent* is the global path planning event.

3. B_L is a collection of blocking events. E_L is the set of request events and blocking events, $R_L \in E_L$, $B_L \in E_L$, R_L and B_L its expression is

$$R_L = \{LParthEvent\} \\ B_L = \{\phi\} \tag{12}$$

where *LParthEvent* is the global path planning event.

4. $\rightarrow_G$ and $\rightarrow_L$ are state transition processes. the mixed state transition process is

$$init_{G1} \xrightarrow{e_{G1}} q_{G2} \xrightarrow{e_{GL}} init_{L1} \xrightarrow{e_{L1}} q_{L2} \tag{13}$$

when $GParthEvent \in e_{G1}$, where initial state $init_{G1}$, enters the next state q_{G2}. When $LParthEvent \in e_{NG2} \wedge GParthEvent \notin eN_{G2}$, enter the next state $init_{L1}$. When $LParthEvent \in e_{L2}$, enter the next state q_{L2}.

4   Implementation of the Navigation System

In this section, we first explain how to implement the behavioral programming approach by using the Java language and BPJ package [4]. Then, we describe the implementation principle of the navigation behavior thread.

4.1   Implementation of Navigation Control

The navigation system is divided into three B-thread implementation classes to complete local path planning function, global path planning function, and navigation functions, respectively. We first complete the behavior thread of the navigation control function. Table 1 is the abstract logic pseudo code. The class name NavigaitionCtrl inherits the BThread class to implement the runBthread() method. The main logic code is implemented in the runBthread() method. GParthEvent is a global path planning event, LParthEvent local path planning event. Coordinate the event thread requesting this event by synchronizing the event function bSync().

Table 1. Navigation control behavior thread.

B-thread 1: Navigation control behavior thread.

Class NavigationCtrl entends BThread {
　　　runBThread ( ) {
　　　　　while (true){
　　　　　　　bSync (none, LParthEvent, GParthEvent);
　　　　　　　bSync (none, GParthEvent, LParthEvent);
　　　　　}
　　　}
}

4.2   Implementation of Global Path Planning

The global path planning function of the mobile robot is to calculate the moving route from the start position to the target position in the known environment. The global path planning of this paper is implemented by the A* algorithm [2, 23, 24]. So it is quite flexible and can be used in many situations. It is an efficient search algorithm [14, 18].

The Implementation of the Behavior Thread: According to the A* algorithm programming principle, we first code the algorithm and then integrate it into the behavior thread GlobalPathPlanning. Table 2 is abstract logic pseudo code.

4.3   Implementation of Local Path Planning

The main purpose of the local path planning function of the mobile robot is to achieve obstacle avoidance of dynamic obstacles. This paper uses fuzzy logic [17] to complete the local path planning function.

The Implementation of the Behavior Thread: According to the fuzzy logic algorithm programming principle, we first code the algorithm and then integrate it into the behavior thread LocalPathPlanning. Table 3 is abstract logic pseudo code.

Table 2. Global path planning behavior thread.

B-thread 2: Global path planning behavior thread.

```
Class GlobalPathPlanning entends BThread {
        runBThread ( ) {
                while ( true ){
                bSync ( GParthEvent,  none ,  none );
                if ( global route does not exist ){
                        load map data;
                        set location information ;
                        compute globalRoute based on A∗ algorithm;
                }
                bSync ( GRuoteEvent ( globalRoute ), none, none );
        }
    }
}
```

Table 3. Local path planning behavior thread.

B-thread 3: Local path planning behavior thread.

```
Class LocalPathPlanning entends BThread {
        runBThread ( ) {
                while ( true ) {
                        globalRoute = watch and capture GRuoteEvent;
                        for (point : globalRoute ) {
                                movement based on based on fuzzy logic;
                        }
                }
        }
}
```

5   The Simulation and Analysis

In this section, we implement the mobile robot navigation function based on behavioral programming approach. We first stimulate the navigation effect of the path planning of the static map and the dynamic map during the navigation process to verify the feasibility of the behavioral programming. And then analyze the impact on the application by adding and removing behavior threads.

5.1   Navigation Simulation

In the simulation experiment, we set a closed indoor environment, giving the start position, target position and static map information to the mobile robot in order to realize the navigation function of the mobile robot autonomously. As shown in the left figure of Fig. 2, the mobile robot completes the navigation simulation experiment in a static environment. The black part is unified as a static obstacle, the yellow marked point is the starting position of the mobile robot, the red marked point is the target position, and the green marked point is the static track point of the mobile robot. As shown in the right figure of Fig. 2, the dynamic obstacles are randomly placed in a closed indoor environment. The blue marked points are dynamic obstacles, and the gray marked points are dynamic track points. The mobile robot can also successfully complete the navigation function when passing through random obstacles.

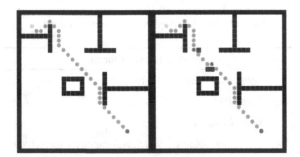

Fig. 2. Navigation simulation diagram, where the left figure is the static environment and the right figure is the dynamic environment.

5.2   Result Analysis

We validate the normal operation of the application and whether the navigation function is implemented through the addition and deletion tests of the behavior thread. As shown in Table 4, symbol "●" represents the thread that has been added to the application, symbol "○" represents the thread that the application has deleted, and the "✓" represents yes, "✗" represents no. We have done a total of seven sets of experiments.

Table 4. Adding or deleting behavior thread test.

Test number	1	2	3	4	5	6	7
NavigationCtrl behavior thread	●	○	○	●	●	○	●
GlobalPathPlanning behavior thread	○	●	○	●	○	●	●
LocalPathPlanning behavior thread	○	○	●	○	●	●	●
Can the application program running?	✓	✓	✓	✓	✓	✓	✓
Implement navigation?	✗	✗	✗	✗	✗	✗	✓

Based on the above-mentioned behavior thread add and delete test experiments, we can see that when the three behavior threads are partially added to the application, it does not affect the normal operation of the application, which means the application will not report an error. The navigation function is only implemented when all the behavior threads are added to the application, which means that the coupling between each behavior thread is low. This low coupling advantage can facilitate the subsequent code modifications and enhancements. We can also implement incremental development through this thread stacking method.

6   Conclusion

The most basic and important function of the mobile robot is the navigation. This paper shows how to use behavior program technique in the navigation design and implementation. We first decompose the navigation of the mobile robot into local path planning and global path planning, and then decouple and incrementally develop the mobile robot navigation function based on the behavior programming. The feasibility and effectiveness of the behavioral programming approach in the navigation system are verified by the simulation experiment and data analysis. In the future, we will conduct more experiments with this technique to show the soundness.

References

1. Berkman-Chardon, A., Harel, D., Goel, Y., Marelly, R., Szekely, S. Weiss, G.: Scenario-based programming for mobile applications. In: International Conference on Mobile Software Engineering and Systems, Texas, USA (2016)
2. Awerbuch, B., Gallager, R.: A new distributed algorithm to find breadth first search trees. IEEE Trans. Inf. Theory **33**(3), 315–322 (1987)
3. Harel, D., Marron, A., Weiss, G.: Behavioral programming. Commun. ACM **55**(7), 90–100 (2012)
4. Harel, D., Marron, A., Weiss, G.: Programming coordinated behavior in Java. In: D'Hondt, T. (ed.) ECOOP 2010. LNCS, vol. 6183, pp. 250–274. Springer, Heidelberg (2010). https://doi.org/10.1007/978-3-642-14107-2_12

5. Harel, D., Marron, A., Wiener, G., Weiss, G.: Behavioral programming, decentralized control, and multiple time scales. In: Proceedings of the Compilation of the Co-located Workshops on DSM'11, TMC'11, AGERE! 2011, AOOPES'11, NEAT'11, & VMIL'11, pp. 171–182. ACM (2011)
6. Harel, D., Kantor, A., Katz, G.: Relaxing synchronization constraints in behavioral programs. In: McMillan, K., Middeldorp, A., Voronkov, A. (eds.) LPAR 2013. LNCS, vol. 8312, pp. 355–372. Springer, Heidelberg (2013). https://doi.org/10.1007/978-3-642-45221-5_25
7. Harel, D., Kantor, A., Katz, G., Marron, A., Weiss, G., Wiener, G.: Towards behavioral programming in distributed architectures. Sci. Comput. Program. **98**, 233–267 (2015)
8. Harel, D., Katz, G., Marelly, R., Marron, A.: An initial wise development environment for behavioral models. In: International Conference on Model-driven Engineering and Software Development, Texas, USA (2017)
9. Harel, D.: On behavioral programming. In: International Conference on Hardware and Software: Verification and Testing, Haifa, Israel (2012)
10. Harel, D., Lampert, R., Marron, A., Weiss, G.: Model-checking behavioral programs. In: ACM International Conference on Embedded Software, Taiwan, China (2011)
11. Harel, D., Nitzan, S.: Programming animation using behavioral programming. In: Roubtsova, E., McNeile, A., Kindler, E., Gerth, C. (eds.) Behavior Modeling – Foundations and Applications. LNCS, vol. 6368, pp. 113–132. Springer, Cham (2015). https://doi.org/10.1007/978-3-319-21912-7_5
12. Katz, G.: On module-based abstraction and repair of behavioral programs. In: McMillan, K., Middeldorp, A., Voronkov, A. (eds.) LPAR 2013. LNCS, vol. 8312, pp. 518–535. Springer, Heidelberg (2013). https://doi.org/10.1007/978-3-642-45221-5_35
13. DeSouza, G.N., Kak, A.C.: Vision for mobile robot navigation: a survey. IEEE Trans. Pattern Anal. Mach. Intell. **24**(2), 237–267 (2002)
14. Gaschig, J.: Performance measurement and analysis of certain search algorithms. Carnegie-Mellon University Pittsburgh Pa Department Of Computer Science, Technical report (1979)
15. Saade, J.J., Diab, H.B.: Defuzzification methods and new techniques for fuzzy controllers. IEEE Trans. Syst. Man Cybern. Part B (Cybern.) **30**(1), 223–229 (2000)
16. Fiadeiro, J.L.: The many faces of complexity in software design. In: Hinchey, M., Coyle, L. (eds.) Conquering Complexity, pp. 3–47. Springer, Heidelberg (2012). https://doi.org/10.1007/978-1-4471-2297-5_1
17. Zadeh, L.A.: Fuzzy sets. Inf. Control **8**(3), 338–353 (1965)
18. Bell, M.G.: Hyperstar: a multi-path astar algorithm for risk averse vehicle navigation. Transp. Res. Part B: Methodol. **43**(1), 97–107 (2009)
19. Noto, M., Sato, H.: A method for the shortest path search by extended dijkstra algorithm. In: IEEE International Conference on Systems, Man, and Cybernetics (2000)
20. Eitan, N., Harel, D.: Adaptive behavioral programming. In: IEEE International Conference on Tools with Artificial Intelligence, Florida, USA (2011)
21. Keller, R.M.: Formal verification of parallel programs. Commun. ACM **19**(7), 371–384 (1976)
22. Tzafestas, S.G.: Mobile robot control and navigation: a global overview. J. Intell. Rob. Syst. **91**(1), 1–24 (2018)
23. Deng, Y., Chen, Y., Zhang, Y., Mahadevan, S.: Fuzzy dijkstra algorithm for shortest path problem under uncertain environment. Appl. Soft Comput. **12**(3), 1231–1237 (2012)
24. Jianya, Y.Y.G.: An efficient implementation of shortest path algorithm based on dijkstra algorithm. J. Wuhan Tech. Univ. Surv. Mapp. (Wtusm), **3**(004) (1999)

Weed Recognition in Wheat Field Based on Sparse Representation Classification

Shanwen Zhang$^{(\boxtimes)}$, Xianfeng Wang, and Zhen Wang

Department of Information Engineering, XiJing University, Xi'an 710123, China
wjdw716@163.com

Abstract. Weed recognition in field is a challenging and hard research field, due to the diversity and changeability of the weed in field. A weed recognition approach is proposed by sparse representation classification (SRC). The method is different from the existing weed recognition methods, instead of extracting a lot of features from each weed image, weed is recognized by SRC directly through the weed image captured in the field, which can reduce the computing cost and recognition time, and improve the recognition performance. The proposed approach is tested on the weed image dataset and is compared with four feature extraction based weed recognition methods. The recognition rate of the proposed algorithm is 94.52%. The experimental result validates that the proposed method is effective for the weed recognition.

Keywords: Weed segmentation · Weed recognition ·
Sparse representation classification (SRC) · Sparse coefficient

1 Introduction

Weed recognition based on image processing technology has become the focus of weed recognition research. In the process of weed recognition based on machine vision technology, feature extraction is one of the key steps, which has a certain impact on the final recognition effect [1]. Robots that can perform targeted weed control offer the potential to contribute to this goal, for example, through specialized weeding actions such as selective spraying or mechanical weed removal [2]. A prerequisite of such systems is a reliable and robust plant classification system that is able to distinguish crop and weed in the field [3]. A major challenge in this context is the fact that different fields show a large variability. Thus, classification systems have to robustly cope with substantial environmental changes with respect to weed pressure and weed types, growth stages of the crop, visual appearance, and soil conditions [4]. Many weed recognition methods have been proposed [5–9]. Bossu et al. [10] proposed testing and validating the accuracy of four image processing algorithms (wavelet transforms and Gabor filtering) for crop/weed discrimination in synthetic and real images. Jones et al. [11] presented a modeling of crop field in presence of different Weed Infestation Rates and a set of simulated agronomic images was used to test and validate the effectiveness of a crop/weed discrimination algorithm. Ch et al. [12] proposed a general method for

© Springer Nature Switzerland AG 2019
D.-S. Huang et al. (Eds.): ICIC 2019, LNCS 11643, pp. 511–519, 2019.
https://doi.org/10.1007/978-3-030-26763-6_49

weed infestation rate estimation for perspective wide-view images dedicated to real-time precision spraying. A colour camera was positioned above crop fields in order to get a wide angle view of crop rows in perspective. To identify differences in reflectance between cruciferous weeds, Castro et al. [13] applied three classification methods: stepwise discriminant (STEPDISC) analysis, two neural networks, and multilayer perceptron (MLP) and radial basis function (RBF). Hyper-spectral and multispectral signatures of cruciferous weeds, and wheat and broad bean crops can be classified using STEPDISC analysis, and MLP and RBF neural networks with different success. Alchanatis et al. [14] developed an algorithm by using spectral reflectance properties and robust statistics features for weed detection. Soil-crop segmentation was done with two spectral channels, chosen from 100 channels available from the hyperspectral sensor. Weed detection was based on texture features, extracted from the segmented images. Siddiqi et al. [15] developed an algorithm for automatic spray control system based on erosion followed by watershed segmentation algorithm. This algorithm can detect weeds and also classify it. Currently the algorithm is tested on two types of weeds: broad and narrow. The developed algorithm has been tested on these two types of weeds in the lab, which gives a very reliable performance.

Above all of the weed recognition methods show that the classical weed recognition methods have two common limitations: (1) the weed and corresponding features are in general sensitive to the illumination, orientation and the scaling of the image, a preprocessing step prior to feature extraction is applied to making correction for varying translation, rotation and scaling factors; (2) each kind of extracted and selected feature is regarded as equally important in classification task, but the truth is quite otherwise. Especially, some features have little contribute and even have side-effect to the weed recognition method.

From the above analysis, the identification results of the existing weed recognition methods rely heavily on feature extraction. It is difficult to extract the optimal features from the weed image, thus many methods have not been applied to the weed intelligent identification system. The reason is that the weeds in the field are complex, various, irregular and overlapped, as shown in Fig. 1. From Fig. 1, it is seen that the same class weeds vary in shape, while the shapes of the different class weeds of Shepherd's-purse and Hemisteptalyrata are very similar.

In recent years, SRC aims to search for the most compact representation of the input sample in terms of linear combination of a small number of elementary samples called atoms, which are usually selected from an over-complete dictionary [16]. SRC has been applied to signal analysis, radar signal formation, images or video compression and reconstruction, and so on, and has been successfully applied to face recognition, human movement recognition, tumor classification and plant species identification [17–20]. Based on SRC, a weed recognition method is proposed in this paper. The proposed method differs from the classical weed recognition methods. Instead of extracting a lot of features from each weed image, the weed recognition task is implemented directly on the color histograms and leaf weed images, and the weed is recognized according to the sparse coefficients.

(A) Gray vegetable

(B) Shepherd's-purse

(C) Hemisteptalyrata

Fig. 1. The weed image examples

2 Sparse Representation Based Classification

Suppose n training samples $X = [x_1, x_2, \ldots, x_n]$ belonging to k classes, where $x_i \in R^m$, generally $m \gg n$, and n_i being the sample number of the i-th class, let us stack the n_i samples associated with subject i as vectors $v_{i,1}, v_{i,2}, \ldots, v_{i,n_i} (v_{i,j} \in R^m, j = 1, 2, \ldots, n_{n_i})$ and make up a matrix $W = [W_1, W_2, \ldots, W_k]$, where $W \in R^{m \times n}$, $W_i = [v_{i,1}, v_{i,2}, \ldots, v_{i,n_i}]$, and assume these vectors are sufficient to span the i-th image subspace. Suppose a new test sample $y \in R^m$ belonging to i-th class, based on the theory of SR, y would lie in the linear span of the training samples W_i. Then the test sample y can be classified according to x. x can be obtained by solving the following ℓ_1-minimization problem [18, 20]:

$$J(x, \lambda) = \min_x \{\|Wx - y\|_2 + \lambda \|x\|_1\} \tag{1}$$

where $\lambda > 0$ is a adjust parameter to balance the degree of noise, and ensure $(W^T W)^{-1}$ is valid, which can be determined experimentally, $\|x\|_2 = \sqrt{\sum_i |x_i|^2}$ denotes the l_2-norm.

Equation (3) mean that the test sample can be approximately represented by a linear combination of all training samples.

$$x' = (W^T W + \lambda I)^{-1} y \tag{2}$$

where I is the identity matrix.

Equation (2) can be solve by least-angle regression (LARS) [20]. Suppose y belong to the i-th class, y can be approximately reconstructed as $y' = W\delta_i(x')$, where $\delta_i(x')$ is the part coefficients of x associated with the i-th class. Then y can be classified into the class with the minimum residual class between y and y', which is defined as follows,

$$\min_i r_i(y) = \left\| y - W\delta_i(x') \right\|_2 \tag{3}$$

Identity the class of y by $\arg \min_i r_i(y)$.

3 Weed Recognition Based SRC

The weed image segmentation is a key process in the weed recognition. The K-means clustering algorithm can be applied to the leaf weed segmentation, which tries to classify pixels based on a set of features into K number of classes. In this paper, we use the K-means clustering algorithm to segment the weed image from wheat [21, 22]. The range 'a*' and 'b*' can be experimentally determined when the most of the weed pixels have its intensity values. The cluster having the mean 'a*' and 'b*' in this range is selected as the weed cluster [23].

According to the basic principle of SRC, a weed recognition method is proposed as follows.

Step 1 Dataset preparation. Segment the weed from background in the field by K-means clustering algorithm.

Step 2 Color feature extraction. Divide the three L*a*b* components of the weed image, and extract histograms of L*a*b* components, and calculate the FFT, and finally extract the log frequency histogram features, denoted as V^L, V^a, V^b, respectively.

Step 3 Shape feature extraction. Convert each weed image into gray scale and reshape as a vector $v \in R^m$, called as vectored image, where m is the dimension of v.

Step 4 Feature combination. As for each weed image, normalize and concatenate shape feature v and the color features V^L, V^a, V^b as a combined vector $[v, V^L, V^a, V^b]$ to describe this weed image. Principal Component Analysis (PCA) is utilized to reduce the dimensionality of the combined vector by retaining 98% energy.

Step 5 Randomly select n combined vector from per class as the training set, the remaining as the testing set. Construct the over-complete dictionary A by the training set $A = [A_1, A_2, \ldots, A_k] \in R^{n \times m}$, where A_i is the sub-matrix formed by the combined vector belonging to the i-th class.

Step 6 Solve the optimization problem. For the given vectored test image $y \in R^m$, solve the optimization problem defined in Eq. (3) by LARS.

Step 7 Check whether the termination condition is satisfied, which is defined as the ratio between the two smallest residuals. A lower ratio indicates that the test image is more effectively approximated by the training samples from one class instead of those from the other classes.

Step 8 Compute the residuals $r_i(y)$ between y and its estimate y' for each category by Eq. (2). Let $\delta_i(x') \in R^n$ keep only nonzero entries in x' that are associated with the class i. Approximate the test vector y as $y' = W\delta_i(x')$ using only the coefficients of x' which corresponds to the i-th class. For each class, compute the residuals $r_i(y) = \left\| y - W\delta_i(x') \right\|_2$, where $i = 1,2, ...,k$.

Step 9 The decision rule of the SR based classification is: if $r_j(y) = \min_i r_i(y)$, y is assigned to the class j.

Repeated the Steps 3 to 7 for each image in the testing set, then the recognition precision is then calculated for each category.

4 Experiments and Analysis

In this section, the performance of SRC based weed recognition method is validated on a weed image dataset, and compared with four state-of-the-art weed recognition algorithms: A novel approach for weed type classification based on shape descriptors and a fuzzy decision-making method (SDFCM) [24], weeds identification using Fast and Efficient Shape Descriptor (FESD) [4], and weed recognition by SVM texture feature classification in outdoor vegetable crops images (SVMTFC) [25]. All experiments are implemented using MATLAB 7.0 software on an Intel Xeon X3430 PC with 2 GB RAM.

Weeds are very common in wheat seedling growth stage. In North China, 8-10 days after wheat sowing is the most concentrated period of weed excavation. The image acquisition equipment is Canon SLR digital camera, model IXUS1000HS (EF-S36-360mmf/3.4-5.6 ISSTM), focal length is set to automatic intelligent focusing, and image resolution is 640×480 pixels. Eight kinds of 1600 weed images per plant in the wheat field were collected when wheat grew to 3 to 5 leaves, forming a weed image dataset, including Bromus, Sargassum spinosa, Curly ear with sticky hair, Gray vegetable, Affiliated vegetables, Sowing Niang Peng, Mud Hu Cabbage and Shepherd's purse. Some weed images are shown in Fig. 2A. The corresponding weeds without background are shown in Fig. 2B. All images were used to train and test weed identification method.

Fig. 2. Eight weed leaves of 8 kinds of weeds and corresponding segmented images

From each weed image, we draw the histograms and log frequency histograms of L*a*b* of a segmented weed image, respectively, as shown in Fig. 3.

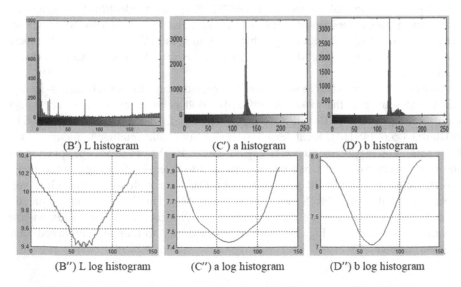

Fig. 3. L*a*b** components of the weed and its histogram and log histogram

We perform ten rounds of five-fold cross validation experiments with random selection of training data, and record the average results as the final recognition accuracy. To ensure the performance not biased from certain random selection of training/testing set, the 5-fold cross validation experiment is repeated independently 50 times. The average recognition rates across these 50 runs with 95% confidence are regarded as the final classification results. The experimental results by SDFCM, FESD, SVMTFC and SRC are shown in Table 1, where PCA preprocessing is employed to avoid the SSS problem.

Table 1. Average recognition rates, deviations and optimal dimension of six methods

Method	SDFCM	FESD	SVMTFC	SRC
Recognition rate (%)	91.84 ± 1.43	90.15 ± 1.52	91.18 ± 1.43	94.52 ± 1.17
Recognition time (ms)	6	5	7	5

From Table 1, it is found that SRC outperforms other three algorithms. The reason may be that SRC is effective for nonlinear, complicated high-dimensionality weed image recognition task. In the experiments by the methods SDFCM and SVMTFC, in order to get a high recognition rate, a lot of features are extracted and selected from each weed image, and the fuzzy decision-making method and SVM are determined by several times, while the parameter selection of the proposed method is simple, only the scalar regularization λ, minimum error and the number of iterations t. Their original values are set to be the same as in the previous works [18, 20]. The parameters can be obtained with higher classification accuracy. In this case, the proposed method is more robust than the four other algorithms. The main computation cost of the proposed methods lie in the iteration procedures. In recognition task, in other three methods, every training weed image is regarded being same important, while in SRC, the sparse coefficients can explain the importance of the every training weed image. The larger the leaf image coefficient is, the more important it is. In addition, the weed images with SRC can be recognized according to the maximum projection coefficient.

5 Conclusions and Future Works

The weed recognition plays an important role in protecting wheat management. Because the weed leaves are very irregular, complex and diversity, many existing weed recognition methods cannot meet the need of the automatic identification system of the weed. As a new data representation method, SRC has received considerable attention in recent years. Based on SR, a weed recognition method is proposed in this paper. The proposed method directly uses the weed images to form the dictionary without training, and then obtains the approximate SR of specific input leaf images by a sparse model solver, which can reduce the computation time of the algorithm and meet the requirements of the real weed recognition system. The experimental results on the weed image database show that the proposed method is effective and feasible. Future work will concentrate on how to select over-complete dictionary to large weed image databases.

References

1. Burks, T.F., Shearer, S.A., Payne, F.A.: Classification of weed species using color texture features and discriminant analysis. Trans. ASAE **43**(2), 441–448 (2000)
2. EI-Faki, M.S., Zhang, N., Peterson, D.E.: Weed detection using color machine vision. Trans. ASAE, **43**(6), 1969–1978 (2000)
3. Granitto, P.M., Verdes, P.F., Ceccatto, H.A.: Large-scale investigation of weed seed identification by machine vision. Comput. Electron. Agric. **47**(1), 15–24 (2005)
4. Tannouche, A., Sbai, K., Rahmoune, M., et al.: A fast and efficient shape descriptor for an advanced weed type classification approach. Int. J. Electr. Comput. Eng. **6**(3), 1168–1175 (2016)
5. Naeem, A.M., Ahmad, I., Islam, M., et al.: Weed classification using angular cross sectional intensities for real-time selective herbicide applications. In: International Conference on Computing: Theory and Applications, pp. 70–74. IEEE (2007)
6. Onyango, C.M., Marchant, J.A.: Segmentation of row crop plants from weeds using colour and morphology. Comput. Electron. Agric. **39**(3), 141–155 (2003)
7. Aitkenhead, M.J., Dalgetty, I.A., Mullins, C.E., et al.: Weed and crop discrimination using image analysis and artificial intelligence methods. Comput. Electron. Agric. **39**(3), 157–171 (2003)
8. Haug, S., Michaels, A., Biber, P., et al.: Plant classification system for crop/weed discrimination without segmentation. In: Applications of Computer Vision. IEEE (2014)
9. Strothmann, W., Ruckelshausen, A., Hertzberg, J., et al.: Plant classification with in-field-labeling for crop/weed discrimination using spectral features and 3D surface features from a multi-wavelength laser line profile system. Comput. Electron. Agric. **134**(C), 79–93 (2017)
10. Bossu, J., Gée, C., Jones, G., et al.: Wavelet transform to discriminate between crop and weed in perspective agronomic images. Comput. Electron. Agric. **65**(1), 133–143 (2009)
11. Jones, G., Gee, C., Truchetet, F.: Crop/weed discrimination in simulated images. In: Proceedings of SPIE - The International Society for Optical Engineering, vol. 6497, pp. 64970E–64970E-7 (2007)
12. Gée, C., Bossu, J., Jones, G., et al.: Crop/weed discrimination in perspective agronomic images. Comput. Electron. Agric. **60**(1), 49–59 (2008)
13. Castro, A.I.D., Juradoexpósito, M., Lópezgranados, F.: Applying neural networks to hyperspectral and multispectral field data for discrimination of cruciferous weeds in winter crops. Sci. World J. **2012**(8), 630390 (2012)
14. Alchanatis, V., Ridel, L., Hetzroni, A., et al.: Weed detection in multi-spectral images of cotton fields. Comput. Electron. Agric. **47**(3), 243–260 (2005)
15. Siddiqi, M.H., Ahmad, W., Ahmad, I.: Weed classification using erosion and watershed segmentation algorithm. In: Elleithy, K. (ed.) Innovations and Advanced Techniques in Systems, Computing Sciences and Software Engineering, pp. 366–369. Springer, Dordrecht (2008). https://doi.org/10.1007/978-1-4020-8735-6_69
16. Wright, J., Ma, Y., Mairal, J., et al.: Sparse representation for computer vision and pattern recognition. Proc. IEEE **98**(6), 1031–1044 (2009)
17. Wagner, A., Wright, J., Ganesh, A., et al.: Towards a practical face recognition system: robust alignment and illumination by sparse representation. IEEE Trans. Pattern Anal. Mach. Intell. (PAMI) **34**(2), 372–386 (2012)
18. Gkalelis, N., Tefas, A., Pitas, I.: Sparse human movement representation and recognition. In: IEEE 10th Workshop Multimedia Signal Processing, pp. 165–169 (2008)
19. Zheng, C.H., Zhang, L., Ng, T.Y., et al.: Metasample-based sparse representation for tumor classification. IEEE/ACM Trans. Comput. Biol. Bioinf. **8**(5), 1273–1282 (2011)

20. Jin, T., Hou, X., Li, P., Zhou, F.: A novel method of automatic plant species identification using sparse representation of leaf tooth features. PLoS ONE **10**(10), 1–20 (2015)
21. Tushar, H.J., Ravindra, D.B., Prashant, G.P.: Weed detection using image segmentation. World J. Sci. Technol. **2**(4), 190–194 (2012)
22. Valliammal, N., Geethalakshmi, S.N.: Crop leaf segmentation using non linear K means clustering. IJCSI Int. J. Comput. Sci. **9**(3), 212–218 (2012)
23. Anil, Z.C., Katiyar, S.K.: Color based image segmentation using k-means clustering. Int. J. Eng. Sci. Technol. **2**(10), 5319–5325 (2010)
24. Herrera, P.J., Dorado, J., Ribeiro, Á.: A novel approach for weed type classification based on shape descriptors and a fuzzy decision-making method. Sensors **14**, 15304–15324 (2014)
25. Rojas, C.P., Guzmán, L.S., Toledo, N.V.: Weed recognition by SVM texture feature classification in outdoor vegetable crops images. Ing. Inv. **37**(1), 68–74 (2017)

Automatic Cloud Segmentation Based on Fused Fully Convolutional Networks

Jie An, Jingfeng Wu, and Jinwen Ma[✉]

Department of Information Science,
School of Mathematical Sciences and LMAM, Peking University,
Beijing 100871, China
{jie.an, pkuwjf}@pku.edu.cn, jwma@math.pku.edu.cn

Abstract. Cloud detection and segmentation of remote sensing images is a pivotal task in the area of weather forecast. Many meteorologic applications such as precipitation forecast, extreme weather forecast, etc., depend on the results of the cloud detection. In this paper, based on the satellite remote sensing image dataset, we propose an image segmentation model to address the cloud detection problem. Our model is derived from the fully convolutional neural network, which achieves pixel-level cloud segmentation results on high resolution, large scale, multi-channel satellite images. We introduce Deep Feature Aggregation and Model Fuse strategies to improve the cloud segmentation results. Compared with the traditional methods, our proposed algorithm has the advantages that is independent of the expert knowledge, totally data motivated, and more robust in hard cases. The testing results show that the proposed model can satisfy the requirements of the weather forecast, thus has a strong potential to be put into business usage.

Keywords: Remote sensing images · Semantic segmentation · FCN · Deep learning · Cloud detection

1 Introduction

There is no need to say more about the crucial role that the remote sensing data has played in people's daily life of contemporary society. As the development of the high-precision sensors, a growing amount of high-resolution remote sensing data is collected every second, raising an increasing demanding on new effective techniques to handle such vast amounts of data of extremely high dimensionality. Among which, meteorological satellite remote sensing data is the satellite images collected by meteorological satellites for weather forecasting missions. Every day, tons of this kind of satellite images are generated by the meteorological satellites in orbit. Since the detection of meteorological satellite remote sensing image is the preliminary of meteorological forecasting, it becomes an important and attractive topic to researchers (Fig. 1).

© Springer Nature Switzerland AG 2019
D.-S. Huang et al. (Eds.): ICIC 2019, LNCS 11643, pp. 520–528, 2019.
https://doi.org/10.1007/978-3-030-26763-6_50

Fig. 1. Satellite images and two types of ground truth masks. Left: the image of visible channel. Middle: the two classes (cloudy/non-cloudy) ground truth. Right: the four classes (cloudy/probably cloudy/clear/probably clear) ground truth.

Concisely, the cloud detection task for meteorological satellite images is to identify the type of each pixel of the image, i.e., cloudy, probably cloudy, clear and probably clear. Or on the other hand, one can treat it as a four-classes semantic segmentation task based on remote sensing data.

Traditionally, cloud detection is treated with the thresholds-based models [1, 16]. The quality of the acquired thresholds depends on the sensor accuracy and the experts' understanding of the physical meaning of the collected signals in addition with the careful statistical analysis. Being simple and reliable, the physical models for cloud segmentation have already been employed in commercial products, e.g., the MODIS cloud product [16]. Such advantages, however, come with price. The reliance on the experts' accumulated experience causes the model too costy to obtain and almost impossible to transfer to other similar datasets. More importantly, threshold methods are unusual sensitive to the data noise. Thus, researchers are looking for effective machine learning models learned purely from the collected data, which are known for robustness.

Classical machine learning models have been well studied in the area of remote sensing data analysis, including cloud segmentation. Viewing segmentation as pixel level classification, various classification machine learning methods can be employed in segmenting remote sensing data directly, e.g., histogram thresholds [4], support vector machine [3], sparse representation classifier [13], extreme learning machine [18], autoencoder [5] and etc. Since these models classify each pixel separately, they use to suffer from high computational burden when it comes to high-resolution remote sensing images, which has large amounts of pixels. Thus, they can hardly satisfy the requirement of real-time weather forecasting.

Recently, there are also works trying to apply deep learning methods into segmenting the remote sensing images, motivated by the success of Fully Convolutional Networks (FCN) [14] and its variants [2, 10, 11, 17, 23], which achieve remarkable performance on the normal RGB images. And it has also been demonstrated that deep learning approaches could indeed outperform classical machine learning models in the segmentation on various types of remote sensing images [7, 9, 20, 22]. Another line is based on super resolution [6, 8, 12, 19, 21, 24]. They proposed to address cloud detection by using CNN to classify the super pixels. Though the super resolution approach helps, it still cannot achieve good pixel-level cloud detection performance [15]. suggests to use FCN [14] for cloud detection. However, they have not carefully designed the network structure for cloud detection task. Also, they model is limited into small input data and it cannot solve the challenge of the exceeding of GPU memory when taking the extremely high-resolution remote sensing data as input.

As far as we know, there is no literature studying the cloud detection on extremely high resolution (5500 × 5500) and multiple channels (16 channels) meteorological satellite remote sensing images.

To bridge the gap, we propose a novel FCN-based model for the cloud detection task on such extremely high resolution and multiple channels images. We use Deep Feature Aggregation (FA) to improve cloud segmentation results by adopting multi-scale features. Moreover, we fused the segmentation results by two structurally-distinct models based on FCN and hereby achieve state-of-the-art performance. Our proposed model is able to obtain pixel-level cloud detection results, i.e., to assign each pixel belonging the image a label of cloud, probably cloud, clear or probably clear. Experiments on practical datasets show that our method outperforms state-of-the-art FCN networks in terms of accuracy, precision, recall, F1 and IoU, while it is also efficient enough to support real-time weather forecasting.

2 Methodology

2.1 Datasets and Cloud Detection

The concerned cloud remote sensing images are collected by Himawari-8 satellite[1], which collects data for the Earth every ten minutes. The original data has 16 spectrum channels (6 visible channels and 10 infrared light channels), and 5500 × 5500 pixels per image. The data is open for downloading. We choose one-month data as the training set, and four-day data from another month as the test set.

To obtain the annotation of the images, we use the expert-corrected label from commercial MODIS [16] cloud product. In our annotation, every pixel of data is labeled as either *cloudy, probably cloudy, clear or probably clear*. Thus, the issue of cloud detection could be viewed as a four categories semantic segmentation problem. And our model is expected to output a label for each pixel. The major challenge of cloud detection is, due to the extremely high resolution and multiple channels of the input data and limited by the hardware resources, one cannot directly apply semantic segmentation strategies to address the problem.

2.2 The Segmentation Model for Remote Sensing Images

Overview of Our Framework. We design a novel FCN based framework to handle the segmentation tasks on extremely high resolution and multiple channels remote sensing images. As shown in Fig. 2, our framework consists of three parts:

---

[1] http://www.data.jma.go.jp/mscweb/en/himawari89/cloud_service/cloud_service.html.

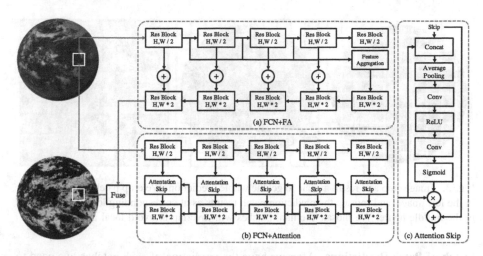

Fig. 2. Our proposed framework and the network structure.

1. Splitting the input images. we cut the original image (5500 × 5500 × 16) into small patches (256 × 256 × 16);
2. Segmentation of patches. We use an FCN-like network to derive the segmentation results of small patches;
3. Fusion of patch predictions. The final output of our model is the fusion of the predictions of the small patches of one original input.

We now turn to elaborate each part.

Cropping the Input Images. Generally, the meteorological satellite remote sensing images is of huge size, e.g., 5500 × 5500 × 16. Thus, due to the limit of GPU memory, usually less than 128 Gb, it is not possible to directly train or evaluate semantic segmentation networks on the whole original images. Therefore, it is necessary to split the original image into small patches and use the small patches as the input of the model.

In practice, to augment the training set and better training the model, we randomly sample 256 × 256 × 16 patches from the original image as our patched training set. There are two remarks. First, in order to eliminate the noise of the patched training set, we delete patches which do not intersect with the Earth. Second, for helping the fusion process, we keep an overlap of boundary pixels for two contiguous patches, as illustrated in Fig. 2.

Segmentation of Patches. The structure of our segmentation networks is shown in Fig. 2. The network is based on FCN [14] and U-Net [9]. We use two networks with Feature Aggregation and Attention Skip strategies separately and fuse the segmentation results of them. The encoder part of each network uses residue network to extract image features, while the decoder part uses symmetrical trans-convolution layers to enlarge features. We add shortcut connection between the encoder and the decoder to make the model as a "U" shape, which is known to be beneficial to semantic segmentation.

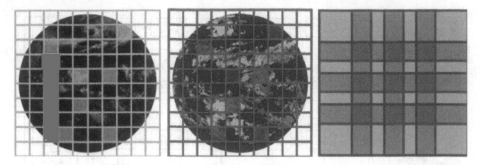

Fig. 3. Image crop and result mosaic to get the whole prediction. We crop patch image as shown in the left image, and mosaic the prediction patch results as at corresponding locations as shown in the middle figure. We mosaic the final patches with overlap to avoid local mismatch.

Stitch of Patch Predictions. After we have the prediction of each patches, we need to fuse them into the original size to make the model valid for evaluation and usage. The fusion process is by combining the patched prediction into whole, and vote the results of the shared boundary pixels of the patches. Figure 3 illustrates this process.

3   Experimental Results

3.1   Settings

In this section we describe the detailed model training and evaluation procedures. As stated before, during training, we use randomly sampled $256 \times 256 \times 16$ patches as the input of our model. We only use the patches intersected with the Earth. During evaluation, we evenly split one $5500 \times 5500 \times 16$ test image into $256 \times 256 \times 16$ small patches with shared boundary pixels. The total number of full training images is $100,000$, and the total number of full test images is 277.

We choose mean square loss as our loss function

$$L := \| \, Prediction - Groundtruth \, \|_2^2 \, .$$

We use Adam to optimize the loss function, with the learning rate adjust strategy as

$$LR_0 = 10^{-4},$$
$$LR_{i+1} \leftarrow LR_i \times 0.95, \quad i \text{ indicates epoch status.}$$

For all experiments, we save model parameters every epoch, and report the best of them in test set as the final results.

3.2 Results Comparison

We measure the performance of our results in multiple indicators, including IoU, accuracy, precision, recall and F1. The IoU of the class i is computed as

$$IoU_i := \frac{Prediction_i \cap Groundtruth_i}{Prediction_i \cup Groundtruth_i}.$$

And mean IoU is the mean of IoU of each class.

To fully compare our model with others, we report the above indicators in two cases: the cloudy/non-cloudy two classes segmentation and the cloudy/probably cloudy/clear/probably clear four classes segmentation.

As illustrated in Table 1, our proposed model outperforms the result by the Vanilla FCN network structure in literature and FCN [14] coupled with feature aggregation operator only. Meanwhile, our algorithm could simulate the segmentation results of commercial software like MODIS [16] cloud product. What is more, driven by data, our approach is more robust in extreme cases, compared with MODIS [16] cloud product. Last but not least, since our method does not rely on expert knowledge, it could be easily transferred into other similar detection tasks on remote sensing data.

Table 1. Testing results of the proposed algorithm. **FA** denotes Feature Aggregation, **Att** represents Attention Skip.

Metrics	IoU	Accuracy	Precision	Recall	F1 value
FCN Class#2	0.8826	0.9376	0.9382	0.9358	0.9368
FCN+FA Class#2	0.8857	0.9394	0.9389	0.9386	0.9387
FCN+FA+Att Class#2	**0.8879**	**0.9406**	**0.9407**	**0.9393**	**0.9400**
FCN Class#4	0.7862	0.9402	0.7964	0.7665	0.7787
FCN+FA Class#4	0.7873	0.9405	0.8002	0.7633	0.7787
FCN+FA+Att Class#4	**0.7938**	**0.9425**	**0.8053**	**0.7741**	**0.7871**

3.3 Correcting the Wrong Annotation

Surprisingly, we find that our algorithm could even correct the wrong annotation of MODIS [16] cloud product in some extreme cases. Figure 4 shows some scenarios where our predictions are better similar to expert's prediction, than the results of MODIS [16] cloud product. This indicates the commercial potential of our model (Fig. 5).

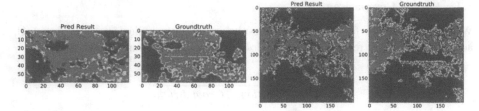

Fig. 4. Our model can improve the results of the MODIS cloud production. As left two image shows, the ground truth image has an artifact that a straight line in the middle of the image. Such an issue is also shown in the right figure.

Fig. 5. Four class prediction results. The left images are the input image. The middle images are four class prediction results. The right images are four class ground truth.

4   Conclusion

The cloud detection task based on meteorological satellite remote sensing data is the key for many follow-up applications. In this work, based on FCN [14], we come up with a novel framework for the cloud detection of extremely large remote sensing images. Specifically, the original image is first split into small patches. Then, the segmentation network outputs the prediction of the small patches. Last, we mosaic the prediction of the small patches along their shared boundaries, hence obtaining the segmentation of the extremely large remote sensing images. As a result, our approach can achieve the state-of-the-art performance in cloudy/non-cloudy two classes segmentation task and cloudy/probably cloudy/clear/probably clear four classes segmentation task. Thanks to the data driven properties, our method does not rely on expert knowledge, and could be easily to extend into other similar problems. Experiments indicates our model has strong commercial potential in business usage.

Acknowledgement. This work is supported by the *Natural Science Foundation of China for Grant U1604153* and *High-performance Computing Platform of Peking University.*

References

1. Chepfer, H., et al.: The GCM-oriented calipso cloud product (CALIPSO-GOCCP). J. Geophy. Res.: Atmos. **115**(D4) (2010)
2. Dai, J., He, K., Sun, J.: BoxSup: exploiting bounding boxes to supervise convolutional networks for semantic segmentation. In: Proceedings of the IEEE International Conference on Computer Vision, pp. 1635–1643 (2015)
3. Dumitru, C.O., Datcu, M.: Information content of very high resolution sar images: study of feature extraction and imaging parameters. IEEE Trans. Geosci. Remote Sens. **51**(8), 4591–4610 (2013)
4. El Zaart, A., Ziou, D., Wang, S., Jiang, Q.: Segmentation of sar images. Pattern Recogn. **35**(3), 713–724 (2002)
5. Geng, J., Fan, J., Wang, H., Ma, X., Li, B., Chen, F.: High-resolution SAR image classification via deep convolutional autoencoders. IEEE Geosci. Remote Sens. Lett. **12**(11), 2351–2355 (2015)
6. Henry, C., Azimi, S.M., Merkle, N.: Road segmentation in SAR satellite images with deep fully-convolutional neural networks. arXiv preprint arXiv:1802.01445 (2018)
7. Jiao, L., Liang, M., Chen, H., Yang, S., Liu, H., Cao, X.: Deep fully convolutional network-based spatial distribution prediction for hyperspectral image classification. IEEE Trans. Geosci. Remote Sens. **55**(10), 5585–5599 (2017)
8. Le Goff, M., Tourneret, J.Y., Wendt, H., Ortner, M., Spigai, M.: Deep learning for cloud detection (2017)
9. Li, R., et al.: DeepUNet: a deep fully convolutional network for pixel-level sea-land segmentation. IEEE J. Sel. Top. Appl. Earth Obs. Remote Sens. **11**(11), 3954–3962 (2018). Fused-FCN for Automatic Cloud Segmentation 9
10. Chen, L.-C., Papandreou, G., Kokkinos, I., Murphy, K., Yuille, A.: Semantic image segmentation with deep convolutional nets and fully connected CRFs. In: International Conference on Learning Representations (2015)

11. Lin, G., Milan, A., Shen, C., Reid, I.: RefineNet: multi-path refinement networks with identity mappings for high-resolution semantic segmentation. arXiv preprint arXiv:1611. 06612 (2016)

12. Liu, H., Zeng, D., Tian, Q.: Super-pixel cloud detection using hierarchical fusion CNN. In: 2018 IEEE Fourth International Conference on Multimedia Big Data (BigMM), September 2018. https://doi.org/10.1109/bigmm.2018.8499091

13. Liu, M., Wu, Y., Zhao, W., Zhang, Q., Li, M., Liao, G.: Dempster–Shafer fusion of multiple sparse representation and statistical property for SAR target configuration recognition. IEEE Geosci. Remote Sens. Lett. **11**(6), 1106–1110 (2014)

14. Long, J., Shelhamer, E., Darrell, T.: Fully convolutional networks for semantic segmentation. In: Proceedings of the IEEE Conference on Computer Vision and Pattern Recognition, pp. 3431–3440 (2015)

15. Mohajerani, S., Krammer, T.A., Saeedi, P.: Cloud detection algorithm for remote sensing images using fully convolutional neural networks. arXiv preprint arXiv:1810.05782 (2018)

16. Platnick, S., et al.: The modis cloud products: algorithms and examples from terra. IEEE Trans. Geosci. Remote Sens. **41**(2), 459–473 (2003)

17. Ronneberger, O., Fischer, P., Brox, T.: U-Net: convolutional networks for biomedical image segmentation. In: Navab, N., Hornegger, J., Wells, W.M., Frangi, A.F. (eds.) MICCAI 2015. LNCS, vol. 9351, pp. 234–241. Springer, Cham (2015). https://doi.org/10.1007/978-3-319-24574-4_28

18. Samat, A., Gamba, P., Du, P., Luo, J.: Active extreme learning machines for quad-polarimetric SAR imagery classification. Int. J. Appl. Earth Obs. Geoinf. **35**, 305–319 (2015)

19. Shi, M., Xie, F., Zi, Y., Yin, J.: Cloud detection of remote sensing images by deep learning. In: 2016 IEEE International Geoscience and Remote Sensing Symposium (IGARSS), pp. 701–704. IEEE (2016)

20. Wang, Y., He, C., Liu, X., Liao, M.: A hierarchical fully convolutional network integrated with sparse and low-rank subspace representations for PolSAR imagery classification. Remote Sens. **10**(2), 342 (2018)

21. Xie, F., Shi, M., Shi, Z., Yin, J., Zhao, D.: Multilevel cloud detection in remote sensing images based on deep learning. IEEE J. Sel. Top. Appl. Earth Obs. Remote Sens. **10**(8), 3631–3640 (2017)

22. Yao, W., Marmanis, D., Datcu, M.: Semantic segmentation using deep neural networks for SAR and optical image pairs. In: Proceedings of the Big Data from Space, pp. 1–4 (2017)

23. Yu, F., Koltun, V.: Multi-scale context aggregation by dilated convolutions. arXiv preprint arXiv:1511.07122 (2015)

24. Zi, Y., Xie, F., Jiang, Z.: A cloud detection method for landsat 8 images based on PCANet. Remote Sens. **10**(6), 877 (2018)

Label Propagation Based Semi-supervised Feature Selection to Decode Clinical Phenotype of Huntington's Disease

Xue Jiang[1,2,3] , Miao Chen[1] , Weidi Wang[1,2,3] ,
Weichen Song[1,2,3] , and Guan Ning Lin[1,2,3(✉)]

[1] School of Biomedical Engineering, Shanghai Jiao Tong University,
Shanghai 200030, China
{jiangxue_s,chenmiao95}@situ.edu.cn,
wwd-swxx@foxmail.com, song628196@gmail.com,
nickgnl@sjtu.edu.cn
[2] Shanghai Key Laboratory of Psychotic Disorders, Shanghai 200030, China
[3] Brain Science of Technology Research Center, Shanghai Jiao Tong University,
Shanghai 200030, China

Abstract. Huntington's disease is a type of neurodegenerative disease caused by gene HTT. To date, its molecular pathogenesis is still unclear. Clinically, behavior, cognitive, and mental function are affected progressively. With the rapid development of sequencing technologies, it is possible to explore the molecular mechanisms at the genome-wide transcriptomic level using computational methods. Our previous studies have shown that it is difficult to distinguish disease genes from non-disease genes. To understand the molecular pathogenesis under complex clinical phenotypes during the disease progression, it is better to identify biomarkers corresponding to different disease stage. Therefore, in this study, we designed a label propagation based semi-supervised feature selection approach (LPFS) to identify disease-associated genes corresponding to different clinical phenotypes. LPFS selects disease-associated genes corresponding to different disease stage through the alternative iteration of label propagation clustering and feature selection. We then conducted an enrichment analysis to understand gene functions and affected pathways during the disease progression, thus to decode the changes in individual behavioral and mental characteristics during neurodegenerative disease progression at the gene expression level. Our results have shown that LPFS performs better in comparison with the-state-of-art methods. We found that TGF-beta signaling pathway, olfactory transduction, cytokine-cytokine receptor interaction, immune response, and inflammatory response were gradually affected during the disease progression. In addition, we found that the expression of Ccdc33, Capsl, Al662270, and Dlgap5 were seriously changed caused by the development of the disease.

Keywords: Label propagation clustering · Feature selection · Biomarkers that corresponding to clinical phenotypes

© Springer Nature Switzerland AG 2019
D.-S. Huang et al. (Eds.): ICIC 2019, LNCS 11643, pp. 529–542, 2019.
https://doi.org/10.1007/978-3-030-26763-6_51

1 Background

Huntington's disease (HD) is a type of chronic progressive disease with complex pathogenic mechanisms caused by a triplet (CAG) repeat elongation in huntingtin (HTT) gene on chromosome 4 that codes for polyglutamine in the huntingtin protein [1], leading to abnormal behavior, mental dysfunction and ultimately death [2–4]. The mutant protein can enter the nucleus and alter gene transcription [5]. With the accumulation of the mutant protein, numerous interactions between molecules and pathways can be affected, resulting in neuronal dysfunction and degeneration [6, 7]. With the connections between neurons get sparse, the neurons finally died during the disease deterioration, and the volumes of striatum decreased markedly [8]. Clinically, motor ability, cognitive, and mental functions are gradually affected.

With the rapid development of the high-throughput sequencing technology, large amounts of omics data and biomedical data have been accumulated, pro-viding both opportunities and challenges to develop computational methods for decoding the molecular mechanisms and conducting pathological analysis under complicated phenotypes of neurodegenerative disease. Mining biomarkers corresponding to the development of the disease with biomedical data and omics data, and correlating the biomarkers to clinical phenotypes are helpful for understanding physiopathology mechanisms under the abnormal behavior, promoting the accurate diagnosis and early interventional treatment of neurodegenerative disease.

Generally, at the transcriptome level, researchers screen key genes affected by disease to get a deep insight of molecular pathogenesis. Nevertheless, the relationship between genes and their functions is complex and multifaceted, namely the same gene can play a role in many different functions. In living organisms, genes interact with each other to produce high-level biological functions, such as motor ability, cognitive ability, memory, emotion, etc. It has been well established that genes that have synergistic effects usually have similar expression patterns, and participate in a same biochemical reaction or in a same pathway [9]. Therefore, searching for gene clusters that are severely affected, and analyzing the biological pathways involved in can be helpful to understand the dynamic process at molecular level during the degeneration of the disease. The screened key genes and pathways can further be related to clinical abnormal behaviors.

Traditional statistical-based differentially expressed gene selection methods cannot effectively select clinical phenotype associated genes for chronic neurodegenerative disease. Besides, our previous studies shown that the expression level of most lethal phenotype genes are not significantly changed during Huntington's disease degeneration [10, 11]. Nevertheless, clustering algorithms often used to classify each data point into a specific group. Data points that belong to the same group would have similar properties, while data points that belong to different groups usually have very different properties. They can be used to detect higher-order biological signals, thus to understand the changes of biological process which are seriously affected by the disease, deepen the understanding of the molecular mechanism of pathology.

Lapel propagation clustering algorithm is a graph-based semi-supervised learning method. It is based on guilt-by-association to predict the label information of unlabeled nodes with a few labeled nodes [12]. When the labels of the data points tend to be stable, the data points with the same label identity are divided into a same category. Since it is costly to make tags of the data, unsupervised and semi-supervised methods have great prospect in this type of applications. Thus, we proposes a semi-supervised feature selection method based on label propagation clustering algorithm (LPFS) to identify key genes which could be matched to the complex clinical phenotypes of different disease stage. LPFS includes two steps: it first conducts the label propagation clustering on the samples with gene expression data, then it conducts feature selection based on the feature selection matrix. We conduct alternative iteration of the two steps to screen key genes which could be matched to the complex clinical phenotypes of different disease stages. To our best knowledge, this is the first time to put disease gene selection and sample clustering in one framework.

To investigate the effectiveness of the biomarkers selected by our LPFS, we also conducted experiments with DESeq 2 [13], edgeR [14], limma [15], t-test [16], fold change method (FC) [16], joint non-negative matrix factorization meta-analysis method (jNMFMA) [17], and flexible non-negative matrix factorization method (FNMF) [11]. Finally, we performed functional enrichment analysis of key genes identified by LPFS, thus to analyze the affected gene functions and high-order biological signals underlying the complex clinical phenotypes, gaining a deep understand of the dynamic molecular mechanisms during the disease progression.

The rest of this paper is organized as follow: In Sect. 2, we present the proposed LPFS in detail. In Sect. 3, we illustrate experiments of different methods with RNA-seq data of Huntington's disease. The enrichment analysis of key genes obtained by LPFS are performed and reported. And the overall discussion of experimental results of various methods are also reported. In Sect. 4, conclusions are presented.

2 Methods

In this section, we present LPFS approach in detail and discuss its parameter setting.

The gene expression data are denoted as $X = [x_{ij}]_{n \times m}$, where x_{ij} represents the expression level of gene j in sample i. $x_{i\cdot}$ denotes sample i, and $x_{\cdot j}$ denotes gene j. $L = \{1, \cdots, c\}$ represents the set of labels, c is the number of cluster number, and l_i is the label for sample $x_{i\cdot}$, $l_i \in L$. The initial category label matrix is denoted as $Y = [y_{ij}]_{n \times c}$, where

$$y_{ij} = \begin{cases} 1, & \text{if } l_i = j, \\ 0, & \text{otherwise.} \end{cases} \tag{1}$$

Y_i is the $i - th$ row in matrix Y, representing the initial category label of sample $x_{i\cdot}$.

H denotes a vector function $H : X \rightarrow R^c$. Each $x_{i\cdot}$ corresponds to a H_i. $H = [H_1^T, \cdots, H_n^T]$ is a $n \times c$ clustering indicator matrix. The category label of $x_{i\cdot}$ is $l_i = \arg\max_{j \leq c} h_{ij}$. $F = [f_{ij}]_{m \times c}$ is feature selection matrix. In this study, we define $\|A\|_F = \sqrt{\sum_i \sum_j a_{ij}^2}$, and the $l_{2,1}$ of matrix A is $\|A\|_{2,1} = \sum_j \left(\sqrt{\sum_i a_{ij}^2} \right)$.

To make precision diagnosis of patient, a key point is to identify the illness state of the patient correctly. To address the problem, we designed a feature selection method based on label propagation clustering, which put feature selection and clustering in one framework. LPFS conduct feature selection during the clustering process, filter out redundant features, and select key features that would well represent different category samples. The selected features should make the distance within one class is closer, and the distance between classes is farther. Biologically, it is to select key genes that can distinguish different stages of the disease, thus to identify the severely affected genes under different clinical phenotypes. Samples of same disease stage should belong to one category. Since not all genes have contribution to sample classification, therefore, we put $l_{2,1}$ constraint on feature selection matrix to sparse each column of it and filter out noise factors [17]. According to mathematical meaning, LPFS can be formulated as the following optimization problem:

$$\min(H, F) \sum_{i,j=1}^{n} w_{ij} \left\| \frac{1}{\sqrt{d_{ii}}} H_i - \frac{1}{\sqrt{d_{jj}}} H_j \right\| + \mu \sum_{i=1}^{n} \|H_i - Y_i\|^2 + \|XF - H\|_F^2 + \beta \|F\|_{2,1}$$

(2)

Here, μ and β are hyper-parameter, balance the importance of the final label and the initial label of a node during label propagation and that of sparse feature selection in the mathematical model, respectively. μ, $\beta \in (0, 1)$. It should be noticed that $\|F\|_{2,1} = \sum_{j=1}^{c} \sqrt{\sum_{i=1}^{m} f_{ij}^2}$. Since there only cluster indicator matrix H is unknown by fixing F in the first there terms of Eq. (2), and there only feature selection matrix F is unknown by fixing H in the last two terms of Eq. (2). So, we compute the solution for the LPFS via an iterative updating algorithm that alternatively updates H and F. The detailed solving processes are shown below.

Step 1. Define an undirected graph $G = (V, E)$ using gene expression data X, where we use Gaussian kernel function to measure the relationship between two nodes. The weight matrix of G is $W = [w_{ij}]_{n \times n}$, where

$$w_{ij} = \begin{cases} \exp(-\|x_{i.} - x_{j.}\|^2 / (2\delta^2)), & \text{if } i \neq j, \\ 0, & \text{otherwise.} \end{cases}$$

(3)

Step 2. Normalize the weight matrix. Let $D = diag\{d_{ii}\}$, where $d_{ii} = \sum_{j=1}^{m} w_{ij}$, therefore, the normalized weight matrix is

$$Z = D^{-1/2} W D^{-1/2}$$

(4)

Step 3. Initialize the initial category label matrix Y, and initialize cluster indicator matrix H to Y.
Step 4. According to the last two terms in Eq. (2), we solve feature selection matrix F

$$\min(F) \, \|XF - H\|_F^2 + \beta\|F\|_{2,1} \tag{5}$$

The elements in F should be non-negative to keep the contribution of genes not be systematically offset. ϕ_{ij} is the Lagrangian multiplier of $f_{ij} \geq 0$. So, we can construct Lagrangian function as follow:

$$L(F) = \alpha Tr(XFF^TX^T - 2XFH^T + HH^T) + \beta Tr(FUF^T) + Tr(\Psi F^T) \tag{6}$$

Here, $U = \mathrm{diag}\{\frac{1}{2\|F^1\|_2}, \cdots, \frac{1}{2\|F^c\|_2}\}$ is an Auxiliary matrix, and F^i is denoted as the $i-th$ column of matrix F, $\psi = [\varphi_{ij}]$.

The derivation of F is

$$\frac{\partial L}{\partial F} = 2X^TXF - 2X^TF + 2\beta FU + \Psi \tag{7}$$

Based on the KKT condition $\varphi_{ij}f_{ij} = 0$, we can get

$$\frac{\partial L}{\partial F} = 2X^TXF - 2X^TH + 2\beta FU + \psi = 0 \tag{8}$$

$$(2X^TXF - 2X^TH + 2\beta FU)_{ij}f_{ij} = -\varphi_{ij}f_{ij} = 0 \tag{9}$$

Equation (9) can be written as

$$(X^TH)_{ij}f_{ij} = (X^TXF + \beta FU)_{ij}f_{ij} \tag{10}$$

Then, we can get the update role of F

$$f_{ij} \leftarrow f_{ij} \frac{(X^TH)_{ij}}{(X^TXF + \beta FU)_{ij}} \tag{11}$$

Step 5. According to the first three terms in Eq. (2), we solve cluster indicator matrix H.

$$Q(H) = \min_{(H)} \sum_{i,j=1}^{n} w_{ij} \left\| \frac{1}{\sqrt{d_{ii}}} H_i - \frac{1}{\sqrt{d_{jj}}} H_j \right\| + \mu \sum_{i=1}^{n} \|H_i - Y_i\|^2 + \|XF - H\|_F^2 \tag{12}$$

Equation (12) is a convex function. The derivation of H is

$$\frac{\partial Q}{\partial H} = 2[(H - ZH) + \mu(H - Y)] - 2(\mathrm{XF} - \mathrm{H}) \tag{13}$$

We can get the global optimal solution at the stationary point.

$$[(H - ZH) + \mu(H - Y)] - (XF - H) = 0 \tag{14}$$

$$H^* = ((1 + \mu)I - Z)^{-1}(\mu Y + XF) \tag{15}$$

The category of sample i is

$$l_i = \arg\max_{j \leq c} h_{ij}^* \tag{16}$$

Therefore, we update the cluster indicator matrix $H = \left[h_{ij}\right]_{n \times c}$, where

$$\mathrm{h}_{ij} = \begin{cases} 1, & \text{if } l_i = j, \\ 0, & \text{otherwise.} \end{cases} \tag{17}$$

Step 6. Conduct loop iteration of Step 4 until the objective function of Eq. (5) converges. Then we can get the feature selection matrix F.

Step 7. Conduct loop iteration of Step 5 until the objective function of Eq. (12) converges. Then we can get cluster indicator matrix H.

Step 8. Conduct iteration of Step 3 to Step 7, until the objective function of Eq. (2) converges. At this points, we get the feature selection matrix F and cluster indicator matrix H.

Step 9. Based on rank-product method [16], we calculate the element fluctuation of each row in the feature selection matrix. The elements in $k - th$ row fluctuate significantly, representing that the corresponding feature k has a stronger ability to distinguish samples of different categories.

Sorting the rank-product value of each row of the feature selection matrix in descending order, high ranking rows were reserved and low ranking rows were removed from the feature selection matrix.

Low ranking row indicates the elements in that row change very little under different columns, i.e. the corresponding gene has no discrimination ability of different category samples. Therefore, to improve prediction precision and reduce computational complexity, we filter out low ranking genes to conduct next iteration.

Step 10. Repeat aforementioned steps from Step 1 to Step 9.

Let function $top(v_s)$ represents the s larger elements of vector v.

Since greater elements in F^j contribute more to specific identification of category j, the genes, whose column number in the gene expression matrix is equal to the row number of the greater element in the feature selection matrix, are seen as key features of category j, i.e. the genes that are severely affected under this condition.

In this study, we use key_j to denote the key gene set of category j

$$key_j = \arg_{i \leq m} top_s f_{ij} \tag{18}$$

The detailed process of LPFS is summarized in Table 1.

It should be noted that when the number of features is too many, it is hard to distinguish connection relationships among Samples. It is di cult to get accurate

Table 1. Algorithm 1: LPFS.

Input: X, Y, μ, β, s,
1: **Repeat**
2:    Construct weight matrix W, and compute the normalized weight matrix Z according to Eq. (3) and Eq. (4);
3:    Initialize initial category label matrix Y and cluster indicator matrix H ;
4:    **Repeat**
5:      Compute feature selection matrix F according to Eq. (11);
6:    **Until** the objective function of Eq. (12) converges;
7:    **Repeat**
8:      Compute cluster indicator matrix H according to Eq. (15);
9:    **Until** the objective function of Eq. (12) converges;
10:    Select key features according to F based on Rank-product approach, and modify X according to the selected features:
11: **Until** the iteration termination condition is met;
12: Select key genes of different disease stage or clinical phenotypes according to Eq. (18).

clustering results since there is no obvious clustering patterns, resulting in unstable and invalid key gene sets. Besides, when the number of clusters is less than the categories, i.e., samples belong to two categories are classified into one cluster in experimental results, it will result in one column of the cluster indicator matrix to 0. Then, some columns in the feature selection matrix will be all equal to 0, eventually leading to instability of the solution. Theoretically, the computational process tends to stable as the number of features decreases. In addition, increase the number of samples is helpful to clarify the module structure in the network.

To ensure the convergence of Eq. (2), we first solve feature selection matrix, and then solve cluster indicator matrix. According to experience and suggestions in paper [18], we set $\mu = 0.2$, and $\beta = 0.2$. Besides, we set $\delta = 200$ to ensure $\|x_i - x_j\|^2 / (2\delta^2) \in (0, 1)$, thus getting a reasonable connection between genes. In each iteration, we remove low ranking 500 genes to modify the gene expression data for next iteration. In this study, we conduct 10 iterations to end the process.

3   Results and Discussion

First, we briefly introduced the gene expression dataset of Huntington's disease. Second, we demonstrated the experimental results of LPFS. Then, to verify the effectiveness of LPFS, we also conducted experiments with DESeq2, edgeR, limma, t-test, FC, jNMFMA, and FNMF. We further analyzed and discussed the disease-associated gene prediction accuracy of different methods. Finally, we conducted function annotation and enrichment analysis of the selected key genes.

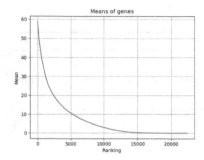

Fig. 1. Ranking of the means of gene expression in all samples.

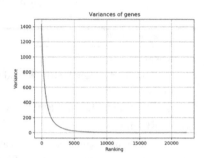

Fig. 2. Ranking of the variances of gene expression values in all samples

3.1   Gene Expression Data

The gene expression data are downloaded from http://www.hdinhd.org, which are obtained from the striatum tissue of Huntington's disease mice through RNA-seq technology. The experimental mice in this data set are of 2-month-old, 6-month-old, and 10-month-old. The genotypes include ploy Q20, poly Q80, poly Q92, poly Q111, poly Q140, and poly Q175. The ploy Q20 is normal one, while the rest genotypes are disease ones. There are 16 2-month-old mice of ploy Q20, 16 10-month-old mice of ploy Q20, and 8 mice for every other genotype at each age. The data set contain 23,351 genes. Since the genes expressed robustly across all samples have little contribution to sample classification, we select top 5000 genes based on the mean (Fig. 1) and variance (Fig. 2) of gene expression data to reduce computational complexity. Besides, to test the accuracy of the selected genes by different methods, we collected 520 modifier genes from the literature [19], including 89 disease genes and 431 non-disease genes. The detailed information of the data set is illustrated in Table 2.

Table 2. Gene expression data of Huntington's disease mice.

Tissue	Striatum
Age	2-month-old, 6-month-old, 10-month-old
Genotype	poly Q20, poly Q80, poly Q92, poly Q111, poly Q140, poly Q175

3.2 Prediction Performance of LPFS

To get robust gene sets of different disease stage, we designed the following experimental flow, see Fig. 3. First, we use normal samples with genotype of ploy Q20 under 3 different time points and case samples with genotype of ploy Qx under 3 different time points, $Qx \in \{Q80,\ Q92,\ Q111,\ Q140,\ Q175\}$, to conduct LPFS. Samples of a genotype at a time point are seen as one category. Thus, there are 6 categories in each experiment. In the 10 iterations of LPFS, we get 10 feature selection matrix. We rank genes in descending order according to the elements in each column of the feature selection matrix. Through the intersection of top 1000 genes of each iteration. We get final key gene set for each category. The overlap number of top 1000 genes in 10 iterations for each category in each experiment is shown in Table 3.

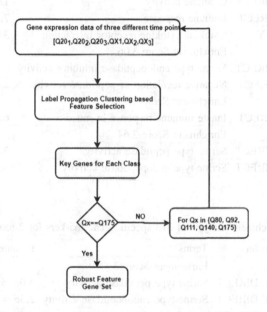

Fig. 3. The Flowchart of LPFS with Huntington's disease RNA-seq data.

Table 3. The overlap number of top 1000 genes in 10 iterations for each category in each experiments.

Experiment	Normal samples			Case samples		
	2-month-old	6-month-old	10-month-old	2-month-old	6-month-old	10-month-old
Q20 vs. Q80	3	4	5	3	10	5
Q20 vs. Q92	11	4	2	6	5	5
Q20 vs. Q111	2	7	4	1	5	6
Q20 vs. Q140	122	143	205	175	158	188
Q20 vs. Q175	151	168	222	183	174	217

Finally, we combined key genes of each category to get a robust gene set. In summary, LPFS screened 951 genes, including 210, 229, 290 specific gene markers for 2-month-old, 6-month-old, 10-month-old normal mice, respectively, and 313, 294, 330 specific gene markers for 2-month-old, 6-month-old, and 10-month-old case mice, respectively. We conducted enrichment analysis of those gene sets to get a deep understanding of the molecular activity for different state [20, 21]. The enrichment analysis results are shown in Tables 4, 5, 6 and 7.

Table 4. The enrichment analysis of 951 genes obtained by LPFS

Annotation cluster	Terms	P-value	Benjamini
Cluster 1	Enrichment Score 4.5		
GOTERM MF DIRECT	Cytokine activity	1.3e−6	8.9e−4
GOTERM BP DIRECT	Immune response	7.4e−5	1.6e−1
KEGG PATHWAY	Cytokine-cytokine receptor interaction	3.4e−4	6.9e−2
Cluster 2	Enrichment Score 3.06		
GOTERM MF DIRECT	Serine-type endopeptidase inhibitor activity	8.1e−5	1.9e−2
GOTERM BP DIRECT	Negative regulation of peptidase activity	2.4e−3	5.0e−1
Cluster 3	Enrichment Score 2.79		
GOTERM BP DIRECT	Innate immune response in mucosa	6.2e−4	5.1e−1
Cluster 4	Enrichment Score 2.64		
GOTERM MF DIRECT	Serine-type peptidase activity	3.2e−6	1.1e−3
GOTERM MF DIRECT	Serine-type endopeptidase activity	3.8e−4	4.3e−2

Table 5. The enrichment analysis of 313 specific gene markers for 2-month-old case mice.

Annotation cluster	Terms	P-value	Benjamini
Cluster 1	Enrichment Score 3		
GOTERM MF DIRECT	Serine-type peptidase activity	3.0e−5	7.9e−3
GOTERM MF DIRECT	Serine-type endopeptidase activity	2.3e−4	1.9e−2
GOTERM MF DIRECT	Peptidase activity	5.1e−4	3.3e−2
Cluster 2	Enrichment Score 2.01		
GOTERM MF DIRECT	Cytokine activity	4.6e−5	5.9e−3
GOTERM BP DIRECT	Protein signal transduction	1.2e−3	4.5e−1
KEGG PATHWAY	TGF-beta signaling pathway	5.3e−2	7.9e−1
Cluster 3	Enrichment Score 1.55		
GOTERM MF DIRECT	Structural molecular activity	8.2e−3	3.5e−1
GOTERM CC DIRECT	Intermediate ament	3.2e−2	5.6e−1

Table 6. The enrichment analysis of 294 specific gene markers for 6-month-old case mice.

Annotation cluster	Terms	P-value	Benjamini
Cluster 1	Enrichment Score 2.11		
GOTERM MF DIRECT	Signal transducer activity	2.4e−5	8.0e−3
GOTERM BP DIRECT	Signal transduction	3.3e−5	3.1e−1
GOTERM BP DIRECT	G protein coupled receptor signaling pathway	9.7e−4	3.1e−1
Cluster 2	Enrichment Score 1.08		
GOTERM MF DIRECT	Cytokine activity	2.0e−2	8.1c−1
GOTERM BP DIRECT	Immune response	2.6e−2	8.8e−1
KEGG PATHWAY	Cytokine-cytokine receptor interaction	4.2e−2	8.0e−1

Table 7. The enrichment analysis of 329 specific gene markers for 10-month-old case mice.

Annotation cluster	Terms	P-value	Benjamini
Cluster 1	Enrichment Score 3.54		
KEGG PATHWAY	Cytokine-cytokine receptor interaction	3.5e−5	5.6e−3
GOTERM BP DIRECT	Immune response	4.4e−5	4.7e−2
GOTERM MF DIRECT	Cytokine activity	1.1e−3	1.5e−1
GOTERM BP DIRECT	Inflammatory response	4.4e−3	7.0e−1
Cluster 2	Enrichment Score 1.89		
GOTERM BP DIRECT	Defense response to Gram-positive bacterium	1.2e−2	4.7e−1
GOTERM BP DIRECT	Innate immune response in mucosa	2.8e−2	9.6e−1
COTERM BP DIRECT	Antibacterial humoral response	6.5e−2	9.8e−1
Cluster 3	Enrichment Score 1.64		
GOTERM BP DIRECT	Negative regulation of cysteine-type endopeptidase activity	1.5e−2	9.1e−1
GOTERM MF DIRECT	Cysteine-type endopeptidase inhibitor activity	1.6e−2	5.7e−1
GOTERM MF DIRECT	Protease binding	5.1e−2	7.7e−1

From Table 4, we can see that cytokine activity, immune response, cytokine-cytokine receptor interaction, serine-type endopeptidase inhibitor activity, and serine-type endopeptidase activity are affected during the disease degeneration. From Table 5 we can know that serine-type peptidase activity, serine-type endopeptidase activity, and peptidase activity are specific prominence within 2-month-old case mice. And Table 6 shows that signal transducer activity, G protein coupled receptor signaling pathway, and olfactory transduction are specific prominence within 6-month-old case mice. Table 7 shows that cytokine-cytokine receptor interaction, immune response, and inflammatory response are specific prominence within 10-month-old case mice.

3.3 Prediction Performance of FC, DESeq2, edgeR, limma, JNMFMA, FNMF, and LPFS

To verify the effectiveness of LPFS, we also conduct experiments with FC, t-test, DESeq2, edgeR, limma, jNMFMA, and FNMF. Area under ROC curve (AUC) and area under precision recall (AUPR) curve are used as evaluative criteria of prediction accuracy. The experimental results are shown in Table 8. The performance of LPFS is comparable to that of the-state-of-art methods. We further choose the best performance result of each method to draw the ROC curves and PR curves. The ROC curves and PR curves of the 8 methods are shown in Figs. 4 and 5, respectively. We can know that LPFS performs a little better than other methods.

In addition, we statistics the overlap degree of top 1000 genes obtained by any two methods (951 genes for LPFS). The details are shown in Table 9. Finally, we get intersection genes of the top 1000 genes obtained by the 8 methods. There are 4 overlapped genes in total, i.e. Ccdc33 (coiled-coil domain containing 33, COG ONTOLOGY: cell division and chromosome partitioning), Capsl (calcyphosine like, GOTERM MF DIRECT: calcium ion binding), Dlgap5 (DLG associated protein 5, GOTERM BP DIRET: cell cycle, signaling), and Al662270 (have no annotation information yet), indicating that the function of cell division, cell cycle, and calcium ion binding are severally affected by the disease.

Table 8. The AUC and AUPR of different methods.

Methods	FC	t-test	DESeq 2	edgeR	limma	jNMFMA	FNMF	LPFS
AUC	0.570	0.509	0.524	0.531	0.497	0.547 ± 0.03	0.548 ± 0.02	0.552 ± 0.05
AUPR	0.227	0.166	0.179	0.180	0.160	0.188 ± 0.02	0.196 ± 0.01	0.197 ± 0.02

Table 9. The overlap degree of the top 1000 genes obtained by any two methods (951 genes for LPFS).

	DESeq 2	edgeR	limma	t-test	FC	jNMFMA	FNMF
edgeR	523						
Limma	312	457					
t-test	463	539	435				
FC	230	362	304	221			
jNMFMA	175	252	304	192	546		
FNMF	120	141	246	147	215	213	
LPFS	120	206	526	159	271	242	277

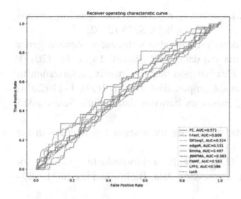

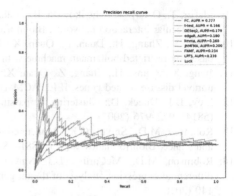

Fig. 4. The ROC curves of FC, t-test, DESeq 2, edgeR, limma, jNMFMA, and LPFS.

Fig. 5. The Precision Recall curves of FC, t-test, DESeq 2, edgeR, limma, jNMFMA, and LPFS.

4 Conclusion

To screen the clinical phenotype associated genes, we designed LPFS to screen key genes that specific identify disease state of different stages. Large amounts of experiments have been conducted to analyze the performance of LPFS. And enrichment analysis was conducted to make a deep understanding of biological function of key genes for each disease stage. Finally, by getting intersection top ranking genes of 8 method, we found 4 genes, including Ccdc33, Capsl, Dlgap5, and Al662270, are seriously affected by Huntington's disease.

References

1. Ross, C.A., et al.: Huntington disease: natural history, biomarkers and prospects for therapeutics. Nat. Rev. Neurol. **10**(4), 204 (2014)
2. Appel, S.H., Smith, R.G., Le, W.D.: Immune-mediated cell death in neurodegenerative disease. Adv. Neurol. **69**, 153–159 (1996)
3. Hardy, J.: Pathways to primary neurodegenerative disease. In: Mayo Clinic Proceedings, pp. 835–837. Elsevier (1999)
4. Gammon, K.: Neurodegenerative disease: brain windfall. Nature **515**(7526), 299–300 (2014)
5. Seredenina, T., LuthiCarter, R.: What have we learned from gene expression proles in huntington's disease? Neurobiol. Dis. **45**(1), 83–98 (2012)
6. Wang, X., Huang, T., Bu, G., Xu, H.: Dysregulation of protein tracking in neurodegeneration. Mol. Neurodegeneration **9**(1), 1–9 (2014)
7. Diglia, M., et al.: Aggregation of huntingtin in neuronal intranuclear inclusions and dystrophic neurites in brain. Science **277**(5334), 1990–1993 (1997)
8. Waldvogel, H.J., Kim, E.H., Thu, D.C., Tippett, L.J., Faull, R.L.: New perspectives on the neuropathology in huntington's disease in the human brain and its relation to symptom variation. J. Huntington's Dis. **1**(2), 143–153 (2012)

9. Ideker, T., Ozier, O., Schwikowski, B., et al.: Discovering regulatory and signalling circuits in molecular interaction networks. Bioinformatics **18**(suppl. 1), S233 (2002)

10. Jiang, X., Zhang, H., Duan, F., Quan, X.: Identify huntington's disease associated genes based on restricted boltzmann machine with rna-seq data. BMC Bioinf. **18**(1), 447 (2017)

11. Jiang, X., Zhang, H., Zhang, Z., Quan, X.: Flexible non-negative matrix factorization to unravel disease-related genes. IEEE/ACM Trans. Comput. Biol. Bioinf. **1**(99), 1–11 (2018)

12. Frey, B.J., Dueck, D.: Clustering by passing messages between data points. Science **315** (5814), 972–976 (2007)

13. Robinson, M.D., Smyth, G.K.: Moderated statistical tests for assessing differences in tag abundance. Bioinformatics **23**(21), 2881–2887 (2007)

14. Robinson, M.D., McCarthy, D.J., Smyth, G.K.: edgeR: a bioconductor package for differential expression analysis of digital gene expression data. Bioinformatics **26**(1), 139–140 (2010)

15. Ritchie, M.E., et al.: LIMMA powers differential expression analyses for rna-sequencing and microarray studies. Nucleic Acids Res. **43**(7), 47 (2015)

16. Hong, F., Breitling, R.: A comparison of meta-analysis methods for detecting differentially expressed genes in microarray experiments. Bioinformatics **24**(3), 374–382 (2008)

17. Ding, C., Zhou, D., He, X., Zha, H.: R1-PCA: rotational invariant L1-norm principal component analysis for robust subspace factorization. In: International Conference on Machine Learning, pp. 281–288 (2006)

18. Liu, H., Shao, M., Fu, Y.: Consensus guided unsupervised feature selection. In: Proceedings of the Association for the Advancement of Artificial Intelligence, Phoenix, AZ, USA, pp. 12–17, February 2016

19. Langfelder, P., et al.: Integrated genomics and proteomics de ne huntingtin cag length-dependent networks in mice. Nat. Neurosci. **19**(4), 623 (2016)

20. Huang, D.W., Sherman, B.T., Lempicki, R.A.: Systematic and integrative analysis of large gene lists using DAVID bioinformatics resources. Nat. Protoc. **4**(1), 44–57 (2009)

21. Huang, D.W., Sherman, B.T., Lempicki, R.A.: Bioinformatics enrichment tools: paths toward the comprehensive functional analysis of large gene lists. Nucleic Acids Res. **37**(1), 1–13 (2009)

Urine Sediment Detection Based on Deep Learning

Xiao-Tao Xu[1], Jun Zhang[1(✉)], Peng Chen[2], Bing Wang[3], and Yi Xia[1]

[1] College of Electrical Engineering and Automation, Anhui University,
Hefei 230601, Anhui, China
wwwzhangjun@163.com
[2] Institute of Health Sciences, Anhui University, Hefei 230601, Anhui, China
[3] School of Electrical and Information Engineering,
Anhui University of Technology, Ma'anshan 243032, China

Abstract. Particle urinary sediment analysis in microscopic images can help doctors assess patients with kidney and urinary tract disease. Manual urine sediment inspection is labor intensive, subjective and time consuming, and traditional automated algorithms often extract handcrafted identification features. In this paper, instead of using manual extraction of features, we use CNN to learn features in an end-to-end manner to identify urine particles. In this paper, urine particle recognition is used as object detection processing, and other advanced target detection algorithms, Faster R-cnn, SSD, and deep learning frameworks such as RestNet and DenseNet, are used to study a new target detection method for urine particle recognition.

Keywords: Urine sediment identification · Target detection · CNN · Faster R-CNN · SSD · RestNet · DenseNet

1 Introduction

Urine sediment examination (USE) is usually performed by microscopic images inspection of centrifuged urine by experienced nephrologists. By qualitatively or quantitatively analyzing the formed components including Red Blood Cells (RBCs), White Blood Cells (WBCs) and other cells in the urine sediment image, it is possible to diagnose the urinary system diseases, which is an important means for routine medical diagnosis. Currently, it is still an important task to detect Red Blood Cells (RBCs) and White Blood Cells (WBCs) from urinary sediment images. General indications for urine analysis include: occult blood caused by erythrocytosis, gross hematuria, etc.; leukocytosis (average number of more than 5 in high power field) caused by pyuria, bladder or urethritis, pyelonephritis, kidney tuberculosis, etc. [1, 2]. Traditionally, urine sediment detection requires professional medical staff to treat the urine in time, but there is a slight delay in the sampling and analysis process. The urine sample may breed bacteria to affect the medical staff's judgment on the disease condition and subsequent treatment. Besides, the operators calculate the number of cells in the urine sediment particles by visual inspection, which is not only time consuming process, but also heavily depend on the operator's professional skills. Therefore, it is difficult to obtain

© Springer Nature Switzerland AG 2019
D.-S. Huang et al. (Eds.): ICIC 2019, LNCS 11643, pp. 543–552, 2019.
https://doi.org/10.1007/978-3-030-26763-6_52

the accurate urine sediment analysis if only use manual microscopy of USE. To deal with the problem, many automated technology for analyzing urine microscope image has become more widespread in recent decades.

As shown in Fig. 1(a), almost all previous automation methods have a fixed process. That is, the microscopic image is first preprocessed and segmented to generate candidate regions, and then features are extracted on the regions for classification. However, the performance of these methods depends to a large extent on the accuracy of the segmentation and the effectiveness of feature extraction.

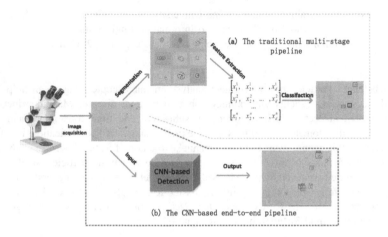

Fig. 1. The pipelines for urinary particles recognition.

Different from traditional image processing methods, convolutional neural network (CNN) is an end-to-end framework, which has been applied to many image processing tasks such as object detection, classification. In this paper, CNN is used to learn hierarchical levels of features from urine microscope image. As shown in Fig. 1(b), We propose an end-to-end framework to detect urinary sediment cells. The proposed framework is different from Faster-RCNN [3], SSD [4] and YOLO series [5–7]. To make the proposed methods more suitable for urine sediment cell identification, a novel network structure and multiple scale features are combined. The detection performance of blood cells is improved while the computational time is reduced.

We highlight the contributions as follows:

- We applied a new target detection method for urine sediment identification to learn characteristics in an end-to-end manner to identify urine sediment cells.
- We have studied a new multi-scale prediction method for the identification of urine sediment cells.
- We designed a network model that combines multiple deep learning frameworks to achieve better performance for urinary sediment cell identification.
- We identified red blood cells and white blood cells in urine sediments, and obtained the best average detection accuracy of 96.2%, and each image was only recognized for 21 ms.

1.1 Related Work

Traditional image processing technology have been applied to the detect various cells in urine samples. In general, the pipelines comprise three steps: cell segmentation, feature extraction and classification. The diagram of the pipeline is shown in Fig. 1(a).

Most existing researches focus on improving the image segmentation method for blood cells in urine images [8]. Mumford-Shah model and simplified Mumford-Shah model [9] combined with some level set methods to segment the microscopic cell image of urinary sediment are introduced..

However, the performance of these methods is very sensitive to the initial boundary condition of the level set function. Therefore, wavelet transform and adaptive threshold segmentation methods are used to detect the edge of WBCs, RBCs, epithelial cells and tubular cells. Among these adaptive threshold segmentation methods are an adaptive bi-threshold segmentation using histogram of the variance mapping image [10] and standard deviation gradient with dual-threshold. Since the real urinary images are much more difficult to segment, some methods based on machine learning are proposed. Cellular neural networks [11] are deployed to segment WBCs and epithelial cells. Gabor filters couple with simulated annealing and K-means clustering [12] are also used for urinary images segmentation. But these methods only work for small patches of size 128 × 128 Pixels, while the real microscopic urine images are much larger in size. Recently, Abdul Aziz et al. use U-net [13] to extract the object from urine microscopy images. This is the first application of Deep Learning architecture applied for extraction of urine objects [14]. Faster R-CNN and its variants are also used as effective pipeline to detect RBCs and WBCs from urinary sediment images. Contrasting traditional USE techniques, deep learning based techniques achieve better detection performance. However, these deep learning based techniques require more computational time, real-time urine sediment detection cannot be obtained. Moreover, most cells located in urinary sediment images are typical small objects, it is not easy to identify by using Faster R-CNN pipeline. Therefore, this paper proposes novel end-to-end pipeline to identify urine particles more effective. The proposed pipeline can improve the detection accuracy and decrease the computational time simultaneously.

2 Data

In this paper, we collected a large number of urine sediment images from the hospital to create a real urine sediment analysis database. Since modern clinical urine sediment analysis mainly focuses on RBCs and WBCs, each image is annotated with these two category cells by professional medical staff. Total 1,560 urine sediment images are obtained. After removing some images with noise, 897 images (image resolution is 720 * 576) are left. 717 pictures were randomly selected as the training set, 180 sheets were used as test sets, some samples are shown in Fig. 2. Three types images are listed, the left images only contrain WBCs, the middle images only contain RBCs and the right images contrain both WBCs and RBCs.

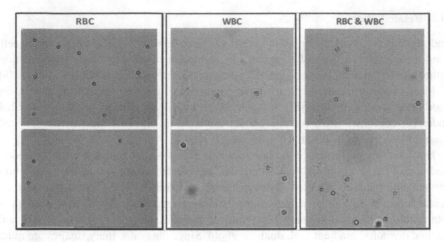

Fig. 2. Selected samples of urinary sediment particle.

3 Method

In this paper, a new target detection algorithm is studied. The object detection task is treated as a regression task. Firstly, the feature extraction network extracts features from the input image to obtain feature maps of different sizes. Then, the multi-scale fusion divides the input image into a specified number of grid cells, and each grid cell predicts a fixed number of bounding boxes. Finally, the bounding box with the largest IOU of bounding box and ground truth is used to predict the object. Its image processing system is shown in Fig. 3 below:

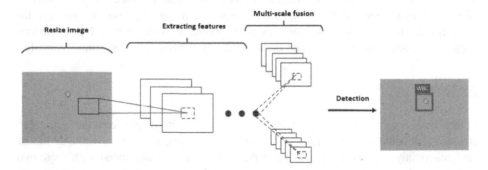

Fig. 3. Urine sediment image processing system.

Next, we will introduce the details of the target recognition algorithm for urine sediment detection proposed in this paper.

3.1   Convolutional with Anchor Boxes

First, feature extraction is performed on the input image feature to achieve a certain size feature map. Subsequently, this paper uses the concept of anchor to introduce the concept of anchor to predict the bounding boxes, but does not use the RPN to select the bounding boxes in the sliding window operation on the convolution feature map, but the N * N generated by the feature extraction. Cells are selected. If the center coordinate of an object in ground truth falls on a grid cell, then the grid cell predicts the object, because each cell predicts three bounding boxes, and the three bounding boxes have the highest confidence. The box is used to predict the object more accurately. The network designed in this paper predicts 4 coordinates, t_x, t_y, t_w, t_h and a confidence score for each bounding box, where the first four are coordinates. If the cell is offset from the upper left corner of the image (c_x, c_y) and the previous bounding box has a width and height pw, ph, the prediction corresponds (Fig. 4).

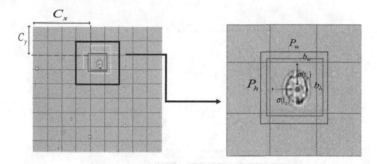

Fig. 4. Bounding boxes with dimension priors and location prediction.

$$b_x = \sigma(t_x) + c_x \tag{1}$$

$$b_y = \sigma(t_y) + c_y \tag{2}$$

$$b_w = p_w e^{t_w} \tag{3}$$

$$b_h = p_h e^{t_h} \tag{4}$$

$$Pr(object) * IOU(b, object) = \sigma(t_0) \tag{5}$$

Among them, σ is sigmod, (1) (2) and (3) (4) respectively represent the position and size of the bounding box with respect to the feature map, and Eq. (5) represents the accuracy of the bounding box.

The confidence score contains two aspects, one is the probability that the bounding box contains the target, and the other is the accuracy of the bounding box. When the bounding box contains the detection target, Pr(object) = 1; otherwise, Pr(object) = 0. The accuracy of the bounding box can be characterized by the prediction box and the intersection truth of the ground truth.

3.2 Prediction Across Scales

This paper uses feature pyramid networks [15], and for the morphological character-istics of urine sediment identification, the high-level features of low-resolution, high-semantic information and the low-level features of high-resolution, low-speech infor-mation are top-down. Edge joins, so that features at all scales have rich semantic information. Faster RCNN adopts (a) this method, that is, only adopts the character-istics of the last layer of the network. SSD (Single Shot Detector) adopts (b) this multi-scale feature fusion method, there is no upsampling process, that is, different layers from the network. Extracting features of different scales for prediction does not add extra computational effort. In this paper, we use (c) this way, the top-level features are fused by upsampling and low-level features, and each layer is independently predicted. Detection on multiple scale feature maps, the detection effect of small targets is still relatively obvious.

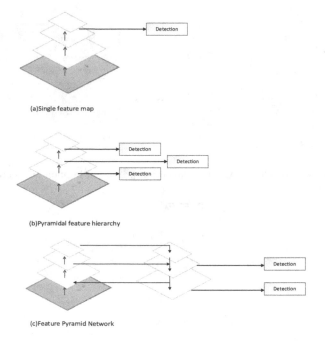

Fig. 5. (a) Use only single scale features for faster detection. (b) An alternative is to reuse the pyramidal feature hierarchy computed by a ConvNet as if it were a featurized image pyramid. (c) Our proposed Feature Pyramid Network (FPN) is fast like (a) and (b), but more accurate.

The specific process is as follows: the high-level feature is double-sampled, and then combined with the corresponding previous layer feature (the previous layer can be used after the 1 * 1 convolution kernel, the purpose is to change the channels, and the latter layer the channels are the same), the combination is to do the addition between pixels. Iterate through the process until the finest feature map is generated. After a series of experiments, since the cells in the urine sediment picture belong to small targets, if the highest prediction layer is retained, the false positive rate will be increased. Therefore, two scale fusion methods are selected for prediction, as shown in Fig. 5(c). Making the feature map have better fine-grained features is equivalent to performing a feature fusion, which is beneficial to the detection of small targets.

3.3 Feature Extractor

This paper uses a new classification network as the feature extraction part, draws on the idea of ResNet [16], introduces the residual module to improve the recognition of small targets, and changes the layer-by-layer training of deep neural network to stage-by-stage training. The residual training is performed by the shortcut connection method to achieve a small loss, which can effectively solve the problems of deep network gradient dispersion and gradient explosion. At the same time, it also introduces the idea of DenseNet [17], which can reduce the disappearance of the gradient like the residual neural network, enhance the transmission of image feature information, make the image features more fully utilized, and reduce the calculation to a certain extent quantity complexity. The optimization scheme designed in this paper uses the characteristics of the dense block to introduce its high degree of multiplexing and fusion of picture features, so that the network can better identify the cell types in the urine sediment image, and the convolutional layers in the network structure are adopted. The 3 * 3 convolution kernel, and the 1 * 1 convolution kernel is placed between the 3 * 3 convolution kernels to compress the features, and batch normalization is also used to stabilize the model training. The resulting basic model is shown below (Fig. 6):

	Type	Filter	Size	Output
	Convolutional	32	3 x 3	416 x 416
	Convolutional	64	3 x 3 / 2	208 x 208
1 x	Convolutional	32	1 x 1	
	Convolutional	64	3 x 3	
	Residual			208 x 208
	Convolutional	128	3 x 3 / 2	104 x 104
2 x	Convolutional	64	1 x 1	
	Convolutional	128	3 x 3	
	Residual			104 x 104
	Convolutional	256	3 x 3 / 2	52 x 52
8 x	Convolutional	128	1 x 1	
	Convolutional	64	3 x 3	
	dense			52 x 52
	Convolutional	512	3 x 3 / 2	26 x 26
8 x	Convolutional	256	1 x 1	
	Convolutional	128	3 x 3	
	dense			26 x 26
	Convolutional	1024		13 x 13
4 x	Convolutional	512	1 x 1	
	Convolutional	256	3 x 3	
	dense			13 x 13
2 x	Convolutional	512	1 x 1	
	Convolutional	1024	3 x 3	13 x 13
	Convolutional	512	1 x 1	13 x 13

Fig. 6. New network structure parameters.

4 Experiments

Network training parameter settings. Data augmentation strategies similar to Faster-RCNN and SSD are used, including random crops, rotations, and hue, saturation, and exposure shifts. The training phase uses an asynchronous stochastic gradient descent with a momentum term of 0.9. Each batch contains 68 images, the initial learning rate of the weight is 0.01, and the attenuation coefficient is set to 0.0005.

Network training strategy. Because the different experimental structures need to be trained in the comparative experiment, the number of iterations of the training to achieve the best weight is different. Therefore, the network weight file is saved every 1000 iterations during training to select the best weight file to prevent over-prevention.

In comparison with the current advanced target detection algorithms, the proposed method has great advantages in the detection of urine sediment images, as shown in Fig. 7:

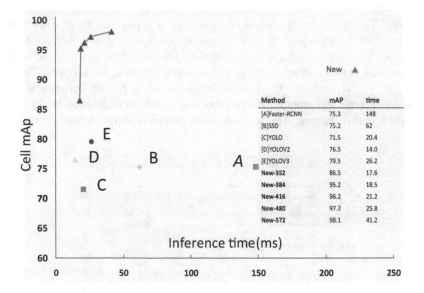

Fig. 7. The performance of urine sediment cell detection proposed in this paper is compared with other target detection algorithms.

As can be seen from Fig. 7, the method of this paper is better than Faster-RCNN, SSD and YOLO. The series has improved the accuracy of detection by more than 10%. Although the speed is inferior to the YOLO series, it does not affect its real-time performance. The reason is that the network of this paper is much deeper than YOLOv1 in YOLOv2, and the amount of calculation and parameters are much higher than them, but the method of this paper is more targeted in detecting small targets. As can be seen from the selection of the image resolution, as the resolution increases, the mAP of the urine sediment image gradually increases, but with the result that the detection speed is greatly reduced, so in order to weigh this Relationship, the image resolution selected in this paper is 416 * 416, which not only ensures the detection accuracy, but also ensures the real-time detection speed.

5 Conclusions

In this paper, we have studied a new end-to-end target detection method. For the detection of urine sediment cell images, we clustered the datasets, defined the network according to the scale of its own dataset, and directly predicted the target cells in the image. Drawing on the ideas of RestNet and DenseNet, a new network framework was studied and cell counts and recognition of urine microscopic images were applied. We also compare our proposed method with the existing target detection algorithm, and prove that the proposed extraction method is very effective in urine object extraction.

Acknowledgement. This work is supported by Anhui Provincial Natural Science Foundation (grant number 1608085MF136) and Natural Science Foundation of China (grant number 61872004).

References

1. Kouri, T., Fogazzi, G., Gant, V., Hallander, H., Hofmann, W., Guder, W.: European urinalysis guidelines. Scand. J. Clin. Lab. Invest. Suppl. **60**(231), 1–96 (2000)
2. Ince, F.D., Ellidağ, H.Y., Koseoğlu, M., Şimşek, N., Yalçın, H., Zengin, M.O.: The comparison of automated urine analyzers with manual microscopic examination for urinalysis automated urine analyzers and manual urinalysis. Pract. Lab. Med. **5**(2), 14–20 (2016)
3. Ren, S., He, K., Girshick, R., Sun, J.: Faster R-CNN: towards real-time object detection with region proposal networks. In: Advances in Neural Information Processing Systems, pp. 91–99 (2015)
4. Liu, W., Anguelov, D., Erhan, D., Szegedy, C., Reed, S., Fu, C.-Y., Berg, Alexander C.: SSD: single shot multibox detector. In: Leibe, B., Matas, J., Sebe, N., Welling, M. (eds.) ECCV 2016. LNCS, vol. 9905, pp. 21–37. Springer, Cham (2016). https://doi.org/10.1007/978-3-319-46448-0_2
5. Redmon, J., Divvala, S., Girshick, R., et al.: You only look once: unified, real time object detection. In: Computer Vision and Pattern Recognition, pp. 779–788 (2016)
6. Redmon, J., Farhadi, A.: YOLO9000: better, faster, stronger. In: IEEE Conference on Computer Vision and Pattern Recognition, pp. 6517-6525 (2017)
7. Redmon, J., Farhadi, A.: YOLOv3: an incremental improvement. In: IEEE Conference on Computer Vision and Pattern Recognition (2018)
8. Luo, H., Ma, S., Wu, D., Xu, Z.: Mumford-shah segmentation for microscopic image of the urinary sediment. In: International Conference on Bioinformatics and Biomedical Engineering, pp. 861–863. IEEE (2007)
9. Chan, T.F., Vese, L.A.: Active contours without edges. IEEE Trans. Image Process. **10**(2), 266–277 (2001)

10. Li, C., Fang, B., Wang, Y., Lu, G., Qian, J., Chen, L.: Automatic detecting and recognition of casts in urine sediment images. In: International Conference on Wavelet Analysis and Pattern Recognition, pp. 26–31. IEEE (2009)

11. Zhang, Z., Xia, S., Duan, H.: Cellular neural network based urinary image segmentation. In: International Conference on Natural Computation, vol. 2, pp. 285–289. IEEE (2007)

12. Zhang, S., Wang, J., Zhao, S., Luan, X.: Urinary sediment images segmentation based on efficient gabor flters. In: International Conference on Complex Medical Engineering, pp. 812–815. IEEE (2007)

13. Ronneberger, O., Fischer, P., Brox, T.: U-net: convolutional networks for biomedical image segmentation. In: International Conference on Medical Image Computing and Computer-Assisted Intervention, pp. 234–241 (2015)

14. Aziz, A., Pande, H., Cheluvaraju, B., Dastidar, T.R.: Improved Extraction of Objects from Urine Microscopy Images with Unsupervise

15. Lin, T.-Y., Dollar, P., Girshick, R., He, K., Hariharan, B., Belongie, S.: Feature pyramid networks for object detection. In: Proceedings of the IEEE Conference on Computer Vision and Pattern Recognition, pp. 2117–2125 (2017)

16. He, K., Zhang, X., Ren, S., et al.: Deep residual learning for image recognition. In: Proceedings of the 2016 IEEE Conference on Computer Vision and Pattern Recognition, pp. 770–778. IEEE Computer Society, Washington, DC (2016)

17. Huang, G., Liu, Z., Weinberger, K.Q., et al.: Densely connected convolutional networks. In: IEEE conference on Computer Vision and Pattern Recognition, pp. 4700-4708 (2016)

Identification of Apple Leaf Diseases Based on Convolutional Neural Network

Tao Fang[1], Peng Chen[1,2(✉)], Jun Zhang[3], and Bing Wang[4(✉)]

[1] School of Computer Science and Technology, Anhui University,
Hefei 230601, Anhui, China
pchen.ustcl0@foxmail.com

[2] Institutes of Physical Science and Information Technology, Anhui University,
Hefei 230601, Anhui, China

[3] School of Electrical Engineering and Automation, Anhui University,
Hefei 230601, China
wwwzhangjun@163.com

[4] School of Electrical and Information Engineering,
Anhui University of Technology, Ma'anshan 243032, Anhui, China
bwang@ahut.edu.cn

Abstract. Accurate identification of apple leaf diseases is key to the prevention and control of insect pests and diseases in apple trees. This paper proposed an improved convolutional neural network combining batch normalization and center loss function based on VGG16 model. Batch normalization is used to normalize the input data of the convolutional layer, which accelerates network convergence, while the use of center loss function in conjunction with softmax loss function makes the network having more cohesive features, thereby improving apple leaf diseases classification accuracy. In addition, by selecting a reasonable initial learning rate, the parameters of the network can reach the optimal value at a faster speed during the training of the neural network, and at the same time, the performance of the network is improved. The experimental results showed that our method achieved higher recognition performance than the-state-of-the-art methods in the identification of apple leaf diseases, compared with several popular convolutional neural networks.

Keywords: Disease identification · Convolutional neural network · Batch normalization · Center loss function

1 Introduction

In the process of planting and production, apples are prone to diseases due to their inadaptability to the external environment and infection by other organisms. The occurrence of diseases will have a serious impact on the yield and quality of the apple. Therefore, early detection and diagnosis of apple diseases is very vital. However, due to the wide variety of diseases, it is easy to be misdiagnosed only by artificial observation and judgment, at the same time, plant diseases cannot be diagnosed and treated in time [1]. The key factor in the management of plant diseases is the rapid and accurate

© Springer Nature Switzerland AG 2019
D.-S. Huang et al. (Eds.): ICIC 2019, LNCS 11643, pp. 553–564, 2019.
https://doi.org/10.1007/978-3-030-26763-6_53

diagnosis of disease types, so that timely and effective control measures are taken to avoid the misuse of pesticides.

With the continuous development of computer technology, the intelligent identification of plant leaf diseases has made good progress. In [2], Wang et al. proposed a discriminant analysis method to identify the type of cucumber lesions, by extracting the characteristics of color, shape and texture in plant leaf lesions, as well as combining with environmental information. Zhang et al. proposed an improved method based on Bernsen algorithm for the detection and segmentation of leaf lesions in plant diseases, which can determine the occurrence of plant diseases by analyzing the color of the plant leaves and segmenting lesion images [3]. Wei et al. adopted computer image processing technology to the preprocessing and feature extraction of cucumber disease images, where 15 characteristic parameters of cucumber downy mildew were extracted from the aspects of statistics, shape and color to identify the disease, and obtained a high recognition rate [4]. Zhang et al. extracted the color, shape and texture features of the lesion by dividing the spots in corn leaves, and then identified the 5 corn leaves by K-nearest neighbor (KNN) classification algorithm [5]. However, all the above works identified plant diseases by extracting the characteristics of plant images. Because it is difficult to select useful features that contribute significantly to the identification of disease types, most identification methods achieved low recognition performance due to the complex diversity of diseased leaf images. Moreover, with the rapid growth of image data, it is more and more hard to artificial design the characteristics of images that meet the needs of actual plant disease identification.

In the field of computer vision, object classification is one of the basic problems of research, and also the basis of other advanced or complex visual problems [6]. Convolutional networks [7] are an efficient tool for classification tasks. Compared with the traditional methods for manually designing features of images, the deep convolutional neural network emerging in recent years is an end-to-end strategy, which can implement efficient and automatic learning and classification of image features. The use of convolutional neural networks to identify early dis ease images has become a new research hotspot in agricultural field. Convolutional neural networks not only reduce the requirements of image preprocessing, but also improve the recognition accuracy of images. Sladojevic et al. proposed a plant disease identification method based on deep neural network, which can effectively distinguish healthy leaves and 13 different disease leaves [8]. Zhang et al. Constructed a deep convolutional neural network (DCNN) model to extract high-level abstract features directly from normalized diseased leaf images, and to identify diseases at the output layer of the CNN-based method [9]. Amara et al. [10] designed a classification method for banana diseases based on deep learning and achieved a high recognition rate. Liu et al. introduced an accurate method for identifying apple leaf disease based on deep convolutional neural network [11]. The method generates enough pathological images and designs a new architecture based on AlexNet's deep convolutional neural network, which yielded an overall accuracy of 97.62% to detect apple leaf disease. Jeon et al. [12] proposed a method for detecting plant diseases based on deep learning which can detect 26 diseases of 14 crops. These works have proven that convolutional neural networks are feasible to identify plant leaf diseases.

This paper proposed an improved VGG16 model to automatically identify apple leaf diseases. To address the issue of the slow convergence of network training and the low recognition rate of complex background pictures in deep learning, a batch normalization layer was added to the original VGG16 model to accelerate the convergence and prevent the gradient dispersion of the model. At the same time, the classification accuracy was also improved. Moreover, for the loss function of our model, center loss [13] function was adopted. The use of softmax loss function is to hope that the learned features have better generalization and discrimination ability. By punishing the samples of each kind and the offset of the center of the sample, the same kind of samples are gathered together as much as possible. In this way, the intra-class distance is reduced and the classification accuracy is improved. The last but not the least, the range of the optimal learning rate is determined experimentally to optimize the loss function and make the network model converging faster.

2 Architecture

The VGG16 [14] network structure consists of 13 convolutional layers and 3 fully connected layers, each with a convolution kernel size of 3 × 3 and a convolution step size of 1. For the sake of certainty that the image size after convolution is unchanged, the image is filled, and each pixel is filled with 1 pixel. All pooling layers use a 2 × 2 core with a step size of 2. Except for the last fully connected layer, all layers in this model use the RELU activation function. This paper proposed an improved neural network structure model based on the VGG16 model, where each convolutional layer followed a batch normalization layer to prevent gradient dispersion. In terms of loss function, the auxiliary function center loss is added, and the overall framework is shown in Fig. 1.

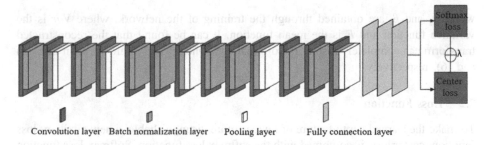

Fig. 1. The model of apple disease recognition based on deep convolutional neural network.

2.1 Feature Representation Network

Batch normalization (BN) was originally proposed in the literature [15], which is to batch normalize the input data of each layer during the training of the neural network. In traditional neural networks, a sample is normalized (subtracted by the standard deviation) before the sample is input to the input layer, thereby reducing the difference between samples. However, BN not only normalizes the data of the input layer, but also normalizes the input of each hidden layer. On the one hand, the addition of BN improves the training speed and speeds up the convergence process of the network. On the other hand, it also improves the classification performance of the network. The algorithm using batch normalization is as follows:

$$\mu = \frac{1}{n}\sum_{i=1}^{n} x_i \tag{1}$$

$$\sigma = \frac{1}{n}\sum_{i=1}^{n}(x_i - \mu)^2 \tag{2}$$

where μ and σ are the batch mean and variance, respectively. Then the data is normalized as,

$$\hat{x}_i = \frac{x_i - \mu}{\sqrt{\sigma^2 + \varepsilon}} \tag{3}$$

A data x_i with a mean of 0 and a variance of 1 is obtained. In the formula, ε is a constant set to avoid that the fractional σ is not satisfied when the variance σ is 0. To avoid of the destruction of feature distribution after data normalization, there is a need to restore the original feature distribution by reconstructing the transform.

$$y_i = \gamma_i x_i + \beta_i \tag{4}$$

$$\gamma_i = \sqrt{Var[x_i]} \tag{5}$$

$$\beta_i = E[x_i] \tag{6}$$

where γ_i and β_i are obtained through the training of the network, where Var is the variance function and E is the mean function. It can be found that the reconstructed transform can completely restore the original data when γ_i and β_i are set as in Eqs. (5) and (6), respectively.

2.2   Loss Function

To make the learned depth feature of images more distinguishable, a new auxiliary loss function, center loss, is combined with the softmax loss function. Softmax loss function is usually used as the loss function for CNNs in solving classification problems such as face recognition. To learn higher discriminative features, Wen *et al.* proposed a new auxiliary loss function, center loss function, which is an auxiliary loss function, i.e., the newly proposed loss function needs to be used together with the softmax loss function instead of replacing the latter.

In the process of feature extraction, in many cases, the intra-class spacing of instances is greater than the inter-class spacing of them. We hope that features are not only separable, but also large different. In training a network, the softmax loss function only encourages features to be separable (not distinguishable), which usually makes the resulting depth features having strong inter-class discriminative power. For the elaborating and complex data of apple leaves, in this work, we hope that the data in the feature space is not only separable between classes of leaves, but also more importantly, it is compacted within each class. In some cases, the intra-class difference of plant leaves in the same class are likely to be greater than the inter-class difference of leaves in different classes, thus only keeping samples in inter-class compact, our model can make a more robust decision for the samples with large variations within the same class, that is, learning a discriminative feature. To address this issue, in the training process, the center loss function is used to learn the center of deep features in each class, which can be simultaneously updated by minimizing the distance between the deep features and the corresponding class centers. The CNNs are trained under the joint supervision of softmax loss function and center loss function, and a hyper-parameter λ, is used to balance the two loss functions. In the combination of the two loss functions, softmax loss function is considered to be responsible for increasing the inter-class distance, and center loss function is for reducing the intra-class distance, which can make the learned features more cohesive, and thereby achieve better classification performance.

Here, the softmax loss formula is shown in below,

$$\mathcal{L}_s = - \sum_{i=1}^{m} \log \frac{e^{W_{y_i}^T x_i + b_{y_i}}}{\sum_{j=1}^{n} e^{W_j^T x_i + b_j}} \tag{7}$$

where $x_i \in \mathbb{R}^d$ represents the ith deep feature, belong to the y_i th class. Feature dimension is d. $W_j \in \mathbb{R}^d$ denotes the jth column of the weights $W \in \mathbb{R}^{d \times n}$ in the last fully connected layer, $b \in \mathbb{R}^n$ is the bias term. The size of mini-batch is m, and the number of class is n. The center loss formula is,

$$\mathcal{L}_c = \frac{1}{2} \sum_{i=1}^{m} \|x_i - c_{y_i}\|_2^2 \tag{8}$$

where $c_{y_i} \in \mathbb{R}^d$ represents the y_ith class center of deep features.

The combination of the two loss functions is indicated below:

$$\mathcal{L} = \mathcal{L}_s + \lambda \mathcal{L}_c = - \sum_{i=1}^{m} \log \frac{e^{W_{y_i}^T x_i + b_{y_i}}}{\sum_{j=1}^{n} e^{W_j^T x_i + b_j}} + \frac{\lambda}{2} \sum_{i=1}^{m} \|x_i - c_{y_i}\|_2^2 \tag{9}$$

where the hyper-parameter λ is used for balancing the two loss functions. The softmax loss can be considered as a special case of this joint supervision, if λ is set to 0.

3   Data Set

This work collected six common apple leaf diseases and some healthy apple leaves. Leaf diseases include anthracnose leaf blight, cedar rust, gray spot, leaf rust, black rot and black spot. There were 5373 diseased leaf images and 1683 healthy leaf images. Since the sizes and formats of the images are different, the images were uniformly converted into JPG format, and all images were adjusted to 256 × 256 by increasing the canvas. All leaf images were randomly divided into two parts: training data and test data, respectively including 5646 pictures and 1410 pictures. Some apple leaf images are shown in Fig. 2.

Fig. 2. Some cases of apple leaf images: (a) apple anthracnose leaf blight; (b) cedar rust; (c) gray spot; (d) leaf rust; (e) black rot; (f) apple scab; (g) healthy.

4   Experiments and Results

For the apple leaf disease recognition based on our proposed CNN-based method, each feature map of one convolutional layer represents the features of one image. The deeper the network layer is, the more abstract the features are. The aim of the fully connected layer is to combine the features of underlying feature maps which are then applied to a classifier for disease type identification. The probabilities that each disease leaf image in the test set belongs to 7 different categories of diseases are created, and the category corresponding to the largest probability is selected as the disease category, to which the disease leaf belongs. The optimal parameters of our model were obtained after fine-tuning 10,000 times on the training set of disease leaf images. The classification rate of the network on the test set is relatively stable, when the network was trained by more iterations.

4.1   The Impact of Learning Rate on Prediction Accuracy

Since gradient descent method used in network always affects the final performance of the network, the learning rate for gradient descent should be set in reasonable value. The learning rate determines how fast the parameters of network move to the optimal values. If the learning rate is too large, it is likely to make the performance of network vibrating; on the contrary, if the learning rate is too small, the optimization efficiency may be too low, and the network cannot be converged for a long time, so the learning rate is critical to affect the performance of the network. Smith described a powerful method for selecting a series of learning rates for neural networks [16], which aims to train a network starting from a low learning rate and increasing the learning rate exponentially in each batch. In the beginning stage, the low learning rate makes the loss function value slowly improved, and then the training process starts to be accelerated until the learning speed becomes too high, which causes the loss function value increasing and the training process being diverged. In the experiments of recognizing apple leaf diseases, the initial learning rate is set to 0.00001. After 2000 iterations, the learning rate is increased by 10 times, as shown in the left graph of Fig. 3. After the training is completed, the curve of learning rate with respect to iteration and that of loss function with respect to learning rate are drawn in Fig. 3. It can be seen from the right graph of Fig. 3 that the loss function changes the fastest, when the learning rate is between 0.01 and 0.001, compared with other range of learning rate, that is, the optimal learning rate is about 0.01 in this work. Therefore, in the subsequent experiments, the initial learning rate *base_lr* is set to 0.01, 3000 times per iteration, the learning rate is reduced to one tenth of the original learning rate.

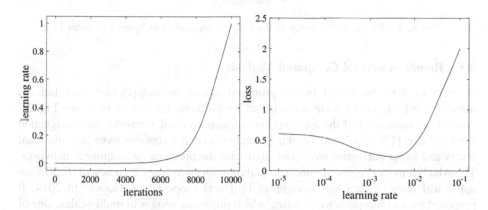

Fig. 3. Illustrator of curves of learning rate and loss function value in this work.

4.2   Selection of Hyper-Parameter λ

In the proposed model, the total loss of the network is integrated by softmax loss function and center loss function. In order to achieve a better recognition effect, control the ratio of softmax loss function to center loss function, different values of hyper-parameter λ that control the weight of softmax loss and center loss are investigated. Figure 4 illustrates the prediction performance of the model with respect to λ. It can be seen from the Fig. 4 that the model performs the best when λ is 0.09.

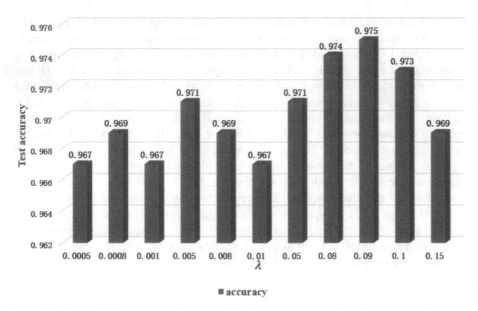

Fig. 4. Prediction performance of the model with respect to hyper-parameter λ.

4.3 Results of Several Compared Methods

In order to show the power of our proposed model, several popular convolutional networks and our model were investigated for performance comparison (see Fig. 5). Nowadays, most state-of-the-art deep convolutional neural networks were originated from AlexNet [17], who's most striking feature is in that it contains more convolutional levels and larger parameter size, compared with the previous convolutional networks. The AlexNet model achieved good recognition with an average accuracy of 92.50% on apple leaf diseases data set. GoogleNet [18] was proposed by Google in 2014. It proposed a novel Inception mechanism, which processes images in multi-scales. One of the benefits of Inception mechanism is that it greatly reduces the number of parameters in the model by integrating multiple convolution kernels with different scales and pooling layers. GoogleNet was able to extracting multi-dimensional features and achieving a recognition rate of 94.12% on apple leaf diseases data set. Residual Network [19] used Shortcut Connections to fit Residual Representations to solve the problem of arduous training in deep networks. The network performed well, and Res50 achieved an accuracy of 95.00% on apple leaf diseases data set. The main innovation of VGG network was the use of small-sized convolution kernels, all of which used 3 × 3 convolution kernels. The VGG16 model simplified the neural network structure and achieved a recognition rate of 95.70% on apple leaf diseases data set. After applying batch normalization to each convolutional layer, the VGG16 model achieved an accuracy of 96.70%. Furthermore, the VGG16 model achieved a recognition rate of 97.58% when adopted batch normalization and center loss function.

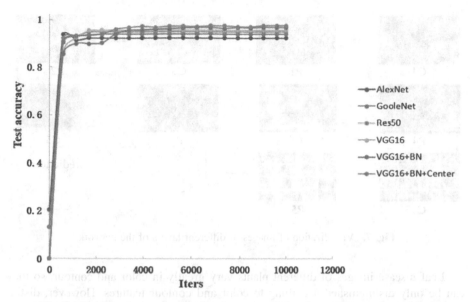

Fig. 5. Classification accuracy of various convolutional neural network models.

To further illustrate the superiority of the proposed model, the predictions of each class of the final proposed model were compared with the original VGG16 model (see Fig. 6). The proposed model got test accuracy ranging from 95.00% to 99.70%, compared with the VGG16 model ranging from 92.27% to 99.35%hile. Because the background of the leaves of anthracnose leaf blight and leaf rust is complex, the noise interference of the background and leaf is relatively large, which makes the identification task is formidable. The recognition rates of VGG16 model on anthracnose leaf blight and leaf rust were 93.00% and 92.27%, respectively, and the accuracy rates of the proposed model on those were 96.50% and 95.45%, respectively. It can be seen that our proposed convolutional neural network model combined with batch normalization and center loss function performed better on apple leaf disease than VGG16 model.

	0	1	2	3	4	5	6	Acc
0	186	0	0	14	0	0	0	93.00%
1	0	153	1	0	0	0	0	99.35%
2	0	2	189	0	3	1	0	96.92%
3	16	1	0	203	0	0	0	92.27%
4	0	0	3	0	122	0	0	96.80%
5	1	2	2	0	0	168	7	93.33%
6	0	1	1	0	1	4	329	97.92%

VGG16

	0	1	2	3	4	5	6	Acc
0	193	0	0	7	0	0	0	96.50%
1	0	153	1	0	0	0	0	99.35%
2	0	0	193	0	2	0	0	98.97%
3	10	0	0	210	0	0	0	95.45%
4	0	0	4	0	121	0	0	96.80%
5	0	2	1	1	0	171	5	95.00%
6	0	0	0	0	0	1	335	99.70%

VGG16+BN+Center loss

Fig. 6. Confusion matrices of two models.

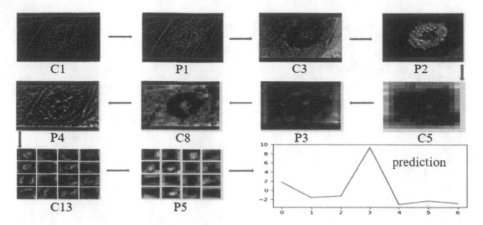

Fig. 7. Visualization of images in different layers of the network.

Leaf disease images of different plants vary greatly in color and contour, so they can be only distinguished according to color and contour features. However, distinguishing the same leaf disease images on the same plants requires further extraction of texture information on the blades of leaves. As shown in Fig. 7, the visualization of images with leaf rust in our network can be clearly seen that in the first few layers of the network, the texture and lesion characteristics of the leaves are clearly visible. As the network became deeply, the feature pictures become more and more abstraction, and finally the leaf disease prediction results are output in the classifier layer.

However, one problem that was overlooked in this paper is that for the same leaf disease, the severity [20] of the disease has an impact on the classification results of the network. In the experiments on apple leaf diseases, the network performed worse on the disease of apple scab (see Fig. 8). The reasons for the poor classifications might be in that the severity of leaf disease caused by black spot disease was different. For leaves with scab in milder degree, the appearance is very similar to that of healthy leaves, which is always misjudged as healthy leaves by classifiers.

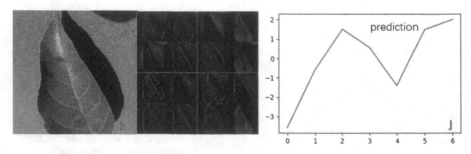

Fig. 8. Visualization for misclassification images: (h) The fifth category of apple scab leaf; (i) The feature map obtained after a series of feature extractions; (j) The classifier misjudged the sixth category, namely healthy leaf.

5 Conclusion

This paper proposed an improved convolutional neural network for apple leaf disease identification, which was inspired from the original VGG16 model. The proposed model combined with batch normalization and center loss function. In choosing the initial learning rate, experiments can be seen that a low learning rate is suitable in training the network, so that the loss function of the network is optimal without decreasing the training speed. Moreover, the proposed model was compared with the state-of-the-art models and the original VGG16, and experimental results showed that our model achieved an improvement on leaf diseases identification. However, deep learning requires the support of massive databases, so the amount of training data will be increased in subsequent research, that is, the model is trained by leaf data of various plants, which will enhance the accuracy of the plant disease identification method based on the depth CNN, and improve the fitting ability [21] and generalization ability [22] of the deep learning model.

Acknowledgments. This work was financially supported by the National Natural Science Foundation of China (Nos. 61672035, 61872004, 61472282 and 31401293), Anhui Province Funds for Excellent Youth Scholars in Colleges (gxyqZD2016068) and Anhui Scientific Research Foundation for Returned Scholars.

References

1. Chen, Z.Y., Liu, Y.F., Liu, Y.Z.: Research progress in biocontrol of bacillus spp. Against plant diseases. Jiangsu J. Agric. Sci. 28(5), 999–1006 (2012)
2. Wang, X., Zhang, S., Wang, Z.: Recognition of cucumber diseases based on leaf image and environmental information. Trans. Chin. Soc. Agric. Eng. 30(14), 148–153 (2014)
3. Zhang, A.W., Huang, W.Z., Shi, Y.: Improved Bernsen binary algorithm for spot detection of plant disease leaves. Guangdong Agric. Sci. 2016(12), 22 (2016)
4. Wei, Y., et al.: A study of image processing on identifying cucumber disease. In: Li, D., Chen, Y. (eds.) CCTA 2011. IAICT, vol. 370, pp. 201–209. Springer, Heidelberg (2012). https://doi.org/10.1007/978-3-642-27275-2_22
5. Zhang, S.W., Shang, Y.J., Wang, L.: Plant disease recognition based on plant leaf image. J. Anim. Plant Sci. 25(3), 42–45 (2015)
6. Huang, K.Q., Ren, W.Q., Tan, T.N.: A review on image object classification and detection. Chin. J. Comput. 37(6), 1225–1240 (2014)
7. Zeiler, Matthew D., Fergus, R.: Visualizing and understanding convolutional networks. In: Fleet, D., Pajdla, T., Schiele, B., Tuytelaars, T. (eds.) ECCV 2014. LNCS, vol. 8689, pp. 818–833. Springer, Cham (2014). https://doi.org/10.1007/978-3-319-10590-1_53
8. Sladojevic, S., Arsenovic, M., Anderla, A., Culibrk, D.: Deep neural networks based recognition of plant diseases by leaf image classification. Comput. Intell. Neurosci. 2016, 1–11 (2016)
9. Zhang, S.W., Xie, Z.Q., Zhang, Q.Q.: Application research on convolutional neural network for cucumber leaf disease recognition. Jiangsu J. Agric. Sci. (2018)
10. Amara, J., Bouaziz, B. Algergawy, A.: A deep learning-based approach for banana leaf diseases classification. In: BTW (Workshops), pp. 79–88 (2017)

11. Liu, B., Zhang, Y., He, D.J., Li, Y.: Identification of apple leaf diseases based on deep convolutional neural networks. Symmetry **10**(1), 11 (2017)
12. Jeon, W.S., Rhee, S.Y.: Plant leaf recognition using a convolution neural network. Int. J. Fuzzy Logic Intell. Syst. **17**(1), 26–34 (2017)
13. Wen, Y., Zhang, K., Li, Z., Qiao, Yu.: A discriminative feature learning approach for deep face recognition. In: Leibe, B., Matas, J., Sebe, N., Welling, M. (eds.) ECCV 2016. LNCS, vol. 9911, pp. 499–515. Springer, Cham (2016). https://doi.org/10.1007/978-3-319-46478-7_31
14. Simonyan, K., Zisserman, A.: Very deep convolutional networks for large-scale image recognition. arXiv preprint arXiv: 1409.1556 (2014)
15. Ioffe, S., Szegedy, C.: Batch normalization: accelerating deep network training by reducing internal covariate shift. arXiv preprint arXiv: 1502.03167 (2015)
16. Smith, L.N.: Cyclical learning rates for training neural networks. In: 2017 IEEE Winter Conference on Applications of Computer Vision (WACV), pp. 464–472. IEEE (2017)
17. Russakovsky, O., Deng, J., Su, H., Krause, J., Satheesh, S.: Imagenet large scale visual recognition challenge. Int. J. Comput. Vis. **115**(3), 211–252 (2015)
18. Szegedy, C., Liu, W., Jia, Y., Sermanet, P., Reed, S., Anguelov, D.: Going deeper with convolutions. In: Proceedings of the IEEE Conference on Computer Vision and Pattern Recognition, pp. 1–9 (2015)
19. He, K., Zhang, X., Ren, S., Sun, J.: Deep residual learning for image recognition. In: Proceedings of the IEEE Conference on Computer Vision and Pattern Recognition, pp. 770–778 (2016)
20. Gao, P., Nan, Z.B., Duan, T.Y., Zhang, F., Liu, Q.T., Meng, F.J.: Effects of spot blight on photosynthesis of Apocynum venetum and the scale system of the disease severity. J. Plant Prot. **42**(4), 531–537 (2015)
21. Wan, L., Zeiler, M., Zhang, S., Le Cun, Y., Fergus, R.: Regularization of neural networks using dropconnect. In: International Conference on Machine Learning, pp. 1058–1066 (2013)
22. Wang, X.Z., Xing, H.J., Li, Y., Hua, Q., Dong, C.R., Pedrycz, W.: A study on relationship between generalization abilities and fuzziness of base classifiers in ensemble learning. IEEE Trans. Fuzzy Syst. **23**(5), 1638–1654 (2015)

Multiomics Data Analysis Using Tensor Decomposition Based Unsupervised Feature Extraction

–Comparison with DIABLO–

Y-h. Taguchi[(⊠)] [iD]

Department of Physics, Chuo University, Tokyo 112-8551, Japan
tag@granular.com

Abstract. Multiomics data analysis is the central issue of genomics science. In spite of that, there are not well defined methods that can integrate multomics data sets, which are formatted as matrices with different sizes. In this paper, I propose the usage of tensor decomposition based unsupervised feature extraction as a data mining tool for multiomics data set. It can successfully integrate miRNA expression, mRNA expression and proteome, which were used as a demonstration example of DIABLO that is the recently proposed advanced method for the integrated analysis of multiomics data set.

Keywords: Tensor decomposition · Feature selection · Multiomics data set

1 Introduction

Multiomics data, including miRNA expression, mRNA expression, promoter methylation and histone modification, have recently come to be measured over the various biological problems. In contrast to the rapid development of measurement technology, the data analysis pipeline developed very slowly. This is principally because we have never faced the flood of data set until very recently; measuring data set has ever been more expensive than analyzing it. Thus, only limited efforts have been spent for analysis of high dimensional data that has ever been rarely available.

Multiomics data is a typical high dimensional dataset; the number of samples (typically $<10^2$) is always less than number of features, i.e., that of mRNAs ($\sim 10^4$), that of miRNAs ($\sim 10^3$) and that of methylation sites ($\sim 10^5$). There are several methods proposed in order to integrate multiomics data formatted as matrices with distinct sizes. Figure 1 shows typical three strategies to integrate three matrices that share the M samples for which three distinct features whose numbers are N_1, N_2, and N_3 are measured. Figure 1(A), contraction, is simply merging three matrices such that they share M samples as rows while N_1, N_2, and N_3 features are aligned as columns. After merging them, all downstream analyses are performed with assuming only one feature whose number is $N_1 + N_2 + N_3$. Although this strategy looks simple, there can be multiple disadvantages. First of all, if the number of individual features, N_1, N_2, and N_3, differ from one another so much, features having the smallest number might be

© Springer Nature Switzerland AG 2019
D.-S. Huang et al. (Eds.): ICIC 2019, LNCS 11643, pp. 565–574, 2019.
https://doi.org/10.1007/978-3-030-26763-6_54

neglected. This might prevent us from considering three features equally. Even if the numbers are almost equal, if some feature has much larger amplitude than others, it also prevents us from dealing with them equally. In this sense, it is very usual to normalize individual features before the contraction. Nevertheless, the normalization might also affect the outcome, because how to normalize them is quite subjective.

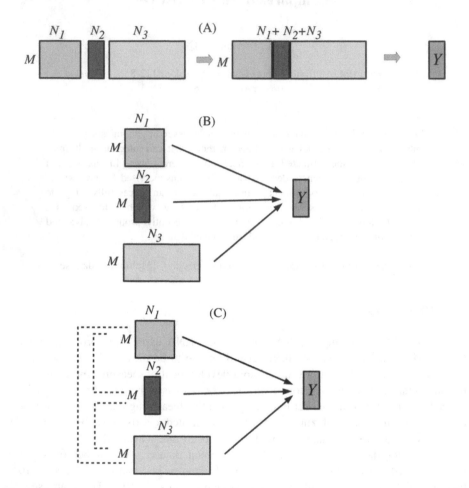

Fig. 1. Three distinct strategies that integrate multiomics formatted as matrices with distinct dimensions, $M \times N_1$, $M \times N_2$, and $M \times N_3$. (A) Contraction (B) Ensemble (C) DIABLO.

In contrast to contraction, ensemble strategy shown in Fig. 1(B) oppositely does not integrate multiomics data until very last stage. The simplest ensemble strategy is to train individual feature independently, and decision is made upon the majority rule. This strategy is also simple because we do not need any new strategies considering integration of multi omics data set. The disadvantage of this strategy is obvious. There is no justification for giving one vote to individual feature. If the majority of features are useless, i.e., do not have any practical relationship with outcome Y, voting system simple increases the noise. In this sense, ensemble can be worse than contraction that can disregard useless features during training.

The third strategy shown in Fig. 1(C), DIABLO [1], which is a part of mixOmics [2] that aims integrated analysis of multiomics data, is more advanced method. In DIABLO strategy, not individual features but sets (pairs) of individual features are employed for training. Then, outcome Y is predicted based upon ensemble strategy of them. Thus, DIABLO strategy has more ability to learn effective features from available multiomics data. One disadvantage is that how to relate individual features must be designed by human beings; this process can be quite subjective.

In this paper, in contrast to these three strategies in Fig. 1, unsupervised strategy based upon tensor decomposition (TD), in short, "TD based unsupervised feature extraction (FE)", is proposed and is applied to multiomics data set. As can be seen later, TD based unsupervised FE achieves performance competitive with that achieved by DIABLO strategy.

2 Materials and Methods

2.1 Multiomics Data Set

Data set used here is included in mixOmics package[1]. As described in the web page "Case study: TCGA"[2], this data set can be loaded into R using data ('breast.TCGA') command after installing mixOmics package. It includes 150 samples composed of 45 Basal, 30 Her2 and 75 LumA subtypes, to which 200 mRNAs, 184 miRNAs and 142 proteome expression are measured.

2.2 Tensor Decomposition

We apply TD with higher order singular value decomposition (HOSVD) [3] algorithm to case I type I tensor [4]. Starting from three matrices, $x_{i_1 j}^{\mathrm{mRNA}} \in \mathbb{R}^{200 \times 150}$, $x_{i_2 j}^{\mathrm{miRNA}} \in \mathbb{R}^{184 \times 150}$, and $x_{i_3 j}^{\mathrm{prot}} \in \mathbb{R}^{142 \times 150}$, we generate four mode tensor

$$x_{i_1 i_2 i_3 j} = x_{i_1 j}^{\mathrm{mRNA}} \cdot x_{i_2 j}^{\mathrm{miRNA}} \cdot x_{i_3 j}^{\mathrm{prot}} \tag{1}$$

and HOSVD is applied to it as

$$x_{i_1 i_2 i_3 j} = \sum_{\ell_1=1}^{200} \sum_{\ell_2=1}^{184} \sum_{\ell_3=1}^{142} \sum_{\ell_4=1}^{150} G(\ell_1, \ell_2, \ell_3, \ell_4) u_{\ell_1 i_1}^{\mathrm{mRNA}} u_{\ell_2 i_2}^{\mathrm{miRNA}} u_{\ell_3 i_3}^{\mathrm{prot}} u_{\ell_4 j} \tag{2}$$

where $u_{\ell_1 i_1}^{\mathrm{mRNA}} \in \mathbb{R}^{200 \times 200}$, $u_{\ell_2 i_2}^{\mathrm{miRNA}} \in \mathbb{R}^{184 \times 184}$, $u_{\ell_3 i_3}^{\mathrm{prot}} \in \mathbb{R}^{142 \times 142}$, and $u_{\ell_4 j} \in \mathbb{R}^{150 \times 150}$, are singular value matrices (they are also orthogonal matrices) and $G \in \mathbb{R}^{200 \times 184 \times 142 \times 150}$ is a core tensor.

---

[1] http://www.bioconductor.org/packages/release/bioc/html/mixOmics.html

[2] http://mixomics.org/mixdiablo/case-study-tcga/

3   Results

3.1   Diablo

Here I briefly summarize how well DIABLO works when it is applied to data set described in Sect. 2.1 as denoted in the web page "Case study: TCGA" (see footnote 2). The interaction assumed is mRNA-miRNA, mRNA-proteome, and miRNA-proteome.

1. Three subtypes can be discriminated with the success rate of 95% with using more than two components generated by DIABLO.
2. 15 mRNAs, 18 miRNAs and 7 proteins are selected.
3. Using features selected in step 2, heatmap is drawn. These three subtypes are well separated in the heatmap. Thus, DIABLO successfully selects limited number of features that discriminate three subtypes.

Thus, the point is if TD based unsupervised FE can achieve similar performance as those by DIABLO or not.

3.2   TD Based Unsupervised FE

As described in Sect. 2.2, HOSVD is applied to case I type I tensor, Eq. (1). Then two singular value vectors, u_{1j} and u_{4j}, turn out to discriminate three subtypes well (Fig. 2). In order to quantitatively evaluate how well these two singular value vector discriminates three subtypes, we apply linear discriminant analysis (LDA) with using leave one out cross validation (LOOCV) (Table 1). It achieved as high as 95% accuracy, which is almost equal to that by DIABLO.

Table 1. The confusion table obtained by applying LDA to three cancer subtypes with u_{1j} and u_{4j}. LOOCV is used. Row: inference, column: true subtypes. Numbers in bold represent those of correctly predicted samples.

	Basel	Her2	LumA
Basel	**42**	4	0
Her2	2	**25**	2
LumA	1	1	**73**

Next, in order to see if the limited number of mRNAs, miRNAs and proteomes can be selected to discriminate three cancer subtypes well, we select subsets of these three features. In order that, we first need to find which $u_{\ell_1 i_1}^{\mathrm{mRNA}}$, $u_{\ell_2 i_2}^{\mathrm{miRNA}}$, and $u_{\ell_3 i_3}^{\mathrm{prot}}$ are most associated with u_{1j} and u_{4j}. This requires the identification of core tensor, $G(\ell_1, \ell_2, \ell_3, \ell_4)$, having the largest absolute values with $\ell_4 = 1, 4$. Table 2 shows the list of those $G(\ell_1, \ell_2, \ell_3, \ell_4)$s with the descending order of absolute values of

$G(\ell_1, \ell_2, \ell_3, \ell_4)$s. It is obvious that $G(\ell_1, \ell_2, \ell_3, \ell_4)$s with $1 \leq \ell_1, \ell_2 \leq 2$ and $1 \leq \ell_3 \leq 4$ have larger absolute values. Then we compute the squared summation of singular value vectors attributed to i_1 th mRNA, i_2 th miRNA, and i_3 th proteome as

$$\sum_{\ell_1=1}^{2} (u_{\ell_1 i_1}^{mRNA})^2$$

$$\sum_{\ell_2=1}^{2} (u_{\ell_2 i_2}^{miRNA})^2$$

$$\sum_{\ell_3=1}^{4} (u_{\ell_3 i_3}^{prot})^2$$

and select top ranked ten mRNAs, miRNAs and proteome with larger squared summation of singular value vectors.

Figure 3 shows the heatmap generated using selected 10 mRNAs, 10 miRNAs and 10 proteome. It is obvious that three subtypes are clustered well separately; it is competitively well as compared with the heatmap generated by DIABLO (see footnote 2). In addition to this, three features that share same profiles are clustered together as in the result by DIABLO (see hierarchical clustering of columns in Fig. 3). This suggests that TD based unsupervised FE has ability to select distinct features sharing same profiles over three subtypes as DIABLO achieved.

Table 2. $G(\ell_1, \ell_2, \ell_3, \ell_4)$s sorted descending order of absolute values among those having $\ell_4 = 1, 4$.

rank	$\ell 1$	$\ell 2$	$\ell 3$	$\ell 4$	$G(\ell 1, \ell 2, \ell 3, \ell 4)$
1	1	1	1	1	−407857.582
2	1	1	4	4	−209720.615
3	2	1	1	4	−20452.480
4	2	1	3	1	−11677.505
5	2	1	4	1	−10428.742
6	2	1	2	1	10157.467
7	1	1	2	1	−8973.774
8	1	2	1	4	8360.976
9	2	1	5	4	−6628.467
10	1	1	3	4	6623.046

4 Discussions

In this paper, I applied recently proposed TD based unsupervised FE, which was applied to wide range of studies [4–34], to multiomics data analysis. Apparently, the performance achieved by TD based unsupervised FE is at most competitive to that of DIABLO. Thus, one might wonder why TD based unsupervised FE is recommended in this study. There are multiple reasons for this recommendation. First, DIABLO used random number seed to perform analysis. This means, every time we select different random number seed, we inevitably have distinct sets of selected mRNAs, miRNAs and proteome, although overall performance remains unchanged. This might be problematic because we might be interested in identification of disease causing genes. If distinct set of features are selected every time we change random number seed, it might prevent us from interpreting the outcome biologically. In contrast to this, TD based unsupervised FE can give us quite stable outcomes. Not only TD based unsupervised FE does not need random number seed, but also it is quite stable even when samples are resampled [4–34]. In this point, TD based unsupervised FE is more suitable to be employed than DIABLO form the biological point of views.

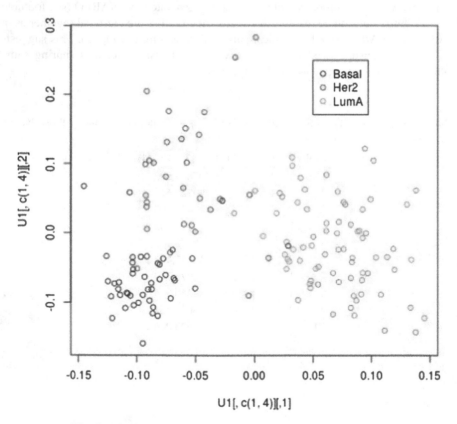

Fig. 2. Scatter plot of u_{1j} (horizontal axis) and u_{4j} (vertical axis).

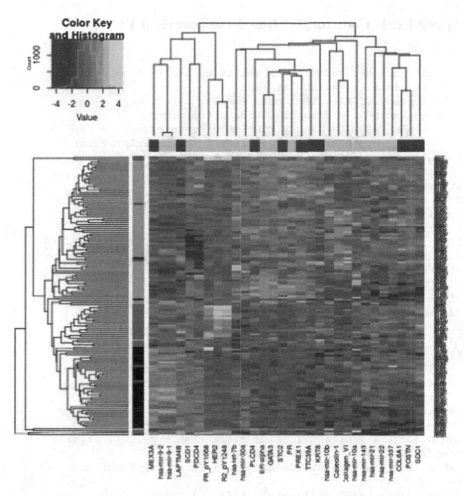

Fig. 3. Heatmap of selected 10 mRNAs (blue), 10 miRNAs (pink), and 10 proteome (cyan) in columns and 150 samples (black:Basel, red:Her2, green:Luma). Yellow: expressed expression, blue: depressed expression. (Color figure online)

Also from the computational point of views, TD based unsupervised FE is recommended more than DIABLO. From the point of computational time, DIABLO requires more time than TD based unsupervised FE, because DIABLO needs to learn from the data set and labeling while TD based unsupervised FE does not require this process due to unsupervised nature. In this sense, if these two achieve equally, TD based unsupervised FE is more recommended method than DIABLO.

Appendix: R Code for TD Based Unsupervised FE

```
install.packages("mixOmics") #mixOmics instlattion
require(mixOmics) #mixOmics load
data('breast.TCGA') #TCGA data loading
data = list(mRNA = breast.TCGA$data.train$mrna,
            miRNA = breast.TCGA$data.train$mirna,
            proteomics = breast.TCGA$data.train$protein)
install.packages("rTensor") #rTensor installation
require(rTensor) #rTensor load
#tensor generation
Z <- array(NA,c(150,200,184,142))
for (i in c(1:150))
{cat(i," ")
Z[i,,,] <-data.matrix(outer(outer(data$mRNA[i,],
data$miRNA[i,],"*"),data$proteomics[i,],"*"))}
#tensor decomposition
HOSVD <- hosvd(as.tensor(Z))
U1 <- HOSVD$U[[1]] #x_{\ell_4,J}
U2 <- HOSVD$U[[2]] #x_{\ell_1,i_1}
U3 <- HOSVD$U[[3]] #x_{\ell_2,i_2}
U4 <- HOSVD$U[[4]] #x_{\ell_3,i_3}
#150 samples scatter plot (x_{\ell_4,j})
plot(U1[,c(1,4)],col=breast.TCGA$data.train$subtype)
legend(0.05,0.25,names(summary(breast.TCGA$data.train
$subtype)),col=1:3,pch=1)
require(MASS) #MASS load
LD <-
lda(U1[,c(1,4)],breast.TCGA$data.train$subtype,CV=T,prior
=rep(1/3,3)) #liner discriminant anaysis
table(LD$class,breast.TCGA$data.train$subtype) #confusion
matrix
ZZ <-order(-abs(HOSVD$Z@data[c(1,4),,,]))
[1:20];data.frame(arrayInd(ZZ,dim(HOSVD$Z@data[c(1,4),,,]
)),HOSVD$Z@data[c(1,4),,,][ZZ]) #sorting G with ascending
order of absolute values of G
P2 <- pchisq(rowSums(scale(U2[,1:2])^2),2,lower.tail=F)
P3 <- pchisq(rowSums(scale(U3[,1:2])^2),2,lower.tail=F)
P4 <- pchisq(rowSums(scale(U4[,1:4])^2),4,lower.tail=F)
U <-
cbind(data$mRNA[,order(P2)[1:10]],cbind(data$miRNA[,order
(P3)[1:10]],data$proteomics[,order(P4)[1:10]])) #select
top 10 with larger squared summation of singular value
vectors
install.packages("gplots") #gplots install
require(gplots) #gplot load
#heatmap plot
heatmap.2(scale(U),col=rgb(seq(0,1,by=0.1),seq(0,1,by=0.1
),seq(1,0,by=-
0.1)),RowSideColors=c(rep("black",45),rep("red",30),rep("
green",75)),hclustfun=function(x){hclust(x,method="averag
e")},trace="none",ColSideColors=c(rep("blue",10),rep("pin
k",10),rep("cyan",10)))
```

References

1. Singh, A., et al.: DIABLO: an integrative approach for identifying key molecular drivers from multi-omics assays. Bioinformatics, bty1054. https://doi.org/10.1093/bioinformatics/bty1054

2. Rohart, F., Gautier, B., Singh, A., Lê Cao, K.-A.: mixOmics: an R package for 'omics feature selection and multiple data integration. PLoS Comput. Biol. **13**(11), e1005752 (2017)

3. Symeonidis, P., Zioupos, A.: HOSVD on tensors and its extensions. Matrix and Tensor Factorization Techniques for Recommender Systems. SCS, pp. 81–93. Springer, Cham (2016). https://doi.org/10.1007/978-3-319-41357-0_6

4. Taguchi, Y-h.: Tensor decomposition-based unsupervised feature extraction applied to matrix products for multi-view data processing. PLoS ONE 12(8): e0183933 (2017)

5. Ishida, S., Umeyama, H., Iwadate, M., Taguchi, Y.H.: Bioinformatic screening of autoimmune disease genes and protein structure prediction with FAMS for drug discovery. Protein Pept. Lett. **21**, 828–839 (2014)

6. Taguchi, Y.-H.: microRNA-mRNA interaction identification in Wilms tumor using principalcomponent analysis based unsupervised feature extraction. In: 2016 IEEE 16th International Conference on Bioinformatics and Bioengineering (BIBE), pp. 71–78 (2016)

7. Murakami, Y., et al.: Comprehensive analysis of transcriptome and metabolome analysis in Intrahepatic Cholangiocarcinoma and Hepatocellular Carcinoma. Sci. Rep. **5**, 16294 (2015)

8. Taguchi, Y.-H.: Identification of more feasible MicroRNA-mRNA interactions within multiple cancers using principal component analysis based unsupervised feature extraction. Int. J. Mol. Sci. **17**, 696 (2016)

9. Murakami, Y., et al.: Comprehensive miRNA expression analysis in peripheral blood can diagnose liver disease. PLoS ONE **7**, e48366 (2012)

10. Taguchi, Y.-H.: Identification of candidate drugs using tensor-decomposition based unsupervised feature extraction in integrated analysis of gene expression between diseases and DrugMatrix datasets. Sci. Rep. **7**, 13733 (2017)

11. Tamori, A., et al.: MicroRNA expression in hepatocellular carcinoma after the eradication of chronic hepatitis virus C infection using interferon therapy. Hepatol. Res. **46**, E26–E35 (2016)

12. Taguchi, Y.-H., Iwadate, M., Umeyama, H., Murakami, Y.: Principal component analysis based unsupervised feature extraction applied to bioinformatics analysis. Comput. Methods Appl. Bioinf. Anal. 153–182 (2017). https://www.worldscientific.com/doi/10.1142/9789813207981_0008

13. Taguchi, Y.H.: Principal components analysis based unsupervised feature extraction applied to gene expression analysis of blood from dengue haemorrhagic fever patients. Sci. Rep. **7**, 44016 (2017)

14. Taguchi, Y.-H., Iwadate, M., Umeyama, H., Murakami, Y., Okamoto, A.: Heuristic principal component analysis-based unsupervised feature extraction and its application to bioinformatics (2014)

15. Taguchi, Y.-H.: Principal component analysis based unsupervised feature extraction applied to publicly available gene expression profiles provides new insights into the mechanisms of action of histone deacetylase inhibitors. Neuroepigenetics **8**, 1–18 (2016)

16. Taguchi, Y.-H., Murakami, Y.: Universal disease biomarker: can a fixed set of blood microRNAs diagnose multiple diseases? BMC Res. Notes **7**, 581 (2014)

17. Taguchi, Y.-H.: Principal component analysis based unsupervised feature extraction applied to budding yeast temporally periodic gene expression. BioData Min. **9**, 22 (2016)

18. Umeyama, H., Iwadate, M., Taguchi, Y.-H.: TINAGL1 and B3GALNT1 are potential therapy target genes to suppress metastasis in non-small cell lung cancer. BMC Genom. **15**, S2 (2014)

19. Taguchi, Y.H., Murakami, Y.: Principal component analysis based feature extraction approach to identify circulating microRNA biomarkers. PLoS ONE **8**, e66714 (2013)
20. Taguchi, Y.-H., Wang, H.: Genetic association between amyotrophic lateral sclerosis and cancer. Genes (Basel) **8**, 243 (2017)
21. Taguchi, Y.-H., Iwadate, M., Umeyama, H.: SFRP1 is a possible candidate for epigenetic therapy in non-small cell lung cancer. BMC Med. Genomics **9**, 28 (2016)
22. Taguchi, Y.-H., Iwadate, M., Umeyama, H.: Principal component analysis-based unsupervised feature extraction applied to in silico drug discovery for posttraumatic stress disorder-mediated heart disease. BMC Bioinf. **16**, 139 (2015)
23. Taguchi, Y.-H., Iwadate, M., Umeyama, H.: Heuristic principal component analysis-based unsupervised feature extraction and its application to gene expression analysis of amyotrophic lateral sclerosis data sets. In: 2015 IEEE Conference on Computational Intelligence in Bioinformatics and Computational Biology (CIBCB), pp. 1–10 (2015)
24. Taguchi, Y-H., Umeyama, H., Iwadate, M., Murakami, Y., Okamoto, A.: Heuristic principal component analysis-based unsupervised feature extraction and its application to bioinformatics. In: Wang, B., Li, R., Perrizo, W. (eds.) Big Data Analytics in Bioinformatics and Healthcare, pp. 138–162. IGI global (2015)
25. Murakami, Y., et al.: Comparison of hepatocellular carcinoma miRNA expression profiling as evaluated by next generation sequencing and microarray. PLoS ONE **9**, e106314 (2014)
26. Taguchi, Y.-h.: Integrative analysis of gene expression and promoter methylation during reprogramming of a non-small-cell lung cancer cell line using principal component analysis-based unsupervised feature extraction. In: Huang, D.-S., Han, K., Gromiha, M. (eds.) ICIC 2014. LNCS, vol. 8590, pp. 445–455. Springer, Cham (2014). https://doi.org/10.1007/978-3-319-09330-7_52
27. Taguchi, Y-H.: One-class differential expression analysis using tensor decomposition-based unsupervised feature extraction applied to integrated analysis of multiple omics data from 26 lung adenocarcinoma cell lines. In: 2017 IEEE 17th International Conference on Bioinformatics and Bioengineering (BIBE), Washington, DC, pp. 131–138 (2017). https://doi.org/10.1109/bibe.2017.00-66
28. Taguchi, Y.-H.: Principal component analysis-based unsupervised feature extraction applied to single-cell gene expression analysis. In: ICIC 2018, pp. 816–826 (2018)
29. Taguchi, Y.-H., Wang, H.: Exploring microrna biomarker for amyotrophic lateral sclerosis. Int. J. Mol. Sci. **19**(5), 131 (2018)
30. Taguchi, Y.-H.: Tensor decomposition-based and principal-component-analysis-based unsupervised feature extraction applied to the gene expression and methylation profiles in the brains of social insects with multiple castes. BMC Bioinf. **19**(S9), 99 (2018)
31. Taguchi, Y.-H.: Tensor decomposition-based unsupervised feature extraction can identify the universal nature of sequence-nonspecific off-target regulation of mRNA mediated by MicroRNA transfection. Cells **7**(6), 54 (2018)
32. Taguchi, Y.-H.: Tensor decomposition–based unsupervised feature extraction for integrated analysis of TCGA data on MicroRNA expression and promoter methylation of genes in ovarian cancer. In: 2018 IEEE 18th International Conference on Bioinformatics and Bioengineering (BIBE), Taichung, Taiwan, pp. 195–200 (2018). https://doi.org/10.1109/bibe.2018.00045
33. Taguchi, Y.-H.: Drug candidate identification based on gene expression of treated cells using tensor decomposition-based unsupervised feature extraction for large-scale data. BMC Bioinf. **19**(S13), 388 (2019)
34. Taguchi, Y.-H., Wang, H.: Exploring MicroRNA Biomarkers for Parkinson's Disease from mRNA Expression Profiles. Cells **7**(12), 245 (2018)

Sequence-Based Prediction of Hot Spots in Protein-RNA Complexes Using an Ensemble Approach

Le Zhao[1], Sijia Zhang[2(✉)], and Junfeng Xia[1,2]

[1] School of Computer Science and Technology, Anhui University,
Hefei 230601, Anhui, China
[2] Institutes of Physical Science and Information Technology, Anhui University,
Hefei 230601, Anhui, China
sijiasj.zhang@foxmail.com

Abstract. RNA-binding hot spots are dominant and fundamental residues that contribute most to the binding free energy of protein-RNA interfaces. As experimental methods for identifying hot spots are expensive and time-consuming, high-efficiency computational approaches are required in predicting hot spots on a large scale. In this work, we proposed a sequence-based machine learning method to predict hot spots in protein-RNA complexes. We extracted 83 relative independent physicochemical features from a set of the 544 properties in AAindex1. Each physicochemical feature was combined with the predicted relative accessible surface area (RASA) and substitution probability feature from Blocks Substitution Matrix (BLOSUM) for training models by support vector machine (SVM) and k-nearest neighbor algorithm (k-NN). The combinations of the 166 individual models were explored and 33 top-performance models were selected to construct the final ensemble classifier by a majority voting technique. The ensemble classifier outperformed the state-of-the-art computational methods, yielding F1 score of 0.742 and AUC of 0.824 on the independent test set.

Keywords: Protein-RNA complexes · Hot spot · Ensemble method · Protein sequence feature

1 Introduction

During most biological processes, proteins work by interacting with other molecules through their interfaces, where protein-RNA interactions play key roles in regulating gene expression and structural recognition [1, 2]. Many previous studies have revealed that the binding free energy of proteins is not substantially distributed over the inter-action surfaces [3, 4]. Only a small and complementary set of interface residues termed hot spots contribute mainly to the binding free energy. As experimental technique for identifying hot spots is slow and labor-intensive, there is a need for researchers to develop alternative approaches to predict hot spots *in silico*.

Due to the crucial role played by hot spots, many studies have been developed to predict RNA-binding sites [5–9]. However, few efforts were made to identify hot spots

© Springer Nature Switzerland AG 2019
D.-S. Huang et al. (Eds.): ICIC 2019, LNCS 11643, pp. 575–582, 2019.
https://doi.org/10.1007/978-3-030-26763-6_55

in protein-RNA complexes. Previously, Barik et al. [10] used evolutionary conservation along with structural and physicochemical attributes to discriminate the binding hot spots at protein-RNA recognition sites, which is the pioneering work in this field. For the lack of public available database to analysis protein-RNA binding hot spots collected from mutagenesis experiments, Pan et al. [11] created a reference protein-RNA hot spots dataset which was manually curated from the literature. In addition, they proposed a feature-based machine-learning method called PrabHot to identify RNA-binding hot spots. Both two methods require structural information of proteins.

In this work, we developed a sequence-based prediction tool, to predict RNA-binding hot spots. In our model, only protein sequences were used as input information. We got 83 physicochemical descriptors from AAindex1 [12] and encoded sequences with each descriptor. Moreover, relative accessible surface area (RASA) and blocks substitution matrix were integrated with each descriptor to encode amino acid residues. Two algorithms radial basis function (RBF)-based support vector machine (SVM) and k-nearest neighbor algorithm (k-NN), were then employed to construct classifiers with each descriptor, and we got 166 individual classifiers. In order to improve the prediction performance, 33 optimal classifiers were selected with the highest AUC ranks. Finally, we built an ensemble vote classifier based on these 33 classifiers. The better prediction performance than the state-of-the-art methods indicates that our sequence-based approach can achieve a comparable prediction accuracy.

2   Method

2.1   Dataset

In this study, we used 47 protein-RNA complexes as our datasets which come from Pan et al.'s work [11]. Among 47 complexes, 32 were selected randomly as the training dataset including 79 hot spots and 72 non-hot spots and the other 15 complexes were used as the test dataset with 28 hot spots and 30 non-hot spots.

2.2   Sequence-Based Features

Physicochemical Features
We employed AAindex1 [12] which contains 544 physicochemical characteristics to encode every residue of our protein sequences. Owing to the highly correlated characteristics may decrease the performance of predictors with bias, we removed a subset of characteristics to ensure the correlation coefficient between any pair of characteristics was less than 0.6, which resulted in 83 descriptors [13]. Next, Hu's encoding approach called the sequence order effect was used for reference to derive physicochemical features for each residue [14], which is original from Chou et al. [15]. To improve prediction quality, both sequence order information and amino acid composition were used. The sequence order effect can be formulized as:

$$\theta_1 = \frac{1}{L-1} \sum_{i=1}^{L-1} [\Phi(R_{i+1}) - \Phi(R_i)]$$

$$\theta_2 = \frac{1}{L-2} \sum_{i=1}^{L-2} [\Phi(R_{i+2}) - \Phi(R_i)]$$

$$\theta_3 = \frac{1}{L-3} \sum_{i=1}^{L-3} [\Phi(R_{i+3}) - \Phi(R_i)] \tag{1}$$

$$\cdots$$

$$\theta_k = \frac{1}{L-k} \sum_{i=1}^{L-k} [\Phi(R_{i+k}) - \Phi(R_i)], (k = 1, 2, 3, \ldots, L-1)$$

where L is the length of sliding window, R represents a residue of protein sequences, k is the distance between two residues and k is less than $L-1$, and $\Phi(R_i)$ shows the numeralization of 83 AAindex1 descriptors on i-th residue. In Eq. (1), θ_1 is called the first-tier correlation factor when the step-size between two residues is 1, θ_2 is the second-tier correlation factor which indicates the sequence order correlation between residues are the second nearest, θ_3 is the third-tier correlation factor that reflects the third nearest sequence order correlation, and so forth. According to Eq. (1), each residue is set as the central residue of sliding window and we calculate properties of them. If the number of left or right-hand neighbors is less than $L/2$, zero is given to these void places. In this work, we applied 11 residues as the length of sliding window, that is to say, 10 properties can be obtained to encode every central residue with each descriptor from AAindex1.

Relative Accessible Surface Area (RASA)
Relative accessible surface area (RASA) of a protein residue is a measure of residue solvent exposure. Here, we applied a sequence-based tool, NetSurfP [16], to calculate RASA.

Blocks Substitution Matrix (BLOSUM)
BLOSUM is a substitution matrix used to score alignments between evolutionarily divergent protein sequences [17]. We obtained BLOSUM62 from AAindex2 database [12] as the encoding feature used in our model.

2.3   Ensemble Classifier Construction

The ensemble vote classifier (EVC) is a meta-classifier for combining similar or conceptually different machine learning classifiers for classification via majority or plurality voting. The sample labels were predicted using average probability values. Allowing for 83 descriptors from AAindex1 were included in our study, we utilized two well-known machine-learning algorithms as follow: RBF-based SVM [18] and k-NN algorithm. To construct EVC, top n classifiers were chosen in terms of AUC performance generated on the training set using 10-fold cross-validation.

2.4   Evaluation Criteria

To assess classification performance of our model, we adopted a few commonly used measures, including sensitivity (SEN), specificity (SPE), precision (PRE), F1 score (F1), Matthew's correlation coefficient (MCC) and accuracy (ACC). These measurements were defined as:

$$SEN = TP/(TP + FN) \tag{2}$$

$$SPE = TN/(TN + FP) \tag{3}$$

$$PRE = TP/(TP + FP) \tag{4}$$

$$F1 = \frac{2 \times SEN \times PRE}{SEN + PRE} \tag{5}$$

$$MCC = \frac{TP \times TN - FP \times FN}{\sqrt{(TP + FP)(TP + FN)(TN + FP)(TN + FN)}} \tag{6}$$

$$ACC = \frac{TP + TN}{TP + FP + TN + FN} \tag{7}$$

where TP, FP, TN, FN represent the number of true positive (correctly predicted hot spot residue), false positive (non-hot spot residue incorrectly predicted as hot spot), true negative (correctly predicted non-hot spot residue) and false negative (hot spot residue incorrectly predicted as non- hot spot), respectively. We also adopted the ROC curve as the evaluation measure in this work. From the ROC curve, we calculated the area under the ROC curve (AUC).

3   Results and Discussion

3.1   Features Evaluation

In our work, three groups of sequence features were used, which are physicochemical properties, RASA, and BLOSUM62. Experientially, RASA is deemed as a useful feature which has been commonly used to investigate hot spot residues in protein-protein compounds [15, 19, 20]. Here, we evaluated the performance of each feature group to find out how they impact on our model. The comparison results on the training set measured by AUC score can be seen in Fig. 1. When BLOSUM62 is removed, the AUC value decreases from 0.857 to 0.722 (ΔAUC = 0.135), and the performance is worse when RASA is excluded, with the AUC score 0.699 (ΔAUC = 0.158). The results show that RASA is an indispensable and discriminative feature to define hot spots.

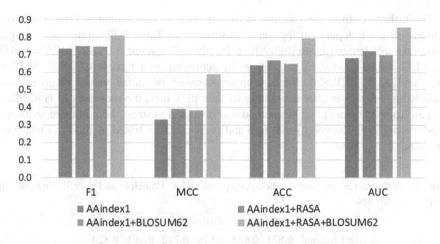

Fig. 1. Importance evaluation of features used in our method.

Table 1. Performance of our method compared with other methods on the training set.

Method	SEN	SPE	PRE	F1	MCC	AUC
Our method	**0.848**	0.736	0.779	**0.812**	**0.589**	0.857
Our method-50	0.847	0.644	0.724	0.780	0.505	0.827
PrabHot	0.784	**0.761**	**0.782**	0.754	0.513	**0.860**
PrabHot-50	0.757	0.748	0.768	0.745	0.502	0.832
HotSPRing	0.681	0.552	0.617	0.667	0.280	0.699

Note: The highest value in each column is shown in bold. Our
method-50 and PrabHot-50 represent the average performance
across 50 times of 10-fold cross-validation.

3.2 Compared with Other Methods

Recently, two computational methods PrabHot and HotSPRing were published to
predict RNA-binding hot spots. In order to make a fair comparison among three
methods, we used 10-fold cross-validation to evaluate predictor performance on 32
complexes (training set). To precisely evaluate the model, Pan et al. iterated 10-fold
cross-validation for 50 times and this resulted in PrabHot-50. For the same purpose, we
used the average performance of 10-fold cross-validation across 50 runs. Meanwhile,
we set the prediction threshold as 0.561 to get a maximized F1 score. As we can see in
Table 1, our method shows similar success rate in comparison with PrabHot. The F1
score, MCC and AUC of our model on the training set is 0.812, 0.589 and 0.857
respectively, while PrabHot correctly predicts hot spots with F1 score = 0.754,
MCC = 0.513 and AUC = 0.860. HotSPRing, which is the first prediction tool in this
field, correctly identifies RNA-binding hot spots with F1 score = 0.667, MCC = 0.280
and AUC = 0.699. From the high sensitivity score we can see that our method performs better in identifying hot spots than non-hot spots on the training set.

To further confirm the robustness of our model, we compared three prediction methods on the independent test set. Performance in Table 2 illustrates that our predictor displays better discernibility than PrabHot (F1 score = 0.742, MCC = 0.453, and AUC = 0.804) on the same dataset by achieving an F1 score of 0.742, MCC of 0.461 and AUC of 0.824. Because there were no predicted values returned from HotSPRing web server after submitting the complex files, the measures of HotSPRing were all from PrabHot [11]. Our method was designed to stress the point that sequence-based method owns as good prediction ability as structure-based method in identifying hot spots.

Table 2. Performance of our method compared with PrabHot and HotSPRing on the independent test set.

Method	SEN	SPE	PRE	F1	MCC	AUC
Our method	**0.821**	0.633	0.676	**0.742**	**0.461**	**0.824**
PrabHot	0.793	**0.655**	**0.697**	0.742	0.453	0.804
HotSPRing	0.655	0.552	0.604	0.633	0.258	0.658

Note: The highest value in each column is shown in bold.

3.3   Case Study: Human HnRNP A2/B1 Protein Bound to 10-mer RNA Complex

Heterogeneous nuclear ribonucleoproteins (hnRNPs) play a vital role in RNA splicing, modification, location and translation. Each hnRNP contains at least one RNA-binding domain (RBD). For this complex (PDB ID: 5HO4), experiments identified two hot spots and four non-hot spots on the protein chain (Fig. 2A). The prediction results of our method and PrabHot can be found in Fig. 2B and C. It is obvious that two non-hot spots (H108 and F24) were wrongly predicted by PrabHot and only one non-hot spot (F24) was wrongly identified by our method.

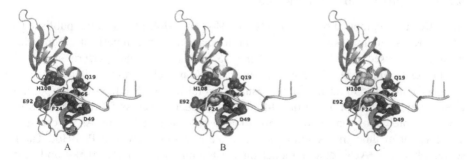

Fig. 2. The hot spot residues identified by experiments (A) compared with the prediction results of two methods, our method (B) and PrabHot (C). The lightblue chain represents the protein sequence (PDB ID: 5HO4, chain A) while the yellow chain represents the RNA sequence (PDB ID: 5HO4, chain B). Red residues in spheres denote experimentally identified hot spots, blue residues in spheres denote experimentally identified non-hot spots and green residues in B and C denote mistakenly predicted residues. (Color figure online)

4 Conclusion

In this article, we proposed a sequence-based method to distinguish hot spots and non-hot spots on protein-RNA interfaces. To develop our model, a total of 83 descriptors were extracted from AAindex1 database. Every residue was encoded by a physico-chemical descriptor using 11-length sliding window, which results in 10 features. Combined with RASA and BLOSUM62, a total of 12-dimensional features were extracted for each residue. Two algorithms RBF-based SVM and k-NN were then used to build the ensemble classifier based on 33 selected optimal classifiers. The prediction results show that the sequence-based approach we proposed can yield a good performance which is comparable to structural methods.

Apart from the distinguished performance of our predictor, there is still room to improve our method. As nowadays most explored features are related to protein and amino acid, we will excavate more RNA-related features and put them into our model. Meanwhile, we aim to construct an optional model for both sequence and structure information provided so that this flexible model can predict potential hot spots and non-hot spots with or without structural information.

Acknowledgement. This work was supported by the National Natural Science Foundation of China (61672037, 21601001, and 11835014), the Anhui Provincial Outstanding Young Talent Support Plan (gxyqZD2017005), the Young Wanjiang Scholar Program of Anhui Province, the Recruitment Program for Leading Talent Team of Anhui Province (2019-16), the China Post-doctoral Science Foundation Grant (2018M630699) and the Anhui Provincial Postdoctoral Science Foundation Grant (2017B325).

References

1. König, J., et al.: Protein-RNA interactions: new genomic technologies and perspectives. Nat. Rev. Genetics **13**(2), 77 (2012)
2. Ellis, J.J., Broom, M., Jones, S.: Protein-RNA interactions: structural analysis and functional classes. Proteins: Struct. Funct. Bioinf. **66**(4), 903–911 (2007)
3. Clackson, T., Wells, J.A.: A hot spot of binding energy in a hormone-receptor interface. Science **267**(5196), 383–386 (1995)
4. Moreira, I.S., Fernandes, P.A., Ramos, M.J.: Hot spots-A review of the protein-protein interface determinant amino-acid residues. Proteins: Struct. Funct. Bioinf. **68**(4), 803–812 (2007)
5. Kumar, M., Gromiha, M.M., Raghava, G.: Prediction of RNA binding sites in a protein using SVM and PSSM profile. Proteins: Struct. Funct. Bioinf. **71**(1), 189–194 (2008)
6. Liu, Z.-P., et al.: Prediction of protein-RNA binding sites by a random forest method with combined features. Bioinformatics **26**(13), 1616–1622 (2010)
7. Tang, Y., et al.: A boosting approach for prediction of protein-RNA binding residues. BMC Bioinf. **18**(13), 465 (2017)
8. Walia, R.R., et al.: RNABindRPlus: a predictor that combines machine learning and sequence homology-based methods to improve the reliability of predicted RNA-binding residues in proteins. PLoS One **9**(5), e97725 (2014)
9. Yang, X., et al.: SNBRFinder: a sequence-based hybrid algorithm for enhanced prediction of nucleic acid-binding residues. PLoS One **10**(7), e0133260 (2015)

10. Barik, A., et al.: Probing binding hot spots at protein-RNA recognition sites. Nucleic Acids Res. **44**(2), e9 (2015)
11. Pan, Y., et al.: Computational identification of binding energy hot spots in protein-RNA complexes using an ensemble approach. Bioinformatics **34**(9), 1473–1480 (2017)
12. Shuichi, K., et al.: AAindex: amino acid index database, progress report 2008. Nucleic Acids Res. **36**(Database issue), D202–D205 (2008)
13. Chen, P., et al.: Accurate prediction of hot spot residues through physicochemical characteristics of amino acid sequences. Proteins: Struct. Funct. Bioinf. **81**(8), 1351–1362 (2013)
14. Hu, S.-S., et al.: Protein binding hot spots prediction from sequence only by a new ensemble learning method. Amino Acids **49**(10), 1773–1785 (2017)
15. Chou, K.C.: Prediction of protein cellular attributes using pseudo-amino acid composition. Proteins: Struct. Funct. Bioinf. **43**(3), 246–255 (2001)
16. Morten, N., et al.: A generic method for assignment of reliability scores applied to solvent accessibility predictions. BMC Struct. Biol. **9**(1), 51 (2009)
17. Henikoff, S., Henikoff, J.G.: Amino acid substitution matrices from protein blocks. Proc. Nat. Acad. Sci. **89**(22), 10915–10919 (1992)
18. Chang, C.-C., Lin, C.-J.: LIBSVM: a library for support vector machines. ACM Trans. Intell. Syst. Technol. (TIST) **2**(3), 27 (2011)
19. Xia, J.-F., et al.: APIS: accurate prediction of hot spots in protein interfaces by combining protrusion index with solvent accessibility. BMC Bioinf. **11**(1), 174 (2010)
20. Zhu, X., Mitchell, J.C.: KFC2: a knowledge-based hot spot prediction method based on interface solvation, atomic density, and plasticity features. Proteins: Struct. Funct. Bioinf. **79**(9), 2671–2683 (2011)

Realtime Computer Vision-Based Accurate Vehicle Counting and Speed Estimation for Highways

C. Shiranthika[1] [ID], P. Premaratne[2]([⊠]) [ID], Z. Zheng[2],
and B. Halloran[2][ID]

[1] Faculty of Information Technology, University of Moratuwa,
Moratuwa, Sri Lanka
[2] School of Electrical, Computer and Telecommunications Engineering,
Faculty of Engineering and Information Sciences, University of Wollongong,
Wollongong, Australia
prashan@uow.edu.au

Abstract. In Australian urban roads, pneumatic tubes are temporarily installed over roads to determine the road usage by vehicles. This is a relatively expensive process and the data cannot be obtained for about two weeks until a manual retrieval of data. This data is collected very randomly in order to determine the road usage in Australia. However, since the manual labor of installing such a device is very expensive in Australia, such deployments are rare and do not provide adequate information to the Road Maritime Services in Australia for future design and management of roads.

We have developed a highly accurate real-time computer vision-based system which relies on back ground subtraction, morphological operations and Gaussian filtering to track centroid of vehicles and accurately determine their speeds and count them. The system also sends speed alerts when congestion lowers the allowable speeds on highways. The real-time processing is achieved through optimization of our algorithms implemented using OpenCV. The code optimization has resulted in real-time operation of our system requiring no more processing power than that is available on a typical modern smartphone. The system is robust against typical lighting variations due to the movement of the sun and can maintain the accuracy in a drizzle or cloud movement making the system very practicable for deployment in Australian highways. In order to avoid the occlusion problem faced by many vision-based traffic monitoring systems, we have placed our cameras strategically above the highways with excellent results.

Keywords: Computer vision · OpenCV · Gaussian filtering

1 Introduction

In many countries, traffic flow monitoring is already a significant issue when thousands of cameras are monitoring parts of their road network. However, almost all these cameras simply relay video of traffic information and human subjects should man them to interpret traffic conditions. In Australia, many urban areas deploy temporally installed

© Springer Nature Switzerland AG 2019
D.-S. Huang et al. (Eds.): ICIC 2019, LNCS 11643, pp. 583–592, 2019.
https://doi.org/10.1007/978-3-030-26763-6_56

pneumatic tubes to count the road usage to determine the number of vehicles on certain stretches of roads which are not monitored through cameras as shown in Fig. 1. Such temporary deployments of pneumatic tubes along with their counters are expensive for local governments and the data they provide can only be collected after a fortnight. The system we have developed to determine the road usage has shown to be very accurate in daytime and operates in real-time. The data that is the speed and the number of vehicles counted are transmitted in real-time to a base station for traffic analysis.

There have been many systems developed in the world to calculate the speed and the number of vehicles travelling on high speed road systems. However, these systems are extremely expensive and only used in major road networks sparingly. This invites small scale low-costs systems to be developed that would measure road usage and speeds of motor vehicles on urban roads. We have developed a system based on computer vision with very high accuracy that operates in real time. Our system utilizes processing power of no more than that is available on a modern smartphone.

Fig. 1. Pneumatic tube-based traffic counters in Australia.

2   Related Work

In 2016, Miller *et al.* described a vehicle counting and speed estimation approach using hidden Markov models [1]. Their approach used tracking of state to take advantage of constrained vehicle motion to detect and count vehicles using a hidden Markov model. Observations for the model were provided by a trained Haar feature vehicle detector. These detections were robust enough in *stop and go traffic* and changes in lighting and camera motion, which would normally interfere with motion-based vehicle detection and counting. They managed to show that their method was able to provide significantly better vehicle volume counts than both multiple targets moving object tracking and virtual detection line (VDL) on a dataset of over 88 h of video. On one of their test sets, the proposed method achieved a median 5 minute-bin error of 0.0686 for this counting task while the multiple target motion tracking and VDL implementations had median errors of 0.0957 and 0.2290 respectively. One of the setbacks of their approach was that it did not achieve real-time operation.

Tamersoy *et al.* describes a method of tracking and speed estimation that also relies on Markovian model with modest success in 2010 [2]. Their approach was tested on high way surveillance video and was not run in real-time. The proposed approach employed vehicle detection and tracking modules. In the detection module, an automatically trained binary classifier detected vehicles while providing robustness against viewpoint, poor quality videos and clutter. Efficient tracking was then achieved using a simplified multi-hypothesis approach. In their implementation, first an over-complete set of tracks is created considering every observed detection within a time interval. As needed, hypothesized detections were generated to force continuous tracks. Finally, a scoring function was used to separate the valid tracks in the overcomplete set. They claimed that their tracking system achieved accurate results in significantly challenging highway surveillance videos.

Subaweh *et al.* describes an implementation based on Pixel Based Adaptive Segmenter Model for Background Subtraction method to perform object tracking and counting [3]. Pixel Based Adaptive Segmenter has been used as a background model for background subtraction method. CvBlob was used as the library to perform vehicle tracking with vehicles that have minimum of 500-pixel areas and 20000 maximum pixel areas in video surveillance. Using background subtraction process, result of segmentation was reported to be influenced by illumination change, weather, outdoor views, shadows, and small object on video surveillance. On the process of vehicle tracking, vehicle tracking accuracy depended on foreground pixel area. Large foreground pixel area resulted in more accurate tracking of vehicles. They reported that the vehicle counting was dependent on the accurate tracking of vehicles.

Seenouvong *et al.* presented a method of using visual surveillance to track and count vehicles [4]. Their approach used background subtraction technique to find foreground objects in a video sequence. In order to detect moving vehicles more accurately, several computer vision techniques, including thresholding, hole filling and adaptive morphological operations were then applied. Finally, vehicle counting was performed using a virtual detection zone. Experimental results showed that the accuracy of the proposed vehicle counting system was around 96%.

Li *et al.* proposed an adaptive subtracted background method to count vehicle and track them in 2014 [5]. They managed to accurately separate the vehicle foreground from the adaptive background model through a combination of Otsu's thresholding method and moving cast shadow detection method. In vehicle tracking and counting, they applied both virtual detector and blob tracking to increase the accuracy of their method. However, their system seems to be accurate only when one vehicle at a time is detected.

In the past, Zhang *et al.* [6] and Yang *et al.* [7] had developed accurate systems which are considered the state-of-the-art which has inspired our work, yet they failed to operate in real-time. The real-time operation of a traffic monitoring system is paramount as without which, the system does not offer any practical solution for traffic analysis. Both Zhang *et al.* and Yang *et al.* used Foreground Time-spatial Images (FTSI) concept where they develop a snapshot of detected images of vehicles into a time referenced graph. We have deviated from Zhang's approach and developed our own centroid tracking of detected blobs (vehicles) passing a VDL with excellent results.

Vehicle counting from an unmanned aerial vehicle (UAV) has become a popular research topic in traffic monitoring. Xiang *et al.* describes a camera mounted on UAV to capture aerial videos to estimate the traffic information [8]. Compared with traditional sensors, the UAV can be flexibly deployed to the areas that need to be monitored and can provide a larger perspective. Their work describes a novel framework for vehicle counting based on aerial videos where the moving-object detector can handle both static background and moving background. A pixel-level video foreground detector is deployed to handle static background which can update background model continuously. Image-registration is employed to estimate the camera motion, which allows the vehicles to be detected in a reference coordinate system in the case of moving background. They deploy an online-learning tracker to overcome the change of scale and shape of vehicle in images which can update the samples used for training. They also designed a multi-object management module which could efficiently analyze and validate the status of the tracked vehicles with multi-threading technique. They reported a success rate of 85% for moving background and 90% for static background for vehicle counting.

3   Vehicle Detection

Vehicle detection is the fundamental step in vehicle counting and speed estimation and has been previously attempted with methods such as frame difference [9], optical flow [10], Background Subtraction (BS) [11] etc. Nevertheless, frame difference and optical flow methods are not able to track the vehicles with low speeds or the stationary vehicles meanwhile BS provides better accuracy for counting vehicles with a stationary camera. Our work uses another method namely foreground detection with VDL, which is widely used to detect and count vehicles [9]. There are several stages for vehicle detection; background initialization, VDL and Region of Interest (ROI) settings, foreground detection and background update. To generate the background, we need several empty frames without vehicles. This is not difficult to achieve with a stationary camera as the background does not change (only minor variation due to lighting conditions). The next step is to set ROI and VDL. By setting ROI, the computer can focus on a specific area for processing rather than the entire frame thereby optimizing the processing power. The VDL is set as a reference line to determining the crossing of a centroid (of a vehicle) across it to determine a vehicle passing. Next step is the foreground detection. The relationship between the foreground component and background component can be explained by the following equation, where $B(x, y)$ refers to the coordinate of background pixel and $I(x, y)$ refers to the new incoming pixel coordinate. $F(x, y) = 1$ indicates that the new incoming value I is closer to the certain pre-determined threshold value $R(x, y)$ than the minimum value of the background samples while $F(x, y) = 0$ shows that there is no foreground component detected [6].

$$F(x,y) = \begin{cases} 1 \ \# \ \{ \text{dist}(I(x,y), B(x,y)) < R(x,y) \} < \# \ \text{min} \\ 0 \quad \text{else} \end{cases}$$

The complete vehicle counting stages are depicted in the flowchart of Fig. 2 where 'Draw Result' stage depicts the centroid based counting approach.

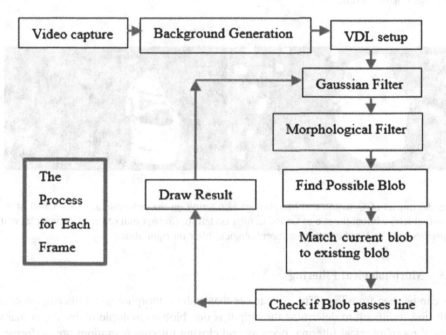

Fig. 2. Flow chart of the proposed system for vehicle counting.

3.1 Pre-processing

Realtime operation of computer vision systems with limited processing power demands removal of unwanted features. The colour of a vehicle offers useful features to recognize vehicle types or makes yet, for vehicle counting, such information is redundant. The purpose of grey scale processing in our approach is to remove the colour information of the original image and only keep the brightness information, which is necessary for applying many filtering techniques. The quality of vehicle detection is seriously affected by various types of image noise and artefacts due to lighting changes, cloud cover, reflection from motor vehicles and appendages attached to vehicles.

3.2 Gaussian Filtering

As we can see from Fig. 3 (a), without Gaussian filtering, there are lot of small noise-related artefacts generated due to slight variations in color in Background Subtraction process. The Gaussian filter is a linear smoothing filter and it produces a new weighted average of the previous image. The value of each pixel is obtained by weighted averaging of itself and other pixel values in the neighborhood. The specific operation of Gaussian filtering is to scan each pixel in the image with a template (or convolution mask), and to replace the value of the center pixel of the template with the weighted average grey value of the pixels in the neighborhood determined by the template. The outcome of this process is to replace any noise affected pixel with an average value of its neighboring pixels.

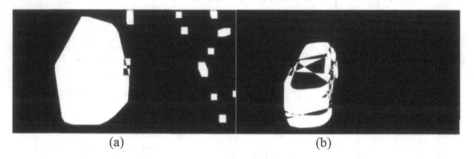

(a)   (b)

Fig. 3. Impact of Gaussian and Morphological filtering on the outcome, a. Convex hull of the blob (vehicle) without the use of Gaussian filter on left. b. Convex hull of the blob (vehicle) with Gaussian filter and without the use morphological filter on right above.

3.3 Morphological Filtering

As can be seen from Fig. 3(b), we can see that without morphological filtering, system will find it difficult to determine the output is one blob or multiple blobs. As in many typical morphological filtering, opening and closing filtering operations are performed with a structural element. We experimentally found an element of size 15 × 15 was ideal for our case. Both opening and closing functions comprise of fundamental erosion and dilation operations. The function of erosion is to eliminate unrelated details from the image, and the function of dilation is to bridge any cracks. The opening operation is to first perform erosion and then dilation, which will generally break the narrow discontinuities and eliminates the fine protrusions, while the closing operation usually eliminates narrow discontinuities and long narrow gaps, eliminates small holes and fills the breaks in the contour. The combination of open and close operations can smooth the contour of the active object.

3.4   Convex Hull of the Blob

After the morphological filtering as shown Fig. 4(c), it is more advantageous to develop it into a convex hull as shown in Fig. 4(d). Convex hull is typically known as the simplest convex polygon; a set of points can create where the points lie in the polygon perimeter. Comparing Fig. 4(b) with (d) clearly points out the advantage of convex hull based centroid calculation where a vehicle will undoubtedly form a solid blob unlike any artefacts due to lighting variations in the process.

Vehicle Counting Based on Centroid Tracking: In order to count vehicles, centroid tracking is proposed in our work. Looking at Fig. 3(d), centroid of this convex hull shape (blob) is simply determined to track its movement over consecutive frames. The main idea of the centroid tracking algorithm is to set up a VDL in every frame and count the vehicle when the centroid of the vehicle passes the line [12]. To track the centroid of the object consecutively, Euclidean distance is used for letting the system assume that two centroids in two consecutive frames belong to the same vehicle if the Euclidean distance is less than a certain threshold. For instance, in our experiment, we have this Euclidean distance threshold at 5 pixels as the stretch of the road we are monitoring have two tracks and with the given speeds on the road, it is unlikely that vehicle on one track veer onto another track in about 75 ms.

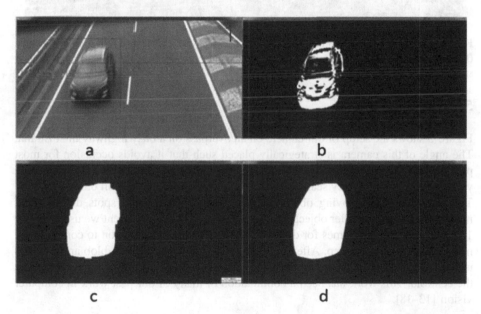

Fig. 4. Capture of a vehicle and its pre-processing stages, a. Vehicle is captured and tracked, b. Thresholded image with Gaussian filtering to remove noise, c. Figure 4(b) after undergoing morphological operations, d. Obtained convex hull or the 'blob' ready for determining the centroid.

4   Speed Estimation of Vehicles

As discussed in the previous section, Euclidean distance can be used to determine the velocity of a vehicle as well. The main idea is to calculate Euclidean distance between two centroids which meets the condition such that they represent the same vehicle in two consecutive frames and then divide this distance by the time difference of the two consecutive frames. The Euclidean distance in pixel coordinates represent a certain scaled value of true distance in metres as the location of the camera (its height above the road and the angle) is unique to each camera deployment.

Fig. 5. Strategic placement of the camera above a highway. a. Urban stretch of road in Australia (left). b. Camera placement to avoid occlusion and count vehicles in real-time and estimate their speed (right).

5   Discussion

Figure 5 shows the setup of our camera on an overpass on a busy highway in Australia. The angle of this camera is strategically placed such that it avoids occlusion for most practical cases. We use Gaussian filter to remove the main image noise. The threshold value we use is 30 for grey scale using 256 levels which works well in our experiment. This determines the moving objects of course with some noisy spots due to road-markings and other smaller objects on the road. The structural element we use is of size 15×15 and is used 3 times for dilation followed by once for erosion to complete our morphological filtering step. After applying the morphological filter, blob analysis was used to find the convex hull and draw the contour of the object and then to determine the centroid. This work has been a continuation of many of our past work in computer vision [13–18].

6   Conclusion

We have developed a vehicle counting method that drew inspiration from the state-of-the-art system developed by Zhang *et al.* [6]. However, our approach provides a real-time vehicle counting ability with the least amount of processing power unlike Zhang *et al.* which relies on Foreground Time-spatial Images (FTSI) which bring unnecessary complexity and suffers from occlusions. Our approach relies on developing a complex hull blob for each vehicle and determining the centroid of consecutive frames to determine whether the centroids belong to the same vehicle and if then, whether they pass a VDL to count the vehicle. We use the time difference between consecutive frames and a scale factor that reflects camera distance and camera angle to determine the speed of the vehicle accurately. We have conducted multiple experiments for hours to determine the accuracy of our system to ascertain its operation in real-time. Our system is very robust yet, simpler than the state-of-the-art requiring minimum processing resources for real-time operation. One of the limitations of our system is that we have not tested its ability to operate during night as low lighting conditions will have a significant impact on our various processing stages. However, this aspect will be investigated in our future research.

References

1. Miller, N., Thomas, M.A., Eichel, J.A., Mishra, A.: A hidden Markov model for vehicle detection and counting. In: 12th Conference on Computer and Robot Vision, pp. 269–276 (2015)
2. Tamersoy, B., Aggarwal, J.K.: Counting vehicles in highway surveillance videos. In: International Conference on Pattern Recognition, pp. 3631–3635 (2010)
3. Subaweh, M.B., Wibowo, E.P.: Implementation of pixel based adaptive segmenter method for tracking and counting vehicles in visual surveillance. In: International Conference on Informatics and Computing (ICIC) (2016)
4. Seenouvong, N., Watchareeruetai, U., Nuthong, C., Khongsomboon, K., Ohnishi, N.: A computer vision-based vehicle detection and counting system. In: 8th International Conference on Knowledge and Smart Technology (KST) (2016)
5. Li, D., Liang, B., Zhang, W.: Real-time moving vehicle detection, tracking, and counting system implemented with OpenCV. In: 4th IEEE International Conference on Information Science and Technology, pp. 631–634 (2014)
6. Zhang, Y., Zhao, C., Zhang, Q.: Counting vehicles in urban traffic scenes using foreground time-spatial images. IET Intel. Trans. Syst. **11**(2), 61–67 (2017)
7. Yang, M., Jhang, R., Hou, J.: Traffic flow estimation and vehicle-type classification using vision-based spatial–temporal profile analysis. IET Comput. Vis. **7**(5), 394–404 (2013)
8. Xiang, X., Zhai, M., Lv, N., Saddik, A.: Vehicle counting based on vehicle detection and tracking from aerial videos. Sensors **18**, 2560 (2018). https://doi.org/10.3390/s18082560
9. Zhan, C., Duan, X., Xu, S., Song, Z., Luo, M.: An improved moving object detection algorithm based on frame difference and edge detection. In: Fourth International Conference on Image and Graphics (ICIG 2007), pp. 519–523 (2007)
10. Haag, M., Nagel, H.: Combination of edge element and optical flow estimates for 3D-model-based vehicle tracking in traffic image sequences. Int. J. Comput. Vis. **35**(3), 295–319 (1999)
11. Niu, L., Jiang, N.: A moving objects detection algorithm based on improved background subtraction. In: 2008 Eighth International Conference on Intelligent Systems Design and Applications, vol. 3, pp. 604–607 (2008)
12. Cheon, M., Lee, W., Yoon, C., Park, M.: Vision-based vehicle detection system with consideration of the detecting location. IEEE Trans. Intell. Transp. Syst. **13**(3), 1243–1252 (2012)

13. Premaratne, P., Yang, S., Zou, Z., Vial, P.: Australian sign language recognition using moment invariants. In: Huang, D.-S., Jo, K.-H., Zhou, Y.-Q., Han, K. (eds.) ICIC 2013. LNCS (LNAI), vol. 7996, pp. 509–514. Springer, Heidelberg (2013). https://doi.org/10.1007/978-3-642-39482-9_59

14. Premaratne, P., Ajaz, S., Premaratne, M.: Hand gesture tracking and recognition system for control of consumer electronics. In: Huang, D.-S., Gan, Y., Gupta, P., Gromiha, M.Michael (eds.) ICIC 2011. LNCS (LNAI), vol. 6839, pp. 588–593. Springer, Heidelberg (2012). https://doi.org/10.1007/978-3-642-25944-9_76

15. Premaratne, P., Premaratne, M.: Image similarity index based on moment invariants of approximation level of discrete wavelet transform. Electron. Lett. **48**(23), 1465–1467 (2012)

16. Premaratne, P., Premaratne, M.: Key-based scrambling for secure image communication. In: Huang, D.-S., Gupta, P., Zhang, X., Premaratne, P. (eds.) ICIC 2012. CCIS, vol. 304, pp. 259–263. Springer, Heidelberg (2012). https://doi.org/10.1007/978-3-642-31837-5_38

17. Premaratne, P., Nguyen, Q., Premaratne, M.: Human computer interaction using hand gestures. In: Huang, D.-S., McGinnity, M., Heutte, L., Zhang, X.-P. (eds.) ICIC 2010. CCIS, vol. 93, pp. 381–386. Springer, Heidelberg (2010). https://doi.org/10.1007/978-3-642-14831-6_51

18. Premaratne, P., Ko, C.C.: Retrieval of symmetrical image blur using zero sheets. In: IEE Proceedings: Vision, Image and Signal Processing, vol. 148, no. 1, pp. 65–69 (2001)

Comparison of Various Weighted K-Nearest Neighbor Methods for Positioning Systems Using Visible LED Lights

Huy Q. Tran[ID] and Cheolkeun Ha[✉]

Robotics and Mechatronics Lab,
Ulsan University, Ulsan 44610, Republic of Korea
cheolkeun@gmail.com

Abstract. K-nearest neighbor (kNN) is one of the most popular methods used in indoor positioning systems. The estimated position is, nevertheless, the center of the area formed by some fingerprints which have the smallest Euclidean distance, regardless of the difference between these distances. This leads to an error in the prediction process. In this paper, to improve the positioning accuracy, some variants of kNN, namely Weighted kNN (WkNN), are suggested. In addition to evaluating the quality of each method, we provide a detailed comparison of all methods together to figure out the optimal solution for the visible LED light positioning system. The obtained results show that all the proposed WkNN methods can significantly improve the positioning accuracy. However, the level of improvement is not exactly the same. In the best case, our proposed solution achieves an improvement by 100-fold compared to traditional kNN method.

Keywords: Indoor positioning · Visible light · Weighted k-nearest neighbor

1 Introduction

In recent years, optical wireless communication (OWC)-based applications have marked an obvious advance as a result of the progress of several advanced OWC technologies such as visible light communication (VLC), light fidelity (LiFi), optical camera communication (OCC), free space optical communication (FSOC), and light detection and ranging (LiDAR) [1]. Among those technologies, VLC has been receiving positive evaluations from researchers because it can provide illumination, data communication, and localization at the same time. VLC can be used for both indoor and outdoor environments. However, the adverse influence of sunlight is a major cause of the limitation of VLC-based outdoor applications [2]. On the contrary, VLC shows outstanding advantages in indoor environment thanks to the availability of light-emitting diode (LED) lighting system and LED's suitability for data communication and positioning purposes.

For VLC-based indoor positioning, many methods have been applied such as angle of arrival (AOA) [3, 4], time of arrival (TOA) [5, 6], time difference of arrival (TDOA) [7], and fingerprinting [8]. Although each method has varying degrees of complexity

© Springer Nature Switzerland AG 2019
D.-S. Huang et al. (Eds.): ICIC 2019, LNCS 11643, pp. 593–603, 2019.
https://doi.org/10.1007/978-3-030-26763-6_57

and accuracy, the fingerprinting method is a preferred choice because of its simplicity and high positioning accuracy.

In deterministic methods, k-nearest neighbor (kNN) is the most commonly used solution [8–10]. In Reference [8], by finding the nearest fingerprints of the received signal strength (RSS), Vongkulbhisal et al. showed that their approach achieved an accuracy of up to centimeters. To improve the positioning accuracy, Van et al. suggested an advanced Weighted kNN (WkNN) solution to overcome the disadvantage of traditional kNN algorithm [9]. In that paper, the authors proved that the performance of location estimation process was very encouraging, despite the negative impact of ambient light. In addition to two-dimensional positioning system, VLC and KNN also worked well in three-dimensional environment [10]. The experimental results proved that their solution reached the accuracy of 7 cm and reduced the estimated location error of 0–6 cm thanks to the combination of kNN and weighted average's estimation.

In this paper, we combine fingerprinting with kNN method to determine the location of the object carrying the photo-detector (PD). To improve the positioning accuracy, the Euclidean distances computed from kNN are weighted and the actual value of weight varies in inverse proportion to its Euclidean distance. However, each WkNN method achieves different estimation results.

The main contribution of this paper are as follows:

- We propose new WkNN methods, which show a noticeable improvement in VLC based indoor positioning system.
- We also provide comparisons of all methods together. The obtained results are the basis for choosing the optimal WkNN solution for further studies.

The rest of this paper is organized as follows: In Sect. 2, the overview of the visible light positioning system and our proposed solutions are provided. In Sect. 3, simulation results and discussion are thoroughly presented. Finally, Sect. 4 offers our conclusion.

2 Overview of Visible Light Positioning and Proposed Solution

2.1 VLC Model Channel

In this paper, a line-of-sight channel was assumed as shown in Fig. 1, where h is the distance between the LED and the optical receiver, d is the distance from LED to the floor surface, Φ and ψ are the irradiance angle and the incident angle, respectively. FOV is the field-of-view angle of the receiver, $\Phi_{1/2}$ is the semi-angle of each LED light.

For simplicity, we only consider the line-of-sight channel, which has the total received optical power given by [11]:

$$P_R = \sum_{i=1}^{4} H_{oi} P_T \tag{1}$$

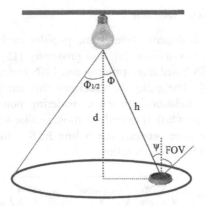

Fig. 1. VLC line-of-sight channel

where P_T is the total transmitted optical power; H_{oi} is the channel DC gain, which is shown as follows [12]:

$$H_o = \begin{cases} \left(\frac{n+1}{2\pi}\right)\left(\frac{A}{h^2}\right)\cos^n(\phi)T_s(\psi)g(\psi)\cos(\psi), & 0 \le \psi \le FOV \\ 0, & \psi > FOV \end{cases} \quad (2)$$

where A is the effective area of the PD; h is the distance between LED light and the PD.

The performance of the VLC-based positioning solution is mainly affected by two kinds of noises, including shot noise and thermal noise. These noises have a negative effect on the signal-to-noise ratio (SNR). The SNR is usually measured in decibels and can be expressed as [12]:

$$SNR = 10log_{10}\frac{R^2P_R^2/A^2}{\sigma_{thermal}^2 + \sigma_{shot}^2} \quad (3)$$

where R is the responsivity of the PD; $\sigma_{thermal}^2$, σ_{shot}^2 are the thermal noise variance and shot noise variance.

2.2 Received Signal Strength (RSS) and Fingerprinting

Indoor positioning systems using VLC can achieve high accuracy based on a number of different algorithms such as AOA, TOA, TDOA, RSS, vision analysis, fingerprinting [13]. Recently, a combination of RSS and fingerprinting has been one of the preferred options due to its simplicity and acceptable positioning accuracy. This solution can be conducted based on two distinct modes: offline mode and online mode. In this paper, a 25×25 fingerprinting grid is assumed. The RSS at each fingerprinting is gathered in the offline mode. Then, these data are used to calculate the Euclidean distance (4) in the online mode.

2.3   Weighted K-Nearest Neighbor

To estimate locations with fingerprinting, some popular methods are used including deterministic [8–10, 14], probabilistic [9], and proximity [15]. In deterministic methods, a combination of RSS-based fingerprinting and kNN is needed to achieve a higher positioning accuracy [9]. The main drawback of this method is that it is time-consuming to find the correlation between considering point and all the reference points. In this paper, the main task is to find the most similar RSS values by computing the nearest Euclidean distance between the online RSS values and the offline RSS values. This distance can be given as follows:

$$d_j = \sqrt{\sum_{i=1}^{n} \left(RSS_i^{online} - RSS_{ij}^{offline} \right)^2} \tag{4}$$

where n is the number of LED; RSS_i^{online} and $RSS_{ij}^{offline}$ are the RSS gathered in the online mode and in the offline mode, respectively.

From the Euclidean distance, the location of the PD can be estimated. However, this location is based on the average value of the nearest points, which does not accurately reflect the actual coordinate of the PD. To achieve higher positioning accuracy, each Euclidean distance is weighted. In Reference [9], the authors proposed a simple but effective WkNN solution for VLC-based indoor positioning system. The weight is calculated as follows:

$$w_i = 1 - \frac{d_i}{\sum_{j=1}^{k} d_j} \tag{5}$$

Besides the method that is proven in VLC-based positioning applications, other approaches are also mentioned. In Reference [16], the authors used the WkNN algorithm as an important part to improve the positioning accuracy for the narrow-band signal in IoT networks. In that paper, the weight is assigned to each nearest point given by:

$$w_i = \frac{1/d_i}{\sum_{j=1}^{k} \left(1/d_j \right)} \tag{6}$$

In this paper, we also propose the third kind of WkNN to create favorable conditions for later comparison process. By inversing the square of Euclidean distance, we have:

$$w_i = \frac{1}{d_i^2} \tag{7}$$

After finding the weight for each neighbor, the estimated location of the PD can be determined as follows:

$$(\tilde{x}, \tilde{y}) = \left(\frac{\sum_{i=1}^{k} w_i x_i}{\sum_{i=1}^{k} w_i}, \frac{\sum_{i=1}^{k} w_i y_i}{\sum_{i=1}^{k} w_i} \right) \qquad (8)$$

where $\tilde{x}, \tilde{y}$ are the estimated location; x_i, y_i are the nearest neighbors.

Summary, we have three distinct approaches to WkNN given as follows (Table 1):

Table 1. WkNN methods

Name	1th weight	2nd weight	3rd weight
Weight equation	$w_i = 1 - \dfrac{d_i}{\sum_{j=1}^{k} d_j}$	$w_i = \dfrac{1/d_i}{\sum_{j=1}^{k} (1/d_j)}$	$w_i = \dfrac{1}{d_i^2}$

3 Simulation and Discussion

3.1 Simulation Configuration

In visible LED light positioning systems, the typical architecture is shown in Fig. 2. In this model, the structure of the room, the distribution of LED lights, and the type of optical receiver are the most important specifications. To achieve the most realistic results, we assume that four LED lights are suspended from the ceiling of a room (5 m × 5 m × 3 m). The power of a LED light is 20 W. The physical detection area of the PD is 1 cm^2. The field of view angle of the PD and the semi-angle of each LED light are 70°. Assume that the original coordinate is in the center of the floor, each LED is attached to the ceiling and is located at a distance of 1.25 m away from the two nearest walls.

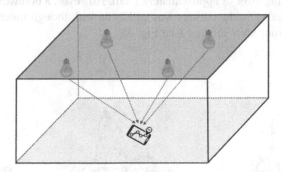

Fig. 2. VLC model

3.2 Performance Evaluation

This section described the simulation results and statistical analyses based on different algorithms including kNN and improved WkNN versions. To accurately evaluate the positioning performance of each method, the positioning errors were determined and depicted from Figs. 3, 4, 5, 6 and 7.

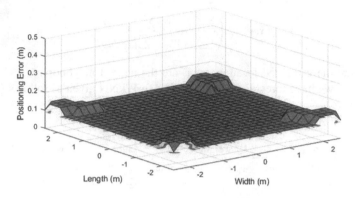

Fig. 3. Positioning error by kNN

After applying kNN method, the estimated positioning error was shown in Fig. 3 and Table 2. It was observed that the estimated locations are consistently distributed. However, the positioning accuracy was relatively low when the average positioning errors were approximately in the range of 10–14 cm. As discussed above, the main drawback of kNN is that it is difficult to determine the exact estimated location when the Euclidean distances between the considering point and the nearest points are not the same, mainly because the estimated position in traditional kNN method is actually the average value of the Euclidean distances despite their actual magnitude. In order to overcome that weakness, the weight of each Euclidean distance was proposed.

By using WkNN methods, Figs. 4, 5 and 6 showed a significant improvement in positioning quality. Although different approaches were applied, similar positioning performances were presented in Figs. 4 and 5. In these Figures, our solutions produced the mean positioning error of approximately 1 cm. However, a noteworthy point is that the positioning quality in the corners was still quite bad, though much better than the results obtained from kNN method (see Fig. 3).

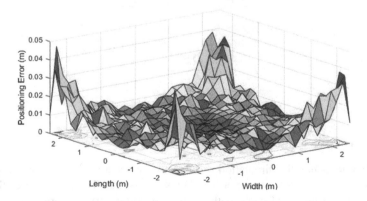

Fig. 4. Positioning error by 1st weight method

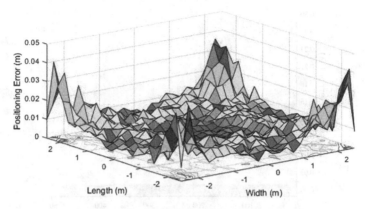

Fig. 5. Positioning error by 2nd weight method

As can be seen in the Fig. 6, the last proposed solution (7) revealed the best positioning accuracy with the average positioning error of 0.65 mm. The outstanding performance of this method was also reflected in the room corners and near the edge areas where the distribution of the signal-to-noise ratio is the lowest. This proposed solution achieved a noticeable improvement by nearly 100-fold compared to traditional kNN method.

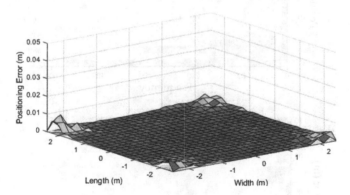

Fig. 6. Positioning error by 3rd weight method

Table 2. Positioning error and standard deviation with kNN and WkNN methods

Compared parameters	kNN	WkNN methods		
		1st weight	2nd weight	3rd weight
Maximum error (mm)	141.42	50.56	42.56	11.19
Minimum error (mm)	100.00	1.59	1.22	3.88×10^{-3}
Mean error (mm)	105.09	9.79	9.63	0.65
Standard deviation (mm)	13.60	5.88	5.86	1.02

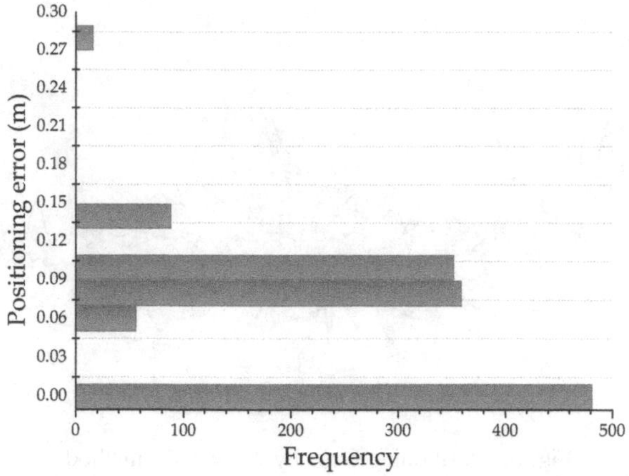

(a)

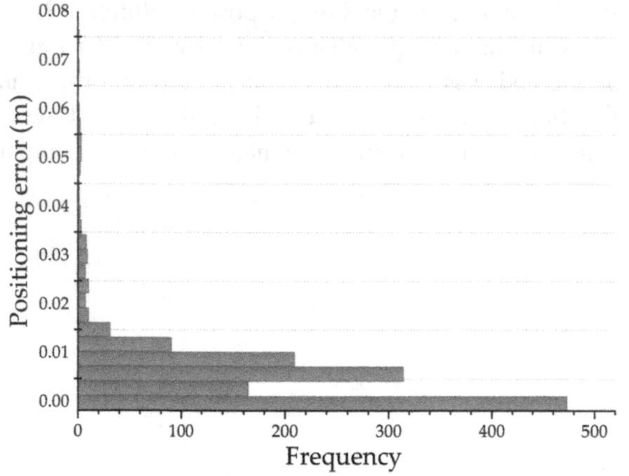

(b)

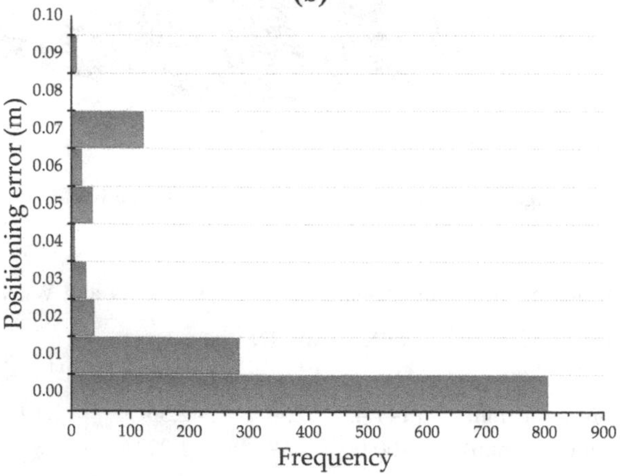

(c)

Fig. 7. Histogram of positioning error by (a) kNN, (b) 1st weight, (c) 2nd weight, (d) 3rd weight

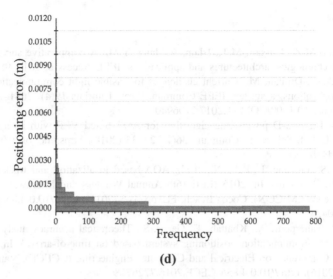

Fig. 7. (*continued*)

To comprehensively evaluate the performance of each proposed method, the histogram of positioning error of each method was surveyed as illustrated in Fig. 7. It can be clearly seen that the positioning accuracy is gradually improved from Fig. 7a to d. Especially, most of the estimated positions in the last WkNN method (7) had extremely low errors and their distribution is almost identical. In addition to the level of positioning accuracy, a noticeable improvement in standard deviation was also an encouraging plus point for the proposed solutions. In Table 2, the figures revealed a modest decrease in the standard deviation from 13.6 mm with kNN to 1.02 mm with the 3rd WkNN method. These results demonstrated that each WkNN method achieved different performance, however all of them provided superior positioning accuracy compared to classic kNN algorithm.

4 Conclusion

In this work, we investigated some improved WkNN methods for visible LED lights based indoor positioning systems. The proposed WkNN algorithms showed outstanding achievements in positioning accuracy compared with traditional kNN method, although each approach achieved a different level of accuracy. The improvement was revealed not only in the positioning error but also in the standard deviation. In the best case, our solution provided a mean positioning accuracy of 0.65 mm. To evaluate the quality of the proposed solution in detail, there are still some issues that need to be addressed in our future work. The impact of multipath reflection, and the changes in the specifications of the optical transmitter and receiver should be thoroughly examined.

Acknowledgments. This work was supported by Korea Hydro & Nuclear Power company through the project "Nuclear Innovation Center for Haeoleum Alliance".

References

1. Chowdhury, M.Z., Hossan, M.T., Islam, A., Jang, Y.M.: A comparative survey of optical wireless technologies: architectures and applications. IEEE Access **6**, 9819–9840 (2018)
2. Căilean, A.M., Dimian, M.: Current challenges for visible light communications usage in vehicle applications: a survey. IEEE Commun. Surv. Tutorials **19**(4), 2681–2703 (2017). https://doi.org/10.1109/COMST.2017.2706940
3. Steendam, H.: A 3-D positioning algorithm for AOA-based VLP with an aperture-based receiver. IEEE J. Sel. Areas Commun. **36**(1), 23–33 (2018). https://doi.org/10.1109/JSAC.2017.2774478
4. Eroglu, Y.S., Guvenc, I., Pala, N., et al.: AOA-based localization and tracking in multi-element VLC systems. In: 2015 IEEE 16th Annual Wireless and Microwave Technology Conference (WAMICON), Cocoa Beach, FL, pp. 1–5 (2015). http://10.0.4.85/WAMICON.2015.7120424
5. Amini, C., Taherpour, A., Khattab, T., Gazor, S.: Theoretical accuracy analysis of indoor visible light communication positioning system based on time-of-arrival. In: 2016 IEEE Canadian Conference on Electrical and Computer Engineering (CCECE), Vancouver, BC, pp. 1–5 (2016). http://10.0.4.85/CCECE.2016.7726718
6. Wang, T.Q., Sekercioglu, Y.A., Neild, A., Armstrong, J.: Position accuracy of time-of-arrival based ranging using visible light with application in indoor localization systems. J. Lightwave Technol. **31**(20), 3302–3308 (2013). https://doi.org/10.1109/JLT.2013.2281592
7. Do, T.-H., Yoo, M.: TDOA-based indoor positioning using visible light. Photon Netw. Commun. **27**(2), 80–88 (2014)
8. Wang, C., Wang, L., Chi, X., Liu, S., Shi, W., Deng, J.: The research of indoor positioning based on visible light communication. China Commun. **12**(8), 85–92 (2015). https://doi.org/10.1109/CC.2015.7224709
9. Vongkulbhisal, J., Chantaramolee, B., Zhao, Y., Mohammed, W.S.: A fingerprinting-based indoor localization system using intensity modulation of light emitting diodes. Microw. Opt. Technol. Lett. **54**(5), 1218–1227 (2012)
10. Van, M.T., Van Tuan, N., Son, T.T., Le-Minh, H., Burton, A.: Weighted k-nearest neighbour model for indoor VLC positioning. IET Commun. **11**, 864–871 (2017). https://doi.org/10.1049/iet-com.2016.0961
11. Xu, M., Xia, W., Jia, Z., Zhu, Y., Shen, L.: A VLC-based 3-D indoor positioning system using fingerprinting and K-nearest neighbor. In: 2017 IEEE 85th Vehicular Technology Conference (VTC Spring), Sydney, NSW, pp. 1–5 (2017). http://10.0.4.85/VTCSpring.2017.8108345
12. Komine, T., Nakagawa, M.: Fundamental analysis for visible-light communication system using LED lights. IEEE Trans. Consum. Electron. **50**(1), 100–107 (2004). https://doi.org/10.1109/TCE.2004.1277847
13. Zhuang, Y., Hua, L., Qi, L., Yang, J., Cao, P., et al.: A survey of positioning systems using visible LED lights. IEEE Commun. Surv. Tutor. **20**, 1963–1988 (2018). https://doi.org/10.1109/COMST.2018.2806558
14. Do, T.H., Yoo, M.: An in-depth survey of visible light communication based positioning systems. Sensors **16**, 678 (2016). https://doi.org/10.3390/s16050678
15. Kail, G., Maechler, P., Preyss, N., Burg, A.: Robust asynchronous indoor localization using LED lighting. In: Proceedings of IEEE International Conference on Acoustics, Speech, and Signal Processing (ICASSP), Florence, Italy, pp. 1866–1870 (2014)

16. Zhao, Y., et al.: Proximity report triggering threshold optimization for network-based indoor positioning. In: Proceedings of 18th International Conference on Information Fusion (Fusion), Washington, DC, USA, pp. 1061–1069 (2015)
17. Li, Z., Braun, T., Zhao, X., Zhao, Z., Hu, F., Liang, H.: A narrow-band indoor positioning system by fusing time and received signal strength via ensemble learning. IEEE Access **6**, 9936–9950 (2018). https://doi.org/10.1109/ACCESS.2018.2794337

Parameters Optimization for Support Vector Regression Based Indoor Visible Light Localization

Huy Q. Tran(iD) and Cheolkeun Ha(⊠)

Robotics and Mechatronics Lab, Ulsan University,
Ulsan 44610, Republic of Korea
cheolkeun@gmail.com

Abstract. In this paper, we optimize parameters of indoor visible light local-ization system based on support vector regression algorithm to achieve higher positioning accuracy. Additionally, some other popular supervised machine learning algorithms such as linear regression, artificial neural networks, and k-nearest neighbors are also implemented. Then, we compare these solutions together to demonstrate the superiority of our approach. This solution is simulated in a hypothetical space of $5 \text{ m} \times 5 \text{ m} \times 3 \text{ m}$. To obtain satisfactory perfor-mance, a system of four LED lights and a photodiode are used to transmit and receive optical power, respectively. In the proposed system, the location estima-tion process is divided into two distinct sub-processes: offline stage and online stage. In the offline stage, data collection and data training are carried out. The results obtained from this stage and the current data in the online stage are the base to determine the current location of the object carrying the photodiode. The simulation results prove that our approach can achieve positioning accuracy of almost 7.4 cm.

Keywords: Support vector regression · Indoor positioning · Visible light

1 Introduction

Recently, Light Emitting Diode (LED) has been widely used in data communication and indoor positioning applications. In data transmission field, LED is highly appre-ciated because visible light communication (VLC) provides high data rates, wide bandwidth, and heightened security [1, 2]. For indoor positioning system (IPS), VLC has initially proved its effectiveness thanks to the use of advanced LED technology which is considered as the main lightning system in the future [2]. VLC-based posi-tioning systems have several outstanding advantages such as working stably in RF sensitive area, being less effected by multipath reflections than other signals (i.e., RF, WiFi), utilizing the availability of LED light sources, obtaining high positioning accuracy [3]. In indoor environment, the limitation of global positioning system (GPS) leads to the development of other alternative technologies such as WiFi [4], RF [5], VLC [6, 7]. In those solutions, VLC is a novel technique that brings high efficiency and VLC is also one of the top choices for real applications which require high accuracy positioning [8–10].

© Springer Nature Switzerland AG 2019
D.-S. Huang et al. (Eds.): ICIC 2019, LNCS 11643, pp. 604–616, 2019.
https://doi.org/10.1007/978-3-030-26763-6_58

Support vector machine (SVM) is a discriminative classifier that belongs to supervised machine learning. SVM can be applied for both classification and regression. In regression field, this algorithm is known as support vector regression (SVR) [11]. In Reference [12], Zhang *et al.* proposed an advanced SVM for indoor localization. By comparison with other popular machine learning algorithms including k-nearest neighbor, back propagation neural network, and traditional SVM, the obtained results proved that their solution achieved higher positioning accuracy and lower computational complexity. In the same way, Shi *et al.* [13] applied SVR to determine the location of the mobile object in IEEE 802.11 environments. Then, these authors compared their approach with the neural network methods. Their solution also improved the error in the positioning process, the demand for storage capacity, and the computation cost.

In indoor visible light localization applications, many researchers have also used machine learning as an affective solution to improve the positioning accuracy. Gradim *et al.* [14] utilized clustering method and outlier removal to achieve an improvement of 35% in accuracy. Similarly, Saadi *et al.* [15] proved that the average localization accuracy of their solution can reach 31 cm by using K-means clustering. Additionally, a combination of a simple regression with linear and nonlinear least square estimator was proposed by Shawky *et al.* [16]. In this approach, the positioning system achieved a mean positioning accuracy in the range from 22 cm to 37 cm. It is clear that machine learning based IPS has recently yielded very positive results.

In this paper, we present a comprehensive analysis and evaluation of the VLC based IPS using SVR which is known as one of the most powerful machine learning algorithms. The key contributions in this work are summarized as follows:

- We optimize specific some important technical parameters in VLC system based upon SVR. Specifically, we investigate the impacts of the half-power semi-angle, the field-of-view (FOV) angle, the transmitted optical power, and the distance between the LED lights and the floor.
- After the optimization process, we perform an assessment of positioning errors with other popular supervised machine learning algorithms, including linear regression (LR), artificial neural networks (ANN), and k-nearest neighbors (KNN). Then, we provide a comparison between our proposed solution and those algorithms. These results serve as a premise for investigation of other advanced SVR in the future.

The rest of this paper is organized as follows: the VLC channel model and the proposed solution are provided in Sect. 2. Section 3 presents simulation results and performance analysis. The conclusion is shown in Sect. 4.

2 VLC Channel Model and Proposed Solution

2.1 VLC Channel Model

The proposed VLC system consists of three following basic sections: transmitter section, optical channel section and receiver section as depicted in Fig. 1. In the transmitter section, the signals were created by a signal generator module, then these signals were transmitted to the LED driver, which was used to regulate the power to each LED. The encoded and modulated signals are sent to the receiver via the line-of-sight channel. After passing through the optical concentrator and optical filter, photodiode or photo-detector (PD) received these data and transferred them into digital data. Finally, the location estimation process could be done thanks to these data and the proposed algorithm.

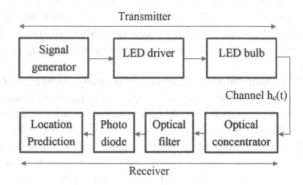

Fig. 1. VLC channel model

In this paper, the received signal strength of each LED at each reference point was collected as shown in Fig. 2. Assume that a 25×25 grid of reference points was applied, the intensity of optical power can be computed as follows.

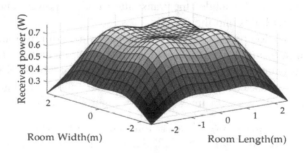

Fig. 2. The distribution of received optical power

The output electrical signal $y(t)$ can be shown as [17]:

$$y(t) = Rx(t) \otimes h_c(t) + N(t) \tag{1}$$

where R is the PD responsibility, $x(t)$ is the input optical signal and convolved with the total channel impulse $h_c(t)$, $N(t)$ is the Gaussian noise.

The total channel impulse consists of the line-of-sight (LOS) link and the non-line-of-sight (NLOS) link. In our work, the NLOS channel was ignored as the room wide enough, thus the total channel impulse is given as [18]:

$$h_c(t) = \frac{n+1}{2\pi d^2} A_{det} cos_\theta^n cos_\varphi \tag{2}$$

where A_{det} is the detector effective area, d is the distance from LED to PD, θ is the irradiance angle, φ is the incidence angle, n is the Lambertian emission order and this component is described as [18]:

$$n = \frac{-\ln(2)}{\ln(cos\theta_{1/2})} \tag{3}$$

Where $cos\theta_{1/2}$ is the half-power semi-angle of an LED

The variance of Gaussian noise is the sum of the shot noise from background radiation, the shot noise from received signal, the shot noise from dark current, and the thermal noise [17]:

$$\sigma_{total}^2 = \sigma_{BR}^2 + \sigma_{RS}^2 + \sigma_{DC}^2 + \sigma_{TN}^2 \tag{4}$$

The shot noise from background radiation is given as:

$$\sigma_{BR} = \sqrt{2\gamma I_p I_{nbf} B} \tag{5}$$

where γ is the electronic charge, I_p is the photocurrent due to background radiation, I_{nbf} is the noise bandwidth factor, B is the equivalent noise-bandwidth of the photodiode.

The shot noise from received signal is given as:

$$\sigma_{RS} = \sqrt{2\gamma R P_R B} \tag{6}$$

where P_R is the received optical power

The shot noise from dark current is given by:

$$\sigma_{DC} = \sqrt{2\gamma I_{dc} B} \tag{7}$$

where I_{dc} is the dark current in photodiode

The thermal noise is given by:

$$\sigma_{TN} = \sqrt{\frac{8\pi\kappa T_a}{G} \eta A I_2 B^2 + \frac{16\pi^2 \kappa T_k \Gamma}{g} \eta^2 A^2 I_3 B^3} \tag{8}$$

where κ is the Boltzmann's constant, T_a is the absolute temperature, G is the open-loop voltage gain, η is the fixed capacitance of PD per unit area, A is the effective area of photodiode, Γ is the FET channel noise factor, g is the FET transconductance, and I_3 is the noise-bandwidth factor.

2.2   Proposed Solution

In this section, the location estimation process is presented. To locate the current position of the PD, this process is divided into two separate modes as shown in Fig. 3. In the offline mode, the intensity of the received signal from all the reference points are gathered, then the data training process using SVR is executed. In the online mode, the received signal strength at the current location are firstly collected k consecutive times by the PD. Next, the location prediction process is conducted by connecting the trained data in the offline mode and the current data in the online mode. Finally, the estimated location of the object carrying the optical sensor is inferred. From this location, we can completely determine the positioning error based on the root mean square error (RMSE) equation as follows:

$$RMSE = \sqrt{\frac{\sum_{i=1}^{N}(y_i - \hat{y}_i)^2}{N}} \tag{9}$$

where y_i is i^{th} real location, $\hat{y}_i$ is the ith estimated location, N is the number of locations.

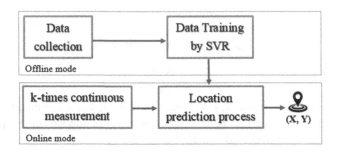

Fig. 3. Proposed SVR based IPS diagram

In this paper, we use SVR as a main key to figure out the optimal parameters of the VLC system because it is one of the most powerful supervised machine learning. The way SVR works similar to SVM. To minimize the error, the margin of the hyperplane is maximized. Assume that (x_i, y_i) is the given training data where x_i denotes the received signal strength, the function f(x) can be found from the obtained target y_i. The linear function f(x) is described as [19]:

$$f(x) = w^T \theta(x) + b \tag{10}$$

where w is the weight, b is the bias, and $\theta(x)$ is a nonlinear mapping function.

To calculate the support vector weight w and the bias b, this can be expressed as a convex optimization problem as follow [13]:

$$\text{minimize } \frac{1}{2}\|w^2\| + C\sum_{i=1}^{n}(\xi_i + \xi_i^*) \tag{11}$$

Subject to

$$\begin{cases} y_i - w^T\theta(x_i) \leq \varepsilon + \xi_i \\ w^T\theta(x_i) - y_i \leq \varepsilon + \xi_i^* \\ \xi_i, \xi_i^* \geq 0, i = 1, \ldots, N \end{cases} \tag{12}$$

where w is the margin, C is a regularization constant, ξ_i and ξ_i^* are upper and lower constrains on the model output, (x_i, y_i) is the training set, ε is empirical parameter.

In this paper, the radial basis function kernel is used and defined as [13]:

$$K_{RBF}(x, x') = exp\left[-\frac{\|x - x'^2\|}{\sigma^2}\right] \tag{13}$$

Where σ is a parameter specified by user.

3 Simulation Results and Analysis

3.1 Simulation Configuration

To execute the proposed solution, a hypothetical environment and a VLC channel are created as shown in Fig. 4. In this Figure, h and d are the distance from four LED suspended on the ceiling to the floor, and the distance between an LED and PD, respectively. θ is the irradiance angle and φ is the incident angle. The value of θ and φ depend on the relative position between LED system and the PD.

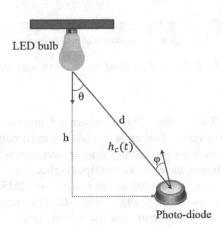

Fig. 4. Line-of-sight channel

3.2   Parameters Optimization

3.2.1   Semi-angle at Half Illuminance

When we steadily increase the semi-angle at half illuminance, the positioning accuracy gradually improve as showed in Table 1 and Fig. 5. The worst circumstance appears corresponding to an angle of 10°. When this angle comes to 40°, the positioning quality reached steady state and the best performance occurs when this angle is 70°. A remarkable point here is that both RMSE and mean accuracy score show a better improvement only if the semi-angle is 20° onwards.

Table 1. Positioning quality according to semi-angle

Semi-angle (degree)	10	20	30	40	50	60	70	80	90
RMSE (m)	1.095	0.334	0.111	0.0899	0.0814	0.0805	0.0751	0.0764	0.0765
Accuracy Score (%)	71.56	99.72	99.73	99.81	99.84	99.85	99.87	99.87	99.86
Standard deviation (m)	0.0583	0.0415	0.0101	0.0035	0.0034	0.0049	0.0056	0.0042	0.0061

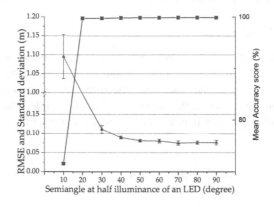

Fig. 5. RMSE and standard deviation vs semi-angle

3.2.2   FOV Angle

It can be seen in the Table 2 and Fig. 6, when we increase the FOV angle, the positioning RMSE lightly varies. This error reaches the maximum value corresponding to a FOV angle of 90°. In this case, the positioning accuracy is less dependent on the FOV angle because we ignore the effect of multipath reflections. The mean errors are in the range of 74.5–81.8 mm. In contrast to the stability of RMSE, the mean accuracy scores gradually decrease as the FOV angle increased. An exception occurs when the FOV angle is 10°. The accuracy score and the RMSE reach the highest value at an angle of 20°.

In addition to RMSE, the standard deviation (StD) of each case of FOV angle is presented in Table 2. The lowest StD value occurs when FOV is 30° and the it receives the highest value when FOV is 90°.

From the above analysis, the worst situation happens when the FOV angle is set to 90°. By contrast, to satisfy high positioning accuracy, low StD, and high score, an angle of 20° is an optimal selection.

Table 2. Positioning quality according to FOV angle

FOV angle (degree)	10	20	30	40	50	60	70	80	90
RMSE (m)	0.0759	0.0745	0.0761	0.0755	0.0751	0.0779	0.7814	0.0788	0.0818
Accuracy Score (%)	92.91	98.54	95.98	92.56	89.15	86.23	84.16	82.78	82.3
Standard deviation (m)	0.0053	0.0045	0.0037	0.0068	0.0055	0.0046	0.0049	0.0063	0.0078

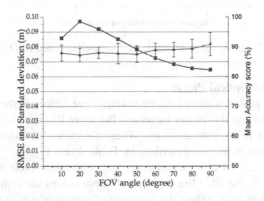

Fig. 6. RMSE and standard deviation *vs.* FOV angle

3.2.3 Distance Between an LED and the Floor

As depicted in Fig. 7, a change in the distance from an LED to the floor can lead to a significant variation in positioning error. It is clear that a very close or very far distance produced a lower positioning accuracy. In this work, the optimal distance is in the range of 3 m to 5 m. In this range, the mean positioning errors is approximately 75 mm.

To evaluate the performance of the proposed algorithm, the mean accuracy score of training process is computed. Although the distance between LED and the floor gradually increases from 1 m to 8 m, the accuracy score remains stable. In this case, this distance does not affect the algorithm's performance (Table 3).

Table 3. Positioning quality according to distance between LED and receiver

Distance (m)	1	2	3	4	5	6	7	8
RMSE (m)	0.2011	0.0912	0.0763	0.0745	0.0751	0.0964	0.1075	0.1541
Accuracy Score (%)	99.21	99.81	99.87	99.87	99.86	99.79	99.742	99.471
Standard deviation (m)	0.0207	0.0046	0.0047	0.00852	0.006	0.0042	0.0077	0.0129

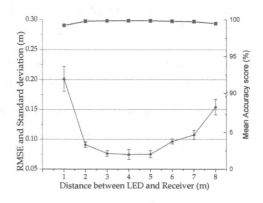

Fig. 7. RMSE and standard deviation *vs.* Distance between LED and receiver

3.2.4   Transmitted Optical Power

Transmitted optical power is one of the most important factors in the VLC system. As shown in Fig. 8, the more this power increases, the more RMSE decreases. From 20 W and more, the errors reach a steady state. When the transmitted optical power is less than 20 W, very large errors are described in Table 4 and Fig. 8.

Similar to the previous case, we also see an equivalent result of training scores, which are depicted by the blue line in Fig. 8. These scores are quite stable and high with approximately 98.18%. When the transmitted optical power is lower than 20 W, the training accuracy scores are also low but not significant. Therefore, we can affirm that the training quality is less affected by transmitted power.

Table 4. Positioning quality according to transmitted optical power

Transmitted power (W)	1	5	10	20	30	40	50
RMSE (m)	0.6905	0.2062	0.1287	0.07769	0.0765	0.0798	0.0808
Accuracy Score (%)	89.04	99.12	99.65	99.86	99.87	99.86	99.85
Standard deviation (m)	0.0457	0.0209	0.0155	0.0043	0.0055	0.0045	0.0039

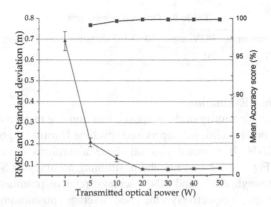

Fig. 8. RMSE and standard deviation *vs* transmitted optical power

3.3 Performance Evaluation

3.3.1 Error Analysis

According to the above experiments in Sect. 3.2, the optimal VLC parameters are shown in Table 5. From these parameters, we carry out an assessment of the error distribution on the entire surface of the room by analyzing the histogram of the positioning errors as illustrated in Fig. 9. It can be found that most of the errors are less than 10 cm. Specifically, the probability of positioning errors in the range of $5 \div 10$ is the largest and accounts for 59%. By contrast, the number of points with the errors greater than 10 cm is negligible. These points often belong to the corners where the received signal strengths is always low.

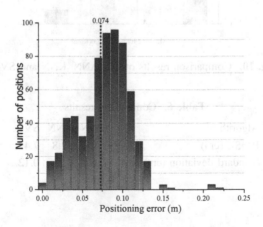

Fig. 9. Histogram of positioning errors

Table 5. Optimal parameters

Parameters	Semi-angle	FOV angle	LED-PD distance (m)	Transmitted power (W)
Optimal value	70	20	3	30

3.3.2   Performance Evaluation

In order to verify the superiority of the proposed solution, we make a direct comparison between SVR and other traditional supervised machine learning algorithms, including LR, ANN, and KNN. It is noted that all these algorithms have been optimized beforehand. From Fig. 10, we find that the positioning accuracy of SVR is superior to the remaining. Although ANN and KNN achieve relative promising accuracy with 25.1 cm and 12.8 cm, respectively, the best average positioning error of these approaches is 7.4 cm, which is achieved by SVR. In addition to positioning error, we also evaluate the StD of each method. We find that both SVR and KNN reveal the same StD value, while the StD of LR and ANN are the worst. Specific values are described in detail in Table 6.

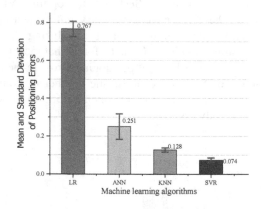

Fig. 10. Comparison results of LR, ANN, KNN and SVR

Table 6. Comparison results

Algorithm	LR	ANN	KNN	SVR
RMSE (cm)	76.7	25.1	12.8	7.4
Standard deviation (cm)	0.4	0.67	0.11	0.12

4   Conclusion

In this paper, we introduced an SVR algorithm based indoor positioning solution using visible LED light. To evaluate the performance of the proposed solution, comprehensive statistical results were presented in turn, such as the impact of semi-angle at half illuminance, FOV, the distance from LED light to the floor, the transmitted optical power. From these results, we selected the most suitable system parameters. In the future, some weighted SVR methods will be studied and applied to improve the positioning accuracy. Besides improving the algorithms, optimizing relevant technical parameters of the proposed system is also an important step to achieve better performance.

Acknowledgments. This work was supported by Korea Hydro & Nuclear Power company through the project "Nuclear Innovation Center for Haeoleum Alliance".

References

1. Vanus, J., Stratil, T., Martinek, R., Bilik, P., Zidek, J.: The possibility of using VLC data transfer in the smart home, vol. 49, no. 25, pp. 176–181. Elsivier (2016). https://doi.org/10.1016/j.ifacol.2016.12.030
2. Pathak, P.H., Feng, X., Hu, P., Mohapatra, P.: Visible light communication, networking, and sensing: a survey, potential and challenges. IEEE Commun. Surv. Tutorials **17**(4), 2047–2077 (2015). https://doi.org/10.1109/comst.2015.2476474
3. Luo, J., Fan, L., Li, H.: Indoor positioning systems based on visible light communication: state of the art. IEEE Commun. Surv. Tutorials **19**(4), 2871–2893 (2017). https://doi.org/10.1109/comst.2017.2743228
4. Zou, H., Jin, M., Jiang, H., Xie, L., Spanos, C.J.: WinIPS: WiFi-based non-intrusive indoor positioning system with online radio map construction and adaptation. IEEE Trans. Wirel. Commun. **16**(12), 8118–8130 (2017). https://doi.org/10.1109/TWC.2017.2757472
5. Haute, T.V., et al.: Platform for benchmarking of RF-based indoor localization solutions. IEEE Commun. Mag. **53**(9), 126–133 (2015). https://doi.org/10.1109/MCOM.2015.7263356
6. Keskin, M.F., Sezer, A.D., Gezici, S.: Localization via visible light systems. Proc. IEEE **106**(6), 1063–1088 (2018). https://doi.org/10.1109/JPROC.2018.2823500
7. Park, J.K., Woo, T., Kim, M., Kim, J.T.: Hadamard matrix design for a low-cost indoor positioning system in visible light communication. IEEE Photon. J. **9**(2), 1–10 (2017). https://doi.org/10.1109/jphot.2017.2667038. Art no. 7801710
8. Xie, B., Chen, K., Tan, G., Lu, M., Liu, Y., Wu, J., et al.: LIPS: a light intensity-based positioning system for indoor environments. ACM Trans. Sen. Netw. **12**, 1–27 (2016)
9. Nadeem, U., Hassan, N.U., Pasha, M.A., Yuen, C.: Highly accurate 3D wireless indoor positioning system using white LED lights. Electron. Lett. **50**, 828–830 (2014)
10. Jung, S.Y., Hann, S., Park, C.S.: TDOA-based optical wireless indoor localization using LED ceiling lamps. IEEE Trans. Consum. Electron. **57**, 1592–1597 (2011)
11. Smola, A.: Regression estimation with support vector learning machines. Technical report, Technische Universität München (1996)
12. Zhang, L., Li, Y., Gu, Y., Yang, W.: An efficient machine learning approach for indoor localization. China Commun. **14**(11), 141–150 (2017). https://doi.org/10.1109/CC.2017.8233657
13. Shi, K., Ma, Z., Zhang, R., Hu, W., Chen, H.: Support vector regression based indoor location in IEEE 802.11 environments. Mob. Inf. Syst. **2015**, 14 p. (2015). https://doi.org/10.1155/2015/295652. Article ID 295652

14. Gradim, P., Fonseca, L.N.A., Mohamed, R.E.: On the usage of machine learning techniques to improve position accuracy in visible light positioning systems. In: 2018 11th International Symposium on Communication Systems, Networks & Digital Signal Processing (CSNDSP), Budapest, pp. 1–6 (2018). https://doi.org/10.1109/csndsp.2018.8471773
15. Saadi, M., Ahmad, T., Zhao, Y., Wuttisttikulkij, L.: An LED based indoor localization system using k-means clustering. In: 2016 15th IEEE International Conference on Machine Learning and Applications (ICMLA), Anaheim, CA, pp. 246–252 (2016). https://doi.org/10.1109/icmla.2016.0048
16. Shawky, S., El-Shimy, M.A., El-Sahn, Z.A., Rizk, M.R.M., Aly, M.H.: Improved VLC-based indoor positioning system using a regression approach with conventional RSS techniques. In: 2017 13th International Wireless Communications and Mobile Computing Conference (IWCMC), Valencia, pp. 904–909 (2017). https://doi.org/10.1109/iwcmc.2017.7986406
17. Zhang, X., Duan, J., Fu, Y., Shi, A.: Theoretical accuracy analysis of indoor visible light communication positioning system based on received signal strength indicator. J. Lightwave Technol. 32(21), 4180–4186 (2014). https://doi.org/10.1109/jlt.2014.2349530
18. Ghassemlooy, Z., Popoola, W., Rajbhandari, S.: Optical Wireless Communications, System and Channel Modeling with MATLAB. CRC Press, Boca Raton (2012). ISBN 9781439851883
19. Smola, J., Schölkopf, B.: A tutorial on support vector regression. NeuroCOLT2 Technical report Series NC2-TR-1998-030 (1998)

A Novel Mechanism of Position Update in Multi-objective Particle Swarm Optimization

Yanmin Liu[1(✉)], Lian Yuan[2], Aijia Ouyang[1], Wei Li[2], Rui Leng[1],
and Tao Huang[1]

[1] College of Mathematics and Computer Science, Zunyi Normal University,
Zunyi 563002, China
yanmin7813@163.com
[2] School of Data Science and Information Engineering,
Guizhou Minzu University, Guiyang 550025, China

Abstract. To balance convergence and diversity of multi-objective particle swarm optimization, a new mechanism of position update in multi-objective particle swarm optimization (PM-MOPSO) is proposed in this paper. In PM-MOPSO, according to the relationship of diversity, we determine the distribution of particles in the population with the iterations. Additionally, the size of the particle's position changes is adjusted in terms of the particle distribution. The experimental results show that PM-MOPSO is better in convergence and distribution compared with other two algorithms.

Keywords: Multi-objective particle swarm optimization ·
Diversity information · Convergence

1 Introduction

Multi-objective optimization problems (MOPs) are a kind of problem widely used in real life [1]. How to solve MOPs is the research hotspot in the field of artificial intelligence. In order to solve this kind of problem effectively, some scholars have proposed multi-objective particle swarm optimization (MOPSO). Coello et al. proposed the multi-objective particle swarm optimization (MOPSO) [2], which Pareto dominance is merged into particle swarm optimization to handle MOPs. Because of the PSO advantages, MOPSO exhibits well performance in solving MOPs compared with other natural calculation methods NSGA-II [3], microGA [4] and so on. Due to its simple form and easy implementation, it has attracted extensive research by many scholars [5, 6]. However every coin has two sides, it is easy to fall into the local optimal solution. To overcome these shortcomings, some mechanisms have been proposed for this problem. For example, Cheng [7] used the multi-dimensional uniform mutation operator to prevent algorithm from trapping into local optimum. Dai and Wang [8] proposed a multi-objective particle swarm optimization based on decomposition, which the objective space of a multi-objective problem is decomposed into a set of sub-regions based on a set of direction vectors to maintain the diversity. However in the

© Springer Nature Switzerland AG 2019
D.-S. Huang et al. (Eds.): ICIC 2019, LNCS 11643, pp. 617–625, 2019.
https://doi.org/10.1007/978-3-030-26763-6_59

existing MOPSO most of them lack the position adjustment mechanism, which will make the swarm fall into the local optimal solution. To balance convergence and diversity in MOPSO, we proposed a new mechanism of position update is proposed where the size of the particle's position changes is adjusted according to the variation of the particle distribution.

2 Related Works

2.1 Multi-objective Optimization Problems

A minimum multi-objective optimization problem can be described as follows:

$$\min y = F(x) = (f_1(x), f_2(x), \dots f_m(x))$$
$$s.t \begin{cases} g_i \geq 0 & i = 1, 2, \dots p \\ h_j = 0 & j = 1, 2, \dots q \end{cases} \tag{1}$$

Where x is an n-dimensional vector in decision space; m is the number of objective functions; $g_i \geq 0$ $(i = 1, 2, \dots p)$ is constraint, of p inequality constraints; $h_j = 0$ $(j = 1, 2, \dots, q)$ is constraint of q equality constraints.

2.2 Multi-objective Particle Swarm Optimization

The specific process of MOPSO is described in [2]. The position and velocity of the i-th particle are denoted by $x_i = (x_{i1}, x_{i2}, \dots x_{iD})$ and $v_i = (v_{i1}, v_{i2}, \dots v_{iD})$ respectively. The particle updates its speed and position according to the following formulas,

$$v_i(t+1) = wv_i(t) + c_1 r_1(t)(pbest_i(t) - x_i(t)) + c_2 r_2(t)(gbest_i(t) - x_i(t)) \tag{2}$$

$$x_i(t+1) = x_i(t) + v_i(t+1) \tag{3}$$

where t is the iteration number; w is the inertial weight; c_1 and c_2 are the learning factors; r_1 and r_2 are random numbers generated uniformly in the range [0, 1].

3 The Details of PM-MOPSO

3.1 Mechanism of Position Update

Definition 1 The diversity information of swarm (_Div_). It measures the distribution of the non-dominated solutions in swarm. A smaller value of _Div_ implies more sparse distribution of non-dominated solutions. The diversity information of population is defined as follows:

$$Div = \sqrt{\frac{\sum_{i=1}^{N}\left(d_i - \overline{d}\right)^2}{N-1}} \tag{4}$$

Where N indicates the number of particle; d_i indicates the Euclidean distance between the non-dominated solutions obtained; $\overline{d}$ indicates the average value of d_i distance.

We use ZDT1, ZDT2 and ZDT6 test functions to observe the relationship between the diversity information of population with the number of iterations (see Fig. 1). From Fig. 1, in the 80th generation, the diversity information value of the population is small, and the distribution of particle in the population is evenly distributed.

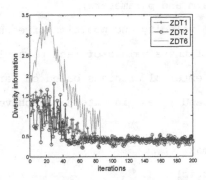

Fig. 1. Graph of the diversity information of population with the number of iterations.

To balance convergence and diversity, we propose a new position update mechanism. When the number of iterations is low, the position of the particles changes greatly, and on the contrary when the number of iterations reaches a given threshold *gen*, the position of the particles changes is little. The formula (5) gives the change process.

$$x_i(t+1) = \begin{cases} x_i(t) + v_i(t+1) & \text{if } t < gen \\ x_i(t) + \lambda \cdot v_i(t+1) & \text{if } t \geq gen \end{cases} \tag{5}$$

Where t is the number of iterations; *gen* is the threshold, here *gen* = 80; λ is the compressibility of the velocity.

Here, the λ values is set as 0.3, 0.4, 0.5, 0.6, 0.7 and 0.8 respectively to carry out the experiment on ZDT1, ZDT2, ZDT3, ZDT4 and ZDT6. Tables 1 and 2 presents the effect of different λ values on the convergence and diversity.

From Table 1, when λ = 0.6 the convergence of the algorithm on ZDT1 is optimal; when λ = 0.5, the convergence on ZDT2 is optimal; when λ = 0.3, the convergence on ZDT3 is optimal; when λ = 0.4 the convergence on ZDT4 is optimal; when λ = 0.8, the convergence on ZDT6 is optimal. From Table 2, when λ = 0.3, the diversity on ZDT1 is optimal; when λ = 0.5, the diversity on ZDT2 is optimal; when λ = 0.5, the diversity on ZDT3 is optimal; when λ = 0.4 the diversity on ZDT4 is optimal; when λ = 0.6 the diversity on ZDT6 is optimal. In summary, when $\lambda = 0.5$, the performance of the algorithm is optimal, so $\lambda = 0.5$ is used in formula (5).

3.2   Procedure of PM-MOPSO

The PM-MOPSO algorithm is as follows:

Algorithm. The pseudocode of PM-MOPSO

---

(1) **Begin**

(2) Initialize swarm and parameters;

(3) Initialize the velocity and position of each particle;

(4) Calculate the fitness values of each particle and sort them;

(5) Build initial external archives based on Pareto dominance;

(6) Assign *pbest* and *gbest* in external archives;

(7) T=0;

(8) **While** T < Tmax

(9)   **For** each particle

(10)   Update particle velocity and position by Eq (2) and (5);

(11)   Evaluate the fitness values of current particle and sort them;

(12)   Update *pbest;*

(13) **End for**

(14)   Update *gbest* in external archives;

(15)   Update and maintain external archives;

(16)   T ++;

(17)   **End While**

(18)   Output the results;

(19) **End Begin**

---

4   Experiments and Results

4.1   Test Function

To test the performance of PM-MOPSO ZDT1, ZDT2, ZDT3, ZDT4 and ZDT6 are selected to test the performance of the PM-MOPSO compared with MOPSO and NSPSO [9]. The parameter settings of MOPSO and NSPSO are consistent with the initially proposed setting and the size of the external archive of PM-MOPSO is set to 200. The parameters of experiment simulation are as follows: the dimensions of test functions are set as 30, the maximum iteration of all test functions is set to 2000 and each algorithm runs independently 30 times on all test functions.

4.2   Experiments Indicators

In this paper, we use the convergence indicators (γ) and diversity indicators (Δ) to evaluate the performance [10]. The convergence indicator measures the degree of approximation between the front of non-dominated solutions obtained by the algorithm and the actual *PF*. The diversity indicator measures the distribution of the non-dominated solutions obtained with the algorithm.

Table 1. The effect of different values of λ on the convergence of the algorithm.

Function	GD	0.3	0.4	0.5	0.6	0.7	0.8
ZDT1	Mean	7.65E−04	1.00E−03	8.35E−04	**7.55E−04**	7.72E−04	7.80E−04
ZDT2	Mean	8.63E−04	1.52E−03	**8.04E−04**	8.27E−04	9.22E−04	1.16E−03
ZDT3	Mean	**4.10E−03**	4.11E−03	4.48E−03	4.78E−03	5.06E−03	1.51E−01
ZDT4	Mean	6.11E−03	**6.91E−04**	7.11E−04	7.33E−04	7.83E−02	7.57E−04
ZDT6	Mean	1.84E−02	5.25E−03	4.12E−03	3.76E−03	2.60E−03	**1.96E−03**

Table 2. The effect of different values of λ on the diversity of the algorithm.

Function	SP	0.3	0.4	0.5	0.6	0.7	0.8
ZDT1	Mean	**1.52E+00**	1.59E+00	1.59E+00	1.63E+00	1.62E+00	1.65E+00
ZDT2	Mean	6.60E−01	6.36E−01	**6.16E−01**	6.79E−01	7.53E−01	8.66E−01
ZDT3	Mean	1.42E+00	1.35E+00	**1.34E+00**	1.36E+00	1.41E+00	1.44E+00
ZDT4	Mean	7.15E−01	**6.00E−01**	6.08E−01	6.68E−01	6.69E−01	8.33E−01
ZDT6	Mean	8.63E−01	6.61E−01	6.06E−01	**5.83E−01**	6.73E−01	7.89E−01

4.3   Experiments Results

Here, MATLAB 2013a is used to carry out a simulation experiment on a PC with Intel (R) Core (TM) i7-6700 @3.40 GHz CPU.

Figure 2 presents the comparison diagram of simulation experiment for three algorithms in five benchmark test functions respectively, and it is clear that PM-MOPSO performs very well both in convergence and diversity on ZDT1-ZDT4 and ZDT6 by comparison with MOPSO and NSPSO. Table 3 gives the indicators for PM-MOPSO, MOPSO and NSPSO where quantitative analysis is made from maximum, minimum, average and standard deviation respectively. From Table 3, it can conclude that the convergence of PM-MOPSO is better than that of MOPSO on ZDT2, ZDT3 and ZDT4. The convergence of PM-MOPSO is better than that of NSPSO on the test functions of ZDT1–ZDT4 and ZDT6. The convergence of PM-MOPSO is not better than that of MOPSO on ZDT1 and ZDT6, but it is also highly competitive compared with other algorithms. On most of test functions, the experimental results in GD indicator show that the GD values of PM-MOPSO are much closer to zero compared with MOPSO and NSPSO, which means that the non-dominated solutions obtained with PM-MOPSO can be close to the actual Pareto front in a better way.

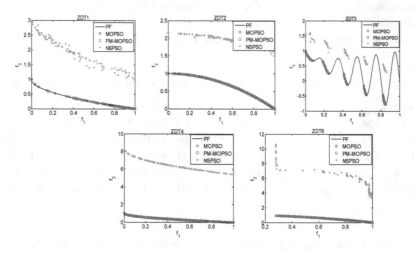

Fig. 2. Convergence characteristics of PM-MOPSO.

In summary it can be seen from Table 3 that the diversity of PM-MOPSO is better than that of MOPSO on ZDT1–ZDT4 and ZDT6 and the diversity of PM-MOPSO is better than that of NSPSO on ZDT2, ZDT4 and ZDT6, but not as good as that of NSPSO on ZDT1 and ZDT3. That is to say, the non-dominated solutions obtained by PM-MOPSO are much more evenly distributed compared with MOPSO and NSPSO.

Table 3. Performance matrices of five test function.

Function		GD			SP		
		PM-MOPSO	MOPSO	NSPSO	PM-MOPSO	MOPSO	NSPSO
ZDT1	Mean	8.19E−04	**7.57E−04**	1.59E+00	1.59E+00	1.62E+00	**6.63E−01**
	Std	2.12E−04	1.47E−04	2.46E−01	6.64E−02	8.53E−02	5.36E−02
ZDT2	Mean	**7.99E−04**	1.51E−03	1.01E+00	**6.16E−01**	1.08E+00	6.91E−01
	Std	3.21E−05	8.92E−05	3.94E−01	3.13E−02	3.67E−02	1.07E−01
ZDT3	Mean	**4.44E−03**	5.13E−03	2.87E−01	1.34E+00	1.52E+00	**6.49E−01**
	Std	2.72E−04	2.26E−04	1.88E−01	3.48E−02	2.65E−02	6.26E−02
ZDT4	Mean	**6.95E−04**	9.10E−04	1.03E+01	**6.09E−01**	1.07E+00	7.04E−01
	Std	4.42E−05	6.20E−05	8.18E+00	2.80E−02	2.04E−02	8.54E−02
ZDT6	Mean	3.99E−03	**1.18E−03**	4.02E+00	**6.02E−01**	9.84E−01	8.74E−01
	Std	3.52E−04	1.86E−04	2.33E+00	2.50E−02	6.18E−02	1.29E−01

Figures 3 and 4 show that the boxplot for convergence and diversity on ZDT1–ZDT4 and ZDT6 for 30 runs. From Fig. 3, it can be seen that PM-MOPSO has achieved good results for convergence on ZDT1, ZDT2, ZDT3, ZDT4 and ZDT6. From Fig. 4 it also can be seen that the diversity of PM-MOPSO is better than that of MOPSO on ZDT1–ZDT4 and ZDT6, and its diversity is better than that of NSOPSO on ZDT2, ZDT4 and ZDT6. Table 3 gives the same results.

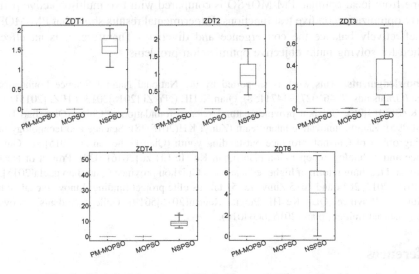

Fig. 3. Statistical boxplot of GD indicator of different algorithms.

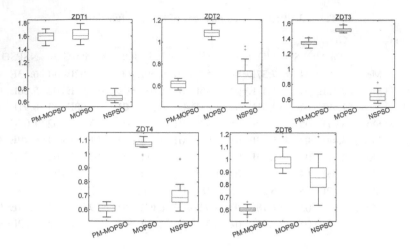

Fig. 4. Statistical boxplot of SP indicator of different algorithms.

5   Conclusion

In this paper, we proposed a new mechanism of position update in multi-objective particle swarm optimization to balance the convergence and diversity of algorithm. In the proposed PM-MOPSO algorithm, the particle position change is adjusted according to the particle distribution in the population with iterations, which make the particle can escape from local optimal. PM-MOPSO is compared with two multi-objective particle swarm optimization on five test functions. Experimental results show that PM-MOPSO can effectively balance the convergence and diversity. Therefore, it is an effective method for solving multi-objective optimization problems

Acknowledgments. This work is supported by the National Natural Science Foundation of China (Grants nos. 71461027, 71471158); Qian KeHE (NY Zi [2016]3013, LH Zi [2015]7033, J Zi LKZS[2014]06); Guizhou province natural science foundation in China (Qian Jiao He KY [2014]295); Zhunyi innovative talent team (Zunyi KH(2015)38); Science and technology talent training object of Guizhou province outstanding youth (Qian ke he ren zi [2015]06); Guizhou science and technology cooperation plan (Qian Ke He LH zi [2016]7028); Project of teaching quality and teaching reform of higher education in Guizhou province (Qian Jiao gaofa[2015]337) and 2016; 2013, 2014 and 2015 Zunyi 15851 talents elite project funding; Innovative talent team in Guizhou Province (Qian Ke HE Pingtai Rencai[2016]5619); College students' innovative entrepreneurial training plan (201510664016).

References

1. Bin, M.Z., Jeevan, K., Huang, C.J., et al.: A multi-objective particle swarm optimization algorithm based on dynamic boundary search for constrained optimization. Appl. Soft Comput. **70**(1), 680–700 (2018)
2. Coello, C.C., Pulido, G.T., Lechuga, M.S.: Handling multiple objectives with particle swarm optimization. IEEE Trans. Evol. Comput. **8**(3), 256–279 (2004)

3. Deb, K., Pratap, A., Agarwal, S., et al.: A fast and elitist multiobjective genetic algorithm: NSGA-II. IEEE Trans. Evol. Comput. **6**(2), 182–197 (2002)
4. Knowles, J., Corne, D.: Approximating the nondominated front using the pareto archived evolution strategy. Evol. Comput. **8**(2), 149–172 (2000)
5. Verma, A., Kaushal, S.: A hybrid multi-objective particle swarm optimization for scientific workflow scheduling. Parallel Comput. **62**, 1–19 (2017)
6. Adewumi, A.O., Popoola, P.A.: A multi-objective particle swarm optimization for the submission decision process. Int. J. Syst. Assur. Eng. Manag. **9**(1), 98–110 (2018)
7. Cheng, S., Zhan, H., Shu, Z.: An innovative hybrid multi-objective particle swarm optimization with or without constraints handling. Appl. Soft Comput. **47**, 370–388 (2016)
8. Dai, C., Wang, Y., Ye, M.: A new multi-objective particle swarm optimization algorithm based on decomposition. Inf. Sci. **325**(12), 541–557 (2015)
9. Li, Xiaodong: A non-dominated sorting particle swarm optimizer for multiobjective optimization. In: Cantú-Paz, Erick, Foster, James A. (eds.) GECCO 2003. LNCS, vol. 2723, pp. 37–48. Springer, Heidelberg (2003). https://doi.org/10.1007/3-540-45105-6_4
10. Deb, K., Thiele, L., Laumanns, M., Zitzler, E.: Scalable test problems for evolutionary multiobjective optimization. In: Abraham, A., Jain, L., Goldberg, R. (eds.) Evolutionary multiobjective optimization. Advanced Information and Knowledge Processing, pp. 105–145. Springer, London (2005)

A New Multi-objective Particle Swarm Optimization Based on Linear Decreasing Velocity Update Mechanism

Yanmin Liu[1(✉)], Lian Yuan[2], Aijia Ouyang[1], Hongyan Ye[2],
Rui Leng[1], and Tao Huang[1]

[1] College of Mathematics and Computer Science, Zunyi Normal University,
Zunyi 563002, China
yanmin7813@163.com
[2] School of Data Science and Information Engineering,
Guizhou Minzu University, Guiyang 550025, China

Abstract. In this paper, a new mechanism of velocity update in multi-objective particle swarm optimization (VM-MOPSO) is proposed. The main goal of the method is to balance local exploration and global exploration of multi-objective particle swarm optimization. In VM-MOPSO, as the number of iterations increases, the learning strength of global optimal solutions is adjusted by a linear decreasing search mechanism, which can make the swarm hold a stronger global search ability in the initial stage of the iteration and better local search ability in the later stage of the iteration. Experimental results in benchmark functions present that our method is better in convergence and diversity by comparison with MOPSO.

Keywords: Multi-objective particle swarm optimization · Local exploration · Global exploration

1 Introduction

Multi-objective particle swarm optimization (MOPSO) [1] is a heuristic method inspired by the study of bird feeding behavior. MOPSO has been found to be successful in a multi-objective optimization problem(MOPs) which has attracted the attention of a large number of researchers [2–6]. In the study of MOPSO, there are two key problems to be addressed. The first problem is how to select an excellent global and personal optimal particle to guide the swarm flight. The second problem is how to balance local and global exploration. In recent years, some strategies have been proposed for these problems. For example, Zhang [7] proposed a competitive strategy, where the particles are updated on the basis of the pairwise competition performed in the current swarm at each generation, but this update mechanism does not consider personal and global optimal particles. Yang [8] introduced a new Pareto-optimal solution searching algorithm for finding the global optimal particle, which assesses the ability of global and local searching and employed Sigma method to improve the local searching ability. The existing MOPSO strategies proposed by scholars are effective to some extent, but

© Springer Nature Switzerland AG 2019
D.-S. Huang et al. (Eds.): ICIC 2019, LNCS 11643, pp. 626–633, 2019.
https://doi.org/10.1007/978-3-030-26763-6_60

it is still difficult to balance local exploration and global exploration. For this reason a new mechanism of velocity update is proposed in our proposed VM-MOPSO where the learning strength of particles to global optimal solutions is adjusted by a linear decreasing search strategy.

2 Related Works

2.1 Multi-objective Optimization Problems

A general minimization objective vector of multi-objective problem with can be described as follows:

$$\min y = F(x) = (f_1(x), f_2(x), \ldots f_m(x))$$
$$s.t \begin{cases} g_i \geq 0 & i = 1, 2, \ldots p \\ h_j = 0 & j = 1, 2, \ldots q \end{cases} \tag{1}$$

Where x is a vector with n decision variables; m is the number of objective functions; g_i is constraint of p inequality constraints; p_i is constraint of q equality constraints.

2.2 Multi-objective Particle Swarm Optimization

Multi-objective particle swarm optimization (MOPSO) is an improvement on the single-objective particle swarm optimization (PSO). The position and velocity of particle i are denoted as $x_i = (x_{i1}, x_{i2}, \ldots x_{iD})$ and $v_i = (v_{i1}, v_{i2}, \ldots v_{iD})$ respectively. The particle is updated according to the following equations:

$$v_i(t+1) = wv_i(t) + c_1 r_1(t)(pbest_i(t) - x_i(t)) + c_2 r_2(t)(gbest_i(t) - x_i(t)) \tag{2}$$

$$x_i(t+1) = x_i(t) + v_i(t+1) \tag{3}$$

where t is the iteration number; w is the inertial weight; c_1 and c_2 are the learning factors; r_1 and r_2 are random numbers generated uniformly in the range [0, 1].

3 The Details of VM-MOPSO

3.1 Mechanism of Velocity Update

Because of the nature of MOPs, in the early stage of the search, a stronger global search ability is needed to find a better solution, and in the late stage of the search, a stronger local search ability is needed to explore a better local solution region. The search process of MOPSO depends on the global optimal and personal optimal particles stored in the external archive to guide the flight direction of the whole swarm. Therefore, in the initial stage of the search, the intensity of particles learned from the global optimal is stronger, so that the particles explored the search space as much as possible to obtain better diversity. Additionally, as the number of iterations increases, the swarm needs stronger local search ability, which can slow the intensity of particles to global optimal in order to improve the local search ability. Considering the characteristics of MOPSO, the learning intensity of particles to the global optimal is linear decreasing in VM-MOPSO. From the above, the proposed algorithms the velocity is updated as follows:

$$v_i(t+1) = wv_i(t) + c_1r_1(t)(pbest_i(t) - x_i(t)) + c_2r_2(t)(\alpha \cdot gbest_i(t) - x_i(t)) \quad (4)$$

Where $\alpha = \beta - (\beta - k) \times t/T_{max}$ is the learning intensity of the individual from the global optimal solution. T_{max} is the maximum iterations; t is the current iteration; β and k are constants, here $\beta = 1$. The k value is determined by experimental simulation as follows.

Table 1. The influence of k value on the GD of the algorithm.

Functions	GD	$k = 0.2$	$k = 0.3$	$k = 0.4$	$k = 0.5$	$k = 0.6$
ZDT1	Mean	2.60E–03	2.47E–03	1.84E–03	1.04E–03	**8.21E–04**
ZDT2	Mean	9.73E–04	1.11E–03	6.81E–04	**6.80E–04**	7.38E–04
ZDT3	Mean	**3.65E–03**	4.17E–03	4.42E–03	4.28E–03	4.16E–03
ZDT4	Mean	9.97E–04	8.85E–04	8.40E–04	**7.73E–04**	8.09E–04
ZDT6	Mean	2.88E–02	**2.40E–04**	5.76E–04	1.06E–03	8.91E–02

Table 2. The influence of k value on the SP of the algorithm.

Function	SP	$k = 0.2$	$k = 0.3$	$k = 0.4$	$k = 0.5$	$k = 0.6$
ZDT1	Mean	**1.36E+00**	1.45E+00	1.46E+00	1.56E+00	1.58E+00
ZDT2	Mean	9.65E–01	9.40E–01	8.06E–01	**7.51E–01**	7.84E–01
ZDT3	Mean	**1.27E+00**	1.34E+00	1.37E+00	1.39E+00	1.38E+00
ZDT4	Mean	7.85E–01	7.86E–01	7.95E–01	**7.66E–01**	7.73E–01
ZDT6	Mean	1.67E+00	1.45E+00	1.16E+00	9.87E–01	**8.38E–01**

Here, k value is set as 0.2, 0.3, 0.4, 0.5 and 0.6 respectively to carry out the experiment in five test functions. By analyzing the impact of different k value, the optimal k value is determined. Table 1 shows the influence of different k values on the convergence GD. From Table 1, when $k = 0.6$, the GD value on ZDT1 is best; when $k = 0.5$, the GD on ZDT2 and ZDT4 is best; when $k = 0.2$, the GD on ZDT3 is best; when $k = 0.3$, the GD on ZDT6 is best. Table 2 shows the influence of different k values on the diversity of the algorithm. From Table 2, when $k = 0.2$, the SP on ZDT1 and ZDT3 is best; when $k = 0.5$, the SP on ZDT2 and ZDT4 is best; when $k = 0.6$, the SP on ZDT6 is best. From the above analysis, when $k = 0.5$, the convergence and diversity of the algorithm are best, so k in Eq. (8) is taken as 0.5.

3.2   Procedure of VM-MOPSO

The VM-MOPSO algorithm is as follows:

Algorithm. The pseudocode of VM-MOPSO

Input: the number of particles *N*, the size of the external archive *rep*, the maximum number of iterations *maxgen*, the dimension size of the decision space *sizex* and the number of mesh divisions *numgrid*.

Output: *Sfit*

(1) Initialize the velocity and position of each particle;

(2) Calculate the fitness values of each particle (*Sfit*);

(3) If the termination conditions are satisfied, then algorithm stops; otherwise, pass on the next step;

(4) Establish external archives based on Pareto dominance;

(5) Assign *pbest* and *gbest* in external archives;

(6) Update particle velocity and position by Eq (4) and (3);

(7) Evaluate the fitness values of current particle and sort them;

(8) Update *pbest*;

(9) Update *gbest* in external archives;

(10) Make t=t+1, transfer to step 3.

---

4   Experiments and Results

4.1   Test Function and Experiments Parameters

To compare the performance of VM-MOPSO and MOPSO, five test functions used in this paper include, i.e., ZDT1, ZDT2, ZDT3, ZDT4 and ZDT6 [9], to test the performance of each algorithm. For each algorithm, the dimension of all test functions is set as 30; the maximum iteration number is 2000; the external archive size is set to 200; the size of the population is 200; all algorithms are run 30 times independently. For VM-MOPSO, the parameters are as follows: $w = 0.4$; $c_1 = c_2 = 2$; the value of k is set according to the experimental results. The parameter settings of MOPSO in the paper are consistent with the initially proposed setting.

4.2   Experiments Indicators

In this paper, convergence (GD, γ) and diversity (spread, Δ) performance indicators are employed to evaluate the performance of VM-MOPSO quantitatively [10].

4.3   Experiments Results and Analysis

The comparison of convergence characteristics for two algorithms in five benchmark test functions are presented as Fig. 1 respectively. Figure 1 shows that VM-MOPSO has good performance both in convergence and diversity in five benchmark test functions by comparison with MOPSO which indicates the solutions of VM-MOPSO are well closer to Pareto front in five test functions.

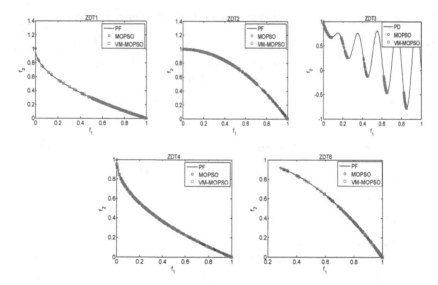

Fig. 1. Convergence characteristics of VM-MOPSO.

Tables 3 shows the indicators of diversity and convergence for VM-MOPSO and MOPSO, a quantitative analysis is made from four aspects. We can conclude that the convergence of VM-MOPSO is better than that of MOPSO on ZDT2-ZDT4 and ZDT6. Additionally in the convergence evaluation results, VM-MOPSO has superior values in four test functions compared with MOPSO, and it found better solutions closely related to the real PF. In a word, it can be seen from Table 3 that the diversity of VM-MOPSO is better than that of MOPSO in five test functions. At the same time, the diversity evaluation results of VM-MOPSO is much more evenly distributed in all test functions by comparison with MOPSO.

To further verify the effectiveness of the algorithm, we uses box plots to present the statistical data of the convergence and diversity metrics where the box plot can present the stability of algorithms for MOPs. Each performance value is calculated through 30 runs in all test functions, and then these experiment results are gathered for statistical analysis which are shown as Figs. 2 and 3. From Fig. 2, it can be seen that VM-

Table 3. Performance matrices of five test function.

Function		GD		SP	
		VM-MOPSO	MOPSO	VM-MOPSO	MOPSO
ZDT1	Min	6.09E−04	5.47E−04	1.39E+00	1.47E+00
	Max	2.10E−03	1.20E−03	1.72E+00	1.79E+00
	Mean	1.11E−03	**7.57E−04**	**1.53E+00**	1.62E+00
	Std	4.34E−04	1.47E−04	8.05E−02	8.53E−02
ZDT2	Min	6.27E−04	1.40E−03	7.30E−01	1.02E+00
	Max	8.02E−04	1.70E−03	8.96E−01	1.17E+00
	Mean	**7.02E−04**	1.51E−03	**7.81E−01**	1.08E+00
	Std	3.84E−05	8.92E−05	3.80E−02	3.67E−02
ZDT3	Min	3.40E−03	4.80E−03	1.32E+00	1.48E+00
	Max	5.10E−03	5.60E−03	1.45E+00	1.60E+00
	Mean	**4.15E−03**	5.13E−03	**1.38E+00**	1.52E+00
	Std	4.17E−04	2.26E−04	3.36E−02	2.65E−02
ZDT4	Min	7.18E−04	8.14E−04	6.95E−01	1.05E+00
	Max	8.74E−04	1.10E−03	9.31E−01	1.13E+00
	Mean	**7.95E−04**	9.10E−04	**7.83E−01**	1.07E+00
	Std	4.37E−05	6.20E−05	4.49E−02	2.04E−02
ZDT6	Min	7.07E−04	8.99E−04	8.89E−01	8.92E−01
	Max	1.60E−03	1.70E−03	1.07E+00	1.18E+00
	Mean	**1.10E−03**	1.18E−03	**9.81E−01**	9.84E−01
	Std	2.11E−04	1.86E−04	4.70E−02	6.18E−02

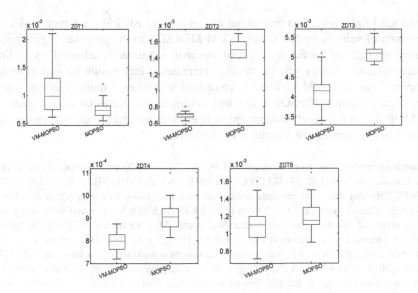

Fig. 2. Statistical box plot of GD indicator of different algorithms.

MOPSO has achieved good results for the convergence on ZDT2-ZDT4 and ZDT6, but was undesirable on ZDT1 compared with MOPSO. From Fig. 3 we can see that the diversity of VM-MOPSO is better than that of MOPSO in all test functions. This is exactly the same as the results analyzed in Table 3. From the results of experiments, VM-MOPSO performed desirably both in convergence and diversity evaluations.

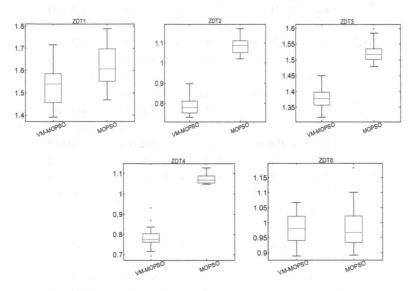

Fig. 3. Statistical boxplot of SP indicator of different algorithms.

5   Conclusion

To balance local exploration and global exploration of MOPSO, we proposed a new mechanism of velocity update strategy (VM-MOPSO). In the proposed algorithm, the learning strength of particles to global optimal solutions is adjusted by a linear decreasing search strategy with the iteration increases, which ensure the swarm flight to the optimal solution. VM-MOPSO is compared with classic multi-objective particle swarm optimization (MOPSO) in five test functions. Experimental results show that VM-MOPSO can effectively balance the local exploration and global exploration and it is an efficient improvement algorithm for MOPSO.

Acknowledgments. This work is supported by the National Natural Science Foundation of China (Grants nos. 71461027, 71471158); Qian KeHE (NY Zi [2016]3013, LH Zi [2015]7033, J Zi LKZS[2014]06); Guizhou province natural science foundation in China (Qian Jiao He KY [2014]295); Zhunyi innovative talent team (Zunyi KH(2015)38); Science and technology talent training object of Guizhou province outstanding youth (Qian ke he ren zi [2015]06); Guizhou science and technology cooperation plan (Qian Ke He LH zi [2016]7028); Project of teaching quality and teaching reform of higher education in Guizhou province (Qian Jiao gaofa[2015]337) and 2016; 2013, 2014 and 2015 Zunyi 15851 talents elite project funding; Innovative talent team in Guizhou Province (Qian Ke HE Pingtai Rencai[2016]5619); College students' innovative entrepreneurial training plan (201510664016).

References

1. Coello, C.C., Pulido, G.T., Lechuga, M.S.: Handling multiple objectives with particle swarm optimization. IEEE Trans. Evol. Comput. **8**(3), 256–279 (2004)
2. He, Z., Zhou, J., Qin, H., Jia, B., Lu, C.: Efficient multi-objective optimization algorithm for hybrid flow shop scheduling problems with setup energy consumptions. Eng. Appl. Artif. Intell. **181**(20), 584–598 (2018)
3. Verma, A., Kaushal, S.: A hybrid multi-objective particle swarm optimization for scientific workflow scheduling. Parallel Comput. **62**, 1–19 (2017)
4. Liang, J., Guo, Q., Yue, C., Qu, B., Yu, K.: A self-organizing multi-objective particle swarm optimization algorithm for multimodal multi-objective problems. In: Tan, Y., Shi, Y., Tang, Q. (eds.) ICSI 2018. LNCS, vol. 10941, pp. 550–560. Springer, Cham (2018). https://doi.org/10.1007/978-3-319-93815-8_52
5. Wu, C.C., Chen, J.Y., Lin, W.C., et al.: A multi-objective particle swarm optimization algorithm for community detection in complex networks. Swarm Evol. Comput. **39**, 297–309 (2018)
6. Lin, Q., Li, J., Du, Z., et al.: A novel multi-objective particle swarm optimization with multiple search strategie. Eur. J. Oper. Res. **247**(3), 732–744 (2015)
7. Zhang, X., Cheng, R., et al.: A competitive mechanism based multi-objective particle swarm optimizer with fast convergence. Inf. Sci. **427**, 63–76 (2018)
8. Yang, J., Zhou, J., Liu, L., et al.: A novel strategy of pareto-optimal solution searching in multi-objective particle swarm optimization (MOPSO). Comput. Math Appl. **57**(11), 1995–2000 (2009)
9. Kennedy, J., Eberhart, R.: Particle swarm optimization. In: IEEE International Conference on Neural Networks, pp. 1942–1948 (1995)
10. Deb, K., Thiele, L., Laumanns, M., Zitzler, E.: Scalable test problems for evolutionary multiobjective optimization. In: Abraham, A., Jain, L., Goldberg, R. (eds.) Evolutionary multiobjective optimization. Advanced Information and Knowledge Processing, pp. 105–145. Springer, London (2005). https://doi.org/10.1007/1-84628-137-7_6

Cluster-Head Selection for Energy-Harvesting IoT Devices in Multi-tier 5G Cellular Networks

Mario R. Camana(iD), Carla E. Garcia(iD), and Insoo Koo$^{(\boxtimes)}$(iD)

University of Ulsan, Ulsan, South Korea
iskoo@ulsan.ac.kr

Abstract. Fifth-generation cellular networks promise to interconnect a wide variety of wireless devices, such as pico cells, femto cells and Internet of Thing devices. In this vision, multiple tiers appear as one of the main solutions to overcome these challenges providing an increase in the spectrum efficiency through the spectrum reuse. In this work, we investigate an approach to increase the lifetime of Internet of Thing devices, equipped with energy-harvesting capabilities, in a heterogeneous network considering a macro-tier and an underlay-tier. The proposed solution considers the k-means algorithm to group the IoT devices and a cluster head selection algorithm to balance the energy consumed in the network based on the residual energy and distance to the regional manager node. To improve the knowledge of the amount of energy harvested, we propose a solar intensity-prediction approach based on a multilayer perceptron algorithm from which the results are used to increase the performance in the cluster head selection scheme. Numerical results show that the proposed approach achieves significant improvement over the baseline Low Energy Adaptive Clustering Hierarchy scheme in increasing the residual energy and the number of IoT devices alive in the network.

Keywords: Internet of Things · 5G networks · Multilayer perceptron · Network lifetime · LEACH

1 Introduction

The Internet of Things (IoT) is becoming one of the potential technologies for services and applications of the future. The IoT is a network composed of a large number of sensors, actuators and wireless devices with the ability to communicate between themselves to perform complex tasks in a cooperative environment. Fifth generation (5G) cellular networks promise cell data rates of 10 Gbps and delays between 2 ms and 5 ms to support future demand for data services [1]. To achieve the 5G performance requirements, one of the main solutions is to use multiple tiers, which consist of the conventional macrocell tier (macro-tier) composed of the macro base station (MBS) and the macro UEs (MUEs), and an underlay-tier, which may include pico and femto cells, relays, sensors, and so on. Since the cellular resources are shared between the macro-tier and underlay-tier, spectral efficiency is increased, and coverage is improved.

© Springer Nature Switzerland AG 2019
D.-S. Huang et al. (Eds.): ICIC 2019, LNCS 11643, pp. 634–645, 2019.
https://doi.org/10.1007/978-3-030-26763-6_61

In IoT networks composed of a wide range of devices, energy consumption becomes one of the main challenges, since it is expensive to regularly replace the battery of an IoT device. Therefore, devices with energy-harvesting (EH) capabilities appear to be the solution for sustaining a perpetual lifetime, since IoT devices can harvest energy from renewable sources, such as solar or radio frequency radiation, to recharge their batteries [2]. However, the random nature of the energy sources leads to adapting the current protocols to EH systems. Furthermore, many techniques have been developed to extend the lifetime of the network, such as multi-hops, cooperative transmission, data aggregation, and clustering [3].

1.1 Related Works

In [1], the authors addressed the resource allocation problem in a heterogeneous network composed of one MBS and a set of MUEs in the macro-tier, and a cluster of several small base stations (SBS) and several device-to-device (D2D) pairs in the underlay-tier. The objective is to obtain the transmit power and assignment of the resource blocks for the underlay transmitters that maximize the sum data rate. The authors proposed three distributed heuristic solutions: stable-matching, factor graph-based message passing, and distributed auction-based approaches.

The Low Energy Adaptive Clustering Hierarchy (LEACH) protocol [4] minimizes global energy usage by performing randomized rotations of the cluster head, distributing the energy load among all the nodes. A cooperative clustering protocol based on LEACH for energy harvesting-based wireless sensor networks (WSNs) was proposed [3] where the authors considered duty cycle-based cluster head selection. A cluster head-selection approach based on a hybrid model with both moth flame and ant lion optimization was proposed [5] where the objective function contains the parameters of delay, distance, load, temperature, and energy consumed. An extension of the LEACH protocol to increase the lifetime of the WSN was proposed [6] where the authors provided three methods considering total and partial energy harvesting, as well as a sleep operation. In [7], the authors considered an energy-harvesting WSN to propose a CH-selection and clustering algorithm based on the energy status and the energy harvested by the nodes, as well as a multi-hop routing scheme. Modified k-means was proposed [8] where three CH candidates are selected in each of the clusters, and the role of CH is rotated between these three CH candidates over time. The algorithm first selects a CH node based on distance from the centroid and energy level in order to finally assign CH candidates to itself and to its two nearest nodes. In [9], the authors proposed a genetic algorithm to obtain the number and selection of CHs as an optimization problem considering distance and the remaining energy of the nodes as parameters. A clustering procedure in a sensor-assisted cognitive radio (CR) network with ad hoc CR was considered [10] where the CR serves as a cluster head, and the sensor nodes join the closest CH in order to form each cluster. The cluster-updating process is performed when there is a change in the number of nodes or when the CR moves to another position.

A smart-city environment with several IoT devices within Long Term Evolution-Advanced (LTE-A) cell coverage was considered [11], where the authors proposed a D2D-based solution to cluster the devices and cooperatively upload their data to an

Evolved Node B (eNodeB) through the CH in each cluster. CH selection is based on the channel quality indicator value and the number of devices within its coverage area. The authors in [12] considered a WSN in a smart city and proposed an energy-efficient clustering protocol where the network is divided into intraclusters, and the data are transmitted by using multi-hop routes over the CHs. CH selection is based on the actual residual energy and the distance to the base station.

Artificial neural network for regression has been widely used in the literature to solve prediction problems achieving high accuracy [13–16]. A neural network approach was applied to predict the stock market in [13], where the authors presented an analysis of the optimal hidden layers and hidden neurons for stock price prediction. In [14], the authors develop a deep neural network approach for short-term wind prediction, where a simple feedforward multilayer perceptron (MLP) algorithm to predict orthogonal wind components on a 3-h horizon. A neural network approach to predict solar energy was proposed in [15], where the parameters are irradiation, atmospheric pressure, relative air humidity, and air temperature. In [16], the authors investigated the prediction for the digital terrestrial television coverage by applying machine regression algorithms, such as random forest regression, AdaBoost regression, and multilayer perceptron regression.

1.2 Main Contributions

Although CH-selection algorithms have been studied in the literature, as mentioned in the previous subsection, the clustering and CH selection in a heterogeneous network considering a macro-tier and underlay-tier is still unsolved. Therefore, with the above motivations, in this paper, we consider a heterogeneous network where several IoT devices are deployed, and they use the available channels in an underlay manner. In this system, our aim is to increase the lifetime of the network by performing clustering to group the IoT devices, and by using a CH-selection algorithm to balance the energy consumed in the network. Thus, the main contributions of this paper are summarized as follows.

- We propose a solar energy–prediction approach based on the MLP algorithm. The actual measurement of solar intensity and target time are used to accurately estimate the solar intensity in the future.
- We propose a clustering algorithm to balance the energy of the IoT devices in the network, and a centralized CH-selection scheme based on the distance to the regional manager node and the residual energy, which is estimated by using the predicted harvested energy.
- The performance of the proposed approach is compared with that of the LEACH protocol. Simulation results show that the proposed scheme outperforms the LEACH scheme in terms of residual energy, the number of IoT devices that are alive, and the total number of packets dropped.

The remaining sections of this paper are organized as follows. The network model is described in Sect. 2. In Sect. 3, we describe the energy-prediction approach based on the MLP algorithm, as well as the proposed CH-selection scheme based on k-means clustering. Numerical evaluations are provided for performance analysis in Sect. 4. Finally, the conclusions are drawn in Sect. 5.

2   Network Model

Let us consider a transmission scenario of a heterogeneous network as shown in Fig. 1. The network consists of one MBS and a set of C cellular MUE. There is also one regional manager node (RMN), M IoT devices and a cluster of S small-cell base stations (SBSs) located within the coverage area of the MBS serving one small-cell user equipment (SUE) per SBS. The IoT devices, SBSs, and SUEs are underlaid within the macro-tier by reusing the same set of radio resources.

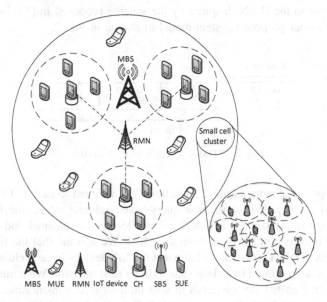

MBS   MUE   RMN   IoT device   CH   SBS   SUE

Fig. 1. Diagram of the heterogeneous network model.

By using the underlying transmission, the macro-tier and the underlay-tier (the IoT devices, SBSs, and SUEs) can use the same set of nonoverlapping and orthogonal channels $\mathcal{C} = \{1, 2, \ldots, C\}$. Following [1], the transmit power of the SBSs and IoT devices is selected from a finite set of power levels $\mathcal{P} = \{1, 2, \ldots, P\}$. Then, each transmitter (SBS or IoT device) is able to use a particular channel with a suitable power level for transmission as long as the cross-tier interference with the MUEs is within the threshold limit. The MBS performs the channel allocation for any underlay transmitter based on the resource allocation problem proposed in [1]. In this paper, we assume that the channel allocation is successfully performed at the MBS and that the transmit power of the IoT devices is available in the RMN. Moreover, perfect synchronization between the RMN, MBS, CHs and IoT devices is assumed.

The proposed system model is a representation of a smart city application where the IoT devices are located over a wide area within the coverage range of the RMN, which has an unlimited energy supply. In order to increase the lifetime of the IoT network, we consider a clustering mechanism to group the IoT devices in proximity and a CH-selection algorithm to reduce the transmit power of the IoT devices. The IoT devices can harvest energy from photovoltaic solar cells, where we use the harvest-store-use protocol which allows storing the energy before using it in the future.

3 Proposed Algorithm Description

Our proposed scheme is based on k-means to group the IoT devices based on their proximity and CH selection in each cluster will be done based on the residual energy and the distance to the RMN. Inspired by the scheme proposed in [17], we adopt the frame format to our proposed system model as shown in Fig. 2.

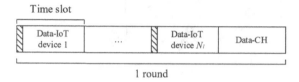

Fig. 2. TDMA schedule in each cluster.

In the proposed scheme a timeslot duration T_s is assigned to each IoT device in the cluster $k \in \{1, \ldots, K\}$. We consider a query-based scheme where the CH sends a control message to the desired IoT device and allocates the channel and power level based on the information obtained from the MBS. We assume that the time division multiple access (TDMA) schedule is known at the IoT devices in each cluster. Then, an IoT device is able to remain in a sleep state until its next timeslot. We define one round as the period that an IoT device needs to wait until its next transmission.

Besides the reporting information, each IoT device forwards its residual energy level to the CH. The CH aggregates and compresses the information received from the IoTs during one round, and sends it to the RMN.

3.1 Clustering Scheme Based on K-means

We assume that the location of the IoT devices is known at the RMN in order to perform clustering by using the k-means algorithm. A detailed description of the k-means algorithm is provided in Sect. II of [18]. The principal parameter for k-means is the number of clusters K, which affects the delay, network throughput, lifetime and so on. In order to guarantee the QoS requirements at the IoT, we need to limit the number of clusters to a minimum and a maximum. First, based on packet arrival rate ρ and maximum delay $D_{\max}$, we can calculate the maximum possible round duration in each cluster as $round_{\max} = \min\left(\frac{1}{\rho}, D_{\max}\right)$, which permits defining the minimum number of clusters as $K_{\min} = \left\lceil \frac{MT_s}{round_{\max}} \right\rceil$. Second, the number of orthogonal channels C defines the maximum number of clusters $K_{\max}$, above which two or more clusters have to share the same channel leading to collisions.

By increasing the number of clusters, we can reduce the distance between the non-CH IoT devices and the CH decreasing the energy consumed by the packet transmission towards the CH. However, this leads to an increase in the amount of information to transmit from the CH to the RMN augmenting the energy consumed by the CH.

3.2 Energy-Harvesting Prediction

In this paper, we consider a solar energy source that fluctuates throughout the day and seasons but remains nearly constant during periods of time shorter than 30 min [3]. In order to improve the accuracy of the information at the RMN about the energy harvested by the IoT devices, we propose a solar intensity–prediction model based on a multilayer perceptron (MLP) regressor [13].

The MLP regressor is a type of feedforward artificial neural network and consists of one input layer, one or more hidden layers, and one output layer. In this paper, we propose an MLP regressor composed of two neurons in the input layer and one hidden layer, as shown in Fig. 3. The basic idea of the proposed scheme is to use the actual measurement of solar intensity to estimate the solar intensity after one period, T.

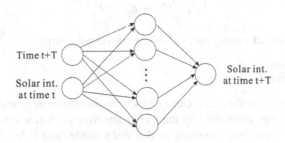

Fig. 3. MLP regressor structure for solar intensity prediction.

In the training phase, we used public solar radiation data available in [19], considering a period T between each measurement. The dataset was created with two features per sample, where the first feature is time t, and the second feature corresponds to the solar intensity at time $t - T$. Furthermore, the target value for each sample is the solar intensity at time t.

With respect to the testing phase, the value of time $t + T$ and the solar intensity at time t and are used to predict the value of the solar intensity in the next time period $t + T$. Then, the harvesting power of IoT device i in cluster k becomes $E_h^{i,l} = \eta_i c_i I_{i,l}$, where η_i is the harvesting efficiency, c_i is the solar cell area, and $I_{i,l}$ is the solar intensity of IoT device i.

3.3   Energy Consumption

The energy consumed by each IoT device is determined by the energy used to transmit and receive packets, as well as, the energy consumed to listen for an arriving packet. Furthermore, we considered a TDMA schedule for each cluster in such a way that only one IoT device is able to transmit during each timeslot, while the other IoT devices switch to sleep mode. The energy consumption of a non-CH IoT device $i \in \{1, .., M\}$ in cluster $k \in \{1, \ldots, K\}$ is

$$E_c^{i,k} = P_{Txi,k} \frac{B}{R} + P_l \left(T_s - \frac{B}{R} \right) + P_{sl}(N_k - 1)T_s, \tag{1}$$

where B is the data payload, R is the data rate, T_s is the timeslot, N_k is the number of IoT devices in cluster k, $P_{Txi,k}$ is the transmit power of IoT device i in cluster k, and P_{sl} and P_l are the power consumed in sleep and listening modes, respectively. On the other hand, the energy consumption of CH IoT device i in cluster k is

$$E_c^{i,k} = P_{Rx}(N_k - 1)\frac{B}{R} + P_l(N_k - 1)\left(T_s - \frac{B}{R} \right) + P_{Txi,k}N_k \left(\frac{\lceil \alpha B \rceil}{R} \right), \tag{2}$$

where P_{Rx} is the power consumed in receiving mode, and α is the compression ratio. The residual energy of IoT device i in cluster k is

$$E_r^{i,k} = E_o^{i,k} - E_c^{i,k} + E_h^{i,k} \tag{3}$$

where $E_o^{i,k}$ is the initial energy and $E_h^{i,k}$ is the harvested energy.

3.4   Cost Metrics

CH selection is performed in each cluster based on residual energy and the distance to the RMN. The energy consumed by the CH is superior to than a non-CH IoT device because the CH is not able to switch to the sleep mode, and it has to send a larger amount of data to the RMN, leading to fast draining of its battery. Therefore, we consider that the CH IoT devices are not fixed and that the role changes after every time interval, γ, in each cluster.

The distance from the IoT device to the RMN affects the energy consumed to transmit a packet, where longer distances lead to using greater amounts of energy per data packet. On the other hand, the residual energy is an essential parameter to take into account to select a CH, because if the energy is not high enough at the CH, its packet and all the packets of the non-CH IoT devices in that cluster will be dropped.

We propose a cost metric to trade off the parameters of distance and residual energy to select the best CH in each cluster as follows:

$$\alpha_{i,k} = \left(\beta \frac{d_{i,RMN}}{\sum\limits_{j=1}^{N_k} d_{j,RMN}} + (1 - \beta) \frac{E_c^{i,k}}{E_r^{i,k}} \right), \tag{4}$$

where $E_c^{i,k}$ and $E_r^{i,k}$ are calculated by the predicted value for the next L rounds, considering the IoT device as a CH, and where β is a tradeoff factor.

In the operation of the network, when a larger amount of residual energy is available in the IoT devices, the distance to the RMN become the parameter with the highest importance. However, when the residual energy is low, the CH needs to be selected based on the IoT device with the largest amount of residual energy to successfully complete the CH task of sending packets to the RMN. Therefore, we iteratively adjust the tradeoff factor β according to the time, starting with an initial value β_o, when the initial energy at the battery is E_o, and reducing its value over time in such a way that the distance parameter has priority at early times and the residual energy parameter has priority when the IoT devices have started draining their batteries.

Furthermore, the RMN starts a new instance of the CH-selection algorithm if the residual energy of the actual CH is less than the energy threshold value E_{th}. Table 1 describes the proposed algorithm for CH selection.

Table 1. Proposed algorithm

1: **Inputs:** Number of clusters K, time interval γ, $\alpha_{\min} = 10^5$, period for prediction L
  and energy threshold value E_{th}.
2: Execute the k-means algorithm to group the IoT devices into K clusters.
3: Get the actual $E_r^{i,k}$ of each IoT device in the RMN.
4: RMN predict $E_h^{i,k}$ by using the MLP regressor for the next L rounds.
5: RMN predict $E_c^{i,k}$ and $E_r^{i,k}$ for the next L rounds.
6: **For each cluster** $k = 1, ..., K$, **do:**
7:     **For each IoT device** i **in the cluster** k, **do:**
8:         Evaluate the cost metric $\alpha_{i,k}$ by (4) for the IoT device i
9:         **if** $E_r^{i,k} > E_{th}$ and $\alpha_{i,k} < \alpha_{\min,k}$ **then**
             IoT device i is selected as CH in the cluster k
             $\alpha_{\min,k} = \alpha_{i,k}$
         end if
10:    **end for**
11: **end for**
12: Repeat the algorithm to select a new CH every time interval γ.

---

4   Simulation Results

In this section, we numerically evaluate the performance of our proposed CH-selection scheme in the heterogeneous network, illustrated in Fig. 1, in comparison with the LEACH approach [4]. In the simulations, we set $M = 100$ for IoT devices randomly deployed in a radius of 50 m around the RMN; the number of clusters was set to $K = 12$, the number of available orthogonal channels was $C = 20$, and the time interval to select the CH was $\gamma = 250T_s$. The transmit power of the IoT devices was determined by the power allocation algorithm at the MBS. The principal simulation parameters are summarized in Table 2.

Table 2. Simulation parameters

Parameter	Symbol	Value	Parameter	Symbol	Value
Traffic (packet/s)	ρ	0.5, 0.3	Solar cell area (cm^2)	c	17
Data payload (bits)	B	1000	Harvesting efficiency	η	0.22
Data rate (Kbps)	R	250	Initial energy (J)	E_o	2
Sleeping (mW)	P_{sl}	0.003	Battery capacity (J)	C_B	20
Idle listening (mW)	P_l	0.06	Energy threshold (J)	E_{th}	0.2
Receive (mW)	P_{Rx}	60	Timeslot duration (ms)	T_s	50

Figure 4 shows the performance comparison of the solar intensity prediction between the proposed scheme based on the MLP regressor and the scheme proposed in [2], which is based on a Kalman filter. For this simulation, we utilized 80 neurons in the hidden layer. We observe that if the period between each measurement is 15 min, the proposed MLP regressor scheme outperforms the Kalman filter approach. Also, if the period between each measurement is one minute, the proposed approach still outperforms the Kalman filter scheme. However, the results under both schemes are close to the real value, because solar intensity remains nearly constant during periods of time shorter than 30 min, and for a period of one minute there is only a slight variation between each measurement.

The simulated LEACH algorithm follows the description in [4] using a probability of 10% for becoming a CH. However, we include a modification to only permit an IoT device to declare itself as the CH if the residual energy is greater than the energy threshold E_{th}.

Figure 5 illustrates the average residual energy by using the proposed algorithm and the LEACH algorithm with traffic rates of 0.5 packets/s and 0.3 packets/s. In general, the average residual energy decreases over time, but in the peak hours of solar intensity, the amount of harvested energy helps to compensate for the energy consumed. We can see that the proposed scheme achieves higher residual energy under both traffic rates. At 0.4 packets/s, the amount of harvested energy allows the IoT devices to save energy to be used in the future, leading to an increase in the residual energy. At 0.5 packets/s, the harvested energy helps to maintain the energy in the IoT devices, but the residual energy decreases over time since the harvested energy from

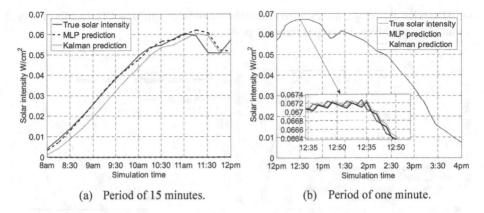

(a) Period of 15 minutes.   (b) Period of one minute.

Fig. 4. Solar intensity prediction over periods of one minute and 15 min.

the solar source varies during the day. This behavior is because the proposed scheme chooses the cluster head by a tradeoff of residual energy and distance to the RMM, selecting an IoT device close to the RMN with enough residual energy to successfully accomplish the CH tasks. In this way, we can reduce the energy consumed for the transmission to the RMN, and avoid packets dropped and retransmissions since the IoT device is selected as CH based on its residual energy being the best option in the cluster to satisfy the role of CH.

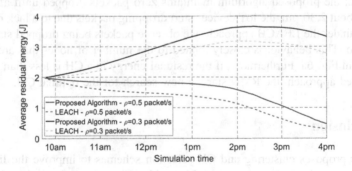

Fig. 5. Average residual energy.

Figure 6a shows the number of live nodes by considering traffic rates of 0.5 packets/s and 0.3 packets/s. Considering the performance at 0.3 packets/s the proposed approach keeps 100% of the nodes alive during the analyzed period, but in the LEACH approach, the first IoT device dies around 12 pm. At 0.5 packets/s, the first IoT device dies around 2:30 pm under the proposed scheme, whereas under the LEACH scheme, the first IoT device dies around 10:30 am, which is a difference of four hours. The reason is that the LEACH protocol selects the CH in a random way, without taking into account the distance to the RMN and the residual energy in that IoT device. In this way, an IoT device at a longer distance from the RMN can be assigned as CH, and its energy is quickly drained by the higher transmit power needed.

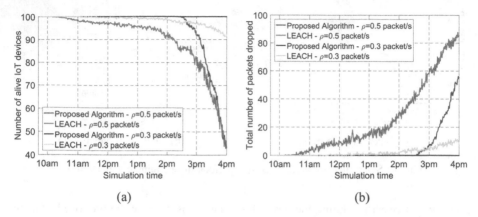

Fig. 6. (a) IoT devices that are alive. (b) Total number of packets dropped.

Figure 6b shows the total number of packets dropped due to a lack of energy in the IoT devices for traffic rates of 0.5 packets/s and 0.3 packet/s. We can see that at 0.3 packet/s, the proposed algorithm drops none of the packets, whereas the LEACH approach drops around 10% by 4 pm. Looking at the performance at 0.5 packets/s, we can see that the proposed algorithm maintains zero packets dropped until after 2 pm, and after about 2:30 pm, the IoT devices start dropping packets due to a lack of energy. However, under the LEACH approach, we observe packets being dropped starting just after 10 am. This behavior is closely related to the number of nodes that are alive, as illustrated in Fig. 6a. Furthermore, if the residual energy in a CH is less than E_{th} under the proposed approach, the RMN starts a new search for the optimal CH.

5   Conclusion

This paper proposes clustering and CH-selection schemes to improve the lifetime of IoT devices in a heterogeneous network considering a macro-tier and underlay-tier. First, an energy-prediction approach is proposed to estimate solar intensity based on a multilayer perceptron algorithm. Second, a k-means algorithm is used to group the IoT devices into clusters, and the CH-selection scheme based on the distance to the RMN and the predicted energy residual in the future is used to select the CH in a rotating manner. The results obtained by the proposed approach demonstrated a significant improvement over the LEACH scheme.

Acknowledgment. This work was supported by the National Research Foundation of Korea (NRF) grant through the Korean Government (MSIT) under Grant NRF-2018R1A2B6001714.

References

1. Hasan, M., Hossain, E.: Distributed resource allocation in 5G cellular networks. In: Towards 5G, pp. 129–161 (2016)
2. Nguyen, T.D., Khan, J.Y., Ngo, D.T.: A distributed energy-harvesting-aware routing algorithm for heterogeneous IoT networks. IEEE Trans. Green Commun. Netw. 2(4), 1115–1127 (2018)
3. Bahbahani, M.S., Alsusa, E.: A cooperative clustering protocol with duty cycling for energy harvesting enabled wireless sensor networks. IEEE Trans. Wirel. Commun. 17(1), 101–111 (2018)
4. Heinzelman, W.R., Chandrakasan, A., Balakrishnan, H.: Energy-efficient communication protocol for wireless microsensor networks. In: Proceedings of the 33rd Annual Hawaii International Conference on System Sciences (2000)
5. Reddy, M.P.K., Babu, M.R.: A hybrid cluster head selection model for internet of things. Clust. Comput. 1–13 (2017). https://doi.org/10.1007/s10586-017-1261-1
6. Onishi, T., Ogose, S.: Lifetime extension of wireless sensor networks with energy harvesting. J. Sig. Process. 22(2), 77–86 (2018)
7. Bozorgi, S.M., Rostami, A.S., Hosseinabadi, A.A.R., Balas, V.E.: A new clustering protocol for energy harvesting-wireless sensor networks. Comput. Electr. Eng. 64, 233–247 (2017)
8. Periyasamy, S., Khara, S., Thangavelu, S.: Balanced cluster head selection based on modified k-means in a distributed wireless sensor network. Int. J. Distrib. Sens. Netw. 12(3), 5040475 (2016). https://doi.org/10.1155/2016/5040475
9. Pal, V., Yogita, Singh, G., Yadav, R.P.: Cluster head selection optimization based on genetic algorithm to prolong lifetime of wireless sensor networks. Procedia Comput. Sci. 57, 1417–1423 (2015)
10. Usman, M., Har, D., Koo, I.: Energy-efficient infrastructure sensor network for ad hoc cognitive radio network. IEEE Sens. J. 16(8), 2775–2787 (2016)
11. Orsino, A., Araniti, G., Militano, L., Alonso-Zarate, J., Molinaro, A., Iera, A.: Energy efficient IoT data collection in smart cities exploiting D2D communications. Sensors 16(6), 836 (2016)
12. Baniata, M., Hong, J.: Energy-efficient unequal chain length clustering for wireless sensor networks in smart cities. Wirel. Commun. Mob. Comput. 2017, 1–12 (2017)
13. Ke, J., Liu, X.: Empirical analysis of optimal hidden neurons in neural network modeling for stock prediction. In: 2008 IEEE Pacific-Asia Workshop on Computational Intelligence and Industrial Application (2008)
14. Dalto, M., Matusko, J., Vasak, M.: Deep neural networks for ultra-short-term wind forecasting. In: 2015 IEEE International Conference on Industrial Technology (ICIT) (2015)
15. Rodríguez, F., Fleetwood, A., Galarza, A., Fontán, L.: Predicting solar energy generation through artificial neural networks using weather forecasts for microgrid control. Renew. Energy 126, 855–864 (2018)
16. Moreta, C.E.G., Acosta, M.R.C., Koo, I.: Prediction of digital terrestrial television coverage using machine learning regression. IEEE Trans. Broadcast. 1–11 (2019). https://doi.org/10.1109/tbc.2019.2901409
17. Aslam, S., Hasan, N., Jang, J., Lee, K.-G.: Optimized energy harvesting, cluster-head selection and channel allocation for IoTs in smart cities. Sensors 16(12), 2046 (2016)
18. Na, S., Xumin, L., Yong, G.: Research on k-means clustering algorithm: an improved k-means clustering algorithm. In: 2010 Third International Symposium on Intelligent Information Technology and Security Informatics (2010)
19. HelioClim-3 Database. http://www.soda-pro.com/web-services/radiation

Segmenting Crop Disease Leaf Image by Modified Fully-Convolutional Networks

Xian-feng Wang, Zhen Wang, and Shan-wen Zhang$^{(\boxtimes)}$

Department of Information Engineering, XiJing University, Xi'an 710123, China
wjdw716@163.com

Abstract. Crop disease leaf image segmentation is an important and challenging step, because the disease leaf image and corresponding lesions are often complex, various, and variant, and the segmenting results directly impact on subsequent disease recognition rate. A segmentation algorithm is proposed by modified fully convolutional networks (FCNs) to deal with the problem of segmenting spots from crop leaf disease image with complicated background. The experimental result shows that the proposed method can be used in complicated field environment with high extracting accuracy.

Keywords: Crop disease leaf image segmentation ·
Fully convolutional networks (FCNs) · Modified FCNs ·
Deconvolutional operator

1 Introduction

Crop diseases cause significant reductions in agricultural productivity worldwide [1]. Crop disease symptoms often first appear on the crop leaves, moreover the different kinds of diseases have different symptoms, which is the important basis to detect disease occurrence and recognize crop types. The image segmentation of diseased leaves is a key step in disease atomic recognition, and the segmentation effect directly affects the subsequent recognition effect. The segmentation of disease leaf image is to subdivide the diseased leaf image into normal area and diseased spot area [1–3]. In the process of disease recognition, the extraction of eigenvalues and the construction of classifiers are based on them. Diseased leaf image segmentation is always one of the most difficult tasks in the crop disease recognition, and it is also a hot research topic in image processing and pattern recognition fields. There are many kinds of image segmentation algorithms for diseased leaf image segmentation, including threshold segmentation, edge detection, segmentation based on mathematical morphology and fuzzy clustering [4–6]. Camargo and Smith [7] successfully segmented the lesion and background of banana leaf black spot in their designed crop disease classification and recognition system, taking the banana leaf black spot as an example, using the optimal threshold histogram threshold segmentation method. The characteristics of threshold segmentation are simple and efficient. The difficulty lies in the selection of threshold. The color and texture of crop pest and disease areas are often different from those of non-disease areas [8, 9]. Baum et al. [10] used Sobel edge detection operator to isolate barley plaque from the background. In the experiment of rice leaf image segmentation,

© Springer Nature Switzerland AG 2019
D.-S. Huang et al. (Eds.): ICIC 2019, LNCS 11643, pp. 646–652, 2019.
https://doi.org/10.1007/978-3-030-26763-6_62

a rice leaf edge detection algorithm based on multi-strategy fusion technology is proposed, which combines minimum outer rectangle algorithm, median filter and Canny operator. The disadvantage is that the segmentation efficiency of the edge detection method depends on the edge detection operator and its robustness is poor [11, 12]. Casady et al. [13] used mathematical morphology to segment rice canopy images, combined with gray median method to extract the height and area of rice canopy, and achieved good results. Combining the linear mathematical morphology segmentation with the non-linear edge detection method, the segmentation of crop leaves is completed. Fuzzy clustering segmentation algorithm belongs to unsupervised learning in pattern recognition [14]. It stipulates that the membership of each pixel in an image is fuzzy and has been widely used in recent years. Jaware et al. [15] used Otsu's algorithm [16] to calculate the shielding threshold of green pixels of disease image, eliminate the zero RGB pixels and edge features of infection, and used the optimized K-means clustering method to segment the image of crop disease leaves. The experiment proved that the algorithm was efficient and high-precision. Li et al. [17] used K-means clustering method based on a and b components of Lab color model to identify red spiders in color images, with remarkable results. A large number of image data of crop diseases images have the characteristics of fuzziness and uncertainty. The membership function in the fuzzy clustering can model the fuzziness and uncertainty in the image, so it can be effectively applied to image segmentation. Fuzzy clustering method also has some shortcomings, such as sensitivity to noise and initialization data, and large amount of computation of the algorithm, which affect its practical application in agricultural production, and need to be further improved and optimized.

In recent years, deep learning has achieved good results in image segmentation and image recognition. Many researchers have applied deep learning technology to crop diseases segmentation and recognition, and achieved some results [18–20]. Hanson et al. [7] proposed a plant disease recognition method based on convolution neural networks (CNNs). The experimental results show that CNNs has high recognition accuracy. Good segmentation results were achieved in the process of grape disease leaves segmentation in natural scenes. Fully convolutional networks (FCNs) is an effective segmentation method, which has been applied to several research fields [19, 21, 22]. Based on FCNs, an improved modified FCNs based crop disease leaf segmentation method is proposed.

2 Modified FCNs

Based on FCNs, a modified FCNs model is constructed for crop disease leaf image segmentation. The network is trained by several images of maize leaf lesions. The features of lesion area in maize leaf lesion images are learned, and the end-to-end image segmentation of crop disease leaf is realized from input to output.

The main steps of crop disease leaf image segmentation by FCNs are described as follows,

(1) The original image is input into the convolution neural network model and the initial feature map is obtained by convolution operation. The convolution layer mainly consists of a convolution kernel of K size N * N * C. After convolution operation between the original image and the convolution kernel, the non-linear activation function is used to enhance the feature extraction ability of the convolution layer. By operation, the feature of K size $(M - N + 1) * M - N + 1)$ graph can be obtained. The concrete operation formulas of convolution layer are as follows:

$$x_i^{(l)} = f(\sum_{i\in\delta_j}^{M} W_i^{(l)} X_i^{(l-1)} + b_i^{(l)}) \tag{1}$$

where $x_i^{(l-1)}$ is the output of the $l - 1$ hidden layer, $x_i^{(l)}$ is the input image of the input layer, $W_i^{(l)}$ is the mapping weight matrix of the lth hidden layer, $b_i^{(l)}$ is the bias matrix of the lth hidden layer, f is the activation function used to solve the problem of the inadequate expressive ability of the original linear function. Its expression is $f(x) = \max(0, x)$.

(2) The maximum pooling is adopted in this study. Activation function is still used to enhance the nonlinearity of the model after the downsampling operation. The concrete formulas for calculating the pooling layer are as follows:

$$x_i^{(l)} = w_i^{(l)} down(a_i^{(l-1)}) + b_s$$
$$a_i^{(l)} = f(x_i^{(l)}) \tag{2}$$

where l denotes the number of current pooling layer, $down$ is a downward operation, W is a weight matrix, and b_s is a biased matrix.

(3) Full-convolution neural network performs the end-to-end pixel-by-pixel classification process. After feature extraction of the input original image using convolution layer, pooling layer and activation function, it is necessary to input the extracted feature map into the pixel-based classification layer for pixel classification. Common classifiers include SoftMax, SVM and so on. The classification level is as follows:

$$\text{soft max}(x_i) = \exp[w_i^T x^{(i)}] / \sum_{j=1}^{C} \exp[w_j^T x^{(i)}] \tag{3}$$

where is w_i the pixel matrix of the convolution layer output feature map is obtained.

(4) After classifying the pixels at the classification level, the loss function is used to evaluate the training effect of the model. The lower the loss values of the training set and the test set, the better the training effect of the model.

The coding network consists of 13 convolution layers and 5 pooling layers, including convolution kernel (CONV), batch normalization layer (Batch Normalization) and activation layer (RELU). The convolution kernel is uniformly set to 3 * 3 size and the stride is set to 1. The maximum pooling layer is used in the pooling layer. The size of the pooling layer is set to 2 * 2 and the step size is set to 2. The decoding network consists of convolution layer, up sampling layer and SoftMax classifier. The scale of upper sampling layer is set to 2. Because the segmentation of maize leaf lesion image is a two-classification problem (normal area and lesion area), the channel number of convolution kernel in the last layer of decoding network is set. Secondly, the dense feature map obtained by decoding network is input into the classification layer to classify the pixels, that is to say, the segmentation of maize leaf lesion image is completed.

Based on the improved FCNs model, the Tensor flow framework in deep learning is constructed, and Python language is used as the programming language. The operating system of the experimental platform is Ubuntu 16.04 and the memory of the computer is 32 GB. The platform uses Nvidia GTX1080Ti 11 GB GPU graphics card and carries Intel (R) Kernel i7 processor. In the process of training the network, the small batch stochastic gradient descent (SGD) algorithm with momentum factor is used to train the network model. In order to guarantee the nonlinearity of the model and improve the learning efficiency of the convolution layer, RELU is used as the activation function. Batch size is set to 32, 64 and 128 due to the large image data set and the limitation of computer memory. In order to ensure the efficiency of network training, the initial learning rate is set to 0.01, the momentum factor is set to 0.9, and the Batch size is set to 128. After 1200 iterations, the training speed of the network model will slow down, so the learning rate will be reduced to 0.001 [23, 24].

3 Experiments and analysis

Different size convolution kernels will affect the feature extraction ability of network model. In order to better understand the network, the type of visual convolution kernels in this study can be seen that smaller convolution kernels (CONV) have smaller local receptive fields, but contain more details, which can better extract the main information contained in the image and remove redundant feature information. In order to verify the effect of convolution kernel size on segmentation accuracy, Batch Size was set to 128, and the default learning rate was 0.01. When pooling type is chosen as average pooling, the convolution kernels of 1 * 1 size are 2.25% points higher than those of 3 * 3 and 5 * 5 in IOU evaluation index, respectively. The convolutional kernels are shown in Fig. 1.

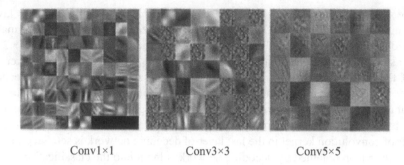

Conv1×1   Conv3×3   Conv5×5

Fig. 1. Visualization of different types of convolutional kernels

In order to test the segmentation performance of this study, different segmentation methods were used to segment maize leaf lesion images. Three different image segmentation network structures were selected in the experiment, namely FCN-8s, DeepLabV3 and PSP Net, and two traditional image segmentation methods, Logic Regression and SVM, were selected. The segmentation effect of different segmentation methods is shown in Fig. 2. From the graph, we can see that FCN-8s has obvious misclassification phenomenon; DeepLabV3 has better segmentation effect than FCN, but can only segment larger lesions, but the segmentation accuracy of small lesions is poor; PSP Net segmentation effect is good, and the details of lesions are more accurate, but there are still some errors in the logical regression and SVM segmentation. The two traditional segmentation methods are basically the same in segmentation effect, and both of them can segment the lesion accurately, but because of the use of mathematical morphology processing, the local edge information of the image is lost, and the small lesion area also appears over-segmentation phenomenon [24]. The segmentation method proposed in this study not only guarantees the integrity of the lesion, but also highlights the small lesion area segmentation. According to different segmentation methods, the segmentation effect is compared on the test set images, and the evaluation index is shown in Table 1.

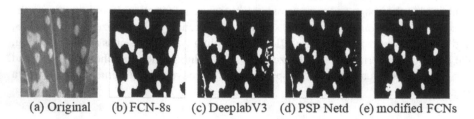

(a) Original   (b) FCN-8s   (c) DeeplabV3   (d) PSP Netd   (e) modified FCNs

Fig. 2. Segmented lesion images by different segmentation methods

Table 1. The segmentation accuracies by different segmentation methods

Method	Training time (h)	Segmenting time (s)	COM (%)	Global Acc (%)	IOU (%)
FCN-8s	3.23	1.43	86.52	87.56	83.45
DeepLabV3	2.89	1.56	88.63	88.32	85.63
PSP Net	3.12	1.51	89.42	89.10	86.10
Modified FCNs	2.31	1.24	96.34	95.87	91.23

From Table 1, it is found that the proposed method outperforms the other methods. In the segmentation experiments on the test set image, the IOU value reaches 0.9123. Compared with the traditional convolution neural network structure, the training time of the traditional segmentation method is shorter because it does not need a lot of convolution operations. But in the early stage of segmentation, a lot of image pre-processing is needed, and the method of feature extraction needs to be set manually, and the end-to-end pixel segmentation is not achieved.

4   Conclusion

An improved FCNs model is proposed for crop disease leaf image segmentation. It mainly includes a coding network and a decoding network. The coding network is improved on the traditional VGG-16 network. The decoding network structure corresponds to the coding network. The main purpose is to deconvolute the pooling layer in the coding network and restore the output characteristics of the coding network. The improved model can segment the crop leaf lesion image more accurately, avoiding the traditional method of artificial design feature extraction, and is simpler than the existing convolution neural network in the structure of the model. This method has better adaptability to different backgrounds in the process of segmentation. It can overcome the influence of complex environment on image segmentation and accurately realize the segmentation of lesion area in maize leaf image. It also has great advantages in the speed of segmentation. It can realize real-time image segmentation and lay a foundation for the subsequent accurate recognition of maize disease types.

References

1. Martinelli, F., Scalenghe, R., Davino, S., et al.: Advanced methods of plant disease detection. A review. Agron. Sustain. Dev. **35**(1), 1–25 (2015)
2. Shelhamer, E., Long, J., Darrell, T.: Fully convolutional networks for semantic segmentation. IEEE Trans. Pattern Anal. Mach. Intell. 1 (2016). https://doi.org/10.1109/tpami.2016.2572683
3. Du, M.G., Zhang, S.W.: Crop disease leaf image segmentation based on genetic algorithm and maximum entropy. Appl. Mech. Mater. 713–715 (2015)
4. Wang, L., Tao, Y., Tian, Y.: Crop disease leaf image segmentation method based on color features. In: International Conference on Computer & Computing Technologies in Agriculture, pp. 713–717 (2007)

5. Guan, H.O., Shao-Hua, X.U., Feng, T.: Fuzzy neural network based on T-S model and its application on image segmentation of plant diseases. J. China Agric. Univ. **16**(3), 145–149 (2011)
6. Zhang, S., You, Z., Wu, X.: Plant disease leaf image segmentation based on superpixel clustering and EM algorithm. Neural Comput. Appl. **5**, 1–8 (2017)
7. Camargo, A., Smith, J.S.: An image-processing based algorithm to automatically identify plant disease visual symptoms. Int. J. Food Eng. **102**(1), 9–21 (2013)
8. Rodriguez, A.V.C., Kim, J.T.: Plant disease symptoms, identification from colored images. In: Gli, J., Horabik, J., Lipiec, J. (eds.) Encyclopedia of Agrophysics. Springer, Dordrecht (2011). https://doi.org/10.1007/978-90-481-3585-1_216
9. Mutka, A.M., Bart, R.S.: Image-based phenotyping of plant disease symptoms. Front. Plant Sci. **5** (2015). https://doi.org/10.3389/fpls.2014.00734
10. Baum, T., Navarro-Quezada, A., Knogge, W., et al.: HyphArea—automated analysis of spatiotemporal fungal patterns. J. Plant Physiol. **168**(1), 72–78 (2011)
11. Dong, P., Wang, X.: Recognition of greenhouse cucumber disease based on image processing technology. Open J. Appl. Sci. **3**(1), 27–31 (2013)
12. Revathi, P., Hemalatha, M.: Advance computing enrichment evaluation of cotton leaf spot disease detection using Image Edge detection. In: Third International Conference on Computing Communication & Networking Technologies. IEEE (2012)
13. Casady, W.W., Singh, N., Costello, T.A.: Machine vision for measurement of rice canopy dimensions. Trans. ASAE **39**(5), 1891–1898 (1996)
14. Guanlin, L., Zhanhong, M., Chong, H., et al.: Segmentation of color images of grape diseases using K_means clustering algorithm. Trans. Chin. Soc. Agric. Eng. **26**(14), 32–37 (2010)
15. Jaware, T.H., Badgujar, R.D., Patil, P.G.: Crop disease detection using image segmentation. World J. Sci. Technol. **2**(4), 190–194 (2012)
16. Otsu, N.: A threshold selection method from gray-level histograms. IEEE Trans. Syst. Man Cybern. **9**(1), 62–66 (2007)
17. Changji, W., Helong, Yu.: An image segmentation method for maize disease based on IGA-PCNN. In: Guo, C., Hou, Z.-G., Zeng, Z. (eds.) ISNN 2013. LNCS, vol. 7951, pp. 602–611. Springer, Heidelberg (2013). https://doi.org/10.1007/978-3-642-39065-4_72
18. Amara, J., Bouaziz, B., Algergawy, A.: A deep learning-based approach for banana leaf diseases classification. In: Mitschang, B., et al. (eds.) BTW 2017 - Workshopband. LNI, pp. 79–88. Springer, Bonn (2017)
19. Hanson, A.M.G.J., Joel, M.G., Joy, A., Francis, J.: Plant leaf disease detection using deep learning and convolutional neural network. Int. J. Eng. Sci. Comput. **7**, 5324–5328 (2017)
20. Liu, B., Zhang, Y., He, D.J., et al.: Identification of apple leaf diseases based on deep convolutional neural networks. Symmetry **10**(11), 1–16 (2018). https://doi.org/10.3390/sym10010011
21. Yu, S., Cheng, Y., Xie, L., et al.: Fully convolutional networks for action recognition. IET Comput. Vis. **11**(8), 744–749 (2017)
22. Long, J., Shelhamer, E., Darrell, T.: Fully convolutional networks for semantic segmentation. IEEE Trans. Pattern Anal. Mach. Intell. **39**(4), 640–651 (2014)
23. Krizhevsky, A., Sutskever, I., Hinton, G.E.: ImageNet classification with deep convolutional neural networks. In: Advances in Neural Information Processing Systems, pp. 1097–1105 (2012)
24. Szegedy, C., Liu, W., Jia, Y., et al.: Going deeper with convolutions. In: IEEE Conference on Computer Vision and Pattern Recognition. IEEE Computer Society, pp. 1–9 (2014)

A Recognition Method for Italian Alphabet Gestures Based on Convolutional Neural Network

Xiaoyu Ji[✉], Qiming Yu, Yunxia Liu, and Shan Kong

College of Information Science and Technology, Zhengzhou Normal University,
Zhengzhou, China
iamjixiaoyu@163.com

Abstract. Convolutional Neural Network(CNN) have achieved great success in image recognition and classification, but most of researches on gesture recognition are for English, there are very few identification studies for other small languages. An recognition method for Italian alphabet gestures based on CNN is proposed in this paper. First, an Italian alphabet gesture data set is created, including 22 letters, of which 4 letters (G, S, J, and Z) are excluded from the data set because of their dynamism, and a CNN model consisting of three blocks is established, convolutional and pooling layers are included in every block. Then weights and biases in the model are trained by the adaptive moment estimation algorithm called Adam to reduce the loss to the minimum step by step. Finally, we build a CNN model based on the proposed method on a deep learning platform named Keras, testing images are selected from the established static dataset randomly, the results of multiple experiments show that the recognition rate can reach up to 94%.

Keywords: Gesture recognition · CNN · Adaptive moment estimation · Keras

1 Introduction

Although most people think that there is only one kind of sign language all over the world, but the fact is that people from different regions use different kind of sign languages [1, 2]. Each country generally has its own sign language, and some even have more than one, although there are many similarities among different sign languages [3].

In Italy, the official sign language called LIS has not been officially recognized yet, although it is estimated that at least 10% of Italians have some form of hearing impairment who are using LIS [4]. However, most existing work projects are based on the American Sign Language (ASL) [5–7], and the scientific community has been studying how to use technology to solve this problem. Therefore, we focus on the LIS and hope to find an effective recognition method for the sign language LIS.

Deep learning is a research field that has been relatively hot in recent years. Compared with shallow models, deep learning has obvious advantages in feature extraction and modeling [8, 9]. Its advantage is that deeper and more comprehensive features can be extracted from the original image conveniently [8, 10]. The feature

© Springer Nature Switzerland AG 2019
D.-S. Huang et al. (Eds.): ICIC 2019, LNCS 11643, pp. 653–664, 2019.
https://doi.org/10.1007/978-3-030-26763-6_63

representations, and these feature maps can be widely used in other fields, of course, these features can also be applied to more aspects of life, it overcomes some of the problems that were considered to be tricky in the field of artificial intelligence in the past [10]. And the more training data sets, the stronger the processing power of the chip, the deep learning has achieved outstanding achievements in natural language processing [11, 12], speech recognition and semantic analysis, which further promotes the development of artificial intelligence [13]. At present, deep neural networks occupy the mainstream, and Convolutional Neural Networks (CNNs), and CNNs were once applied by researchers to image recognition and achieved great success. CNNs are robust and well tolerated [14], and are also easily trained and optimized.

2   Convolutional Neural Network Model

2.1   Global Structure

CNN usually consists of input layer, convolution layer, excitation layer and fully connected layer. The global structure of established CNN model is given in Fig. 1.

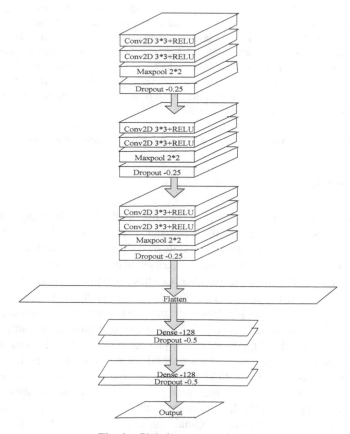

Fig. 1. Global structure of CNN

The size of every static Italian alphabet image is 64 * 64 * 3, the first 64 is the number of rows of the image, the second 64 is the number of columns, and the parameter of 3 is the number of channels.

2.2 Convolution Layers

The essence of the convolution operation is a weighted summation process, which is equivalent to multiplying the values of image and convolutional kernel, a region of the same size as the convolutional kernel is formed when the image is covered by the kernel every time, there are two values at every position in this region, one is from the image and the other is from the kernel, product of two values at every position is calculated and the sum of all the products is taken as the final result of the central position of the region.

Suppose the convolution kernel is an N × N matrix, where the value of N is generally odd, and the values of the kernel can be continuously updated as the learning progresses. This allows it to continually reinforce sample features during training iterations, bringing the final data closer to the correct output. Figure 2 and (1) gives out the chart and formula of convolutional operation respectively.

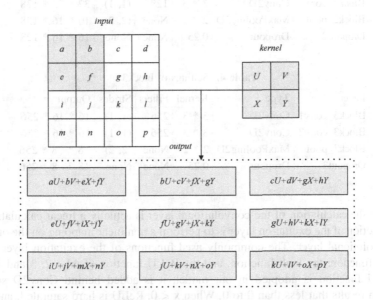

Fig. 2. Computation process of convolutional operation

There are totally 18 layers including Dropout and Dense operations, and these layers are divided into 7 blocks, block1, block2 and block3 have the same components but different parameters. They are all made up of 2 Conv2D layers, 1 Maxpooling2D layer and 1 Dropout layer, every Conv2D layer is followed by an activation function called "relu" so that the results of convolutional operation can be limited between 0 and 1. The numbers of these three blocks' parameters are shown in Table 1.

Table 1. Parameters of convolution layers

	Conv1	Conv2	Pool	Dropout
Block1	1792	36928	0	0
Block2	73856	147584	0	0
Block3	295168	590080	0	0

Table 2. Settings of block1

Layer	Type	Kernel	Filters	Strides	Output
Block1_conv1	Conv2D	3 * 3	64	(1, 1)	64 * 64 * 64
Block1_conv2	Conv2D	3 * 3	64	(1, 1)	64 * 64 * 64
Block1_pool	MaxPooling2D	2 * 2	None	(2, 2)	32 * 32 * 64
Dropout1	Dropout	0.25	None	None	32 * 32 * 64

Table 3. Settings of block2

Layer	Type	Kernel	Filters	Strides	Output
Block2_conv1	Conv2D	3 * 3	128	(1, 1)	32 * 32 * 128
Block2_conv2	Conv2D	3 * 3	128	(1, 1)	32 * 32 * 128
Block2_pool	MaxPooling2D	2 * 2	None	(2, 2)	16 * 16 * 128
Dropout2	Dropout	0.25	None	None	16 * 16 * 128

Table 4. Settings of block3

Layer	Type	Kernel	Filters	Strides	Output
Block3_conv1	Conv2D	3 * 3	256	(1, 1)	16 * 16 * 256
Block3_conv2	Conv2D	3 * 3	256	(1, 1)	16 * 16 * 256
Block3_pool	MaxPooling2D	2 * 2	None	(2, 2)	8 * 8 * 256
Dropout3	Dropout	0.25	None	None	8 * 8 * 256

Since the calculation of the convolutional layer is actually a linear calculation, the main function of the excitation layer is to perform a nonlinear mapping on the output of the convolutional layer. The commonly used functions of the excitation layer are the sigmoid function, the tanh function, and the ReLU function (Tables 2, 3 and 4).

ReLU function is adopted in our model, it is added behind Conv2D so as to transform results that less than 0 to 0. When $x < 0$, ReLU is hard saturated, and when $x > 0$, there is no saturation problem. ReLU can keep the gradient from decaying when $x > 0$, which fundamentally alleviates the problem of gradient disappearance. The advantage is that it allows the experimenter to train the deep neural network directly in a supervised manner without relying on unsupervised layer-by-layer pre-training. ReLU is expressed as Formula (1) or (2).

$$f(x) = \begin{cases} 0, & if\ x<0 \\ x, & if\ x\geq 0 \end{cases} \tag{1}$$

$$f(x) = max(0, x) \tag{2}$$

And ReLU can be expressed in another way as Fig. 3 for intuition.

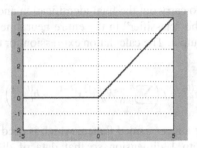

Fig. 3. Curve of ReLU

The feature maps produced by the convolution layer are usually with large scales, in this case, the pooling layers are added to divide the feature maps into several regions, then maximum pooling or averaging pooling is used on these regions, a single maximum or average is produced so as to replace all values of current region. Furthermore, the important feature values of the local regions input by the convolutional layer are extracted to achieve dimensionality reduction.

And make it maintain spatial invariance, translation is not deformed, rotation invariance and scale are not deformed to avoid overfitting. That is to say, through pooling, the lower learning neurons get new, smaller dimensions. Max pooling is the most popular method that usually used in image processing, Fig. 4 shows the process of max pooling and average pooling with a region size of 2 * 2, which can reduce the amount of data to 1/4 of the original feature maps.

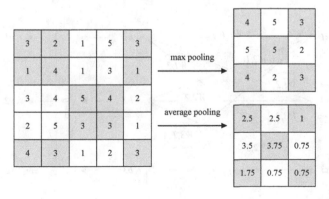

Fig. 4. Process of max pooling and average pooling

2.3   Fully Connected and Output Layers

As mentioned above, double convolutional layers are used to extract various deep feature maps from current image, then excitation layer and pooling layer are added to extract a small amount of important data from feature maps, maybe we lost some unimportant information, but significant reduction in data volume is gained. Different convolutional kernels produce different feature maps and different feature maps just express different kind of information, so all the feature maps need to be integrated from partial to global in order to carry out the final identification and data classification. The fully connected layer is the "classifier" in the entire neural network, and it is also the last layer just before the output. The calculation expression for the fully connected layer is shown in (3).

$$a_i^{(l)} = f\left(\sum\nolimits_{i=0}^{n} W_{ij}^{(l-1)} x_i^{(l-1)} + b_i^{(l-1)}\right) \tag{3}$$

Block3 is followed by a layer named flatten, which is used to transform the current data from 3 dimensions to 1 dimension so that data of different channels can be combined into 1 channel. In our model, 8 * 8 * 256 feature maps go out of block3 into flatten layer, so we can get a 1 * 16384 sized vector finally.

Block5 and block6 share common structures including 1 fully connection layer and 1 dropout. In block5, we get a 16384 numbers from block4 named flatten layer, we need to calculate 128 outputs based on these 16384 numbers by using the linear formula with 16384 * 128 + 128 = 2097280 parameters, so well as block6, there are 128 * 128 + 128 = 16512 parameters.

Softmax function is adopted in block7, so that we can get probabilities of 22 alphabets, one of these alphabets who reach the maximum of the probabilities will be recognized as the final result. So as to the block5 and block6 above, there are 128 * 22 + 22 = 2838 parameters. As shown in Fig. 5, 1 sample vector is combined with 3 features($x1$, $x2$, $x3$), and 1 output vector is combined with 3 features which are treated as probabilities of different categories, we take the largest probability as the final recognition result.

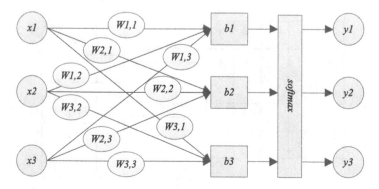

Fig. 5. Simple softmax case

Usually the flow chart above will be transformed to Eq. (4) or vector matrix (5) so as to gain higher efficiency.

$$\begin{bmatrix} y_1 \\ y_2 \\ y_3 \end{bmatrix} = softmax \begin{pmatrix} W_{1,1}x_1 + W_{1,2}x_2 + W_{1,3}x_3 + b_1 \\ W_{2,1}x_1 + W_{2,2}x_2 + W_{2,3}x_3 + b_2 \\ W_{3,1}x_1 + W_{3,2}x_2 + W_{3,3}x_3 + b_3 \end{pmatrix} \tag{4}$$

$$\begin{bmatrix} y_1 \\ y_2 \\ y_3 \end{bmatrix} = softmax \left(\begin{bmatrix} W_{1,1} & W_{1,2} & W_{1,3} \\ W_{2,1} & W_{2,2} & W_{2,3} \\ W_{3,1} & W_{3,2} & W_{3,3} \end{bmatrix} \begin{bmatrix} x_1 \\ x_2 \\ x_3 \end{bmatrix} + \begin{bmatrix} b_1 \\ b_2 \\ b_3 \end{bmatrix} \right) \tag{5}$$

3 Back Propagation Method

If the whole neural network plus the structure of the cost function is treated as a function of a series of functions (each layer corresponds to a function), the derivative of each of the functions can be obtained by mathematical expression analysis.

$$h_\theta(x) = \left(f^{(l+1)} \cdot f^{(l)} \cdots f^{(3)} \cdot f^{(2)} \cdot f^{(1)} \right) \tag{6}$$

In (6) where θ is the parameter of current CNN, and $f^{(1)} = x$, $f^{(L+1)} = h_q(x)$, and for every l, the derivatives of the functions (7) between adjacent layers are known.

$$\partial = \frac{\partial f^{(l+1)}}{\partial f^{(l)}} \tag{7}$$

According to the chain guide law, the cost function is applied to the derivative of any one layer J about l, that is, the error signal is backwardly transmitted to the first layer by numerical calculation in (8).

$$\delta_l = \frac{\partial}{\partial f^{(l)}} J(\theta, x, y) = \frac{\partial J}{\partial f^{(l+1)}} \frac{\partial f^{(l+1)}}{\partial f^{(l)}} = \delta_{l+1} \frac{\partial f^{(l+1)}}{\partial f^{(l)}} \tag{8}$$

In the l layer, calculate the gradient from J to the parameter $\theta^{(l)}$ according to (9).

$$\nabla_{\theta^{(l)}} J(\theta, x, y) = \frac{\partial J}{\partial \theta^{(l)}} = \frac{\partial J}{\partial f^{(l)}} \frac{\partial f^{(l)}}{\partial \theta^{(l)}} = \delta_l \frac{\partial f^{(l)}}{\partial \theta^{(l)}} \tag{9}$$

Finally, the gradients of all samples were added to give a total gradient as given in (10).

$$\nabla_{\theta^{(l)}} J(\theta) = \sum_{i=1}^{m} \nabla_{\theta^{(l)}} J\left(\theta, x^{(i)}, y^{(i)} \right) \tag{10}$$

Adam (Adaptive Moment Estimation) is an effective random optimization method that requires only a step to meet memory requirements. The method actually calculates the adaptive learning rate of the individual, and different parameters can be obtained from the gradients of the first and second moments. The advantage is that the size of the parameter update is constant, it does not require a fixed target, and uses sparseness, the gradient is performed naturally, and the basic formula is given as follow.

$$m_t = \mu \cdot m_{t-1} + (1 - \mu) \cdot g_t \tag{11}$$

In (11), m_t is the first moment estimation for gradient, as the estimation for $E[g_t]$.

$$n_t = v \cdot n_{t-1} + (1 - v) \cdot g_t^2 \tag{12}$$

In (12), n_t: second moment estimation for gradient, as the estimation for $E[g_t^2]$.

$$\hat{m}_t = \frac{m_t}{1 - \mu^t} \tag{13}$$

$$\hat{n}_t = \frac{n_t}{1 - v^t} \tag{14}$$

We calculate the correction value of m_t according to (13), and the correction value of n_t according to (14). Use m_t as the unbiased estimation for $E[g_t]$ approximately and n_t as the unbiased estimation for $E[g_t^2]$ approximately.

The weight training method of convolutional neural networks uses a method based on a stepwise optimization of stochastic objective functions. Assume the cost function of the convolutional neural network to be $J(W, b)$, we can get the result from (15) as follow.

$$J(W,b) = \frac{1}{m}\sum_{i=1}^{m} J(W, b; x_i, y_i) = \frac{1}{m}\sum_{i=1}^{m} \left(\frac{1}{2}\|h_{W,b}(x_i) - y_i\|^2\right) \tag{15}$$

In (15), W is connection parameters between units in a convolutional neural network, b is the bias, m is the number of training samples, $h_{w,b}(x_t)$ is output of the last layer, that is the softmax layer in our convolutional network model, and y_i is the real label of the i th sample.

$$\theta_{t+1} = \theta_t - \frac{\eta}{\sqrt{\hat{n}_t} + \varepsilon}\hat{m}_t \tag{16}$$

Here, the correction value of m_t and n_t have been given above, and we set η as 0.9 as learning rate, set ε as 10^{-8} so as to avoid the case when the denominator is 0 according to (16).

Then, we can find the minimum value of the cost function $J(W, b)$ by constantly updating the parameters W and b.

4   Case Study for Italian Alphabets

The LIS gesture database in this article is collected from the internet by our team. The created data set includes 11008 photos, including 22 letters. The four letters (G, S, J, and Z) are excluded from the data set because the corresponding symbols need to be moved, and Fig. 6 shows the collection of gesture pictures from different directions.

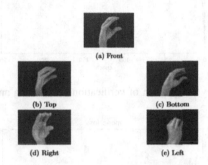

Fig. 6.   Images of gesture c collected from different directions

As shown in Fig. 7, we observed 87% of the final training accuracy and 98% of the verification accuracy. The verification accuracy is higher than the training accuracy, so the training loss is much higher than the verification loss. In addition, because the model changes over time, the loss of the first batch of an epoch is usually higher than the second batch, and we remember that the training loss is the average loss per batch of training data.

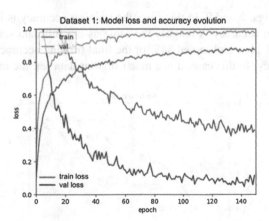

Fig. 7.   Comparison of accuracy and loss rate of training set training and verification

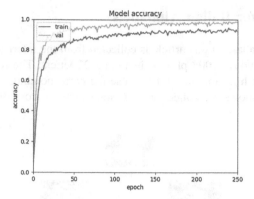

Fig. 8. Accuracy comparison of verification set training and verification

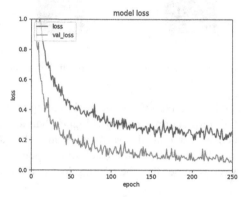

Fig. 9. Loss Rate comparison of training and verification in verification set

As shown in Figs. 8 and 9, in this case, the training accuracy is increased to 91%, and the verification accuracy is roughly the same as the full data set (97%).

In Figs. 10 and 11, we observed 84% of the final training accuracy and 94% of the verification accuracy. In this case, it is a much smaller data set: the internal differences

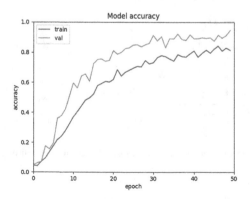

Fig. 10. Accuracy comparison of test set training and verification

of the small data set are relatively small, so this means that the model correctly captures the internal data of the pattern and the training error is greater.

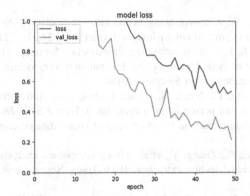

Fig. 11. Loss Rate comparison of test set training and verification

5 Conclusion

In this paper, only static letter gesture recognition is studied. The vocabulary is limited, the number and scope of samples are limited, the recognition rate is not very ideal, and it is still in the testing stage. Follow-up hope to do the following work: semantic definition of sign language gestures, so that it can be more intuitive recognition, and try to interact with the development of the system. The next step is to use C++ language to implement a widely used gesture recognition system to meet the needs of real life.

Acknowledgement. This paper is sponsored by the 9th Key Subject Construction Project of Henan (Zhengzhou Normal University) & National Education Ministry, School and Research Cooperation Project (NEMSRC, Grant 201801329013).

References

1. Huang, J., Zhou, W., Zhang, Q., et al.: Video-based sign language recognition without temporal segmentation. In: 32nd AAAI Conference on Artificial Intelligence (AAAI 2018) (2018)
2. Anantha Rao, G., Kishore, P.V.V., Sastry, A.S.C.S., Anil Kumar, D., Kiran Kumar, E.: Selfie continuous sign language recognition with neural network classifier. In: Satapathy, S. C., Bhateja, V., Chowdary, P.S.R., Chakravarthy, V.V.S.S.S., Anguera, J. (eds.) Proceedings of 2nd International Conference on Micro-Electronics, Electromagnetics and Telecommunications. LNEE, vol. 434, pp. 31–40. Springer, Singapore (2018). https://doi.org/10.1007/978-981-10-4280-5_4
3. Hu, Y., Zhao, H.F., Wang, Z.G.: Sign language fingerspelling recognition using depth information and deep belief networks. Int. J. Pattern Recogn. Artif. Intell. **32**(06), 13 (2018)

4. Aristodemo, V., Geraci, C.: Visible degrees in Italian sign language. Nat. Lang. Linguist. Theory **2**, 1–15 (2017)
5. Islam, M.M., Siddiqua, S., Afnan, J.: Real time hand gesture recognition using different algorithms based on American sign language. In: IEEE International Conference on Imaging (2017)
6. Ameen, S., Vadera, S.: A convolutional neural network to classify American sign language fingerspelling from depth and colour images. Expert Syst. **34**(3), e12197 (2017)
7. Mei, S., Jiang, R., Ji, J., et al.: Invariant feature extraction for image classification via multi-channel convolutional neural network. In: International Symposium on Intelligent Signal Processing and Communication Systems (2018)
8. Schetinin, V., Jakaite, L., Nyah, N., et al.: Feature extraction with GMDH-type neural networks for EEG-based person identification. Int. J. Neural Syst. **28**(6), 1750064 (2018)
9. Li, Z., Lu, X.: Feature extraction based on support vector data description. Neural Process. Lett. **1**, 1–17 (2018)
10. Zhou, G., Cichocki, A., Zhang, Y., et al.: Group component analysis for multiblock data: common and individual feature extraction. IEEE Trans. Neural Netw. Learn. Syst. **27**(11), 2426–2439 (2016)
11. Chan, W., Ke, N.R., Lane, I.: Transferring knowledge from a RNN to a DNN. Comput. Sci. (2015)
12. Lecun, Y., Bengio, Y., Hinton, G.: Deep learning. Nature **521**(7553), 436 (2015)
13. Wei, Y., Sun, X., Yang, K., et al.: Hierarchical semantic image matching using CNN feature pyramid. Comput. Vis. Image Underst. **169**, S1077314218300018 (2018)
14. Ren, S., He, K., Girshick, R., et al.: Faster R-CNN: towards real-time object detection with region proposal networks. IEEE Trans. Pattern Anal. Mach. Intell. **39**(6), 1137–1149 (2017)

Two-Stage Algorithm for Solving Multi-depot Green Vehicle Routing Problem with Time Window

Yang Li[1], Bin Qian[1,2(✉)], Rong Hu[1,2], Li-Ping Wu[1], and Bo Liu[3]

[1] School of Information Engineering and Automation,
Kunming University of Science and Technology, Kunming 650500, China
bin.qian@vip.163.com
[2] School of Mechanical and Electronic Engineering,
Kunming University of Science and Technology, Kunming 650500, China
[3] Academy of Mathematics and Systems Science,
Chinese Academy of Sciences, Beijing 100190, China

Abstract. This paper proposes a two-stage algorithm (TSA) for solving the Multi-Depot Green VRP with time window (MDGVRPTW). The problem is np-hard. Firstly, the first stage is the decomposition stage. In this stage, Edge balanced algorithm (EBA) is combined with K-means clustering algorithm to decompose MDGVRPTW into multiple GVRP to reduce the complexity of solving the problem. Then, the second stage is the problem-solving stage, in which the improved hybrid ant colony algorithm (IHACO) is used to search the solution space of each decomposed subproblem in parallel. In order to obtain the solution of the original problem, an adaptive pheromone incremental updating strategy is proposed to improve the efficiency of ant colony algorithm. Finally, the effectiveness of the proposed algorithm is verified by comparing the simulation results with the relevant algorithms.

Keywords: Green vehicle routing problem (GVRP) · Multiple depots · Time window · K-means · Hybrid ant colony algorithm

1 Introduction

The traditional Vehicle Routing Problem (VRP) was first proposed by Dantzig and Ramser in 1959 [1]. This problem is mainly described as the intelligent scheduling of vehicle travel quantity, route and travel time to optimize the total transportation cost while meeting the requirements of vehicle load, volume, mileage and customer service. With the increasingly prominent environmental problems, Green VRP (GVRP), which takes into account carbon emissions and other factors, has been gradually studied in recent years [2]. One branch of research on GVRP is multi-depot GVRP (MDGVRPTW). In terms of MDGVRPTW, Jabir et al. considered factors such as carbon dioxide emissions in the objective function and solved the problem by combining the ant colony algorithm with Variable Neighborhood Search (VNS). Experiments have proved that the algorithm was useful not only for small-scale problems but also for the large-scale issues [3]. Kaabachi established a multi-objective optimization

© Springer Nature Switzerland AG 2019
D.-S. Huang et al. (Eds.): ICIC 2019, LNCS 11643, pp. 665–675, 2019.
https://doi.org/10.1007/978-3-030-26763-6_64

model which took into account factors such as distance, carbon emissions, and fuel consumptions in the objective function. Ant colony algorithm was used to solve the problem. Although MDVRP has been widely studied, the literature research on MDVRP which takes carbon emissions, fuel emissions and time windows into account is still minimal. Since VRP is the np-hard problem and MDGVRPTW can reduced to GVRPTW, MDGVRPTW also belongs to the np-hard problem, so it is of great theoretical significance to study. Previous studies have shown that the traditional mathematical programming method for solving the small-scale VRP with only 20 customers requires a long time [5]. Therefore, this paper designed an intelligent optimization algorithm to solve large-scale MDGVRPTW.

In the existing MDGVRPTW research, most of the problems are solved as a whole, but due to the complexity of the problem, the designed encoding and decoding methods which are complex and inefficient reduces the search efficiency of the algorithm. In recent years, some scholars use clustering strategy to decompose the problem first and then put forward an algorithm to solve the corresponding subproblem and then achieved excellent results. For example, Geetha added the nearest neighbor algorithm in the initialized process of the solution algorithm to cluster the customers and classify the customers close to a certain depot into a customer group, and then used the hybrid genetic algorithm to solve the problem [6]. Ho adopted the similar processing methods that added the nearest neighbor algorithm to cluster customers in the process of genetic algorithm initialization, and then grouped customers through CW saving algorithm. Finally, the original problem converted into the multiple TSP [7]. Geetha improved the method of literature [7] by using the improved K-means algorithm to cluster customers first and then using the PSO algorithm combined with the genetic operation to solve it [8]. However, there is no algorithm to solve the green vehicle routing problem (MDGVRPTW) by using the clustering strategy.

Referring to the idea of "decomposition first, optimization second" mentioned above, this paper proposes a two-stage algorithm (TSA) to solve MDGVRPTW. Firstly, IBKA (Improved balanced K-means algorithm) submitted in the decomposition stage of the problem which is used to assign a certain number of customers (or customer groups) to each depot thus forming a series of GVRP. IBKA extended the application range of the existing balanced K-means clustering algorithm [9] from 2 to 3 depots that made the distribution between depots and customers more reasonable. Then, in the solving stage of the problem, the improved ant colony algorithm was used to conduct a parallel global search for the solution space of each subproblem (GVRP) and then found the high-quality solution area. Meanwhile, a local search based on a variety of neighborhood structures was designed to search the high-quality solution region in detail. Finally, the effectiveness of the proposed TSA is verified by simulation and algorithm comparison.

2 Problem Description

2.1 MDGVRPTW Problem Description and Related Assumptions

The vehicle routing problem studied in this paper mainly considers the model with multiple depots, time window constraints, carbon emission, and fuel emission. The customer's location coordinates, depots location coordinates, customer's time window and customer's goods demands has been given by the data.

2.2 Establishment of MDGVRPTW Mathematical Model

$$\text{min}Z = F_1 + F_2 + F_3 + F_4 + F_5$$

$$F_1 = \sum_{p=1}^{P_t} \sum_{k=1}^{K_P} \sum_{i=0}^{N} \sum_{j=0}^{N} C_1 * x_{pijk} * d_{ij}$$

$$F_2 = \sum_{p=1}^{P_t} \sum_{k=1}^{K_P} \sum_{i=0}^{N} \sum_{j=0}^{N} C_2 * FU_{ij} * x_{pijk}$$

$$F_3 = \sum_{p=1}^{P_t} \sum_{k=1}^{K_P} \sum_{i=0}^{N} \sum_{j=0}^{N} C_3 * E_{ij} * x_{pijk} \qquad (1)$$

$$F_4 = \sum_{p=1}^{P_t} \sum_{k=1}^{K_P} \sum_{i=0}^{N} \sum_{j=0}^{N} C_4 * x_{pijk}$$

$$F_5 = \sum_{i=1}^{N} \max\{pe * (ET_i - t_i), 0, pl * (t_i - LT_i)\}$$

The calculation method of fuel emission and carbon emission adopts the comprehensive fuel consumption model [9]:

$$FU_{ij} = \psi * \left(\lambda * N * V_s + \frac{P_{tr}}{\eta}\right) * d_{ij}/(\mu * \xi * v)$$

$$E_{ij} = \psi * \left(\lambda * N * V_s + \frac{P_{tr}}{\eta}\right) * d_{ij} * e/(\mu * \xi * v)$$

$$s.t \quad \sum_{j=1}^{N} \sum_{k=1}^{K_P} x_{P0jk} = \sum_{j=1}^{N} \sum_{k=1}^{K_P} x_{Pj0k} \leq K_P (\forall P \in P_s) \qquad (2)$$

$$\sum_{p=1}^{P_t} \sum_{i=1}^{N} \sum_{k=1}^{K_P} x_{Pijk} = 1 \quad (i \neq j, \forall j \in V \backslash \{0\}) \qquad (3)$$

$$\sum_{p=1}^{P_t} \sum_{j=1}^{N} \sum_{k=1}^{K_P} x_{Pijk} = 1 \quad (i \neq j, \forall i \in V \backslash \{0\}) \qquad (4)$$

$$\sum_{j=1}^{N} x_{P0jk} = \sum_{j=1}^{N} x_{Pj0k} \leq 1, \ (\forall P \in P_s, \forall k \in K_P) \qquad (5)$$

$$\sum_{j=1}^{N} \sum_{i=1}^{N} x_{Pijk} * q_i \leq Q \ (i \neq j, \forall k \in K_P, \forall P \in P_s) \qquad (6)$$

$$t_j = \sum_{i=0}^{N} x_{Pijk} * \left(t_i + \frac{d_{ij}}{v} + s_i\right), (j \in V\backslash\{0\}, \forall P \in P_s, \forall k \in K_P) \tag{7}$$

$$x_{Pijk} = \begin{cases} 1 \\ 0 \end{cases} \quad (i \neq j, j, i \in V, \forall k \in K_P, \forall P \in P_s) \tag{8}$$

Where the objective function (1) is expressed as minimizing the total transportation cost which includes five types of costs. Constraint (2) means that the number of vehicles started from a certain depot is equal to the number of vehicles returning to the same depot, and must be less than or equal to the total number of vehicles in a certain depot; Constraints (3) and (4) mean that any customer can only be served by one vehicle and only once; Constraint (5) means that all vehicles started from a certain depot must return to the same depot. If constraint (5) equals to zero, it means that this vehicle is not used; Constraint (6) means that the vehicle cannot exceed its rated load in the distribution process. If the left hand of the constraint (5) less than Q, that means the load of the vehicle is underload; Constraint (7) represents the time when the vehicle arrives at customer j. Constraint (8) represents the decision variable in the objective function, whose value range is 0 or 1 (Table 1).

Table 1. Symbols and definitions

Symbol	Definition	Symbol	Definition
F_1	Distance cost	K_P	P depots contain Kp car
F_2	Fuel costs	N	N customers total
F_3	Carbon cost	V	The set of customer Numbers $\{0,1,2...,N\}$ (0 represents depot)
F_4	Fixed vehicle cost	d_{ij}	The distance from i to j
F_5	Time window penalty fee	x_{Pijk}	Decision variable
C_1	Distance cost coefficient	pe	A Unit penalty for the early arrival of vehicles
C_2	The fuel cost coefficient	pl	A Unit penalty for the late arrival of vehicles
C_3	Carbon emission cost coefficient	ET_i	The earliest time of customer i
C_4	Fixed departure cost coefficient	LT_i	The latest time of customer i
i	Number i customer	S_i	The unloading time required by customer i
j	Number j customer	q_i	The demand for goods required by customer i
P_s	P_s represents the set $\{1,2...P_t\}$,	t_i	When the vehicle arrives at customer i
P_t	P_t depots in total	Q	The maximum carrying capacity of a vehicle

(continued)

Table 1. (*continued*)

Symbol	Definition	Symbol	Definition
P	Number P depot	FU_{ij}	The fuel consumption of the vehicle from customer i to customer j
E_{ij}	The carbon emission of the vehicle from customer i to customer j		

Note: references for setting other relevant parameters in the comprehensive fuel consumption model [10]

3 The First Stage (The Decomposition Stage)

To guide the intelligent algorithm searching in the high-quality solution space and improving the efficiency of the algorithm effectively, this paper first adopts the improved balanced K-means clustering algorithm.

3.1 Improved Balanced K-means Algorithm (IBKA)

Due to the literature [11] the balance algorithm applies only for the two groups of customers. While the number of depots is more than two, customers need to be clustered forming more than two groups which are balanced. In this paper, the balanced K-means algorithm is extended to balance among three types of customer groups. The balanced algorithm steps and related pseudo-codes among three groups of customers are as follows:

> **Step 1:** Perform the standard K-means clustering algorithm for all customers and take the clustering center of gravity as the coordinate position of each depot when initializing. Initialize the number of clustering (three categories) as the number of depot (three categories). Take Euclidean distance as the evaluation index and the number of iterations as the termination condition.
>
> **Step 2:** When the above steps were finished, the balance algorithm is performed among the three types of customer groups, as shown in Table 2.
>
> **Step 3:** Calculate the distance from each depot to each clustering center of gravity and list the distance matrix A. A is the two-dimensional matrix of m(row) * n (column). The matrix represents the distance from a depot to a clustering center of gravity, m is the number of depots, and n is the number of clustering center.
>
> **Step 4:** Add the elements of A with different rows and columns. Diverse results can be figured out by this method. Select the smallest value of the results as the final selection.

$$A_{(m*n)} = \begin{pmatrix} d(1,1) & d(1,2) & d(1,3) \\ d(2,1) & d(2,2) & d(2,3) \\ d(3,1) & d(3,2) & d(3,3) \end{pmatrix} \tag{9}$$

$$d_i = \min(d_1, d_2, d_3, d_4, d_5, d_6) \tag{10}$$

Table 2. Pseudo-code for K-means balance algorithm of three depots

---

```
// The clustering results of the above K-means algorithm: A, B and C represent three types of customers
//
    Begin
        sort_client(A, B, C);      // The number of customers in the three customer groups A, B and C is
    sorted and exchanged accordingly, so that the number of customers in the three categories A>, B> C//
        sort_distance(A, B, C);   // Calculate the edge distance between A, B;A, C;B and C respectively, and
    sort them accordingly (algorithm of edge distance from [11]).//
        While (condition 1)      // Condition 1 means that the number of customers in A,B, and C is no
    more than 1//
            if (condition 2)     // Condition 2 represents the minimum distance from A customer in category
    A to an edge in class B//
                Move (A, B) ;    // Move the client with the smallest edge distance in class A to class B//
            elseif (condition3)  // Condition 3 represents the minimum distance from A customer in
    category A to an edge in class C//
            Move (A, C) ;    // Same as above //
            else
            Move (B, C) ;    // Same as above//
            end // The number of any two types of customers in A,B and C is equal
            if (condition4)    // Condition 4 indicates that if the difference between the most customer class
    and the least customer class is greater than N after balancing the two above//
            equal_ distribution(A,B,C) ;  // Among the three types of customers, A, B and C move the most
    customers to the other two types in A balanced way, and finally make the difference between the most
    customers and the least customers less than N (N is the setting value, which is set as 10 in this paper).//
            end
    end
```

The matrix A including $d(m, n)$ that expressed the distance from m to n. The values of different row and column elements in matrix A calculated respectively and the number of calculations is m! times in total. The addition method is:

$$d_1 = d(1, 1) + d(2, 2) + d(3, 3)$$
$$d_2 = d(1, 1) + d(2, 3) + d(3, 2)$$
$$\cdots\cdots$$
$$d_3 = d(1, 3) + d(2, 2) + d(3, 1)$$

Select the minimum value of $d_1 \ldots d_k$ (k = m!). According to formula (10), if d_1 is the minimum, then class A will be selected by depot1 for serving.

4   The Second Stage (The Solving Stage)

4.1   Encoding Method and Decoding Method

This paper adopted the encoding method that including all customers in a depot after clustering. The depot was defined by the number 0 that did not add to paths, and each ant represented the path including all customers of a depot [12]. For example, a total of 10 customers for vehicles in a depot was encoded by 1-4-9-5-10-2-3-6-7-8.

The decoding method was used by the Beasley's that decoded the ant's path [13]. Every client's node of the ant's path should be considered successively until the sum of the clients' demands was higher than the load capacity of the vehicle. Then it would be formed one route of the vehicle by these clients' nodes. Simultaneously, kept finding the rest of the clients' nodes of ant's path until the path dividing had been finished.

4.2   Initialization

(1) Pheromone concentration initialization

Scan method was used to construct a route of all customers' points served by vehicles [14], and the constructed the route that was the ant's path is used to initialize the pheromone concentration that defined τ_{ij}:

$$\tau_{ij} = \begin{cases} P_m & \textit{if } i, j \textit{ is the ant's path constructed by scanning method} \\ 1 & \textit{else} \end{cases} \tag{11}$$

Where $P_m > 1$. To prevent the algorithm from getting trapped into local optimization earlier, the maximum and minimum values of pheromone concentration of τ_{ij} are set during the algorithm process [15].

$$\tau_{ij}\_\min = \frac{Q_m}{2 \sum_i^N d_{0i}}, \ 0 < \tau_{ij}\_\min < 1 \tag{12}$$

$$\tau_{ij}\_\max = \frac{Q_m}{\sum_i^N d_{0i}}, \ \tau_{ij}\_\max > P_m \tag{13}$$

Where N is the number of all customers, P_m is the initial pheromone concentration parameter, d_{0i} is the distance between the depot and customer i, and Q_m is a constant.

(2) The initialization of the increment of pheromone concentration and the number of ants

Set $\Delta\tau_{ij} = 0\,(i, j \in V, V$ defined all customer collection), $\Delta\tau_{ij}$ which is described the increment of pheromone concentration from the customer i to the customer j. Set the total number of ants as m, and set $m = 2/3 * N$, N denotes that there are N customers in total.

4.3   Route Search

(1) Tour construction

Tour construction was realized by this formula:

$$P_{ou}^t = \begin{cases} \dfrac{\tau_{ou}^\alpha * \eta_{ou}^\beta}{\sum \tau_{os}^\alpha * \eta_{os}^\beta} & \textit{if } u \notin tabu \\ 0 & \textit{else} \end{cases} \tag{14}$$

The P_{ou}^t represents the transition probability of t ant from o site to u site and operates by roulette in order to select the next site of the ant; α represents the importance of residual information from site o to site u, and β represents the importance of heuristic information from site o site u; *tabu* represents location that the ants have been searched,

s represents the customer location that the ant has not been searched, τ_{ou} represents the pheromone concentration under the current iteration times between o to u, η_{ou} represents the reciprocal of distance from o to u, τ_{os} represents the pheromone concentration under the current iteration times between o to s, η_{os} represents the reciprocal of distance from o to s.

(2) Local search
The path of each ant had decoded before the local search. After decoding, the route of each vehicle was generated, and the value of the objective function of each vehicle was calculated. The cumulative amount of the objective function of each vehicle was the total value. The VNS strategies of "2-opt", "or-opt", "Exchange" and "Swap" were used successively. If the route of each vehicle had been searched and the new route was better than the original route, then the original route would be replaced by the new route, otherwise, no replacement would be taken place. Figure 1 shows more details.

(3) Pheromone concentration update
The pheromone concentration update of the ant path performed as follows: If the customer sequence of the optimal solution generated under the current iteration time corresponds to the optimization target value M times without change, then execute formula (15) to calculate the $\rho(e)$, and perform (16–17); Otherwise, execute formula (16–17) to update the pheromone concentration directly:

$$\rho(e) = \begin{cases} 0.95\rho(e-1), & if\ 0.95\rho(e-1) \geq \rho_{min} \\ \rho_{min} & else \end{cases} \tag{15}$$

$$\tau_{ij}(e+1) = \rho(e) * \tau_{ij}(e) + \Delta\tau_{ij}(e),\ \rho(e) \in (0,1) \tag{16}$$

$$\Delta\tau_{ij}(e) = \begin{cases} \frac{W}{L_B} & if\ i,j\ is\ the\ ant\ passes\ by\ the\ customer\ site \\ 0 & else \end{cases} \tag{17}$$

Where defining $\rho(e_0) = 1$ as the initial value of $\rho(e)$; $\rho(e)$ represents *the* update coefficient of $\tau_{ij}(e)$, ρ_{min} represents the minimum value of $\rho(e)$, M represents the set value, e_0 represents the initial iteration times, e represents the current iteration time $(1 \leq e)$; $\tau_{ij}(e+1)$ represents the next iteration of the pheromone concentration, $\Delta\tau_{ij}(e)$ represents pheromone increment under the current iteration time; L_B represents the best value of the route traveled by the ant, and W represents the pheromone increment constant.

(4) Termination conditions
Setting the termination condition as the running time of the algorithm. If the running time requirement is met, the route of each vehicle serving customers and the corresponding total driving cost will be output.

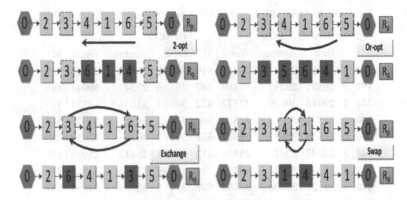

Fig. 1. Schematic diagram of local search strategy

5 Simulation Result and Comparisons

In this section, all the tests of the algorithm run on 3.2 GHz Intel I7 processor, 8G RAM, programming environment for matlab2018a, each the size of the case independent running 20 times, each algorithm in the 20 times shown the optimal, average and the worst (unit: yuan) in Table 3, the algorithm compared to the other at the same running time. The MDVRPTW problems in test data come from the web site (http://neo.lcc.uma.es/vrp/) of pr09, pr12, pr13, pr14, pr15, pr16.

To verify the effectiveness of this solution, IHACO_IBKA is compared with the effective algorithm for solving the MDGVRPTW in international journals. This algorithm is the Improved Hybrid ant colony-variable neighborhood search algorithm (IHACO) [3]. The parameters of IHACO_IBKA proposed are set as follows: Cpu_time = $0.5 * N(s)$, $\alpha = 1.25$, $\beta = 2.5$, $P_m = 1.1$, W = 500. The run time of CPU is also set to $0.5 * N(s)$ and its other parameters are set to the same values in literature [3].

5.1 TSA Performance Test

According to the test results in Table 3, except for the two cases, the average values of IHACO_IBKA are better than IHACO. Simultaneously, with the increase of the problem scale, the advantage of the algorithm is more obvious. The data shows that when the problem size increases, the solution space area of the problem also increases, and it is difficult to obtain the high-quality solution of the problem in a short time by using the intelligent optimization algorithm alone. IBKA was used to decompose the MDGVRPTW reasonably before IHACO was used to solve its subproblems. The standard deviations (SD) of the algorithm is better than IHACO in the most cases also. Finally, the experiment verifies the validity of solving MDGVRPTW by IHACO_IBKA.

Table 3. IHACO_IBKA and IHACO performance verification table

N_P	IHACO_IBKA				IHACO			
	Best	Average	Worst	SD	Best	Average	Worst	SD
144_2	24912	26011	**27162**	**519**	24287	**26002**	27568	539
192_2	**28581**	**29212**	31163	547	28886	29542	**30041**	**416**
216_2	**29616**	**30639**	**31572**	**422**	30907	31643	32551	475
240_2	**31371**	**31963**	**32834**	**540**	33462	34259	34922	588
288_2	**37828**	**38687**	**39371**	**552**	39697	40773	42052	733
144_3	24947	25423	**25990**	**312**	24111	**25412**	25999	320
192_3	32905	**33122**	**33759**	293	**31999**	33376	33860	**273**
216_3	33127	**33906**	**34784**	**587**	**33111**	33965	34869	687
240_3	**35888**	**37194**	38684	**835**	35947	37856	38751	866
288_3	**42516**	**43647**	**44271**	**566**	42586	43904	44327	766

Note: N represents the number of customers, P represents the number of depots

6   Conclusion

In this paper, TSA is proposed for solving MDGVRPTW. TSA algorithm consists of two stages. The first stage is the problem decomposition stage, in which IBKA is designed to decompose MDGVRPTW, so as to control the solution scale of the problem effectively. IBKA aims to shorten the transportation cost of vehicles, which is consistent with the optimization objective of the original problem. The second stage is the problem-solving stage. In this stage, an improved hybrid ant colony algorithm is proposed to solve each subproblem in parallel. Firstly, the improved ant colony algorithm is used to obtain a high-quality solution area of the subproblems, and then the local search using the designed VNS is performed in the high-quality solution area detailly. Through the simulation experiment and algorithm comparison, the proposed TSA is proved to be an effective algorithm for MDGVRPTW. In the next step, MDGVRPTW with uncertain factors will be considered and will design a new clustering strategy combining the problem information.

Acknowledgements. This research is partially supported by the National Science Foundation of China (51665025), and the Applied Basic Research Key Project of Yunnan, China.

References

1. Dantzig, R.: The truck dispatching problem. Manag. Sci. **1**(6), 80–81 (1959)
2. Erdoğan, S., Miller, H.E.: A green vehicle routing problem. Transp. Res. Part E: Logistics Transp. Rev. **48**(1), 100–114 (2012)
3. Jabir, E., Panicker, V., Sridharan, R.: Design and development of a hybrid ant colony-variable neighbourhood search algorithm for a multi-depot green vehicle routing problem. Transp. Res. Part D: Transp. Environ. **57**, 422–457 (2017)

4. Kaabachi, I., Jriji, D., Krichen, S.: An improved ant colony optimization for green multi-depot vehicle routing problem with time windows. IEEE (2017)
5. Schneider, M., Stenger, A., Goeke, D.: The electric vehicle-routing problem with time windows and recharging stations. Transp. Sci. 1–21 (2014)
6. Geetha, S., et al.: Metaheuristic approach for the multi-depot vehicle routing problem. Appl. Artif. Intell. Int. J. **26**, 878–901 (2012)
7. Ho, W., et al.: A hybrid genetic algorithm for the multi-depot vehicle routing problem. Eng. Appl. Artif. Intell. **21**, 548–557 (2008)
8. Geetha, S., Poonthalir, G., Vanathi, P.T.: Nested particle swarm optimization for multi-depot vehicle routing problem. Oper. Res. **16**(3), 329–348 (2013)
9. Ma, J., et al.: Mutation ant colony algorithm for multiple-depot multiple-types vehicle routing problems with shortest finish time. Syst. Eng. Theory Pract. **31**, 1508–1516 (2011)
10. Bektaş, T., Laporte, G.: The pollution-routing problem. Transp. Res. Part B: Methodol. **45** (8), 1232–1250 (2011)
11. He, R., et al.: Balanced K-means algorithm for partitioning areas in large-scale vehicle routing problem. IEEE (2009)
12. Bell, J.E., McMullen, P.R.: Ant colony optimization techniques for the vehicle routing problem. Adv. Eng. Inform. **18**, 41–48 (2004)
13. Beasley, J.E.: Route first—cluster second methods for vehicle routing. OMEGA **11**(4), 403–408 (1983)
14. Gillett, B.E., Miller, L.R.: A heuristic algorithm for the vehicle-dispatch problem. Oper. Res. **22**(2), 340–349 (1974). INFORMS Stable: https://www.jstor.org/stable/169591. Accessed 06 Oct 2018
15. Bin, Yu., Yang, Z.-Z., Yao, B.: An improved ant colony optimization for vehicle routing problem[J]. Eur. J. Oper. Res. **196**, 171–176 (2009)

Hybrid Cross-entropy Algorithm for Mixed Model U-shaped Assembly Line Balancing Problem

Yi-Fan Zheng[1], Rong Hu[1(✉)], Bin Qian[1], Ling Wang[2], and Feng-Hong Xiang[1]

[1] School of Information Engineering and Automation,
Kunming University of Science and Technology, Kunming 650500, China
ronghu@vip.163.com
[2] Department of Automation, Tsinghua University, Beijing 10084, China

Abstract. Assembly line balancing problem are widespread in manufacturing industries such as electronics or auto parts. As an efficient metaheuristic, cross-entropy (CE) method can be applied to solve mixed model U-shaped assembly line balancing problem (MMUALBP). First, a higher efficient task encoding method called task selection factor based (TSFB) encoding is proposed. Then, a hybrid cross-entropy algorithm (HCEA) is proposed, in the global phase of the algorithm, new individuals are generated through the cross-entropy probability matrix; and in the local phase, variable neighborhood search (VNS) strategy is used to improve the problem that the algorithm is easy to converge quickly and fall into local optimum. Finally, the effectiveness of HCEA in solving the MMUALBP is verified by experiments and comparisons.

Keywords: U-shaped assembly line balancing problem · Mixed model · Cross-entropy · Variable neighborhood search

1 Introduction

Assembly line is a special manufacturing system, generally as the last stage of production. In the manufacturing industry, assembly produce accounts for about 11%–40% of the total labor resources, and about 30%–50% of the total cost in the entire production [1]. Therefore, assembly produce plays a very important role in manufacturing. A system with such a function can be called an assembly line system: according to the specific process flow, each product passes through each workstation in the specified speed sequence, and all the operation steps are completed in sequence.

Assembly line balancing problem (ALBP) was first proposed in 1995 by Salveson [2] and has been proved to be an NP-hard problem [3], which research the problem of allocating a series of tasks with priority constraints to different workstations reasonable to improve the assembly line efficiency. Due to the higher space utilization rate and flexibility comparing to straight assembly line, U-shaped assembly line balancing problem (UALBP) has become a hot issue in the field of dispatching research in recent years. UALBP is introduced and modeled by Miltenburg et al. [4], and then be studied

© Springer Nature Switzerland AG 2019
D.-S. Huang et al. (Eds.): ICIC 2019, LNCS 11643, pp. 676–685, 2019.
https://doi.org/10.1007/978-3-030-26763-6_65

widely by many researchers. Urban et al. [5] established a 0–1 integer programming model for solving UALBP, and targeting the minimum number of workstations. Hadi et al. [6] designed a shortest path planning model to solve UALBP. Mathematical programming methods is not suitable for solving large-scale UALBP due to the high computational complexity, metaheuristic algorithms are considered to be a more effective way, such as genetic algorithm (GA) [7], simulated annealing algorithms (SA) [8], ant colony algorithm (ACO) [9] et al. Mixed-model assembly lines(MMUAL) produce several models which are the variations of a same base product on the same line. Rabbani et al. [10] proposed an objective of weighting maximizing line efficiency and minimizing the variation of workload to evaluate the MMUALBP, and using genetic algorithm based on 10 allocation rules encoding which proposed in [7]. Zhang [11] proposed an improved genetic algorithm using a multi-level random allocation encoding for solving large-scale MMUALBP.

Cross-entropy (CE) method was first proposed by Rubinstein [12] to estimate the probability of occurrence of rare events in complex random networks, whose key operation is to update the probability parameters of rare events and use the effective sampling method to approximate the problem to its optimal or suboptimal solution. CE method has been applied to solve combined optimization problem. Chepuri et al. [13] used the CE method to deal with vehicle routing problems. Santosa et al. [14] combine the CE method with the genetic algorithm to solve the no-wait job shop scheduling problem with the maximum makespan. Wadhawan et al. [15] used CE optimization method to solve the logistics scheduling problem of transport grain trains. As far as we know, there is no any published paper in CE method for MMUALBP.

In this paper, we proposed a hybrid cross-entropy algorithm (HCEA) for MMULBP, the optimization objective is weighting maximizing line efficiency and minimizing the variation of workload which proposed in [10]. The MMUALPB is described in the Sect. 2. In Sect. 3, the framework of HECA for solving it is proposed. Experiments and comparisons are provided to verify the effectiveness of HCEA. Finally, we put an end to the paper with some conclusions.

2 Problem Description

2.1 General UALBP Description

Compared with the straight assembly line, each workstation on the U-shaped assembly line contains both the start and the end of line, workers can operate both sides of the assembly line by moving around. As shown in Fig. 1, the cycle time is set to 10, follow the same production sequence, the assembly line with U-shaped layout requires fewer workstations than which with straight layout. Therefore, U-shaped assembly line has higher efficiency and flexibility.

While in straight lines a task could be allocated to a workstation only if all of its predecessors are allocated before, U-lines allow both the forward and backward allocation of tasks to stations. The concepts of combined precedence graph and phantom precedence diagram are employed to describe the precedence relationship between tasks for both sides of the line, as shown in Fig. 2. Generally, UALBP model is described as follow:

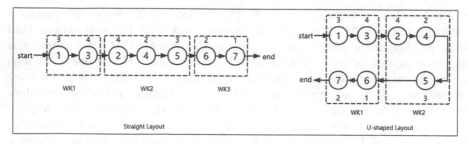

Fig. 1. The difference between U-type and strait assembly line

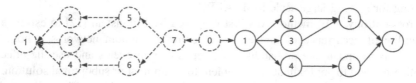

Fig. 2. Precedence graph and phantom precedence diagram

$$\sum_{j=1}^{J} (X_{ij} + Y_{ij}) = 1, \forall i \in \{i_1, i_2, \ldots, I\} \tag{1}$$

$$\sum_{j=1}^{J=1} (X_{\bar{i}j} - X_{\tilde{i}j}) + (Y_{\bar{i}j} - Y_{\tilde{i}j}) \geq 0, \forall (\tilde{i}, \bar{i}) \in PR \tag{2}$$

$$\sum_{i=1}^{I} t_i(X_{ij} + Y_{ij}) \leq CT, \forall j \in \{j_1, j_2, \ldots, J\} \tag{3}$$

Formula (1) indicates that each task must be allocated and can only be allocated to one side of the station, X_{ij} (Y_{ij}) shows if task i is allocated to workstation j from the precedence (phantom) graph. Formula (2) indicates the precedence relationship between tasks in two sides of line, $\forall(\tilde{i}, \bar{i}) \in PR$ shows that task $\bar{i}$ must be started after the finish of task $\tilde{i}$. Formula (3) is the cycle time constraint, the cycle time is defined as the specified total operating time for each station in a producing cycle. The actual total operating time cannot be greater than the cycle time in each station.

2.2 MMUALBP Description

Mixed-model U-shaped assembly lines (MMUAL) are common in assembly lines of small-volume products with similar processes, such as electronic components. Since there are different precedence relationships between tasks for several products, it is necessary to establish a joint precedence diagram of all products to describe the precedence relationship of the MMUAL, as shown in Fig. 3.

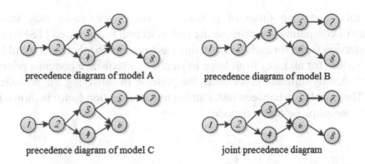

Fig. 3. The joint precedence diagram of MMUAL

$$\text{Maximize } \frac{1}{M} \times \sum_{m=1}^{M} \left(\frac{\sum_{i=1}^{I} t_{im}}{CT \times J} + \left[1 - \sqrt{\frac{1}{J} \times \sum_{j=1}^{J} (u_{m,j} - a_m)^2} \right] \right) \tag{4}$$

$$\frac{1}{M} \times \sum_{m=1}^{M} \left(\frac{\sum_{i=1}^{I} t_{im}}{CT \times J} \right) \tag{5}$$

$$1 - \frac{1}{M} \times \sum_{m=1}^{M} \sqrt{\frac{1}{J} \times \sum_{j=1}^{J} (u_{m,j} - a_m)^2} \tag{6}$$

$$u_{m,j} = \frac{1}{CT} \times \sum_{i=1}^{I} t_{im} (X_{ij} + Y_{ij}) \tag{7}$$

$$a_m = \frac{1}{J} \times \sum_{j=1}^{J} u_{m,j} \tag{8}$$

Formula (4) is the optimization objective of MMUALBP proposed by Rabbani et al. [10]. Actually, it is weighted by two parts shown in (5) and (6). Formula (5) is the calculation of line efficiency (LE) which is defined as ratio of the actual total operating time to the cycle time, M is the number of models, I is the total number of tasks, and J is the workstation number. Formula (6) is to maximize the difference between 1 and variation of workload (VOW) due to the VOW is a minimized objective, VOW is the standard deviation of the actual efficiency of each workstation, the smaller the value is means that the MMUAL has stronger stability, $u_{m,j}$ is the utilization of workstation j and a_m is the average utilization of all workstations. The calculation of $u_{m,j}$ and a_m shown in (7) and (8).

3 HCEA for MMUALBP

3.1 Encoding and Decoding

Due to the complex precedence relationship between tasks of MMUAL, encoding and decoding are important problems for MMUALBP research. Consider that the Multiple-rule Based (MRB) encoding proposed by [7], which needs to calculate the number (total operating time) of predecessor (successor) tasks may increase the complexity of computing, we propose the task selection factor based (TSFB) encoding.

The selection factor for each task is defined as a real number between 0 and 1. Sort the selection factors for all tasks from large to small, this sequence contains priority information selected by different tasks under the premise of satisfying the precedence relationship. The correlation between task number and its selection factor is shown in Fig. 4.

Follow the steps below to decode:

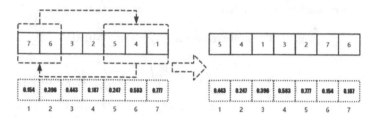

Fig. 4. The correlation between task number and its selection factor

Step 1: Initialize the current workstation $j = 1$, the current allocation number $n = 1$, task set $D = \{i_1, i_2, \ldots, I\}$;

Step 2: Establishing the precedence matrix for the joint precedence relationship, including a forward matrix and a background matrix. For example, the precedence matrix for the precedence diagram shown in Fig. 2 can be express as follow, if the kth row and lth column of the matrix equal to 1 that means task l is the predecessor for task k:

$$
\begin{bmatrix}
0 & 0 & 0 & 0 & 0 & 0 & 0 \\
1 & 0 & 0 & 0 & 0 & 0 & 0 \\
1 & 0 & 0 & 0 & 0 & 0 & 0 \\
1 & 0 & 0 & 0 & 0 & 0 & 0 \\
0 & 1 & 1 & 0 & 0 & 0 & 0 \\
0 & 0 & 0 & 1 & 0 & 0 & 0 \\
0 & 0 & 0 & 0 & 1 & 1 & 0
\end{bmatrix}
\begin{bmatrix}
0 & 1 & 1 & 1 & 0 & 0 & 0 \\
0 & 0 & 0 & 0 & 1 & 0 & 0 \\
0 & 0 & 0 & 0 & 1 & 0 & 0 \\
0 & 0 & 0 & 0 & 0 & 1 & 0 \\
0 & 0 & 0 & 0 & 0 & 0 & 1 \\
0 & 0 & 0 & 0 & 0 & 0 & 1 \\
0 & 0 & 0 & 0 & 0 & 0 & 0
\end{bmatrix}
$$

Step 3: Make the assignable task set $D_i = [\,]$, search for forward and background precedence matrix, if all the element in k th row of both matrixes equal to 0, do $D_i = D_i + i_k$ when i_k is still in set D.

Step 4: Comparing all the selection factors of tasks selected in Step 3, the task i_s which has the largest selection factor number will be allocated to the current workstation j.

Step 5: Set i_s the longest operating time in all M models.

Step 6: Determine whether the cycle time constraint shown in (3) is met, if the total operating time of the current workstation is over the cycle time, do $j = j + 1$, then move to Step 3; if not, do $D = D - i_s$, then move to Step 3.

Step 7: Do $n = n + 1$, if $n \leq N$, N is the max number of tasks, move to Step 3 to Step 6; if $n > N$, end.

3.2   Cross-entropy Method

Cross entropy (CE) is inspired by the concept of Kullback-Leibler distance which was developed to measure the distance between an ideal reference distribution and the actual distribution. CE method generally two key steps: generating samples with specific mechanism and updating parameters based on elite sample. Suppose that there is a maximize function $S(x)$ over all x in set X:

$$\gamma^* = \max_{x \in X} S(x) \tag{9}$$

Where X is the solution space for all task allocation schemes, γ^* is the optimal objective by function $S(x)$. The sample x needs obey the probability distribution $f(;\mu)$ of the parameter μ, so γ^* can be solved by determine the optimal probability distribution $f(;\mu)$. Using the probability estimation:

$$l(\gamma) = P_\mu(S(x) \geq \gamma) = \sum_x I_{\{S(x) \geq \gamma\}} \bullet f(x;\mu) = E_\mu I_{\{S(x) \geq \gamma\}} \tag{10}$$

The estimation of $l(\gamma)$ uses the method of important sampling, according to the distribution of g which can make $S(x)$ close to γ:

$$\hat{l} = \frac{1}{N} \sum_{i-1}^{N} I_{\{S(x_i) \geq \gamma_1\}} \frac{f(x_i;\mu)}{g(x_i)} \tag{11}$$

In order to estimate $l(\gamma)$, it is necessary to determine the probability parameter μ to minimize the difference between the optimal distribution g^* of the distribution g and $f(;\mu)$. Measure the Kullback-Leible (K-L) distances of two probability distributions to determine the similarity between them, and minimize the K-L distance equivalence to minimize the cross entropy. The problem eventually translates into a probability parameter μ that minimizes the cross entropy of the sample distribution $f(;\mu)$ and g^* from the sample distribution $f(;\mu)$:

$$\mu^* = \max_\mu E_\mu I_{\{S(x) \geq \gamma\}} \ln f(x;\mu) \tag{12}$$

The probability parameter μ is represented by a probability expression p, which can be expressed as follows:

$$p_{il} = \frac{E_p I_{\{S(X) \geq \gamma\}} I_{\{x_i=l\}}}{E_p I_{\{S(X) \geq \gamma\}}} = \frac{\sum\limits_{v=1}^{m} I_{\{S(X_v) \geq \gamma\}} I_{\{x_{vi}=l\}}}{\sum\limits_{v=1}^{m} I_{\{S(X_v) \geq \gamma\}}} \tag{13}$$

Expression p_{il} indicates the probability that task i is at the l th position.

3.3   VNS for Local Search

For combinatorial optimization problems, there are generally multiple high quality solutions in the vicinity. Therefore, the algorithm performs a variable neighborhood strategy (VNS) for local search on π_{gen} to achieve a detailed search for the region near π_{gen}.

For a certain arrangement $\pi = (\pi_1, \pi_2, \cdots \pi_n)$, Interchange (π, μ, v) represents the element at the position of the μ th position in the solution π and the element at the v th position. Swap (π, μ) operation is the element at the μ position and the element at the $\mu + 1$ position. Insert (π, μ, v) indicates the v position in the solution π The upper element is placed at the μ position and the element at the μ position is pushed back one position.

In this paper, the search strategy of variable neighborhood is mainly to use the Interchange operation to perform the interference operation, so that it can jump out of the local optimum, and select the swap operation and the insert operation by probability. According to the experimental results, the performance of the Insert operation is stronger. Therefore, the probability that the Insert operation is selected is slightly larger than the swap operation. Assume that $\pi_{gen} = (\pi_1, \pi_2, \cdots \pi_n)$ represents a better solution in contemporary populations. The specific experimental steps for neighborhood search are as follows:

Step 1: Interference operation. Randomly generate two numbers μ and v, and $\mu \neq v$, perform an Interchange operation on π_{gen} to generate π'_{gen}.
Step 2: Set $loop = 1$, randomly generate a number p of $[0, 1]$, if $p \leq 0.3$, proceed to Step 2.1, otherwise proceed to Step 2.2.
    Step 2.1: The number μ is randomly generated, and a Swap operation is performed on π'_{gen} to generate π''_{gen}.
    Step 2.2: Randomly generate two numbers μ and v, and $\mu \neq v$, perform an Interchange operation on π'_{gen} to generate π''_{gen}.
Step 3: If $f\left(\pi''_{gen}\right) < f\left(\pi'_{gen}\right)$, then $\pi'_{gen} = \pi''_{gen}$, if $loop < n$, $loop = loop + 1$.
Step 4: If $f\left(\pi'_{gen}\right) < f(\pi_{gen})$, then $\pi_{gen} = \pi'_{gen}$.

3.4   Proposed Algorithm

Proposed HCEA design not only utilizes the CE method itself to have a strong global search ability to solve the solution to the optimal solution, but also uses the processing technique based on the spatial characteristics of the random problem to improve the local search ability of the algorithm. Due to the balance of global and local search capabilities, it is helpful to obtain a better solution for MMUALBP.

A new solution can be generated by sampling the probability parameter determined by (13), and the specific steps of the CE method for probability sampling are given as follows:

Step 1: The probability distribution parameter of task coding in the k th iteration is $\mu(k - 1)$, and a certain number of individuals are randomly generated by the sampling method of roulette to constitute a set of random samples $\{x_1, x_2, \ldots, x_n\}$ of this iteration.

Step 2: The probability parameter $\mu(k-1)$ of this iteration is determined by the random sample generated in Step1 according to Eq. (13). In the single-objective optimization problem, by ordering the objective function value $\{S(x_1), S(x_2), \ldots, S(x_n)\}$ of the sample $\{x_1, x_2, \ldots, x_n\}$, the ρ-quantile of the sample is calculated such that $P(S(x) \leq \gamma^*) = \rho$, to select elite samples.

Step 3: For the probability parameter of the $(k+1)$ th iteration task coding, the following update strategy is introduced to introduce the smoothing coefficient α:

$$\mu(k) = \alpha\mu(k) + (1-\alpha)\mu(k-1) \tag{14}$$

In order to maintain the diversity and dispersion of the population, this paper uses the randomly generated method to initialize the population, and generates the task sequence by randomly generating the selection factors of different processes and sorting them. In addition, to avoid oversaturation of the probability parameters, the probability parameters are reset every 20 iterations. The algorithm flow is shown in Fig. 5.

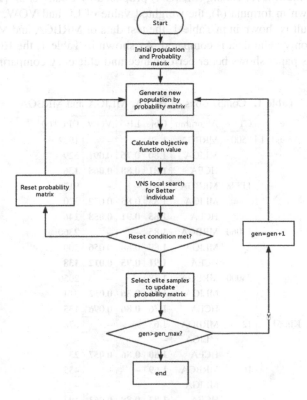

Fig. 5. Framework of HCEA

4   Simulation Result and Comparisons

4.1   Experimental Setup

HCEA are coded in Delphi 2010 and run on a PC with Intel i5-7300HQ 2.80 GHz. The proposed HCEA's parameters are set as follows: the population size $P = 50$, the smoothing parameter $\alpha = 0.2$, the swap (π, μ) operation probability of the variable neighborhood in the local search mechanism is 0.3, and the Insert (π, μ, v) operation is 0.7.

The experimental data comes from the assembly line balance data support website: http://alb.mansci.de/, which selects MMUALBP's medium-sized and large-scale two benchmark cases: Kim 61 and Arcus 111 to test the effect of HCEA for different scale problems. Each group of experiments runs independently for 10 times to average.

4.2   Results and Comparison

To test the performances of HCEA, we compare with a multi-rule based genetic algorithm (MRBGA) proposed by Rabbani et al. [10] and an improved genetic algorithm based on multi-level coding (MLIGA) proposed by Zhang et al. [11]. Objective function is shown in formula (4), the weighted value of LE and VOW. Experimental comparison result is shown in in Table 1, the test data of MRBGA and MLIGA comes from [10, 11], only valid data is compared. As shown in Table 1, the HCEA which is proposed in this paper shows better performance and efficiency comparing to MLIGA and MRBGA.

Table 1. Comparisons of HCEA, MLIGA and MRBGA

Case	CT	Algorithm	Obj	LE	VOW	CPUT(s)
Arcus111	8500	MRBGA	1.79	–	–	1902
		MLIGA	1.80	0.76	0.091	329
		HCEA	**1.81**	**0.88**	**0.068**	**136**
	11378	MRBGA	1.82	–	–	917
		MLIGA	1.83	0.85	0.072	320
		HCEA	**1.85**	**0.91**	**0.058**	**146**
	17060	MRBGA	1.85	–	–	2360
		MLIGA	1.89	0.88	0.056	300
		HCEA	**1.91**	**0.95**	**0.012**	**138**
	34000	MRBGA	1.78	–	–	2050
		MLIGA	**1.81**	**0.86**	**0.052**	314
		HCEA	1.76	**0.86**	0.096	**135**
Kim61	12	MRBGA	1.63	–	–	678
		MLIGA	–	–	–	–
		HCEA	**1.80**	**0.86**	**0.057**	**23**
	16	MRBGA	1.69	–	–	455
		MLIGA	–	–	–	–
		HCEA	**1.82**	**0.88**	**0.063**	**19**
	24	MRBGA	1.64	–	–	332
		MLIGA	–	–	–	–
		HCEA	**1.65**	**0.81**	**0.16**	**20**

5   Conclusion

This paper proposes a hybrid cross-entropy algorithm (HCEA) for MMULBP, The MMUALBP problem is transformed into a sorting model of the associated process after being coded by the selection factor, which greatly reduces the complexity of using intelligent algorithms to solve such problems. The proposed HCEA adopts a variable neighborhood search strategy to make the algorithm search in the neighborhood, and balance the global search and the local search through the maintenance operation. Simulation experiments verify the effectiveness of the coding method for improving computation time and the robustness of HCEA in solving such problems.

Acknowledgements. This research is partially supported by the National Science Foundation of China (51665025), and the Applied Basic Research Key Project of Yunnan, China, and National Natural Science Fund for Distinguished Young Scholars of China (61525304).

References

1. Du, Y.P., Yang, Y.X.: The research into the problem of assembly line balance. Mach. Des. Manuf. **2**, 1001–3997 (2003)
2. Salveson, M.E.: The assembly line balancing problem. J. Ind. Eng. **29**(10), 55–101 (1955)
3. Scholl, A.: Balancing and Sequencing of Assembly Lines, 2nd edn, pp. 34–351. Physica-Verlag, Heidelberg (1999)
4. Miltenburg, G.J., Wijngaard, J.: The U-line balancing problem. INFORMS (1994)
5. Urban, T.L.: Note. Optimal balancing of U-shaped assembly lines. Manag. Sci. **44**(5), 738–741 (1998)
6. Gencer, C., et al.: A shortest route formulation of simple U-type assembly line balancing problem. Appl. Math. Model. **29**(4), 373–380 (2005)
7. Baykasoğlu, A., Özbakır, L.: Stochastic U-line balancing using genetic algorithms. Int. J. Adv. Manuf. Technol. **32**(1–2), 139–147 (2007)
8. Jayaswal, S., Agarwal, P.: Balancing U-shaped assembly lines with resource dependent task times: a simulated annealing approach. J. Manuf. Syst. **33**(4), 522–534 (2014)
9. Sabuncuoglu, I., Erel, E., Alp, A.: Ant colony optimization for the single model U-type assembly line balancing problem. Int. J. Prod. Econ. **120**(2), 287–300 (2009)
10. Rabbani, M., Kazemi, S.M., Manavizadeh, N.: Mixed model U-line balancing type-1 problem: A new approach. J. Manuf. Syst. **31**(2), 131–138 (2012)
11. Zhang, Z.-K., et al.: Balancing large-size mixed-model U-type assembly lines via improved genetic algorithm. Mach. Des. Manuf. **1**, 137–139 (2016)
12. Rubinstein, R.Y., Kroese, D.P.: The Cross-Entropy Method: A Unified Approach to Combinatorial Optimization. Monte-Carlo Simulation and Machine Learning. Springer Verlag, New York (2004). https://doi.org/10.1007/978-1-4757-4321-0
13. Chepuri, K., Homem-De-Mello, T.: Solving the vehicle routing problem with stochastic demands using the cross-entropy method. Ann. Oper. Res. **134**(1), 153–181 (2005)
14. Santosa, B., Budiman, M.A., Wiratno, S.E.: A cross entropy-genetic algorithm for m-machines no-wait job-shop scheduling problem. J. Intell. Learn. Syst. Appl. **3**, 171–180 (2011)
15. Wadhawan, I.B., Pudney, P.J., Howlett, P.G., et al.: Scheduling trains with cross entropy optimisation. Anziam J. **51**, 332–346 (2010)

Study on Medical Image Report Generation Based on Improved Encoding-Decoding Method

Li Sun[1], Weipeng Wang[1], Jiyun Li[1(✉)], and Jingsheng Lin[2(✉)]

[1] School of Computer Science and Technology, DongHua University,
Shanghai 201620, China
jyli@dhu.edu.cn
[2] Rui Jin Hospital, Shanghai 200000, China
jasonlin@rjh.com.cn

Abstract. The automatic description of images has made good advances, but limited by the little-sample dataset, that the automatic generation of medical imaging reports is still a challenging problem. Aiming at the problem of training the joint model (CNN-RNN) on little-sample datasets, this paper proposes an improved encoding-decoding mode, in which the encoder uses less parameter in FCN (Fully Convolutional Network) for identifying lesions in mammography, and encoding it into a semantic vector. The decoder uses a LSTM (Long Short-Term Memory network) for solving, thereby reducing sample requirements. In addition, this paper combines multi-label classification (MLC) to assist the semantic coding process and uses post-processing such as the beam search to make the output fit in the natural language description better. Compared to existing models, our improved model on public mammography dataset (INbreast) with real-world data supplement achieved the BLEU score improvements by two points.

Keywords: Deep learning · Mammography · Semantic description · Fully Convolutional Network

1 Introduction

In recent years, generating images descriptions using natural language sentences have gradually become a hot topic. This is a challenging task because it requires not only understanding the image but also transforming the visual semantics of the image into sentences. In order to establish a semantic relationship between the two different forms, it is necessary to map them into one space so as to understand the connection between them, which means, to establish a multi-task joint model. And deep learning has a good capability on this task.

Different from early sentence templates or methods based on sorting retrieval, deep neural networks can summarize the results on training samples, forming new grammatically correct sentences rather than template-based combinations, and it has a good ability of generalization. Our work is inspired by the latest advances in image description generation [1–8], as well as some early pioneering work [9–11]. However, most of the

© Springer Nature Switzerland AG 2019
D.-S. Huang et al. (Eds.): ICIC 2019, LNCS 11643, pp. 686–696, 2019.
https://doi.org/10.1007/978-3-030-26763-6_66

study on the automatic generation of image text is limited by the three-channel RGB image dataset of natural scenes such as MSCOCO [12]. In the field of medical imaging, this topic has not been popularized. Obviously, there are a number of problems in describing medical images. Compared with natural images, the semantic information of medical images tend to be concentrated on the detail area. There are many challenging difficulties in standardizing this unobtrusive but important information.

In this work, we use a joint framework based on CNN (Convolutional Neural Networks) and RNN (Recurrent Neural Networks) to generate semantically described sentences. Our deep neural network is trained to perform two tasks: (1) Identify suspicious area entities in medical images (2) Generate semantic descriptions of lesions based on the semantic features of the images. The network adopts joint-loss function, shares the weights in detecting and describing tasks, and learns the individual representations and associated dependencies of semantic descriptors.

2   Related Works

2.1   Image Caption

The Image Caption is a type of task that is automatically described for image generation in the field of machine vision. Learning from the research progress of machine translation [13], Vinyals et al. [6] provided the image features extracted by CNN's last hidden layer to RNN to generate descriptions. Most of the image description generation models are based on a CNN-RNN framework, and CNN is responsible for decoding image information to semantic vector, and RNN decodes it into text content. In addition, Aneja et al. [14] used CNN to replace the RNN for decoding tasks and achieved similar performance.

In addition to introduce attention mechanisms [7] for this task, Johnson et al. [3] also introduced the Dense Caption task, which requires a description for each detected image region, Krause et al. [4] and Liang et al. [15] used multi-LSTM for generation topic paragraph. This paper also use LSTM for text generation, rather than multi-title segment generation and attention mechanism, we combined the FCN and MLC (multi-label classification) to improve the coding part of the picture description, and the model output was optimized by beam search in the post-processing.

2.2   Textual Label Generating for Medical Images

Medical images and image reports have many different features and difficulties in the task of image recognition and semantic text generation. Medical images always has a low signal-to-noise ratio, and it is difficult to identify lesions and abnormal regions. It is also hard to generate text descriptions for these regions.

There are several works currently aiming at mapping textual descriptions into medical images [16, 17]. In their study, the target text is fully structured or semi-structured (e.g. labels, attributes, templates) rather than natural language. Among them, Shin et al. [16] studied the prediction methods of radiological images and markers of reports. However, these labels are mostly limited to the name of the disease and there is not much information about the lesion. Kisilev et al. [17] established a process to predict the properties of medical images, some of which are text labels. Given a medical image, they first perform image segmentation, then extract local visual features, and finally construct a classifier model to classify it into a predetermined (text) category. Jing et al. [2] proposed a similar method with our work, but they focus on public chest x-ray dataset which has m ore clear lesion and regular report, and they used a VGG19 to extract image feature that does not benefit on few shot learning.

Our method based on deep neural networks can learn a complete expression for the whole image, meanwhile, it can focus on detail information by using MLC layers. In addition, most cases in their dataset are diseased cases, and in fact, most radiological examinations are normal. Therefore, detecting relatively rare cases in this imbalance data is also a challenge.

3   Method

3.1   Encoding-Decoding Model (CNN-RNN)

Similar to the principle of machine translation, CNN-RNN model has encoding and decoding part that can transfer information to another form. CNN-RNN model replaces the encoding part with CNN which has been widely used in object recognition and detection tasks in image processing, and finally producing a vector that obtains a global feature of the image. The decoding part still uses RNN for decoding text matching. So the joint framework combining CNN and RNN is also called the CNN-RNN framework, whose advantage not only can eliminate the template-based language design process via the end-to-end training, but also both deep learning models can be fully pretrained from other databases, to reduce training burden and improve the generalization performance. The CNN-RNN model architecture is shown in Fig. 1.

The image is encoded by a CNN and then decoded by a RNN. In the process of RNN chain-solving decoding, x_t represents a variable-length input vector for word encoding of the sentence description, h_t is the hidden layer unit for the RNN, and p_{t+1} is a expected word probability that will output at the next step.

We directly maximize the probability of a correct description of a given image via the following formula:

$$\theta^* = arg\,max \sum\nolimits_{(I,S)} log\,p(S|I;\theta) \tag{1}$$

where θ is the model parameter, I represents the input image, and S represents the corresponding description of the sentence. Usually, we use the chained rule to simulate the joint probability on $S_0, S_1, \ldots S_N$, where N is the length of the sentence (number of words) for each sample:

$$log\,p(S|I) = \sum\nolimits_{t=1}^{N} log\,p(S_t|I, S_0, \ldots, S_{t-1}) \tag{2}$$

In the training process, (S, I) is used as a training sample pair, and the sum of the logarithmic probabilities of the words constituting each sentence is calculated.

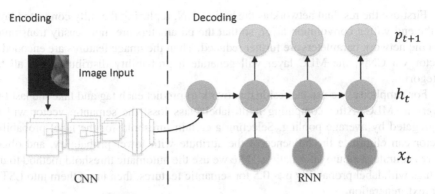

Fig. 1. CNN-RNN model, the left part shows the encoding process that always CNN work and the right part is decoding process using RNN.

The input of the RNN model needs to include both image and text information. The training process can be understood as the conditional probability $p(S_t|I, S_0, \ldots, S_{t-1})$ for predicting the current word in the condition where the precursor words probability distribution has known. The image information is derived from the CNN's output. As for the text information, it is represented by the word embedding after the sentence segmentation.

There are problems with gradient disappearance and gradient explosion during RNN training. In order to solve this problem in the process of error back propagation, a special form of the RNN named LSTM is usually introduced, which has achieved good results in translation [13] and sequence prediction [18].

3.2 Improved Codec Model (FCN-MLC-LSTM)

Apart from adopting LSTM as the decoder, we also take the specific application of the CNN and the depth of the VGG and GoogLeNet networks into account. It is difficult to train the parameters on a little-scale dataset, so we adjust the CNN of the encoding part, replacing it with a FCN. In order to focus on the global and local information of medical images, the FCN and MLC are combined to generate a probability distribution for different attributes of the image to guide the generation of description statements. Thus, we proposed an improved CNN-RNN model called FCN-MLC-LSTM model, as shown in Fig. 2:

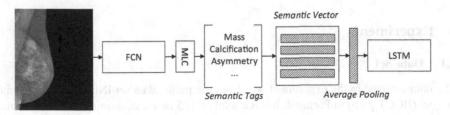

Fig. 2. Between CNN output layer and LSTM, we added an MLC layer to predict tags that each image may belong to. That semantic features can be used in LSTM.

First use the residual network as the basic CNN, replacing the fully connected layer at the end with a convolution layer, so that the parameters are more easily transmitted and the network parameters are further reduced. Then the image features are encoded in vector via CNN, the MLC layer will generate a probability distribution on all tag categories.

For simplicity, we use the residual network to predict each tag and take the last two layers as MLC. After computing multi-label class loss, the semantic vector will be aggregated by average pooling. Selecting a certain threshold for the label probability vector can eliminate the influence of the attribute with lower probability, and obtain more accurate attribute information. Here we use the automatic threshold method to use M tags with label probability $p > 0.5$ for semantic features, then input them into LSTM for text generation.

In order to further reduce the parameters and adapt to the characteristics of medical images, we learned from U-net [19] and truncated its down-sampling part as the CNN for decoding, whose network structure is shown in Fig. 3. We also added a 1×1 size convolution to decode the semantic vector after the output layer of the network.

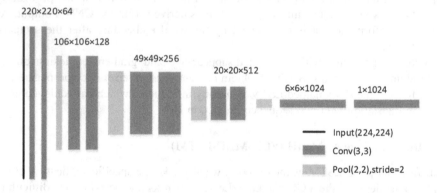

Fig. 3. U-net's down-sampling part. Input image thought the first Conv layer the tensor size changed to $220 \times 220 \times 64$, each tensor size in above is convolutional layers output.

The convolution kernel and the pooled kernel are general size of 3×3 and 2×2 respectively. And the tensor size marked in the figure is the convolution layer's input after each pooling.

4 Experiment

4.1 Data Set

The data set used in the experiment was from the public data set INbreast of a national project (BCCT.plan) in Portugal. It has a total of 115 cases, containing 410 images and corresponding 117 reports. The data includes the complete Bi-Rads classification and five types of the label (Mass, Micros, Multiple, Distortion, Asymmetry). There are duplicate reports in the dataset, but these different-date reports have only one example target images. We use these reports to base on the last inspection report and use the remaining reports to supplement it. The post text is translated and used as a report for final training. To further verify the effectiveness of the proposed method in real-world data we got a hundred breast cancer cases supported by a cooperative hospital in Shanghai. It contains 400 mammography with the label and reports target that written by trained physicians, same as INbreast.

4.2 Data Preprocessing

Data preprocessing involves two aspects of image and text: the processing of images used a usual method of medical image enhancement: Contrast Limited Adaptive histogram equalization (CLAHE). At the same time, we used a threshold segmentation (Otsu) to reduce the background area noise. Before embedding the word vector, every image description needs segments to word list for sequence input. Considering that the Chinese word segmentation tool jieba has a poor effect on the medical field that could make model hard to convergence, this paper adds a custom dictionary and a stop-word list in the process of word segmentation. Our custom dictionary is organized by the relevant vocabulary in two medical dictionaries: ICD-10 and MedDRA, to reduce the word segmentation mistake. Stop-word list is a general Chinese stop-word vocabulary that can be found in https://github.com/goto456/stopwords.

4.3 Training

If using I to represent the input image and $S = (S_0, \ldots, S_N)$ to represent the real sentence describing of the image, the expansion process is as follows:

$$x_{-1} = CNN(I) \tag{3}$$

$$x_t = W_e(S_t), \; t \in \{0, 1, \ldots, N-1\} \tag{4}$$

$$p_{t+1} = LSTM(x_t), \; t \in \{-1, 0, \ldots, N-1\} \tag{5}$$

Here we represent each word as a one-hot representation of the word vector S_t, and W_e represents the word embedding model. For a sentence of length N, S_0 represents the first word of the sentence, and S_N is the end of the sentence (defined as "<EOS>"). The generation of "<EOS>" means the model has produced a complete sentence, LSTM will not predict the next word. As input to the LSTM, images and words are mapped to vectors in the same size. We map the image semantics by fixing the output layer dimensions of the convolutional neural network, and the words are mapped by word embedding. The high-dimensional semantic vector of the image is used as the initial input to the LSTM and only entered once at -1th time step. We don't input image semantic vector in the nodes predicted by each word, because this does not produce better predictions, the network can make full use of the information in the image and pass it back to each time step input.

We use the Adam strategy to iteratively optimize across the entire training set, with the batch size set to 12, and the training loss is the sum of the negative log-likelihoods of the correct words in each time step, as shown below:

$$L(I, S) = -\sum\nolimits_{t=1}^{N} \log p_t(S_t) \tag{6}$$

In addition, we have adopted some general strategies to make the generated sentences of a given image closer to natural representation. We use packed sequence for sentence filling. The length of each batch in the training process is not uniform. We need to pad these long sentences to facilitate the training data input into LSTM. Take care of both the accuracy and training is guaranteed, the filled part does not participate in the transmission of the parameter update. In addition, we use beam search to iteratively consider the set of Kth best sentences up to time t as candidates for generating sentences of size $t + 1$, and only retain the best K. This will make the sentences we generated closer to the real report description for a given input image. In order to improve the diversity of sentences and avoid over-fitting, we set the beam size to 3 in the experiment.

4.4   Evaluation Criteria and Results

The main optimal parameter settings summarized from repeatedly experiments are listed in Table 1:

Table 1. Model parameters set.

Parameter name	Iteration times	Batch size	Optimization function	Embedding size	Beam size
Value	1000	12	Adam	256	3

We compared two existing Image Caption models with our improvements on the public dataset. In the process of model training iteration 1000 rounds, the number of parameters and training time of each model are shown in Table 1:

Table 2. Models of parameters amount and training cost time.

	VGG-RNN [8]	GoogLe-LSTM [6]	Res-MLC-LSTM	FCN-MLC-LSTM
Parameters	140M	96M	92M	14M
Run time	12 h	8 h	6 h	2 h

Since the RNN hidden layer node based on batch sentences length, the number of parameters listed in Table 1 is the number of parameters about the CNN network. The model runtime is based on the 1070Ti GPU hardware and the CUDA 9.0 version of the driver. For simplicity, the versions of the comparison convolution network are VGG16, InceptionV3, and Resnet50, respectively, and the number of parameters is only a rough expression (M, Million) on the same order of magnitude.

In addition to evaluating the generation of our model's report descriptions that are more suitable for medical imaging, we have adopted two general evaluation criteria:

1. BLEU (Bilingual evaluation understudy) [20] is a popular machine translation evaluation index, which is later cited in the evaluation of the picture description results. It is a criterion for the accuracy of word-based n-grams and is used to analyze the degree of similarity between generated sentence and reference sentence. Calculated as follows:

$$P_n = \frac{\sum_{C \in \{Candidates\}} \sum_{n-gram \in C} Count_{clip}(n - gram)}{\sum_{C' \in \{Candidates\}} \sum_{n-gram' \in C'} Count(n - gram')} \quad (7)$$

The numerator of the expression represents the minimum number of occurrences of the n-gram in the generate sentence and reference sentence, and the denominator represents the number of occurrences of the n-gram in generating a sentence.

2. CIDEr (Consensus-based Image Description Evaluation) [21], this indicator represents each sentence in the form of a TF-IDF vector and then calculates the score by referring to the cosine similarity between generate caption and reference caption. The average value of CIDEr's calculation of cosine similarity is calculated by the following formula:

$$CIDEr_n(c_i, S_i) = \frac{1}{m} \sum_j \frac{g^n(c_i)^T g^n(s_{ij})}{\|g^n(c_i)\| \cdot \|g^n(s_{ij})\|} \quad (8)$$

S_i and c_i represent the set of reference and generated sentences, respectively, and $g^n(c_i)$ and $g^n(s_{ij})$ are their corresponding TF-IDF vectors.

We used cross-validation to divide the data set by 10-fold and test it on each of the divided test sets to get an average score. Compared with several existing models, the experimental results on two datasets are shown in Tables 3 and 4. The numbers in B-1 to B-4 in the header represent the length of the n-gram match.

Table 3. BLEU and CIDER scores of the experimental results.

	B-1	B-2	B-3	B-4	CIDEr
VGG-RNN [8]	31.2	25.2	16.3	9.6	15.5
GoogLe-LSTM [6]	58.0	28.8	23.5	11.0	30.9
Res-MLC-LSTM	60.2	40.0	32.2	22.8	56.6
FCN-MLC-LSTM	60.7	41.2	32.6	23.7	61.7

The scores in Table 2 can be understood as the matching degree between the generated sentence and reference sentence. It can be seen in Tables 2 and 3 that in the medical images of fewer samples and their report data, fully convolutional network with fewer parameters can effectively improve the efficiency and accuracy on encoding-decoding medical image report generation task. In another way, MLC task also can obviously improve model performance, that can be seen in line 3, MLC overcomes partial convolution feature reduce and make model achieved a similar effect with GoogLe-LSTM.

Different configurations of the machine, lead to differences in the hardware environment and initialization, the simulation results are not the same, the data listed in the table are referenced to the same machine. Here we list some samples in Table 4 that can be compared with another method.

Table 4. Sentence generate results.

	Groud True	GoogLe-LSTM[6]	Res-MLC-LSTM	FCN-MLC-LSTM
	Breast asymmetry was observed, breast volume was reduced, with sig-ns of densification and destruction of matrix structure and skin thickening, with a history of surgery and a history of referrals. No noxious tumors, suspicious microcalcificati ons or other significant changes in nodular images were found on either side	Breast asymmetry was found, breast volume decreased, signs of bone densification, structural distortion and skin thickening, dense breast parenchyma, unsuspecting malignant tumors, and benign microcalcifica tion.	Breast asymmetry was found, breast volume was reduced, with signs of densification and matrix structure distortion and skin thickening. No signs of malignancy of opaque nodules were found, as well as suspected microcalcifica tions or other significant lesions.	Breast asymmetry was found, breast volume was reduced, with signs of densification and matrix structure distortion and skin thickening. No potential malignancy, suspected microcalcifica tion or other obvious nodule signs were found.

5 Conclusion

In this article, we examine how to automatically generate text reports of medical images aims to help medical professionals generate reports more accurately and efficiently. Deep learning on public medical image data sets is more difficult due to the lack of sample and the complex CNN weight training. Choosing a good model structure and certain pre-training can alleviate this problem. In the mixed data set we demonstrate the effectiveness of the proposed method through comparative experiments. Our future research direction is the analysis of breast MR sequence images, based on the three-dimensional spatial volume information, which will be more precise expressed on the higher-dimensional convolution kernel.

Acknowledgment. This work was supported by the Science and Technology Development Foundation of Shanghai (18511102703, 16JC1400802, 16JC1400803), the Special Fund of Shanghai Municipal Commission of Economy and Informatization (RX-RJJC-08-16-0483, 2017-RGZN-01004, XX-XXFZ-02-18-2666, XX-XXFZ-01-18-2604).

References

1. Wang, W., Ding, Y., Tian, C.: A novel semantic attribute-based feature for image caption generation. In: 2018 IEEE International Conference on Acoustics, Speech and Signal Processing (ICASSP), pp. 3081–3085. IEEE (2018)
2. Jing, B., Xie, P., Xing, E.: On the automatic generation of medical imaging reports. arXiv preprint arXiv:1711.08195 (2017)
3. Johnson J., Karpathy, A., Fei-Fei, L.: DenseCap: fully convolutional localization networks for dense captioning. In: Proceedings of the IEEE Conference on Computer Vision and Pattern Recognition, pp. 4565–4574 (2016)
4. Krause, J., Johnson, J., Krishna, R., et al.: A hierarchical approach for generating descriptive image paragraphs. In: Proceedings of the IEEE Conference on Computer Vision and Pattern Recognition, pp. 317–325 (2017)
5. Chen, X., Zitnick, C.L.: Learning a recurrent visual representation for image caption generation. arXiv preprint arXiv:1411.5654 (2014)
6. Vinyals, O., Toshev, A., Bengio, S., et al.: Show and tell: a neural image caption generator. In: Proceedings of the IEEE Conference on Computer Vision and Pattern Recognition, pp. 3156–3164 (2015)
7. He, X., Yang, Y., Shi, B., et al.: VD-SAN: visual-densely semantic attention network for image caption generation. Neurocomputing **328**, 48–55 (2019)
8. Karpathy, A., Fei-Fei, L.: Deep visual-semantic alignments for generating image descriptions. In: Proceedings of the IEEE Conference on Computer Vision and Pattern Recognition, pp. 3128–3137 (2015)
9. Kulkarni, G., Premraj, V., Ordonez, V., et al.: BabyTalk: understanding and generating simple image descriptions. IEEE Trans. Pattern Anal. Mach. Intell. **35**(12), 2891–2903 (2013)
10. Feng, Y., Lapata, M.: How many words is a picture worth? Automatic caption generation for news images. In: Proceedings of the 48th Annual Meeting of the Association for Computational Linguistics, pp. 1239–1249. Association for Computational Linguistics (2010)

11. Farhadi, A., et al.: Every picture tells a story: generating sentences from images. In: Daniilidis, K., Maragos, P., Paragios, N. (eds.) ECCV 2010. LNCS, vol. 6314, pp. 15–29. Springer, Heidelberg (2010). https://doi.org/10.1007/978-3-642-15561-1_2

12. Lin, T.-Y., et al.: Microsoft COCO: common objects in context. In: Fleet, D., Pajdla, T., Schiele, B., Tuytelaars, T. (eds.) ECCV 2014. LNCS, vol. 8693, pp. 740–755. Springer, Cham (2014). https://doi.org/10.1007/978-3-319-10602-1_48

13. Sutskever, I., Vinyals, O., Le, Q.V.: Sequence to sequence learning with neural networks. In: Advances in Neural Information Processing Systems, pp. 3104–3112 (2014)

14. Aneja, J., Deshpande, A., Schwing, A.G.: Convolutional image captioning. In: Proceedings of the IEEE Conference on Computer Vision and Pattern Recognition, pp. 5561–5570 (2018)

15. Liang, X., Hu, Z., Zhang, H., et al.: Recurrent topic-transition GAN for visual paragraph generation. In; Proceedings of the IEEE International Conference on Computer Vision, pp. 3362–3371 (2017)

16. Shin, H.C., Roberts, K., Lu, L., et al.: Learning to read chest x-rays: recurrent neural cascade model for automated image annotation. In: Proceedings of the IEEE conference on computer vision and pattern recognition, pp. 2497–2506 (2016)

17. Kisilev, P., Walach, E., Barkan, E., et al.: From medical image to automatic medical report generation. IBM J. Res. Dev. 59(2/3), 2:1–2:7 (2015)

18. Graves, A.: Generating sequences with recurrent neural networks. arXiv preprint arXiv: 1308.0850 (2013)

19. Ronneberger, O., Fischer, P., Brox, T.: U-Net: convolutional networks for biomedical image segmentation. In: Navab, N., Hornegger, J., Wells, W., Frangi, F. (eds.) MICCAI 2015. LNCS, vol. 9351, pp. 234–241. Springer, Cham (2015). https://doi.org/10.1007/978-3-319-24574-4_28

20. Papineni, K., Roukos, S., Ward, T., et al.: IBM research report Bleu: a method for automatic evaluation of machine translation. IBM Research Division Technical Report, RC22176 (W0109-022), Yorktown Heights, New York (2001)

21. Vedantam, R., Lawrence Zitnick, C., Parikh, D.: CIDEr: consensus-based image description evaluation. In: Proceedings of the IEEE Conference on Computer Vision and Pattern Recognition, pp. 4566–4575 (2015)

Multi-verse Optimization Algorithm for Solving Two-Dimensional TSP

Guo Zhou[1(✉)], Wei Pan[2], and Yongquan Zhou[2]

[1] Department of Science and Technology Teaching,
China University of Political Science and Law, Beijing 100088, China
guo.zhou@live.com
[2] College of Information Science and Engineering,
Guangxi University for Nationalities, Nanning 530006, China

Abstract. Multi-verse optimization (MVO) algorithm is proposed as a new metaheuristic optimization algorithm, which is successfully applied to function optimization and engineering computation, and shows good performance. The Traveling Salesperson Problem (TSP) is an NP-complete combinatorial optimization problem of substantial importance in many scheduling applications. In this paper, we use the MVO for solving two-dimensional TSP, and compared with the particle swarm optimization (PSO), genetic algorithm (GA) and Cuckoo Search (CS) Algorithm. The ten test instance results show that the proposed solving two-dimensional TSP algorithm performs better in terms of convergence rate and solution quality.

Keywords: Multi-verse optimization algorithm · Metaheuristics optimization · Two-dimensional traveling salesman problem

1 Introduction

Traveling Salesperson Problem (TSP) finds a shortest tour for a traveling salesperson who starts from a city, visits all other cities in an order, and finally returns back to the home city with a condition that she or he visits each city exactly once in her/his tour and optimizes on the cost of the travel [1–3]. Clearly, the distance traveled by a salesperson depends on the order in which (s) he travels the cities. Thus, the problem is to find an optimal ordering of the cities which optimizes cost objective(s). It does not take much mathematical skill to understand the problem but it is typically a hard combinatorial optimization problem. Tracing back the history, TSP (though not by this name) was documented as early as in 1759 by Euler whose interest was in solving Knights' tour problem.

A Knight's tour is a Hamiltonian cycle for the graph whose nodes are the 64 squares of a chessboard, with two nodes adjacent if and only if a knight could move in one stop from one square to the other. The term traveling salesman was first coined possibly in 1932 in a German book titled, "The traveling salesman, how and what he should do to get commission and be successful in his business", written by a salesperson [4–8]. As a precursor, Menger first demonstrated that an exhaustive search is a possible way to compute an optimal solution and concluded that a nearest neighbor

© Springer Nature Switzerland AG 2019
D.-S. Huang et al. (Eds.): ICIC 2019, LNCS 11643, pp. 697–706, 2019.
https://doi.org/10.1007/978-3-030-26763-6_67

algorithm does not guarantee an optimal solution [9]. However, systematic study of the TSP as a combinatorial optimization problem started with the work of Dantzig et al. [10]. Since then, many algorithms have been proposed to solve this combinatorial hard problem for both single as well as multiple objective optimization. Almost all sorts of heuristic and stochastic searches have been applied to effectively solve this problem, and the remains an interesting and challenging problem.

Multi-verse optimization (MVO) is one of the metaheuristic methods proposed by Mirjalili in 2015 [11]. The main inspirations of the algorithm is based on three concepts in cosmology. The MVO algorithm has many advantages such as a simple structure, immediately accessible for practical application, ease of implementation. In this paper, we use the MVO for solving two-dimensional TSP, and compared with the particle swarm optimization (PSO), genetic algorithm (GA) and Cuckoo Search (CS) Algorithm. The results of the ten tests instance show that the proposed for solving TSP algorithm performs better in terms of convergence rate and solution quality.

2 Two-Dimensional TSP

So-called TSP problem, given graph $G = (V, A)$, where V is the vertex set, A is the arc set composed by interconnected vertex, knowing connection distance between the vertex, required to identify a Hamilton circuit which has the shortest length, that is the shortest circuit that through all the vertices once and only once. To the city set $V = \{s_1, s_2, s_3 \ldots s_n\}$, supposing an access order of which is $T = \{t_1, t_2, t_3 \ldots t_n\}$, where $t_i \in V$ $(i = 1, 2, \ldots, N)$, agreeing $t_n + 1 = t_1$, For example, let problem space: $X = \{\text{Beijing, Chengdu, Guangzhou, Shanghai}\}$, $F(x) = dist(Hefei, x[0]) + \sum_{i=0}^{2} dist$ $(x[i], x[i+1]) + dist(x[3], Hefei)$. Let us assume that the tour always starts and ends in Hefei. The TSP problem as follow (see Fig. 1).

Fig. 1. A TSP example for the problem of city [12]

3 Basic MVO

Multi-verse optimization algorithm (MVO) is inspired by the theory of multi-verse in physics [13]. Three main concepts of the multi-verse theory (white hole, black hole, and wormhole) are mathematically modeled to construct the MVO. We utilize the concepts of white hole and black hole in order to explore search spaces [14, 15] by MVO. In contrast, the wormholes assist MVO in exploiting the search spaces. We assume that each solution is analogous to a universe and each variable in the solution is an object in that universe. In addition, we assign each solution an inflation rate, which is proportional to the corresponding fitness function value of the solution. We also use the term time instead of the iteration since it is a common term in multi-verse theory and cosmology. The following riles are applied to the universes of MVO:

(1) The higher inflation rate, the higher probability of having white hole.
(2) The higher inflation rate, the lower probability of having black holes.
(3) Universes with higher inflation rate tend to send objects through white holes.
(4) Universes with lower inflation rate tend to receive more objects through black holes.
(5) The objects in all universes may face random movement towards the best universe via wormholes regardless of the inflation rate.

In order to mathematically model the white/black holes tunnels and exchange the objects of universes, we utilized a roulette wheel mechanism (Fig. 2).

Fig. 2. White hole, black hole, and wormhole [16, 17]

At the each iteration, we sort the universe based of their inflation rates and chose one of them by the roulette wheel to have a white hole [18]. The following steps are done in order to do these. Assume that

$$
u = \begin{bmatrix}
x_1^1 & x_1^2 & \cdots & x_1^d \\
x_2^1 & x_2^2 & \cdots & x_2^d \\
\vdots & \vdots & \vdots & \vdots \\
x_n^1 & x_n^2 & \cdots & x_n^d
\end{bmatrix}
$$

where d is the number of variables and n is the number of universes.

$$x_i^j = \begin{cases} x_k^j & r1 < NI(Ui) \\ x_i^j & r1 \geq NI(Ui) \end{cases}$$

where x_i^j indicates the *jth* variable of the *ith* universe, U_i shows the *ith* universe, $NI(U_i)$ is normalized inflation rate of the *ith* universe, r_1 is a random number in (0, 1), x_k^j indicates the *jth* variable of *kth* universe selected by a roulette wheel selection mechanism. Procedure of the basic MVO as follows:

SU = Sorted universes
NI = Normalize inflation rate (fitness) of the universes
   for each universe indexed by i
     Black_hole_index = i;
   for each object indexed by j;
     $r_1 = rand([0,1]);$
  if $r_1 < NI(U_i)$
       white_hole_index = Roulete_Wheel_Selection(−NI);
       U(Black_hole_index, j) = SU(White_hole_index, j);
  endif
 endfor
endfor

To provide local changes for each universe and have high probability of improving the inflation rate using wormholes, assuming that wormhole tunnels are always established between a universe and the best universe formed so far. The mechanism is as follows:

$$x_i^j = \begin{cases} X_j + TDR * \left((ub_j - lb_j) * r_4 + lb_j\right) & r_3 < 0.5 \\ X_j - TDR * \left((ub_j - lb_j) * r_4 + lb_j\right) & r_3 \geq 0.5 \end{cases}$$

where X_j indicates the *jth* variable of the best universe formed so far, TDR (Travelling distance rate) is a coefficient, WEP (Wormhole existence probability) is another coefficient, lb_j is the lower bound of *jth* variable, ub_j is the upper bound of *jth* variable, r_2, r_3, r_4 are random numbers in (0, 1) (Fig. 3).

$$WEP = \min + l * \left(\frac{\max - \min}{L}\right)$$

min(minimum) = 0.2, max(maximum) = 1, l is the current iteration, L shows the maximum iterations.

$$TDR = 1 - \frac{l^{\frac{1}{p}}}{L^{\frac{1}{p}}}$$

where p defines the exploitation accuracy over the iterations.

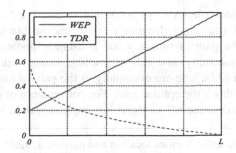

Fig. 3. WEP versus TDR

Procedure of the basic MVO is as follows:

for each universe indexed by i

    for each object indexed by j

        $r_2 = random([0,1]);$

        if $r_2 <$ Wormhole _ existance _ probability

        $r_3 = random([0,1]);$

        $r_4 = random([0,1]);$

if $r_3 < 0.5$

$U(i,j) = Best\_universe(j) + Travelling\_distance\_rate*((ub(j)-lb(j))*r_4 + lb(j));$

else

$U(i,j) = Best\_universe(j) - Travelling\_distance\_rate*((ub(j)-lb(j))*r_4 + lb(j));$

endif

  endif

*end*for

*end*for

4   MVO for Solving Two-Dimensional TSP

In the MVO algorithm, we all know that universes with higher inflation rate tend to send objects through white holes and Universes with lower inflation rate tend to receive more objects through black holes. The objects in all universes may face random movement towards the best universe via wormholes regardless of the inflation rate. In the TSP, We assume that from A city to B City as Particles from the white hole to black hole through wormhole. In MVO, The higher inflation rate, the higher probability of having white hole. The higher inflation rate, The lower probability of having black holes.

Particles from white hole (A city) according to the WEP (wormhole existence probability) and TDR (travelling distance rate) to choose black hole (B/next city). Then, according to the path of fitness value constantly updated the path of WEP wormhole existence probability) and TDR (travelling distance rate). We make most of the particles that from white hole are eventually in the path of maximum fitness value (black hole), we think this is the optimal path. For convenience of description, To solve the TSP problem, We describe MVO algorithm implementation steps are as follows.

Step 1. Initialization the N cities location and particle number m. then, We calculate the Euclidean distance between two cities. (this paper, we suppose the maximum iteration $iter\_\max = 200, m = 60$);

    while ($iter <= iter\_\max$)

Step 2. Particles from white hole(A city) according to the WEP（wormhole existence probability）and TDR(travelling distance rate) to choose the optimal Black hole(next city).

    Step 2.1 Randomly placed the n particles in the N cities;

    Step 2.2 The selection and determination of white holes are done by the roulette wheel, which is based on the normalized inflation rate. The less inflation rate, the higher probability of sending objects though white/black hole tunnels; and Then use roulette method selected at random to move to the next city.

    Step 2.3 Repeat Step 2, until meet the stop condition.

Step 3. Calculating the shortest distance and the average distance after the iteration.

    for $j = 1 : N$; computation

$$DL\ N(i,j) = ((cityN(i,1) - cityN(j,1))^2 + (city\ N(i,2) - city\ N(j,2))^2)^{0.5};$$

(where DL is distance matrix)).

---

5 Simulation Experiments and Result Analysis

5.1 Experimental Setup

The experimental environment are implemented using MATLAB 2012Ra, the algorithms are run on the same AMD A10-6700APU with Redeo(tm) HD Graphics @3.70 GHz with 4.00 GB RAM in Window 7.

5.2   Experimental Results Comparison

(1) Cities number = 30 (See Table 1)

Table 1. The experiment parameter coordinates and N (cities number) = 30

City1: (41, 94)	City2: (37, 84)	City3: (54, 67)
City4: (25, 62)	City5: (7, 64)	City6: (2, 99)
City7: (68, 58)	City8: (71, 44)	City9: (54, 62)
City10: (83, 69)	City11: (64, 60)	City12: (18, 54)
City13: (22, 60)	City14: (83, 46)	City15: (91, 38)
City16: (25, 38)	City17: (24, 42)	City18: (58, 69)
City19: (71, 71)	City20: (74, 78)	City21: (87, 76)
City22: (18, 40)	City23: (13, 40)	City24: (82, 7)
City25: (62, 32)	City26: (58, 35)	City27: (45, 21)
City28: (41, 26)	City29: (44, 35)	City30: (4, 50)

(a)   **(b)**

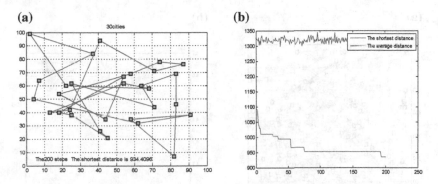

Fig. 4. (a) Optimal roadmap with N = 30 (PSO). (b) Shortest distance and average distance (PSO)

We get (PSO, N = 30), the shortest_route is:

$14 \rightarrow 24 \rightarrow 26 \rightarrow 15 \rightarrow 25 \rightarrow 30 \rightarrow 5 \rightarrow 2 \rightarrow 6 \rightarrow 13 \rightarrow 7 \rightarrow 9 \rightarrow 23 \rightarrow 17 \rightarrow 1 \rightarrow$ $19 \rightarrow 21 \rightarrow 20 \rightarrow 18 \rightarrow 12 \rightarrow 29 \rightarrow 3 \rightarrow 22 \rightarrow 16 \rightarrow 27 \rightarrow 28 \rightarrow 4 \rightarrow 8 \rightarrow 11 \rightarrow 10.$

The shortest length is 934.4096. It takes 32.965 s when used PSO to solve TSP (Fig. 4).

We get (MVO, N = 30), the shortest route is

$10 \rightarrow 21 \rightarrow 20 \rightarrow 19 \rightarrow 11 \rightarrow 7 \rightarrow 8 \rightarrow 14 \rightarrow 15 \rightarrow 24 \rightarrow 25 \rightarrow 26 \rightarrow 29 \rightarrow 28 \rightarrow$ $27 \rightarrow 16 \rightarrow 17 \rightarrow 22 \rightarrow 23 \rightarrow 30 \rightarrow 12 \rightarrow 13 \rightarrow 4 \rightarrow 5 \rightarrow 6 \rightarrow 1 \rightarrow 2 \rightarrow 3 \rightarrow 9 \rightarrow 18.$

The shortest length is 429.5107. It takes 3.785 s when used MVO to solve TSP (Fig. 5).

(a)   **(b)**

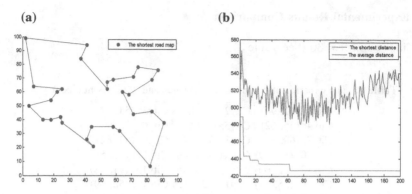

Fig. 5. (a) Optimal road map with $N = 30$ (MVO). (b) Shortest distance and average distance (MVO)

(2) Cities number = 130

(a)   **(b)**

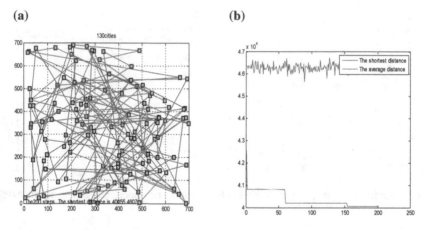

Fig. 6. (a) Optimal road map with $N = 130$ (PSO). (b) Shortest distance and average distance (PSO)

We get (PSO, $N = 130$), the shortest route is:

$42 \rightarrow 53 \rightarrow 18 \rightarrow 51 \rightarrow 54 \rightarrow 1 \rightarrow 76 \rightarrow 93 \rightarrow 66 \rightarrow 95 \rightarrow 37 \rightarrow 115 \rightarrow 114 \rightarrow$
$38 \rightarrow 100 \rightarrow 12 \rightarrow 113 \rightarrow 124 \rightarrow 58 \rightarrow 73 \rightarrow 91 \rightarrow 9 \rightarrow 15 \rightarrow 105 \rightarrow 31 \rightarrow 70 \rightarrow 97$
$\rightarrow 6 \rightarrow 16 \rightarrow 129 \rightarrow 104 \rightarrow 24 \rightarrow 116 \rightarrow 80 \rightarrow 28 \rightarrow 59 \rightarrow 20 \rightarrow 4 \rightarrow 25 \rightarrow 89 \rightarrow$
$122 \rightarrow 126 \rightarrow 22 \rightarrow 87 \rightarrow 102 \rightarrow 21 \rightarrow 23 \rightarrow 40 \rightarrow 43 \rightarrow 125 \rightarrow 127 \rightarrow 120 \rightarrow 79$
$\rightarrow 107 \rightarrow 65 \rightarrow 84 \rightarrow 92 \rightarrow 55 \rightarrow 56 \rightarrow 7 \rightarrow 98 \rightarrow 72 \rightarrow 99 \rightarrow 62 \rightarrow 64 \rightarrow 48 \rightarrow 77$
$\rightarrow 6 \rightarrow 123 \rightarrow 4 \rightarrow 11 \rightarrow 128 \rightarrow 101 \rightarrow 36 \rightarrow 35 \rightarrow 74 \rightarrow 29 \rightarrow 60 \rightarrow 82 \rightarrow 111 \rightarrow$
$13 \rightarrow 119 \rightarrow 88 \rightarrow 49 \rightarrow 10 \rightarrow 27 \rightarrow 96 \rightarrow 90 \rightarrow 50 \rightarrow 71 \rightarrow 41 \rightarrow 85 \rightarrow 32 \rightarrow 63$
$\rightarrow 8 \rightarrow 52 \rightarrow 118 \rightarrow 109 \rightarrow 45 \rightarrow 78 \rightarrow 108 \rightarrow 103 \rightarrow 33 \rightarrow 67 \rightarrow 39 \rightarrow 83 \rightarrow 121$
$\rightarrow 110 \rightarrow 94 \rightarrow 68 \rightarrow 57 \rightarrow 75 \rightarrow 34 \rightarrow 86 \rightarrow 3 \rightarrow 130 \rightarrow 47 \rightarrow 19 \rightarrow 17 \rightarrow 5 \rightarrow 14$
$\rightarrow 61 \rightarrow 106 \rightarrow 81 \rightarrow 2 \rightarrow 117 \rightarrow 26 \rightarrow 30 \rightarrow 46 \rightarrow 112.$

The shortest length is 39090.8747. It takes 277. 121 s when used PSO solve TSP (Fig. 6).

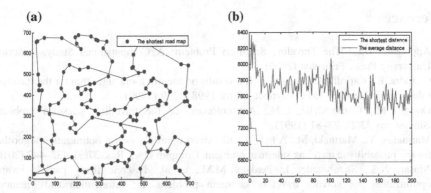

(a) The shortest road map

(b) The shortest distance / The average distance

Fig. 7. (a) Optimal road map with $N = 130$ (MVO). (b) Shortest distance and average distance (MVO)

We get (MVO, $N = 130$), the shortest route is:
$12 \rightarrow 87 \rightarrow 81 \rightarrow 103 \rightarrow 77 \rightarrow 94 \rightarrow 89 \rightarrow 110 \rightarrow 98 \rightarrow 68 \rightarrow 63 \rightarrow 70 \rightarrow 97 \rightarrow 26 \rightarrow 7 \rightarrow 88 \rightarrow 69 \rightarrow 64 \rightarrow 86 \rightarrow 124 \rightarrow 129 \rightarrow 61 \rightarrow 109 \rightarrow 76 \rightarrow 11 \rightarrow 5 \rightarrow 45 \rightarrow 16 \rightarrow 128 \rightarrow 105 \rightarrow 62 \rightarrow 112 \rightarrow 117 \rightarrow 39 \rightarrow 71 \rightarrow 41 \rightarrow 1 \rightarrow 130 \rightarrow 50 \rightarrow 2 \rightarrow 118 \rightarrow 80 \rightarrow 46 \rightarrow 20 \rightarrow 93 \rightarrow 37 \rightarrow 22 \rightarrow 47 \rightarrow 40 \rightarrow 23 \rightarrow 122 \rightarrow 55 \rightarrow 60 \rightarrow 51 \rightarrow 42 \rightarrow 44 \rightarrow 4 \rightarrow 35 \rightarrow 54 \rightarrow 17 \rightarrow 31 \rightarrow 27 \rightarrow 19 \rightarrow 100 \rightarrow 116 \rightarrow 24 \rightarrow 15 \rightarrow 29 \rightarrow 95 \rightarrow 79 \rightarrow 38 \rightarrow 92 \rightarrow 73 \rightarrow 99 \rightarrow 74 \rightarrow 75 \rightarrow 52 \rightarrow 9 \rightarrow 57 \rightarrow 56 \rightarrow 65 \rightarrow 82 \rightarrow 101 \rightarrow 123 \rightarrow 111 \rightarrow 119 \rightarrow 84 \rightarrow 36 \rightarrow 32 \rightarrow 113 \rightarrow 25 \rightarrow 48 \rightarrow 43 \rightarrow 104 \rightarrow 107 \rightarrow 127 \rightarrow 34 \rightarrow 18 \rightarrow 8 \rightarrow 108 \rightarrow 114 \rightarrow 3 \rightarrow 83 \rightarrow 30 \rightarrow 59 \rightarrow 121 \rightarrow 78 \rightarrow 90 \rightarrow 125 \rightarrow 85 \rightarrow 66 \rightarrow 28 \rightarrow 115 \rightarrow 126 \rightarrow 21 \rightarrow 33 \rightarrow 96 \rightarrow 67 \rightarrow 13 \rightarrow 14 \rightarrow 10 \rightarrow 102 \rightarrow 6 \rightarrow 91 \rightarrow 72 \rightarrow 49 \rightarrow 58 \rightarrow 53 \rightarrow 120 \rightarrow 106.$

The shortest length is 6.7760E+03. It takes 63.027 s when used MVO to solve TSP (Fig. 7).

6 Conclusions

The Traveling Salesperson Problem (TSP) is an NP-complete combinatorial optimization problem of substantial importance in many scheduling applications. In this paper, we use the MVO to solving ten two-dimensional TSP, and compared with the particle swarm optimization (PSO). The tests results show that the proposed solving two-dimensional TSP algorithm performs better in terms of convergence rate and solution quality. In future, we hope applying MVO algorithm to solve many practical problems.

Acknowledgment. This work is supported by Project of Young Scholar Fund of China University of Political Science and Law under Grants No. 10819144. Project of China University of Political Science and Law Research Innovation under Grant No. 10818441.

References

1. Applegate, D.L.: The Traveling Salesman Problem: A Computational Study. Princeton University Press, Princeton (2006)
2. Chandra, B., Karloff, H., Tovey, C.: New results on the old k-opt algorithm for the traveling salesman problem. SIAM J. Comput. **28**(6), 1998–2029 (1999)
3. Dorigo, M., Gambardella, L.M.: Ant colonies for the travelling salesman problem. Biosystems **43**(2), 73–81 (1997)
4. Marinakis, Y., Marinaki, M.: A hybrid multi-swarm particle swarm optimization algorithm for the probabilistic traveling salesman problem. Comput. Oper. Res. **37**(3), 432–442 (2010)
5. Niasar, N.S., Shanbezade, J., Perdam, M.M., et al.: Discrete fuzzy particle swarm optimization for solving traveling salesman problem. In: Information and Financial Engineering 2009, pp. 162–165. IEEE Press, New York (2009)
6. Potvin, J.Y.: Genetic algorithms for the traveling salesman problem. Ann. Oper. Res. **63**(3), 337–370 (1996)
7. Shi, X.H., Liang, Y.C., Lee, H.P., et al.: Particle swarm optimization-based algorithms for TSP and generalized TSP. Inf. Process. Lett. **103**(5), 169–176 (2007)
8. Lawler, E.L., Lenstra, J.K., Rinnooy Kan, A.H.G., Shmoys, D.B.: The Traveling Salesman Problem: A Guided Tour of Combinatorial Optimization. Wiley, New York (1985)
9. Menger, K.: Das botenproblem. Ergebnisse Eines Mathema tischen Kolloquiums **2**, 11–12 (1932)
10. Dantzig, G.B., Fulkerson, D.R., Johnson, S.M.: Solution of a large scale traveling salesman problem. Oper. Res. **2**, 393–410 (1954)
11. Mirjalili, S.: Multi-verse optimizer: a nature-inspired algorithm for global optimization. Neural Comput. Appl. **27**, 495–513 (2016)
12. http://blog.csdn.net/zjujqq/article/details/8829879
13. Khour, J., Ovrut, B.A., Seiberg, N., Steinhardt, P.J., Turok, N.: From big crunch to big bang. Phys. Rev. D **65**, 086007 (2002)
14. Davies, P.C.: Thermodynamics of black holes. Rep. Prog. Phys. **41**, 1313 (1978)
15. Morris, M.S., Thorne, K.S.: Wormholes in spacing and their use for interstellar travel: a tool for teaching general relativity. Am. J. Phys. **56**, 395–412 (1998)
16. Guth, A.H.: Eternal inflation and its implications. J. Phys. A Math. Theor. **40**, 43–57 (2007)
17. Holliday, D., Resnick, R., Walker, J.: Fundamentals of Physics. Wiley, Hoboken (1993)
18. Schutz, B.: Gravity from the Ground Up. Cambridge University Press, Cambridge (2003)

A Quaternion's Encoding Sine Cosine Algorithm

Li Lv, Dengxu He$^{(\boxtimes)}$, Miao Lu, and Yundi Rao

College of Science, Guangxi University for Nationalities,
Nanning 530006, China
dengxuhe@126.com

Abstract. Sine cosine algorithm (SCA) is a new meta-heuristic algorithm based on sines and cosines. This paper presents quaternion sine cosine algorithm (QSCA). QSCA algorithm introduces the idea of coding individuals with quaternions. Each individual is composed of a real part and three imaginary parts, extending the search space from one dimension to four dimensions, which increases the diversity of the population in the algorithm, further enhances the ability of the algorithm to find the global optimal value, and improves the accuracy of the algorithm. QSCA has been tested using five standard benchmark functions. The results show that the algorithm has better global optimization ability and higher precision.

Keywords: Meta-heuristic algorithm · Sine cosine algorithm ·
Quaternion coding · Benchmark test functions · P-Values

1 Introduction

Optimization is the process of finding one or more solutions and minimizing or maximizing one or more objectives in a problem by satisfying certain constraints. Optimization problem is involved in various research fields, which makes optimization technology develop. Because of the insufficiency of traditional optimization method, it is easy to be trapped in local optimization, and it is necessary to deduce the search space [1]. In the past 20 years, Meta-heuristic algorithms (MAs) which is a optimization method that imitates natural behavior to find the optimal solution is widely regarded by researchers as an effective method to solve most complex optimization problems [2]. Therefore, many meta-heuristic algorithms have been proposed, such as the particle swarm optimization (PSO) [3], the artificial bee colony (ABC) [4], the moth-flame optimization (MFO) [5], the bat algorithm (BA) [6] and the dragonfly algorithm (DA) [7] which are based on insects and other animals. There are also physics-based algorithms, such as the sine cosine algorithm (SCA) [8].

The sine cosine algorithm, which uses sine and cosine functions to explore and exploit the space between two solutions in search space, was proposed by Mirjalili. The sine and cosine algorithm is an optimization algorithm based on the sine and cosine operators in simple mathematical functions to update the motion. The SCA's parameters determine the search individual's movement step size and the direction of random movement. The SCA algorithm has the characteristics of simple structure, few parameters and easy to understand, but the algorithm also has many short comings.

D.-S. Huang et al. (Eds.): ICIC 2019, LNCS 11643, pp. 707–718, 2019.
https://doi.org/10.1007/978-3-030-26763-6_68

Aiming at the disadvantage that parameter setting in SCA can only affect specific regions, Issa [9] proposed an enhanced version combining SCA and PSO algorithm, which exploits search space better than standard SCA. For SCA to be easily trapped in local optimality, Elaziz [10] proposes an SCA with the opposition based learning, which can better explore the search space and generate more accurate solutions than standard SCA. The hybrid sine-cosine algorithm with teaching learning-based optimization algorithm (SCA-TLBO) proposed by Nenavath [11] is compared with the standard SCA algorithm, which can better avoid falling into local optimum and has a faster convergence speed. In order to solve the classification problem of high-dimensional and large capacity data sets. Sindhu [12] proposed a sine cosine algorithm using elite strategy and new update mechanism to improve the classification accuracy.

The original SCA algorithm uses real number coding to encode the algorithm, which limits the application scope of the algorithm to the real number range, limits the diversity of the population and is not conducive to the optimization of the algorithm. This paper presents a novel quaternion sine cosine algorithm (QSCA). Although the quaternion search space is much larger than the original search space, the fitness value determined by the fitness function in the quaternion space is not complicated, so it is easy to explore the space [13]. The contribution of this paper is to introduce the idea of quaternion coding into SCA algorithm, introduce one real part and three imaginary parts of quaternion into SCA algorithm, and map the one-dimensional coding space of real number to the four-dimensional coding space of quaternion. A real part and three imaginary parts of quaternion are used to represent an individual in the population, and the real part and three imaginary parts are updated respectively to obtain the optimal value of the algorithm. The improved method not only increases the diversity of individuals in the population, but also improves the possibility of obtaining the optimal solution and the optimization performance of the algorithm.

2   Quaternion's Algebra

Quaternions [14] are simple supercomplex numbers whose standard form is

$$q = x_0 + x_1 i + x_2 j + x_3 k, \tag{1}$$

where x_0, x_1, x_2, x_3 are real numbers i, j and k are imaginary parts. Actually i, j, k geometric meaning can be understood as a kind of rotation, which i represents the rotation in the positive direction of the X-axis to the positive direction of the Y-axis in the plane between the X-axis and the Y-axis, j represents the rotation in the positive direction of the Z-axis to the positive direction of the X-axis in the plane between the Z-axis and the X-axis, k represents the rotation in the positive direction of the Y-axis to the positive direction of the Z-axis in the plane between the Y-axis and the Z-axis. And the following relationships exist between each imaginary part:

$$ij = k; jk = i; ki = j; ji = -k; kj = -i; ik = -j; i^2 = j^2 = k^2 = -1. \tag{2}$$

Assuming q_0 and q_1 are quaternions and β is a real number, then the representations of q_0 and q_1 are $q_0 = x_0 + x_1 i + x_2 j + x_3 k$ and $q_1 = y_0 + y_1 i + y_2 j + y_3 k$ respectively. Here are some common operations for quaternions [15].

Definition of the addition operation of two quaternions is expressed as following

$$q_0 + q_1 = (x_0 + y_0) + (x_1 + y_1)i + (x_2 + y_2)j + (x_3 + y_3)k, \tag{3}$$

while the definition of subtraction operation represented by

$$q_0 - q_1 = (x_0 - y_0) + (x_1 - y_1)i + (x_2 - y_2)j + (x_3 - y_3)k. \tag{4}$$

Finally, the number multiplication operation is defined as

$$\beta q_0 = \beta(x_0 + x_1 i + x_2 j + x_3 k) = \beta x_0 + \beta x_1 i + \beta x_2 j + \beta x_3 k, \tag{5}$$

Where $\beta \in R$.

The quaternion q_0 can also be expressed as $q_0 = a + bj$, where a and b both are complex number, j is an imaginary part [16]. Let $a = x_0 + x_1 i$, $b = x_2 + x_3 i$. Then the quaternion number q_0 is shown in following equation

$$q_0 = a + bj = x_0 + x_1 i + x_2 j + x_3 k. \tag{6}$$

Finally, quaternions have an important operation of the norm. That can map quaternion from quaternion space to real space, as follows:

$$N(q_0) = \sqrt{x_0^2 + x_1^2 + x_2^2 + x_3^2}. \tag{7}$$

3 Sine Cosine Algorithm (SCA)

The sine cosine algorithm is a meta-heuristic algorithm, which is started with a set of random solutions. Then the global optimal solution is approached continuously through exploration and exploitation.

Firstly, a set of random solutions are generated. Next, the individual positions are updated by

$$X_i^{t+1} = \begin{cases} X_i^t + r_1 \times \sin(r_2) \times \left| r_3 P_i^t - X_i^t \right|, r_4 < 0.5, \\ X_i^t + r_1 \times \cos(r_2) \times \left| r_3 P_i^t - X_i^t \right|, r_4 \geq 0.5, \end{cases} \tag{8}$$

where X_i^t is the position of the current solution in $i\text{-}th$ dimension at $t\text{-}th$ iteration, r_2 is the random number in $[0, 2\pi]$, r_3 is the random number in $[0, 2]$ and r_4 is the random number in $[0, 1]$. P_i is the target solution in $i\text{-}th$ dimension, and $|.|$ indicates the absolute value (Fig. 1).

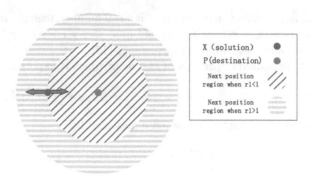

Fig. 1. Effects of sine and cosine in Eq. (8) on the next position

Another important random parameter r_1 is used to balance exploration and exploitation. Its expression is shown as

$$r_1 = a - t\frac{a}{T},\qquad(9)$$

where a is a constant, the t represents the current iteration number, and the maximum number of iterations is denoted by T.

SCA has four important parameters, each of which has a different function. The next position of solution (or direction of movement) is dictated by r_1. The parameter r_2 determines the distance to move. And the parameter r_3 is a random weight that influences the movement towards the target position randomly, emphasizing the influence on the movement distance when $r_3 > 1$ or $r_3 < 1$. The r_4 is a random value deciding whether to use sine function or cosine function in Eq. (8). The algorithm steps for SCA are shown below.

Algorithm 1. Sine cosine optimization algorithm

1. Initialize a set of search agents (solutions)(X)
2. **Repeat**
3.   Evaluate each of the search agents by the objective function
4.   Update the best solution obtiled so far (P = X*)
5.   Update r_1, r_2, r_3 and r_4.
6.   Update the position of search agents using Eq. (8)
7. **Until** t < maximum number of iterations
8. **Return** the best solution obtained so far as the global optimum

4   Quaternion Encoding Sine Cosine Algorithm (QSCA)

The original SCA was the basis for quaternion encoding SCA, which was to move individuals from Euclidean space to quaternion space. Each individual of SCA algorithm in Euclidean space is represented as a n-dimensional real value vector $s = s_0, \cdots, s_n$, where $s_k = R^n, (k = 0, 1, \cdots, n)$, and the quaternion space of n-dimensional vector expressed as $S = S_0, \cdots, S_n$, where $S_k \in H^n \wedge H \in R^4$, $(k = 0, 1, \cdots, n)$. Although quaternion space is more complex, it is easier to find the optimal solution in the search process.

4.1   Initializing the Quaternion Encoding Population

According to Eq. (6), an quaternion encoding individual S can be represented by two complex numbers S_R and S_I. They are given by

$$S_R = S_{RR} + S_{RI}i = \rho_R(\cos\theta_R + \sin\theta_R i), \tag{10}$$

$$S_I = S_{IR} + S_{II}i = \rho_I(\cos\theta_I + \sin\theta_I i), \tag{11}$$

$$S = S_R + S_I j = \rho_R\cos\theta_R + \rho_R\sin\theta_R i + \rho_I\cos\theta_I j + \rho_I\sin\theta_I k, \tag{12}$$

According to the problem's definition domain $[L, U]$, the modules and amplitudes that determine the individual X are randomly generated, shown in Eqs. (13) and (14).

$$\begin{cases} \rho_R \in \left[0, \frac{L-U}{2}\right] \\ \rho_I \in \left[0, \frac{L-U}{2}\right] \end{cases}, \tag{13}$$

$$\begin{cases} \theta_R \in [-2\pi, 2\pi] \\ \theta_I \in [-2\pi, 2\pi] \end{cases}. \tag{14}$$

After the above steps, the population has been initialized.

4.2   The Updating Method of QSCA

Update real part

$$S_{RR}^{t+1} = \begin{cases} S_{RR}^t + r_1 \times \sin(r_2) \times \left|r_3 P_{RR}^t - S_{RR}^t\right|, r_4 < 0.5, \\ S_{RR}^t + r_1 \times \cos(r_2) \times \left|r_3 P_{RR}^t - S_{RR}^t\right|, r_4 \geq 0.5. \end{cases} \tag{15}$$

Update three imaginary parts

$$S_{RI}^{t+1} = \begin{cases} S_{RI}^t + r_1 \times \sin(r_2) \times \left|r_3 P_{RI}^t - S_{RI}^t\right|, r_4 < 0.5, \\ S_{RI}^t + r_1 \times \cos(r_2) \times \left|r_3 P_{RI}^t - S_{RI}^t\right|, r_4 \geq 0.5. \end{cases} \tag{16}$$

$$S_{IR}^{t+1} = \begin{cases} S_{IR}^t + r_1 \times \sin(r_2) \times \left|r_3 P_{IR}^t - S_{IR}^t\right|, r_4 < 0.5, \\ S_{IR}^t + r_1 \times \cos(r_2) \times \left|r_3 P_{IR}^t - S_{IR}^t\right|, r_4 \geq 0.5. \end{cases} \tag{17}$$

$$S_{II}^{t+1} = \begin{cases} S_{II}^t + r_1 \times \sin(r_2) \times \left|r_3 P_{II}^t - S_{II}^t\right|, r_4 < 0.5, \\ S_{II}^t + r_1 \times \cos(r_2) \times \left|r_3 P_{II}^t - S_{II}^t\right|, r_4 \geq 0.5. \end{cases} \tag{18}$$

Among them, P_{RR}, P_{RI}, P_{IR} and P_{II} represent the quaternion individuals at the position of the four-part optimal solution respectively. The current solution is represented by S_{RR}, S_{RI}, S_{IR} and S_{II}. Random parameters r_1, r_2, r_3, r_4 have the same meaning as the value range of SCA.

4.3   The Calculation Method of Fitness Value

Since quaternions are composed of four parts, it is necessary to convert quaternions into real numbers to calculate fitness function values. The steps are as follows. Firstly, taking the norm of complex number ρ_R, ρ_I and quaternion ρ

$$\rho = N(S), \tag{19}$$

$$\rho_R = \sqrt{S_{RR}^2 + S_{RI}^2}, \tag{20}$$

$$\rho_I = \sqrt{S_{IR}^2 + S_{II}^2}. \tag{21}$$

Next, an quaternion encoded individual S is represented by complex shown in Eq. (12). So, the individuals encoded by the quaternion can be decoded by

$$X_R = \rho_R \, \text{sgn} \left(\sin \left(\frac{S_{RR}}{\rho_R} \right) \right) + \frac{U+L}{2}, \tag{22}$$

$$X_I = \rho_I \, \text{sgn} \left(\sin \left(\frac{S_{II}}{\rho_I} \right) \right) + \frac{U+L}{2}, \tag{23}$$

$$X = \sqrt{X_R^2 + X_I^2}, \tag{24}$$

where the X_R and X_I are both real-value converted from the complex number [17] in Eqs. (10) and (11). The X represents the real variable transformed from the quaternion encoded individual. Next, the corresponding fitness function values are calculated and evaluated. If it is better than the current global optimum, the current global optimum is replaced. Otherwise, the next iteration is executed.

4.4   Pseudocode of QSCA

QSCA is to transfer search agents in the Euclidean space of SCA to quaternion space, so that an search agent is updated by a real part and three imaginary parts respectively. The diversity of the population was enriched, and the global search ability and performance of the algorithm was greatly improved. The pseudocode for the QSCA algorithm is shown in Algorithm 2.

Algorithm 2. Quaternion sine cosine optimization algorithm

1. Initialize a set of quaternion encoded search agents using Eq. (13)-(14) (solutions)(S)
2. **Repeat**
3.　　　Convert quaternion-encoded search agents to real-value using Eq. (22)-(24)
4.　　　Evaluate each of the search agents by the objective function
5.　　　Update the best solution obtiled so far (P = S*)
6.　　　Update r_1, r_2, r_3 and r_4 .
7.　　　Update the position of search agents using Eq. (15)-(18)
8. **Until** t < maximum number of iterations
9. **Return** the best solution obtained so far as the global optimum

5 Simulation Experiments and Result Analysis

The purpose of our experimental work is to prove the rationality of the quaternion encoding method for the individual in the sine cosine algorithm. In essence, this paper focuses on whether this encoding method can improve the global search ability of sine cosine algorithm. Therefore, the QSCA proposed in this article is applied to the function optimization problem. Secondly, QSCA is compared with six meta-heuristics in the four indexes of best value, worst value, average value and standard deviation.

5.1 Experimental Setup

The experiment was done on Windows 10 (64-bit) and ran on the CPU Core i5-8250U with 8 GB of ram. Matlab 2017a software was used.

5.2 Comparison of Each Algorithm Performance

Table 1 is the parameter setting of these algorithms in the experimental test of the benchmark function. The population number is 30 and the iteration number is 100. In this paper, three kinds of standard reference functions (single-mode reference function, multi-mode reference function and fixed-dimensional multi-mode reference function) in the Table 2 were tested 30 times independently, in order to compare with other optimization algorithms in terms of solution quality and convergence speed.

Table 1. The parameters of the algorithm and their values.

Algorithm	Parameter	Value	Algorithm	Parameter	Value
SCA	a	2.0	DA	Inertia weight (w)	0.9
BA	A	0.9		Separation weight (s)	0.1
	r	0.5		Alignment weight (a)	0.1
	α	0.95		Cohesion weight (c)	0.7
	Qmin	−1.0		Food factor (f)	1.0
	Qmax	1.0		Enemy factor (e)	1.0

(continued)

Table 1. (*continued*)

Algorithm	Parameter	Value	Algorithm	Parameter	Value
ABC	The maximum cycle number	100	PSO	Vmax	1.0
				Vmin	−1.0
	Modification rate (MR)	0.8		C1	0.5
MFO	B	1.0		C2	0.5
	L	[−1, 1]			

The benchmark function test results are shown in Table 3. In the table, Best, Worst, Mean and Std were used to represent the best fitness value, worst fitness value, Mean of fitness value and standard deviation of the experiment after 30 independent operation, respectively.

Table 2. Benchmark functions used in this study (Type: M: Multimodal, U: Unimodal, F: Fixed-dimension multimodal, Dim: Dimension, Scope: Upper bound, Lower bound, f_{min}: Optimal value).

No.	Type	Benchmark	Dim	Scope	f_{min}
f_1	U	$f(x) = \sum_{i=1}^{n} x_i^2$	30	$x_i \in [-100, 100]$	0
f_2	U	$f(x) = \sum_{i=1}^{D} \left[100(x_{i+1} - x_i^2)^2 + (1 - x_i^2)^2 \right]$	30	$x_i \in [-30, 30]$	0
f_3	M	$f(x) = \sum_{i=1}^{n} \left[x_i^2 - 10\cos(2\pi x_i) + 10 \right]$	30	$x_i \in [-5.12, 5.12]$	0
f_4	M	$f(x) = \frac{1}{4000} \sum_{i=1}^{n} x_i^2 - \prod_{i=1}^{n} \cos\left(\frac{x_i}{\sqrt{i}}\right) + 1$	30	$x_i \in [-600, 600]$	0
f_5	F	$f(x) = 0.5 + \frac{\sin^2(\sqrt{x_1^2 + x_2^2}) - 0.5}{(1 + 0.001(x_1^2 + x_2^2))^2}$	2	$x_i \in [-100, 100]$	−1

The test results in Table 3 show that QSCA is superior to the other six algorithms in the four indicators tested. As can be seen from the mean value and standard deviation, QSCA is highly robust to unimodal benchmark function, multimodal benchmark function and fixed-dimension multimodal benchmark function and the theoretical optimal value can be searched on the f_1, f_3 and f_4. It can be seen from the convergence accuracy diagram in Figs. 2, 3, 4, 5 and 6 that QSCA is superior to the other six algorithms in the convergence accuracy and speed. It can be seen from the anova test of global minimum of Figs. 2, 3, 4, 5 and 6 that QSCA has strong robustness.

Table 3. Simulation results for test functions (D: dimensional).

Functions		QSCA	SCA	PSO	BA	ABC	DA	MFO
$f_1(D = 30)$	Best	0.00000	105.359	987.444	5.1E+04	3.2E+03	1.0E+03	5.3E+03
	Worst	0.00000	1.0E+04	3.6E+03	7.6E+04	1.2E+04	6.8E+03	3.4E+04
	Mean	0.00000	3.5E+03	2.0E+03	6.4E+04	7.8E+03	3.3E+03	1.2E+04
	Std	0.00000	2.4E+03	723.475	6.5E+03	2.5E+03	1.5E+03	6.4E+03
$f_2(D = 30)$	Best	27.2702	6.3E+04	5.8E+04	7.4E+07	1.7E+03	2.5E+04	2.6E+06
	Worst	29.0000	6.3E+04	8.5E+05	1.8E+08	2.7E+07	3.8E+06	8.4E+07
	Mean	28.9052	1.4E+07	3.7E+05	1.3E+08	1.0E+07	1.4E+06	1.4E+07
	Std	0.31560	8.8E+06	2.3E+05	1.3E+08	7.1E+06	1.1E+06	1.4E+07
$f_3(D = 30)$	Best	0.00000	26.4960	137.883	155.544	100.157	108.031	145.223
	Worst	0.00000	299.153	265.858	283.049	159.816	268.196	292.742
	Mean	0.00000	148.209	193.459	208.308	128.151	180.538	214.139
	Std	0.00000	54.4576	35.3294	28.3256	15.1651	39.8588	34.7997
$f_4(D = 30)$	Best	0.00000	3.71197	5.77940	435.569	26.0279	12.0197	41.1379
	Worst	0.00000	121.626	37.9545	726.765	95.9734	74.0855	174.649
	Mean	0.00000	32.7974	19.6004	602.846	61.6121	35.7159	92.5580
	Std	0.00000	24.6412	6.88610	63.0268	19.5924	14.3589	37.8693
$f_5(D = 2)$	Best	0.00000	0.00000	1.3E−08	0.07819	0.00388	0.00000	0.00972
	Worst	0.00000	0.00972	0.00972	0.48254	0.03786	0.00972	0.00972
	Mean	0.00000	0.00403	0.00753	0.29402	0.01232	0.00712	0.00972
	Std	0.00000	0.00432	0.00404	0.14128	0.01232	0.00437	4.1E−15

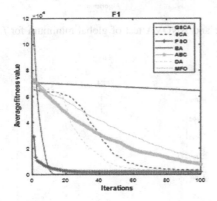 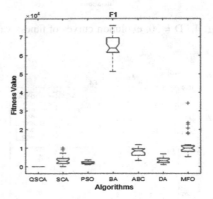

Fig. 2. D = 30, evolution curves of fitness value and ANOVA test of global minimum for f_1.

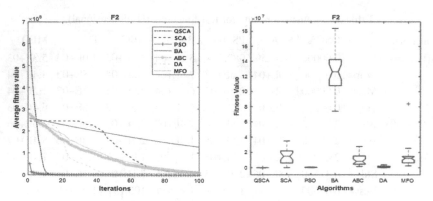

Fig. 3. D = 30, evolution curves of fitness value and ANOVA test of global minimum for f_2.

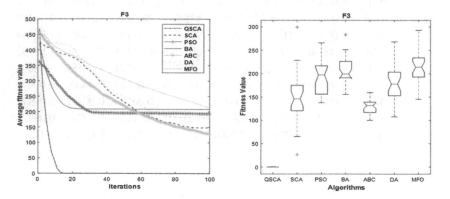

Fig. 4. D = 30, evolution curves of fitness value and ANOVA test of global minimum for f_3.

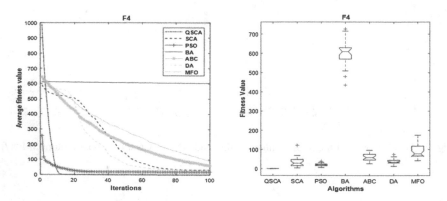

Fig. 5. D = 30, evolution curves of fitness value and ANOVA test of global minimum for f_4.

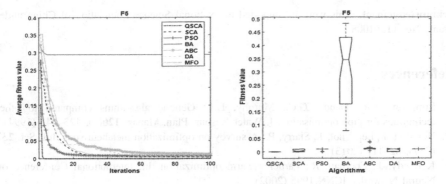

Fig. 6. D = 2, evolution curves of fitness value and ANOVA test of global minimum for f_5.

5.3 P-values of the Wilcoxon Rank-Sum Test

This paper verifies the relationship between the QSCA algorithm and other algorithms by using the Wilcoxon rank-sum test. P = 0.05 is used as the test standard, and the test results are shown in Table 4. In Table 4, none of the p-values are greater than 0.05. Therefore, it can be proved that QSCA is significantly different from other algorithms, and experimental data are not obtained accidentally.

Table 4. P-Values of the Wilcoxon rank-sum test results

Functions	QSCAvsSCA	QSCAvsPSO	QSCAvsBA	QSCAvsABC	QSCAvsDA	QSCAvsMFO
f_1	1.21E−12	1.21E−12	1.21E−12	1.21E−12	1.21E−12	1.21E−12
f_2	3.02E−11	3.02E−11	3.02E−11	3.02E−11	3.02E−11	3.02E−11
f_3	3.02E−12	3.02E−12	3.02E−12	3.02E−12	3.02E−12	3.02E−12
f_4	3.02E−12	3.02E−12	3.02E−12	3.02E−12	3.02E−12	3.02E−12
f_5	4.57E−12	5.34E−13	1.21E−12	1.21E−12	1.93E−10	4.46E−13

6 Conclusion

In this paper, the idea of quaternion coding is introduced into sine cosine algorithm. QSCA takes advantage of the characteristics of quaternion coding, that is, four-dimensional coding space maps one-dimensional coding space, and one real part and three imaginary parts are updated respectively. Each individual has inherent parallelism, which increases the population diversity and enhances the ability of the algorithm to find the global minimum. QSCA extends the scope of standard SCA applications from Euclidean space to quaternion space. The test results of five standard benchmark functions show that the optimization accuracy and stability of QSCA are superior to other six algorithms. In future studies, it is suggested to apply QSCA to more practical engineering problems and solve NP hard problems in some literatures.

Acknowledgement. This work is supported by National Science Foundation of China under Grants No. 11561008.

References

1. Simpson, A.R., Dandy, G.C., Murphy, L.J.: Genetic algorithms compared to other techniques for pipe optimisation. J. Water Resour. Plan. Manag. **120**(4), 423–443 (1994)
2. Boussad, I., Lepagnot, J., Siarry, P.: A survey on optimization metaheuristics. Inf. Sci. **237** (237), 82–117 (2013)
3. Kennedy, J., Eberhart, R.: Particle swarm optimization. In: International Conference on Neural Networks, ICNN 1995 (2002)
4. Karaboga, D., Akay, B.: A comparative study of artificial bee colony algorithm. Appl. Math. Comput. **214**(1), 108–132 (2009)
5. Mirjalili, S.: Moth-flame optimization algorithm: a novel nature-inspired heuristic paradigm. Knowl.-Based Syst. **89**, 228–249 (2015)
6. Yang, X.S., Gandomi, A.H.: Bat algorithm: a novel approach for global engineering optimization. Eng. Comput. **29**(5), 464–483 (2012)
7. Mirjalili, S.: Dragonfly algorithm: a new meta-heuristic optimization technique for solving single-objective, discrete, and multi-objective problems. Neural Comput. Appl. **27**(4), 1053–1073 (2016)
8. Mirjalili, S.: SCA: a sine cosine algorithm for solving optimization problems. Knowl. Based Syst. **96**, 120–133 (2016)
9. Issa, M., Hassanien, A.E., Oliva, D., Helmi, A., Ziedan, I., Alzohairy, A.: ASCA-PSO: adaptive sine cosine optimization algorithm integrated with particle swarm for pairwise local sequence alignment. Expert Syst. Appl. **99**, 56–70 (2018)
10. Elaziz, M.A., Oliva, D., Xiong, S.: An improved opposition-based sine cosine algorithm for global optimization. Expert Syst. Appl. **90**, 484–500 (2017)
11. Nenavath, H., Jatoth, R.K.: Hybrid SCA–TLBO: a novel optimization algorithm for global optimization and visual tracking. Neural Comput. Appl. 1–30 (2018)
12. Sindhu, R., Ngadiran, R., Yacob, Y.M., Zahri, N.A.H., Hariharan, M.: Sine cosine algorithm for feature selection with elitism strategy and new updating mechanism. Neural Comput. Appl. 1–12 (2017)
13. Fister, I., Yang, X.-S., Brest, J., Fister, I.: Modified firefly algorithm using quaternion representation. Expert Syst. Appl. **40**(18), 7220–7230 (2013)
14. Kc, G.: Elements of quaternions. Science **2**(75), 564 (1969)
15. Schwartz, C.: Calculus with a quaternionic variable. J. Math. Phys. **50**(1), 307 (2009)
16. Zhang, F.: Quaternion and matrices of quaternions. Linear Algebra Appl. **251**(2), 21–57 (1997)
17. Miao, F., Zhou, Y., Luo, Q.: Complex-valued encoding symbiotic organisms search algorithm for global optimization. Knowl. Inf. Syst. **3**, 1–40 (2018)

A Complex-Valued Encoding Moth-Flame Optimization Algorithm for Global Optimization

Pengchuan Wang[1], Yongquan Zhou[1,2(✉)], Qifang Luo[1,2],
Chencheng Fan[1], and Zhehong Xiang[1]

[1] College of Information Science and Engineering,
Guangxi University for Nationalities, Nanning 530006, China
yongquanzhou@126.com
[2] Guangxi High School Key Laboratory of Complex System
and Computational Intelligence, Nanning 530006, China

Abstract. The real-valued moth-flame optimization algorithm (MFO) is a new bio-inspired algorithm. It simulates the navigation mechanism of moth lateral positioning under moonlight. MFO has excellent performance in solving optimization problems and has strong ability in solving power optimization combination. In order to improve the global search ability of the algorithm, a complex-valued encoding moth-flame optimization algorithm (CMFO) is proposed. The real and imaginary parts of the population are updated by using the diploid structure of complex-valued encoding. The diversity of the population was increased. The effectiveness of CMFO algorithm has been verified by 4 benchmark problems, Statistically significant results and analysis show that the proposed complex-valued encoding moth-flame optimization algorithm is very promising and occasionally competitive compared with other well-established meta-heuristic techniques.

Keywords: Moth-flame optimization algorithm · Complex-valued encoding · Benchmark functions · Diploid structure

1 Introduction

Meta-heuristic algorithm is a special heuristic-based method. Its design idea is that it can solve many different problems without changing the basic framework of the algorithm [1]. Nature is a perfect example of adaptive problem solving. Natural heuristic method (usually called bio-heuristic method) is a special meta-heuristic method, which develops ideas to simulate biological or physical phenomena to solve problems. According to the inspiration sources of these algorithms, natural heuristic methods can be divided into four categories: evolutionary, swarm-based, physical-based and human-based methods [2, 3]. The evolutionary method has been developed under the enlightenment of the law of natural evolution. Among these methods, the most popular one is undoubtedly the genetic algorithm method which simulates Darwin's evolutionism [4]. On the other hand, a swarm-based technology is designed to simulate the social and collective behavior of animal groups (such as birds, insects,

D.-S. Huang et al. (Eds.): ICIC 2019, LNCS 11643, pp. 719–728, 2019.
https://doi.org/10.1007/978-3-030-26763-6_69

fish, etc.). Particle swarm optimization [5] algorithm inspired by the social behavior of bird flocking is the most representative and successful example in this field. Other related methods include artificial bee colony [6], whale optimization algorithm [2], etc. In addition, there are some physics-based algorithms that have been developed on the basis of imitating the laws of physics observed in our universe. The most popular methods in this category are simulated annealing [7], gravity search algorithm [8]. Finally, we can mention human-based algorithms. These methods of natural inspiration are unique because they derive inspiration from phenomena that are usually associated with human behavior, lifestyle or perception. The most famous methods in literature include Teaching learning based optimization algorithm [9], and many more.

In 2015, Australian scholar Mirjalili proposed a new swarm intelligence algorithm moth-flame optimization algorithm [10]. The algorithm simulates the lateral positioning navigation mechanism of moths flying in moonlight, and is an optimization method based on helical flight. Moth-flame optimization algorithm is simple in principle, does not need gradient information of the problem, and has strong robustness. However, moth-flame optimization algorithm also has some drawbacks, such as low precision and vulnerability to local optimum. Therefore, it is necessary to further expand and improve the algorithm.

It is well known that the individual MFO algorithm uses real coding. Complex-valued encoding uses its diploid structure to express individuals, and uses real part and imaginary part to represent individuals respectively. Its advantage is to expand the information capacity of individuals. In this paper, the complex-valued encoding method is used for MFO algorithm. The complex number corresponds to the actual variables of the moth population. The real part and imaginary part of the complex number are still represented by the real number. Because of the two-dimensional nature of complex number itself, the new complex-value encoding greatly expands the characteristic space of the population and enhances the diversity of the population. The search accuracy and convergence speed of complex-valued encoded moth-flame optimization algorithm (CMFO) have been greatly improved compared with the efficiency of MFO.

2 Moth-Flame Optimization Algorithm (MFO)

2.1 Inspiration

Moths are winged insects belonging to the family Butterflies. At night, moths fly by moonlight. For the purpose of flying, they use the special navigation mechanism of lateral positioning. According to this method, moths keep a fixed angle with the moon when flying, as shown in Fig. 1. However, moths have been observed to fly around light in a spiral manner, rather than horizontally. This is because lateral positioning is effective only when the light source is far away from the moth. Because the light source is far from the moon, the straight path becomes a spiral path as shown in Fig. 2.

Fig. 1. Transverse orientation [10]   **Fig. 2.** Spiral flying path [10]

2.2 Mathematical Model

In the basic moth optimization algorithm, the position of moth in space is the variable of the problem, assuming that moth is the candidate solution. By changing the moth's position vector, the algorithm can solve the low-dimensional and multi-dimensional space problems. In addition, it is worth noting that moth and flame are both candidates in moth optimization algorithm. The moth is the main moving body in the solution space, and the flame is the optimal value obtained by the moth in the current iteration. The flame can be understood as the location marker at the end of the moth's final search. When the algorithm is locally exploited, moths will search for the optimal position in the field of flame. Under this mechanism, the optimization accuracy of moths is improved.

As mentioned above, the algorithm is inspired by lateral positioning. We use the following equation to update the moth's position:

$$M_i = S(M_i, F_j) \tag{1}$$

Here M_i denotes the ith moth, F_j denotes the jth flame, and S is a spiral function.

Based on the above, the logarithmic helix function of moth optimization algorithm is defined as follows:

$$S(M_i, F_j) = D_i \cdot e^{bt} \cdot \cos(2\pi t) + F_j \tag{2}$$

Here the distance between the ith moth and the jth flame is denoted by D_i. b is a constant defining the logarithmic helix and t is a random number between [−1, 1]. D_i is calculated by the following formula:

$$D_i = |F_j - M_i| \tag{3}$$

In the whole search space, the position of moth is updated relative to n different positions, which results in the decrease of the search accuracy and easy to fall into local optimum. Therefore, an adaptive mechanism based on the number of flames is proposed. The formula is as follows:

$$flame\,no = round\left(N - l * \frac{N-1}{T}\right) \tag{4}$$

Here l is the current iteration number, N is the maximum number of flames and T is the maximum number of iterations.

3 Complex-Valued Moth-Flame Optimization Algorithm

In the biological world, the chromosomes of complex biological tissues generally use double or multi-stranded structures. Due to the two-dimensional characteristic of complex-valued encoding, this paper naturally applies it to represent diploid. In recent years, there are many algorithms that use complex coding to represent individuals. This article is inspired by this. In particular, a plurality of alleles can be used to describe a pair of alleles in the chromosome pair, complex real and imaginary parts are called real genes and virtual genes [11]. For a problem with N arguments, there are N complex numbers, the corresponding N complex numbers are recorded as follows (9):

$$x_p = R_p + iI_p \qquad p = 1, 2, 3, \cdots, N \tag{5}$$

Individuals of the population can be expressed as diploid structures and recorded as Table 1, where RN and IN represent the real part and imaginary part of the complex number, respectively. Therefore, the nth individual can be represented as shown in Table 1.

Table 1. Individual structure of population

$Individual_1$	$Individual_2$	$Individual_i$	$Individual_n$
(R_{P1}, I_{p1})	(R_{P2}, I_{p2})	...	(R_{PN}, I_{pN})

3.1 Initializing Complex-Valued Encoding Population

According to the definition interval $[A_k, B_k]$, $k = 1, 2, \ldots, 2M$, of the problem, $2M$ modules and $2M$ amplitudes [12] are randomly generated:.

$$\rho_k \in \left[0, \frac{A_k - B_k}{2}\right], \; k = 1, 2, \cdots, 2M \tag{6}$$

$$\theta_k \in [-2\pi, 2\pi], \; k = 1, 2, \cdots, 2M \tag{7}$$

According to formula (4) we get M complex numbers:

$$X_{Rk} + iX_{Ik} = \rho_k(\cos\theta_k + i\sin\theta_k), \; k = 1, 2, \cdots, 2M \tag{8}$$

Through the above process, we can get 2M real part and 2M imaginary part at the same time, and then update them respectively in the following way.

3.2 The Updating Method of CMFO

For the double structure of CMFO complex-valued encoding, we need complex-valued encoding for the logarithmic helix function definition formula of the original moth optimization algorithm. The up-date methods of CMFO are as follows:

$$S(M^i_{real}, F^j_{real}) = D^i_{real} \cdot e^{bt} \cdot \cos(2\pi t) + F^j_{real} \qquad (9)$$

$$S\left(M^i_{imaginary}, F^j_{imaginary}\right) = D^i_{imaginary} \cdot e^{bt} \cdot \cos(2\pi t) + F^j_{imaginary} \qquad (10)$$

Here D^i_{real} denotes the distance between the real part of the ith moth and the jth flame, $D^i_{imaginary}$ denotes the distance between the imaginary part of the ith moth and the jth flame, b and t have the same meaning as the original version of MFO.

The distance formula between the real moth and the flame D^i_{real} is calculated by the following formula (11), while the distance formula between the imaginary moth and the flame $D^i_{imaginary}$ is calculated by the following formula (12).

$$D^i_{real} = \left| F^i_{real} - M^i_{real} \right| \qquad (11)$$

$$D^i_{imaginary} = \left| F^i_{imaginary} - M^i_{imaginary} \right| \qquad (12)$$

The updated formula of flame self-adaptive mechanism does not change in complex-valued encoding moth-flame optimization algorithm.

3.3 The Calculation Method of Fitness Value

Because the complex number is composed of two parts: the real part and the imaginary part, we need to transform the coding space in the computation of fitness [12]. Therefore, before calculating the fitness value, we need to convert the complex number to real number, and then calculate the fitness function value. The concrete practices are as follows:

$$\rho_k = \sqrt{X^2_{Rk} + X^2_{IR}}, k = 1, 2, \cdots, M \qquad (13)$$

$$X_k = \rho_k \text{sgn}\left(\sin\left(\frac{X_{Ik}}{\rho_k}\right)\right) + \frac{A_k + B_k}{2}, k = 1, 2, \cdots, M \qquad (14)$$

where X_k is the real variable argument after conversion. According to the real variable, the corresponding fitness function value is calculated and evaluated. If it is better than the current optimal value, it is replaced. Otherwise, the next iteration is carried out.

3.4 CMFO Algorithm

The CMFO introduces complex diploid structure. The strategy of updating real part and imaginary part at the same time increases the diversity of information space, enhances the global search ability of searching individuals, and optimizes the performance of the algorithm of CMFO is as follows:

CMFO algorithm

Initialize the position of n moths: [Eq.(6) and Eq.(7)]

Get the real and imaginary part of complex [Eq. (8)]

Convert to real variables [Eq.(13) and Eq.(14)]

$$OM_{real} = FitnessFunction(M_{real});$$

$$OM_{imaginary} = FitnessFunction(M_{imaginary});$$

If iteration $==1$

$$F_{real} = sort(M_{real});$$

$$F_{imaginary} = sort(M_{imaginary});$$

$$OF_{real} = sort(OM_{real});$$

$$OF_{imaginary} = sort(OM_{imaginary});$$

Else

$$F_{real} = sort(M_{real}^{t-1}, M_{real}^{t});$$

$$F_{imaginary} = sort(M_{imaginary}^{t-1}, M_{imaginary}^{t});$$

$$OF_{real} = sort(M_{real}^{t-1}, M_{real}^{t});$$

$$OF_{imaginary} = sort(M_{imaginary}^{t-1}, M_{imaginary}^{t});$$

End

For $i=1:n$

    For $j=1:d$

        Update r and t

        Calculate D_{real} using Eq. (11) with respect to the corresponding moth

        Calculate $D_{imaginary}$ using Eq. (12) with respect to the corresponding moth

        Update $M_{real}(i,j)$ using Eq. (9) with respect to the corresponding moth

        Update $M_{imaginary}(i,j)$ using Eq. (10) with respect to the corresponding moth

    End

End

---

4 Simulation Experiments and Result Analysis

In this section, 4 test functions are selected, as shown in Table 2. In order to verify the optimization performance of CMFO, 4 different standard set test functions were simulated. These test functions can judge whether the various features of these algorithms are excellent, such as fast convergence, falling into local optimum, jumping out of local optimum and avoiding premature convergence.

4.1 Experimental Setup

All the simulation experiments are based on MATLAB. The integrated development environment is MATLAB2017a. All simulation experiments are carried out on a computer with Inter (R) Core (TM) i5_7200, main frequency 2.50 GHz and memory 8.00G.

4.2 Benchmark Function and Parameter Setting

In this section, we choose five mainstream meta-heuristic algorithms to compare with CFMO. Including the artificial bee colony optimization algorithm (ABC) [5], cuckoo search optimizer (CS) [13], sine cosine algorithm (SCA) [14] and the original version moth-flame optimization algorithm (MFO) [10]. 4 benchmark functions are used to verify the performance of CMFO. These classical test functions are mainly divided into single-peak test function, multi-peak test function and fixed-dimensional test function. These reference functions are shown in Table 2 below. Range is the boundary of the problem search space. The convergence accuracy of the 4 benchmark functions is 0 and 4 benchmark functions are simulated under 30-dimensional conditions.

Table 2. Benchmark function

Benchmark function	Range
$f_1(x) = \sum_{i=1}^{D-1} [100(x_{i+1} - x_i^2)^2 + (x_i - 1)^2]$	$x_i \in [-30, 30]$
$f_2(x) = \sum_{i=1}^{n} (\lvert x_i + 0.5 \rvert)^2$	$x_i \in [-100, 100]$
$f_3(x) = -20 \exp\left(-0.2\sqrt{\frac{1}{n}\sum_{i=1}^{n} x_i^2} - \exp\left(\frac{1}{n}\sum_{i=1}^{n} \cos 2\pi x_i\right)\right) + 20 + e$	$x_i \in [-32, 32]$
$f_4(x) = \frac{1}{4000}\sum_{i=1}^{n} (x_i^2) - \prod_{i=1}^{n} \cos(\frac{x_i}{\sqrt{i}}) + 1$	$x_i \in [-600, 600]$

4.3 Result Analysis

In this section, the performance of CMFO algorithm is simulated and the experimental results are shown in Table 3. Best, Mean, Worst and Std. represent the optimal solution, the average solution, the worst solution and the standard deviation of the results of 30 independent experiments. As shown in the table, we rank CMFO according to the optimal value. CMFO always ranks first. It can be concluded that CMFO performs better than other algorithms in optimization performance and is more competitive. Figures 3, 4, 5, 6, 7, 8, 9, 10 show the convergence curve and variance diagram of the algorithm. It can be seen from the graph that CMFO has faster convergence speed and better optimization accuracy than other mainstream algorithms when convergence accuracy is the same. So it proves that CMFO algorithm is competitive.

Table 3. Simulation results for test functions

Benchmark functions	Method	Results				Rank
		Best	Worst	Mean	Std.	
F1 (D = 30)	ABC	2.7E+02	1.0E+04	2.96E+03	2.5E+03	1
	CS	1.78E+01	1.2E+02	4.9E+01	3.1E+01	
	SCA	2.74E+01	9.7E+02	1.04E+02	1.9E+02	
	MFO	8.07E+01	8.0E+02	2.7E+02	146E+02	
	CMFO	8.1152	9.9E+01	1.1E+01	2.8E+01	
F2 (D = 30)	ABC	1.81E−03	19.3512	4.2721	5.4432	1
	CS	0.69E−03	6.6089	0.6027	1.36E−03	
	SCA	3.603	7.2692	4.6246	0.6382	
	MFO	1.72E−05	1.0E+04	2.3E+03	4.3E+03	
	CMFO	0.91E−05	1.97E−03	1.47E−03	0.25E−04	
F3 (D = 30)	ABC	6.7845	1.6E+01	1.3E+01	2.2319	1
	CS	0.8306	5.1003	2.8419	1.0911	
	SCA	0.64E−04	20.3133	14.9286	8.5088	
	MFO	6.0025	19.9657	15.0501	7.452	
	CMFO	0.47E−04	15.1294	2.4009	0.3541	
F4 (D = 30)	ABC	1.29E−03	1.3978	0.7478	0.3455	1
	CS	0.86E−03	0.2005	0.0889	0.0569	
	SCA	2.53E−16	0.8426	6.1977	0.2684	
	MFO	1.4E−04	9.1E+01	1.21E+01	3.1E+01	
	CMFO	5.37E−65	1.06E−04	7.67E−05	1.29E−05	

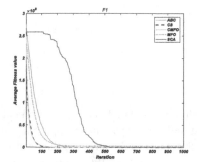

Fig. 3. Evolution curve of fitness value for F_1

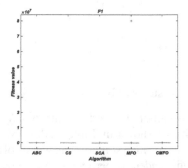

Fig. 4. Standard test of global minimum for F_1

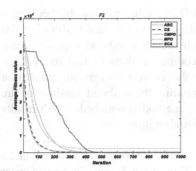

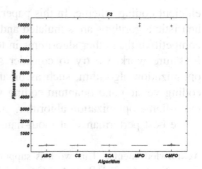

Fig. 5. Evolution curve of fitness value for F_3

Fig. 6. Standard test of global minimum for F_2

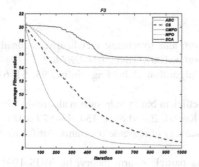

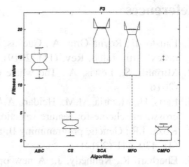

Fig. 7. Evolution curve of fitness value for F_3

Fig. 8. Standard test of global minimum for F_3

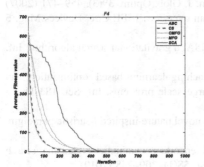

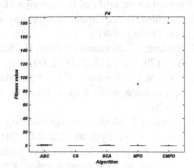

Fig. 9. Evolution curve of fitness value for F_4

Fig. 10. Standard test of global minimum for F_4

5 Conclusions and Future Research

In this paper, a complex-valued encoding moth-flame optimization algorithm (CMFO) is proposed. Using the idea of its diploid structure, the algorithm divides the moth population into real part and virtual part for updating, and obtains a new and more efficient coding scheme. In this paper, CMFO, MFO and other well-established meta-heuristic algorithms are simulated and validated. The results show that CMFO is more competitive than other algorithms in terms of search accuracy and convergence speed. In future work, we try to consider some other coding versions of real moth-flame optimization algorithm, such as binary version, polar coordinate version, quaternion coding version and quantum coding version. Comparing the different versions of the moth-flame optimization algorithm, the best coding method is obtained, which results in the best performance of moth-flame optimization algorithm.

Acknowledgments. This work is supported by National Science Foundation of China under Grant No. 61563008. Project of Guangxi University for Nationalities Science Foundation under Grant No. 2018GXNSFAA138146.

References

1. Fausto, F., Reyna-Orta, A., Cuevas, E., et al.: From ants to whales: metaheuristics for all tastes. Artif. Intell. Rev. (11) (2019). https://doi.org/10.1007/s10462-018-09676-2
2. Mirjalili, S., Lewis, A.: The whale optimization algorithm. Adv. Eng. Softw. **95**, 51–67 (2016)
3. Faris, H., Mafarja, M.M., Heidari, A.A., et al.: An efficient binary salp swarm algorithm with crossover scheme for feature selection problems. Knowl.-Based Syst. **154**, 43–67 (2018)
4. Koza, J.R.: Genetic programming II: automatic discovery of reusable programs. Artif. Life **1**(4), 439–441 (2014)
5. Eberhart, R., Kennedy, J.: A new optimizer using particle swarm theory. In: MHS 1995, Sixth International Symposium on Micro Machine and Human Science (2002)
6. Karaboga, D., Basturk, B.: A powerful and efficient algorithm for numerical function optimization: artificial bee colony (ABC) algorithm. J. Glob. Optim. **39**(3), 459–471 (2007)
7. Rutenbar, R.A.: Simulated annealing algorithms: an overview. IEEE Circ. Devices Mag. **5**(1), 19–26 (1989)
8. Rashedi, E., Nezamabadi-Pour, H., Saryazdi, S.: GSA: a gravitational search algorithm. Inf. Sci. **179**(13), 2232–2248 (2009)
9. Rao, R.V., Savsani, V.J., Vakharia, D.P.: Teaching–learning-based optimization: an optimization method for continuous non-linear large scale problems. Inf. Sci. **183**(1), 1–15 (2012)
10. Mirjalili, S.: Moth-flame optimization algorithm: a novel nature-inspired heuristic paradigm. Knowl.-Based Syst. **89**, 228–249 (2015)
11. Miao, F., Zhou, Y., Luo, Q.: Complex-valued encoding symbiotic organisms search algorithm for global optimization. Knowl. Inf. Syst. **58**(1), 209–248 (2019)
12. Chen, D.-B., Li, H.-J., Li, Z.: Particle swarm optimization based on complex-valued encoding and application in function optimization. Comput. Eng. Appl. **45**, 59–61 (2009)
13. Gandomi, A.H., Yang, X.S., Alavi, A.H.: Cuckoo search algorithm: a metaheuristic approach to solve structural optimization problems. Eng. Comput. **29**(2), 245 (2013)
14. Mirjalili, S.: SCA: a sine cosine algorithm for solving optimization problems. Knowl.-Based Syst. **96**, 120–133 (2016)

An Enhanced Whale Optimization Algorithm with Simplex Method

Yanbiao Niu[1,2], Zhonghua Tang[1,2], Yongquan Zhou[1,2(✉)],
and Zhongmin Wang[1,2]

[1] College of Information Science and Engineering,
Guangxi University for Nationalities, Nanning 530006, China
yongquanzhou@126.com
[2] Guangxi High School Key Laboratory of Complex System and Computational
Intelligence, Nanning 530006, China

Abstract. This paper proposes an enhanced whale optimization algorithm with the simplex method named SMWOA algorithm. SMWOA make WOA faster, more robust, and avoid premature convergence. The simplex method (SM) iteratively optimizes the current worst step size, avoids the population search at the edge, and improves the convergence accuracy and speed of the algorithm. The SMWOA algorithm is compared with other well-known meta-heuristic algorithms on 5 benchmarks and 1 classical engineering design problem. The experimental results show that the SMWOA algorithm has better performance than other meta-heuristic optimization algorithms in low and high dimensions.

Keywords: An enhanced whale optimization algorithm · Simplex method · Benchmark function · Meta-heuristic optimization algorithms

1 Introduction

In recent years, a great many nature-inspired meta-heuristic algorithms have been developed and applied to many optimization problems [1]. Swarm-based techniques have become popular, with the main inspiration coming from a collection of decentralized, self-organizing, collaborative search agent systems [2]. Compared with the traditional precise algorithm, the stochastic optimization algorithm can not only deal with a large number of decision variables but also has strong competitiveness and close to the optimal results. Among many kinds of research, some famous swarm-based optimizers are genetic algorithm (GA) [3], differential evolution (DE) [4] and particle swarm optimization (PSO) [5]. The success of these algorithms in addressing problems of large scale and complexity has encouraged other researchers to develop many new swarm algorithms such as salp swarm algorithm (SSA) [6], grasshopper optimization algorithm (GOA) [7] and grey wolf optimizer (GWO) [8].

The whale optimization algorithm is proposed by Mirjalili et al. in 2016 [9]. It is a new efficient meta-heuristic algorithm inspired by the search and hunting activities of humpback whales in the ocean. However, similar to other swarm-based meta-heuristics, this algorithm also has random operators to explore and exploit the search space. Therefore, when solving the optimization problem, it may rapidly converge to

D.-S. Huang et al. (Eds.): ICIC 2019, LNCS 11643, pp. 729–738, 2019.
https://doi.org/10.1007/978-3-030-26763-6_70

the local optimal solution rather than the global optimal solution. In order to solve the above problems, this paper proposes an enhanced WOA algorithm with simplex method named SMWOA which aimed at enhance the precision of the convergence of basic WOA algorithm. The simplex method [10] has strong ability to avoid local optimization and improve the ability of global optimal search. Experimental results show that the SMWOA algorithm is feasible and effective, and emphasize its superior approximation ability in high dimensional space.

2 Whale Optimization Algorithm (WOA) and Simplex Method

2.1 Whale Optimization Algorithm

WOA is a new meta-heuristic swarm intelligence optimization algorithm to solve optimization problems. It is derived from the feeding behavior of humpback whales in the bubble net. The hunt for humpback whales can be modeled mathematically in two stages [9].

The humpback whales searching prey is represented by the following Eqs. (1) and (2)

$$\vec{D} = \left| \vec{C} \cdot \overrightarrow{X_{rand}} - \vec{X} \right| \tag{1}$$

$$\vec{X}(t+1) = \overrightarrow{X_{rand}} - \vec{A} \cdot \vec{D} \tag{2}$$

Where $\overrightarrow{X_{rand}}$ is the random vector (a random whale) selected from the current population. $\vec{A}$ and $\vec{C}$ are coefficient vectors, and the calculation formula is as follows:

$$\vec{A} = 2\vec{a} \cdot \vec{r} - \vec{a} \tag{3}$$

$$\vec{C} = 2 \cdot \vec{r} \tag{4}$$

Where vector $\vec{a}$ is decreasing linearly from 2 to 0 during the iteration, and $\vec{r}$ is a random vector, within the range of 0 and 1.

$$\vec{D} = \left| \vec{C} \cdot \overrightarrow{X^*}(t) - \vec{X}(t) \right| \tag{5}$$

$$\vec{X}(t+1) = \overrightarrow{X^*}(t) - \vec{A} \cdot \vec{D} \tag{6}$$

Where t is the current iteration, X^* is the position vector of the current optimal solution, and $\vec{X}$ is the position vector. Here, if $|A| > 1$, Eqs. (1) and (2) express the searching prey, otherwise Eqs. (5) and (6) express the encircling prey, which shows the shrinking mechanism.

Humpback whales prey on fish groups with a logarithmic conical spiral motion. The mathematical model is as follows:

$$\overrightarrow{X}(t+1) = \overrightarrow{D} \cdot e^{bl} \cdot \cos(2\pi l) + \overrightarrow{X^*}(t) \tag{7}$$

Where $\overrightarrow{D} = \left| \overrightarrow{X^*}(t) - \overrightarrow{X}(t) \right|$ represents the distance from the ith whale to its prey (the best solution so far), l is a random number in $[-1, 1]$, b is the constant that defines the shape of the logarithmic spiral.

In the process of attacking, whales show both attack modes. Therefore, assuming that they have a 50% probability of contracting and enveloping mechanism, and their positions are updated by a spiral model with the same probability, the model can be modeled as:

$$\overrightarrow{X}(t+1) = \begin{cases} \overrightarrow{X^*}(t) - \overrightarrow{A} \cdot \overrightarrow{D} & \text{if } p < 0.5 \\ \overrightarrow{D'} \cdot e^{bl} \cdot \cos(2\pi l) + \overrightarrow{X^*}(t) & \text{if } p > 0.5 \end{cases} \tag{8}$$

Where p is a random number in $[0, 1]$.

2.2 Simplex Method

The simplex method has unique advantages in local search and often gets higher search precision through optimization. The method, proposed by Spendley et al., is a simple linear search method to find local minima of functions. It is based on the idea of comparing the values of the objective function at the N + 1 vertices of a polytope (simplex) in N-dimensional space and moving the polyhedron towards the minimum point as the optimization progress. Subsequently, simplex method have been used for optimization and optimal search, and the preliminary results show it's promising capability [10].

3 An Enhanced Whale Optimization Algorithm with Simplex Method

In order to improve the accuracy and convergence speed of the algorithm, the SMWOA algorithm is proposed. The simplex method has good performance, makes the algorithm jump out of the local optimum, and avoids the population searching at the edge, leading it to the global optimization. This means that the method helps achieve a better balance between exploration and exploitation of WOA. Therefore, after each iteration, we use the simplex method to update the position of the worst search agent. This makes the algorithm closer to the optimal solution, improves exploit ability of the algorithm, and speed it up to find the optimal solution. The modified Algorithm 1 showed as follows:

Algorithm 1. SMWOA pseudo-code
1.   Initialize the whales population $X_i (i = 1,2,...n)$
2.   Initialize a, A, and C l, and p
3.   Calculate the fitness of each search agent
4. X^* =the best search agent
5.   **while** $(t < \text{max\_}iteration)$
6.   **for** each search agent
7.   Update a, A, and C l, and p
8.   **if1** $(p < 0.5)$
9.   **if2** $(|A| < 1)$
10.   Update the position of the current search agent by Eq. (6)
11.   **else if2** $(|A| \geq 1)$
12.   Select a random search agent (X_{rand})
13.   Update the position of the current search agent by Eq. (2)
14.   **end if2**
15.   **else if1** $(p \geq 0.5)$
16.   Update the position of the current search by Eq. (7)
17.   **end if1**
18.   **end for**
19.   Update the position of the worst search agent using the simplex method [Eqs. (9)-(13)]
20.   Check if any search agent goes beyond the search space and amend it
21.   Calculate the fitness of each search agent
22.   Update X^* if there is a better solution
23. $t = t + 1$
24.   **end while**
25.   Return X*

4 Simulation Experiments

In this section, we selected 5 benchmark functions with different characteristics to verify the performance of SMWOA algorithm from different perspectives. In general, benchmark functions can be segmented into three categories: high-dimension unimodal test functions ($f_1 \sim f_2$), high-dimension multi-modal test functions ($f_3 \sim f_4$) and fixed-dimensional multi-modal test functions (f_5), as shown in Table 1.

Table 1. Benchmark functions.

Benchmark function	Dim	Range	F_{min}
$f_1(x) = \sum\limits_{i=1}^{n} x_i^2$	50	$x_i \in [-100, 100]$	0
$f_2(x) = \sum\limits_{i=1}^{n} \|x_i\| + \prod\limits_{i=1}^{n} \|x_i\|$	50	$x_i \in [-10, 10]$	0
$f_3(x) = \sum\limits_{i=1}^{n} x_i \sin(x_i) + 0.1 x_i$	50	$x_i \in [-10, 10]$	0
$f_4(x) = \sum\limits_{i=1}^{n} [x_i^2 - 10\cos(2\pi x_i) + 10]$	50	$x_i \in [-5.12, 5.12]$	0
$f_5(x) = -\frac{1 + \cos(12\sqrt{x_1^2 + x_2^2})}{0.5(x_1^2 + x_2^2) + 2}$	2	$x_i \in [-5.12, 5.12]$	-1

4.1 Results of the Algorithms

To better validate the performance of SMWOA, seven of the most advanced meta-heuristic algorithms are adopted: MFO [11], PSOGSA [12], BA [13], ABC [14], SBO [18], SCA [19], and WOA [9]. To make a fair comparison, each algorithm runs 30 times on the benchmark function, plus the standard deviation of the last generation of the best approximate solution. This feature presents us which algorithm behaves much more stable. The main parameter settings for all algorithms are shown in Table 2. The statistical results include Best, Worst, Mean, and Std values of the target function values. All algorithms are ranked according to the value of std.

Table 2. The parameters setting for six algorithms.

Algorithm	Parameter values
MFO [11]	The population size is 30, the maximum iteration number is 1000
PSOGSA [12]	The population size is 30, the maximum iteration number is 1000
BA [13]	$A = 0.9$, $r = 0.5$, $f \in [-1, 1]$ the population size is 30, the maximum iteration number is 1000
ABC [14]	The population size is 30, the maximum iteration number is 1000
SBO [18]	Parameter values of α and Z are considered, 0.94 and 0.02, respectively. The mutation probability is 0.05. The population size is 30, the maximum iteration number is 1000
SCA [19]	α Linearly decreased from 2 to 0 in [19], the population size is 30. The maximum iteration number is 1000
WOA [9]	$\vec{\alpha}$ Linearly decreased from 2 to 0 in [9], the population size is 30. The maximum iteration number is 1000
SMWOA	$\vec{\alpha}$ Linearly decreased from 2 to 0 in [9], the population size is 30. The maximum iteration number is 1000

Table 3. Results of benchmark functions.

Functions result		MFO	PSO-GSA	BA	ABC	SBO	SCA	WOA	SMW-OA
f1	Best	5.457	0.213	$4.1e^{+4}$	$5.6e^{-3}$	0.153	0.845	$1.0e^{-165}$	0
	Worst	$3.0e^{+4}$	$2.0e^{+4}$	$6.5e^{+4}$	0.45	0.408	$9.7e^{+2}$	$7.6e^{-145}$	$5.9e^{-323}$
	Mean	$6.6e^{+3}$	$9.3e^{+3}$	$5.4e^{+4}$	$8.8e^{-2}$	0.282	$1.3e^{+2}$	$2.5e^{-146}$	$9.8e^{-323}$
	Std	$8.0e^{+3}$	$8.2e^{+3}$	$6.1e^{+3}$	0.106	0.058	$2.5e^{+2}$	$1.3e^{-145}$	0
	Rank	7	8	6	4	3	5	2	1
f2	Best	20.21	$7.6e^{-6}$	$2.3e^{+11}$	$2.9e^{-2}$	0.166	$2.6e^{-5}$	$6.3e^{-122}$	$1.9e^{-260}$
	Worst	$1.1e^{+2}$	$1.8e^{+2}$	$3.7e^{+20}$	0.136	0.290	6.9e-2	$7.6e^{-100}$	$8.1e^{-244}$
	Mean	70.87	47.01	$1.7e^{+19}$	$7.5e^{-2}$	0.229	9.9e-3	$2.5e^{-101}$	$2.9e^{-245}$
	Std	29.59	63.16	$7.6e^{+29}$	$2.5e^{-2}$	0.028	1.4e-2	$1.3e^{-100}$	0
	Rank	6	7	8	4	5	3	2	1
f3	Best	$7.2e^{-2}$	2.24	7.94	$4.9e^{-2}$	0.101	$1.4e^{-4}$	$1.1e^{-113}$	$4.6e^{-261}$
	Worst	32.65	14.09	39.6	0.70	0.341	16.21	$2.1e^{-103}$	$1.9e^{-238}$
	Mean	11.32	6.96	17.1	0.27	0.206	2.34	$9.4e^{-105}$	$8.1e^{-240}$
	Std	8.99	3.28	7.85	0.153	0.058	3.46	$3.9e^{-104}$	0
	Rank	8	5	7	4	3	6	2	1
f4	Best	$1.7e^{+2}$	$1.4e^{+2}$	$2.9e^{+2}$	11.39	76.74	0.41	0	0
	Worst	$3.9e^{+2}$	$3.8e^{+2}$	$4.6e^{+2}$	24.10	$1.3e^{+2}$	$2.4e^{+2}$	0	0
	Mean	$3.1e^{+2}$	$2.4e^{+2}$	$3.6e^{+2}$	16.8	$1.0e^{+2}$	73.31	0	0
	Std	50.40	48.82	38.27	2.92	14.57	58.20	0	0
	Rank	6	5	4	2	3	7	1	1
f5	Best	−1	−1	−0.936	−0.99	−1	−1	−1	−1
	Worst	−0.93	−0.93	−0.229	−0.97	−0.93	−1	−0.936	−0.936
	Mean	−0.96	−0.99	−0.657	−0.99	−0.97	−1	−0.976	−0.997
	Std	$3.2e^{-2}$	0.019	0.225	5.8e-3	$3.2e^{-2}$	0	0.0297	0.0116
	Rank	7	4	8	2	6	1	5	3

The results of f_1–f_2 in Table 3 shows that the SMWOA algorithm can provide very competitive results on unimodal functions. From Figs. 1 and 2, we can clearly see that SMWOA has the fastest convergence rate when searching the global optimum. As can be seen from Figs. 6 and 7, the standard deviation of SMWOA is significantly less than that of the other seven algorithms.

The results of f_3–f_4 in Table 3 shows that the SMWOA outperforms all the other algorithms. Moreover, for f_4, WOA and SMWOA can achieve the theoretical global optimum. As can be seen from the curves in the figures, SMWOA has the fastest convergence speed and higher convergence accuracy. Figures 8 and 9, the standard deviations of the SMWOA are smaller than those of the other algorithms. It can be concluded that SMWOA can avoid local minimum and has a good convergence rate for high-dimensional multimodal test functions.

The SMWOA failed to show the best standard deviation on f_5, while at the same time, the SMWOA can find the best fitness value. Figure 5 show the convergence curves of all the algorithms on fixed-dimension multimodal benchmark functions. In

Fig. 5, SMWOA is the third best and obtains the same final optimum. SMWOA is the third best standard deviations in all algorithms.

In summary, the experimental results show that SMWOA algorithm is highly competitive and superior to other well-known algorithms (Figs. 3, 4 and 10).

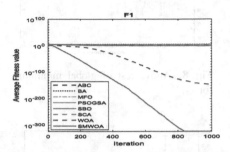

Fig. 1. Evolution curves of fitness value for f_{01}

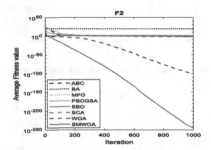

Fig. 2. Evolution curves of fitness value for f_{02}

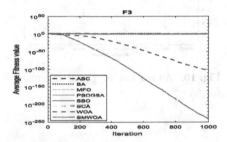

Fig. 3. Evolution curves of fitness value for f_{03}

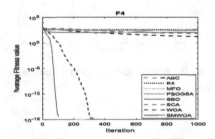

Fig. 4. Evolution curves of fitness value for f_{04}

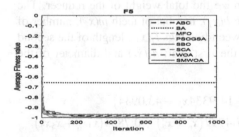

Fig. 5. Evolution curves of fitness value for f_{05}

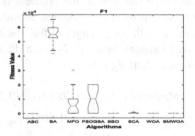

Fig. 6. Anova test of global minimum for f_{01}

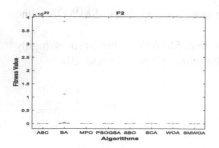

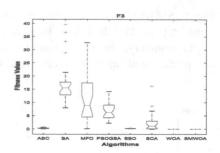

Fig. 7. Anova test of global minimum for f_{02}

Fig. 8. Anova test of global minimum for f_{03}

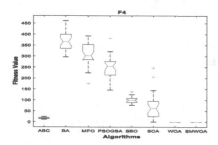

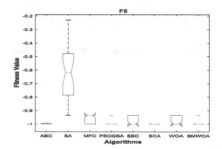

Fig. 9. Anova test of global minimum for f_{04}

Fig. 10. Anova test of global minimum for f_{05}

5   Constrained Optimization Using the SMWOA Algorithm

Reducer design problem is one of the basic structural engineering problems. The objective function of the problem is to minimize the total weight of the reducer. The problem involves 7 variables, including width $b(x_1)$, number of teeth $m(x_2)$, number of pinion teeth $z(x_3)$, length of the first shaft between bearings $l_1(x_4)$, length of the second shaft between bearings $l_2(x_5)$, a diameter of the first shaft $d_1(x_6)$ and diameter of the second shaft $d_2(x_7)$.

$$\text{Minimize} f(\overrightarrow{x}) = 0.7854x_1x_2^2(3.3333x_3^2 + 14.9334x_3 - 43.0934)$$
$$- 1.508x_1(x_6^2 + x_7^2) + 7.4777(x_6^3 + x_7^3) + 0.7854(x_4x_6^2 + x_5x_7^2)$$

Subject to $g_1(\overrightarrow{x}) = -x_1 + 0.0193x_3 \leq 0,$ $g_2(\overrightarrow{x}) = \dfrac{397.5}{x_1 x_2^2 x_3^2} - 1 \leq 0,$

$$g_3(\overrightarrow{x}) = \frac{1.93x_4^3}{x_2 x_6^4 x_3} - 1 \leq 0, \qquad g_4(\overrightarrow{x}) = \frac{1.93x_5^3}{x_2 x_7^5 x_3} - 1 \leq 0,$$

$$g_5(\overrightarrow{x}) = \frac{\left[(745x_4/x_2x_3)^2 + 16.9 \times 10^6\right]^{1/2}}{110x_6^3} - 1 \leq 0,$$

$$g_6(\overrightarrow{x}) = \frac{\left[(745x_5/x_2x_3)^2 + 157.5 \times 10^6\right]^{1/2}}{85x_7^3} - 1 \leq 0,$$

$$g_7(\overrightarrow{x}) = \frac{x_2 x_3}{40} - 1 \leq 0, g_8(\overrightarrow{x}) = \frac{5x_2}{x_1} - 1 \leq 0, g_9(\overrightarrow{x}) = \frac{x_1}{12x_2} - 1 \leq 0,$$

$$g_{10}(\overrightarrow{x}) = \frac{1.5x_6 + 1.9}{x_4} - 1 \leq 0, g_{11}(\overrightarrow{x}) = \frac{1.1x_6 + 1.7}{x_5} - 1 \leq 0,$$

Where $2.6 \leq x_1 \leq 3.6, 0.7 \leq x_2 \leq 0.8, 17 \leq x_3 \leq 28, 7.3 \leq x_4 \leq 8.3,$
$7.3 \leq x_5 \leq 8.3, 2.9 \leq x_6 \leq 3.9, 5.0 \leq x_7 \leq 5.5.$

Table 4. Comparison results of the speed reducer design problem.

Algorithms	Optimal values for variables							Optimal cost
	b	m	z	l_1	l_2	d_1	d_2	
CS [15]	3.501	0.7	17	7.605	7.818	3.352	5.287	3000.98
HCPS [16]	3.5	0.7	17	7.3	7.715	3.350	5.286	2994.47
SCA [17]	3.5	0.7	17	7.327	7.715	3.350	5.286	2994.74
ABC [14]	3.499	0.7	17	7.3	7.8	3.350	5.287	2997.05
SMWOA	3.5	0.7	17	7.3	7.3	3.350	5.286	**2985.13**

Table 4 shows that SMWOA can obtain the optimal cost value and is superior to all algorithms.

6 Conclusions

An enhanced WOA algorithm, SMWOA algorithm, is proposed to solve the optimization problem. To evaluate the performance of SMWOA, we used 5 benchmark functions and compared them with the other seven most advanced meta-heuristic algorithms. As shown in Sect. 4, it proves that SMWOA is superior to all algorithms in most test cases and that SMWOA is a feasible and quite effective method in global optimization problems. What's more, We solved one classical engineering problems with our proposed SMWOA method, as shown in Sect. 5. The results show that SMWOA performs well in unknown and challenging search space.

Acknowledgment. This work is supported by National Science Foundation of China under Grant No. 61563008. Project of Guangxi University for Nationalities Science Foundation under Grant No. 2018GXNSFAA138146.

References

1. Abdel-Basset, M., El-Shahat, D., El-Henawy, I., et al.: A modified flower pollination algorithm for the multidimensional knapsack problem: human-centric decision making. Soft. Comput. **22**(13), 4221–4239 (2018)
2. Heidari, A.A., Abbaspour, R.A., Jordehi, A.R.: Gaussian bare-bones water cycle algorithm for optimal reactive power dispatch in electrical power systems. Appl. Soft Comput. **57**, 657–671 (2017)
3. Hossam, F., Al-Zoubi, A.M., Asghar, H.A., et al.: An intelligent system for spam detection and identification of the most relevant features based on evolutionary random weight networks. Inf. Fusion **48**, 67–83 (2018). S1566253518303968
4. Wang, L., Zeng, Y., Chen, T.: Back propagation neural network with adaptive differential evolution algorithm for time series forecasting. Expert Syst. Appl. **42**(2), 855–863 (2015)
5. Jordehi, A.R.: A review on constraint handling strategies in particle swarm optimisation. Neural Comput. Appl. **26**(6), 1265–1275 (2015)
6. Faris, H., Mafarja, M.M., Heidari, A.A., et al.: An efficient binary salp swarm algorithm with crossover scheme for feature selection problems. Knowl.-Based Syst. **154**, 43–67 (2018)
7. Asghar, H.A., Hossam, F., Ibrahim, A., et al.: An efficient hybrid multilayer perceptron neural network with grasshopper optimization. Soft Comput. (2018). https://doi.org/10.1007/s00500-018-3424-2
8. Mirjalili, S., Mirjalili, S.M., Lewis, A.: Grey wolf optimizer. Adv. Eng. Softw. **69**, 46–61 (2014)
9. Mirjalili, S., Lewis, A.: The whale optimization algorithm. Adv. Eng. Softw. **95**, 51–67 (2016)
10. Davoodi, E., Hagh, M.T., Zadeh, S.G.: A hybrid improved quantum-behaved particle swarm optimization-simplex method (IQPSOS) to solve power system load flow problems. Appl. Soft Comput. **21**, 171–179 (2014)
11. Mirjalili, S.: Moth-flame optimization algorithm: a novel nature-inspired heuristic paradigm. Knowl.-Based Syst. **89**, 228–249 (2015)
12. Mirjalili, S., Hashim, S.Z.M.: A new hybrid PSOGSA algorithm for function optimization. In: International Conference on Computer and Information Application, pp. 374–377 (2010)
13. Yang, X.S.: A new metaheuristic bat-inspired algorithm. Comput. Knowl. Technol **284**, 65–74 (2010)
14. Karaboga, D., Basturk, B.: A powerful and efficient algorithm for numerical function optimization: artificial bee colony (ABC) algorithm. J Glob Optim **39**(3), 459–471 (2007)
15. Gandomi, A.H., Yang, X.-S., Alavi, A.H.: Cuckoo search algorithm: a metaheuristic approach to solve structural optimization problems. Eng. Comput. **29**, 17–35 (2013)
16. Long, W., et al.: A hybrid cuckoo search algorithm with feasibility-based rule for constrained structural optimization. J. Central South Univ. **21**(8), 3197–3204 (2014)
17. Ray, T., Liew, K.M.: Society and civilization: an optimization algorithm based on the simulation of social behavior. IEEE Trans. Evol. Comput. **7**(4), 386–396 (2003)
18. Moosavi, S.H.S., Bardsiri, V.K.V.: Satin bowerbird optimizer: a new optimization algorithm to optimize ANFIS for software development effort estimation. Eng. Appl. Artif. Intell. **60**, 1–15 (2017)
19. Mirjalili, S.: SCA: a sine cosine algorithm for solving optimization problems. Knowl. Based. Syst. **96**, 120–133 (2016)

BFPA: Butterfly Strategy Flower Pollination Algorithm

Mengyi Lei[1,2], Qifang Luo[1,2(✉)], Yongquan Zhou[1,2],
Chengmei Tang[1,2], and Yuanyuan Gao[1,2]

[1] College of Information Science and Engineering,
Guangxi University for Nationalities, Nanning 530006, China
l.qf@163.com
[2] Key Laboratory of Guangxi High Schools Complex System
and Computational Intelligence, Nanning 530006, China

Abstract. Aiming at the shortcomings of slow convergence and low precision of flower pollination algorithm, a flower pollination algorithm based on butterfly pollination strategy (BFPA) was proposed. The algorithm first uses the butterfly pollination strategy to accelerate the convergence speed of the global search phase. Second, in the local search phase, the beetle antenna search help algorithm is used to jump out of the local optimum. The experiment uses five Benchmark test functions to test, and the results show that the BFPA algorithm has better performance than other versions of the pollination algorithm.

Keywords: Flower pollination algorithm · Butterfly optimization algorithm · Global optimization · Metaheuristic algorithm

1 Introduction

Intelligent optimization algorithm is a method of solving complex optimization problems by simulating a natural phenomenon or process in nature. Many types of intelligent optimization algorithms have been proposed, such as particle swarm optimization (PSO) [1], genetic algorithm (GA) [2], and ant colony algorithm (ACO) [3]. In 2012, X. S. Yang simulated the process of flower pollination in nature, and proposed a metaheuristic bionic optimization algorithm-Flower Pollination Algorithm (FPA) [4]. Although there are thousands of flowers in nature, they are mainly pollinated by asexual pollination or sexual pollination. Asexual pollination is often referred to as self-pollination, which is mainly done by wind, water and other media; sexual pollination is generally called alienation pollination, often relying on butterflies, bees, etc. to complete pollination. Since butterflies, bees, etc. can fly long distances, alienation pollination is considered a global search, while self-pollination is a local search. In this paper, the butterfly algorithm is introduced into the global search stage of the pollination algorithm to improve the convergence speed of the FPA algorithm. Introduce the beetle antenna strategy into the local search phase and give it to improve the ability to jump out of local optimum.

The rest of the paper is organized as follows: Sect. 2 briefly introduces the original pollination algorithm; Sect. 3 introduces a novel butterfly pollination strategy for

© Springer Nature Switzerland AG 2019
D.-S. Huang et al. (Eds.): ICIC 2019, LNCS 11643, pp. 739–748, 2019.
https://doi.org/10.1007/978-3-030-26763-6_71

flower pollination; Sect. 4 simulation experiments and results analysis; Sect. 5 conclusions and future work.

2   Flower Pollination Algorithm (FPA)

The flower pollination algorithm is a group intelligent bionic optimization algorithm that simulates the pollination process of flowering plants in nature. In the real world of nature, every flowering plant can produce many flowers, each flower can produce millions of pollen gametes. In order to simplify the pollination process and make the algorithm more efficient, it is set to open only one flower per flowering plant, and each flower produces only one pollen gamete. A flower or a pollen gamete corresponds to a feasible solution in the problem, and each flower is switched by the conversion probability p. The FPA algorithm is now subjected to four idealized conditional assumptions:

Alienation pollination requires butterfly or bird to carry pollen for pollination, with a large pollination range, which is regarded as a global search process, and the pollinator obeys *Lèvy* flight;

Self-pollination is carried out by natural factors, and the pollination range is small, which is regarded as a local search process;

The probability of pollen reproduction is proportional to the similarity of the two flowers;

The transition probability p controls the switching probability of the global search and the local search.

First, the initial population is generated randomly, assuming the population size is n and the search space dimension is d. Then, the initial population is evaluated to determine the current optimal solution. When a new solution is produced, the pollination type is first determined based on a preset probability P. When $rand < P$, pollen i was cross-pollinated at t time. The location update formula is as follows:

$$x_i^{t+1} = x_i^t + L(\lambda)(x_i^t - gbest) \tag{1}$$

Among them, x_i^{t+1} denotes the position of pollen i at $t + 1$, *gbest* denotes the position of the best pollen in the current population, and L is a control parameter. Its essence is a random step size obeying the *Lèvy* distribution, which satisfies the formula (2):

$$L \sim \frac{\lambda \Gamma(\lambda) \sin(\pi\lambda/2)}{\pi} \frac{1}{S^{1+\lambda}}, \ (S \geq S_0 > 0) \tag{2}$$

In the above formula, $\Gamma(\lambda)$ is a standard gamma function. When the step size $S > 0$, the distribution is valid. The empirical value $\lambda = 1.5$ is obtained from many experiments. On the contrary, when $rand < P$, self-pollination is carried out. The formula for updating the pollen position pollen i at t time is as follows:

$$x_i^{t+1} = x_i^t + \varepsilon(x_j^t - x_k^t) \tag{3}$$

Among them, x_j^t and x_k^t represent the positions of two pollens in the population different from pollen i, respectively. $\varepsilon \in [0,1]$ is a proportional coefficient that is subject to uniform distribution. To better simulate the two different stages of pollination, we took advantage of the conversion probabilities of the four idealized rules to switch between cross-pollination and self-pollination. According to previous experimental results, $p = 0.8$ is more suitable [4]. The implementation of pollination is embodied in the pseudo code of Algorithm 1.

Algorithm 1.   Flower Pollination Algorithm

Define Objective function $f(x)$, $x = (x_1, x_2, \ldots \ldots x_d)$

Initialize a population of n flowers/pollen gametes with random solutions
Find the best solution **gbest** in the initial population
Define a switch probability $P \in [0,1]$
Define a stopping criterion (either a fixed number of generations/iterations or accuracy)
While (t <MaxGeneration)
    For $i = 1 : n$ (all n flowers in the population)
        If $rand < P$
            Draw a (d -dimensional) step vector L which obeys a $L\acute{e}vy$ distribution
            Global pollination via equation (1) and get new solution x_i
        Else
            Draw ε form a uniform distribution in (0,1)
            Do local pollination via equation (3) and get new solution x_i
        End If
        Evaluate the new solutions
        If new solutions are better, update them in the population
    End For
    Find the current best solution **gbest**
End While
Output the best solution found

---

3   Butterfly Strategy Flower Pollination Algorithm (BFPA)

3.1   Butterfly Optimization Algorithm

Butterflies use their sense of smell, sight, taste, touch and hearing to find food that help them move from one place to another. In all these senses, the sense of smell is the most important sense of helping the butterfly find food. According to scientific observations, butterflies can accurately locate the source of the scent, which is often emitted by the flowers. When a butterfly can feel the smell of any flower, it will move toward it. This algorithm is called global search. In another case, when the butterfly can't smell of the surrounding flowers, it will rely on the beetle search strategy to give it a direction. This phase is called local search.

The Butterfly Optimization Algorithm (BOA) [5] is divided into three phases, first performing the initialization phase, defining the objective function and its solution space, setting the parameter values, creating the initial population, then searching in an iterative manner, and finally finding the best solution and terminating the algorithm. The butterfly algorithm uses formula (4) to produce a scent at their location, and the butterfly moves to a better position using Eq. (5).

$$f = cI^a \tag{4}$$

$$x_i^{t+1} = x_i^t + (r^2 \times g^* - x_i^t) \times f_i \tag{5}$$

Here, f is the size of the perceived scent, c is the sensory form, I is the stimulus intensity, and a is the power index of the dependent form, indicating the different degrees of absorption. Both c and a belong to [0, 1], x_i^t is the solution vector x_i of the first butterfly in the t iteration. g^* represents the best solution currently found, f_i is the fragrance of the first butterfly, and r is a random number in [0, 1].

The local search phase is as follows:

$$x_i^{t+1} = x_i^t + (r^2 \times x_j^t - x_k^t) \times f_i \tag{6}$$

where x_j^t and x_k^t are the jth and kth butterflies in the solution space. The implementation of butterfly algorithm is embodied in the pseudo code of Algorithm 2.

Algorithm 2. Butterfly Optimization Algorithm

Define Objective function $f(x)$, $x = (x_1, x_2, \ldots \ldots x_{dim})$,*dim*=no. of dimensions

Generate initial population of n Butterfly $x_i = (i = 1,2, \ldots, n)$

Stimulus Intensity I_i at x_i is determined by $f(x_i)$

Define sensor modality c, power exponent a and switch probability p

While   stopping criteria not met **do**

    For each butterfly *bf* in population **do**

        Calculate fragrance for *bf* using Eq. (4)

    end For

    Find the best *bf*

    For each butterfly *bf* in population **do**

        Generate a random number *r* from [0,1]

      If $r < p$ **then**

        Move toward best butterfly/solution using Eq. (5)

      else

        Move randomly using Eq. (6)

      end If

    End For

    Update the value of a

End While

Output the best solution found

3.2   Beetle Antennae Search

Beetle antennae search is an intelligent optimization algorithm proposed in 2017 [6]. It does not need to know the specific form of the function to achieve efficient optimization.

The bionic principle of the beetle search is that the cow does not know the specific location of the food when it is eating, and it can find food according to the smell of the food. If the antennae on the left side of the beetle receive a larger scent than the right side, the hornbill moves to the left and vice versa. In order to establish the model, the following describes the random direction of the Beetle antennae search.

$$\vec{b} = \frac{rnd(k, 1)}{\|rnd(k, 1)\|} \tag{7}$$

where rnd (.) denotes a random function, and k presents the dimension of position. In addition, search behaviors that move to the left and right sides are given, such as formula (8) and (9).

$$x_r = x^t + d^t \vec{b} \tag{8}$$

$$x_l = x^t - d^t \vec{b} \tag{9}$$

where x_r represents the location in the search space on the right and x_l represents the location of the search space on the left. d represents the sensing length of the antenna corresponding to the development capability.

3.3   Butterfly Strategy Flower Pollination Algorithm

The nectar produced by the colorful flowers, as well as the aroma of the released flowers, can attract pollinators such as butterflies to complete pollination and pollination. The original flower pollination algorithm can easily solve the low-dimensional problem, but it will fall into the local optimum when solving the high-dimensional problem. In order to solve this problem, a flower pollination algorithm for butterfly pollination is proposed to reduce the problem of late localization and improve its mining capacity.

The butterfly flower pollination algorithm self-pollination update formula is as follows:

$$x_r^{t+1} = x_i^t + L(\lambda)(x_i^t - gbest) + d^t \vec{b} \tag{10}$$

$$x_l^{t+1} = x_i^t + L(\lambda)(x_i^t - gbest) - d^t \vec{b} \tag{11}$$

where x_r^{t+1} denotes the position to move to the right, x_l^{t+1} denotes the position to move to the left. The location update formula for the alienation pollination process is as follows:

$$x_i^{t+1} = x_i^t + \varepsilon(x_j^t - x_k^t) \times f_i \tag{12}$$

where f_i denotes the fragrance of the first flower.

4 Simulation Experiments and Result Analysis

4.1 Comparison of Each Algorithm Performance

In order to verify the validity of the BFPA algorithm, it is compared with the original flower pollination algorithm (FPA) and other improved versions of pollination algorithm, including dimensional Evolution Flower Pollination Algorithm (MFPA) [7], quantum coding Flower Pollination Algorithm (QFPA) [8] and bee Flower Pollination Algorithm (BPFPA) [9] comparative experiment was carried out.

The population size of each algorithm is 30, the number of iterations is 500, and p is 0.8, and each algorithm runs 30 times independently. The five test functions selected for the experiment are shown in Table 1.

Table 1. Benchmark functions

Benchmark function	Dim	Range	f_{min}
$f_1(x) = \sum_{i=1}^{n} x_i^2$	50	$x_i \in [-100, 100]$	0
$f_2(x) = \sum_{i=1}^{n} (\sum_{j=1}^{i} x_j)^2$	50	$x_i \in [-100, 100]$	0
$f_3(x) = \max_i \{|x_i|, 1 \leq i \leq D\}$	50	$x_i \in [-100, 100]$	0
$f_4(x) = \sum_{i=1}^{D-1} [100(x_{i+1} - x_i^2)^2 + (x_i - 1)^2]$	50	$x_i \in [-30, 30]$	0
$f_5(x) = \sum_{i=1}^{n} (|x_i + 0.5|)^2$	50	$x_i \in [-100, 100]$	0

The test results of the five test functions are shown in Table 2. Among them, Best, Mean, Worst and Std respectively represent the optimal value, mean value, worst value and variance in 30 experiments independently. Here, the Rank in Table 2 is ranked according to the optimal value. From the experimental results data in Table 2, the BFPA algorithm has better performance than the improved pollination algorithm in other versions.

In the results of the five test functions, it is the optimal value or the worst value, or the average value, the BFPA algorithm ranks better than the other four algorithms, which shows the stability of the algorithm. In general, the BFPA algorithm has better demonstrated its better performance and stability, which fully demonstrates its effectiveness and feasibility in solving optimization problems.

Figures 1, 2, 3, 4 and 5 are the convergence values of the fitness values of the five comparison algorithms FPA QFPA MFPA BPFPA BFPA. All the convergence curves are averaged. It can be seen from Figs. 1, 2, 3, 4 and 5 that the BFPA algorithm can obtain the global optimal value faster than the other four algorithms. Although the convergence accuracy of the BFPA algorithm in Figs. 1 and 3 is slightly inferior to the BPFPA algorithm, the overall performance is better than other algorithms. Figures 6, 7, 8, 9, and 10 is the variance diagram corresponding to the test results. It can be seen

Table 2. Results of benchmark functions

Benchmark function	Results	Algorithms					Rank
		FPA	MFPA	QFPA	BPFPA	BFPA	
f_1	Best	1076.4	3220.8	2.2E+04	5.04	1.76	1
	Worst	2470.95	8810.44	3.6E+04	31.60	9.68	
	Mean	2117.2	5541.19	2.9E+04	15.70	5.23	
	Std	374.77	149.76	3.9E+03	7.70	2.04	
f_2	Best	7.1E+03	2.98	8.8E+04	1.9E+03	0	1
	Worst	2.6E+03	2.45E+04	1.1E+05	5.6E+03	0	
	Mean	1.5E+03	1.04E+04	1.0E+05	3.8E+03	0	
	Std	5.1 E+03	4.09+03	7.6E+03	999.42	0	
f_3	Best	14.92	17.79	74.62	11.36	14.34	1
	Worst	26.47	27.32	85.49	21.97	24.15	
	Mean	19.48	22.52	80.31	15.88	19.32	
	Std	2.44	2.80	2.74	2.91	2.29	
f_4	Best	6.3E+04	2.04E+05	1.9E+07	699.09	0	1
	Worst	6.9E+05	2.79E+06	4.9E+07	4848.11	0	
	Mean	3.3E+05	9.99E+05	3.5E+07	2384.71	0	
	Std	1.5E+05	5.90E+05	7.2E+06	1164.29	0	
f_5	Best	1207.64	3237.54	2.0E+04	3.87	2.09	1
	Worst	3232.32	9743.57	3.9E+04	51.20	8.06	
	Mean	2175.96	5319.35	2.8E+04	18.64	5.04	
	Std	567.54	1406.33	3482.92	10.04	2.12	

from the five variance graphs that the variance of the BFPA algorithm is much smaller than other comparison algorithms. All the above experimental results are a good proof that the BFPA algorithm can effectively solve the optimization problem and reflect its strong search ability.

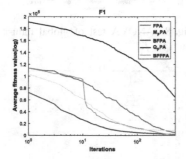

Fig. 1. Evolution curves of fitness value for f_1

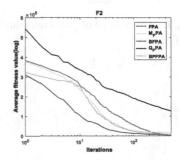

Fig. 2. Evolution curves of fitness value for f_2

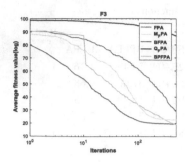

Fig. 3. Evolution curves of fitness value for f_3

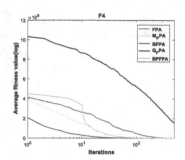

Fig. 4. Evolution curves of fitness value for f_4

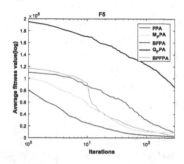

Fig. 5. Evolution curves of fitness value for f_5

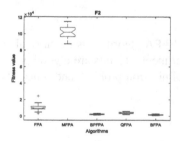

Fig. 6. ANOVA test of global minimum for f_1

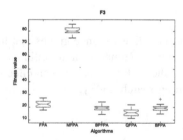

Fig. 7. ANOVA test of global minimum for f_2

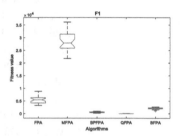

Fig. 8. ANOVA test of global minimum for f_3

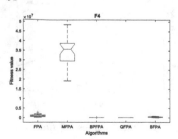

Fig. 9. ANOVA test of global minimum for f_4

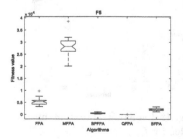

Fig. 10. ANOVA test of global minimum for f_5

4.2 Result Analysis

Five test functions were selected in Sect. 4.1 for simulation experiments to illustrate the performance of the BFPA algorithm. The experimental result data is shown in Table 2. The experimental results simulation convergence diagram is shown in Figs. 1, 2, 3, 4 and 5, and the variance diagram is shown in Figs. 6, 7, 8, 9, and 10. All the data in the above table and the result graphs show that BFPA has the characteristics of fast convergence and high stability, which proves the feasibility and effectiveness of the algorithm in solving optimization problems.

5 Conclusions and Future Works

In order to overcome the shortcomings of the original pollination algorithm mentioned in the abstract, a butterfly strategy pollination algorithm was introduced for this purpose, and the butterfly optimization algorithm helps to improve its search speed and exploration ability. From the results of the tests, the performance of BFPA is better or at least comparable to the comparison algorithm mentioned in this paper. For the BFPA algorithm, there are still many applications to be studied in the future, such as medical aspects and chemical aspects.

Acknowledgments. This work is supported by National Science Foundation of China under Grant No. 61563008. Project of Guangxi University for Nationalities Science Foundation under Grant No. 2018GXNSFAA138146.

References

1. Kennedy, J., Eberhart, R.: Particle swarm optimization. In: Proceedings of the IEEE International Conference on Neural Networks, Perth, Australia, vol. IV, pp. 1942–1948 (1995)
2. Srinivas, M., Patnaik, L.M.: Adaptive probabilities of crossover and mutation in genetic algorithms. IEEE Trans. Syst. Man Cybern. **24**(4), 656–667 (1994)
3. Socha, K., Dorigo, M.: Ant colony optimization for continuous domains. Eur. J. Oper. Res. **185**(3), 1155–1173 (2008)
4. Yang, X.-S.: Flower pollination algorithm for global optimization. In: Durand-Lose, J., Jonoska, N. (eds.) UCNC 2012. LNCS, vol. 7445, pp. 240–249. Springer, Heidelberg (2012). https://doi.org/10.1007/978-3-642-32894-7_27
5. Sankalap, A., Satvir, S.: Butterfly optimization algorithm: a novel approach for global optimization. Soft Comput. **23**(3), 715–734 (2018). https://doi.org/10.1007/s00500-018-3102-4
6. Jiang, X., Li, S.: BAS: beetle antennae search algorithm for optimization problems. Int. J. Robot. Control, **1**(1), 1–5 (2018)
7. Lu, K., Li, H.: Quantum-behaved flower pollination algorithm. In: 14th International Symposium on Distributed Computing and Applications for Business Engineering and Science (2015). https://doi.org/10.1109/dcabes.2015.24

8. Ram, J.P., Babu, T.S., Dragicevic, T., Rajasekar, N.: A new hybrid bee pollinator flower pollination algorithm for solar PV parameter estimation. Energy Convers. Manag. **135**, 463–476 (2017)
9. Sayed, S.A.F., Nabil, E., Badr, A.: A binary clonal flower pollination algorithm for feature selection. Pattern Recogn. Lett. **77**, 21–27 (2016)

Artificial Neural Network Hyperparameter Optimisation for Network Intrusion Detection

Marek Pawlicki[(✉)], Rafał Kozik, and Michał Choraś

UTP University of Science and Technology, Bydgoszcz, Poland
marek.pawlicki@utp.edu.pl

Abstract. Intrusion Detection is crucial in cybersecurity. So is the ability to identify the myriad of attacks. Artificial Neural Networks are an established and proven method of accurate classification. There are approaches to make ANN models faster by applying Principal Component Analysis as a feature extractor. However, ANNs are extremely versatile, a wide range of setups can achieve significantly different classification results. The main contribution of this paper is the evaluation of the way the hyperparameters can influence the final classification result. In this paper, a wide range of ANN setups is put to comparison, and the finest arrangement achieves the multi-class classification accuracy of 99.909% on an established benchmark dataset.

Keywords: Cybersecurity · Artificial Neural Network · Hyperparameter tuning

1 Introduction

Every single day the modern citizen is under siege by a wide array of cyberthreats including malware, worms, trojan horses, spyware, SQLI, XSS, ransomware, adversarial AI [1], and many, many more. In a sense all those malicious instances simply became part of our daily routine. A short while ago, at the beginning of 2018, a banking malware geared towards android has plundered the wallets of unsuspecting bank app users [2]. The new BankBot strain was altered to such a degree that it was granted passage through the Google Play Store antivirus protection, even though BankBot is a well-known malware. The trojan operated under the guise of what was a benevolent application at a first glance, but once set up on an Android device, it proceeded to appropriate the bank's access credentials.

A very well known case of cross-site scripting (XSS) took place when eBay turned out to be vulnerable to attack [3]. In 2014 JavaScript code was being included in costly item's listings. The user only had to click a malicious, but benign-looking listing to have the script seize control of his browser, get redirected to a site that looked exactly like eBay, and have their credit card credentials stolen. A recent report [4] suggests that the vulnerability has not been fixed after all those years.

Early 2018 was marked by a security violation that touched over 150 million users of a popular fitness app, MyFitnessPal. The media coverage of the breach tried to pass the event as "just another day on the Internet" [5]. With the prevailing risk of both new and known cybersecurity threats it is very tempting to just nod in agreement with that assertion.

© Springer Nature Switzerland AG 2019
D.-S. Huang et al. (Eds.): ICIC 2019, LNCS 11643, pp. 749–760, 2019.
https://doi.org/10.1007/978-3-030-26763-6_72

The wide range of cybersecurity violations resulted in spurring an array of different detection methods. Two main trends of research and development emerged, namely signature-based and anomaly-based. Signature-based IDS (Intrusion Detection Systems) operate utilising a storehouse of recognised attacks, while anomaly-based methods form a model of 'normal' traffic and go into alert whenever there has been spotted a divergence from the model [6].

The black-hat society utilises numerous obfuscation techniques to deceive the signature-based detectors. According to a recent analysis, known malevolent software can be made absolutely invisible to contemporary anti-malware applications [7].

The structure of the paper is as follows: Sect. 2 provides the summary of the related work, Sect. 3 elaborates on the theory behind ANNs and various ways the algorithm can be tuned. Section 4 focuses on experimental setup and results, including also a short description of the benchmark dataset. The conclusion is given thereafter.

2   Related Work

The application of Artificial Neural Networks (ANN) for intrusion detection systems (IDS) is hardly a new concept. There have been evaluations of the notion of using ANN to aid anomaly detection as far as 2009 [8]. In [9] the authors try to address the problems of overfitting, high memory consumption and high overhead of standard IDS with a feed-forward ANN. Specifically, a 2-layered feedforward ANN was recommended. The aforementioned problems were handled through conjugated training function and validation dataset. The authors claim that their method achieves similar results to classical procedures, but with less computational overhead. The procedure was tested on the benchmark KDD'99 dataset. The conclusion of the paper states that less data is better because of the time the machine needs to crunch it.

In [10] pruning of the ANN is evaluated as part of the optimisation of the network. It is basically the deletion of neural nodes of either the input or the hidden layers. This makes the ANN faster, as less computations have to be processed. In [11] an Artificial Neural Network also showed promise as an IDS when evaluated. The results were, in fact, very encouraging.

In [12] Principal Component Analysis (PCA) is employed as a feature extractor, before feeding the data to the ANN, as opposed to providing the inputs directly form the dataset. As the article illustrates, this drops the memory requirements of the method significantly, along with the time of training necessary. The two evaluated methods displayed comparable results as far as the accuracy is concerned. This makes applying PCA the clearly better option. Using a Kernel PCA betters the training time of ANN, but uses significantly more memory than traditional PCA. Both methods have similar accuracy measures, so the authors of [13] using a mix of different algorithms is preferable.

There has been research on utilising Graphical Processing Units to accelerate ANN based IDS, since GPU's are a good fit for ANN computations. An increase in performance has been proven. [14] The authors of [15] evaluate an ANN with one hidden layer in comparison with a Support Vector Machine, a Naive Bayes and a C4.5 algorithm. The ANN achieves comparable, or better results, but thanks to the simpler nature of a 3-layer ANN framework requires less computations than other tested algorithms. The experiments were performed on the NSL-KDD dataset, which is the current benchmark, and the successor of KDD'99. In [16] the researches focus on accelerating their Deep Neural Network model for IDS through the use of different hardware setups. The results state that utilising multicore CPU's achieves better training times than a serial setup. In this particular experiment the GPU underperformed, and authors state that this is the case because of the type of data used. The authors plan on expanding the set of features of the NSL-KDD dataset to improve accuracy.

3 Artificial Neural Network

Artificial Neural Networks (ANN) are an all-purpose utility for modeling. With a myriad of applications, they are an accepted and renowned tool for data mining, with classification, regression, clustering and time series analysis abilities. The basic assumption of an ANN is that it imitates, to a certain extent, the learning competences of a biological neural network, stressing by principle the properties of neural networks found in human brains, although strongly streamlined. [17]

The surprising modeling capacity of ANN in pattern recognition derives from its strong malleability as it fits to data. This extensive approximation capacity is markedly important when handling real-world data, when the information is plentiful, but the patterns buried in it remain uncovered.

In an ANN knowledge is gained through updating weights with consecutive batches of data instances. The algorithm can recognise the associations among the variables, as well as generalise in a way that allows for high performance on new, unforseen data. [18] It is basically like fitting a line, or a plane, or a hyper-plane through a set [19].

An artificial neural network with a sole computational layer is dubbed a perceptron. It consists of and input and an output, computational layer. After the data points are fed to the input layer, they are issued to the computational layer. The input layer contains d nodes that speak for d features $X = [x_1 \ldots x_d]$ and edges of weight $W = [w_1 \ldots w_d]$. The output neuron computes $W \cdot X = \sum_{i=1}^{d} (w_i x_i)$.

In case of the perceptron, the forecast is binary, and is delineated by the sign of the value that is the result of the output layer computation. To help deal with distribution imbalance, bias can be added.

The prediction of $\widehat{y}$ is the result of the following equation:

$$\widehat{y} = sign\{W \cdot X + b\} = sign\{\sum_{i=1}^{d} w_i x_i + b\}$$

As seen in the equation, the sign is the activation function $\phi(v)$. Numerous activation functions can be utilised in artificial neural networks with multiple hidden layers. For ease of training it is commonly either the Rectified Linear Unit (ReLU) or Hard Tanh in multilayered networks. The error of the regression can be indicated as the difference between the real-life test value and the predicted value, so $E(X) = y - \hat{y}$ If the error is not equal to 0 the weights should be amended. Thus, the purpose of the perceptron is to minimise the least-squares between y and $\hat{y}$, for all data points in dataset D. This objective is dubbed the loss function.

$$\sum_{(X,y)\in D} (y - sign\{W \cdot X\})$$

The loss function is defined over the whole dataset X, the weights W are updated with the learning rate α, and the algorithm iterates over the entire dataset until it converges. This algorithm was named stochastic gradient-descent, also expressed by:

$$W \Leftarrow W + \alpha E(X)X$$

[20] A multi-layer neural network is created via multiple computational layers, also named the hidden layers. The title itself hints to the black-box character of those layers, as the computations are shrouded from the users perspective. The data points are carried from the input layer subsequent layers with computations at every stage, down to the output layer.

The aforementioned procedure is referred to as the feed-forward neural network [20]. The exact count of nodes in the foremost computational layer usually does not reach the count of nodes of the input layer. The particular number of neurons and the number of hidden layers is in proportion to the intricacy of the necessary model and, of course, on the data. [18]. While in some special cases utilising a fully-connected layer is the norm, the use of hidden layers with the count of neurons below that of the inputs grants a loss in representation, which often times increases the network's performance. This is very likely as a result of getting rid of the noise in data [20].

A network built with too many neurons can display unwanted behavior known as overfitting. Also named overtraining, this particular phenomenon happens when the artificial neural network fitted the exact patterns found in the training dataset so tightly that it has trouble performing on unforseen data, as the approximation is not generalised enough [20].

3.1   Backpropagation

Having to train a single-layer perceptron is quite simple - the loss function is simply a function of the weights. With multiple layers the procedure gets messy as it has many layers of weights influence one another. Backpropagation calculates the Error Gradient as the sum of local-gradients over multiple paths to the output node. [20] The algorithm consists of two phases - the forward and the backward phase. In the forward phase the data points are served to the input nodes, and one after one the results at consecutive layers are computed with the current weights. The result of this prediction is compared to the training instance. The backward phase uncovers the gradient of the loss function for all the weights. The gradients update the weights, starting from the output layer, stepping back all the way to the first layer. This weight updating process iterates over the training data - each iteration is called an epoch - ANN's can often take thousands of those iterations to attain convergence.

3.2   TensorFlow and Keras

In this article TensorFlow has been used, which is a high performance, open source library, provided by the developers and engineers of the Google Brain team. It serves as a capable support for machine and deep learning, ad it is currently implemented in an array of scientific and industry applications. [21] Keras, which operates on top of TensorFlow and a myriad of other machine learning libraries, brings an astounding speed of experimentation along with incomparable user experience. This is attained via modular, expandable design. Keras was brought into existence more as an interface than an autonomous library. Keras received full support in the TensorFlow library, and makes possible intuitive coding of both machine and deep learning procedures [22].

3.3   Hyperparameter Optimization

A most important part of the Artificial Neural Network design comes in the role of the activation function, as the effect it carries over the achievable results is straight forward. One can have diverse types of activation functions. The decision on the type of an activation function plays a crucial role especially in multi-layer networks, as each layer can have it's own non-linear activation function. [20] Each distinctive function can have a special influence on the results of the ANN, as well as how the ANN converges, and the comprehensive nature of the network. Out of a wide range of activation functions $\phi(v)$ four were selected:

- Sigmoid
- Hard Sigmoid
- Rectified Linear Unit (ReLU)
- Hyperbolic Tangent (tanh)

The optimal network setup is found by using a grid search procedure, which completes an all-encompassing search over the hyperparameter's space. The grid search parameters included:

- the epoch count
- the batch size
- the activation function
- the optimiser
- in some tests the number of hidden layers
- in some tests the number of neuron nodes

The full cycle of learning and adapting the weights of the network is called and epoch. The particular count of samples utilised in one iteration is called batch size [20]. The grid search can test different activation functions and optimisers. The optimisers evaluated in this paper are:

- Adaptive Moment Estimation (adam)
- Root Mean Square Propagation (rmsprop)
- Stochastic gradient descent (SGD)

An example of the results the grid search method offers is found in Table 1 in the results section.

3.4   Principal Component Analysis

The search for a feature vector which communicates the nature of the dataset, but without having to represent every single feature is named dimensionality reduction.

It is about the construction of an n-dimensional projection that explains the data of a k-dimensional space. Computational benefits are the first ones that come to mind, followed by preventing the 'curse of dimensionality'. It makes ML classifiers fall short of the expected results with the increase of dimensions. [17] Exponential increase of samples is necessary for the algorithms to be back on track.

One of the go-to methods of dimensionality reduction is Principal Component Analysis (PCA). To put it shortly, PCA looks for a view of the data where the variance is maximised. An example introduced in [17] shows that if the data creates a line, performing PCA would immediately indicate that the variance over but one dimensions equals 0. Thus, since the features of those dimensions are useless, they can be gotten rid of. Even though data-gathering could suggest a high signal strength in one direction, the data will most likely contain noise in a lot of features. Provided the signal overpowers the noise to high enough extent, the elicited projection containing maximum variance is highly likely to convey the essence of the data.

4   Experimental Setup and Results

4.1   Dataset Description

NSL-KDD is a data set created to address the problems of the KDD'99 data, which were repeatedly raised in the literature. It is now an established benchmark dataset, even though it still displays some of the unwanted characteristics. Still, the lack of open IDS datasets and the difficulty of collecting the data makes NSL-KDD the go-to solution for intrusion detection research.

The set contains almost 5.000.000 records, which makes it both suitable for machine learning, and not overbearingly humongous so as to force researches to pick parts of the set randomly. This makes the results more easily comparable.

The NSL-KDD is cleared of redundant data, to prevent ML algorithms bias, which is an improvement over the original KDD'99 dataset.

4.2   Experimental Setup

The experiments were set up on the same 7th generation Intel Core i7-7500U CPU with two cores of 2.7 and 2.9 GHz and 16 GB RAM. The testing environment was set up using the Keras interface for the TensorFlow library running on Python 3.5. Multiple architecture setups were tested, ranging from 1 hidden layer of 25 neurons, which constitute a half of the count of neurons in the input layer. 2 to 1 a network of 4 layers 25 neurons each. The NSL-KDD dataset provides 41 features, 3 of them are categorical, or discrete variables. These are one-hot encoded to convert them to a form which is usable in the ANN algorithm, and then all the features are normalised. This process inflates the number of features to 118. PCA is then performed to get the number of features down to 50. The number of extracted features was an arbitrary decision based on initial tests of the setup. This reduced feature vector constitutes the feature-set fed to the input layer of the Artificial Neural Network. The pipeline of the process is illustrated on Fig. 1.

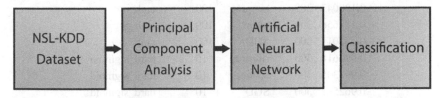

Fig. 1. The process pipeline

4.3 Results

Hyperparameter optimisation is performed on each of the setups. The gridsearch method evaluates each of possible permutations of the selected hyperparameters. Namely, the used epochs count, the batch size, the optimiser and the activation function are consecutively permutated in order to achieve the highest accuracy. The tables below illustrate the way the accuracy fluctuates on various ANN setups. The Table 1 displays the results of the gridsearch of an ANN with 4 hidden layers, 25 neurons on each layer. Table 2 shows how the gridsearch fared for a 1-hidden layer, 25 neural nodes ANN. The remaining Tables 3, 4 and 5 illustrate the gridsearch of ANN with 2 hidden layers and 25 neurons, 1 hidden layer and 10 neurons and an ANN with 2 layers, 25 neurons and dropout of 0.2 applied respectively.

Table 1. 4 dense computational layers, 25 neurons each and output

Accuracy	Epochs	Optimizer	Batch-size	Activation
0.998983	300	adam	10	sigmoid
0.953717	300	rmsprop	10	relu
0.954267	300	adam	10	relu
0.949774	300	SGD	10	relu
0.954515	300	rmsprop	100	relu
0.955097	300	adam	10	relu
0.859187	300	SGD	100	relu
0.998591	300	rmsprop	10	sigmoid
0.998983	300	adam	10	sigmoid
0.992189	300	SGD	10	sigmoid
0.998779	300	rmsprop	100	sigmoid
0.998957	300	adam	100	sigmoid
0.957635	300	SGD	100	sigmoid
0.204583	300	rmsprop	10	tanh

(continued)

Table 1. (*continued*)

Accuracy	Epochs	Optimizer	Batch-size	Activation
0.056442	300	adam	10	tanh
0.420010	300	SGD	10	tanh
0.120043	300	rmsprop	100	tanh
0.122656	300	adam	100	tanh
0.620011	300	SGD	100	tanh
0.996618	300	rmsprop	10	hard_sigmoid
0.997305	300	adam	10	hard_sigmoid
0.962501	300	SGD	10	hard_sigmoid
0.998516	300	rmsprop	100	hard_sigmoid
0.998512	300	adam	100	hard_sigmoid
0.957635	300	SGD	100	hard_sigmoid

Table 2. 1 layer of 25 neurons and output

Accuracy	Activation	Batch-size	Epochs	Optimizer
0.998607	relu	10	300	rmsprop
0.998925	relu	10	300	adam
0.998324	relu	10	300	SGD
0.998897	relu	100	300	rmsprop
0.998925	relu	100	300	adam
0.995683	relu	100	300	SGD
0.998713	sigmoid	10	300	rmsprop
0.999044	sigmoid	10	300	adam
0.996074	sigmoid	10	300	SGD
0.998935	sigmoid	100	300	rmsprop
0.999060	sigmoid	100	300	adam
0.992068	sigmoid	100	300	SGD
0.998641	tanh	10	300	rmsprop
0.999022	tanh	10	300	adam
0.997957	tanh	10	300	SGD
0.998996	tanh	100	300	rmsprop
0.999128	tanh	100	300	adam
0.995365	tanh	100	300	SGD
0.998727	hard_sigmoid	10	300	rmsprop
0.999014	hard_sigmoid	10	300	adam
0.996134	hard_sigmoid	10	300	SGD
0.998905	hard_sigmoid	100	300	rmsprop
0.999074	hard_sigmoid	100	300	adam
0.991900	hard_sigmoid	100	300	SGD

Table 3. 2 layers 25 neurons

Accuracy	Optimizer	Batch-size	Epochs	Activation
0.999090	adam	10	300	relu
0.998773	rmsprop	10	300	relu
0.999090	adam	10	300	relu
0.998857	rmsprop	100	300	relu
0.999020	adam	100	300	relu
0.995717	SGD	100	300	relu
0.998719	rmsprop	10	300	sigmoid
0.999022	adam	10	300	sigmoid
0.995391	SGD	10	300	sigmoid
0.999070	rmsprop	100	300	sigmoid
0.999084	adam	100	300	sigmoid
0.990065	SGD	100	300	sigmoid
0.998827	rmsprop	10	300	tanh
0.998947	adam	10	300	tanh
0.998603	SGD	10	300	tanh
0.999028	rmsprop	100	300	tanh
0.999022	adam	100	300	tanh
0.995403	SGD	100	300	tanh
0.998819	rmsprop	10	300	hard_sigmoid
0.999036	adam	10	300	hard_sigmoid
0.995310	SGD	10	300	hard sigmoid
0.998979	rmsprop	100	300	hard_sigmoid
0.998987	adam	100	300	hard_sigmoid
0.989853	SGD	100	300	hard_sigmoid

Table 4. 1 layer 10 neurons

Accuracy	Optimizer	Epochs	Activation	Batch-size
0.998915	adam	300	sigmoid	10
0.998516	rmsprop	300	relu	10
0.998761	adam	300	relu	10
0.997432	SGD	300	relu	10
0.998775	rmsprop	300	relu	100
0.998881	adam	300	relu	100
0.995214	SGD	300	relu	100
0.998450	rmsprop	300	sigmoid	10
0.998915	adam	300	sigmoid	10
0.995691	SGD	300	sigmoid	10
0.998709	rmsprop	300	sigmoid	100
0.998717	adam	300	sigmoid	100

(continued)

Table 4. (*continued*)

Accuracy	Optimizer	Epochs	Activation	Batch-size
0.990996	SGD	300	sigmoid	100
0.998562	rmsprop	300	tanh	10
0.998829	adam	300	tanh	10
0.996776	SGD	300	tanh	10
0.998765	rmsprop	300	tanh	100
0.998771	adam	300	tanh	100
0.994085	SGD	300	tanh	100
0.998522	rmsprop	300	hard_sigmoid	10
0.998833	adam	300	hard_sigmoid	10
0.995639	SGD	300	hard_sigmoid	10
0.998683	rmsprop	300	hard_sigmoid	100
0.998845	adam	300	hard_sigmoid	100
0.991385	SGD	300	hard_sigmoid	100

Table 5. 2 layers/25 neurons + dropout rate 0.2

Accuracy	Activation	Optimizer	Epochs	Batch-size
0.999074	relu	adam	300	10
0.999074	relu	adam	300	10
0.998701	relu	SGD	300	10
0.998919	relu	rmsprop	300	100
0.998994	relu	adam	300	100
0.995760	relu	SGD	300	100
0.998657	sigmoid	rmsprop	300	10
0.998987	sigmoid	adam	300	10
0.995268	sigmoid	SGD	300	10
0.998921	sigmoid	rmsprop	300	100
0.998949	sigmoid	adam	300	100
0.990065	sigmoid	SGD	300	100
0.998787	tanh	rmsprop	300	10
0.999066	tanh	adam	300	10
0.998518	tanh	SGD	300	10
0.998969	tanh	rmsprop	300	100
0.999054	tanh	adam	300	100
0.995393	tanh	SGD	300	100
0.998763	hard_sigmoid	rmsprop	300	10
0.999004	hard_sigmoid	adam	300	10
0.995260	hard_sigmoid	SGD	300	10
0.999034	hard_sigmoid	adam	300	100
0.989977	hard_sigmoid	SGD	300	100

5   Conclusions

As it is apparent from the provided tables, the final setup of the ANN can have a significant effect on the performance. For example, the very best accuracy attained was 0.999090 using the Adam optimiser, the batch size of 10, 300 epochs and the Rectified Linear Unit activation function. This comes in stark contrast with the worst result of accuracy of 0.056442 with the Adam optimiser, 300 epochs, 10 batches and the hyperbolic tangent activation function in an ANN of 4 hidden layers, 25 neurons each. This basically means that the model picked the wrong answer almost every single time.

References

1. McGraw, G., Morrisett, G.: Attacking malicious code: a report to the Infosec Research Council. IEEE Softw. **17**(5), 33–41 (2000)
2. Bielec, A.: Analysis of a polish bankbot (2018)
3. Kelion, L.: eBay redirect attack puts buyers' credentials at risk (2014)
4. Mutton, P.: Hackers still exploiting eBay's stored XSS vulnerabilities in 2017 (2017)
5. Lee, D.: MyFitnessPal breach affects millions of under armour users (2018)
6. Idika, N., Mathur, A.: A survey of malware detection techniques. Purdue University, March 2007
7. Canfora, G., Di Sorbo, A., Mercaldo, F., Visaggio, C.A.: Obfuscation techniques against signature-based detection: a case study. In: 2015 Mobile Systems Technologies Workshop (MST), pp. 21–26, May 2015
8. Sani, Y., Mohamedou, A., Ali, K., Farjamfar, A., Azman, M., Shamsuddin, S.: An overview of neural networks use in anomaly intrusion detection systems. In: 2009 IEEE Student Conference on Research and Development (SCOReD), pp. 89–92, November 2009
9. Haddadi, F., Khanchi, S., Shetabi, M., Derhami, V.: Intrusion detection and attack classification using feed-forward neural network. In: 2010 Second International Conference on Computer and Network Technology, pp. 262–266, April 2010
10. Gong, W., Fu, W., Cai, L.: A neural network based intrusion detection data fusion model. In: 2010 Third International Joint Conference on Computational Science and Optimization, vol. 2, pp. 410–414, May 2010
11. Mukhopadhyay, I., Chakraborty, M., Chakrabarti, S., Chatterjee, T.: Back propagation neural network approach to intrusion detection system. In: 2011 International Conference on Recent Trends in Information Systems, pp. 303–308, December 2011
12. Sonawane, H.A., Pattewar, T.A.: A comparative performance evaluation of intrusion detection based on neural network and PCA. In: 2015 International Conference on Communications and Signal Processing (ICCSP), pp. 0841–0845, April 2015
13. Pattewar, T.M., Sonawane, H.A.: Neural network based intrusion detection using Bayesian with PCA and KPCA feature extraction. In: 2015 IEEE International Conference on Computer Graphics, Vision and Information Security (CGVIS), pp. 83–88, November 2015
14. Van, N.T.T., Thinh, T.N.: Accelerating anomaly-based IDS using neural network on GPU. In: 2015 International Conference on Advanced Computing and Applications (ACOMP), pp. 67–74, November 2015
15. Subba, B., Biswas, S., Karmakar, S.: A neural network based system for intrusion detection and attack classification. In: 2016 Twenty Second National Conference on Communication (NCC), pp. 1–6, March 2016

16. Potluri, S., Diedrich, C.: Accelerated deep neural networks for enhanced intrusion detection system. In: 2016 IEEE 21st International Conference on Emerging Technologies and Factory Automation (ETFA), pp. 1–8, September 2016
17. Maimon, O., Rokach, L.: Data Mining and Knowledge Discovery Handbook, 2nd edn. Springer, Boston (2010). https://doi.org/10.1007/978-0-387-09823-4
18. Nunes, I., et al.: Artificial Neural Networks A Practical Course. Springer, Cham (2017). https://doi.org/10.1007/978-3-319-43162-8
19. Bassis, S., Esposito, A., Morabito, F.C., Pasero, E.: Advances in Neural Networks. Springer, Cham (2016). https://doi.org/10.1007/978-3-319-18164-6
20. Charu, C.A.: Neural Networks and Deep Learning a Textbook (2018)
21. Abadi, M., et al.: TensorFlow: large-scale machine learning on heterogeneous systems (2015). Software: tensorflow.org
22. Chollet, F., et al.: Keras (2015). https://github.com/fchollet/keras

Author Index

Printed in the United States
by Baker & Taylor Publisher Services

Printed in the United States
by Baker & Taylor Publisher Services